FOUNDATIONS OF MANAGERIAL MATHEMATICS

GM 400

Edited by
Michael P. Wegman

Elementary Algebra for College Students, Fourth Edition
Allen R. Angel

Business Mathematics: A collegiate Approach, Seven Edition
Nelda W. Roueche and Virginia H. Graves

Statistics for Business and Economics, Sixth Edition
James T. McClave and P. George Benson

Pearson
Custom
Publishing

Excerpts taken from:

Elementary Algebra for College Students, Fourth Edition, by Allen R. Angel
Copyright © 1996, 1992, 1988, 1985 by Prentice-Hall, Inc.
A Pearson Education Company
Upper Saddle River, New Jersey 07458

Business Mathematics: A Collegiate Approach, Seventh Edition,
by Nelda W. Roueche and Virginia H. Graves
Copyright © 1997, 1993, 1988, 1983, 1978, 1973, 1969 by Prentice-Hall, Inc.

Statistics for Business and Economics, Sixth Edition,
James T. McClave and P. George Benson
Copyright © 1994 Prentice-Hall, Inc.

This special edition published in cooperation with
Pearson Custom Publishing.

Printed in the United States of America

10 9 8 7

Please visit our website at www.pearsoncustom.com

ISBN 0–536–59839–8

BA 990605

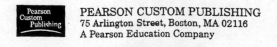

PEARSON CUSTOM PUBLISHING
75 Arlington Street, Boston, MA 02116
A Pearson Education Company

Contents

I From: *Elementary Algebra for College Students*, Fourth Edition, by Allen R. Angel
   Chapter 1 Real Numbers
   1.1   Study Skills for Success in Mathematics   2
   1.2   Fractions   9
   1.3   The Real Number System   21
   1.4   Inequalities   26
   1.5   Addition of Real Numbers   29
   1.6   Subtraction of Real Numbers   36
   1.7   Multiplication and Division of Real Numbers   44
   1.8   An Introduction to Exponents   52
   1.9   Use of Parentheses and Order of Operations   57
   1.10 Properties of the Real Number System   64
         Summary   69
         Review Exercises   71
         Practice Test   73

II From: *Business Mathematics: A Collegiate Approach*, Seventh Edition, by Nelda W. Roueche and Virginia H. Graves
    Chapter 3 Review of Percent   75
    1   Basic Percent   76
    2   Percent Equation Forms   82
    3   Word Problems Using Percents   87

III From: *Elementary Algebra for College Students*, Fourth Edition, by Allen R. Angel
     Chapter 2 Solving Linear Equations and Inequalities   95
     2.1   Combining Like Terms   96
     2.2   The Addition Property of Equality   105
     2.3   The Multiplication Property of Equality   115
     2.4   Solving Linear Equations with a Variable on Only One Side of the Equation   124
     2.5   Solving Linear Equations with the Variable on Both Sides of the Equation   131
     2.6   Ratios and Proportions   140
     2.7   Inequalities in One Variable   152
           Summary   158
           Review Exercises   159
           Practice Test   161

IV From: *Elementary Algebra for College Students*, Fourth Edition, by Allen R. Angel
    Chapter 3 Formulas and applications of Algebra   163
    3.1   Formulas   164
    3.2   Changing Application Problems into Equations   175
    3.3   Solving Application Problems   185
    3.4   Geometric Problems   198
          Summary   202
          Review Exercises   203
          Practice Test   205

V From: *Elementary Algebra for College Students*, Fourth Edition, by Allen R. Angel
   Chapter 7 Graphing Linear Equations   207
   7.1   Pie, Bar, and Line Graphs   208
   7.2   The Cartesian Coordinate System and Linear Equations in Two Variables   221
   7.3   Graphing Linear Equations   229
   7.4   Slope of a Line   244
   7.5   Slope-Intercept and Point-Slope Forms of a Linear Equation   250
   7.6   Functions   262
   7.7   Graphing Linear Inequalities   272
         Summary   276
         Review Exercises   278
         Practice Test   283

VI   From: *Elementary Algebra for College Students*, Fourth Edition, by Allen R. Angel

Chapter 8   Systems of Linear Equations   285

    8.1   Solving Systems of Equations Graphically   286
    8.2   Solving Systems of Equations by Substitution   296
    8.3   Solving Systems of Equations by the Addition Method   303
    8.4   Applications of Systems of Equations   311
    8.5   Systems of Linear Inequalities   323
        Summary   327
        Review Exercises   327
        Practice Test   329
        Cumulative Review Test   330

VII   From: *Business Mathematics: A Collegiate Approach*, Seventh Edition, by Nelda W. Roueche and Virginia H. Graves

Chapter 15   Simple Interest   331

    1   Basic Simple Interest   332
    2   Ordinary Time and Exact Time   337
    3   Ordinary Interest and Exact Interest   340
    4   Simple Interest Notes   344
    5   Present Value   351

VIII   From: *Business Mathematics: A Collegiate Approach*, Seventh Edition, by Nelda W. Roueche and Virginia H. Graves

Chapter 18   Compound Interest   361

    1   Compound Interest (by Computation)   362
    2   Compound Amount (Using Tables)   367
    3   Interest Compounded Daily   374
    4   Present Value (at Compound Interest)   381

IX   From: *Business Mathematics: A Collegiate Approach*, Seventh Edition, by Nelda W. Roueche and Virginia H. Graves

Chapter 19   Annuities   389

    1   Amount of an Annuity   391
    2   Present Value of an Annuity   393

X   From: *Business Mathematics: A Collegiate Approach*, Seventh Edition, by Nelda W. Roueche and Virginia H. Graves

Chapter 20   Sinking Funds and Amortization   401

    1   Sinking Funds and Bonds   402
    2   Amortization   409
    3   Review   419

XI   From: *Statistics for Business and Economics*, Sixth Edition, by James T. McClave and P. George Benson

Chapter 1   What Is Statistics?   425

    1.1   Statistics: What Is It?   426
    1.2   The Elements of Statistics   430
    1.3   Statistics: Witchcraft or Science?   433
    1.4   Processes (Optional)   435
    1.5   The Role of Statistics in Managerial Decision-Making   439

XII   From: *Statistics for Business and Economics*, Sixth Edition, by James T. McClave and P. George Benson

Chapter 2   Methods for Describing Sets of Data   445

    2.1   Types of Data   446
    2.2   Graphical Methods for Describing Quantitative Data: Histograms and Stem-and-Leaf Displays   452
    2.3   Graphical Methods for Describing Quantitative Data Produced Over Time: The Time Series Plot (Optional)   471
    2.4   Numerical Methods for Measuring Variability   479
    2.5   Numerical Methods for Measuring Variability   487

2.6   Interpreting the Standard Deviation   499

2.7   Calculating a Mean and Standard Deviation from Grouped Data (Optional)   508

2.8   Measures of Relative Standing   509

2.9   Box Plots: Graphical Descriptions Based on Quartiles (Optional)   517

2.10   Distorting the Truth with Descriptive Techniques   527

XIII   From: *Statistics for Business and Economics*, Sixth Edition, by James T. McClave and P. George Benson

Chapter Three   Probability   551

3.1   Events, Sample Spaces, and Probability   552

3.2   Unions and Intersections   566

3.3   The Additive Rule and Mutually Exclusive Events   569

3.4   Complimentary Events   571

3.5   Conditional Probability   578

3.6   The Multiplicative Rule and Independent Events   583

3.7   Random Sampling   591

XIV   From: *Elementary Algebra for College Students*, Fourth Edition, by Allen R. Angel

Appendices   605

A   Review of Decimals and Percent   605

B   Finding the Greatest Common Factor and Least Common Denominator   608

XV   From: *Business Mathematics: A Collegiate Approach*, Seventh Edition, by Nelda W. Roueche and Virginia H. Graves

Tables   611

XVI   **Answers 667**

I   667

II   670

III   674

VII   677

VIII   686

III   691

XV   693

XVIII   695

XIX   697

XX   699

Answers to Selected Exercises

1,2   703

3,4   704

Chapter 1

Real Numbers

1.1 Study Skills for Success in Mathematics
1.2 Fractions
1.3 The Real Number System
1.4 Inequalities
1.5 Addition of Real Numbers
1.6 Subtraction of Real Numbers
1.7 Multiplication and Division of Real Numbers
1.8 An Introduction to Exponents
1.9 Use of Parentheses and Order of Operations
1.10 Properties of the Real Number System

SUMMARY
REVIEW EXERCISES
PRACTICE TEST

See Section 1.2, Exercise 73

Preview and Perspective

In this chapter we provide the building blocks for this course and all other mathematics courses you may take.

A review of addition, subtraction, multiplication, and division of numbers containing decimal points is provided in Appendix A. Percents are also discussed in Appendix A. You may wish to review this material now.

For many students, Section 1.1, Study Skills for Success in Mathematics, may be the most important one in this book. Read it carefully and follow the advice given. Following the study skills presented will greatly increase your chance of success in this course and in all other mathematics courses.

In Section 1.2 we discuss fractions, including reducing fractions; addition, subtraction, multiplication, and division of fractions; and mixed numbers. *It is essential that you understand fractions* because we will work with fractions throughout the course. Furthermore, we will soon be discussing algebraic fractions, which we call rational expressions, and the same rules and procedures that apply to arithmetic fractions apply to rational expressions.

In Section 1.3 we introduce the structure of the real number system. In Section 1.4 we introduce inequalities and discuss absolute value informally. Both of these topics are important, especially if you plan on taking another mathematics course. In Sections 1.5 through 1.7 we discuss the operations on the real numbers. *Addition, subtraction, multiplication, and division of real numbers must be clearly understood before you finish this chapter* because you will use real numbers in Chapter 2 and throughout the book.

Exponents are introduced in Section 1.8. We discuss exponents in more depth in Section 4.1. You must master the order of operations to follow when evaluating expressions and formulas. We explain how to do this in Section 1.9.

In Section 1.10, we discuss the properties of the real number system, which we shall use throughout the book.

1.1　Study Skills for Success in Mathematics

Tape 1

1 Recognize the goals of this text.
2 Learn proper study skills.
3 Prepare for and take exams.
4 Learn to manage time and seek help when needed.
5 Purchase a scientific calculator.

This section is extremely important. Take the time to read it carefully and follow the advice given. For many of you this section may be the most important section of the text.

Most of you taking this course fall into one of three categories: (1) those who did not take algebra in high school, (2) those who took algebra in high school but did not understand the material, or (3) those who took algebra in high school and were successful but have been out of school for some time and need a refresher course. Whichever the case, you will need to acquire study skills for mathematics courses.

Before we discuss study skills I will present the goals of this text. These goals may help you realize why certain topics are covered in the text and why they are covered as they are.

Goals of This Text   **1** The goals of this text include:

1. Presenting traditional algebra topics
2. Preparing you for more advanced mathematics courses
3. Building your confidence in, and your enjoyment of, mathematics
4. Improving your reasoning and critical thinking skills
5. Increasing your understanding of how important mathematics is in solving real-life problems
6. Encouraging you to think mathematically, so that you will feel comfortable translating real-life problems into mathematical equations, and then solving the problems.

It is important to realize that this course is the foundation for more advanced mathematics courses. A thorough understanding of algebra will make it easier for you to succeed in later mathematics courses.

2 Now we will consider study skills and other items of importance.

Have a Positive Attitude

You may be thinking to yourself, "I hate math," or "I wish I did not have to take this class." You may have heard of "math anxiety" and feel you fit this category. The first thing to do to be successful in this course is to change your attitude to a more positive one. You must be willing to give this course, and yourself, a fair chance.

Based on past experiences in mathematics, you may feel this is difficult. However, mathematics is something you need to work at. Many of you are more mature now than when you took previous mathematics courses. Your maturity and desire to learn are extremely important, and can make a tremendous difference in your ability to succeed in mathematics. I believe you can be successful in this course, but you also need to believe it.

Preparing for and Attending Class

To be prepared for class, you need to do your homework. If you have difficulty with the homework, or some of the concepts, write down questions to ask your instructor. If you were given a reading assignment, read the appropriate material carefully before class. If you were not given a reading assignment, spend a few minutes previewing any new material in the textbook before class. At this point you don't have to understand everything you read. Just get a feeling for the definitions and concepts that will be discussed. This quick preview will help you understand what your instructor is explaining during class.

After the material is explained in class, read the corresponding sections of the text slowly and carefully, word by word.

You should plan to attend every class. Most instructors agree that there is an inverse relationship between absences and grades. That is, the more absences you have, the lower your grade will be. Every time you miss a class, you miss important information. If you must miss a class, contact your instructor ahead of time, and get the reading assignment and homework. If possible, before the next class try to borrow and copy a friend's notes to help you understand the material you missed.

To be successful in this course, you must thoroughly understand the material in this chapter, especially fractions and adding and subtracting real numbers. If you are having difficulty after covering these topics, see your instructor for help.

In algebra and other mathematics courses, the material you learn is cumulative. That is, the new material is built on material that was presented previously. You must understand each section before moving on to the next section, and each chapter before moving on to the next chapter. Therefore, do not let yourself fall behind. Seek help as soon as you need it—do not wait! Make sure that you do all your homework assignments completely and study the text carefully. You will greatly increase your chance of success in this course by following the study skills presented in the next section.

While in class, pay attention to what your instructor is saying. If you don't understand something, ask your instructor to repeat the material. If you have read the assigned material before class and have questions that have not been answered, ask your instructor. If you don't ask questions, your instructor will not know that you have a problem understanding the material.

In class, take careful notes. Write numbers and letters clearly, so that you can read them later. It is not necessary to write down every word your instructor says. Copy the major points and the examples that do not appear in the text. You should not be taking notes so frantically that you lose track of what your instructor is saying. It is a mistake to believe that you can copy material in class without understanding it, and then figure it out later.

Reading the Text

A mathematics text is not a novel. Mathematics textbooks should be read slowly and carefully, word by word. If you don't understand what you are reading, reread the material. When you come across a new concept or definition, you may wish to underline it, so that it stands out. Then it will be easier to find later. When you come across an example, read and follow it line by line. Don't just skim it. Then work out the example on another sheet of paper. Make notes of anything you don't understand to ask your instructor.

This textbook has special features to help you. I suggest that you pay particular attention to these highlighted features, including the Common Student Error boxes, the Helpful Hint boxes, and important procedures and definitions identified by color. The **Common Student Error** boxes point out the most common errors made by students. Read and study this material very carefully and make sure that you understand what is explained. If you avoid making these common errors, your chances of success in this and other mathematics classes will be increased greatly. The **Helpful Hints** offer many valuable techniques for working certain problems. They may also present some very useful information or show an alternative way to work a problem.

Doing Homework

Two very important commitments that you must make to be successful in this course are attending class and doing your homework regularly. Your assignments must be worked conscientiously and completely. Do your homework as soon as possible, so the material presented in class will be fresh in your mind. Research has shown that for mathematics courses, studying and doing homework shortly after learning the material improves retention and performance. Mathematics cannot be learned by observation. You need to practice what you have heard in class. It is through doing homework that you truly learn the material. While working homework you will become aware of the types of problems that you need further help with. If you do not work the assigned exercises, you will not know what questions to ask in class.

When you do your homework, make sure that you write it neatly and carefully. List the exercise number next to each problem and work each problem in a step-by-step manner. Then you can refer to it later and understand what is written. Pay particular attention to copying signs and exponents correctly.

Don't forget to check the answers to your homework assignments. This book contains the answers to the odd-numbered exercises in the back of the book. In addition, the answers to all the cumulative review and end-of-chapter review exercises, practice tests, and cumulative review tests are in the back of the book. Answers to selected Group Activity/Challenge Problems are also provided.

Ask questions in class about homework problems you don't understand. You should not feel comfortable until you understand all the concepts needed to work every assigned problem successfully.

Studying for Class

Study in the proper atmosphere, in an area where you will not be constantly disturbed, so that your attention can be devoted to what you are reading. The area where you study should be well ventilated and well lit. You should have sufficient desk space to spread out all your materials. Your chair should be comfortable. There should be no loud music to distract you from studying.

Before you begin studying, make sure that you have all the materials you need (pencils, markers, calculator, etc.). You may wish to highlight the important points covered in class or in the book.

It is recommended that students study and do homework for at least two hours for each hour of class time. Some students require more time than others. It is important to spread your studying time out over the entire week rather than studying during one large block of time.

When studying, you should not only understand how to work a problem, but also know *why* you follow the specific steps you do to work the problem. If you do not have an understanding of why you follow the specific process, you will not be able to transfer the process to solve similar problems.

This book has **Cumulative Review Exercises** at the end of every section after this section. Even if these exercises are not assigned for homework, I urge you to work them as part of your studying process. These exercises reinforce material presented earlier in the course, and you will be less likely to forget the material if you review it repeatedly throughout the course. They will also help prepare you for the final exam. If you forget how to work one of the Cumulative Review Exercises, turn to the section indicated in blue next to the problem and review that section. Then try the problem again.

Preparing for an Exam

3 If you study a little bit each day you should not need to cram the night before an exam. Begin your studying early. If you wait until the last minute, you may not have time to seek the help you may need if you find you cannot work a problem.

To review for an exam:

1. Read your class notes.
2. Review your homework assignments.
3. Study formulas, definitions, and procedures given in the text.
4. Read the Common Student Error boxes and Helpful Hint boxes carefully.

5. Read the summary at the end of each chapter.

6. Work the review exercises at the end of each chapter. If you have difficulties, restudy those sections. If you still have trouble, seek help.

7. Work the chapter practice test.

Midterm and Final Exams

When studying for a comprehensive midterm or final exam follow the procedures discussed for preparing for an exam. However, also:

1. Study all your previous tests carefully. Make sure that you have learned to work the problems you may have previously missed.

2. Work the cumulative review tests at the end of each even-numbered chapter. These tests cover the material from the beginning of the book to the end of that chapter.

3. If your instructor has given you a worksheet or practice exam, make sure that you complete it. Ask questions on any problems you do not understand.

4. Begin your studying process early so that you can seek all the help you need in a timely manner.

Taking an Exam

Make sure you get sufficient sleep the night before the test. If you studied properly, you should not have to stay up late preparing for a test. Arrive at the exam site early so that you have a few minutes to relax before the exam. If you rush into the exam, you will start out nervous and anxious. After you are given the exam, you should do the following:

1. Carefully write down any formulas or ideas that you need to remember.

2. Look over the entire exam quickly to get an idea of its length. Also make sure that no pages are missing.

3. Read the test directions carefully.

4. Read each question carefully. Answer each question completely, and make sure that you have answered the specific question asked.

5. Work the questions you understand best first; then go back and work those you are not sure of. Do not spend too much time on any one problem or you may not be able to complete the exam. Be prepared to spend more time on problems worth more points.

6. Attempt each problem. You may get at least partial credit even if you do not obtain the correct answer. If you make no attempt at answering the question, you will lose full credit.

7. Work carefully in a step-by-step manner. Copy all signs and exponents correctly when working from step to step, and make sure to copy the original question from the test correctly.

8. Write clearly so that your instructor can read your work. If your instructor cannot read your work, you may lose credit. Also, if your writing is not clear, it is easy to make a mistake when working from one step to the next. When appropriate, make sure that your final answer stands out by placing a box around it.

9. If you have time, check your work and your answers.

10. Do not be concerned if others finish the test before you or if you are the last to finish. Use all your extra time to check your work.

Stay calm when taking your test. Do not get upset if you come across a problem you can't figure out right away. Go on to something else and come back to that problem later.

Time Management   ▐4▌ As mentioned earlier, it is recommended that students study and do homework for at least two hours for each hour of class time. Finding the necessary time to study is not always easy. Below are some suggestions that you may find helpful.

1. Plan ahead. Determine when you will study and do your homework. Do not schedule other activities for these periods. Try to space these periods evenly over the week.

2. Be organized, so that you will not have to waste time looking for your books, your pen, your calculator, or your notes.

3. If you are allowed to use a calculator, use it for tedious calculations.

4. When you stop studying, clearly mark where you stopped in the text.

5. Try not to take on added responsibilities. You must set your priorities. If your education is a top priority, as it should be, you may have to reduce time spent on other activities.

6. If time is a problem, do not overburden yourself with too many courses. Consider taking fewer credits. If you do not have sufficient time to study, your understanding and all your grades may suffer.

Using Supplements   This text comes with a large variety of supplements. Find out from your instructor early in the semester which supplements are available and might be beneficial for you to use. Supplements should not replace reading the text, but should be used to enhance your understanding of the material.

Seeking Help   Be sure to get help as soon as you need it! Do not wait! In mathematics, one day's material is often based on the previous day's material. So, if you don't understand the material today, you will not be able to understand the material tomorrow.

Where should you seek help? There are often a number of resources on campus. Try to make a friend in the class with whom you can study. Often, you can help one another. You may wish to form a study group with other students in your class. Discussing the concepts and homework with your peers will reinforce your own understanding of the material.

You should know your instructor's office hours, and you should not hesitate to seek help from your instructor when you need it. Make sure that you have read the assigned material and attempted the homework before meeting with your instructor. Come prepared with specific questions to ask.

There are often other sources of help available. Many colleges have a mathematics lab or a mathematics learning center, where tutors are available. Ask your instructor early in the semester where and when tutoring is available. Arrange for a tutor as soon as you need one.

The Calculator **5** I strongly urge you to purchase a scientific calculator as soon as possible. One can be purchased for under $15 and can be used in many courses. Ask your instructor if you may use a calculator in class, on homework, and on tests. If so, you should use your calculator whenever possible to save time. Also ask your instructor if he or she recommends a particular calculator for this or a future mathematics class.

If a calculator contains a $\boxed{\text{LOG}}$ key or $\boxed{\text{SIN}}$ key, it is a scientific calculator. You *cannot* use the square root key $\boxed{\sqrt{x}}$ to identify scientific calculators since both scientific calculators and nonscientific calculators may have this key. You should pay particular attention to the **Calculator Corners** in this book. The Calculator Corners explain how to use your calculator to solve problems.

A Final Word You can be successful at mathematics if you attend class regularly, pay attention in class, study your text carefully, do your homework daily, review regularly, and seek help as soon as you need it. Good luck in your course.

Exercise Set 1.1

Do you know:

1. Your professor's name and office hours?
2. Your professor's office location and telephone number?
3. Where and when you can obtain help if your professor is not available?
4. The name and phone number of a friend in your class?
5. What supplements are available to assist you in learning?
6. If your instructor is recommending the use of a particular calculator?
7. When you can use your calculator in this course?

If you do not know the answer to any of the questions just asked, you should find out as soon as possible.

8. What are your reasons for taking this course?
9. What are your goals for this course?
10. Are you beginning this course with a positive attitude? It is important that you do!
11. List the things you need to do to prepare properly for class.

12. Explain how a mathematics text should be read.
13. For each hour of class time, how many hours outside of class are recommended for studying and doing homework?
14. When studying, you should not only understand how to work a problem, but also why you follow the specific steps you do. Why is this important?
15. Two very important commitments that you must make to be successful in this course are (a) doing homework regularly and completely and (b) attending class regularly. Explain why these commitments are necessary.
16. Write a summary of the steps you should follow when taking an exam.
17. Have you given any thought to studying with a friend or a group of friends? Can you see any advantages in doing so? Can you see any disadvantages in doing so?

1.2   Fractions

Tape 1

1. Learn multiplication symbols.
2. Recognize factors.
3. Reduce fractions to lowest terms.
4. Multiply fractions.
5. Divide fractions.
6. Add and subtract fractions.
7. Convert mixed numbers to fractions.

Students taking algebra for the first time often ask, "What is the difference between arithmetic and algebra?" When doing arithmetic, all the quantities used in the calculations are known. In algebra, however, one or more of the quantities are unknown and must be found.

EXAMPLE 1   A recipe calls for 3 cups of flour. Mrs. Clark has 2 cups of flour. How many additional cups does she need?

Solution: The answer is 1 cup.

Although very elementary, this is an example of an algebraic problem. The unknown quantity is the number of additional cups of flour needed.

An understanding of decimal numbers (see Appendix A) and fractions is essential to success in algebra. You will need to know how to reduce a fraction to its lowest terms and how to add, subtract, multiply, and divide fractions. We will review these topics in this section. We will also explain the meaning of factors.

Multiplication Symbols

1. In algebra we often use letters called **variables** to represent numbers. Letters commonly used as variables are **x, y,** and **z.** So that we do not confuse the variable x with the times sign, we use different notation to indicate multiplication.

Multiplication Symbols

If a and b stand for (or represent) any two mathematical quantities, then each of the following may be used to indicate the product of a and b ("a times b").

$$ab \qquad a \cdot b \qquad a(b) \qquad (a)b \qquad (a)(b)$$

Examples

3 times 4 may be written:	3 times x may be written:	x times y may be written:
	$3x$	xy
3(4)	3(x)	$x(y)$
(3)4	(3)x	(x)y
(3)(4)	(3)(x)	(x)(y)
3 · 4	3 · x	$x \cdot y$

A word commonly used in algebra is "expression." An **expression** is a general term for any collection of numbers, variables, grouping symbols, such as parentheses ( ) or brackets [ ], and *operations,* such as addition, subtraction, multiplication, and division. Some examples of expressions are $5 - 2$, $x + 7$, $2x - 3y$, and $2(x + 3)$. We will discuss expressions further in Chapter 2.

Factors

2 The numbers or variables multiplied in a multiplication problem are called factors.

> If $a \cdot b = c$, then a and b are **factors** of c.

For example, in $3 \cdot 5 = 15$, the numbers 3 and 5 are factors of the product 15. In $2 \cdot 15 = 30$, the numbers 2 and 15 are factors of the product 30. Note that 30 has many other factors. Since $5 \cdot 6 = 30$, the numbers 5 and 6 are also factors of 30. Since $3x$ means 3 times x, both the 3 and the x are factors of $3x$.

Reduce Fractions

3 Now we have the necessary information to discuss fractions. The top number of a fraction is called the **numerator,** and the bottom number is called the **denominator.** In the fraction $\frac{3}{5}$, the 3 is the numerator and the 5 is the denominator.

A fraction is **reduced to its lowest terms** when the numerator and denominator have no common factors other than 1. To reduce a fraction to its lowest terms, follow these steps.

> **To Reduce a Fraction to Its Lowest Terms**
>
> 1. Find the largest number that will divide into (without remainder) both the numerator and the denominator. This number is called the **greatest common factor** (GCF).
> 2. Then divide both the numerator and the denominator by the greatest common factor.

If you do not remember how to find the greatest common factor of two or more numbers, read Appendix B.

EXAMPLE 2 Reduce $\dfrac{10}{25}$ to its lowest terms.

Solution: The largest number that divides both 10 and 25 is 5. Therefore, 5 is the greatest common factor. Divide both the numerator and the denominator by 5 to reduce the fraction to its lowest terms.

$$\frac{10}{25} = \frac{10 \div 5}{25 \div 5} = \frac{2}{5}$$

EXAMPLE 3   Reduce $\dfrac{6}{18}$ to its lowest terms.

Solution: Both 6 and 18 can be divided by 1, 2, 3, and 6. The largest of these numbers, 6, is the greatest common factor. Divide both the numerator and the denominator by 6.

$$\frac{6}{18} = \frac{6 \div 6}{18 \div 6} = \frac{1}{3}$$

Note in Example 3 that both the numerator and denominator could have been written with a factor of 6. Then the common factor 6 could be divided out.

$$\frac{6}{18} = \frac{1 \cdot \cancel{6}}{3 \cdot \cancel{6}} = \frac{1}{3}$$

When you work with fractions you should give your answers in lowest terms.

Multiplication of Fractions

4 To multiply two or more fractions, multiply their numerators together and then multiply their denominators together.

> ### Multiplication of Fractions
>
> $$\frac{a}{b} \cdot \frac{c}{d} = \frac{ac}{bd}$$

EXAMPLE 4   Multiply $\dfrac{6}{13}$ by $\dfrac{5}{12}$.

Solution: $\dfrac{6}{13} \cdot \dfrac{5}{12} = \dfrac{6 \cdot 5}{13 \cdot 12} = \dfrac{30}{156} = \dfrac{5}{26}$

In Example 4, reducing $\frac{30}{156}$ to its lowest terms, $\frac{5}{26}$, is for many students more difficult than the multiplication itself. Before multiplying fractions, to help avoid having to reduce an answer to its lowest terms, we often divide both a numerator and a denominator by a common factor. **This process can be used only when multiplying fractions; it cannot be used when adding or subtracting fractions.**

EXAMPLE 5   Divide a numerator and a denominator by a common factor and then multiply.

$$\frac{6}{13} \cdot \frac{5}{12}$$

Solution: Since the numerator 6 and the denominator 12 can both be divided by the common factor 6, we divide out the 6 first.

$$\frac{6}{13} \cdot \frac{5}{12} = \frac{\overset{1}{\cancel{6}}}{13} \cdot \frac{5}{\underset{2}{\cancel{12}}} = \frac{1 \cdot 5}{13 \cdot 2} = \frac{5}{26}$$

Note that the answer obtained in Example 5 is identical to the answer obtained in Example 4.

EXAMPLE 6   Multiply $\dfrac{27}{40} \cdot \dfrac{16}{9}$.

Solution: $\dfrac{27}{40} \cdot \dfrac{16}{9} = \dfrac{\overset{3}{\cancel{27}}}{40} \cdot \dfrac{16}{\underset{1}{\cancel{9}}}$ **Divide both 27 and 9 by 9.**

$= \dfrac{\overset{3}{\cancel{27}}}{\underset{5}{\cancel{40}}} \cdot \dfrac{\overset{2}{\cancel{16}}}{\underset{1}{\cancel{9}}}$ **Divide both 40 and 16 by 8.**

$= \dfrac{3 \cdot 2}{5 \cdot 1} = \dfrac{6}{5}$

The numbers 0, 1, 2, 3, 4, . . . are called **whole numbers.** The three dots after the 4 indicate that the whole numbers continue indefinitely in the same manner. Thus the numbers 468 and 5043 are also whole numbers. Whole numbers will be discussed further in Section 1.3. To multiply a whole number by a fraction, write the whole number with a denominator of 1 and then multiply.

EXAMPLE 7   Multiply $5 \cdot \dfrac{2}{15}$.

Solution: $\dfrac{5}{1} \cdot \dfrac{2}{15} = \dfrac{\overset{1}{\cancel{5}}}{1} \cdot \dfrac{2}{\underset{3}{\cancel{15}}} = \dfrac{2}{3}$

Division of Fractions   ⑤ To divide one fraction by another, invert the divisor (the second fraction if written with ÷) and proceed as in multiplication.

> ### Division of Fractions
>
> $$\dfrac{a}{b} \div \dfrac{c}{d} = \dfrac{a}{b} \cdot \dfrac{d}{c} = \dfrac{ad}{bc}$$

EXAMPLE 8   Divide $\dfrac{3}{5} \div \dfrac{5}{6}$.

Solution: $\dfrac{3}{5} \div \dfrac{5}{6} = \dfrac{3}{5} \cdot \dfrac{6}{5} = \dfrac{3 \cdot 6}{5 \cdot 5} = \dfrac{18}{25}$

Sometimes, rather than being asked to obtain the answer to a problem by adding, subtracting, multiplying, or dividing, you may be asked to evaluate an expression. To **evaluate** an expression means to obtain the answer to the problem using the operations given.

EXAMPLE 9 Evaluate $\dfrac{4}{7} \div \dfrac{5}{12}$.

Solution: $\dfrac{4}{7} \div \dfrac{5}{12} = \dfrac{4}{7} \cdot \dfrac{12}{5} = \dfrac{48}{35}$

EXAMPLE 10 Evaluate $\dfrac{3}{8} \div 9$.

Solution: Write 9 as $\dfrac{9}{1}$.

$$\frac{3}{8} \div 9 = \frac{3}{8} \div \frac{9}{1} = \frac{3}{8} \cdot \frac{1}{\underset{3}{\cancel{9}}} = \frac{1}{24}$$

Addition and Subtraction of Fractions

6 *Only fractions that have the same* (or a common) *denominator can be added or subtracted.* To add (or subtract) fractions with the same denominator, add (or subtract) the numerators and keep the common denominator.

> **Addition and Subtraction of Fractions**
>
> $$\frac{a}{c} + \frac{b}{c} = \frac{a+b}{c} \quad \text{or} \quad \frac{a}{c} - \frac{b}{c} = \frac{a-b}{c}$$

EXAMPLE 11 Evaluate $\dfrac{9}{15} + \dfrac{2}{15}$.

Solution: $\dfrac{9}{15} + \dfrac{2}{15} = \dfrac{9+2}{15} = \dfrac{11}{15}$

EXAMPLE 12 Evaluate $\dfrac{8}{13} - \dfrac{5}{13}$.

Solution: $\dfrac{8}{13} - \dfrac{5}{13} = \dfrac{8-5}{13} = \dfrac{3}{13}$

To add (or subtract) fractions with unlike denominators, we must first rewrite each fraction with the same, or a common, denominator. The smallest number that is divisible by two or more denominators is called the **least common denominator.** *If you have forgotten how to find the least common denominator, or LCD, review Appendix B now.*

EXAMPLE 13   Add $\dfrac{1}{2} + \dfrac{1}{5}$.

Solution: We cannot add these fractions until we rewrite them with a common denominator. Since the lowest number that both 2 and 5 divide into (without remainder) is 10, we will first rewrite both fractions with the least common denominator of 10.

$$\frac{1}{2} = \frac{1}{2} \cdot \frac{5}{5} = \frac{5}{10} \quad \text{and} \quad \frac{1}{5} = \frac{1}{5} \cdot \frac{2}{2} = \frac{2}{10}$$

Now add.

$$\frac{1}{2} + \frac{1}{5} = \frac{5}{10} + \frac{2}{10} = \frac{7}{10}$$

Note that multiplying both the numerator and denominator by the same number is the same as multiplying by 1. Thus the value of the fraction does not change.

EXAMPLE 14   Subtract $\dfrac{3}{4} - \dfrac{2}{3}$.

Solution: The least common denominator is 12. Therefore, we rewrite both fractions with a denominator of 12.

$$\frac{3}{4} = \frac{3}{4} \cdot \frac{3}{3} = \frac{9}{12} \quad \text{and} \quad \frac{2}{3} = \frac{2}{3} \cdot \frac{4}{4} = \frac{8}{12}$$

Now subtract.

$$\frac{3}{4} - \frac{2}{3} = \frac{9}{12} - \frac{8}{12} = \frac{1}{12}$$

COMMON STUDENT ERROR   It is important that you realize that dividing out a common factor in the numerator of one fraction and the denominator of a different fraction can be performed only when multiplying fractions. **This process cannot be performed when adding or subtracting fractions.**

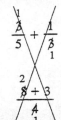

Correct	*Incorrect*
Multiplication problems	Addition problems

Mixed Numbers   **7** Consider the number $5\frac{2}{3}$. This is an example of a **mixed number.** A mixed number consists of a whole number followed by a fraction. The mixed number $5\frac{2}{3}$ means $5 + \frac{2}{3}$. The mixed number $5\frac{2}{3}$ may be changed to a fraction as follows:

$$5\frac{2}{3} = 5 + \frac{2}{3} = \frac{15}{3} + \frac{2}{3} = \frac{17}{3}$$

Any fraction whose numerator is greater than its denominator* may be changed to a mixed number. For example, $\frac{17}{3}$ may be changed to

$$\frac{17}{3} = \frac{15}{3} + \frac{2}{3} = 5 + \frac{2}{3} = 5\frac{2}{3}$$

The procedure used to change from a mixed number to a fraction can be simplified as follows.

> ### To Change a Mixed Number to a Fraction
>
> 1. Multiply the denominator of the fraction in the mixed number by the whole number preceding it.
> 2. Add the numerator of the fraction in the mixed number to the product obtained in step 1. This sum represents the numerator of the fraction we are seeking. The denominator of the fraction we are seeking is the same as the denominator of the fraction in the mixed number.

EXAMPLE 15   Change the mixed number $5\dfrac{2}{3}$ to a fraction.

Solution: Multiply the denominator, 3, by the whole number, 5, to get a product of 15. To this product add the numerator, 2. This sum, 17, represents the numerator of the fraction. The denominator of the fraction we are seeking is the same as the denominator of the fraction in the mixed number, 3. Thus, $5\dfrac{2}{3} = \dfrac{17}{3}$.

$$5\frac{2}{3} = \frac{15 + 2}{3} = \frac{17}{3}$$

EXAMPLE 16   Change $6\dfrac{5}{9}$ to a fraction.

Solution: Multiply 9 by 6 to get 54; then add 5 to get 59. This is the numerator of the fraction we are seeking.

$$6\frac{5}{9} = \frac{54 + 5}{9} = \frac{59}{9}$$

*A fraction such as $\frac{17}{3}$, whose numerator is greater than its denominator, is sometimes referred to as an *improper fraction.* However, this is misleading because there is nothing "improper" about such fractions. In fact, such fractions are used in all mathematics, and they are generally preferred to mixed numbers.

> **To Change a Fraction Greater Than 1 to a Mixed Number**
>
> 1. Divide the numerator by the denominator. Note the quotient and remainder.
> 2. Write the mixed number. The quotient found in step 1 is the whole number part of the mixed number. The remainder is the numerator of the fraction in the mixed number. The denominator in the fraction of the mixed number will be the same as the denominator in the original fraction.

EXAMPLE 17   Change $\dfrac{17}{3}$ to a mixed number.

Solution:

$$
\begin{array}{r}
5 \quad \longleftarrow \text{ whole number}\\
\text{Denominator} \longrightarrow \; 3\overline{)17}\\
\underline{15}\\
2 \quad \longleftarrow \text{ remainder}
\end{array}
$$

$$
\frac{17}{3} = 5\frac{2}{3}
$$

$\longleftarrow$ remainder
$\longleftarrow$ denominator (or divisor)
whole number

Thus, $\dfrac{17}{3}$ changed to a mixed number is $5\dfrac{2}{3}$.

EXAMPLE 18   Change $\dfrac{21}{5}$ to a mixed number.

Solution:

$$
\begin{array}{r}
4\\
5\overline{)21}\\
\underline{20}\\
1
\end{array}
\qquad \text{therefore} \qquad \frac{21}{5} = 4\frac{1}{5}
$$

To add, subtract, multiply, or divide mixed numbers, we often change the mixed numbers to fractions.

EXAMPLE 19   Add $2\dfrac{1}{4} + \dfrac{1}{2}$.

Solution: Change $2\dfrac{1}{4}$ to $\dfrac{9}{4}$; then add.

$$
2\frac{1}{4} + \frac{1}{2} = \frac{9}{4} + \frac{1}{2}
$$

$$
= \frac{9}{4} + \frac{2}{4}
$$

$$
= \frac{11}{4} \text{ or } 2\frac{3}{4}
$$

EXAMPLE 20 Multiply $\left(3\frac{3}{4}\right)\left(4\frac{3}{5}\right)$.

Solution: Change both mixed numbers to fractions; then multiply.

$$\left(3\frac{3}{4}\right)\left(4\frac{3}{5}\right) = \frac{\overset{3}{\cancel{15}}}{4} \cdot \frac{23}{\underset{1}{\cancel{5}}} = \frac{69}{4} \quad \text{or} \quad 17\frac{1}{4}$$

EXAMPLE 21 Divide $\frac{4}{5} \div 2\frac{5}{8}$.

Solution: Change $2\frac{5}{8}$ to a fraction; then follow the procedure for dividing fractions.

$$\frac{4}{5} \div 2\frac{5}{8} = \frac{4}{5} \div \frac{21}{8}$$

$$= \frac{4}{5} \cdot \frac{8}{21} = \frac{32}{105}$$

Exercise Set 1.2

Reduce each fraction to its lowest terms. If a fraction is already in its lowest terms, so state.

1. $\dfrac{4}{16}$ **2.** $\dfrac{5}{20}$ **3.** $\dfrac{10}{15}$ **4.** $\dfrac{3}{8}$

5. $\dfrac{15}{30}$ **6.** $\dfrac{9}{30}$ **7.** $\dfrac{15}{35}$ **8.** $\dfrac{36}{72}$

9. $\dfrac{40}{64}$ **10.** $\dfrac{15}{120}$ **11.** $\dfrac{9}{14}$ **12.** $\dfrac{6}{42}$

13. $\dfrac{96}{72}$ **14.** $\dfrac{14}{28}$ **15.** $\dfrac{50}{35}$ **16.** $\dfrac{84}{28}$

Indicate any parts where a common factor can be divided out as a first step in solving the problem. Explain your answer.

17. (a) $\dfrac{3}{5} \cdot \dfrac{10}{11}$ **(b)** $\dfrac{3}{5} + \dfrac{10}{11}$ **(c)** $\dfrac{3}{5} - \dfrac{10}{11}$ **(d)** $\dfrac{3}{5} \div \dfrac{10}{11}$

18. (a) $\dfrac{4}{5} + \dfrac{1}{4}$ **(b)** $\dfrac{4}{5} - \dfrac{1}{4}$ **(c)** $\dfrac{4}{5} \cdot \dfrac{1}{4}$ **(d)** $\dfrac{4}{5} \div \dfrac{1}{4}$

19. (a) $6 + \dfrac{5}{12}$ **(b)** $6 \cdot \dfrac{5}{12}$ **(c)** $6 - \dfrac{5}{12}$ **(d)** $6 \div \dfrac{5}{12}$

20. (a) $4 + \dfrac{3}{4}$ **(b)** $4 - \dfrac{3}{4}$ **(c)** $4 \div \dfrac{3}{4}$ **(d)** $4 \cdot \dfrac{3}{4}$

Find the product or quotient. Write the answers in lowest terms.

21. $\dfrac{1}{2} \cdot \dfrac{3}{4}$ **22.** $\dfrac{3}{5} \cdot \dfrac{4}{7}$ **23.** $\dfrac{5}{4} \cdot \dfrac{2}{7}$ **24.** $\dfrac{5}{12} \cdot \dfrac{6}{5}$

25. $\dfrac{3}{8} \cdot \dfrac{2}{9}$ **26.** $\dfrac{15}{16} \cdot \dfrac{4}{3}$ **27.** $\dfrac{1}{4} \div \dfrac{1}{5}$ **28.** $\dfrac{2}{3} \cdot \dfrac{3}{5}$

29. $\dfrac{5}{12} \div \dfrac{4}{3}$ **30.** $\dfrac{2}{9} \div \dfrac{12}{5}$ **31.** $\dfrac{10}{3} \div \dfrac{5}{9}$ **32.** $\dfrac{12}{5} \div \dfrac{3}{7}$

33. $\dfrac{5}{12} \cdot \dfrac{16}{15}$ **34.** $\dfrac{3}{10} \cdot \dfrac{5}{12}$ **35.** $\dfrac{4}{15} \div \dfrac{13}{12}$ **36.** $\dfrac{15}{16} \div \dfrac{1}{2}$

37. $\dfrac{12}{7} \cdot \dfrac{19}{24}$ **38.** $\dfrac{28}{13} \cdot \dfrac{2}{7}$ **39.** $1\dfrac{4}{5} \cdot \dfrac{20}{3}$ **40.** $4\dfrac{4}{5} \div \dfrac{8}{15}$

41. $\left(\dfrac{3}{5}\right)\left(1\dfrac{2}{3}\right)$ **42.** $\left(\dfrac{5}{8}\right)\left(3\dfrac{1}{3}\right)$ **43.** $3\dfrac{2}{3} \div 1\dfrac{5}{6}$ **44.** $3\dfrac{1}{4} \div \dfrac{5}{6}$

Add or subtract. Write the answers in lowest terms.

45. $\dfrac{2}{7} + \dfrac{3}{7}$ **46.** $\dfrac{3}{10} + \dfrac{5}{10}$ **47.** $\dfrac{7}{12} - \dfrac{5}{12}$ **48.** $\dfrac{18}{36} - \dfrac{1}{36}$

49. $\dfrac{5}{14} + \dfrac{9}{14}$ **50.** $\dfrac{9}{10} - \dfrac{3}{10}$ **51.** $\dfrac{19}{26} - \dfrac{5}{26}$ **52.** $\dfrac{1}{3} + \dfrac{1}{5}$

53. $\dfrac{2}{5} + \dfrac{5}{6}$ **54.** $\dfrac{1}{9} - \dfrac{1}{18}$ **55.** $\dfrac{4}{12} - \dfrac{2}{15}$ **56.** $\dfrac{5}{6} - \dfrac{3}{7}$

57. $\dfrac{2}{10} + \dfrac{1}{15}$ **58.** $\dfrac{5}{8} - \dfrac{1}{6}$ **59.** $\dfrac{5}{8} - \dfrac{4}{7}$ **60.** $\dfrac{3}{8} + \dfrac{5}{12}$

61. $\dfrac{5}{6} + \dfrac{9}{24}$ **62.** $\dfrac{7}{15} - \dfrac{12}{30}$ **63.** $\dfrac{4}{7} - \dfrac{1}{4}$ **64.** $3\dfrac{1}{2} + \dfrac{1}{4}$

65. $4\dfrac{1}{4} + \dfrac{2}{5}$ **66.** $\dfrac{3}{10} + 2\dfrac{1}{3}$ **67.** $2\dfrac{1}{2} + 1\dfrac{1}{3}$ **68.** $\dfrac{4}{5} - \dfrac{2}{7}$

69. $4\dfrac{2}{3} - 1\dfrac{1}{5}$ **70.** $3\dfrac{1}{8} - \dfrac{3}{4} - \dfrac{1}{2}$ **71.** $1\dfrac{4}{5} - \dfrac{3}{4} + 3$ **72.** $2\dfrac{2}{3} + 1\dfrac{3}{5} - \dfrac{3}{12}$

In many problems you will need to subtract a fraction from 1, where 1 represents "the whole" or the "total amount." Exercises 73–76 are answered by subtracting the fraction given from 1.

73. On Earth, $\dfrac{1}{6}$ of all fresh water is in the Antarctic. How much of Earth's supply of fresh water is elsewhere?

74. The probability that an event does not occur may be found by subtracting the probability that the event does occur from 1. If the probability that global warming is occurring is $\dfrac{7}{9}$, find the probability that global warming is not occurring.

75. An article in your local newspaper states that the chance of a person in your tax bracket being audited by the Internal Revenue Service is $\dfrac{1}{12}$. What is the chance of a person in this tax bracket not being audited?

76. Of all oats grown in the United States, $\dfrac{19}{20}$ is fed to animals. How much of the total crop is not fed to animals?

Solve.

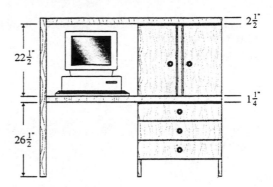

77. Paul, a drapemaker, wishes to make 3 identical pairs of drapes. If each pair needs $6\frac{3}{4}$ yards of material, how much material will Paul need?

78. A board is $22\frac{1}{2}$ feet long. What is the length of each piece when cut in five equal lengths? (Ignore the thickness of the cuts.)

79. A length of $3\frac{1}{16}$ inches is cut from a piece of wood $16\frac{3}{4}$ inches long. What is the length of the remaining piece of wood?

80. At the beginning of the day a stock was selling for $11\frac{7}{8}$ dollars. At the close of the session it was selling for $13\frac{3}{4}$ dollars. How much did the stock gain that day?

81. Ellen soldered two pieces of pipe measuring $3\frac{3}{8}$ feet and $5\frac{1}{16}$ feet. What is the total length of these two pieces of pipe?

82. A recipe calls for $2\frac{1}{2}$ cups of flour and another $1\frac{1}{3}$ cups of flour to be added later. How much flour does the recipe require?

83. At high tide the water level at a measuring stick is $20\frac{3}{4}$ feet. At low tide the water level dropped to $8\frac{7}{8}$ feet. How much did the water level fall?

84. The inseam on a new pair of pants is 30 inches. If Leland's inseam is $28\frac{3}{8}$ inches, how much will the cuffs need to be shortened?

85. The instructions on a turkey indicate that a 12- to 16-pound turkey should bake at 325°F for about 22 minutes per pound. Donna is planning to bake a $13\frac{1}{2}$ pound turkey. Approximately how long should the turkey be baked?

86. A recipe calls for $\frac{3}{4}$ teaspoon of teriyaki seasoning for each pound of beef. To cook $4\frac{1}{2}$ pounds of beef, how many teaspoons of teriyaki are needed?

87. Dawn cuts a piece of wood measuring $3\frac{1}{8}$ inches into two equal pieces. How long is each piece?

88. Tom wishes to subdivide a $4\frac{5}{8}$-acre lot into three equal-size lots. What will be the acreage of each lot?

89. A nurse must give $\frac{1}{16}$ milligram of a drug for each kilogram of patient weight. If Mr. Duncan weighs (or has a mass of) 80 kilograms, find the amount of the drug Mr. Duncan should be given.

90. Find the total height of the computer desk shown in the figure.

91. Marcinda is considering purchasing a mail order computer. The catalog describes the computer as $7\frac{1}{2}$ inches high and the monitor as $14\frac{3}{8}$ inches high.
Marcinda is hoping to place the monitor on top of the computer and to place the computer and monitor together in the opening where the computer is shown in the desk in Exercise 90.
(a) Will there be sufficient room to do this?
(b) If so, how much extra height will she have?

92. A mechanic wishes to use a bolt to fasten a piece of wood $4\frac{1}{2}$ inches thick with a metal tube $2\frac{1}{3}$ inches thick. If the thickness of the nut is $\frac{1}{8}$ inch, find the length of the shaft of the bolt so that the nut fits flush with the end of the bolt (see the figure).

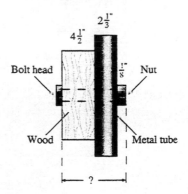

93. Find:

   (a) $\frac{5}{6} \cdot \frac{3}{8}$

   (b) $\frac{5}{6} \div \frac{3}{8}$

   (c) $\frac{5}{6} + \frac{3}{8}$

   (d) $\frac{5}{6} - \frac{3}{8}$

94. What are numbers or variables being multiplied called?

95. What is an expression?

96. In a fraction, what is the name of the **(a)** top number and **(b)** bottom number?

97. Consider parts (a) and (b) below.

(a) $\dfrac{\overset{1}{\cancel{3}}}{5} \cdot \dfrac{1}{\underset{2}{\cancel{6}}}$ (b) $\dfrac{\overset{1}{\cancel{3}}}{\underset{2}{\cancel{6}}}$

Which part shows reducing a fraction to its lowest terms? Explain.

98. Explain how to reduce a fraction to its lowest terms.

99. Explain how to multiply fractions.

100. Explain how to divide fractions.

101. Explain how to add or subtract fractions.

102. Explain how to convert a mixed number to a fraction.

103. Explain how to convert a fraction whose numerator is greater than its denominator into a mixed number.

Group Activity/ Challenge Problems

1. The directions below show how to make either two or four servings of Minute Rice.

(a) Write down three different methods that can be used to find the amount of each ingredient needed to make three servings of Minute Rice.

(b) Find the amount of each ingredient using each of the three methods.

(c) Do the answers from each of the three methods agree?

	AMOUNTS OF RICE AND WATER. USE EQUAL AMOUNTS RICE AND WATER. MINUTE RICE DOUBLES IN VOLUME.		
To Make	**Rice & Water (equal measures)**	**Salt**	**Butter or Margarine (if desired)**
2 servings	$\frac{2}{3}$ cup	$\frac{1}{4}$ tsp.	1 tsp.
4 servings	$1\frac{1}{3}$ cups	$\frac{1}{2}$ tsp.	2 tsp.

MINUTE® is a registered trademark of General Foods Corporation, White Plains, N.Y.

2. An allopurinal pill comes in 300-milligram doses. Dr. Duncan wants a patient to get 450 milligrams each day by cutting the pills in half and taking $\frac{1}{2}$ pill three times a day. If she wants to prescribe enough pills for a 6-month period (assume 30 days per month), how many pills should she prescribe?

Evaluate

3. $\dfrac{\frac{1}{2}+\frac{3}{4}}{\frac{3}{4}-\frac{1}{3}}$

4. $\dfrac{\frac{12}{5}-\frac{5}{4}}{\frac{5}{9}\div\frac{2}{3}}$

5. $\left(\dfrac{5}{12}+\dfrac{3}{5}\right)\div\left(\dfrac{5}{7}\cdot\dfrac{3}{10}\right)$

1.3   The Real Number System

1 Identify some important sets of numbers.
2 Know the structure of the real numbers.

Tape 1

We will be talking about and using various types of numbers throughout the text. This section introduces you to some of those numbers and to the structure of the real number system. This section is a quick overview. Some of the sets of numbers we mention in this section, such as rational and irrational numbers, are discussed in greater depth later in the text.

Sets of Numbers

1 A **set** is a collection of **elements** listed within braces. The set {*a, b, c, d, e*} consists of five elements, namely *a, b, c, d,* and *e*. A set that contains no elements is called an **empty set** (or **null set**). The symbol { } or the symbol ϕ is used to represent the empty set.

There are many different sets of numbers. Two important sets are the natural numbers and the whole numbers. The whole numbers were introduced earlier.

Natural numbers: {1, 2, 3, 4, 5, . . .}

Whole numbers: {0, 1, 2, 3, 4, 5, . . .}

An aid in understanding sets of numbers is the real number line (Fig. 1.1).

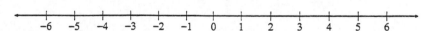

FIGURE 1.1

The real number line continues indefinitely in both directions. The numbers to the right of 0 are positive and those to the left of 0 are negative. Zero is neither positive nor negative (Fig. 1.2).

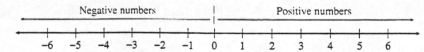

FIGURE 1.2

Figure 1.3 illustrates the natural numbers marked on the number line. The natural numbers are also called the **positive integers** or the **counting numbers.**

FIGURE 1.3

Another important set of numbers is the integers.

Integers: {. . . , −5, −4, −3, −2, −1, 0, 1, 2, 3, 4, 5, . . .}

negative integers   positive integers

The integers consist of the negative integers, 0, and the positive integers. The integers are marked on the number line in Figure 1.4.

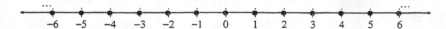

FIGURE 1.4

Can you think of any numbers that are not integers? You probably thought of "fractions" or "decimal numbers." Fractions and decimal numbers belong to the set of rational numbers. The set of **rational numbers** consists of all the numbers that can be expressed as a quotient of two integers, with the denominator not 0.

> **Rational numbers:**   {quotient of two integers, denominator not 0}

The fraction $\frac{1}{2}$ is a quotient of two integers with the denominator not 0. Thus, $\frac{1}{2}$ is a rational number. The decimal number 0.4 can be written $\frac{4}{10}$ and is therefore a rational number. All integers are also rational numbers since they can be written with a denominator of 1: for example, $3 = \frac{3}{1}$, $-12 = \frac{-12}{1}$, and $0 = \frac{0}{1}$. Some rational numbers are illustrated on the number line in Figure 1.5.

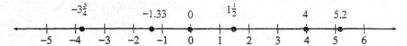

FIGURE 1.5

Most of the numbers that we use are rational numbers; however, some numbers are not rational. Numbers such as the square root of 2, written $\sqrt{2}$, are not rational numbers. Any number that can be represented on the number line that is not a rational number is called an **irrational number.** The $\sqrt{2}$ is *approximately* 1.41. Some irrational numbers are illustrated on the number line in Figure 1.6. Rational and irrational numbers will be discussed further in later chapters.

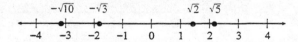

FIGURE 1.6

Structure of the Real Numbers

❷ Notice that many different types of numbers can be illustrated on the number line. Any number that can be represented on the number line is a **real number.**

Real numbers: {all numbers that can be represented on the real number line}

The symbol $\mathbb{R}$ is used to represent the set of real numbers. All the numbers mentioned thus far are real numbers. The natural numbers, the whole numbers, the integers, the rational numbers, and the irrational numbers are all real numbers. There are some types of numbers that are not real numbers, but these numbers are beyond the scope of this book. Figure 1.7 illustrates the relationship between the various sets of numbers within the set of real numbers.

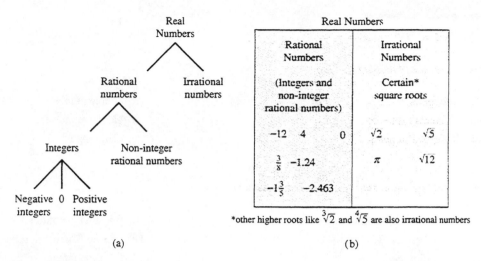

FIGURE 1.7

In Figure 1.7(a), we can see that when we combine the rational numbers and the irrational numbers we get the real numbers. When we combine the integers with the non-integer rational numbers (such as $\frac{1}{2}$ and 0.42), we get the rational numbers. When we combine the positive integers (or natural numbers), 0, and the negative integers, we get the integers.

Consider the positive integer 5. If we follow the positive integer branch in Figure 1.7(a) upward, we see that the number 5 is also an integer, a rational number, and a real number. Now consider the number $\frac{1}{2}$. It belongs to the non-integer rational numbers. If we follow this branch upward, we can see that $\frac{1}{2}$ is also a rational number and a real number.

EXAMPLE 1 Consider the following set of numbers:

$$\left\{ -6, -0.5, 4\frac{1}{2}, -96, \sqrt{3}, 0, 9, -\frac{4}{7}, -2.9, \sqrt{7}, -\sqrt{5} \right\}$$

List the elements of the set that are:
(a) Natural numbers.   **(b)** Whole numbers.
(c) Integers.   **(d)** Rational numbers.
(e) Irrational numbers.   **(f)** Real numbers.

Solution: **(a)** 9   **(b)** 0, 9   **(c)** $-6, -96, 0, 9$

   (d) $-6, -0.5, 4\frac{1}{2}, -96, 0, 9, -\frac{4}{7}, -2.9$

   (e) $\sqrt{3}, \sqrt{7}, -\sqrt{5}$

   (f) $-6, -0.5, 4\frac{1}{2}, -96, \sqrt{3}, 0, 9, -\frac{4}{7}, -2.9, \sqrt{7}, -\sqrt{5}$

Exercise Set 1.3

List each set of numbers.

1. Integers.

3. Natural numbers.

5. Positive integers.

2. Whole numbers.

4. Negative integers.

6. Counting numbers.

In Exercises 7–38, state whether each statement is true or false.

7. -1 is a negative integer.

9. 0 is an integer.

11. $\frac{1}{2}$ is an integer.

13. $\sqrt{2}$ is a rational number.

15. $-\frac{3}{5}$ is a rational number.

17. $-4\frac{1}{3}$ is a rational number.

19. $-\frac{5}{3}$ is an irrational number.

21. 0 is a positive number.

22. When zero is added to the set of counting numbers, the set of whole numbers is formed.

23. The natural numbers, counting numbers, and positive integers are different names for the same set of numbers.

24. When the negative integers, the positive integers, and 0 are combined, the integers are formed.

25. Any number to the left of zero on the number line is a negative number.

26. Every negative integer is a real number.

27. Every integer is a rational number.

28. Every rational number is a real number.

29. Every real number is a rational number.

30. Every negative number is a negative integer.

31. Some real numbers are not rational numbers.

32. Some rational numbers are not real numbers.

33. The symbol $\mathbb{R}$ is used to represent the set of real numbers.

34. Every integer is positive.

35. The symbol ϕ is used to represent the empty set.

36. All real numbers can be represented on the number line.

37. Every number greater than zero is a positive integer.

38. Irrational numbers cannot be represented on the number line.

8. 0 is a whole number.

10. -1.36 is a real number.

12. 0.5 is an integer.

14. $\sqrt{7}$ is a real number.

16. 0 is a rational number.

18. -5 is both a rational number and a real number.

20. $2\frac{5}{8}$ is an irrational number.

39. Consider the set of numbers.

$$\left\{ -6, 7, 12.4, -\frac{9}{5}, -2\frac{1}{4}, \sqrt{3}, 0, 9, \sqrt{7}, 0.35 \right\}$$

List those numbers that are:

(a) Positive integers.

(b) Whole numbers.

(c) Integers.

(d) Rational numbers.

(e) Irrational numbers.

(f) Real numbers.

40. Consider the set of numbers.

$$\left\{ -\frac{5}{3}, 0, -2, 5, 5\frac{1}{2}, \sqrt{2}, -\sqrt{3}, 1.63, 207 \right\}$$

List those numbers that are:

(a) Positive integers.

(b) Whole numbers.

(c) Integers.

(d) Rational numbers.

(e) Irrational numbers.

(f) Real numbers.

41. Consider the set of numbers

$$\left\{\frac{1}{2}, \sqrt{2}, -\sqrt{2}, 4\frac{1}{2}, \frac{5}{12}, -1.67, 5, -300, -9\frac{1}{2}\right\}$$

List those numbers that are:

(a) Positive integers.

(b) Whole numbers.

(c) Negative integers.

(d) Integers.

(e) Rational numbers.

(f) Irrational numbers.

(g) Real numbers.

In Exercises 42–53, give three examples of numbers that satisfy the conditions.

42. A real number but not an integer.

43. A rational number but not an integer.

44. An integer but not a negative integer.

45. A real number but not a rational number.

46. An irrational number and a positive number.

47. An integer and a rational number.

48. A negative integer and a real number.

49. A negative integer and a rational number.

50. A real number but not a positive rational number.

51. A rational number but not a negative number.

52. An integer but not a positive integer.

53. A real number but not an irrational number.

54. (a) What is a rational number?

(b) Explain why every integer is a rational number.

55. Write a paragraph or two describing the structure of the real number system. Explain how whole numbers, counting numbers, integers, rational numbers, irrational numbers, and real numbers are related.

CUMULATIVE REVIEW EXERCISES

[1. 2] **56.** Convert $4\frac{2}{3}$ to a fraction.

57. Write $\frac{16}{3}$ as a mixed number.

58. Add $\frac{3}{5} + \frac{5}{8}$.

59. Multiply $\left(\frac{5}{9}\right)\left(4\frac{2}{3}\right)$.

Group Activity/ Challenge Problems

1. (a) Does the set of natural numbers have a last number? If so, what is it?

(b) Do you know what a set that has no last number is called?

2. How many decimal numbers are there **(a)** between 1.0 and 2.0; **(b)** between 1.4 and 1.5? Explain your answer.

3. How many fractions are there **(a)** between 1 and 2; **(b)** between $\frac{1}{3}$ and $\frac{1}{5}$? Explain your answer.

*Set A **union** set B, symbolized A∪B, consists of the set of elements that belong to set A or set B (or both sets). Set A **intersection** set B, symbolized A∩B, consists of the set of elements common to both Set A and set B. For each of the given pair of sets find A∪B and A∩B.*

4. A = {2, 3, 4, 6, 8, 9}   B = {1, 2, 3, 5, 7, 8}

5. A = {a, b, c, d, g, i, j}   B = {b, c, d, h, m, p}

6. A = {red, blue, green, yellow}   B = {pink, orange, purple}

1.4   Inequalities

1 Determine which is the greater of two numbers.
2 Find the absolute value of a number

Comparing Numbers

1 The number line (Fig. 1.8) can be used to explain inequalities. When comparing two numbers, **the number to the right on the number line is the greater number, and the number to the left is the lesser number.** The symbol > is used to represent the words "is greater than." The symbol < is used to represent the words "is less than."

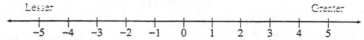

FIGURE 1.8

The statement that the number 3 is greater than the number 2 is written $3 > 2$. Notice that 3 is to the right of 2 on the number line. The statement that the number 0 is greater than the number -1 is written $0 > -1$. Notice that 0 is to the right of -1 on the number line.

Instead of stating that 3 is greater than 2, we could state that 2 is less than 3, written $2 < 3$. Notice that 2 is to the left of 3 on the number line. The statement that the number -1 is less than the number 0 is written $-1 < 0$. Notice that -1 is to the left of 0 on the number line.

EXAMPLE 1 Insert either > or < in the shaded area between the paired numbers to make a true statement.

(a) -4 -2 **(b)** $-\frac{3}{2}$ 2.5 **(c)** $\frac{1}{2}$ $\frac{1}{4}$ **(d)** -2 4

Solution: The points given are shown on the number line (Fig. 1.9).

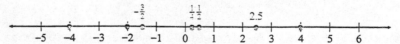

FIGURE 1.9

(a) $-4 < -2$; notice that -4 is to the left of -2.
(b) $-\frac{3}{2} < 2.5$; notice that $-\frac{3}{2}$ is to the left of 2.5.
(c) $\frac{1}{2} > \frac{1}{4}$; notice that $\frac{1}{2}$ is to the right of $\frac{1}{4}$.
(d) $-2 < 4$; notice that -2 is to the left of 4.

EXAMPLE 2 Insert either > or < in the shaded area between the paired numbers to make a true statement.

(a) -1 -2 **(b)** -1 0 **(c)** -2 2 **(d)** -4.09 -4.9

Solution: The numbers given are shown on the number line (Fig. 1.10).

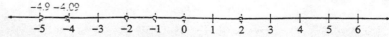

FIGURE 1.10

(a) $-1 > -2$; notice that -1 is to the right of -2.
(b) $-1 < 0$; notice that -1 is to the left of 0.
(c) $-2 < 2$; notice that -2 is to the left of 2.
(d) $-4.09 > -4.9$; notice that -4.09 is to the right of -4.9.

Absolute Value   2 The concept of absolute value can be explained with the help of the number line shown in Figure 1.11. The **absolute value** of a number can be considered the distance between the number and 0 on the number line. Thus, the absolute value of 3, written $|3|$, is 3 since it is 3 units from 0 on the number line. Similarly, the absolute value of -3, written $|-3|$, is also 3 since -3 is 3 units from 0.

$$|3| = 3 \quad \text{and} \quad |-3| = 3$$

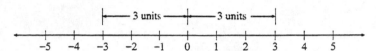

FIGURE 1.11

Since the absolute value of a number measures the distance (without regard to direction) of a number from 0 on the number line, **the absolute value of every number will be either positive or zero.**

Number	*Absolute Value of Number*
6	$\|6\| = 6$
-6	$\|-6\| = 6$
0	$\|0\| = 0$
$-\dfrac{1}{2}$	$\left\|-\dfrac{1}{2}\right\| = \dfrac{1}{2}$

The negative of the absolute value of a nonzero number will always be a negative number.

For example:

$$-|2| = -(2) = -2 \quad \text{and} \quad -|-3| = -(3) = -3$$

EXAMPLE 3 Insert either $>$, $<$, or $=$ in the shaded area to make a true statement.

(a) $|3| \quad 3$ (b) $|-2| \quad |2|$ (c) $-2 \quad |-4|$
(d) $|-5| \quad 0$ (e) $|12| \quad |-18|$

Solution: (a) $|3| = 3$.
(b) $|-2| = |2|$, since both $|-2|$ and $|2|$ equal 2.
(c) $-2 < |-4|$, since $|-4| = 4$.
(d) $|-5| > 0$, since $|-5| = 5$.
(e) $|12| < |-18|$, since $|12| = 12$ and $|-18| = 18$.

The concept of absolute value is very important in higher-level mathematics courses. If you take a course in intermediate algebra, you will learn a more formal definition of absolute value. We will use absolute value in Section 1.5 to add and subtract real numbers.

Exercise Set 1.4

Evaluate.

1. $|4|$ **2.** $|-3|$ **3.** $|-15|$ **4.** $|-12|$ **5.** $|0|$

6. $|54|$ **7.** $-|-8|$ **8.** $-|92|$ **9.** $-|65|$ **10.** $-|-34|$

Insert either $<$ or $>$ in the shaded area to make a true statement.

11. $2 \quad 3$

12. $4 \quad -2$

13. $-3 \quad 0$

14. $-6 \quad -4$

15. $\dfrac{1}{2} \quad -\dfrac{2}{3}$

16. $\dfrac{3}{5} \quad \dfrac{4}{5}$

17. $0.2 \quad 0.4$

18. $-0.2 \quad -0.4$

19. $-\dfrac{1}{2} \quad -1$

20. $0 \quad -0.9$

21. $4 \quad -4$

22. $-\dfrac{3}{4} \quad -1$

23. $-2.1 \quad -2$

24. $-1.83 \quad -1.82$

25. $\dfrac{5}{9} \quad -\dfrac{5}{9}$

26. $-9 \quad -12$

27. $-\dfrac{3}{2} \quad \dfrac{3}{2}$

28. $-4.09 \quad -5.3$

29. $0.49 \quad 0.43$

30. $-1.0 \quad -0.7$

31. $5 \quad -7$

32. $0.001 \quad 0.002$

33. $-0.006 \quad -0.007$

34. $\dfrac{1}{2} \quad -\dfrac{1}{2}$

35. $-5 \quad -2$

36. $\dfrac{5}{3} \quad \dfrac{3}{5}$

37. $-\dfrac{2}{3} \quad -3$

38. $\dfrac{5}{2} \quad \dfrac{7}{2}$

39. $-\dfrac{1}{2} \quad -\dfrac{3}{2}$

40. $-0.4 \quad -0.5$

Insert either $<$, $>$, or $=$ in the shaded area to make a true statement.

41. $8 \quad |-7|$

42. $|-8| \quad |-7|$

43. $|0| \quad \dfrac{2}{3}$

44. $|-4| \quad -3$

45. $|-3| \quad |-4|$

46. $|-1.9| \quad -1.8$

47. $4 \quad \left|-\dfrac{9}{2}\right|$

48. $-5 \quad |5|$

49. $\left|-\dfrac{6}{2}\right| \quad \left|-\dfrac{2}{6}\right|$

50. $\left|\dfrac{2}{5}\right| \quad |-0.40|$

Insert either >, <, *or* = *in the shaded area to make a true statement.*

51. $\frac{2}{3} + \frac{2}{3} + \frac{2}{3} + \frac{2}{3}$ $4 \cdot \frac{2}{3}$

52. $\frac{2}{3} \cdot \frac{2}{3}$ $\frac{2}{3} + \frac{2}{3}$

53. $\frac{1}{2} \cdot \frac{1}{2}$ $\frac{1}{2} \div \frac{1}{2}$

54. $5 \div \frac{2}{3}$ $\frac{2}{3} \div 5$

55. $\frac{5}{8} - \frac{1}{2}$ $\frac{5}{8} \div \frac{1}{2}$

56. $2\frac{1}{3} \cdot \frac{1}{2}$ $2\frac{1}{3} + \frac{1}{2}$

57. What numbers are 4 units from 0 on the number line?

58. What numbers are 5 units from 0 on the number line?

59. What numbers are 2 units from 0 on the number line?

60. Are there any real numbers whose absolute value is not a positive number? Explain your answer.

61. What is the absolute value of a number?

CUMULATIVE REVIEW EXERCISES

[1.2] **62.** Subtract $1\frac{2}{3} - \frac{3}{8}$.

63. List the set of whole numbers.

64. List the set of counting numbers.

[1.3] **65.** Consider the set of numbers

$$\{5, -2, 0, \tfrac{1}{3}, \sqrt{3}, -\tfrac{5}{9}, 2.3\}.$$

List the numbers in the set that are:

(a) Natural numbers.

(b) Whole numbers.

(c) Integers.

(d) Rational numbers.

(e) Irrational numbers.

(f) Real numbers.

Group Activity/ Challenge Problems

1. A number greater than 0 and less than 1 (or between 0 and 1) is multiplied by itself. Will the product be less than, equal to, or greater than the original number selected? Explain why this is always true.

2. A number between 0 and 1 is divided by itself. Will the quotient be less than, equal to, or greater than the original number selected? Explain why this is always true.

3. What two numbers can be substituted for x to make $|x| = 3$ a true statement?

4. Are there any values for x that would make $|x| = -|x|$ a true statement?

5. (a) To what is $|x|$ equal if x represents a real number greater than or equal to 0? **(b)** To what is $|x|$ equal if x represents a real number less than 0? **(c)** Fill in the shaded areas to make a true statement.

$$\text{(c) } |x| = \begin{cases} \underline{}, & x \geq 0 \\ \underline{}, & x < 0 \end{cases}$$

1.5 Addition of Real Numbers

Tape 1

1 Add real numbers using the number line.
2 Identify opposites or additive inverses.
3 Add using absolute values.

There are many practical uses for negative numbers. A submarine diving below sea level, a bank account that has been overdrawn, a business spending more than it earns, and a temperature below zero are some examples. In some

European hotels, the floors below the registration lobby are given negative numbers.

The four basic **operations** of arithmetic are addition, subtraction, multiplication, and division. In the next few sections we will explain how to add, subtract, multiply, and divide numbers. We will consider both positive and negative numbers. In this section we discuss the operation of addition.

Add Real Numbers Using the Number Line

1 To add numbers, we make use of the number line. Represent the first number to be added (first *addend*) by an arrow starting at 0. The arrow is drawn to the right if the number is positive. If the number is negative, the arrow is drawn to the left. From the tip of the first arrow, draw a second arrow to represent the second addend. The second arrow is drawn to the right or left, as just explained. The sum of the two numbers is found at the tip of the second arrow. Note that *any number except 0 without a sign in front of it is positive.* For example, 3 means +3 and 5 means +5.

EXAMPLE 1   Evaluate $3 + (-4)$ using the number line.

Solution: *Always begin at 0.* Since the first addend, the 3, is positive, the first arrow starts at 0 and is drawn 3 units to the right (Fig. 1.12).

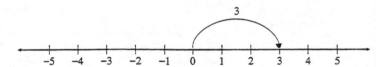

FIGURE 1.12

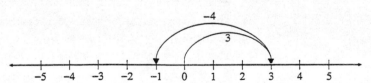

FIGURE 1.13

The second arrow starts at 3 and is drawn 4 units to the left, since the second addend is negative (Fig. 1.13). The tip of the second arrow is at -1. Thus

$$3 + (-4) = -1$$

EXAMPLE 2   Evaluate $-4 + 2$ using the number line.

Solution: Begin at 0. Since the first addend is negative, -4, the first arrow is drawn 4 units to the left. From there, since 2 is positive, the second arrow is drawn 2 units to the right. The second arrow ends at -2 (Fig. 1.14).

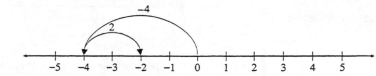

FIGURE 1.14

$$-4 + 2 = -2$$

EXAMPLE 3 Evaluate $-3 + (-2)$ using the number line.

Solution: Start at 0. Since both numbers being added are negative, both arrows will be drawn to the left (Fig. 1.15).

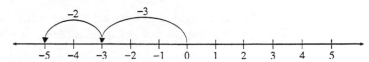

FIGURE 1.15

$$-3 + (-2) = -5$$

In Example 3, we can think of the expression $-3 + (-2)$ as combining a *loss* of 3 and a *loss* of 2 for a total *loss* of 5, or -5.

EXAMPLE 4 Add $5 + (-5)$.

Solution: The first arrow starts at 0 and is drawn 5 units to the right. The second arrow starts at 5 and is drawn 5 units to the left. The tip of the second arrow is at 0. Thus, $5 + (-5) = 0$ (Fig. 1.16).

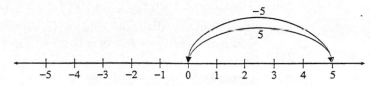

FIGURE 1.16

$$5 + (-5) = 0$$

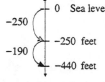

FIGURE 1.17

EXAMPLE 5 A submarine dives 250 feet. Later it dives an additional 190 feet. Find the depth of the submarine (assume that depths below sea level are indicated by negative numbers).

Solution: A vertical number line (Fig. 1.17) may help you visualize this problem.

$$-250 + (-190) = -440 \text{ feet}$$

Identify Opposites   **2**

> Any two numbers whose sum is zero are said to be **opposites** (or **additive inverses**) of each other. In general, if we let a represent any real number, then its opposite is $-a$ and $a + (-a) = 0$.

In Example 4 the sum of 5 and -5 is zero. Thus -5 is the opposite of 5 and 5 is the opposite of -5.

EXAMPLE 6   Find the opposite of each number.

(a) 3   (b) -4

Solution: (a) The opposite of 3 is -3, since $3 + (-3) = 0$.
(b) The opposite of -4 is 4, since $-4 + 4 = 0$.

Add Using Absolute Value   **3**

Now that we have had some practice adding signed numbers on the number line, we give a rule (in two parts) for using absolute value to add signed numbers. Remember that the absolute value of a nonzero number will always be positive. The first part follows.

> **To add real numbers with the same sign** (either both positive or both negative), add their absolute values. The sum has the same sign as the numbers being added.

EXAMPLE 7   Add $4 + 8$.

Solution: Since both numbers have the same sign, both positive, we add their absolute values: $|4| + |8| = 4 + 8 = 12$. Since both numbers being added are positive, the sum is positive. Thus $4 + 8 = 12$.

EXAMPLE 8   Add $-6 + (-9)$.

Solution: Since both numbers have the same sign, both negative, we add their absolute values: $|-6| + |-9| = 6 + 9 = 15$. Since both numbers being added are negative, their sum is negative. Thus $-6 + (-9) = -15$.

The sum of two positive numbers will always be positive and the sum of two negative numbers will always be negative.

> **To add two signed numbers with different signs** (one positive and the other negative), find the difference between the larger absolute value and the smaller absolute value. The answer has the sign of the number with the larger absolute value.

EXAMPLE 9   Add $10 + (-6)$.

Solution: The two numbers being added have different signs; thus we find the difference between the larger absolute value and the smaller: $|10| - |-6|$ $= 10 - 6 = 4$. Since $|10|$ is greater than $|-6|$ and the sign of 10 is positive, the sum is positive. Thus, $10 + (-6) = 4$.

EXAMPLE 10   Add $12 + (-18)$.

Solution: The numbers being added have different signs; thus we find the difference between the larger absolute value and the smaller: $|-18| - |12| =$ $18 - 12 = 6$. Since $|-18|$ is greater than $|12|$ and the sign of -18 is negative, the sum is negative. Thus, $12 + (-18) = -6$.

EXAMPLE 11   Add $-24 + 19$.

Solution: The two numbers being added have different signs; thus we find the difference between the larger absolute value and the smaller: $|-24| - |19|$ $= 24 - 19 = 5$. Since $|-24|$ is greater than $|19|$, the sum is negative. Therefore, $-24 + 19 = -5$.

The sum of two signed numbers with different signs may be either positive or negative. The sign of the sum will be the same as the sign of the number with the larger absolute value.

Helpful Hint

Architects often make a scale model of a building before starting construction of the building. This "model" helps them visualize the project and often helps them avoid problems.

Mathematicians also construct models. A mathematical *model* may be a physical representation of a mathematical concept. It may be as simple as using tiles or chips to represent specific numbers. For example, below we use a model to help explain addition of real numbers. This may help some of you understand the concepts better.

We let a red chip represent $+1$ and a green chip represent -1.

$$● = +1 \qquad ◐ = -1$$

If we add $+1$ and -1, or a red and a green chip, we get 0.

Now consider the addition problem $3 + (-5)$. We can represent this as

$$\underbrace{●\,●\,●}_{3} + \underbrace{◐\,◐\,◐\,◐\,◐}_{-5}$$

If we remove 3 red chips and 3 green chips, or three zeros, we are left with 2 green chips, which represents a sum of -2. Thus, $3 + (-5) = -2$,

$$\cancel{●}\,\cancel{●}\,\cancel{●} + \cancel{◐}\,\cancel{◐}\,\cancel{◐}\,◐\,◐$$

Now consider the problem $-4 + (-2)$. We can represent this as

$$\underbrace{◐\,◐\,◐\,◐}_{-4} + \underbrace{◐\,◐}_{-2}$$

Since we end up with 6 green chips, and each green chip represents -1, the sum is -6. Therefore, $-4 + (-2) = -6$.

EXAMPLE 12 The ABC Company had a loss of $4000 for the first 6 months of the year and a profit of $15,500 for the second 6 months of the year. Find the net profit or loss for the year.

Solution: This problem can be represented as $-4000 + 15,500$. Since the two numbers being added have different signs, find the difference between the larger absolute value and the smaller.

$$|15,500| - |-4000| = 15,500 - 4000 = 11,500$$

Thus, the net profit for the year was $11,500.

Calculator Corner

USE OF A SCIENTIFIC CALCULATOR AND ADDITION OF REAL NUMBERS

It is important that you understand the procedures for adding, subtracting, multiplying, and dividing real numbers *without* using a calculator. To do so, you must understand the basic concepts presented in this and the following two sections. You should not need to rely on a calculator to work problems. You can, however, use the calculator to help save time in difficult calculations. If you have an understanding of the basic concepts, you should be able to tell if you have made an error entering information on the calculator by seeing if the answer is reasonable. In each respective section we show how to add, subtract, multiply, and divide real numbers using a calculator. We strongly urge you to purchase or borrow a *scientific calculator.* Ask your instructor if he or she is recommending a specific calculator. You will find it very useful in this and many other mathematics and science courses. The cost of a scientific calculator is not much more than the cost of the nonscientific calculator. A picture of a typical scientific calculator is shown on the left.

ENTERING NEGATIVE NUMBERS

Scientific calculators contain a ⁺/- key, which is used to enter a negative number. To enter the number -5 we press 5 ⁺/- and a -5 will be displayed. Now we show how to evaluate some addition problems on a calculator.

ADDITION OF REAL NUMBERS

Evaluate	Keystrokes	Answer
$5 + (-2)$	5 + 2 +/- = 3	3
$-3 + (-8)$	3 +/- + 8 +/- = -11	-11
$52 + (-97)$	52 + 97 +/- = -45	-45
$-127 + (-82)$	127 +/- + 82 +/- = -209	-209

Exercise Set 1.5

Write the opposite of each number.

1. 12

2. -7

3. -40

4. 3

5. 0

6. 6

7. $\dfrac{5}{3}$

8. $-\dfrac{1}{2}$

9. $\dfrac{3}{5}$

10. -1

11. 0.63

12. -0.721

13. $3\dfrac{1}{5}$

14. $-5\dfrac{1}{4}$

15. -3.1

16. 5.26

Add.

17. $4 + 3$

18. $-4 + 3$

19. $4 + (-3)$

20. $4 + (-2)$

21. $-4 + (-2)$

22. $-3 + (-5)$

23. $6 + (-6)$

24. $-6 + 6$

25. $-4 + 4$

26. $-3 + 5$

27. $-8 + (-2)$

28. $6 + (-5)$

29. $-3 + 3$

30. $-8 + 2$

31. $-3 + (-7)$

32. $0 + (-3)$

33. $0 + 0$

34. $0 + (-0)$

35. $-6 + 0$

36. $-9 + 13$

37. $22 + (-19)$

38. $-13 + (-18)$

39. $-45 + 36$

40. $40 + (-25)$

41. $18 + (-9)$

42. $-7 + 7$

43. $-14 + (-13)$

44. $-27 + (-9)$

45. $-35 + (-9)$

46. $34 + (-12)$

47. $4 + (-30)$

48. $-16 + 9$

49. $-35 + 40$

50. $-12 + 17$

51. $180 + (-200)$

52. $-33 + (-92)$

53. $-105 + 74$

54. $183 + (-183)$

55. $184 + (-93)$

56. $-42 + 129$

57. $-452 + 312$

58. $-94 + (-98)$

59. $-60 + (-38)$

60. $49 + (-63)$

For each of the following, (a) determine by observation whether the sum will be a positive number, zero, or a negative number; (b) find the sum using your calculator; and (c) examine your answer to part (b) to see if it is reasonable and makes sense.

61. $463 + (-197)$

62. $-140 + (-629)$

63. $-84 + (-289)$

64. $-593 + 624$

65. $-947 + 495$

66. $762 + (-762)$

67. $-496 + (-804)$

68. $-354 + 1090$

69. $-285 + 263$

70. $1035 + (-972)$

71. $-1833 + (-2047)$

72. $-138 + 648$

73. $4793 + (-6060)$

74. $-9095 + (-647)$

75. $-1025 + (-1025)$

76. $7625 + (-1938)$

77. $-8276 + (-6283)$

78. $-4693 + 6773$

79. $-9042 + 7827$

80. $-4067 + (-3078)$

81. $1046 + (-8540)$

82. $-625 + (-9248)$

83. $8364 + (-906)$

84. $-436 + 8954$

Answer true or false.

85. The sum of two negative numbers is always a negative number.

86. The sum of two positive numbers is never a negative number.

87. The sum of a positive number and a negative number is always a positive number.

88. The sum of a negative number and a positive number is sometimes a negative number.

89. The sum of a positive number and a negative number is always a negative number.

90. The sum of a number and its opposite is always equal to zero.

Write an expression that can be used to solve each problem and then solve.

91. Mr. Yelserp owed $67 on his bank credit card. He charged another item costing $107. Find the amount that Mr. Yelserp owed the bank.

92. Mr. Weber charged $193 worth of goods on his charge card. Find his balance after he made a payment of $112.

93. Mrs. Petrie paid $1424 in federal income tax. When she was audited, Mrs. Petrie had to pay an additional $503. What was her total tax?

94. Mr. Vela hiked 847 meters down the Grand Canyon. He climbed back up 385 meters and then rested. Find his distance from the rim of the canyon.

SEE EXERCISE 94

95. A company is drilling a well. During the first week they drilled 22 feet, and during the second week they drilled another 32 feet before they struck water. How deep is the well?

96. A football team lost 18 yards on one play and then lost 3 yards on the following play. What was the total loss in yardage?

97. In 1992, there were approximately 141 million births and 49 million deaths worldwide. What was the change in the world's population in 1992?

98. An airplane at an altitude of 2400 feet above sea level drops a package into the ocean. The package settles at a point 200 feet below sea level. How far did the object fall?

99. Explain in your own words how to add two numbers with like signs.

100. Explain in your own words how to add two numbers with unlike signs.

CUMULATIVE REVIEW EXERCISES

[1.1] **101.** Multiply $\left(\frac{3}{5}\right)\left(1\frac{2}{3}\right)$

102. Subtract $3 - \frac{5}{16}$

[1.3] *Insert either $<$, $>$, or $=$ in the shaded area to make the statement true.*

103. $|-3|$ ▨ 2

104. 8 ▨ $|-7|$

Group Activity/ Challenge Problems

Evaluate each exercise by adding the numbers from left to right. We will discuss problems like this shortly.

1. $(-4) + (-6) + (-12)$ **2.** $5 + (-7) + (-8)$ **3.** $29 + (-46) + 37$

Find the following sums. Explain how you determined your answer. Hint: pair small numbers with large numbers from the ends inward.

4. $1 + 2 + 3 + \cdots + 10$

5. $1 + 2 + 3 + \cdots + 20$

6. $1 + 2 + 3 + \cdots + 100$

7. $1 + 2 + 3 + \cdots + 5000$

1.6 Subtraction of Real Numbers

1 Subtract real numbers.
2 Subtract real numbers mentally.

Tape 2

Subtraction

1 Any subtraction problem can be rewritten as an addition problem using the additive inverse.

Subtraction of Real Numbers

In general, if a and b represent any two real numbers, then

$$a - b = a + (-b)$$

This rule says that to subtract b from a, add the opposite or additive inverse of b to a.

EXAMPLE 1 Evaluate $9 - (+4)$.

Solution: We are subtracting a positive 4 from 9. To accomplish this we add the opposite of $+4$, which is -4, to 9.

$$9 - (+4) = 9 + (-4) = 5$$

subtract positive 4   add   negative 4

We evaluated $9 + (-4)$ using the procedures for *adding* real numbers presented in Section 1.5.

Often in a subtraction problem, when the number being subtracted is a positive number, the $+$ sign preceding the number being subtracted is not illustrated. For example, in the subtraction $9 - 4$,

$$9 - 4 \text{ means } 9 - (+4)$$

Thus, to evaluate $9 - 4$, we must add the opposite of 4 (or $+4$), which is -4, to 9.

$$9 - 4 = 9 + (-4) = 5$$

subtract positive 4 add negative 4

This procedure is illustrated in Example 2.

EXAMPLE 2 Evaluate $5 - 3$.

Solution: We must subtract a positive 3 from 5. To change this problem to an addition problem, add the opposite of 3, which is -3, to 5.

subtraction   addition
problem   problem
$$5 - 3 = 5 + (-3) = 2$$

subtract   positive 3   add   negative 3

EXAMPLE 3 Evaluate $4 - 9$.

Solution: Add the opposite of 9, which is -9, to 4.

$$4 - 9 = 4 + (-9) = -5$$

EXAMPLE 4 Evaluate $-4 - 2$.

Solution: Add the opposite of 2, which is -2, to -4.

$$-4 - 2 = -4 + (-2) = -6$$

EXAMPLE 5   Evaluate $4 - (-2)$.

Solution: We are asked to subtract a negative 2 from 4. To do this, add the opposite of -2, which is 2, to 4.

$$4 - (-2) = 4 + 2 = 6$$

subtract   negative 2   add   positive 2

Helpful Hint

By examining Example 5 we see that

$$4 - (-2) = 4 + 2$$

two negative   + sign
signs together

Whenever we subtract a negative number, we can replace the two negative signs with a plus sign.

EXAMPLE 6   Evaluate $6 - (-3)$.

Solution: Since we are subtracting a negative number, adding the opposite of -3, which is 3, to 6 will result in the two negative signs being replaced by a plus sign.

$$6 - (-3) = 6 + 3 = 9$$

EXAMPLE 7   Evaluate $-15 - (-12)$.

Solution: $-15 - (-12) = -15 + 12 = -3$

Helpful Hint

We will now indicate how we may illustrate subtraction using colored chips. Remember from the preceding section that a red chip represents $+1$ and a green chip -1.

$$\bullet = +1 \qquad \circ = -1$$

Consider the subtraction problem $2 - 5$. If we change this to an addition problem we get $2 + (-5)$. We can then add, as was done in the preceding section. The figure below shows that $2 + (-5) = -3$.

$$\bullet\bullet + \circ\circ\circ\circ\circ$$

Now consider $-2 - 5$. This means $-2 + (-5)$, which can be represented as follows:

$$\circ\circ + \circ\circ\circ\circ\circ$$

Thus, $-2 - 5 = -7$.

Now consider the problem $-3 - (-5)$. This can be rewritten as $-3 + 5$, which can be represented as follows:

$$\circ\circ\circ + \bullet\bullet\bullet\bullet\bullet$$

Thus, $-3 - (-5) = 2$.

Some students still have difficulty understanding why when you subtract a negative number you obtain a positive number. Let us look at the problem $3 - (-2)$. This time we will look at it from a little different point of view. Let us start with 3:

●●●

From this we wish to subtract a negative two. To the $+3$ shown above we will add two zeros by adding two $+1$ -1 combinations. Remember, $+1$ and -1 sum to 0.

$\underbrace{●●●}_{+3}$ + $\underbrace{●◖}_{0}$ + $\underbrace{●◖}_{0}$

Now we can subtract or "take away" the two -1's as shown:

●●● + ● ∉ + ● ∉

From this we see that we are left with $3 + 2$ or 5. Thus, $3 - (-2) = 5$.

EXAMPLE 8 Subtract 12 from 3.

Solution: $3 - 12 = 3 + (-12) = -9$

Helpful Hint

Example 8 asked us to "subtract 12 from 3." Some of you may have expected this to be written as $12 - 3$ since you may be accustomed to getting a positive answer. However, the correct method of writing this is $3 - 12$. Notice that the number following the word "from" is our starting point. That is where the calculation begins. For example:

Subtract 5 from -1, means $-1 - 5$.   From 6 subtract 2, means $6 - 2$.

Subtract -3 from 2, means $2 - (-3)$.   From -6 subtract -3, means $-6 - (-3)$.

Subtract a from b, means $b - a$.   From a subtract b, means $a - b$.

EXAMPLE 9 Subtract 5 from 5.

Solution: $5 - 5 = 5 + (-5) = 0$

EXAMPLE 10 Subtract -6 from 4.

Solution: $4 - (-6) = 4 + 6 = 10$

EXAMPLE 11 Evaluate.

(a) $8 - (-5)$ **(b)** $-3 - (-9)$

Solution: **(a)** $8 - (-5) = 8 + 5 = 13$
         (b) $-3 - (-9) = -3 + 9 = 6$

EXAMPLE 12 Mary Jo Morin's checkbook indicated a balance of $125 before she wrote a check for $183. Find the balance in her checkbook.

Solution: $125 - 183 = 125 + (-183) = -58$. The negative indicates a deficit. Therefore, Mary Jo is overdrawn by $58.

EXAMPLE 13 Janet made $4200 in the stock market, while Mateo lost $3000. How much further ahead is Janet than Mateo financially?

Solution: Janet's gain is represented as a positive number. Mateo's loss is represented as a negative number.

$$4200 - (-3000) = 4200 + 3000 = 7200$$

Janet is therefore $7200 ahead of Mateo financially.

EXAMPLE 14 Evaluate.

(a) $12 + (-4)$ (b) $-16 - 3$ (c) $5 + (-4)$
(d) $6 - (-5)$ (e) $-12 - (-3)$ (f) $8 - 13$

Solution: Parts (a) and (c) are addition problems, while the other parts are subtraction problems. We can rewrite each subtraction problem as an addition problem to evaluate.

(a) $12 + (-4) = 8$ (b) $-16 - 3 = -16 + (-3) = -19$
(c) $5 + (-4) = 1$ (d) $6 - (-5) = 6 + 5 = 11$
(e) $-12 - (-3) = -12 + 3 = -9$ (f) $8 - 13 = 8 + (-13) = -5$

Subtract Mentally   **2** In the previous examples, we changed subtraction problems to addition problems. We did this because we know how to add real numbers. After this chapter, when we work out a subtraction problem, we will not show this step. *You need to practice and thoroughly understand how to add and subtract real numbers. You should understand this material so well that, when asked to evaluate an expression like $-4 - 6$, you will be able to compute the answer mentally. You should understand that $-4 - 6$ means the same as $-4 + (-6)$, but you should not need to write the addition to find the value of the expression, -10.*

Let us evaluate a few subtraction problems without showing the process of changing the subtraction to addition.

EXAMPLE 15 Evaluate.

(a) $-7 - 5$ (b) $4 - 12$ (c) $18 - 25$ (d) $-20 - 12$

Solution: (a) $-7 - 5 = -12$ (b) $4 - 12 = -8$
            (c) $18 - 25 = -7$ (d) $-20 - 12 = -32$

In Example 15 we may have reasoned that $-7 - 5$ meant $-7 + (-5)$, which is -12, but we did not need to show it.

In evaluating expressions involving more than one addition and subtraction, work from left to right unless parentheses or other grouping symbols appear.

EXAMPLE 16 Evaluate.

(a) $-6 - 12 - 4$ (b) $-3 + 1 - 7$ (c) $8 - 10 + 2$

Solution: We work from left to right.

(a) $\underbrace{-6 - 12}\; - 4$ (b) $\underbrace{-3 + 1}\; - 7$ (c) $\underbrace{8 - 10}\; + 2$

$= \quad -18 \quad - 4$ $= \quad -2 \quad - 7$ $= \quad -2 \quad + 2$

$= -22$ $= -9$ $= 0$

After this section you will generally not see an expression like $3 + (-4)$. Instead, the expression will be written as $3 - 4$. Recall that $3 - 4$ means $3 + (-4)$ by our definition of subtraction. **Whenever we see an expression of the form $a + (-b)$, we can write the expression as $a - b$.** For example, $12 + (-15)$ can be written $12 - 15$ and $-6 + (-9)$ can be written $-6 - 9$.

EXAMPLE 17   Evaluate.

(a) $-3 - (-4) + (-10) + (-5)$ (b) $-3 - (-4) - 10 - 5$

Solution: (a) Again we work from left to right.

$$-3 - (-4) + (-10) + (-5) = -3 + 4 + (-10) + (-5)$$
$$= 1 + (-10) + (-5)$$
$$= -9 + (-5)$$
$$= -14$$

(b) This part is really the same problem as part (a), since $+(-10)$ can be written -10 and $+(-5)$ can be written -5.

$$-3 - (-4) - 10 - 5 = -3 + 4 - 10 - 5$$
$$= 1 - 10 - 5$$
$$= -9 - 5$$
$$= -14$$

Calculator Corner

SUBTRACTION OF REAL NUMBERS

In the calculator corner on page 34 we indicated that the $^+\!/\!_-$ key is used to enter a negative number. Below we show some examples of subtracting real numbers on a scientific calculator. The number following the $=$ is the answer.

Evaluate	*Keystrokes*
$6 - 10$	$6 \;-\; 10 \;=\; -4$
$-5 - 8$	$5 \;^+\!/\!_-\; -\; 8 \;=\; -13$ *Note:* $^+\!/\!_-$ is pressed *after* the number to be made negative.

You can subtract a negative number on the calculator as shown below.

Evaluate	*Keystrokes*
$2 - (-7)$	$2 \;-\; 7 \;^+\!/\!_-\; =\; 9$
$-9 - (-3)$	$9 \;^+\!/\!_-\; -\; 3 \;^+\!/\!_-\; =\; -6$

Exercise Set 1.6

Evaluate.

1. $6 - 3$
2. $-6 - 4$
3. $8 - 9$
4. $5 - 3$
5. $3 - 3$
6. $-4 - 2$
7. $(-7) - (-4)$
8. $-4 - (-3)$
9. $-3 - 3$
10. $-4 - 4$
11. $3 - (-3)$
12. $4 - 4$
13. $0 - 6$
14. $6 - 6$
15. $0 - (-6)$
16. $9 - (-3)$
17. $-3 - 5$
18. $-5 - (-3)$
19. $-5 + 7$
20. $-7 - 9$
21. $5 - 3$
22. $5 - 12$
23. $6 - (-3)$
24. $6 - 10$
25. $8 - 8$
26. $-8 - 8$
27. $-8 - 10$
28. $4 - 12$
29. $-4 - (-2)$
30. $7 - 9$
31. $(-4) - (-4)$
32. $15 - 8$
33. $6 - 6$
34. $(-8) - (-12)$
35. $9 - 9$
36. $-6 - (-2)$
37. $4 - 5$
38. $-9 - 2$
39. $-2 - 3$
40. $9 - (-12)$
41. $-25 - 16$
42. $-20 - (-15)$
43. $37 - 40$
44. $40 - 37$
45. $-100 - 80$
46. $80 - 100$
47. $-20 - 90$
48. $-45 - 37$
49. $-50 - (-40)$
50. $70 - (-70)$
51. $130 - (-90)$
52. $40 - 62$
53. $87 - 87$
54. $93 - (-93)$
55. $-53 - (-7)$
56. $-75 - (-16)$

57. Subtract 3 from -15.
58. Subtract -4 from -5.
59. Subtract 8 from -8.
60. Subtract 10 from -20.
61. Subtract 8 from 18.
62. Subtract 5 from -5.
63. Subtract -3 from -5.
64. Subtract 10 from -3.
65. Subtract -4 from 9.
66. Subtract 18 from -18.
67. Subtract 18 from 18.
68. Subtract 5 from 5.
69. Subtract 12 from 8.
70. Subtract -9 from 12.
71. Subtract -15 from -4.
72. Subtract -12 from 3.
73. Subtract -36 from 45.
74. Subtract 17 from -12.

For each of the following, (a) determine by observation whether the difference will be a positive number, zero, or a negative number; (b) find the difference using your calculator; and (c) examine your answer to part (b) to see if it is reasonable and makes sense.

75. $296 - 197$
76. $483 - 569$
77. $102 - 697$
78. $-372 - 195$
79. $349 - (-498)$
80. $843 - (-745)$
81. $950 - (-762)$
82. $575 - (-462)$
83. $-408 - (-604)$
84. $-776 - 358$
85. $-1024 - (-576)$
86. $-1047 - 376$
87. $165.7 - 49.6$
88. $-40.2 - (-12.6)$
89. $-37.2 - (-37.2)$
90. $597.3 - (-64.72)$

91. Subtract 364 from 295.
92. Subtract -387 from -932.
93. Subtract 647 from -1023.
94. Subtract 2432 from -6771.
95. Subtract -7.62 from 89.7.
96. Subtract 16.2 from -87.7.

Evaluate.

97. $6 + 5 - (+4)$
98. $9 - (+6) - (+5)$
99. $-3 + (-4) + 5$
100. $9 - 7 + (-2)$
101. $-13 - (+5) + 3$
102. $7 - (+4) - (-3)$
103. $-9 - (-3) + 4$
104. $15 + (-7) - (-3)$
105. $5 - (+3) + (-2)$
106. $12 + (-5) - (-4)$
107. $25 + (+12) - (-6)$
108. $-7 + 6 - 3$
109. $-4 - 7 + 5$
110. $20 - 4 - 25$
111. $-4 + 7 - 12$
112. $-36 - 5 + 9$
113. $45 - 3 - 7$
114. $-2 + 7 - 9$
115. $-9 - 4 - 8$
116. $25 - 19 + 27$
117. $-4 - 13 + 5$
118. $(-4) + (-3) + 5 - 7$
119. $-9 - 3 - (-4) + 5$
120. $17 + (-3) - 9 - (-7)$
121. $32 + 5 - 7 - 12$
122. $-19 + (-3) - (-5) - (-2)$
123. $6 - 9 - (-3) + 12$
124. $-7 - 4 - 3 + 5$
125. $19 + 4 - 20 - 25$
126. $37 - (-19) + 7 - 12$

127. A Girl Scout troop received 920 boxes of thin mint Girl Scout cookies. They sold 1246 boxes of thin mints. How many more boxes will the troop need to order?

128. An airplane is 2000 feet above sea level. A submarine is 1500 feet below sea level. How far above the submarine is the airplane?

129. Mike made $750 in the stock market while Kirk lost $496. What is the difference in their performance?

130. The highest point on Earth, Mt. Everest, is 29,028 feet above sea level. The lowest point on Earth, the Marianas Trench, is 36,198 feet below sea level. How far above the Marianas Trench is the top of Mt. Everest?

See Exercise 130

131. The greatest change in temperature ever recorded within a 24-hour period occurred at Browning,

Montana, on January 23, 1916. The temperature fell from 44°F to −56°F. How much did the temperature drop?

132. **(a)** Is the statement $a + (−b) = a − b$ true for all real numbers a and b?

  (b) If $a = −3$ and $b = 5$, determine if $a + (−b) = a − b$.

133. **(a)** Explain how to subtract −2 from 6.

  (b) Subtract −2 from 6 following the procedure given in part (a).

134. **(a)** Explain how to subtract 6 from −9.

  (b) Subtract 6 from −9 using the procedure given in part (a).

135. Two trains start at the same station at the same time. The Amtrak travels 68 miles in 1 hour. The Pacific Express travels 80 miles in 1 hour. **(a)** If the two trains travel in opposite directions, how far apart will they be in 1 hour? Explain.

  (b) If the two trains travel in the same direction, how far apart will they be in 1 hour? Explain.

136. Consider the expression $6 − 4 + 3 − 5 − 2$, which contains only additions and subtractions.

  (a) State the order we follow to evaluate the expression. Explain why we follow this order.

  (b) Evaluate the expression using the order you gave in part (a).

CUMULATIVE REVIEW EXERCISES

[1.3] **137.** List the set of integers.

138. Explain the relationship between the set of rational numbers, the set of irrational numbers, and the set of real numbers.

[1.4] *Insert either $>$, $<$, or $=$ in the shaded area to make each statement true.*

139. $|−3|$ ▨ $−5$

140. $|−6|$ ▨ $|−7|$

Group Activity/ Challenge Problems

Find the sum.

1. $1 − 2 + 3 − 4 + 5 − 6 + 7 − 8 + 9 − 10$

2. $1 − 2 + 3 − 4 + 5 − 6 + \cdots + 99 − 100$

3. $−1 + 2 − 3 + 4 − 5 + 6 − \cdots − 99 + 100$

4. Consider a number line.

  (a) What is the distance, in units, between −2 and 5?

  (b) Write a subtraction problem to represent this distance (the distance is to be positive).

5. A model rocket is on a hill near the ocean. The hill's height is 62 feet above sea level. When ignited, the rocket climbs upward to 128 feet above sea level, then it falls and lands in the ocean and settles 59 feet below sea level. Find the total distance traveled by the rocket.

Evaluate each of the following.

6. $(−5 − 4 − 3 − 2 − 1) − (−5 − 4 − 3 − 2 − 1)$

7. $−5 + 4 − 3 + 2 − 1 + 5 − 4 + 3 − 2 + 1$

1.7 Multiplication and Division of Real Numbers

Tape 2

1. Multiply real numbers.
2. Divide real numbers.
3. Remove negative signs from denominators.
4. Understand the difference between 0 in the numerator and 0 in the denominator of a fraction.

Multiplication of Real Numbers

1. The following rules are used in determining the sign of the product when two numbers are multiplied.

> ## Multiplication of Real Numbers
>
> 1. The product of two numbers with **like** signs is a **positive** number.
> 2. The product of two numbers with **unlike** signs is a **negative** number.

By this rule, the product of two positive numbers or two negative numbers will be a positive number. The product of a positive number and a negative number will be a negative number.

EXAMPLE 1 Evaluate $3(-5)$.

Solution: Since the numbers have unlike signs, the product is negative.

$$3(-5) = -15$$

EXAMPLE 2 Evaluate $(-6)(7)$.

Solution: Since the numbers have unlike signs, the product is negative.

$$(-6)(7) = -42$$

EXAMPLE 3 Evaluate $(-7)(-5)$.

Solution: Since the numbers have like signs, both negative, the product is positive.

$$(-7)(-5) = 35$$

EXAMPLE 4 Evaluate each expression.

    (a) $-6 \cdot 3$ **(b)** $(-4)(-8)$ **(c)** $4(-9)$
    (d) $0 \cdot 4$ **(e)** $0(-2)$ **(f)** $-3(-6)$

Solution: **(a)** $-6 \cdot 3 = -18$ **(b)** $(-4)(-8) = 32$ **(c)** $4(-9) = -36$
        (d) $0 \cdot 4 = 0$ **(e)** $0(-2) = 0$ **(f)** $-3(-6) = 18$

Note that zero multiplied by any real number equals zero.

EXAMPLE 5   Multiply $\left(\dfrac{-1}{8}\right)\left(\dfrac{-3}{5}\right)$.

Solution: $\left(\dfrac{-1}{8}\right)\left(\dfrac{-3}{5}\right) = \dfrac{(-1) \cdot (-3)}{8 \cdot 5} = \dfrac{3}{40}$

EXAMPLE 6   Evaluate $\left(\dfrac{3}{20}\right)\left(\dfrac{-3}{10}\right)$.

Solution: $\left(\dfrac{3}{20}\right)\left(\dfrac{-3}{10}\right) = \dfrac{3(-3)}{20\,(10)} = \dfrac{-9}{200}$

Sometimes you may be asked to perform more than one multiplication in a given problem. When this happens, the sign of the final product can be determined by counting the number of *negative* numbers being multiplied. **The product of an even number of negative numbers will always be positive. The product of an odd number of negative numbers will always be negative.** Can you explain why?

EXAMPLE 7   Evaluate $(-2)(3)(-2)(-1)$.

Solution: Since there are three negative numbers (an odd number of negatives), the product will be negative, as illustrated.

$$\begin{aligned}
(-2)(3)(-2)(-1) &= (-6)(-2)(-1) \\
&= (12)(-1) \\
&= -12
\end{aligned}$$

EXAMPLE 8   Evaluate $(-3)(2)(-1)(-2)(-4)$.

Solution: Since there are four negative numbers (an even number), the product will be positive.

$$\begin{aligned}
(-3)(2)(-1)(-2)(-4) &= (-6)(-1)(-2)(-4) \\
&= (6)(-2)(-4) \\
&= (-12)(-4) \\
&= 48
\end{aligned}$$

Division of Real Numbers

The rules for dividing numbers are very similar to those used in multiplying numbers.

> **Division of Real Numbers**
>
> **1.** The quotient of two numbers with **like** signs is a **positive** number.
> **2.** The quotient of two numbers with **unlike** signs is a **negative** number.

Therefore, the quotient of two positive numbers or two negative numbers will be a positive number. The quotient of a positive and a negative number will be a negative number.

EXAMPLE 9 Evaluate $\dfrac{20}{-5}$.

Solution: Since the numbers have unlike signs, the quotient is negative.

$$\frac{20}{-5} = -4$$

EXAMPLE 10 Evaluate $\dfrac{-36}{4}$.

Solution: Since the numbers have unlike signs, the quotient is negative.

$$\frac{-36}{4} = -9$$

EXAMPLE 11 Evaluate $\dfrac{-30}{-5}$.

Solution: Since the numbers have like signs, both negative, the quotient is positive.

$$\frac{-30}{-5} = 6$$

EXAMPLE 12 Evaluate $-16 \div (-2)$.

Solution: $\dfrac{-16}{-2} = 8$

EXAMPLE 13 Evaluate $\dfrac{-2}{3} \div \dfrac{-5}{7}$.

Solution: Invert the *divisor*, $\dfrac{-5}{7}$, and then multiply.

$$\frac{-2}{3} \div \frac{-5}{7} = \left(\frac{-2}{3}\right)\left(\frac{7}{-5}\right)$$

$$= \frac{-14}{-15}$$

$$= \frac{14}{15}$$

**Remove Negative
Sign in the
Denominator**

3 We now know that the quotient of a positive and a negative number is a negative number. The fractions $-\frac{3}{4}$, $\frac{-3}{4}$, and $\frac{3}{-4}$ all represent the same negative number, negative three-fourths.

If a and b represent any real numbers, $b \neq 0$, then

$$\frac{a}{-b} = \frac{-a}{b} = -\frac{a}{b}$$

In mathematics we generally do not write a fraction with a negative sign in the denominator. When a negative sign appears in a denominator, we can move it to the numerator or place it in front of the fraction. For example, the fraction $\frac{5}{-7}$ should be written as either $-\frac{5}{7}$ or $\frac{-5}{7}$.

EXAMPLE 14 Evaluate $\dfrac{2}{5} \div \dfrac{-8}{15}$.

Solution: $\dfrac{2}{5} \div \dfrac{-8}{15} = \dfrac{\overset{1}{\cancel{2}}}{\underset{1}{\cancel{5}}} \cdot \dfrac{\overset{3}{\cancel{15}}}{\underset{4}{-\cancel{8}}} = \dfrac{1(3)}{1(-4)} = \dfrac{3}{-4} = -\dfrac{3}{4}$

The operations on real numbers are summarized in Table 1.1.

TABLE 1.1   Summary of Operations on Real Numbers

Signs of Numbers	Addition	Subtraction	Multiplication	Division
Both Numbers Are Positive	Sum Is Always Positive	Difference May Be Either Positive or Negative	Product Is Always Positive	Quotient Is Always Positive
Examples				
6 and 2	$6 + 2 = 8$	$6 - 2 = 4$	$6 \cdot 2 = 12$	$6 \div 2 = 3$
2 and 6	$2 + 6 = 8$	$2 - 6 = -4$	$2 \cdot 6 = 12$	$2 \div 6 = \frac{1}{3}$
One Number Is Positive and the Other Number Is Negative	Sum May Be Either Positive or Negative	Difference May Be Either Positive or Negative	Product Is Always Negative	Quotient Is Always Negative
Examples				
6 and −2	$6 + (-2) = 4$	$6 - (-2) = 8$	$6(-2) = -12$	$6 \div (-2) = -3$
−6 and 2	$-6 + 2 = -4$	$-6 - (2) = -8$	$-6(2) = -12$	$-6 \div 2 = -3$
Both Numbers Are Negative	Sum Is Always Negative	Difference May Be Either Positive or Negative	Product Is Always Positive	Quotient Is Always Positive
Examples				
−6 and −2	$-6 + (-2) = -8$	$-6 - (-2) = -4$	$-6(-2) = 12$	$-6 \div (-2) = 3$
−2 and −6	$-2 + (-6) = -8$	$-2 - (-6) = 4$	$-2(-6) = 12$	$-2 \div (-6) = \frac{1}{3}$

Helpful Hint

At this point some students begin confusing problems like $-2 - 3$ with $(-2)(-3)$ and problems like $2 - 3$ with problems like $2(-3)$. If you do not understand the difference between problems like $-2 - 3$ and $(-2)(-3)$, make an appointment to see your instructor as soon as possible.

Subtraction Problems

$-2 - 3 = -5$

$2 - 3 = -1$

Multiplication Problems

$(-2)(-3) = 6$

$(2)(-3) = -6$

Helpful Hint
....

For multiplication and division of real numbers:

$$(+)(+) = + \quad \frac{(+)}{(+)} = +$$

$$(-)(-) = + \quad \frac{(-)}{(-)} = +$$

Like signs give positive products and quotients.

$$(+)(-) = - \quad \frac{(+)}{(-)} = -$$

$$(-)(+) = - \quad \frac{(-)}{(+)} = -$$

Unlike signs give negative products and quotients

Division Involving 0   **4**   Now let us look at division involving the number 0. What is $\frac{0}{1}$ equal to? Note that $\frac{6}{3} = 2$ because $3 \cdot 2 = 6$. We can follow the same procedure to determine the value of $\frac{0}{1}$. Suppose that $\frac{0}{1}$ is equal to some number, which we will designate by **?** .

$$\text{If } \frac{0}{1} = \text{ ? } \text{ then } 1 \cdot \text{ ? } = 0$$

Since only $1 \cdot 0 = 0$, the **?** must be 0. Thus, $\frac{0}{1} = 0$. Using the same technique, we can show that zero divided by any nonzero number is zero.

> If a represents any real number except 0, then
> $$\frac{0}{a} = 0$$

Now what is $\frac{1}{0}$ equal to?

$$\text{If } \frac{1}{0} = \text{ ? } \text{ then } 0 \cdot \text{ ? } = 1$$

But since 0 multiplied by any number will be 0, there is no value that can replace **?** . We say that $\frac{1}{0}$ is *undefined*. Using the same technique, we can show that any real number, except 0, divided by 0 is undefined.

> If a represents any real number except 0, then
> $$\frac{a}{0} \text{ is } \textbf{undefined}.$$

What is $\frac{0}{0}$ equal to?

$$\text{If } \frac{0}{0} = \text{ ? } \text{ then } 0 \cdot \text{ ? } = 0$$

But since the product of any number and 0 is 0, the   ?   can be replaced by any real number. Therefore the quotient $\frac{0}{0}$ cannot be determined, and so we will not use it in this course.*

> ### Summary of Division Involving Zero
>
> If a represents any real number except 0, then
>
> $$\frac{0}{a} = 0. \qquad \frac{a}{0} \text{ is undefined.}$$

---

*At this level, some professors prefer to call $\frac{0}{0}$ *indeterminate* while others prefer to call $\frac{0}{0}$ *undefined*. In higher level mathematics courses $\frac{0}{0}$ is sometimes referred to as the *indeterminate form*.

Calculator Corner

MULTIPLICATION OF REAL NUMBERS

Below we illustrate how real numbers may be multiplied on a calculator.

Evaluate	Keystrokes
$6(-23)$	6 $\times$ 23 $^+/_-$ = -138
$(-14)(-37)$	14 $^+/_-$ $\times$ 37 $^+/_-$ = 518

Since you know that a positive number multiplied by a negative number will be negative, to obtain the product of $6(-23)$, you can multiply 6×23 and write a negative sign before the answer. Similarly, since you know that a negative number multiplied by a negative number is positive, you can obtain the answer to $(-14)(-37)$ simply by multiplying $(14)(37)$.

DIVISION OF REAL NUMBERS

Below we illustrate how real numbers may be divided on a calculator.

Evaluate	Keystrokes
$\dfrac{-40}{8}$	40 $^+/_-$ $\div$ 8 = -5
$\dfrac{85}{-5}$	85 $\div$ 5 $^+/_-$ = -17
$\dfrac{-240}{-16}$	240 $^+/_-$ $\div$ 16 $^+/_-$ = 15

A positive number divided by a negative number, or a negative number divided by a positive number, is a negative number. Therefore, the first two examples could have been done using only positive numbers and then placing a negative sign before the value obtained to get the correct answer. Since a negative number divided by a negative number is positive, the third quotient could have been found by dividing 240/16.

EXAMPLE 15 Indicate whether the quotient is 0 or undefined.

(a) $\dfrac{0}{2}$ (b) $\dfrac{5}{0}$ (c) $\dfrac{0}{-4}$ (d) $\dfrac{-2}{0}$

Solution: The answer to parts (a) and (c) is 0. The answer to parts (b) and (d) is undefined.

Exercise Set 1.7

Find the product.

1. $(-4)(-3)$
2. $-4 \cdot 2$
3. $3(-3)$
4. $6(-2)$
5. $(-4)(8)$
6. $(-3)(2)$
7. $9(-1)$
8. $-1(8)$
9. $-4(-3)$
10. $0(4)$
11. $-9(-4)$
12. $(-12)(-3)$
13. $8(12)$
14. $(-5)(-6)$
15. $-9(-9)$
16. $(15)(-4)$
17. $-2(5)$
18. $6(-12)$
19. $(-6)(2)(-3)$
20. $5(-2)(-8)$
21. $0(3)(8)$
22. $2(-3)(7)$
23. $(-1)(-1)(-1)$
24. $2(4)(-2)(-5)$
25. $-5(-3)(8)(-1)$
26. $(-3)(-4)(-5)(-1)$
27. $(-4)(3)(-7)(1)$
28. $4(3)(1)(-1)$
29. $(-3)(2)(5)(3)$
30. $(-1)(3)(0)(-7)$
31. $(-5)(-6)(-3)(-4)$
32. $(-1)(-1)(9)(8)$

Find the product.

33. $\left(\dfrac{-1}{2}\right)\left(\dfrac{3}{5}\right)$
34. $\left(\dfrac{2}{3}\right)\left(\dfrac{-3}{5}\right)$
35. $\left(\dfrac{-8}{9}\right)\left(\dfrac{-7}{12}\right)$
36. $\left(\dfrac{-5}{12}\right)\left(\dfrac{-6}{11}\right)$
37. $\left(\dfrac{6}{-3}\right)\left(\dfrac{4}{-2}\right)$
38. $\left(\dfrac{8}{-11}\right)\left(\dfrac{6}{-5}\right)$
39. $\left(\dfrac{5}{-7}\right)\left(\dfrac{6}{8}\right)$
40. $\left(\dfrac{9}{10}\right)\left(\dfrac{7}{-8}\right)$

Find the quotient.

41. $\dfrac{6}{2}$
42. $9 \div (-3)$
43. $-16 \div (-4)$
44. $\dfrac{-24}{8}$
45. $\dfrac{-36}{-9}$
46. $-45 \div 5$
47. $\dfrac{-16}{4}$
48. $\dfrac{36}{-2}$
49. $\dfrac{18}{-1}$
50. $\dfrac{-12}{-1}$
51. $-15 \div (-3)$
52. $12 \div (-6)$
53. $\dfrac{-6}{-1}$
54. $\dfrac{60}{-12}$
55. $\dfrac{-25}{-5}$
56. $\dfrac{36}{-4}$
57. $\dfrac{1}{-1}$
58. $\dfrac{-1}{1}$
59. $\dfrac{-48}{12}$
60. $\dfrac{50}{-5}$
61. $\dfrac{0}{1}$
62. $-40 \div (-8)$
63. $-64 \div (-4)$
64. $(-120) \div (-120)$
65. Divide 0 by 4.
66. Divide 20 by -5.
67. Divide 30 by -10.
68. Divide -30 by -10.
69. Divide -180 by 30.
70. Divide -60 by 5.
71. Divide -25 by -5.
72. Divide 80 by -20.

Find the quotient.

73. $\dfrac{5}{12} \div \left(\dfrac{-5}{9}\right)$

74. $(-3) \div \dfrac{5}{19}$

75. $\dfrac{3}{-10} \div (-8)$

76. $\dfrac{-4}{9} \div \left(\dfrac{-6}{7}\right)$

77. $\dfrac{-15}{21} \div \left(\dfrac{-15}{21}\right)$

78. $\dfrac{8}{-15} \div \left(\dfrac{-9}{10}\right)$

79. $(-12) \div \dfrac{5}{12}$

80. $\dfrac{-16}{3} \div \left(\dfrac{5}{-9}\right)$

Evaluate.

81. $-6 \cdot 5$

82. $-9(-3)$

83. $\dfrac{-18}{-2}$

84. $\dfrac{100}{-5}$

85. $-50 \div (-10)$

86. $-3(0)$

87. $-5(-12)$

88. $56 \div (-8)$

89. $\dfrac{0}{5}$

90. Divide 60 by -2.

91. $(-1)(-5)(-9)$

92. Divide -120 by -10.

93. $-100 \div 5$

94. $4(-2)(-1)(-5)$

95. Divide 60 by -60.

96. $(6)(-1)(-3)(4)$

Indicate whether each of the following is 0 or undefined.

97. $0 \div 6$

98. $-4 \div 0$

99. $\dfrac{5}{0}$

100. $\dfrac{-2}{0}$

101. $\dfrac{0}{1}$

102. $0 \div (-2)$

103. $0 \div 6$

104. $6 \div 0$

105. $\dfrac{0}{-6}$

106. $\dfrac{0}{-1}$

107. 3 divided by 0

108. 0 divided by 12

For each of the following, (a) determine by observation whether the product or quotient will be a positive number, 0, a negative number, or undefined; (b) find the product or quotient on your calculator (an error message indicates that the quotient is undefined); (c) examine your answer in part (b) to see if it is reasonable and makes sense.

109. $96(-15)$

110. $(-212)(-87)$

111. $-168 \div 42$

112. $204 \div (-17)$

113. $-240/15$

114. $190/(-5)$

115. $243 \div (-27)$

116. $(-323) \div (-17)$

117. $(-15)(-170)$

118. $-440 \div 22$

119. $(-406)(-42)$

120. $(18)(-27)$

121. $(1530)(0)$

122. $0 \div 1935$

123. $(-19)(10.5)$

124. $-86.4 \div (-36)$

125. $7.2 \div 0$

126. $-37.74 \div 37$

127. $0 \div (-5260)$

128. $(4.3)(-2.1)(6.3)$

129. $(-90)(-1.2)(-1.6)$

130. $-288.86/1.43$

131. $(9.6)(-12.2)(-60)$

132. $0.48020/(-19.6)$

In Exercises 133–145, answer true or false.

133. The product of a positive number and a negative number is a negative number.

134. The product of two negative numbers is a negative number.

135. The quotient of two negative numbers is a positive number.

136. The quotient of two numbers with unlike signs is a positive number.

137. The product of an even number of negative numbers is a positive number.

138. The product of an odd number of negative numbers is a negative number.

139. Zero divided by 1 is 1.

140. Six divided by 0 is 0.

141. One divided by 0 is 0.

142. Zero divided by 1 is undefined.

143. Five divided by 0 is undefined.

144. The product of 0 and any real number is 0.

145. Division by 0 does not result in a real number.

146. Write out the rules for determining the sign of the product or quotient of two numbers.

147. Explain why the product of an even number of negative numbers is a positive number.

148. Will the product of $(1)(-2)(3)(-4)(5)(-6) \cdots (33)(-34)$ be a positive number or a negative number? Explain how you determined your answer.

CUMULATIVE REVIEW EXERCISES

[1.1] **149.** Find the quotient $\dfrac{5}{7} \div \dfrac{1}{5}$.

[1.5] **150.** Subtract -18 from -20.

Evaluate.

151. $6 - 3 - 4 - 2$

152. $5 - (-2) + 3 - 7$

Group Activity/ Challenge Problems

We will learn in the next section that $2^3 = 2 \cdot 2 \cdot 2$ and $x^m = \underbrace{x \cdot x \cdot x \cdot \cdots \cdot x}_{m \text{ factors of } x}$.

Using this information evaluate each of the following.

1. 3^4 **2.** $(-2)^3$ **3.** $\left(\dfrac{2}{3}\right)^3$ **4.** 1^{100} **5.** $(-1)^{81}$

Find the quotient.

6. $\dfrac{1 - 2 + 3 - 4 + 5 - \cdots + 99 - 100}{1 - 2 + 3 - 4 + 5 - \cdots + 99 - 100}$

7. $\dfrac{-1 + 2 - 3 + 4 - 5 + \cdots - 99 + 100}{1 - 2 + 3 - 4 + 5 - \cdots + 99 - 100}$

8. $\dfrac{5 \cdot 4 \cdot 3 \cdot 2 \cdot 1}{(-5)(-4)(-3)(-2)(-1)}$ **9.** $\dfrac{6 \cdot 5 \cdot 4 \cdot 3 \cdot 2 \cdot 1}{(-6)(-5)(-4)(-3)(-2)(-1)}$

10. $\dfrac{(-5)(-4)(-3)(-2)(-1)}{(-1)(2)(-3)(4)(-5)} \cdot (-1)(-2)(-3)$

1.8   An Introduction to Exponents

Tape 2

1. Learning the meaning of exponents.
2. Evaluate expressions containing exponents.
3. Learn the difference between $-x^2$ and $(-x)^2$.

Exponents

1. To understand certain topics in algebra, you must understand exponents. Exponents are introduced in this section and are discussed in more detail in Chapter 4.

In the expression 4^2, the 4 is called the **base,** and the 2 is called the **exponent.** The number 4^2 is read "4 squared" or "4 to the second power" and means

$$\underbrace{4 \cdot 4}_{\textbf{2 factors of 4}} = 4^2$$

The number 4^3 is read "4 cubed" or "4 to the third power" and means

$$\underbrace{4 \cdot 4 \cdot 4}_{\textbf{3 factors of 4}} = 4^3$$

In general, the number b to the nth power, written b^n, means

$$\underbrace{b \cdot b \cdot b \cdot \cdots \cdot b}_{n \text{ factors of } b} = b^n$$

Thus, $b^4 = b \cdot b \cdot b \cdot b$ or $bbbb$ and $x^3 = x \cdot x \cdot x$ or xxx.

Evaluate Expressions Containing Exponents **2**

EXAMPLE 1 Evaluate.

(a) 3^2 (b) 2^5 (c) 1^5 (d) 4^3 (e) $(-3)^2$ (f) $(-2)^3$ (g) $\left(\frac{2}{3}\right)^2$

Solution: (a) $3^2 = 3 \cdot 3 = 9$
(b) $2^5 = 2 \cdot 2 \cdot 2 \cdot 2 \cdot 2 = 32$
(c) $1^5 = 1 \cdot 1 \cdot 1 \cdot 1 \cdot 1 = 1$ (1 raised to any power equals 1; why?)
(d) $4^3 = 4 \cdot 4 \cdot 4 = 64$
(e) $(-3)^2 = (-3)(-3) = 9$
(f) $(-2)^3 = (-2)(-2)(-2) = -8$
(g) $\left(\frac{2}{3}\right)^2 = \left(\frac{2}{3}\right)\left(\frac{2}{3}\right) = \frac{4}{9}$

Other examples of exponential notation are:

(a) $x \cdot x \cdot x \cdot x = x^4$ (b) $aabbb = a^2b^3$
(c) $x \cdot x \cdot y = x^2y$ (d) $aaabb = a^3b^2$
(e) $xyxx = x^3y$ (f) $xyzzy = xy^2z^2$
(g) $3 \cdot x \cdot x \cdot y = 3x^2y$ (h) $5xyyyy = 5xy^4$
(i) $3 \cdot 3 \cdot x \cdot x = 3^2x^2$ (j) $5 \cdot 5 \cdot 5 \cdot xxy = 5^3x^2y$

Notice in parts **(e)** and **(f)** that the order of the factors does not matter.

Helpful Hint

Do you know the difference between **(a)** $x + x + x + x + x + x$ and **(b)** $x \cdot x \cdot x \cdot x \cdot x \cdot x$? Can you write a simplified expression for both parts **(a)** and **(b)**? The simplified expression for part **(a)** is $6x$ and the simplified expression for part **(b)** is x^6. Note that $x + x + x + x + x + x = 6x$ and $x \cdot x \cdot x \cdot x \cdot x \cdot x = x^6$.

It is not necessary to write exponents of 1. Thus, when writing xxy, we write x^2y and not x^2y^1. **Whenever we see a letter or number without an exponent, we always assume that letter or number has an exponent of 1.**

EXAMPLE 2 Write each expression as a product of factors.

(a) x^2y (b) xy^3z (c) $3x^2yz^3$ (d) 2^3xy (e) $3^2x^3y^2$

Solution: (a) $x^2y = xxy$ (b) $xy^3z = xyyyz$ (c) $3x^2yz^3 = 3xxyzzz$
(d) $2^3xy = 2 \cdot 2 \cdot 2xy$ (e) $3^2x^3y^2 = 3 \cdot 3xxxyy$

−x² and (−x)² ❸ **An exponent refers to only the number or letter that directly precedes it unless parentheses are used to indicate otherwise.** For example, in the expression $3x^2$, only the x is squared. In the expression $-x^2$ only the x is squared. We can write $-x^2$ as $-1x^2$ because any real number may be multiplied by 1 without affecting its value.

$$-x^2 = -1x^2$$

By looking at $-1x^2$ we can see that only the x is squared, not the -1. If the entire expression $-x$ was to be squared, we would need to use parentheses and write $(-x)^2$. Note the difference in the following two examples:

$$-x^2 = -(x)(x)$$
$$(-x)^2 = (-x)(-x)$$

Consider the expressions -3^2 and $(-3)^2$. How do they differ?

$$-3^2 = -(3)(3) = -9$$
$$(-3)^2 = (-3)(-3) = 9$$

EXAMPLE 3 Evaluate.

(a) -5^2 (b) $(-5)^2$ (c) -2^3 (d) $(-2)^3$

Solution: (a) $-5^2 = -(5)(5) = -25$ (b) $(-5)^2 = (-5)(-5) = 25$

(c) $-2^3 = -(2)(2)(2) = -8$ (d) $(-2)^3 = (-2)(-2)(-2) = -8$

EXAMPLE 4 Evaluate (a) -2^4 and (b) $(-2)^4$.

Solution: (a) $-2^4 = -(2)(2)(2)(2) = -16$
(b) $(-2)^4 = (-2)(-2)(-2)(-2) = 16$

EXAMPLE 5 Evaluate (a) x^2 and (b) $-x^2$ for $x = 3$.

Solution: Substitute 3 for x.

(a) $x^2 = 3^2 = 3 \cdot 3 = 9$ (b) $-x^2 = -3^2 = -(3)(3) = -9$

EXAMPLE 6 Evaluate (a) y^2 and (b) $-y^2$ for $y = -4$.

Solution: Substitute -4 for y.

(a) $y^2 = (-4)^2 = (-4)(-4) = 16$
(b) $-y^2 = -(-4)^2 = -(-4)(-4) = -16$

Note that $-x^2$ will always be a negative number for any nonzero value of x, and $(-x)^2$ will always be a positive number for any nonzero value of x. Can you explain why? See Exercises 104 and 105.

COMMON STUDENT ERROR The expression $-x^2$ means $-(x^2)$. When asked to evaluate $-x^2$ for any real number x, many students will incorrectly treat $-x^2$ as $(-x)^2$.
Evaluate $-x^2$ when $x = 5$.

Correct	*Incorrect*
$-5^2 = -(5^2) = -(5)(5)$	$-5^2 = (-5)(-5)$
$= -25$	$= 25$

USE OF x^2 AND y^x KEYS

The x^2 key is used to square a value. For example, to evaluate 5^2 we would press.

$$5 \;\; \boxed{x^2} \;\; 25$$

After the x^2 key is pressed the answer 25 is displayed.
To evaluate $(-5)^2$ on a calculator, we press

$$5 \;\; \boxed{+/-} \;\; \boxed{x^2} \;\; 25$$

Note that $(-5)^2$ has a value of 25.

To raise a value to a power greater than 2 we use the y^x or x^y key. Some calculators have a y^x key while others have an x^y key. To use these keys you enter the number, then press either the y^x or x^y key, then enter the exponent. After the $\boxed{=}$ key is pressed the answer will be displayed.

Evaluate	Keystrokes
2^5	$2 \; \boxed{y^x} \; 5 \; \boxed{=} \; 32$
$(13)^4$	$13 \; \boxed{y^x} \; 4 \; \boxed{=} \; 28561$

Even when using the parentheses keys *some* scientific calculators cannot directly raise a negative number to a power greater than 2. For example, if you evaluate $(-2)^5$ using the keystrokes $\boxed{(} \; 2 \; \boxed{+/-} \; \boxed{)} \; \boxed{y^x} \; 5 \; \boxed{=}$ *some* calculators will give an *error* message. The correct answer is -32. Possibly the easiest way to raise negative numbers to a power may be to raise the positive number to the power and then write a negative sign before the final answer if needed. *A negative number raised to an odd power will be negative, and a negative number raised to an even power will be positive.* Can you explain why this is true?

Evaluate	Keystrokes	Correct Answer
$(-2)^5$	$2 \; \boxed{y^x} \; 5 \; \boxed{=} \; 32$	-32 (since the exponent is odd)
$(-13)^4$	$13 \; \boxed{y^x} \; 4 \; \boxed{=} \; 28561$	28561 (since the exponent is even)

RAISING FRACTIONS TO POWERS

To raise fractions to powers we may use the $\boxed{=}$ key before using the x^2 or y^x key, or we may use parentheses.

Evaluate	Keystrokes
$\left(\dfrac{2}{5}\right)^2$	$2 \; \boxed{\div} \; 5 \; \boxed{=} \; \boxed{x^2} \; .16$ or $\boxed{(} \; 2 \; \boxed{\div} \; 5 \; \boxed{)} \; \boxed{x^2} \; .16$
$\left(\dfrac{2}{5}\right)^6$	$2 \; \boxed{\div} \; 5 \; \boxed{=} \; \boxed{y^x} \; 6 \; \boxed{=} \; .004096$ or $\boxed{(} \; 2 \; \boxed{\div} \; 5 \; \boxed{)} \; \boxed{y^x} \; 6 \; \boxed{=} \; .004096$

When evaluating $\left(\dfrac{2}{5}\right)^2$ what would happen if we did not use either the $\boxed{=}$ or the parentheses keys? That is, what would the calculator display if you keyed in $2 \; \boxed{\div} \; 5 \; \boxed{x^2}$ and $2 \; \boxed{\div} \; 5 \; \boxed{x^2} \; \boxed{=}$? Try this now on your calculator and explain the results. See Group Activity Exercise 5.

Exercise Set 1.8

Evaluate.

1. 5^2
2. 3^2
3. 2^3
4. 1^5
5. 3^3
6. -5^2
7. 6^3
8. $(-2)^2$
9. $(-2)^3$
10. -3^4
11. $(-1)^3$
12. 6^2
13. 3^3
14. 2^5
15. -6^2
16. 5^3
17. $(-6)^2$
18. $(-3)^3$
19. 2^4
20. $(-3)^4$
21. 4^1
22. -3^2
23. $(-2)^4$
24. -1^4
25. -2^4
26. $(-1)^4$
27. $(-4)^3$
28. $3^2(4)^2$
29. $5^2 \cdot 3^2$
30. $(-1)^4(3)^3$
31. $5(4^2)$
32. $2^3 \cdot 5^1$
33. $2^1 \cdot 4^2$
34. $(-2)^4(-1)^3$
35. $3(-5^2)$
36. $9(-2)^2$

Express in exponential form.

37. $x \cdot\ x \cdot y \cdot y$
38. $x \cdot y \cdot z \cdot z$
39. $xyyyz$
40. $xxxxz$
41. $yyzzz$
42. $aabbab$
43. $xyxyz$
44. $x \cdot x \cdot y \cdot z \cdot z$
45. $a \cdot x \cdot a \cdot x \cdot y$
46. $x \cdot x \cdot x \cdot y \cdot y$
47. $x \cdot y \cdot y \cdot z \cdot z \cdot z$
48. $xyyyy$
49. $3xyy$
50. $2 \cdot 2 \cdot 2xyyyy$

Express as a product of factors.

51. x^2y
52. y^2z
53. xy^3
54. x^2yz
55. xy^2z^3
56. $2x^2y^2$
57. 3^2yz
58. 2^3y^3
59. 2^3x^3y
60. 3^3xy^3
61. $(-2)^2y^3z$
62. $(-1)^2x^3y^2$

Evaluate (a) x^2 and (b) $-x^2$ for each of the following values of x.

63. 3
64. 2
65. 4
66. 1
67. -2
68. 5
69. 7
70. 8
71. -1
72. -5
73. $-\dfrac{1}{2}$
74. $\dfrac{3}{4}$

In Exercises 75–94 (a) determine by observation whether the answer should be positive or negative, (b) evaluate the expression on your calculator, and (c) determine if your answer in part (b) is reasonable and makes sense.

75. 3^5
76. 4^6
77. $(-2)^3$
78. 5^4
79. -2^5
80. $(-6)^3$
81. -5^6
82. 10^4
83. $(-6)^4$
84. $(1.3)^3$
85. $(8.4)^3$
86. $(5.3)^4$
87. $(-2.3)^3$
88. $(-4.5)^4$
89. $(-1/2)^4$
90. $-(1/2)^4$
91. $(2/5)^4$
92. $(3/4)^3$
93. $(-2/3)^4$
94. $-\left(\dfrac{3}{5}\right)^3$

In Exercises 95–103, answer true or false.

95. $(-4)^{20}$ is a negative number.
96. $(-4)^{19}$ is a negative number.
97. $-(-3)^{15}$ is a negative number.
98. $-(-2)^{14}$ is a negative number.
99. x^2y means x^2y^1.
100. $3xy^4$ means $3^1x^1y^4$.
101. $2x^5y$ means $2^1x^5y^1$.

102. When a number is written without an exponent, the exponent on the number is 0.

103. When a variable is written without an exponent, the exponent on the variable is 1.

104. Explain why $-x^2$ will always be a negative number for any nonzero value of x.

105. Explain why $(-x)^2$ will always be a positive number for any nonzero value of x.

106. Will the expression $(-6)^{15}$ be a positive or a negative number? Explain.

107. Will the expression $(-1)^{100}$ be a positive or a negative number? Explain.

108. Will the expression -8^{14} be a positive or a negative number? Explain.

109. We will discuss using zero as an exponent in Section 4.1. On your scientific calculator find the value of 4^0 by using your y^x or x^y key and record its value. Evaluate a few other numbers raised to the zero power. Can you make any conclusions about a real number (other than 0) raised to the zero power?

CUMULATIVE REVIEW EXERCISES

[1.6] **110.** Subtract -6 from 12.

111. Evaluate $-4 - 3 + 9 - 7$.

112. Evaluate $-4672 - 5692$ on your calculator.

[1.7] *Evaluate.*

113. $\left(\dfrac{-5}{7}\right) \div \left(\dfrac{-3}{14}\right)$

114. $\dfrac{0}{4}$

Group Activity/ Challenge Problems

*In Exercises 1–4, simplify parts (**a**) to (**c**), and leave the answer in exponential form. Using parts (**a**) to (**c**), and other examples, determine the answer to part (**d**).*

1. (a) $2^2 \cdot 2^3$ (b) $3^2 \cdot 3^3$ (c) $2^3 \cdot 2^4$ (d) $x^m \cdot x^n$

2. (a) $\dfrac{2^3}{2^2}$ (b) $\dfrac{3^4}{3^2}$ (c) $\dfrac{4^5}{4^3}$ (d) $\dfrac{x^m}{x^n}$

3. (a) $(2^3)^2$ (b) $(3^3)^2$ (c) $(4^2)^2$ (d) $(x^m)^n$

4. (a) $(2x)^2$ (b) $(3x)^2$ (c) $(4x)^3$ (d) $(ax)^m$

General rules that may be used to solve problems like 1 through 4 will be discussed in Chapter 4.

5. In the Calculator Corner in this section we showed that to evaluate $\left(\dfrac{2}{5}\right)^2$ we press the following keys:

$$2 \div 5 = x^2 \;.16$$

Therefore, $(2/5)^2 = 0.16$. Using a scientific calculator, perform the set of keystrokes below. Explain each result.

(a) $2 \div 5\; x^2$ (b) $2 \div 5\; x^2\; =$

Tape 2

Order of Operations

1.9   Use of Parentheses and Order of Operations

1 Learn the order of operations.
2 Learn the use of parentheses.
3 Evaluate expressions for given values of the variable.

1 Evaluate $2 + 3 \cdot 4$. Is it 20? Is it 14? To answer this question you must know the order of operations to follow when evaluating a mathematical expression. You will often have to evaluate expressions containing multiple operations.

> **To Evaluate Mathematical Expressions, Use the Following Order**
> 1. First, evaluate the information within **parentheses** ( ), or brackets [   ]. If the expression contains nested parentheses (one pair of parentheses within another pair), evaluate the information in the innermost parentheses first.
> 2. Next, evaluate all **exponents**.
> 3. Next, evaluate all **multiplications** or **divisions** in the order in which they occur, working from left to right.
> 4. Finally, evaluate all **additions** or **subtractions** in the order in which they occur, working from left to right.

We can now evaluate $2 + 3 \cdot 4$. Since multiplications are performed before additions,

$$2 + 3 \cdot 4 \text{ means } 2 + (3 \cdot 4) = 2 + 12 = 14$$

Calculator Corner

We now know that $2 + 3 \cdot 4$ means $2 + (3 \cdot 4)$ and has a value of 14. What will a calculator display if you key in the following?

$$\boxed{2} + \boxed{3} \times \boxed{4} =$$

The answer depends on your calculator. *Scientific calculators* will evaluate an expression following the rules just stated.

Scientific calculator: $\boxed{2} + \boxed{3} \times \boxed{4} = 14$

Nonscientific calculators will perform operations in the order they are entered.

Nonscientific calculator: $\boxed{2} + \boxed{3} \times \boxed{4} = 20$

Remember that in algebra, unless otherwise instructed by parentheses, we always perform multiplications and divisions before additions and subtractions. Is your calculator a scientific calculator?

To calculate $2 + (3 \times 4)$ on a nonscientific calculator, we first enter the multiplication and then the addition, as follows:

$$\boxed{3} \times \boxed{4} + \boxed{2} = 14$$

Scientific calculators are not much more expensive than nonscientific calculators. We recommend that you purchase a scientific calculator, especially if you plan to take more mathematics or science courses.

Use of Parentheses   **2** Parentheses or brackets may be used (1) to change the order of operations to be followed in evaluating an algebraic expression or (2) to help clarify the understanding of an expression.

To evaluate the expression $2 + 3 \cdot 4$, we would normally perform the multiplication, $3 \cdot 4$, first. If we wished to have the addition performed before the multiplication, we could indicate this by placing parentheses about the $2 + 3$:

$$(2 + 3) \cdot 4 = 5 \cdot 4 = 20$$

Consider the expression $1 \cdot 3 + 2 \cdot 4$. According to the order, multiplications are to be performed before additions. We can rewrite this expression as $(1 \cdot 3) + (2 \cdot 4)$. Note that the order of operations was not changed. The parentheses were used only to help clarify the order to be followed.

Helpful Hint

If parentheses are not used to change the order of operations, multiplications and divisions are always performed before additions and subtractions. When a problem has only multiplications and divisions, work from left to right. Similarly, when a problem has only additions and subtractions, work from left to right.

EXAMPLE 1   Evaluate $2 + 3 \cdot 5^2 - 7$.

Solution: Color shading is used to indicate the order in which the expression is to be evaluated.

$$2 + 3 \cdot 5^2 - 7$$
$$= 2 + 3 \cdot 25 - 7$$
$$= 2 + 75 - 7$$
$$= 77 - 7$$
$$= 70$$

EXAMPLE 2   Evaluate $6 + 3[(12 \div 4) + 5]$.

Solution: $6 + 3[(12 \div 4) + 5]$
$$= 6 + 3[3 + 5]$$
$$= 6 + 3(8)$$
$$= 6 + 24$$
$$= 30$$

EXAMPLE 3   Evaluate $(4 \div 2) + 4(5 - 2)^2$.

Solution: $(4 \div 2) + 4(5 - 2)^2$
$$= 2 + 4(3)^2$$
$$= 2 + 4 \cdot 9$$
$$= 2 + 36$$
$$= 38$$

EXAMPLE 4   Evaluate $5 + 2^2 \cdot 3 - 3^2$.

Solution: $5 + 2^2 \cdot 3 - 3^2$
$$= 5 + 4 \cdot 3 - 9$$
$$= 5 + 12 - 9$$
$$= 17 - 9$$
$$= 8$$

EXAMPLE 5 Evaluate $-8 - 81 \div 9 \cdot 2^2 + 7$.

Solution:

$$8 - 81 \div 9 \cdot 2^2 + 7$$
$$= -8 - 81 \div 9 \cdot 4 + 7$$
$$= -8 - 9 \cdot 4 + 7$$
$$= -8 - 36 + 7$$
$$= -44 + 7$$
$$= -37$$

EXAMPLE 6 Evaluate.

(a) $-4^2 + 6 \div 3$ (b) $(-4)^2 + 6 \div 3$

Solution:

(a) $\quad -4^2 + 6 \div 3$ (b) $\quad (-4)^2 + 6 \div 3$

$\quad = -16 + 6 \div 3 \qquad = 16 + 6 \div 3$

$\quad = -16 + 2 \qquad\qquad = 16 + 2$

$\quad = -14 \qquad\qquad\qquad = 18$

EXAMPLE 7 Evaluate $\dfrac{3}{8} - \dfrac{2}{5} \cdot \dfrac{1}{12}$.

Solution: First perform the multiplication.

$$\frac{3}{8} - \left(\frac{\overset{1}{\cancel{2}}}{5} \cdot \frac{1}{\underset{6}{\cancel{12}}} \right)$$

$$= \frac{3}{8} - \frac{1}{30}$$

$$= \frac{45}{120} - \frac{4}{120}$$

$$= \frac{41}{120}$$

EXAMPLE 8 Write the following statements as mathematical expressions using parentheses and brackets and then evaluate: Multiply 5 by 3. To this product add 6. Multiply this sum by 7.

Solution:

$\quad 5 \cdot 3$ **Multiply 5 by 3.**

$\quad (5 \cdot 3) + 6$ **Add 6.**

$\quad 7[(5 \cdot 3) + 6]$ **Multiply the sum by 7.**

Now evaluate the expression.

$$7[(5 \cdot 3) + 6]$$
$$= 7[15 + 6]$$
$$= 7(21)$$
$$= 147$$

Sometimes brackets are used in place of parentheses to help avoid confusion. If only parentheses had been used, the preceding expression would appear as $7((5 \cdot 3) + 6)$.

EXAMPLE 9 Write the following statements as mathematical expressions using parentheses and brackets and then evaluate: Subtract 3 from 15. Divide this difference by 2. Multiply this quotient by 4.

Solution: $15 - 3$ **Subtract 3 from 15.**
               $(15 - 3) \div 2$ **Divide by 2.**
             $4[(15 - 3) \div 2]$ **Multiply the quotient by 4.**

Now evaluate.

$$4[(15 - 3) \div 2]$$
$$= 4[12 \div 2]$$
$$= 4(6)$$
$$= 24$$

Calculator Corner

USING PARENTHESES

When evaluating an expression on a calculator where the order of operations is to be changed, you will need to use parentheses. If you are not sure whether or not they are needed, it will not hurt to add them. Consider $\dfrac{8}{4 - 2}$. Since we wish to divide 8 by the difference $4 - 2$, we need to use parentheses.

Evaluate   *Keystrokes*

$\dfrac{8}{4 - 2}$ $8 \div (4 - 2) = 4$

What would you obtain if you evaluated $8 \div 4 - 2 =$ on a calculator? Why would you get that result? Here is another example.

Evaluate   *Keystrokes*

$-5(20 - 46) - 12$ $5 \;{}^{+\!/_-} \times (20 - 46) - 12 = 118$

Evaluating Expressions Containing Variables

▣ Now we will evaluate some expressions for given values of the variables.

EXAMPLE 10 Evaluate $7x - 2$ when $x = 2$.

Solution: Substitute 2 for x in the expression.

$$7x - 2 = 7(2) - 2 = 14 - 2 = 12$$

EXAMPLE 11   Evaluate $(3x + 1) + 2x^2$ when $x = 4$.

Solution: Substitute 4 for each x in the expression.

$$\begin{aligned}
(3x + 1) + 2x^2 &= [3(4) + 1] + 2(4)^2 \\
&= [12 + 1] + 2(4)^2 \\
&= 13 + 2(16) \\
&= 13 + 32 \\
&= 45
\end{aligned}$$

EXAMPLE 12   Evaluate $-y^2 + 3(x + 2) - 5$ when $x = -3$ and $y = -2$.

Solution:
$$\begin{aligned}
-y^2 + 3(x + 2) - 5 &= -(-2)^2 + 3(-3 + 2) - 5 \\
&= -(-2)^2 + 3(-1) - 5 \\
&= -(4) + 3(-1) - 5 \\
&= -4 - 3 - 5 \\
&= -7 - 5 \\
&= -12
\end{aligned}$$

Calculator Corner

EVALUATING EXPRESSIONS

Later in this course you will need to evaluate an expression like $3x^2 - 2x + 5$ for various values of x. Below we show how to evaluate such expressions.

Evaluate	*Keystrokes*
(a) $3x^2 - 2x + 5$, for $x = 4$ $3(4)^2 - 2(4) + 5$	$3 \times 4\;x^2\; - 2 \times 4 + 5 = 45$
(b) $3x^2 - 2x + 5$, for $x = -6$ $3(-6)^2 - 2(-6) + 5$	$3 \times 6^{+/_-}\;x^2\; - 2 \times 6^{+/_-} + 5 = 125$
(c) $-x^2 - 3x - 5$, for $x = -2$ $-(-2)^2 - 3(-2) - 5$	$1^{+/_-} \times 2^{+/_-}\;x^2\; - 3 \times 2^{+/_-} - 5 = -3$

Remember in part (c) that $-x^2 = -1x^2$.

Exercise Set 1.9

Evaluate.

1. $3 + 4 \cdot 5$

2. $3 - 5^2 - 2$

3. $6 - 6 + 8$

4. $(6^2 \div 3) - (6 - 4)$

5. $1 + 3 \cdot 2^2$

6. $4 \cdot 3^2 - 2 \cdot 5$

7. $-4^2 + 6$

8. $(-2)^3 + 8 \div 4$

9. $(4 - 3) \cdot (5 - 1)^2$

10. $20 - 6 - 3 - 2$

11. $3 \cdot 7 + 4 \cdot 2$

12. $8 + 5(6 - 1)$

13. $[1 - (4 \cdot 5)] + 6$

14. $[12 - (4 \div 2)] - 5$

15. $4^2 - 3 \cdot 4 - 6$

16. $5 - 3 + 4^2 - 6$

17. $-2[-5 + (3 - 4)]$

18. $(-3)^2 + (3 - 4)^3 - 5$

19. $(6 \div 3)^3 + 4^2 \div 8$

20. $5^2 - 2^2(4 - 2)^2$

21. $-4^2 + 8 \div 2 \cdot 5 + 3$

22. $-4 - (-12 + 4) \div 2 + 1$

23. $3 + (4^2 - 10)^2 - 3$

24. $[-2(2 - 4)^2]^2 - 6$

25. $[6 - (-2 - 3)]^2$

26. $(-2)^2 + 4^2 \div 2^2 + 3$

27. $(3^2 - 1) \div (3 + 1)^2$

28. $-4(5 - 2)^2 + 5$

29. $-[(56 \div 7) - 6 \div 2]$

30. $4[6 + (6 \div 2)^2] - 1$

31. $2[3(8 - 2^2) - 6]$

32. $(13 + 5) - (4 - 2)^2$

33. $10 - [8 - (3 + 4)]^2$

34. $6 - 8 \cdot 2 \div 4 \div 2 + 5$

35. $[4 + ((5 - 2)^2 \div 3)^2]^2$

36. $2[((6 \div 3)^2 + 4)^2 - 3]$

37. $[-3(4 - 2)^2]^2 - [-3(3 - 5)^2]$

38. $[7 - [3(8 \div 4)]^2 + 9 \cdot 4]^2$

39. $(14 \div 7 \cdot 7 \div 7 - 7)^2$

40. $2.5 + 7.56 \div 2.1 + (9.2)^2$

41. $(8.4 + 3.1)^2 - (3.64 - 1.2)$

42. $2[1.63 + 5(4.7)] - 3.15$

43. $(4.3)^2 + 2(5.3) - 3.05$

44. $\frac{2}{3} + \frac{3}{8} \cdot \frac{4}{5}$

45. $\left(\frac{2}{7} + \frac{3}{8}\right) - \frac{3}{112}$

46. $\left(\frac{5}{6} \cdot \frac{4}{5}\right) + \left(\frac{2}{3} \cdot \frac{5}{8}\right)$

47. $\frac{3}{4} - 4 \cdot \frac{5}{40}$

48. $\frac{2}{3} + 4 \div 3^2$

49. $2\left(3 + \frac{2}{5}\right) \div \left(\frac{3}{5}\right)^2$

50. $64 \cdot \frac{1}{2} \div 8 + \frac{3}{4}$

Write the following statements as mathematical expressions using parentheses and brackets and then evaluate.

51. Multiply 6 by 3. From this product, subtract 4. From this difference, subtract 2.

52. Add 4 to 9. Divide this sum by 2. Add 10 to this quotient.

53. Divide 20 by 5. Add 12 to this quotient. Subtract 8 from this sum. Multiply this difference by 9.

54. Multiply 6 by 3. To this product, add 27. Divide this sum by 8. Multiply this quotient by 10.

55. Add $\frac{4}{5}$ to $\frac{3}{7}$. Multiply this sum by $\frac{2}{3}$.

56. Multiply $\frac{3}{8}$ by $\frac{4}{5}$. To this product, add $\frac{7}{120}$. From this sum, subtract $\frac{1}{60}$.

Evaluate for the values given.

57. $x + 4$, when $x = -2$.

58. $2x - 4x + 5$, when $x = 1$.

59. $3x - 2$, when $x = 4$.

60. $3(x - 2)$, when $x = 5$.

61. $x^2 - 6$, when $x = -3$.

62. $x^2 + 4$, when $x = 5$.

63. $-3x^2 - 4$, when $x = 1$.

64. $2x^2 + x$, when $x = 3$.

65. $-4x^2 - 2x + 5$, when $x = -3$.

66. $-3x^2 + 6x + 5$, when $x = 5$.

67. $3(x - 2)^2$, when $x = 7$.

68. $4(x + 1)^2 - 6x$, when $x = 5$.

69. $2(x - 3)(x + 4)$, when $x = 1$.

70. $3x^2(x - 1) + 5$, when $x = -4$.

71. $-6x + 3y$, when $x = 2$ and $y = 4$.

72. $6x + 3y^2 - 5$, when $x = 1$ and $y = -3$.

73. $x^2 - y^2$, when $x = -2$, and $y = -3$.

74. $x^2 - y^2$, when $x = 2$ and $y = -4$.

75. $4(x + y)^2 + 4x - 3y$, when $x = 2$ and $y = -3$.

76. $(4x - 3y)^2 - 5$, when $x = 4$ and $y = -2$.

77. $3(a + b)^2 + 4(a + b) - 6$, when $a = 4$ and $b = -1$.

78. $4xy - 6x + 3$, when $x = 5$ and $y = 2$.

79. $x^2y - 6xy + 3x$, when $x = 2$ and $y = 3$.

80. $\frac{6x^2}{3} + \frac{2x^2}{2}$, when $x = 2$.

81. $6x^2 + 3xy - y^2$, when $x = 2$ and $y = -3$.

82. $3(x - 4)^2 - (3x - 4)^2$, when $x = -1$.

83. $5(2x - 3)^2 - 4(6 - y)^2$, when $x = -2$ and $y = -1$.

84. $[2(x - 3) + (y + 2)]^2 - 6x^2$, when $x = 3$ and $y = -2$.

🖩 *Later in the text we will need to evaluate expressions like $ax^2 + bx + c$ where a, b, and c are real numbers for various values of the variable x. In Exercises 85–100, determine the value of the expression for the value of the variable given (a) without using a calculator and (b) using a scientific calculator. If parts (a) and (b) do not agree, determine why. (See the Calculator Corner on page 62.)*

85. $x^2 + 3x - 5$, $x = 2$

86. $2x^2 - 5x + 3$, $x = 1$

87. $x^2 - 4x + 7$, $x = -3$

88. $3x^2 - 6x - 4$, $x = 2$

89. $-x^2 + 6x - 5$, $x = 3$

90. $4x^2 - 5x$, $x = -6$

91. $-x^2 - 2x - 5$, $x = -3$

92. $-3x^2 - 12$, $x = -3$

93. $2x^2 - 4x - 10$, $x = 5$

94. $6x^2 - 3x + 2$, $x = 4$

95. $-x^2 - 6x + 8$, $x = 5$

96. $-5x^2 - 3x + 12$, $x = -3$

97. $x^2 - 16x + 5$, $x = 5$

98. $4x^2 + 5x - 3$, $x = -2$

99. $x^2 + 8x - 10$, $x = 4$

100. $x^2 - 4x + 12$, $x = 6$

101. In your own words, write the order of operations to follow to evaluate a mathematical expression.

102. (a) Write in your own words the procedure you would use to evaluate $[9 - (8 \div 2)]^2 - 6^3$.

(b) Evaluate the expression in part (a).

103. (a) Write in your own words the procedure you would use to evaluate the expression $-4x^2 + 3x - 6$ when x is 5.

(b) Evaluate the expression in part (a) when $x = 5$.

CUMULATIVE REVIEW EXERCISES

[1.7] **104.** Evaluate $(-2)(-4)(6)(-1)(-3)$.

[1.8] **105.** When $x = -5$ evaluate (a) x^2 and (b) $-x^2$.

Evaluate.

106. $(-2)^4$

107. -2^4

Group Activity/ Challenge Problems

Evaluate for the values given.

1. $4([3(x - 2)]^2 + 4)$, when $x = 4$.

2. $[(3 - 6)^2 + 4]^2 + 3 \cdot 4 - 12 \div 3$.

3. $-2[(3x^2 + 4)^2 - (3x^2 - 2)^2]$, when $x = -2$.

Insert one pair of parentheses to make the statement true.

4. $14 + 6 \div 2 \times 4 = 40$

5. $12 - 4 - 6 + 10 = 24$

6. $24 \div 6 \div 2 + 2 = 1$

7. $30 + 15 \div 5 + 10 \div 2 = 38$

8. $18 \div 3^2 - 3 + 5 = 8$

1.10 Properties of the Real Number System

Tape 3

1 Identify the commutative property.

2 Identify the associative property.

3 Identify the distributive property.

Here, we introduce various properties of the real number system. We will use these properties throughout the text.

The Commutative Property

1 The *commutative property of addition* states that the order in which any two real numbers are added does not matter.

> **Commutative Property of Addition**
>
> If a and b represent any two real numbers, then
> $$a + b = b + a$$

Notice the commutative property involves a change in *order*. For example,

$$4 + 3 = 3 + 4$$
$$7 = 7$$

The *commutative property of multiplication* states that the order in which any two real numbers are multiplied does not matter.

> ### Commutative Property of Multiplication
>
> If a and b represent any two real numbers. then
>
> $$a \cdot b = b \cdot a$$

For example,

$$6 \cdot 3 = 3 \cdot 6$$
$$18 = 18$$

The commutative property **does not hold** *for subtraction or division.* For example, $4 - 6 \neq 6 - 4$ and $6 \div 3 \neq 3 \div 6$.

The Associative Property

2 The *associative property of addition* states that, in the addition of three or more numbers, parentheses may be placed around any two adjacent numbers without changing the results.

> ### Associative Property of Addition
>
> If a, b. and c represent any three real numbers. then
>
> $$(a + b) + c = a + (b + c)$$

Notice that the associative property involves a change of *grouping*. For example,

$$(3 + 4) + 5 = 3 + (4 + 5)$$
$$7 + 5 = 3 + 9$$
$$12 = 12$$

In this example the 3 and 4 are grouped together on the left, and the 4 and 5 are grouped together on the right.

The *associative property of multiplication* states that, in the multiplication of three or more numbers, parentheses may be placed around any two adjacent numbers without changing the results.

> ### Associative Property of Multiplication
>
> If a, b. and c represent any three real numbers. then
>
> $$(a \cdot b) \cdot c = a \cdot (b \cdot c)$$

For example,

$$(6 \cdot 2) \cdot 4 = 6 \cdot (2 \cdot 4)$$
$$12 \cdot 4 = 6 \cdot 8$$
$$48 = 48$$

Notice that the associative property involves a change of grouping. When the associative property is used, the content within the parentheses changes.

The associative property **does not hold** *for subtraction or division.* For example, $(4 - 1) - 3 \neq 4 - (1 - 3)$ and $(8 \div 4) \div 2 \neq 8 \div (4 \div 2)$.

The Distributive Property

3 A very important property of the real numbers is the *distributive property of multiplication over addition.*

> **Distributive Property**
>
> If a, b, and c represent any three real numbers, then
>
> $$a(b + c) = ab + ac$$

For example, if we let $a = 2$, $b = 3$, and $c = 4$, then

$$2(3 + 4) = (2 \cdot 3) + (2 \cdot 4)$$
$$2 \cdot 7 = 6 + 8$$
$$14 = 14$$

Therefore, we may either add first and then multiply, or multiply first and then add. The distributive property will be discussed in more detail in Chapter 2.

Helpful Hint
....

The *commutative property* changes *order.*

The *associative property* changes *grouping.*

The *distributive property* involves two operations, multiplication and addition.

The following are additional illustrations of the commutative, associative, and distributive properties. If we assume that x represents any real number, then:

$x + 4 = 4 + x$ by the commutative property of addition.
$x \cdot 4 = 4 \cdot x$ by the commutative property of multiplication.
$(x + 4) + 7 = x + (4 + 7)$ by the associative property of addition.
$(x \cdot 4) \cdot 6 = x \cdot (4 \cdot 6)$ by the associative property of multiplication.
$3(x + 4) = (3 \cdot x) + (3 \cdot 4)$ or $3x + 12$ by the distributive property.

EXAMPLE 1   Name the properties.

(a) $4 + (-2) = -2 + 4$ (b) $x + y = y + x$
(c) $x \cdot y = y \cdot x$ (d) $(-12 + 3) + 4 = -12 + (3 + 4)$

Solution: (a) Commutative property of addition
(b) Commutative property of addition
(c) Commutative property of multiplication
(d) Associative property of addition

EXAMPLE 2   Name the properties.

(a) $2(x + 2) = (2 \cdot x) + (2 \cdot 2) = 2x + 4$
(b) $4(x + y) = (4 \cdot x) + (4 \cdot y) = 4x + 4y$
(c) $3x + 3y = (3 \cdot x) + (3 \cdot y) = 3(x + y)$
(d) $(3 \cdot 6) \cdot 5 = 3 \cdot (6 \cdot 5)$

Solution: (a) Distributive property
        (b) Distributive property
        (c) Distributive property (in reverse order)
        (d) Associative property of multiplication

EXAMPLE 3   Name the properties.

(a) $(3 + 4) + 5 = (4 + 3) + 5$
(b) $(2 + 3) + (4 + 5) = (4 + 5) + (2 + 3)$
(c) $3(x + 4) = 3(4 + x)$ (d) $3(x + 4) = (x + 4)3$

Solution: (a) Commutative property of addition. The $3 + 4$ was changed to $4 + 3$. The same numbers remain within parentheses; therefore, it is not the associative property.
        (b) Commutative property of addition. The order of parentheses was changed; however, the same numbers remain within the parentheses.
        (c) Commutative property of addition. $x + 4$ was changed to $4 + x$.
        (d) Commutative property of multiplication. The expression within parentheses is not changed.

Helpful Hint

Do not confuse the distributive property with the associative property of multiplication. Make sure you understand the difference.

Distributive Property	*Associative Property of Multiplication*
$3(4 + x) = 3 \cdot 4 + 3 \cdot x$	$3(4 \cdot x) = (3 \cdot 4)x$
$= 12 + 3x$	$= 12x$

For the distributive property to be used, there must be two *terms*, separated by a plus or minus sign, within the parentheses, as in $3(4 + x)$.

EXAMPLE 4   Name the property used to go from one step to the next.

(a) $9 + 4(x + 5)$
(b) $= 9 + 4x + 20$
(c) $= 9 + 20 + 4x$
(d) $= 29 + 4x$ **addition facts**
(e) $= 4x + 29$

Solution: (**a to b**) Distributive property
        (**b to c**) Commutative property of addition; $4x + 20 = 20 + 4x$
        (**d to e**) Commutative property of addition; $29 + 4x = 4x + 29$

The distributive property can be expanded in the following manner:

$$a(b + c + d + \cdots + n) = ab + ac + ad + \cdots + an$$

For example, $3(x + y + 5) = 3x + 3y + 15$.

Exercise Set 1.10

Name the property illustrated.

1. $4(3 + 5) = 4(3) + 4(5)$
2. $3 + y = y + 3$
3. $5 \cdot y = y \cdot 5$
4. $1(x + 3) = (1)(x) + (1)(3) = x + 3$
5. $2(x + 4) = 2x + 8$
6. $3(4 + x) = 12 + 3x$
7. $x \cdot (y \cdot z) = (x \cdot y) \cdot z$
8. $1(x + 4) = x + 4$
9. $1(x + 3) = x + 3$
10. $3 + (4 + x) = (3 + 4) + x$

Complete using the property given.

11. $3 + 4 =$
    commutative property of addition
12. $-3 + 4 =$
    commutative property of addition
13. $-6 \cdot (4 \cdot 2) =$
    associative property of multiplication
14. $-4 + (5 + 3) =$
    associative property of addition
15. $(6)(y) =$
    commutative property of multiplication
16. $4(x + 3) =$
    distributive property
17. $1(x + y) =$
    distributive property
18. $6(x + y) =$
    distributive property
19. $4x + 3y =$
    commutative property of addition
20. $3(x + y) =$
    distributive property
21. $5x + 5y =$
    distributive property (in reverse order)
22. $(3 + x) + y =$
    associative property of addition
23. $(x + 2)3 =$
    commutative property of multiplication
24. $2x + 2z =$
    distributive property (in reverse order)
25. $(3x + 4) + 6 =$
    associative property of addition
26. $3(x + y) =$
    commutative property of addition
27. $3(x + y) =$
    commutative property of multiplication
28. $(3x)y =$
    associative property of multiplication
29. $4(x + y + 3) =$
    distributive property
30. $3(x + y + 2) =$
    distributive property

Name the property illustrated to go from one step to the next. See Example 4.

31. $(3 + x) + 4 = (x + 3) + 4$
32. $ = x + (3 + 4)$
    $ = x + 7$
33. $6 + 5(x + 3) = 6 + 5x + 15$
34. $ = 6 + 15 + 5x$
    $ = 21 + 5x$

35. $ = 5x + 21$
36. $(x + 4)5 = 5(x + 4)$
37. $ = 5x + 20$
38. $ = 20 + 5x$

In Exercises 39–42, indicate if the given processes are commutative. That is, does changing the order in which the items are done result in the same final outcome? Explain.

39. Putting sugar and then cream in coffee; putting cream and then sugar in coffee.

40. Applying suntan lotion and then sunning yourself; sunning yourself and then applying suntan lotion.

41. Putting on your socks and then your shoes; putting on your shoes and then your socks.

42. Brushing your teeth and then washing your face; washing your face and then brushing your teeth.

43. Explain how you can tell the difference between the associative property of multiplication and the distributive property.

CUMULATIVE REVIEW EXERCISES

[1.2] **44.** Add $2\frac{3}{5} + \frac{2}{3}$.

45. Subtract $3\frac{5}{8} - 2\frac{3}{16}$.

[1.9] *Evaluate.*

46. $12 - 24 \div 8 + 4 \cdot 3^2$

47. $-4x^2 + 6xy + 3y^2$, when $x = 2$ and $y = -3$

Group Activity/ Challenge Problems

Indicate if the property displayed is the commutative, associative, or distributive property. Explain.

1. $2 + (3 + 4) = (3 + 4) + 2$

2. $(a + b) + (c + d) = (c + d) + (a + b)$

3. $3 + (x + y) + z = 3 + x + (y + z)$

Summary

GLOSSARY

Absolute value (27): The distance between a number and 0 on the number line. The absolute value of any nonzero number will be positive.

Additive inverses or opposites (32): Two numbers whose sum is zero.

Denominator (10): The bottom number of a fraction.

Empty Set (21): A set that contains no elements.

Evaluate (13): To evaluate an expression means to find its value.

Expression (10): An expression is any collection of numbers, letters, grouping symbols, and operations.

Factor (10): If $a \cdot b = c$, then a and b are factors of c.

Greatest common factor (GCF) (10): The largest number that divides into two or more numbers.

Least common denominator (LCD) (13): The smallest number divisible by two or more denominators.

Numerator (10): The top number of a fraction.

Operation (30): The basic operations of arithmetic are addition, subtraction, multiplication, and division.

Reduced to its lowest terms (10): A fraction is reduced to its lowest terms when its numerator and denominator have no common factor other than 1.

Set (21): A collection of elements listed within braces.

Variable (9): A letter used to represent a number.

IMPORTANT FACTS

Fractions: $\dfrac{a}{c} + \dfrac{b}{c} = \dfrac{a+b}{c}$ $\qquad$ $\dfrac{a}{c} - \dfrac{b}{c} = \dfrac{a-b}{c}$

$\dfrac{a}{b} \cdot \dfrac{c}{d} = \dfrac{ac}{bd}$ $\qquad$ $\dfrac{a}{b} \div \dfrac{c}{d} = \dfrac{a}{b} \cdot \dfrac{d}{c} = \dfrac{ad}{bc}$

Sets of Numbers

Natural numbers: $\{1, 2, 3, 4, \ldots\}$

Whole numbers: $\{0, 1, 2, 3, 4, \ldots\}$

Integers: $\{\ldots, -3, -2, -1, 0, 1, 2, 3, \ldots\}$

Rational numbers: {quotient of two integers, denominator not 0}

Irrational numbers: {real numbers that are not rational numbers}

Real numbers: {all numbers that can be represented on the number line}

Operations on the Real Numbers

To *add real numbers with the same sign,* add their absolute values. The sum has the same sign as the numbers being added.

To *add real numbers with different signs,* find the difference between the larger absolute value and the smaller absolute value. The answer has the sign of the number with the larger absolute value.

To *subtract b from a,* add the opposite of b to a.

$$a - b = a + (-b)$$

The *products* and *quotients* of numbers with *like signs* will be *positive.* The *products* and *quotients* of numbers with *unlike signs* will be *negative.*

Division Involving 0

If a represents any real number except 0, then

$$\frac{0}{a} = 0$$

$$\frac{a}{0} \text{ is undefined}$$

Exponents

$$b^n = \underbrace{b \cdot b \cdot b \cdot \cdots \cdot b}_{n \text{ factors of } b}$$

Order of Operations

1. Evaluate expressions within parentheses.
2. Evaluate all expressions with exponents.
3. Perform multiplications or divisions working left to right.
4. Perform additions or subtractions working left to right.

PROPERTIES OF THE REAL NUMBER SYSTEM

Property	Addition	Multiplication
Commutative	$a + b = b + a$	$ab = ba$
Associative	$(a + b) + c = a + (b + c)$	$(ab)c = a(bc)$
Distributive	$a(b + c) = ab + ac$	

Review Exercises

[1.2] *Perform the operations indicated. Reduce answers to lowest terms.*

1. $\dfrac{3}{5} \cdot \dfrac{5}{6}$

2. $\dfrac{2}{5} \div \dfrac{10}{9}$

3. $\dfrac{5}{12} \div \dfrac{3}{5}$

4. $\dfrac{5}{6} + \dfrac{1}{3}$

5. $\dfrac{3}{8} - \dfrac{1}{9}$

6. $2\dfrac{1}{3} - 1\dfrac{1}{5}$

[1.3] 7. List the set of natural numbers.

8. List the set of whole numbers.

9. List the set of integers.

10. Describe the set of rational numbers.

11. Describe the set of real numbers.

12. Consider the set of numbers
$$\left\{ 3, -5, -12, 0, \frac{1}{2}, -0.62, \sqrt{7}, 426, -3\frac{1}{4} \right\}$$

List those that are

(a) Positive integers.

(b) Whole numbers.

(c) Integers.

(d) Rational numbers.

(e) Irrational numbers.

(f) Real numbers.

13. Consider the set of numbers
$$\left\{ -2.3, -8, -9, 1\frac{1}{2}, \sqrt{2}, -\sqrt{2}, 1, -\frac{3}{17} \right\}$$

List those that are

(a) Natural numbers.

(b) Whole numbers.

(c) Negative integers.

(d) Integers.

(e) Rational numbers.

(f) Real numbers.

[1.4] *Insert either <, >, or = in the shaded area to make a true statement.*

14. $-3 \quad\quad -5$

15. $-2 \quad\quad 1$

16. $0.6 \quad\quad -1.3$

17. $-2.6 \quad\quad -3.6$

18. $0.50 \quad\quad 0.509$

19. $4.6 \quad\quad 4.06$

20. $-3.2 \quad\quad -3.02$

21. $5 \quad\quad |-3|$

22. $-3 \quad\quad |-7|$

23. $|-2.5| \quad\quad \left|\dfrac{5}{2}\right|$

[1.5, 1.6] *Evaluate.*

24. $-3 + 6$

25. $-4 + (-5)$

26. $-6 + 6$

27. $4 + (-9)$

28. $0 + (-3)$

29. $-10 + 4$

30. $-8 - (-2)$

31. $-9 - (-4)$

32. $4 - (-4)$

33. $0 - 2$

34. $-8 - 1$

35. $2 - 12$

36. $7 - 2$

37. $2 - 7$

38. $0 - (-4)$

39. $-7 - 5$

Evaluate.

40. $6 - 4 + 3$

41. $-5 + 7 - 6$

42. $-5 - 4 - 3$

43. $-2 + (-3) - 2$

44. $-(-4) + 5 - (+3)$

45. $7 - (+4) - (-3)$

46. $5 - 2 - 7 + 3$

47. $4 - (-2) + 3$

[1.7] *Evaluate.*

48. $-4(7)$

49. $(-9)(-3)$

50. $4(-9)$

51. $-2(3)$

52. $\left(\dfrac{3}{5}\right)\left(\dfrac{-2}{7}\right)$

53. $\left(\dfrac{10}{11}\right)\left(\dfrac{3}{-5}\right)$

54. $\left(\dfrac{-5}{8}\right)\left(\dfrac{-3}{7}\right)$

55. $0 \cdot \dfrac{4}{9}$

56. $4(-2)(-6)$

57. $(-1)(-3)(4)$

58. $-5(2)(7)$

59. $(-3)(-4)(-5)$

60. $-1(-2)(3)(-4)$

61. $(-4)(-6)(-2)(-3)$

Evaluate.

62. $15 \div (-3)$

63. $6 \div (-2)$

64. $-20 \div 5$

65. $-36 \div (-2)$

66. $0 \div 4$

67. $0 \div (-4)$

68. $72 \div (-9)$

69. $-40 \div (-8)$

70. $-4 \div \left(\dfrac{-4}{9}\right)$

71. $\dfrac{15}{32} \div (-5)$

72. $\dfrac{3}{8} \div \left(\dfrac{-1}{2}\right)$

73. $\dfrac{28}{-3} \div \dfrac{9}{-2}$

74. $\dfrac{14}{3} \div \left(\dfrac{-6}{5}\right)$

75. $\left(\dfrac{-5}{12}\right) \div \left(\dfrac{-5}{12}\right)$

Indicate whether each of the following is 0 or undefined.

76. $0 \div 4$

77. $0 \div (-6)$

78. $8 \div 0$

79. $-4 \div 0$

80. $\dfrac{8}{0}$

81. $\dfrac{0}{-5}$

[1.5–1.7, 1.9] *Evaluate.*

82. $-4(2 - 8)$

83. $2(4 - 8)$

84. $(3 - 6) + 4$

85. $(-4 + 3) - (2 - 6)$

86. $[4 + 3(-2)] - 6$

87. $(-4 - 2)(-3)$

88. $[4 + (-4)] + (6 - 8)$

89. $9[3 + (-4)] + 5$

90. $-4(-3) + [4 \div (-2)]$

91. $(-3 \cdot 4) \div (-2 \cdot 6)$

92. $(-3)(-4) + 6 - 3$

93. $[-2(3) + 6] - 4$

[1.8] *Evaluate.*

94. 4^2

95. 6^2

96. 9^3

97. 1^5

98. 3^4

99. 2^4

100. $(-3)^3$

101. $(-1)^9$

102. $(-2)^5$

103. $\left(\dfrac{2}{7}\right)^2$

104. $\left(\dfrac{-3}{5}\right)^2$

105. $\left(\dfrac{2}{5}\right)^3$

Express in exponential form.

106. xxy

107. xyy

108. $xxyyx$

109. $yyzz$

110. $2 \cdot 2 \cdot 3 \cdot 3 \cdot 3xyy$

111. $5 \cdot 7 \cdot 7 \cdot xxy$

112. $xyxyz$

Express as a product of factors.

113. x^2y

114. xz^3

115. y^3z

116. $2x^3y^2$

Evaluate for the values given.

117. $-x^2$, when $x = 3$

118. $-x^2$, when $x = -4$

119. $-x^3$, when $x = 3$

120. $-x^4$, when $x = -2$

[1.9] *Evaluate.*

121. $3 + 5 \cdot 4$

122. $7 - 3^2$

123. $3 \cdot 5 + 4 \cdot 2$

124. $(3 - 7)^2 + 6$

125. $6 + 4 \cdot 5$

126. $8 - 36 \div 4 \cdot 3$

127. $6 - 3^2 \cdot 5$

128. $2 - (8 - 3)$

129. $[6 - (3 \cdot 5)] + 5$

130. $3[9 - (4^2 + 3)] \cdot 2$

131. $(-3^2 + 4^2) + (3^2 \div 3)$

132. $2^3 \div 4 + 6 \cdot 3$

133. $(4 \div 2)^4 + 4^2 \div 2^2$

134. $(15 - 2^2)^2 - 4 \cdot 3 + 10 \div 2$

135. $4^3 \div 4^2 - 5(2 - 7) \div 5$

Evaluate for the values given.

136. $4x - 6$, when $x = 5$

137. $8 - 3x$, when $x = 2$

138. $6 - 4x$, when $x = -5$

139. $x^2 - 5x + 3$, when $x = 6$

140. $5y^2 + 3y - 2$, when $y = -1$

141. $-x^2 + 2x - 3$, when $x = 2$

142. $-x^2 + 2x - 3$, when $x = -2$

143. $-3x^2 - 5x + 5$, when $x = 1$

144. $3xy - 5x$, when $x = 3$ and $y = 4$

145. $-x^2 - 8x - 12$, when $x = -3$

.5–1.9] ▦ *(a) Use a scientific calculator to evaluate the expression and (b) check to see if your answer is reasonable.*

146. $158 + (-493)$

147. $324 - (-29.6)$

148. $\dfrac{-17.28}{6}$

149. $(-62)(-1.9)$

150. 5^7

151. $(-3)^6$

152. $-(4.2)^3$

153. $3x^2 - 4x + 3$, when $x = 5$

154. $-2x^2 - 6x - 3$, when $x = -2$

.10] *Name the property illustrated.*

155. $(4 + 3) + 9 = 4 + (3 + 9)$

156. $6 \cdot x = x \cdot 6$

157. $4(x + 3) = 4x + 12$

158. $(x + 4)3 = 3(x + 4)$

159. $6x + 3x = 3x + 6x$

160. $(x + 7) + 4 = x + (7 + 4)$

161. $-6x + 3 = 3 + (-6x)$

....

Practice Test

1. Consider the set of numbers

$$\left\{ -6, 42, -3\frac{1}{2}, 0, 6.52, \sqrt{5}, \frac{5}{9}, -7, -1 \right\}$$

List those that are:

(a) Natural numbers.

(b) Whole numbers.

(c) Integers.

(d) Rational numbers.

(e) Irrational numbers.

(f) Real numbers.

Insert either $<$, $>$, or $=$ in the shaded area to make a true statement.

2. $-6 \quad\quad -3$

3. $|-3| \quad\quad |-2|$

Evaluate.

4. $-4 + (-8)$

5. $-6 - 5$

6. $4 - (-12)$

7. $5 - 12 - 7$

8. $(-4 + 6) - 3(-2)$

9. $(-4)(-3)(2)(-1)$

10. $\left(\dfrac{-2}{9}\right) \div \left(\dfrac{-7}{8}\right)$

11. $\left(-12 \cdot \dfrac{1}{2}\right) \div 3$

12. $3 \cdot 5^2 - 4 \cdot 6^2$

13. $(4 - 6^2) \div [4(2 + 3) - 4]$

14. $-6(-2 - 3) \div 5 \cdot 2$

15. $(-3)^4$

16. $\left(\dfrac{3}{5}\right)^3$

17. Write $2 \cdot 2 \cdot 5 \cdot 5 \cdot yyzzz$ in exponential form.

18. Write $2^2 3^3 x^4 y^2$ as a product of factors.

Evaluate for the values given.

19. $2x^2 - 6$, when $x = -4$

20. $6x - 3y^2 + 4$, when $x = 3$ and $y = -2$

21. $-x^2 - 6x + 3$, when $x = -2$

Name the property illustrated.

22. $x + 3 = 3 + x$

23. $4(x + 9) = 4x + 36$

24. $(2 + x) + 4 = 2 + (x + 4)$

25. $5(x + y) = (x + y)5$

....

REVIEW OF PERCENT

OBJECTIVES

Upon completion of Chapter 3, you will be able to:

1. Define and use correctly the terminology associated with each topic.

2. **a.** Change a percent to its equivalent decimal or fraction (Section 1: Examples 1, 2; Problems 1–32).

   b. Change a decimal or fraction to its equivalent percent (Section 1: Examples 3, 4; Problems 33–64).

3. Use an equation to find the missing element in a percentage relationship (examples: What percent of 30 is 25? 60 is 120% of what number?) (Section 2: Example 1; Problems 1–36).

4. Use the basic equation form "__% of Original = Change?" to find the percent of change (increase or decrease) (example: $33 is what percent more than $27?) (Section 2: Example 2; Problems 37–48).

5. Use an equation to find the original number when the percent of change (increase or decrease) and the result are both known (example: What number increased by 25% of itself gives 30?) (Section 2: Example 3; Problems 49–60).

6. Given a word problem containing percents, express the problem in a concise sentence which translates into an equation that solves the problem (Section 3: Examples 1–5; Problems 1–50).

Percent is a fundamental topic with which everyone has some familiarity. We use a percent like a ratio to make a comparison. A ratio is often expressed as a fraction, such as $\frac{18}{24}$ or $\frac{3}{4}$, whereas a percent would express a relationship using 100 as the denominator of the fraction, such as $\frac{75}{100}$. Percent compares the number of parts out of 100 to which the fraction is equivalent.

Because percent is one of the most frequently applied mathematical concepts in all areas of business, it is extremely important for anyone entering business to be capable of accurate percent calculations.

For a further discussion of percents, fractions, and decimals, see Appendix A.

SECTION 1

BASIC PERCENT

The use of percent will be easier if you remember that **percent** means **hundredths.** That is, the expression "46%" may just as correctly be read "46 hundredths." The word "hundredths" denotes either a common fraction with 100 as denominator or a decimal fraction of two decimal places. Thus,

$$46\% = 46\text{ hundredths} = \frac{46}{100} \quad \text{or} \quad 0.46$$

A percent must first be changed to either a fractional or decimal form before that percent of any number can be found. These conversions are simplified by applying the fact that "percent" means "hundredths."

A. CHANGING A PERCENT TO A DECIMAL

When people think of percent, they normally think of the most common percents, those between 1% and 99%. These are the percents that occupy the first two places in the decimal representation of a percent. (For example, 99% = 99 hundredths = 0.99, and 1% = 1 hundredth = 0.01.)

> A.1 *When converting percents to decimals, write the whole percents between 1% and 99% in the first two decimal places.*

When this rule is followed, the other digits will then naturally fall into their correct places, as demonstrated next.

Example 1   **% to Decimal**

Express each of the following percents as a decimal.

(a) 5% = 5 hundredths = 0.05
(b) 86% = 86 hundredths = 0.86
(c) 16.3% = 0.163   (since 16% = 0.16)
(d) 131% = 1.31   (since 31% = 0.31)

(e) 122.75% = 1.2275   (since 22% = 0.22)

(f) 6.09% = 0.0609   (since 6% = 0.06)

(g) 0.4% = 0.004   (since 0% = 0.00)

(h) 0.03% = 0.0003   (since 0% = 0.00)

Some percents are written using common fractions. To change a fraction to a decimal, you must divide the numerator by the denominator.

$$\frac{n}{d}\overline{)}\qquad \text{or}\qquad d\overline{)n}$$

A.2 *When a fractional percent is to be changed to a decimal, first convert the fractional percent to a decimal percent, and then convert the decimal percent to an ordinary decimal.*

(Machine calculations of the decimal percent may be rounded to the third decimal place.)

Example 1   **Fractional % to Decimal**
(cont.)

Express each of the following percents as a decimal.

(i) $\frac{7}{8}$%:   Recall that $\frac{7}{8}$ means $8\overline{)7.000} = 0.875$ ($.875$)

And since $\frac{7}{8} = 0.875$

then $\frac{7}{8}\% = 0.875\% = 0.00875$

(j) $\frac{4}{7}$%:   First, $\frac{4}{7}$ means $7\overline{)4.00} = 0.57\frac{1}{7}$ (or 0.571) ($.57\frac{1}{7}$)

Then $\frac{4}{7} = 0.57\frac{1}{7}$

implies that $\frac{4}{7}\% = 0.57\frac{1}{7}\% = 0.0057\frac{1}{7}$ (or 0.00571)

A fractional percent always indicates a percent less than 1% (or it indicates that fractional part of 1%). Thus, $\frac{1}{4}\% = \frac{1}{4}$ of 1%; $\frac{3}{5}\% = \frac{3}{5}$ of 1%.

When the given fraction is a common one for which the decimal equivalent is known, the process of *converting a fractional percent to a decimal* may be shortened:

A.3 *Write two zeros to the right of the decimal point (0.00) to indicate that the percent is less than 1%, and then write the digits that are normally used to denote the decimal equivalent of the fraction.*

Example 1
(cont.)

(k) $\frac{1}{4}\%$: $\left(\frac{1}{4}\% = \frac{1}{4}\text{ of }1\%\right)$

To show that the percent is less than 1%, write: 0.00

To indicate $\frac{1}{4}$, affix the digits "25" $\left(\frac{1}{4} = 25\text{ hundredths}\right)$:   0.0025

Thus, $\frac{1}{4}\% = 0.0025$.

(This may be easily verified, since $4 \times 0.0025 = 0.0100 = 1\%$.)

(l) $\frac{2}{3}\%$: $\left(\frac{2}{3}\% = \frac{2}{3}\text{ of }1\%\right)$

Indicate a percent less than 1%:   0.00

Affix the digits $66\frac{2}{3}$: $0.0066\frac{2}{3}$

B. CHANGING A PERCENT TO A FRACTION

The procedure for changing a percent to a fraction is summarized as follows:

B.1 *After an ordinary percent has been changed to hundredths (by dropping the percent sign and placing the number over a denominator of 100), the resulting fraction should be reduced to lowest terms.*

An improper fraction—one in which the numerator is greater than the denominator—is considered to be in lowest terms provided that it cannot be further reduced.

Example 2   **% to Fraction**

Convert each percent to its fractional equivalent in lowest terms.

(a) $45\% = 45\text{ hundredths} = \frac{45}{100} = \frac{9}{20}$

(b) $8\% = 8\text{ hundredths} = \frac{8}{100} = \frac{2}{25}$

(c) $175\% = 175\text{ hundredths} = \frac{175}{100} = \frac{7}{4}$

Percents containing fractions may be converted to their ordinary fractional equivalents by altering the above procedure slightly. The fact that "percent" means "hundredths" may also be shown as

$$\% = \text{hundredth} = \frac{1}{100}$$

B.2 *Percents containing fractions are changed to ordinary fractions by substituting $\dfrac{1}{100}$ for the % sign and multiplying.*

Now let us apply this fact to change some fractional percents to common fractions.

Example 2
(cont.)

% with Fraction to Fraction

(d) $12\dfrac{1}{2}\% = 12\dfrac{1}{2} \times \dfrac{1}{100} = \dfrac{25}{2} \times \dfrac{1}{100} = \dfrac{25}{200} = \dfrac{1}{8}$

(e) $55\dfrac{5}{9}\% = 55\dfrac{5}{9} \times \dfrac{1}{100} = \dfrac{500}{9} \times \dfrac{1}{100} = \dfrac{500}{900} = \dfrac{5}{9}$

(f) $\dfrac{1}{3}\% = \dfrac{1}{3} \times \dfrac{1}{100} = \dfrac{1}{300}$

B.3 *Decimal percents may be converted to fractions by applying the following procedure:*

1. *Change the percent to its decimal equivalent.*
2. *Pronounce the value of the decimal; then write this number as a fraction and reduce it.*

Example 2
(cont.)

Decimal % to Fraction

(g) 22.5%:
  1. Since 22% = 0.22, then 22.5% = 0.225.
  2. $0.225 = 225$ thousandths $= \dfrac{225}{1,000} = \dfrac{9}{40}$.

(h) 0.56%: Since 0% = 0.00, then

$$0.56\% = 0.0056$$

$$= 56 \text{ ten-thousandths}$$

$$= \dfrac{56}{10,000}$$

$$= \dfrac{7}{1,250}$$

(i)   0.6%:

$$0.6\% = 0.006$$

$$= 6 \text{ thousandths}$$

$$= \frac{6}{1,000}$$

$$= \frac{3}{500}$$

C. CHANGING A DECIMAL TO A PERCENT

Just as "percent" means "hundredths," so is the opposite also true—that is, *hundredths = percent.* Rule C states an important concept that should be remembered when working with decimals and percents.

> **C.** *When a decimal number is to be changed to a percent, the hundredths places of the decimal indicate the whole "percents" between 1% and 99% (0.01 = 1%, and 0.99 = 99%).*

By first isolating the whole percents between 1% and 99%, you will have no difficulty in placing the other digits correctly.

If there is to be a decimal point in the percent, it will come after the hundredth's place of the decimal number. (This is why it is sometimes said: "To change a decimal to a percent, move the decimal point two places to the right and add a percent sign.")

Example 3   **Decimal to %**

Express each of these decimals as a percent.

(a) $0.67 = 67$ hundredths $= 67\%$
(b) $0.82\frac{1}{2} = 82\frac{1}{2}$ hundredths $= 82\frac{1}{2}\%$
(c) $0.08 = 8$ hundredths $= 8\%$
(d) 0.721:   Since $0.72 = 72\%$, then $0.721 = 72.1\%$.

It may prove helpful to circle the first two decimal places, as an aid in identifying the percents between 1% and 99%.

(e) $1.\underline{45}9$:   Given 1.459, the .45 indicates 45%.

Thus, $1.459 = 145.9\%$.

(f) 0.$\widehat{9}$:   Given 0.9, the .9 or .90 denotes 90%.

$$\text{So, } 0.9 = 90\%.$$

(g) 0.$\widehat{00}$26:   Given 0.0026, the 0.00 represents 0%.

$$\text{Hence, } 0.0026 = 0.26\%.$$

D. Changing a Fraction to a Percent

The procedure for changing a fraction to a percent is summarized in Rule D.

D. *To change a fraction to a percent, apply the following steps:*

1. *Convert the fraction to its decimal equivalent by dividing the numerator by the denominator:*

$$\frac{n}{d}\overline{)} \quad or \quad d\overline{)n}$$

(Machine calculations may be rounded to the third decimal place.)

2. *Then change the decimal to a percent, as illustrated in the preceding example.*

Example 4   **Fraction to %**

Change each fraction to its equivalent percent.

(a) $\dfrac{5}{8} = \dfrac{.625}{8\overline{)5.000}} = 0.625 = 62.5\%$

(b) $\dfrac{7}{18} = \dfrac{.38\frac{16}{18}}{18\overline{)7.00}} = 0.38\dfrac{8}{9} = 38\dfrac{8}{9}\%$ (or 38.9%)

(c) $\dfrac{5}{4} = \dfrac{1.25}{4\overline{)5.00}} = 1.25 = 125\%$

(d) $1\dfrac{4}{5} \left(\text{since } \dfrac{4}{5} = \dfrac{.80}{5\overline{)4.00}} = 0.80 \right) = 1.80 = 180\%$

or $1\dfrac{4}{5} = \dfrac{9}{5} = \dfrac{1.80}{5\overline{)9.00}} = 1.80 = 180\%$

(e) $2\dfrac{3}{4} \left(\text{since } \dfrac{3}{4} = 0.75 \right) = 2.75 = 275\%$

or $2\dfrac{3}{4} = \dfrac{11}{4} = 2.75 = 275\%$

SECTION 1   PROBLEMS

Express each percent both as a decimal and as a fraction in lowest terms.

1. 35%	**2.** 11%	**3.** 16%	**4.** 32%
5. 3%	**6.** 2%	**7.** 52.25%	**8.** 30.5%
9. 4.5%	**10.** 6.25%	**11.** 250%	**12.** 174%
13. 137.5%	**14.** 128.4%	**15.** 0.8%	**16.** 0.48%
17. 1.75%	**18.** 1.3%	**19.** 145%	**20.** 105%
21. ¾%	**22.** ⅛%	**23.** ⅖%	**24.** 1/20%
25. ⅜%	**26.** ⅘%	**27.** 1⅗%	**28.** 2¼%
29. 87½%	**30.** 16⅗%	**31.** 12½%	**32.** 8⅕%

Express each of the following as a percent.

33. 0.07	**34.** 0.09	**35.** 0.35	**36.** 0.41
37. 0.36	**38.** 0.52	**39.** 0.165	**40.** 0.232
41. 2.11	**42.** 1.45	**43.** 1.06	**44.** 4.38
45. 0.001	**46.** 0.022	**47.** 0.5	**48.** 0.8
49. 0.005	**50.** 0.008	**51.** 3.1	**52.** 2.88
53. 4.6	**54.** 5.5	**55.** 0.03	**56.** 0.01
57. 4/9	**58.** 5/6	**59.** ⅗	**60.** 5/12
61. 1¾	**62.** 3½	**63.** 4⅘	**64.** 1⅛

SECTION 2
PERCENT EQUATION FORMS

All problems that involve the use of percent are some variation of the basic percent form: "Some percent of one number equals another number." This basic **percent equation form** may be abbreviated as:

$$\_\_\_\% \text{ of } \_\_\_ = \_\_\_$$

Given in reverse order, the equation form is:

$$\_\_\_ = \_\_\_\% \text{ of } \_\_\_$$

Another way of expressing the preceding formula is:

$$\text{rate} \times \text{base} = \text{percentage} \qquad (r \cdot b = p)$$

Because there can be only one unknown in an elementary equation, there are only three variations of the basic equation form: The unknown can be either (1) the percent (or **rate**), (2) the first number (or **base**), or (3) the second number (the **percentage**). For instance, consider

$$70\% \text{ of } 52 = 36.4$$

Here, 70% is the rate, 52 is the base, and 36.4 is the percentage. (This is somewhat confusing because the percentage is not a percent; the rate is the percent. This confusion, however, is avoided by using the percent equation form above.)

Equation-solving procedures that were studied earlier will be applied to solve percentage problems. *Recall that before a percent of any number can be computed, the percent must first be changed to either a fraction or a decimal.* Conversely, if the unknown represents a percent, the solution to the equation will be a decimal or fraction that must then be converted to the percent.

Example 1   (a)   16% of 45 is what number?

$$0.16 \times 45 = n$$

$$7.2 = n$$

(b)   What percent of 30 is 6?

$$r \times 30 = 6$$

$$30r = 6$$

$$\frac{30r}{30} = \frac{6}{30}$$

$$r = \frac{1}{5}$$

$$r = 20\%$$

(c) $66\frac{2}{3}\%$ of what number is 12?

Because $66\frac{2}{3}\%$ is exactly $\frac{2}{3}$, we will use $\frac{2}{3}$:

$$\frac{2}{3} \times n = 12$$

$$\frac{2n}{3} = 12$$

$$\frac{3}{2} \times \frac{2n}{3} = 12 \times \frac{3}{2}$$

$$n = 18$$

Many of the formulas used to solve mathematical problems in business are nothing more than the basic percent equation form with different words (or variables) substituted for the percent and the first and second numbers. The methods used to solve the formulas are identical to those of Example 1.

One such formula is used to find **percent of change** (that is, percent of increase or decrease). In words, the formula can be stated, "What percent of the original number is the change?" In more abbreviated form it is

$$\underline{}\% \text{ of Original} = \text{Change?}$$

Example 2   (a)   What percent more than 24 is 33?

> 1. *Original number.* To have "more than 24" implies that we originally had 24; thus, 24 is the original number. In general, it can be said that the "original number" is the number that follows the words "more than" or "less than" in the stated problem.
>
> 2. *Change.* The "change" is the amount of increase or decrease that occurred. That is, the change is the numerical difference between the two numbers in the problem. (The fact that it may be a negative difference is not important to this formula.) Thus, the change in this example is $33 - 24 = 9$.

$$\underline{}\% \text{ of Original} = \text{Change}$$
$$\underline{}\% \text{ of} \qquad 24 = 9$$

$$24x = 9$$

$$\frac{24x}{24} = \frac{9}{24}$$

$$x = \frac{3}{8}$$

$$x = 37\tfrac{1}{2}\%$$

Thus, 24 increased by $37\tfrac{1}{2}\%$ of itself gives 33.

(b)   12 is what percent less than 18?

Original $= 18$	$\underline{}\%$ of Original $=$ Change
Change $= 18 - 12$	$18r = 6$
$\qquad = 6$	$\dfrac{18r}{18} = \dfrac{6}{18}$
	$r = \tfrac{1}{3}$
	$r = 33\tfrac{1}{3}\%$

Thus, 18 decreased by $33\tfrac{1}{3}\%$ of itself is 12.

This formula is often applied to changes in the prices of merchandise or stocks and to changes in volume of business from one year to the next. Other applications include increase in cost of living or unemployment and decrease in expenses or net profit.

A third type of problem is a variation of the "percent of change" type. In this application we know the percent of change (percent increase or decrease) and the result, and we compute the amount of the original number. The original number is either increased or decreased by a percent of itself. The number is expressed as 100%n or 1n so that the variables can be combined.

Example 3   (a)   What number decreased by 12% of itself gives 66?

What number <u>decreased by</u> (12% of itself) <u>gives</u> <u>66</u>?

$$n \quad - \quad (0.12 \times n) \quad = \quad 66$$

$$n^* \quad - \quad 0.12n \quad = \quad 66$$

$$0.88n \quad = \quad 66$$

$$\frac{0.88n}{0.88} = \frac{66.00}{0.88}$$

$$n \quad = \quad 75$$

(b)   What number increased by $33\frac{1}{3}\%$ of itself gives 28?

When the percent contains a repeating decimal, it is easier to work with the fraction equivalent instead of the decimal equivalent.

$$\frac{3}{3}n + \frac{1n}{3} = 28$$

$$\frac{4n}{3} = 28$$

$$\frac{3}{4} \times \frac{4n}{3} = \overset{7}{28} \times \frac{3}{4}$$

$$n = 21$$

*Recall that $n = 1n$; thus,

$$n - 0.12n = 1n - 0.12n$$

$$= 1.00n - 0.12n$$

$$= 0.88n$$

SECTION 2   PROBLEMS

Use equations to obtain the following solutions. Express percent remainders either as fractions or rounded to hundredths (example: $28\frac{4}{7}$% or 28.57%).

Part One

1. 5% of 120 is what amount?
2. 8% of 700 is what number?
3. 12% of 900 is what number?
4. 20% of 640 is how much?
5. 25% of 78 is how much?
6. 42% of 90 is what amount?
7. What is ⅗% of 37,000?
8. What is ¾% of 6,000?
9. What is 37½% of 88?
10. How much is 12½% of 560?
11. What is 4½% of 600?
12. ¼% of 14,000 is what amount?
13. What percent of 48 is 12?
14. What percent of 90 is 63?
15. 18 is what percent of 96?
16. What percent of 100 is 13?
17. 28 is what percent of 80?
18. 240 is what percent of 4,000?
19. 5.4 is what percent of 180?
20. 45 is what percent of 900?
21. What percent of 9 is 2?
22. What percent of 18 is 4.5?
23. 15% of what number is 48?
24. 120% of what amount is 78?
25. 44% of what number is 33?
26. 11½% of what number is 115?
27. 18 is 2¼% of what amount?
28. 90 is 33⅓% of what amount?
29. 42⁶⁄₇% of what number is 9?
30. 16⅔% of what amount is 45?
31. 84% of what amount is 105?
32. 100 is 1¼% of what amount?
33. 49.5 is 5.5% of what number?
34. 3.5 is 0.7% of what number?
35. 4.5 is 0.6% of what amount?
36. 48 is 22²⁄₉% of what amount?

Part Two

37. What percent more than 5 is 7?
38. What percent more than 150 is 180?
39. 44 is what percent less than 55?
40. What percent less than 150 is 105?
41. 130 is what percent less than 325?
42. 195 is what percent less than 260?
43. 132 is what percent more than 108?
44. 300 is what percent more than 200?
45. $54 is what percent more than $42?
46. $210 is what percent more than $180?
47. What percent less than $600 is $597?
48. What percent less than $800 is $794?

Part Three

49. What number increased by 30% of itself gives 78?
50. What number increased by 25% of itself gives 90?
51. What amount decreased by 25% of itself gives 36?
52. What amount decreased by 11⅑% of itself gives 48?
53. What number increased by 50% of itself gives 108?
54. What number increased by 26.5% of itself gives 253?
55. What amount decreased by 16⅔% of itself gives 540?
56. What amount decreased by 33⅓% of itself gives 150?
57. What number increased by 83⅓% of itself gives 121?
58. What number increased by 0.4% of itself gives 1,004?
59. What amount decreased by 11⅑% gives 56?
60. What amount decreased by 37½% gives 120?

SECTION 3
WORD PROBLEMS USING PERCENTS

Three primary types of percent applications are illustrated by the following five examples. These types are:

1. The basic percent equation form: ____% of ____ = ____ (Examples 1–3).
2. Finding *percent* of change (increase or decrease), using ____% of Original = Change (Example 4).
3. Finding an *amount* that has been increased or decreased by a percent of itself (Example 5).

Example 1   A direct-mail campaign by a magazine produced $16,000 in renewals and new subscriptions. If renewals totaled $10,000, what percent of the subscriptions were renewals?

$$\underline{\text{What percent of subscriptions were renewals?}}$$

$$\underline{}\% \ \times \ \$16,000 \ = \ \$10,000$$

$$16{,}000r \ = \ 10{,}000$$

$$\frac{\cancel{16{,}000}r}{\cancel{16{,}000}} \ = \ \frac{10{,}000}{16{,}000}$$

$$r \ = \ 0.625$$

$$r \ = \ 62.5\%$$

Example 2   Thirty-five percent of a payment made to a partnership land purchase was tax deductible. If a partner receives a notice that he qualifies for a $700 tax deduction, how much was his total payment?

$$\underline{35\% \text{ of payment was tax deduction}}$$

$$35\% \times \quad p \quad = \quad \$700$$

$$0.35p \ = \ 700$$

$$\frac{\cancel{0.35}p}{\cancel{0.35}} \ = \ \frac{700.00}{0.35}$$

$$p \ = \ \$2{,}000$$

Example 3 A quarterback completed 40% of his attempted passes in a professional football game. If he attempted 65 passes, how many did he complete?

$$\underline{40\% \text{ of}} \ \underline{\text{attempted passes}} \ \underline{\text{were}} \ \underline{\text{completed passes}}$$

$$0.4 \times \qquad 65 \qquad = \qquad c$$

$$0.4(65) \qquad = \qquad c$$

$$26 \qquad = \qquad c$$

Example 4 Last year's sales were $45,000; sales for this year totaled $48,600. What was the percent of increase in sales?

Original = $45,000   ____% of Original = Change?

Change = $48,600 − $45,000   ____% of $45,000 = $3,600

= $3,600 $45,000r = 3,600

$$\frac{\cancel{45,000}r}{\cancel{45,000}} = \frac{3,600}{45,000}$$

$$r = 0.08$$

$$r = 8\%$$

Example 5 Labor expenses (wages) at a construction project increased by 10% this month. If wages totaled $13,200 this month, how much were last month's wages?

$$\underline{\text{Old wages}} \ \underline{\text{increased by}} \ \underline{10\% \text{ (of itself)}} \ \underline{\text{equals}} \ \underline{\text{new wages}}$$

$$w \qquad + \qquad (10\% \times w) \qquad = \qquad \$13,200$$

$$w \qquad + \qquad 0.1w \qquad = \qquad 13,200$$

$$\frac{\cancel{1.1}w}{\cancel{1.1}} \qquad = \qquad \frac{13,200.0}{1.1}$$

$$w \qquad = \qquad \$12,000$$

Note. Percents are never used just by themselves. In an equation, any percent that is included must be a percent *of* ("times") some other number or variable.

For convenience, the following problems are divided into two parts, each of which covers all the given examples. Part 1 covers the three types of problems presented: (1) Examples 1–3, see Problems 1–16; (2) Example 4, see Problems 17–22; (3) Example 5, see Problems 23–32. Additional practice is provided in Part 2, but the order is scrambled.

PERCENT EQUIVALENTS OF COMMON FRACTIONS

The following percents (many with fractional remainders) will be given in many problems so that students without calculators can conveniently use the exact fractional equivalents. (Students using calculators may also use the fractional equivalents by entering the numerators and denominators separately.)

$$\frac{1}{2} = 50\%$$

$$\frac{1}{3} = 33\frac{1}{3}\% \qquad \frac{2}{3} = 66\frac{2}{3}\%$$

$$\frac{1}{4} = 25\% \qquad \frac{3}{4} = 75\%$$

$$\frac{1}{5} = 20\% \qquad \frac{2}{5} = 40\% \qquad \frac{3}{5} = 60\% \qquad \frac{4}{5} = 80\%$$

$$\frac{1}{6} = 16\frac{2}{3}\% \qquad \frac{5}{6} = 83\frac{1}{3}\%$$

$$\frac{1}{7} = 14\frac{2}{7}\% \qquad \frac{2}{7} = 28\frac{4}{7}\% \qquad \frac{3}{7} = 42\frac{6}{7}\%$$

$$\frac{1}{8} = 12\frac{1}{2}\% \qquad \frac{3}{8} = 37\frac{1}{2}\% \qquad \frac{5}{8} = 62\frac{1}{2}\% \qquad \frac{7}{8} = 87\frac{1}{2}\%$$

$$\frac{1}{9} = 11\frac{1}{9}\% \qquad \frac{2}{9} = 22\frac{2}{9}\% \qquad \frac{4}{9} = 44\frac{4}{9}\% \qquad \frac{5}{9} = 55\frac{5}{9}\%$$

$$\frac{1}{10} = 10\% \qquad \frac{3}{10} = 30\% \qquad \frac{7}{10} = 70\% \qquad \frac{9}{10} = 90\%$$

$$\frac{1}{12} = 8\frac{1}{3}\%$$

SECTION 3   PROBLEMS

Part One

1. A real estate agent earned a commission of $5,760 on a house sale of $144,000. What percent of the house sale was the commission?

2. A yogurt store's overhead last quarter was $6,750 while sales were $15,000. The store's overhead was what percent of its sales?

3. An office manager finds that she spends 3 hours each day on personnel problems. If she works an 8-hour day, what percent of her day is spent on personnel problems?

4. Out of its total budget of $60,000, the human resources department spent $51,600 on wages. What percent of the budget was spent on wages?

5. A salesclerk makes a 7% commission on his net sales. If his net sales last week were $5,618, what was his commission?

6. Income from advertisements placed in the Montana Ledger newspaper amounted to 75% of total revenue. What were the receipts from advertising if revenues totaled $150,000 last month?

7. A taxpayer pays 1½% of the assessed value of his real estate for real property tax. If the assessed value of the property is $75,000, how much must he pay in property tax?

8. Jana spends about 12½% of her weekly wages for lunches. If she earns $360 a week, how much does she spend on average for lunches?

9. A candidate in a state senate race won 52% of the votes cast. If the candidate received 64,272 votes, how many votes were cast for all candidates in this race?

10. Charles receives 20% of his income from investments. What was his total income, if his investment income was $10,200?

11. There are 16 employees at Cranshaw Co. who chose the group health insurance plan. This number represents 33⅓% of all Cranshaw employees. How many people are employed by the company?

12. Inventory represents 60.25% of a hardware store's total assets. What are the total assets if the inventory is valued at $180,750?

13. Eight percent of a stock's cost was paid in dividends last year. If the stock cost $85, what dividend did it yield?

14. A collection agency charges 33⅓% of accounts receivable collections as a fee. The agency collected $186,000 last month. What fee did it earn for these collections?

15. Thirty percent of the selling price of a battery charger is the markup. If the markup is $7.50, how much is the selling price?

16. The raw material cost to manufacture a pair of safety boots is $10. The raw materials run 22⅔% of the total production cost. What is the total cost?

17. The population of Jackson City in 1980 was 54,000. By 1990, the population had jumped to 78,000. What percent increase does this represent?

18. Monthly cable charges last year were $36 while the same charges this year amount to $37.98. What percent increase does this represent?

19. Accounting majors who were hired after graduating last spring received an average of $27,000. Accounting majors this year received an average of $27,810. What percent increase does this represent?

20. Jack made 12 account calls on Monday and 8 calls on Tuesday. What percent decrease in calls is this?

21. At a holiday sale, the price of a dress was $76.80. Before the sale, it had a list price of $96. What was the percent decrease in price?

22. Sandy's travel expense vouchers totaled $570 last month compared to $595.65 this month. What is the percent increase in her travel expenses?

23. What number increased by 25% of itself yields 35?

24. What number increased by 40% of itself yields 4,200?

25. What amount decreased by 16⅔% of itself leaves 25?

26. What amount decreased by 2% of itself equals $19.60?

27. It is estimated that by the year 2000 there will be 39 million Americans over the age of 65. This number represents a 30% increase from the year 1990. How many people were over 65 in 1990?

28. Within the past two years, the average price of a haircut has increased by 11⅑%. If a haircut costs $20 today, what was the cost two years ago?

29. A local union's membership decreased by 12% over a 5-year period. At the end of this period, there were 5,632 members. How many members were there at the beginning of the period?

30. During a special promotion, the price of a multimedia system was reduced by 30%. What was the price before the reduction if the sales price was $2,100?

31. The current selling price of a blender is 15% higher than it was last year. If this year's price is $41.40, what was the price last year?

32. This year, the Simmons Co. showed $93,960 in current liabilities on its annual balance sheet. This was an 8% increase from the previous year. What was the total of the current liabilities for the previous year?

Part Two

33. Thrifty Stores Inc. estimates that ½% of its credit sales of $243,000 will be uncollectible. How much is its estimated uncollectible accounts expense?

34. At its grand opening, Rossbach Co. estimated that 16⅔% of its cutomers were teenagers. Nine hundred and thirty customers visited the store during this time. How many were teenagers?

35. The average price for a new home in Crystal City decreased from $120,000 to $112,800. What was the percent decrease in the price of a home?

36. The cost of coffee to a grocery store has increased from $200 per case to $206 per case over the past six months. What is the percent increase in cost?

37. The price of a photocopier was reduced by 25%, making the sales price $600. What was the price before the reduction?

38. Monthly expenses for courier service at Campanella Co. have increased by 4½% since last year. The current month's expense is $209. How much was the courier expense during the same month last year?

39. Twelve percent of merchandise sold was returned to the store. If $5,520 of goods was returned, how much were the total sales?

40. Seventeen percent of recent graduates of Parker College had secured jobs before graduation. If 68 people had jobs before graduation, how many graduates were there?

41. Enrollment in a tax seminar decreased from 130 to 117 over a 2-year period. What percent change does this represent?

SUMMARY OF CONVERSIONS

Given:	To Convert to:	
PERCENT	A. DECIMAL	B. FRACTION
Basic % (1% to 99%)	Basic percents become the first two (hundredths) decimal places. (Other digits align accordingly.) (Example: 76% = 76 hundredths = 0.76)	Percent sign is dropped and given number is placed over a denominator of 100; reduce. (Example: 76% = 76 hundredths = $\frac{76}{100} = \frac{19}{25}$)
Decimal % (125.73%; 0.45%)	Digits representing percents greater than 99% or less than 1% are aligned around the first two (hundredths) decimal places (see also Section 1, "Basic Percent"). (Example: 0.45% = 0.0045)	Convert the percent to a decimal (as indicated at left). Pronounce the decimal value; then write this as a fraction and reduce. (Example: 0.45% = 0.0045 = 45 ten-thousandths = $\frac{45}{10,000}$ = $\frac{9}{2,000}$)
Fractional % ($\frac{1}{4}$%; $\frac{7}{5}$%; $1\frac{2}{3}$%)	Convert the fractional percent to a decimal percent (by dividing the numerator by the denominator). Then convert this decimal percent to an ordinary decimal (as shown above). (Example: $\frac{7}{5}$% = 1.4% = 0.014)	Percent sign is replaced by $\frac{1}{100}$; multiply and reduce. (Example: $\frac{7}{5}$% = $\frac{7}{5} \times \frac{1}{100} = \frac{7}{500}$)

	To Convert to Percent
C. *Decimals* (0.473; 1.2; 0.0015)	Isolate the first two (hundredths) decimal places to identify the basic percent (1% to 99%). Other digits will then be aligned correctly. (Example: 0.473 = 0.㊼3 = 47.3%)
D. *Fractions* ($\frac{2}{9}$; $\frac{7}{3}$; $1\frac{1}{2}$)	Convert the fraction to a decimal (by dividing the numerator by the denominator). Then follow the above procedure for converting a decimal to percent. (Example: $\frac{2}{9}$ = 0.22$\frac{2}{9}$ = 0.㉒$\frac{2}{9}$ = 22$\frac{2}{9}$%)

42. The price of an oriental rug dropped from $5,400 to $3,294. What percent decrease is this?

43. The value of a store's inventory increased from $50,000 to $62,000. By what percent did the value increase?

44. Orders for a statistics textbook increased from 4,800 to 5,760 at a publishing company this year. What was the percent increase in textbooks ordered?

45. A car dealership saw a 3.8% increase in sales of new cars in May over April. If 519 new cars were sold in May, how many were sold in April?

46. The price of the latest edition of a word-processing software package increased 8$\frac{1}{3}$% over a previous edition. The new software costs $104. What was the previous edition's price?

47. The owner of a small business has total assets of $840,000 while her net worth is $336,000. What percent of her total assets is her net worth?

48. Office equipment purchased by an accounting firm for $6,000 has been depreciated by $4,000. What percent of the purchase price has been depreciated?

49. Find a newspaper or magazine article that includes percents, and bring it to class for discussion. Does the use of percents clarify or enhance the information in the article? Why or why not? Are the percents presented in a way that would enable you to compute additional data not specifically stated in the article?

50. Continue with the newspaper or magazine article from Problem 49. Create a word problem using information from the article, and solve the problem using techniques you have used for earlier problems in this assignment. Repeat this with a second word problem.

CHAPTER 3 GLOSSARY

Base. The number that a percent multiplies: the first number in the basic percent equation form. (The base represents 100%.)

Hundredths. Equals percent; a value associated with the first two decimal places or with a common fraction having a denominator of 100.

Percent. Means hundredths; indicates a common fraction with a denominator of 100 or a decimal fraction of two decimal places.

Percentage. A part of the base (a number or an amount) that is determined by multiplying the given percent (rate) times the base. (See the accompanying figure.)

Percent equation form. The basic equation, ____% of ____ = ____; in words, what % of a first number (base) is a second number (percentage)?

Percent of change. The equation, ____% of original = change; a variation of the basic equation form, used to find a percent of increase or decrease.

Rate. The percent that multiplies a base. (See the accompanying figure.)

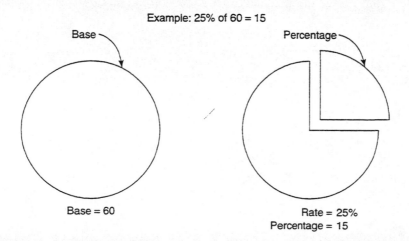

Example: 25% of 60 = 15

Base → Base = 60

Percentage → Rate = 25%
Percentage = 15

Chapter 2

Solving Linear Equations and Inequalities

2.1 Combining Like Terms

2.2 The Addition Property of Equality

2.3 The Multiplication Property of Equality

2.4 Solving Linear Equations with a Variable on Only One Side of the Equation

2.5 Solving Linear Equations with the Variable on Both Sides of the Equation

2.6 Ratios and Proportions

2.7 Inequalities in One Variable

SUMMARY
REVIEW EXERCISES
PRACTICE TEST
CUMULATIVE REVIEW TEST

See Section 2.6, Exercise 43

Preview and Perspective

When many students describe algebra they use the words "solving equations." Solving equations is an important part of algebra and of most other mathematics courses you may take. The major emphasis of this chapter is to teach you how to solve linear equations. We will be using the principles learned in this chapter throughout the book. For example, in Chapter 3, when we study applications of algebra, we will write the applications as linear equations and then solve them. Later in the book we will discuss other types of equations, such as quadratic equations. The procedures presented in this chapter will also be used when solving quadratic equations.

To be successful in solving linear equations, you need to have a thorough understanding of adding, subtracting, multiplying, and dividing real numbers. This material was discussed in Chapter 1. The material presented in the first four sections of this chapter are the building blocks for solving linear equations. In Section 2.5 we combine the material presented previously to solve a variety of linear equations.

In Section 2.6 we discuss ratios and proportions and how to set up and solve them. For many students, proportions may be the most common type of equation used to solve real-life application problems. Once you learn to set up and solve proportions you will see that they have a tremendous number of real-life applications.

In Section 2.7 we discuss solving linear inequalities. Solving linear inequalities is an extension to solving linear equations. The procedure used to solve linear inequalities is basically the same as the procedure used to solve linear equations. The material presented in this section will be helpful in Section 8.6 when we graph linear inequalities in two variables. Linear and other types of inequalities will be discussed in more depth in an intermediate algebra course.

2.1 Combining Like Terms

Tape 3

1 Identify terms.
2 Identify like terms.
3 Combine like terms.
4 Use the distributive property to remove parentheses.
5 Remove parentheses when they are preceded by a plus or minus sign.
6 Simplify an expression.

Identify Terms

1 In Section 1.2 and other sections of the text, we indicated that letters called **variables** (or **literal numbers**) are used to represent numbers.

As was indicated in Chapter 1, an **expression** (sometimes referred to as an **algebraic expression**) is a collection of numbers, variables, grouping symbols, and operation symbols. Examples of expressions are:

$$5, \quad x^2 - 6, \quad 4x - 3, \quad 2(x + 5) + 6, \quad \frac{x + 3}{4}$$

When an algebraic expression consists of several parts, the parts that are added or subtracted are called the **terms** of the expression. The expression $2x - 3y - 5$ has three terms: $2x$, $-3y$, and -5. The expression

$$3x + 2xy + 5(x + y)$$

also has three terms: $3x$, $2xy$, and $5(x + y)$.

The + and − signs that break the expression into terms are a part of the term. However, when listing the terms of an expression, it is not necessary to list the + sign at the beginning of a term.

Expression	*Terms*
$-2x + 3y - 8$	$-2x, \quad 3y, \quad -8$
$3y - 2x + \dfrac{1}{2}$	$3y, \quad -2x, \quad \dfrac{1}{2}$
$7 + x + 4 - 5x$	$7, \quad x, \quad 4, \quad -5x$
$3(x - 1) - 4x + 2$	$3(x -1), \quad -4x, \quad 2$
$\dfrac{x + 4}{3} - 5x + 3$	$\dfrac{x + 4}{3}, \quad -5x, \quad 3$

The numerical part of a term is called its **numerical coefficient** or simply its **coefficient.** In the term $6x$, the 6 is the numerical coefficient. Note that $6x$ means the variable x is multiplied by 6.

Term	*Numerical Coefficient*
$3x$	3
$-\dfrac{1}{2}x$	$-\dfrac{1}{2}$
$4(x - 3)$	4
$\dfrac{2x}{3}$	$\dfrac{2}{3}$, since $\dfrac{2x}{3}$ means $\dfrac{2}{3}x$
$\dfrac{x + 4}{3}$	$\dfrac{1}{3}$, since $\dfrac{x + 4}{3}$ means $\dfrac{1}{3}(x + 4)$

Whenever a term appears without a numerical coefficient, we assume that the numerical coefficient is 1.

Examples

x means $1x$	$-x$ means $-1x$
x^2 means $1x^2$	$-x^2$ means $-1x^2$
xy means $1xy$	$-xy$ means $-1xy$
$(x + 2)$ means $1(x + 2)$	$-(x + 2)$ means $-1(x + 2)$

If an expression has a term that is a number (without a variable), we refer to that number as a **constant term,** or simply a **constant.** In the expression $x^2 + 3x - 4$, the -4 is a constant term, or a constant.

Identify Like Terms   **2** **Like terms** are terms that have the same variables with the same exponents. The following are examples of like terms and unlike terms. Note that if two terms are like terms, only their numerical coefficients may differ.

Like Terms	Unlike Terms	
$3x, \quad -4x$	$3x, \quad 2$	(One term has a variable, the other is a constant)
$4y, \quad 6y$	$3x, \quad 4y$	(Variables differ)
$5, \quad -6$	$x, \quad 3$	(One term has a variable, the other is a constant)
$3(x+1), \quad -2(x+1)$	$2x, \quad 3xy$	(Variables differ)
$3x^2, \quad 4x^2$	$3x, \quad 4x^2$	(Exponents differ)

EXAMPLE 1 Identify any like terms.

(a) $2x + 3x + 4$ (b) $2x + 3y + 2$ (c) $x + 3 + y - \frac{1}{2}$

Solution: (a) $2x$ and $3x$ are like terms.

(b) There are no like terms.

(c) 3 and $-\frac{1}{2}$ are like terms.

EXAMPLE 2 Identify any like terms.

(a) $5x - x + 6$ (b) $3 - 2x + 4x - 6$ (c) $12 + x + 7$

Solution: (a) $5x$ and $-x$ (or $-1x$) are like terms.

(b) 3 and -6 are like terms; $-2x$ and $4x$ are like terms.

(c) 12 and 7 are like terms.

Combine Terms   **3** We often need to simplify expressions by combining like terms. **To combine like terms** means to add or subtract the like terms in an expression. To combine like terms, we can use the procedure that follows.

To Combine Like Terms

1. Determine which terms are like terms.
2. Add or subtract the coefficients of the like terms.
3. Multiply the number found in step 2 by the common variables.

Examples 3 through 9 illustrate this procedure.

EXAMPLE 3 Combine like terms: $4x + 3x$.

Solution: $4x$ and $3x$ are like terms with the common variable x. Since $4 + 3 = 7$, then $4x + 3x = 7x$.

EXAMPLE 4 Combine like terms: $\frac{3}{5}x - \frac{2}{3}x$.

Solution: Since $\frac{3}{5} - \frac{2}{3} = \frac{9}{15} - \frac{10}{15} = -\frac{1}{15}$, then $\frac{3}{5}x - \frac{2}{3}x = -\frac{1}{15}x$.

EXAMPLE 5 Combine like terms: $5.23a - 7.45a$.

Solution: Since $5.23 - 7.45 = -2.22$, then $5.23a - 7.45a = -2.22a$.

EXAMPLE 6 Combine like terms: $3x + x + 5$.

Solution: The $3x$ and x are like terms.

$$3x + x + 5 = 3x + 1x + 5 = 4x + 5$$

EXAMPLE 7 Combine like terms: $12 + x + 7$.

Solution: The 12 and 7 are like terms. We can rearrange the terms to get

$$x + 12 + 7 \quad \text{or} \quad x + 19$$

EXAMPLE 8 Combine like terms: $3y + 4x - 3 - 2x$.

Solution: The only like terms are $4x$ and $-2x$.

$$\text{Rearranging terms: } 4x - 2x + 3y - 3$$
$$\text{Combine like terms: } 2x + 3y - 3$$

EXAMPLE 9 Combine like terms: $-2x + 3y - 4x + 3 - y + 5$.

Solution: $-2x$ and $-4x$ are like terms.

$3y$ and $-y$ are like terms.

3 and 5 are like terms.

Grouping the like terms together gives

$$-2x - 4x + 3y - y + 3 + 5$$
$$-6x + 2y + 8$$

The commutative and associative properties were used to rearrange the terms in Examples 7, 8, and 9. The order of the terms in the answer is not critical. Thus $2y - 6x + 8$ is also an acceptable answer to Example 9. When writing answers, we generally list the terms containing variables in alphabetical order from left to right, and list the constant term on the right.

COMMON STUDENT ERROR Students often misinterpret the meaning of a term like $3x$. What does $3x$ mean?

Correct | *Incorrect*
$3x = x + x + x$ | ~~$3x = x \cdot x \cdot x$~~

Just as $2 + 2 + 2$ can be expressed as $3 \cdot 2$, $x + x + x$ can be expressed as $3 \cdot x$ or $3x$. Note that when we combine like terms in $x + x + x$ we get $3x$. Also note that $x \cdot x \cdot x = x^3$, not $3x$.

Distributive Property We introduced the distributive property in Section 1.10. Because this property is so important, we will study it again. But before we do, let us go back briefly to the subtraction of real numbers. Recall from Section 1.6 that

$$6 - 3 = 6 + (-3)$$

For any real numbers a and b,

$$a - b = a + (-b)$$

We will use the fact that $a + (-b)$ means $a - b$ in discussing the distributive property.

Distributive Property

For any real numbers a, b, and c,

$$a(b + c) = ab + ac$$

EXAMPLE 10   Use the distributive property to remove parentheses.

(a) $2(x + 4)$ (b) $-2(x + 4)$

Solution: (a) $2(x + 4) = 2x + 2(4) = 2x + 8$

(b) $-2(x + 4) = -2x + (-2)(4) = -2x + (-8) = -2x - 8$

Note in part (b) that, instead of leaving the answer $-2x + (-8)$, we wrote it as $-2x - 8$, which is the proper form of the answer.

EXAMPLE 11   Use the distributive property to remove parentheses.

(a) $3(x - 2)$ (b) $-2(4x - 3)$

Solution: (a) By the definition of subtraction, we may write $x - 2$ as $x + (-2)$.

$$3(x - 2) = 3[x + (-2)] = 3x + 3(-2)$$
$$= 3x + (-6)$$
$$= 3x - 6$$

(b) $-2(4x - 3) = -2[4x + (-3)] = -2(4x) + (-2)(-3) = -8x + 6$

The distributive property is used often in algebra, so you need to understand it well. You should understand it so well that you will be able to simplify an expression using the distributive property without having to write down all the steps that we listed in working Examples 10 and 11. Study closely the Helpful Hint on the top of page 81.

The distributive property can be expanded as follows:

$$a(b + c + d + \cdots + n) = ab + ac + ad + \cdots + an$$

Examples of the expanded distributive property are

$$3(x + y + z) = 3x + 3y + 3z$$
$$2(x + y - 3) = 2x + 2y - 6$$

Helpful Hint

With a little practice, you will be able to eliminate some of the intermediate steps when you use the distributive property. When using the distributive property, there are eight possibilities with regard to signs. Study and learn the eight possibilities that follow.

Positive Coefficient

$2(x) = 2x$

(a) $2(x + 3) = 2x + 6$

$2(+3) = +6$

$2(x) = 2x$

(b) $2(x - 3) = 2x - 6$

$2(-3) = -6$

$2(-x) = -2x$

(c) $2(-x + 3) = -2x + 6$

$2(+3) = +6$

$2(-x) = -2x$

(d) $2(-x - 3) = -2x - 6$

$2(-3) = -6$

Negative Coefficient

$(-2)(x) = -2x$

(e) $-2(x + 3) = -2x - 6$

$(-2)(+3) = -6$

$(-2)(x) = -2x$

(f) $-2(x - 3) = -2x + 6$

$(-2)(-3) = +6$

$(-2)(-x) = 2x$

(g) $-2(-x + 3) = 2x - 6$

$(-2)(+3) = -6$

$(-2)(-x) = 2x$

(h) $-2(-x - 3) = 2x + 6$

$(-2)(-3) = +6$

EXAMPLE 12 Use the distributive property to remove parentheses.

(a) $4(x - 3)$ **(b)** $-2(2x - 4)$ **(c)** $-\dfrac{1}{2}(4x + 5)$ **(d)** $-2(3x - 2y + 4z)$

Solution:

(a) $4(x - 3) = 4x - 12$ **(b)** $-2(2x - 4) = -4x + 8$

(c) $-\dfrac{1}{2}(4x + 5) = -2x - \dfrac{5}{2}$ **(d)** $-2(3x - 2y + 4z) = -6x + 4y - 8z$

The distributive property can also be used from the right, as in Example 13.

EXAMPLE 13 Use the distributive property to remove parentheses from the expression $(2x - 8y)4$.

Solution: We distribute the 4 on the right side of the parentheses over the terms within the parentheses.

$$(2x - 8y)4 = 2x(4) - 8y(4)$$
$$= 8x - 32y$$

Example 13 could have been rewritten as $4(2x - 8y)$ by the commutative property of multiplication, and then the 4 could have been distributed from the left to obtain the same answer, $8x - 32y$.

Plus or Minus Sign Before Parentheses

5 In the expression $(4x + 3)$, how do we remove parentheses? Recall that the coefficient of a term is assumed to be 1 if none is shown. Therefore, we may write

$$(4x + 3) = 1(4x + 3)$$
$$= 1(4x) + (1)(3)$$
$$= 4x + 3$$

Note that $(4x + 3) = 4x + 3$. **When no sign or a plus sign precedes parentheses, the parentheses may be removed without having to change the expression inside the parentheses.**

Examples
$$(x + 3) = x + 3$$
$$(2x - 3) = 2x - 3$$
$$+(2x - 5) = 2x - 5$$
$$+(x + 2y - 6) = x + 2y - 6$$

Now consider the expression $-(4x + 3)$. How do we remove parentheses? Here, the number in front of the parentheses is -1, and we write

$$-(4x + 3) = -1(4x + 3)$$
$$= -1(4x) + (-1)(3)$$
$$= -4x + (-3)$$
$$= -4x - 3$$

Thus, $-(4x + 3) = -4x - 3$. **When a negative sign precedes parentheses, the signs of all the terms within the parentheses are changed when the parentheses are removed.**

Examples
$$-(x + 4) = -x - 4$$
$$-(-2x + 3) = 2x - 3$$
$$-(5x - y + 3) = -5x + y - 3$$
$$-(-2x - 3y - 5) = 2x + 3y + 5$$

Simplify an Expression   **6**

> **To Simplify an Expression**
> 1. Use the distributive property to remove any parentheses.
> 2. Combine like terms.

EXAMPLE 14   Simplify $6 - (2x + 3)$.

Solution: $6 - (2x + 3) = 6 - 2x - 3$ Use the distributive property.

$= -2x + 3$ Combine like terms.

Note: $3 - 2x$ is the same as $-2x + 3$; however, we generally write the term containing the variable first.

EXAMPLE 15   Simplify $6x + 4(2x + 3)$.

Solution: $6x + 4(2x + 3) = 6x + 8x + 12$ Use the distributive property.

$= 14x + 12$ Combine like terms.

EXAMPLE 16   Simplify $2(x - 1) + 9$.

Solution: $2(x - 1) + 9 = 2x - 2 + 9$ Use the distributive property.

$= 2x + 7$ Combine like terms.

EXAMPLE 17   Simplify $2(x + 3) - 3(x - 2) - 4$.

Solution: $2(x + 3) - 3(x - 2) - 4 = 2x + 6 - 3x + 6 - 4$ Use the distributive property.

$= 2x - 3x + 6 + 6 - 4$ Rearrange terms.

$= -x + 8$ Combine like terms.

Helpful Hint

It is important for you to have a clear understanding of the concepts of *term* and *factor*. When two or more expressions are **multiplied,** each expression is a **factor** of the product. For example, since $4 \cdot 3 = 12$, the 4 and the 3 are factors of 12. Since $3 \cdot x = 3x$, the 3 and the x are factors of $3x$. Similarly, in the expression $5xyz$, the 5, x, y, and z are all factors.

In an expression, the parts that are **added or subtracted** are the **terms** of the expression. For example, the expression $2x^2 + 3x - 4$, has three terms, $2x^2$, $3x$, and -4. Note that the terms of an expression may have factors. For example, in the term $2x^2$, the 2 and the x^2 are factors because they are multiplied.

Exercise Set 2.1

Combine like terms when possible.

1. $2x + 3x$
2. $3x + 6$
3. $4x - 5x$
4. $4x + 3y$
5. $12 + x - 3$
6. $-2x - 3x$
7. $-2x + 5x$
8. $4x - 7x + 4$
9. $x + 3x - 7$
10. $3 + 2x - 5$
11. $6 - 3 + 2x$
12. $2 + 2x + 3x$
13. $-4 + 5x + 12$
14. $-2x - 3x - 2 - 3$
15. $5x + 2y + 3 + y$

16. $-x + 2 - x - 2$

17. $4x - 2x + 3 - 7$

18. $x - 4x + 3$

19. $5 + x + 3$

20. $x + 2x + y + 2$

21. $-3x + 2 - 5x$

22. $x + 4 - 6$

23. $5 + 2x - 4x + 6$

24. $3x + 4x - 2 + 5$

25. $x - 2 - 4 + 2x$

26. $2x + 4 - 3 + x$

27. $2 - 3x - 2x + 1$

28. $3x - x + 4 - 6$

29. $2y + 4y + 6$

30. $6 - x - x$

31. $x - 6 + 3x - 4$

32. $-2x + 4x - 3$

33. $4 - x + 4x - 8$

34. $x + 4 + \frac{3}{5}$

35. $x + \frac{3}{4} - \frac{1}{3}$

36. $5.23x + 1.42 - 4.61x$

37. $68.2x - 19.7x + 8.3$

38. $\frac{1}{2}x + 3y + 1$

39. $x + \frac{1}{2}y - \frac{3}{8}y$

40. $2x + 3 + 4x + 5$

41. $-4x - 3.1 - 5.2$

42. $-x + 2x + y$

43. $1 + x + 6 - 3x$

44. $2x - 7 - 5x + 2$

45. $3x - 7 - 9 + 4x$

46. $x - y - 2y + 3$

47. $4x + 6 + 3x - 7$

48. $-y - 6 - 3y - y$

49. $-4 + x - 6 + 2$

50. $x - 3y + 2x + 4$

51. $-19.36 + 40.02x + 12.25 - 18.3x$

52. $52x - 52x - 63.5 - 63.5$

53. $\frac{3}{5}x - 3 - \frac{7}{4}x - 2$

54. $\frac{1}{5}y + 3x - 2x - \frac{2}{3}y$

Use the distributive property to remove parentheses.

55. $2(x + 6)$

56. $3(x - 2)$

57. $5(x + 4)$

58. $-2(x + 3)$

59. $-2(x - 4)$

60. $3(-x + 5)$

61. $-\frac{1}{2}(2x - 4)$

62. $-4(x + 6)$

63. $1(-4 + x)$

64. $4(y + 3)$

65. $\frac{1}{4}(x - 12)$

66. $5(x + y + 4)$

67. $-0.6(3x - 5)$

68. $-(x - 3)$

69. $\frac{1}{2}(-2x + 6)$

70. $-2(x + y - z)$

71. $0.4(2x - 0.5)$

72. $-(x + 4y)$

73. $-(-x + y)$

74. $(3x + 4y - 6)$

75. $-(2x - 6y + 8)$

76. $-(-2x + 6 - y)$

77. $4.6(3.1x - 2.3y + 1.8)$

78. $-2(-x + 3y + 5)$

79. $2\left(\frac{1}{2}x - 4y + \frac{1}{4}\right)$

80. $2\left(3 - \frac{1}{2}x + 4y\right)$

81. $(x + 3y - 9)$

82. $(-x + 5 - 2y)$

83. $-(-x + 4 + 2y)$

84. $2.3(1.6x - 5.9y + 4.8)$

Simplify when possible.

85. $4(x - 2) - x$

86. $2 - (x + 3)$

87. $-2(3 - x) + 1$

88. $-(2x + 3) + 5$

89. $6x + 2(4x + 9)$

90. $3(x + y) + 2y$

91. $2(x - y) + 2x + 3$

92. $6 + (x - 8) + 2x$

93. $(2x + y) - 2x + 3$

94. $4 - (2x + 3) + 5$

95. $8x - (x - 3)$

96. $-(x - 5) - 3x + 4$

97. $2(x - 3) - (x + 3)$

98. $3y - (2x + 2y) - 6x$

99. $4(x - 3) + 2(x - 2) + 4$

100. $4(x + 3) - 2x$

101. $2(x - 4) - 3x + 6$

102. $6 - 2(x + 3) + 5x$

103. $-3(x - 4) + 2x - 6$

104. $-(x + 2) + 3x - 6$

105. $4(x - 3) + 4x - 7$

106. $-3(x + 2y) + 3y + 4$

107. $0.4 + (x + 5) - 0.6 + 2$

108. $4 - (2 - x) + 3x$

109. $9 - (-3x + 4) - 5$

110. $2y - 6(y - 2) + 3$

111. $4(x + 2) - 3(x - 4) - 5$

112. $4 - (y - 5) + 2x + 3$

113. $-0.2(2 - x) + 4(y + 0.2)$

114. $-5(-y + 2) + 3(2 - x) - 4$

115. $-6x + 3y - (6 + x) + (x + 3)$

116. $(x + 3) + (x - 4) - 6x$

117. $-(x + 3) + (2x + 4) - 6$

118. $\frac{1}{2}(x + 3) + \frac{1}{3}(3x + 6)$

119. $\frac{2}{3}(x - 2) - \frac{1}{2}(x + 4)$

120. When no sign or a plus sign precedes an expression within parentheses, explain how to remove the parentheses.

121. When a minus sign precedes an expression within parentheses, explain how to remove the parentheses.

122. Explain the difference between a factor and a term.

123. Consider the expression $2x^2 + 3x - 5$.

(a) List the terms of this expression. Explain why each is a term.

(b) List the positive factors of the term $2x^2$. Explain why each is a factor of the term.

[1.4] *Evaluate.*

124. $|-7|$

125. $-|-16|$

📝 [1.9] **126.** Write a paragraph explaining the order of operations.

127. Evaluate $-x^2 + 5x - 6$ when $x = -1$.

Group Activity/ Challenge Problems

Simplify.

1. $4x + 5y + 6(3x - 5y) - 4x + 3$

2. $2x^2 - 4x + 8x^2 - 3(x + 2) - x^2 - 2$

3. $x^2 + 2y - y^2 + 3x + 5x^2 + 6y^2 + 5y$

4. $2[3 + 4(x - 5)] - [2 - (x - 3)]$

5. Consider the expression $3x^2 - 10x + 8$. **(a)** List each term of the expression. **(b)** List the positive factors of $3x^2$, and **(c)** List all factors of the constant 8, including the negative factors. Note that a term may have many factors.

2.2 The Addition Property of Equality

Tape 3

1️⃣ Identify linear equations.

2️⃣ Check solutions to equations.

3️⃣ Identify and define equivalent equations.

4️⃣ Use the addition property to solve equations.

5️⃣ Solve equations doing some steps mentally.

Linear Equations

1️⃣ A statement that shows two algebraic expressions are equal is called an **equation**. For example, $4x + 3 = 2x - 4$ is an equation. In this chapter we learn to solve **linear equations in one variable.**

> A **linear equation** in one variable is an equation that can be written in the form
> $$ax + b = c$$
> for real numbers a, b, and c, $a \neq 0$.

Examples of linear equations in one variable are

$$x + 4 = 7$$
$$2x - 4 = 6$$

Check Solutions to Equations

2️⃣ The **solution of an equation** is the number or numbers that make the equation a true statement. For example, the solution to $x + 4 = 7$ is 3. We will shortly learn how to find the solution to an equation, or to **solve an equation.** But before we do this we will learn how to *check* the solution of an equation.

The solution to an equation may be **checked** by substituting the value that is believed to be the solution into the original equation. If the substitution results in a true statement, your solution is correct. If the substitution results in a false statement, then either your solution or your check is incorrect, and you need to go back and find your error. Try to check all your solutions.

To check whether 3 is the solution to $x + 4 = 7$, we substitute 3 for each x in the equation.

Check: $x = 3$

$$x + 4 = 7$$
$$3 + 4 = 7$$
$$7 = 7 \quad \text{true}$$

Since the check results in a true statement, 3 is a solution.

EXAMPLE 1 Consider the equation $2x - 4 = 6$. Determine whether

(a) 3 is a solution.

(b) 5 is a solution.

Solution: (a) To determine whether 3 is a solution to the equation, substitute 3 for x.

Check: $x = 3$

$$2x - 4 = 6$$
$$2(3) - 4 = 6$$
$$6 - 4 = 6$$
$$2 = 6 \quad \text{false}$$

Since we obtained a false statement, 3 is not a solution.

(b) Substitute 5 for x in the equation.

Check: $x = 5$

$$2x - 4 = 6$$
$$2(5) - 4 = 6$$
$$10 - 4 = 6$$
$$6 = 6 \quad \text{true}$$

Since the value 5 checks, 5 is a solution to the equation.

We can use the same procedures to check more complex equations, as shown in Examples 2 and 3.

EXAMPLE 2 Determine whether 18 is a solution to the equation $3x - 2(x + 3) = 12$.

Solution: To determine whether 18 is a solution, substitute 18 for each x in the equation. If the substitution results in a true statement, then 18 is the solution.

$$3x - 2(x + 3) = 12$$
$$3(18) - 2(18 + 3) = 12$$
$$54 - 2(21) = 12$$
$$54 - 42 = 12$$
$$12 = 12 \quad \text{true}$$

Since we obtain a true statement, 18 is the solution.

EXAMPLE 3 Determine whether $-\dfrac{3}{2}$ is a solution to the equation
$$3(x + 3) = 6 + x.$$

Solution: Substitute $-\dfrac{3}{2}$ for each x in the equation.

$$3(x + 3) = 6 + x$$

$$3\left(-\frac{3}{2} + 3\right) = 6 + \left(-\frac{3}{2}\right)$$

$$3\left(-\frac{3}{2} + \frac{6}{2}\right) = \frac{12}{2} - \frac{3}{2}$$

$$3\left(\frac{3}{2}\right) = \frac{9}{2}$$

$$\frac{9}{2} = \frac{9}{2} \qquad \text{true}$$

Thus, $-\dfrac{3}{2}$ is the solution.

Calculator Corner

CHECKING SOLUTIONS

Calculators can be used to check solutions to equations. For example, to check to see if $\frac{-10}{3}$ is a solution to the equation $2x + 3 = 5(x + 3) - 2$, we perform the following steps:

1. Substitute $\frac{-10}{3}$ for each x.

$$2x + 3 = 5(x + 3) - 2$$

$$2\left(\frac{-10}{3}\right) + 3 = 5\left(\frac{-10}{3} + 3\right) - 2$$

2. Evaluate each side of the equation separately using your calculator. If you obtain the same value on both sides, your solution checks. The procedures for evaluating the left and right sides of the equation depend on whether or not your calculator is a scientific calculator (see page 34). If you do not have a scientific calculator, remember that you need to work within parentheses first, and then do your multiplications and divisions from left to right before your additions and subtractions. In the following steps we assume that you have a scientific calculator.

To evaluate the left side of the equation, $2\left(\frac{-10}{3}\right) + 3$, press the following keys:

$$\boxed{2} \ \boxed{\times} \ \boxed{(} \ \boxed{10} \ \boxed{^{+}/_{-}} \ \boxed{\div} \ \boxed{3} \ \boxed{)} \ \boxed{+} \ \boxed{3} \ \boxed{=} \ -3.6666667$$

To evaluate the right side of the equation, $5\left(\frac{-10}{3} + 3\right) - 2$, press the following keys:

$$\boxed{5} \ \boxed{\times} \ \boxed{(} \ \boxed{10} \ \boxed{^{+}/_{-}} \ \boxed{\div} \ \boxed{3} \ \boxed{+} \ \boxed{3} \ \boxed{)} \ \boxed{-} \ \boxed{2} \ \boxed{=} \ -3.6666667$$

Since both sides give the same value the solution checks. Note that because calculators differ in their electronics, sometimes the last digit of a calculation will differ.

Equivalent Equations

3 Now that we know how to check a solution to an equation we will discuss solving equations. Complete procedures for solving equations will be given shortly. For now, you need to understand that **to solve an equation, it is necessary to get the variable alone on one side of the equal sign. We say that we isolate the variable.** To isolate the variable, we make use of two properties: the addition and multiplication properties of equality. Look first at Figure 2.1.

Think of an equation as a balanced statement whose left side is balanced by its right side. When solving an equation, we must make sure that the equation remains balanced at all times. That is, both sides must always remain equal. **We ensure that an equation always remains equal by doing the same thing to both sides of the equation.** For example, if we add a number to the left side of the equation, we must add exactly the same number to the right side. If we multiply the right side of the equation by some number, we must multiply the left side by the same number.

When we add the same number to both sides of an equation or multiply both sides of an equation by the same nonzero number, we do not change the solution to the equation, just the form. Two or more equations with the same solution are called **equivalent equations.** The equations $2x - 4 = 2$, $2x = 6$, and $x = 3$ are equivalent, since the solution to each is 3.

| Left side of equation | = | Right side of equation |

FIGURE 2.1

Check: $x = 3$

$$2x - 4 = 2 \qquad\qquad 2x = 6 \qquad\qquad x = 3$$
$$2(3) - 4 = 2 \qquad\qquad 2(3) = 6 \qquad\qquad 3 = 3 \quad \text{true}$$
$$6 - 4 = 2 \qquad\qquad 6 = 6 \quad \text{true}$$
$$2 = 2 \quad \text{true}$$

When solving an equation, we use the addition and multiplication properties to express a given equation as simpler equivalent equations until we obtain the solution.

Before stating the addition property of equality, I would like to give you an intuitive and visual introduction to solving equations using the addition property. The multiplication property of equality will be discussed in Section 2.3.

We stated that both sides of an equation must always stay balanced. That is, what you do to one side of the equation you must also do to the other side. Consider Figure 2.2.

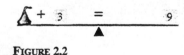

FIGURE 2.2

In this figure and in other figures involving a balance we use the symbol ⚊ to represent a chocolate "kiss," which is a piece of candy. We could have used a box, a tree, a whale, or any other symbol in place of the kiss. The symbol used is not important in understanding the addition property of equality. The kiss is a symbol that is being used to represent some number. Earlier we stated that in algebra we use letters called variables, such as x and y, to represent numbers. Therefore, if you wished you could replace the kiss with an x or y or some other letter. Whenever we use more than one kiss on a balance the kisses all represent the same value. The value of the kiss may change with each example. We will use the balance to show how the addition property of equalities may be used to solve equations.

In Figure 2.2, can you determine the number the kiss represents if both sides of the equation are to be balanced? If you answered 6, you answered correctly.

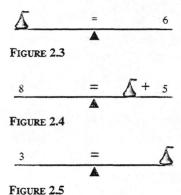

FIGURE 2.3

FIGURE 2.4

FIGURE 2.5

How did you determine your answer? Note that one kiss plus 3 equals 9. If you subtract 3 from both sides of the equation (or scale) you will be left with one kiss equals 6 (Fig. 2.3).

Now consider Figure 2.4.

What is the value of the kiss if both sides are to be balanced? If you answered 3, you are correct. How did you determine your answer? If you subtract 5 from both sides of the balance (Fig. 2.5) you see that one kiss equals 3.

In both of these problems we have actually used the addition property of equality to solve equations. Below we show the balances from Figures 2.2 and 2.4 and the equations that can be determined from the figures. We also indicate the solution to the equations. In the equations we have used the letter x to represent the value of a kiss. However, we could have used k, for kiss, or any other letter. In algebra, we often use the letter x to represent the value of the unknown quantity. To find the value of a kiss, we subtract the amount on the same side of the balance as the kiss from both sides of the balance. To solve each equation for the variable x, we subtract the amount on the same side of the equal sign as the variable from both sides of the equation.

Figure	*Equation*	*Solution*
	$x + 3 = 9$	$x = 6$
	$8 = x + 5$	$x = 3$

Use the Addition Property to Solve Equations

4 Now that we have provided an informal introduction, let us define the addition property of equality.

> **Addition Property of Equality**
>
> If $a = b$, then $a + c = b + c$ for any real numbers a, b, and c.

This property implies that the same number can be added to both sides of an equation without changing the solution. **The addition property is used to solve equations of the form $x + a = b$.** To isolate the variable x in equations of this form, add the opposite or additive inverse of a, $-a$, to both sides of the equation.

To isolate the variable when solving equations of the form $x + a = b$, we use the addition property to eliminate the number **on the same side of the equal sign as the variable.** (This is like isolating the kiss on the balance.) Study the following examples carefully.

Equation	*To Solve, Use the Addition Property to Eliminate the Number*
$x + 8 = 10$	8
$x - 7 = 12$	-7
$5 = x - 12$	-12
$-4 = x + 9$	9

Now let us work some problems.

EXAMPLE 4 Solve the equation $x - 4 = 3$.

Solution: To isolate the variable, x, we must eliminate the -4 from the left side of the equation. To do this we add 4, the opposite of -4, to *both sides* of the equation.

$$x - 4 = 3$$
$$x - 4 + 4 = 3 + 4 \qquad \text{Add 4 to both sides of the equation.}$$
$$x + 0 = 7$$
$$x = 7$$

Note how the process helps to isolate x.

Check: $x - 4 = 3$
$$7 - 4 = 3$$
$$3 = 3 \qquad \text{true}$$

EXAMPLE 5 Solve the equation $y - 3 = -5$.

Solution: To solve this equation, we must isolate the variable, y. To eliminate the -3 from the left side of the equation, we add its opposite, 3, to *both sides* of the equation.

$$y - 3 = -5$$
$$y - 3 + 3 = -5 + 3 \qquad \text{Add 3 to both sides of the equation.}$$
$$y + 0 = -2$$
$$y = -2$$

Note that we did not check the solution to Example 5. Space limitations prevent us from showing all checks. However, *you should check all of your answers.*

EXAMPLE 6 Solve the equation $x + 5 = 9$.

Solution: To solve this equation, we must isolate the variable, x. Therefore, we must eliminate the 5 from the left side of the equation. To do this, we add the opposite of 5, -5, to both sides of the equation.

$$x + 5 = 9$$
$$x + 5 + (-5) = 9 + (-5) \qquad \text{Add } -5 \text{ to both sides of the equation.}$$
$$x + 0 = 4$$
$$x = 4$$

In Example 6 we added -5 to both sides of the equation. From Section 1.6 we know that $5 + (-5) = 5 - 5$. Thus, we can see that adding a negative 5 to both sides of the equation is equivalent to subtracting a 5 from both sides of the equation. According to the addition property, the same number may be *added* to both sides of an equation. **Since subtraction is defined in terms of addition, the addi-**

tion property also allows us to *subtract* the same number from both sides of the equation. Thus, Example 6 could have also been worked as follows:

$$x + 5 = 9$$
$$x + 5 - 5 = 9 - 5 \qquad \text{Subtract 5 from both sides of the equation.}$$
$$x + 0 = 4$$
$$x = 4$$

In this text, unless there is a specific reason to do otherwise, rather than adding a negative number to both sides of the equation, we will subtract a number from both sides of the equation.

EXAMPLE 7   Solve the equation $x + 7 = -3$.

Solution: $x + 7 = -3$

$$x + 7 - 7 = -3 - 7 \qquad \text{Subtract 7 from both sides of the equation.}$$
$$x + 0 = -10$$
$$x = -10$$

Check: $x + 7 = -3$
$$-10 + 7 = -3$$
$$-3 = -3 \qquad \text{true}$$

Helpful Hint

Some students may not fully understand which number to add or subtract when solving equations. Remember that our goal in solving equations is to get the variable alone on one side of the equation. To do this, we add or subtract **the number on the same side of the equation as the variable** to both sides of the equation.

Equation	Must Eliminate	Number to Add (or Subtract) to (or from) Both Sides of the Equation	Correct Results	Solution
$x - 5 = 8$	-5	add 5	$x - 5 \;\boxed{+5} = 8 \;\boxed{+5}$	$x = 13$
$x - 3 = -12$	-3	add 3	$x - 3 \;\boxed{+3} = -12 \;\boxed{+3}$	$= -9$
$2 = x - 7$	-7	add 7	$2 \;\boxed{+7} = x - 7 \;\boxed{+7}$	$9 = x$
$x + 12 = -5$	$+12$	subtract 12	$x + 12 \;\boxed{-12} = -5 \;\boxed{-12}$	$x = -17$
$6 = x + 4$	$+4$	subtract 4	$6 \;\boxed{-4} = x + 4 \;\boxed{-4}$	$2 = x$
$13 = x + 9$	$+9$	subtract 9	$13 \;\boxed{-9} = x + 9 \;\boxed{-9}$	$4 = x$

Notice that under the *Correct Results* column, when the equation is simplified by combining terms, the x will become isolated because the sum of a number and its opposite is 0, and $x + 0$ equals x.

EXAMPLE 8   Solve the equation $4 = x - 5$.

Solution: The variable x is on the right side of the equation. To isolate the x, we must eliminate the -5 from the right side of the equation. This can be accomplished by adding 5 to both sides of the equation.

$$4 = x - 5$$
$$4 + 5 = x - 5 + 5 \qquad \text{Add 5 to both sides of the equation.}$$
$$9 = x + 0$$
$$9 = x$$

Thus, the solution is 9.

EXAMPLE 9   Solve the equation $-6.25 = x + 12.78$.

Solution: The variable is on the right side of the equation. Subtract 12.78 from both sides of the equation to isolate the variable.

$$-6.25 = x + 12.78$$
$$-6.25 - 12.78 = x + 12.78 - 12.78 \qquad \text{Subtract 12.78 from both sides of the equation.}$$
$$-19.03 = x + 0$$
$$-19.03 = x$$

The solution is -19.03.

COMMON STUDENT ERROR When solving equations, our goal is to get the variable alone on one side of the equal sign. Consider the equation $x + 3 = -4$. How do we solve it?

	Correct	*Wrong*

Correct

Remove the 3 from the left side of the equation.

$$x + 3 = -4$$
$$x + 3 - 3 = -4 - 3$$
$$x = -7$$

Variable is now isolated.

Wrong

Remove the -4 from the right side of the equation.

$$x + 3 = -4$$
$$x + 3 \div 4 = -4 \div 4$$
$$x + 7 = 0$$

Variable is not isolated.

Remember, use the addition property to **remove the number that is on the same side of the equation as the variable.**

Performing Some Steps Mentally

5 Consider the following two problems:

(a)
$$x - 5 = 12$$
$$x - 5 + 5 = 12 + 5$$
$$x + 0 = 12 + 5$$
$$x = 17$$

(b)
$$15 = x + 3$$
$$15 - 3 = x + 3 - 3$$
$$15 - 3 = x + 0$$
$$12 = x$$

Note how the number on the same side of the equal sign as the variable is transferred to the opposite side of the equal sign when the addition property is used.

Also note that the sign of the number changes when transferred from one side of the equal sign to the other.

When you feel comfortable using the addition property, you may wish to do some of the steps mentally to reduce some of the written work. For example, the preceding two problems may be shortened as follows.

Shortened Form

(a) $x - 5 = 12$ $x - 5 = 12$

$x - 5 + 5 = 12 + 5$ ⟵ Do this step mentally. $x = 12 + 5$

$x = 12 + 5$ $x = 17$

$x = 17$

Shortened Form

(b) $15 = x + 3$ $15 = x + 3$

$15 - 3 = x + 3 - 3$ ⟵ Do this step mentally. $15 - 3 = x$

$15 - 3 = x$ $12 = x$

$12 = x$

Exercise Set 2.2

By checking, determine if the number following the equation is a solution to the equation.

1. $2x - 3 = 5, 4$

2. $2x + 1 = x - 5, -6$

3. $2x - 5 = 5(x + 2), -3$

4. $2(x - 3) = 3(x + 1), 1$

5. $3x - 5 = 2(x + 3) - 11, 0$

6. $-2(x - 3) = -5x + 3 - x, -2$

7. $5(x + 2) - 3(x - 1) = 4, 2.3$

8. $x + 3 = 3x + 2, \frac{1}{2}$

9. $4x - 4 = 2x - 3, \frac{1}{2}$

10. $3x + 4 = -2x + 9, \frac{1}{2}$

11. $3(x + 2) = 5(x - 1), \frac{11}{2}$

12. $-(x + 3) - (x - 6) = 3x - 4, 5$

(a) *In Exercises 13–20, represent each figure as an equation using x, and* **(b)** *solve the equation. Refer to page 89 for examples.*

13. △ + 5 = 8

14. △ + 2 = 9

15. 12 = △ + 3

16. 15 = △ + 4

17. 10 = △ + 7

18. △ + 9 = 10

19. △ + 6 = 4 + 11

20. 12 + 4 = △ + 3

Solve each equation and check your solution.

21. $x + 2 = 6$

22. $x - 4 = 9$

23. $x + 7 = -3$

24. $x - 4 = -8$

25. $x + 4 = -5$

26. $x - 16 = 36$

27. $x + 43 = -18$

28. $6 + x = 9$

29. $-8 + x = 14$

30. $7 = 9 + x$

31. $27 = x - 16$

32. $-9 = x - 25$

33. $-13 = x - 1$

34. $4 = 11 + x$

35. $29 = -43 + x$

36. $-18 = -14 + x$

37. $7 + x = -19$

38. $9 + x = 9$

39. $x + 29 = -29$

40. $4 + x = -9$

41. $9 = x - 3$

42. $5 + x = 12$

43. $x + 7 = -5$

44. $6 = 4 + x$

45. $9 + x = 12$

46. $-4 = x - 3$

47. $-5 = 4 + x$

48. $12 = 16 + x$

49. $40 = x - 13$

50. $15 + x = -5$

51. $x - 12 = -9$

52. $x + 6 = -12$

53. $4 + x = 9$

54. $-6 = 9 + x$

55. $-8 = -9 + x$

56. $-12 = 8 + x$

57. $5 = x - 12$

58. $2 = x + 9$

59. $-50 = x - 24$

60. $-29 + x = -15$

61. $16 + x = -20$

62. $-25 = 18 + x$

63. $40.2 + x = -7.3$

64. $-27.23 + x = 9.77$

65. $-37 + x = 9.5$

66. $7.2 + x = 7.2$

67. $x - 8.42 = -30$

68. $6.2 + x = 5.7$

69. $9.75 = x + 9.75$

70. $139 = x - 117$

71. $600 = x - 120$

72. What is an equation?

73. (a) What is meant by the "solution of an equation"? (b) What does it mean to "solve an equation"?

74. Explain how the solution to an equation may be checked.

75. In your own words explain the Addition Property of Equality.

76. What are equivalent equations?

77. To solve an equation we "isolate the variable." (a) Explain what this means, and (b) explain how to isolate the variable in the equations discussed in this section.

78. When solving the equation $x - 4 = 6$, would you add 4 to both sides of the equation or subtract 6 from both sides of the equation? Explain.

79. When solving the equation $5 = x + 3$, would you subtract 5 from both sides of the equation or subtract 3 from both sides of the equation? Explain.

CUMULATIVE REVIEW EXERCISES

[1.9] *Evaluate.*

80. $3x + 4(x - 3) + 2$ when $x = 4$.

81. $6x - 2(2x + 1)$ when $x = -3$.

[2.1] *Simplify.*

82. $4x + 3(x - 2) - 5x - 7$.

83. $-(x - 3) + 7(2x - 5) - 3x$.

Group Activity/ Challenge Problems

1. By checking, determine which of the following are solutions to the equation $2(x + 3) = 2x + 6$.

(a) -1 (b) 5 (c) $\dfrac{1}{2}$

(d) Select any number not given in parts (a), (b), or (c) and determine if that number is a solution to the equation.

(e) Will every real number be a solution to this equation? Explain.

2. By checking, determine which of the following are solutions to $2x^2 - 7x + 3 = 0$.

   (a) 3   **(b)** 2   **(c)** $\dfrac{1}{2}$

3. In the next section we introduce the multiplication property. When discussing the multiplication property we will use a figure like the one that follows.

$$\triangle + \triangle \quad = \quad \underline{\hspace{3cm}} \quad 8$$
$$\blacktriangle$$

   (a) Write an equation using the variable x, that can be used to represent this figure.

   (b) Solve the equation.

Follow the instructions in Exercise 3 for the following figures.

$$\triangle + \triangle + \triangle \quad = \quad \underline{\hspace{2cm}} \quad 12 \qquad\qquad 20 \quad \underline{\hspace{2cm}} \quad = \triangle + \triangle + \triangle + \triangle$$
4. $\qquad\qquad\quad \blacktriangle \qquad\qquad\qquad\qquad$ **5.** $\qquad\quad \blacktriangle$

2.3   The Multiplication Property of Equality

Tape 3

1 Identify reciprocals.

2 Use the multiplication property of equality to solve equations.

3 Solve equations of the form $-x = a$.

4 Do some steps mentally when solving equations.

Identify Reciprocals

1 Before we discuss the multiplication property, let us discuss what is meant by the **reciprocal** of a number. Two numbers are reciprocals of each other when their product is 1. Some examples of numbers and their reciprocals follow.

Number	*Reciprocal*	*Product*
3	$\dfrac{1}{3}$	$(3)\left(\dfrac{1}{3}\right) = 1$
$-\dfrac{3}{5}$	$-\dfrac{5}{3}$	$\left(-\dfrac{3}{5}\right)\left(-\dfrac{5}{3}\right) = 1$
-1	-1	$(-1)(-1) = 1$

The reciprocal of a positive number is a positive number and the reciprocal of a negative number is a negative number. Note that 0 has no reciprocal.

In general, if a represents any number, its reciprocal is $\frac{1}{a}$. For example, the reciprocal of 3 is $\frac{1}{3}$ and the reciprocal of -2 is $\frac{1}{-2}$ or $-\frac{1}{2}$.

The reciprocal of $-\frac{3}{5}$ is $\dfrac{1}{-\frac{3}{5}}$, which can be written as $1 \div \left(-\frac{3}{5}\right)$. Simplifying, we get $\left(\frac{1}{1}\right)\left(-\frac{5}{3}\right) = -\frac{5}{3}$. Thus, the reciprocal of $-\frac{3}{5}$ is $-\frac{5}{3}$.

Use the Multiplication Property to Solve Equations

2 In Section 2.2 we used the addition property of equality to solve equations of the form $x + a = b$ where a and b represent real numbers. In this section we will solve equations of the form $ax = b$, where a and b represent real numbers. Equations of the form $ax = b$ are solved using the multiplication property of equality. It is important that you recognize the difference between equations like $x + 2 = 8$ and $2x = 8$. In $x + 2 = 8$ the 2 is being added to x, so we use the addition property to solve the equation. In $2x = 8$ the 2 is multiplying the x, so we use the multiplication property to solve the equation. The multiplication property is used to solve linear equations where the coefficient of the x term is a number other than 1. Below we give a visual interpretation of the difference between the equations. To write the equation we have used x to represent the value of a kiss.

Figure	*Equation*	*Property to Use to Solve Equation*	*Solution*
	$x + 2 = 8$	Addition (the equation contains only one x)	6
	$x + x = 8$ or $2x = 8$	Multiplication (the left side of the equation contains more than one x)	4
	$15 = x + x + x$ or $15 = 3x$	Multiplication (the right side of the equation contains more than one x).	5

To help you understand the multiplication property of equality we will give a visual interpretation of the property before stating it.

Consider Figure 2.6. To find the value of one kiss, we need to redraw the balance with only one kiss on one side of the balance. We need to eliminate one of the two kisses on the left side of the balance. We can accomplish this by either multiplying the two kisses by $\frac{1}{2}$ to get $\frac{1}{2}(2) = 1$, or by dividing the two kisses by 2 to get $\frac{2}{2} = 1$. The two processes are equivalent. We must remember that whatever we do to one side of the balance we must do to the other side. Thus, if we multiply the two kisses by $\frac{1}{2}$, we need to multiply the 8 by $\frac{1}{2}$ to get $\frac{1}{2}(8) = 4$. If we divide the two kisses by 2, we need to divide the 8 by 2 to get $\frac{8}{2} = 4$. Either procedure results in the balance shown in Figure 2.7, where we can see that the value of a kiss is 4.

FIGURE 2.6

FIGURE 2.7

FIGURE 2.8

Now consider the balance in Figure 2.8. There are 4 kisses of equal value on the right side of the balance. To find the value of one kiss we need to redraw the balance so that only one kiss appears on the right side. We can do this by multiplying the 4 kisses by $\frac{1}{4}$ to get $4(\frac{1}{4}) = 1$, or by dividing the 4 kisses by 4 to get $\frac{4}{4} = 1$. If we multiply the kisses on the right side of the balance by $\frac{1}{4}$, we need to multiply the 9 on the left side of the balance by $\frac{1}{4}$. This gives $\frac{1}{4}(9) = \frac{9}{4}$. If we divide the kisses on the right side of the balance by 4, we need to divide the 9 on the left side of the balance by 4. This gives $\frac{9}{4}$. Either method results in the kiss on the right side of the balance having a value of $\frac{9}{4}$ (Fig. 2.9).

FIGURE 2.9

Below we illustrate how Figure 2.8 may be represented as an equation if we let x represent the value of a kiss.

Figure	*Equation*	*Solution*
9 $= $ ⬦+⬦+⬦+⬦ ▲	$9 = x + x + x + x$ or $9 = 4x$	$\dfrac{9}{4}$

To solve the equation $9 = 4x$ we perform a similar process used in finding the value of one kiss on the balance. To find the value of x in the equation $9 = 4x$ we can *multiply* both sides of the equation *by the reciprocal of the number of x's that appear.* Since the right side of the equation contains 4 x's we can multiply both sides of the equation by $\frac{1}{4}$. We can also solve the equation by *dividing* both sides of the equation *by the number of x's that appear,* 4. Using either method we find that $x = \frac{9}{4}$.

The information presented above may help you in solving equations using the multiplication property of equality. Now we present the multiplication property of equality.

Multiplication Property of Equality

If $a = b$, then $a \cdot c = b \cdot c$ for any numbers a, b, and c.

The multiplication property implies that both sides of an equation can be multiplied by the same number without changing the solution. **The multiplication property can be used to solve equations of the form $ax = b$.** We can isolate the variable in equations of this form by multiplying both sides of the equation by the reciprocal of a, which is $\frac{1}{a}$. By doing so the numerical coefficient of the variable, x, becomes 1, which can be omitted when we write the variable. By following this process, we say that we *eliminate* the coefficient from the variable.

Equation	*To Solve, Use the Multiplication Property to Eliminate the Coefficient*
$4x = 9$	4
$-5x = 20$	-5
$15 = \dfrac{1}{2}x$	$\dfrac{1}{2}$
$7 = -9x$	-9

Now let us work some problems.

EXAMPLE 1   Solve the equation $3x = 6$.

Solution: To isolate the variable, x, we must eliminate the 3 from the left side of the equation. To do this, we multiply both sides of the equation by the reciprocal of 3, which is $\frac{1}{3}$.

$$3x = 6$$

$$\frac{1}{3} \cdot 3x = \frac{1}{3} \cdot 6 \qquad \text{Multiply both sides of the equation by } \frac{1}{3}.$$

$$\frac{1}{\underset{1}{\cancel{3}}} \cdot \overset{1}{\cancel{3}}x = \frac{1}{\underset{1}{\cancel{3}}} \cdot \overset{2}{\cancel{6}} \qquad \text{Divide out the common factors.}$$

$$1x = 2$$

$$x = 2$$

Notice in Example 1 that $1x$ is replaced by x in the next step. Usually we do this step mentally. How would you represent and solve the equation $3x = 6$ using a balance? Try this now.

EXAMPLE 2   Solve the equation $\frac{x}{2} = 4$.

Solution: Since dividing by 2 is the same as multiplying by $\frac{1}{2}$, the equation $\frac{x}{2} = 4$ is the same as $\frac{1}{2}x = 4$. We will therefore multiply both sides of the equation by the reciprocal of $\frac{1}{2}$, which is 2.

$$\frac{x}{2} = 4$$

$$\overset{1}{\cancel{2}}\left(\frac{x}{\underset{1}{\cancel{2}}}\right) = 2 \cdot 4 \qquad \text{Multiply both sides of the equation by 2.}$$

$$x = 2 \cdot 4$$

$$x = 8$$

Check: $\dfrac{x}{2} = 4$

$$\frac{8}{2} = 4$$

$$4 = 4 \qquad \text{true}$$

EXAMPLE 3   Solve the equation $\frac{2}{3}x = 6$.

Solution: The reciprocal of $\frac{2}{3}$ is $\frac{3}{2}$. Multiply both sides of the equation by $\frac{3}{2}$.

$$\frac{2}{3}x = 6$$

$$\frac{3}{2} \cdot \frac{2}{3}x = \frac{3}{2} \cdot 6$$

$$1x = 9$$

$$x = 9$$

Check: $\dfrac{2}{3}x = 6$

$$\dfrac{2}{3}(9) = 6$$

$$6 = 6 \qquad \text{true}$$

In Example 1, $3x = 6$, we multiplied both sides of the equation by $\frac{1}{3}$ to isolate the variable. We could have also isolated the variable by dividing both sides of the equation by 3, as follows:

$$3x = 6$$

$$\dfrac{\overset{1}{\cancel{3}}x}{\underset{1}{\cancel{3}}} = \dfrac{\overset{2}{\cancel{6}}}{\underset{1}{\cancel{3}}} \qquad \text{Divide both sides of the equation by 3.}$$

$$x = 2$$

We can do this because dividing by 3 is equivalent to multiplying by $\frac{1}{3}$. **Since division can be defined in terms of multiplication ($\frac{a}{b}$ means $a \cdot \frac{1}{b}$), the multiplication property also allows us to divide both sides of an equation by the same nonzero number.** This process is illustrated in Examples 4 through 6.

EXAMPLE 4 Solve the equation $8p = 5$.

Solution: $8p = 5$

$$\dfrac{8p}{8} = \dfrac{5}{8} \qquad \text{Divide both sides of the equation by 8.}$$

$$p = \dfrac{5}{8}$$

EXAMPLE 5 Solve the equation $-12 = -3x$.

Solution: In this equation the variable, x, is on the right side of the equal sign. To isolate x, we divide both sides of the equation by -3.

$$-12 = -3x$$

$$\dfrac{-12}{-3} = \dfrac{-3x}{-3} \qquad \text{Divide both sides of the equation by } -3.$$

$$4 = x$$

EXAMPLE 6 Solve the equation $0.32x = 1.28$.

Solution: We begin by dividing both sides of the equation by 0.32 to isolate the variable x.

$$0.32x = 1.28$$

$$\dfrac{0.32x}{0.32x} = \dfrac{1.28}{0.32} \qquad \text{Divide both sides of the equation by 0.32.}$$

$$x = 4$$

Working problems involving decimal numbers on a calculator will probably save you time.

Helpful Hint

When solving an equation of the form $ax = b$, we can isolate the variable by

1. Multiplying both sides of the equation by the reciprocal of a, $\dfrac{1}{a}$, as was done in Examples 1, 2, and 3, or
2. Dividing both sides of the equation by a, as was done in Examples 4, 5, and 6.

Either method may be used to isolate the variable. However, if the equation contains a fraction, or fractions, you will arrive at a solution more quickly by multiplying by the reciprocal of a. This is illustrated in Examples 7 and 8.

EXAMPLE 7 Solve the equation $-2x = \dfrac{3}{5}$.

Solution: Since this equation contains a fraction, we will isolate the variable by multiplying both sides of the equation by $-\frac{1}{2}$, which is the reciprocal of -2.

$$-2x = \frac{3}{5}$$

$$\left(-\frac{1}{2}\right)(-2x) = \left(-\frac{1}{2}\right)\left(\frac{3}{5}\right) \qquad \textbf{Multiply both sides of the equation by } \quad \frac{1}{2}.$$

$$1x = \left(-\frac{1}{2}\right)\left(\frac{3}{5}\right)$$

$$x = -\frac{3}{10}$$

In Example 7, if you wished to solve the equation by dividing both sides of the equation by -2, you would have to divide the fraction $\frac{3}{5}$ by -2.

EXAMPLE 8 Solve the equation $-6 = -\dfrac{3}{5}x$.

Solution: Since this equation contains a fraction, we will isolate the variable by multiplying both sides of the equation by the reciprocal of $-\frac{3}{5}$, which is $-\frac{5}{3}$.

$$-6 = -\frac{3}{5}x$$

$$(-6)\left(-\frac{5}{3}\right) = \left(-\frac{5}{3}\right)\left(-\frac{3}{5}x\right)$$

$$10 = x$$

In Example 8 the equation was written as $-6x = -\frac{3}{5}x$. This equation is equivalent to the equations $-6 = \frac{-3}{5}x$ and $-6 = \frac{3}{-5}x$. Can you explain why? All three equations have the same solution, 10.

Solve Equations of the Form $-x = a$

3 When solving an equation we may obtain an equation like $-x = 7$. This is not a solution since $-x = 7$ means $-1x = 7$. The solution to an equation is of the form $x =$ some number. When an equation is of the form $-x = 7$, we can solve for x by multiplying both sides of the equation by -1, as illustrated in the following example.

EXAMPLE 9   Solve the equation $-x = 7$.

Solution: $-x = 7$ means that $-1x = 7$. We are solving for x, not $-x$. We can multiply both sides of the equation by -1 to get x on the left side of the equation.

$$-x = 7$$
$$-1x = 7$$
$$(-1)(-1x) = (-1)(7) \qquad \text{Multiply both sides of the equation by } -1.$$
$$1x = -7$$
$$x = -7$$

Check:
$$-x = 7$$
$$-(-7) = 7$$
$$7 = 7 \qquad \text{true}$$

Thus, the solution is -7.

Example 9 may also be solved by dividing both sides of the equation by -1. Try this now and see that you get the same solution. Whenever we have the opposite (or negative) of a variable equal to a quantity, as in Example 9, we can solve for the variable by multiplying (or dividing) both sides of the equation by -1.

EXAMPLE 10   Solve the equation $-x = -5$.

Solution:
$$-x = -5$$
$$-1x = -5$$
$$(-1)(-1x) = (-1)(-5) \qquad \text{Multiply both sides of the equation by } -1.$$
$$1x = 5$$
$$x = 5$$

Helpful Hint

For any real number a, $a \neq 0$,
If $-x = a$, then $x = -a$

Examples: $\quad -x = 7 \qquad\qquad -x = -2$
$$x = -7 \qquad\qquad x = -(-2)$$
$$x = 2$$

Performing Some Steps Mentally

4 When you feel comfortable using the multiplication property, you may wish to do some of the steps mentally to reduce some of the written work. Now we present two examples worked out in detail, along with their shortened form.

EXAMPLE 11 Solve the equation $-3x = -21$.

Solution:

$$-3x = -21$$

$$\frac{-3x}{-3} = \frac{-21}{-3} \longleftarrow \text{Do this step mentally.}$$

$$x = \frac{-21}{-3}$$

$$x = 7$$

Shortened Form

$$-3x = -21$$

$$x = \frac{-21}{-3}$$

$$x = 7$$

EXAMPLE 12 Solve the equation $\frac{1}{3}x = 9$.

Solution:

$$\frac{1}{3}x = 9$$

$$3\left(\frac{1}{3}x\right) = 3(9) \longleftarrow \text{Do this step mentally.}$$

$$x = 3(9)$$

$$x = 27$$

Shortened Form

$$\frac{1}{3}x = 9$$

$$x = 3(9)$$

$$x = 27$$

In Section 2.2 we discussed the addition property and in this section we discussed the multiplication property. It is important that you understand the difference between the two. The following Helpful Hint should be studied carefully.

Helpful Hint

The **addition property** is used to solve equations of the form $x + a = b$. The *addition property* is used when a number is *added to or subtracted from* a variable.

$$x + 3 = -6 \qquad\qquad x - 5 = -2$$

$$x + 3 - 3 = -6 - 3 \qquad x - 5 + 5 = -2 + 5$$

$$x = -9 \qquad\qquad x = 3$$

The **multiplication property** is used to solve equations of the form $ax = b$. It is used when a variable is *multiplied or divided by a number.*

$$3x = 6 \qquad\qquad \frac{x}{2} = 4 \qquad\qquad \frac{2}{5}x = 12$$

$$\frac{3x}{3} = \frac{6}{3} \qquad\qquad 2\left(\frac{x}{2}\right) = 2(4) \qquad \left(\frac{5}{2}\right)\left(\frac{2}{5}x\right) = \left(\frac{5}{2}\right)(12)$$

$$x = 2 \qquad\qquad x = 8 \qquad\qquad x = 30$$

Exercise Set 2.3

(a) *Express the figure as an equation in the variable x, and,* (b) *solve the equation.*

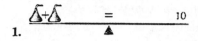

1.   △+△ = 10   ▲

2.   △+△+△+△ = 4   ▲

3.   6 = △+△+△   ▲

4.   △+△+△ = 21   △

5.   △+△ = 5   ▲

6.   △+△+△+△ = 8   ▲

7.   4 = △+△+△   ▲

8.   △+△+△ = 30   ▲

Solve each equation and check your solution.

9. $2x = 6$

10. $5x = 20$

11. $\dfrac{x}{2} = 4$

12. $\dfrac{x}{3} = 12$

13. $-4x = 8$

14. $8 = 16y$

15. $\dfrac{x}{6} = -2$

16. $\dfrac{x}{3} = -2$

17. $\dfrac{x}{5} = 1$

18. $-2x = 12$

19. $-32x = -96$

20. $16 = -4y$

21. $-6 - 4z$

22. $\dfrac{x}{8} = -3$

23. $-x = -6$

24. $-x = 9$

25. $-2 = -y$

26. $-3 = \dfrac{x}{5}$

27. $-\dfrac{x}{7} = -7$

28. $4 = \dfrac{x}{9}$

29. $4 = -12x$

30. $12y = -15$

31. $-\dfrac{x}{3} = -2$

32. $-\dfrac{a}{8} = -7$

33. $13x = 10$

34. $-24x = -18$

35. $-4.2x = -8.4$

36. $-3.72 = 1.24y$

37. $7x = -7$

38. $3x = \dfrac{3}{5}$

39. $5x = -\dfrac{3}{8}$

40. $-2b = -\dfrac{4}{5}$

41. $15 = -\dfrac{x}{5}$

42. $\dfrac{x}{16} = -4$

43. $-\dfrac{x}{5} = -25$

44. $-x = -\dfrac{5}{9}$

45. $\dfrac{x}{5} = -7$

46. $-3r = -18$

47. $5 = \dfrac{x}{4}$

48. $-3 = \dfrac{x}{-5}$

49. $6d = -30$

50. $\dfrac{2}{7}x = 7$

51. $\dfrac{y}{-2} = -6$

52. $-2x = \dfrac{3}{5}$

53. $\dfrac{-3}{8}w = 6$

54. $-x = \dfrac{4}{7}$

55. $\dfrac{1}{3}x = -12$

56. $6 = \dfrac{3}{5}x$

57. $-4 = -\dfrac{2}{3}z$

58. $-8 = \dfrac{-4}{5}x$

59. $-1.4x = 28.28$

60. $-0.42x = -2.142$

61. $2x = -\dfrac{5}{2}$

62. $6x = \dfrac{8}{3}$

63. $\dfrac{2}{3}x = 6$

64. $-\dfrac{1}{2}x = \dfrac{2}{3}$

65. (a) If $-x = a$, where a represents any real number, what does x equal?
(b) If $-x = 5$, what is x?
(c) If $-x = -5$, what is x?

66. When solving the equation $3x = 5$, would you divide both sides of the equation by 3 or by 5? Explain.

67. When solving the equation $-2x = 5$, would you add 2 to both sides of the equation or divide both sides of the equation by -2? Explain.

68. Consider the equation $\frac{2}{3}x = 4$. This equation could be solved by multiplying both sides of the equation by $\frac{3}{2}$, the reciprocal of $\frac{2}{3}$, or by dividing both sides of the equation by $\frac{2}{3}$. Which method do you feel would be easier? Explain your answer. Find the solution to the equation.

69. Consider the equation $4x = \frac{3}{5}$. Would it be easier to solve this equation by dividing both sides of the equation by 4 or by multiplying both sides of the equation

by $\frac{1}{4}$, the reciprocal of 4? Explain your answer. Find the solution to the problem.

70. Consider the equation $\frac{3}{7}x = \frac{4}{5}$. Would it be easier to solve this equation by dividing both sides of the equation by $\frac{3}{7}$ or by multiplying both sides of the equation by $\frac{7}{3}$, the reciprocal of $\frac{3}{7}$? Explain your answer. Find the solution to the equation.

CUMULATIVE REVIEW EXERCISES

[1.6] **71.** Subtract -4 from -8.

72. Evaluate $6 - (-3) - 5 - 4$.

[2.1] **73.** Simplify $-(x + 3) - 5(2x - 7) + 6$.

[2.2] **74.** Solve the equation $-48 = x + 9$.

Group Activity/ Challenge Problems

In the next section we will solve equations using both the addition and multiplication properties. We can use figures like those in Exercises 1–4 to illustrate such problems. For each exercise,

(a) Find the value of a kiss. Hint: Use the addition property first to get the kisses by themselves on one side of the balance. Then use the multiplication property to find the value of a kiss.

(b) Write an equation in variable x that can be used to represent the figure.

(c) Solve the equation and find the value of x. (The value of x should be the same as the value of a kiss. Follow the hint presented in part (a).)

1. $\triangle + \triangle + 6 = 14$

2. $9 = \triangle + \triangle + \triangle + 9$

3. $6 = \triangle + 4 + \triangle$

4. $7 = \triangle + \triangle + 2 + \triangle$

2.4 Solving Linear Equations with a Variable on Only One Side of the Equation

Tape 4

Solve Linear Equations

1 Solve linear equations that contain a variable on only one side of the equal sign.

1 In this section we discuss how to solve linear equations using **both** the addition and multiplication properties of equality when a variable appears on only one side of the equal sign. In Section 2.5 we will discuss how to solve linear equations using both properties when a variable appears on both sides of the equal sign.

Below we show some illustrations that have been represented as equations. In the equations we represented the value of a kiss with the letter x. In each of these equations the variable appears on only one side of the equal sign. We also give the solution to each equation. You probably cannot determine the solutions yet. Do not worry about this. The purpose of this section is to teach you the procedures for finding the solution to such problems.

Figure	Equation	Solution
△+△+ 4 = 14	$2x + 4 = 14$	5
△+△+△+ 6 = 27	$3x + 6 = 27$	7
12 = △+△+ 5	$12 = 2x + 5$	$\dfrac{7}{2}$

The general procedure we use to solve equations is to "isolate the variable." That is, we must get the variable, x, alone on one side of the equal sign. If you consider the balance, we will need to eliminate all the numbers from the same side of the balance as the kisses. No one method is the "best" to solve all linear equations. Following is a general procedure that can be used to solve linear equations when the variable appears on only one side of the equation and the equation does not contain fractions.

> **To Solve Linear Equations with a Variable on Only One Side of the Equal Sign**
>
> 1. Use the distributive property to remove parentheses.
> 2. Combine like terms on the same side of the equal sign.
> 3. Use the addition property to obtain an equation with the term containing the variable on one side of the equal sign and a constant on the other side. This will result in an equation of the form $ax = b$.
> 4. Use the multiplication property to isolate the variable. This will give a solution of the form $x = \dfrac{b}{a}\left(\text{or } 1x = \dfrac{b}{a}\right)$.
> 5. Check the solution in the *original* equation.

When solving an equation you should always check your solution, as is indicated in step 5. We will not show all checks because of lack of space. We solved some equations containing fractions in Section 2.3. More complex equations containing fractions will be solved by a different procedure in Section 6.6.

When solving an equation remember that our goal is to obtain the variable alone on one side of the equation.

To help you visualize the boxed procedure consider the figure and corresponding equation below.

Figure	Equation
△+△+ 4 = 10	$2x + 4 = 10$

The equation $2x + 4 = 10$ contains no parentheses and no like terms on the same side of the equal sign. Therefore, we start with step 3, using the addition property. Remember from Section 2.2 that the addition property allows us to add (or subtract) the same quantity to (or from) both sides of an equation without changing its solution. Here we subtract 4 from both sides of the equation to isolate the term containing the variable.

Figure		*Equation*	

△+△+ 4　=　10 $2x + 4 = 10$

△+△　=　6 $2x + 4 - 4 = 10 - 4$　**Addition property**

                    or　　$2x = 6$

Notice how the term containing the variable, $2x$, is now by itself on one side of the equal sign. Now we use the multiplication property, step 4, to isolate the variable and obtain the solution. Remember from Section 2.3 that the multiplication property allows us to multiply or divide both sides of the equation by the same nonzero number without changing its solution. Here we divide both sides of the equation by 2, the coefficient of the term containing the variable, to obtain the solution, 3.

$$2x = 6$$

△　=　3 $$\frac{\overset{1}{\cancel{2}x}}{\underset{1}{\cancel{2}}} = \frac{\overset{3}{\cancel{6}}}{\underset{1}{\cancel{2}}}$$　**Multiplication property**

$$x = 3$$

EXAMPLE 1　Solve the equation $2x - 5 = 9$.

Solution:　We will follow the procedure outlined for solving equations. Since the equation contains no parentheses and since there are no like terms to be combined, we start with step 3.

Step 3　　　　　$2x - 5 = 9$

　　　　　　　$2x - 5 \boxed{+ 5} = 9 \boxed{+ 5}$　**Add 5 to both sides of the equation.**

　　　　　　　　　$2x = 14$

Step 4　　　　　$\dfrac{2x}{2} = \dfrac{14}{2}$　**Divide both sides of the equation by 2.**

　　　　　　　　　$x = 7$

Step 5 Check:　　$2x - 5 = 9$

　　　　　　　$2(7) - 5 = 9$

　　　　　　　$14 - 5 = 9$

　　　　　　　　$9 = 9$　**true**

Since the check is true, the solution is 7. Note that after completing step 3 we obtain $2x = 14$, which is an equation of the form $ax = b$. After completing step 4 we obtain the answer in the form $x = $ a real number.

Helpful Hint

When solving an equation that does not contain fractions, **the addition property (step 3) is to be used before the multiplication property (step 4).** If you use the multiplication property before the addition property, it is still possible to obtain the correct answer. However, you will usually have to do more work, and you may end up working with fractions. What would happen if you tried to solve Example 1 using the multiplication property before the addition property?

EXAMPLE 2 Solve the equation $-2x - 6 = -3$.

Solution: $\qquad\qquad -2x - 6 = -3.$

    Step 3 $\qquad -2x - 6 + 6 = -3 + 6$ Add 6 to both sides of the equation.

$$-2x = 3$$

    Step 4 $\qquad\qquad \dfrac{-2x}{-2} = \dfrac{3}{-2}$ Divide both sides of the equation by -2.

$$x = -\dfrac{3}{2}$$

    Step 5 Check: $\qquad -2x - 6 = -3$

$$-2\left(-\dfrac{3}{2}\right) - 6 = -3$$

$$3 - 6 = -3$$

$$-3 = -3 \qquad \text{true}$$

The solution is $-\dfrac{3}{2}$.

Note that checks are always made with the original equation. In some of the following examples the check will be omitted to save space.

EXAMPLE 3 Solve the equation $16 = 4x + 6 - 2x$.

Solution: Again we must isolate the variable x. Since the right side of the equation has two like terms containing the variable x, we will first combine these like terms.

    Step 2 $\qquad\qquad 16 = 4x + 6 - 2x$

$$16 = 2x + 6 \qquad \text{Like terms were combined.}$$

    Step 3 $\qquad 16 - 6 = 2x + 6 - 6$ Subtract 6 from both sides of equation.

$$10 = 2x$$

    Step 4 $\qquad\qquad \dfrac{10}{2} = \dfrac{2x}{2}$ Divide both sides of equation by 2.

$$5 = x$$

The preceding solution can be condensed as follows.

$16 = 4x + 6 - 2x$

$16 = 2x + 6$ Like terms were combined.

$10 = 2x$ 6 was subtracted from both sides of equation.

$5 = x$ Both sides of equation were divided by 2.

In Chapter 3 we will be solving many equations that contain decimal numbers. To solve such equations we follow the same procedure as outlined earlier. Example 4, on page 109, illustrates the solution to an equation that contains decimal numbers.

Helpful Hint

In the first two chapters you have been introduced to a variety of mathematics terms. Some of the most commonly used terms are "evaluate," "simplify," "solve," and "check." Make sure you understand what each term means and when each term is used.

Evaluate: To *evaluate an expression* means to find its numerical value.

Evaluate: $16 \div 2^2 + 36 \div 4$
$= 16 \div 4 + 36 \div 4$
$= 4 + 36 \div 4$
$= 4 + 9$
$= 13$

Evaluate: $-x^2 + 3x - 2$ when $x = 4$
$= -4^2 + 3(4) - 2$
$= -16 + 12 - 2$
$= -4 - 2$
$= -6$

Simplify: To *simplify an expression* means to perform the operations and combine like terms.

Simplify: $3(x - 2) - 4(2x + 3)$
$3(x - 2) - 4(2x + 3) = 3x - 6 - 8x - 12$
$= -5x - 18$

Note that when you simplify an expression containing variables you do not generally end up with just a numerical value unless all the variable terms happen to add to zero.

Solve: To *solve an equation* means to find the value or the values of the variables that make the equation a true statement.

Solve: $2x + 3(x + 1) = 18$
$2x + 3x + 3 = 18$
$5x + 3 = 18$
$5x = 15$
$x = 3$

Check: To *check an equation,* we substitute the value believed to be the solution into the original equation. If this substitution results in a true statement, then we say the answer checks. For example, to check the solution of the equation just solved, we substitute 3 for x in the equation.

Check: $2x + 3(x + 1) = 18$
$2(3) + 3(3 + 1) = 18$
$6 + 3(4) = 18$
$6 + 12 = 18$
$18 = 18$ true

Since we obtained a true statement, the 3 checks.

It is important to realize that *expressions may be evaluated or simplified* (depending on the type of problem) and *equations are solved and then checked.*

EXAMPLE 4   Solve the equation $x + 1.24 - 0.07x = 4.96$.

Solution: $x + 1.24 - 0.07x = 4.96$

$$0.93x + 1.24 = 4.96$$ Like terms were combined, $1x - 0.07x = 0.93x$.

$$0.93x + 1.24 - 1.24 = 4.96 - 1.24$$ Subtract 1.24 from both sides of equation.

$$0.93x = 3.72$$

$$\frac{0.93x}{0.93} = \frac{3.72}{0.93}$$ Divide both sides of equation by 0.93.

$$x = 4$$

EXAMPLE 5   Solve the equation $2(x + 4) - 5x = -3$.

Solution: $2(x + 4) - 5x = -3$.

$$2x + 8 - 5x = -3$$ The distributive property was used.

$$-3x + 8 = -3$$ Like terms were combined.

$$-3x + 8 - 8 = -3 - 8$$ Subtract 8 from both sides of equation.

$$-3x = -11$$

$$\frac{-3x}{-3} = \frac{-11}{-3}$$ Divide both sides of equation by -3.

$$x = \frac{11}{3}$$

The solution to Example 5 can be condensed as follows:

$$2(x + 4) - 5x = -3$$

$$2x + 8 - 5x = -3$$ The distributive property was used.

$$-3x + 8 = -3$$ Like terms were combined.

$$-3x = -11$$ 8 was subtracted from both sides of equation.

$$x = \frac{11}{3}$$ Both sides of equation were divided by -3.

EXAMPLE 6   Solve the equation $2x - (x + 2) = 6$.

Solution: $2x - (x + 2) = 6$

$$2x - x - 2 = 6$$ The distributive property was used.

$$x - 2 = 6$$ Like terms were combined.

$$x = 8$$ 2 was added to both sides of equation.

Exercise Set 2.4

(a) *Represent the figure as an equation in the variable x and* **(b)** *solve the equation.*

1. △ + △ + 4   =   16

2. △ + △ + △ + 8 =   20

3. $30 \quad = \triangle + \triangle + 12$

4. $27 \quad = \triangle + \triangle + \triangle + 9$

5. $\triangle + \triangle + 10 + \triangle = \quad 4$

6. $3 \quad = \triangle + 6 + \triangle + \triangle$

7. $5 + \triangle + \triangle + \triangle = \quad 12$

8. $9 \quad = \triangle + \triangle + 12$

Solve each equation. You may wish to use a calculator for equations containing decimal numbers.

9. $2x + 4 = 10$

10. $2x - 4 = 8$

11. $-2x - 5 = 7$

12. $-4x + 5 = -3$

13. $5x - 6 = 19$

14. $6 - 3x = 18$

15. $5x - 2 = 10$

16. $-9x + 3 = 15$

17. $-x - 4 = 8$

18. $6 = 2x - 3$

19. $12 - x = 9$

20. $-3x - 3 = -12$

21. $8 + 3x = 19$

22. $-2x + 7 = -10$

23. $16x + 5 = -14$

24. $19 = 25 + 4x$

25. $-4.2 = 2x + 1.6$

26. $-24 + 16x = -24$

27. $6x - 9 = 21$

28. $-x + 4 = -8$

29. $12 = -6x + 5$

30. $15 = 7x + 1$

31. $-2x - 7 = -13$

32. $-2 - x = -12$

33. $x + 0.05x = 21$

34. $x + 0.07x = 16.05$

35. $2.3x - 9.34 = 6.3$

36. $-2.3 = -1.4 + 0.6x$

37. $28.8 = x - 0.10x$

38. $32.76 = 2.45x - 8.75x$

39. $3(x + 2) = 6$

40. $3(x - 2) = 12$

41. $4(3 - x) = 12$

42. $-2(x + 3) = -9$

43. $-4 = -(x + 5)$

44. $-3(2 - 3x) = 9$

45. $12 = 4(x + 3)$

46. $-2(x + 4) + 5 = 1$

47. $5 = 2(3x + 6)$

48. $-2 = 5(3x + 1) - 12x$

49. $2x + 3(x + 2) = 11$

50. $4 = -2(x + 3)$

51. $x - 3(2x + 3) = 11$

52. $3(4 - x) + 5x = 9$

53. $5x + 3x - 4x - 7 = 9$

54. $-(x + 2) = 4$

55. $0.7(x + 3) = 4.2$

56. $12 + (x + 9) = 7$

57. $1.4(5x - 4) = -1.4$

58. $0.1(2.4x + 5) = 1.7$

59. $3 - 2(x + 3) + 2 = 1$

60. $2(3x - 4) - 4x = 12$

61. $1 - (x + 3) + 2x = 4$

62. $5x - 2x - 7x = -20$

63. $4.22 - 6.4x + 9.60 = 0.38$

64. $-4(x + 2) - 3x = 20$

65. $5.76 - 4.24x - 1.9x = 27.864$

66. **(a)** In your own words, write the general procedure for solving an equation where the variable appears on only one side of the equal sign.

(b) Refer to page 105 to see if you omitted any steps.

67. When solving equations that do not contain fractions, do we normally use the addition or multiplication property first in the process of isolating the variable? Explain your answer.

68. **(a)** Explain, in a step-by-step manner, how to solve the equation $2(3x + 4) = -4$.

(b) Solve the equation by following the steps listed in part (a).

69. **(a)** Explain, in a step-by-step manner, how to solve the equation $4x - 2(x + 3) = 4$.

(b) Solve the equation by following the steps listed in part (a).

CUMULATIVE REVIEW EXERCISES

[1.2] **70.** Add $\dfrac{5}{8} + \dfrac{3}{5}$.

[1.9] **71.** Evaluate $[5(2 - 6) + 3(8 \div 4)^2]^2$.

[2.2] **72.** To solve an equation, what do you need to do to the variable?

[2.3] **73.** To solve the equation $7 = -4x$, would you add 4 to both sides of the equation or divide both sides of the equation by -4? Explain your answer.

Group Activity/ Challenge Problems

Solve each equation.

1. $3(x - 2) - (x + 5) - 2(3 - 2x) = 18.$

2. $-6 = -(x - 5) - 3(5 + 2x) - 4(2x - 4).$

3. $4[3 - 2(x + 4)] - (x + 3) = 13.$

In Chapter 3 we will discuss procedures for writing application problems as equations. Let us see if you can figure out how to write an equation for Exercises 4–6. For each exercise, (a) draw a balance that represents the problem; (b) using the balance in part (a), write an equation that represents the problem; (c) solve the equation, (d) check your answer.

4. John and Mary purchased 2 large chocolate kisses and a birthday card. The birthday card cost $2. The total amount for the 3 items cost $8. What was the price of a single chocolate kiss?

5. Eduardo purchased 3 boxes of stationary. He also purchased wrapping paper and thank you cards. If the wrapping paper and thank you cards together cost $6, and the total he paid was $42, find the cost of a box of stationary.

6. Mahandi purchased three rolls of peppermint candies and the local newspaper. The newspaper cost 50 cents. He paid $2.75 in all. What did a roll of candies cost?

In Section 2.5 we will solve equations in which the variable appears on both sides of the equation. In Exercises 7 – 10, (a) express the figure as an equation, (b) solve the equation, and (c) explain how you determined the solution. We will give step-by-step procedures for solving such equations in the next section, but you should start thinking about this now. Hint: To solve use the addition property to get all terms containing the variable on one side of the equation and all constant terms on the other side of the equation. Then use the multiplication property.

7. $\triangle + \triangle \quad = \quad \triangle + 3$

8. $\triangle + \triangle + 6 \quad = \quad \triangle + \triangle + \triangle + 4$

9. $\triangle + \triangle + 3 \quad = \triangle + \triangle + \triangle + \triangle + 2$

10. $\triangle + \triangle + \triangle + 1 = \quad \triangle + 4$

2.5 Solving Linear Equations with the Variable on Both Sides of the Equation

Tape 4

1 Solve equations when the variable appears on both sides of the equal sign.

2 Identify identities and contradictions.

Variable on Both Sides of Equation

1 Below we show some figures that have been represented as equations. We have once again let the value of a kiss be represented by the letter x. In each of these equations the variable appears on both sides of the equation. We also give the solution to each equation. At this time you probably cannot determine the solutions. Do not worry about this. In this section we will teach you the procedure to solve equations of this type.

Figure	*Equation*	*Solution*
△+△+ 3 = △ + 6	$2x + 3 = x + 6$	3
△+ 4 = △+△+ 2	$x + 4 = 2x + 2$	2
△+△+△+ 5 = △+ 20	$3x + 5 = x + 20$	$\dfrac{15}{2}$

Following is a general procedure, similar to the one outlined in Section 2.4, to solve linear equations with the variable on both sides of the equal sign.

> ### To Solve Linear Equations with the Variable on Both Sides of the Equal Sign
>
> 1. Use the distributive property to remove parentheses.
> 2. Combine like terms on the same side of the equal sign.
> 3. Use the addition property to rewrite the equation with all terms containing the variable on one side of the equal sign and all terms not containing the variable on the other side of the equal sign. It may be necessary to use the addition property twice to accomplish this goal. You will eventually get an equation of the form $ax = b$.
> 4. Use the multiplication property to isolate the variable. This will give a solution of the form $x =$ some number.
> 5. Check the solution in the original equation.

The steps listed here are basically the same as the steps listed in the boxed procedure on page 105, except that in step 3 you may need to use the addition property more than once to obtain an equation of the form $ax = b$.

Remember that our goal in solving equations is to isolate the variable, that is, to get the variable alone on one side of the equation. To help you visualize the boxed procedure, consider the figure and corresponding equation that follow.

Figure	*Equation*
△+△+△+ 4 = △+ 12	$3x + 4 = x + 12$

The equation $3x + 4 = x + 12$ contains no parentheses and no like terms on the same side of the equal sign. Therefore, we start with step 3, the addition property. We will use the addition property twice in order to obtain an equation where the variable appears on only one side of the equal sign. We begin by subtracting x from both sides of the equation to get all the terms containing the variable on the left side of the equation. This will give the following:

Figure *Equation*

△+△+△+ 4 = △+ 12 $3x + 4 = x + 12$

$3x - x + 4 = x - x + 12$ **Addition property**

△+△+ 4 = 12   or $2x + 4 = 12$

Notice that the variable, x, now appears on only one side of the equation. However, $+4$ still appears on the same side of the equal sign as the $2x$. We use the addition property a second time to get the term containing the variable by itself on one side of the equation. Subtracting 4 from both sides of the equation gives $2x = 8$, which is an equation of the form $ax = b$.

Figure	*Equation*	
	$2x + 4 = 12$	
	$2x + 4 - 4 = 12 - 4$ $2x = 8$	**Addition property**

Now that the $2x$ is by itself on one side of the equation we can use the multiplication property to isolate the variable and solve the equation for x. Divide both sides of the equation by 2 to isolate the variable and solve the equation.

$$2x = 8$$

$$\frac{\overset{1}{\cancel{2}}x}{\cancel{2}} = \frac{\overset{4}{\cancel{8}}}{\cancel{2}}$$ **Multiplication property**

$$x = 4$$

The solution to the equation is 4.

EXAMPLE 1   Solve the equation $4x + 6 = 2x + 4$.

Solution: Remember that our goal is always to get all terms with the variable on one side of the equal sign and all terms without the variable on the other side. The terms with the variable may be collected on either side of the equal sign. Many methods can be used to isolate the variable. We will illustrate two. In method 1, we will isolate the variable on the left side of the equation. In method 2, we will isolate the variable on the right side of the equation. In both methods, we will follow the steps given in the box on page 112. Since this equation does not contain parentheses and there are no like terms on the same side of the equal sign, we begin with step 3.

Method 1:   Isolating the variable on the left

$$4x + 6 = 2x + 4$$

Step 3 $4x - 2x + 6 = 2x - 2x + 4$ Subtract $2x$ from both sides of the equation.
$$2x + 6 = 4$$

Step 3 $2x + 6 - 6 = 4 - 6$ Subtract 6 from both sides of the equation.
$$2x = -2$$

Step 4 $\dfrac{2x}{2} = \dfrac{-2}{2}$ Divide both sides of the equation by 2.

$$x = -1$$

Method 2:   Isolating the variable on the right

$$4x + 6 = 2x + 4$$

Step 3 $4x - 4x + 6 = 2x - 4x + 4$ **Subtract 4x from both sides of the equation.**

$$6 = -2x + 4$$

Step 3 $6 - 4 = -2x + 4 - 4$ **Subtract 4 from both sides of the equation.**

$$2 = -2x$$

Step 4 $\dfrac{2}{-2} = \dfrac{-2x}{-2}$ **Divide both sides of the equation by −2.**

$$-1 = x$$

The same answer is obtained whether we isolate the variable on the left or right.

Step 5   Check: $4x + 6 = 2x + 4$

$$4(-1) + 6 = 2(-1) + 4$$

$$-4 + 6 = -2 + 4$$

$$2 = 2 \quad \text{true}$$

EXAMPLE 2   Solve the equation $2x - 3 - 5x = 13 + 4x - 2$.

Solution: We will choose to collect the terms containing the variable on the right side of the equation. Since there are like terms *on the same side of the equal sign,* we will begin by combining these like terms.

Step 2 $2x - 3 - 5x = 13 + 4x - 2$

$$-3x - 3 = 4x + 11$$ **Like terms were combined.**

Step 3 $-3x + 3x - 3 = 4x + 3x + 11$ **Add 3x to both sides of the equation.**

$$-3 = 7x + 11$$

Step 3 $-3 - 11 = 7x + 11 - 11$ **Subtract 11 from both sides of the equation.**

$$-14 = 7x$$

Step 4 $\dfrac{-14}{7} = \dfrac{7x}{7}$ **Divide both sides of the equation by 7.**

$$-2 = x$$

Step 5   Check: $2x - 3 - 5x = 13 + 4x - 2$

$$2(-2) - 3 - 5(-2) = 13 + 4(-2) - 2$$

$$-4 - 3 + 10 = 13 - 8 - 2$$

$$-7 + 10 = 5 - 2$$

$$3 = 3 \quad \text{true}$$

Since the check is true, the solution is −2.

The solution to Example 2 could be condensed as follows:

$$2x - 3 - 5x = 13 + 4x - 2$$

$$-3x - 3 = 4x + 11 \qquad \text{Like terms were combined.}$$

$$-3 = 7x + 11 \qquad 3x \text{ was added to both sides of equation.}$$

$$-14 = 7x \qquad 11 \text{ was subtracted from both sides of equation.}$$

$$-2 = x \qquad \text{Both sides of equation were divided by 7.}$$

We solved Example 2 by moving the terms containing the variable to the right side of the equation. Now rework the problem moving the terms containing the variable to the left side of the equation. You should obtain the same answer.

EXAMPLE 3   Solve the equation $5.74x + 5.42 = 2.24x - 9.28$.

Solution: We first notice that there are no like terms on the same side of the equal sign that can be combined. We will elect to collect the terms containing the variable on the left side of the equation.

$$5.74x + 5.42 = 2.24x - 9.28$$

Step 3 $5.74x - 2.24x + 5.42 = 2.24x - 2.24x - 9.28$ Subtract 2.24x from both sides of equation.

$$3.5x + 5.42 = -9.28$$

Step 3 $3.5x + 5.42 - 5.42 = -9.28 - 5.42$ Subtract 5.42 from both sides of equation.

$$3.5x = -14.7$$

Step 4 $\dfrac{3.5x}{3.5} = \dfrac{-14.7}{3.5}$ Divide both sides of equation by 3.5.

$$x = -4.2$$

EXAMPLE 4   Solve the equation $2(p + 3) = -3p + 10$.

Solution: $\qquad 2(p + 3) = -3p + 10$

Step 1 $\qquad 2p + 6 = -3p + 10$ Distributive property was used.

Step 3 $\quad 2p + 3p + 6 = -3p + 3p + 10$ Add 3p to both sides of equation.

$$5p + 6 = 10$$

Step 3 $\quad 5p + 6 - 6 = 10 - 6$ Subtract 6 from both sides of equation.

$$5p = 4$$

Step 4 $\qquad \dfrac{5p}{5} = \dfrac{4}{5}$ Divide both sides of equation by 5.

$$p = \dfrac{4}{5}$$

The solution to Example 4 could be condensed as follows:

$$2(p + 3) = -3p + 10$$

$$2p + 6 = -3p + 10 \qquad \text{Distributive property was used.}$$

$$5p + 6 = 10 \qquad \text{3p was added to both sides of equation.}$$

$$5p = 4 \qquad \text{6 was subtracted from both sides of equation.}$$

$$p = \frac{4}{5} \qquad \text{Both sides of equation were divided by 5.}$$

Helpful Hint

After the distributive property was used in step 1, Example 4, we obtained the equation $2p + 6 = -3p + 10$. Then we had to decide whether to collect terms with the variable on the left or the right side of the equal sign. If we wish the sum of the terms containing a variable to be positive, we use the addition property to eliminate the variable, with the *smaller* numerical coefficient from one side of the equation. Since -3 is smaller than 2, we added $3p$ to both sides of the equation. This eliminated $-3p$ from the right side of the equation and resulted in the sum of the variable terms on the left side of the equation, $5p$, being positive.

EXAMPLE 5   Solve the equation $2(x - 5) + 3 = 3x + 9$.

Solution: $2(x - 5) + 3 = 3x + 9$

Step 1	$2x - 10 + 3 = 3x + 9$	Distributive property was used.
Step 2	$2x - 7 = 3x + 9$	Like terms were combined.
Step 3	$-7 = x + 9$	2x was subtracted from both sides of equation.
Step 3	$-16 = x$	9 was subtracted from both sides of equation.

EXAMPLE 6   Solve the equation $7 - 2x + 5x = -2(-3x + 4)$.

Solution: $7 - 2x + 5x = -2(-3x + 4)$

Step 1	$7 - 2x + 5x = 6x - 8$	Distributive property was used.
Step 2	$7 + 3x = 6x - 8$	Like terms were combined.
Step 3	$7 = 3x - 8$	3x was subtracted from both sides of equation.
Step 3	$15 = 3x$	8 was added to both sides of equation.
Step 4	$5 = x$	Both sides of equation were divided by 3.

The solution is 5.

Identities and Contradictions

2 Thus far all the equations we have solved have had a single value for a solution. Equations of this type are called **conditional equations,** for they are only true under specific conditions. Some equations, as in Example 7, are true for all values of x. Equations that are true for all values of x are called **identities.** A third type of equation, as in Example 8, has no solution and is called a **contradiction.**

EXAMPLE 7   Solve the equation $2x + 6 = 2(x + 3)$.

Solution: $2x + 6 = 2(x + 3)$
$2x + 6 = 2x + 6$

Since the same expression appears on both sides of the equal sign, the statement is true for all values of x. If we continue to solve this equation further, we might obtain

$2x = 2x$ **6 was subtracted from both sides of equation.**

$0 = 0$ **2x was subtracted from both sides of equation.**

Note: The solution process could have been stopped at $2x + 6 = 2x + 6$. Since one side is identical to the other side, the equation is true for all values of x. **Therefore, the solution to this equation is all real numbers.**

COMMON STUDENT ERROR   Some students confuse combining like terms with using the addition property. Remember that *when combining terms you work on only one side of the equal sign at a time,* as in

$3x + 4 - x = 4x - 8$

$2x + 4 = 4x - 8$ **The 3x and −x were combined.**

When using the addition property, you add (or subtract) the same quantity to (from) **both sides of the equation,** *as shown below.*

Correct
$2x + 4 = 4x - 8$
$2x - 2x + 4 = 4x - 2x - 8$ **2x was subtracted from *both sides of equation.***
$4 = 2x - 8$
$4 + 8 = 2x - 8 + 8$ **8 was added to *both sides of equation.***
$12 = 2x$
$x = 6$

Incorrect

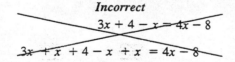

$3x + 4 - x = 4x - 8$

$3x + x + 4 - x + x = 4x - 8$ **Wrong use of the addition property; note *x* was not added to *both* sides of the equation.**

Ordinarily, when solving an equation, combining like terms is done before using the addition property.

EXAMPLE 8   Solve the equation $-3x + 4 + 5x = 4x - 2x + 5$.

Solution: $-3x + 4 + 5x = 4x - 2x + 5$
$2x + 4 = 2x + 5$ **Like terms were combined.**
$2x - 2x + 4 = 2x - 2x + 5$ **Subtract 2x from both sides of equation.**
$4 = 5$ **false**

When solving an equation, if you obtain an obviously false statement, as in this example, the equation has no solution. No value of x will make the equation a true statement. **Therefore, when giving the answer to this problem, you should use the words** *no solution.* An answer left blank may be marked wrong.

Helpful Hint

Some students start solving equations correctly but do not complete the solution. Sometimes they are not sure that what they are doing is correct and they give up for lack of confidence. You must have confidence in yourself. As long as you follow the procedure on page 112 you should obtain the correct solution, even if it takes quite a few steps. Remember two important things: (1) Our goal is to isolate the variable, and (2) whatever you do to one side of the equation you must also do to the other side. That is, you must treat both sides of the equation equally.

Exercise Set 2.5

(a) *Represent the figure as an equation in the variable* x *and* **(b)** *solve the equation.*

1.
2.
3.
4.
5.
6.
7.
8.

Solve each equation. You may wish to use a calculator to solve the equations containing decimal numbers.

9. $4x = 3x + 5$
10. $x + 6 = 2x - 4$
11. $-4x + 10 = 6x$
12. $6x = 4x + 8$
13. $5x + 3 = 6$
14. $-6x = 2x + 16$
15. $15 - 3x = 4x - 2x$
16. $8 - 6x = 4x + 10$
17. $2x - 4 = 3x - 6$
18. $-5x = -4x + 9$
19. $3 - 2y = 9 - 8y$
20. $124.8 - 9.4x = 4.8x + 32.5$
21. $4 - 0.6x = 2.4x - 8.48$
22. $8 + y = 2y - 6 + y$
23. $5x = 2(x + 6)$
24. $8x - 4 = 3(x - 2)$
25. $x - 25 = 12x + 9 + 3x$
26. $5y + 6 = 2y + 3 - y$
27. $2(x + 2) = 4x + 1 - 2x$
28. $4r = 10 - 2(r - 4)$
29. $-(w + 2) = -6w + 32$
30. $15(4 - x) = 5(10 + 2x)$
31. $4 - (2x + 5) = 6x + 31$
32. $4(2x - 3) = -2(3x + 16)$
33. $0.1(x + 10) = 0.3x - 4$
34. $3y - 6y + 2 = 8y + 6 - 5y$
35. $2(x + 4) = 4x + 3 - 2x + 5$
36. $5(2.9x - 3) = 2(x + 4)$
37. $9(-y + 3) = -6y + 15 - 3y + 12$
38. $-4(-y + 3) = 12y + 8 - 2y$

39. $-(3 - p) = -(2p + 3)$

40. $12 - 2x - 3(x + 2) = 4x + 6 - x$

41. $-(x + 4) + 5 = 4x + 1 - 5x$

42. $19x + 3(4x + 9) = -6x - 38$

43. $35(2x + 12) = 7(x - 4) + 3x$

44. $10(x - 10) + 5 = 5(2x - 20)$

45. $0.4(x + 0.7) = 0.6(x - 4.2)$

46. $3(x - 4) = 2(x - 8) + 5x$

47. $-(x - 5) + 2 = 3(4 - x) + 5x$

48. $1.2(6x - 8) = 2.4(x - 5)$

49. $2(x - 6) + 3(x + 1) = 4x + 3$

50. $-2(-3x + 5) + 6 = 4(x - 2)$

51. $5 + 2x = 6(x + 1) - 5(x - 3)$

52. $4 - (6x + 3) = -(-2x + 3)$

53. $5 - (x - 5) = 2(x + 3) - 6(x + 1)$

54. $12 - 6x + 3(2x + 3) = 2x + 5$

55. (a) In your own words, write the general procedure for solving an equation that does not contain fractions where the variable appears on both sides of the equation. **(b)** Refer to page 112 to see if you omitted any steps.

56. When solving an equation, how will you know if the equation is an identity?

57. When solving an equation, how will you know if the equation has no real solution?

58. (a) Explain, in a step-by-step manner, how to solve the equation $4(x + 3) = 6(x - 5)$.

(b) Solve the equation by following the steps listed in part (a).

59. (a) Explain, in a step-by-step manner, how to solve the equation $4x + 3(x + 2) = 5x - 10$.

(b) Solve the equation by following the steps listed in part (a).

CUMULATIVE REVIEW EXERCISES

[1.8] **60.** Evaluate $\left(\dfrac{2}{3}\right)^5$ on your calculator.

[2.1] **61.** Explain the difference between a factor and a term.

[2.4] **62.** Simplify $2(x - 3) + 4x - (4 - x)$.

63. Solve $2(x - 3) + 4x - (4 - x) = 0$.

64. Solve $(x + 4) - (4x - 3) = 16$.

Group Activity/ Challenge Problems

1. Solve $-2(x + 3) + 5x = -3(5 - 2x) + 3(x + 2) + 6x$.

2. Solve $4(2x - 3) - (x + 7) - 4x + 6 = 5(x - 2) - 3x + 7(2x + 2)$.

3. Solve $4 - [5 - 3(x + 2)] = x - 3$.

*In the next chapter we will be discussing procedures for writing application problems as equations. Can you write equations for Exercises 4–6? For each exercise **(a)** make a sketch using a balance like those in Exercises 1–8 that represents the problem; **(b)** represent the sketch as an equation in the variable x. **(c)** solve the equation and **(d)** check your answer to make sure that it makes sense.*

4. Mary Kay purchased 2 large chocolate kisses. The total cost of the two kisses was equal to the cost of 1 kiss plus $6. Find the cost of one chocolate kiss.

5. Three identical boxes are weighed. Their total weight is the same as (or equals) the weight of one of the boxes plus 20 pounds. Find the weight of a box.

6. Isaac purchased 4 gallons of skim milk. The price of the 4 gallons of milk is the same as the price of 2 gallons of milk plus some other groceries that cost $5.20. What is the price of a gallon of skim milk?

2.6   Ratios and Proportions

Tape 4

1 Understand ratios.
2 Solve proportions using cross multiplication.
3 Solve practical application problems.
4 Use proportions to change units.
5 Use proportions in geometric problems.

Ratios

1 A **ratio** is a quotient of two quantities. Ratios provide a way to compare two numbers or quantities. The ratio of the number a to the number b may be written

$$a \text{ to } b, \qquad a{:}b, \qquad \text{or} \qquad \frac{a}{b}$$

where *a* and *b* are called the **terms** of the ratio.

EXAMPLE 1   An algebra class consists of 11 males and 15 females.

(a) Find the ratio of males to females.

(b) Find the ratio of females to the entire class.

Solution: (a) 11:15   (b) 15:26

In Example 1, part (a) could also have been written $\frac{11}{15}$ or "11 to 15." Part (b) could also have been written $\frac{15}{26}$ or "15 to 26."

EXAMPLE 2   There are two types of cholesterol, low-density lipoprotein, (LDL—considered the harmful type of cholesterol) and high-density lipoprotein (HDL—considered the healthful type of cholesterol). Some doctors recommend that the ratio of low- to high-density cholesterol be less than or equal to 4:1. Mr. Kane's cholesterol test showed that his low-density cholesterol measured 167 milligrams per deciliter, and his high-density cholesterol measured 40 milligrams per deciliter. Is Mr. Kane's ratio of low- to high-density cholesterol less than or equal to the recommended 4:1 ratio?

Solution: The ratio of low- to high-density cholesterol is $\frac{167}{40}$. If we divide 167 by 40, we obtain 4.175. Thus, Mr. Kane's ratio is equivalent to 4.175:1. Therefore, his ratio is not less than or equal to the desired 4:1 ratio.

EXAMPLE 3   Find the ratio of 8 feet to 20 yards.

Solution: To express this as a ratio, both quantities must be in the same units. Since 1 yard equals 3 feet, 20 yards equals 60 feet. Thus, the ratio is $\frac{8}{60}$. The ratio in lowest terms is $\frac{2}{15}$ (or 2:15).

EXAMPLE 4   The *gear ratio* of two gears is defined as

$$\text{gear ratio} = \frac{\text{number of teeth on the driving gear}}{\text{number of teeth on the driven gear}}$$

Find the gear ratio of the gears shown in Figure 2.10.

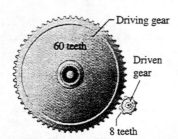

Driving gear

60 teeth

Driven gear

8 teeth

FIGURE 2.10

Solution: Gear ratio $= \dfrac{60}{8} = \dfrac{15}{2}$. Thus, the gear ratio is 15:2. Gear ratios are generally given as some quantity to 1. If we divide both parts of the ratio by the second number, we will obtain a ratio of some number to 1. Dividing both 15 and 2 by 2 gives a gear ratio of 7.5:1. (A typical first gear ratio on a passenger car may be 3.545:1).

Solve Proportions   **2** A **proportion** is a special type of equation. It is a statement of equality between two ratios. One way of denoting a proportion is $a:b = c:d$, which is read "a is to b as c is to d." In this text we write proportions as

$$\frac{a}{b} = \frac{c}{d}$$

The a and d are referred to as the **extremes,** and the b and c are referred to as the **means** of the proportion. One method that can be used in evaluating proportions is **cross-multiplication:**

Cross-Multiplication

If $\dfrac{a}{b} = \dfrac{c}{d}$ then $ad = bc$.

Note that the product of the means is equal to the product of the extremes.

If any three of the four quantities of a proportion are known, the fourth quantity can easily be found.

EXAMPLE 5   Solve for x by cross-multiplying $\dfrac{x}{3} = \dfrac{25}{15}$.

Solution: $\dfrac{x}{3} = \dfrac{25}{15}$ *Check:* $\dfrac{x}{3} = \dfrac{25}{15}$

$\quad x \cdot 15 = 3 \cdot 25$ $\dfrac{5}{3} = \dfrac{25}{15}$

$\qquad 15x = 75$ $\dfrac{5}{3} = \dfrac{25}{15}$

$\qquad x = \dfrac{75}{15} = 5$ $\dfrac{5}{3} = \dfrac{5}{3}$ **true**

EXAMPLE 6   Solve for x by cross-multiplying $\dfrac{-8}{3} = \dfrac{64}{x}$.

Solution: $\dfrac{-8}{3} = \dfrac{64}{x}$ *Check:* $\dfrac{-8}{3} = \dfrac{64}{x}$

$\quad -8 \cdot x = 3 \cdot 64$ $\dfrac{-8}{3} = \dfrac{\overset{8}{\cancel{64}}}{\underset{3}{\cancel{-24}}}$

$\qquad -8x = 192$

$\qquad \dfrac{-8x}{-8} = \dfrac{192}{-8}$ $\dfrac{-8}{3} = \dfrac{8}{-3}$

$\qquad x = -24$ $\dfrac{-8}{3} = \dfrac{-8}{3}$ **true**

Applications   **3** Often, practical applications can be solved using proportions. To solve such problems, use the following procedure.

To Solve Problems Using Proportions

1. Represent the unknown quantity by a variable (a letter).

2. Set up the proportion by listing the given ratio on the left side of the equal sign, and the unknown and the other given quantity on the right side of the equal sign. When setting up the right side of the proportion, the same respective quantities should occupy the same respective positions on the left and the right. For example, an acceptable proportion might be

$$\text{Given ratio} \left\{ \frac{\text{miles}}{\text{hour}} = \frac{\text{miles}}{\text{hour}} \right.$$

3. Once the proportion is correctly written, drop the units and cross-multiply.

4. Solve the resulting equation.

5. Answer the questions asked.

Note that the two ratios* must have the same units. For example, if one ratio is given in miles/hour and the second ratio is given in feet/hour, one of the ratios must be changed before setting up the proportion.

EXAMPLE 7   A 30-pound bag of fertilizer will cover an area of 2500 square feet.

(a) How many pounds are needed to cover an area of 16,000 square feet?

(b) How many bags of fertilizer are needed?

Solution: **(a)** The given ratio is 30 pounds per 2500 square feet. The unknown quantity is the number of pounds necessary to cover 16,000 square feet.

Step 1   Let x = number of pounds.

Step 2   Given ratio $\left\{ \dfrac{30 \text{ pounds}}{2500 \text{ square feet}} = \dfrac{x \text{ pounds}}{16{,}000 \text{ square feet}} \right.$ ←— Unknown
← Given quantity

Note how the pounds and the area are given in the same relative positions.

Step 3
$$\frac{30}{2500} = \frac{x}{16{,}000}$$

$$30(16{,}000) = 2500x$$

---

* Strictly speaking, a quotient of two quantities with different units, such as $\dfrac{6 \text{ miles}}{1 \text{ hour}}$, is called a *rate*. However, few books make the distinction between ratios and rates when discussing proportions.

Step 4

$$480,000 = 2500x$$

$$\frac{480,000}{2500} = x$$

$$192 = x$$

Step 5   One hundred ninety-two pounds of fertilizer are needed.

(b)   Since each bag weighs 30 pounds, the number of bags is found by division.

$$192 \div 30 = 6.4 \text{ bags}$$

The number of bags needed is therefore 7, since you must purchase whole bags.

EXAMPLE 8   In Washington County the property tax rate is $8.065 per $1000 of assessed value. If a house and its property have been assessed at $124,000, find the tax the owner will have to pay.

Solution: The unknown quantity is the tax the property owner must pay. Let us call this unknown x.

$$\frac{\text{tax}}{\text{assesed value}} = \frac{\text{tax}}{\text{assessed value}}$$

Given tax rate $\begin{cases} \dfrac{8.065}{1000} = \dfrac{x}{124,000} \end{cases}$

$$(8.065)(124,000) = 1000x$$

$$1,000,060 = 1000x$$

$$\$1000.06 = x$$

The owner will have to pay $1000.06 tax.

EXAMPLE 9   A doctor asks a nurse to give a patient 250 milligrams of the drug simethicone. The drug is available only in a solution whose concentration is 40 milligrams of simethicone per 0.6 milliliter of solution. How many milliliters of solution should the nurse give the patient?

Solution: We can set up the proportion using the medication on hand as the given ratio and the number of milliliters needed to be given as the unknown.

Given ratio (medication on hand) $\begin{cases} \dfrac{40 \text{ milligrams}}{0.6 \text{ milliliter}} = \dfrac{250 \text{ milligrams}}{x \text{ milliliters}} \end{cases}$ ⟵ Desired medication
⟵ Unknown

Now solve for x.

$$\frac{40}{0.6} = \frac{250}{x}$$

$$40x = 0.6(250)$$

$$40x = 150$$

$$x = \frac{150}{40} = 3.75$$

Thus, the nurse should administer 3.75 milliliters of the simethicone solution.

COMMON STUDENT ERROR   When you set up a proportion the same units should not be multiplied by themselves during cross-multiplication.

Correct   *Incorrect*

$$\frac{\text{miles}}{\text{hour}} = \frac{\text{miles}}{\text{hour}} \qquad \frac{\cancel{\text{miles}}}{\cancel{\text{hour}}} \cancel{=} \frac{\cancel{\text{hour}}}{\cancel{\text{miles}}}$$

Conversions   ▣ Proportions can also be used to convert from one quantity to another. For example, you can use a proportion to convert a measurement in feet to a measurement in meters, or to convert from U.S. dollars to Mexican pesos. The following examples illustrate converting units.

EXAMPLE 10   Convert 18.36 inches to feet.

Solution: We know that 1 foot is 12 inches. We use this known fact in one ratio of our proportion. In the second ratio we set the quantities with the same units in the same respective positions.

$$\text{Known ratio} \left\{ \frac{1 \text{ foot}}{12 \text{ inches}} = \frac{x \text{ feet}}{18.36 \text{ inches}} \right.$$

Since we are given 18.36 inches, we place this quantity in the denominator of the second ratio. The unknown quantity is the number of feet, which we will call x. Note that both numerators contain the same units and both denominators contain the same units. Now drop the units and solve for x by cross-multiplying.

$$\frac{1}{12} = \frac{x}{18.36}$$
$$1(18.36) = 12x$$
$$18.36 = 12x$$
$$\frac{18.36}{12} = \frac{12x}{12}$$
$$1.53 = x$$

Thus, 18.36 inches equals 1.53 feet.

EXAMPLE 11   One kilogram is equal to 2.2 pounds.

(a) Find the weight in pounds of a poodle that weighs 7.48 kilograms.

(b) Mary Jo weighs 121 pounds. How many kilograms does she weigh?

Solution: **(a)** We use the fact that 1 kilogram = 2.2 pounds for our known ratio. The unknown quantity is the number of pounds. We will call this quantity x.

$$\text{Known ratio} \left\{ \frac{1 \text{ kilogram}}{2.2 \text{ pounds}} = \frac{7.48 \text{ kilograms}}{x \text{ pounds}} \right.$$
$$\frac{1}{2.2} = \frac{7.48}{x}$$
$$1x = (2.2)(7.48)$$
$$x = 16.456$$

Thus, the poodle weighs 16.456 pounds.

(b) The unknown quantity is the number of kilograms. We will call the unknown quantity x.

$$\frac{1 \text{ kilogram}}{2.2 \text{ pounds}} = \frac{x \text{ kilograms}}{121 \text{ pounds}}$$

$$\frac{1}{2.2} = \frac{x}{121}$$

$$1(121) = 2.2x$$

$$121 = 2.2x$$

$$\frac{121}{2.2} = x$$

$$55 = x$$

Thus, Mary Jo weighs 55 kilograms.

EXAMPLE 12   Marisa exchanged 15 U.S. dollars for 46.75 Mexican pesos at a bank in Cancun, Mexico.

(a) What is the conversion rate per U.S. dollar (that is, what is 1 U.S. dollar worth in pesos)?

(b) At the straw market in downtown Cancun, Marisa purchased a hand-made Mayan calendar for 385 pesos. What is the cost of the calendar in U.S. dollars?

Solution: **(a)** We know that 15 U.S. dollars equals 46.75 Mexican pesos. We use this fact in our proportion. The unknown quantity is the number of pesos equal to 1 U.S. dollar.

$$\text{Known}\left\{ \frac{15 \text{ dollars}}{46.75 \text{ pesos}} = \frac{1 \text{ dollar}}{x \text{ pesos}} \right.$$

$$15x = 46.75$$

$$x = \frac{46.75}{15} = 3.1167$$

Thus, $1 can be converted to 3.1167 pesos.

(b) We need to convert 385 pesos to U.S. dollars. We will call the amount of U.S. dollars x.

$$\frac{15 \text{ dollars}}{46.75 \text{ pesos}} = \frac{x \text{ dollars}}{385 \text{ pesos}}$$

$$(15)(385) = 46.75x$$

$$5775 = 46.75x$$

$$\frac{5775}{46.75} = x$$

$$123.53 = x$$

Thus, the cost of the Mayan calendar is 123.53 U.S. dollars or $123.53.

Helpful Hint

Some of the problems we have just worked using proportions could have been done without using proportions. However, when working problems of this type, students often have difficulty in deciding whether to multiply or divide to obtain the correct answer. By setting up a proportion, you may be better able to understand the problem and have more success at obtaining the correct answer.

Similar Figures   Proportions can also be used to solve problems in geometry and trigonometry. The following examples illustrate how proportions may be used to solve problems involving **similar figures.** Two figures are said to be similar when their corresponding angles are equal and their corresponding sides are in proportion.

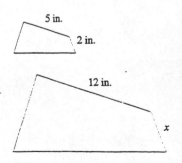

EXAMPLE 13   The figures to the left are similar. Find the length of the side indicated by the x.

Solution: We set up a proportion of corresponding sides to find the length of side x.

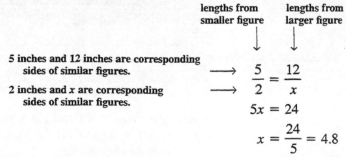

5 inches and 12 inches are corresponding sides of similar figures. $\longrightarrow$

2 inches and x are corresponding sides of similar figures. $\longrightarrow$

$$\frac{5}{2} = \frac{12}{x}$$

$$5x = 24$$

$$x = \frac{24}{5} = 4.8$$

Thus, the side is 4.8 inches in length.

Note in Example 13 that the proportion could have also been set up as

$$\frac{5}{12} = \frac{2}{x}$$

because one pair of corresponding sides is in the numerator and another pair is in the denominator.

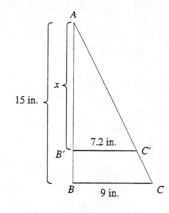

EXAMPLE 14 Triangles ABC and $AB'C'$ are similar triangles. Use a proportion to find the length of side AB'.

Solution: We set up a proportion of corresponding sides to find the length of side AB'. We will let x represent the length of side AB'. One proportion we can use is

$$\frac{\text{length of } AB}{\text{length of } BC} = \frac{\text{length of } AB'}{\text{length of } B'C'}$$

Now insert the proper values and solve for the variable x.

$$\frac{15}{9} = \frac{x}{7.2}$$
$$(15)(7.2) = 9x$$
$$108 = 9x$$
$$12 = x$$

Thus, the length of side AB' is 12 inches.

Exercise Set 2.6

The results of an English examination are 5 A's, 6 B's, 8 C's, 4 D's, and 2 F's. Write the following ratios.

1. A's to C's.
2. A's to total grades.
3. D's to F's.
4. Grades better than C to total grades.
5. Total grades to D's.
6. Grades better than C to grades less than C.

Determine the following ratios. Write each ratio in lowest terms.

7. 5 feet to 3 feet.
8. 60 dollars to 80 dollars.
9. 20 hours to 60 hours.
10. 100 people to 80 people.
11. 4 hours to 40 minutes.
12. 6 feet to 4 yards.
13. 26 ounces to 4 pounds.
14. 7 dimes to 12 nickels.

Find the gear ratio. See Example 4.

15. Driving gear, 40 teeth; driven gear, 5 teeth.
16. Driven gear, 8 teeth; driving gear, 30 teeth.

In Exercises 17–20 **(a)** *determine the indicated ratio, and* **(b)** *write the ratio as some quantity to 1*

17. In 1970 the world population was 3.6 billion people. In 1990 the world population had increased to 5.3 billion. What is the ratio of the 1990 world population to the 1970 world population?

18. In 1970 in the United States, 72,700 metric tons of aluminum was used for soft-drink and beer containers. In 1990 this amount had increased to 1,251,900 metric tons. Find the ratio of the amount of aluminum used for beer and soft-drink containers in 1990 to the amount used in 1970.

19. The Department of Agriculture has estimated that an acre of land in the United States can produce about 20,000 pounds of potatoes. The same acre of land, if used to raise cattle feed, can produce about 165 pounds of beef. Find the ratio of pounds of potatoes to pounds of beef that can be produced on an acre of land.

20. The U.S. population is about 256,560,000. About 635,000 of these persons are medical doctors. The population of China is 1,169,620,000, including about 1,810,000 medical doctors. Find the ratio of persons to doctors for the United States and for China.

Solve for the variable by cross-multiplying.

21. $\dfrac{4}{x} = \dfrac{5}{20}$

22. $\dfrac{x}{4} = \dfrac{12}{48}$

23. $\dfrac{5}{3} = \dfrac{75}{x}$

24. $\dfrac{x}{32} = \dfrac{-5}{4}$

25. $\dfrac{90}{x} = \dfrac{-9}{10}$

26. $\dfrac{-3}{8} = \dfrac{x}{40}$

27. $\dfrac{1}{9} = \dfrac{x}{45}$

28. $\dfrac{y}{6} = \dfrac{7}{42}$

29. $\dfrac{3}{z} = \dfrac{2}{-20}$

30. $\dfrac{3}{12} = \dfrac{-1.4}{z}$

31. $\dfrac{15}{20} = \dfrac{x}{8}$

32. $\dfrac{12}{3} = \dfrac{x}{-100}$

Write a proportion that can be used to solve the problem, then solve the problem. Use a calculator where appropriate.

33. A car can travel 32 miles on 1 gallon of gasoline. How far can it travel on 12 gallons of gasoline?

34. A quality control worker can check 12 parts in 2.5 minutes. How long will it take her to check 60 parts?

35. A gallon of paint covers 825 square feet. How much paint is needed to cover a house with a surface area of 5775 square feet?

36. If 100 feet of wire has an electrical resistance of 7.3 ohms, find the electrical resistance of 40 feet of wire.

37. A blueprint of a shopping mall is in the scale of 1:150. Thus 1 foot on a blueprint represents 150 feet of actual length. One part of the mall is to be 190 feet long. How long will it appear on the blueprint?

38. The property tax in the town of Plainview, Texas, is $8.235 per $1000 of assessed value. If the Litton's house is assessed at $122,000, how much property tax will they owe?

39. A photograph shows a boy standing next to a tall cactus. If the boy, who is actually 48 inches tall, measures 0.6 inch in the photograph, how tall is the cactus that measures 3.25 inches in the photo?

40. If a 40-pound bag of fertilizer covers 5000 square feet, how many pounds of fertilizer are needed to cover an area of 26,000 square feet?

41. The instructions on a bottle of liquid insecticide say "use 3 teaspoons of insecticide per gallon of water." If your sprayer has an 8-gallon capacity, how much insecticide should be used to fill the sprayer?

42. A recipe for McGillicutty stew calls for $4\frac{1}{2}$ pounds of beef. If the recipe is for 20 servings, how much beef is needed to make 12 servings?

43. Every ton of recycled paper saves approximately 17 trees. (It also saves dumping cost, landfill space, about 7000 gallons of water, and 4100 kilowatt-hours of electricity that would be used in new paper products. Furthermore, to collect and recycle paper provides five times as many jobs as to harvest virgin timber.) If your college recycles 20 tons of paper in a year, how many trees has it saved?

See Exercise 39.

44. A recipe for pancake mix calls for two eggs for each 6 cups of pancake mix. The Mesa County Fire Department is planning a Sunday brunch for the community. How many eggs will they use if they plan to use 120 cups of the pancake mix?

45. A nurse must administer 220 micrograms of atropine sulfate. The drug is available in solution form. The concentration of the atropine sulfate solution is 400 micrograms per milliliter. How many milliliters should be given?

46. A doctor asks a nurse to administer 0.7 gram of meprobamate per square meter of body surface. The patient's body surface is 0.6 square meter. How much meprobamate should be given?

47. While on fast forward, the counter of your VCR goes from 0 to 250 in 30 seconds. Your videocassette tape contains two movies. The second movie starts at 800 on the VCR counter. If you are at the beginning of the tape, approximately how long will you keep the VCR on fast forward to reach the beginning of the second movie?

48. Mary read 40 pages of a novel in 30 minutes. **(a)** If she continues reading at the same rate, how long will it take her to read the entire 760-page book? **(b)** How long will it take her to finish the book from page 31?

Solve using a proportion. Round your answers to two decimal places.

51. Convert 57 inches to feet.

52. Convert 17,952 feet to miles (5280 feet = 1 mile).

53. Convert 26.1 square feet to square yards (9 square feet = 1 square yard).

54. Convert 146.4 ounces to pounds.

55. One inch equals 2.54 centimeters. Find the length of a book in inches if it measures 26.67 centimeters.

56. One liter equals approximately 1.06 quarts. Find the volume in quarts of a 5-liter container.

57. One mile equals approximately 1.6 kilometers. Find the distance in miles of a 25-kilometer kangaroo crossing.

58. One mile equals approximately 1.6 kilometers. Find the distance in kilometers from San Diego, California, to San Francisco, California, a distance of 520 miles.

59. If gold is selling for $400 per 480 grains (a troy ounce), what is the cost per grain?

60. In chemistry we learn that 100 torr (a unit of measurement) equals 0.13 atmosphere. Find the number of torr in 0.39 atmosphere.

49. In the United States in 1990, the birth rate was 16 per one thousand people. In the United States in 1990, there were approximately 4,179,200 births. What was the U.S. population in 1990?

50. It is estimated that each year 1 in every 15,000 (1:15,000) people are born with a genetic disorder called Prader–Willi syndrome. If there were approximately 4,179,200 births in the United States in 1990, approximately how many children were born with Prader–Willi syndrome?

61. In a statistics course, we find that for one particular set of scores 16 points equals 3.2 standard deviations. How many points equals 1 standard deviation?

62. When Fong visited the United States from Canada, he exchanged 10 Canadian dollars for 7.40 U.S. dollars. If he exchanges his remaining 2000 Canadian dollars for U.S. dollars, how much more will he receive?

63. Antonio, who is visiting the United States from Italy, wishes to obtain U.S. currency. If one Italian lira can be converted to 0.00059 U.S. dollar, how many lire will be need to obtain 1200 U.S. dollars?

64. Ms. Johnson spent an evening in a hotel in London, England. When she checked out, she was charged 90 pounds. What was the U.S. dollar equivalence of her hotel bill if 1 English pound could be converted to 1.64 U.S. dollars?

The figures below are similar. For each pair, find the length of the side indicated with an x.

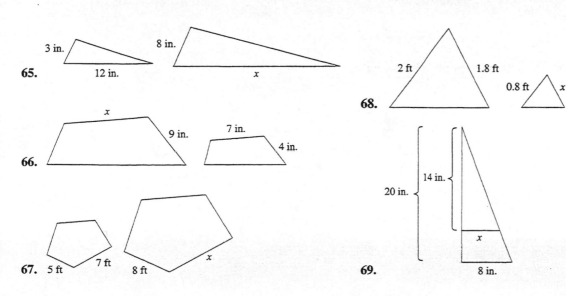

70.

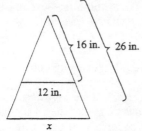

16 in. 26 in.

12 in.

x

71. Mrs. Sanchez's low-density cholesterol level is 127 milligrams per deciliter (mg/dL). Her high-density cholesterol level is 60 mg/dL. Is Mrs. Sanchez's ratio of low-density to high-density cholesterol level less than or equal to the 4:1 recommended level? See Example 2.

72. (a) Another ratio used by some doctors when measuring cholesterol level is the ratio of total cholesterol to high-density cholesterol.* Is this ratio increased or decreased if the total cholesterol remains the same but the high-density level is increased? Explain.

(b) Doctors recommend that the ratio of total cholesterol to high-density cholesterol be less than or equal to 4.5:1. If Mike's total cholesterol is 220 mg/dL and his high-density cholesterol is 50 mg/dL, is his ratio less than or equal to the 4.5:1? Explain.

73. (a) Find the ratio of your height to your arm span when your arms are extended horizontally outward. You will need help in getting these measurements.

(b) If a box were to be drawn about your body with your arms extended, would the box be a square or a rectangle? If a rectangle, would the larger length be your arm span or your height measurement? Explain.

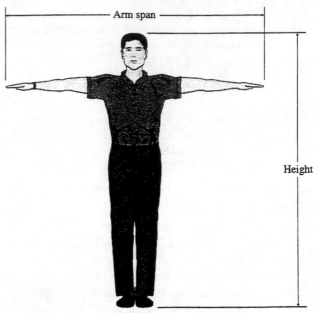

Arm span

Height

See Exercise 7.3

74. A special ratio in mathematics is called the golden ratio. Do research in a history of mathematics book, or another book recommended by your professor, and explain what the golden ratio is and why it is important.

75. As you have learned, proportions can be used to solve a wide variety of problems. What information is needed for a problem to be set up and solved using a proportion?

CUMULATIVE REVIEW EXERCISES

[1.10] *Name the properties illustrated.*

76. $x + 3 = 3 + x$

77. $3(xy) = (3x)y$

78. $2(x - 3) = 2x - 6$

[2.5] **79.** Solve $-(2x + 6) = 2(3x - 6)$.

*Total cholesterol includes both low- and high-density cholesterol, plus other types of cholesterol.

Group Activity/ Challenge Problems

1. A GE Soft White A-19 incandescent bulb has an average life of about 750 hours. A fluorescent bulb, the Phillips SL 18, produces equivalent light. Its average life is 10,000 hours. **(a)** Express the ratio of the life of the incandescent bulb to the life of the fluorescent bulb. **(b)** Express this ratio as some number to 1.

2. The recipe for the filling for an apple pie calls for:

   12 cups sliced apples $\frac{1}{4}$ teaspoon salt
   $\frac{1}{2}$ cup flour   2 tablespoons butter or margarine
   1 teaspoon nutmeg $1\frac{1}{2}$ cups sugar
   1 teaspoon cinnamon

   Determine the amount of each of the other ingredients that should be used if only 8 cups of apples are available.

3. Insulin comes in 10-cubic-centimeter (cc) vials labeled in the number of units of insulin per cubic centimeter. Thus a vial labeled U40 means there are 40 units of insulin per cubic centimeter of fluid. If a patient needs 25 units of insulin, how many cubic centimeters of fluid should be drawn up into a syringe from the U40 vial?

4. In 1938, about 12,000 nesting pairs of wood storks lived in the Everglades. By 1988, 50 years later, their numbers had decreased to about 1200 pairs, partly because of the loss of peripheral wetlands. If the decrease in population continues at the present rate, in what year would the wood storks become extinct in the Everglades?

5. In 1992, according to the world population data sheet, the world population was 5420 million people. The world birth rate that year was 26 per 1000 people and the world death rate was 9 per 1000 people. **(a)** Find the number of births worldwide in 1992. **(b)** Find the number of deaths worldwide in 1992. **(c)** Find the world population increase in 1992.

6. An important concept that we will discuss in Chapter 7 is "slope." The slope of a straight line may be defined as *a ratio* of the vertical change to the horizontal change between any two points on the line. Determine the slope of the line below.

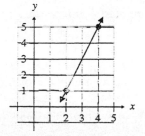

7. Recent legislation requires new nutritional information on food packages. This information can be used to calculate the *percent of calories from fat* in a product. In all foods, each gram of carbohydrates has 4 calories, each gram of protein has 4 calories, and each gram of fat has 9 calories. The percent of calories from fat is found by taking the *ratio* of the calories from fat to the total calories of the food and multiplying this value, in decimal form, by 100. For example, if a food product contains 7 grams of carbohydrates, 2 grams of protein, and 5 grams of fat, we compute the percent of calories from fat as follows:

$$\text{calories from carbohydrates} = 7 \times 4 = 28$$
$$\text{calories from protein} = 2 \times 4 = 8$$
$$\text{calories from fat} = 5 \times 9 = \underline{45}$$
$$\text{total calories} = 81$$

$$\text{percent of calories from fat} = \frac{\text{calories from fat}}{\text{total calories}} \times 100$$

$$= \frac{45}{81}(100) = 0.556(100) = 55.6\%$$

Thus, this product contains about 56% calories from fat. Most medical associations recommend that human diets contain no more than 30% calories from fat.

According to its label, a 4-ounce serving of Healthy Choice Rocky Road Frozen Dairy Dessert contains less than 160 calories, 3 grams of protein, 32 grams of carbohydrates, and 2 grams of fat. It also indicates that the percent of calories from fat is 11%. Use the procedure presented above to determine if the manufacturer's claim regarding the number of calories and percent of calories from fat is correct.

2.7   Inequalities in One Variable

① Solve linear inequalities.
② Solve linear inequalities that have all real numbers as their solution or have no solution.

Tape 4

Solve Linear Inequalities

① The greater-than symbol, $>$, and less-than symbol, $<$, were introduced in Section 1.4. The symbol $\geq$ means greater than or equal to and $\leq$ means less than or equal to. A mathematical statement containing one or more of these symbols is called an **inequality**. The direction of the symbol is sometimes called the **sense** or **order** of the inequality.

Examples of Inequalities in One Variable

$$x + 3 < 5, \qquad x + 4 \geq 2x - 6, \qquad 4 > -x + 3$$

To solve an inequality, we must get the variable by itself on one side of the inequality symbol. To do this, we make use of properties very similar to those used to solve equations. Here are four properties used to solve inequalities. Later in this section we will introduce two additional properties.

> **Properties Used to Solve Inequalities**
> For real numbers, a, b, and c:
> 1. If $a > b$, then $a + c > b + c$.
> 2. If $a > b$, then $a - c > b - c$.
> 3. If $a > b$ and $c > 0$, then $ac > bc$.
> 4. If $a > b$ and $c > 0$, then $\dfrac{a}{c} > \dfrac{b}{c}$.

Property 1 says the same number may be added to both sides of an inequality. Property 2 says the same number may be subtracted from both sides of an inequality. Property 3 says the same *positive* number may be used to multiply both sides of an inequality. Property 4 says the same *positive* number may be used to divide both sides of an inequality. When any of these four properties is used, the direction of the inequality symbol does not change.

EXAMPLE 1 Solve the inequality $x - 4 > 7$, and graph the solution on the real number line.

Solution: To solve this inequality, we need to isolate the variable, x. Therefore, we must eliminate the -4 from the left side of the inequality. To do this, we add 4 to both sides of the inequality.

$$x - 4 > 7$$
$$x - 4 + 4 > 7 + 4 \qquad \text{Add 4 to both sides of the inequality.}$$
$$x > 11$$

The solution is all real numbers greater than 11. We can illustrate the solution on the number line by placing an open circle at 11 on the number line and drawing an arrow to the right (Fig. 2.11).

The open circle at the 11 indicates that the 11 is *not* part of the solution. The arrow going to the right indicates that all the values greater than 11 are solutions to the inequality.

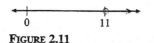

FIGURE 2.11

EXAMPLE 2 Solve the inequality $2x + 6 \le -2$, and graph the solution on the real number line.

Solution: To isolate the variable, we must eliminate the $+6$ from the left side of the inequality. We do this by subtracting 6 from both sides of the inequality.

$$2x + 6 \le -2$$
$$2x + 6 - 6 \le -2 - 6 \qquad \text{Subtract 6 from both sides of the inequality.}$$
$$2x \le -8$$
$$\frac{2x}{2} \le \frac{-8}{2} \qquad \text{Divide both sides of the inequality by 2.}$$
$$x \le -4$$

FIGURE 2.12

The solution is all real numbers less than or equal to -4. We can illustrate the solution on the number line by placing a closed, or darkened, circle at -4 and drawing an arrow to the left (Fig. 2.12).

The darkened circle at -4 indicates that -4 *is* a part of the solution. The arrow going to the left indicates that all the values less than -4 are also solutions to the inequality.

Notice in properties 3 and 4 that we specified that $c > 0$. What happens when an inequality is multiplied or divided by a negative number? Examples 3 and 4 will illustrate this.

EXAMPLE 3   Multiply both sides of the inequality $8 > -4$ by -2.

Solution: $8 > -4$

$$-2(8) < -2(-4)$$

$$-16 < 8$$

EXAMPLE 4   Divide both sides of the inequality $8 > -4$ by -2.

Solution: $8 > -4$

$$\frac{8}{-2} < \frac{-4}{-2}$$

$$-4 < 2$$

Examples 3 and 4 illustrate that **when an inequality is multiplied or divided by a negative number, the direction of the inequality symbol changes.**

Additional Properties Used to Solve Inequalities

5. If $a > b$ and $c < 0$, then $ac < bc$.

6. If $a > b$ and $c < 0$, then $\dfrac{a}{c} < \dfrac{b}{c}$.

EXAMPLE 5   Solve the inequality $-2x > 6$, and graph the solution on the real number line.

Solution: To isolate the variable, we must eliminate the -2 on the left side of the inequality. To do this, we can divide both sides of the inequality by -2. When we do this, however, we must remember to change the direction of the inequality symbol.

$$-2x > 6$$

$$\frac{-2x}{-2} < \frac{6}{-2} \qquad \text{Divide both sides of the inequality by } -2 \text{ and change the direction of the inequality symbol.}$$

$$x < -3$$

FIGURE 2.13

The solution is all real numbers less than -3. The solution is graphed on the number line in Figure 2.13.

EXAMPLE 6 Solve the inequality $4 \geq -5 - x$, and graph the solution on the real number line.

Solution: *Method 1:*

$$4 \geq -5 - x$$
$$4 + 5 \geq -5 + 5 - x \qquad \text{Add 5 to both sides of the inequality.}$$
$$9 \geq -x$$
$$-1(9) \leq -1(-x) \qquad \text{Multiply both sides of the inequality by } -1 \text{ and}$$
$$-9 \leq x \qquad\qquad\qquad \text{change the direction of the inequality symbol.}$$

The inequality $-9 \leq x$ can also be written $x \geq -9$.

Method 2:

$$4 \geq -5 - x$$
$$4 + x \geq -5 - x + x \qquad \text{Add } x \text{ to both sides of the inequality.}$$
$$4 + x \geq -5$$
$$4 - 4 + x \geq -5 - 4 \qquad \text{Subtract 4 from both sides of the inequality.}$$
$$x \geq -9$$

FIGURE 2.14

The solution is graphed on the number line in Figure 2.14. Other methods could also be used to solve this problem.

Notice in Example 6, method 1, we wrote $-9 \leq x$ as $x \geq -9$. Although the solution $-9 \leq x$ is correct, it is customary to write the solution to an inequality with the variable on the left. One reason we write the variable on the left is that it often makes it easier to graph the solution on the number line. How would you graph $-3 > x$? How would you graph $-5 \leq x$? If you rewrite these inequalities with the variable on the left side, the answer becomes clearer.

$$-3 > x \qquad \text{means} \qquad x < -3$$
$$\text{and} \quad -5 \leq x \qquad \text{means} \qquad x \geq -5$$

Notice that you can change an answer from a greater-than statement to a less-than statement or from a less-than statement to a greater-than statement. When you change the answer from one form to the other, remember that the inequality symbol must point to the letter or number to which it was pointing originally.

Helpful Hint

....

$a > x$ means $x < a$ (Note that both inequality symbols point to x.)
$a < x$ means $x > a$ (Note that both inequality symbols point to a.)

Examples: $-3 > x$ means $x < -3$

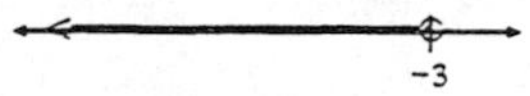

$-5 \leq x$ means $x \geq -5$

Let us now solve inequalities where the variable appears on both sides of the inequality symbol. To solve these inequalities we use the same basic procedure that we used to solve equations. However, we must remember that whenever we multiply or divide both sides of an inequality by a negative number, we must change the direction of the inequality symbol.

EXAMPLE 7   Solve the inequality $2x + 4 < -x + 12$, and graph the solution on the real number line.

Solution: $2x + 4 < -x + 12$

$2x + x + 4 < -x + x + 12$ **Add x to both sides of the inequality.**

$3x + 4 < 12$

$3x + 4 - 4 < 12 - 4$ **Subtract 4 from both sides of the inequality.**

$3x < 8$

$\dfrac{3x}{3} < \dfrac{8}{3}$ **Divide both sides of the inequality by 3.**

$x < \dfrac{8}{3}$

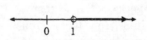

FIGURE 2.15

The solution is graphed on the number line in Figure 2.15.

EXAMPLE 8   Solve the inequality $-5x + 9 < -2x + 6$, and graph the solution on the real number line.

Solution: $-5x + 9 < -2x + 6$

$-5x < -2x - 3$ **9 was subtracted from both sides of the inequality.**

$-3x < -3$ **2x was added to both sides of the inequality.**

$x > 1$ **Both sides of inequality were divided by -3 and direction of inequality symbol was changed.**

FIGURE 2.16

The solution is graphed in Figure 2.16.

Special Cases   **2** In Examples 9 and 10 we illustrate two special types of inequalities. Example 9 is an inequality that is always true for all real numbers, and Example 10 is an inequality that is never true for any real number.

EXAMPLE 9   Solve the inequality $2(x + 3) \le 5x - 3x + 8$, and graph the solution on the real number line.

Solution: $2(x + 3) \le 5x - 3x + 8$

$2x + 6 \le 5x - 3x + 8$ **Distributive property was used.**

$2x + 6 \le 2x + 8$ **Like terms were combined.**

$2x - 2x + 6 \le 2x - 2x + 8$ **Subtract 2x from both sides of the inequality.**

$6 \le 8$

FIGURE 2.17

Since 6 is always less than or equal to 8, the solution is **all real numbers** (Fig. 2.17).

EXAMPLE 10   Solve the inequality $4(x + 1) > x + 5 + 3x$, and graph the solution on the real number line.

Solution: $4(x + 1) > x + 5 + 3x$

$\qquad\quad 4x + 4 > x + 5 + 3x$ Distributive property was used.

$\qquad\qquad 4x + 4 > 4x + 5$ Like terms were combined.

$\quad 4x - 4x + 4 > 4x - 4x + 5$ Subtract $4x$ from both sides of the
inequality.

$\qquad\qquad\qquad 4 > 5$

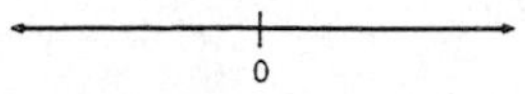

FIGURE 2.18

Since 4 is never greater than 5, the answer is **no solution** (Fig. 2.18). There is no real number that makes the statement true.

Exercise Set 2.7

Solve each inequality and graph the solution on the real number line.

1. $x + 3 > 7$

2. $x - 4 > -3$

3. $x + 5 \geq 3$

4. $4 - x \geq 3$

5. $-x + 3 < 8$

6. $4 < 3 + x$

7. $6 > x - 4$

8. $-4 \leq -x - 3$

9. $8 \leq 4 - x$

10. $2x < 4$

11. $-2x < 3$

12. $6 \geq -3x$

13. $2x + 3 \leq 5$

14. $-4x - 3 > 5$

15. $12x + 24 < -12$

16. $3x - 4 \leq 9$

17. $4 - 6x > -5$

18. $8 < 4 - 2x$

19. $15 > -9x + 50$

20. $3x - 4 < 5$

21. $4 < 3x + 12$

22. $-4x > 2x + 12$

23. $6x + 2 \leq 3x - 9$

24. $-2x - 4 \leq -5x + 12$

25. $x - 4 \leq 3x + 8$

26. $-3x - 5 \geq 4x - 29$

27. $-x + 4 < -3x + 6$

28. $2(x - 3) < 4x + 10$

29. $-3(2x - 4) > 2(6x - 12)$

30. $-(x + 3) \leq 4x + 5$

31. $x + 3 < x + 4$

32. $x + 5 \geq x - 2$

33. $6(3 - x) < 2x + 12$

34. $2(3 - x) + 4x < -6$

35. $-21(2 - x) + 3x > 4x + 4$

36. $-(x + 3) \geq 2x + 6$

37. $4x - 4 < 4(x - 5)$

38. $-2(-5 - x) > 3(x + 2) + 4 - x$

39. $5(2x + 3) \geq 6 + (x + 2) - 2x$

40. $-3(-2x + 12) < -4(x + 2) - 6$

41. When solving an inequality, if you obtain the result $3 < 5$, what is the solution?

42. When solving an inequality, if you obtain the result $4 \geq 2$, what is the solution?

43. When solving an inequality, if you obtain the result $5 < 2$, what is the solution?

44. When solving an inequality, if you obtain the result $-4 \geq -2$, what is the solution?

45. When solving an inequality, under what conditions will it be necessary to change the direction of the inequality symbol?

46. List the six rules used to solve inequalities.

CUMULATIVE REVIEW EXERCISES

[1.8] 47. Evaluate $-x^2$ for $x = 3$.

48. Evaluate $-x^2$ for $x = -5$.

[2.5] 49. Solve $4 - 3(2x - 4) = 5 - (x + 3)$.

[2.6] 50. The Milford electric company charges $0.174 per kilowatt-hour of electricity. The Cisneros's monthly electric bill was $87 for the month of July. How many kilowatt-hours of electricity did the Cisneros use in July?

Group Activity/ Challenge Problems

1. Solve the inequality
   $$3(2 - x) - 4(2x - 3) \le 6 + 2x - 6(x - 5) + 2x.$$
2. Solve the inequality
   $$-(x + 4) + 6x - 5 > -4(x + 3) + 2(x + 6) - 5x.$$
3. The inequality symbols discussed so far are $<$, $\le$, $>$, and $\ge$. Can you name an inequality symbol that we have not mentioned in this section?
4. Reproduced below is a portion of the Florida Individual and Joint Intangible Tax Return for 1995.

TAX CALCULATION WORKSHEET

(COMPLETE ONLY ONE (1) COLUMN BELOW)

FILING STATUS (Step 1)	INDIVIDUAL		JOINT	
	BOX A	BOX B	BOX C	BOX D
IF YOUR TAXABLE ASSETS FROM SCHEDULE A LINE 5 ARE:	$100,000 or LESS	GREATER than $100,000	$200,000 or LESS	GREATER than $200,000
6A. TAXABLE ASSETS (SCHEDULE A, LINE 5) (Step 2)	$_____	$_____	$_____	$_____
6B. TIMES TAX RATE	x .001	x .002	x .001	x .002
6C. GROSS TAX (Step 3) (MULTIPLY LINE 6A x LINE 6B)	$_____	$_____	$_____	$_____
6D. LESS EXEMPTION	- $20.00	-$120.00	-$40.00	-$240.00
6E. TOTAL TAX DUE (Step 4) (SUBTRACT LINE 6D FROM LINE 6C IF LESS THAN ZERO ENTER 0)	$_____	$_____	$_____	$_____
CARRY TOTAL TAX DUE AMOUNT TO SCHEDULE A, LINE 6				

Use the Tax Calculation Worksheet to determine your total tax due (line 6e) if your total taxable assets from Schedule A line 5 are as follows.

(a) $30,000 and your filing status is individual.

(b) $175,000 and your filing status is individual.

(c) $200,000 and your filing status is joint.

(d) $300,000 and your filing status is joint.

Summary

GLOSSARY

Algebraic expression (76): A collection of numbers, variables, grouping symbols, and operation symbols.

Check (85): A procedure where the value believed to be the solution to an equation is substituted back into the equation.

Coefficient or numerical coefficient (77): The numerical part of a term.

Constant or constant term (77): A term in an expression that does not contain a variable.

Equation (85): A statement that two algebraic expressions are equal.

Equivalent equations (88): Two or more equations that have the same solution.

Identity (116): An equation that is true for all values of the variable.

Inequality (132): A mathematical statement containing one or more inequality symbols ($>$, $\ge$, $<$, $\le$).

Like terms (77): Terms that have the same variables with the same exponents.

Proportion (121): A statement of equality between two ratios.

Ratio (120): A quotient of two quantities with the same units.

Reciprocal of real number a (95): $\dfrac{1}{a}$, $a \neq 0$.

Similar figures (126): Two figures are similar when their corresponding angles are equal and their corresponding sides are in proportion.

Simplify (82): To simplify an expression means to combine like terms in the expression.

Solution (85): The value or values of the variable that make an equation a true statement.

Solve (85): To find the solution to an equation.

Term (76): The parts that are added or subtracted in an algebraic expression.

IMPORTANT FACTS

Distributive property:

$a(b + c) = ab + ac$.

Addition property:

If $a = b$, then $a + c = b + c$.

Multiplication property:

If $a = b$, then $a \cdot c = b \cdot c$.

Cross-multiplication:

If $\dfrac{a}{b} = \dfrac{c}{d}$, then $ad = bc$.

Properties used to solve inequalities

1. If $a > b$, then $a + c > b + c$.
2. If $a > b$, then $a - c > b - c$.
3. If $a > b$ and $c > 0$, then $ac > bc$.
4. If $a > b$ and $c > 0$, then $\dfrac{a}{c} > \dfrac{b}{c}$.
5. If $a > b$ and $c < 0$, then $ac < bc$.
6. If $a > b$ and $c < 0$, then $\dfrac{a}{c} < \dfrac{b}{c}$.

Review Exercises

[2.1] *Use the distributive property to simplify.*

1. $2(x + 4)$
2. $3(x - 2)$
3. $2(4x - 3)$
4. $-2(x + 4)$
5. $-(x + 2)$
6. $-(x - 2)$
7. $-4(4 - x)$
8. $3(6 - 2x)$
9. $4(5x - 6)$
10. $-3(2x - 5)$
11. $6(6x - 6)$
12. $4(-x + 3)$
13. $-3(x + y)$
14. $-2(3x - 2)$
15. $-(3 + 2y)$
16. $-(x + 2y - z)$
17. $3(x + 3y - 2z)$
18. $-2(2x - 3y + 7)$

Simplify where possible.

19. $2x + 3x$
20. $4y + 3y + 2$
21. $4 - 2y + 3$
22. $1 + 3x + 2x$
23. $6x + 2y + y$
24. $-2x - x + 3y$
25. $2x + 3y + 4x + 5y$
26. $6x + 3y + 2$
27. $2x - 3x - 1$
28. $5x - 2x + 3y + 6$
29. $x + 8x - 9x + 3$
30. $-4x - 8x + 3$
31. $3(x + 2) + 2x$
32. $-2(x + 3) + 6$
33. $2x + 3(x + 4) - 5$
34. $4(3 - 2x) - 2x$
35. $6 - (-x + 3) + 4x$
36. $2(2x + 5) - 10 - 4$
37. $-6(4 - 3x) - 18 + 4x$
38. $6 - 3(x + y) + 6x$
39. $3(x + y) - 2(2x - y)$
40. $3x - 6y + 2(4y + 8)$
41. $3 - (x - y) + (x - y)$
42. $(x + y) - (2x + 3y) + 4$

[2.2–2.5] *Solve.*

43. $2x = 4$
44. $x + 3 = -5$
45. $x - 4 = 7$
46. $\dfrac{x}{3} = -9$
47. $2x + 4 = 8$
48. $14 = 3 + 2x$
49. $8x - 3 = -19$
50. $6 - x = 9$
51. $-x = -12$

52. $2(x + 2) = 6$

53. $-3(2x - 8) = -12$

54. $4(6 + 2x) = 0$

55. $3x + 2x + 6 = -15$

56. $4 = -2(x + 3)$

57. $27 = 46 + 2x - x$

58. $4x + 6 - 7x + 9 = 18$

59. $4 + 3(x + 2) = 12$

60. $-3 + 3x = -2(x + 1)$

61. $3x - 6 = -5x + 30$

62. $-(x + 2) = 2(3x - 6)$

63. $2x + 6 = 3x + 9$

64. $-5x + 3 = 2x + 10$

65. $3x - 12x = 24 - 6x$

66. $2(x + 4) = -3(x + 5)$

67. $4(2x - 3) + 4 = 9x + 2$

68. $6x + 11 = -(6x + 5)$

69. $2(x + 7) = 6x + 9 - 4x$

70. $-5(3 - 4x) = -6 + 20x - 9$

71. $4(x - 3) - (x + 5) = 0$

72. $-2(4 - x) = 6(x + 2) + 3x$

[2.6] *Determine the following ratios. Write each ratio in lowest terms.*

73. 15 feet to 20 feet.

74. 80 ounces to 12 pounds.

75. 32 ounces to 2 pounds.

Solve each proportion.

76. $\dfrac{x}{9} = \dfrac{6}{18}$

77. $\dfrac{15}{10} = \dfrac{x}{20}$

78. $\dfrac{3}{x} = \dfrac{15}{45}$

79. $\dfrac{20}{45} = \dfrac{15}{x}$

80. $\dfrac{6}{5} = \dfrac{-12}{x}$

81. $\dfrac{x}{9} = \dfrac{8}{-3}$

82. $\dfrac{-4}{9} = \dfrac{-16}{x}$

83. $\dfrac{x}{-15} = \dfrac{30}{-5}$

Each of the following pairs of figures are similar. Find the length of the side indicated by x.

84.

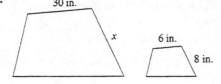

30 in.   x   6 in.   8 in.

85.

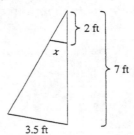

2 ft   x   7 ft   3.5 ft

[2.7] *Solve each inequality, and graph the solution on the real number line.*

86. $2x + 4 \geq 8$

87. $6 - 2x > 4x - 12$

88. $6 - 3x \leq 2x + 18$

89. $2(x + 4) \leq 2x - 5$

90. $2(x + 3) > 6x - 4x + 4$

91. $x + 6 > 9x + 30$

92. $x - 2 \leq -4x + 7$

93. $-(x + 2) < -2(-2x + 5)$

94. $2(x + 3) < -(x + 3) + 4$

95. $-6x - 3 \geq 2(x - 4) + 3x$

96. $-2(x - 4) \leq 3x + 6 - 5x$

97. $2(2x + 4) > 4(x + 2) - 6$

[2.6] *Set up a proportion and solve each problem.*

98. If a 4-ounce piece of cake has 160 calories, how many calories does a 6-ounce piece of that cake have?

99. If a copy machine can copy 5 pages per minute, how many pages can be copied in 22 minutes?

100. If the scale of a map is 1 inch to 60 miles, what distance on the map represents 380 miles?

101. Bryce builds a model car to a scale of 1 inch to 0.9 feet. If the completed model is 10.5 inches, what is the size of the actual car?

102. If one U.S. dollar can be exchanged for 3.1165 Mexican pesos, find the value of 1 peso in terms of U.S. dollars.

103. If 3 radians equal 171.9 degrees, find the number of degrees in 1 radian.

104. If a machine can fill and cap 80 bottles of catsup in 50 seconds, how many bottles of catsup can it fill and cap in 2 minutes?

Practice Test

Use the distributive property to simplify.

1. $-2(4 - 2x)$

2. $-(x + 3y - 4)$

Simplify.

3. $3x - x + 4$

4. $4 + 2x - 3x + 6$

5. $y - 2x - 4x - 6$

6. $x - 4y + 6x - y + 3$

7. $2x + 3 + 2(3x - 2)$

Solve.

8. $2x + 4 = 12$

9. $-x - 3x + 4 = 12$

10. $4x - 2 = x + 4$

11. $3(x - 2) = -(5 - 4x)$

12. $2x - 3(-2x + 4) = -13 + x$

13. $3x - 4 - x = 2(x + 5)$

14. $-3(2x + 3) = -2(3x + 1) - 7$

15. $\dfrac{9}{x} = \dfrac{3}{-15}$

Solve and graph the solution on the real number line.

16. $2x - 4 < 4x + 10$

17. $3(x + 4) \geq 5x - 12$

18. $4(x + 3) + 2x < 6x - 3$

19. The following figures are similar figures. Find the length of side x.

20. If 6 gallons of insecticide can treat 3 acres of land, how many gallons of insecticide are needed to treat 75 acres?

x

4 ft

8 ft   3 ft

Cumulative Review Test

1. Multiply $\dfrac{16}{20} \cdot \dfrac{4}{5}$.

2. Divide $\dfrac{8}{24} \div \dfrac{2}{3}$.

3. Insert $<$, $>$, or $=$ in the shaded area to make a true statement: $|-2|$ ___ 1.

4. Evaluate $-6 - (-3) + 5 - 8$.

Simplify.

10. $6x + 2y + 4x - y$

Solve.

12. $4x - 2 = 10$

5. Subtract -4 from -12.

6. Evaluate $16 - 6 \div 2 \cdot 3$.

7. Evaluate $3[6 - (4 - 3^2)] - 30$.

8. Evaluate $-3x^2 - 4x + 5$ when $x = -2$.

9. Name the property illustrated:
$(x + 4) + 6 = x + (4 + 6)$.

11. $3x - 2x + 16 + 2x$

13. $\dfrac{1}{4}x = -10$

14. $6x + 5x + 6 = 28$

15. $3(x - 2) = 5(x - 1) + 3x + 4$

16. $\dfrac{15}{30} = \dfrac{3}{x}$

Solve, and graph the solution on the number line.

17. $x - 4 > 6$

18. $2x - 7 \leq 3x + 5$

19. A 36-pound bag of fertilizer can fertilize an area of 5000 square feet. How many pounds of fertilizer will Marisa need to fertilize her 22,000-square-foot lawn?

20. If Samuel earns $10.50 after working for 2 hours scrubbing boats at the marina, how much does he earn after 8 hours?

Chapter 3

Formulas and Applications of Algebra

3.1 Formulas
3.2 Changing Application Problems into Equations
3.3 Solving Application Problems
3.4 Geometric Problems

SUMMARY
REVIEW EXERCISES
PRACTICE TEST

See Section 3.2, Group Activity 2

Preview and Perspective

The major goal of this chapter is to teach you the terminology and techniques to write real-life application problems as equations. The equations are then solved using the techniques taught in Chapter 2. For mathematics to be relevant it must be useful. In this chapter we explain and illustrate the tremendous number of real-life applications of algebra. Since this is such an important topic, and since we want you to learn it well and feel comfortable applying mathematics to real-world situations, we cover this chapter especially slowly. You need to have confidence in your work, and you need to do all your homework. The more problems you attempt, the better you will become at setting up and solving application (or word) problems. After completing this chapter, whenever a real-life application of mathematics comes up, try to set it up and solve it algebraically.

We begin this chapter with a discussion of formulas. We explain how to evaluate a formula and how to solve for a variable in a formula. We will be using formulas throughout this course, so you must understand their use. You probably realize that most mathematics and science courses use a wide variety of formulas. Formulas are also used in many other disciplines, including the arts, business and economics, medicine, and technology, to name just a few.

In Section 3.2 we explain how to write real-life applications as equations. In Section 3.3 we continue writing application problems as equations. We then solve the equations to determine the answers to the problems. The general procedures discussed in Sections 3.2 and 3.3 are then applied to specific geometric applications in Section 3.4. Since application problems are so important, we cover them in many different sections throughout the book. For example, we discuss applications of motion problems and mixture problems in Section 4.7.

3.1 Formulas

Tape 5

1. Use the simple interest formula.
2. Use geometric formulas.
3. Solve for a variable in a formula.

A **formula** is an equation commonly used to express a specific relationship mathematically. For example, the formula for the area of a rectangle is

$$\text{area} = \text{length} \cdot \text{width} \quad \text{or} \quad A = lw$$

To **evaluate a formula,** substitute the appropriate numerical values for the variables and perform the indicated operations.

Simple Interest Formula

1. A formula used in banking is the *simple interest formula.*

> ### Simple Interest Formula
>
> $$\text{interest} = \text{principal} \cdot \text{rate} \cdot \text{time} \quad \text{or} \quad i = prt$$

This formula is used to determine the simple interest, i, earned on some savings accounts, or the simple interest an individual must pay on certain loans. In the simple interest formula $i = prt$, p is the principal (the amount invested or borrowed), r is the interest rate in decimal form, and t is the amount of time of the investment or loan.

EXAMPLE 1   Avery borrows $2000 from a bank for 3 years. The bank charges 12% simple interest per year for the loan. How much interest will Avery owe the bank?

Solution: The principal, p, is $2000, the rate, r, is 12% or 0.12 in decimal form, and the time, t, is 3 years. Substituting these values in the simple interest formula gives

$$i = prt$$
$$i = 2000(0.12)(3) = 720$$

The simple interest is $720. After 3 years when Avery repays his loan he will pay the principal, $2000, plus the interest, $720, for a total of $2720.

EXAMPLE 2   Amber invests $5000 in a savings account which earns simple interest for 2 years. If the interest earned from the account is $800, find the rate.

Solution: We use the simple interest formula, $i = prt$. We are given the principal, p, the time, t, and the interest, i. We are asked to find the rate, r. We substitute the given values in the simple interest formula and solve the resulting equation for r.

$$i = prt$$
$$800 = 5000(r)(2)$$
$$800 = 10{,}000r$$
$$\frac{800}{10{,}000} = \frac{10{,}000r}{10{,}000}$$
$$0.08 = r$$

Thus, the simple interest rate is 0.08, or 8% per year.

Geometric Formulas

2   The **perimeter**, P, is the sum of the lengths of the sides of a figure. Perimeters are measured in the same common unit as the sides. For example, perimeter may be measured in centimeters, inches, or feet. The **area,** A, is the total surface within the figure's boundaries. Areas are measured in square units. For example, area may be measured in square centimeters, square inches, or square feet. Table 3.1 on page 146 gives the formulas for finding the areas and perimeters of triangles and quadrilaterals. **Quadrilateral** is a general name for a four-sided figure.

EXAMPLE 3   Kim's rectangular vegetable garden is 12 feet long and 6 feet wide (Fig. 3.1).

(a) If Kim wants to put fencing around the garden to keep the animals out, how much fencing will she need?

(b) What is the area of Kim's garden?

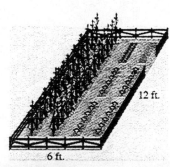

12 ft.

6 ft.

FIGURE 3.1

Solution: **(a)** To find the amount of fencing needed we need to find the perimeter of the garden. Substitute 12 for l and 6 for w in the formula for the perimeter of a rectangle.

$$P = 2l + 2w$$
$$P = 2(12) + 2(6) = 24 + 12 = 36 \text{ feet}$$

Thus, Kim will need 36 feet of fencing.

(b) Substitute 12 for l and 6 for w in the formula for the area of a rectangle.

$$A = lw$$
$$A = (12)(6) = 72 \text{ square feet (or 72 ft}^2)$$

Kim's vegetable garden has an area of 72 square feet.

TABLE 3.1   FORMULAS FOR AREAS AND PERIMETERS OF QUADRILATERALS AND TRIANGLES

Figure	Sketch	Area	Perimeter
Square		$A = s^2$	$P = 4s$
Rectangle		$A = lw$	$P = 2l + 2w$
Parallelogram		$A = lh$	$P = 2l + 2w$
Trapezoid		$A = \frac{1}{2}h(b + d)$	$P = a + b + c + d$
Triangle		$A = \frac{1}{2}bh$	$P = a + b + c$

EXAMPLE 4 Find the length of a rectangle whose perimeter is 22 inches and whose width is 3 inches.

Solution: Substitute 22 for P and 3 for w in the formula $P = 2l + 2w$; then solve for the length, l.

$$P = 2l + 2w$$
$$22 = 2l + 2(3)$$
$$22 = 2l + 6$$
$$22 - 6 = 2l + 6 - 6$$
$$16 = 2l$$
$$\frac{16}{2} = \frac{2l}{2}$$
$$8 = l$$

The length is 8 inches.

EXAMPLE 5 The area of a triangle is 30 square feet and its base is 12 feet (Fig. 3.2). Find its height.

Solution: $A = \dfrac{1}{2}bh$

$$30 = \dfrac{1}{2}(12)h$$

$$30 = 6h$$

$$\dfrac{30}{6} = \dfrac{6h}{6}$$

$$5 = h$$

FIGURE 3.2

The height of the triangle is 5 feet.

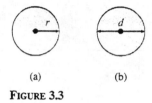

(a)   (b)

FIGURE 3.3

Another figure that we see and use daily is the circle. The **circumference,** C, is the length (or perimeter) of the curve that forms a circle. The **radius,** r, is the line segment from the center of the circle to any point on the circle (Fig. 3.3a). The **diameter** of a circle is a line segment through the center whose end points both lie on the circle (Fig. 3.3b). *Note that the length of the diameter is twice the length of the radius.*

The formulas for both the area and the circumference of a circle are given in Table 3.2.

TABLE 3.2 FORMULAS FOR CIRCLES		
Circle	**Area**	**Circumference**
	$A = \pi r^2$	$C = 2\pi r$

The value of pi, symbolized by the Greek lowercase letter π, is *approximately* 3.14.

Calculator Corner

Most scientific calculators have a key for the value of π. If you press $\boxed{\pi}$, your calculator will display 3.1415927. This is only an approximation of π since π is an irrational number. If you own a scientific calculator, use the π key instead of using 3.14 when working problems that involve π. In this book we will use 3.14 for π since not every student owns a scientific calculator. If you use the π key, your answers will be slightly more accurate than ours, but still approximate.

EXAMPLE 6 Determine the area and circumference of a circle whose diameter is 16 inches.

Solution: The radius is half the diameter, so $r = \dfrac{16}{2} = 8$ inches.

$$A = \pi r^2 \qquad\qquad C = 2\pi r$$
$$A = 3.14(8)^2 \qquad\qquad C = 2(3.14)(8)$$
$$A = 3.14(64) \qquad\qquad C = 50.24 \text{ inches}$$
$$A = 200.96 \text{ square inches}$$

If you used a scientific calculator and used the π key, your answer for the area would be 201.06193 and for the circumference would be 50.265482.

Table 3.3 gives formulas for finding the volume of certain three-dimensional figures. Volume is measured in cubic units, such as cubic centimeters or cubic feet.

TABLE 3.3 FORMULAS FOR VOLUMES OF THREE-DIMENSIONAL FIGURES

Figure	Sketch	Volume
Rectangular solid		$V = lwh$
Right circular cylinder		$V = \pi r^2 h$
Right circular cone		$V = \dfrac{1}{3}\pi r^2 h$
Sphere		$V = \dfrac{4}{3}\pi r^3$

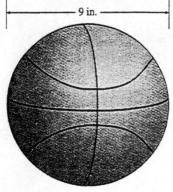

FIGURE 3.4

EXAMPLE 7 Find the volume of a basketball if its diameter is 9 inches (Fig. 3.4).

Solution: Since its diameter is 9 inches, its radius is 4.5 inches.

$$V = \frac{4}{3}\,\pi r^3$$

$$V = \frac{4}{3}\,(3.14)(4.5)^3 = \frac{4}{3}\,(3.14)(91.125) = 381.51$$

Therefore, a basketball has a volume of 381.51 cubic inches. If you used the π key on your calculator, your answer would be 381.7035074.

EXAMPLE 8 Find the height of a right circular cylinder if its volume is 904.32 cubic inches and its radius is 6 inches (Fig. 3.5)

Solution: $V = \pi r^2 h$

$904.32 = (3.14)(6)^2 h$

$904.32 = (3.14)(36)h$

$904.32 = 113.04h$

$\dfrac{904.32}{113.04} = \dfrac{113.04h}{113.04}$

$8 = h$

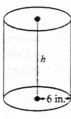

FIGURE 3.5

Thus, the height is 8 inches.

Let us do one more problem that involves evaluating a formula.

EXAMPLE 9   The number of diagonals, d, in a polygon of n sides is given by the formula $d = \frac{1}{2}n^2 - \frac{3}{2}n$.

(a) How many diagonals does a quadrilateral (4 sides) have?

(b) How many diagonals does an octagon (8 sides) have?

Check: for (a)

Solution: (a) $n = 4$ (b) $n = 8$

$d = \dfrac{1}{2}(4)^2 - \dfrac{3}{2}(4)$ $d = \dfrac{1}{2}(8)^2 - \dfrac{3}{2}(8)$

$= \dfrac{1}{2}(16) - 6$ $= \dfrac{1}{2}(64) - 12$

$= 8 - 6 = 2$ $= 32 - 12 = 20$

Solving for a Variable in a Formula or Equation

3 Often in this course and in other mathematics and science courses, you will be given an equation or formula solved for one variable and have to solve it for a different variable. We will now learn how to do this. This material will reinforce what you learned about solving equations in Chapter 2. We will use the procedures learned here to solve problems in many other sections of the text.

To solve for a variable in a formula, treat each of the quantities, except the one you are solving for, as if they were constants. Then solve for the desired variable by isolating it on one side of the equation, as you did in Chapter 2.

EXAMPLE 10   Solve the formula $A = lw$ for w.

Solution: We must get w by itself on one side of the equation. We begin by removing the l from the right side of the equation to isolate the w.

$A = lw$

$\dfrac{A}{l} = \dfrac{lw}{l}$ **Divide both sides of the equation by l.**

$\dfrac{A}{l} = w$

EXAMPLE 11 Solve the formula $P = 2l + 2w$ for l.

Solution: We must get l all by itself on one side of the equation. We begin by removing the $2w$ from the right side of the equation to isolate the term containing the l.

$$P = 2l + 2w$$
$$P - 2w = 2l + 2w - 2w \qquad \text{Subtract } 2w \text{ from both sides of the equation.}$$
$$P - 2w = 2l$$
$$\frac{P - 2w}{2} = \frac{2l}{2} \qquad \text{Divide both sides of the equation by 2.}$$
$$\frac{P - 2w}{2} = l \qquad \left(\text{or } l = \frac{P}{2} - w\right)$$

EXAMPLE 12 An equation we use in Chapter 7 is $y = mx + b$. Solve for m.

Solution: We must get the m all by itself on one side of the equal sign.

$$y = mx + b$$
$$y - b = mx + b - b \qquad \text{Subtract } b \text{ from both sides of the equation.}$$
$$y - b = mx$$
$$\frac{y - b}{x} = \frac{mx}{x} \qquad \text{Divide both sides of the equation by } x.$$
$$\frac{y - b}{x} = m \qquad \left(\text{or } m = \frac{y}{x} - \frac{b}{x}\right)$$

EXAMPLE 13 Solve the simple interest formula $i = prt$ for p.

Solution: We must isolate the p. Since p is multiplied by both r and t, we divide both sides of the equation by rt.

$$i = prt$$
$$\frac{i}{rt} = \frac{prt}{rt}$$
$$\frac{i}{rt} = p$$

In Chapter 7 when discussing graphing we will need to solve many equations for the variable y. This procedure is illustrated in Example 14.

EXAMPLE 14 **(a)** Solve the equation $2x + 3y = 12$ for y.

(b) Find the value of y when $x = 6$.

Solution: **(a)** Begin by isolating the term containing the variable y.

$$2x + 3y = 12$$

$$2x - 2x + 3y = 12 - 2x \qquad \text{Subtract } 2x \text{ from both sides of equation.}$$

$$3y = 12 - 2x$$

$$\frac{3y}{3} = \frac{12 - 2x}{3} \qquad \text{Divide both sides of equation by 3.}$$

$$y = \frac{12 - 2x}{3} \qquad \left(\text{or } y = \frac{12}{3} - \frac{2x}{3} = 4 - \frac{2}{3}x \right)$$

(b) To find the value of y when x is 6, substitute 6 for x in the equation solved for y in part (a).

$$y = \frac{12 - 2x}{3}$$

$$y = \frac{12 - 2(6)}{3} = \frac{12 - 12}{3} = \frac{0}{3} = 0$$

We see that when $x = 6$, $y = 0$.

Some formulas contain fractions. When a formula contains a fraction, we can eliminate the fraction by multiplying both sides of the equation by the denominator, as illustrated in Example 15.

EXAMPLE 15 Solve the formula $A = \dfrac{m + n}{2}$ for m.

Solution: We begin by multiplying both sides of the equation by 2 to eliminate the fraction. Then we isolate the variable m.

$$A = \frac{m + n}{2}$$

$$2A = 2 \left(\frac{m + n}{2} \right) \qquad \text{Multiply both sides of equation by 2.}$$

$$2A = m + n$$

$$2A - n = m + n - n \qquad \text{Subtract } n \text{ from both sides of equation.}$$

$$2A - n = m$$

Thus, $m = 2A - n$.

Exercise Set 3.1

Use the formula to find the value of the variable indicated. Use a calculator to save time. Round answers off to hundredths.

1. $A = s^2$; find A when $s = 5$.

2. $P = a + b + c$; find P when $a = 4$, $b = 3$, and $c = 7$.

3. $P = 2l + 2w$; find P when $l = 6$ and $w = 5$.

4. $A = \dfrac{1}{2}bh$; find A when $b = 12$ and $h = 8$.

5. $A = \frac{1}{2}h(b + d)$; find A when $h = 6$, $b = 18$, and $d = 24$

6. $A = \pi r^2$; find A when $r = 6$. Use $\pi = 3.14$.

7. $C = 2\pi r$; find C when $r = 2$. Use $\pi = 3.14$.

8. $p = i^2 r$; find r when $p = 4000$ and $i = 2$.

9. $A = \frac{1}{2}bh$; find h when $A = 30$ and $b = 6$.

10. $V = \frac{1}{3}Bh$; find h when $V = 40$ and $B = 12$.

11. $V = lwh$; find l when $V = 18$, $w = 1$ and $h = 3$.

12. $T = \frac{RS}{R + S}$; find T when $R = 50$ and $S = 50$.

13. $A = P(1 + rt)$; find A when $P = 1000$, $r = 0.08$, and $t = 1$.

14. $P = 2l + 2w$; find l when $P = 28$ and $w = 6$.

15. $M = \frac{a + b}{2}$; find b when $M = 36$ and $a = 16$.

16. $F = \frac{9}{5}C + 32$; find F when $C = 10$.

17. $C = \frac{5}{9}(F - 32)$; find C when $F = 41$.

18. $z = \frac{x - m}{s}$; find z when $x = 115$, $m = 100$, and $s = 15$.

19. $z = \frac{x - m}{s}$; find x when $z = 2$, $m = 50$, and $s = 5$.

20. $z = \frac{x - m}{s}$; find s when $z = 3$, $x = 80$, and $m = 59$.

21. $K = \frac{1}{2}mv^2$; find m when $K = 288$ and $v = 6$.

22. $A = P(1 + rt)$; find r when $A = 1500$, $t = 1$, and $P = 1000$.

23. $V = \pi r^2 h$; find h when $V = 678.24$, and $r = 6$. Use $\pi = 3.14$.

24. $V = \frac{4}{3}\pi r^3$; find V when $r = 6$. Use $\pi = 3.14$.

Solve each equation for y; then find the value of y for the given value of x. See Example 14.

25. $2x + y = 8$, when $x = 2$.

26. $6x + 2y = -12$, when $x = -3$.

27. $2x = 6y - 4$, when $x = 10$.

28. $-3x - 5y = -10$, when $x = 0$.

29. $2y = 6 - 3x$, when $x = 2$.

30. $15 = 3y - x$, when $x = 3$.

31. $-4x + 5y = -20$, when $x = 4$.

32. $3x - 2y = -18$, when $x = -1$.

33. $-3x = 18 - 6y$, when $x = 0$.

34. $-12 = -2x - 3y$, when $x = -2$.

35. $-8 = -x - 2y$, when $x = -4$.

36. $2x + 5y = 20$, when $x = -5$.

Solve for the variable indicated.

37. $d = rt$, for t

38. $d = rt$, for r

39. $i = prt$, for p

40. $i = prt$, for r

41. $C = \pi d$, for d

42. $V = lwh$, for w

43. $A = \frac{1}{2}bh$, for b

44. $E = IR$, for I

45. $P = 2l + 2w$, for w

46. $PV = KT$, for T

47. $4n + 3 = m$, for n

48. $3t - 4r = 25$, for t

49. $y = mx + b$, for b

50. $y = mx + b$, for x

51. $I = P + Prt$, for r

52. $A = \frac{m + d}{2}$, for m

53. $A = \frac{m + 2d}{3}$, for d

54. $R = \frac{l + 3w}{2}$, for w

55. $d = a + b + c$, for b

56. $A = \frac{a + b + c}{3}$, for b

57. $ax + by = c$, for y

58. $ax + by + c = 0$, for y

59. $V = \pi r^2 h$, for h

60. $V = \frac{1}{3}\pi r^2 h$, for h

Use the formula in Example 9, $d = \frac{1}{2}n^2 - \frac{3}{2}n$, to find the number of diagonals in a figure with the given number of sides.

61. 10 sides   **62.** 6 sides

Use the formula $C = \frac{5}{9}(F - 32)$ to find the Celsius temperature (C) equivalent to the given Fahrenheit temperature (F).

63. $F = 50°$ **64.** $F = 86°$

Use the formula $F = \frac{9}{5}C + 32$, to find the Fahrenheit temperature (F) equivalent to the given Celsius temperature (C).

65. $C = 35°$ **66.** $C = 10°$

In chemistry the ideal gas law is $P = KT/V$, where P is pressure, T is temperature, V is volume, and K is a constant. Find the missing quantity.

67. $T = 10, K = 1, V = 1$

68. $T = 30, P = 3, K = 0.5$

69. $P = 80, T = 100, V = 5$

70. $P = 100, K = 2, V = 6$

The sum of the first n even numbers can be found by the formula $S = n^2 + n$. Find the sum of the numbers indicated.

71. First 5 even numbers.

72. First 10 even numbers.

In Exercises 73 through 76, use the simple interest formula. See Examples 1 and 2.

73. Mr. Thongsophaporn borrowed $4000 for 3 years at 12% simple interest per year. How much interest did he pay?

74. Ms. Rodriguez lent her brother $4000 for a period of 2 years. At the end of the 2 years, her brother repaid the $4000 plus $640 interest. What simple interest rate did her brother pay?

75. Ms. Levy invested a certain amount of money in a savings account paying 7% simple interest per year.

When she withdrew her money at the end of 3 years, she received $1050 in interest. How much money did Ms. Levy place in the savings account?

76. Mr. O'Connor borrowed $6000 at $7\frac{1}{2}$% simple interest per year. When he withdrew his money, he received $1800 in interest. How long had he left his money in the account?

Use the formulas given in Tables 3.1, 3.2, and 3.3 to work Exercises 77–90. See Examples 3–8.

77. Find the perimeter of a triangle whose sides are 5 inches, 12 inches, and 13 inches.

78. Find the area of a rectangle whose length is 9 inches and whose width is 4 inches.

79. Find the area of a triangle whose base is 6 centimeters and whose height is 8 centimeters.

80. Find the perimeter of a rectangle whose length is 5 meters and whose width is 3 meters.

81. Find the area of a circle whose radius is 4 inches. Use 3.14 for π.

82. Find the area of a circle whose diameter is 6 centimeters.

83. Find the circumference of a circle whose diameter is 8 inches.

84. Find the area of a trapezoid whose height is 2 feet and whose bases are 6 feet and 4 feet.

85. The area of the smallest post office in America (in Ochopee, Florida) is 48 square feet. If the length of the post office is 6 feet, find the width of the post office.

86. A sail on a sailboat is in the shape of a triangle. If the area of the sail is 36 square feet and the height of the sail is 12 feet, find the base of the sail.

87. The largest banyon tree in the continental United States is at the Edison House in Fort Myers, Florida. The circumference of the aerial roots of the tree is 390 feet. Find **(a)** the radius of the aerial roots to the nearest tenth of a foot, and **(b)** the diameter of the aerial roots to the nearest tenth of a foot.

See Exercise 87.

88. Donovan's garden is in the shape of a trapezoid. If the height of the trapezoid is 12 meters, one base is 15 meters, and the area is 126 square meters, find the length of the other base..

89. An oil drum has a height of 4 feet and a diameter of 22 inches. Find the volume of the drum in cubic inches.

90. Find the volume of an ice cream cone (cone only) if its diameter is 3 inches and its height is 5 inches.

91. By using any formula for area, explain why area is measured in square units.

CUMULATIVE REVIEW EXERCISES

[1.9] **94.** Evaluate $[4(12 \div 2^2 - 3)^2]^2$.

[2.6] **95.** A stable has 4 Morgan and 6 Arabian horses. Find the ratio of Arabians to Morgans.

96. It takes 3 minutes to siphon 25 gallons of water out of a swimming pool. How long will it take to empty a

92. By using any formula for volume, explain why volume is measured in cubic units.

93. (a) Consider the formula for the circumference of a circle, $C = 2\pi r$. If you solve this formula for π, what will you obtain?

(b) If you take the ratio of the circumference of a circle to its diameter, about what numerical value will you obtain? Explain how you determined your answer.

(c) Carefully draw a circle, make it at least 4 inches in diameter. Use a piece of string and a ruler to determine the circumference and diameter of the circle. Find the ratio of the circumference to the diameter. When you divide the circumference by the diameter, what value do you obtain?

13,500-gallon swimming pool by siphoning? Write a proportion that can be used to solve the problem, and then find the desired value.

[2.7] **97.** Solve $2(x - 4) \geq 3x + 9$

Group Activity/ Challenge Problems

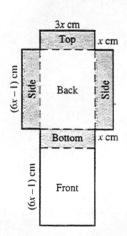

1. (a) Using the formulas presented in this section, write an equation in d that can be used to find the shaded area in the figure shown.

(b) Find the shaded area when $d = 4$ feet.

(c) Find the shaded area when $d = 6$ feet.

2. A cereal box is to be made by folding the cardboard along the dashed lines as shown in the figure on the left.

(a) Using the formula

$$\text{volume} = \text{length} \cdot \text{width} \cdot \text{height}$$

write an equation for the volume of the box.

(b) Find the volume of the box when $x = 7$ cm.

(c) Write an equation for the surface area of the box.

(d) Find the surface area when $x = 7$ cm.

3. Earth's diameter is 3963 miles and the moon's diameter is 2160 miles. The moon travels in an elliptical orbit around the Earth. From the center of Earth to the center of the moon the minimum distance is 221,463 miles and the maximum distance is 252,710 miles. Assuming that Earth and the moon are spheres, find **(a)** the nearest approach of their surfaces, **(b)** the farthest approach of their surfaces, and **(c)** the circumference of the moon.

4. The Pantheon is an ancient building in Rome constructed about A.D. 126. It is shaped like a circular cylinder with a dome on top. The outside circumference of the cylinder is about 446 feet.

(a) Find the radius and diameter of the cylindrical part of the Pantheon.

(b) If the walls of the Pantheon are 4 feet thick, find the inside diameter of the floor of the Pantheon.

(c) Find the surface area of the marble floor inside the Pantheon.

(d) If the height of the cylindrical part of the Pantheon (excluding the domed portion) is 120 feet, find its inside volume.

3.2   Changing Application Problems into Equations

Tape 5

1 Translate phrases into mathematical expressions.
2 Write expressions involving percent.
3 Express the relationship between two related quantities.
4 Write expressions involving multiplication.
5 Translate application problems into equations.

Translate Phrases into Mathematical Expressions

1 One practical advantage of knowing algebra is that you can use it to solve everyday problems involving mathematics. For algebra to be useful in solving everyday problems, you must first be able to transform application problems into mathematical language. The purpose of this section is to help you take a verbal or word problem and write it as a mathematical equation.

Often the most difficult part of solving an application problem is translating it into an equation. Before you can translate a problem into an equation, you must understand the meaning of certain statements and how they are expressed mathematically. Here are examples of statements represented as algebraic expressions.

Verbal	*Algebraic*
5 more than a number	$x + 5$
a number increased by 3	$x + 3$
7 less than a number	$x - 7$
a number decreased by 12	$x - 12$
twice a number	$2x$
the product of 6 and a number	$6x$
one-eighth of a number	$\frac{1}{8}x$ or $\frac{x}{8}$
a number divided by 3	$\frac{1}{3}x$ or $\frac{x}{3}$
4 more than twice a number	$2x + 4$
5 less than three times a number	$3x - 5$
3 times the sum of a number and 8	$3(x + 8)$
twice the difference of a number and 4	$2(x - 4)$

To give you more practice with the mathematical terms, we will also convert some algebraic expressions into verbal expressions. Often an algebraic expression can be written in several different ways. Following is a list of some of the possible verbal expressions that can be used to represent the given algebraic expression.

Algebraic	*Verbal*
$2x + 3$	Three more than twice a number The sum of twice a number and three Twice a number, increased by three Three added to twice a number
$3x - 4$	Four less than three times a number Three times a number, decreased by four The difference of three times a number and four Four subtracted from three times a number

EXAMPLE 1   Express each phrase as an algebraic expression.

(a) The distance, d, increased by 10 miles.

(b) 6 less than twice the area.

(c) 3 pounds more than four times the weight.

(d) Twice the sum of the height plus 3 feet.

Solution: (a) $d + 10$ (b) $2a - 6$

(c) $4w + 3$ (d) $2(h + 3)$

In Example 1, the letter x (or any other letter) could have been used in place of those selected.

EXAMPLE 2   Write three different verbal statements to represent the following expressions.

(a) $5x - 2$ (b) $2x + 7$

Solution: (a) **1.** Two less than five times a number.

   2. Five times a number, decreased by two.

   3. The difference of five times a number and two.

(b) **1.** Seven more than twice a number.

   2. Two times a number, increased by seven.

   3. The sum of two times a number and seven.

EXAMPLE 3 Write a verbal statement to represent each expression.

   (a) $3x - 4$ **(b)** $3(x - 4)$

Solution: **(a)** One possible statement is: four less than three times a number.

   (b) Three times the difference of a number and four.

Write Expressions Involving Percent

2 Since percents are used so often, you must have a clear understanding of how to write expressions involving percent. Study Example 4 carefully.

EXAMPLE 4 Express each phrase as an algebraic expression.

   (a) The cost increased by 6%.

   (b) The population decreased by 12%.

Solution: **(a)** When shopping we may see a "25% off" sales sign. We assume that this means 25% off *the original cost*, even though this is not stated. This question asks for the cost increased by 6%. We assume that this means the cost increased by 6% of the original cost, and write

$$c + 0.06c$$

original cost ——⌐   increased by   ⌐—— 6% of the original cost

Thus, the answer is $c + 0.06c$.

   (b) Using the same reasoning as in part **(a)**, the answer is $p - 0.12p$.

COMMON STUDENT ERROR In Example 4(a) we asked you to represent a cost increased by 6%. Note the answer is $c + 0.06c$. Often, students write the answer to this question as $c + 0.06$. It is important to realize that a percent of a quantity must always be a percent multiplied by some number or letter. Some phrases involving the word percent and the correct and incorrect interpretations follow.

Phrase	*Correct*	*Incorrect*
A $7\frac{1}{2}\%$ sales tax on c dollars	$0.075c$	~~0.075~~
The cost, c, increased by a $7\frac{1}{2}\%$ sales tax	$c + 0.075c$	~~$c + 0.075$~~
The cost, c, reduced by 25%	$c - 0.25c$	~~$c - 0.25$~~

Express Relationships between Two Related Quantities

3 Sometimes in a problem, two numbers are related to each other in a certain way. We often represent the simplest, or most basic number that needs to be expressed, as a variable, and the other as an expression containing that variable. Some examples follow.

Verbal	*One Number*	*Second Number*
two numbers differ by 3	x	$x + 3$
John's age now and John's age in 6 years	x	$x + 6$
one number is six times the other number	x	$6x$
one number is 12% less than the other	x	$x - 0.12x$

Note that often more than one pair of expressions can be used to represent the two numbers. For example, "two numbers differ by 3" can also be expressed as x and $x - 3$. Let us now look at two more verbal statements.

Verbal	*One Number*	*Second Number*
the sum of two numbers is 10	x	$10 - x$
a 25-foot length of wood cut in two pieces	x	$25 - x$

It may not be obvious why in "the sum of two numbers is 10" the two numbers are represented as x and $10 - x$. Suppose that one number is 2; what is the other number? Since the sum is 10, the second number must be $10 - 2$ or 8. Suppose that one number is 6; the second number must be $10 - 6$, or 4. In general, if the first number is x, the second number must be $10 - x$. Note that the sum of x and $10 - x$ is 10 (Fig. 3.6).

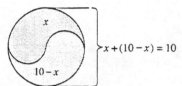

FIGURE 3.6

Consider the phrase "a 25-foot length of wood cut in two pieces." If we call one length x, then the other length must be $25 - x$. For example, if one length is 6 feet, the other length must be $25 - 6$ or 19 feet, (Fig. 3.7).

EXAMPLE 5 For each relationship select a variable to represent one quantity and state what that quantity represents. Then express the second quantity in terms of the variable.

(a) A boy is 15 years older than his brother.

(b) The speed of one car is 1.4 times the speed of another.

(c) Two business partners share $75.

(d) John has $5 more than three times the amount that Dee has.

(e) The length of a rectangle is 3 feet less than four times its width.

(f) A number is increased by 6%.

Solution:

(a) Let x be the age of the younger brother; then $x + 15$ is the age of the older brother.

(b) Let s be the speed of the slower car; then $1.4s$ is the speed of the faster car.

(c) Let d be the amount in dollars one partner receives; then $75 - d$ is the amount in dollars the other partner receives.

(d) Let d be Dee's money in dollars; then $3d + 5$ is John's money in dollars.

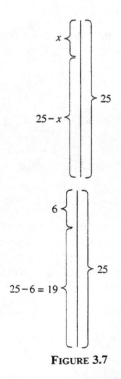

FIGURE 3.7

(e) Let w be the width of the rectangle; then $4w - 3$ is the length of the rectangle.

(f) Let n be the number. Then that number increased by 6% is $n + 0.06n$.

Write Expressions Involving Multiplication

4 Consider the statement "the cost of 3 items at \$5 each." How would you represent this quantity using mathematical symbols? You would probably reason that the cost would be 3 times \$5 and write $3 \cdot 5$ or $3(5)$.

Now consider the statement "the cost of x items at \$5 each." How would you represent this statement using mathematical symbols? If you use the same reasoning, you might write $x \cdot 5$ or $x(5)$. Another way to write this product is $5x$. Thus, the cost of x items at \$5 each could be represented as $5x$.

Finally, consider the statement "the cost of x items at y dollars each." How would you represent this statement using mathematical symbols? Following the reasoning used in the previous two illustrations, you might write $x \cdot y$ or $x(y)$. Since these products can be written as xy, the cost of x items at y dollars each can be represented as xy.

EXAMPLE 6 Write each of the following as an algebraic expression.

(a) The cost of purchasing x items at \$2 each.

(b) A 5% commission on x dollars in sales.

(c) The number of calories in x potato chips, where each potato chip has 8 calories.

(d) The increase in population in n years for a city growing at a rate of 300 per year.

(e) The distance traveled in t hours when 55 miles are traveled each hour.

Solution:

(a) We can reason like this: one item would cost $1(2)$ dollars, two items would cost $2(2)$ dollars, three items $3(2)$, four items $4(2)$, and so on. Continuing this reasoning process, we can see that x items would cost $x(2)$ or $2x$ dollars.

(b) A 5% commission on \$1 sales would be $0.05(1)$, on \$2 sales $0.05(2)$, on \$3 sales $0.05(3)$, on \$4 sales $0.05(4)$, and so on. Therefore, the commission on sales of x dollars would be $0.05(x)$ or $0.05x$.

(c) $8x$

(d) $300n$

(e) $55t$

EXAMPLE 7 A slice of white bread contains 65 calories and a slice of whole-wheat bread contains 55 calories. Write an algebraic expression to represent the total number of calories in x slices of white and y slices of whole-wheat bread.

Solution: x slices of white bread contain $65x$ calories.

y slices of whole-wheat bread contain $55y$ calories.

Together they contain $65x + 55y$ calories.

EXAMPLE 8   Write an algebraic expression for each phrase.

(a) The number of ounces in x pounds.

(b) The number of cents in a dimes and b nickels.

(c) The number of seconds in x hours, y minutes, and z seconds (3600 seconds = 1 hour).

Solution:

(a) Since each pound contains 16 ounces, x pounds is $16 \cdot x$ or $16x$ ounces.

(b) $10a + 5b$

(c) $3600x + 60y + z$

Some terms that we will be using are consecutive integers, consecutive even integers, and consecutive odd integers. **Consecutive integers** are integers that differ by 1 unit. For example, the integers 6 and 7 are consecutive integers. Two consecutive integers may be represented as x and $x + 1$. **Consecutive even integers** are even integers that differ by 2 units. For example, 6 and 8 are consecutive even integers. **Consecutive odd integers** are odd integers that differ by 2 units. For example, 7 and 9 are consecutive odd integers. Two consecutive even integers, or two consecutive odd integers, may be represented as x and $x + 2$.

Translate Application Problems into Equations

5 The word *is* in a verbal problem often means *is equal to* and is represented by an equal sign. Some examples of verbal problems written as equations follow:

Verbal	*Equation*
6 more than twice a number *is* 4	$2x + 6 = 4$
a number decreased by 4 *is* 3 more than twice the number	$x - 4 = 2x + 3$
the product of two consecutive integers *is* 56	$x(x + 1) = 56$
one number is 4 more than three times the other number; their sum *is* 60	$x + (3x + 4) = 60$
a number increased by 15% *is* 120	$x + 0.15x = 120$
the sum of two consecutive odd integers *is* 24	$x + (x + 2) = 24$

Now let us translate some equations into verbal statements. Some examples of equations written as verbal statements follow. We will write only two verbal statements for each equation, but remember there are other ways these equations can be written.

Equation	*Verbal*
$3x - 4 = 4x + 3$	Four less than three times a number *is* three more than four times the number.
	Three times a number, decreased by four *is* four times the number, increased by three.
$3(x - 2) = 6x - 4$	Three times the difference of a number and two *is* four less than six times the number.
	The product of three and the difference of a number and two *is* six times the number, decreased by four.

EXAMPLE 9   Write two verbal statements to represent the equation $x - 2 = 3x - 5$.

Solution:

1. A number decreased by two *is* five less than three times the number.

2. The difference of a number and two *is* the difference of three times the number and five.

EXAMPLE 10   Write a verbal statement to represent the equation $x + 2(x - 4) = 6$.

Solution: The sum of a number and twice the difference of the number and four *is* six.

EXAMPLE 11   Write each problem as an equation.

(a) One number is four less than twice the other. Their sum is 14.

(b) For two consecutive integers, the sum of the smaller and three times the larger is 23.

Solution:

(a) First, express the two numbers in terms of the variable.

Let x = one number

then $2x - 4$ = second number

Now we write the equation using the information given.

First number + second number = 14

$$x + (2x - 4) = 14$$

(b) First, express the two consecutive integers in terms of the variable.

Let x = smaller consecutive integer

then $x + 1$ = larger consecutive integer

Now we write the equation using the information given.

Smaller + three times the larger = 23

$$x + 3(x + 1) = 23$$

EXAMPLE 12   Write the following problem as an equation. One train travels 3 miles more than twice the distance another train travels. The total distance traveled by both trains is 800 miles.

Solution: First express the distance traveled by each train in terms of the variable.

Let x = distance traveled by one train

then $2x + 3$ = distance traveled by second train

Now write the equation using the information given.

distance of train 1 + distance of train 2 = total distance

$$x + (2x + 3) = 800$$

EXAMPLE 13   Express each of the following as an equation.

(a) The cost of renting a snow blower for x days at \$12 per day is \$60.

(b) The population of the town of Newton is increasing at a rate of 500 people per year. The increase in population in t years is 2500.

(c) The distance Dawn and Jack traveled for x days at 600 miles per day is 1500 miles.

(d) The number of cents in d dimes is 120.

Solution: (a) $12x = 60$ (b) $500t = 2500$

(c) $600x = 1500$ (d) $10d = 120$

Exercise Set 3.2

Write as an algebraic expression.

1. Five more than a number.
2. Seven less than a number.
3. Four times a number.
4. The product of a number and eight
5. 70% of a number x.
6. 8% of a number y.
7. A 10% sales tax on a piano costing c dollars.
8. A $7\frac{1}{2}$% sales tax on a car costing p dollars.
9. The 16% of the U.S. population, p, who do not receive adequate nourishment.
10. Only 7% of all U.S. tires, t, are recycled.
11. Three less than six times a number.
12. Six times the diffference of a number and 3.
13. Seven plus three-fourths of a number.
14. Four times a number, decreased by two.
15. Twice the sum of a number and 8.
16. Seventeen decreased by x.

17. The cost of purchasing x rolls of electrical tape at \$4 each.
18. The rental fee for subscribing to Home Box Office for x months at \$12 per month.
19. The cost in dollars of traveling x miles at 23 cents per mile.
20. The distance traveled in t hours when traveling 30 miles per hour.
21. The cost of renting a mailbox for b months at a cost of \$8.20 per month.
22. The cost of waste disposal for y months at \$16 per month.
23. The population growth of a city in n years if the city is growing at a rate of 300 persons per year.
24. The number of calories in x grams of carbohydrates if each gram of carbohydrate contains 4 calories.
25. The number of cents in x quarters.
26. The number of cents in x quarters and y dimes.
27. The number of inches in x feet.

28. The number of inches in x feet and y inches.

29. The number of ounces in c pounds.

30. The number of ounces in c pounds and d ounces.

31. An average chicken egg contains 275 milligrams (mg) of cholesterol and an ounce of chicken contains about 25 mg of cholesterol. Write an expression for the amount of cholesterol in x chicken eggs and y ounces of chicken.

32. According to U.S. guidelines, each gram of carbohydrates contains 4 calories, each gram of protein contains 4 calories, and each gram of fat contains 9 calories. Write an expression for the number of calories in a serving of a product that contains x grams of carbohydrates, y grams of protein, and z grams of fat.

Express as a verbal statement. (There are many acceptable answers.)

33. $x - 6$

34. $x + 3$

35. $4x + 1$

36. $3x - 4$

37. $5x - 7$

38. $2x - 3$

39. $4x - 2$

40. $5 - x$

41. $2 - 3x$

42. $4 + 6x$

43. $2(x - 1)$

44. $3(x + 2)$

Select a variable to represent one quantity and state what that variable represents. Then express the second quantity in terms of the variable.

45. Eileen's salary is \$45 more than Martin's salary.

46. A boy is 12 years older than his brother.

47. A number is one-third of another.

48. Two consecutive integers.

49. Two consecutive even integers.

50. One hundred dollars divided between two people.

51. Two numbers differ by 12.

52. A number is 5 less than four times another number.

53. A number is 3 more than one-half another number.

54. A Cadillac costs 1.7 times as much as a Ford.

55. A number is 4 less than three times another number.

56. An 80-foot tree cut into two pieces.

57. Two consecutive odd integers.

58. A number and the number increased by 12%.

59. A number and the number decreased by 15%.

60. The cost of an item and the cost increased by a 7% sales tax.

Use the given variable to represent one quantity. Express the second quantity in terms of the first.

61. The cost of an item, c, and the cost decreased by 10%.

62. The president's salary, s, and the president's salary increased by 3%.

63. The pollution level, p, and the pollution level reduced by 50%.

64. The federal deficit, d, and the federal deficit reduced by 5%.

65. The world population, w, and double the world population.

66. The sales of compact disks, s, and the sales cut in half.

67. The mileage of a car, m, and the mileage increased by 15%.

68. The number of students, n, earning a grade of A in this course, and that number increased by 100%.

Express as an equation.

69. One number is five times another. The sum of the two numbers is 18.

70. Marie is 6 years older than Denise. The sum of their ages is 48.

71. The sum of two consecutive integers is 47.

72. The product of two consecutive even integers is 48.

73. Twice a number, decreased by 8 is 12.

74. For two consecutive integers, the sum of the smaller and twice the larger is 29.

75. One-fifth of the sum of a number and 10 is 150.

76. One train travels six times as far as another. The total distance traveled by both trains is 700 miles.

77. One train travels 8 miles less than twice the other. The total distance traveled by both trains is 1000 miles.

78. One number is 3 greater than six times the other. Their product is 408.

79. A number increased by 8% is 92.

80. The cost of a car plus a 7% tax is $13,600.

81. The cost of a jacket at a 25%-off sale is $65.

82. The cost of a meal plus a 15% tip is $18.

83. The cost of a videocassette recorder reduced by 20% is $215.

84. The product of a number and the number plus 5% is 120.

85. One number is 3 less than twice another number. Their sum is 21.

86. The cost of renting a phone at a cost of $2.37 per month for x months is $27.

87. The distance traveled by a car going 40 miles per hour for t hours is 180 miles.

88. The cost of traveling x miles at 23 cents per mile is $12.80.

89. The number of calories in y french fried potatoes at 15 calories per french fry is 215.

90. Milltown is increasing at a rate of 200 per year. The increase in population in t years is 2400.

91. The number of cents in q quarters is 150.

92. The number of ounces in p pounds is 64.

In Exercises 93–104, express each equation as a verbal statement. (There are many acceptable answers.)

93. $x + 3 = 6$

94. $x - 5 = 2x$

95. $3x - 1 = 2x + 4$

96. $x - 3 = 2x + 3$

97. $4(x - 1) = 6$

98. $3x + 2 = 2(x - 3)$

99. $5x + 6 = 6x - 1$

100. $x - 3 = 2(x + 1)$

101. $x + (x + 4) = 8$

102. $x + (2x + 1) = 5$

103. $2x + (x + 3) = 5$

104. $2x - (x + 3) = 6$

105. Explain why the cost of purchasing x items at 6 dollars each is represented as $6x$.

106. Explain why the cost of purchasing x items at y dollars each is represented as xy.

CUMULATIVE REVIEW EXERCISES

[2.6] *Write a proportion that can be used to solve each problem. Solve each problem and find the desired values.*

107. A recipe for chicken stew calls for $\frac{1}{2}$ teaspoon of thyme for each pound of poultry. If the poultry for the stew weighs 6.7 pounds, how much thyme should be used?

108. Melinda mixes water with dry cat chow for her cat Max. If the directions say to mix 1 cup of water with every 3 cups of dry cat chow, how much water will Melinda add to $\frac{1}{2}$ cup of dry cat chow?

[3.1] **109.** $P = 2l + 2w$; find l when $P = 40$ and $w = 5$

110. Solve $3x - 2y = 6$ for y. Then find the value of y when x has a value of 6.

Group Activity/ Challenge Problems

1. (a) Write an algebraic expression for the number of seconds in d days, h hours, m minutes, and s seconds.

(b) Use the expression found in part **(a)** to determine the number of seconds in 4 days, 6 hours, 15 minutes, and 25 seconds.

2. At the time of this writing, the toll for southbound traffic on the Golden Gate Bridge is $1.50 per vehicle axle (there is no toll for northbound traffic).

(a) If the number of 2-, 3-, 4-, 5-, and 6-axle vehicles are represented with the letters r, s, t, u, and v, respectively, write an *expression* that represents the daily revenue of the Golden Gate Bridge Authority.

(b) Write an *equation* that can be used to determine the daily revenue, *d*.

In Exercises 3–7, (a) write down the quantity you are being asked to find and represent this quantity with a varible, and (b) write an equation containing that variable that can be used to solve the problem. Do not solve the equation. We will discuss problems like those that follow in the next section.

3. An average bath uses 30 gallons of water and an average shower uses 6 gallons of water per minute. How long a shower would result in the same water usage as a bath?

4. A subway token costs $1.20. It takes one token to go to work and one token to return from work daily. A monthly subway pass costs $50 and provides for unlimited use of the subway. How long would it take for the daily subway cost to equal the cost of the monthly pass?

5. The average American produces 40,000 pounds of carbon dioxide each year by driving a car, running air conditioners, lighting, and using appliances and other items that require the burning of fossil fuels. How long would it take for the average American to produce 1,000,000 pounds of carbon dioxide?

6. An employee has a choice of two salary plans. Plan A provides a weekly salary of $200 plus a 5% commission on the employee's sales. Plan B provides a weekly salary of $100 plus an 8% commission on the employee's sales. What must be the weekly sales for the two plans to give the same weekly salary?

7. The cost of renting an 18-foot truck from Mertz is $20 a day plus 60 cents a mile. The cost of renting a similar truck from U-Hail is $30 a day plus 45 cents a mile. How far would you have to drive the rental truck in 1 day for the total cost to be the same with both companies?

3.3   Solving Application Problems

1 Set up and solve verbal problems.
2 Selecting a mortgage.
3 Solving application problems containing large numbers.

Tape 5

There are many types of application problems that can be solved using algebra. In this section we introduce several types. In Section 3.4, we introduce additional types of application problems. Application problems are also presented in many other sections and exercise sets throughout the book. Your instructor may not have time to cover all the applications given in this book. If not, you may still wish to spend a little time on your own reading those problems just to get a feel for the types of applications presented.

To be prepared for this section, you must understand the material presented in Section 3.2. The best way to learn to set up a verbal or word problem is to practice. The more verbal problems you study and attempt, the easier it will become to solve them.

Set Up and Solve Verbal Problems

1 We often transform verbal problems into mathematical terms without realizing it. For example, if you need 3 cups of milk for a recipe and the measuring cup holds only 2 cups, you reason that you need 1 additional cup of milk after the initial 2 cups. You may not realize it, but when you do this simple operation, you are using algebra.

Let x = number of additional cups of milk needed

Thought process: (initial 2 cups) + $\left(\begin{array}{c}\text{number of}\\\text{additional cups}\end{array}\right)$ = total milk needed

Equation to represent problem: $2 + x = 3$

When we solve for x, we get 1 cup of milk.

You probably said to yourself: Why do I have to go through all this when I know that the answer is $3 - 2$ or 1 cup? When you perform this subtraction, you have mentally solved the equation $2 + x = 3$.

$$2 + x = 3$$
$$2 - 2 + x = 3 - 2$$
$$x = 3 - 2$$
$$x = 1$$

Let's look at another example.

EXAMPLE 1 Suppose that you are at a supermarket, and your purchases so far total $13.20. In addition to groceries, you wish to purchase as many packages of gum as possible, but you have a total of only $18. If a package of gum costs $1.15, how many can you purchase?

Solution: How can we represent this problem as an equation? We might reason as follows. We need to find the number of packages of gum. Let us call this unknown quantity x.

Let x = number of packages of gum

Thought process: cost of groceries + cost of gum = total cost

Substitute $13.20 for the cost of groceries and $18 for the total cost to get

$$13.20 + \text{cost of gum} = 18$$

At this point you might be tempted to replace the cost of gum with the letter x. But look at what x represents. The variable x represents the *number* of packages of gum, *not the cost of the gum*. In Section 3.2 we learned that the cost of x packages of gum at $1.15 per package is $1.15x$. Now substitute the cost of the x packages of gum, $1.15x$, into the equation to obtain

Equation to represent problem: $13.20 + 1.15x = 18$

When we solve this equation, we obtain $x = 4.2$ packages (to the nearest tenth). Since you cannot purchase a part of a pack of gum, only 4 packages of gum can be purchased.

Now let us look at the procedure for setting up and solving a word problem.

To Solve a Word Problem

1. Read the question carefully.
2. If possible, draw a sketch to help visualize the problem.
3. Determine which quantity you are being asked to find. Choose a letter to represent this unknown quantity. Write down exactly what this letter represents. If there is more than one unknown quantity, represent all unknown quantities in terms of this variable.

4. Write the word problem as an equation.
5. Solve the equation for the unknown quantity.
6. Answer the question or questions asked.
7. Check the solution in the original stated problem.

Let us now set up and solve some word problems using this procedure.

EXAMPLE 2 Two subtracted from four times a number is 10. Find the number.

Solution: We are asked to find the number. We designate the unknown number by the letter x.
Let x = unknown number.

2 subtracted
from 4 times
a number is 10

Write the equation:	$4x - 2 = 10$
Solve the equation:	$4x = 12$
Answer the question:	$x = 3$

Check: Substitute 3 for the number in the original problem. Two subtracted from four times a number is 10.

$$4(3) - 2 = 10$$
$$10 = 10 \qquad \textbf{true}$$

Since the solution checks, the unknown number is 3.

EXAMPLE 3 The sum of two numbers is 17. Find the two numbers if the larger is five more than twice the smaller number.

Solution: We are asked to find *two* numbers. We will call the smaller number x. Then we will represent the larger number in terms of x.

$$\text{Let } x = \text{smaller number}$$
$$\text{then } 2x + 5 = \text{larger number}$$

The sum of the two numbers is 17. Therefore, we write the equation

$$\text{smaller number} + \text{larger number} = 17$$
$$x + (2x + 5) = 17$$

Now solve the equation.

$$3x + 5 = 17$$
$$3x = 12$$
$$x = 4$$

Answer the questions:

$$\text{smaller number} = 4$$
$$\text{larger number} = 2x + 5$$
$$= 2(4) + 5 = 13$$

Check: The sum of the two numbers $= 17$

$$4 + 13 = 17$$
$$17 = 17 \quad \textbf{true}$$

EXAMPLE 4 Doug and Mila's roller blade company manufactures 10,000 pairs of roller blades each year. They wish to increase production by 1250 pairs of roller blades each year until their yearly production is 25,000 pairs. How long will it take for them to reach their goal?

Solution: We are asked to find the number of years.

Let $n = $ number of years

then $1250n = $ increase in production over n years

$$(\text{present production}) + \left(\begin{array}{c}\text{increased production} \\ \text{over } n \text{ years}\end{array}\right) = \text{future production}$$

$$10,000 + 1250n = 25,000$$
$$1250n = 15,000$$
$$n = \frac{15,000}{1250}$$
$$n = 12 \text{ years}$$

A check will show that 12 years is the correct answer.

EXAMPLE 5 A 32-fluid-ounce container of fruit punch contains 3.84 fluid ounces of pure fruit juice. Find the percent by volume of pure fruit juice in the punch.

Solution: We are asked to find the percent of pure juice.

Let $x = $ percent of pure juice

We use the formula

total volume $\times$ percent of pure juice $=$ amount of pure juice

Since 32 is the total volume, x is the percent of pure juice, and 3.84 is the amount of pure juice, the equation is $32x = 3.84$.

$$32x = 3.84$$
$$\frac{32x}{32} = \frac{3.84}{32}$$
$$x = 0.12 \quad \text{or} \quad 12\%$$

Therefore, the punch is 12% pure fruit juice by volume.

EXAMPLE 6   John is considering buying a copier for his small business run from his home. He currently pays 8 cents a copy at his local copy center. A new copier is on sale for $360. How many copies would John need to make at the copy center for the copying cost to equal the cost of the new copier?

Solution: We are asked to find the number of copies.

Let x = number of copies

then $0.08x$ = cost for making x copies

cost for making x copies = cost of the new copier

$$0.08x = 360$$

$$x = \frac{360}{0.08} = 4500$$

Thus, after 4500 copies are made the cost would be equal. Of course, other factors, such as the cost of paper, convenience, and distance to the copy center, must be considered when deciding whether to purchase the copier.

EXAMPLE 7   The cost of renting a Me-Haul 24-foot truck for local moving is $50 a day plus 40 cents a mile. Find the maximum distance that Mrs. Ahmed can travel if she has only $80.

Solution: We are asked to find the number of miles Mrs. Ahmed can drive.

Let x = number of miles

then $0.40x$ = cost of driving x miles

daily cost + mileage cost = total cost

$$50 + 0.40x = 80$$

$$0.40x = 30$$

$$\frac{0.40x}{0.40} = \frac{30}{0.40}$$

$$x = 75$$

Therefore, Mrs. Ahmed can drive 75 miles in one day.

EXAMPLE 8   At A$^+$ Auto the new owner is giving her sales staff a choice of salary plans. Plan 1 is a $200 per week base salary plus a 2% commission on sales. Plan 2 is a straight 8% commission on sales.

(a) Maria must select one of the plans but is not sure of the sales needed for her weekly salary to be the same under the two plans. Can you determine it?

(b) If Maria is certain that she can make $6000 sales per week, which plan should she select?

Solution: **(a)** We are asked to find the dollar sales.

Let x = dollar sales

then $0.02x$ = commission from plan 1 sales

and $0.08x$ = commission from plan 2 sales

$$\text{salary from plan 1} = \text{salary from plan 2}$$
$$\text{base salary} + 2\% \text{ commission} = 8\% \text{ commission}$$
$$200 + 0.02x = 0.08x$$
$$200 = 0.06x$$
$$0.06x = 200$$
$$\frac{0.06x}{0.06} = \frac{200}{0.06}$$
$$x = 3333.33$$

If Maria's sales are about $3333 dollars, both plans would give her about the same salary.

(b) If Maria's sales are $6000, she would earn more weekly by working on straight commission, plan 2. Check this out yourself by computing Maria's salary under both plans and comparing them.

EXAMPLE 9   Allied Airlines wishes to keep its airfare, including a 7% tax, between Dallas, Texas, and Los Angeles, California, at exactly $160. Find the cost of the ticket before tax.

Solution: We are asked to find the cost of the ticket before tax.

Let x = cost of the ticket before tax

then $0.07x$ = tax on the ticket

$$\left(\begin{array}{c}\text{cost of ticket}\\\text{before tax}\end{array}\right) + \left(\begin{array}{c}\text{tax on}\\\text{the ticket}\end{array}\right) = 160$$
$$x + 0.07x = 160$$
$$1.07x = 160$$
$$x = \frac{160}{1.07}$$
$$x = 149.53$$

Thus, if Allied prices the ticket at $149.53, the total cost including a 7% tax will be $160.

EXAMPLE 10   According to a will an estate is to be divided among two grandchildren and two charities. The two grandchildren, Alisha and Rayanna, are each to receive twice as much as each of the two charities, the Red Cross and the Salvation Army. If the estate is valued at $240,000, how much will each grandchild and each charity receive?

Solution: We are asked how much each grandchild and each charity will receive. Since the grandchildren will each receive twice as much as the charities, we will let x represent the amount each charity receives.

Let x = amount each charity receives

then $2x$ = amount each grandchild receives

The total received by the two grandchildren and two charities is $240,000. Thus, the equation we use is:

each charity   each grandchild
receives x receives $2x$

$$x + x \quad + \quad 2x + 2x \quad = 240{,}000$$
$$6x \quad = 240{,}000$$
$$x \quad = \quad 40{,}000$$

Thus, the American Red Cross and Salvation Army will receive $40,000, and each grandchild will receive 2(40,000), or $80,000.

EXAMPLE 11   Mr. and Mrs. Frank plan to install a security system in their house. They have narrowed down their choices to two security dealers: Moneywell and Doile security systems. Moneywell's system costs $3360 to install and their monitoring fee is $17 per month. Doile's equivalent system costs only $2260 to install, but their monitoring fee is $28 per month.

(a) Assuming that their monthly monitoring fees do not change, in how many months would the total cost of Moneywell's and Doile's system be the same?

(b) If both dealers guarantee not to raise monthly fees for 10 years, and if you plan to use the system for 10 years, which system would be the least expensive?

Solution: **(a)** Doile's system has a smaller initial cost ($2260 vs. $3360); however, their monthly monitoring fees are greater ($28 vs. $17). We are asked to find the number of months after which the total cost of the two systems will be the same.

Let n = number of months

then $17n$ = monthly monitoring cost for Moneywell's system for n months

and $28n$ = monthly monitoring cost for Doile's system for n months

total cost of Moneywell = total cost of Doile

$$\left(\begin{array}{c} \text{initial} \\ \text{cost} \end{array} \right) + \left(\begin{array}{c} \text{monthly cost} \\ \text{for } n \text{ months} \end{array} \right) = \left(\begin{array}{c} \text{initial} \\ \text{cost} \end{array} \right) + \left(\begin{array}{c} \text{monthly cost} \\ \text{for } n \text{ months} \end{array} \right)$$

$$3360 + 17n = 2260 + 28n$$
$$1100 + 17n = 28n$$
$$1100 = 11n$$
$$100 = n$$

The total cost would be the same in 100 months or about 8.3 years.

(b) Over a 10-year period Moneywell's system would be less expensive. After 8.3 years Moneywell will be less expensive because of their lower monthly cost. Determine the cost for both Moneywell and Doile for 10 years of use now.

Selecting a Mortgage   **2**   Many of you will purchase a house. Choosing the wrong mortgage can cost you thousands of extra dollars. Table 3.4 is used to determine monthly mortgage payments of principal and interest. The table gives the monthly mortgage payment per $1000 of mortgage at different mortgage rates for various terms of the loan. For example, for a mortgage for 30 years at 7.5%, the monthly payment of principal and interest is $7.00 per $1000 borrowed (circled in table). Thus, for a $50,000 mortgage for 30 years at 7.5% the monthly mortgage payment would be 50 times $7.00 or $350.

$$50(7.00) = \$350$$

TABLE 3.4 ANY BANK, USA: EQUAL MONTHLY PAYMENT TO AMORTIZE A LOAN OF $1,000

Rate	Payment for a Mortgage Period (years) of:				Rate	Payment for a Mortgage Period (years) of:			
(%)	15	20	25	30	(%)	15	20	25	30
4.500	7.65	6.33	5.56	5.07	8.625	9.93	8.76	8.14	7.78
4.625	7.71	6.39	5.63	5.14	8.750	10.00	8.84	8.23	7.87
4.750	7.78	6.46	5.70	5.22	8.875	10.07	8.92	8.31	7.96
4.875	7.84	6.53	5.77	5.29	9.000	10.15	9.00	8.40	8.05
5.000	7.91	6.60	5.85	5.37	9.125	10.22	9.08	8.48	8.14
5.125	7.97	6.67	5.92	5.44	9.250	10.30	9.16	8.57	8.23
5.250	8.04	6.73	6.00	5.52	9.375	10.37	9.24	8.66	8.32
5.375	8.10	6.81	6.07	5.60	9.500	10.45	9.33	8.74	8.41
5.500	8.17	6.88	6.14	5.68	9.625	10.52	9.41	8.83	8.50
5.625	8.24	6.95	6.22	5.76	9.750	10.60	9.49	8.92	8.60
5.750	8.30	7.02	6.29	5.84	9.875	10.67	9.57	9.00	8.69
5.875	8.37	7.09	6.37	5.92	10.000	10.75	9.66	9.09	8.78
6.000	8.44	7.16	6.44	6.00	10.125	10.83	9.74	9.18	8.87
6.125	8.51	7.24	6.52	6.08	10.250	10.90	9.82	9.27	8.97
6.250	8.57	7.31	6.60	6.16	10.375	10.98	9.90	9.36	9.06
6.375	8.64	7.38	6.67	6.24	10.500	11.06	9.99	9.45	9.15
6.500	8.71	7.46	6.75	6.32	10.625	11.14	10.07	9.54	9.25
6.625	8.78	7.53	6.83	6.40	10.750	11.21	10.16	9.63	9.34
6.750	8.85	7.60	6.91	6.49	10.875	11.29	10.24	9.72	9.43
6.875	8.92	7.68	6.99	6.57	11.000	11.37	10.33	9.81	9.53
7.000	8.99	7.76	7.07	6.66	11.125	11.45	10.41	9.90	9.62
7.125	9.06	7.83	7.15	6.74	11.250	11.53	10.50	9.99	9.72
7.250	9.13	7.91	7.23	6.83	11.375	11.61	10.58	10.08	9.81
7.375	9.20	7.98	7.31	6.91	11.500	11.69	10.67	10.17	9.91
7.500	9.28	8.06	7.39	7.00	11.625	11.77	10.76	10.26	10.00
7.625	9.35	8.14	7.48	7.08	11.750	11.85	10.84	10.35	10.10
7.750	9.42	8.21	7.56	7.17	11.875	11.93	10.93	10.44	10.20
7.875	9.49	8.29	7.64	7.26	12.000	12.01	11.02	10.54	10.29
8.000	9.56	8.37	7.72	7.34	12.125	12.09	11.10	10.63	10.39
8.125	9.63	8.45	7.81	7.43	12.250	12.17	11.19	10.72	10.48
8.250	9.71	8.53	7.89	7.52	12.375	12.25	11.28	10.82	10.58
8.375	9.78	8.60	7.97	7.61	12.500	12.33	11.37	10.91	10.68
8.500	9.85	8.68	8.06	7.69					

This payment does not include taxes or insurance, which are sometimes added to the mortgage payment and sometimes paid separately. Also, these figures may be slightly inaccurate because of round-off error.

Sometimes banks charge "points" when they give a loan. One point is 1% of the mortgage. Thus for a $50,000 mortgage, one point is 0.01(50,000) = $500 and 3 points is 0.03(50,000) = $1500.

EXAMPLE 12   Kristen needs a 30-year $50,000 mortgage. Banc One is charging 7.5% with no points and Collier's Bank is charging 7.125% with 3.00 points.

(a) How long would it take for the total cost of both mortgages to be the same?

(b) If Kristen is planning to sell the house after 5 years, which mortgage should she select?

(c) If Kristen is planning on paying off the loan in 30 years, how much will she save by selecting the 7.125% mortgage?

Solution: **(a)** With the 7.5% mortgage, Kristen's monthly payment is 50(7) = $350. With the 7.125% mortgage, Kristen's monthly payment is 50(6.74) = $337. In addition, Kristen must pay 0.03(50,000) = $1500 because of the 3 points.

Let x = number of months when total payments from both mortgages are equal

then $350x$ = monthly payments for x months with 7.5% loan

and $337x$ = monthly payments for x months with 7.125% loan

Now set up an equation and solve.

$$\left(\begin{array}{c} \text{monthly payments} \\ \text{for 7.5\% mortgage} \end{array} \right) = \left(\begin{array}{c} \text{monthly payments} \\ \text{for 7.125\% mortgage} \end{array} \right) + \left(\text{points} \right)$$

$$350x = 337x + 1500$$

$$13x = 1500$$

$$x = 115.4 \text{ months}$$

Thus, the two mortgages would be the same after about 115 months or about 9 years 7 months.

(b) Because of the lower initial cost Banc One's total cost will be lower until about 9 years 7 months. After this, Collier's Bank will have the lower total cost because of their lower monthly payment. For five years Kristen should select the one with the lower initial cost. That is the 7.5% Banc One mortgage.

(c) Over 30 years (360 months) the total cost of each plan is as follows:

7.5%	*7.125%*
350(360) = $126,000	337(360) + 1500 = 121,320 + 1500
	= 122,820

Thus, over 30 years Kristen would save 126,000 − 122,820 = $3180 with the 7.125% Collier's Bank mortgage.

Large Numbers   ❸ **EXAMPLE 13**   In 1990 there were about 800 million hectares of rain forest on the earth (about 32 million square miles). That same year 17 million hectares of rain forest were destroyed (an area about twice the size of Ireland). If the deforestation were to continue at the same rate, when would the rain forest be destroyed completely?

Solution: We are asked to find the number of years when the rain forest would be destroyed.

Let x = number of years

then $17x$ = millions of hectares of rain forest lost in x years

area of rain forest in 1990 − area lost in x years = area remaining

$$800 - 17x = 0$$
$$800 = 17x$$
$$\frac{800}{17} = \frac{17x}{17}$$
$$47 = x$$

Thus, at the current rate the rain forest would be destroyed in about 47 years from 1990, which is the year 2037.

Notice in Example 13 that the numbers given were 800 million and 17 million. Since both numbers were given in millions it was not necessary to write the numbers as 800,000,000 and 17,000,000, respectively, to set up and solve the equation. Had we written the equation as $800,000,000 - 17,000,000x = 0$ and solved this equation we would have obtained the same answer.

Exercise Set 3.3

For Exercises 1–45, set up an equation that can be used to solve the problem. Solve the equation and answer the question asked. Use a calculator where you feel it is appropriate.

1. The sum of two consecutive integers is 45. Find the numbers.

2. The sum of two consecutive even integers is 106. Find the numbers.

3. The sum of two consecutive odd numbers is 68. Find the numbers.

4. One number is 3 more than twice a second number. Their sum is 27. Find the numbers.

5. One number is 5 less than three times a second number. Their sum is 43. Find the numbers.

6. The sum of three consecutive integers is 39. Find the three integers.

7. The sum of three consecutive odd integers is 87. Find the three integers.

8. The sum of the two facing page numbers in an open book is 149. What are the page numbers?

9. The larger of two integers is 8 less than twice the smaller. When the smaller number is subtracted from the larger, the difference is 17. Find the two numbers.

10. The sum of three integers is 29. Find the three numbers if one number is twice the smallest and the third number is 4 more than twice the smallest.

11. In 1993 the most fuel-efficient car on highways was the Geo Metro xFi and the least efficient was the Vector Acromotive V8. The Geo gets 3 miles per gallon (mpg) more than 5 times that of the Vector. Find the number of miles per gallon of each car if the sum of the miles per gallon for the two cars is 69 mpg.

12. The total number of medals won by Norway in the 1994 Winter Olympic games was twice the amount the United States won. If both countries together won 39 medals, how many medals did each team win?

13. The number of operating nuclear reactors in Canada in 1994 is 6 more than 15 times the number in Mexico. If the sum of the nuclear reactors in 1994 in these two countries is 22, find the number of reactors in each country. (The United States presently has 109 of the world's 424 reactors in use today.)

14. A small town has a population of 4000. If its population increases by 200 per year, how long will it be before the population reaches 5800?

15. Caldwell Banker sold a house for Mrs. Sanchez. The amount that Mrs. Sanchez received after the real estate broker subtracted her 6% commission was $65,800. Find the selling price of the house.

16. A 4-ounce glass of table wine has an alcohol content of 0.48 ounce (14 grams). What is the percent alcohol by volume of the wine?

17. An 18-karat gold bracelet weighing 20 grams contains 15 grams of pure gold. What is the percent of pure gold by weight contained in 18-karat gold?

18. It cost Teshanna $5.75 a week to wash and dry her clothing at the corner laundry. If a washer and dryer cost a total of $747.50, how many weeks would it take for Teshanna's laundry cost to equal the cost of purchasing a washer and dryer?

19. The rock group Purple Finger received $1500 plus $2.00 per head for their performance at the Big Mac Arena. If the total they received for their performance was $3100, how many people were in attendance?

20. The cost of renting a truck is $39 a day plus 40 cents per mile. How far can Milt drive in one day if he has only $75?

21. A tennis star was hired to sign autographs at a convention. She was paid $2000 plus 2% of all admission fees collected at the door. If the total amount she received for the day was $2400, find the total amount collected at the door.

22. State College reimburses its employees $40 a day plus 21 cents a mile when they use their own vehicles on college business. If Professor Kohn takes a 1-day trip and is reimbursed $103 how far did she travel?

23. At Ace Warehouse, for a yearly fee of $60 you save 8% of the price of all items purchased in the store. What would be the total Mary would need to spend during the year so that her savings equal the yearly fee?

24. At a one-day 20%-off sale, Tan purchased a hat for $15.99. What is the regular price of the hat?

25. During the 1995 contract negotiations the city school board approved an 8% pay increase for its teachers effective in 1996. If Paul, a first-grade teacher, projects his 1996 annual salary to be $37,800, what is his present salary?

26. Mr. Murphy receives a weekly salary of $210. He also receives a 6% commission on the total dollar volume of all sales he makes. What must his dollar volume be in a week if he is to make a total of $450?

27. Eunice, a hot dog vendor, wishes to price her hot dogs such that the total cost of the hot dog, including a 7% tax, is $1.50. What will be the price of a hot dog before tax?

28. Essex County has an 8% sales tax. How much does Karita's car cost before tax if the total cost of the car plus its sales tax is $12,800?

29. Mr. Wironowski left his estate of $210,000 to his two children and his favorite charity. If each child is to receive three times the amount left to his favorite charity, how much did each child and the charity receive?

30. Ninety-one hours of overtime must be split among four workers. The two younger workers are to be assigned the same number of hours. The third worker is to be assigned twice as much as each of the younger workers. The fourth worker is to be assigned three times as much as each of the younger workers. How much overtime should be assigned to each worker?

31. Presently only about 4000 landfills are operating in the United States (down from 14,000 in 1978). This number is expected to drop by 300 per year. How long will it take for the number of landfills to drop to 2000?

32. Gary Gutchell worked a 55-hour week last week. He is not sure of his hourly rate, but knows that he is paid $1\frac{1}{2}$ times his regular hourly rate for all hours over a 40-hour week. His pay last week was $400. What was his hourly rate?

33. Installing a water-saving showerhead saves about 60% of the water when you shower. If a 10-minute shower with a water-saving showerhead uses 24 gallons of water, how much water would a 10-minute shower without the special showerhead use?

34. The Midtown Tennis Club has two payment plans for its members. Plan 1 has a monthly fee of $20 plus $8 per hour court rental time. Plan 2 has no monthly fee, but court time is $16.25 per hour. If court time is rented in 1-hour intervals, how many hours would you have to play per month so that plan 1 becomes a better buy?

35. The fine for speeding in Boomtown is $5 per mile per hour over the speed limit plus a $15 administrative charge. Michelle received a speeding ticket and had to pay a fine of $65. How many miles per hour over the speed limit was she traveling?

36. Miss Dunn is on vacation and stops at a store to buy some film and other items. Her total bill before tax was $22. After tax the bill came to $23.76. Find the local sales tax rate.

37. The *World Almanac* identifies Punta Gorda, Florida as the fastest-growing metropolitan area in the United States from 1980 to 1990. From 1980 to 1990 the population grew about 90%. The almanac gives the 1990 population as 110,000 people but does not give the 1980 population. Can you find the 1980 population?

38. The city with the largest population loss from 1980 to 1990 according to the *World Almanac* was Gary, Indiana. Gary lost about 23% of its population during

this period. If Gary's 1990 population was about 116,000, find the population of Gary, Indiana in 1980.

39. After Mrs. Egan is seated in a restaurant, she realizes that she has only $20. If from this $20 she must pay a 7% tax and she wishes to leave a 15% tip, what is the maximum price for a meal that she can afford to pay?

40. During the first week of a going-out-of-business sale, the Alpine ski shop reduced the price of all items by 20%. During the second week of the sale, they reduced the price of all items over $100 by an additional $25. If Helga purchases a pair of Head skis during the second week for $231, what is the regular price of the skis?

41. The Holiday Health Club has reduced its annual membership fee by 10%. In addition, if you sign up on a Monday, they will take an additional $20 off the already reduced price. If Jorge purchases a year's membership on a Monday and pays $250, what is the regular membership fee?

42. Refer to Example 11. Assume that Moneywell's security system cost $4200 and their monthly monitoring fee is $16. Also assume that Doile's system cost $2500 and their monthly monitoring fee is $25. When will the total cost of these systems be the same?

43. A chain saw uses a mixture of gasoline and oil. For each part oil, you need 15 parts gasoline. If a total of 4 gallons of the oil–gas mixture is to be made, how much oil and how much gas will need to be mixed?

44. The number of divorces granted in 1992 was 2% higher than in 1991. If 1.215 million divorces were granted in 1992, approximately how many divorces were granted in 1991?

45. The number of marriages performed in the United States in 1992 was 1% lower than in 1991. If the number of marriages in 1992 was 2.362 million, approximately how many marriages were performed in 1991? (See Example 13).

Solve the following problems

46. The SavUmor mail order prescription drug suppliers provide two membership plans. Under plan A you pay an annual $200 membership plus 50% of the manufacturer's list price of each drug. Under plan B you pay a $50 annual membership fee plus 75% of the manufacturer's list price of any drug.

   (a) How much per year must a family's drug bill total for the two plans to result in the same cost?

   (b) If Mr. Renaud's allopurinol treatment has a manufacturer's list price of $7.50 for a month's supply, and Mrs. Renaud's monthly treatment of Premarin and Medroxyprogesterone together have a list price of $48, and they expect to average an additional $10 per month for other prescriptions, which plan would be the least expensive?

47. The Yearstons are considering two banks for a 20-year $50,000 mortgage. M&T is charging 9.50% interest with no points, and Citibank is charging 8.00% interest with 4 points.

    (a) How long would it take for the total cost of the two mortgages to be the same?

    (b) If they plan to live in their house for the 20 years, which mortgage would be the least expensive?

48. Song is considering two banks for a 30-year $60,000 mortgage. Marine Midland is charging 8.25% interest with no points and Chase Bank is charging 8.00% interest with 3 points.

    (a) How long would it be for the total cost of the two mortgages to be the same?

    (b) If she plans to sell her house in 10 years, which mortgage would be the less expensive?

49. John is considering two banks for a 20-year $100,000 mortgage. Key Mortgage Corp. is charging 9.00% interest with no points, and Countrywide Mortgage Corp. is charging 8.875% interest, also with no points. However, the credit check and application fee at Countrywide is $150 greater than that at Key Mortgage Corp.

    (a) How long would it take for the total cost of the two mortgages to be the same?

    (b) If John plans to live in the house for 10 years, which mortgage would be less expensive?

50. Lisa is considering two banks for a 30-year $75,000 mortgage. NationsBank is charging 9.5% interest with 1 point and Bank America is charging 9.25% interest with 2 points. The Bank America application fee is also $150 greater than NationsBank.

    (a) How long would it take for the total cost of the two mortgages to be the same?

    (b) If Lisa plans to sell her house in 8 years, which mortgage would be less expensive?

51. Because interest rates are low, the Appletons are considering refinancing their house. They presently have $50,000 of their mortgage remaining and they are making monthly mortgage payments of prinicpal and interest of $740. The bank they are considering will refinance their $50,000 mortgage for 20 years at 7.875% interest with no points. However, the closing cost for refinancing the house is $3000 (the closing costs are paid by the borrower when refinancing).

    (a) If the Appletons refinance, how long will it take for the money they save from the lower payment to equal the closing cost?

    (b) How much lower will their monthly payments be?

52. The Smiths are considering refinancing their house. They presently have $40,000 of their mortgage remaining and they are making monthly mortgage payments of $450. The bank they are considering will refinance their house for a 30-year period at 9.25% interest with 2 points. The closing cost is $2500.

    (a) If they refinance, how long will it take for the money they save from the lower monthly payments to equal the closing cost and points?

    (b) If they plan to live in the house for only 6 more years, does it pay for them to refinance?

53. Make up your own realistic word problem that can be solved using algebra. Express the problem as an equation and solve the equation. Make sure you answer the question that was asked in the problem.

CUMULATIVE REVIEW EXERCISES

1.9] **54.** Evaluate $\dfrac{1}{4} + \dfrac{3}{4} \div \dfrac{1}{2} - \dfrac{1}{3}$.

Name the property used.

1.10] **55.** $(x + y) + 5 = x + (y + 5)$

56. $xy = yx$

57. $x(x + y) = x^2 + xy$

[2.6] **58.** At a firemen's chicken barbecue, the chef estimates that he will need $\frac{1}{2}$ pound of coleslaw for each 5 people. If he expects 560 residents to attend, how many pounds of coleslaw will he need?

[3.1] **59.** Solve the formula $M = \dfrac{a + b}{2}$ for b.

Group Activity/ Challenge Problems

1. To find the **average** of a set of values, you find the sum of the values and divide the sum by the number of values. **(a)** If Paul's first three test grades are 74, 88, and 76, write an equation that can be used to find the grade that Paul must get on his fourth exam to have an 80 average. **(b)** Solve the equation from part (a) and determine the grade Paul must receive.

2. At a basketball game Duke University scored 78 points. Duke made 12 free throws (1 point each). Duke also made 4 times as many 2-point field goals as 3-point field goals (field goals made from more than 18 feet from the basket). How many 2-point field goals and how many 3-point field goals did Duke make?

3. Pick any number, say 9.   9

   Multiply the number by 4: $9 \cdot 4 = 36$

   Add 6 to the product: $36 + 6 = 42$

   Divide the sum by 2: $42 \div 2 = 21$

   Subtract 3 from the quotient: $21 - 3 = 18$

   The solution is twice the number you started with. Show that when you select n to represent the given number the solution will always be $2n$.

For Exercises 4–6, (a) set up an equation that can be used to solve the problem and (b) solve the equation and answer the question asked.

4. In 1992 14,000 metric tons of uranium waste were produced. By the year 2000 this amount is expected to increase to 40,000. Find the percent increase from 1992 to 2000.

5. A driver education course costs $45 but saves those under age 25 10% of their annual insurance premiums until they reach age 25. Dan has just turned 18, and his insurance costs $600 per year.

   (a) How long will it take for the amount saved from insurance to equal the price of the course?

   (b) When Dan turns 25, how much will he have saved?

6. The world's most densely populated country (measured in people per square mile) is Hong Kong. Hong Kong has one of the lowest population growth rates in Southeast Asia, 0.8%. If the population density of Hong Kong was 253,488 people per square mile in 1994, find its 1993 population density. (New York City has a population density of about 11,480 people per square mile and Tokyo has a population density of about 25,019 people per square mile.)

3.4 Geometric Problems

Tape 5

1 Solve geometric problems.

Geometric Problems   **1** This section serves two purposes. One is to reinforce the geometric formulas introduced in Section 3.1. The second is to reinforce procedures for setting up and solving word problems discussed in Sections 3.2 and 3.3. The more

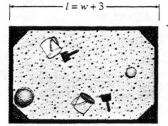

FIGURE 3.8

practice you have at setting up and solving the word problems, the better you will become at solving them.

EXAMPLE 1   Mrs. O'Connor is planning to build a sandbox for her daughter. She has 26 feet of lumber to build the perimeter. What should the dimensions of the rectangular sandbox be if the length is to be 3 feet longer than the width?

Solution: We are asked to find the dimensions of the sandbox.

Let x = width of sandbox

then $x + 3$ = length of sandbox (Fig. 3.8)

From Section 3.1 we know that $P = 2l + 2w$. We have called the width of the sandbox x, and the length $x + 3$. We substitute these expressions into the equation.

$$P = 2l + 2w$$
$$26 = 2(x + 3) + 2x$$
$$26 = 2x + 6 + 2x$$
$$26 = 4x + 6$$
$$20 = 4x$$
$$5 = x$$

Thus, the width is 5 feet, and the length is $x + 3 = 5 + 3 = 8$ feet.

Check: $P = 2l + 2w$
$$26 = 2(8) + 2(5)$$
$$26 = 16 + 10$$
$$26 = 26 \quad \text{true}$$

EXAMPLE 2   The sum of the angles of a triangle measure 180 degrees (180°). If two angles are the same and the third is 30° greater than the other two, find all three angles.

Solution: We are asked to find the three angles.

Let x = each smaller angle

then $x + 30$ = larger angle (Fig. 3.9)

FIGURE 3.9

$$\text{Sum of the 3 angles} = 180$$
$$x + x + (x + 30) = 180$$
$$3x + 30 = 180$$
$$3x = 150$$
$$x = \frac{150}{3} = 50°$$

Therefore, the three angles are 50°, 50°, and 50° + 30° or 80°.

Check: $50° + 50° + 80° = 180°$
$$180° = 180° \quad \text{true}$$

Recall from Section 3.1 that a quadrilateral is a four-sided figure. Quadrilaterals include squares, rectangles, parallelograms, and trapezoids. The sum of the measures of the angles of any quadrilateral is 360°. We use this information in Example 3.

EXAMPLE 3 In a parallelogram the opposite angles have the same measures. If each of the two larger angles in a parallelogram is 20° less than three times the smaller angles, find the measure of each angle.

Solution: Let x = the measure of each of the two smaller angles

then $3x - 20$ = the measure of each of the two larger angles

A diagram of the parallelogram is given in Figure 3.10.

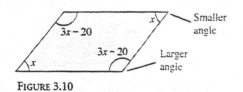

FIGURE 3.10

$$\left(\begin{array}{c} \text{measure of the} \\ \text{two smaller angles} \end{array} \right) + \left(\begin{array}{c} \text{measure of the} \\ \text{two larger angles} \end{array} \right) = 360$$

$$x + x + (3x - 20) + (3x - 20) = 360$$

$$x + x + 3x - 20 + 3x - 20 = 360$$

$$8x - 40 = 360$$

$$8x = 400$$

$$x = 50$$

Thus, each of the two smaller angles is 50° and each of the two larger angles is $3x - 20 = 3(50) - 20 = 130°$. As a check, $50° + 50° + 130° + 130° = 360°$.

EXAMPLE 4 A bookcase is to have four shelves, including the top, as shown in Figure 3.11. The height of the bookcase is to be 3 feet more than the width. Find the dimensions of the bookcase if only 30 feet of lumber is available.

Solution: We are asked to find the dimensions of the bookcase.

Let x = length of a shelf

then $x + 3$ = height of bookcase

4 shelves + 2 sides = total lumber available

$$4x + 2(x + 3) = 30$$

$$4x + 2x + 6 = 30$$

$$6x + 6 = 30$$

$$6x = 24$$

$$x = 4$$

The length of each shelf is 4 feet and the height of the bookcase is 4 + 3 or 7 feet.

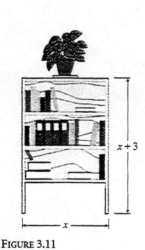

FIGURE 3.11

Check: $4 + 4 + 4 + 4 + 7 + 7 = 30$

$$30 = 30 \quad \textbf{true}$$

Exercise Set 3.4

Solve the following geometric problems.

1. An **equilateral triangle** is a triangle that has three sides of the same length. If the perimeter of an equilateral triangle is 28.5 inches, find the length of each side. Equilateral triangles are discussed in Appendix C.

2. Two angles are **complementary angles** if the sum of their measures is 90°. If angle *A* and angle *B* are complementary angles, and angle *A* is 21° more than twice angle *B*, find the measures of angle *A* and angle *B*. Complementary angles are discussed in Appendix C.

3. Two angles are **supplementary angles** if the sum of their measures is 180°. If angle *A* and angle *B* are supplementary angles, and angle *B* is 8° less than three times angle *A*, find the measures of angle *A* and angle *B*. Supplementary angles are discussed in Appendix C.

4. If one angle of a triangle is 20° larger than the smallest angle, and the third angle is six times as large as the smallest angle, find the measures of the three angles.

5. If one angle of a triangle is 10° greater than the smallest angle, and the third angle is 30° less than twice the smallest angle, find the measures of the three angles.

6. The length of a rectangle is 8 feet more than its width. What are the dimensions of the rectangle if the perimeter is 48 feet?

7. In an **isosceles triangle,** two sides are equal. The third side is 2 meters less than each of the other sides. Find the length of each side if the perimeter is 10 meters. Isosceles triangles are discussed in Appendix C.

8. The perimeter of a rectangle is 120 feet. Find the length and width of the rectangle if the length is twice the width.

9. The perimeter of a basement floor of a house is 240 feet. Find the length and width of the rectangular floor if the length is 24 feet less than twice the width.

10. If the two smaller angles of a parallelogram have equal measures and the two larger angles are each 30° larger than each smaller angle, find the measure of each angle.

11. If the two smaller angles of a parallelogram have equal measures and the two larger angles each measure 27° less than twice each smaller angle, find the measure of each angle.

12. The measure of one angle of a quadrilateral is 10° greater than the smallest angle, the third angle is 14° greater than twice the smallest angle, and the fourth angle is 21° greater than the smallest angle. Find the measures of the four angles of the quadrilateral.

13. A bookcase is to have four shelves as shown. The height of the bookcase is to be 2 feet more than the width, and only 20 feet of lumber is available. What should be the dimensions of the bookcase?

14. What should the dimensions of the bookcase in Exercise 13 be if the height is to be twice its width?

15. Betty McKane plans to build storage shelves as shown. If she has only 45 feet of lumber for the entire unit and wishes the length to be 3 times the height, find the length and height of the unit.

16. An area is to be fenced in along a straight river bank as illustrated. If the length of the fenced-in area is to be 4 feet greater than the width, and the total amount of fencing used is 64 feet, find the width and length of the fenced-in area.

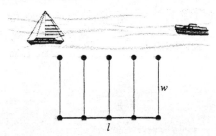

17. In the equation $A = l \cdot w$, what happens to the area if the length is doubled and the width is halved? Explain your answer.

18. In the equation $A = s^2$, what happens to the area if the length of a side, *s*, is doubled? Explain your answer.

19. In the equation $V = l \cdot w \cdot h$, what happens to the volume if the length, width, and height are all doubled? Explain your answer.

20. In the equation $V = \dfrac{4}{3}\pi r^3$, what happens to the volume if the radius is tripled? Explain your answer.

21. Create your own realistic geometric word problem that can be solved using algebra. Write the problem as an equation and solve it. Answer the question asked in the original problem.

CUMULATIVE REVIEW EXERCISES

Insert either $>$, $<$, or $=$ in the shaded area to make the statement true.

[1.3] **22.** $-|-6|$ ▢ $|-4|$

23. $|-3|$ ▢ $-|3|$

[1.6] **24.** Evaluate $-6 - (-2) + (-4)$.

[2.1] **25.** Simplify $-6y + x - 3(x - 2) + 2y$.

[3.1] **26.** Solve $2x + 3y = 9$ for y; then find the value of y when $x = 3$.

Group Activity/ Challenge Problems

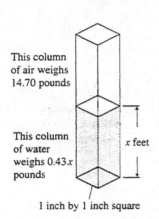

This column of air weighs 14.70 pounds

This column of water weighs $0.43x$ pounds

x feet

1 inch by 1 inch square

1. Consider the accompanying figure. **(a)** Write a formula for determining the area of the shaded region. **(b)** Find the area of the shaded region when $S = 9$ inches and $s = 6$ inches.

2. One way to express the area of the figure on the right is $(a + b)(c + d)$. Can you determine another expression, using the area of the four rectangles, to represent the area of the figure?

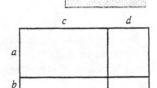

3. The total pressure, P, in pounds per square inch, exerted on an object x feet below sea level is given by the formula $P = 14.70 + 0.43x$. As shown in the accompanying diagram, the 14.70 represents the weight in pounds of the column of air (from sea level to the top of the atmosphere) standing over a 1-inch by 1-inch square of seawater. The $0.43x$ represents the weight, in pounds, of a column of water 1 inch by 1 inch by x feet.

   (a) A submarine can withstand a total pressure of 162 pounds per square inch. How deep can the submarine go?

   (b) If the pressure gauge in the submarine registers a pressure of 97.26 pounds per square inch, how deep is the submarine?

Summary

GLOSSARY

Area (145): The total surface area within a figure's boundaries.

Circumference (147): The length of the curve that forms a circle.

Complementary angles (181): Two angles whose measures sum to 90°.

Diameter (147): A line segment through the center whose endpoints both lie on the circle.

Equilateral triangle (181): A triangle whose three sides have the same length.

Formula (144): An equation commonly used to express a specific physical concept mathematically.

Perimeter (145): The sum of the lengths of the sides of a figure.

Quadrilateral (145): A four-sided figure.

Radius (147): A line segment from the center of a circle to any point on the circle.

Supplementary angles (181): Two angles whose measures sum to 180°.

IMPORTANT FACTS

Simple interest formula: $i = prt$

The sum of the measures of the angles in any triangle is 180°.

The sum of the measures of the angles of a quadrilateral is 360°.

To Solve a Word Problem

1. Read the question carefully.

2. If possible, draw a sketch to help visualize the problem.

3. Determine which quantity you are being asked to find. Choose a letter to represent this unknown quantity; write down exactly what this letter represents. If there is more than one unknown quantity, express all unknown quantities in terms of the variable selected.

4. Write the word problem as an equation.

5. Solve the equation for the unknown quantity.

6. Answer the question or questions asked.

7. Check the solution in the original problem.

Review Exercises

[3.1] *Find the value of the variable indicated.*

1. $C = \pi d$; find C when $d = 4$. Use $\pi = 3.14$.

3. $P = 2l + 2w$; find P when $l = 6$ and $w = 4$.

5. $E = IR$; find E when $I = 0.12$ and $R = 2000$.

7. $V = \dfrac{4}{3}\pi r^3$; find V when $r = 3$. Use $\pi = 3.14$.

9. $y = mx + b$; find b when $y = 15$, $m = 3$, and $x = -2$.

11. $4x - 3y = 15 + x$; find y when $x = -3$.

13. $IR = E + Rr$; find r when $I = 5$, $E = 100$, and $R = 200$.

2. $A = \frac{1}{2}bh$; find A when $b = 12$ and $h = 8$.

4. $i = prt$; find i when $p = 1000$, $r = 15\%$, and $t = 2$.

6. $A = \pi r^2$; find A when $r = 3$. Use $\pi = 3.14$.

8. $Fd^2 = km$; find k when $F = 60$, $m = 12$, and $d = 2$.

10. $2x + 3y = -9$; find y when $x = 12$.

12. $2x = y + 3z + 4$; find y when $x = 5$ and $z = -3$.

Solve the equation for y; then find the value of y for the given value of x.

14. $2x - y = 12$, $x = 10$

16. $3x = 5 + 2y$, $x = -3$

18. $6 = -3x - 2y$, $x = -6$

15. $3x - 2y = -4$, $x = 2$

17. $-6x - 2y = 20$, $x = 0$

19. $3y - 4x = -3$, $x = 2$

Solve for the variable indicated.

20. $F = ma$, for m

22. $i = prt$, for t

24. $2x - 3y = 6$, for y

26. $V = \pi r^2 h$, for h

21. $A = \frac{1}{2}bh$, for h

23. $P = 2l + 2w$, for w

25. $A = \dfrac{B + C}{2}$, for B

Solve.

27. How much interest will Karen pay if she borrows $600 for 2 years at 15% simple interest? (Use $i = prt$.)

[3.2, 3.3] *Solve each problem.*

29. One number is 4 more than the other. Find the two numbers if their sum is 62.

30. The sum of two consecutive integers is 255. Find the two integers.

31. The larger of two integers is 3 more than five times the smaller integer. Find the two numbers if the smaller subtracted from the larger is 31.

32. What is the cost of a car before tax if the total cost including a 5% tax is $8400?

33. In Paul's present position as a salesman he receives a base salary of $500 per week plus a 3% commission on all sales he makes. He is considering moving to another company where he would sell the same goods. His base salary would be only $400 per week, but his commission would be 8% on all sales he makes. What weekly dollar sales would he have to make for the total salary of each company to be the same?

34. During the first week of a going-out-of-business sale, all prices are reduced by 20%. During the second week of the sale, all prices that still cost more than $100 are reduced by an additional $25. During the second week of the sale, Kathy purchased a camcorder for $495. What was the original price of the camcorder?

35. The Johnsons are considering two banks for a 30-year $60,000 mortgage. Comerica Bank is offering 8.875% interest with no points and Mellon Bank is offering 8.625% interest with 3 points.

   (a) How long would it take for the total payments from each bank to be the same?

   (b) If the Johnsons plan on keeping the house for 20 years, to which bank should they apply?

36. Debra Houy is considering refinancing her house. The present balance on her mortgage is $70,000 and her monthly payment of principal and interest is $750. First Chicago Corporation is offering her a 20-year $70,000 mortgage with 8.50% interest and one point. The closing cost, in addition to the one point, is $3200.

   (a) How long would it take for the money she saves in monthly payments to equal the cost of the point and the closing cost?

   (b) If she plans to live in the house for only 10 more years, does it pay for her to refinance?

[3.3] **28.** The perimeter of a rectangle is 16 inches. Find the length of the rectangle if the width is 2 inches.

[3.4] **37.** If one angle of a triangle measures 10° greater than the smallest angle, and the third angle measures 10° less than twice the smallest angle, find the measures of the three angles.

38. One angle of a trapezoid measures 10° greater than the smallest angle. A third angle measures five times the smallest angle. The fourth angle measures 20° greater than four times the smallest angle. Find the measure of the four angles.

39. Mrs. Appleby wants a garden whose length is 4 feet longer than its width. The perimeter of the garden is to be 70 feet. What will be the dimensions of the garden?

[3.1–3.4]

40. The sum of two consecutive odd integers is 208. Find the two integers.

41. What is the cost of a television set before tax if the total cost, including a 6% tax, is $477?

42. Mr. McAdams sells water softeners. He receives a weekly salary of $300 plus a 5% commission on the sales he makes. If Mr. McAdams earned $900 last week, what were his sales in dollars?

43. One angle of a triangle is 8° greater than the smallest angle. The third angle is 4° greater than twice the smallest angle. Find the measure of the three angles of the triangle.

44. Dreyel Company plans to increase its number of employees by 25 per year. If the company presently has 427 employees, how long will it take before they reach 627 employees?

45. If the two larger angles of a parallelogram each measure 40° greater than the two smaller angles, find the measure of the four angles.

46. Two copy centers across the street from one another are competing for business and both have made special offers. Under Copy King's plan, for a monthly fee of $20 each copy made in that month costs only 4 cents. King Kopie charges a monthly fee of $25 plus 3 cents a copy.

   (a) How many copies made in a month would result in both copy centers charging the same amount?

   (b) If you belong to both plans, and intend to make 1000 copies of an advertisement for your band, which center would cost less, and by how much?

Practice Test

1. *Use* $P = 2l + 2w$ to find P when $l = 6$ feet and $w = 3$ feet.

2. Use $A = P + Prt$ to find A when $P = 100$, $r = 0.15$, and $t = 3$.

3. Use $V = \frac{1}{3}\pi r^2 h$ to find V when $r = 4$ and $h = 6$. Use $\pi = 3.14$.

Solve for the variable indicated.

4. $P = IR$, for R

5. $3x - 2y = 6$, for y

6. $A = \dfrac{a + b}{3}$, for a

7. $D = R(c + a)$, for c

8. The sum of two integers is 158. Find the two integers if the larger is 10 less than twice the smaller.

9. The sum of three consecutive integers is 42. Find the three integers.

10. Mr. Herron has only $20. If he wishes to leave a 15% tip and must pay 7% tax, find the price of the most expensive meal that he can order.

11. A triangle has a perimeter of 75 inches. Find the three sides if one side is 15 inches larger than the smallest side, and the third side is twice the smallest side.

12. The sum of the angles of a parallelogram is 360°. If the two smaller angles are equal and the two larger angles are each 30° greater than twice the smaller angles, find the measure of each angle.

Chapter 7

Graphing Linear Equations

7.1 Pie, Bar, and Line Graphs

7.2 The Cartesian Coordinate System and Linear Equations in Two Variables

7.3 Graphing Linear Equations

7.4 Slope of a Line

7.5 Slope–Intercept and Point–Slope Forms of a Linear Equation

7.6 Functions

7.7 Graphing Linear Inequalities

SUMMARY

REVIEW EXERCISES

PRACTICE TEST

See Section 7.1, Group Activities 1.

Preview and Perspective

In this chapter we explain how to graph linear equations. The graphs of linear equations are straight lines. We will graph linear equations further in Chapter 8, when we graph systems of equations. The material presented in this chapter will be used again in Chapter 10 when we graph other types of equations, whose graphs are not straight lines.

Graphing is one of the most important topics in mathematics, and each year its importance increases. If you take additional mathematics courses you will graph many different types of equations. The material presented in this chapter should give you a good background for graphing in later courses. Graphs are also used in many professions and industries. They are used to display information and to make projections about the future.

In Section 7.1 we introduce and discuss pie, bar, and line graphs. You see graphs of this type daily in newspapers and magazines, yet many students do not understand how to interpret them. Once you are able to interpret these graphs you will be in a better position to make important personal decisions.

In Section 7.2 we introduce the Cartesian coordinate system and explain how to plot points. In Section 7.3 we discuss two methods for graphing linear equations: by plotting points and by using the x and y intercepts. The slope of a line is discussed in Section 7.4. In Section 7.5 we discuss a third procedure, using slope, for graphing a linear equation.

Functions are discussed in Section 7.6. Functions are a unifying concept in mathematics. In this chapter we give a brief and somewhat informal introduction to functions. Functions will be discussed in much more depth in later mathematics courses.

We solved inequalities in one variable in Section 2.7. In Section 7.7 we will solve and graph linear inequalities in two variables. Graphing linear inequalities is an extension of graphing linear equations. In later mathematics courses, you may graph other types of inequalities in two variables.

This is an important chapter. If you plan on taking another mathematics course, graphs and functions will probably be a significant part of that course.

7.1 Pie, Bar, and Line Graphs

1 Learn to interpret pie graphs.
2 Learn to interpret bar and line graphs.

In this section we discuss pie graphs, bar graphs, and line graphs. You see such graphs daily in newspapers and magazines.

Tape 11

Pie Graphs

1 A *pie graph*, also called a *circle graph*, displays information using a circle. The circle is divided into pieces called *sectors*. Figure 7.1 illustrates a pie graph showing sources of business start-up capital.

In Figure 7.1, notice that 73% of the $82,300 used to start the average new business in the survey came from the individuals themselves and their family and friends. The sector of the circle that represents the individuals, their family, and friends should be 73% of the area of the entire circle. Outside investors should be 13% of the area of the entire circle, and so on. The total percent indicated in the circle should be 100%. Note that 73% + 13% + 8% + 6% = 100%. How much

Founders of businesses risked an average of $82,300 to start their companies. The money came from:

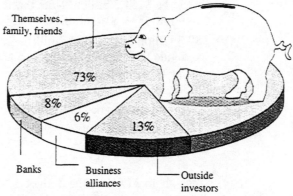

FIGURE 7.1

money of the $82,300 came from the individuals, their family, and friends? To determine this amount, we find 73% of $82,300 as follows:

$$(0.73)(82,300) = 60,079$$

Thus, $60,079 came from the individuals, their family, and friends. The amount from outside investors, banks, and business alliances is determined as follows:

Outside investors:	$(0.13)(82,300) = 10,699$
Banks:	$(0.08)(82,300) = 6584$
Business alliances:	$(0.06)(82,300) = 4938$

Notice that the sum of the four amounts is $82,300. That is, $60,079 + $10,699 + $6584 + $4938 = $82,300.

EXAMPLE 1   Consider the pie graph in Figure 7.2, which shows federal health care spending in 1993.

(a) What should the sum of the amounts in the four sectors equal? Explain.

(b) What percent of the total budget went to Medicaid?

(c) What percent of the area of the circle should be designated as Medicaid?

(d) Redraw the pie graph so that it lists percents rather than dollar amounts.

Where federal health-care spending goes ('93, in billions)

Total $254.2

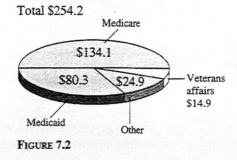

FIGURE 7.2

Solution:

(a) Since the total budget is $254.2 billion, the sum of the four sectors should be $254.2 billion. Note that $134.1 billion + $80.3 billion + $24.9 billion + $14.9 billion = $254.2 billion.

(b) $80.3 billion of the $254.2 billion goes to Medicaid. To find the percent, we divide the amount that goes to Medicaid by the total budget, then change the decimal answer to a percent. The procedure follows.

$$\text{Percent that goes to Medicaid} = \frac{\text{amount for Medicaid}}{\text{total budget}}$$

$$= \frac{80.3}{254.2} \approx 0.316 \approx 31.6\%$$

(c) Since about 31.6% of the budget is for Medicaid, the portion of the circle illustrating Medicaid should be about 31.6% of the area of the circle.

(d) To redraw this circle with percents, we need to determine the percent of the total for each sector. We follow the same procedure we used to find the percent that goes for Medicaid to find the other percents.

$$\text{Percent that goes to Medicare} = \frac{134.1}{254.2} \approx 0.528 \approx 52.8\%$$

$$\text{Percent that goes to veterans' affairs} = \frac{14.9}{254.2} \approx 0.059 \approx 5.9\%$$

$$\text{Percent that goes to other} = \frac{24.9}{254.2} \approx 0.098 \approx 9.8\%$$

Notice that 31.6% + 52.8% + 5.9% + 9.8% = 100.1%. We get slightly more than 100% because of roundoff error. The circle graph is illustrated with percents in Figure 7.3.

Where federal health-care spending goes ('93, in billions)

Total $254.2

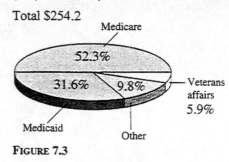

FIGURE 7.3

Bar and Line Graphs **2** Now we discuss bar and line graphs. A typical bar graph is shown in Figure 7.4. This bar graph shows the net income of Blockbuster Entertainment. In a bar graph, one of the axes indicates amounts. Bars are used to show the amounts of each item. The amounts may be listed on either the vertical or horizontal axis. The other axis will give additional information, such as the years the amounts were recorded.

Blockbuster net income

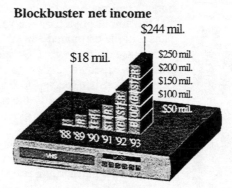

FIGURE 7.4

Consider the bar graph in Figure 7.4. To determine the annual income of Blockbuster Entertainment in any year, find the bar for that year and estimate where the top of the bar would intersect the vertical axis if the top of the bar were extended. For example, in 1989 we see that the income was slightly under $50 million, but in 1992 the income had grown to about $150 million. From this graph we see that the annual income of Blockbuster has grown each year since 1988. This is due primarily to the increase in movie rentals. Can you estimate the total income of Blockbuster from 1988 up to and including 1993? Since each bar represents the annual income for a specific year, the total income can be found by adding the income for each of the six years. Estimate the total income of Blockbuster from 1988 to 1993 now. Your total should be about $620 million. Answers will differ somewhat based on individual estimates. For example, one student might estimate 1990 income to be $60 million, while another might estimate it to be $70 million.

Bar graphs can be used to illustrate trends. However, you need to be aware that trends change. For example, by looking at this graph you might be led to believe that Blockbuster Entertainment will continue to increase its annual income year after year. However, you might form a different opinion after looking at the *line graph* indicated in Figure 7.5.

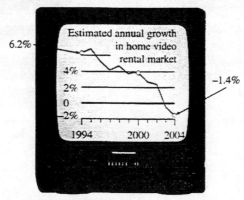

FIGURE 7.5

A line graph generally has amounts indicated on the vertical axis, and some measure of time, such as years or months, listed on its horizontal axis. To construct a line graph, mark the corresponding amounts above the respective time pe-

FIGURE 7.6

FIGURE 7.7

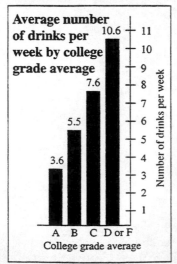

FIGURE 7.8

riods. Then connect the marks consecutively with straight-line segments. Notice that the amount listed on the vertical axis in Figure 7.5 is percent. This graph indicates that the estimated annual growth in the home video market rental is expected to increase by 6.2% in 1994 and peak in 1995. By the year 2000 the increase in growth is expected to slow to about 4%. Between 2002 and 2003 the rental home video market is expected to begin decreasing in size. The decrease in the growth from 1995 may be due to the increase in the use of cable television and the number of television channels available.

EXAMPLE 2   Consider the graphs indicated in Figures 7.6 and 7.7. The information for these graphs was provided by the Southern Illinois University Core Alcohol and Drug Survey.

(a) Explain why both of these figures may be considered bar graphs.

(b) Redraw Figure 7.6 as a bar graph with a vertical axis indicating the number of drinks on the right side of the graph.

(c) Explain what Figure 7.6 shows.

(d) Redraw Figure 7.7 as a bar graph with the horizontal axis indicating the number of drinks.

(e) Explain what Figure 7.7 shows.

Solution:

(a) In Figures 7.6 and 7.7, pictures of cans are used instead of bars. Pictures are often used in place of bars to make the graph more interesting or appealing. However, the same information is indicated whether bars or cans are used.

(b) Figure 7.8 shows the same information as illustrated in Figure 7.6.

(c) Figure 7.6 indicates that, in general, college students who achieve better grades drink less.

(d) Figure 7.9 illustrates the same information as illustrated in Figure 7.7.

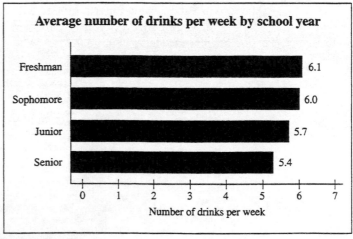

FIGURE 7.9

(e) Figure 7.7 illustrates that the average number of drinks consumed decreases from the freshmen year through the senior year.

Figure 7.10 illustrates a line graph showing the increase in global temperature from 1960 to 1990. The information for this graph was provided by the U.S. Department of Agriculture. Notice the break above the zero in the

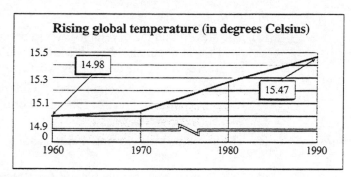

FIGURE 7.10

vertical axis. If all the values from 0 to 15.5 were to be shown, this line graph would be very high and require more space. To save space we "break the axis," as illustrated in this figure. The break indicates that a part of the axis has been omitted.

In Figure 7.11 we have redrawn the bar graph in Figure 7.9 with a break in the horizontal axis. The break gives the graph a different appearance and makes the difference between the classes appear greater.

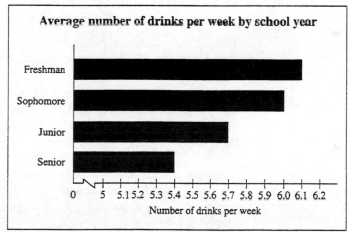

FIGURE 7.11

Some bar and line graphs are formed by placing individual parts on top of one another as illustrated in Example 3.

EXAMPLE 3 The line graph in Figure 7.12 shows Bureau of the Census data for past, present, and projected population for both the developed and developing world.

(a) Explain how to find the developing world population for any given year. Estimate:

(b) the world's population in 1994 (indicated by the vertical dashed line),

(c) the developed world's population in 1994,

(d) the developing world's population in 1994, and,

(e) the increase in the world's population from 1950 to 2010.

(f) Explain what this graph shows.

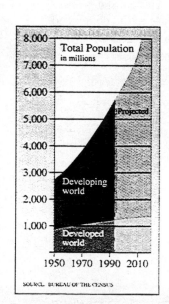

FIGURE 7.12

Solution:

(a) One way to find the developing world population is to subtract the developed world population from the total population for the given year. This difference will be the developing world population.

(b) The 1994 world population is about 5700 million or 5.7 billion people (the article indicates that in 1994 the world's population is increasing by 94 million per year).

(c) The developed world's population is about 1300 million or 1.3 billion people.

(d) The developing world population for 1994 can be found by subtracting the developed world population from the total population:

developing world population in 1994 = 5.7 billion − 1.3 billion = 4.4 billion

(e) The increase in the world's population can be found by subtracting the world's population in 1950 from the projected world's population in 2010. The world's population in 1950 was about 2.7 billion and the projected world population in 2010 is about 7.9 billion:

increase in the world's population from 1950 to 2010

= 7.9 billion − 2.7 billion = 5.2 billion

Many people do not realize how large 5.2 billion is. To give you some idea, if you counted by seconds, it would take about 165 years to count to 5.2 billion.

(f) The line graph shows that the world's population is increasing rapidly. The greatest increase is in the developing countries and regions (such as the Gaza Strip, Ethiopia, and Somalia, where the average number of births per woman are 7.9, 7.5, and 6.8, respectively). The developed countries are growing at a much slower rate (the average number of births per woman in Hong Kong, Italy, Japan, and the United States are 1.2, 1.3, 1.6, and 2.0 respectively). By 2010 the increase in the developed countries will be about 120 million and the increase in the developing countries will be about 1.7 billion.

Exercise Set 7.1

1. Use the circle graph below to answer the following questions.

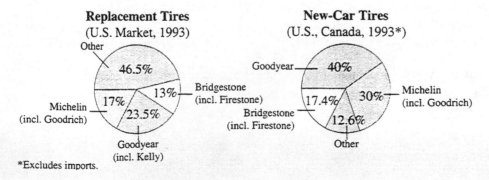

Replacement Tires
(U.S. Market, 1993)

Other
46.5%
Michelin (incl. Goodrich) — 17%
13% — Bridgestone (incl. Firestone)
23.5%
Goodyear (incl. Kelly)
*Excludes imports.

New-Car Tires
(U.S., Canada, 1993*)

Goodyear — 40%
17.4%
30% — Michelin (incl. Goodrich)
Bridgestone (incl. Firestone)
12.6%
Other

(a) In 1993, what percent of replacement tires were manufactured by Goodyear, Michelin, or Bridgestone?

(b) By observing the graph, is it possible to determine whether Goodyear sold more replacement tires or more new car tires in 1993? Explain.

(c) By observing the graph, is it possible to determine the number of new tires sold by Michelin in 1993? Explain.

(d) By observing the graphs, is it possible to determine whether Goodyear, Michelin, or Bridgestone made the greatest profit in 1993? Explain.

2. Use the circle graph below to answer the following questions.

Distribution of Federal Spending (1993)

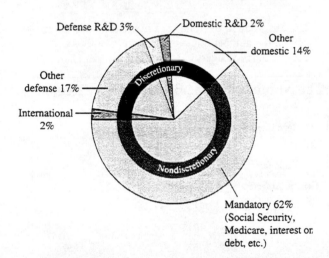

What percent of the federal budget was for

(a) discretionary spending?

(b) nondiscretionary spending?

(c) research and development (total)?

(d) If the total 1993 federal spending was $1.47 trillion, what was the total spent on research and development?

(e) How much was spent on mandatory items?

3. The following graph shows a breakdown of revenue from the 1993 Virginia State Fair held at Strawberry Hill in Richmond.

How much money was collected from

(a) ticket sales?

(b) fees from concessionaires and vendors?

State Fair 1993 Revenue: $3.6 Million

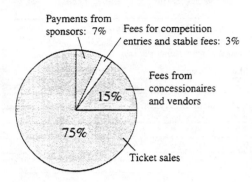

(c) Redraw this pie graph using dollar amounts collected rather than percents.

4. Consider the bar graph illustrated below (computers). Information for this graph was obtained by Motorola.

Average Number of Microcontrollers in:

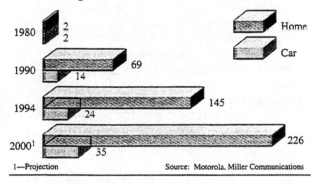

1—Projection   Source: Motorola. Miller Communications

(a) What was the increase in the number of microcomputers in the typical house from 1990 to 1994?

(b) What was the increase in the number of microcomputers in the typical car from 1990 to 1994?

(c) List at least 10 places where microcomputers may be found in a home.

(d) Do you believe that this explosive growth in the use of microcomputers will continue in the typical house? Explain.

5. The following bar graph shows changes in the record time, for the world's men 100 meter race.

From	To	Difference	Length of time
Fastest Record Slow to Change			
It took more than 26 years to shave one-tenth of a second from the world men's 100-meter record.			
9.95	9.93	.02	15 years
9.93	9.92	.01	5 years
9.92	9.90	.02	3 years
9.90	9.86	.04	2.5 months
9.86	9.85	.01	3 years

Note: Canada's Ben Johnson ran times of 9.83 and 9.79, but both were invalidated because of drug use.

(a) How long was the men's 100-meter record at 9.95 seconds?

(b) How long did it take for the record to be reduced from 9.95 seconds to 9.90 seconds, and by what part of a second had the record been reduced during this time period?

(c) Explain how this graph shows that it took more than 26 years for one-tenth of a second to be shaved from the world's 100-meter record.

(d) If next year, the record is reduced by three hundredths of a second, what will be the new record time?

6. Consider the following bar graph. Information for this graph was gathered by the Gallup Organization.

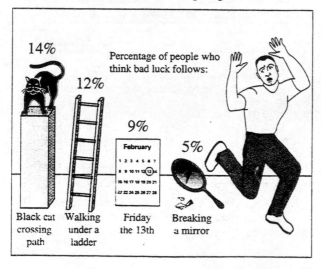

(a) Do more people believe that walking under a ladder is more likely to bring bad luck than breaking a mirror? Explain.

(b) If we add the four percents, we get a total of 40%. Does this mean that 40% of the population believe that bad luck will follow the occurrence of one these items? Explain.

See Exercise 5.

(c) Redraw this bar graph listing percent on the horizontal.

7. The bar graph in the following figure provides information on the number of cinema screens worldwide. Source: Screen Digest.

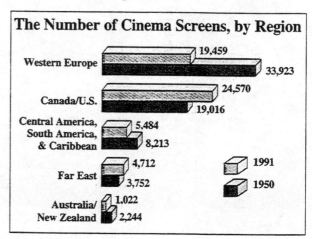

(a) Has the number of cinema screens increased or decreased in western Europe from 1950 to 1991, and by how much?

(b) Has the number of cinema screens increased or decreased in Canada/U.S. from 1950 to 1991, and by how much?

(c) What was the total number of cinema screens in 1950? What was the total number in 1991?

See Exercise 7.

8. The bar graph below shows 1993 military expenditures as a percentage of gross domestic product in selected countries. *Source:* United Nations.

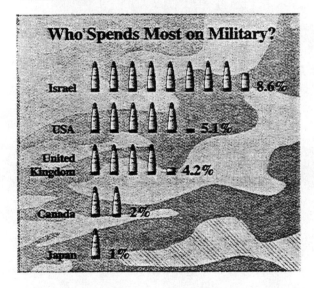

(a) By observing the graph, is it possible to determine how many dollars were spent by the United States on military expenditures in 1993? Explain.

(b) In 1993 the U.S. gross domestic product was $6377.9 billion. Determine the amount the United States spent on military expenditures in 1993.

(c) In 1993, Israel's gross domestic product was $74 billion. Determine the amount Israel spent on military expenditures in 1993.

9. The following graph illustrates new AIDS cases reported worldwide.

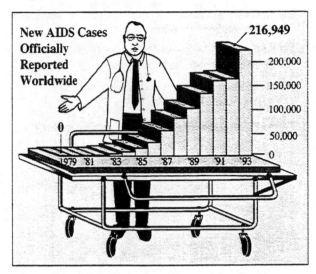

Estimate the number of new AIDS cases reported in

(a) 1986

(b) 1987

(c) 1992.

(d) Estimate the number of AIDS cases reported to the World Health Organization from 1979 through 1993. (The World Health Organization suspects that in 1993 the number of AIDS cases was much higher than that reported: about 4 million people with AIDS, plus 17 million people infected with HIV.)

10. The following line graph shows legal U.S. immigration by decades, beginning 1901 to 1910 and ending 1981 to 1990. For example, from the graph we can see that during the decade 1901-1910 there were 8,795,386 immigrants to legally enter the United States.

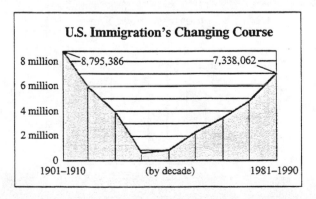

(a) Describe the trend in U.S. immigration from 1901–1910 to 1981–1990.

(b) During which decade was there the greatest decrease in the number of legal immigrants?

(c) During which decade was there the greatest increase in the number of legal immigrants?

(d) Estimate the increase in the number of legal immigrants from 1971–1980 to 1981–1990.

11. Use the line graph to answer the following questions.

Savings as a Percent of GDP

(a) Estimate savings as a percent of gross domestic product for Japan, for the European Union, and for the United States in 1984.

(b) Describe the savings trend in the United States from 1984 to 1994.

(c) Describe the savings trend in Japan from 1984 to 1994.

12. Consider the following graph, with information supplied by the Aerospace Industry Association.

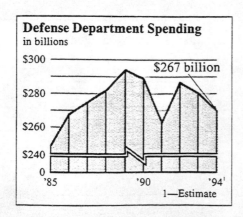

Defense Department Spending
in billions

$267 billion

1—Estimate

Estimate the amount the United States spent on defense in

(a) 1989

(b) 1991

(c) 1992.

(d) Estimate the difference in the amount spent in 1991 and 1994.

(e) Estimate the total spent on defense from 1985 through 1994.

13. Consider the line graph that follows.

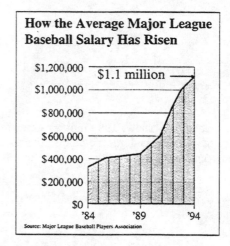

How the Average Major League Baseball Salary Has Risen

$1.1 million

Source: Major League Baseball Players Association

(a) Estimate the average baseball player's salary in 1984.

(b) When did baseball players' salaries start to increase rapidly?

(c) Estimate the average baseball player's salary in 1989.

(d) Estimate the increase in salary from 1989 to 1994.

(e) Estimate the percent increase in salary from 1989 to 1994 by dividing the increase in salary from 1989 to 1994 [part (d)] by the 1989 salary.

(f) Estimate the average yearly percent increase from 1989 to 1994 by dividing the percent increase [part (e)] by the number of years from 1989 to 1994, which is 5 years.

14. Consider the following text and line graphs.

Population and the Environment

The world's demand for wood — half of which is used as the primary source of energy in developing countries — has continued to climb. The use of wood is threatening the world's forests and raising the amount of carbon dioxide in the air. Some scientists say carbon dioxide is the prime contributor to global warming, the theoretical "greenhouse effect." Even though developed nations are working to cut carbon dioxide emissions, levels are expected to continue upward because of activities in developing countries.

Wood production (millions of cubic meters)

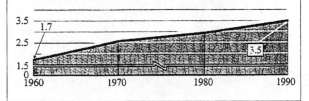

More carbon dioxide (parts per million)

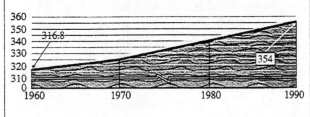

(a) Find the difference in wood production from 1960 to 1990.

(b) Estimate the percent increase in wood production by dividing the increase from 1960 to 1990 found in part (a) by the amount of wood produced in 1960.

(c) Estimate the annual percent increase in wood production from 1960 to 1990 by dividing the percent increase found in part (b) by the number of years from 1960 to 1990, which is 30.

(d) Using information provided in parts (a)–(c), determine the annual percent increase in carbon dioxide from 1960 to 1990.

15. The information for the following graph is provided by the World Bank.

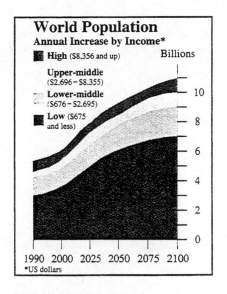

(a) In 1990, estimate the world population classified as having a low income.

(b) In 2100, estimate the projected world population classified as having a low income.

(c) In 1990 estimate the world population classified as having a high income.

(d) In 2100 estimate the world population classified as having a high income.

(e) In 2100 estimate the world population classified as having a lower–middle income.

(f) Explain what this graph shows.

See Exercise 15.

16. Describe a pie graph.
17. Describe a bar graph.
18. Describe a line graph.
19. Find two pie graphs in newspapers or magazines, cut them out and paste them in your notebook, and explain what they show.

20. Find two bar graphs in newspapers or magazines, cut them out and paste them in your notebook, and explain what they show.
21. Find two line graphs in newspapers or magazines, cut them out and paste them in your notebook, and explain what they show.

CUMULATIVE REVIEW EXERCISES

[4.4] 22. Simplify $3x - \dfrac{2}{3} + \dfrac{3}{5}x - \dfrac{1}{2}$

[4.6] 23. Divide $3x^2 - 4x + 6$ by $x - 2$.

[5.5] 24. Factor $4x^2 - 16$.

[6.6] 25. Solve $x - \dfrac{2}{3} = \dfrac{3}{5}x - \dfrac{1}{2}$

Group Activity/ Challenge Problems

1. The Disney Corporation receives its income from theme parks and resorts, films, and consumer products. The percent income from each source in 1992 is indicated below. Construct a pie graph which indicates the percent of total income from each source. Explain how you drew the sectors so that they contain the correct percent of the area. (*Hint:* A circle contains 360°.)

Theme parks and resorts	45%
Films	35%
Consumer products	20%

2. The average cost of making a movie, in millions of dollars, in a variety of countries in 1991, is indicated below.

U.S.	7.63
U.K.	5.32
France	3.86
Belgium	3.44
Australia	3.34
Italy	2.70
Germany	1.86
India	0.12

Illustrate this information using a bar graph with the cost on the horizontal axis. (The average cost of making a movie in only U.S. major studios exceeds $24 million.)

3. The following chart indicates the number of TV households and the number of cable households for various countries.

(a) For each country determine the cable households as a percentage of total TV households. Round answers to the nearest percent.

(b) Illustrate the percent of cable households relative to total TV households for the countries indicated using a bar graph with percent on the vertical axis.

Country	TV Households	Cable Households
Belgium	3,700,000	3,400,000
Netherlands	6,100,000	4,900,000
Canada	9,756,000	7,537,000
United States	92,740,000	54,890,000
Germany	33,281,000	9,900,000
Japan	40,000,000	6,170,000
United Kingdom	21,600,000	490,000

4. The number of cellular telephone subscribers from 1984 to 1993 is indicated below. Draw a line graph indicating the information.

Year	84	85	86	87	88	89	90	91	92	93
Subscribers (millions)	0.1	0.3	0.7	1.2	2.1	3.5	5.3	7.6	11.0	16.0

7.2 The Cartesian Coordinate System and Linear Equations in Two Variables

Tape 11

1 Plot points in the Cartesian coordinate system.
2 Determine whether an ordered pair is a solution to a linear equation.

The Cartesian Coordinate System

1 In this chapter we discuss several procedures that can be used to draw graphs. A **graph** shows the relationship between two variables in an equation. Many algebraic relationships are easier to understand if we can see a picture of them. We draw graphs using the **Cartesian (or rectangular) coordinate system.** The Cartesian coordinate system is named for its developer, the French mathematician and philosopher René Descartes (1596–1650).

The Cartesian coordinate system provides a means of locating and identifying points just as the coordinates on a map help us find cities and other locations. Consider the map of the Great Smoky Mountains (see Fig. 7.13 on page 376). Can you find Cades Cove on the map? If I tell you that it is in grid A3, you can probably find it much quicker and easier.

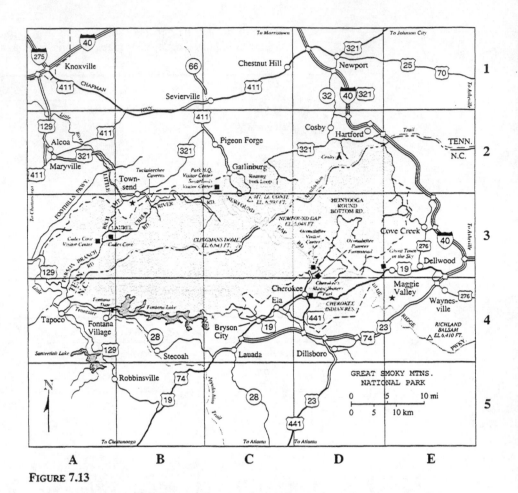

FIGURE 7.13

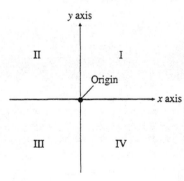

FIGURE 7.14

The Cartesian coordinate system is a grid system, like that of a map, except that it is formed by two axes (or number lines) drawn perpendicular to each other. The two intersecting axes form four **quadrants** (Fig. 7.14).

The horizontal axis is called the *x* **axis.** The vertical axis is called the *y* **axis.** The point of intersection of the two axes is called the **origin.** At the origin the value of *x* is 0 and the value of *y* is 0. Starting from the origin and moving to the right along the *x* axis, the numbers increase. Starting from the origin and moving to the left, the numbers decrease (Fig. 7.15). Starting from the origin and moving up the *y* axis, the numbers increase. Starting from the origin and moving down, the numbers decrease.

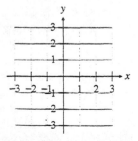

FIGURE 7.15

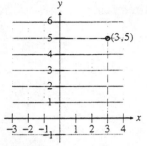

Figure 7.16

To locate a point, it is necessary to know both the value of x and the value of y, or the **coordinates,** of the point. When the x and y coordinates of a point are placed in parentheses, *with the x coordinate listed first,* we have an **ordered pair.** In the ordered pair (3, 5) the x coordinate is 3 and the y coordinate is 5. The point corresponding to the ordered pair (3, 5) is plotted in Figure 7.16. The phrase "the point corresponding to the ordered pair (3, 5)" is often abbreviated "the point (3, 5)". For example, if we write "the point (-1, 2)" it means "the point corresponding to the ordered pair (-1, 2)."

Example 1 Plot each point on the same axes.

(a) $A(4, 2)$ (b) $B(2, 4)$ (c) $C(-3, 1)$

(d) $D(4, 0)$ (e) $E(-2, -5)$ (f) $F(0, -3)$

(g) $G(0, 3)$ (h) $H(6, -\frac{7}{2})$ (i) $I(-\frac{3}{2}, -\frac{5}{2})$

Solution: The first number in each ordered pair is the x coordinate and the second number is the y coordinate. The points are plotted in Figure 7.17.

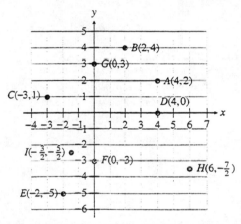

Figure 7.17

Note that when the x coordinate is 0, as in Example 1(f) and (g), the point is on the y axis. When the y coordinate is 0, as in Example 1(d), the point is on the x axis.

Example 2 List the ordered pairs for each point shown in Figure 7.18.

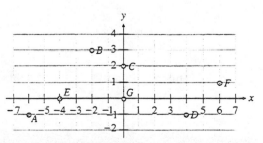

Figure 7.18

Solution: Remember to give the x value first in the ordered pair.

Point	Ordered Pair
A	$(-6, -1)$
B	$(-2, 3)$
C	$(0, 2)$
D	$(4, -1)$
E	$(-4, 0)$
F	$(6, 1)$
G	$(0, 0)$

Linear Equations

2 In Section 7.3 we will learn to graph linear equations in two variables. Below we explain how to identify a linear equation in two variables.

> A **linear equation in two variables** is an equation that can be put in the form
>
> $$ax + by = c$$
>
> where a, b, and c are real numbers.

The graphs of equations of the form ax + by = c *are straight lines. For this reason such equations are called linear.* Linear equations may be written in various forms, as we will show later. A linear equation in the form $ax + by = c$ is said to be in **standard form.**

Examples of Linear Equations

$$3x - 2y = 4$$
$$y = 5x + 3$$
$$x - 3y + 4 = 0$$

Note in the examples that only the equation $3x - 2y = 4$ is in standard form. However, the bottom two equations can be written in standard form, as follows:

$$y = 5x + 3 \qquad x - 3y + 4 = 0$$
$$-5x + y = 3 \qquad\qquad x - 3y = -4$$

Most of the equations we have discussed thus far have contained only one variable. Exceptions to this include formulas used in application sections. Consider the linear equation in *one* variable, $2x + 3 = 5$. What is its solution?

$$2x + 3 = 5$$
$$2x = 2$$
$$x = 1$$

This equation has only one solution, 1.

Check: $2x + 3 = 5$
$$2(1) + 3 = 5$$
$$5 = 5 \qquad \textbf{true}$$

Now consider the linear equation in *two* variables, $y = x + 1$. What is the solution? Since the equation contains two variables, its solutions must contain two numbers, one for each variable. One pair of numbers that satisfies this equation is $x = 1$ and $y = 2$. To see that this is true, we substitute both values into the equation and see that the equation checks.

Check: $y = x + 1$

$\qquad$ $2 = 1 + 1$

$\qquad$ $2 = 2$ $\quad$ true

We write this answer as an ordered pair by writing the x and y values within parentheses separated by a comma. Remember the x value is always listed first since the form of an ordered pair is (x, y). Therefore, one possible solution to this equation is the ordered pair $(1, 2)$. The equation $y = x + 1$ has other possible solutions, as follows.

Solution	*Solution*	*Solution*
$x = 2, y = 3$	$x = -1, y = 0$	$x = -3, y = -2$

Check: $\quad$ $y = x + 1$ $\qquad\qquad$ $y = x + 1$ $\qquad\qquad$ $y = x + 1$

$\qquad\qquad$ $3 = 2 + 1$ $\qquad\qquad$ $0 = -1 + 1$ $\qquad\qquad$ $-2 = -3 + 1$

$\qquad\qquad$ $3 = 3$ $\quad$ true $\qquad\quad$ $0 = 0$ $\quad$ true $\qquad\quad$ $-2 = -2$ $\quad$ true

Solution Written as an Ordered Pair

$\qquad$ $(2, 3)$ $\qquad\qquad\qquad$ $(-1, 0)$ $\qquad\qquad\qquad$ $(-3, -2)$

How many possible solutions does the equation $y = x + 1$ have? The equation $y = x + 1$ has an unlimited or *infinite number* of possible solutions. Since it is not possible to list all the specific solutions, the solutions are illustrated with a graph. **A graph of an equation is an illustration of a set of points whose coordinates satisfy the equation.** Figure 7.19a shows the points $(2, 3)$, $(-1, 0)$, and $(-3, -2)$ plotted in the Cartesian coordinate system. Figure 7.19b shows a straight line drawn through the three points. Every point on this line will satisfy the equation $y = x + 1$, so this graph illustrates all the solutions of $y = x + 1$. Check to see if the ordered pair $(1, 2)$, which is on the line, satisfies the equation.

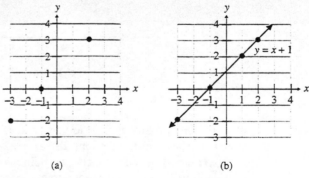

$\qquad\qquad$ (a) $\qquad\qquad\qquad\qquad\qquad$ (b)

FIGURE 7.19

EXAMPLE 3 Determine which of the following ordered pairs satisfy the equation $2x + 3y = 12$.

(a) $(2, 3)$ $\qquad$ **(b)** $(3, 2)$ $\qquad$ **(c)** $(8, -\frac{4}{3})$

Solution: To determine if the ordered pairs are solutions, we substitute them into the equation.

(a) $2x + 3y = 12$
$2(2) + 3(3) = 12$
$4 + 9 = 12$
$13 = 12$, false

(b) $2x + 3y = 12$
$2(3) + 3(2) = 12$
$6 + 6 = 12$
$12 = 12$, true

(c) $2x + 3y = 12$
$2(8) + 3(-\frac{4}{3}) = 12$
$16 - 4 = 12$
$12 = 12$, true

$(2, 3)$ is *not* a solution $(3, 2)$ is a solution $(8, -\frac{4}{3})$ is a solution.   ●····

In Example 3, if we plotted the two solutions $(3, 2)$ and $(8, -\frac{4}{3})$ and connected the two points with a straight line, we would get the graph of the equation $2x + 3y = 12$. The coordinates of every point on this line would satisfy the equation.

In Figure 7.19b, what do you notice about the points $(2, 3)$, $(1, 2)$, $(-1, 0)$, and $(-3, -2)$? You probably said that they are in a straight line. A set of points that are in a straight line are said to be **collinear**. *In Section 7.3 when you graph linear equations by plotting points, the points you plot should all be collinear.*

EXAMPLE 4   Determine if the three points given are collinear.

(a) $(2, 7)$, $(0, 3)$, and $(-2, -1)$

(b) $(0, 5)$, $(\frac{5}{2}, 0)$, and $(5, -5)$

(c) $(-2, -5)$, $(0, 1)$, and $(5, 8)$

Solution: We plot the points to determine if they are collinear. The solution is shown in Figure 7.20.

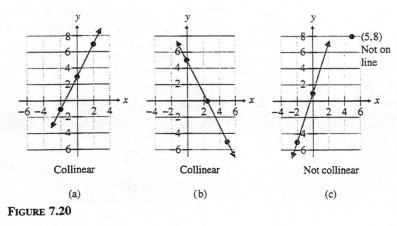

(a)	(b)	(c)
Collinear	Collinear	Not collinear

FIGURE 7.20

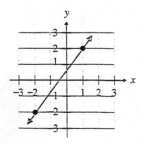

FIGURE 7.21

How many points do you need to graph a linear equation? As mentioned earlier, **the graph of every linear equation of the form $ax + by = c$ will be a straight line.** Since only two points are needed to draw a straight line (Fig. 7.21), only two points are needed to graph a linear equation. However, if you graph a linear equation using only two points and you have made an error in determining or plotting one of those points, your graph will be wrong and you will not know it. If you use at least three points to plot your graph, as in Figure 7.19b and they are collinear, you probably have not made a mistake.

EXAMPLE 5

(a) Determine which of the following ordered pairs satisfy the equation $2x + y = 4$.

$$(2, 0), \ (0, 4), \ (3, -1), \ (-1, 6)$$

(b) Plot all the points on the same axes and draw a straight line through the three points that are collinear.

(c) Does the graph support your answer in part (a)? Explain.

(d) What does this straight line represent?

Solution:

(a) We substitute values for x and y into the equation $2x + y = 4$ and determine if they check.

Check:

$(2, 0)$		$(0, 4)$	
$2x + y = 4$		$2x + y = 4$	
$2(2) + 0 = 4$		$2(0) + 4 = 4$	
$4 = 4$	true	$4 = 4$	true

$(3, -1)$		$(-1, 6)$	
$2x + y = 4$		$2x + y = 4$	
$2(3) - 1 = 4$		$2(-1) + 6 = 4$	
$6 - 1 = 4$		$-2 + 6 = 4$	
$5 = 4$	false	$4 = 4$	true

All the points except $(3, -1)$ check and are solutions to the equation.

(b) See Figure 7.22

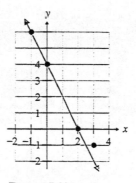

FIGURE 7.22

(c) Yes, the three points that are solutions are collinear. The point $(3, -1)$, which is not a solution, is not collinear with the other points.

(d) The straight line represents all solutions of $2x + y = 4$. The coordinates of every point on this line satisfy the equation $2x + y = 4$.

Exercise Set 7.2

Indicate the quadrant in which each of the points belong.

1. $(2, 5)$
2. $(-3, 6)$
3. $(-4, -2)$
4. $(5, -3)$
5. $(-8, 5)$
6. $(-6, 30)$
7. $(7, 93)$
8. $(83, -57)$
9. $(-124, -132)$
10. $(75, -200)$
11. $(-8, 42)$
12. $(-46, -192)$

13. List the ordered pairs corresponding to each point.

14. List the ordered pairs corresponding to each point.

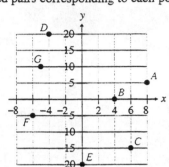

Plot each point on the same set of axes.

15. (a) $(4, 2)$
    (b) $(-3, 2)$
    (c) $(0, -3)$
    (d) $(-2, 0)$
    (e) $(-3, -4)$
    (f) $(-4, -2)$

16. (a) $(-3, -1)$
    (b) $(2, 0)$
    (c) $(-3, 2)$
    (d) $(\frac{1}{2}, -4)$
    (e) $(-4, 2)$
    (f) $(0, 4)$

17. (a) $(4, 0)$
    (b) $(-1, 3)$
    (c) $(2, 4)$
    (d) $(0, -2)$
    (e) $(-3, -3)$
    (f) $(2, -3)$

Plot the following points. Then determine if they are collinear.

18. (a) $(1, -1)$
    (b) $(5, 3)$
    (c) $(-3, -5)$
    (d) $(0, -2)$
    (e) $(2, 0)$

19. (a) $(1, -2)$
    (b) $(0, -5)$
    (c) $(3, 1)$
    (d) $(-1, -8)$
    (e) $(\frac{1}{2}, -\frac{7}{2})$

20. (a) $(0, 2)$
    (b) $(-1, 3)$
    (c) $(-2, 4)$
    (d) $(3, 0)$
    (e) $(4, -2)$

In Exercises 21–26, (a) determine which three of the four ordered pairs satisfy the given equation. (b) Plot all the points on the same axes and draw a straight line through the three points that are collinear. (c) Does the graph support your answer in part (a)? Explain. (d) What does this straight line represent? (See Example 5.)

21. $y = x + 1$,   (a) $(0, 1)$ (b) $(-1, 0)$ (c) $(2, 3)$ (d) $(1, 1)$
22. $2x + y = -4$,   (a) $(-2, 0)$ (b) $(-2, 1)$ (c) $(0, -4)$ (d) $(-1, -2)$
23. $3x - 2y = 6$,   (a) $(4, 0)$ (b) $(2, 0)$ (c) $(\frac{2}{3}, -2)$ (d) $(\frac{4}{3}, -1)$
24. $2x - 4y = 6$,   (a) $(3, 0)$ (b) $(2, -\frac{1}{2})$ (c) $(0, -\frac{3}{2})$ (d) $(-1, -1)$
25. $2x + 4y = 4$,   (a) $(2, 3)$ (b) $(1, \frac{1}{2})$ (c) $(0, 1)$ (d) $(-2, 2)$
26. $y = \frac{1}{2}x + 2$,   (a) $(0, 2)$ (b) $(2, 0)$ (c) $(-2, 1)$ (d) $(4, 4)$

27. In an ordered pair, which coordinate is always listed first?

28. What is another name for the Cartesian coordinate system?

29. (a) Is the *horizontal axis* the x or y axis in the Cartesian coordinate system?
    (b) Is the *vertical axis* the x or y axis?

30. What is the *origin* in the Cartesian coordinate system?

31. We can refer to the *x axis* and we can refer to the *y axis*. We can also refer to the *x* and *y axes*. Explain when we use the word *axis* and when we use the word *axes*.

32. Explain how to plot the point $(-3, 5)$ in the Cartesian coordinate system.

33. What does the graph of a linear equation illustrate?

34. Why are arrowheads added to the ends of graphs of linear equations?

35. What will the graph of a linear equation look like?

36. (a) How many points are needed to graph a linear equation? (b) Why is it always a good idea to use three or more points when graphing a linear equation?

37. What is the standard form of a linear equation?

38. When graphing linear equations the points that are plotted should all be *collinear*. Explain what this means.

CUMULATIVE REVIEW EXERCISES

[4.4] **39.** Subtract $6x^2 - 4x + 5$ from $-2x^2 - 5x + 9$.

[4.5] **40.** Multiply $(3x^2 - 4x + 5)(2x - 3)$.

[5.2] **41.** Factor by grouping $x^2 - 2x + 3xy - 6y$.

[6.4] **42.** Subtract $\dfrac{3}{x + 2} - \dfrac{4}{x + 1}$.

Group Activity/ Challenge Problems

In Section 7.3 we discuss how to find ordered pairs to plot when graphing linear equations. Let us see if you can draw some graphs now. For the following (a) select any three values for x and find the corresponding values of y; (b) plot the points (they should be collinear); (c) draw the graph.

1. $y = x$ **2.** $y = 2x$ **3.** $y = x + 1$ **4.** $2x + y = 4$

5. Another type of coordinate system that is used to identify a location or position on the Earth's surface involves *latitude and longitude*. Do research and write a report explaining how a specific location on the surface of the Earth can be represented using latitude and longitude. In your report approximate the location of your college using latitude and longitude.

7.3 Graphing Linear Equations

Tape 12

1 Graph linear equations by plotting points.
2 Graph linear equations of the form $ax + by = 0$.
3 Graph linear equations using the *x* and *y* intercepts.
4 Graph horizontal and vertical lines.

In Section 7.2 we explained the Cartesian Coordinate System, how to plot points, and how to recognize linear equations in two variables. Now we are ready to graph linear equations. *In this section we discuss two methods that can be used to graph linear equations: (1) graphing by plotting points, and (2) graphing using the x and y intercepts.* In Section 7.4 we discuss graphing using the slope and the *y* intercept. We begin by discussing graphing by plotting points.

Graphing by Plotting Points

❶ Graphing by plotting points is the most versatile method of graphing because we can also use it to graph second- and higher-degree equations. We will graph quadratic equations, which are second-degree equations, by plotting points in Chapter 10.

Graphing Linear Equations by Plotting Points

1. Solve the linear equation for the variable *y*. That is, get the variable *y* by itself on the left side of the equal sign.

2. Select a value for the variable *x*. Substitute this value in the equation for *x* and find the corresponding value of *y*. Record the ordered pair (*x, y*).

3. Repeat step 2 with two different values of *x*. This will give you two additional ordered pairs.

4. Plot the three ordered pairs. The three points should be collinear. If they are not collinear, recheck your work for mistakes.

5. *With a straightedge*, draw a straight line through the three points. Draw arrowheads on each end of the line to show that the line continues indefinitely in both directions.

In step 1, you need to solve the equation for *y*. If you have forgotten how to do this, review Section 3.1. In steps 2 and 3, you need to select values for *x*. The values you choose to select are up to you. However, you should choose values small enough so that the ordered pairs obtained can be plotted on the axes. Since *y* is often easy to find when $x = 0$, 0 is always a good value to select for *x*.

EXAMPLE 1   Graph the equation $y = 3x + 6$.

Solution: First we determine that this is a linear equation. Its graph must therefore be a straight line. The equation is already solved for *y*. Select three values for *x*, substitute them in the equation, and find the corresponding values for *y*. We will arbitrarily select the values 0, 2, and −3 for *x*. The calculations that follow show that when $x = 0$, $y = 6$, when $x = 2$, $y = 12$, and when $x = -3$, $y = -3$.

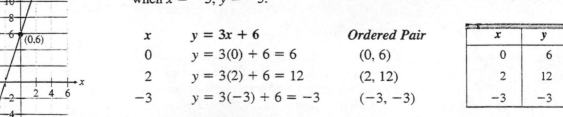

x	$y = 3x + 6$	*Ordered Pair*	*x*	*y*
0	$y = 3(0) + 6 = 6$	(0, 6)	0	6
2	$y = 3(2) + 6 = 12$	(2, 12)	2	12
−3	$y = 3(-3) + 6 = -3$	(−3, −3)	−3	−3

It is sometimes convenient to list the *x* and *y* values in a table. Then plot the three ordered pairs on the same axes (Fig. 7.23).

Since the three points are collinear, the graph appears correct. Connect the three points with a straight line. Place arrowheads at the ends of the line to show that the line continues infinitely in both directions.

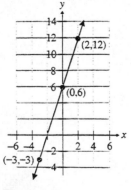

FIGURE 7.23

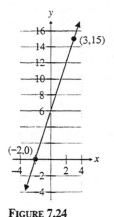

FIGURE 7.24

To graph the equation $y = 3x + 6$, we arbitrarily used the three values $x = 0$, $x = 2$, and $x = -3$. We could have selected three entirely different values and obtained exactly the same graph. When selecting values to substitute for x, use values that make the equation easy to evaluate.

The graph drawn in Example 1 represents the set of *all* ordered pairs that satisfy the equation $y = 3x + 6$. If we select any point on this line, the ordered pair represented by that point will be a solution to the equation $y = 3x + 6$. Similarly, any solution to the equation will be represented by a point on the line. Let us select some points on the graph, say, (3, 15) and (−2, 0), and verify that they are solutions to the equation (Fig. 7.24).

$$\text{Check } (3, 15): \quad y = 3x + 6 \qquad\qquad \text{Check } (-2, 0): \quad y = 3x + 6$$
$$15 = 3(3) + 6 \qquad\qquad\qquad\qquad 0 = 3(-2) + 6$$
$$15 = 9 + 6 \qquad\qquad\qquad\qquad\quad 0 = -6 + 6$$
$$15 = 15 \quad \text{true} \qquad\qquad\qquad\quad 0 = 0 \quad \text{true}$$

Remember, a graph of an equation is an illustration of the set of points whose coordinates satisfy the equation.

EXAMPLE 2 Graph the equation $2y = 4x - 12$.

Solution: We begin by solving the equation for y. This will make it easier to determine ordered pairs that satisfy the equation. To solve the equation for y, divide both sides of the equation by 2.

$$2y = 4x - 12$$
$$y = \frac{4x - 12}{2} = \frac{4x}{2} - \frac{12}{2} = 2x - 6$$

Now select three values for x and find the corresponding values for y using the equation $y = 2x - 6$.

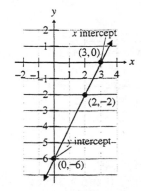

FIGURE 7.25

	$y = 2x - 6$		x	y
Let $x = 0$,	$y = 2(0) - 6 = -6$		0	−6
Let $x = 2$,	$y = 2(2) - 6 = -2$		2	−2
Let $x = 3$,	$y = 2(3) - 6 = 0$		3	0

Plot the points and draw the straight line (Fig. 7.25).

Graphing Linear Equations of the Form $ax + by = 0$

2 In Example 3 we graph an equation of the form $ax + by = 0$, which is a linear equation whose constant is 0.

EXAMPLE 3 Graph the equation $2x + 5y = 0$.

Solution: We begin by solving the equation for y.

$$2x + 5y = 0$$
$$5y = -2x$$
$$y = -\frac{2x}{5} \quad \text{or} \quad y = -\frac{2}{5}x$$

Now we select values for x and find the corresponding values of y. Which values shall we select for x? Notice that the coefficient of the x term is a fraction, with the denominator 5. If we select values for x that are multiples of the denominator, such as $\ldots -15, -10, -5, 0, 5, 10, 15, \ldots$, the 5 in the denominator will divide out. This will give us integer values for y. We will arbitrarily select the values $x = -5$, $x = 0$, and $x = 5$.

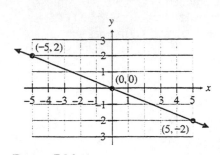

$$y = -\frac{2}{5}x$$

Let $x = -5$, $y = \left(-\frac{2}{5}\right)(-5) = 2$

Let $x = 0$, $y = \left(-\frac{2}{5}\right)(0) = 0$

Let $x = 5$, $y = -\frac{2}{5}(5) = -2$

x	y
-5	2
0	0
5	-2

FIGURE 7.26

Now plot the points and draw the graph (Fig. 7.26).

The graph in Example 3 passes through the origin. The graph of every linear equation with a constant of 0 (equations of the form $ax + by = 0$) will pass through the origin.

Graphing Using Intercepts

3 Now we discuss graphing linear equations using the x and y intercepts. Let us examine two points on the graph in Figure 7.25. Note that the graph crosses the x axis at 3. Therefore, $(3, 0)$ is called the **x intercept**. Note that the x intercept has an x coordinate of 3 and a y coordinate of 0. In general, an x intercept will be of the form $(x, 0)$. The x in the ordered pair is the value where the graph crosses the x axis.

The graph in Figure 7.25 crosses the y axis at -6. Therefore, $(0, -6)$ is called the **y intercept**. Note that the y intercept has an x coordinate of 0 and a y coordinate of -6. In general, a y intercept will be of the form $(0, y)$. The y in the ordered pair represents the value where the graph crosses the y axis.

Note that the graph in Figure 7.26 crosses both the x and y axes at the origin. Thus, both the x and y intercepts of this graph are $(0, 0)$.

It is often convenient to graph linear equations by finding their x and y intercepts. To graph an equation using the x and y intercepts, use the procedure that follows.

> **Graphing Linear Equations Using the x and y Intercepts**
> 1. **Find the y intercept by setting x in the given equation equal to 0 and finding the corresponding value of y.**
> 2. **Find the x intercept by setting y in the given equation equal to 0 and finding the corresponding value of x.**

3. Determine a check point by selecting a nonzero value for x and finding the corresponding value of y.

4. Plot the y intercept (where the graph crosses the y axis), the x intercept (where the graph crosses the x axis), and the check point. The three points should be collinear. If not, recheck your work.

5. *Using a straightedge,* draw a straight line through the three points. Draw an arrowhead at both ends of the line to show that the line continues indefinitely in both directions.

Helpful Hint

Since only two points are needed to determine a straight line, it is not absolutely necessary to determine and plot the check point in step 3. However, *if you use only the x and y intercepts to draw your graph and one of those points is wrong, your graph will be incorrect and you will not know it.* It is always a good idea to use three points when graphing a linear equation.

EXAMPLE 4 Graph the equation $3y = 6x + 12$ by plotting the x and y intercepts.

Solution: To find the y intercept (where the graph crosses the y axis), set $x = 0$ and find the corresponding value of y.

$$3y = 6x + 12$$
$$3y = 6(0) + 12$$
$$3y = 0 + 12$$
$$3y = 12$$
$$y = \frac{12}{3} = 4$$

The graph crosses the y axis at 4. The ordered pair representing the y intercept is $(0, 4)$. To find the x intercept (where the graph crosses the x axis), set $y = 0$ and find the corresponding value of x.

$$3y = 6x + 12$$
$$3(0) = 6x + 12$$
$$0 = 6x + 12$$
$$-12 = 6x$$
$$\frac{-12}{6} = x$$
$$-2 = x$$

The graph crosses the x axis at -2. The ordered pair representing the x intercept is $(-2, 0)$. Now plot the intercepts (Fig. 7.27).

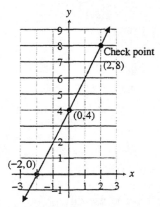

FIGURE 7.27

Before we graph the equation, we will select a nonzero value for x, find the corresponding value of y, and make sure that it is collinear with the x and y intercepts. This third point is our check point.

$$\text{Let } x = 2$$
$$3y = 6x + 12$$
$$3y = 6(2) + 12$$
$$3y = 12 + 12$$
$$3y = 24$$
$$y = \frac{24}{3} = 8$$

Plot the check point (2, 8). Since the three points are collinear, draw the straight line through all three points.

EXAMPLE 5 Graph the equation $2x + 3y = 9$ by finding the x and y intercepts.

Solution:

Find y Intercept	Find x Intercept	Check Point
Let $x = 0$	Let $y = 0$	Let $x = 2$
$2x + 3y = 9$	$2x + 3y = 9$	$2x + 3y = 9$
$2(0) + 3y = 9$	$2x + 3(0) = 9$	$2(2) + 3y = 9$
$0 + 3y = 9$	$2x + 0 = 9$	$4 + 3y = 9$
$3y = 9$	$2x = 9$	$3y = 5$
$y = 3$	$x = \dfrac{9}{2}$	$y = \dfrac{5}{3}$

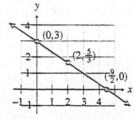

FIGURE 7.28

The three ordered pairs are $(0, 3,)$, $\left(\frac{9}{2}, 0\right)$, and $\left(2, \frac{5}{3}\right)$.

The three points appear to be collinear. Draw a straight line through all three points (Fig. 7.28).

EXAMPLE 6 Graph the equation $y = 20x + 60$.

Solution:

Find y Intercept	Find x Intercept	Check Point
Let $x = 0$	Let $y = 0$	Let $x = 3$
$y = 20x + 60$	$y = 20x + 60$	$y = 20x + 60$
$y = 20(0) + 60$	$0 = 20x + 60$	$y = 20(3) + 60$
$y = 60$	$-60 = 20x$	$y = 60 + 60$
	$-3 = x$	$y = 120$

The three ordered pairs are (0, 60), (−3, 0), and (3, 120). Since the values of y are large, we let each interval on the y axis be 15 units rather than 1 (Fig. 7.29). In addition, the length of the intervals on the y axis will be made smaller than those on the x axis. Sometimes you will have have to use different scales on the x and y axes, as illustrated, to accommodate the graph. Now plot the points and draw the graph.

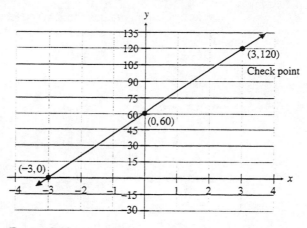

FIGURE 7.29

When selecting the scales for your axes, you should realize that different scales will result in the same equation having a different appearance. Consider the graphs shown in Figure 7.30. Both graphs represent the same equation, $y = x$. In Figure 7.30a, both the x and y axes have the same scale. In Figure 7.30b, the x and y axes do not have the same scale. Both graphs are correct in that each represents the graph of $y = x$. The difference in appearance is due to the difference in scales on the x axis. When possible, keep the scales on the x and y axis the same, as in Figure 7.30a.

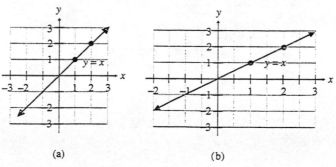

FIGURE 7.30

EXAMPLE 7   Graph the equation $3y + 2x = -4$.

(a) By solving the equation for y, selecting three values of x, and finding the corresponding values of y.

(b) By using the x and y intercepts.

Solution:

$$\text{(a)} \quad 3y + 2x = -4$$
$$3y = -2x - 4$$
$$y = \frac{-2x - 4}{3} = -\frac{2}{3}x - \frac{4}{3}$$

When selecting values for x, we select those that are multiples of 3 so that the arithmetic will be easier. Let us select 0, 3, and -3.

$$y = -\frac{2}{3}x - \frac{4}{3}$$

Let $x = 0$, $y = -\frac{2}{3}(0) - \frac{4}{3} = 0 - \frac{4}{3} = -\frac{4}{3}$

Let $x = 3$, $y = -\frac{2}{3}(3) - \frac{4}{3} = -\frac{6}{3} - \frac{4}{3} = -\frac{10}{3}$

Let $x = -3$, $y = -\frac{2}{3}(-3) - \frac{4}{3} = \frac{6}{3} - \frac{4}{3} = \frac{2}{3}$

x	y
0	$-\frac{4}{3}$
3	$-\frac{10}{3}$
-3	$\frac{2}{3}$

The graph is shown in Figure 7.31. Note that the coordinates are not always integers.

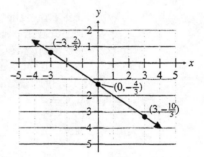

FIGURE 7.31

(b) $3y + 2x = -4$

Find y Intercept	*Find x Intercept*	*Check Point*
Let $x = 0$	Let $y = 0$	Let $x = 3$, then
$3y + 2x = -4$	$3y + 2x = -4$	$y = -\frac{10}{3}$
$3y + 2(0) = -4$	$3(0) + 2x = -4$	from part (a).
$3y = -4$	$2x = -4$	$\left(3, -\frac{10}{3}\right)$
$y = -\frac{4}{3}$	$x = -2$	

The graph is shown in Figure 7.32. Note that the graphs in Figures 7.31 and 7.32 are the same.

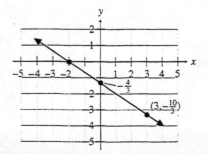

FIGURE 7.32

Horizontal and Vertical Lines

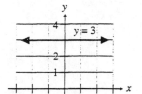

FIGURE 7.33

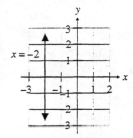

FIGURE 7.34

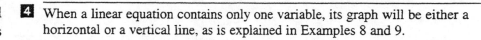 When a linear equation contains only one variable, its graph will be either a horizontal or a vertical line, as is explained in Examples 8 and 9.

EXAMPLE 8   Graph the equation $y = 3$.

Solution: This equation can be written as $y = 3 + 0x$. Thus, for any value of x selected, y will be 3. The graph of $y = 3$ is illustrated in Figure 7.33.

> **The graph of an equation of the form $y = b$ is a horizontal line whose y intercept is $(0, b)$**

EXAMPLE 9   Graph the equation $x = -2$.

Solution: This equation can be written as $x = -2 + 0y$. Thus, for any value of y selected, x will have a value of -2. The graph of $x = -2$ is illustrated in Figure 7.34.

> **The graph of an equation of the form $x = a$ is a vertical line whose x intercept is $(a, 0)$.**

Before we leave this section, let us look at an application of graphing. We will see additional applications of graphing linear equations in Sections 7.6 and 8.4.

EXAMPLE 10   The salary, R, received by a salesperson is $200 per week plus a 7% commission on all sales, s.

(a) Write an equation for the salary, R, in terms of the sales, s.

(b) Graph the salary for sales of $0 up to and including $20,000.

(c) From the graph estimate the salary if the salesperson's weekly sales are $15,000.

(d) By observing the graph, estimate the sales needed for the salesperson to earn a salary of $800.

Solution:

(a) Since s is the amount of sales, a 7% commission on s dollars in sales is $0.07s$.

$$\text{Salary received} = \$200 + \text{commission}$$
$$R = 200 + 0.07s$$

(b) We select three values for s and find the corresponding values of R.

	$R = 200 + 0.07s$		s	R
Let $s = 0$	$R = 200 + 0.07(0) = 200$		0	200
Let $s = 10,000$	$R = 200 + 0.07(10,000) = 900$		10,000	900
Let $s = 20,000$	$R = 200 + 0.07(20,000) = 1600$		20,000	1600

The graph is illustrated in Figure 7.35. Notice that since we only graph the equation for values of s from 0 to 20,000, we do not place arrowheads on the ends of the graph.

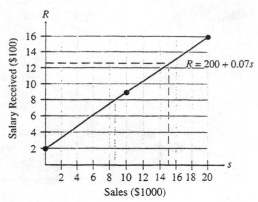

FIGURE 7.35

(c) To determine the weekly salary earned on sales of $15,000, locate $15,000 on the sales axis. Then draw a vertical line up to where it intersects the graph, the *red* line in Figure 7.35. Now draw a horizontal line across to the salary axis. Since the horizontal line crosses the salary axis at about $1250, weekly sales of $15,000 would result in a weekly salary of about $1250. You can find the exact salary by substituting 15,000 for s in the equation $R = 200 + 0.07s$ and finding the value of R. Do this now.

(d) To find the sales needed for the salesperson to earn a weekly salary of $800, we find $800 on the salary axis. We then draw a horizontal line from the point to the graph, as shown with the *green* line in Figure 7.35. We then draw a vertical line from the point of intersection of the graph to the sales axis. This value on the sales axis represents the sales needed for the salesperson to earn $800. Thus, sales of about $8600 per week would result in a salary of $800. An exact answer can be found by substituting 800 for R in the equation $R = 200 + 0.07s$ and solving the equation for s. Do this now.

Helpful Hint

In Chapter 2 we solved linear equations in one variable. Consider the solution to the equation $3x + 5 = x + 9$.

$$3x + 5 = x + 9$$
$$2x + 5 = 9$$
$$2x = 4$$
$$x = 2$$

A check will show that 2 makes the statement true, so 2 is the solution to the equation.

Consider the equation $3x + 5 = x + 9$ again. This time let us set one side of the equation equal to zero, as follows.

$$3x + 5 = x + 9$$
$$2x + 5 = 9$$
$$2x - 4 = 0$$

Now if we replace the 0 with y, we get $y = 2x - 4$. The graph of $y = 2x - 4$ follows.

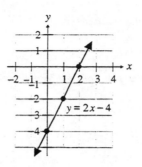

Notice the x intercept of this graph is at 2, the value obtained for the solution of the equation $3x + 5 = x + 9$. Is this just a coincidence, or will this process always result in the x intercept of the graph being the solution to the linear equation in one variable? This process will always result in the x intercept being the solution to the linear equation in one variable. Let's discuss why.

Consider the two equations $3x + 5 = x + 9$ and $2x - 4 = 0$. These equations are equivalent since they have the same solution. The solution to the equation $2x - 4 = 0$ is the value of x that makes the expression $2x - 4$ have a value of 0. If we replace the 0 in the equation with y, we get $y = 2x - 4$. The value of y is 0 where the graph crosses the x axis, or at the x intercept. Thus, the value of x where the graph crosses the x axis is the solution to both $2x - 4 = 0$ and $3x + 5 = x + 9$.

Calculator Corner

Calculators are available that will graph equations on the calculator display. Such calculators are called graphing calculators or graphers. Some graphing calculators available at this time include:

Casio	*Hewlett-Packard*	*Sharp*	*Texas Instruments*
FX7000	HP 48S/Sx	EL-9200	TI 81
FX7700	HP 48G/Gx	EL-9300	TI 82
FX 8700			TI 85

The TI 82 is pictured on the left.

The cost of graphing calculators start at about \$65 and increase, depending on the model and features you select. Using graphing calculators in mathematics courses is becoming more and more common. You may find yourself using a graphing calculator if you take additional mathematics courses.

Since each calculator functions a little differently, you should consult with your mathematics instructor before you purchase one. A particular graphing calculator may be required in a later course.

Exercise Set 7.3

Find the missing coordinate in the solutions for $2x + y = 6$.

1. $(2, ?)$ **2.** $(-1, ?)$ **3.** $(?, -5)$

4. $(?, -3)$ **5.** $(?, 0)$ **6.** $(\frac{1}{2}, ?)$

Find the missing coordinate in the solutions for $3x - 2y = 8$.

7. $(2, ?)$ **8.** $(0, ?)$ **9.** $(?, 0)$

10. $(?, -\frac{1}{2})$ **11.** $(-3, ?)$ **12.** $(?, -5)$

Graph each equation.

13. $y = 4$ **14.** $x = -2$ **15.** $x = 3$ **16.** $y = 2$

Graph by plotting points. Plot at least three points for each graph.

17. $y = 4x - 2$ **18.** $y = -x + 3$ **19.** $y = 6x + 2$ **20.** $y = x - 4$

21. $y = -\dfrac{1}{2}x + 3$ **22.** $2y = 2x + 4$ **23.** $6x - 2y = 4$ **24.** $4x - y = 5$

25. $5x - 2y = 8$ **26.** $3x + 2y = 0$ **27.** $6x + 5y = 30$ **28.** $-2x - 3y = 6$

29. $-4x + 5y = 0$ **30.** $8y - 16x = 24$ **31.** $y = 20x + 40$ **32.** $2y - 50 = 100x$

33. $y = \dfrac{2}{3}x$

34. $y = -\dfrac{3}{5}x$

35. $y = \dfrac{1}{2}x + 4$

36. $y = -\dfrac{2}{5}x + 2$

37. $2y = 3x + 6$

38. $-4x - y = -2$

39. $-4x + 8y = 16$

40. $4x - 6y = 10$

Graph using the x and y intercepts.

41. $y = 2x + 4$

42. $y = -2x + 6$

43. $y = 4x - 3$

44. $y = -3x + 8$

45. $y = -6x + 5$

46. $y = 4x + 16$

47. $2y + 3x = 12$

48. $-2x + 3y = 10$

49. $4x = 3y - 9$

50. $7x + 14y = 21$

51. $\dfrac{1}{2}x + y = 4$

52. $30x + 25y = 50$

53. $6x - 12y = 24$　　**54.** $25x + 50y = 100$　　**55.** $8y = 6x - 12$　　**56.** $-3y - 2x = -6$

57. $30y + 10x = 45$　　**58.** $120x - 360y = 720$　　**59.** $40x + 6y = 40$　　**60.** $20x - 240 = -60y$

61. $\dfrac{1}{3}x + \dfrac{1}{4}y = 12$　　**62.** $\dfrac{1}{5}x - \dfrac{2}{3}y = 60$　　**63.** $\dfrac{1}{2}x = \dfrac{2}{5}y - 80$　　**64.** $\dfrac{2}{3}y = \dfrac{5}{4}x + 120$

Write the equation represented by the given graph. (See Examples 8 and 9.)

65.
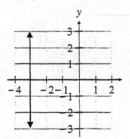

66.
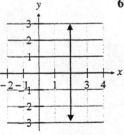

67.
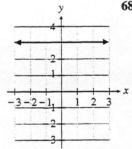

68.
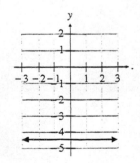

Study Example 10 before working Exercises 69–72.

69. The cost, C, of renting a large truck is $25 per day plus $1 per mile, m.

(a) Write an equation for the cost in terms of the miles driven.

(b) Graph the equation for values up to and including 100 miles.

(c) Estimate the cost of driving 50 miles in one day.

(d) Estimate the miles driven if the cost for one day is $60.

70. Simple interest is calculated by the simple interest formula, interest = principal x rate x time or $I = prt$. If the principal is $10,000 and the rate is 5%

   (a) Write an equation for simple interest in terms of time.

   (b) Graph the equation for times of 0 to 20 years inclusive.

   (c) What is the simple interest for 10 years?

   (d) If the simple interest is $500, find the length of time.

71. The weekly profit, P, of a video rental store can be approximated by the formula $P = 1.5n - 200$, where n is the number of tapes rented weekly.

   (a) Draw a graph of profit in terms of tape rentals for up to and including 1000 tapes.

   (b) Estimate the weekly profit if 500 tapes are rented.

   (c) Estimate the number of tapes rented if the week's profit is $1000.

72. The cost, C, of playing tennis in the Downtown Tennis Club includes an annual $200 membership fee plus $10 per hour, h, of court time.

   (a) Write an equation for the annual cost of playing tennis at the Downtown Tennis Club in terms of hours played.

   (b) Graph the equation for up to and including 300 hours.

   (c) Estimate the cost for playing 200 hours in a year.

   (d) If the annual cost for playing tennis was $1200, estimate how many hours of tennis were played.

73. Explain how to find the x and y intercepts of a line.

74. How many points are needed to graph a straight line? How many points should be used? Why?

75. What will the graph of $y = b$ look like for any real number b?

76. What will the graph of $x = a$ look like for any real number a?

77. In Example 10 (c) and (d), we made an estimate. Why is it sometimes not possible to obtain an exact answer from a graph?

78. In Example 10 does the salary, R, depend on the sales, s, or do the sales depend on the salary? Explain.

Determine the coefficients to be placed in the shaded areas so that the graph of the equation will be a line with the x and y intercepts specified. Explain how you determined your answer.

79. $x +$ $y = 20$; x intercept of 4, y intercept of 5

80. $x +$ $y = 18$; x intercept of -3, y intercept of 6

81. $x -$ $y = -12$; x intercept of -2, y intercept of 3

82. $x -$ $y = 30$; x intercept of -5, y intercept of -15

CUMULATIVE REVIEW EXERCISES

[2.5] **83.** Solve the equation $4(x - 2) - (3 - x) = 2x + 4$.

[4.7] **84.** Two cyclists are 18 miles apart headed toward each other. One is traveling at a speed of 3 miles per hour faster than the other. If they meet in 1.5 hours, find the speed of each.

[5.6] **85.** Solve the equation $2x^2 = -23x + 12$.

[6.6] **86.** Solve the equation $x - 14 = \dfrac{-48}{x}$.

Group Activity/ Challenge Problems

1. (a) Graph each of the following equations on the same axes:
$$y = 2x + 4, \quad y = 2x + 2, \quad y = 2x - 2.$$

   (b) What do you notice about the graphs?

   (c) Explain why you think this happens. We discuss this material further in Section 7.5.

2. (a) Carefully graph the following equations on the same axes: $y = 2x - 1$, $y = -x + 5$.

(b) Determine the point of intersection of the two graphs.

(c) Substitute the values for x and y at the point of intersection into each of the two equations and determine if the point of intersection satisfies each equation.

(d) Do you believe there are any other ordered pairs that satisfy both equations? Explain your answer. We will study equations like these, called systems of equations, in Chapter 8.

3. A straight line has an x intercept of $(2, 0)$ and a y intercept of $(0, 4)$.

(a) Draw the line.

(b) Determine the equation of the line. Explain how you determined your answer. We study problems like this in Section 7.5.

In chapter 10 we will be graphing quadratic equations. The graphs of quadratic equations are *not* straight lines. Graph each of the following quadratic equations by selecting values for x and find the corresponding values of y, then plot the points. Make sure you plot a sufficient number of points to get an accurate graph.

4. $y = x^2 - 4$ **5.** $y = x^2 - 2x - 8$

7.4   Slope of a Line

Tape 12

1   Find the slope of a line.
2   Recognize positive and negative slopes.
3   Examine the slopes of horizontal and vertical lines.

Slope   **1**   The slope of a line is an important concept in many areas of mathematics. A knowledge of slope is helpful in understanding linear equations.

The slope of a line is a measure of the *steepness* of the line. The **slope of a line** is a ratio of the vertical change to the horizontal change between any two selected points on the line. As an example, consider the two points $(3, 6)$ and $(1, 2)$, (Fig. 7.36a).

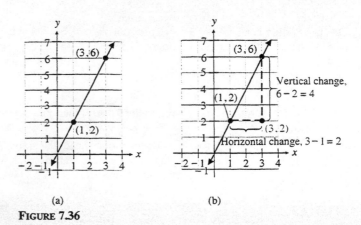

(a)   (b)

FIGURE 7.36

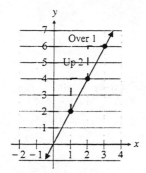

FIGURE 7.37

If we draw a line parallel to the x axis through the point (1, 2) and a line parallel to the y axis through the point (3, 6), the two lines intersect at (3, 2), (Fig. 7.36b). From the figure we can determine the slope of the line. The vertical change (along the y axis) is $6 - 2$, or 4 units. The horizontal change (along the x axis) is $3 - 1$, or 2 units.

$$\text{Slope} = \frac{\text{vertical change}}{\text{horizontal change}} = \frac{4}{2} = 2$$

Thus, the slope of the line through these two points is 2. By examining the line connecting these two points, we can see that as the graph moves up 2 units on the y axis it moves to the right 1 unit on the x axis (Fig. 7.37).

Now we present the procedure to find the slope of a line between any two points (x_1, y_1) and (x_2, y_2). Consider Figure 7.38.

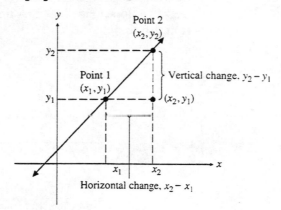

FIGURE 7.38

The vertical change can be found by subtracting y_1 from y_2. The horizontal change can be found by subtracting x_1 from x_2.

Slope of a Line Through the Points (x_1, y_1) and (x_2, y_2)

$$\text{Slope} = \frac{\text{change in } y \text{ (vertical change)}}{\text{change in } x \text{ (horizontal change)}} = \frac{y_2 - y_1}{x_2 - x_1}$$

It makes no difference which two points are selected when finding the slope of a line. It also makes no difference which point you label (x_1, y_1) or (x_2, y_2). The Greek capital letter delta, Δ, is often used to represent the words "the change in." Thus, the slope, which is symbolized by the letter m, is indicated as

$$m = \frac{\Delta y}{\Delta x} = \frac{y_2 - y_1}{x_2 - x_1}$$

EXAMPLE 1   Find the slope of the line through the points $(-6, -1)$ and $(3, 5)$.

Solution: We will designate $(-6, -1)$ as (x_1, y_1) and $(3, 5)$ as (x_2, y_2).

$$m = \frac{y_2 - y_1}{x_2 - x_1} = \frac{5 - (-1)}{3 - (-6)} = \frac{5 + 1}{3 + 6} = \frac{6}{9} = \frac{2}{3}$$

Thus, the slope is $\frac{2}{3}$.

If we had designated (3, 5) as (x_1, y_1) and $(-6, -1)$ as (x_2, y_2), we would have obtained the same results.

$$m = \frac{y_2 - y_1}{x_2 - x_1} = \frac{-1 - 5}{-6 - 3} = \frac{-6}{-9} = \frac{2}{3}$$

Positive and Negative Slopes

A straight line for which the value of y increases as x increases has a **positive slope** (Fig. 7.39a). A line with a positive slope rises as it moves from left to right. A straight line for which the value of y decreases as x increases has a **negative slope** (Fig. 7.39b). A line with a negative slope falls as it moves from left to right.

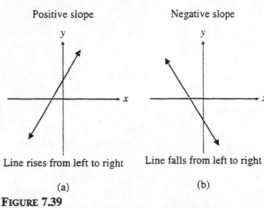

Positive slope   Negative slope

Line rises from left to right   Line falls from left to right

(a)   (b)

FIGURE 7.39

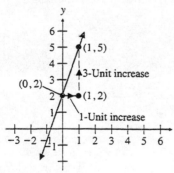

FIGURE 7.40

EXAMPLE 2   Consider the line in Figure 7.40.

(a) Determine its slope by observing the vertical change and horizontal change between the points (1, 5) and (0, 2).

(b) Calculate the slope of the line using the two given points.

Solution:

(a) The first thing you should notice is that the slope is positive since the line rises from left to right. Now determine the vertical change between the two points. The vertical change is +3 units. Next determine the horizontal change between the two points. The horizontal change is +1 unit. Since the slope is the ratio of the vertical change to the horizontal change between any two points, and since the slope is positive, the slope of the line is $\frac{3}{1}$ or 3.

(b) We can use any two points on the line to determine its slope. Since we are given the ordered pairs (1, 5) and (0, 2) we will use them.

Let (x_2, y_2) be (1, 5)   Let (x_1, y_1) be (0, 2)

$$m = \frac{y_2 - y_1}{x_2 - x_1} = \frac{5 - 2}{1 - 0} = \frac{3}{1} = 3$$

Note that the slope obtained in part (**b**) agrees with the slope obtained in part (**a**). If we had designated $(1, 5)$ as (x_1, y_1) and $(0, 2)$ as (x_2, y_2), the slope would not have changed. Try reversing (x_1, y_1) and (x_2, y_2) and see that you will still obtain a slope of 3.

EXAMPLE 3   Find the slope of the line in Figure 7.41 by observing the vertical change and horizontal change between the two points shown.

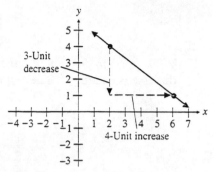

FIGURE 7.41

Solution: Since the graph falls from left to right we should realize that the line has a negative slope. The vertical change between the two given points is -3 units since it is decreasing. The horizontal change between the two given points is 4 units since it is increasing. Since the ratio of the vertical change to the horizontal change is -3 units to 4 units, the slope of this line is

$$\frac{-3}{4} \text{ or } -\frac{3}{4}.$$

Using the two points shown in Fig. 7.41 and the definition of slope, calculate the slope of the line. You should obtain the same answer as we did in Example 3.

Slope of Horizontal and Vertical Lines

3 Now we consider the slope of horizontal and vertical lines.

Consider the graph of $y = 3$ (Fig. 7.42). What is its slope?

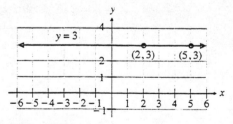

FIGURE 7.42

The graph is parallel to the x axis and goes through the points $(2, 3)$ and $(5, 3)$. Select $(5, 3)$ as (x_2, y_2) and $(2, 3)$ as (x_1, y_1). Then the slope of the line is

$$m = \frac{y_2 - y_1}{x_2 - x_1} = \frac{3 - 3}{5 - 2} = \frac{0}{3} = 0$$

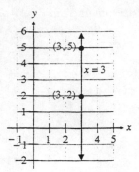

FIGURE 7.43

Since there is no change in y, this line has a slope of 0. **Every horizontal line has a slope of 0.**

Now we discuss vertical lines. Consider the graph of $x = 3$ (Fig. 7.43). What is its slope?

The graph is parallel to the y axis and goes through the points (3, 2) and (3, 5). Select (3, 5) as (x_2, y_2) and (3, 2) as (x_1, y_1). Then the slope of the line is

$$m = \frac{y_2 - y_1}{x_2 - x_1} = \frac{5 - 2}{3 - 3} = \frac{3}{0}$$

We learned in Section 1.7 that $\frac{3}{0}$ is undefined. Thus, we say that the slope of this line is undefined. **The slope of any vertical line is undefined.**

Exercise Set 7.4

Find the slope of the line through the given points.

1. (4, 1) and (5, 6)

2. (8, −2) and (6, −4)

3. (9, 0) and (5, −2)

4. (5, −6) and (6, −5)

5. (3, 8) and (−3, 8)

6. (−4, 2) and (6, 5)

7. (−4, 6) and (−2, 6)

8. (9, 3) and (5, −6)

9. (3, 4) and (3, −2)

10. (−7, 5) and (3, −4)

11. (−4, 2) and (5, −3)

12. (−9, −6) and (−3, −1)

13. (−1, 7) and (4, −3)

14. (0, 4) and (6, −2)

By observing the vertical and horizontal change of the line between the two points indicated, determine the slope of the line.

15.

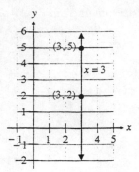

16.

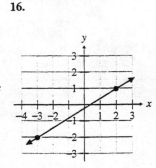

17.

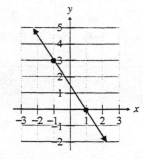

18.

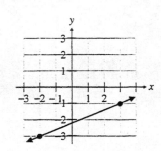

19.

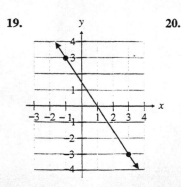

20.

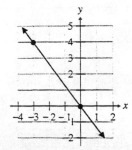

21.

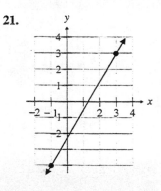

22.

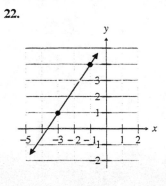

23.

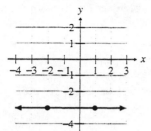

24.

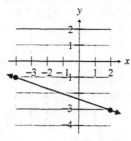

25.

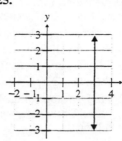

26.

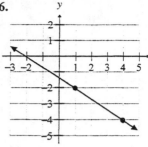

27. Explain what is meant by the slope of a line.

28. Explain how to find the slope of a line.

29. What does it mean when a line has a positive slope?

30. What does it mean when a line has a negative slope?

31. Explain how to tell by observation if the line has a positive slope or negative slope.

32. What is the slope of any horizontal line? Explain your answer.

33. Do vertical lines have a slope? Explain.

CUMULATIVE REVIEW EXERCISES

We have spent a great deal of time discussing and solving equations. For each type of equation that follows (**a**) *give a general description of the equation, and* (**b**) *give a specific example of the equation (answers will vary).*

[2.2] **34.** A linear equation in one variable.

[5.6] **35.** A quadratic equation in one variable.

[6.6] **36.** A rational equation in one variable.

[7.2] **37.** A linear equation in two variables.

Group Activity/ Challenge Problems

1. Find the slope of the line through the points $(\frac{1}{2}, -\frac{3}{8})$ and $(-\frac{4}{9}, -\frac{7}{2})$.

2. If one point on a line is $(6, -4)$ and the slope of the line is $-\frac{5}{3}$, identify another point on the line.

3. One point on a line is $(-5, 2)$ and the slope of the line is $-\frac{3}{4}$. A second point on the line has a y coordinate of -7. Find the x coordinate of the point.

4. The slope of a hill and the slope of a line both measure steepness. However, there are several important differences.

(a) Explain how you think the slope of a hill is determined.

(b) Is the slope of a line, graphed in the Cartesian coordinate system, measured in any specific unit? Is the slope of a hill measured in any specific unit?

5. A quadrilateral (a four-sided figure) has four vertices (the points where the sides meet). Vertex A is at $(0, 1)$, vertex B is at $(6, 2)$, vertex C is at $(5, 4)$, and vertex D is at $(1, -1)$.

   (a) Graph the quadrilateral in the Cartesian coordinate system.

   (b) Find the slope of sides AC, CB, DB, and AD.

   (c) Do you believe this figure is a parallelogram? Explain.

6. The following graph shows the world's population estimated to the year 2016.

   (a) Find the slope of the line segment between each pair of points, that is, ab, bc, and so on. Remember, the second coordinate is in billions. Thus, for example, 0.5 billion is actually 500,000,000.

   (b) Would you say that this graph represents a linear equation? Explain.

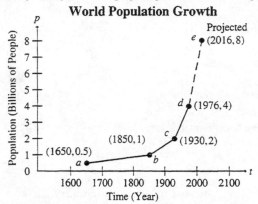

7. Consider the graph on the left.

   (a) Do you believe that the slope of the dashed line from a to d will be the same as the average of the slopes of the three solid lines?

   (b) Find the slope of the dashed line from a to d.

   (c) Find the slope of each of the three solid lines.

   (d) Find the average of the three slopes found in part (c).

   (e) Determine if your answer in part (a) appears correct.

   (f) What do you think this means?

7.5 Slope–Intercept and Point–Slope Forms of a Linear Equation

Tape 12

1 Write a linear equation in slope–intercept form.
2 Graph a linear equation using the slope and y intercept.
3 Use the slope and y intercept to determine the equation of a line.
4 Determine if two lines are parallel.
5 Use the slope and a point on the line or two points on a line to determine the equation of the line.
6 Compare the three methods of graphing linear equations.

In Section 7.2 we introduced the **standard form** of a linear equation, $ax + by = c$. In this section we introduce two more forms, the slope–intercept form and the point–slope form. We begin our discussion with the slope–intercept form.

Slope–Intercept Form   **1** A very important form of a linear equation is the **slope–intercept form,** $y = mx + b$. The graph of an equation of the form $y = mx + b$ will always be a straight line with a **slope of m** and a **y intercept of b.** For example, the graph of the equation $y = 3x - 4$ will be a straight line with a slope of 3 and a y intercept of -4. The graph of $y = -2x + 5$ will be a straight line with a slope of -2 and a y intercept of 5.

> ### Slope–Intercept Form of a Linear Equation
>
> $$y = mx + b$$
>
> where m is the slope, and b* is the y intercept of the line.

$$\overset{\text{slope}}{\underset{}{}} \quad \overset{y\text{ intercept}}{\underset{}{}}$$
$$y = mx + b$$

Equations in Slope–Intercept Form	Slope	y Intercept
$y = 3x - 6$	3	-6
$y = \dfrac{1}{2}x + \dfrac{3}{2}$	$\dfrac{1}{2}$	$\dfrac{3}{2}$
$y = -5x + 3$	-5	3
$y = -\dfrac{2}{3}x - \dfrac{3}{5}$	$-\dfrac{2}{3}$	$-\dfrac{3}{5}$

> **To write a linear equation in slope–intercept form,** solve the equation for y.

Once the equation is solved for y, the numerical coefficient of the x term will be the slope, and the constant term will be the y intercept.

EXAMPLE 1 Write the equation $-3x + 4y = 8$ in slope–intercept form. State the slope and y intercept.

Solution: To write this equation in slope–intercept form, we solve the equation for y.

$$-3x + 4y = 8$$
$$4y = 3x + 8$$
$$y = \frac{3x + 8}{4}$$
$$y = \frac{3}{4}x + \frac{8}{4}$$
$$y = \frac{3}{4}x + 2$$

The slope is $\frac{3}{4}$, and the y intercept is 2.

---

*In this section, when we refer to b as the y intercept, it means that the y intercept is $(0, b)$.

Graphing Linear Equations Using the Slope and *y* Intercept

2 In Section 7.4 we discussed two methods of graphing a linear equation. They were (1) by plotting points and (2) using the *x* and *y* intercepts. Now we present a third method. This method makes use of the slope and the *y* intercept. Remember that when we solve an equation for *y* we put the equation in slope–intercept form. Once in this form we can determine the slope and the *y* intercept of the graph from the equation. The procedure to use to graph by this method follows.

> **To Graph Linear Equations Using the Slope and *y* Intercept**
> 1. Solve the linear equation for *y*. That is, get the equation in slope–intercept form, $y = mx + b$.
> 2. Note the slope, *m*, and *y* intercept, *b*.
> 3. Plot the *y* intercept on the *y* axis.
> 4. Use the slope to find a second point on the graph.
>   (a) If the slope is **positive,** a second point can be found by moving **up and to the right.** Thus, if the slope is of the form $\dfrac{p}{q}$, we can find a second point by moving *up p* units and to the *right q* units.
>   (b) If the slope is **negative,** a second point can be found by moving **down and to the right** (or **up and to the left**). Thus, if the slope is of the form $-\dfrac{p}{q}$ $\left(\text{or } \dfrac{-p}{q} \text{ or } \dfrac{p}{-q}\right)$, we can find a second point by moving *down p* units and to the *right q* units (or *up p* units and to the *left q* units).
> 5. With a straightedge, draw a straight line through the two points. Draw arrowheads at the ends of the line to show that the line continues indefinitely in both directions.

EXAMPLE 2 Write the equation $-3x + 4y = 8$ in slope–intercept form; then use the slope and *y* intercept to graph $-3x + 4y = 8$.

Solution: In Example 1 we solved $-3x + 4y = 8$ for *y*. We found that

$$y = \frac{3}{4}x + 2$$

The slope of the line is 3/4 and the *y* intercept is 2. Mark the first point, the *y* intercept, at 2 on the *y* axis (Fig. 7.44). Now we use the slope 3/4 , to find a second point. Since the slope is positive, we move up 3 units and to the right 4 units to find the second point. A second point will be at (4, 5). We can continue this process to obtain a third point at (8, 8). Now draw a straight line through the three points. Notice that the line has a positive slope, which is what we expected.

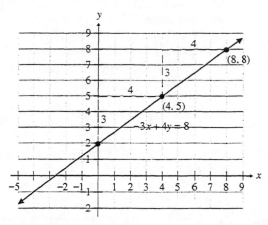

FIGURE 7.44

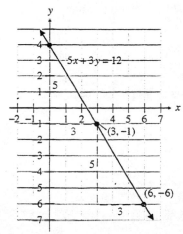

FIGURE 7.45

EXAMPLE 3 Graph the equation $5x + 3y = 12$ by using the slope and y intercept.

Solution: Solve the equation for y.

$$5x + 3y = 12$$
$$3y = -5x + 12$$
$$y = \frac{-5x + 12}{3}$$
$$y = -\frac{5}{3}x + 4$$

Thus, the slope is $-5/3$ and the y intercept is 4. Begin by marking a point at 4 on the y axis (Fig. 7.45). Then move down 5 units and to the right 3 units to determine the next point. We move down and to the right (or up and to the left) because the slope is negative and a line with a negative slope must fall as it goes from left to right. Finally, draw the straight line between the plotted points.

Determine the Equation of a Line

☒ Now that we know how to use the slope–intercept form of a line, we can use it to write the equation of a given line. To do so, we need to determine the slope, m, and y intercept, b, of the line. Once we determine these values we can write the equation in slope–intercept form, $y = mx + b$. For example, if we determine the slope of a line is -4 and the y intercept is 6, the equation of the line is $y = -4x + 6$.

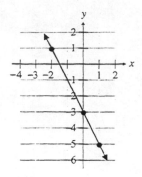

FIGURE 7.46

EXAMPLE 4   Determine the equation of the line shown in Figure 7.46.

Solution: The graph shows that the y intercept is -3. Now we need to determine the slope of the line. Since the graph falls from left to right, it has a negative slope. We can see that the vertical change is 2 units for each horizontal change of 1 unit. Thus, the slope of the line is -2. The slope can also be determined by selecting any two points on the line and calculating the slope. Let us use the point $(-2, 1)$ to represent (x_2, y_2) and the point $(0, -3)$ to represent (x_1, y_1).

$$m = \frac{\Delta y}{\Delta x} = \frac{y_2 - y_1}{x_2 - x_1} = \frac{1 - (-3)}{-2 - 0} = \frac{1 + 3}{-2} = \frac{4}{-2} = -2$$

Again we obtain a slope of -2. The slope–intercept form of a line is $y = mx + b$, where m is the slope and b is the y intercept. Substituting -2 for m and -3 for b gives us the equation of the line in Figure 7.46, which is $y = -2x - 3$.

Parallel Lines

4 We will discuss the meaning of parallel lines shortly, but before we do we will work Example 5.

EXAMPLE 5   Determine if both equations represent lines that have the same slope.

$$6x + 3y = 8$$
$$-4x - 2y = -3$$

Solution: Solve each equation for y to get the equations in slope–intercept form.

$$6x + 3y = 8 \qquad\qquad -4x - 2y = -3$$
$$3y = -6x + 8 \qquad\qquad -2y = 4x - 3$$
$$y = \frac{-6x + 8}{3} \qquad\qquad y = \frac{4x - 3}{-2}$$
$$y = -2x + \frac{8}{3} \qquad\qquad y = -2x + \frac{3}{2}$$

Both lines have the same slope of -2. Notice, however, that their y intercepts are different.

Two lines are **parallel** when they do not intersect no matter how far they are extended. Figure 7.47 illustrates two parallel lines. **Lines with the same slope are parallel** (or identical) **lines.** The graphs of the equations in Example 5 are parallel lines since they both have the same slope, -2. Note that the two equations represent different lines since their y intercepts are different.

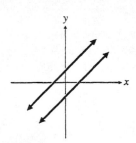

FIGURE 7.47

To Determine If Two Lines Are Parallel
Write both equations in slope–intercept form and compare the slopes of the two lines. If both lines have the same slope, but different y inter-

cepts, then the lines are parallel. If the slopes are not the same, the lines are not parallel. If both equations have the same slope and the same y intercept then both equations represent the same line.

EXAMPLE 6

(a) Determine whether or not the following equations represent parallel lines.
(b) Graph both equations on the same set of axes.

$$y = 2x + 4$$
$$-4x + 2y = -2$$

Solution:

(a) Write each equation in slope–intercept form and compare their slopes. The equation $y = 2x + 4$ is already in slope–intercept form.

$$-4x + 2y = -2$$
$$2y = 4x - 2$$
$$y = \frac{4x - 2}{2} = 2x - 1$$

The two equations are now

$$y = 2x + 4$$
$$y = 2x - 1$$

Since both equations have the same slope, 2, but different y intercepts, the equations represent parallel lines.

(b) We now graph $y = 2x + 4$ and $y = 2x - 1$ on the same axes (Fig. 7.48). Remember that $y = 2x - 1$ is the equation $-4x + 2y = -2$ in slope-intercept form.

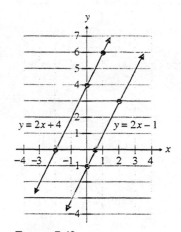

FIGURE 7.48

Point–Slope Form of a Linear Equation

5 Thus far we have discussed the standard form of a linear equation, $ax + by = c$, and the slope–intercept form of a linear equation, $y = mx + b$. Now we will discuss another form, called the *point–slope form.*

When the slope of a line and a point on the line are known, we can use the point–slope form to determine the equation of the line. The point–slope form can be obtained by beginning with the slope between any selected point (x, y) and a fixed point (x_1, y_1) on a line.

$$m = \frac{y - y_1}{x - x_1} \quad \text{or} \quad \frac{m}{1} = \frac{y - y_1}{x - x_1}$$

Now cross-multiply to obtain

$$m(x - x_1) = y - y_1 \quad \text{or} \quad y - y_1 = m(x - x_1)$$

Point–Slope Form of a Linear Equation

$$y - y_1 = m(x - x_1)$$

where m is the slope of the line and (x_1, y_1) is a point on the line.

EXAMPLE 7 Write an equation of the line that goes through the point (2, 3) and has a slope of 4.

Solution: The slope m is 4. The point on the line is (2, 3); use this point for (x_1, y_1) in the formula. Substitute 4 for m, 2 for x_1, and 3 for y_1 in the point–slope form of a linear equation.

$$y - y_1 = m(x - x_1)$$
$$y - 3 = 4(x - 2)$$
$$y - 3 = 4x - 8$$
$$y = 4x - 5$$

The graph of $y = 4x - 5$ has a slope of 4 and passes through the point (2, 3). •....

The answer to Example 7 was given in slope–intercept form. The answer could have also been given in standard form. Therefore, two other acceptable answers are $-4x + y = -5$ and $4x - y = 5$. Your instructor may specify the form in which the equation is to be given.

Helpful Hint

We have discussed three forms of a linear equation. We summarize the three forms below:

Standard Form	Examples
$ax + by = c$	$2x - 3y = 8$
	$-5x + y = -2$

Slope–Intercept Form	Examples
$y = mx + b$	$y = 2x - 5$
(m is the slope, b is the y intercept)	$y = -\dfrac{3}{2}x + 2$

Point–Slope Form	Examples
$y - y_1 = m(x - x_1)$	$y - 3 = 2(x + 4)$
(m is the slope, (x_1, y_1) is a point on the line)	$y + 5 = -4(x - 1)$

We now discuss how to use the point–slope form to determine the equation of a line when two points on the line are known.

EXAMPLE 8 Find an equation of the line through the points $(-1, -3)$ and $(4, 2)$. Write the equation in slope–intercept form.

Solution: To use the point–slope form, we must first find the slope of the line through the two points. To determine the slope, let us designate $(-1, -3)$ as (x_1, y_1) and $(4, 2)$ as (x_2, y_2).

$$m = \frac{y_2 - y_1}{x_2 - x_1} = \frac{2 - (-3)}{4 - (-1)} = \frac{2 + 3}{4 + 1} = \frac{5}{5} = 1$$

We can use either point (one at a time) in determining the equation of the line. This example will be worked out using both points to show that the solutions obtained are identical.

Using the point $(-1, -3)$ as (x_1, y_1),

$$y - y_1 = m(x - x_1)$$
$$y - (-3) = 1[x - (-1)]$$
$$y + 3 = x + 1$$
$$y = x - 2$$

Using the point $(4, 2)$ as (x_1, y_1),

$$y - y_1 = m(x - x_1)$$
$$y - 2 = 1(x - 4)$$
$$y - 2 = x - 4$$
$$y = x - 2$$

Note that the equations for the line are identical.

Helpful Hint

In the exercise set at the end of this section, you will be asked to write a linear equation in slope–intercept form. Even though you will eventually write the equation in slope–intercept form, you may need to start your work with the point–slope form. Below we indicate the initial form to use to solve the problem.

Begin with the **slope–intercept form** if you know:

The slope of the line and the y intercept

Begin with the **point–slope form** if you know:

(a) The slope of the line and a point on the line, or

(b) Two points on the line (first find the slope, then use the point–slope form)

Summary of Three Methods of Graphing Linear Equations

6 We have discussed three methods to graph a linear equation: (1) plotting points, (2) using the x and y intercepts, and (3) using the slope and y intercept. In Example 9 we graph an equation using all three methods. No single method is always the easiest to use. If the equation is given in slope–intercept form, $y = mx + b$, then graphing by plotting points or by using the slope and y intercept might be easier. If the equation is given in standard form, $ax + by = c$, then graphing using the intercepts might be easier. Unless your teacher specifies that you should graph by a specific method, you may use the method that you feel most comfortable with. Graphing by plotting is the most versatile method since it can also be used to graph equations that are not straight lines.

EXAMPLE 9 Graph $3x - 2y = 8$ **(a)** by plotting points; **(b)** using the x and y intercepts; and **(c)** using the slope and y intercept.

Solution: For parts **(a)** and **(c)** we must write the equation in slope–intercept form.

$$3x - 2y = 8$$

$$-2y = -3x + 8$$

$$y = \frac{-3x + 8}{-2} = \frac{3}{2}x - 4$$

(a) *Plotting points:* Substitute values for x and find the corresponding values of y. Then plot the ordered pairs and draw the graph (Fig. 7.49).

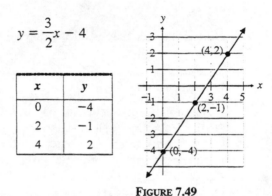

$$y = \frac{3}{2}x - 4$$

x	y
0	-4
2	-1
4	2

FIGURE 7.49

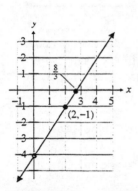

FIGURE 7.50

(b) *Intercepts:* Find the x and y intercepts and a check point. Then plot the points and draw the graph (Fig. 7.50).

$$3x - 2y = 8$$

x Intercept Let $y = 0$	*y Intercept* Let $x = 0$	*Check Point* Let $x = 2$
$3x - 2y = 8$	$3x - 2y = 8$	$3x - 2y = 8$
$3x - 2(0) = 8$	$3(0) - 2y = 8$	$3(2) - 2y = 8$
$3x = 8$	$-2y = 8$	$6 - 2y = 8$
$x = \dfrac{8}{3}$	$y = -4$	$-2y = 2$
		$y = -1$

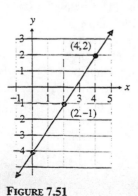

FIGURE 7.51

(c) *Slope and y intercept:* Start by plotting the y intercept -4. Since the slope is $\frac{3}{2}$, we obtain a second point by moving up 3 units and moving to the right 2 units. The graph is illustrated in Figure 7.51.

Notice that we get the same line by all three methods.

Exercise Set 7.5

Determine the slope and y intercept of the line represented by each equation. Graph the line using the slope and y intercept. (See Examples 2 and 3.)

1. $y = 2x - 1$

2. $y = 3x + 2$

3. $y = -x + 5$

4. $y = 2x$

5. $y = -4x$

6. $2x + y = 5$

7. $-2x + y = -3$

8. $3x - y = -2$

9. $3x + 3y = 9$

10. $5x - 2y = 10$

11. $-x + 2y = 8$

12. $5x + 10y = 15$

13. $4x = 6y + 9$

14. $4y = 5x - 12$

15. $-6x = -2y + 8$

16. $6y = 5x - 9$

17. $-3x + 8y = -8$

18. $16y = 8x + 32$

19. $3x = 2y - 4$

20. $20x = 80y + 40$

Determine the equation of each line. (See example 4.)

21.

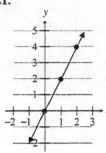

22.

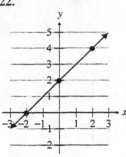

23.

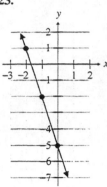

24.

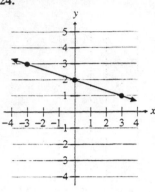

25.

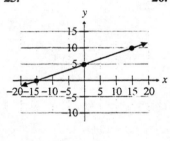

26.

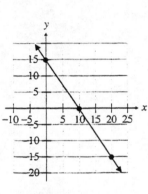

27.

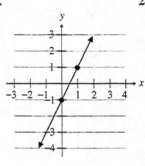

28.

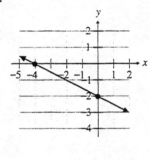

Determine if the lines are parallel. (See Examples 5 and 6.)

29. $y = 2x - 4$
$y = 2x + 3$

30. $2x + 3y = 8$

$y = -\dfrac{2}{3}x + 5$

31. $4x + 2y = 9$
$8x = 4 - 4y$

32. $3x - 5y = 7$
$5y + 3x = 2$

33. $2x + 5y = 9$
$-x + 3y = 9$

34. $6x + 2y = 8$
$4x - 9 = -y$

35. $y = \dfrac{1}{2}x - 6$

$3y = 6x + 9$

36. $2y - 6 = -5x$

$y = -\dfrac{5}{2}x - 2$

Write the equation of the line, with the given properties, in slope–intercept form. (See the Helpful Hint on page 410 and Examples 7 and 8.)

37. Slope = 5, through (0, 4)

38. Slope = 4, through (2, 3)

39. Slope = −2, through (−4, 5)

40. Slope = −1, through (6, 0)

41. Slope = $\frac{1}{2}$, through (−1, −5)

42. Slope = $-\frac{2}{3}$, through (−1, −2)

43. Slope = $\frac{3}{5}$, y intercept = 7

44. Slope = $\frac{1}{2}$, y intercept = −3

45 Through (−4, −2) and (−2, 4)

46. Through (6, 3) and (5, 2)

47. Through (−4, 6) and (4, −6)

48. Through (1, 0) and (−2, 4)

49. Through (10, 3) and (0, −2)

50. Through (−6, −2) and (5, −3)

51. Slope = 5.2, y intercept = −1.6

52. Slope = $-\frac{5}{8}$, y intercept = $-\frac{7}{10}$

Graph the equation by (a) plotting points, (b) using the x and y intercepts, and (c) using the slope and y intercept. (See Example 9.)

53. $3x - 2y = 4$

54. $4x + 3y = 6$

55. $2x - 3y = -6$

56. When you are given an equation in a form other than slope–intercept form, how can you change it to slope–intercept form?

57. Explain how you can determine if two lines are parallel without actually graphing them.

58. Consider the two equations $40x - 60y = 100$ and $-40x + 60y = 80$.

   (a) When these equations are graphed, will the two lines have the same slope? Explain how you determined your answer.

   (b) Will these two equations when graphed be parallel lines?

59. Write **(a)** the standard form of a linear equation, **(b)** the slope–intercept form of a linear equation, and **(c)** the point–slope form of a linear equation.

60. Suppose that you were asked to write the equation of a line with the properties given below. Which form of a linear equation—standard form, slope–intercept form, or point–slope form—would you start with? Explain your answer.

   (a) The slope of the line and the y intercept of the line

   (b) The slope and a point on the line

   (c) Two points on the line

61. **(a)** Explain in your own words, in a step-by-step manner, how to graph a linear equation using each of the three methods discussed: plotting points, using the x and y intercepts, and using the slope and y intercept.

   (b) Graph $-3x + 2y = 4$ using each of the three methods.

CUMULATIVE REVIEW EXERCISES

[4.6] **62.** Divide $\dfrac{9x^3 - 3x^2 - 9x + 4}{3x + 2}$.

[4.7] **63.** Consuella has 1 liter of a 5% saltwater solution. How much pure water, without salt, will Consuella need to add to the 5% solution to obtain a 2% saltwater solution?

[6.2] **64.** Divide $\dfrac{x^2 + 2x - 8}{x^2 - 16} \div \dfrac{2x^2 - 5x - 3}{x^2 - 7x + 12}$.

[6.4] **65.** Add $\dfrac{3}{x - 2} + \dfrac{5}{x + 2}$.

[6.6] **66.** Solve the equation $x + \dfrac{30}{x} = 11$.

[6.7] **67.** The area of a triangle is 36 square feet. Find the base and height if its height is 7 feet less than twice its base.

Group Activity/ Challenge Problems

1. Determine the equation of the line with y intercept at 4 that is parallel to the line $2x + y = 6$. Explain how you determined your answer.

2. Determine if the line with x intercept at 5 and y intercept at -2 is parallel to the line $4x + 10y = 20$. Explain how you determined your answer.

3. Will a line through the points (60, 30) and (20, 90) be parallel to the line with x intercept at 2 and y intercept at 3? Explain how you determined your answer.

4. Write an equation of the line parallel to $3x - 4y = 6$ that passes through the point $(-4, -1)$.

5. Two lines are **perpendicular** and cross at right angles when their slopes are negative reciprocals of each other. The negative reciprocal of any number a is $-1/a$. For example, the negative reciprocal of 2 is $-\frac{1}{2}$ and the negative reciprocal of $-\frac{3}{4}$ is $\frac{4}{3}$. Write an equation of the line perpendicular to $-5x + 2y = -4$ that passes through the point $(2, \frac{1}{2})$.

6. Write the equation $3x = 4y + 6$ in point–slope form. Explain how you obtained your answer. There is more than one acceptable answer.

7. Determine the equation of the straight line that intersects the greatest number of shaded points on the following graph.

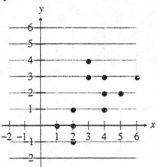

7.6   Functions

Tape 13

1. Identify relations.
2. Find the domain and range of a relation.
3. Use the vertical line test to determine if a relation is a function.
4. Graph linear functions.

In this section we introduce relations and functions. As you will learn shortly, a function is a special type of relation. Functions are a common thread in mathematics courses from algebra through calculus. In this section we give an informal introduction to relations and functions. The information given here will prove very valuable to you if you plan on taking additional mathematics courses. We will also be discussing functions in Chapter 10, when we graph quadratic equations.

Recall from Section 1.3 that a set is a collection of **elements.** In this section the elements will be numbers or ordered pairs. Remember that sets are indicated by using braces, { }. For example, in the set {1, 2, 3, 4, 5} the elements are 1, 2, 3, 4, and 5. Three dots at the end of a set indicate that the set continues in the same manner. For example, {1, 2, 3, 4, 5, . . . } represents the set of all natural numbers.

Relations   1   Now we will discuss relations. A **relation** is any set of ordered pairs. A relation may be indicated by (1) an equation in two variables, (2) a set of ordered pairs, or (3) a graph. Consider the equation $y = x + 2$, where x is an integer between 1 and 4 inclusive. This equation and every other equation in two variables is a relation. We can obtain some ordered pairs that satisfy the equation by selecting values for x and finding the corresponding values of y.

	$y = x+2$	*Ordered Pair*
Let $x = 1$	$y = 1 + 2 = 3$	(1, 3)
Let $x = 2$	$y = 2 + 2 = 4$	(2, 4)
Let $x = 3$	$y = 3 + 2 = 5$	(3, 5)
Let $x = 4$	$y = 4 + 2 = 6$	(4, 6)

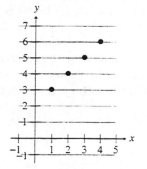

FIGURE 7.52

The set of ordered pairs $\{(1, 3), (2, 4), (3, 5), (4, 6)\}$ is a relation. In fact, every set of ordered pairs is a relation. If we plot the set of ordered pairs, we get the graph in Figure 7.52. The graph in Figure 7.52 is a relation. In fact, every graph drawn in the Cartesian coordinate system is a relation. As you can see, the word *relation* is a general term that can be used to describe any relationship between two variables.

Suppose that you are buying navel oranges at the supermarket. The cost of each orange is 20¢. If you purchase 1 orange, your cost will be 20¢. If you purchase 2 oranges, your cost will be 2(20¢), or 40¢. Three oranges cost 3(20¢), or 60¢, and so on (see Table 7.1). In general, if you purchase n oranges your cost will be 20¢ times the number of oranges. We can express this relationship with the equation $c = 0.20n$, where c is the cost, in dollars, of n oranges. In the equation $c = 0.20n$ the cost, c, depends on the number of oranges, n. Thus, we call c the **dependent variable** and n the **independent variable**.

TABLE 7.1

Number of Oranges, n	Cost in Dollars, c
0	0.00
1	0.20
2	0.40
3	0.60
.	.
.	.
.	.
n	$0.20n$

Domain and Range

In a relation the set of values that can be used for the independent variable is called the **domain**. The set of values that represent the dependent variable is called the **range**. Since the values in the domain are substituted into the equation, the values in the domain determine the values in the range. Consider the equation for the cost of n oranges, $c = 0.20n$. What is the domain and what is the range? The domain is the set of "input values" that can be used for n, the number of oranges. Since we cannot purchase a fractional part of an orange, or a negative number of oranges, the domain is the set of whole numbers $\{0, 1, 2, 3, 4, \ldots\}$. We can purchase from 0 oranges to any fixed number of oranges. The three dots at the end of the set indicate that the set continues indefinitely. Notice that the numbers in the left column of Table 7.1 are the numbers that made up the domain.

When the values in the domain 0, 1, 2, 3, . . . are substituted for n in the formula $c = 0.20n$, the values we get are 0.00, 0.20, 0.40, 0.60, ... The set of these "output values" form the range. Thus the range is $\{0.00, 0.20, 0.40, 0.60, 0.80, \ldots\}$. Notice that the values in the right column of Table 7.1 are the numbers that make up the range.

If we list the values in Table 7.1 as a set of ordered pairs, we get $\{(0, 0.00), (1, 0.20), (2, 0.40), (3, 0.60), \ldots\}$. Note that the *domain is the set of first coordinates in the set of ordered pairs,* and the *range is the set of second coordinates in the set of ordered pairs.*

If we refer back to the equation $y = x + 2$, where x is an integer between 1 and 4 inclusive, we see that the domain, the set of values of x, is $\{1, 2, 3, 4\}$. The range, the set of values of y, is $\{3, 4, 5, 6\}$.

When a graph is given, its domain and range may be determined by observation. The domain is the set of values of x, the first coordinate in each ordered pair, and the range is the set of values of y, the second coordinate in each ordered pair.

EXAMPLE 1   State the domain and the range of the relation shown in Figure 7.53.

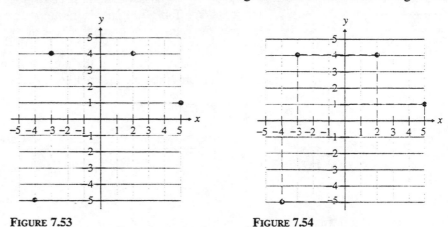

FIGURE 7.53   FIGURE 7.54

Solution: The domain is the set of values of x, which are indicated in red on the x axis in Figure 7.54. The domain is $\{-4, -3, 2, 5\}$. The range is the set of values of y, which are indicated in blue on the y axis in Figure 7.54. The range is $\{-5, 1, 4\}$.

In our discussions thus far the domains have been limited to integer values. In Example 2 we present a relation whose domain is not limited to integer values.

EXAMPLE 2   Determine the domain and range of the relation shown in Figure 7.55.

Solution: The arrowheads on the line indicate that the graph continues indefinitely in both directions. From the graph we can see that any real value of x can be used in the domain. Therefore, we say that the domain is *the set of real numbers*. Since the symbol $\mathbb{R}$ is used to represent the set of real numbers, we can write, domain: $\mathbb{R}$. Similarly, every value of y will be included in the range, and the range is also *the set of real numbers*. Therefore, we may write, range: $\mathbb{R}$.

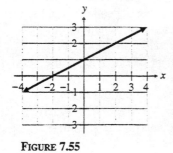

FIGURE 7.55

Functions   **3** Now we discuss functions. A **function** is a special type of relation. For a relation to be a function, each first coordinate in the set of ordered pairs must have a *unique* second coordinate. Is the set of ordered pairs $\{(4, 5), (3, 2), (-2, -3), (2, 5), (1, 6)\}$ a function? Do any of the ordered pairs have the same first coordinates and a different second coordinate? If so, this relation would not be a function. *Since no two ordered pairs have the same first coordinate and a different second coordinate, this set of ordered pairs is a function.* Now consider the set of ordered pairs $\{(4, 5), (3, 2), (-2, -3), (4, 1), (5, -2)\}$. Is this set of ordered pairs a function? Since the two ordered pairs $(4, 5)$ and $(4, 1)$ have the same first coordinate and a different second coordinate, this set of ordered pairs is *not a function*. Note that the second coordinates in the set of ordered pairs may repeat. However, the first coordinates cannot repeat if the set of ordered pairs is to be a function.

Function

A function is a relation in which no two ordered pairs have the same first coordinate and a different second coordinate.

A function may also be defined as a relation in which each element of the domain corresponds to exactly one element in the range. In other words, each value of x must correspond to a unique value of y. This may sound a bit confusing but the following graph can help in your understanding. Let us graph the two sets of ordered pairs $\{(4, 5), (3, 2), (-2, -3), (2, 5), (1, 6)\}$ and $\{(4, 5), (3, 2), (-2, -3), (4, 1), (5, -2)\}$ on different axes (Fig. 7.56 (a) and (b) respectively).

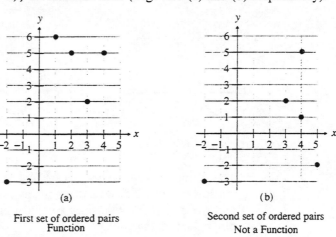

(a)

First set of ordered pairs
Function

(b)

Second set of ordered pairs
Not a Function

FIGURE 7.56

Notice that in Figure 7.56a, if a vertical line is drawn through each point, no vertical line intersects more than one point. This indicates that no two ordered pairs have the same first (or x) coordinate. This also indicates that for each element in the domain (the values of x) there is a unique element in the range (the values of y). Thus, each value of x corresponds to a unique value of y. Therefore, this set of points is a function.

Now look at Figure 7.56b. If a vertical line is drawn through each point, one vertical line passes through two points. The red vertical line intersects both $(4, 5)$ and $(4, 1)$. This indicates that there are two ordered pairs that have the same first (or x) coordinate and a different second coordinate. Therefore, this set of ordered pairs is *not* a function. Also notice that each element in the domain *does not* correspond to a unique element in the range. The number 4 in the domain corresponds to two numbers, 5 and 1, in the range.

To determine if a graph is a function, we can use the **vertical line test** which we just introduced. **If a vertical line can be drawn through any part of a graph and the vertical line intersects another part of the graph, then each value of x does not have a unique value of y and the graph is not a function. If a vertical line cannot be drawn to intersect the graph at more than one point, each value of x has a unique value of y, and the graph is a function.**

EXAMPLE 3

Using the vertical line test, determine whether or not the following graphs are functions.

(a)   **(b)**   **(c)**

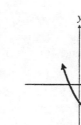 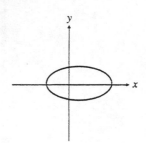

Solution:

(a)   **(b)**   **(c)**

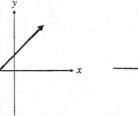 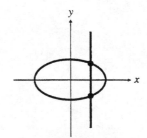

The graphs in parts **(a)** and **(b)** are functions since it is not possible to draw a vertical line that intersects the graph at more than one point. The graph in part **(c)** is not a function since a vertical line can be drawn to intersect the graph at more than one point.

Let us return to the equation $y = x + 2$, where x is an integer in the set $\{1, 2, 3, 4\}$. Study its graph (Fig. 7.52). This relation is a function since its graph passes the vertical line test. Since the graph is a function the equation $y = x + 2$ for $x = 1, 2, 3, 4$ is also a function. Since the value of y in the equation or function depends on the value of x, we say that y *is a function of x*. The notation $y = f(x)$ is used to show that y is a function of the variable x. For this function we can write

$$y = f(x) = x + 2$$

The notation $f(x)$ is read "f of x" and *does not mean f times x*.

To evaluate a function for a specific value of x, substitute that value for x everywhere the x appears in the function. For example, to evaluate the function $f(x) = x + 2$ at $x = 1$, we do the following:

$$y = f(x) = x + 2$$
$$y = f(1) = 1 + 2 = 3$$

Thus, when x is 1, y is 3. When $x = 4$, $y = 6$, as illustrated below.

$$y = f(x) = x + 2$$
$$y = f(4) = 4 + 2 = 6$$

The notation $f(1)$ is read "f of 1" and $f(4)$ is read "f of 4."

Recall that the domain of the function $y = x + 2$ was the integers 1, 2, 3, and 4. Figure 7.57 displays how the function assigns each value of x in the domain to exactly one value of y in the range.

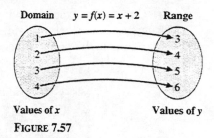

FIGURE 7.57

Sometimes we may use the notation $f(x)$ in place of y. For example, the function $y = x + 2$ may sometimes be written as $f(x) = x + 2$. Always keep in mind that $f(x)$ is the same as y.

EXAMPLE 4   For the function $f(x) = x^2 + 2x - 3$, find **(a)** $f(4)$ and **(b)** $f(-5)$. **(c)** If $x = -1$, determine the value of y.

Solution:

(a) Substitute 4 for each x in the function, and then evaluate.

$$f(x) = x^2 + 2x - 3$$
$$f(4) = 4^2 + 2(4) - 3 = 16 + 8 - 3 = 21$$

(b) $f(x) = x^2 + 2x - 3$
$$f(-5) = (-5)^2 + 2(-5) - 3 = 25 - 10 - 3 = 12$$

(c) Since $y = f(x)$ we evaluate $f(x)$ at -1.
$$f(x) = x^2 + 2x - 3$$
$$f(-1) = (-1)^2 + 2(-1) - 3 = 1 - 2 - 3 = -4$$

Thus, when $x = -1$, $y = -4$.

Graph Linear Functions

4 The graphs of all equations of the form $y = ax + b$ will be straight lines that are functions. Therefore, we may refer to equations of the form $y = ax + b$ as **linear functions**. Equations of the form $f(x) = ax + b$ are also linear functions since $f(x)$ is the same as y. We may graph linear functions as shown in Example 5.

EXAMPLE 5   Graph $f(x) = 2x + 4$.

Solution: Since $f(x)$ is the same as y, write $y = f(x) = 2x + 4$. Select values for x and find the corresponding values for y or $f(x)$.

$$y = f(x) = 2x + 4$$

		x	y
$x = -3$	$y = f(-3) = 2(-3) + 4 = -2$	-3	-2
$x = 0$	$y = f(0) = 2(0) + 4 = 4$	0	4
$x = 1$	$y = f(1) = 2(1) + 4 = 6$	1	6

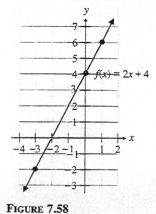

FIGURE 7.58

Now plot the points and draw the graph of the function (Fig. 7.58).

EXAMPLE 6   The weekly profit, p, of an ice skating rink is a function of the number of skaters per week, n. The function approximating the profit is $p = f(n) = 8n - 600$, where $0 \leq n \leq 400$.

(a) Construct a graph showing the relationship between the number of skaters and the weekly profit.
(b) Estimate the profit if there are 200 skaters in a given week.

FIGURE 7.59

Solution:

(a) Select values for n, and find the corresponding values for p. Then draw the graph (Fig. 7.59). Notice there are no arrowheads on the line because the function is defined only for values of n between 0 and 400 inclusive.

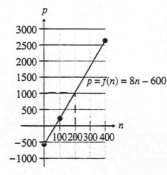

FIGURE 7.59

$$p = f(n) = 8n - 600$$

Let $n = 0$ $p = f(0) = 8(0) - 600 = -600$

Let $n = 100$ $p = f(100) = 8(100) - 600 = 200$

Let $n = 400$ $p = f(400) = 8(400) - 600 = 2600$

n	p
0	−600
100	200
400	2600

(b) Using the red dashed line on the graph, we can see that if there are 200 skaters the weekly profit is $1000.

We will discuss functions further in Section 10.4, when graphing quadratic equations.

Exercise Set 7.6

Determine which of the relations are also functions. Give the range and domain of each relation or function.

1. $\{(4, 4), (2, 2), (3, 5), (1, 3), (5, 1)\}$

2. $\{(2, 1), (4, 0), (3, 5), (2, 2), (5, 1)\}$

3. $\{(5, -2), (3, 0), (1, 2), (1, 4), (2, 4), (7, 5)\}$

4. $\{(-2, 1), (1, -3), (3, 4), (4, 5), (-2, 0)\}$

5. $\{(5, 0), (3, -4), (0, -1), (3, 2), (1, 1)\}$

6. $\{(-1, 3), (-3, 4), (0, 3), (5, 2), (3, 5), (2, 5)\}$

7. $\{(4, 0), (0, -3), (1, 5), (1, 0), (1, 2)\}$

8. $\{(4, -3), (3, -7), (4, -9), (3, 5)\}$

9. $\{(0, 3), (1, 3), (2, 3), (3, 3), (4, 3)\}$

10. $\{(3, 5), (2, 4), (1, 0), (0, 1), (-1, 5)\}$

The domain and range of a relation are illustrated. **(a)** *Construct a set of ordered pairs that represent the relation.* **(b)** *Determine if the relation is a function. Explain your answer.*

11.

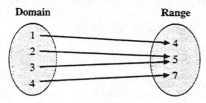

12.

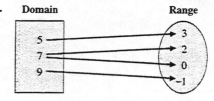

13.

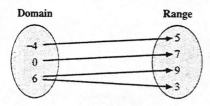

14.

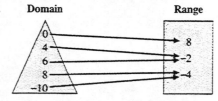

Use the vertical line test to determine if the relation is also a function.

15.

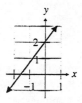

16.

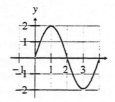

17.

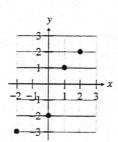

18.

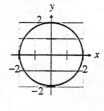

19.

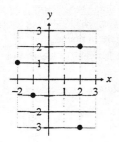

20.

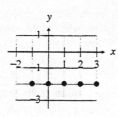

21.

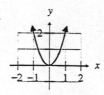

22.

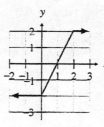

23.

24.

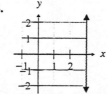

25.

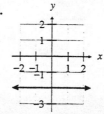

26.

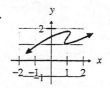

Evaluate the functions at the values indicated.

27. $f(x) = 2x + 3$; find **(a)** $f(2)$ **(b)** $f(-2)$

28. $f(x) = -3x + 5$; find **(a)** $f(0)$ **(b)** $f(1)$

29. $f(x) = x^2 - 4$; find **(a)** $f(2)$ **(b)** $f(3)$

30. $f(x) = 2x^2 + 3x - 4$ **(a)** $f(1)$ **(b)** $f(-3)$

31. $f(x) = 3x^2 - x + 5$ **(a)** $f(0)$ **(b)** $f(2)$

32. $f(x) = \dfrac{1}{2}x - 4$; find **(a)** $f(10)$ **(b)** $f(-4)$

33. $f(x) = \dfrac{x + 4}{2}$; find **(a)** $f(2)$ **(b)** $f(6)$

34. $f(x) = \dfrac{1}{2}x^2 + 6$; find **(a)** $f(2)$ **(b)** $f(-2)$

Graph each function.

35. $f(x) = 2x + 1$

36. $f(x) = -x + 4$

37. $f(x) = 3x - 1$

38. $f(x) = 4x + 2$

39. $f(x) = -2x + 4$

40. $f(x) = -x + 5$

41. $f(x) = -3x - 3$

42. $f(x) = -4x$

43. The cost, c, in dollars, of repairing a highway can be estimated by the formula $c = 2000 + 6000m$, where m is the number of miles to be repaired.

(a) Draw a graph of the function for up to and including 6 miles.

(b) Estimate the cost of repairing 2 miles of road.

See Exercise 43.

44. The cost, c, in dollars, of a cross-country train trip can be estimated by the function $c = 50 + 0.15m$, where m is the distance traveled in miles.

(a) Draw a graph of the function for up to and including 3000 miles traveled.

(b) Estimate the cost of a 1000-mile trip.

45. A discount stock broker commission, c, on stock trades is $25 plus 2% of the sales value, s. Therefore, the broker's commission is a function of the sales, $c = 25 + 0.02s$.

(a) Draw a graph illustrating the broker's commission on sales up to and including $10,000.

(b) If the sales value of a trade is $8000, estimate the broker's commission.

46. A state's auto registration fee, f, is $20 plus $15 per 1000 pounds of the vehicle's gross weight. The registration fee is a function of the vehicle's weight, $f = 20 + 0.015w$, where w is the weight of the vehicle in pounds.

(a) Draw a graph of the function for vehicle weights up to and including 10,000 pounds.

(b) Estimate the registration fee of a vehicle whose gross weight is 4000 pounds.

47. A new singing group, The Three Bugs, sign a recording contract with the Squash Record label. Their contract provides them with a signing bonus of $10,000, plus an 8% royalty on the sales, s, of their new record, Hey Jud! Their income, i, is a function of their sales, $i = 10,000 + 0.08s$.

(a) Draw a graph of the function for sales of up to and including $100,000.

(b) Estimate their income if their sales are $20,000.

48. A monthly electric bill, m, in dollars, consists of a $20 monthly fee plus $0.07 per kilowatthour, k, of electricity used. The amount of the bill is a function of the kilowatthours used, $m = 20 + 0.07k$.

(a) Draw a graph for up to and including 3,000 kilowatthours of electricity used in a month.

(b) Estimate the bill if 1500 kilowatthours of electricity are used.

49. The 1994 Internal Revenue Tax Rate Schedule indicates that the income tax, t, for a single person earning no more than $22,100 is 15% of their taxable income, i. The tax is a function of their income, $t = 0.15i$.

(a) Draw a graph of the function for taxable incomes up to and including $22,100.

(b) Estimate the tax if a single person's taxable income is $15,000.

50. What is a relation?

51. What is a function?

52. What is the domain of a relation or function?

53. What is the range of a relation or function?

54. (a) Is every relation a function?

(b) Is every function a relation? Explain your answer.

55. If two distinct ordered pairs in a relation have the same first coordinate, can the relation be a function? Explain.

56. If a relation consists of six ordered pairs and the domain of the relation consists of five values of x, can the relation be a function? Explain.

57. If a relation consists of six ordered pairs and the range of the relation consists of five values of y, can the relation be a function? Explain.

58. In a function is it necessary for each value of y in the range to have a unique value of x in the domain? Explain.

Consider the following graphs. Recall from Section 2.7 that an open circle at the end of a line segment means that the endpoint is not included in the answer. A solid circle at the end of a line segment indicates that the endpoint is included in the answer. Determine whether the following graphs are functions. Explain your answer.

59.

60.

61.

62.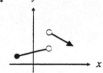

CUMULATIVE REVIEW EXERCISES

[.5] **63.** Solve the equation $3x - 4 = 5(x - 2) - 1$.

[.6] **64.** If it requires $15 worth of gas to travel 280 miles, how much will it cost to travel 1000 miles?

[2.7] **65.** Solve the inequality $3x + 9 < -x + 5$ and graph the solution on the number line.

[3.1] **66.** Solve the formula $A = 2l + 2w$, for w.

Group Activity/ Challenge Problems

1. Give three real-life examples (different from those already given) of a quantity that is a function of another. Write each as a function, and indicate what each variable represents.

2. $f(x) = \frac{1}{2}x^2 - 3x + 5$; find (a) $f\left(\frac{1}{2}\right)$ (b) $f\left(\frac{2}{3}\right)$ (c) $f(0.2)$

3. $f(x) = x^2 + 2x - 3$; find (a) $f(1)$ (b) $f(2)$ (c) $f(a)$. Explain how you determined your answer to part (c).

4. The cost of mailing a first-class letter at the time of this writing is 32 cents for the first ounce and 23 cents for each additional ounce. A graph showing the cost of mailing a letter first class is pictured on the right.

(a) Does this graph represent a function? Explain your answer.

(b) What is the cost of mailing a 4-ounce package first class?

(c) What is the cost of mailing a 3.6-ounce package first class?

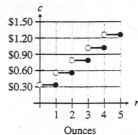

7.7 Graphing Linear Inequalities

1 Graph linear inequalities in two variables.

Tape 13

Graphing Inequalities in Two Variables

1 A linear inequality results when the equal sign in a linear equation is replaced with an inequality sign. Examples of linear inequalities in two variables are

$$3x + 2y > 4 \qquad -x + 3y < -2$$
$$-x + 4y \geq 3 \qquad 4x - y \leq 4$$

To Graph a Linear Inequality

1. Replace the inequality symbol with an equal sign.

2. Draw the graph of the equation in step 1. If the original inequality contained the symbol $\geq$ or $\leq$, draw the graph using a solid line. If the original inequality contained the symbol $>$ or $<$, draw the graph using a dashed line.

3. Select any point not on the line and determine if this point is a solution to the original inequality. If the selected point is a solution, shade the region on the side of the line containing this point. If the selected point does not satisfy the inequality, shade the region on the side of the line not containing this point.

EXAMPLE 1 Graph the inequality $y < 2x - 4$.

Solution: First graph the equation $y = 2x - 4$ (Fig. 7.60). Since the original inequality contains a less than sign, $<$, use a dashed line when drawing the graph. The dashed line indicates that the points on this line are not solutions to the inequality $y < 2x - 4$.

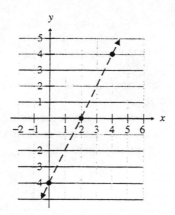

FIGURE 7.60

Next select a point not on the line and determine if this point satisfies the inequality. Often the easiest point to use is the origin, (0, 0).

Check:

$$y < 2x - 4$$
$$0 < 2(0) - 4$$
$$0 < 0 - 4$$
$$0 < -4 \qquad \text{false}$$

Since 0 is not less than -4, the point (0, 0) does not satisfy the inequality. The solution will therefore be all the points on the opposite side of the line from the point (0, 0). Shade in this region (Fig. 7.61).

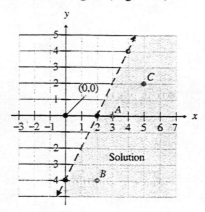

FIGURE 7.61

Every point in the shaded area satisfies the given inequality. Let us check a few selected points A, B, and C.

Point A	*Point B*	*Point C*
(3, 0)	(2, −4)	(5, 2)
$y < 2x - 4$	$y < 2x - 4$	$y < 2x - 4$
$0 < 2(3) - 4$	$-4 < 2(2) - 4$	$2 < 2(5) - 4$
$0 < 2$ true	$-4 < 0$ true	$2 < 6$ true

All points in the shaded area in Figure 7.61 satisfy the inequality $y < 2x - 4$. The points in the unshaded area to the left of the dashed line would satisfy the inequality $y > 2x - 4$.

EXAMPLE 2 Graph the inequality $y \geq -\frac{1}{2}x$.

Solution: Graph the equation $y = -\frac{1}{2}x$. Since the inequality symbol is $\geq$, we use a solid line to indicate that the points on the line are solutions to the inequality (Fig. 7.62).

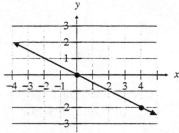

FIGURE 7.62

Since the point $(0, 0)$ is on the line, we cannot select it as our test point. Let us select the point $(3, 1)$.

$$y \geq -\frac{1}{2}x$$

$$1 \geq -\frac{1}{2}(3)$$

$$1 \geq -\frac{3}{2} \qquad \textbf{true}$$

Since the ordered pair $(3, 1)$ satisfies the inequality, every point on the same side of the line as $(3, 1)$ will also satisfy the inequality $y \geq -\frac{1}{2}x$. Shade this region (Fig. 7.63). Every point in the shaded region as well as every point on the line satisfies the inequality.

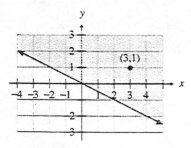

FIGURE 7.63

In some of the exercises you may need to solve the inequality for y before graphing. For example, to graph $-2x + y < -4$ you would solve the inequality for y to obtain $y < 2x - 4$. Then you would graph the inequality $y < 2x - 4$. Note that $y < 2x - 4$ was graphed in Figure 7.61.

Exercise Set 7.7

Graph each inequality.

1. $x > 3$

2. $y < -2$

3. $x \geq \dfrac{5}{2}$

4. $y < x$

5. $y \geq 2x$

6. $y > -2x$

7. $y < x - 4$

8. $y < 2x + 1$

9. $y < -3x + 4$

10. $y \geq 2x + 4$

11. $y \geq \dfrac{1}{2}x - 4$

12. $y < 3x + 4$

13. $y \leq \dfrac{1}{3}x + 3$

14. $y > 4x + 1$

15. $3x + y \leq 5$

16. $3x - 2 < y$

17. $2x + y \leq 3$

18. $3y > 2x - 3$

19. $y - 4 \leq -x$

20. $4x - 2y \leq 6$

21. $2y - 5x < -6$

22. $-2x \leq -3y + 9$

23. $y \geq -4x + 3$

24. $y > -\dfrac{x}{2} + 2$

25. When graphing inequalities that contain either $\leq$ or $\geq$, explain why the points on the line will be solutions to the inequality.

26. When graphing inequalities that contain either $<$ or $>$, explain why the points on the line will not be solutions to the inequality.

CUMULATIVE REVIEW EXERCISES

[2.7] **27.** Solve the inequality $2(x - 3) < 4(x - 2) - 4$ and graph the solution on the number line.

[3.1] **28.** Use the simple interest formula $i = prt$ to find the principal if the simple interest Manuel gained over a 3-year period at a rate of 8% is $300.

[6.6] **29.** Solve the formula $C = \frac{5}{9}(F - 32)$ for F.

[7.5] **30.** The equation of a line is $6x - 5y = 9$. Find the slope and y intercept of the line.

Group Activity/ Challenge Problems

1. Indicate whether the phrase given means less than, less than or equal to, greater than, or greater than or equal to.

   (a) no more than   (b) no less than   (c) at most   (d) at least

2. Which of the following inequalities have the same graphs? Explain how you determined your answer.

   (a) $2x - y > 4$ (b) $-2x + y < -4$ (c) $y < 2x - 4$ (d) $-2y + 4x < -8$

3. How do the graphs of $2x + 3y > 6$ and $2x + 3y < 6$ differ?

4. Consider the two inequalities $2x + 1 > 5$ and $2x + y > 5$.

   (a) How many variables does the inequality $2x + 1 > 5$ contain?

   (b) How many variables does the inequality $2x + y > 5$ contain?

   (c) What is the solution to $2x + 1 > 5$? Indicate the solution on the number line.

   (d) Graph $2x + y > 5$.

   Graph the inequality in the first quadrant only, that is, where $x \geq 0$ and $y \geq 0$.

5. A toy company must ship x toy cars to one outlet and y toy cars to a second outlet. The maximum number of toy cars that the manufacturer can produce and ship is 200. We can represent this situation with the inequality $x + y \leq 200$. Graph the inequality.

6. An auto dealer wishes to sell x cars and y trucks this year and he needs to sell a total of at least 100 vehicles.

   (a) Represent this situation as an inequality.

   (b) Graph the inequality.

7. Each newly released videotape cost $2 to rent and each older videotape cost $1 to rent. James wishes to rent x new and y older tapes, but he can spend no more than $10.

   (a) Represent this situation with an inequality.

   (b) Graph the inequality.

Summary

GLOSSARY

Bar graph (364): A graph that displays information using either horizontal or vertical bars.

Cartesian (or rectangular) coordinate system (375): Two axes intersecting at right angles that are used when drawing graphs.

Collinear (380): A set of points in a straight line is collinear.

Domain (417): The set of values that can be used for the independent variable in a relation or function.

Function (418): A relation in which no two ordered pairs have the same first coordinate and a different second coordinate.

Graph (379): An illustration of the set of points whose coordinates satisfy an equation or an inequality.

Line graph (365): A graph that displays information using connected line segments. The horizontal axis is usually some measure of time.

Linear equation in two variables (378): An equation that can be written in the form $ax + by = c$.

Negative slope (400): A line has a negative slope if the values of y decrease as the values of x increase.

Origin (376): The point of intersection of the x and y axes.

Parallel lines (408): Lines that never intersect.

Pie (or circle) graph (362): A graph that displays information in the form of a circle.

Positive slope (400): A line has a positive slope if the values of y increase as the values of x increase.

Range (417): The set of values that represent the dependent variable in a relation or function.

Relation (416): Any set of ordered pairs.

Slope of a line (398): The ratio of the vertical change to the horizontal change between any two points on the line.

x axis (376): The horizontal axis in the Cartesian coordinate system.

x intercept (386): The value of x at the point where the graph crosses the x axis.

y axis (376): The vertical axis in the Cartesian coordinate system.

y intercept (386): The value of y at the point where the graph crosses the y axis.

IMPORTANT FACTS

To find the x intercept: Set $y = 0$ and find the corresponding value of x.

To find the y intercept: Set $x = 0$ and find the corresponding value of y.

Slope of line, m, through points (x_1, y_1) and (x_2, y_2):

$$m = \frac{y_2 - y_1}{x_2 - x_1}$$

Methods of Graphing
$$y = 3x - 4$$

By Plotting Points	*Using Intercepts*	*Using Slope and y Intercept*
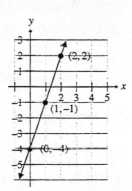	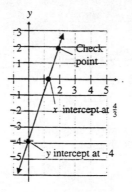	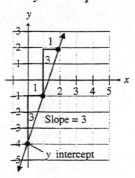

Standard form of a linear equation: $ax + by = c$.

Slope-intercept form of a linear equation: $y = mx + b$.

Point-slope form of a linear equation: $y - y_1 = m(x - x_1)$.

Review of slope

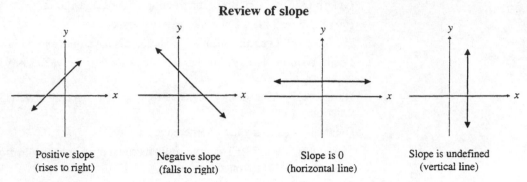

| Positive slope (rises to right) | Negative slope (falls to right) | Slope is 0 (horizontal line) | Slope is undefined (vertical line) |

Vertical line test: If a vertical line can be drawn through any part of a graph and the vertical line intersects another part of the graph, the graph is not a function.

Review Exercises

[7.1] **1.** The following pie graph illustrates the percent of dollars charged to credit cards in the United States in 1994.

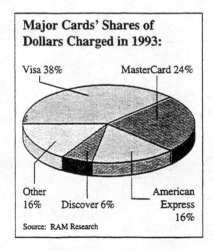

Major Cards' Shares of Dollars Charged in 1993:

Visa 38%   MasterCard 24%

Other 16%   Discover 6%   American Express 16%

Source: RAM Research

(a) What percent of all charges were charged to Visa?

(b) What percent of all charges were charged to either Visa or MasterCard?

(c) In 1994, $635 billion dollars were charged to credit cards. How much was charged to American Express cards?

(d) Redraw the pie graph using dollar figures rather than percents in the sectors.

2. The following chart shows how consumer shopping habits have changed over the past five years.

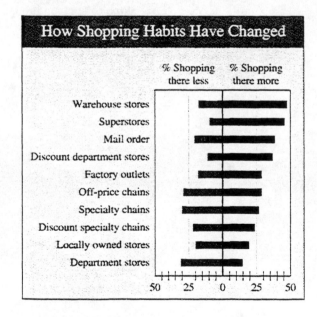

How Shopping Habits Have Changed

% Shopping there less   % Shopping there more

Warehouse stores
Superstores
Mail order
Discount department stores
Factory outlets
Off-price chains
Specialty chains
Discount specialty chains
Locally owned stores
Department stores

50   25   0   25   50

(a) Estimate the percent who said they shopped more at a warehouse store.

(b) Estimate the percent who said they shopped less at a warehouse store.

(c) Overall, is there a greater or smaller percent of people shopping at a warehouse store? List the percent increase or decrease.

(d) Which category had the biggest percent gain over-all? Explain your answer.

(e) Describe the general change in our shopping habits from 1987 to 1994.

3. The following line graph indicates the worldwide market share, in percent, of DOS (disk operating system) software, Windows software, and Macintosh software from 1990 to 1994.

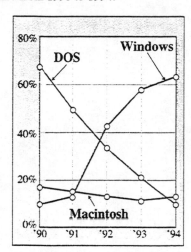

(a) Estimate the market share of software for DOS in 1990 and 1994.

(b) Estimate when the market share of Windows software equaled the market share for DOS.

(c) Estimate the total market share of all software for Windows, DOS, or Macintosh in 1990.

(d) Estimate the total market share of all software for Windows, DOS, or Macintosh in 1994.

4. The following two graphs show changes in the US prison population and the crimes committed since 1979.

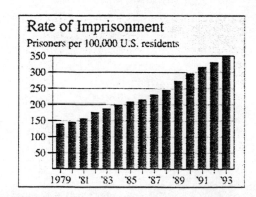

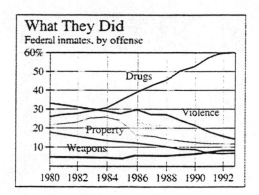

(a) Estimate the rate of imprisonment in 1979 and in 1993, and estimate the increase.

(b) Estimate the percent of inmates imprisoned because of drug charges in 1980 and 1992.

(c) Estimate the sum of the percents for the five categories in the line graph in 1980. Does your answer seem reasonable? Explain.

(d) Repeat part **(c)** for 1992.

(e) Describe the general change in the prison population from 1980 to 1992.

[7.2] 5. Plot each ordered pair on the same axes.
  (a) $A(5, 3)$
  (b) $B(0, 6)$
  (c) $C(5, \frac{1}{2})$
  (d) $D(-4, 3)$
  (e) $E(-6, -1)$
  (f) $F(-2, 0)$

6. Determine if the points given are collinear: $(0, -4)$, $(6, 8)$, $(-2, 0)$, $(4, 4)$

7. Which of the following ordered pairs satisfy the equation $2x + 3y = 9$?
  (a) $(4, 3)$ **(b)** $(0, 3)$
  (c) $(-1, 4)$ **(d)** $(2, \frac{5}{3})$

[7.3] 8. Find the missing coordinate in the following solutions for $3x - 2y = 8$ **(a)** $(2, ?)$ **(b)** $(0, ?)$ **(c)** $(?, 4)$
  (d) $(?, 0)$

Graph each equation using the method of your choice.

9. $y = 2$ **10.** $x = -3$ **11.** $y = 3x$

12. $y = 2x - 1$ **13.** $y = -3x + 4$ **14.** $y = -\dfrac{1}{2}x + 4$

15. $2x + 3y = 6$ **16.** $3x - 2y = 12$ **17.** $2y = 3x - 6$

18. $4x - y = 8$ **19.** $-5x - 2y = 10$ **20.** $3x = 6y + 9$

21. $25x + 50y = 100$ **22.** $3x - 2y = 270$ **23.** $\dfrac{2}{3}x = \dfrac{1}{4}y + 20$

[7.4] *Find the slope of the line through the given points.*

24. $(3, -7)$ and $(-2, 5)$

25. $(-4, -2)$ and $(8, -3)$

26. $(-2, -1)$ and $(-4, 3)$

27. What is the slope of a horizontal line?

28. What is the slope of a vertical line?

29. Define the slope of a straight line.

Find the slope of the lines graphed below.

30.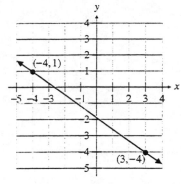

31.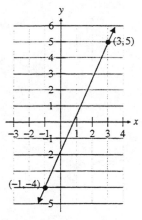

32.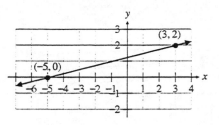

7.5] *Determine the slope and y intercept of the graph of each equation.*

33. $y = -x + 4$

34. $y = -4x + \frac{1}{2}$

35. $2x + 3y = 8$

36. $3x + 6y = 9$

37. $4y = 6x + 12$

38. $3x + 5y = 12$

39. $9x + 7y = 15$

40. $4x - 8 = 0$

41. $3y + 9 = 0$

Write the equation of each line.

42.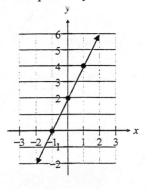

43.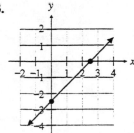

44.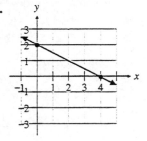

Determine if the two lines are parallel.

45. $y = 3x - 6$

$6y = 18x + 6$

46. $2x - 3y = 9$

$3x - 2y = 6$

47. $y = \frac{4}{9}x + 5$

$4x = 9y + 2$

48. $4x = 6y + 3$

$-2x = -3y + 10$

Find the equation of the line with the properties given.

49. Slope $= 2$, through $(3, 4)$

50. Slope $= -3$, through $(-1, 5)$

51. Slope $= -\frac{2}{3}$, through $(3, 2)$

52. Slope $= 0$, through $(4, 2)$

53. Slope is undefined, through $(3, 5)$

54. Slope $= -2$, y-intercept $= -4$

55. Through $(-2, 3)$ and $(0, -4)$

56. Through $(-4, -2)$ and $(-4, 3)$

7.6] *Determine which of these relations are also functions. Give the domain and range of each.*

57. $\{(0, 2), (4, -3), (1, 5), (2, -1), (6, 4)\}$

58. $\{(3, 1), (4, 2), (4, 5), (6, 1), (7, 0)\}$

59. $\{(3, 1), (4, 1), (5, 1), (6, 2), (3, -3)\}$

60. $\{(5, -2), (3, -2), (4, -2), (9, -2), (-2, -2)\}$

The domain and range of a relation are illustrated. **(a)** *Construct a set of ordered pairs that represent the relation.* **(b)** *Determine if the relation is a function. Explain your answer.*

61. Domain   Range

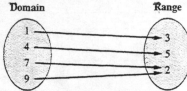

62. Domain   Range

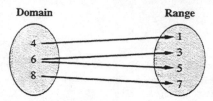

Use the vertical line test to determine if the relation is also a function.

63.

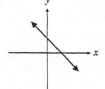

64.

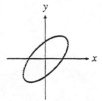

65.

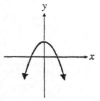

66.

Evaluate the functions at the values indicated.

67. $f(x) = 3x - 4$; find **(a)** $f(2)$ **(b)** $f(-5)$

68. $f(x) = -4x - 5$; find **(a)** $f(-4)$ **(b)** $f(8)$

69. $f(x) = \frac{1}{3}x - 5$; find **(a)** $f(3)$ **(b)** $f(-9)$

70. $f(x) = 2x^2 - 4x + 6$; find **(a)** $f(3)$ **(b)** $f(-5)$

Graph the following functions.

71. $f(x) = 3x - 5$ **72.** $f(x) = -2x + 3$ **73.** $f(x) = -4x$ **74.** $f(x) = -3x - 1$

75. A discount stockbroker charges $25 plus 3 cents per share of stock bought or sold. The broker's commission, c, in dollars, is a function of the number of shares, n, bought or sold, $c = 25 + 0.03n$.

   (a) Draw a graph illustrating the broker's commission for up to and including 10,000 shares of stock.

   (b) Estimate the commission if 1000 shares of a stock are purchased.

76. The monthly profit, p, of an Everything For A Dollar store can be estimated by the function $p = 4x - 1600$, where x represents the number of items sold.

   (a) Draw a graph of the function for up to and including 1000 items sold.

   (b) Estimate the profit if 400 items are sold.

[7.7] *Graph each inequality.*

77. $y \geq -3$ **78.** $x < 4$ **79.** $y < 3x$ **80.** $y > 2x + 1$

Graph each inequality.

81. $y \leq 4x - 3$ **82.** $-6x + y \geq 5$ **83.** $y < -x + 4$ **84.** $3y + 6 \leq x$

Practice Test

1. The following bar graph shows the 1994 market shares, in percent, of over-the-counter pain-reliever drugs.

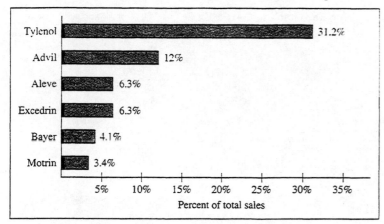

Percent of total sales

(a) If a bar was to be added for "other," what percent would correspond to it? Explain how you determined your answer.

(b) By what percent does sales of Advil exceed sales of Excedrin?

(c) In 1994 the annual sales for pain relievers was $2.6 billion. What was the annual dollar sales of Tylenol?

2. Which of the following ordered pairs satisfy the equation $3y = 5x - 9$?

(a) $(3, 2)$ **(b)** $(\frac{9}{5}, 0)$

(c) $(-2, -6)$ **(d)** $(0, 3)$

3. Find the slope of the line through the points $(-4, 3)$ and $(2, -5)$.

4. Find the slope and y intercept of $4x - 9y = 15$.

5. Write an equation of the graph in the accompanying figure.

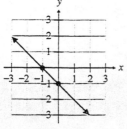

6. Write, in slope–intercept form, an equation of the line with a slope of 3 passing through the point $(1, 3)$.

7. Write, in slope–intercept form, an equation of the line passing through the points $(3, -1)$ and $(-4, 2)$.

8. Determine if the following equations represent parallel lines. Explain how you determined your answer.

$$2y = 3x - 6 \text{ and } y - \frac{3}{2}x = -5.$$

9. Graph $x = -5$.   **10.** Graph $y = 3x - 2$.

11. Graph $3x + 5y = 15$.   **12.** Graph $3x - 2y = 8$.

13. Define a function.

14. **(a)** Determine whether the relation that follows is a function. Explain your answer.

$$\{(1, 2), (3, -4), (5, 3), (1, 0), (6, 5)\}$$

(b) Give the domain and range of the relation or function.

15. Determine if the following graphs are functions. Explain how you determined your answer.

(a)

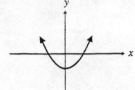

(b)

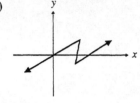

16. Graph the function $f(x) = 2x - 4$.

17. Graph $y \geq -3x + 5$.

18. Graph $y < 4x - 2$.

Chapter 8

Systems of Linear Equations

8.1 Solving Systems of Equations Graphically

8.2 Solving Systems of Equations by Substitution

8.3 Solving Systems of Equations by the Addition Method

8.4 Applications of Systems of Equations

8.5 Systems of Linear Inequalities

SUMMARY

REVIEW EXERCISES

PRACTICE TEST

CUMULATIVE REVIEW TEST

See Section 8.2, Exercise 23.

Preview and Perspective

In this chapter we learn how to express application problems as systems of linear equations and how to solve systems of linear equations. People in business work with many variables and unknown quantities. For example, a company considers overhead cost, cost of material, labor cost, maximum possible production, selling price of the item, and a host of other items when seeking to maximize their profit. The business may express the relationships between the variables in several equations or inequalities. These equations or inequalities form a *system* of equations or inequalities. The solution of the system of equations or inequalities gives the value of the variables (such as production, price, labor cost) for which the company can maximize profits. Such problems are sometimes called linear programming problems. Computers may be used to solve complex systems of equations but first someone must develop the system of equations.

In this chapter we explain three procedures for solving systems of equations. In Section 8.1 we solve systems using graphs. In Section 8.2 we solve systems using substitution. In Section 8.3 we solve systems using the addition (or elimination) method. In Section 8.4 we explain how to express real life application problems as systems of linear equations. Lastly, in Section 8.5 we build on the graphical solution presented in Section 8.1, and solve systems of linear *inequalities* graphically.

Systems of linear equations may also be solved using matrices, determinants, or graphing calculators. You may solve systems of linear equations using one or more of these techniques in intermediate algebra. In this course we deal only with linear systems of equations in two variables. The graphs of such equations are straight lines. In more advanced courses, you may solve systems of nonlinear equations. In a nonlinear system the graph of at least one of the equations is not a straight line.

To be successful with Section 8.1, solving systems of equations graphically, you need to understand the procedure for graphing straight lines presented in Sections 7.3 through 7.5. To be successful with Section 8.5, systems of inequalities, you need to understand how to graph linear inequalities, which was presented in Section 7.7.

8.1   Solving Systems of Equations Graphically

Tape 13

1 Determine whether or not an ordered pair is a solution to a system of equations.

2 Determine if a system of equations is consistent, inconsistent, or dependent.

3 Solve a system of equations graphically.

Solutions to a System of Linear Equations

1 When we seek a common solution to two or more linear equations, the equations are called **simultaneous linear equations** or a **system of linear equations.** An example of a system of linear equations follows:

$$\left.\begin{array}{l}(1) \; y = x + 5 \\ (2) \; y = 2x + 4\end{array}\right\} \quad \text{system of linear equations}$$

The **solution to a system of equations** is the ordered pair or pairs that satisfy all equations in the system. The solution to the system above is (1, 6).

Check:

In Equation (1)	*In Equation (2)*
(1, 6)	(1, 6)
$y = x + 5$	$y = 2x + 4$
$6 = 1 + 5$	$6 = 2(1) + 4$
$6 = 6$ true	$6 = 6$ true

Because the ordered pair (1, 6) satisfies *both* equations, it is a solution to the system of equations. Notice that the ordered pair (2, 7) satisfies the first equation but does not satisfy the second equation.

Check:

In Equation (1)	*In Equation (2)*
(2, 7)	(2, 7)
$y = x + 5$	$y = 2x + 4$
$7 = 2 + 5$	$7 = 2(2) + 4$
$7 = 7$ true	$7 = 8$ false

Since the ordered pair (2, 7) does not satisfy both equations, it is *not* a solution to the system of equations.

EXAMPLE 1 Determine which of the following ordered pairs satisfy the system of equations.

$$y = 2x - 8$$
$$2x + y = 4$$

(a) $(2, -4)$ **(b)** $(4, -4)$ **(c)** $(3, -2)$

Solution:

(a) Substitute 2 for x and -4 for y in each equation.

$y = 2x - 8$	$2x + y = 4$
$-4 = 2(2) - 8$	$2(2) + (-4) = 4$
$-4 = 4 - 8$	$4 - 4 = 4$
$-4 = -4$ true	$0 = 4$ false

Since $(2, -4)$ does not satisfy both equations, it is not a solution to the system of equations.

(b) Substitute 4 for x and -4 for y in each equation.

$y = 2x - 8$	$2x + y = 4$
$-4 = 2(4) - 8$	$2(4) + (-4) = 4$
$-4 = 8 - 8$	$8 - 4 = 4$
$-4 = 0$ false	$4 = 4$ true

Since $(4, -4)$ does not satisfy both equations it is not a solution to the system of equations.

(c) Substitute 3 for x and -2 for y in each equation.

$$y = 2x - 8 \qquad\qquad 2x + y = 4$$
$$-2 = 2(3) - 8 \qquad\qquad 2(3) + (-2) = 4$$
$$-2 = 6 - 8 \qquad\qquad 6 - 2 = 4$$
$$-2 = -2 \quad \text{true} \qquad\qquad 4 = 4 \quad \text{true}$$

Since $(3, -2)$ satisfies both equations, it is a solution to the system of linear equations.

In this chapter we discuss three methods for finding the solution to a system of equations: the graphical method, the substitution method, and the addition method. In this section we discuss the graphical method.

Consistent, Inconsistent and Dependent Systems

2 The **solution to a system of linear equations** is the ordered pair (or pairs) common to all lines in the system when the lines are graphed. When two lines are graphed, three situations are possible, as illustrated in Figure 8.1.

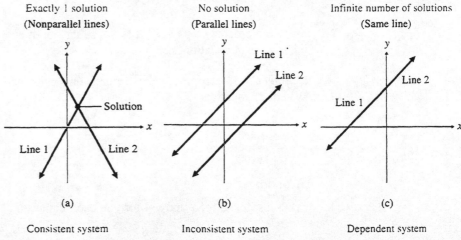

Exactly 1 solution
(Nonparallel lines)

No solution
(Parallel lines)

Infinite number of solutions
(Same line)

(a)   (b)   (c)

Consistent system   Inconsistent system   Dependent system

FIGURE 8.1

In Figure 8.1a, lines 1 and 2 are not parallel lines. They intersect at exactly one point. This system of equations has *exactly one solution*. This is an example of a **consistent system of equations.** A consistent system of equations is a system of equations that has a solution.

In Figure 8.1b, lines 1 and 2 are two different parallel lines. The lines do not intersect, and this system of equations has *no solution*. This is an example of an **inconsistent system of equations.** An inconsistent system of equations is a system of equations that has no solution.

In Figure 8.1c, lines 1 and 2 are actually the same line. In this case, every point on the line satisfies both equations and is a solution to the system of equations. This system has *an infinite number of solutions*. This is an example of a **dependent system of equations.** A dependent system of linear equations is a system of equations that has an infinite number of solutions. If a system of two linear equations is dependent, then both equations represent the same line. *Note that a dependent system is also a consistent system since it has a solution.*

We can determine if a system of linear equations is consistent, inconsistent, or dependent by writing each equation in slope–intercept form and comparing the slopes and y intercepts. If the slopes of the lines are different (Fig. 8.1a), the system is consistent. If the slopes are the same but the y intercepts are different (Fig. 8.1b), the system is inconsistent. If both the slopes and the y intercepts are the same (Fig. 8.1c), the system is dependent.

EXAMPLE 2 Determine whether the system is consistent, inconsistent, or dependent.

$$3x + 4y = 8$$
$$6x + 8y = 4$$

Solution: Write each equation in slope–intercept form and then compare the slopes and the y intercepts.

$$3x + 4y = 8 \qquad\qquad 6x + 8y = 4$$
$$4y = -3x + 8 \qquad\qquad 8y = -6x + 4$$
$$y = \frac{-3x + 8}{4} \qquad\qquad y = \frac{-6x + 4}{8}$$
$$y = \frac{-3}{4}x + 2 \qquad\qquad y = \frac{-6}{8}x + \frac{4}{8}$$
$$y = \frac{-3}{4}x + \frac{1}{2}$$

Since the equations have the same slope, $-\frac{3}{4}$, and different y intercepts, the lines are parallel. This system of equations is therefore inconsistent and has no solution.

Solve Systems Graphically **3**

> To obtain the solution to a system of equations graphically, graph each equation and determine the point or points of intersection.

EXAMPLE 3 Solve the following system of equations graphically.

$$2x + y = 11$$
$$x + 3y = 18$$

Solution: Find the x and y intercepts of each graph; then draw the graphs.

$2x + y = 11$	*Ordered Pair*	$x + 3y = 18$	*Ordered Pair*
Let $x = 0$; then $y = 11$	$(0, 11)$	Let $x = 0$; then $y = 6$	$(0, 6)$
Let $y = 0$; then $x = \dfrac{11}{2}$	$\left(\dfrac{11}{2}, 0\right)$	Let $y = 0$; then $x = 18$	$(18, 0)$

The two graphs (Fig. 8.2) appear to intersect at the point (3, 5). The point (3, 5) may be the solution to the system of equations. To be sure, however, we must check to see that (3, 5) satisfies *both* equations.

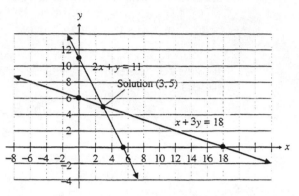

FIGURE 8.2

Check:

$$2x + y = 11 \qquad\qquad x + 3y = 18$$
$$2(3) + 5 = 11 \qquad\qquad 3 + 3(5) = 18$$
$$11 = 11 \quad \text{true} \qquad\qquad 18 = 18 \quad \text{true}$$

Since the ordered pair (3, 5) checks in both equations, it is the solution to the system of equations. This system of equations is consistent.

EXAMPLE 4   Solve the following system of equations graphically.

$$2x + y = 3$$
$$4x + 2y = 12$$

Solution:

$2x + y = 3$	*Ordered Pair*	$4x + 2y = 12$	*Ordered Pair*
Let $x = 0$; then $y = 3$	$(0, 3)$	Let $x = 0$; then $y = 6$	$(0, 6)$
Let $y = 0$; then $x = \dfrac{3}{2}$	$\left(\dfrac{3}{2}, 0\right)$	Let $y = 0$; then $x = 3$	$(3, 0)$

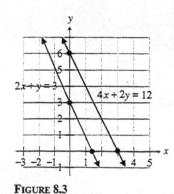

FIGURE 8.3

The two lines (Fig. 8.3) appear to be parallel.

To show that the two lines are indeed parallel, write each equation in slope–intercept form.

$$2x + y = 3 \qquad\qquad 4x + 2y = 12$$
$$y = -2x + 3 \qquad\qquad 2y = -4x + 12$$
$$\qquad\qquad\qquad\qquad\qquad y = -2x + 6$$

Both equations have the same slope, -2, and different y intercepts; thus the lines must be parallel. Since parallel lines do not intersect, this system of equations has no solution. This system of equations is inconsistent.

EXAMPLE 5   Solve the following system of equations graphically.

$$x - \frac{1}{2}y = 2$$

$$y = 2x - 4$$

Solution:

$x - \frac{1}{2}y = 2$	*Ordered Pair*	$y = 2x - 4$	*Ordered Pair*
Let $x = 0$; then $y = -4$	$(0, -4)$	Let $x = 0$; then $y = -4$	$(0, -4)$
Let $y = 0$; then $x = 2$	$(2, 0)$	Let $y = 0$; then $x = 2$	$(2, 0)$

Because the lines have the same x and y intercepts, both equations represent the same line (Fig. 8.4). When the equations are changed to slope–intercept form, it becomes clear that the equations are identical and the system is dependent.

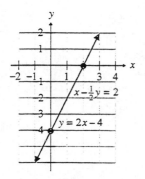

FIGURE 8.4

$$x - \frac{1}{2}y = 2 \qquad\qquad y = 2x - 4$$

$$2\left(x - \frac{1}{2}y\right) = 2(2)$$

$$2x - y = 4$$

$$-y = -2x + 4$$

$$y = 2x - 4$$

The solution to this system of equations is all the points on the line.

When graphing a system of equations, the intersection of the lines is not always easy to read on the graph. For example, the solution to a system of equations may be the ordered pair $(\frac{5}{9}, -\frac{4}{11})$. In cases like this, it is not easy to find the exact value of the solution by observation, but you should be able to give an approximate answer. An approximate answer to this system might be $(\frac{1}{2}, -\frac{1}{3})$ or $(0.6, -0.3)$. The accuracy of your answer will depend on how carefully you draw the graphs and on the scale of the graph paper used.

In Section 3.3 we solved a problem involving security systems using only one variable. In the example that follows, we will work that same problem using two variables and illustrate the solution in the form of a graph. Although an answer may sometimes be easier to obtain using only one variable, a graph of the situation may help you to visualize the total picture better. Before you read Example 6, you may wish to review the solution to Example 11 in Section 3.3.

EXAMPLE 6   Mr. and Mrs. Frank plan to install a security system in their house. They have narrowed down their choices to two security dealers: Moneywell and Doile security systems. Moneywell's system cost $3660 to install and their monitoring fee is $17 per month. Doile's equivalent system cost only $2260 to install, but their monitoring fee is $28 per month.

(a) Assuming that their monthly monitoring fees do not change, in how many months would the total cost of Moneywell's and Doile's system be the same?

(b) If both dealers guarantee not to raise monthly fees for 10 years, and if you plan to use the system for 10 years, which system would be the least expensive?

Solution:

(a) We need to determine the number of months when both systems will have the same total cost.

Let n = number of months
  c = total cost of the security system over n months

Now write an equation to represent the cost of each system using the two variables c and n.

	Moneywell		*Doile*

$$\text{Total cost} = \binom{\text{initial}}{\text{cost}} + \binom{\text{fees over}}{n \text{ months}} \qquad \text{Total cost} = \binom{\text{initial}}{\text{cost}} + \binom{\text{fees over}}{n \text{ months}}$$

$$c = 3360 + 17n \qquad\qquad c = 2260 + 28n$$

Thus, our system of equations is

$$c = 3360 + 17n$$
$$c = 2260 + 28n$$

Now graph each equation.

$c = 3360 + 17n$

Let $n = 0$	$c = 3360 + 17(0) = 3360$
Let $n = 100$	$c = 3360 + 17(100) = 5060$
Let $n = 150$	$c = 3360 + 17(150) = 5910$

n	c
0	3360
100	5060
150	5910

$c = 2260 + 28n$

Let $n = 0$	$c = 2260 + 28(0) = 2260$
Let $n = 100$	$c = 2260 + 28(100) = 5060$
Let $n = 150$	$c = 2260 + 28(150) = 6460$

n	c
0	2260
100	5060
150	6460

Security systems

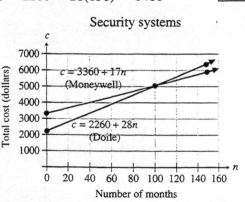

FIGURE 8.5

The graph (Fig. 8.5) shows that the total cost of the two security systems would be the same in 100 months. This is the same answer obtained in Example 11 in Section 3.3.

(b) Since 10 years is 120 months, draw a dashed vertical line at $n = 120$ months and see where it intersects the two lines. Since at 120 months the Doile line is higher than the Moneywell line, the cost for the Doile system for 120 months is more than the cost of the Moneywell system. Therefore, the cost of the Moneywell system would be less expensive for 10 years.

Applications of systems of equations are discussed further in Section 8.5

Helpful Hint

In the Helpful Hint in Section 7.3 we gave one graphical interpretation of the solution of a linear equation in one variable. Now we will give another. Consider the equation $3x - 1 = x + 1$. Its solution is 1, as is illustrated below.

$$3x - 1 = x + 1$$
$$2x - 1 = 1$$
$$2x = 2$$
$$x = 1$$

Let us set each side of the equation $3x - 1 = x + 1$ equal to y to obtain the following system of equations:

$$y = 3x - 1$$
$$y = x + 1$$

The graphical solution of this system of equations is illustrated below.

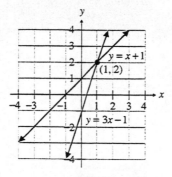

A check will show that the solution to the system is (1, 2). Notice that the x coordinate of the solution of the system, 1, is the solution to the linear equation in one variable, $3x - 1 = x + 1$. Thus, you can solve a linear equation in one variable by changing it to a system of linear equation in two variables. The x coordinate of the solution to the system will be the solution to the linear equation in one variable.

Exercise Set 8.1

Determine which, if any, of the following ordered pairs satisfy each system of linear equations.

1. $y = 3x - 4$
$y = -x + 4$
   (a) $(-2, 2)$ **(b)** $(-4, -8)$ **(c)** $(2, 2)$

2. $y = -4x$
$y = -2x + 8$
   (a) $(0, 0)$ **(b)** $(-4, 16)$ **(c)** $(2, -8)$

3. $y = 2x - 3$
$y = x + 5$
   (a) $(8, 13)$ **(b)** $(4, 5)$ **(c)** $(4, 9)$

4. $x + 2y = 4$
$y = 3x + 3$
   (a) $(0, 2)$ **(b)** $(-2, 3)$ **(c)** $(4, 15)$

5. $3x - y = 6$
$2x + y = 9$
   (a) $(3, 3)$ **(b)** $(4, -2)$ **(c)** $(-6, 3)$

6. $y = 2x + 4$
$y = 2x - 1$
   (a) $(0, 4)$ **(b)** $(3, 10)$ **(c)** $(-2, 0)$

7. $2x - 3y = 6$
$y = \dfrac{2}{3}x - 2$
   (a) $(3, 0)$ **(b)** $(3, -2)$ **(c)** $(6, 2)$

8. $y = -x + 4$
$2y = -2x + 8$
   (a) $(2, 5)$ **(b)** $(0, 4)$ **(c)** $(5, -1)$

9. $3x - 4y = 8$
$2y = \dfrac{2}{3}x - 4$
   (a) $(0, -2)$ **(b)** $(1, -6)$ **(c)** $\left(-\dfrac{1}{3}, -\dfrac{9}{4}\right)$

10. $2x + 3y = 6$
$-2x + 5 = y$
   (a) $\left(\dfrac{1}{2}, \dfrac{5}{3}\right)$ **(b)** $(2, 1)$ **(c)** $\left(\dfrac{9}{4}, \dfrac{1}{2}\right)$

Identify each system of linear equations (lines are labeled 1 and 2) as consistent, inconsistent, or dependent. State whether the system has exactly one solution, no solution, or an infinite number of solutions.

11.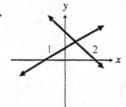

12.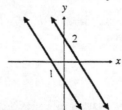

13.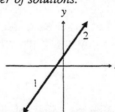

14.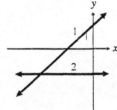

15.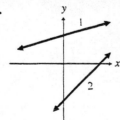

16.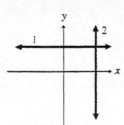

17.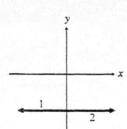

18.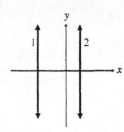

Express each equation in slope–intercept form. Without graphing the equations, state whether the system of equations has exactly one solution, no solution, or an infinite number of solutions.

19. $y = 3x - 2$
$2y = 4x - 6$

20. $x + y = 6$
$x - y = 6$

21. $3y = 2x + 3$
$y = \dfrac{2}{3}x - 2$

22. $y = \dfrac{1}{2}x + 4$
$2y = x + 8$

23. $4x = y - 6$
$3x = 4y + 5$

24. $x + 2y = 6$
$2x + y = 4$

25. $2x = 3y + 4$
$6x - 9y = 12$

26. $x - y = 2$
$2x - 2y = -2$

27. $y = \dfrac{3}{2}x + \dfrac{1}{2}$
$3x - 2y = -\dfrac{1}{2}$

28. $x - y = 3$
$\dfrac{1}{2}x - 2y = -6$

29. $3x + 5y = -7$
$-3x - 5y = -7$

30. $3x = 7y - 9$
$3x = -7y + 9$

Determine the solution to each system of equations graphically. If the system is dependent or inconsistent, so state.

31. $y = x + 2$
$y = -x + 2$

32. $y = 2x + 4$
$y = -3x - 6$

33. $y = 3x - 6$
$y = -x + 6$

34. $y = 2x - 1$
$2y = 4x + 6$

35. $2x = 4$
$y = -3$

36. $x + y = 5$
$2y = x - 2$

37. $y = x + 2$
$x + y = 4$

38. $2x + y = 6$
$2x - y = -2$

39. $y = -\dfrac{1}{2}x + 4$
$x + 2y = 6$

40. $x + 2y = -4$
$2x - y = -3$

41. $x + 2y = 8$
$2x - 3y = 2$

42. $4x - y = 5$
$2y = 8x - 10$

43. $2x + 3y = 6$
$4x = -6y + 12$

44. $2x + 3y = 6$
$2x + y = -2$

45. $y = 3$
$y = 2x - 3$

46. $x - 3$
$y = 2x - 2$

47. $x - 2y = 4$
$2x - 4y = 8$

48. $3x + y = -6$
$2x = 1 + y$

49. $2x + y = -2$
$6x + 3y = 6$

50. $y = 2x - 3$
$y = -x$

51. $4x - 3y = 6$
$2x + 4y = 14$

52. $2x + 6y = 6$
$y = -\dfrac{1}{3}x + 1$

53. $2x - 3y = 0$
$x + 2y = 0$

54. $2x = 4y - 12$
$-4x + 8y = 8$

In Exercises 55–57, find the solution by graphing the system of equations.

55. In Example 6, if Moneywell's system cost $4400 plus $15 per month and Doile's system cost $3400 plus $25 per month, after how many months would the total cost of the two systems be the same?

56. A college is considering purchasing one of two computer systems. In system A the host computer costs $3600 and the terminals cost $400 each. In system B the host computer costs $2400 but the terminals cost $600 each. We can represent this situation with the system of equations

$$c = 3600 + 400n$$
$$c = 2400 + 600n$$

where c is the total cost and n is the number of terminals. Find the number of terminals for which the systems cost the same.

57. The Evergreen Landscape Service charges a consultation fee of $200 plus $60 per hour for labor. The Out of Sight Landscape Service charges a consultation fee of $300 plus $40 per hour for labor. We can represent this situation with the system of equations

$$c = 200 + 60h$$
$$c = 300 + 40h$$

SEE EXERCISE 57.

where c is the total cost and h is the number of hours of labor. Find the number of hours of labor for the two services to have the same total cost.

58. What does the solution to a system of equations represent?

59. Given the system of equations $5x - 4y = 10$ and $12y = 15x - 20$, determine without graphing if the graphs of the two equations will be parallel lines. Explain how you determined your answer.

60. (a) What is a consistent system of equations? (b) What is an inconsistent system of equations? (c) What is a dependent system of equations?

61. Explain how to determine without graphing if a system of linear equations has exactly one solution, no solution, or an infinite number of solutions.

62. When a dependent system of two linear equations is graphed, what will be the results?

CUMULATIVE REVIEW EXERCISES

[1.3] **63.** Consider this set of numbers

$$\{6, -4, 0, \sqrt{3}, 2\tfrac{1}{2}, -\tfrac{9}{5}, 4.22, -\sqrt{7}\}$$

List the numbers that are:

(a) Natural numbers

(b) Whole numbers

(c) Integers

(d) Rational numbers

(e) Irrational numbers

(f) Real numbers

[5.2] **64.** Factor $xy - 4x + 3y - 12$.

[5.4] **65.** Factor $8x^2 + 2x - 15$.

[6.4] **66.** Subtract $\dfrac{x}{x+3} - 2$.

[6.6] **67.** Solve $\dfrac{x}{x+3} - 2 = 0$.

Group Activity/ Challenge Problems

Suppose that a system of three linear equations is graphed on the same axes. Find the maximum number of points where two or more of the lines can intersect if:

1. The three lines have the same slope but different y intercepts

2. The three lines have the same slope and the same y intercept

3. Two lines have the same slope but different y intercepts and the third line has a different slope

4. The three lines have different slopes but the same y intercept

5. The three lines have different slopes but two have the same y intercept

6. The three lines have different slopes and different y intercepts

---

Tape 13

8.2 Solving Systems of Equations by Substitution

1 Solve systems of equations by substitution.

Often, a graphic solution to a system of equations may be inaccurate since you must estimate the coordinates of the point of intersection. For example, can you determine the solution to the system of equations shown in Figure 8.6? You may estimate the solution to be $\left(\dfrac{7}{10}, \dfrac{3}{2}\right)$ when it may actually be $\left(\dfrac{4}{5}, \dfrac{8}{5}\right)$. When an exact solution is necessary, the system should be solved algebraically, either by substitution or by addition of equations.

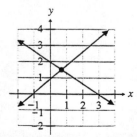

FIGURE 8.6

Solving Systems by Substitution

1 The procedure for solving a system of equations by substitution is illustrated in Example 1. The procedure for solving by addition is presented in Section 8.3. Regardless of which of the two algebraic techniques is used to solve a system of equations, our immediate goal remains the same, that is, to obtain one equation containing only one unknown.

EXAMPLE 1 Solve the following system of equations by substitution.

$$2x + y = 11$$
$$x + 3y = 18$$

Solution: Begin by solving for one of the variables in either of the equations. You may solve for any of the variables; however, if you solve for a variable with a numerical coefficient of 1, you may avoid working with fractions. In this system the y term in $2x + y = 11$ and the x term in $x + 3y = 18$ both have a numerical coefficient of 1.

Let us solve for y in $2x + y = 11$.

$$2x + y = 11$$
$$y = -2x + 11$$

Next, substitute $-2x + 11$ for y in the *other equation*, $x + 3y = 18$, and solve for the remaining variable, x.

$$x + 3y = 18$$
$$x + 3(-2x + 11) = 18$$
$$x - 6x + 33 = 18$$
$$-5x + 33 = 18$$
$$-5x = -15$$
$$x = 3$$

Finally, substitute $x = 3$ in the equation that is solved for y and find the value of y.

$$y = -2x + 11$$
$$y = -2(3) + 11$$
$$y = -6 + 11$$
$$y = 5$$

The solution is the ordered pair $(3, 5)$.

Note that this solution is identical to the graphical solution obtained in Example 3 of Section 8.1.

To Solve a System of Equations by Substitution

1. Solve for a variable in either equation. (If possible, solve for a variable with a numerical coefficient of 1 to avoid working with fractions.)

continued on top of next page

2. Substitute the expression found for the variable in step 1 into the other equation.
3. Solve the equation determined in step 2 to find the value of one variable.
4. Substitute the value found in step 3 into the equation obtained in step 1 to find the other variable.

EXAMPLE 2 Solve the following system of equations by substitution.

$$2x + y = 3$$
$$4x + 2y = 12$$

Solution: Solve for y in $2x + y = 3$.

$$2x + y = 3$$
$$y = -2x + 3$$

Now substitute the expression $-2x + 3$ for y in the *other equation*, $4x + 2y = 12$, and solve for x.

$$4x + 2y = 12$$
$$4x + 2(-2x + 3) = 12$$
$$4x - 4x + 6 = 12$$
$$6 = 12 \qquad \textbf{false}$$

Since the statement 6 = 12 is false, the system has no solution. (Therefore, the graphs of the equations will be parallel lines and the system is inconsistent because it has no solution.)

Note that the solution in Example 2 is identical to the graphical solution obtained in Example 4 of Section 8.1. Figure 8.3 on page 444 shows the parallel lines.

EXAMPLE 3 Solve the following system of equations by substitution.

$$x - \frac{1}{2}y = 2$$
$$y = 2x - 4$$

Solution: The equation $y = 2x - 4$ is already solved for y. Substitute $2x - 4$ for y in the other equation, $x - \frac{1}{2}y = 2$, and solve for x.

$$x - \frac{1}{2}y = 2$$
$$x - \frac{1}{2}(2x - 4) = 2$$
$$x - x + 2 = 2$$
$$2 = 2 \qquad \textbf{true}$$

Notice that the sum of the x terms is 0, and when simplified x is no longer part of the equation. *Since the statement $2 = 2$ is true, this system has an infinite number of solutions. Therefore, the graphs of the equations represent the same line and the system is dependent.*

Note that the solution in Example 3 is identical to the solution obtained graphically in Example 5 of Section 8.1. Figure 8.4 on page 445 shows the graphs of both equations are the same line.

EXAMPLE 4   Solve the following system of equations by substitution.

$$2x + 4y = 6$$
$$4x - 2y = -8$$

Solution: None of the variables in either equation has a numerical coefficient of 1. However, since the numbers 4 and 6 are both divisible by 2, if we solve the first equation for x, we will avoid having to work with fractions.

$$2x + 4y = 6$$
$$2x = -4y + 6$$
$$\frac{2x}{2} = \frac{-4y + 6}{2}$$
$$x = -2y + 3$$

Now substitute $-2y + 3$ for x in the other equation, $4x - 2y = -8$, and solve for the remaining variable y.

$$4x - 2y = -8$$
$$4(-2y + 3) - 2y = -8$$
$$-8y + 12 - 2y = -8$$
$$-10y + 12 = -8$$
$$-10y = -20$$
$$y = 2$$

Finally, solve for x by substituting $y = 2$ in the equation previously solved for x.

$$x = -2y + 3$$
$$x = -2(2) + 3 = -4 + 3 = -1$$

The solution is $(-1, 2)$.

Helpful Hint

Remember that a solution to a system of linear equations must contain both an x and a y value. Don't solve the system for one of the variables and forget to solve for the other.

EXAMPLE 5 Solve the following system of equations by substitution.

$$4x + 4y = 3$$
$$2x = 2y + 5$$

Solution: We will elect to solve for x in the second equation.

$$2x = 2y + 5$$
$$x = \frac{2y + 5}{2}$$
$$x = y + \frac{5}{2}$$

Now substitute $y + \frac{5}{2}$ for x in the other equation.

$$4x + 4y = 3$$
$$4\left(y + \frac{5}{2}\right) + 4y = 3$$
$$4y + 10 + 4y = 3$$
$$8y + 10 = 3$$
$$8y = -7$$
$$y = -\frac{7}{8}$$

Finally, find the value of x.

$$x = y + \frac{5}{2}$$
$$x = -\frac{7}{8} + \frac{5}{2} = -\frac{7}{8} + \frac{20}{8} = \frac{13}{8}$$

The solution is the ordered pair $\left(\frac{13}{8}, -\frac{7}{8}\right)$.

Exercise Set 8.2

Find the solution to each system of equations using substitution.

1. $x + 2y = 4$
$2x - 3y = 1$

2. $y = x + 3$
$y = -x - 5$

3. $x + y = -2$
$x - y = 0$

4. $2x + y = 3$
$2y = 6 - 4x$

5. $2x + y = 3$
$2x + y + 5 = 0$

6. $y = 2x + 4$
$y = -2$

7. $x = 4$
$x + y + 5 = 0$

8. $y = 2x - 13$
$-4x - 7 = 9y$

9. $x - \frac{1}{2}y = 2$
$y = 2x - 4$

10. $2x + 3y = 7$
$6x - y = 1$

11. $3x + y = -1$
$y = 3x + 5$

12. $y = -2x + 5$
$x + 3y = 0$

13. $y = \dfrac{1}{3}x - 2$

$x - 3y = 6$

14. $x = y + 4$

$3x + 7y = -18$

15. $2x + 3y = 7$

$6x - 2y = 10$

16. $4x - 3y = 6$

$2x + 4y = 5$

17. $3x - y = 14$

$6x - 2y = 10$

18. $5x - 2y = -7$

$5 = y - 3x$

19. $4x - 5y = -4$

$3x = 2y - 3$

20. $3x + 4y = 10$

$4x + 5y = 14$

21. $5x + 4y = -7$

$x - \dfrac{5}{3}y = -2$

22. $\dfrac{1}{2}x + y = 4$

$3x + \dfrac{1}{4}y = 6$

23. In Seattle, Washington, the temperature is 82°F, but it is decreasing by 2 degrees an hour. The temperature, T, at time t, in hours, is represented by $T = 82 - 2t$. In Spokane, Washington, the temperature is 64°F, but it is increasing by 2.5 degrees per hour. The temperature, T, can be represented by $T = 64 + 2.5t$. **(a)** If the temperature continues decreasing and increasing at the same rate in these cities, how long it will be before both cities have the same temperature? **(b)** When both cities have the same temperature, what will that temperature be?

24. John, a salesperson for an entertainment company, earns a weekly salary of $300 plus $3 for each video tape he sells. His weekly salary can be represented by $S = 300 + 3n$. He is being offered a chance to change salary plans. Under the new plan he will earn a weekly salary of $400 plus $2 for each video tape he sells. His weekly salary under this new plan can be represented by $S = 400 + 2n$. How many tapes would John need to sell in a week for his salary to be the same under both plans?

25. Jim's car is at the 100 mile marker on the interstate highway 15 miles behind Kathy's car. Jim's car is traveling at 65 miles per hour and Kathy's car is traveling at 60 miles per hour. The mile marker that Jim will be at in t hours can be found by $m = 100 + 65t$ and the mile marker that Kathy will be at in t hours can be found by $m = 115 + 60t$. **(a)** Determine the time it will take for Jim to catch Kathy. **(b)** At what mile marker will they be when they meet?

26. When solving the system of equations

$$3x + 6y = 9$$
$$4x + 3y = 5$$

by substitution, which variable, in which equation, would you choose to solve for to make the solution easier? Explain your answer.

27. When solving a system of linear equations by substitution, how will you know if the system is inconsistent?

28. When solving a system of linear equations by substitution, how will you know if the system is dependent?

CUMULATIVE REVIEW EXERCISES

[1.8] *Evaluate.*

29. -3^3

30. $(-3)^3$

31. -3^4

32. $(-3)^4$

[2.6] **33.** If the directions on a box of Quik-Bake Brownie Mix state that 2 eggs must be added to every 3 cups of brownie mix, how many eggs must be added to 9 cups of brownie mix?

34. If triangles ABC and $A'B'C'$ are similar triangles, find the length of side x.

[4.1] *Simplify.*

35. $\left(\dfrac{3x^2y^4}{x^3y^2}\right)^2$

36. $(4x^2y^3)^3 (3x^4y^5)^2$

[6.6] **37.** Solve the equation

$$\dfrac{3}{x - 12} + \dfrac{5}{x - 5} = \dfrac{5}{x^2 - 17x + 60}.$$

B

6 in 7 in

A 8 in C

B'

4 in

A' x C'

Group Activity/ Challenge Problems

1. For the system of equations

$$y = ax + b$$
$$y = cx + d$$

where $a \neq c$, (a) find the x coordinate of the solution. (b) Use your answer to part (a) to find the x coordinate of the system of equations

$$y = 3x + 2$$
$$y = x + 6$$

(c) Find the solution to the system of equations in part (b).

2. (a) Solve the system of equations

$$2y = 4x + 600$$
$$2y = 2x + 1200$$

(b) Suppose that both sides of each equation in the system are divided by 2, to obtain the following system.

$$y = 2x + 300$$
$$y = x + 600$$

Do you believe the solution to this system will be the same as the solution in part (a)? If not, do you believe the solution to this system will be related in any way to the solution obtained in part (a)? Explain your answer without solving the system.

(c) Solve the system in part (b) and compare the solution with the answer you gave in part (b).

3. (a) Solve the system of equations

$$y = 4x + 600$$
$$y = 2x + 1200$$

(b) Suppose that the right side of each equation in the system is divided by 2, to obtain the following system.

$$y = 2x + 300$$
$$y = x + 600$$

Do you believe the solution to this system will be the same as the solution in part (a)? If not, do you believe the solution to this system will be related in any way to the solution obtained in part (a)? Explain your answer without solving the system.

(c) Solve the system in part (b) and compare your solution to the answer you gave in part (b).

4. In a laboratory a large metal ball is heated to a temperature of 180° F. This metal ball is then placed in a gallon of oil at a temperature of 20° F. When placed in the oil the ball loses temperature at the rate of 10° per minute while the oil's temperature rises at a rate of 6° per minute.

(a) How long will it take for the ball and oil to reach the same temperature?

(b) When the ball and oil reach the same temperature, what will that temperature be?

5. In intermediate algebra you may solve systems containing three equations with three variables. Solve the following system of equations.

$$x = 4$$
$$2x - y = 6$$
$$-x + y + z = -3$$

Tape
14

8.3 Solving Systems of Equations by the Addition Method

1 Solve systems of equations by addition.

The Addition Method

1 A third, and often the easiest, method of solving a system of equations is by the addition (or elimination) method. *The object of this process is to obtain two equations whose sum will be an equation containing only one variable.* Always keep in mind that our immediate goal is to obtain one equation containing only one unknown.

EXAMPLE 1 Solve the following system of equations using the addition method.

$$x + y = 6$$
$$2x - y = 3$$

Solution: Note that one equation contains $+y$ and the other contains $-y$. By adding the equations, we can eliminate the variable y and obtain one equation containing only one variable, x. When added, $+y$ and $-y$ sum to 0, and so the variable y is eliminated.

$$
\begin{aligned}
x + y &= 6 \\
\underline{2x - y} &= \underline{3} \\
3x &= 9
\end{aligned}
$$

Now solve for the remaining variable, x.

$$\frac{3x}{3} = \frac{9}{3}$$
$$x = 3$$

Finally, solve for y by substituting $x = 3$ in either of the original equations.

$$x + y = 6$$
$$3 + y = 6$$
$$y = 3$$

The solution is (3, 3).
Check the answer in *both* equations.

Check:

$x + y = 6$	$2x - y = 3$
$3 + 3 = 6$	$2(3) - 3 = 3$
$6 = 6$ **true**	$6 - 3 = 3$
	$3 = 3$ **true**

EXAMPLE 2 Solve the following system of equations using the addition method.

$$-x + 3y = 8$$
$$x + 2y = -13$$

Solution: By adding the equations we can eliminate the variable x.

$$
\begin{array}{rcr}
-x + 3y = & & 8 \\
x + 2y = & & -13 \\
\hline
5y = & & -5 \\
\end{array}
$$

$$\frac{5y}{5} = \frac{-5}{5}$$

$$y = -1$$

Now solve for x by substituting $y = -1$ in either of the original equations.

$$x + 2y = -13$$
$$x + 2(-1) = -13$$
$$x - 2 = -13$$
$$x = -11$$

The solution is $(-11, -1)$.

Now we state the procedure for solving a system of equations by the addition method.

> **To Solve a System of Equations by the Addition (or Elimination) Method**
>
> 1. If necessary, rewrite each equation so that the terms containing variables appear on the left side of the equal sign and any constants appear on the right side of the equal sign.
> 2. If necessary, multiply one or both equations by a constant(s) so that when the equations are added the resulting sum will contain only one variable.
> 3. Add the equations. This will result in a single equation containing only one variable.
> 4. Solve for the variable in the equation in step 3.
> 5. Substitute the value found in step 4 into either of the original equations. Solve that equation to find the value of the remaining variable.

In step 2 we indicate it may be necessary to multiply one or both equations by a constant. In this text we will use brackets [ ], to indicate that both sides of the equation within the brackets are to be multiplied by some constant. Thus, for example, $2[x + y = 1]$ means that both sides of the equation $x + y = 1$ are to be multiplied by 2. We write

$$2[x + y = 1] \qquad \text{gives} \qquad 2x + 2y = 2$$

Similarly, $-3[4x - 2y = 5]$ means both sides of the equation $4x - 2y = 5$ are to be multiplied by -3. We write

$$-3[4x - 2y = 5] \qquad \text{gives} \qquad -12x + 6y = -15$$

The use of this notation may make it easier for you to follow the procedure used to solve the problem.

EXAMPLE 3   Solve the following system of equations using the addition method.

$$2x + y = 6$$
$$3x + y = 5$$

Solution: The object of the addition process is to obtain two equations whose sum will be an equation containing only one variable. If we add these two equations, none of the variables will be eliminated. However, if we multiply either equation by -1 and then add, the terms containing y will sum to zero, and we will accomplish our goal. We will multiply the top equation by -1.

$$-1[2x + y = 6] \qquad \text{gives} \qquad -2x - y = -6$$
$$3x + y = 5 \qquad\qquad\qquad\qquad 3x + y = 5$$

Remember that both sides of the equation must be multiplied by -1. This process changes the sign of each term in the equation being multiplied without changing the solution to the system of equations. Now add the two equations on the right.

$$-2x - y = -6$$
$$\underline{3x + y = 5}$$
$$x = -1$$

Solve for y in either of the original equations.

$$2x + y = 6$$
$$2(-1) + y = 6$$
$$-2 + y = 6$$
$$y = 8$$

The solution is $(-1, 8)$.

EXAMPLE 4   Solve the following system of equations using the addition method.

$$2x + y = 11$$
$$x + 3y = 18$$

Solution: To eliminate the variable x, we multiply the second equation by -2 and add the two equations.

$$2x + y = 11 \qquad \text{gives} \qquad 2x + y = 11$$
$$-2[x + 3y = 18] \qquad\qquad\qquad -2x - 6y = -36$$

Now add:

$$2x + y = 11$$
$$\underline{-2x - 6y = -36}$$
$$-5y = -25$$
$$y = 5$$

Solve for x.

$$2x + y = 11$$
$$2x + 5 = 11$$
$$2x = 6$$
$$x = 3$$

The solution $(3, 5)$ is the same as the solution obtained graphically in Example 3 of Section 8.1 and by substitution in Example 1 of Section 8.2.

In Example 4, we could have multiplied the first equation by -3 to eliminate the variable y.

$$-3[2x + y = 11] \qquad \text{gives} \qquad -6x - 3y = -33$$
$$x + 3y = 18 \qquad\qquad\qquad\qquad x + 3y = 18$$

Now add:

$$-6x - 3y = -33$$
$$\underline{x + 3y = 18}$$
$$-5x = -15$$
$$x = 3$$

Solve for y.

$$2x + y = 11$$
$$2(3) + y = 11$$
$$6 + y = 11$$
$$y = 5$$

The solution remains the same, $(3, 5)$.

EXAMPLE 5 Solve the following system of equations using the addition method.

$$4x + 2y = -18$$
$$-2x - 5y = 10$$

Solution: To eliminate the variable x, we can multiply the second equation by 2 and then add.

$$4x + 2y = -18 \qquad \text{gives} \qquad 4x + 2y = -18$$
$$2[-2x - 5y = 10] \qquad\qquad\qquad -4x - 10y = 20$$

$$4x + 2y = -18$$
$$\underline{-4x - 10y = 20}$$
$$-8y = 2$$
$$y = -\frac{1}{4}$$

Solve for x:

$$4x + 2y = -18$$

$$4x + 2\left(-\frac{1}{4}\right) = -18$$

$$4x - \frac{1}{2} = -18$$

$$2\left(4x - \frac{1}{2}\right) = 2(-18)$$ **Multiply both sides of the equation by 2 to remove fractions.**

$$8x - 1 = -36$$

$$8x = -35$$

$$x = -\frac{35}{8}$$

The solution is $\left(-\frac{35}{8}, -\frac{1}{4}\right)$.

Check the solution $\left(-\frac{35}{8}, -\frac{1}{4}\right)$ in both equations.

Check:

$$4x + 2y = -18 \qquad\qquad -2x - 5y = 10$$

$$4\left(-\frac{35}{8}\right) + 2\left(-\frac{1}{4}\right) = -18 \qquad -2\left(-\frac{35}{8}\right) - 5\left(-\frac{1}{4}\right) = 10$$

$$-\frac{35}{2} - \frac{1}{2} = -18 \qquad\qquad \frac{35}{4} + \frac{5}{4} = 10$$

$$-\frac{36}{2} = -18 \qquad\qquad \frac{40}{4} = 10$$

$$-18 = -18 \quad \text{true} \qquad\qquad 10 = 10 \quad \text{true}$$

Note that the solution to Example 5 contains fractions. You should not always expect to get integers as answers.

EXAMPLE 6   Solve the following system of equations using the addition method.

$$2x + 3y = 6$$

$$5x - 4y = -8$$

Solution: The variable x can be eliminated by multiplying the first equation by -5 and the second by 2 and then adding the equations.

$$-5[2x + 3y = 6] \qquad \text{gives} \qquad -10x - 15y = -30$$

$$2[5x - 4y = -8] \qquad\qquad\qquad 10x - 8y = -16$$

$$-10x - 15y = -30$$

$$\underline{10x - 8y = -16}$$

$$-23y = -46$$

$$y = 2$$

The same value could have been obtained for y by multiplying the first equation by 5 and the second by -2 and then adding. Try it now and see.

Solve for x.

$$2x + 3y = 6$$
$$2x + 3(2) = 6$$
$$2x + 6 = 6$$
$$2x = 0$$
$$x = 0$$

The solution to this system is $(0, 2)$.

EXAMPLE 7   Solve the following system of equations using the addition method.

$$2x + y = 3$$
$$4x + 2y = 12$$

Solution: The variable y can be eliminated by multiplying the first equation by -2 and then adding the two equations.

$$-2[2x + y = 3] \qquad \text{gives} \qquad -4x - 2y = -6$$
$$4x + 2y = 12 \qquad\qquad\qquad 4x + 2y = 12$$

$$\begin{aligned} -4x - 2y &= -6 \\ \underline{4x + 2y} &= \underline{12} \\ 0 &= 6 \quad \text{false} \end{aligned}$$

Since $0 = 6$ is a false statement, this system has no solution. The system is inconsistent. The graphs of the equations will be parallel lines.

This solution is identical to the solutions obtained by graphing in Example 4 of Section 8.1 and by substitution in Example 2 of Section 8.2.

EXAMPLE 8   Solve the following system of equations using the addition method.

$$x - \frac{1}{2}y = 2$$
$$y = 2x - 4$$

Solution: First align the x and y terms on the left side of the equation.

$$x - \frac{1}{2}y = 2$$
$$-2x + y = -4$$

Now proceed as in the previous examples.

$$2\left[x - \frac{1}{2}y = 2\right] \qquad \text{gives} \qquad 2x - y = 4$$
$$-2x + y = -4 \qquad\qquad\qquad -2x + y = -4$$

$$\begin{array}{r} 2x - y = 4 \\ -2x + y = -4 \\ \hline 0 = 0 \quad \text{true} \end{array}$$

Since 0 = 0 is a true statement, the system is dependent and has an infinite number of solutions. When graphed, both equations will be the same line. This solution is the same as the solutions obtained by graphing in Example 5 of Section 8.1 and by substitution in Example 3 of Section 8.2.

EXAMPLE 9 Solve the following system of equations using the addition method.

$$2x + 3y = 7$$
$$5x - 7y = -3$$

Solution: We can eliminate the variable x by multiplying the first equation by -5 and the second by 2.

$$-5[2x + 3y = 7] \qquad \text{gives} \qquad -10x - 15y = -35$$
$$2[5x - 7y = -3] \qquad\qquad\qquad 10x - 14y = -6$$

$$\begin{array}{r} -10x - 15y = -35 \\ 10x - 14y = -6 \\ \hline -29y = -41 \end{array}$$

$$y = \frac{41}{29}$$

We can now find x by substituting $y = \frac{41}{29}$ into one of the original equations and solving for x. If you try this, you will see that although it can be done, the calculations are messy. An easier method of solving for x is to go back to the original equations and eliminate the variable y.

$$7[2x + 3y = 7] \qquad \text{gives} \qquad 14x + 21y = 49$$
$$3[5x - 7y = -3] \qquad\qquad\qquad 15x - 21y = -9$$

$$\begin{array}{r} 14x + 21y = 49 \\ 15x - 21y = -9 \\ \hline 29x = 40 \end{array}$$

$$x = \frac{40}{29}$$

Thus, the solution is $\left(\frac{40}{29}, \frac{41}{29}\right)$.

Helpful Hint
....
We have illustrated three methods for solving a system of linear equations: graphing, substitution, and addition. When you are given a system of equations, which method should you use to solve the system? When you need an exact solution, graphing should not be used. Of the two algebraic methods, the addition method may be easier to use if there are no numerical coefficients of 1 in the system. If one or more of the variables has a coefficient of 1, you may wish to use either method.

Exercise Set 8.3

Solve each system of equations using the addition method.

1. $x + y = 8$
$x - y = 4$

2. $x - y = 6$
$x + y = 4$

3. $-x + y = 5$
$x + y = 1$

4. $x + y = 10$
$-x + y = -2$

5. $x + 2y = 15$
$x - 2y = -7$

6. $3x + y = 10$
$4x - y = 4$

7. $4x + y = 6$
$-8x - 2y = 20$

8. $5x + 3y = 30$
$3x + 3y = 18$

9. $-5x + y = 14$
$-3x + y = -2$

10. $2x - y = 7$
$3x + 2y = 0$

11. $3x + y = 10$
$3x - 2y = 16$

12. $-4x + 3y = 0$
$5x - 6y = 9$

13. $4x - 3y = 8$
$2x + y = 14$

14. $2x - 3y = 4$
$2x + y = -4$

15. $5x + 3y = 6$
$2x - 4y = 5$

16. $6x - 4y = 9$
$2x - 8y = 3$

17. $4x - 2y = 6$
$y = 2x - 3$

18. $5x - 2y = -4$
$-3x - 4y = -34$

19. $3x - 2y = -2$
$3y = 2x + 4$

20. $5x + 4y = 10$
$-3x - 5y = 7$

21. $3x - 4y = 6$
$-6x + 8y = -4$

22. $2x - 3y = 11$
$-3x = -5y - 17$

23. $3x - 5y = 0$
$2x + 3y = 0$

24. $5x - 2y = 8$
$4y = 10x - 16$

25. $5x - 4y = 20$
$-3x + 2y = -15$

26. $5x = 2y - 4$
$3x - 5y = 6$

27. $6x + 2y = 5$
$3y = 5x - 8$

28. $4x - 3y = -4$
$3x - 5y = 10$

29. $4x + 5y = 0$
$3x = 6y + 4$

30. $4x - 3y = 8$
$-3x + 4y = 9$

31. $x - \frac{1}{2}y = 4$
$3x + y = 6$

32. $2x - \frac{1}{3}y = 6$
$5x - y = 4$

 33. When solving a system of linear equations by the addition method, how will you know if the system is inconsistent?

34. When solving a system of linear equations by the addition method, how will you know if the system is dependent?

35. (a) In your own words explain the procedure to follow to solve a system of linear equations by the addition method.

(b) Solve the system that follows by the procedure given in part **(a)**.
$$3x - 2y = 10$$
$$2x + 5y = 13$$

CUMULATIVE REVIEW EXERCISES

[4.1] **36.** Simplify $\left(\dfrac{16x^4y^6z^3}{4x^6y^5z^7} \right)^3$.

[4.7] **37.** A highway crew is paving a new highway. On average, they pave 110 feet of highway each day. How long will it take the crew to pave 2420 feet?

[6.2] **38.** Simplify $\dfrac{2x^2 - x - 6}{x^2 - 7x + 10} \div \dfrac{2x^2 - 7x - 4}{x^2 - 9x + 20}$.

[6.4] **39.** Simplify $\dfrac{x}{x^2 - 1} - \dfrac{3}{x^2 - 16x + 15}$.

Group Activity/ Challenge Problems

Create a system of linear equations in two variables that has the listed solution. Explain how you obtained your system.

1. (2, 3)

2. (4, −2)

Solve each system of equations using the addition method. (Hint: First remove all fractions.)

3. $\dfrac{x+2}{2} - \dfrac{y+4}{3} = 4.$

$\dfrac{x+y}{2} = \dfrac{1}{2} + \dfrac{x-y}{3}$

4. $\dfrac{5x}{2} + 3y = \dfrac{9}{2} + y$

$\dfrac{1}{4}x - \dfrac{1}{2}y = 6x + 12$

5. (a) Solve the system of equations

$$4x + 2y = 1000$$
$$2x + 4y = 800$$

(b) If we divide all the terms in the top equation by 2 we get the following system.

$$2x + y = 500$$
$$2x + 4y = 800$$

How will the solution to this system compare to the solution in part **(a)**? Explain and then check your explanation by solving this system.

(c) If we divided all the terms in both equations given in part **(a)** by 2 we obtain the following system.

$$2x + y = 500$$
$$x + 2y = 400$$

How will the solution to this system compare to the solution in part **(a)**? Explain and then check your explanation by solving the system.

6. In intermediate algebra you may solve systems of three equations with three unknowns. Solve the following system.

$$x + 2y - z = 2$$
$$2x - y + z = 3$$
$$2x + y + z = 7$$

Hint: work with one pair of equations to get two equations in two unknowns. Then work with a different pair of equations to get two equations in the same two unknowns. Then solve the system of two equations in two unknowns.

8.4 Applications of Systems of Equations

1️⃣ Use systems of equations to solve application problems.

Applications

1️⃣ The method you use to solve a system of equations may depend on whether you wish to see "the entire picture" or are interested in finding the exact solution. If you are interested in the trend as the variable changes, you might decide to graph the equations. If you want only the solution, that is, the ordered pair common to both equations, you might use one of the two algebraic methods to find the common solution. Many of the application problems solved in earlier chapters using only one variable can also be solved using two variables.

EXAMPLE 1   Two angles are **complementary angles** when the sum of their measures is 90°. Angles x and y are complementary and angle x is 24° more than angle y. Find angles x and y.

Solution: Since the angles are complementary, the sum of their measures must be 90°. Thus one equation in the system is $x + y = 90$. Since angle x is 24° greater than angle y, the second equation is $x = y + 24$.

$$\text{system of equations} \qquad \begin{cases} x + y = 90 \\ x = y + 24 \end{cases}$$

Subtract y from each side of the second equation. Then use the addition method to solve.

$$
\begin{array}{r}
x + y = 90 \\
x - y = 24 \\
\hline
2x = 114 \\
x = 57
\end{array}
$$

Now substitute 57 for x in the first equation and solve for y.

$$
\begin{aligned}
x + y &= 90 \\
57 + y &= 90 \\
y &= 33
\end{aligned}
$$

Angle x is 57° and angle y is 33°. Note that their sum is 90° and angle x is 24° greater than angle y.

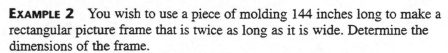

EXAMPLE 2   You wish to use a piece of molding 144 inches long to make a rectangular picture frame that is twice as long as it is wide. Determine the dimensions of the frame.

Solution: The formula for the perimeter of a rectangle is $P = 2l + 2w$.

Let w = width of the frame

l = length of the frame

Since the perimeter is to be 144 inches, one equation in the system is

$$144 = 2l + 2w$$

Since the length is to be twice the width, $l = 2w$.

$$\text{system of equations} \qquad \begin{cases} 144 = 2l + 2w \\ l = 2w \end{cases}$$

We will solve this system by substitution. Substitute $2w$ for l in the equation $144 = 2l + 2w$ to obtain

$$
\begin{aligned}
144 &= 2l + 2w \\
144 &= 2(2w) + 2w \\
144 &= 4w + 2w \\
144 &= 6w \\
24 &= w
\end{aligned}
$$

Therefore, the width is 24 inches. Since the length is twice the width, the length is 2(24) or 48 inches.

EXAMPLE 3   A plane can fly 600 miles per hour with the wind and 450 miles per hour against the wind. Find the speed of the wind and the speed of the plane in still air.

Solution: Let p = speed of the plane in still air

w = speed of the wind

If p equals the speed of the plane in still air and w equals the speed of the wind, then $p + w$ equals the speed of the plane flying with the wind, and $p - w$ equals the speed of the plane flying against the wind. We make use of this information when writing the system of equations.

Speed of plane flying with wind: $p + w = 600$ } system of
Speed of plane flying against wind: $p - w = 450$ } equations

We will use the addition method because the sum of the terms containing w is zero.

$$
\begin{array}{r}
p + w = 600 \\
\underline{p - w = 450} \\
2p = 1050 \\
p = 525
\end{array}
$$

The plane's speed is 525 miles per hour in still air. Now substitute 525 for p in the first equation and solve for w.

$$
\begin{array}{r}
p + w = 600 \\
525 + w = 600 \\
w = 75
\end{array}
$$

The wind's speed is 75 miles per hour.

EXAMPLE 4   Only two-axle vehicles are permitted to cross a bridge that leads to a state park on an island. The toll for the bridge is 50 cents for motorcycles and $1.00 for cars and trucks. On Saturday, the toll booth attendant collected a total of $150, and the vehicle counter recorded 170 vehicles crossing the bridge. How many motorcycles and how many cars and trucks crossed the bridge that day?

Solution: Let x = number of motorcycles

y = number of cars and trucks

Since a total of 170 vehicles crossed the bridge, one equation is $x + y = 170$. The second equation comes from the tolls collected.

Tolls from motorcycles + tolls from cars and trucks = 150
$0.50x$ + $1.00y$ = 150

system of equations $\begin{cases} x + y = 170 \\ 0.50x + 1.00y = 150 \end{cases}$

Since the first equation can be easily solved for y, we will solve this system by substitution. Solving for y in $x + y = 170$ gives $y = 170 - x$. Substitute $170 - x$ for y in the second equation and solve for x.

$$0.50x + 1.00y = 150$$
$$0.50x + 1.00(170 - x) = 150$$
$$0.50x + 170 - 1.00x = 150$$
$$170 - 0.5x = 150$$
$$-0.5x = -20$$
$$\frac{-0.5x}{-0.5} = \frac{-20}{-0.5}$$
$$x = 40$$

Forty motorcycles crossed the bridge. The total number of vehicles that crossed the bridge is 170. Therefore, $170 - 40$ or 130 cars and trucks crossed the bridge that Saturday.

EXAMPLE 5 Mrs. Beal needs to purchase a new engine for her car and have it installed by a mechanic. She is considering two garages: Sally's garage and Scotty's garage. At Sally's garage, the parts cost $800 and the labor cost is $25 per hour. At Scotty's garage, the parts cost $575 and labor cost is $50 per hour.

(a) How many hours would the repairs need to take for the total cost at each garage to be the same?

(b) If both garages estimate that the repair will take 8 hours, which garage would be the least expensive?

Solution: **(a)** Let $n =$ number of hours of labor
$c =$ total cost of repairs

Sally's	*Scotty's*
total cost = parts + labor	total cost = parts + labor
$c = 800 + 25n$	$c = 575 + 50n$

system of equations $\begin{cases} c = 800 + 25n \\ c = 575 + 50n \end{cases}$

total cost at Sally's = total cost at Scotty's
$$800 + 25n = 575 + 50n$$
$$225 + 25n = 50n$$
$$225 = 25n$$
$$9 = n$$

If 9 hours of labor is required, the cost from both garages would be equal.

(b) If repairs take 8 hours, Scotty's would be less expensive as shown below.

Sally's	*Scotty's*
$c = 800 + 25n$	$c = 575 + 50n$
$c = 800 + 25(8)$	$c = 575 + 50(8)$
$c = 1000$	$c = 975$

For 8 hours labor, the cost of repairs at Sally's is $1000 and the cost of repair at Scotty's is $975.

Simple Interest Problems

We introduced the simple interest formula, interest = principal × rate × time or $i = prt$ in Section 3.1. Now we will use this formula to solve a simple interest problem using a system of equations. In Example 6 and the examples that follow, we organize the information in a table.

EXAMPLE 6 Emil has invested a total of $12,000 in two savings accounts. One account earns 5% simple interest and the other earns 8% simple interest. Find the amount invested in each account if he receives a total of $840 interest after 1 year.

Solution: Let x = principal invested at 5%

y = principal invested at 8%

	Principal	Rate	Time	Interest
5% account	x	0.05	1	$0.05x$
8% account	y	0.08	1	$0.08y$

Since the total interest is $840, one of our equations is

$$0.05x + 0.08y = 840$$

Because the total principal invested is $12,000, our second equation is

$$x + y = 12,000$$

$$\left.\begin{array}{r} 0.05x + 0.08y = 840 \\ x + y = 12,000 \end{array}\right\} \text{ system of equations}$$

We will multiply our first equation by 100 to eliminate the decimal numbers. This gives the system

$$5x + 8y = 84,000$$
$$x + y = 12,000$$

To eliminate the x, we will multiply the second equation by -5 and then add the results to the first equation.

$$
\begin{array}{lll}
5x + 8y = 84,000 & \text{gives} & 5x + 8y = 84,000 \\
-5[x + y = 12,000] & & \underline{-5x - 5y = -60,000} \\
& & 3y = 24,000 \\
& & y = 8000
\end{array}
$$

Now solve for x.

$$x + y = 12,000$$
$$x + 8000 = 12,000$$
$$x = 4000$$

Thus, $4000 is invested at 5% and $8000 is invested at 8%.

Motion Problems with Two Rates

We introduced the distance formula, distance = rate · time or $d = rt$, in Section 4.7 and worked additional motion problems in Section 6.7. Now we introduce a method, using two variables and a system of equations, to solve motion problems that involve two rates. When working problems using this method, we use the information given to write two equations in two variables. Then we proceed to solve the system of equations using one of the three methods introduced in this chapter. Often when working motion problems with two different rates it is helpful to construct a table indicating the information given. We do this in Examples 7 and 8.

EXAMPLE 7 It takes Malcolm 3 hours in his motorboat to make a 48-mile trip downstream with the current. The return trip against the current takes him 4 hours. Find **(a)** the speed of the motorboat in still water, and **(b)** the speed of the current.

Solution: **(a)** Let us make a sketch of the situation (Fig. 8.7).

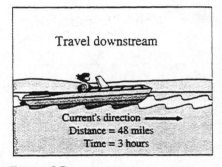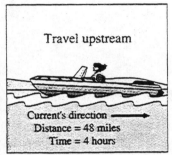

FIGURE 8.7

Let m = speed of the motorboat in still water

c = speed of the current

Boat's Direction	Rate	Time	Distance
With current	$m + c$	3	$3(m + c)$
Against current	$m - c$	4	$4(m - c)$

Since the distances traveled downstream and upstream are both 48 miles, our system of equations is

$$3(m + c) = 48$$
$$4(m - c) = 48$$

If we divide both sides of the top equation by 3 and both sides of the bottom equation by 4, we obtain a simplified system of equations.

$$\frac{3(m + c)}{3} = \frac{48}{3} \qquad\qquad \frac{4(m - c)}{4} = \frac{48}{4}$$
$$m + c = 16 \qquad\qquad\qquad m - c = 12$$

Now we solve the simplified system of equations.

$$
\begin{array}{r}
m + c = 16 \\
\underline{m - c = 12} \\
2m = 28 \\
m = 14
\end{array}
$$

Therefore, the speed of the boat in still water is 14 miles per hour.

(b) The speed of the current may be found by substituting 14 for m in either of the simplified equations. We will use $m + c = 16$.

$$m + c = 16$$
$$14 + c = 16$$
$$c = 2$$

Thus, the speed of the current is 2 miles per hour.

EXAMPLE 8 Dawn and Chris go hiking down the Grand Canyon. Chris begins hiking 0.5 hour before Dawn. Chris travels at 2 miles per hour and Dawn travels at 1.5 miles per hour. How long will it take, after Chris begins hiking, for Chris and Dawn to be 2 miles apart?

Solution: We need to find the time it takes for Chris and Dawn to become separated by 2 miles.

Let x = time Chris is hiking

   y = time Dawn is hiking

Hiker	Rate	Time	Distance
Chris	2	x	$2x$
Dawn	1.5	y	$1.5y$

Since Chris begins hiking 0.5 hour before Dawn, our first equation is

$$x = y + 0.5$$

Note that if we add 0.5 hour to Dawn's time we get the time Chris has been hiking.

Our second equation is obtained from the fact that the distance between the two hikers must be 2 miles. Since the hikers are traveling in the same direction, we must subtract their distances to obtain a difference of 2 miles. Since Chris is traveling at a faster speed and started first, we subtract Dawn's distance from Chris's distance.

$$\text{Chris's distance} - \text{Dawn's distance} = 2 \text{ miles}$$
$$2x - 1.5y = 2$$

The system of equations is

$$x = y + 0.5$$
$$2x - 1.5y = 2$$

The first equation is already solved for x. Substituting $y + 0.5$ for x in the second equation, we get

$$2(y + 0.5) - 1.5y = 2$$
$$2y + 1 - 1.5y = 2$$
$$0.5y + 1 = 2$$
$$0.5y = 1$$
$$y = \frac{1}{0.5} = 2$$

Thus, the time Dawn has been hiking is 2 hours. Since Chris has been hiking 0.5 hour longer than Dawn, Chris has been hiking for 2.5 hours when the distance between them is 2 miles.

Mixture Problems   Mixture problems were solved with one variable in Section 4.7. Now we will solve mixture problems using two variables and systems of equations. Recall that any problem in which two or more quantities are combined to produce a different quantity, or a single quantity is separated into two or more quantities, may be considered a mixture problem.

EXAMPLE 9   Deborah, who owns a coffee shop, wishes to mix Amaretto coffee that sells for $6 per pound with 12 pounds of Kona coffee that sells for $7.50 per pound.

(a) How many pounds of Amaretto coffee must be mixed with the 12 pounds of Kona coffee to obtain a mixture worth $6.50 per pound?

(b) How much of the mixture will be produced?

Solution:

(a) We are asked to find the number of pounds of Amaretto coffee.

Let x = number of pounds of Amaretto coffee

y = number of pounds of mixture

Often it is helpful to make a sketch of the situation. After we draw a sketch we will construct a table. In our sketch we will use barrels to mix the coffee in (Fig. 8.8).

FIGURE 8.8

The value of the coffee is found by multiplying the number of pounds by the price per pound.

Coffee	Price	Number of Pounds	Value of Coffee
Amaretto	6	x	$6x$
Kona	7.50	12	7.50(12)
Mixture	6.50	y	$6.50y$

Our two equations come from the following information:

$$\left(\begin{array}{c}\text{number of pounds}\\\text{of Amaretto coffee}\end{array}\right) + \left(\begin{array}{c}\text{number of pounds}\\\text{of Kona coffee}\end{array}\right) = \left(\begin{array}{c}\text{number of pounds}\\\text{in mixture}\end{array}\right)$$

$$x + 12 = y$$

value of Amaretto coffee + value of Kona coffee = value of mixture

$$6x + 7.50(12) = 6.50y$$

system of equations $\begin{cases} x + 12 = y \\ 6x + 7.50(12) = 6.50y \end{cases}$

Now substitute $x + 12$ for y in the bottom equation and solve for x.

$$6x + 7.50(12) = 6.50y$$
$$6x + 7.50(12) = 6.50(x + 12)$$
$$6x + 90 = 6.50x + 78$$
$$90 = 0.50x + 78$$
$$12 = 0.50x$$
$$24 = x$$

Thus, 24 pounds of Amaretto coffee must be mixed with 12 pounds of Kona coffee.

(b) The total mixture will be $24 + 12$ or 36 pounds.

EXAMPLE 10   A 50% sulfuric acid solution is to be mixed with a 75% sulfuric acid solution to get 60 liters of a 60% sulfuric acid solution. How many liters of the 50% solution and the 75% solution should be mixed?

Solution: Let x = number of liters of 50% solution

y = number of liters of 75% solution

The problem is displayed in Figure 8.9.

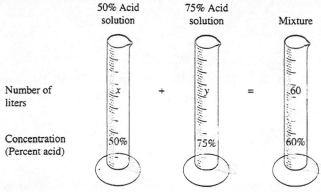

50% Acid solution   75% Acid solution   Mixture

Number of liters x + y =   60

Concentration (Percent acid)   50%   75%   60%

FIGURE 8.9

The acid content of a solution is found by multiplying the volume of the solution by the concentration of the solution.

	Number of Liters	**Concentration**	**Acid Content**
50% Solution	x	0.50	$0.50x$
75% Solution	y	0.75	$0.75y$
Mixture	60	0.60	$0.60(60)$

Because the total volume of the combination is 60 liters, we have

$$x + y = 60$$

From the table we see that

$$\begin{pmatrix} \text{acid content of} \\ \text{50\% solution} \end{pmatrix} + \begin{pmatrix} \text{acid content of} \\ \text{75\% solution} \end{pmatrix} = \begin{pmatrix} \text{acid content} \\ \text{of mixture} \end{pmatrix}$$

$$0.5x + 0.75y = 0.6(60)$$

system of equations $\begin{cases} x + y = 60 \\ 0.5x + 0.75y = 0.6(60) \end{cases}$

We will solve this system by substitution. Solve for y in the first equation.

$$x + y = 60$$
$$y = 60 - x$$

Substitute $60 - x$ for y in the second equation.

$$0.5x + 0.75y = 0.6(60)$$
$$0.5x + 0.75(60 - x) = 36$$
$$0.5x + 45 - 0.75x = 36$$
$$-0.25x + 45 = 36$$
$$-0.25x = -9$$
$$x = \frac{-9}{-0.25} = 36$$

Now solve for y.

$$y = 60 - x$$
$$y = 60 - 36$$
$$y = 24$$

Thus, 36 liters of a 50% acid solution should be mixed with 24 liters of a 75% acid solution to obtain 60 liters of a 60% acid solution.

Exercise Set 8.4

Express each exercise as a system of linear equations, and then find the solution. Use a calculator where appropriate.

1. The sum of two integers is 26. Find the numbers if one number is 2 greater than twice the other.

2. The difference of two integers is 25. Find the two numbers if the larger is 1 less than three times the smaller.

3. Angles A and B are complementary angles. If angle B is 18° greater than angle A, find the measure of each angle. (See Example 1.)

4. Two angles are **supplementary angles** when the sum of their measures is 180°. If angles A and B are supplementary angles, and angle A is four times as large as angle B, find the measure of each angle.

5. If angles A and B are supplementary angles and angle A is 52° greater than angle B, find the measure of each angle.

6. A rectangular picture frame will be made from a piece of molding 60 inches long. What dimensions will the frame have if the length is to be 6 inches greater than the width? (See Example 2.)

7. The perimeter of a rectangular plot of land is 800 feet. If the length is 100 feet greater than the width, find the dimensions of the piece of land.

8. Paul has 25 rare currency bills in his safe deposit box. If their face values total $101 and Paul has only $2 and $5 bills, find the number of each type of currency in his collection.

9. Robin collects 1-ounce gold dollar coins. Her collection consists of 14 coins, which are either gold United States Eagles or gold Canadian Maple Leafs. The total value of her collection is $6560. If the value of the Eagles is $480 each and the value of the Maple Leafs is $460 each, find the number of Eagles and Maple Leafs that Robin owns.

10. Max Cisneros plants corn and wheat on his 62-acre farm in Albuquerque. He estimates that his income before deducting expenses is $3000 per acre of corn and $2200 per acre of wheat. Find the number of acres of corn and wheat planted if his total income before expenses is $158,800.

11. Karla bought five times as many shares of BancOne stock as she did of Microsoft stock. The BancOne stock cost $37 a share and the Microsoft stock cost $75 a share. If her total cost for all the stock was $7,800, how many shares of each did she purchase?

12. A plane can fly 540 miles per hour with the wind and 490 miles per hour against the wind. Find the speed of the plane in still air and the speed of the wind. (See Example 3.)

13. Carlos can paddle a kayak 4.5 miles per hour with the current and 3.2 miles per hour against the current. Find the speed of the kayak in still water and the speed of the current.

14. The population of Alpine Mountain is 40,000 and it is growing by 800 per year. The population of Beautiful Valley is 66,000 and it is decreasing by 500 per year. How long will it take for both areas to have the same population?

15. Sol's Club Discount Warehouse has two membership plans. Under plan A the customer pays a $50 annual membership and 85% of the manufacturer's recommended list price. Under plan B the annual membership fee is $100 and the customer pays 80% of the manufacturer's recommended list price. How much merchandise, in dollars, would one have to purchase to pay the same amount under both plans?

16. Condita, a salesperson, is considering two job offers. She would be selling the same product at each company. At the AMEXI Company, Condita's salary would be $300 per week plus a 5% commission on sales. At the ROMAX company, her salary would be $200 per week plus an 8% commission of sales.

    (a) What weekly dollar volume of sales would Condita need to make for the total income from both companies to be the same?

    (b) If she expects to make sales of $4000, which company would give the greater salary?

17. Jerry is a Financial Planner for Gnocci & Co. His salary is a flat 40% commission of sales. As an employee he has no overhead. He is considering starting his own company. Then 100% of sales would be income to him. However, he estimates his monthly overhead for office rent, secretary, utilities, and so on, would be about $1500 per month.

    (a) How much in sales would Jerry's own company need to make in a month for him to make the same income he did as an employee of Gnocci & Co.?

    (b) Suppose when Jerry opens his own office that in addition to the $1500 per month overhead, he has a one-time cost of $6000 for the purchase of office equipment. If he estimates his monthly sales at $3000, how long would it take to recover the initial $6000 cost?

Review Example 6 before working Exercises 18–20.

18. Mr. and Mrs. McAdams invest a total of $8000 in two savings accounts. One account gives 10% simple interest and the other 8% simple interest. Find the amount placed in each account if they receive a total of $750 in interest after 1 year.

19. The Websters wish to invest a total of $12,500 in two savings accounts. One account pays 10% simple inter-

est and the other, $5\frac{1}{4}$% simple interest. The Websters wish their interest from the two accounts to be at least $1200 at the end of the year. Find the minimum amount that can be placed in the account giving 10% interest.

20. The Cohens invested a total of $10,000. Part of the money was placed in a savings account paying 5% simple interest. The rest was placed in a fixed annuity paying 6% simple interest. If the total interest received for the year was $540, how much had been invested in each account?

Review Examples 7 and 8 before working Exercises 21–26.

21. During a race, Teresa's speed boat travels 4 miles per hour faster than Jill's speed boat. If Teresa's boat finishes the race in 3 hours and Jill finishes the race in 3.2 hours, find the speed of each boat.

22. Bob started to drive from Columbus, Ohio, toward Chicago, Illinois, a distance of 903 miles. At the same time Bob started, Mickey starts driving to Columbus, Ohio, from Chicago, Illinois. If the two meet after 7 hours, and Mickey's speed averages 15 miles per hour greater than Bob's speed, find the speed of each car.

23. A United Airlines jet leaves New York's Kennedy Airport headed for Los Angeles International Airport, a distance of 2700 miles. At the same time, a Delta Airlines jet leaves the Los Angeles Airport headed for Kennedy Airport. Due to headwinds and tailwinds, the United jet's average speed is 100 miles per hour greater than that of the Delta jet. If the two jets pass one another after 3 hours, find the speed of each plane.

24. Two cars start at the same time 240 miles apart and travel toward each other. One car travels 6 miles per hour faster than the other. If they meet after 2 hours, what was the average speed of each car?

25. Micki and Petra go jogging along the same trail. Micki starts 0.3 hour before Petra. If Micki jogs at a rate of 5 miles per hour and Petra jogs at 8 miles per hour, how long after Petra starts would it take for Petra to catch up to Micki?

26. Simon trots his horse Chipmunk east at 8 miles per hour. One half-hour later, Michelle starts at the same point and canters her horse Buttermilk west at 16 miles per hour. How long will it take after Michelle starts riding for Michelle and Simon to be separated by 10 miles?

Review Examples 9 and 10 before working Exercises 27–32.

27. Marie, a chemist, has a 25% hydrochloric acid solution and a 50% hydrochloric acid solution. How many liters of each should she mix to get 10 liters of a hydrochloric acid solution with a 40% acid concentration?

28. Moura Williams, a druggist, needs 1000 milliliters of a 10% phenobarbital solution. She has only 5% and 25% phenobarbital solutions available. How many milliliters of each solution should she mix to obtain the desired solution?

29. Janet wishes to mix 30 pounds of coffee that will sell for $160. To obtain the mixture, she will mix coffee that sells for $5 per pound with coffee that sells for $7 per pound. How many pounds of each type coffee should she use?

30. Jason has milk that is 5% butterfat and skim milk without butterfat. How much 5% milk and how much skim milk should he mix to make 100 gallons of milk that is 3.5% butterfat?

31. The All Natural Juice Company sells apple juice for 12 cents an ounce and apple drink for 6 cents an ounce. They wish to market and sell for 10 cents an ounce cans of juice drink that are part juice and part drink. How many ounces of each will be used if the juice drink is to be sold in 8-ounce cans?

32. Pierre's recipe for Quiche Lorraine calls for 16 ounces (or 2 cups) of light cream, which is 20% milk fat. It is often difficult to find light cream with 20% milk fat at the supermarket. What is commonly found is heavy cream, which is 36% milk fat, and half and half, which is 10.5% milk fat. How many ounces of the heavy cream and how much of the half and half should be mixed to obtain 16 ounces of light cream that is 20% milkfat?

[1.9] 33. Evaluate $3(4x - 3)^2 - 2y^2 - 1$ when $x = 3$ and $y = -2$.

[4.2] 34. Simplify $(3x^4)^{-2}$.

[4.4] 35. Indicate whether or not each of the following is a polynomial. If it is not a polynomial explain why. Give the degree of each polynomial.

(a) $3x^3 + 2x - 6$ (b) $\frac{1}{2}x^4 - 3x^2 - 2$

(c) $x^3 - 2x^2 - x^{-1}$

[4.6] 36. Divide $(2x^2 + 5x - 10) \div (x + 4)$.

Group Activity/ Challenge Problems

1. Two pressurized tanks are connected by a controlled pressure valve as shown in the figure.

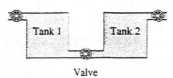

Valve

Initially, the internal pressure in tank 1 is 200 pounds per square inch, and the internal pressure in tank 2 is 20 pounds per square inch. The pressure valve is opened slightly to reduce the pressure in tank 1 by 2 pounds per square inch per minute. This increases the pressure in tank 2 by 2 pounds per square inch per minute. At this rate, how long will it take for the pressure to be equal in both tanks?

2. Mrs. O'Neil is considering cars for purchase. Car A has a list price of $10,500 and gets an average of 40 miles per gallon. Car B has a list price of $9500 and gets an average of 20 miles per gallon. Being a conservationist, Mrs. O'Neil wishes to purchase car A but is concerned about its greater initial cost. She plans to keep the car for many years. If she purchases car A, how many miles would she need to drive for the total cost of car A to equal the total cost of car B? Assume gasoline costs of $1.25 per gallon.

3. Two brothers jog to school daily. The older jogs at 9 miles per hour, the younger, at 5 miles per hour. When the older brother reaches the school, the younger brother is $\frac{1}{2}$ mile away. How far is the school from the boys' house?

4. By weight, an alloy of brass is 70% copper and 30% zinc. Another alloy of brass is 40% copper and 60% zinc. How many grams of each of these alloys must be melted and combined to obtain 300 grams of a brass alloy that is 60% copper and 40% zinc?

8.5   Systems of Linear Inequalities

Tape 14

1 Solve systems of linear inequalities graphically.

Solve Graphically

1 In Section 7.7, we learned how to graph linear inequalities in two variables. In Section 8.1, we learned how to solve systems of equations graphically. In this section, we discuss how to solve systems of linear inequalities graphically. The **solution to a system of linear inequalities** is the set of points that satisfies all inequalities in the system. Although a system of linear inequalities may contain more than two inequalities, in this book, except in the Group Activity Exercises, we will consider systems with only two inequalities.

> **To Solve a System of Linear Inequalities**
> Graph each inequality on the same axes. The solution is the set of points that satisfies all the inequalities in the system.

EXAMPLE 1 Determine the solution to the system of inequalities.

$$x + 2y \leq 6$$
$$y > 2x - 4$$

Solution: First graph the inequality $x + 2y \leq 6$ (Fig. 8.10).

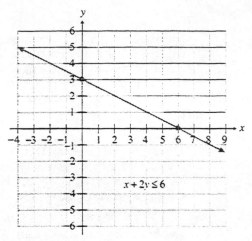

FIGURE 8.10

Now, on the same axes, graph the inequality $y > 2x - 4$ (Fig. 8.11). Note that the line is dashed. Why?

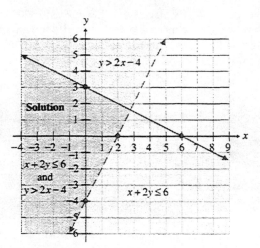

FIGURE 8.11

The solution is the set of points common to both inequalities. It is the part of the graph that contains both shadings. The dashed line is not part of the solution. However, the part of the solid line that satisfies both inequalities is part of the solution.

EXAMPLE 2 Determine the solution to the system of inequalities.

$$2x + 3y \geq 4$$
$$2x - y > -6$$

Solution: Graph $2x + 3y \geq 4$ (Fig. 8.12). Graph $2x - y > -6$ on the same axes (Fig. 8.13). The solution is the part of the graph with both shadings and the part of the solid line that satisfies both inequalities.

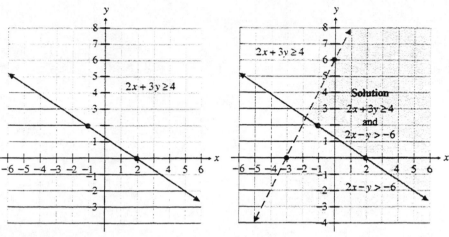

FIGURE 8.12   **FIGURE 8.13**

EXAMPLE 3   Determine the solution to the system of inequalities.

$$y < 2$$
$$x > -3$$

Solution: Graph both inequalities on the same axes (Fig. 8.14).

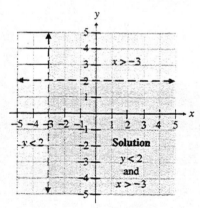

FIGURE 8.14

Exercise Set 8.5

Determine the solution to each system of inequalities.

1. $x + y > 2$
    $x - y < 2$

2. $y \leq 3x - 2$
    $y > -4x$

3. $y \leq x$
    $y < -2x + 4$

4. $2x + 3y < 6$
$4x - 2y \geq 8$

5. $y > x + 1$
$y \geq 3x + 2$

6. $x + 3y \geq 6$
$2x - y > 4$

7. $x - 2y < 6$
$y \leq -x + 4$

8. $y \leq 3x + 4$
$y < 2$

9. $4x + 5y < 20$
$x \geq -3$

10. $3x - 4y \leq 12$
$y > -x + 4$

11. $x \leq 4$
$y \geq -2$

12. $x \geq 0$
$y \leq 0$

13. $x > -3$
$y > 1$

14. $4x + 2y > 8$
$y \leq 2$

15. $-2x + 3y \geq 6$
$x + 4y \geq 4$

16. Can a system of linear inequalities have no solution? Explain your answer with the use of your own example.

17. Is it possible to construct a system of two nonparallel linear inequalities that has no solution? Explain.

CUMULATIVE REVIEW EXERCISES

[4.5] **18.** Multiply $(x^2 - 2x + 7)(3x - 4)$.

[5.2] **19.** Factor $xy + x - 3y - 3$.

[5.3] **20.** Factor $x^2 - 13x + 42$.

[5.4] **21.** Factor $6x^2 - x - 2$.

Group Activity/ Challenge Problems

Determine the solution to the following system of inequalities.

1. $x + 2y \leq 6$
$2x - y < 2$
$y > 2$

2. $x \geq 0$
$y \geq 0$
$y \leq 2x + 4$
$y \leq -x + 6$

3. $x \geq 0$
$y \geq 0$
$5x + y \leq 40$
$10x + y \leq 60$
$x \leq 4$

Summary

GLOSSARY

Consistent system of linear equations (442): A system of linear equations that has a solution.

Dependent system of linear equations (442): A system of linear equations that has an infinite number of solutions.

Inconsistent system of linear equations (442): A system of linear equations that has no solution.

Simultaneous linear equations or a system of linear equations (440): Two or more linear equations considered together.

Solution to a system of equations (441): The ordered pair or pairs that satisfy all equations in the system.

Solution to a system of inequalities (477): The set of ordered pairs that satisfies all inequalities in the system.

IMPORTANT FACTS

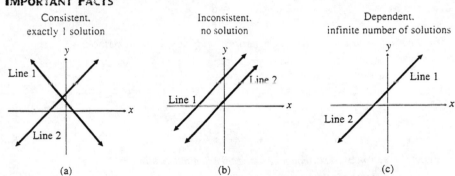

Consistent.
exactly 1 solution

Inconsistent.
no solution

Dependent.
infinite number of solutions

(a)   (b)   (c)

Three methods that can be used to solve a system of linear equations are the (1) graphical method, (2) substitution method, and (3) addition (or elimination) method.

Review Exercises

8.1] *Determine which, if any, of the ordered pairs satisfy each system of equations.*

1. $y = 3x - 2$
$2x + 3y = 5$
(a) $(0, -2)$ (b) $(2, 4)$ (c) $(1, 1)$

2. $y = -x + 4$
$3x + 5y = 15$
(a) $\left(\dfrac{5}{2}, \dfrac{3}{2}\right)$ (b) $(0, 4)$ (c) $\left(\dfrac{1}{2}, \dfrac{3}{5}\right)$

Identify each system of linear equations as consistent, inconsistent, or dependent. State whether the system has exactly one solution, no solution, or an infinite number of solutions.

3.
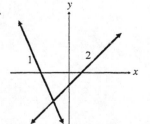

4.
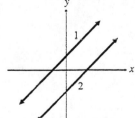

5.
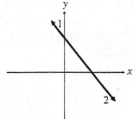

6.
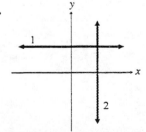

Write each equation in slope–intercept form. Without graphing or solving the system of equations, state whether the system of linear equations has exactly one solution, no solution, or an infinite number of solutions.

7. $x + 2y = 8$
$3x + 6y = 12$

8. $y = -3x - 6$
$2x + 3y = 8$

9. $y = \dfrac{1}{2}x - 4$
$x - 2y = 8$

10. $6x = 4y - 8$
$4x = 6y + 8$

Determine the solution to each system of equations graphically.

11. $y = x + 3$
$y = 2x + 5$

12. $x = -2$
$y = 3$

13. $y = 3$
$y = -2x + 5$

14. $x + 3y = 6$
$y = 2$

15. $x + 2y = 8$
$2x - y = -4$

16. $y = x - 3$
$2x - 2y = 6$

17. $2x + y = 0$
$4x - 3y = 10$

18. $x + 2y = 4$
$\dfrac{1}{2}x + y = -2$

[8.2] *Find the solution to each system of equations using substitution.*

19. $y = 2x - 8$
$2x - 5y = 0$

20. $x = 3y - 9$
$x + 2y = 1$

21. $2x + y = 5$
$3x + 2y = 8$

22. $2x - y = 6$
$x + 2y = 13$

23. $3x + y = 17$
$2x - 3y = 4$

24. $x = -3y$
$x + 4y = 6$

25. $4x - 2y = 10$
$y = 2x + 3$

26. $2x + 4y = 8$
$4x + 8y = 16$

27. $2x - 3y = 8$
$6x + 5y = 10$

28. $4x - y = 6$
$x + 2y = 8$

[8.3] *Find the solution to each system of equations using the addition method.*

29. $x + y = 6$
$x - y = 10$

30. $x + 2y = -3$
$2x - 2y = 6$

31. $2x + 3y = 4$
$x + 2y = -6$

32. $x + y = 12$
$2x + y = 5$

33. $4x - 3y = 8$
$2x + 5y = 8$

34. $-2x + 3y = 15$
$3x + 3y = 10$

35. $2x + y = 9$
$-4x - 2y = 4$

36. $2x + 2y = 8$
$y = 4x - 3$

37. $3x + 4y = 10$
$-6x - 8y = -20$

38. $2x - 5y = 12$
$3x - 4y = -6$

[8.4] *Express as a system of linear equations, and then find the solution.*

39. The sum of two integers is 48. Find the two numbers if the larger is 3 less than twice the smaller.

40. A plane flies 600 miles per hour with the wind and 530 miles per hour against the wind. Find the speed of the wind and the speed of the plane in still air.

41. ABC Truck Rental charges $20 per day plus 50 cents per mile, while Murtz Truck Rental charges $35 per day plus 40 cents per mile. How far would you have to travel in one day for the total cost of both rental companies to be the same?

42. The Hackets invested a total of $16,000. Part of the money was placed in a savings account paying 4% simple interest. The rest was placed in a savings account paying 6% simple interest. If the total interest received for the year was $760, how much had they invested in each account?

43. Ron drives from Charleston, South Carolina to Louisville, Kentucky, a distance of 600 miles. At the same time, Audra starts driving from Louisville to Charleston along the same route. If the two meet after driving 5 hours and Audra's average speed was 6 miles per hour greater than Ron's, find the average speed of each car.

44. Green Turf's grass seed costs 60 cents a pound and Agway's grass seed costs 45 cents a pound. How many pounds of each were used to make a 40-pound mixture that cost $20.25?

45. A chemist has a 30% acid solution and a 50% acid solution. How much of each must be mixed to get 6 liters of a 40% acid solution?

[8.5] *Determine the solution to each system of inequalities.*

46. $x + y > 2$
$2x - y \le 4$

47. $2x - 3y \le 6$
$x + 4y > 4$

48. $2x - 6y > 6$
$x > -2$

49. $x < 2$
$y \ge -3$

Practice Test

1. Determine which, if any, of the ordered pairs satisfy the system of equations.

   (a) $(0, -6)$ **(b)** $\left(-3, -\dfrac{3}{2}\right)$ **(c)** $(2, -4)$

$$x + 2y = -6$$
$$3x + 2y = -12$$

Identify each system as consistent, inconsistent, or dependent. State whether the system has exactly one solution, no solution, or an infinite number of solutions.

2.
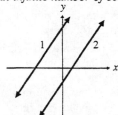

3.
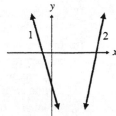

4.
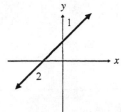

Write each equation in slope–intercept form. Then determine, without solving the system, whether the system of equations has exactly one solution, no solution, or an infinite number of solutions.

5. $3y = 6x - 9$
   $2x - y = 6$

6. $3x + 2y = 10$
   $3x - 2y = 10$

Solve each system of equations graphically.

7. $y = 3x - 2$
   $y = -2x + 8$

8. $3x - 2y = -3$
   $3x + y = 6$

Solve each system of equations using substitution.

9. $3x + y = 8$
   $x - y = 6$

10. $4x - 3y = 9$
    $2x + 4y = 10$

Solve each system of equations using the addition method.

11. $2x + y = 5$
    $x + 3y = -10$

12. $3x + 2y = 12$
    $-2x + 5y = 8$

Express the problem as a system of linear equations, and then find the solution.

13. Budget Rent a Car Agency charges $40 per day plus 8 cents per mile to rent a certain model car. Hertz charges $45 per day plus 3 cents per mile to rent the same car. How many miles will have to be driven in one day for the cost of Budget's car to equal the cost of Hertz's car?

14. Albert's Grocery sells cashews for $6.00 a pound and peanuts for $4.50 a pound. How much of each must Albert mix to get 20 pounds of a mixture that he can sell for $5.00 per pound?

15. Determine the solution to the system of inequalities.

$$2x + 4y < 8$$
$$x - 3y \geq 6$$

Cumulative Review Test

1. Evaluate $\dfrac{|-4| + |-16| \div 2^2}{3 - [2 - (4 \div 2)]}$.

2. Solve the equation $4(x - 2) + 6(x - 3) = 2 - 4x$.

3. Solve the equation $3x^2 - 13x + 12 = 0$.

4. Solve the equation $\dfrac{1}{3}(x + 2) + \dfrac{1}{4} = 8$.

5. Solve the equation $\dfrac{1}{x - 3} + \dfrac{1}{x + 3} = \dfrac{1}{x^2 - 9}$.

6. Find the length of side x if the two figures are similar.

7. Simplify $(x^5 y^3)^4 (2x^3 y^5)$.

8. Factor $6x^2 - 11x + 4$.

9. Subtract $\dfrac{4}{x^2 - 9} - \dfrac{3}{x^2 - 9x + 18}$.

10. Divide $\dfrac{x^2 - 7x + 12}{2x^2 - 11x + 12} \div \dfrac{x^2 - 9}{x^2 - 16}$.

11. Graph the equation $2x - 3y = 6$ by plotting points.

12. Graph the equation $3x + 2y = 9$ using the x and y intercepts.

13. Graph the inequality $2x - y < 6$.

14. Without graphing the equation, determine if the following system of equations has exactly one solution, no solutions, or an infinite number of solutions. Explain.

$$3x = 2y + 8$$
$$-4y = -6x + 12$$

15. Solve the system of equations graphically.

$$x + 2y = 2$$
$$2x - 3y = -3$$

16. Solve the system of equations using the addition method.

$$2x + 3y = 4$$
$$x - 4y = 6$$

17. A factory worker can inspect 40 units in 15 minutes. How long will it take her to inspect 160 units?

18. (a) An author is trying to decide between two publishing contract offers. The PCR Publishing Company offers an initial grant of $20,000 plus a 10% royalty rate on sales. The ARA Publishing Company offers an initial grant of $10,000 plus a 12% royalty rate on sales. How many dollars of sales are needed for the author's total income to be the same from both companies?

(b) If the author expects total dollar sales of $200,000, which company would result in the higher income?

19. How many liters of a 20% hydrochloric acid solution and how many liters of a 35% hydrochloric acid solution should be mixed to get 10 liters of a 25% hydrochloric acid solution?

20. Mr. and Mrs. Pontilo own a pizza shop. Mr. Pontilo can clean the pizza shop by himself in 50 minutes. Mrs. Pontilo can clean the pizza shop by herself in 60 minutes. How long will it take them to clean the pizza shop if they work together?

Mathematics of Finance

C H A P T E R 15

SIMPLE INTEREST

OBJECTIVES

Upon completing Chapter 15, you will be able to:

1. Define and use correctly the terminology associated with each topic.

2.
   a. Use the simple interest formula $I = Prt$ to find any variable, when the other items are given (Section 1: Examples 1, 3, 4; Problems 1, 2, 5–10, 13, 14).

   b. Use the amount formula $M = P + I$ to find the amount or interest (Examples 1, 2, 4; Problems 1–4, 7–10).

   c. Use the amount formula $M = P(1 + rt)$ to find the amount or principal (Examples 2, 5; Problems 3, 4, 11, 12).

3.
   a. Compute ordinary or exact interest using exact time (Section 2: Examples 1–4; Problems 1–6; Section 3: Examples 1–3; Problems 1–8, 13–16).

   b. Predict how a given change in rate or time will affect the amount of interest (Section 3: Problems 9–12).

4. Given information about a simple interest note, use any of the above formulas to compute the unknown (Section 4: Examples 1–3; Problems 1–20):

   a. Interest

   b. Maturity value

   c. Rate

   d. Time

   e. Principal.

5. Compute the present value of a simple interest note, either

   a. On the original day (Section 5: Examples 1, 2; Problems 1–4, 7–14), or

   b. On some other given day prior to maturity (Example 3; Problems 5, 6, 15–20).

The borrowing and lending of money is a practice that dates far back into history. Never, however, has the practice of finance been more widespread than it is today. Money may be loaned at a simple interest or a simple discount rate. The loan may be repaid in a single payment or a series of payments, depending upon the type of loan. When money is invested with a financial institution, compound interest is usually earned on the deposits. The following chapters explain the basic types of loans, important methods of loan repayments, and fundamental investment procedures. Before you proceed, a review of operations with parentheses found in Chapter 1 (p. 5) would be helpful.

SECTION 1
BASIC SIMPLE INTEREST

Persons who rent buildings or equipment expect to pay for the use of someone else's property. Similarly, those who borrow money must pay rent for the use of that money. Rent paid for the privilege of borrowing another's money is called **interest.** The amount of money that was borrowed is the **principal** of a loan.

A certain percentage of the principal is charged as interest. The percent or **rate** is quoted on a yearly (per annum) basis, unless otherwise specified. The **time** is the number of days, months, or years for which the money will be loaned. In order to make rate and time correspond, time is always converted to years, since rate is always given on a yearly basis.

When **simple interest** is being charged, interest is calculated on the whole principal for the entire length of the loan. Simple interest is found using the formula

$$I = Prt$$

where I = interest, P = principal, r = rate, and t = time. The **amount** due on the ending date of the loan (also called **maturity value**) is the sum of the principal plus the interest. This is expressed by the formula

$$M = P + I$$

where M = amount (or maturity value or sum), P = principal, and I = interest.

Example 1   A loan of $900 is made at 16% for 5 months. Determine (a) the interest and (b) the maturity value of this loan.

(a) $P = \$900$

$r = 16\%$ or 0.16 or $\dfrac{16}{100}$

$t = 5 \text{ months}^* = \dfrac{5}{12} \text{ year}$

$I = Prt$

$= \$\overset{3}{\cancel{900}} \times \dfrac{\overset{4}{\cancel{16}}}{\cancel{100}} \times \dfrac{5}{\underset{3}{\cancel{12}}}$

$I = \$60$

*Keep in mind that, for periods less than 1 year, time must be expressed as a fraction of a year.

(b) $M = P + I$

$= \$900 + \$60$

$M = \$960$

The two formulas in Example 1 can be combined, allowing the maturity value to be found in one step. Since $I = Prt$, by substitution in the formula

$$M = P + I$$
$$\downarrow$$
$$= P + Prt$$

$$M = P(1 + rt)$$

If the formula $M = P(1 + rt)$ is used to calculate the amount, the interest may be found by taking the difference between maturity value and principal.

Example 2   Rework Example 1, using the maturity value formula $M = P(1 + rt)$. As before, $P = \$900$, $r = \frac{16}{100}$, and $t = \frac{5}{12}$ year.

(a) $M = P(1 + rt)$

$$= \$900\left(1 + \frac{\overset{4}{\cancel{16}}}{100} \times \frac{5}{\underset{3}{\cancel{12}}}\right)$$

$$= 900\left(1 + \frac{20}{300}\right)$$

$$= 900\left(\frac{300}{300} + \frac{20}{300}\right)$$

$$= \overset{3}{\cancel{900}}\left(\frac{320}{\cancel{300}}\right)$$

$$M = \$960$$

(b) $P + I = M$

$I = M - P$

$= \$960 - \$900$

$I = \$60$

Calculator techniques . . . FOR EXAMPLE 2

When a formula contains parentheses, compute that value and place it into memory; then multiply by the number preceding the parentheses.

Note. To store the value in parentheses, you can perform the "1 M+ " step either before or after you M+ the "$r \times t$" calculation.

0.16 ✕ 5 ÷ 12 M+ ⟶ 0.0666666;   1 M+ ⟶ 1

MR ⟶ 1.0666666 ✕ 900 = ⟶ 959.99994

Rounded to the nearest cent, this equals $960. This technique will apply for many problems in this chapter and the next one.

Note. The "$r \times t$" can be computed as: 5 ✕ 16 % ⟶ 0.8 ÷ 12 M+ , if you prefer to use the % key rather than converting the 16% interest rate to its decimal equivalent.

Example 3   At what rate will $480 earn $28 in interest after 10 months?

$$P = \$480 \qquad\qquad I = Prt$$

$$r = ?$$

$$\$28 = \$480r \times \frac{5}{6}$$

$$t = \frac{10}{12} \ \text{ or } \ \frac{5}{6} \text{year}$$

$$28 = \overset{80}{\cancel{480}} \left(\frac{5}{\cancel{6}} \right) r$$

$$I = \$28$$

$$28 = 400r$$

$$r = \frac{28}{400} \ \text{ or } \ \frac{7}{100} \ \text{ or } \ 0.07$$

$$r = 7\%$$

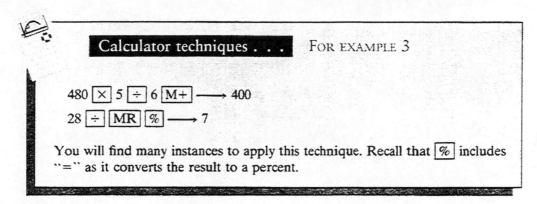

Calculator techniques . . .   FOR EXAMPLE 3

480 $\boxed{\times}$ 5 $\boxed{\div}$ 6 $\boxed{\text{M+}}$ —→ 400

28 $\boxed{\div}$ $\boxed{\text{MR}}$ $\boxed{\%}$ —→ 7

You will find many instances to apply this technique. Recall that $\boxed{\%}$ includes "=" as it converts the result to a percent.

Example 4   How long will it take at an 8% simple interest rate for $950 to amount to $988?

This problem may be worked using the maturity value formula $M = P(1 + rt)$. However, the simple interest formula $I = Prt$ is easier to work with and should be used whenever possible. Notice that the formula $I = Prt$ may be used to find a missing variable whenever the interest is given or can be found quickly.

In this case, the interest may be computed easily, since

$$I = M - P \qquad\qquad I = Prt$$

$$= \$988 - \$950$$

$$\$38 = \$950\left(\frac{8}{100}\right)t$$

$$I = \$38$$

$$38 = 76t$$

$$P = \$950 \qquad\qquad \frac{38}{76} = t$$

$$r = 8\% \quad \text{or} \quad \frac{8}{100}$$

$$t = \frac{38}{76} \quad \text{or} \quad \frac{1}{2}$$

$$t = ?$$

$$t = \frac{1}{2}\text{year} \quad \text{or} \quad 6\,\text{months}$$

Example 5   What principal would have a maturity value of $636 in 8 months if the interest rate is 9%?

In this problem the interest is not given and is impossible to determine because the maturity value and principal are not both known. Thus, the amount formula $M = P(1 + rt)$ must be used to find the principal.

$$P = \$?$$

$$M = P(1 + rt)$$

$$r = 9\% \quad \text{or} \quad \frac{9}{100}$$

$$\$636 = P\left(1 + \frac{\overset{3}{\cancel{9}}}{100} \times \frac{2}{\cancel{3}}\right)$$

$$t = \frac{8}{12} \quad \text{or} \quad \frac{2}{3}\text{year}$$

$$= P\left(1 + \frac{6}{100}\right)$$

$$M = \$636$$

$$= P\left(\frac{100}{100} + \frac{6}{100}\right)$$

$$= P\left(\frac{106}{100}\right)$$

$$\frac{100}{\cancel{106}} \times \overset{6}{\cancel{636}} = P\left(\frac{\cancel{106}}{100}\right)\left(\frac{100}{\cancel{106}}\right)$$

$$\$600 = P$$

Section 1   Problems

Find the interest and amount.

1. a. $500 at 9% for 1 year   b. $500 at 9% for 6 months   c. $780 at 12% for 10 months
   d. $900 at 10.5% for 8 months   e. $840 at 14% for 5 months

2. a. $600 at 10% for 1 year   b. $600 at 10% for 6 months   c. $1,200 at 8% for 4 months
   d. $900 at 8.5% for 3 months   e. $2,400 at 9% for 9 months

3. Find the interest and amount for parts a, c, and e in Problem 1 using the maturity value formula $M = P(1 + rt)$.

4. Utilize the amount formula $M = P(1 + rt)$ to find the interest and amount for parts a, c, and e in Problem 2.

5. What was the interest rate on a note with a principal of $800 for 3 months if the interest was $18?

6. What was the interest rate if the interest due on a 9-month loan of $3,000 was $180?

7. How many months would it take $1,440 to amount to $1,537.20 if an interest rate of 9% was charged?

8. How many months would it take for a loan of $1,500 at 7% interest to acquire a maturity value of $1,587.50?

9. What interest rate was charged on a note with a principal of $4,000 and a time of 3 months if the maturity value was $4,160?

10. If $6,000 is worth $6,300 after 6 months, what interest rate was charged?

11. What principal will have a maturity value of $8,400 after 24 months at 10%?

12. What principal will amount to $9,680 after 18 months at 14%?

13. At what simple interest rate will an investment double itself in 10 years? (Hint: Choose any principal; what is the interest in 10 years?)
14. How long will it take for an investment to double at 16% simple interest? (Hint: Choose any principal; what will be the interest when the investment matures?)

SECTION 2
ORDINARY TIME AND EXACT TIME

The problems given in Section 1 were limited to those with time periods of even months or years. This is not always the case, as many loans are made for a certain number of days. Suppose that a loan is made on July 5 for 60 days; do we consider 60 days to be 2 months and consider the loan due on September 5, or do we take the 60 days literally and consider the amount due on September 3? Suppose this loan made on July 5 is for a time of 2 months; would we consider the time to be $\frac{2}{12} = \frac{1}{6}$ year or should we use the actual 62 days between July 5 and September 5? The answers to these questions depend upon whether ordinary time or exact time is being used.

When **ordinary time** is being used, each month is assumed to have 30 days. Thus, any 5-month period would be considered as $5 \times 30 = 150$ days. Similarly, 90 days would be considered as 3 months. In actual practice, however, ordinary time is seldom used, as we shall see later.

If **exact time** is being used, the specific number of days within the time period is calculated. Thus, 90 days would usually be slightly less than 3 months. Exact time may be calculated most conveniently using Table C-14, The Number of Each Day of the Year, in Appendix C. In this table, each day of the year is listed in consecutive order and assigned a number from 1 to 365. The following examples demonstrate use of the table.

Example 1   Using exact time, find (a) the due date of a loan made on April 15 for 180 days and (b) the exact time from March 10 to July 23.

(a)   From the table of each day of the year, we see that April 15 is the 105th day. Thus,

$$
\begin{array}{rl}
\text{April 15} = & 105 \text{ day} \\
+ & \underline{180 \text{ days}} \\
& 285\text{th day} \quad \text{is October 12, the due date} \\
& \phantom{285\text{th day}} \quad \text{of the note using exact time}
\end{array}
$$

(b)   From March 10 to July 23:

$$
\begin{array}{rl}
\text{July 23} = & 204 \text{ day} \\
\text{March 10} = - & \underline{69 \text{ day}} \\
& 135 \text{ days} \quad \text{between March 10 and July 23,} \\
& \phantom{135 \text{ days}} \quad \text{using exact time}
\end{array}
$$

Example 2   A loan is taken out on June 1 for 5 months. Determine (a) the due date and (b) the number of days in the term of the loan, using both ordinary and exact time.

(a)   Five months after June 1 is November 1. The loan (principal plus interest) will be due on November 1 regardless of which kind of time is used.*

(b)   From June 1 to November 1:

Ordinary Time	*Exact Time*
5 months = 5 × 30	November 1 = 305 day
= 150 days	June 1 = −152 day
	153 days

Sometimes the time period of a loan includes a leap year. This does not affect the calculation of ordinary time, of course, since all months are considered to have 30 days. The leap year must be given consideration, however, when exact time is being used. During a leap year, February 29 becomes the 60th day of the year; thus, from March 1 on, the number of each day is one greater than is shown in Table C-14. For example, during a leap year, March 15 is the 75th day, instead of the 74th day as the table shows. This change in the number of the day must be made before the exact time is calculated.

A simple test allows you to determine whether any given year is a leap year: Leap year always falls on a year evenly divisible by 4. That is, 1996 is divisible by 4, so 1996 is a leap year. The year 1998 is not divisible by 4; thus, 1998 is not a leap year. Presidential elections also fall on leap years.

Example 3   Find the exact time from January 16, 1996 to May 7, 1996.

Since 1996 is a leap year, May 7 is the 128th day.

May 7 = 128 day	
January 16 = − 16 day	
112 days	from January 16, 1996
	to May 7, 1996

Example 4   Find the exact time between November 16 of one year and April 3 of the next (assuming no leap year is involved).

---

*Note.   If the given number of months would end on a day that does not exist, the due date is the last day of the month. For example, a loan on March 31 for 8 months would be due on November 30, since there is no November 31.

We must find the remaining days in the present year and then add the days in the following year:

Present year =   365 days
November 16 = −320 day
45 days remaining in present year
April 3 = + 93 day
138 days from November 16 to April 3

SECTION 2   PROBLEMS

If no year is given in the following problems, assume that it is not a leap year.

Find the exact time from the first date to the second date.

1. a. October 8 to December 5
   b. April 11 to November 11
   c. May 15 to December 23
   d. January 8 to September 8
   e. February 16, 1996, to June 16, 1996
   f. November 23, 1997, to April 15, 1998
   g. August 16, 1998, to January 16, 1999
   h. October 7, 1995, to March 7, 1996
2. a. March 6 to May 31
   b. June 5 to September 15
   c. July 10 to December 10
   d. January 14 to November 28
   e. February 12, 1996, to May 31, 1996
   f. September 23, 1997, to April 1, 1998
   g. July 4, 1998, to March 4, 1999
   h. November 15, 1999, to June 6, 2000

Determine the due date, using exact time.

3. a. 60 days after July 12
   b. 90 days after September 5
   c. 180 days after May 20
   d. 240 days after April 30
   e. 270 days after January 15
   f. 120 days after October 31
4. a. 30 days after August 21
   b. 60 days after October 14
   c. 120 days after June 18
   d. 200 days after March 1
   e. 150 days after July 17
   f. 180 days after November 23

Find the due date and the exact time (in days) for loans made on the given dates.

5. a. October 2 for 2 months
   b. July 7 for 4 months
   c. January 12, 1996, for 8 months
   d. June 18, 1997, for 4 months
   e. February 3, 1996, for 3 months
6. a. February 18 for 6 months
   b. May 24 for 3 months
   c. January 26, 2000, for 9 months
   d. March 30, 1998, for 4 months
   e. January 13, 1996, for 5 months

SECTION 3
ORDINARY INTEREST AND EXACT INTEREST

It has been seen that the time of a loan is frequently a certain number of days. As stated previously, a time of less than one year must be expressed as a fraction of a year. The question then arises: When converting days to fractional years, are the days placed over a denominator of 360 or 365? It is this question with which ordinary and exact interest are concerned.

The term "interest" here refers to the number of days representing one year. Just as ordinary time indicated 30 days per month, **ordinary interest** indicates interest calculated using 360 days per year. Similarly, the term **exact interest** indicates interest calculated using 365 days per year. (A 366-day year is not often used in business even for leap years.)

We have now discussed two ways of determining time (days in the loan period) and two types of interest (days per year). There are four possible combinations of these to obtain t for the interest formula:

I. Exact time over ordinary interest: $t = \dfrac{\text{Exact days}}{360}$

II. Exact time over exact interest: $t = \dfrac{\text{Exact days}}{365}$

III. Ordinary time over ordinary interest: $t = \dfrac{\text{Approximate days}}{360}$

IV. Ordinary time over exact interest: $t = \dfrac{\text{Approximate days}}{365}$

Type 1. The combination of exact time and ordinary interest is known as the **Banker's Rule**, a name derived from the fact that banks (as well as other financial institutions) generally compute their interest in this way:

$$\frac{\text{Exact days}}{360}$$

Example 1 A $730 loan is made on March 1 at 12% for 9 months. Compute the interest by the Bankers' Rule (that is, using exact time and ordinary interest).

Nine months after March 1 is December 1. The exact time is

$$
\begin{aligned}
\text{December 1} &= 335 \text{ day} \\
\text{March 1} &= \underline{60 \text{ day}} \\
& 275 \text{ days}
\end{aligned}
$$

$$P = \$730 \qquad\qquad I = Prt$$

$$r = \frac{12}{100} \qquad\qquad = \$730 \times \frac{\overset{1}{\cancel{12}}}{\cancel{100}} \times \frac{55}{\underset{6}{\cancel{72}}}$$

$$t = \frac{275}{360} \quad \text{or} \quad \frac{55}{72} \qquad\qquad I = \$66.92 \quad \text{(exact time/ordinary interest)}$$

$$I = \,?$$

Calculator techniques . . .   FOR EXAMPLE 1

When using a calculator, there is no particular need to reduce the time fraction in an interest problem:

730 ☒ 0.12 ☒ 275 ÷ 360 − ⟶ 66.916666

This applies throughout the simple interest and discount chapters. Also, the interest rate can be entered as 12 ☒%, if you wish, rather than as its decimal equivalent. (Recall, however, that a percent cannot be the first value entered, since the ☒% key also functions as an =.)

Type II. The combination of exact time and exact interest is gaining in usage by financial institutions and has been used extensively in certain parts of the country during periods when interest rates have been quite high. This is partly to ensure that they do not exceed legal maximum (usury) rates on interest charges and partly because this method results in slightly less interest paid to depositors.

Another major application is by the Federal Reserve Bank and the United States government, which use this method when computing interest:

$$\frac{\text{Exact days}}{365 \text{ or } 366}$$

This exact-time/exact-interest method applies both for interest owed to the government (such as interest for late payment of taxes) and for interest paid by the government to purchasers of certain U.S. interest-bearing certificates. (For example, earnings on U.S. Treasury Notes are computed using a half-year variation of exact interest.)

Example 2   Compute Example 1 using type II (exact time and exact interest).

$$P = \$730 \qquad\qquad I = Prt$$

$$r = \frac{12}{100} \qquad\qquad = \$\overset{10}{\cancel{730}} \times \frac{12}{\cancel{100}} \times \frac{\cancel{55}}{\cancel{73}}$$

$$t = \frac{275}{365} \quad\text{or}\quad \frac{55}{73} \qquad\qquad I = \$66.00 \quad \text{(exact time/exact interest)}$$

$$I = \,?$$

Type III.   The combination of ordinary time and ordinary interest is equivalent to the calculations used in the first section of this chapter. (For example, any 6-month period is equivalent to 180 days or $\frac{1}{2}$ year.) This method of interest calculation is not used commercially, but it is commonly used in private loans between individuals: $\dfrac{\text{Approx. days}}{360}$ or $\dfrac{\text{Months}}{12}$.

Example 3   Rework Example 1 using ordinary time (9 months or 270 days) and ordinary interest (360 days or 12 months).

$$P = \$730 \qquad\qquad I = Prt$$

$$r = \frac{12}{100} \qquad\qquad = \$730 \times \frac{\overset{3}{\cancel{12}}}{\cancel{100}} \times \frac{3}{\cancel{4}}$$

$$t = \frac{9}{12} \quad\text{or}\quad \frac{270}{360} \qquad\qquad I = \$65.70 \quad \text{(ordinary time/ordinary interest)}$$

$$= \frac{3}{4}$$

$$I = \,?$$

Type IV.   The other possible combination of ordinary time and exact interest is not customarily used. (Example 1 reworked using 270 days over a 365-day year yields interest of $64.80.)

Comparing Examples 1 through 3 reveals that type I, the combination of *exact time over ordinary interest* (a 360-day year), produces the most interest on a loan. Since this combination results in the most interest due to the lender, it is therefore the method most often used historically—which accounts for its name, the Bankers' Rule. From this point on, our problems will emphasize this type I method (Bankers' Rule), with supporting use of the type II method.

SECTION 3   PROBLEMS

Find the ordinary interest (type I) and exact interest (type II).

1. a. On $2,400 for 90 days at 12%   b. On $1,500 for 120 days at 10%
2. a. On $2,190 for 45 days at 8%   b. On $2,920 for 60 days at 9%
3. A 3-month note dated August 4 for $2,200 had an interest rate of 9%. Determine the interest due using the three combinations of time and interest (types I, II, and III).
4. A loan of $8,000 was made on June 6 for 4 months at 14%. Calculate the interest on this loan using the three combinations of time and interest (types I, II, and III).

   Use the Bankers' Rule (type I) to compute ordinary interest.

5. Find the ordinary interest on $3,000 for 60 days at each of the given interest rates. Carefully observe the relationships among your answers.
   a. 12%   b. 6%   c. 18%   d. 9%
6. Compute the ordinary interest on $3,000 for 90 days at each of the given rates. Observe carefully the relationships between rates and interest due.
   a. 5%   b. 10%   c. 15%   d. 7.5%
7. Compute the ordinary interest on a $2,800 loan at 15% for each of the given time periods. Notice how a change in time affects the interest due.
   a. 30 days   b. 90 days   c. 45 days   d. 180 days
8. Find the ordinary interest on a $4,000 loan at 12% for each of the given time periods. Carefully observe the relationships among your answers.
   a. 90 days   b. 30 days   c. 120 days   d. 270 days
9. The ordinary interest on a loan for a certain number of days at 10% was $24. What was the ordinary interest on the same principal and for the same time at the following rates? Apply what you learned in Problem 5.
   a. 5%   b. 15%   c. 18%
10. The ordinary interest on a loan for a certain number of days at 8% was $36. Using what you learned in Problem 6, compute the ordinary interest on this loan for the same time at
    a. 16%   b. 10%   c. 12%
11. The ordinary interest on a loan at a certain rate was $75 for 180 days. Applying what you learned in Problem 7, compute the interest on the same principal at the same rate if the times were as follows:
    a. 60 days   b. 45 days   c. 120 days
12. When interest was computed at a certain rate, the interest due on a 120-day loan was $40. Using your conclusions from Problem 8, determine the interest due on the same principal and at the same rate if the time periods were as follows:
    a. 60 days   b. 300 days   c. 240 days

    Use type II to compute exact interest.

13. A 3-month note was taken out on March 6 for $1,825. Calculate the exact interest due on the note
    a. At 14%   b. At 7%   c. At 10%
14. On April 5, a loan of $2,190 was taken out for 2 months. Find the exact interest due on the loan
    a. At 10%   b. At 5%   c. At 15%

15. A loan for $1,460 was made at 8%. Determine the exact interest for

    a. 120 days   b. 30 days   c. 90 days

16. A 9.5% note for $1,460 was made. Determine the exact interest for

    a. 150 days   b. 180 days   c. 270 days

SECTION 4

SIMPLE INTEREST NOTES

A person who borrows money usually signs a written promise to repay the loan; this document is called a **promissory note,** or just a **note.** The money value that is specified on a note is the **face value** of the note. If an interest rate is mentioned in the note, the face value of this simple interest note is the **principal** of the loan. Interest is computed on the whole principal for the entire length of the loan, and the **maturity value** (principal plus interest) is repaid in a single payment on the **due date** (or maturity date) stated in the note. If no interest is mentioned, the face value is the maturity value of the note. The person who borrows the money is called the **maker** of the note, and the one to whom the money will be repaid is known as the **payee.**

The use of simple interest notes varies from state to state; the banks in some states issue simple interest notes, whereas others normally use another type of note. Figure 15-1 shows a simple interest bank note. [The face value of this note is $1,200. Notice that the maturity value ($1,208.88) is also entered for convenience.] Notes between individuals are usually simple interest notes also.

Before loaning money, a bank may require the borrower to provide **collateral**—some item of value that is used to secure the note. Thus, if the loan is not repaid, the bank is entitled to obtain its money by selling the collateral. (Any excess funds above the amount owed would be returned to the borrower.) Some items commonly used as collateral are cars, real estate, insurance policies, stocks and bonds, as well as savings accounts. Figure 15-2 illustrates a simple interest note in which a certificate of deposit is the collateral.

Most promisory notes are short-term notes—for 1 year or less. The most common time period for notes is one quarter (or 90 days). When a note matures after one quarter, the interest due must be paid and the note may usually be renewed for another quarter at the rate then in effect for new loans.

In many localities, short-term loans from banks are almost exclusively either installment loans or simple discount loans. For an installment loan, the maturity value is calculated as for a simple interest loan; however, this amount is repaid in weekly or monthly payments rather than being repaid in one lump sum, as is the case for simple interest notes. (The simple discount loan and the installment loan are both discussed in detail in later topics.)

The bank is required by law to provide the borrower with information about the annual percentage rate and the finance charge. Some banks provide this information on the promissory note itself, as shown in Figure 15-1. Other

(FIXED OR VARIABLE RATE/SINGLE PAYMENT OR INSTALLMENTS) (365) (NATIONAL OR STATE BANK)   NOTE NO. X4-10436

Anything appearing below this block shall control if it conflicts with anything above or in this block.			
MATURITY: Sept. 29, 19X4	RATE: 9%	TERM: 30 days	COLLATERAL: none

PROMISSORY NOTE	NORTH AUSTIN STATE BANK	DATE OF NOTE Aug. 30, 19X4
AMOUNT OF NOTE $1,200.00	TOTAL OF PAYMENTS $1,208.88	AUSTIN, TEXAS	OFFICER GKW
MAKER: ADDRESS: Stanley L. Warren 11208 Apache Trail Round Rock, Texas 78626		ACCT. NO. OR CUST. NO. 029-75-3643 TELEPHONE NO. 528-4117

For value received, each of the undersigned (called Maker whether one or more) jointly and severally promises to pay to the order of the bank named above (called Bank) at its office in the city named above in immediately available current funds of the United States of America the principal sum of One thousand two hundred and no/100!-- Dollars, together with interest on such principal sum, or so much thereof as may be advanced and outstanding, at the rate checked below:

☑ A fixed rate of ____9%____ percent per annum.

☐ A variable rate (called the Variable Rate) based on the prime or base percent per annum rate of interest (called the Base Rate) charged by _____

for short-term loans to substantial and responsible commercial borrowers, each change in the Variable Rate to be effective, without notice to Maker, on the effective date of each change in the Base Rate. The Variable Rate shall be:

☐ The Base Rate plus _____ percentage points.

☐ _____

Interest charges will be calculated for actual days elapsed on the basis of a 365-day year. In no event shall the rate charged hereunder exceed the maximum rate of interest permitted by applicable law, and if application of any variable rate or any other circumstance would cause the rate of interest hereunder to exceed such maximum rate, the rate of interest hereunder automatically shall be reduced to such maximum rate.

Payment shall be due as checked below:

☑ Principal and interest shall be due on demand or, if no demand is made, on Sept. 29, 19X4

☐ Principal shall be due _____. Interest shall be due _____.

☐ Payment shall be due in _____ installments, with the first installment of $_____ due _____ and installments of the same amount due on the _____ day of each _____ thereafter until a final installment equal to the total unpaid balance is due on _____.

☐ _____

Interest:

☐ Is included in above installments.

☐ Is in addition to above installments and shall be due _____, beginning _____.

☐ _____

Purpose: _____

Bank may require payment by Maker and any surety, indorser or guarantor without first resorting to any security. Maker and all other parties liable hereon consent to the release or discharge of any party liable hereon (including any of the undersigned) and to the release, impairment or substitution of any collateral for this note by Bank.

If default occurs in the payment of any principal or interest when due hereunder, or upon the occurrence of any default or failure to perform any covenant, agreement or obligation to be performed under any document or instrument executed in connection with or as security for this note, or if Bank in good faith believes that the prospect of payment of this note is impaired, Bank may declare the entirety of this note, principal and interest, immediately due and payable, but failure to do so at any time shall not constitute a waiver of Bank's right to do so at any other time.

All past due principal and interest shall bear interest from maturity of such principal or interest at the maximum rate of interest permitted by applicable law. If default occurs in the payment of this note at maturity, whether maturity may occur by acceleration or otherwise, or this note is collected through probate, bankruptcy or other proceedings. Maker promises to pay all costs and expenses of collection and enforcement. If this note is placed in the hands of an attorney for collection. Maker promises to pay, in addition to all other costs and expenses of collection and enforcement, an additional amount equal to 15% of the principal and interest then due, as attorney's fees.

Maker and every surety, indorser and guarantor of this note waive presentment for payment, protest, notice of dishonor, grace and notice of acceleration and all other notice, filing of suit and diligence in collecting this note and the enforcing of any of the security rights of Bank, and consent and agree that time of payment hereof may be extended without notice at any time and from time to time, and for periods of time whether or not for a term or terms in excess of the original term hereof, without notice or consideration to, or consent from, any of them.

Stanley L. Warren

Courtesy of North Austin State Bank, Austin, Texas

FIGURE 15-1   Interest-Bearing Note

Consumer Note - Crestar Bank

CRESTAR

William J. McDaniel

Borrower

Co-Borrower

3001 Dawes Avenue; Alexandra, Va 22311

Borrower's Address

Loan Amount Five thousand and no/100 dollars

Dollars ($ 5,000.00)

Date May 1, 19x4

Account No. 4651-9121

Originating Office Old Town

Note No. A2-22341

> In this Note, the words "you" and "your" mean the Borrower and any Co-Borrower. "We," "our," "us" and "the Bank" mean Crestar Bank. "Scheduled Payment" means any payment specified in this Note, whether it is a payment of principal plus interest or a payment of interest only.

This Note covers your loan with the Bank. When you sign it, each one of you is fully responsible for fulfilling all of the promises you make in this Note. By signing this Note, you acknowledge that you received a loan from us in the Loan Amount shown above and agree to pay to us at any of our offices, or at such place as the Bank may in writing designate, the Loan Amount shown above, plus or including interest, and any other amounts due, upon the terms described below.

Terms of Note

☐ **Simple Interest Installment Loan**

You will make a total of _____ monthly payments of principal and interest beginning on _____ , 19 _____ and continuing on the same day of each succeeding month until this Note is paid in full. You will make _____ monthly payments of principal and interest equal to $ _____ and then a final payment equal to the unpaid principal balance plus interest and any other amounts due.

☐ Payment will be by the Alternative Payment Schedule specified below.

☐ **Principal Plus Installment Loan**

You will make a total of _____ monthly payments of principal and interest beginning on _____ , 19 _____ and continuing on the same day of each succeeding month until this Note is paid in full. Each month for _____ months you will make a payment equal to $ _____ in principal plus all interest accrued on the unpaid balance, and then a final payment equal to $ _____ in principal plus all accrued interest and any other amounts due.

☐ Payment will be by the Alternative Payment Schedule specified below.

☒ **Single Payment Loan** due on May 31, , 19 X4 (30 days from the date of this Note).

You will make one payment in full of principal plus accrued interest from the date of this Note until this Note is paid in full plus any other amounts due.

☒ New obligation ☐ Renewal - New disclosure required ☐ Renewal - Same terms and no new disclosure required.

Interest

Interest on an Installment Loan will accrue on a 30/360 day basis. On all other loan types, interest will accrue daily on the basis of a 360-day year. Interest will accrue at the stated interest rate on the unpaid balance from the date of this Note until paid in full. Interest will continue to accrue after maturity, whether by acceleration or otherwise, at the stated interest rate until this Note has been paid in full.

Subject to the above, the interest rate applicable to this Note (the "Rate") is:

☒ 9.0 % per annum, fixed for the term of this Note.

☐ The initial Rate is _____ % per annum, subject to change with changes in the Index identified below. This Rate is based upon the Index plus _____ % per annum.

☐ The Bank's prime rate, which is the rate established from time to time by the Bank and recorded in its Credit Administration Division as a reference for fixing the lending rate on commercial loans. It is not necessarily the lowest rate charged by the Bank for commercial borrowings.

☐ The Bank's personal rate, which is the rate established from time to time by the Bank and recorded in its Credit Administration Division as a reference for fixing the lending rate on personal loans. It is not necessarily the lowest rate charged by the Bank for personal borrowings.

Collateral

We will have a security interest in the property described below (the "Collateral"). The Collateral is described more fully in a

☐ Security Agreement dated _____ ☐ Assignment of Deposit dated _____

☐ Deed of Trust dated _____ ☐ Credit Line Deed of Trust dated _____

☒ Other Certificate of Deposit for $5,000.00 at Crestar dated March 1, 19x4

Covering: _____

You also give us the right of set-off, which means we can apply any funds you have on deposit with us to any amount due and unpaid on this Note. We may use the Collateral (except your dwelling(s)) to secure other loans you have with us and the collateral we are holding for your other loans (except your dwelling(s) and household goods) may also secure this Note. If credit insurance is obtained with this loan, we will have a security interest in all unearned credit insurance premiums.

> **There Are Important Additional Terms And Conditions On The Reverse Side Of This Note. Be Sure To Read Them Before You Sign.**

By signing below, you agree to all the terms of this Note and acknowledge receipt of a completed copy.

William J. McDaniel _____ (Seal)

Borrower's Signature

_____ (Seal)

Co-Borrower's Signature

By signing below, you agree to be bound by all the terms of this Note and acknowledge receipt of a copy of the "Notice to Co-Signer" form.

_____ (Seal)

Endorser's Signature

Endorser's Address

_____ (Seal)

Endorser's Signature

Endorser's Address

CRE-0301 VA (1/91) For use by Crestar Bank only

Distribution: Original - Note File; Canary - Quality Control; Pink - Customer Copy

Courtesy of Crestar Bank, Alexandria, Virginia

FIGURE 15-2 Note with Collateral

Truth-in-Lending Disclosure Statement

CRESTAR

Creditor: ☒ Crestar Bank ☐ Crestar Bank N.A. ☐ Crestar Bank MD

Borrower: William J. McDaniel

Co-Borrower: ______

Loan Type: ☐ Variable Rate Instalment Loan ☐ Fixed Rate Instalment Loan ☐ Single Payment Loan ☐ Demand Loan

Originating Office: Old Town

Use of Terms: In this Disclosure, the words "you" and "your" mean any Borrower or Co-Borrower. "We," "our," and "us" mean the Creditor. "Scheduled Payment" means any payment disclosed in this disclosure or specified in the Note to which this disclosure applies, whether such payment is a payment of principal and interest or a payment of interest only.

Estimates: The Finance Charge and Total of Payments disclosed below are estimates. These amounts have been computed on the assumption that all payments will be received on their scheduled due date. Any other estimate is noted with an asterisk (*) and is based on the best information reasonably available.

ANNUAL PERCENTAGE RATE The cost of your credit as a yearly rate	FINANCE CHARGE The dollar amount the credit will cost you	AMOUNT FINANCED The amount of credit provided to you or on your behalf	TOTAL OF PAYMENTS Amount you will have paid after you have made all payments as scheduled
9.0%	$ 37.50	$ 5,000.00	$ 5,037.50

Payment Schedule:

Number of Payments	Amount of Payments	When Payments Are Due
		Monthly Beginning 19

☒ In one payment of $ 5,037.50 * due on May 31 19 x4

☒ This obligation is payable on demand.

☐ All disclosures are based on an "assumed maturity" of one year. Scheduled interest payments for the first year: ______

☐ Alternate payment schedule for a Demand Loan: ______

Variable Rate: ☐ The Annual Percentage Rate will increase during the term of the loan if the index identified below increases:

☐ The Creditor's Prime Rate, which is the rate established from time to time by the Creditor and recorded in its Credit Administration Division as a reference for fixing the lending rate on commercial loans.

☐ The Creditor's personal rate, which is the rate established from time to time by the Creditor and recorded in its Credit Administration Division as a reference for fixing the lending rate on personal loans.

☐ The lowest prime rate published in the "Money Rates" section of *The Wall Street Journal*.

☐ ______

The maximum interest rate will not exceed the maximum permitted by law or 24%, whichever is less. If the specified index ceases to be published, we will substitute a similar index and send you notice of it. On an Instalment Loan, the effect of an increase in the Annual Percentage Rate may be more payments of the same amount, an increased final payment, or an increase in the amount of your payments. For example, if your loan were for $5,000 at 12% for three years, your monthly payment would be $166.07. If after six months your rate increased to 13% for the remainder of the loan term, your final payment would increase to $237.62; you would have to make one additional partial payment of $72.33; or your regular monthly payments would increase to $168.10. On a Single Payment or Demand Loan, the effect of an increase in the Annual Percentage Rate would be an increase in the amount of your payments. For example, if your loan were for $10,000 at 14% payable on demand with an alternate payment schedule of $1,000 per month plus interest and the rate increased to 16% at the end of the first month, the payment due at the end of the second month would increase from $1,103.56 to $1,118.36.

Late Charge: If any portion of a Scheduled Payment is late, you will have to pay us a late charge of 5% of the amount which is late.

Security: ☐ You are giving a security interest in ☐ the goods or property being purchased. ☐ other property described as follows:

Collateral securing other loans with us (except your consumer dwelling(s),) may also secure this loan.

Assumption (applicable only to loans secured by a principal dwelling): Someone buying your house cannot assume the remainder of the loan on the original terms.

Filing Fees: $______

Property Insurance: You may obtain any required property insurance from an insurance company of your choice.

Prepayment: If you pay off early, you will not have to pay a penalty and will not be entitled to a rebate of any prepaid Finance Charge.

Read all your loan documents for additional information about nonpayment, default, late charges, any required payment in full before the scheduled date, security interests and other matters pertaining to the credit transaction.

Credit Insurance - CREDIT INSURANCE IS NOT REQUIRED FOR THIS LOAN. If you would like Credit Life insurance on your Single Payment or Instalment Loan, or Credit Disability for your Instalment Loan, we can provide it for you. You must specify any insurance protection you want by checking the appropriate blocks below. No insurance protection will be provided unless you sign your request on this disclosure. **Credit Insurance is not available on demand loans.**

☐ Credit Life for: ☐ Borrower ☐ Co-Borrower.

The premium is $ ______ for the term of the loan.

☐ Credit Disability for: ☐ Borrower ☐ Co-Borrower.

The premium is $ ______ for the term of the loan. Credit Life coverage must be provided for you to be eligible for Credit Disability protection

Term Insurance - TERM INSURANCE IS NOT REQUIRED FOR THIS LOAN. If term insurance is desired, you must specify any insurance protection you want by checking the appropriate blocks below and complete an application. The coverage will not be effective unless and until your application is accepted by the insurance company. **This coverage is not offered in the District of Columbia or Maryland.**

☐ Single-Premium Term Life for: ☐ Borrower ☐ Co-Borrower.

The premium is $ ______ for ______ months.

☐ Single-Premium Disability for: ☐ Borrower ☐ Co-Borrower.

The premium is $ ______ for ______ months.

______
SIGNATURE OF PARTY REQUESTING INSURANCE

☐ If checked, a RESPA Estimated Closing Costs form was provided in place of the Itemization of the Amount Financed.

ITEMIZATION OF AMOUNT FINANCED

Paid directly to you or deposited in your account # ______ $ 5,000.00

Used to pay off other loans with us:

______ $ ______

______ $ ______

______ $ ______

______ $ ______

Paid to others on your behalf:
Credit and/or term insurance premium(s) paid to insurance company $ ______

______ $ ______

______ $ ______

______ $ ______

______ $ ______

Amount Financed $ 5,000.00

Prepaid Finance Charge $ ______

Acknowledgement of Receipt: The undersigned acknowledge receipt of a completed copy of this disclosure before entering into any agreement with Creditor concerning this credit transaction.

William J. McDaniel 5/1/x4

Borrower Date Co-Borrower Date Date

CRE-0279 SYS (1/91) Distribution Instructions: White To Borrower; Canary To Disclosure File; Pink To Quality Control

Courtesy of Crestar Bank, Alexandria, Virginia

FIGURE 15-3 Truth-in-Lending Disclosure Statement

banks provide a separate statement, the "Truth-in-Lending Disclosure Statement" (Figure 15-3).

Example 1   A note for $450 was dated June 12 and repaid in 3 months with interest at 12%. Find (a) the due date and (b) the amount repaid.

(a)   The due date was September 12.

(b)   Using the Bankers' Rule, interest and maturity value were as follows:

$$\begin{aligned}
\text{Sept. 12} &= 255 \text{ day} \\
\text{June 12} &= \underline{163 \text{ day}} \\
t &= 92 \text{ days} \quad \text{or} \quad \tfrac{92}{360} \text{ year}
\end{aligned}$$

$$P = \$450$$
$$r = 12\%$$

Interest

$$I = Prt$$

$$= \overset{15}{\cancel{450}} \times \frac{\cancel{12}}{\cancel{100}} \times \frac{.\cancel{92}}{\underset{20}{\cancel{360}}}$$

$$I = \$13.80$$

Maturity Value

$$M = P + I$$

$$= \$450 + \$13.80$$

$$M = \$463.80$$

Example 2   The maturity value of a 60-day simple interest note was $976, including interest at 10%. What was the face value of the note?

$$M = \$976$$

$$r = \frac{10}{100}$$

$$t = \frac{60}{360} \quad \text{or} \quad \frac{1}{6}$$

$$P = ?$$

$$M = P(1 + rt)$$

$$\$976 = P\left(1 + \frac{\overset{5}{\cancel{10}}}{100} \cdot \frac{1}{\underset{3}{\cancel{6}}}\right)$$

$$976 = P\left(1 + \frac{5}{300}\right)$$

$$976 = P\left(\frac{305}{300}\right)$$

$$\left(\frac{300}{305}\right)976 = P\left(\frac{\cancel{305}}{\cancel{300}}\right)\!\left(\frac{\cancel{300}}{\cancel{305}}\right)$$

$$\$960 = P$$

Calculator techniques . . .   FOR EXAMPLE 2

Here, since you can't multiply the value in parentheses times P, you must divide by the parenthetical value (using $\boxed{MR}$) to find P:

$0.1 \boxed{\div} 6 \boxed{M+} \longrightarrow 0.0166666; \quad 1 \boxed{M+} \longrightarrow 1$

$976 \boxed{\div} \boxed{MR} \boxed{=} \longrightarrow 960.00006$

Recall that the "$1 \boxed{M+}$" can be done first, if you prefer.

Example 3 A \$750 note drawn at 15% exact interest had a maturity value of \$795. What was the exact time of the note?

$$M = \ \ \$795$$
$$P = - \ \ 750$$
$$I = \ \ \ \$ \ 45$$

$$r = \frac{15}{100}$$

$$t = ?$$

$$I = Prt$$

$$\$45 = \$750 \times \frac{15}{100} \times t$$

$$45 = 112.5t$$

$$\frac{45}{112.5} = t$$

$$0.4 \text{ year} = t$$

$$t = 0.4 \text{ year} \times 365 \text{ days per year}$$

$$t = 146 \text{ days}$$

SECTION 4   PROBLEMS

Note. You should use exact days in all problems unless exact time is impossible to determine from the information given. For example, if a problem involves a 3-month loan but no date is included, it is impossible to compute exact time; thus, ordinary time would have to be used. However, if a problem states that a 3-month loan began on some specific date, then the exact days during that particular 3-month interval would be used.

Further, ordinary interest should normally be computed, using the Bankers' Rule (exact days over 360). However, a 365-day year should be observed when the loan problem specifies "exact interest."

1. Identify each part of the note shown in Figure 15-1.

   a. Face value   b. Maker   c. Payee   d. Date

   e. Due date   f. Principal   g. Rate   h. Time

   i. Interest   j. Maturity value

2. Answer Problem 1 for the note shown in Figure 15-2 and the Truth-in-Lending Disclosure Statement shown in Figure 15-3.

Complete the following simple interest problems, using the Bankers' Rule whenever possible.

	PRINCIPAL	RATE	DATE	DUE DATE	TIME	INTEREST	MATURITY VALUE
3. a.	$ 400	15%	4/12	5/27			
b.	650	12	9/1		120 days		
c.	720	10	7/13		4 months		
d.		8		6/15	150 days	$36	
4. a.	$4,800	9%	2/12	11/9			
b.	900	11	4/22		60 days		
c.	4,500	12	8/21		3 months		
d.		10		7/13	100 days	$20	

In completing the following problems, use exact days if possible. Find ordinary interest (360-day year) unless exact interest (365-day year) is indicated.

5. A 3-month note dated January 16, 1997, for $1,460 had interest at 15%. Find the exact interest and the maturity value of the note.

6. A note dated January 24, 1997, was made for 4 months at 9%. If the principal of the note was $6,000, find the exact interest and maturity value of the note.

7. A note dated June 6, 1996, reads: "One month from date, I promise to pay $2,400 with interest at 8.5%." Find the maturity value.

8. A note dated October 5, 1996, read: "Two months from date, I promise to pay $400 with interest at 10.5%." What was the maturity value of the note?

9. An 8-month note is drawn for $4,800 with interest at 10%. What maturity value will be paid?

10. Find the maturity value of a 9%, 10-month note with a face value of $2,000.

11. A note dated August 21, 1998, will be due in 3 months. If the face value of the note is $1,095 and $1,128.12 will be paid to discharge the debt, what exact interest rate will be charged?

12. A 6-month note dated February 14, 1998, has a face value of $2,190 and a maturity value of $2,298.60. Determine the exact interest rate charged.

13. How long will it take $1,800 to earn $72 interest at a 10% exact interest rate?

14. How long will it take $730 to earn $18 interest at 10% exact interest?

15. How long will it take $1,600 to earn $64 interest at an 8% interest rate?

16. What time is required for $400 to earn $36 at 12% interest?

17. The interest on a 150-day note is $48.75. If interest was computed at 9%, find the principal of the note.

18. Find the principal of a 180-day note made at 14% if the interest was $105.

19. If $5,230 is paid on November 10 to discharge a note dated May 10, find the face value of the 9% note.

20. Find the face value of a 10% note dated September 7 that matures on December 6. The maturity value on the note is $3,075.

SECTION

PRESENT VALUE

In Problems 19 and 20 of Section 4, we were told the maturity value of a note and asked to find what principal had been loaned. When the principal is being found, this is often referred to as finding the **present value.** Present value can also be explained by answering the question: What amount would have to be invested today (at the present) in order to obtain a given maturity value? This "X" amount that would have to be invested is the present value.

Present value at simple interest can be found using the same maturity value formula that has been used previously: $M = P(1 + rt)$. However, when present value is to be found repeatedly, the formula is usually altered slightly by dividing by the quantity in parentheses.

$$M = P(1 + rt)$$

$$\frac{M}{1 + rt} = \frac{P(\cancel{1 + rt})}{(\cancel{1 + rt})}$$

$$\frac{M}{1 + rt} = P$$

or

$$P = \frac{M}{1 + rt}$$

The formula can be used more conveniently in this form, since it is set up to solve for the principal or present value. However, Example 1 illustrates a present-value problem solved with both versions of the formula, and either form may be used for this type of problem.

Example 1   If the maturity value of a 12%, 3-month note dated March 11 was $618.40, find the present value (or principal, or face value) of the note.

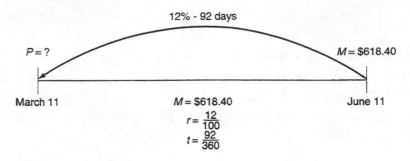

$$M = \$618.40$$
$$r = \frac{12}{100}$$
$$t = \frac{92}{360}$$

$$M = P(1 + rt)$$

$$\$618.40 = P\left(1 + \frac{\cancel{12}}{\cancel{100}} \times \frac{.92}{\cancel{360}_{30}}\right)$$

$$618.40 = P\left(1 + \frac{92}{30}\right)$$

$$618.40 = P\left(\frac{30}{30} + \frac{.92}{30}\right)$$

$$618.40 = P\left(\frac{30.92}{30}\right)$$

$$\frac{30}{30.92}(\overset{20}{\cancel{618.40}}) = P\left(\frac{\cancel{30.92}}{\cancel{30}}\right)\left(\frac{\cancel{30}}{\cancel{30.92}}\right)$$

$$\$600 = P$$

$$P = \frac{M}{1 + rt}$$

$$= \frac{\$618.40}{1 + \frac{\cancel{12}}{\cancel{100}} \times \frac{.92}{\cancel{360}_{30}}}$$

$$= \frac{618.40}{\frac{30}{30} + \frac{.92}{30}}$$

$$= \frac{618.40}{\frac{30.92}{30}}$$

$$= \overset{20}{\cancel{618.40}}\left(\frac{30}{\cancel{30.92}}\right)$$

$$P = \$600$$

Calculator techniques . . . FOR EXAMPLE 1

This technique illustrates the equation on the right, where the formula is set up to solve for the present value, P:

0.12 ⊠ 92 ÷ 360 M+ ⟶ 0.0306666;   1 M+ ⟶ 1

618.40 ÷ MR = ⟶ 600.00003

You will use this technique for many subsequent problems.

Example 1 involves only one interest rate. Many investments, however, involve two interest rates. To illustrate present value at two interest rates, consider the following case.

Suppose that I find a place where I can earn 20% on my investment. The most I have been offered any other place is 12%, so I immediately invest $1,000 in this "gold mine." On the way home, I meet a friend who offers to buy this investment for the same $1,000 I just deposited. Would I sell the investment for $1,000, knowing I could not earn 20% interest on any other investment I might make? No! My $1,000 is really worth more than $1,000 to me, because I would have to deposit more than $1,000 elsewhere in order to earn the same amount of interest.

This case demonstrates that an investment is not always worth its exact face value; it may be worth more or less than its face value when compared to the average rate of interest being paid by most financial institutions. This typical, or average, interest rate is referred to as the **rate money is worth.** Thus, if most financial institutions are paying 8%, then money is worth 8%.

The rate money is worth varies considerably, depending on whether one is borrowing or depositing—and on the kind of deposit made. An ordinary **savings account,** where the money can be withdrawn at any time, earns less interest than a **certificate of deposit** (or CD). A CD usually requires a minimum deposit (often $1,000), and the money must remain on deposit for a specified period of time (usually a 3-month minimum) in order to earn interest at the higher rate. CD rates increase when more money is deposited and/or longer time periods are established.

Another popular account, the **money-market account,** shares some characteristics with each of the others. The money-market account may also require a minimum deposit (often $500), but it allows a limited number of withdrawals or checks (usually three per month) without penalty so long as the minimum balance remains met. Its rate of interest usually falls between that of the other two accounts.

As would be expected, institutions must charge higher rates for notes and other loans than they pay on deposits, or they could not cover expenses and return a profit to their owners.

If an investment is made at a rate that is not the prevailing rate money is worth, then the present value of the investment is different—either greater or less—than the principal. We therefore find what investment, made at the rate money is worth, would have the same maturity value that the actual investment has. The size of this "rate-money-is-worth investment" is the present or true value of the actual investment.

Example 2   A 90-day note for $1,000 is drawn on November 12 at 8%. If money is worth 12%, find the present value of the note on the day it is drawn.

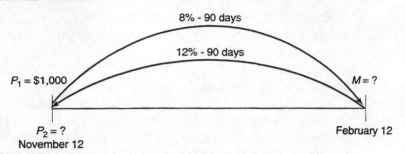

P₁ = $1,000

8% - 90 days

12% - 90 days

M = ?

P₂ = ?
November 12

February 12

The solution to this kind of problem involves two steps: (a) Find the *actual maturity value* of the note, and (b) find the *present value at the rate money is worth* of that calculated amount.

(a) $P_1 = \$1,000$

$r = 8\%$

$t = \dfrac{90}{360}$ or $\dfrac{1}{4}$

$M = ?$

$M = P(1 + rt)$

$= \$1,000\left(1 + \dfrac{\overset{2}{\cancel{8}}}{100} \times \dfrac{1}{\cancel{4}}\right)$

$= 1,000\left(1 + \dfrac{2}{100}\right)$

$= \overset{10}{\cancel{1,000}}\left(\dfrac{102}{\cancel{100}}\right)$

$M = \$1,020$

(b) $M = \$1,020$

$r = 12\%$

$t = \dfrac{90}{360}$ or $\dfrac{1}{4}$

$P_2 = ?$

$P_2 = \dfrac{M}{1 + rt}$

$= \dfrac{\$1,020}{1 + \dfrac{\overset{3}{\cancel{12}}}{100} \times \dfrac{1}{\cancel{4}}}$

$= \dfrac{1,020}{1 + \dfrac{3}{100}}$

$= \dfrac{1,020}{\dfrac{103}{100}}$

$= 1,020\left(\dfrac{100}{103}\right)$

$P_2 = \$990.29$

The present value of the note on the day it was drawn was $990.29. This means that the lender (payee) could have invested only $990.29 at the rate money is worth (12%) and would achieve the same maturity value ($1,020) that will be obtained on the $1,000 note at only 8% interest. That is, $990.29 invested at 12% would earn $29.71 interest ($990.29 + $29.71 = $1,020), producing the same $1,020 maurity value as $1,000 plus $20 interest. Thus, the $1,000 is really worth only $990.29 to the lender.

When computing present value of an investment where two interest rates are involved, you should know beforehand whether the present value is more or less than the principal. In general, the present value is less than the principal when the investment rate is less than the rate money is worth. That is, when the actual rate is less, then the present value is less. The reverse is also true: If the actual rate is more than the rate money is worth, then the present value is more than the principal.

Previous examples have required finding the present value on the day a note was drawn. It is often desirable to know the worth of an investment on some day nearer the due date. The worth of an investment on any day prior to the due date is also called present value. The procedure for finding this present value is the same as that already discussed, except that in the second step the time as well as the rate will be different. It should be emphasized that present value is

1. Computed using the maturity value.
2. Computed for an exact number of days *prior* to the due date.
3. Computed using the rate money is worth.

Example 3 Find the (present) value on October 11 of a $720, 4-month note taken out on July 10 at 15%, if money is worth 12%.

15% - 123 days

$P_1 = \$720$ 12% - 30 days $M = ?$

July 10 $P_2 = ?$ Nov. 10
                         Oct. 11

(a) $P_1 = \$720$ $I = Prt$ $M = P + I$

   $r = 15\%$ $= \$\overset{2}{\cancel{720}} \times \dfrac{15}{\cancel{100}} \times \dfrac{1.23}{\cancel{360}}$ $= \$720 + \$36.90$

   $t = \dfrac{123}{360}$ $I = \$36.90$ $M = \$756.90$

   $M = ?$

(b) $M = \$756.90$

$r = 12\%$

$t = \dfrac{30}{360}$ or $\dfrac{1}{12}$

$P_2 = ?$

$P_2 = \dfrac{M}{1 + rt}$

$= \dfrac{\$756.90}{1 + \dfrac{\cancel{12}}{100} \times \dfrac{1}{\cancel{12}}}$

$= \dfrac{756.90}{1 + \dfrac{1}{100}}$

$= \dfrac{756.90}{\dfrac{101}{100}}$

$= 756.90\left(\dfrac{100}{101}\right)$

$P_2 = \$749.41$

This means that if the note were sold on October 11, it would be sold for $749.41; this money could then be invested at 12% interest, and on November 10 the maturity value of the new investment ($749.41 plus $7.49 interest) would also be $756.90.

SECTION 5 PROBLEMS

Any convenient method may be used to find the amount in the following problems: $I = Prt$ and $M = P + I$, or $M = P(1 + rt)$.

Determine the present value, using the Bankers' Rule.

		MATURITY VALUE	RATE	TIME (DAYS)	PRESENT VALUE
1.	a.	$ 936	12%	120	
	b.	812	9	60	
2.	a.	$ 735	12%	150	
	b.	2,484	14	90	

Complete the following, finding the present value on the day of investment.

		PRINCIPAL	RATE	TIME (DAYS)	MATURITY VALUE	RATE MONEY IS WORTH	PRESENT VALUE
3.	a.	$1,200	10%	180		8%	
	b.	1,500	12	30		9	
4.	a.	$6,000	10%	90		9%	
	b.	8,000	12	120		15	

Complete the following, finding the present value on the day indicated.

		PRINCIPAL	RATE	TIME (DAYS)	MATURITY VALUE	RATE MONEY IS WORTH	DAYS BEFORE MATURITY	PRESENT VALUE
5.	a.	$2,000	9%	270		10%	90	
	b.	2,500	15	180		12	45	
6.	a.	$9,000	12%	300		10%	180	
	b.	7,500	15	120		18	60	

7. On June 3, $4,084 was paid in settlement of a note dated March 23. If interest was charged at 10.5%, what was the principal of the note?

8. The maturity value was $4,062 on a 9% note dated July 15. If the note was due on September 15, what had been the face value?

9. On September 6, $2,080 was paid at the maturity of a note dated May 9. If money is worth 12%, what was the present value of the note on the date it was made?

10. The maturity value of $6,165 was paid on April 15 to discharge a simple interest note dated January 15. If money is worth 11%, what was the present value of the note on the day it was made?

11. A 3-month note for $3,800 was drawn on January 13 at 8%. If money is worth 10%, find the present value of the note on the day it was made.

12. A 4-month note for $3,500 was drawn on February 8 at 15%. If money is worth 18%, find the present value of the note on the day it was issued.

13. Determine the present value of a 6%, 5-month note with a face value of $15,000 made on February 13, if money is worth 7.5%.

14. A 4-month note dated February 12 was made at 11% for $6,000. What is the present value of the note on the day it was made, if money is worth 12%?

15. A 9-month note for $1,440 was made at 9% on March 23. If money is worth 12%, find the present value of the note on November 23.

16. A 3-month note dated May 16 was made at 15% for $12,000. Find the present value of the note on July 17 if money is worth 12%.

17. A 6-month, 12% note for $6,000 was dated March 5. What is the present value on August 16 if money is worth 10%?

18. A 4-month, 9% note dated January 17 had a face value of $2,500. Find the present value on April 17 if money is worth 8%.

124,878.04   *123,503.70*

19. The following offers were made on a house: $123,000 cash, $128,000 in 3 months, or $133,000 in 9 months. Which offer should be accepted if money is worth 10%? Hint: Compare the present value of the three amounts.

20. A contractor is considering three payment options for a contract: $30,000 on signing the contract today, $30,700 in 3 months, or $31,500 on the completion of the contract in 6 months. Money is worth 12%. Which is the best offer? Hint: Compare the present value of each payment.

CHAPTER GLOSSARY

Amount. (See "Maturity value at simple interest.")

Bankers' Rule. The most commonly used method of interest calculation, where time is expressed in exact days over 360 days per year.

Certificate of deposit (CD). A savings investment that earns a higher interest rate than savings accounts because the money is committed for a set period of time (usually a 3-month minimum); may also require a minimum investment (often $1,000).

Collateral. An item of value that is pledged by a borrower in order to insure that a note will be repaid or equivalent value received.

Date (of a note). The date on which a note is drawn (or signed).

Due date (of a note). The date on which a note is to be repaid; the maturity date.

Exact interest. Interest calculated using 365 days per year.

Exact time. The time period of a loan expressed in the specific number of calendar days.

Face value. The money value specified on a promissory note; the principal of a simple interest note.

Interest. Rent paid for the privilege of borrowing money: $I = Prt$, where I = interest, P = principal, r = rate, and t = time.

Maker. A person who signs a note promising to repay a loan.

Maturity value (at simple interest). The total amount (principal plus interest) due on a simple interest loan; also called "amount" or "sum": $M = P + I$, or $M = P(1 + rt)$, where M = maturity value, P = principal, I = interest, r = rate, and t = time.

Maturity value (of a note). The amount to be repaid on the due date of a note (which may or may not include interest).

Money-market account. A combined savings/CD account that requires a minimum balance (often $500) but allows a limited number of checks or withdrawals. Pays higher interest than regular savings, lower than CDs.

Note. A written promise to repay a loan (either with or without interest, and with or without collateral).

Ordinary interest. Interest calculated using 360 days per year.

Ordinary time. The time period of a loan where each month is assumed to have 30 days.

Payee. The person (or bank or firm) to whom the maturity value of a note will be paid.

Present value. (1) Principal; also (2) the value of another investment which, if made (on any given date) at the rate money is worth, would have the same maturity value as has an actual, given investment:

$$P = \frac{M}{1 + rt}$$

where P = principal or present value, M = maturity value, r = rate, and t = time.

Principal.   The original amount of money that is loaned or borrowed; the investment value on which interest is computed.

Promissory note.   (See "Note.")

Rate.   An annual percent at which simple interest is computed.

Rate money is worth.   An average or typical rate currently being used at most financial institutions.

Savings account.   A low-interest account where any amount may be deposited or withdrawn at any time; also called an open account.

Simple interest.   Interest that is computed on the original principal of a loan for the entire time of the loan, and is then added to the principal to obtain the maturity value. (See also "Interest.")

Sum.   (See "Maturity value at simple interest.")

Time.   The duration of a simple-interest investment. (Time must be expressed as a fractional year, in order to correspond with the annual percentage rate at which interest is calculated.)

18

COMPOUND INTEREST

OBJECTIVES

Upon completion of Chapter 18, you will be able to:

1. Define and use correctly the terminology associated with each topic.

2. Compute compound amount without use of a table for short periods (Section 1: Examples 1–4; Problems 1–10).

3. Compute compound interest and amount using the formula $M = P(1 + i)^n$ and the compound amount table (Section 2: Examples 1–3; Problems 1–20).

4.   a. Find compound interest and amount at institutions paying interest compounded daily from date of deposit to date of withdrawal (Section 3: Examples 1–4; Problems 1–10).

   b. Also, compare this with interest and amount that would be earned if interest were not compounded daily (Problems 3, 4).

   c. Use the formulas $I = P \times$ Dep. tab. and $I = W \times$ W/D tab. for computing interest compounded daily (Examples 1–4; Problems 7–10).

5. Compute present value at compound interest on investments made at either simple or compound interest. The formula $P = M(1 + i)^{-n}$ and the present value table will be used (Section 4: Examples 1–3; Problems 1–14).

It was previously noted that money invested with a financial institution earns compound interest. Compound interest is more profitable than simple interest to the investor, because, at compound interest, "interest is earned on interest." That is, interest is earned, not only on the principal, but also on all interest accumulated since the original deposit. Most compound interest is calculated using prepared tables or computer programs. To be certain that you clearly understand compound interest, however, you should compute a few problems yourself.

Note. Pages 521–522 contain a summary of Chapters 18 through 20, which all contain topics involving interest at a compound rate. As you study the forthcoming chapters, you may also refer to the summary to identify the characteristics of each topic.

SECTION 1

COMPOUND INTEREST (BY COMPUTATION)

Recall that for a simple interest investment, interest is paid on the *original principal* only; at the end of the time, the maturity value is the total of the principal plus the simple interest. Now consider the following example.

Example 1　Suppose that Mr. A makes a $1,000 investment for 3 years at 7% simple interest. Then

$$P = \$1,000 \qquad I = Prt \qquad\qquad M = P + I$$

$$r = 7\% \qquad\qquad = \$1,000 \times \frac{7}{100} \times \frac{3}{1} \qquad = \$1,000 + \$210$$

$$t = 3 \text{ years} \qquad I = \$210 \qquad\qquad M = \$1,210$$

Mr. A would earn $210 interest on this investment, making the total maturity value $1,210.

　　Now suppose that Ms. B invests $1,000 for only 6 months, also at 7% interest. Then

$$P = \$1,000 \qquad\quad I = Prt \qquad\qquad M = P + I$$

$$r = 7\% \qquad\qquad = \$1,000 \times \frac{7}{100} \times \frac{1}{2} \qquad = \$1,000 + \$35$$

$$t = 6 \text{ months or} \qquad I = \$35 \qquad\qquad M = \$1,035$$

$$\frac{1}{2} \text{ year}$$

Ms. B would have $1,035 at the end of this 6-month investment.

Assume that Ms. B then reinvests this $1,035 for another 6 months at 7%; she would earn $36.23 on her second investment, making the total amount $1,071.23. If this total were then deposited for another 6 months, the interest earned would be $37.49 and Ms. B would have $1,108.72. If this procedure were repeated each 6 months until 3 years had passed, Ms. B would have made six investments, and the computations would be as follows:

First 6 Months

$$I = Prt$$

$$= \$1,000 \times \frac{7}{100} \times \frac{1}{2}$$

$$I = \$35$$

$$M = \$1,035$$

Second 6 Months

$$I = Prt$$

$$= \$1,035 \times \frac{7}{100} \times \frac{1}{2}$$

$$I = \$36.23$$

$$M = \$1,071.23$$

Third 6 Months

$$I = Prt$$

$$= \$1,071.23 \times \frac{7}{100} \times \frac{1}{2}$$

$$I = \$37.49$$

$$M = \$1,108.72$$

Fourth 6 Months

$$I = Prt$$

$$= \$1,108.72 \times \frac{7}{100} \times \frac{1}{2}$$

$$I = \$38.81$$

$$M = \$1,147.53$$

Fifth 6 Months

$$I = Prt$$

$$= \$1,147.53 \times \frac{7}{100} \times \frac{1}{2}$$

$$I = \$40.16$$

$$M = \$1,187.69$$

Sixth 6 Months

$$I = Prt$$

$$= \$1,187.69 \times \frac{7}{100} \times \frac{1}{2}$$

$$I = \$41.57$$

$$M = \$1,229.26$$

Thus, after 3 years, Ms. B's original principal would have amounted to $1,229.26. Because Mr. A had only $1,210 after his single, 3-year investment, Ms. B made $1,229.26 − $1,210.00, or $19.26 more interest by making successive, short-term investments.

The above example illustrates the idea of **compound interest:** Each time that interest is computed, the interest is added to the previous principal; that total then becomes the principal for the next interest period. Thus, money accumulates faster at compound interest because *interest is earned on interest* as well as on the principal.

Interest is said to be "compounded" whenever interest is computed and added to the previous principal. This is done at regular intervals known as **conversion periods** (or just **periods**). Interest is commonly compounded annually (once a year), semiannually (twice a year), quarterly (four times a year), or monthly. The total value at the end of the investment (original principal plus all interest) is the **compound amount.** The *compound interest* earned is the difference between the compound amount and the original principal. The length of the investment is known as the **term.** The quoted interest rate is always the nominal (or yearly) rate.

Before compound interest can be computed, (1) the term must be expressed as its total number of periods and (2) the interest rate must be converted to its corresponding rate per period.

Example 2   Determine the number of periods for each of the following investments: (a) 7 years compounded annually, (b) 5 years compounded semiannually, (c) 6 years compounded quarterly, and (d) 3 years compounded monthly.

In general, the number of periods is found in this way:

Years × Number of periods per year = Total number of periods

Thus,

(a)   7 years compounded annually = 7 years × 1 period per year
= 7 periods

(b)   5 years compounded semiannually = 5 years × 2 periods per year
= 10 periods

(c)   6 years compounded quarterly = 6 years × 4 periods per year
= 24 periods

(d)   3 years compounded monthly = 3 years × 12 periods per year
= 36 periods

Example 3   Determine the rate per period for each investment: (a) 6% compounded annually, (b) $8\frac{1}{2}$% compounded semiannually, (c) 5% compounded quarterly, and (d) 4% compounded monthly.

Keep in mind that the stated interest rate is always the yearly rate. Thus, if the rate is 8% compounded quarterly, the rate per period is 2% (since 2% paid four times during the year is equivalent to 8% annually).

You can find rate per period as follows:

$$\frac{\text{Yearly rate}}{\text{Number of periods per year}} = \text{Rate per period}$$

Hence,

(a) 6% compounded annually $= \dfrac{6\%}{1\,\text{period per year}}$

$= 6\%$ per period (or 6% each year)

(b) $8\frac{1}{2}\%$ compounded semiannually $= \dfrac{8\frac{1}{2}\%}{2\,\text{periods per year}}$

$= 4\frac{1}{4}\%$ per period (or $4\frac{1}{4}\%$ each 6 months)

(c) 5% compounded quarterly $= \dfrac{5\%}{4\,\text{periods per year}}$

$= 1\frac{1}{4}\%$ per period (or $1\frac{1}{4}\%$ each quarter)

(d) 4% compounded monthly $= \dfrac{4\%}{12\,\text{periods per year}}$

$= \frac{1}{3}\%$ per period (or $\frac{1}{3}\%$ each month)

Now let us compute a problem at compound interest:

Example 4   Find the compound amount and the compound interest for the following investments:

(a) $1,000 for 3 years at 8% compounded annually:

3 years × 1 period per year = 3 periods

$$\frac{8\%}{1\,\text{period per year}} = 8\% \text{ per period}$$

First period:	Principal	$1,000.00	
	Interest	+ 80.00	(8% of $1,000)
Second period:	Principal	$1,080.00	
	Interest	+ 86.40	(8% of $1,080)
Third period:	Principal	$1,166.40	
	Interest	+ 93.31	(8% of $1,166.40)
	Compound amount	$1,259.71	

Compound amount	$1,259.71
Less: Original principal	− 1,000.00
Compound interest	$ 259.71

(b) $1,000 for 1 year at 7% compounded quarterly:

1 year × 4 periods per year = 4 periods

$$\frac{7\%}{4\,\text{periods per year}} = 1\frac{3}{4}\% \text{ per period}$$

		First period:	Principal	$1,000.00	
			Interest	+ 17.50	($1\frac{3}{4}$% of $1,000)
		Second period:	Principal	$1,017.50	
			Interest	+ 17.81	($1\frac{3}{4}$% of $1,017.50)
		Third period:	Principal	$1,035.31	
			Interest	+ 18.12	($1\frac{3}{4}$% of $1,035.31)
		Fourth period:	Principal	$1,053.43	
			Interest	+ 18.44	($1\frac{3}{4}$% of $1,053.43)
		Compound amount		$1,071.87	

Compound amount	$1,071.87
Less: Original principal	− 1,000.00
Compound interest	$ 71.87

Note. Compare this $1,071.87 compound amount with Example 1, in which the compound amount after 1 year at 7% compounded *semiannually* was $1,071.23.

SECTION 1 PROBLEMS

Determine the number of periods and the rate per period for each of the following.

	RATE	COMPOUNDED	YEARS	NO. OF PERIODS	RATE PER PERIOD
1. a.	7%	Annually	5		
b.	6	Monthly	3		
c.	8.5	Semiannually	6		
d.	8	Quarterly	9		
e.	5.5	Semiannually	8		
2. a.	4.5%	Annually	6		
b.	9	Monthly	2		
c.	7.5	Semiannually	5		
d.	6	Quarterly	8		
e.	5	Semiannually	9		

Find the compound amount and the compound interest for each of the following.

3. $5,000 invested for 2 years at 8% compounded
   a. Semiannually   b. Quarterly
4. $4,000 invested for 4 years at 7% compounded
   a. Annually   b. Semiannually
5. $2,000 invested for 3 years at 9% compounded
   a. Annually   b. Semiannually

6. $3,000 invested for 1 year at 5% compounded
   a. Semiannually   b. Quarterly
7. $8,000 invested for 6 months at 6% compounded
   a. Quarterly   b. Monthly
8. $7,000 invested for 9 months at 6% compounded
   a. Quarterly   b. Monthly
9. Study carefully your answers to parts a and b of the preceding problems. What conclusion seems to be indicated?
10. Suppose you are given the principal, rate, and years of a compound interest problem. What else must you know in order to work the problem?

SECTION 2
COMPOUND AMOUNT (USING TABLES)

Example 1 in Section 1 illustrated the advantage of a compound interest investment over a simple interest investment. All financial institutions in the United States pay compound interest on savings. There are several factors that an investor should consider before opening an account, however, as various types of accounts are available, often at considerably different rates and under different conditions.

In an **open account,** the owner may deposit or withdraw funds at any time. The most common type of open account is the **statement account.** The owner of a statement account receives a statement periodically from the bank to show deposits, withdrawals, and interest credited to the account for the period. (Deposits to the bank savings account are made using deposit slips similar to those for checking accounts.) Today, financial institutions pay interest on savings accounts from the date of deposit to the date of withdrawal.

Funds deposited for a specific period of time may be used to purchase a **certificate of deposit** (commonly called a **CD**). CDs offer higher rates than open accounts, and their rates increase as funds are committed for longer periods of time. CDs are commonly purchased for 30 days, 90 days (one quarter), 6 months, and 1 year. Periods of 2 or 3 years are available but are not popular during times of low interest rates, as investors hope rates will rise before then. Minimum deposits of $1,000 or more are usually required for CDs. If funds are withdrawn early from a CD, the owner forfeits the higher interest rate and is usually paid only at the institution's open-account rate on the withdrawn amount. Some institutions offer a no-penalty CD at a slightly lower interest rate than the traditional CD, which allows the owner to withdraw funds early without being assessed a penalty. These CDs are attractive to investors since a low interest rate is not locked in on a long-term investment. Figure 18-1 illustrates a certificate of deposit.

Money-market accounts offer interest rates comparable to certificates of deposits. Unlike CDs, money can be withdrawn from the money-market ac-

Certificate of Deposit   *First National Bank*

May 02, 19X1   May 02, 19X2
Issue Date   Maturity Date

Virginia A. Jenkins   111111111
Name   Taxpayer Number

7000006570746   12 MONTHS $2,800.00
Account Number   Initial Term   Amount

TWO THOUSAND EIGHT HUNDRED DOLLARS AND 00 CENTS
Amount Written Out

4.000%   4.06%   TO THIS ACCOUNT QUARTERLY
Interest Rate   Annual Percentage Yield   Payable

SEMINARY PLAZA   6471   ALEXANDRIA VA
Branch Name   RU#   City/State

The Annual Percentage Yield assumes interest remains on deposit until maturity. A withdrawal will reduce earnings.

By signing this:
■ You acknowledge the receipt of a copy of the Rules and Regulations For Savings Certificates and accept the terms described therein.
■ You understand this time deposit is subject to such Rules and Regulations and as amended from time to time.
■ You acknowledge that the Bank's statement of early withdrawal penalities for time deposits was called to your attention. If this Savings Certificate is designated as a No Penalty certificate, one penalty-free withdrawal of all or part of your deposit may be made after funds have been on deposit seven (7) calendar days.
■ You understand that this Savings Certificate will renew automatically for like successive periods unless you redeem this certificate on the maturity date or within ten (10) calendar days beginning with the maturity date. Certificates which earn a fixed rate of interest will renew at the interest rate in effect on the maturity date. For variable rate certificates which have a floor rate, the rate in effect on the maturity date will be the floor rate for the renewal term.
■ If joint, this Savings Certificate shall be a (choose one):

(   ) Joint account with survivorship (See Rules and Regulations)   (   ) Joint account with no survivorship

Virginia A. Jenkins
Signature   Signature

Signature   Signature

Estate or Trust Account Certification

I hereby certify that I am the executor/executrix or administrator/administratrix or trustee of the Estate/Trust of

_____ ("Estate"/"Trust"). I also hereby certify

that all beneficiaries of the Estate/Trust, irrespective of any possible remainder interests or powers of appointments,

are natural persons. In Witness thereof, this _____ day of _____, 19 _____.

Signature   Signature

Prepared By *Angela Nut*   Authorized By *CB*

Non-Transferable - Initial Deposit Receipt
Member FDIC

SCT-0200 PC (7/93)   COPY 1:   CUSTOMER

Courtesy of First Virginia Bank, Arlington

FIGURE 18-1   Certificate of Deposit

count at any time without penalty, although normally a limit of only two or three checks per month can be written on the account without charge. The interest rate on the money-market account may change daily, weekly, or monthly, whereas the rate on the CD remains the same throughout the term.

Historically, the rates that financial institutions paid to depositors were controlled by federal regulations. The phasing out of those rates caused increased competition among financial institutions for investors' deposits, and the rates now fluctuate with the general economic climate. The mid-1980s and early 1990s experienced an extreme drop in interest rates overall, however, despite competition, and rates still remain low compared to earlier years. The standard by which interest rates are compared is known as the **prime rate**—the lowest rate that large financial institutions charge their "best" customers for loans. Investors earn somewhat less than the prime rate on deposits, and small borrowers pay considerably more than the prime rate when they take out loans or mortgages.

Problems in the preceding section of this chapter demonstrated the advantage of more frequent compounding. Thus, if two accounts offer $5\frac{1}{4}\%$ interest, but one compounds daily and the other compounds quarterly, the depositor would earn slightly more interest in the account compounded daily. (Most CDs have their interest compounded quarterly, even though the CD is for a longer period of time.)

While computing the problems in Section 1, it no doubt became obvious to you that this procedure can become quite long and tedious. Compound amount can also be found using the formula

$$M = P(1 + i)^n$$

where M = compound amount, P = original principal, i = interest rate per period, and n = number of periods.

Example 1   (a) Using the formula for compound amount, compute the compound amount and compound interest on $1,000 invested for 3 years at 8% compounded semiannually.

$$P = \$1,000 \qquad\qquad M = P(1 + i)^n$$

$$i = 4\% \text{ per period} \qquad = \$1,000(1 + 4\%)^6$$

$$n = 6 \text{ periods} \qquad = 1,000(1 + 0.04)^6$$

$$M = ? \qquad\qquad M = 1,000(1.04)^6$$

Recall that the exponent (here, "6") tells how many times the factor 1.04 should be written down before being multiplied. Thus, 1.04 should be used as a factor 6 times:

$$M = \$1{,}000(1.04)^6$$

$$= 1{,}000\underbrace{(1.04)(1.04)(1.04)(1.04)(1.04)(1.04)}$$

$$= 1{,}000 \quad \times \quad (1.2653190\ldots)$$

$$= \cancel{1{,}000} \, (1.2653190\ldots)$$

$$M = \$1{,}265.32$$

Therefore, the maturity value (compound amount) would be $1,265.32. The compound interest is $1,265.32 − $1,000, or $265.32.

Even using this formula, however, the calculation of compound amount would still be quite tedious if the number of periods (the exponent) were very large. The computation is greatly simplified through the use of a compound amount table—a list of the values obtained when the parenthetical expression $(1 + i)$ is used as a factor for the indicated numbers of periods.

Example 1 (cont.)
(b) Using the compound amount formula and the table, rework part (a).

$$P = \$1{,}000 \qquad M = P(1 + i)^n$$

$$i = 4\% \qquad\qquad = \$1{,}000(1 + 4\%)^6$$

$$n = 6$$

To find compound amount, turn to Table C-18, Amount of 1 (at Compound Interest); Appendix C. Various interest rates per period are given at the top left-hand margin of each page; find the page headed by 4%. The lines of the columns correspond to the number of periods, and these are numbered on both the right-hand and left-hand sides of the page. Go down to line 6 (for 6 periods) of the Amount column on the 4% page and there read "1.2653190185"; this is the value of $(1.04)^6$. Now,

$$M = P(1 + i)^n \qquad\qquad I = M - P$$

$$= \$1{,}000(1 + 4\%)^6 \qquad\qquad = \quad \$1{,}265.32$$
$$\qquad\qquad\qquad\qquad\qquad\qquad\quad - \quad 1{,}000.00$$
$$= 1{,}000(1.2653190185) \qquad I = \quad \$\ \ 265.32$$

$$M = \$1{,}265.32$$

Note. The value in the table includes the "1" from the parenthetical expression $(1 + i)$. It is *not* correct to add "1" to the tabular value before multiplying by the principal. (Students should now review Section 1, "Accuracy of Computation," in Chapter 1, which demonstrates how many digits from the table must be used in order to ensure an answer correct to the nearest penny.)

Example 2   Find the compound amount and compound interest on $2,000 invested at 7% compounded quarterly for 6 years.

$$P = \$2,000 \qquad M = P(1 + i)^n \qquad\qquad I = M - P$$

$$i = 1\frac{3}{4}\% \qquad\quad = \$2,000\left(1 + 1\frac{3}{4}\%\right)^{24} \qquad \begin{aligned} &= \quad \$3,032.89 \\ &- \quad 2,000.00 \\ \hline I &= \quad \$1,032.89 \end{aligned}$$

$$n = 24 \qquad\qquad = 2,000(1.516443)$$

$$\qquad\qquad\qquad\quad = 3,032.886$$

$$\qquad\qquad M = \$3,032.89$$

After 6 years, the $2,000 investment would thus be worth $3,032.89, of which $1,032.89 is interest.

Example 3   Ray Copeland opened a savings account on April 1, 19X1, with a deposit of $800. The account paid 4% compounded quarterly. On October 1, 19X1, Ray closed that account and added enough additional money to purchase a $1,000 6-month CD earning interest at 6% compounded monthly. (a) How much more did Ray deposit on October 1? (b) What was the maturity value of his CD on April 1, 19X2? (c) How much total interest was earned?

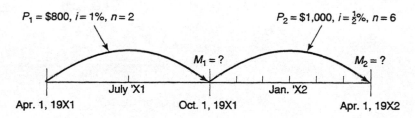

(a)   Banking quarters usually begin on the first days of January, April, July, and October. This means that Ray's $800 deposit earned interest for two quarters. Hence,

$$P_1 = \$800 \qquad M_1 = P(1 + i)^n \qquad\qquad \begin{aligned} \$1,000.00 \\ - \quad 816.08 \\ \hline \$\quad 183.92 \end{aligned} \text{ Additional}$$

$$i = 1\% \qquad\qquad = \$800(1 + 1\%)^2 \qquad\qquad\qquad\qquad\qquad \text{deposit}$$

$$n = 2 \qquad\qquad\quad = 800(1.020100)$$

$$\qquad\qquad\qquad = 816.080$$

$$\qquad\qquad M_1 = \$816.08$$

(b) On October 1, Ray's savings account had a closing balance of $816.08. An additional $183.92 was required to purchase a $1,000 CD. There were then 6 months (two quarters) until the CD matured on April 1, 19X2, during which time the $1,000 principal earned interest at 6% compounded monthly.

$$P_2 = \$1,000 \qquad M_2 = P(1 + i)^n$$

$$i = \frac{1}{2}\% \qquad = \$1,000\left(1 + \frac{1}{2}\%\right)^6$$

$$n = 6 \qquad = 1,000(1.030378)$$

$$= 1,030.378$$

$$M_2 = \$1,030.38$$

The maturity value of Ray's CD was $1,030.38 on April 1, 19X2.

(c) The total interest may be found in either of two ways:

1. By adding the interest paid on each of the principals.
2. By finding the difference between the final balance and the total of all deposits.

(1)

$I = M - P$	$I = M - P$		
$= \quad \$816.08$	$= \quad \$1,030.38$	$\$16.08$	Interest$_1$
$- \quad 800.00$	$- \quad 1,000.00$	$+ \quad 30.38$	Interest$_2$
$I_1 = \quad \$ \ 16.08$	$I_2 = \quad \$ \quad 30.38$	$\$46.46$	Total interest

(2)

$\$800.00$	Deposit$_1$	$\$1,030.38$	Final balance
$+ \ 183.92$	Deposit$_2$	$- \quad 983.92$	Total deposits
$\$983.92$	Total deposits	$\$ \quad 46.46$	Total interest

How Long Does It Take to Double an Investment?

For a sum of money invested at various interest rates compounded quarterly, the following table shows how long it takes to double (to the nearest quarter after the money doubles):

QUARTERLY RATE	YEARS TO DOUBLE	QUARTERLY RATE	YEARS TO DOUBLE	QUARTERLY RATE	YEARS TO DOUBLE
5%	14	$7\frac{1}{2}\%$	$9\frac{1}{2}$	10%	$7\frac{1}{4}$
$5\frac{1}{2}$	$12\frac{3}{4}$	8	9	$10\frac{1}{2}$	$6\frac{3}{4}$
6	$11\frac{3}{4}$	$8\frac{1}{2}$	$8\frac{1}{4}$	11	$6\frac{1}{2}$
$6\frac{1}{2}$	11	9	8	$11\frac{1}{2}$	$6\frac{1}{4}$
7	10	$9\frac{1}{2}$	$7\frac{1}{2}$	12	6

SECTION 2   PROBLEMS

1–6. Rework Problems 3–8 of Section 1 using the compound amount formula and Table C-18. (Some answers may vary by a few cents because the tables are not rounded off after each period.)

Compute the following compound amounts and compound interest, using Table C-18.

	PRINCIPAL	RATE	COMPOUNDED	YEARS
7. a.	$ 300	7%	Monthly	2
b.	6,400	8	Quarterly	4
c.	1,500	5	Semiannually	10
d.	4,800	9	Monthly	8
e.	900	10	Quarterly	6
8. a.	$ 500	5%	Monthly	3
b.	1,700	6	Quarterly	5
c.	3,200	7	Semiannually	6
d.	4,500	8	Monthly	4
e.	8,100	9	Quarterly	7

9. Compute compound amount and interest on the following investments at 6% compounded monthly for 2 years.
   a. $800   b. $1,600   c. $3,200   d. What conclusion can be reached about the principal?

10. Compute compound amount and interest on the following deposits at 5% compounded monthly for 3 years.
   a. $500   b. $1,000   c. $2,000   d. What can be concluded regarding the principal?

11. Determine compound amount and interest on $1,000 earning interest compounded quarterly for 4 years at the following rates:
   a. 3%   b. 6%   c. 12%   d. Does doubling the rate exactly double the interest?

12. Calculate compound amount and interest on $1,000 drawing interest compounded semiannually for 2 years at the following rates:
   a. $3\frac{1}{2}$%   b. 7%   c. 14%   d. Does doubling the rate exactly double the interest?

13. Compute compound amount and interest on $1,000 at 9% compounded semiannually for
   a. 5 years   b. 10 years   c. 20 years   d. Does the interest exactly double when the time is doubled?

14. Determine compound amount and interest on $1,000 at 6% compounded semiannually for
   a. 2 years   b. 4 years   c. 8 years   d. Does the interest exactly double when the time is doubled?

15. Mike Bracy opened a savings account on January 1, 19X1, with a deposit of $800. The account earned interest at 5% compounded quarterly.
   a. What was the value of his account on October 1, 19X1?
   b. On October 1, 19X1, Mike deposited enough money to make his account total $1,000. What amount did he deposit?

   c. How much was Mike's account worth on July 1, 19X2?

   d. How much total interest did Mike earn?

16. On January 1, 19X6, Patricia Humble opened a savings account with a deposit of $1,000. Her bank paid 4% interest compounded quarterly.

   a. What was the value of Humble's account on July 1, 19X6?

   b. On that day, Humble made a deposit sufficient to bring the value of the account to $1,200. What amount did she deposit?

   c. How much was her account worth on July 1, 19X7?

   d. How much total interest did her account earn?

17. On January 2, Tom Ford purchased a $1,000, 90-day CD earning interest at 6% compounded monthly.

   a. What was the maturity value of the CD?

   b. On April 2, Ford added enough money to buy a $1,500, 6-month CD that paid interest at 7% compounded quarterly. How much was his additional deposit?

   c. What was the maturity value of the second CD?

   d. What total amount of interest did the two CDs earn?

18. On March 1, Elena Ticer purchased a $1,000, 90-day CD earning interest at 5% compounded monthly.

   a. What was the maturity value of the CD?

   b. On June 1, Ticer added enough money to purchase a $1,400, 1-year CD that paid interest at 6% compounded quarterly. How much was her additional deposit?

   c. What was the maturity value of this 1-year CD?

   d. How much total interest did Ticer earn?

19. On July 3, 19X1, Sarah Hodges purchased a $1,000, 6-month CD that earned 7% compounded monthly.

   a. What was the maturity value of this CD?

   b. On January 3, 19X2, Sarah added enough money to purchase a $1,300, 2-year CD paying 8% compounded quarterly. How much additional money was deposited?

   c. What was the maturity value of this 2-year CD?

   d. How much interest was earned on the two CDs?

20. On May 1, Ed Grant purchased a $1,000, 6-month CD that earned interest at 5% compounded monthly.

   a. What was the maturity value of the CD?

   b. On November 1, Grant added enough funds to purchase a $1,400 2-year CD paying 7% compounded quarterly. How much additional deposit was made?

   c. What was the maturity value of this 2-year CD?

   d. How much interest was earned on the two CDs?

SECTION 3
INTEREST COMPOUNDED DAILY

Financial institutions also pay "daily interest" (interest compounded daily) on all open accounts where deposits or withdrawals may be made at any time.

That is, financial institutions pay interest for the exact number of days that money has been on deposit.

Interest on deposits is compounded daily, but to eliminate excessive book-keeping, most institutions enter interest in the depositor's account only once each quarter. For this reason, a daily interest table contains factors for one quarter. In accordance with the practice followed by most savings institutions, it is a 90-day quarter; deposits made on the 31st of any month earn interest as if they were made on the 30th. Recall that quarters begin in January, April, July, and October.

Interest on Deposits

As pointed out in the preceding section, interest rates on deposits in savings accounts and regular CDs have remained low in recent years, despite the termination of federal regulations controlling them.

Our study will be limited to $4\frac{1}{2}\%$ interest compounded daily, which approximates the historic passbook interest rate. Interest is found by multiplying the principal (deposit) times the appropriate value from Table C-16, Interest from Day of Deposit, Appendix C. That is,

$$\text{Interest} = \text{Principal} \times \text{Deposit table}$$

which might be abbreviated

$$I = P \times \text{Dep. tab.}$$

In the daily interest deposit table, there is a column for each of the three months of the quarter; each column (month) contains entries for 30 days. To use the table, you look for the date on which a deposit was made; the factor beside that date is the number to be multiplied by the amount of deposit in order to obtain the interest (provided the money remained on deposit until the quarter ended).

Example 1 Find the interest that would be earned at $4\frac{1}{2}\%$ compounded daily, if $1,000 were deposited in a savings and loan association on July 17.

July is the first month of the quarter; therefore, we refer to the "1st Month" column of the deposit table and to the 17th line under that heading:

$$I = P \times \text{Dep. tab.}$$

$$= \$1,000(0.0092923)$$

$$= \ \ 9.2923$$

$$I = \$9.29$$

When the quarter ends, interest of $9.29 will be added to the depositor's account, bringing the total to $1,009.29.

Example 2   Richard Chiles has an account in a financial institution where deposits earn interest at $4\frac{1}{2}$% compounded daily. When the quarter began on January 1, Chiles's account contained $1,000. During the quarter, he made deposits of $200 on February 7 and $300 on March 13. (a) How much interest will the account earn during the quarter? (b) What will be the balance in Chiles's account at the end of the quarter?

For any deposits made after a quarter begins, interest must be computed separately for each deposit. The total interest for the quarter is the sum of all interest for the various deposits.

(a)   Chiles's initial balance of $1,000 will earn interest for the entire quarter:

$$I = P \times \text{Dep. tab.}$$

$$= \$1{,}000(0.0113128)$$

$$= 11.3128$$

$$I = \$11.31$$

The $200 deposit on February 7 would earn interest from the 7th day of the second month:

$$I = P \times \text{Dep. tab.}$$

$$= \$200(0.0067724)$$

$$= 1.35448$$

$$I = \$1.35$$

Interest on the $300 deposit made March 13 (the third month) is

$$I = P \times \text{Dep. tab.}$$

$$= \$300(0.0022524)$$

$$= 0.67572$$

$$I = \$0.68$$

The transactions for the entire quarter would thus be summarized as follows:

Principal	Interest
$1,000	$11.31
200	1.35
+ 300	+ 0.68
$1,500 +	$13.34 = $1,513.34 Balance, end of quarter

The account would earn total interest of $13.34 during the quarter.

(b)   Chiles's account would have a balance of $1,513.34 at the end of the quarter.

INTEREST ON WITHDRAWALS

When withdrawals are involved, interest may be calculated in the following manner:

1. Subtract the withdrawals from the opening principal. Compute interest on this remaining balance for the entire quarter.

2. Determine the interest that would be earned on the withdrawn funds until the date they were withdrawn. This interest is found as follows, using Table C-17, Interest to Day of Withdrawal, Appendix C:

$$Interest = Withdrawal \times Withdrawal\ table$$

which may be abbreviated

$$I = W \times W/D\ tab.$$

(The daily interest withdrawal table is similar to the daily interest deposit table in that it is divided into the 3 months of the quarter, and you use the factor beside the appropriate date.)

3. Total interest for the quarter is the sum of the various amounts of interest found in steps 1 and 2.

Example 3   On July 1, a savings account in a credit union contained $1,250. A withdrawal of $250 was made on September 15. (a) How much interest did the account earn for the quarter, if interest was paid at $4\frac{1}{2}\%$ compounded daily? (b) What was the ending balance in the account?

(a)   Since $250 was withdrawn from the $1,250 account, only $1,000 earned interest for the entire quarter. In Example 2 we found that the interest on $1,000 for one quarter is $11.31.

Next, we compute interest on the $250 between the beginning of the quarter and September 15, when the funds were withdrawn. Since September is the third month of the quarter, we use the 15th line in the "3rd Month" column in the withdrawal table:

$$I = W \times W/D \text{ tab.}$$

$$= \$250(0.0094185)$$

$$= 2.3546$$

$$I = \$2.35$$

The $250 will earn interest of $2.35 before it is withdrawn on September 15. Total interest for the quarter is thus

Interest

$$\begin{array}{r} \$11.31 \\ +\ \ \underline{2.35} \\ \$13.66 \quad \text{Total interest for the quarter} \end{array}$$

(b) The balance in this account at the end of the quarter was

Opening balance	$1,250.00	
Withdrawal	− 250.00	
	$1,000.00	
Interest	+ 13.66	
	$1,013.66	Balance, end of quarter

Example 4 Compute the (a) interest and (b) balance at the end of the quarter after the following transactions, when daily interest is compounded at $4\frac{1}{2}\%$.

Balance	April 1	$1,800
Withdrawal	May 18	200
Deposit	June 14	400
Withdrawal	June 21	200

(a) The account would earn interest on $1,800 for the entire quarter, if there had been no withdrawals. Since there were two withdrawals of $200, however, only $1,800 − $400, or $1,400 will earn interest for the whole quarter:

Withdrawals

May 18	$200	Opening balance	$1,800
June 21	200	Withdrawals	− 400
	$400	Principal earning interest for entire quarter	$1,400

Interest for the quarter is thus computed as follows:

$1,400 principal for entire quarter:	$400 deposit on June 14 (third month):
$I = P \times$ Dep. tab.	$I = P \times$ Dep. tab.
$= \$1,400(0.0113128)$	$= \$400(0.0021271)$
$= 15.8379$	$= 0.8508$
$I = \$15.84$	$I = \$0.85$

The following interest was earned prior to the two withdrawals:

$200 withdrawal on May 18 (second month):	$200 withdrawal on June 21 (third month):
$I = W \times$ W/D tab.	$I = W \times$ W/D tab.
$= \$200(0.0060177)$	$= \$200(0.0101758)$
$= 1.2035$	$= 2.0352$
$I = \$1.20$	$I = \$2.04$

Thus, total interest for the quarter is

	Interest
Interest on funds on deposit for entire quarter	$15.84
Interest on $400 deposited June 14	0.85
Interest on $200 withdrawn May 18	1.20
Interest on $200 withdrawn June 21	2.04
Total interest for quarter	$19.93

(b)   The balance after the quarter ended would be

Deposits   *Withdrawals*

$400	$200	Opening balance	$1,800.00
	200	Deposits	+ 400.00
	$400		$2,200.00
		Withdrawals	− 400.00
			$1,800.00
		Interest	+ 19.93
		Balance,	$1,819.93
		end of quarter	

The savings account would contain $1,819.93 after the quarter ended.

SECTION 3   PROBLEMS

The following problems are all for interest paid at $4\frac{1}{2}$% compounded daily. Find (1) the amount of interest and (2) the balance at the end of the quarter for the following deposits.

1. a. $1,000 on April 15   b. $500 on September 5   c. $1,500 on February 21
   d. $2,000 on October 10

2. a. $1,000 on May 3   b. $800 on July 6   c. $4,000 on September 16   d. $600 on October 8

Compute the interest that would be earned for one quarter (1) at $4\frac{1}{2}$% compounded daily and (2) at $4\frac{1}{2}$% compounded quarterly on the given principals. The factor for $4\frac{1}{2}$% compounded quarterly for one quarter is 0.01125.

3. a. $10,000   b. $4,500

4. a. $7,500   b. $12,000

Find (1) the total amount of interest and (2) the balance after the quarter ended for the following accounts.

OPENING BALANCE	DEPOSITS
5. a. $1,000 on July 1	$ 300 on July 5
	$ 200 on August 21
	$ 400 on September 9
b. $3,700 on April 1	$ 500 on April 6
	$1,000 on May 15
	$ 600 on June 24
6. a. $700 on October 1	$ 500 on October 22
	$ 300 on November 15
	$ 400 on December 5
b. $600 on January 1	$ 200 on January 30
	$ 400 on February 13
	$ 300 on March 9

Compute (1) the interest for the quarter and (2) the balance when the quarter ended for the following problems.

	OPENING BALANCE	WITHDRAWALS
7. a.	$7,400 on January 1	$300 on March 8
b.	$6,800 on October 1	$400 on October 15
		$200 on November 20
8. a.	$10,000 on April 1	$1,000 on May 4
b.	$5,500 on July 1	$100 on August 10
		$400 on September 1

Transactions for an entire quarter are given below. Calculate (1) the total interest each account would earn and (2) the balance in each account after the quarter ends.

	OPENING BALANCE	DEPOSITS	WITHDRAWALS
9. a.	$3,500 on January 1	$ 400 on January 18	$ 200 on March 3
b.	$5,500 on October 1	$ 200 on November 6	$ 400 on October 8
		$ 100 on December 8	$ 300 on December 23
c.	$8,800 on April 1	$ 300 on April 8	$ 200 on April 29
		$ 100 on May 26	$1,000 on June 1
10. a.	$5,600 on October 1	$ 500 on October 30	$1,000 on November 11
b.	$4,900 on January 1	$ 800 on February 5	$ 600 on January 15
		$1,000 on March 12	$ 400 on March 20
c.	$5,100 on April 1	$ 400 on April 8	$ 200 on April 27
		$ 100 on May 9	$ 900 on June 20

SECTION 4
PRESENT VALUE (AT COMPOUND INTEREST)

It often happens that someone wishes to know how much would have to be deposited now (at the present) in order to obtain a certain maturity value. The principal that would have to be deposited is the **present value.**

The formula for obtaining present value at compound interest is a variation of the compound amount formula. The formula is rearranged to solve for P rather than M, by dividing both sides of the equation by the parenthetical expression $(1 + i)^n$:

$$M = P(1 + i)^n$$

$$\frac{M}{(1 + i)^n} = \frac{P\cancel{(1 + i)^n}}{\cancel{(1 + i)^n}}$$

$$\frac{M}{(1 + i)^n} = P$$

or, reversing the order,

$$P = \frac{M}{(1 + i)^n}$$

Therefore, present value could be found by dividing the known maturity value M by the appropriate value from the compound amount table (Table C-18) that we have already been using. However, division using such long decimal numbers would be extremely tedious (without a calculator); hence, present value tables have been developed which allow present value to be computed by multiplication.

Just as $\frac{12}{3} = 12 \cdot \frac{1}{3}$, so

$$\frac{M}{(1 + i)^n} = M \cdot \frac{1}{(1 + i)^n}$$

The entries in Table C-21, Present Value, Appendix C, are the quotients obtained when the numbers from the compound amount table are divided into 1. These quotients (the present value entries) can then be multiplied by the appropriate maturity value to obtain the present value.

Since present value is usually computed using multiplication, the formula is commonly written in a form that indicates multiplication and uses a negative exponent. Recall that a negative exponent indicates that the factor actually belongs in the opposite part of the fraction. $\left(\text{That is, } 3x^{-2} \text{ means } \frac{3}{x^2}. \right)$ Thus,

$$P = \frac{M}{(1 + i)^n}$$

is usually written

$$P = M(1 + i)^{-n}$$

The following examples will illustrate that present value may be found using either the compound amount table (Table C-18) or the present value table (Table C-21). As a general rule, however, you should use the present value table when computing present value at compound interest.

Example 1   An investment made for 6 years at 9% compounded monthly is to have a maturity value of $1,000. Determine the present value using (a) the compound amount table (Table C-18) and (b) the present value table (Table C-21). Also, (c) find how much interest will be included.

(a) $M = \$1,000$ $\qquad P = \dfrac{M}{(1 + i)^n}$

$i = \dfrac{3}{4}\%$ $\qquad\qquad = \dfrac{\$1,000}{\left(1 + \dfrac{3}{4}\%\right)^{72}}$

$n = 72$

$P = ?$ $\qquad\qquad = \dfrac{\$1,000}{1.712553}$

$\qquad\qquad\qquad = 583.924$

$\qquad\qquad\quad P = \$583.92$

(b) $P = M(1 + i)^{-n}$ $\qquad\qquad$ (c) $I = M - P$

$\qquad = \$1,000\left(1 + \dfrac{3}{4}\%\right)^{-72}$ $\qquad\qquad = \quad \$1,000.00$
$\qquad\qquad\qquad\qquad\qquad\qquad\qquad\qquad -\quad\underline{\quad 583.92}$
$\qquad\qquad\qquad\qquad\qquad\qquad\qquad I = \quad\$\ \ 416.08$

$\qquad = 1,000(0.583924)$

$\qquad P = \$583.92$

Thus, $583.92 invested now at 9% compounded monthly will earn $416.08 interest and mature to $1,000 after 6 years.

Example 2 Charles and Sue Baker would like to have $6,000 in 4 years for a down payment on a condominium. (a) What single deposit would have this maturity value if CDs earn 7% compounded quarterly? (b) How much of the final amount will be interest?

(a) $M = \$6,000$ $\qquad P = M(1 + i)^{-n}$ $\qquad\qquad$ (b) $I = M - P$

$n = 16$ $\qquad\qquad = \$6,000\left(1 + 1\dfrac{3}{4}\%\right)^{-16}$ $\qquad\qquad = \quad\$6,000.00$
$\qquad\qquad\qquad\qquad\qquad\qquad\qquad\qquad\qquad\qquad -\quad\underline{4,545.70}$
$i = 1\dfrac{3}{4}\%$ $\qquad\qquad\qquad\qquad\qquad\qquad\qquad\qquad I = \quad\$1,454.30$
$\qquad\qquad\qquad = 6,000(0.7576163)$

$P = ?$ $\qquad\qquad\quad = 4,545.698$

$\qquad\qquad P = \$4,545.70$

If the Bakers purchase a $4,545.70 CD now, it will earn interest of $1,454.30 during 4 years at 7% compounded quarterly and have a $6,000 maturity value.

As was true of simple interest problems, present value (or present worth) may on occasion differ from principal. The actual amount of money that is invested is always the principal; it may or may not be invested at the interest rate currently being paid by most financial institutions. The present value of the investment is the amount that would have to be invested at the rate money is worth (the rate being paid by most financial institutions) in order to obtain the same maturity value that the actual investment will have. If an investment is sold before its maturity date, it should theoretically be sold for its present value at that time.

Example 3   Arthur Levy made a $12,000 real estate investment that he expects will have a maturity value equivalent to interest at 8% compounded monthly for 5 years. If most savings institutions are currently paying 6% compounded quarterly on 5-year CDs, what is the least amount for which Levy should sell his property?

This is a two-part problem. We must first determine the maturity value of the $12,000 investment. Then, using the rate money is actually worth, we must compute the present worth of the maturity value obtained by step 1.

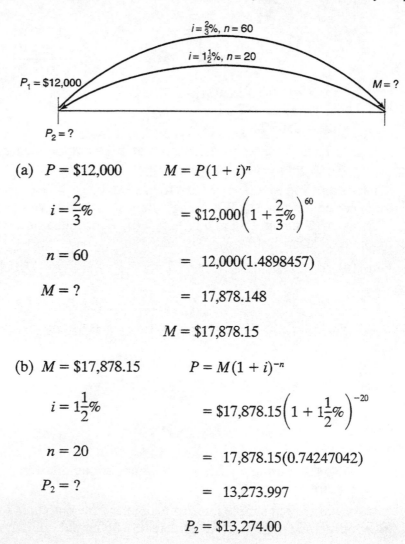

(a) $P = \$12,000$ $M = P(1 + i)^n$

$i = \dfrac{2}{3}\%$ $= \$12,000\left(1 + \dfrac{2}{3}\%\right)^{60}$

$n = 60$ $= 12,000(1.4898457)$

$M = ?$ $= 17,878.148$

                    $M = \$17,878.15$

(b) $M = \$17,878.15$ $P = M(1 + i)^{-n}$

$i = 1\dfrac{1}{2}\%$ $= \$17,878.15\left(1 + 1\dfrac{1}{2}\%\right)^{-20}$

$n = 20$ $= 17,878.15(0.74247042)$

$P_2 = ?$ $= 13,273.997$

                    $P_2 = \$13,274.00$

Levy should not sell the $12,000 property for less than $13,274, because he would have to purchase a CD of this value, paying interest at 6% compounded quarterly, in order to have $17,878.15 in 5 years.

Calculator Tip. For most calculators, the value of i that you use from the interest tables must be rounded to a maximum of 7 decimal places (or a maximum of 8 digits altogether). For instance, in part (b) of this example you would use (0.7424704). In most problems, your result will be within a cent or two of the correct answer. Frequently you will obtain exactly the same amount, to the nearest cent, which happens here.

SECTION 4   PROBLEMS

Compute present value at compound interest, using the data given in Problems 1 and 2. Also determine the amount of interest that will be earned before maturity.

	MATURITY VALUE	RATE	COMPOUNDED	YEARS
1. a.	$1,000	4%	Quarterly	9
b.	4,100	5	Monthly	6
c.	8,000	6	Semiannually	4
d.	1,500	7	Quarterly	15
e.	3,000	6	Monthly	8
2. a.	$3,200	4%	Semiannually	2
b.	2,500	5	Quarterly	5
c.	6,800	7	Monthly	4
d.	1,800	5	Semiannually	1
e.	4,400	6	Quarterly	3

3. Bradford and Maria Quinn want to have $50,000 in savings when their son graduates from high school in 12 years. If their bank will pay 7% compounded quarterly on long-term CDs,
   a. What single deposit now will obtain their goal?
   b. How much interest will their investment earn during this time?
4. Bill and Beth Reno want to have $5,000 in savings in 1 year for a family vacation. If they can make an investment that pays 6% compounded monthly,
   a. How much should the Renos invest now in order to have this maturity value?
   b. How much interest will their investment earn?
5. The Chavez Co. plans to replace its office furniture in 3 years. The business wants to have $30,000 available for this project.
   a. What single deposit must be made now in a 3-year CD that earns 6% interest compounded monthly?
   b. How much interest will the CD earn?
6. The Capitol Plumbing Co. plans to increase the size of its warehouse in 2 years. The business will need $75,000 for the project.

a. What single deposit must be made now in an investment earning 8% interest compounded quarterly?

b. How much interest will the investment earn?

7. Kent Construction Co. expects to expand its operations into other cities in 3 years at a cost of $80,000. Its bank pays 8% interest compounded quarterly.

a. What single deposit now would produce this maturity value?

b. How much interest will be included?

8. Dominion Rentals, Inc., expects to remodel its offices in 6 years at a cost of $100,000. If the company can make an investment paying 9% compounded semiannually,

a. What single deposit made now will produce this maturity value?

b. How much interest will be included?

9. A $6,000 investment is made at 5% compounded semiannually for a 5-year period.

a. What is the maturity value of the investment? (Round the maturity value to the nearest $10 for use in part b.)

b. If money is generally worth 4% compounded quarterly, what is the present value of the investment?

10. A $7,000 investment is made at 6% compounded quarterly for a 4-year period.

a. What is the maturity value of the investment? (Round the maturity value to the nearest $10 for use in part b.)

b. If money is generally worth 5% compounded monthly, what is the present value of the investment?

11. Simon Chong is the payee of a 5-year, 10% simple interest note for $5,400. Money invested in a 5-year CD is worth 6% compounded quarterly.

a. How much will be due when the note matures?

b. If Simon had sold the note on the day it was drawn, how much would he have received?

12. Maggie Clifford is the payee of a 2-year, 11% simple interest note for $6,000. Most financial institutions are currently paying 7% compounded monthly.

a. How much will be the maturity value of the note?

b. How much would Maggie have received if she had sold the note on the day it was originated?

13. A 9% simple interest rate was earned on a 6-month CD for $10,000. Savings accounts are earning 5% compounded monthly.

a. What will be the maturity value of the CD?

b. Using the savings account rate, what is the present worth of the CD?

14. A $5,000, 1-year CD was purchased at a 9% simple interest rate.

a. What maturity value will the CD have?

b. If inflation is increasing at a rate equivalent to 6% compounded monthly (the rate money is worth), what was the value of the CD on the day it was purchased?

CHAPTER *18* GLOSSARY

Certificate of deposit (CD). A savings contract that offers a slightly higher rate when a (usually $1,000 minimum) deposit is made for a specified time period. (An early withdrawal would forfeit the higher rate.)

Compound amount.   The total value at the end of a compound interest investment (original principal plus all interest).

Compound interest.   Interest computed periodically and then added to the previous principal, so that this total then becomes the principal for the next interest period. "Interest earned on (previous) interest." The difference between final maturity value and original principal.

Conversion period.   A regular time interval at which interest is compounded (or computed and added to the previous principal). Interest is commonly compounded daily, monthly, quarterly, semiannually, or annually.

Money-market account.   A savings contract similar to a CD that pays higher interest rates than open accounts, permits the withdrawal of funds at any time, and allows up to three checks per month to be written.

Open account.   A savings account upon which deposits or withdrawals may be made at any time.

Period.   (See "Conversion period.")

Present value.   The amount of money that would have to be deposited (on some given date prior to maturity) in order to obtain a specified maturity value.

Prime rate.   The interest rate banks charge on loans to their "best" customers.

Statement account.   An open account for which the bank sends periodic statements showing transactions that have occurred since the last statement.

Term.   The length of time for a compound interest investment.

ANNUITIES

OBJECTIVES

Upon completion of Chapter 19, you will be able to:

1. Define and use correctly the terminology associated with each topic.

2. Determine amount and compound interest earned on an annuity, using the procedure $M = $ Pmt. $\times$ Amt. ann. tab.$_{\overline{n}|i}$ and the amount of annuity table (Section 1: Example 1; Problems 1–10).

3. **a.** Compute present value of an annuity, using the procedure P.V. = Pmt. $\times$ P.V. ann. tab.$_{\overline{n}|i}$ and the present value of annuity table. (That is, determine the original value required in order for one to withdraw the given annuity payments). (Section 2: Examples 1, 2; Problems 1–12).

b. Also, determine the total amount received and the interest included.

4. Use the same procedure (Objective 3) to determine (Section 2: Example 3, Problems 13–16):

a. The total amount paid for a real estate purchase

b. The equivalent cash price.

Notice that the compound interest problems in the previous chapter basically involved making a *single deposit* which remained invested for the entire time. There are few people, however, who have large sums available to invest in this manner. Most people must attain their savings goals by making a series of regular deposits. This leads to the idea of annuities.

An **annuity** is a series of payments (normally equal in amount) that are made at regular intervals of time. Most people think of an annuity as the regular payment received from an insurance policy when it is cashed in after retirement. This is one good example, but there are many other everyday examples that are seldom thought of as annuities. Besides savings deposits, other common examples are rent, salaries, Social Security payments, installment plan payments, loan payments, insurance payments—in fact, any payment made at regular intervals of time.

There are several time variables that may affect an annuity. For instance, some annuities have definite beginning and ending dates; such an annuity is called an **annuity certain.** Examples of an annuity certain are installment plan payments or the payments from a life insurance policy converted to an annuity of a specified number of years.

If the beginning and/or ending dates are uncertain, the annuity is called a **contingent annuity.** Monthly Social Security retirement benefits and the payments on an ordinary life insurance policy are examples of contingent annuities for which the ending dates are unknown, because both will terminate when the person dies. If a person provides in a will that following death a beneficiary is to receive an annuity for a fixed number of years, this is a contingent annuity for which the beginning date is uncertain. A man with a large estate might provide that his surviving wife receive a specified yearly income for the remainder of her life and that the balance then be donated to some charity; this contingent annuity would then be uncertain on both the beginning and ending dates.

Another factor affecting annuities is whether the payment is made at the beginning of each time interval (such as rent and insurance premiums, which are normally paid in advance) or at the end of the period (such as salaries and Social Security retirement benefits). An annuity for which payments are made at the beginning of each period is known as an **annuity due.** When payments come at the end of each period, the annuity is called an **ordinary annuity.**

We shall be studying *investment annuities*—annuities that earn compound interest (rather than rent or installment payments, for example, which earn no interest). An annuity is said to be a **simple annuity** when the date of payment coincides with the conversion date of the compound interest.

The study of contingent annuities requires some knowledge of probability, which is not within the scope of this text. Thus, since our purpose is just to give you a basic introduction to annuities, our study of annuities will be limited to simple, ordinary annuities certain—annuities for which both the beginning and ending dates are fixed, and for which the payments are made on the conversion date at the end of each period.

SECTION 1
AMOUNT OF AN ANNUITY

The **amount of an annuity** is the maturity value that an account will have after a series of equal payments into it. As in the case of other compound interest problems, amount of an annuity is usually found by using the appropriate table for the appropriate rate per period and the number of periods. Thus, we shall compute amount of an annuity by using Table C-19, Amount of Annuity, Appendix C, and the following procedure:

$$\text{Amount} = \text{Payment} \times \text{Amount of annuity table}_{\overline{n}|i}$$

where n = number of periods and i = interest rate per period. For simplicity, the procedure* might be abbreviated as

$$M = \text{Pmt.} \times \text{Amt. ann. tab.}_{\overline{n}|i}$$

The total amount of deposits is found by multiplying the periodic payment times the number of periods. Total interest earned is then the difference between the maturity value and the total deposits made into the account.

Example 1 (a) Determine the amount (maturity value) of an annuity if Leonard Feldman deposits $100 each quarter for 6 years into an account earning 8% compounded quarterly. (b) How much of this total will Feldman deposit himself? (c) How much of the final amount is interest?

(a)   (Notice that deposits are made each quarter to coincide with the interest conversion date at the bank; we would not be able to compute the annuity if they were otherwise.)

Pmt. = $100	$M = \text{Pmt.} \times \text{Amt. ann. tab.}_{\overline{n}|i}$
$n = 24$	$= \$100 \times \text{Amt. ann. tab.}_{\overline{24}|2\%}$
$i = 2\%$	$= 100(30.42186)$
	$= 3{,}042.186$
	$M = \$3{,}042.19$

Feldman's account will contain $3,042.19 after 6 years.

---

* Many texts give the procedure for amount of an annuity in the form $M = Pm_{\overline{n}|i}$, where M = maturity value, P = payment, and $m_{\overline{n}|i}$ indicates use of the amount of annuity table. Strictly speaking, $M = Pm_{\overline{n}|i}$ is also a procedure, not a formula. The actual formula is $M = P \times \dfrac{(1+i)^n - 1}{i}$.

(b) There will be 24 deposits of $100 each, totaling 24 × $100 or $2,400.

(c) The interest earned during this annuity period is

Amount of annuity	$3,042.19
Total deposits	− 2,400.00
Interest	$ 642.19

SECTION 1 PROBLEMS

Using the amount-of-annuity procedure, find the maturity value that would be obtained if one makes the payments given below. Also determine the total deposits and the total interest earned. Assume that all problems are ordinary annuities, where payments are made at the end of the period, as in Table C-19.

		PERIODIC PAYMENT	RATE	COMPOUNDED	YEARS
1.	a.	$ 200	7%	Semiannually	4
	b.	400	6	Monthly	5
	c.	400	8	Quarterly	8
	d.	1,000	9	Monthly	6
	e.	1,200	5	Semiannually	10
2.	a.	$ 500	6%	Quarterly	7
	b.	800	7	Quarterly	3
	c.	300	8	Semiannually	8
	d.	1,500	5	Quarterly	6
	e.	1,100	6	Monthly	3

3. Edwin Brice deposited $200 each quarter for 3 years into his savings account which paid 6% compounded quarterly.

a. What was the value of his account after 3 years?

b. How much did Mr. Brice invest?

c. How much interest was earned?

4. Erin Anderson deposited $500 each quarter for 2 years into a savings account that paid 7% compounded quarterly.

a. What was the value of her account after 2 years?

b. How much had actually been deposited?

c. How much interest was earned?

5. Maria James deposits $100 every month into an account that earns 5% compounded monthly.

a. What will be the value of her account after 6 years?

b. How much of this total will Ms. James have invested herself?

c. How much interest will her account have earned?

6. Paul Smith Mattress Co. invested $500 each month into an account that earned 6% compounded monthly.

   a. How much was the company's account worth in 5 years?

   b. How much of the total had the company deposited?

   c. How much was interest?

7. The grandparents of Lizzy Grieves deposited $500 into her savings account each year for 15 years. The account earned 5% compounded annually.

   a. How much did they deposit altogether?

   b. What was the amount in the account after the 15th deposit?

   c. How much interest was earned during this time?

8. Strickland Printing Co. invested $6,000 each year for 5 years into an account earning 8% compounded annually.

   a. How much did the company invest in 5 years?

   b. What was the maturity value of the annuity?

   c. How much interest did the annuity earn?

9. The Waters Corp. invested $5,000 each quarter for 4 years into an account paying 8% compounded quarterly.

   a. How much did Waters invest during this time?

   b. What was the amount in the account after the 4th year?

   c. How much interest did they earn?

10. Jones Telecommunications, Inc., invested $8,000 each quarter for 5 years into an account paying 6% compounded quarterly.

    a. How much did the company invest?

    b. What was the amount in the account after 5 years?

    c. How much interest did the maturity value include?

SECTION 2
PRESENT VALUE OF AN ANNUITY

Observe that our study of amount of an annuity involved starting with an empty account and making payments into it so that the account contained its largest amount at the end of the term. The study of present value of an annuity is exactly the reverse: The account contains its largest balance at the beginning of the term and someone receives payments from the account until it is empty. This balance which an account must contain at the beginning of the term is the **present value** or **present worth of an annuity.**

Rather than studying the actual formula for present value of an annuity, we will use an informal procedure as we did for amount of an annuity. By consulting Table C-22, Present Value of Annuity, Appendix C, present value can be computed as follows:

$$\text{Present value} = \text{Payment} \times \text{Present value of annuity table}_{\overline{n}|i}$$

where, as before, n = number of payments and i = interest rate per period. The procedure* can be abbreviated

$$\text{P.V.} = \text{Pmt.} \times \text{P.V. ann. tab.}_{\overline{n}|i}$$

The total amount to be received from an annuity is found by multiplying the payment times the number of periods. As long as there are still funds in the account, it will continue to earn interest; thus, even though the balance of the account is declining during the term of the annuity, the account will still continue to earn some interest until the final payment is received. The total interest that the account will earn is found by subtracting the beginning balance (the present value) from the total payments to be received.

Example 1 Elaine Shaw wishes to receive a $100 annuity each quarter for 6 years while attending college and graduate school. Her account earns 8% compounded quarterly. (a) What must be the (present) value of Elaine's account when she starts college? (b) How much total will Elaine actually receive? (c) How much interest will these annuity payments include?

(a) $\text{Pmt.} = \$100$ $\quad\text{P.V.} = \text{Pmt.} \times \text{P.V. ann. tab.}_{\overline{n}|i}$

$\quad n = 24$ $\quad\quad\quad = \$100 \times \text{P.V. ann. tab.}_{\overline{24}|2\%}$

$\quad i = 2\%$ $\quad\quad\quad = 100(18.91393)$

$\quad\quad\quad\quad\quad\quad\quad = 1{,}891.393$

$\quad\quad\quad\quad\text{P.V.} = \$1{,}891.39$

Elaine's account must contain $1,891.39 when she enters college.

(b) She will receive 24 annuity payments of $100 each, for a total of $2,400.

(c) The account will earn interest of

Total payments	$2,400.00
Present value	− 1,891.39
Interest	$ 508.61

Thus, from an account containing $1,891.39, Elaine may withdraw $100 each quarter until a total of $2,400 has been withdrawn. During this time, the declining fund will have earned $508.61 interest. After the final payment is received, the balance in her account will be exactly $0.

---

* The procedure for present value of an annuity is often indicated as $A = Pa_{\overline{n}|i}$, where A = present value, P = payment, and $a_{\overline{n}|i}$ indicates use of the present value of annuity table.

Example 2   Grover Campbell would like to receive an annuity of $5,000 semiannually for 10 years after he retires; he will retire in 18 years. Money is worth 6% compounded semiannually. (a) How much must Campbell have when he retires in order to finance this annuity? (b) What single deposit made now would provide the funds for the annuity? (c) How much will Campbell actually receive in payments from the annuity? (d) How much interest will the single deposit earn before the annuity ends?

This is a two-part problem: (1) to find the beginning balance (present value) required for the 10-year annuity, and (2) to find what single deposit made now (present value at compound interest) would produce a maturity value equal to the answer obtained in step 1.

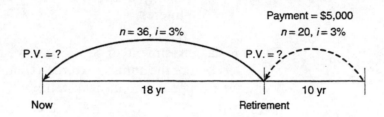

(a)   Pmt. = $5,000   P.V. = Pmt. $\times$ P.V. ann. tab.$_{\overline{n}|i}$

$n = 20$ = $5,000 $\times$ P.V. ann. tab.$_{\overline{20}|3\%}$

$i = 3\%$ = 5,000(14.877475)

                             = 74,387.375

                        P.V. = $74,387.38

The account must contain $74,387.38 at Campbell's retirement, in order for him to receive $5,000 each 6 months for 10 years.

(b)   We next find what single deposit, made now, would reach a maturity value of $74,387.38 when Campbell retires in 18 years.

$M = \$74,387.38$ $P = M(1 + i)^{-n}$

$n = 36$ = $74,387.38(1 + 3\%)^{-36}$

$i = 3\%$ = $74,387.38(0.3450324)$

                     = 25,666.056

                 $P = \$25,666.06$

A single deposit of $25,666.06 now will be worth $74,387.38 after 18 years at 6% compounded semiannually. Notice that $i = 0.3450324251$ was rounded to 7 decimal places in accordance with the Calculator Tip on p. 487.

(c) Campbell will receive 20 payments of $5,000 each, for a total of $100,000 during the term of his annuity.

(d) The total interest is the difference between what he will actually receive from the annuity ($100,000) and the original amount invested ($25,666.06):

Total received	$100,000.00
Principal invested	− 25,666.06
Interest	$ 74,333.94

The original investment of $25,666.06 would produce interest of $74,333.94 before the annuity expires. (Campbell will receive nearly 4 times the original amount invested.)

Equivalent Cash Price. Keep in mind that "present value" often refers to the value of an investment on the first day of the term. (It always refers to the value on some day prior to the maturity date.) This fact will help clarify the following example.

Example 3 A homebuyer made a down payment of $20,000 and will make payments of $7,500 semiannually for 25 years. Money is worth 7% compounded semiannually. (a) What would have been the equivalent cash price of the house? (b) How much will the buyer actually pay for the house?

(a) The "cash price" would have been the cost on the original day. This value on the beginning day of the term indicates that present value is required.

Cash price = Down payment + Present value of periodic payments

$$\text{Pmt.} = \$7,500 \qquad \text{P.V.} = \text{Pmt.} \times \text{P.V. ann. tab.}_{\overline{n}|i}$$

$$n = 50 \qquad = \$7,500 \times \text{P.V. ann. tab.}_{\overline{50}|3\frac{1}{2}\%}$$

$$i = 3\tfrac{1}{2}\% \qquad = 7,500(23.455618)$$

$$= 175,917.13$$

$$\text{P.V.} = \$175,917.13$$

(1) *Calculate the* amount *of an annuity (as in Section 1) and the interest included if one* makes deposits *as given below. Also, (2) determine the* present value *(as in Section 2) required in order to* receive *the given* annuity payments, *and the total interest that would be included in the annuity.*

		PAYMENT	RATE	COMPOUNDED	YEARS
3.	a.	$3,000	6%	Quarterly	6
	b.	4,000	5	Semiannually	8
	c.	5,000	7	Monthly	5
4.	a.	$6,000	8	Quarterly	8
	b.	300	7	Semiannually	12
	c.	4,900	6	Monthly	4

5. Janice Strauss wants to receive a quarterly annuity of $900 while she takes a 2-year nursing course. She has an investment paying 9% compounded quarterly.
   a. How much must she have in her investment account when the annuity begins?
   b. How much will the annuity pay?
   c. How much interest will she earn before the account is exhausted?

6. Bill Jefferson wishes to purchase an annuity of $450 quarterly for 3 years. If the current interest rate is 6% compounded quarterly,
   a. How much would be required to finance the annuity?
   b. How much will Jefferson actually receive from the annuity?
   c. How much total interest will the annuity include?

7. Susan Moody wants to receive an annuity of $300 a month during the first two years of her child's life. If money is compounded at 5% per month,
   a. How much must she have in a savings account to finance the annuity?
   b. How much will she receive over the life of the annuity?
   c. How much interest will the annuity payments include?

8. Sam Wallace wants to receive an annuity of $600 per quarter for a 2-year period. If his investment account pays 5% compounded quarterly,
   a. How much must Wallace have in his account to finance the annuity?
   b. How much will he actually receive from the annuity?
   c. How much interest will his investment earn?

   In problems 9–12, round your solution to each part to the nearest $100 for use in succeeding parts.

9. Jake and Greta Hogan want to receive a $6,000 annuity quarterly for 5 years after they retire. They can invest money at 6% compounded quarterly.
   a. How much money must the Hogans have when they retire in order to receive the annuity?
   b. The Hogans retire in 8 years. What single deposit could they make today in order to finance the annuity?
   c. How much interest will the account earn before the annuity ends?

(1) *Calculate the* amount *of an annuity (as in Section 1) and the interest included if one* makes deposits *as given below. Also,* (2) *determine the* present value *(as in Section 2) required in order to* receive *the given* annuity payments, *and the total interest that would be included in the annuity.*

		PAYMENT	RATE	COMPOUNDED	YEARS
3.	a.	$3,000	6%	Quarterly	6
	b.	4,000	5	Semiannually	8
	c.	5,000	7	Monthly	5
4.	a.	$6,000	8	Quarterly	8
	b.	300	7	Semiannually	12
	c.	4,900	6	Monthly	4

5. Janice Strauss wants to receive a quarterly annuity of $900 while she takes a 2-year nursing course. She has an investment paying 9% compounded quarterly.

   a. How much must she have in her investment account when the annuity begins?

   b. How much will the annuity pay?

   c. How much interest will she earn before the account is exhausted?

6. Bill Jefferson wishes to purchase an annuity of $450 quarterly for 3 years. If the current interest rate is 6% compounded quarterly,

   a. How much would be required to finance the annuity?

   b. How much will Jefferson actually receive from the annuity?

   c. How much total interest will the annuity include?

7. Susan Moody wants to receive an annuity of $300 a month during the first two years of her child's life. If money is compounded at 5% per month,

   a. How much must she have in a savings account to finance the annuity?

   b. How much will she receive over the life of the annuity?

   c. How much interest will the annuity payments include?

8. Sam Wallace wants to receive an annuity of $600 per quarter for a 2-year period. If his investment account pays 5% compounded quarterly,

   a. How much must Wallace have in his account to finance the annuity?

   b. How much will he actually receive from the annuity?

   c. How much interest will his investment earn?

   In problems 9–12, round your solution to each part to the nearest $100 for use in succeeding parts.

9. Jake and Greta Hogan want to receive a $6,000 annuity quarterly for 5 years after they retire. They can invest money at 6% compounded quarterly.

   a. How much money must the Hogans have when they retire in order to receive the annuity?

   b. The Hogans retire in 8 years. What single deposit could they make today in order to finance the annuity?

   c. How much interest will the account earn before the annuity ends?

10. Eric Walton wants to receive a $700 annuity semiannually for 4 years after he retires. He can invest his money at 8% compounded semiannually.

   a. What amount must be on deposit when he starts receiving the annuity?

   b. Walton will retire in 10 years. What single deposit must be made today to provide the funds for the annuity?

   c. How much interest will his deposit earn until the annuity ends?

11. Linn Yann wants to take a 2-year interior design course at the local college, starting in 3 years. During the time she is in school, she wants to receive an annuity of $200 per month. Money can be invested at 8% compounded monthly.

   a. What amount must be on deposit when she starts the courses in order to receive this annuity?

   b. How much would Linn Yann have to deposit today in order to provide for the annuity?

   c. How much interest will she earn before the annuity expires?

12. Jenny Miller plans to send her daughter to college in 6 years. Miller wants to provide for an annuity of $350 monthly during her daughter's 4 years in college. Her money can be invested at 6% compounded monthly.

   a. What amount must be on deposit when the daughter enters college in order to receive this annuity?

   b. How much would Miller have to deposit today in order to provide for the annuity?

   c. How much total interest will this deposit earn during the 10-year period?

13. The MacArthur Group, Inc., bought land for $50,000 down and monthly payments of $1,500 for 7 years.

   a. How much will MacArthur pay altogether for the land?

   b. What cash price invested at 9% compounded monthly would give the seller of the land the same total after 7 years that (s)he would have by depositing MacArthur's payments?

14. Cavett Enterprises purchased property for $25,000 down and monthly payments of $3,000 for 6 years.

   a. What was the total cost to the business?

   b. What cash price deposited at 10% compounded monthly would yield the seller of the property the same maturity value (s)he would have after 6 years of depositing Cavett's payments?

15. A family purchased a home by making a $10,000 down payment and payments of $6,000 quarterly for 20 years.

   a. What was the total cost of the home under this plan?

   b. What would have been the equivalent cash price, if money were worth 8% compounded quarterly?

16. A local area network (LAN) system was purchased by making a $5,000 down payment and quarterly payments of $2,000 for 3 years.

   a. What was the total cost of the LAN system?

   b. What would have been the equivalent cash price, if money were worth 9% compounded quarterly?

CHAPTER 19 GLOSSARY

Amount (of an annuity).   The maturity value of an account after a series of equal (annuity) payments into it.

Annuity.   A series of equal payments made at regular intervals of time (either with or without interest).

Annuity certain. An annuity with definite beginning and ending dates.

Annuity due. An annuity paid (or received) at the beginning of each time interval. (Example: Rent or insurance premiums.)

Contingent annuity. An annuity for which the beginning and/or ending dates are uncertain.

Ordinary annuity. An annuity paid (or received) at the end of each time period. (Example: Salaries or stock dividends.)

Present value (of an annuity). The beginning balance an account must contain in order to receive a given annuity from it.

Simple annuity. An annuity in which the date of payment coincides with the conversion date of the compound interest.

20

SINKING FUNDS AND AMORTIZATION

OBJECTIVES

Upon completion of Chapter 20, you will be able to:

1. Define and use correctly the terminology associated with each topic.

2. Using the procedure Pmt. = $M \times$ S.F. tab.$_{\overline{n}|i}$ and the sinking fund table, determine (Section 1: Example 1; Problems 1, 2, 5–10):

    a. The regular payment required to finance a sinking fund

    b. The total amount deposited

    c. The interest earned.

3. Prepare a sinking fund schedule to verify that the payments (Objective 2) will result in the required maturity value (Section 1: Example 2; Problems 13, 14).

4. Given the quoted price of a bond and its interest rate, determine its (Section 1: Examples 3, 4; Problems 3, 4, 11, 12):

    a. Purchase price   **b.** Premium or discount

    c. Annual interest   **d.** Current yield.

5. Using the procedure Pmt. = P.V. $\times$ Amtz. tab.$_{\overline{n}|i}$ and the amortization table, compute (Section 2: Examples 1, 2; Problems 1–14):

    a. The periodic payment required to amortize a loan

    b. The total amount paid

    c. The interest included.

6. Prepare an amortization schedule to verify that the payments (Objective 5) pay off the loan correctly (Section 2: Example 3; Problems 15, 16).

7. Explain the characteristics of the six basic types of compound interest and annuity problems (Section 3: Problems 1–24).

Far-sighted investors may wish to establish a savings plan whereby regular deposits will achieve a specified savings goal by a certain time. An account of this type is known as a *sinking fund.*

In the loan plans studied in previous chapters, either simple interest or simple discount was charged. For large loans that take many years to repay, however, ordinary simple interest would not be profitable to lenders, as later examples will show. Thus, long-term loans must be repaid in a series of payments that include all interest due since the previous payment. This loan repayment procedure is known as **amortization.**

Sinking funds and amortization are the subjects of the following sections; both topics involve finding a required periodic payment (or annuity).

SECTION 1
SINKING FUNDS AND BONDS

Section 1 of Chapter 19, on the amount of an annuity, dealt with making given periodic payments into an account (at compound interest) and finding what the maturity value of that account would be. It frequently happens that businesses know what amount will be needed on some future date and are concerned with determining what periodic payment (annuity) would have to be invested in order to obtain this amount.

When a special account is established so that the maturity value (equal periodic deposits plus compound interest) will exactly equal a specific amount, such a fund is called a **sinking fund.** Sinking funds are often used to finance the replacement of machinery, equipment, facilities, and so forth, or to finance the redemption of bonds.

Bonds are somewhat similar to promissory notes in that they are written promises to repay a specified debt on a certain date. Both notes and bonds earn simple interest. The primary difference is that interest on bonds is typically paid periodically, whereas the interest on a note is all repaid on the maturity date. Large corporations, municipalities, and state governments usually finance long-term improvements by selling bonds. (A term of 10 years or more is typical.) We shall be concerned first with setting up a sinking fund to provide the *face value* (or **par value** or redemption value) of the bonds at maturity, as well as sinking funds to provide significant maturity values for other purposes.

SINKING FUND PROCEDURES

The object of a sinking fund problem, then, is to determine what periodic payment, invested at compound interest, will produce a given maturity value. Since amount-of-annuity problems also involve building a fund that would contain its largest amount at maturity, we can see that sinking fund problems are a variation of amount-of-annuity problems. The difference is that in this case we are concerned with finding the periodic payment of the annuity rather than the maturity value. (The periodic payment to a sinking fund is often called the **rent.**)

The period payment to a sinking fund can be found using the amount-of-annuity procedure $M = $ Pmt. $\times$ Amt. ann. tab.$_{\overline{n}|i}$ and solving for Pmt. Since use of this procedure would involve long and tedious division, however, you will normally find the periodic payment by using Table C-20, Sinking Fund, Appendix C, and the following procedure:

$$\text{Payment} = \text{Maturity value} \times \text{Sinking fund table}_{\overline{n}|i}$$

where $n = $ number of payments and $i = $ interest rate per period. This procedure* may be abbreviated

$$\text{Pmt.} = M \times \text{S.F. tab.}_{\overline{n}|i}$$

Example 1   Brandon County issued bonds totaling $1,000,000 in order to build an addition to the courthouse. The county commissioners set up a sinking fund at 9% compounded quarterly in order to redeem the 5-year bonds. (a) What quarterly rent must be deposited to the sinking fund? (b) How much of the maturity value will be deposits? (c) How much interest will the sinking fund earn?

(a) $M = \$1,000,000$ Pmt. $= M \times$ S.F. tab.$_{\overline{n}|i}$

$n = 20$ $= \$1,000,000 \times$ S.F. tab.$_{\overline{20}|2\frac{1}{4}\%}$

$i = 2\frac{1}{4}\%$ $= 1,000,000(0.04014207)$

Pmt. $= \$40,142.07$

A payment of $40,142.07 must be deposited into the sinking fund quarterly in order to have $1,000,000 at maturity.

(b)   There will be 20 deposits of $40,142.07 each, making the total deposits $20 \times \$40,142.07$, or $802,841.40.

(c)   The interest earned is thus

Maturity value	$1,000,000.00
Total deposits	− 802,841.40
Interest	$ 197,158.60

---

*The procedure for finding the payment to a sinking fund is often given as $P = M \times \dfrac{1}{m_{\overline{n}|i}}$, where $P = $ payment, $M = $ maturity value, and $\dfrac{1}{m_{\overline{n}|i}}$ indicates use of the sinking fund table. The procedure $P = M \times \dfrac{1}{m_{\overline{n}|i}}$ is a variation of the amount-of-annuity procedure $M = Pm_{\overline{n}|i}$.

When a sinking fund is in progress, businesses often keep a **sinking fund schedule.** The schedule shows how much interest the fund has earned during each period and what the current balance is. The schedule also verifies that the periodic payments will result in the desired maturity value.

Example 2 Prepare a sinking fund schedule to show that semiannual payments of $949 for 2 years will amount to $4,000 when invested at 7% compounded semiannually.

The periodic "interest" earned is found by multiplying the previous "balance at end of period" by the periodic interest rate i. (Example: $949 × $3\frac{1}{2}$% = $33.22)

PAYMENT	PERIODIC INTEREST ($i = 3\frac{1}{2}$%)	PERIODIC PAYMENT	TOTAL INCREASE	BALANCE AT END OF PERIOD
1	$ 0	$ 949.00	$ 949.00	$ 949.00
2	33.22	949.00	982.22	1,931.22
3	67.59	949.00	1,016.59	2,947.81
4	103.17	949.00	1,052.17	3,999.98
Totals	$203.98	$3,796.00		

$3,999.98 Final balance

Notice that the final balance in the sinking fund will be $0.02 less than the $4,000 needed, because of rounding.

BOND PROCEDURES

As described at the beginning of this topic, bonds are similar to promissory notes. The issuers of bonds (usually governmental bodies or large corporations) must pay periodic interest on the face (par) value at a rate specified on the bonds. For *registered bonds,* the bond owners are recorded, and checks are mailed directly. For *coupon bonds,* the owner collects the interest by clipping an attached coupon and submitting it (to the company or specified trustee) on the indicated date. A registered bond is shown in Figure 20-1.

If the Brandon County bonds in Example 1 pay 7% semiannual interest, then each 6 months the county must pay the bond owners interest that collectively totals (by $I = Prt$)

$$\$1,000,000 \times \frac{7}{100} \times \frac{1}{2} = \$35,000 \quad \text{Semiannual interest}$$

This $35,000 interest (the total for all bonds) is in addition to the semiannual payment Brandon County makes to the sinking fund in order to redeem the bonds at maturity.

Most bonds are issued with a par (redemption) value of $1,000 each. Buyers are willing to pay more or less than this face value, depending on the issuer's

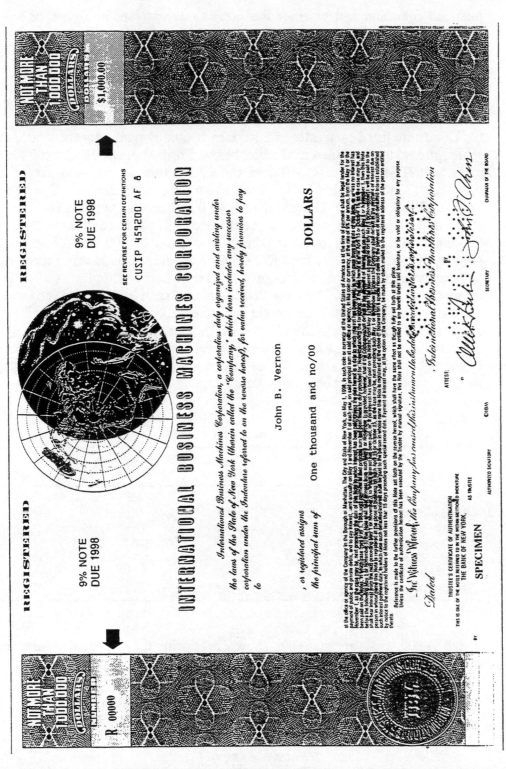

Courtesy of International Business Machines Corporation

FIGURE 20-1 Registered Bond

financial condition and whether the bond's interest rate is higher or lower than the prevailing market rate. Thus, if a financially sound company issues bonds at a higher-than-normal interest rate, the bonds may sell at a **premium** (more than face value). Low-interest bonds would probably sell at a **discount** (less than redemption value). If sold for face value, the bonds are sold at **par.** Generally, as interest rates increase, bond prices decrease, and as interest rates decrease, bond prices increase.

Bonds are listed on a sales exchange by company name, interest rate, and redemption date, as shown in the box below. For instance, "IBM $6\frac{3}{8}00$" indicates that IBM bonds pay $6\frac{3}{8}\%$ interest and mature in the year 2000. The optional "s" in "SouBell 6s04" is merely a plural form of reference. The initials "cv" in "PacSci $7\frac{3}{4}03$cv" indicate that these bonds are convertible to common stock under certain terms. A "current yield" of 6.5 is read as 6.5%. The "volume" indicates the number of bonds sold per $1,000 of face value. A volume of 328 thus stands for $328,000 in face value. Bonds are quoted as a percentage of face value, which also indicates whether they are selling at a premium or a discount. Thus, the "close" figure, such as $98\frac{1}{2}$ (or $985), is the bond price at the close of the previous business day. The "net change," such as $\frac{3}{8}$ (or $3.75), is the change in the price of the bond from the previous trading day. The "vj" preceding a bond name indicates that trading has been suspended by the Securities and Exchange Commission and that the company is in bankruptcy, receivership, or being reorganized under the Bankruptcy Act.

CORPORATION BONDS

BONDS	CURRENT YIELD	VOLUME	CLOSE	NET CHANGE
vjColuG $10\frac{1}{4}11$	. . .	50	$145\frac{1}{8}$	. . .
IBM $6\frac{3}{8}00$	6.5	328	$98\frac{1}{2}$	$+\frac{3}{8}$
Kroger 9s99	8.8	90	$101\frac{7}{8}$	. . .
MobilCp $8\frac{3}{8}01$	7.8	35	108	+1
PacSci $7\frac{3}{4}03$cv	7.2	5	108	−1
Revlon $10\frac{7}{8}10$	11.0	474	$98\frac{1}{2}$	$-1\frac{1}{2}$
SouBell 6s04	6.5	6	$92\frac{3}{4}$	$+1\frac{3}{4}$

Example 3 Three $1,000 bonds are quoted as shown, producing the indicated selling price and premium (or discount):

QUOTE	FACE VALUE	SELLING PRICE	PREMIUM/DISCOUNT
104	$1,000	104% × $1,000 = $1,040	$40 premium
97	1,000	97% × 1,000 = 970	30 discount
$108\frac{1}{2}$	1,000	$108\frac{1}{2}\%$ × 1,000 = 1,085	85 premium

The buyer of a bond normally also pays the previous owner for interest accrued (earned) since the last interest payment. This amount will be reimbursed to the new owner, who will receive full interest at the end of the period. A small (insignificant for our purposes) brokerage commission is also added to a bond's quoted price when the bond is purchased.

Bond purchases are made to provide income for the investor. Certain government bonds pay tax-free income, which makes these bonds desirable even at reduced interest rates. When bonds sell at a discount or a premium, the stated interest rate will differ from the **current yield** (the rate of interest based on the amount actually paid).

Example 4   Two $1,000 bonds each pay 6% simple interest annually. The quoted price of bond A was 98 and of bond B was 114. Find the current annual yield on each.

Annual interest on each bond, by $I = Prt$, is

$$\$1,000 \times \frac{6}{100} \times 1 = \$60$$

Bond A cost $980 and bond B was $1,140. Thus,

$$\text{Current yield} = \frac{\text{Annual interest}}{\text{Market or purchase price}}$$

$$\text{Bond A} = \frac{\$60}{\$980} = 6.12\% \text{ current yield}$$

$$\text{Bond B} = \frac{\$60}{\$1,140} = 5.26\% \text{ current yield}$$

SECTION 1 PROBLEMS

Using the sinking fund table, determine the periodic payment necessary to finance each sinking fund. Also calculate the total deposits and the total amount of interest contained in the maturity value.

	MATURITY VALUE	RATE	COMPOUNDED	YEARS
1. a.	$ 20,000	6%	Quarterly	8
b.	10,000	5	Semiannually	10
c.	40,000	8	Monthly	5
d.	130,000	9	Quarterly	15
e.	400,000	7	Monthly	7
2. a.	$ 30,000	7%	Quarterly	5
b.	50,000	8	Semiannually	6
c.	75,000	6	Monthly	7
d.	100,000	5	Quarterly	4
e.	200,000	9	Monthly	3

For each bond below, assume that the face value is $1,000. Compute the additional information related to each. Express current yield as a percent correct to 2 decimal places.

		PRICE QUOTE	PURCHASE PRICE	PREMIUM (P) OR DISCOUNT (D)	INTEREST RATE	ANNUAL INTEREST	CURRENT YIELD
3.	a.	105			$5\frac{1}{4}\%$		
	b.	92			$5\frac{3}{4}$		
	c.	100			$7\frac{1}{4}$		
	d.	$96\frac{1}{4}$			7.7		
	e.	$101\frac{1}{4}$			$10\frac{1}{8}$		
4.	a.	101			$6\frac{1}{4}\%$		
	b.	88			$5\frac{1}{8}$		
	c.	100			$9\frac{3}{4}$		
	d.	$95\frac{1}{2}$			$8\frac{1}{2}$		
	e.	$106\frac{1}{4}$			10		

5. Yucci Enterprises plans to spend $50,000 in 3 years for new factory equipment. To finance the purchase, the firm will establish a sinking fund at 8% compounded quarterly.

   a. What periodic payment must Yucci make to the sinking fund each quarter?

   b. What will be the total of these payments?

   c. How much interest will the fund contain at maturity?

6. The Osteopathic Medical Center plans to remodel its offices in 4 years. The directors expect to need $75,000.

   a. What quarterly payment is required to be invested in a sinking fund earning 9% compounded quarterly?

   b. What part of the maturity value will be deposits?

   c. How much interest will the fund draw?

7. Miller Shopping Center plans in 4 years to add a parking deck that will cost $1,000,000. Miller can set up a sinking fund at 8% compounded semiannually.

   a. What periodic payment will be made?

   b. What will be the total of these payments?

   c. What will be the total amount of interest earned?

8. The First Edition Bookstore wants $25,000 to upgrade its computer system in 2 years. The store can set up a sinking fund at 7% compounded semiannually.

   a. What semiannual payment must be made to finance the fund?

   b. What total amount will the store invest?

   c. How much interest will the account accumulate?

9. The city of Pleasant Grove voted to issue bonds totaling $700,000 to build an addition to the community center. The bonds will mature in 5 years. If a sinking fund is established earning 6% compounded monthly,

   a. How much must be deposited each month to finance the fund?

   b. How much will the city invest?

   c. How much of the maturity value will be interest?

10. The city of Boise sold bonds totaling $1,000,000 to finance an addition to a recreation center. The bonds mature in 8 years. To provide for redemption of the bonds, a sinking fund was established at 9% compounded monthly.

    a. What will be the monthly payment to the fund?

    b. How much will the city invest?

    c. How much interest will the mature fund include?

11. Boyd Corp. sold 300 bonds of $1,000 par value at 94. The bonds pay 9.4% interest annually to the bondholder.

    a. How much did each bond cost?

    b. What was the premium or discount?

    c. What total amount did Boyd receive from the sale?

    d. How much interest is paid on each bond each year?

    e. What is the current yield to the bondholder?

    f. How much total interest must Boyd pay to all bondholders each year?

12. Austin Enterprises, Inc., sold 500 bonds of $1,000 par value at 104. The bonds pay $8\frac{1}{4}$% interest annually to the bondholders.

    a. What was the cost of each bond?

    b. What was the premium or discount?

    c. What total amount did Austin receive from the sale?

    d. How much interest is paid on each bond each year?

    e. What is the current yield for each bond?

    f. How much total interest must the corporation pay to all bondholders each year?

Find the periodic payment necessary to finance each of the following sinking funds. Then prepare a sinking fund schedule to verify that these periodic payments will result in the desired maturity value.

		MATURITY VALUE	RATE	COMPOUNDED	YEARS
13.	a.	$ 5,000	5%	Semiannually	4
	b.	20,000	6	Annually	5
14.	a.	$ 8,000	8%	Quarterly	2
	b.	50,000	9	Semiannually	3

AMORTIZATION

BANK LOANS

In our study of simple interest, it was pointed out that simple interest notes are usually for short periods of time—a year or less. Example 1 in Section 1 of Chapter 18 (p. 464) was given to illustrate the advantage to the depositor of compound interest over simple interest. The same example can be used to illustrate that simple interest notes for long periods are not profitable to bankers. Suppose that the investors in that example are replaced by bankers who are each lending $1,000. Banker A lends $1,000 at 7% simple interest for 3 years, for which he would receive $210 interest.

Banker B, on the other hand, lends $1,000 at 7% for only 6 months. When the borrower repays the loan after 6 months, banker B then lends both the principal and the interest for another 6 months. This process is repeated for 3 years; so, in effect, banker B earns compound interest on the $1,000 she originally lent.

That is, banker B would earn $229.26 total interest, or $19.26 more than banker A. You can easily understand that banks would prefer to invest their money in successive short-term loans rather than tying it up in single long-term loans. If carried to its logical conclusion, the result would be that no one could borrow money for long-term projects such as building a home or starting a business.

Therefore, a borrower who receives a large bank loan makes periodic, partial payments. That is, at regular intervals payments are made that include both a payment to reduce the principal and also the interest due on the principal still owed. This procedure is the same as paying on the installment plan at an annual percentage rate required by the Truth-in-Lending Law (that is, an effective interest rate—interest paid only on the balance due). At the same time, it enables the bank, in effect, to earn compound interest (by reloaning the interest just repaid).

Note. It should be emphasized that the interest rates associated with amortization are effective rates; that is, the interest rate each period is applied to the outstanding balance only. To put it another way: The borrower receives credit for the principal that has been repaid, and interest is paid only on the amount still owed.

Since the bulk of the debt exists at the beginning of the time period, and the problem is to determine what periodic payment is necessary to discharge the debt, amortization is thus a variation of the present-value-of-annuity problem already studied. The debt itself is the present (beginning) value of the annuity. The payment may be found by using the present-value-of-annuity procedure, P.V. = Pmt. $\times$ P.V. ann. tab.$_{\overline{n}|i}$, and solving for Pmt.

This procedure, however, necessitates dividing by the number from the present-value-of-annuity table. To simplify the calculations, financial institutions usually use Table C-23, Amortization, Appendix C, which is an amortization table for regular payments scheduled each period. This table can be used in the following procedure:

$$\text{Payment} = \text{Present value} \times \text{Amortization table}_{\overline{n}|i}$$

where, as before, n = number of periods and i = interest rate per period. The procedure* may be abbreviated

$$\text{Pmt.} = \text{P.V.} \times \text{Amtz. tab.}_{\overline{n}|i}$$

The total amount paid to amortize a loan is found by multiplying the periodic payment by the number of payments. The total amount of interest is then the difference between the total paid and the original loan (present value).

Example 1   Marge and Gary Thomas bought a $30,000 residential lot by making a $3,000 down payment and making equal semiannual payments for 4 years. (a) How much was each payment if they had a 9% loan? (b) What was the total of their payments? (c) How much interest did the payments include? (d) How much did they pay altogether for the lot?

(a)   Following the $3,000 down payment, the principal (or present value) of the loan was $27,000.

$$\text{P.V.} = \$27,000 \qquad \text{Pmt.} = \text{P.V.} \times \text{Amtz. tab.}_{\overline{n}|i}$$

$$n = 8 \qquad\qquad\qquad = \$27,000 \times \text{Amtz. tab.}_{\overline{8}|4\frac{1}{2}\%}$$

$$i = 4\tfrac{1}{2}\% \qquad\qquad\qquad = \$27,000(0.1516097)$$

$$\text{Pmt.} = \$4,093.46$$

A payment of $4,093.46 each 6 months would repay both the principal and the interest due on a $27,000 loan.

(b)   There were 8 payments of $4,093.46 each, making a total (principal plus interest) of $32,747.68.

(c)   Interest would be computed each 6 months on the balance still owed (balance times $4\tfrac{1}{2}\%$). The total interest would be

Total payments	$32,747.68
Principal	− 27,000.00
Interest	$ 5,747.68

---

*This procedure may also be indicated by $P = A \times \dfrac{1}{a_{\overline{n}|i}}$, where P = payment, A = present value,

and $\dfrac{1}{a_{\overline{n}|i}}$ denotes use of the amortization table. (This table is often entitled "Annuity Whose Present

Value is 1.") The form $P = A \times \dfrac{1}{a_{\overline{n}|i}}$ is a variation of the present-value-of-annuity procedure $A = Pa_{\overline{n}|i}$.

(d) The total cost of the lot, including the down payment, was thus

Total cost of loan	$32,747.68
Down payment	+ 3,000.00
Total cost of lot	$35,747.68

MORTGAGES

Monthly payments on home mortgages are probably the most familiar amortization payment. Since our amortization table (Table C-23) contains only 100 periods, it can only be used to determine monthly payments for loans with terms no longer than $8\frac{1}{3}$ years. However, tables similar to the one below are used by real estate agents and mortgage bankers to determine monthly mortgage payments required at various prevailing rates on home loans of 20, 25, or 30 years.

MONTHLY PAYMENT PER $1,000
OF MORTGAGE[a]

RATE	20 YEARS	25 YEARS	30 YEARS
8%	$ 8.37	$7.72	$7.34
$8\frac{1}{4}$	8.53	7.89	7.52
$8\frac{1}{2}$	8.68	8.06	7.69
$8\frac{3}{4}$	8.84	8.23	7.87
9	9.00	8.40	8.05
$9\frac{1}{4}$	9.16	8.57	8.23
$9\frac{1}{2}$	9.33	8.74	8.41
$9\frac{3}{4}$	9.49	8.92	8.60
10	9.66	9.09	8.78
11	10.33	9.81	9.53

[a] Monthly payments including principal and interest.

The following example illustrates the cost of purchasing a home. As in Example 1, these mortgage payments include interest computed only on the balance due.

Example 2   The Townsends purchased a $98,000 home by making an $8,000 down payment and signing a 10% mortgage with monthly payments for 25 years. (a) Determine the Townsends' monthly payment. (b) What was the total of their payments, and how much of this was interest? (c) What was the total cost of their home?

(a) After their $8,000 down payment, the mortgage principal was $90,000. Their payment was thus

$ 9.09	per $1,000 at 10% for 25 years
× 90	
$818.10	monthly payment on $90,000 mortgage

(b) Twelve payments per year for 25 years equal 300 payments required to repay the mortgage. Their total payments and interest included would be

Monthly payment	$ 818.10
	$\times$ ___300
Total payments	$245,430
Principal	− 90,000
Interest	$155,430

(c) Including their down payment, the Townsends' $98,000 home cost them

Total cost of loan	$245,430
Down payment	+ ___8,000
Total cost of home	$253,430

The **fixed-rate mortgage** has been the traditional home mortgage in the United States. This mortgage has a fixed or set rate of interest, such as 8%, for a fixed time period, such as 20, 25, or 30 years. During the late 1970s and early 1980s, a period of rapid increases in interest rates, the fixed-rate mortgage lost popularity to the **adjustable-rate mortgage (ARM)** or **renegotiable-rate mortgage.** Typically, the interest rate on these mortgages was below market rates initially but then rose after a few years to a maximum rate that remained in force thereafter.

By the mid-1980s, interest rates decreased substantially throughout the economy, and fixed-rate mortgages once more became standard on new loans. As interest rates continued to fall through the early 1990s, many people who had taken out the adjustable-rate mortgages refinanced their homes at the lower interest rate, thereby reducing their monthly payments.

About the same time, the price of new homes increased, making it more difficult for buyers to qualify for financing. Some building contractors arranged financing plans which for the first two or three years were 2% to 3% below the conventional rates. When the rates and monthly payments of these mortgages subsequently increased, and when the economy moved into the recession of 1990–1991, many families were unable to meet their obligations, and the number of foreclosures rose dramatically. Attempting to halt this trend, the Federal Housing Administration (FHA), which underwrites the loans for a large portion of U.S. veterans, greatly tightened their requirements for applicants' proof of financial ability—including proof that the applicants had saved their own down payment and had not borrowed it or even accepted it as a gift.

At the time this edition went to press, mortgage interest rates were approximately 8% for an average 30-year fixed-rate mortgage.

AMORTIZATION SCHEDULES

Persons making payments to amortize a loan are often given an **amortization schedule,** which is a period-by-period breakdown showing how much of each payment goes toward the principal, how much is interest, the total amount of principal and interest that has been paid, the principal still owed, and so forth. Figure 20-2 illustrates an actual amortization schedule of a $50,000 loan at 10% interest for 10 years, which will be repaid in monthly payments of $633.38. Observe that a total of $76,005.46 will be repaid altogether—the $50,000 principal plus $26,005.46 interest.

Example 3   Prepare a simplified amortization schedule for Example 1, which found that a semiannual payment of $4,093.46 would amortize a $27,000 loan at 9% for 4 years.

The "interest" due each period is found by multiplying the "principal owed" by the periodic interest rate i. (Example: $27,000 $\times$ $4\frac{1}{2}$% = $1,215.) The next period's principal is found by subtracting the "payment to principal" from the "principal owed." (Example: $27,000 − $2,878.46 = $24,121.54)

PAYMENT	PRINCIPAL OWED	INTEREST ($i = 4\frac{1}{2}$%)	PAYMENT TO PRINCIPAL ($4,093.46 − INTEREST)
1	$27,000.00	$1,215.00	$ 2,878.46
2	24,121.54	1,085.47	3,007.99
3	21,113.55	950.11	3,143.35
4	17,970.20	808.66	3,284.80
5	14,685.40	660.84	3,432.62
6	11,252.78	506.38	3,587.08
7	7,665.70	344.96	3,748.50
8	3,917.20	176.27	3,917.19
Totals		$5,747.69	$26,999.99

Total cost of loan $32,747.68

Since interest is rounded to the nearest cent each period, the totals on an amortization schedule like this are often off by a few cents. In actual practice, the final loan payment is usually slightly different from the regular payment in order to have the total amounts come out exact.

The discussion at the beginning of this section pointed out that long-term simple interest notes (with a single payment at maturity) would not be profitable to bankers. We now see that such notes would also be unreasonably expensive to borrowers. Thus, effective interest with periodic payments works to the advantage of both the borrower and the lender. If financial institutions could charge simple interest and also receive periodic payments—as is frequently done on installment purchases and loans (although the Truth-in-Lending Law does require that the equivalent effective annual percentage rate be dis-

MORTGAGE AMORTIZATION SCHEDULE

PRIN. 50000	PERIOD RATE	.0075	AMOUNT OF	
APR. .0900	NO. OF PYTS	120	PAYMENT	633.38
TERM 10				
PPA 12	TOTAL AMOUNT PAID			76005.46
MONTH 10	TOTAL INTEREST PAID			26005.46
YEAR 1996				

PAYMENT	INTEREST	PRINCIPAL	PRINCIPAL BALANCE
#	PYT	PYT	
			50000.00
1	375.00	258.38	49741.62
2	373.06	260.32	49481.30
3	371.11	262.27	49219.04
4	369.14	264.24	48954.80
5	367.16	266.22	48688.58
6	365.16	268.21	48420.37
7	363.15	270.23	48150.14
8	361.13	272.25	47877.89
9	359.08	274.29	47603.59
10	357.03	276.35	47327.24
11	354.95	278.42	47048.82
12	352.87	280.51	46768.30
22	331.10	302.28	43844.82
23	328.84	304.54	43540.28
24	326.55	306.83	43233.45
25	324.25	309.13	42924.32
37	295.25	338.13	39020.00
38	292.72	340.66	38688.22
39	290.16	343.22	38345.00
40	287.59	345.79	37999.21
41	284.99	348.38	37650.83
42	282.38	351.00	37299.83
60	231.85	401.53	30512.00
61	228.84	404.54	30107.46
62	225.81	407.57	29699.88
63	222.75	410.63	29289.26
64	219.67	413.71	28875.55
65	216.57	416.81	28458.73
66	213.44	419.94	28038.80
67	210.29	423.09	27615.71
68	207.12	426.26	27189.45
69	203.92	429.46	26759.99
70	200.70	432.68	26327.31
101	87.92	545.46	11177.13
102	83.83	549.55	10627.58
103	79.71	553.67	10073.91
104	75.55	557.82	9516.08
105	71.37	562.01	8954.07
106	67.16	566.22	8387.85
107	62.91	570.47	7817.38
108	58.63	574.75	7242.63
109	54.32	579.06	6663.57
113	36.75	596.63	4303.58
114	32.28	601.10	3702.48
115	27.77	605.61	3096.87
116	23.23	610.15	2486.72
117	18.65	614.73	1871.99
118	14.04	619.34	1252.65
119	9.39	623.98	628.66
120	4.71	628.66	0.00

FIGURE 20-2   Schedule of Direct-Reduction Loan

closed)—this would be the most profitable arrangement for the lender; however, this is not done on long-term loans from banking institutions.

Calculator techniques . . . FOR EXAMPLE 3

This is a technique you have seen before, for paying off a revolving charge account. Loan amortization is an identical process, illustrated here for the first two payments of $4,903.46 each, made on a loan with a beginning principal of $27,000. (As previously, parentheses appear around displayed values that you will use without reentering.)

27,000 $\boxed{M+}$

(27,000) $\boxed{\times}$ 4.5 $\boxed{\%}$ $\longrightarrow$ 1215

$\quad$ 4,093.46 $\boxed{-}$ 1215 $\boxed{M-}$ $\longrightarrow$ 2,878.46; $\quad$ $\boxed{MR}$ $\longrightarrow$ 24,121.54

(24,121.54) $\boxed{\times}$ 4.5 $\boxed{\%}$ $\longrightarrow$ 1,085.47

$\quad$ 4,093.46 $\boxed{-}$ 1,085.47 $\boxed{M-}$ $\longrightarrow$ 3,007.99; $\quad$ $\boxed{MR}$ $\longrightarrow$ 21,113.55

and so forth.

The six remaining payments are calculated in a similar manner. Then, total the columns of interest and the payments to principal, to verify your calculations.

EFFECTIVE VS. SIMPLE INTEREST

The advantage to the borrower of effective interest over simple interest is obvious from the following example, which compares 12% simple interest ($I = Prt$) with effective interest at 12% compounded semiannually ($i = 6\%$) on a $25,000 loan for 10, 20, and 30 years.

Effective versus Simple Interest on a $25,000 Loan at 12%

TERM (YEARS)	TOTAL EFFECTIVE INTEREST ($i = 6\%$)	TOTAL SIMPLE INTEREST (12%)	EXTRA INTEREST AT SIMPLE RATE
10	$18,592.20	$30,000	$11,407.80
20	41,461.60	60,000	18,538.40
30	67,813.40	90,000	22,186.60

Observe on the 10-year loan that there would be over 60% more interest at the simple rate. The percentage difference decreases with longer terms, but on the 30-year loan there would still be 45% more interest at the simple rate. The simple interest alone on the 30-year loan would be 3.6 times as much as the principal that was borrowed. It is easy to see that no one could afford to buy a home or start a business if it were necessary to borrow money at simple interest.

SECTION 2   PROBLEMS

Using the amortization table, C-23, find the payment necessary to amortize each loan. Also compute the total amount that will be repaid, and determine how much interest is included.

		PRINCIPAL (P.V.)	RATE	COMPOUNDED (PAID)	TERM (YEARS)
1.	a.	$400,000	9%	Semiannually	15
	b.	180,000	8	Quarterly	20
	c.	70,000	10	Monthly	6
	d.	200,000	7	Semiannually	12
	e.	60,000	6	Monthly	5
2.	a.	$300,000	8%	Semiannually	15
	b.	150,000	9	Quarterly	10
	c.	80,000	7	Monthly	5
	d.	500,000	10	Semiannually	7
	e.	20,000	9	Monthly	8

Using the table of Monthly Payments per $1,000 of Mortgage, determine the monthly payment required for each mortgage below. Also find the total amount of those payments and the amount of interest included.

		MORTGAGE PRINCIPAL	RATE	TERM (YEARS)
3.	a.	$150,000	$8\frac{1}{4}$%	20
	b.	80,000	$9\frac{1}{4}$	25
	c.	250,000	9	30
	d.	400,000	10	30

		MORTGAGE PRINCIPAL	RATE	TERM (YEARS)
4.	a.	$200,000	8%	30
	b.	300,000	$8\frac{3}{4}$	20
	c.	60,000	$9\frac{1}{4}$	25
	d.	90,000	9	20

5. Jack Daniels borrowed $75,000 in order to go into partnership with his brother. His loan was made at 7% with monthly payments for 5 years.

   a. What is his monthly payment?

   b. How much total interest will Daniels pay?

6. Paul Martin borrowed $30,000 to build an addition to his home. He will repay the 9% loan with monthly payments for 3 years.

   a. What is Martin's monthly payment?

   b. How much total interest will be paid?

7. One Day Cleaners, Inc., borrowed $50,000 to purchase new drycleaning equipment. Quarterly payments will be made for 8 years in order to amortize the 8% loan.

   a. What is the amount of each payment?

   b. How much total interest will be charged?

8. Wooten Veterinarian Supply signed a $60,000 loan to purchase a new inventory system. The company will make quarterly payments at 8% interest for 7 years.

   a. What quarterly payment is necessary to discharge the loan?

   b. How much interest will be included in the payments?

9. Mr. and Mrs. Talkington purchased a $98,000 townhouse by paying $8,000 down and signing a 9% mortgage with quarterly payments for 20 years.

   a. How much is each quarterly payment?

   b. How much interest will the Talkingtons pay?

   c. What will be the total cost of the townhouse?

10. The Dumas Co. purchased real property for a building site for $145,000. It paid $25,000 down and financed the balance at 8% quarterly for 5 years.

    a. What quarterly payment was necessary to repay the loan?

    b. How much interest was included in the payments?

    c. What was the actual total cost of the property?

11. Additions to the offices of Hodges Construction Co. cost $300,000. The firm paid $50,000 down and financed the balance with monthly payments for 6 years at 8%.

    a. What monthly payment was necessary to repay the loan?

    b. How much interest was included in the payments?

    c. What was the actual total cost to Hodges Construction?

12. A new automated distribution system cost Davis Delivery Co. $175,000. Davis paid $25,000 down and financed the remainder at 7% monthly for 5 years.

    a. What monthly payment is required to repay the loan?

    b. How much interest will Davis pay?

    c. What will be the total cost of the system?

13. Mr. and Mrs. Blood purchased a $320,000 home by making a $20,000 down payment. The interest rate was $9\frac{1}{4}\%$.

    a. Compare monthly payments for 25 years to those for 30 years.

    b. What would be the total payments in each case?

    c. Including down payment, how much would the house cost altogether in each case?

    d. Determine how much extra the Bloods would pay under the 30-year mortgage.

14. Jane and Tom Brown purchased a $245,000 home by making a $15,000 down payment. Their mortgage rate is $9\frac{1}{2}\%$.

    a. Compare the monthly payment required for a 20-year mortgage with that for a 25-year mortgage.

    b. How much would each mortgage cost altogether?

    c. What would be the total cost of the house in each case?

    d. How much more would the house cost with the 25-year mortgage?

Find the periodic payment required for each of the following loans. Then verify your answer by preparing an amortization schedule similar to the one in Example 3, showing how much of each payment is interest and how much applies toward principal.

		PRINICPAL (P.V.)	RATE	COMPOUNDED (PAID)	TERM (YEARS)
15.	a.	$8,000	6%	Annually	4
	b.	4,000	9	Semiannually	2
16.	a.	$5,000	7%	Annually	5
	b.	6,000	8	Semiannually	3

SECTION 3
REVIEW

The following criteria may help enable you to distinguish between the basic types of problems studied in Chapters 18 through 20.

1. Determine whether the problem is a compound interest problem or an annuity problem: If a series of *regular payments* is involved, it is an *annuity;* otherwise, it is a compound interest problem.

2. Then, decide whether amount or present value is required: In general, if the question in the problem refers to the *end* of the time period, it is an *amount* problem; if the question relates to the *beginning* of the time period, it is a *present value* problem.

Note. This review includes only the basic problems of each type so that students can confidently identify each without its being listed under a section heading. This is not intended to be a complete review of the entire unit; your personal review should also include the variations of the basic problems studied in each section. The accompanying chart identifies each basic type of problem and the corresponding procedure for each.

COMPOUND INTEREST	ANNUITY
The basic problem involves a *single* deposit invested for the entire time.	The problem involves a *series* of *regular* payments (or deposits).
1. *Amount* at compound interest: A single deposit is made, and you wish to know how much it will be worth at the *end* of the time.	1. *Amount* of an annuity: Regular deposits are *made,* and you wish to know the value of the account at the *end* of the time.
$$M = P(1 + i)^n$$	$$M = \text{Pmt.} \times \text{Amt. ann. tab.}_{\overline{n}|i}$$
2. *Present value* at compound interest: You wish to find what single deposit must be invested at the *beginning* of the time period in order to obtain a given maturity value.	2. *Present value* of an annuity: Regular payments are to be *received,* and you want to find how much must be on deposit at the *beginning* from which to withdraw the payments.
$$P = M(1 + i)^{-n}$$	$$\text{P.V.} = \text{Pmt.} \times \text{P.V. ann. tab.}_{\overline{n}|i}$$
	If the problem involves *finding a periodic payment,* one of the following applies:
	3. *Sinking fund:* You are asked to find what regular payment must be made to *build up* an account to a given amount.
	$$\text{Pmt.} = M \times \text{S.F. tab.}_{\overline{n}|i}$$
	4. *Amortization:* You are asked to determine what regular payment must be made to *discharge* a debt.
	$$\text{Pmt.} = \text{P.V.} \times \text{Amtz. tab.}_{\overline{n}|i}$$

SECTION 3   PROBLEMS

Use the following information to complete Problems 1, 3, 5, and 7.

	VALUE	RATE	COMPOUNDED	TERM (YEARS)
a.	$10,000	8%	Semiannually	8
b.	7,000	7	Monthly	5

Use the following information to complete Problems 2, 4, 6, and 8.

a.	$ 5,000	9	Quarterly	7
b.	20,000	10	Monthly	4

1–2. Assume that each value given above is the principal of an investment. Find the (1) compound amount and (2) compound interest.

3–4. Assume that each value given above is the maturity value of an investment. Compute the (1) present value and (2) compound interest.

5–6. Assume that each value given above is the desired maturity value of a sinking fund. (1) Find the periodic payment required to finance the fund. (2) How much of the final value will be actual deposits? (3) How much interest will be included?

7–8. Assume that each value given above is the principal (present value) of a loan. (1) Compute the periodic payment required to amortize each debt. (2) What total amount will be paid to discharge each obligation? (3) How much interest will be included?

Use the following information to complete Problems 9 and 11.

	PAYMENTS	PERIODIC RATE	COMPOUNDED	TERM (YEARS)
a.	$1,000	6%	Quarterly	20
b.	100	8	Monthly	6

Use the following information to complete Problems 10 and 12.

a.	$100,000	5%	Quarterly	5
b.	10,000	7	Monthly	3

9–10. (1) Determine the maturity value if one makes (invests) each annuity payment above. (2) How much would be deposited during the time period? (3) How much of the maturity value is interest?

11–12. (1) Find the present value required in order to receive each annuity payment above. (2) How much would be received during the term of the annuity? (3) How much interest would be included?

13. Mariana Anderson graduates from college in 2 years. She would like to have $5,000 at that time for a vacation. Money is worth 6% compounded monthly.

a. How much must she invest now in order to achieve her savings goal?

b. How much interest will she earn?

14. Sam Levett wants to have $15,000 in 4 years to make a down payment on a house. His savings can earn 6% compounded monthly.

a. How much must he deposit now to achieve his goal?

b. How much of the $15,000 will be interest?

15. Rich Dairy, Inc., is investing $6,000 each quarter to enlarge its processing plant in 5 years. The dairy's investment earns 8% compounded quarterly.

a. What amount will the account contain in 4 years?

b. How much total interest will the account earn?

16. BBB Trucking Co. is investing $7,000 each quarter to purchase a new refrigerated truck in 4 years. The investment earns 7% compounded quarterly.

a. What amount will the company have after 4 years?

b. How much of this amount will be interest?

17. William Bingham borrowed $70,000 to buy his sisters' shares of stock in the family business. He signed a 9%, 10-year loan, making semiannual payments.

a. How much does he pay each 6 months?

b. How much total interest will he pay on the loan?

18. Lock Manufacturing Co. borrowed $50,000 to purchase furniture for its new headquarters. The company signed a 10%, 3-year loan, making semiannual payments.
    a. What was the semiannual payment?
    b. How much total interest did the company pay on the loan?

19. Ken Atwater would like to receive $500 monthly for 8 years after he retires. He can invest in savings certificates earning 7% compounded monthly.
    a. How much must Atwater's account contain at retirement in order to provide these payments?
    b. How much will he receive before the fund is exhausted?
    c. How much interest will be earned on the account?

20. Instructor George Hamid plans to return to graduate school for 2 years, and he would like to receive $400 each month during this time. He can invest his money at 6% compounded monthly.
    a. What amount must Hamid's account contain when he returns to school?
    b. How much will he receive while he is in school?
    c. What part of these payments will be interest?

21. The Tyler family wants to travel around the United States beginning in 3 years. To make this trip, they anticipate a need for $15,000. Money is currently worth 8% compounded monthly.
    a. How much must the Tylers save each month to reach their goal?
    b. How much of the $15,000 will be their deposits?
    c. How much interest will the account contain?

22. Beltway Equipment Co. sold bonds worth $800,000 at maturity in order to expand its operations. Beltway will make deposits each 6 months for 10 years to provide the funds to redeem the bonds. It can invest money at 9% compounded semiannually.
    a. What semiannual payment will be required to finance the fund?
    b. How much of the $800,000 will be actual deposits?
    c. How much interest will the deposits earn?

23. Beth Coleman invested $5,000 in a savings account which earns 6% compounded quarterly.
    a. How much will the account be worth in 2 years?
    b. How much interest will she earn?

24. Maria Rodman purchased a $1,000 CD that pays 5% compounded quarterly when held for 3 years.
    a. How much will the CD be worth at maturity?
    b. How much interest will the certificate earn?

CHAPTER 20 GLOSSARY

Adjustable-rate mortgage (ARM). A mortgage in which the interest rate may change annually but the amount and time are fixed for the entire loan period.

Amortization. The process of repaying a loan (principal plus interest) by equal periodic payments.

Amortization schedule. A listing of the principal and interest included in each periodic loan payment, as well as a statement of the balance still owed.

Bond. A written promise to repay a specified debt on a certain date, with periodic interest to be paid during the term of the bond. Bonds are typically sold by large corporations and by city and state governments when they borrow money.

Current yield. A rate of interest based on the amount actually paid for a bond (rather than its stated rate based on the par value).

Discount. The amount by which the purchase price of a bond is less than its par value.

Fixed-rate mortgage. A mortgage in which the amount, time, and interest rate are fixed at the beginning of the loan and do not change.

Par value. Face value or redemption value of a bond. The value upon which interest is computed.

Premium. The excess amount above par value that is paid for a bond.

Renegotiable-rate mortgage. (See "Adjustable-rate mortgage.")

Rent. The periodic payment to a sinking fund.

Sinking fund. An annuity account established so that the maturity value (equal periodic deposits plus interest) will exactly equal a specific amount.

Sinking fund schedule. A periodic listing of the growth (in principal and interest) of a sinking fund.

CHAPTER ONE
What Is Statistics?

Contents

1.1 Statistics: What Is It?
1.2 The Elements of Statistics
1.3 Statistics: Witchcraft or Science?
1.4 Processes (Optional)
1.5 The Role of Statistics in Managerial
    Decision-Making

Case Studies

Case Study 1.1 The Consumer Price Index
Case Study 1.2 Taste-Preference Scores for Beer
Case Study 1.3 Monitoring the Unemployment Rate
Case Study 1.4 Auditing Parts and Equipment for
               Airline Maintenance
Case Study 1.5 The Decennial Census of the United
               States
Case Study 1.6 Quality Improvement: U.S. Firms
               Respond to the Challenge from Japan

Where We're Going

What is statistics? Is it a field of study, a group of numbers that summarize a business operation, or—as the title of a popular book (Tanur et al., 1989) suggests—"a guide to the unknown"? We will begin to see in Chapter 1 that each of these descriptions has some applicability in understanding statistics. We will see that *descriptive statistics* focuses on developing numerical summaries that describe some business phenomenon, whereas *inferential statistics* uses numerical summaries to assist in making business decisions. Our main objective is to show how statistics can be useful to you in business decision-making, so the primary theme of this text is inferential statistics.

1.1 Statistics: What Is It?

What does statistics mean to you? Does it bring to mind batting averages, the Dow Jones Industrial Average, unemployment figures, numerical distortions of facts (lying with statistics!), or simply a college requirement you have to complete? We hope to convince you that statistics is a meaningful, useful science with a broad, almost limitless scope of application to business and economic problems. We also want to show that statistics lie only when they are misapplied. Finally, our objective is to paint a unified picture of statistics to leave you with the impression that your time was well spent studying a subject that will prove useful to you in many ways.

Statistics means "numerical descriptions" to most people. The Dow Jones Industrial Average, monthly unemployment figures, and the fraction of women executives in a particular industry are all statistical descriptions of large sets of data. Often, the purpose of calculating these numbers goes beyond the description of the particular set of data. Frequently, the data are regarded as a sample selected from some larger set of data whose characteristics we wish to estimate. For example, a sampling of unpaid accounts for a large merchandiser would allow you to calculate an estimate of the average value of unpaid accounts. This estimate could be used as an audit check on the total value of all unpaid accounts held by the merchandiser. So, the applications of statistics can be divided into two broad areas: **descriptive** and **inferential** statistics.

Descriptive statistics utilizes numerical and graphical methods to look for patterns, summarize, and present the information in a set of data.

Inferential statistics utilizes sample data to make estimates, predictions, or other generalizations about a larger set of data, frequently as an aid to decision making.

Although both descriptive and inferential statistics are discussed in the following chapters, the primary theme of the text is **inference**. Let us examine some case studies that illustrate applications of descriptive and inferential statistics in business and government.

CASE STUDY 1.1 / The Consumer Price Index

A data set of interest to virtually all Americans is the set of prices charged for goods and services in the U.S. economy. The general upward movement in this set of prices is referred to as *inflation*; the general downward movement is referred to as *deflation*. In order to *estimate* the change in prices over time, the Bureau of Labor Statistics (BLS) of the U.S. Department of Labor developed the Consumer Price Index (CPI). Each month, the BLS collects price data about a specific collection of goods and services (called a *market basket*) from 85 urban areas around the country. Statistical procedures are used to compute the CPI (a descriptive statistic) from this sample price data and other information about consumers' spending habits. By comparing the level of the CPI at different points in time, it is possible to *estimate* (make an inference about) the rate of inflation over particular time intervals and to compare the purchasing power of a dollar at different points in time.

One major use of the CPI as an index of inflation is as an indicator of the success or failure of government economic policies. A second use of the CPI is to esca-late income payments. Millions of workers have *escalator clauses* in their collective bargaining contracts; these clauses call for increases in wage rates based on increases in the CPI. In addition, the incomes of Social Security beneficiaries and retired military and federal civil service employees are tied to the CPI. It has been estimated that a 1% increase in the CPI can trigger an increase of over $1 billion in income payments. Thus, it can be said that the very livelihoods of millions of Americans depend on the behavior of a statistical estimator, the CPI (U.S. Department of Labor, 1978). [*Note:* We discuss the Consumer Price Index in greater detail in Chapter 14.]

CASE STUDY 1.2 / Taste-Preference Scores for Beer

Two sets of data of interest to the marketing department of a food-products firm are (1) the set of taste-preference scores given by consumers to its product and to competitors' products when all brands are clearly labeled and (2) the taste-preference scores given by the same set of consumers when all brand labels have been removed and the consumer's only means of product identification is taste. With such information, the marketing department should be able to determine whether taste preference arose because of perceived physical differences in the products or as a result of the consumer's image of the brand. (Brand image is, of course, largely a result of a firm's marketing efforts.) Such a determination should help the firm develop marketing strategies for its product.

A study using these two types of data was conducted by Ralph Allison and Kenneth Uhl (1965) to determine whether beer drinkers could distinguish among major brands of unlabeled beer. A sample of 326 beer drinkers was randomly selected from the set of beer drinkers identified as males who drank beer at least three times a week. During the first week of the study, each of the 326 participants was given a six-pack of unlabeled beer containing three major brands and was asked to taste-rate each beer on a scale from 1 (poor) to 10 (excellent). During the second week, the same set of drinkers was given a six-pack containing six major brands. This time, however, each bottle carried its usual label. Again, the drinkers were asked to taste-rate each beer from 1 to 10. From a statistical analysis of the two sets of data yielded by the study, Allison and Uhl concluded that the 326 beer drinkers studied could not distinguish among brands by taste on an overall basis. This result enabled them to *infer* statistically that such was also the case for beer drinkers in general. Their results also indicated that brand labels and their associations did significantly influence the tasters' evaluations. These findings suggest that physical differences in the products have less to do with their success or failure in the marketplace than the image of the brand in the consumers' minds. As to the benefits of such a study, Allison and Uhl note, "to the extent that product images, and their changes, are believed to be a result of advertising . . . the ability of firms' advertising programs to influence product images can be more thoroughly examined."

CASE STUDY 1.3 / Monitoring the Unemployment Rate

The employment status (employed or unemployed) of each individual in the U.S. work force is a set of data that is of interest to economists, businesspeople, and sociologists. These data provide information on the social and economic health of our society. To obtain information about the employment status of the work force, the U.S. Bureau of the Census conducts what is known as the *Current Population Survey*. Each month approximately 1,500 interviewers visit about 59,000 of the 91.9 million households in the United States and question the occupants over 14 years of age about their employment status. Their responses enable the Bureau of the Census to *estimate* the percentage of people in the labor force who are unemployed (the *unemployment rate*). Thus, a *statistical estimator* serves as a monthly indicator of the nation's economic welfare.

Perhaps you are wondering how a reliable estimate of this percentage can be obtained from a sample that includes only about .1% of the households in the United States. The answer lies in the method used to select the sample of households. The method was designed to enable the Bureau of the Census to control the precision of its estimate while obtaining a sample that is representative of the set of all households in the country. That reliable estimates of nationwide characteristics can be obtained from relatively small sample sizes is an illustration of the power of statistics (U.S. Department of Commerce, 1978). [*Note:* We discuss sampling methods in detail in Chapter 20.]

CASE STUDY 1.4 / Auditing Parts and Equipment for Airline Maintenance

The United Airlines Maintenance Base in San Francisco is responsible for the maintenance and overhaul of all United Airlines aircraft. Its storeroom receives, stores, and distributes all the parts needed for maintenance of the aircraft. To control the stock of spare parts and to determine the value of parts on hand, *inventory counts* (a descriptive statistic) of the number of each item in stock are taken. It is the responsibility of the Auditing Division of United Airlines to verify the accuracy of the inventory counts. Rather than verifying the accuracy of the counts by recounting all of the inventory item groups, the accountants sample a small number of these groups and recount them. If they find a large number of discrepancies between the original counts and their sample counts, they *infer* that many of the rest of the item counts (those not sampled and recounted) are also in error. They conclude that the original inventory counts are unacceptable and must be recounted. On the other hand, if they find only a small number of discrepancies, they *infer* that most of the item counts not rechecked are accurate, and conclude that the original inventory counts are satisfactory.

Before this inferential statistical procedure was implemented, the Auditing Division verified inventory counts by recounting all the items in stock. The inferential procedure enables the accountants to maintain the quality of their verifications with a substantial reduction in work-hours (Hunz, 1956).

CASE STUDY 1.5 / The Decennial Census of the United States

The following description is quoted from the U.S. Bureau of the Census, *Statistical Abstract of the United States: 1992*:

The U.S. Constitution provides for a census of the population every 10 years, primarily to establish a basis for apportionment of members of the House of Representatives among the States. For over a century after the first census in 1790, the census organization was a temporary one, created only for each decennial census. In 1902, the Bureau of the Census was established as a permanent Federal agency, responsible for enumerating the population and also for compiling statistics on other subjects.

The census of the population is a complete count. That is, an attempt is made to account for every person, for each person's residence, and for other characteristics (sex, age, family relationships, etc.). Since the 1940 census, in addition to the complete count information, some data have been obtained from representative samples of the

population. In the 1990 census, variable sampling rates were employed. For most of the country, one in every six households (about 17%) received the long form or sample questionnaire; in governmental units estimated to have fewer than 2500 inhabitants, every other household (50%) received the sample questionnaire to enhance the reliability of sample data for small areas. Exact agreement is not to be expected between sample data and the complete census count.

Census statistics regarding total numbers of people in various age groups are examples of numerical *descriptions* that require no statistical inference, since they are (purportedly) complete counts. However, income data collected by the Bureau of the Census from "representative samples" might be used to make *inferences* about the incomes of *all* persons. You will learn that the reliability of statistical inferences is dependent on the sampling procedure, characteristics of the data, and the methodology employed to make the inferences.

Why study statistics in a business program? The quantification of business research and business operations (quality control, statistical auditing, forecasting, etc.) has been truly astounding over the past several decades. Econometric modeling, market surveys, and the creation of indexes such as the Consumer Price Index all represent relatively recent attempts to quantify economic behavior. It is extremely important that today's business graduate understand the methods and language of statistics, since the alternative is to be swamped by a flood of numbers that are more confusing than enlightening to the untutored mind. The business student should develop a discerning sense of rational thought that will distill the information contained in these numbers so it can be used to make intelligent decisions, inferences, and generalizations. We believe that the study of statistics is essential to the ability to operate effectively in the modern business environment.

1.2   The Elements of Statistics

Statistical methods are particularly useful for studying, analyzing, and learning about **populations**.

***

Definition 1.1

A **population** is a set of existing units (usually people, objects, transactions, or events).

***

Examples of populations include (1) all employed workers in the United States, (2) all registered voters in California, (3) everyone who has purchased a particular brand of cellular telephone, (4) all the cars produced last year by a particular assembly line, (5) the current stock of spare parts at United Airlines' maintenance facility, (6) all sales made at the drive-in window of a fast-food restaurant during a given year, and (7) the set of all accidents occurring on a particular stretch of interstate highway during a holiday period. Notice that the first three population examples (1–3) are sets (groups) of people; the next two (4–5) are sets of objects; the next (6) is a set of transactions; and the last (7) is a set of events.

In studying a population, we focus on one or more characteristics or properties of the units in the population. For example, we may be interested in the age, income, or the number of years of education of the people currently unemployed in the United States. We call such characteristics **variables**.

***

Definition 1.2

A **variable** is a characteristic or property of an individual population unit. The name *variable* is derived from the fact that any particular characteristic may *vary* among the units in a population.

***

In studying a particular variable, it is helpful—as we will see in forthcoming chapters—to be able to obtain a numerical representation for the variable. Thus, when numerical representations are not readily available, the process of measurement plays an important supporting role in statistical studies. **Measurement** is the process by which numbers are assigned to variables of individual population units. Measurement may entail asking a consumer to rate the taste of a product on a scale from 1 to 10 or simply asking a worker how old she is. Frequently, however, it involves the use of instruments such as stopwatches, scales, calipers, etc. We discuss measurement in more detail in the next chapter.

If the population you wish to study is small in size, then it is feasible to measure a variable for every unit in the population. For example, if you are measuring the starting salary for all University of Michigan MBA graduates in 1993, it is at least feasible to obtain every salary. When we measure a variable for every unit of a population, it is called a **census** of the population. However, the populations of interest in business problems are typically much larger, involving perhaps many thousands of units. Some examples of large populations were given after Definition 1.1; others are all invoices produced in the last year by a Fortune 500 company, all potential buyers of a new facsimile machine, and all stockholders of a firm listed on the New York Stock Exchange. In studying such populations it would typically be too time-consuming or too costly to conduct a census. A more reasonable alternative would be to select and study a subset (a portion) of the units in the population.

Thus, for example, instead of examining all 15,472 invoices produced by a company during a given year, an auditor may select and examine a **sample** of only 100 invoices. If he is interested in the variable *dollar value*, then he would record (measure) the dollar value of each invoice.

Definition 1.3

A **sample** is a subset of the units of a population.

The method of selecting the sample is called the sampling procedure, or sampling plan. One very important sampling procedure is **random sampling**, one that assures that every subset of units in the population has the same chance of being included in the sample. Thus, if an auditor samples 100 of the 15,472 invoices in the population so that every invoice (and subset of invoices) has an equal chance of being included in the sample, he has devised a random sample. Random sampling is discussed in Chapter 3, and various other sampling procedures are discussed in Chapter 20.

After selecting the sample and measuring the variable(s) of interest for every sampled unit, the information contained in the sample is used to make *inferences* about the population.

Definition 1.4

A **statistical inference** is an estimate, prediction, or other generalization about a population based on information contained in a sample.

That is, *we use the information contained in the smaller sample to learn about the larger population*.* Thus, from an examination of the sample of 100 invoices, the auditor may estimate the total number of invoices containing errors in the population

---

*The terms *population* and *sample* are often used to refer to the sets of measurements themselves, in addition to the units on which the measurements are made. For applications in which a single variable of interest is being measured, this will cause little confusion. When the terminology is potentially ambiguous, the measurements will be referred to as *population data sets* and *sample data sets*, respectively.

of 15,472 invoices or predict the total number of invoices with errors in next year's population of invoices.

Managers use statistical inferences to guide and support their decisions. For example, the auditor's inference about the quality of the firm's invoices can be used in deciding whether to modify the firm's billing operations. The decision to market a new product may hinge on an inference about the willingness of a population of consumers to buy the product—an inference based on the results of testing the product on a sample of consumers.

The preceding definitions identify four of the five elements of an inferential statistical problem: a population, one or more variables of interest, a sample, and an inference. The fifth—and perhaps most important—is a measure of reliability for the inference. This is the topic of Section 1.3.

EXAMPLE 1.1

A large paint retailer has had numerous complaints from customers about underfilled paint cans. As a result, the retailer has begun inspecting incoming shipments of paint from suppliers. Shipments with underfill problems will be returned to the supplier. A recent shipment contained 2,440 gallon-size cans. The retailer randomly selected 100 cans and weighed each on a scale capable of measuring weight to four decimal places. Properly filled cans weigh 10 pounds.

a. Describe the population.
b. Describe the variable of interest.
c. Describe the sample.
d. Describe the inference.

Solution

a. The population is the set of units of interest to the retailer, which is the shipment of 2,440 cans of paint.

b. The weight of the paint cans is the variable the retailer wishes to evaluate.

c. The sample must be a subset of the population. In this case, it is the 100 cans of paint selected by the retailer. If the 100 cans represent a random sample, then the sampling procedure used must be such that each of the 2,440 cans had an equal chance of being included in the sample.

d. The inference of interest involves the *generalization* of the information contained in the weights of the sample of paint cans to the population of paint cans. In particular, the retailer wants to learn about the extent of the underfill problem (if any) in the population. This might be accomplished by finding the average* weight of the cans in the sample and using it to estimate the average weight of the cans in the population.

---

*Although we will not formally define the term *average* until Chapter 2, *typical* or *middle* can be substituted here without confusion.

EXAMPLE 1.2

Cola wars is the popular media term for the intense competition between the marketing campaigns of Coca-Cola and Pepsi. The campaigns have featured movie and television stars, rock videos, athletic endorsements, and claims of consumer preference based on taste tests. Suppose a particular Pepsi bottler gives 1,000 cola consumers in the bottler's marketing region a "blind" taste test (i.e., a taste test in which the two brand names are disguised). Each consumer is asked to state a preference for brand A or brand B.

a. Describe the population.
b. Describe the variable of interest.
c. Describe the sample.
d. Describe the inference.

Solution

a. The population of interest to the Pepsi bottler is the collection or set of all cola consumers in the marketing region.

b. The characteristic of each cola consumer that the bottler wishes to study is the consumer's cola preference as revealed under the conditions of a blind taste test. Thus, cola preference is the variable of interest.

c. The sample is the group of 1,000 cola consumers from the bottler's marketing region.

d. The inference of interest is the *generalization* of the cola preferences of the 1,000 sampled consumers to the population of all cola consumers in the bottler's marketing region. In particular, the preferences of the consumers in the sample can be used to *estimate* the percentage of all cola consumers in the region who prefer each brand.

1.3 Statistics: Witchcraft or Science?

The primary objective of statistics is inference. In the previous section, we described inference as making generalizations about populations based on information contained in a sample. But making the inference is only part of the story. We also need to know how good the inference is. The only way we could be reasonably certain that an inference about a population is correct would be to include the entire population in our sample. But, due to resource constraints (i.e., insufficient time or money), this is generally not an option. In basing inferences on only a portion of the population (a sample), we introduce an element of uncertainty into our inferences. In general, the smaller the sample size, the less certain we are about the inference. Thus, an inference based on a sample of size 5 is (usually) less reliable than an inference based on a sample of size 100. Consequently, whenever possible, it is important to determine and report the **reliability** of each inference made; this is the fifth element of a statistical problem.

The measure of reliability that accompanies an inference separates the science of statistics from the art of fortune-telling. A palm reader, like a statistician, may examine a sample (your hand) and make inferences about the population (your life). However, unlike statistical inferences, no measure of reliability can be attached to the palm reader's inferences.

Suppose, as in Example 1.1, we are interested in estimating the average weight of a population of paint cans from the average weight of a sample of cans. Using statistical methods, we can determine a *bound on the estimation error*. This bound is simply a number that our estimation error (the difference between the average weight of the sample and the average weight of the population of cans) is not likely to exceed. We will see in later chapters that this bound is a measure of the uncertainty of our inference. The reliability of statistical inferences is discussed throughout this text. For now, we simply want you to realize that an inference is incomplete without a measure of its reliability.

We conclude this section with a summary of the elements of inferential statistical problems and an example to illustrate a measure of reliability.

Five Elements of Inferential Statistical Problems

1. The population of interest
2. One or more variables (characteristics of the population units) that are to be investigated
3. The sample of population units
4. The inference about the population based on information contained in the sample
5. A measure of reliability for the inference

EXAMPLE 1.3

Refer to Example 1.2, in which 1,000 consumers indicated their cola preferences in a taste test. Describe how the reliability of an inference concerning the preferences of all cola consumers in the Pepsi bottler's marketing region could be measured.

Solution

When the preferences of 1,000 consumers are used to estimate the preferences of all consumers in the region, the estimate will not exactly mirror the preferences of the population. For example, if the taste test shows that 56% of the 1,000 consumers preferred Pepsi, it does not follow (nor is it likely) that exactly 56% of all cola drinkers in the region prefer Pepsi. Nevertheless, we may be able to use sound statistical reasoning (which is presented later in the text) to ensure that the sampling procedure used will generate estimates that are almost certainly within a specified limit of the true percentage of all consumers who prefer Pepsi. For example, such reasoning might assure us that the estimate of the preference for Pepsi is almost certainly within 5% of the actual population preference. The implication is that the actual preference for

Pepsi is between 51% [i.e., (56 − 5)%] and 61% [i.e., (56 + 5)%]. This interval represents a measure of reliability for the inference.

1.4   Processes (Optional)

Sections 1.2 and 1.3 focused on the use of statistical methods to analyze and learn about populations, which are sets of *existing* units. Statistical methods are equally useful for analyzing and making inferences about **processes**.

Definition 1.5

A **process** is a series of actions or operations that transforms inputs to outputs. A process produces or generates output over time.

The most obvious processes that are of interest to businesses are production or manufacturing processes. A manufacturing process uses a series of operations performed by people and machines to convert inputs, such as raw materials and parts, to finished products (the outputs). Examples include the process used to produce the paper on which these words are printed, automobile assembly lines, and oil refineries.

Figure 1.1 presents a general description of a process and its inputs and outputs. In the context of manufacturing, the process in the figure (i.e., the transformation process) could be a depiction of the overall production process or it could be a depiction of one of the many processes (sometimes called subprocesses) that exist within an overall production process. Thus, the output shown could be finished goods that will be shipped to an external customer or merely the output of one of the steps or subprocesses of the overall process. In the latter case, the output becomes input for the next subprocess. For example, Figure 1.1 could represent the overall automobile assembly process, with its output being fully assembled cars ready for shipment to dealers. Or, it could depict the windshield-assembly subprocess, with its output of partially assembled cars with windshields ready for "shipment" to the next subprocess in the assembly line.

FIGURE 1.1 ▶
Graphical depiction of a manufacturing process

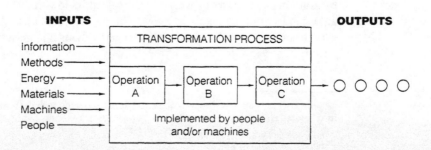

Besides physical products and services, businesses and other organizations generate streams of numerical data over time that are used to evaluate the performance of the organization. Examples include weekly sales figures, quarterly earnings, and yearly profits. The U.S. economy (a complex organization) can be thought of as generating streams of data that include the Gross National Product (GNP), stock prices, and the Consumer Price Index. Statisticians and other analysts conceptualize these data streams as being generated by processes. Typically, however, the series of operations or actions that cause particular data to be realized are either unknown or so complex (or both) that the processes are treated as **black boxes**.

Definition 1.6

A process whose operations or actions are unknown or unspecified is called a **black box**.

Frequently, when a process is treated as a black box, its inputs are not specified either. The entire focus is on the output of the process. A black box process is illustrated in Figure 1.2.

FIGURE 1.2 ▶
A black box process with numerical output

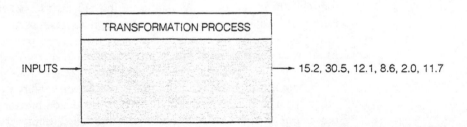

In studying a process, we generally focus on one or more characteristics, or properties, of the output. For example, we may be interested in the weight or the length of the units produced or even the time it takes to produce each unit. As with characteristics of population units, we call these characteristics **variables**. In studying processes whose output is already in numerical form (i.e., a stream of numbers), the characteristic, or property, represented by the numbers (e.g., sales, GNP, or stock prices) is typically the variable of interest. If the output is not numeric, we use **measurement processes** to assign numerical values to variables.* For example, if in the automobile assembly process the weight of the fully assembled automobile is the variable of interest, a measurement process involving a large scale will be used to assign a numerical value to each automobile.

---

*A process whose output is already in numerical form necessarily includes a measurement process as one of its subprocesses.

As with populations, we use sample data to analyze and make inferences (estimates, predictions, or other generalizations) about processes. But the concept of a sample is defined differently when dealing with processes. Recall that a population is a set of existing units and that a sample is a subset of those units. In the case of processes, however, the concept of a set of existing units is not relevant or appropriate. Processes generate or create their output *over time*—one unit after another. For example, a particular automobile assembly line produces a completed vehicle every 4 minutes. We define a sample from a process in the box.

Definition 1.7
....

Any set of output (objects or numbers) produced by a process is called a **sample**.

Thus, the next 10 cars turned out by the assembly line constitute a sample from the process, as do the next 100 cars or every fifth car produced today.

....

EXAMPLE 1.4

A particular fast-food restaurant chain has 6,289 outlets with drive-through windows. To attract more customers to its drive-through services, the company is considering offering a 50% discount on the price of an order that a customer must wait more than a specified number of minutes to receive. To help determine what the time limit should be, the company decided to estimate the average waiting time at a particular drive-through window in Dallas, Texas. For 7 consecutive days, the worker taking customers' orders recorded the time that every order was placed. The worker who handed the order to the customer recorded the time of delivery. In both cases, workers used synchronized digital clocks that reported the time to the nearest second. At the end of the 7-day period, 2,109 orders had been timed.

a. Describe the process of interest at the Dallas restaurant.

b. Describe the variable of interest.

c. Describe the sample.

d. Describe the inference of interest.

e. Describe how the reliability of the inference could be measured.

Solution

a. The process of interest is the drive-through window at a particular fast-food restaurant in Dallas, Texas. It is a process because it "produces," or "generates," meals over time. That is, it services customers over time.

b. The variable the company monitored is customer waiting time, the length of time a customer waits to receive a meal after placing an order. Since the study is focusing only on the output of the process (the time to produce the output) and not the internal operations of the process (the tasks required to produce a meal for a customer), the process is being treated as a black box.

c. The sampling plan was to monitor every order over a particular 7-day period. The sample is the 2,109 orders that were processed during the 7-day period.

d. The company's immediate interest is in learning about the drive-through window in Dallas. They plan to do this by using the waiting times from the sample to make a statistical inference about the drive-through process. In particular, they might use the average waiting time for the sample to estimate the average waiting time at the Dallas facility.

e. As for inferences about populations, measures of reliability can be developed for inferences about processes. The reliability of the estimate of the average waiting time for the Dallas restaurant could be measured by a bound on the error of estimation. That is, we might find that the average waiting time is 4.2 minutes, with a bound on the error of estimation of .5 minute. The implication would be that we could be reasonably certain that the true average waiting time for the Dallas process is between 3.7 and 4.7 minutes.

Notice that there is also a population described in this example: the company's 6,289 existing outlets with drive-through facilities. In the final analysis, the company will use what it learns about the process in Dallas and, perhaps, similar studies at other locations to make an inference about the waiting times in its populations of outlets.

Note that output already generated by a process can be viewed as a population. Suppose a soft-drink canning process produced 2,000 twelve-packs yesterday, all of which were stored in a warehouse. If we were interested in learning something about those 2,000 packages—such as the percentage with defective cardboard packaging—we could treat the 2,000 packages as a population. We might draw a sample from the population in the warehouse, measure the variable of interest, and use the sample data to make a statistical inference about the 2,000 packages, as described in Sections 1.2 and 1.3.

CASE STUDY 1.6 / Quality Improvement: U.S. Firms Respond to the Challenge from Japan

Over the last 2 decades, U.S. firms have been seriously challenged by products of superior quality from overseas, particularly from Japan. Japan currently produces 26% of the cars sold in the United States, and some predict this figure will climb to 40% within a decade. Only one U.S. firm still manufactures televisions; the rest are made in Japan.

To meet this competitive challenge, more and more U.S. firms—both manufacturing and service firms—have begun quality-improvement initiatives of their own. Many of these firms now stress the management of quality in all phases and aspects of their business, from the design of their products to production, distribution, sales, and service.

Broadly speaking, quality-improvement programs are concerned with (1) finding out what the customer wants, (2) translating those wants into a product design, and (3) producing and delivering a product or service that meets or exceeds the specifications of the product design. In all these areas, but particularly in the third, *improvement of quality requires improvement of processes*—including production processes, distribution processes, and service processes.

But what does it mean to say that a process has been improved? Generally speaking, it means that the customer of the process (i.e., the user of the output) indicates a greater satisfaction with the output. Frequently, such increases in satisfaction require a reduction in the variation of one or more process variables. That is, a reduction in the variation of the output stream of the process is needed.

But how can process variation be monitored and reduced? In the mid-1920s, Walter Shewhart of the Bell Telephone Laboratories made perhaps the most significant breakthrough of this century for the improvement of processes. He recognized that variation in process output was inevitable. No two parts produced by a given machine are the same; no two transactions performed by a given bank teller are the same. He also recognized that variation could be understood, monitored, and controlled using statistical methods. He developed a simple graphical technique—called a **control chart**—for determining whether product variation is within acceptable limits. This method provides guidance for when to adjust or change a production process and when to leave it alone. It can be used at the end of the production process or, most significantly, at different points within the process. We discuss control charts and other tools for improving processes in Chapter 13.

In recent years, largely as a result of the Japanese challenge to the supremacy of U.S. products, control charts and other statistical tools have gained widespread use in the United States. As evidence for the claim that U.S. firms are responding well to Japan's competitive challenge, consider this: The most prestigious quality improvement prize in the world that a firm can win is the Deming Prize. It is awarded by the Japanese. In 1989 it was won for the first time by an American company—Florida Power and Light Company.

In this section we have presented a brief introduction to processes and the use of statistical methods to analyze and learn about processes. In Chapters 13, 14, and 15 we present an in-depth treatment of these subjects. If you would like further amplification now of the ideas presented in this section, we suggest that you read Section 13.4 "Systems and Systems Thinking."

1.5 The Role of Statistics in Managerial Decision-Making

Managers frequently rely on input from statistical analyses to help them make decisions. The role statistics can play in managerial decision-making is indicated in the flow diagram in Figure 1.3. Every managerial decision-making problem begins with a real-world problem. This problem is then formulated in managerial terms and framed as a managerial question. The next sequence of steps (proceeding counterclockwise around the flow diagram) identifies the role that statistics can play in this process. The managerial question is translated into a statistical question, the sample data are collected and analyzed, and the statistical question is answered. The next step in the process is using the answer to the statistical question to reach an answer to the managerial question. The answer to the managerial question may suggest a reformulation of the original managerial problem, suggest a new managerial question, or lead to the solution of the managerial problem.

FIGURE 1.3 ►
Flow diagram showing the role of statistics in managerial decision-making
Source: Chervany, Benson, and Iyer (1980)

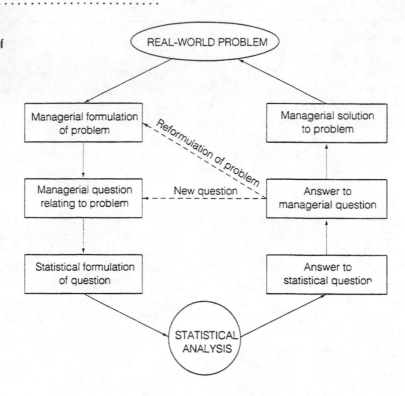

One of the most difficult steps in the decision-making process—one that requires a cooperative effort among managers and statisticians—is the translation of the managerial question into statistical terms (for example, into a question about a population). This statistical question must be formulated so that, when answered, it will provide the key to the answer to the managerial question. Thus, as in the game of chess, you must formulate the statistical question with the end result, the solution to the managerial question, in mind.

Exercises 1.1 – 1.18

Note: Starred (*) exercises refer to the optional section.

Learning the Mechanics

1.1   Explain the difference between descriptive and inferential statistics.

1.2   List and define the five elements of an inferential statistical problem.

1.3   Explain how populations and variables differ.

1.4   Explain how populations and samples differ.

1.5   Why would a statistician consider an inference incomplete without an accompanying measure of its reliability?

*1.6   Explain the difference between a population and a process.

1.7   Consider the set of all students enrolled in your statistics course this term. Suppose you are interested in learning about the current grade point averages (GPAs) of this group.
   a. Define the population and variable of interest.
   b. Suppose you determine the GPA of every member of the class. What would this represent, a census or a sample?
   c. Suppose you determine the GPA of 10 members of the class. Would this represent a census or a sample?
   d. If you determine the GPA of every member of the class and then calculate the average, how much reliability does this have as an "estimate" of the class average GPA?
   e. If you determine the GPA of ten members of the class and then calculate the average, will the number you get necessarily be the same as the average GPA for the whole class? On what factors would you expect the reliability of the estimate to depend?

1.8   Refer to Exercise 1.7. What must be true in order for the sample of 10 students you select from your class to be considered a random sample?

Applying the Concepts

1.9   Pollsters regularly conduct opinion polls to determine the popularity rating of the current president. Suppose a poll is to be conducted tomorrow in which 2,000 individuals will be asked whether the president is doing a good or poor job.
   a. What is the relevant population?
   b. What is the variable of interest? Is it numerical or nonnumerical?
   c. What is the sample?
   d. What is the inference of interest to the pollster?

1.10   Refer to Exercise 1.9. Suppose the poll is conducted as described therein, except that each of the 2,000 individuals polled is asked to rate the job performance of the president on a scale from 0 to 100. How do your answers to parts a–d change, if at all?

1.11   *Fortune* publishes a list of the 500 industrial corporations in the United States with the largest annual sales volume ("The Fortune 500," 1992). Throughout the year, each of these companies is then referred to as a *Fortune 500 company*. Assume a researcher with limited time and money wants to predict the number of new employees these 500 companies anticipate hiring next year. She selects 50 of the 500 companies, and asks a representative of each company how many new employees the company is likely to hire in the coming year.
   a. Identify the population from which the sample was drawn.
   b. What is the variable of interest?
   c. Identify the sample.
   d. What could we infer about the population from the sample data?
   e. When answering part d, are we employing descriptive or inferential statistics? Explain.
   f. *Fortune* lists the net profit of each of the 500 companies. If we compute the average of these 500 net profits to learn more about the Fortune 500 companies, are we employing descriptive or inferential statistics? Explain.

*1.12   Coca-Cola and Schweppes Beverages Limited (CCSB), which was formed in 1987, is 49% owned by the Coca-Cola Company. David Nellist (1992) reports that CCSBs new Wakefield plant can produce 4,000 cans of soft drink per minute. The automated process consists of measuring and dispensing the raw ingredients into storage vessels to create the syrup, and then injecting the syrup, along with carbon dioxide, into the beverage cans. Suppose that to monitor the subprocess that adds carbon dioxide to the cans, five filled cans are pulled off the line every 15 minutes and the amount of carbon dioxide in each of these five is measured to determine whether the amounts are within prescribed limits.
   a. Describe the process studied.
   b. Describe the variable of interest.
   c. Describe the sample.
   d. Describe the inference of interest.
   e. *Brix* is a unit for measuring sugar concentration. If a technician is assigned the task of estimating the average brix level of all 240,000 cans of beverage stored in a warehouse near Wakefield, will the technician be examining a process or a population? Explain.

1.13   An insurance company would like to determine the proportion of all medical doctors who have been involved in one or more malpractice suits. The company selects 500 doctors at random from a professional directory and determines the number in the sample who have ever been involved in a malpractice suit.
   a. Identify the population and variable of interest to the insurance company.
   b. Describe the sample and identify the type of inference the insurance company wishes to make.
   c. What is meant by the phrase *at random* in the context of this exercise?

1.14   *Corporate merger* is a means through which one firm (the bidder) acquires control of the assets of another firm (the target). Carol E. Eger (1982) identified a total of 497 mergers between firms listed on the New York Stock Exchange that resulted in the delisting of the acquired (target) firm's stock during the period 1958–1980. She sampled 38 of these mergers and evaluated the effects of the merger on the value of the holdings of the bidder firm's bondholders. In particular, she wanted to learn whether the value of the holdings increased or decreased as a result of the merger.
   a. Identify the population studied.
   b. Identify the variable of interest.
   c. Describe the sample.
   d. Discuss types of inferences we might wish to make about the population.

1.15   *Job-sharing* is an innovative employment alternative that originated in Sweden and is becoming very popular in the United States. Firms that offer job-sharing plans allow two or more persons to work part-time, sharing one full-time job. For example, two job-sharers might alternate work weeks, with one working while the other is off. Job-sharers never work at the same time and may not even know each other. Job-sharing is particularly attractive to working mothers and to people who frequently lose their jobs due to fluctuations in the economy ("Your Job in the 1980's," 1980). To evaluate employers' satisfaction with job-sharing plans, a government agency contacted 100 firms that offer job-sharing. Each firm's director of personnel was asked whether the firm was satisfied with the productivity of workers with shared jobs.
   a. Identify the population from which the sample was selected.
   b. Identify the variable measured.
   c. Identify the sample selected.
   d. What type of inference is of interest to the government agency?

1.16   Myron Gable and Martin T. Topol (1988) sampled 218 department-store executives to study the relationship between job satisfaction and the degree of Machiavellian orientation. Briefly, the Machiavellian orientation is one in which the executive exerts very strong control—even to the point of deception and cruelty—over the employees supervised. The authors administered a questionnaire to each of the sampled executives and obtained both a job satisfaction score and a Machiavellian rating. They concluded that those with higher satisfaction scores are likely to have a lower "Mach" rating.
   a.   What is the population from which the sample was selected?
   b.   What variables were measured by the authors?
   c.   Identify the sample.
   d.   What inference was made by the authors?

1.17   Manufacturers of consumer goods rely on the information provided by consumer preference surveys to guide both the design and the marketing of new products. In the winter of 1986, Onan Corporation, a manufacturer of built-in generators for recreational vehicles (RVs), was considering developing and marketing a portable generator. Such a product could potentially be marketed both to RV owners and RV manufacturers. To determine RV owners' preferences with respect to the features of a portable generator (e.g., size and manual or electric start), 3,000 questionnaires were mailed to RV owners in the continental United States. One thousand fifty-two (1,052) responses were received by Onan.*
   a.   Identify the population, the variables, the sample, and the inferences of interest to Onan.
   b.   Chapters 6–9 indicate that the reliability of an inference is related to the size of the sample used. In addition to sample size, what other factors might affect the reliability of inferences based on the responses to a mailed questionnaire?

1.18   The Wallace Company of Houston is a distributor of pipes, valves, and fittings to the refining, chemical, and petrochemical industries. The company was one of four winners of the Malcolm Baldrige National Quality Award in 1990. Don Nichols (1991) explains that one of the steps the company takes to monitor the quality of its distribution process is to send out a survey twice a year to a subset of its current customers, asking the customers to rate the speed of deliveries, the accuracy of invoices, and the quality of the packaging of the products they have received from Wallace.
   a.   Describe the process studied.
   b.   Describe the variables of interest.
   c.   Describe the sample.
   d.   Describe the inferences of interest.
   e.   What are some of the factors that are likely to affect the reliability of the inferences?

On Your Own

If you could start your own business right now, what kind would it be? Identify a large population and a characteristic of the units in the population (i.e., a variable) that would be of interest to you and your firm. How would you measure the variable of interest for a sample of units drawn from the population? Is the data set you identified a sample data set or a population data set? How could you use this data set in the operation of your business?

---

*Information by personal communication with Thomas J. Roess, Manager, Market Analysis, Onan Corporation, Fridley, Minnesota.

References

Allison, R. I. and Uhl, K. P. "Influence of beer brand identification on taste perception." *Journal of Marketing Research*, Aug. 1965, pp. 36–39.

Careers in Statistics. Washington, D.C.: American Statistical Association and the Institute of Mathematical Statistics, 1974.

Chervany, N. L., Benson, P. G., and Iyer, R. K. "The planning stage in statistical reasoning." *The American Statistician*, Nov. 1980, pp. 222–226.

Eger, C. E. "Corporate mergers: An analytical analysis of the role of risky debt." Unpublished Ph.D. dissertation. University of Minnesota, 1982.

"The Fortune 500." *Fortune*, Apr. 20, 1992, pp. 220–239.

Gable, M. and Topol, M. T. "Machiavellianism and the department-store executive." *Journal of Retailing*, Spring 1988, pp. 68–84.

Hunz, E. "Application of statistical sampling to inventory audits." *The Internal Auditor*, 1956, 13, p. 38.

Nellist, David. "Quality teamwork at Wakefield." *Industrial Management and Data Systems*, 1992, Vol. 92, No. 2, pp. 21–23.

Nichols, Don. "Quality wins." *Small Business Reports*, May 1991, pp. 26–35.

Tanur, J. M., Mosteller, F., Kruskal, W. H., Link, R. F., Pieters, R. S., and Rising, G. R. *Statistics: A Guide to the Unknown*. San Francisco: Holden-Day, 1989.

U.S. Bureau of the Census. *Statistical Abstract of the United States: 1989*. Washington, D.C.: U.S. Government Printing Office, 1989.

U.S. Department of Commerce. *An Error Profile: Employment as Measured by the Current Population Survey*. Statistical Policy Working Paper 3. Washington, D.C.: U.S. Government Printing Office, 1978.

U.S. Department of Labor. *The Consumer Price Index: Concepts and Content over the Years*. Bureau of Labor Statistics, Report 517. Washington, D.C.: U.S. Government Printing Office, May 1978.

Willis, R. E. and Chervany, N. L. *Statistical Analysis and Modeling for Management Decision-making*. Belmont, Calif.: Wadsworth, 1974, Chapter 1.

"Your job in the 1980's." *Consumer's Digest*, Nov.–Dec. 1980, pp. 32–36.

CHAPTER TWO

Methods for Describing Sets of Data

Contents

2.1 Types of Data

2.2 Graphical Methods for Describing Quantitative Data: Histograms and Stem-and-Leaf Displays

2.3 Graphical Methods for Describing Quantitative Data Produced Over Time: The Time Series Plot (Optional)

2.4 Numerical Methods for Measuring Central Tendency

2.5 Numerical Methods for Measuring Variability

2.6 Interpreting the Standard Deviation

2.7 Calculating a Mean and Standard Deviation from Grouped Data (Optional)

2.8 Measures of Relative Standing

2.9 Box Plots: Graphical Descriptions Based on Quartiles (Optional)

2.10 Distorting the Truth with Descriptive Techniques

Case Studies

Case Study 2.1 Pareto Analysis

Case Study 2.2 Appraising the Market Value of an Asset

Case Study 2.3 Deming Warns Against Knee-Jerk Use of Histograms

Case Study 2.4 Hotels: A Rational Method for Overbooking

Case Study 2.5 The Delphi Technique for Obtaining a Consensus of Opinion

Case Study 2.6 More on the Delphi Technique

Case Study 2.7 Becoming More Sensitive to Customer Needs

Case Study 2.8 Deciding When to Respond to Consumer Complaints

Where We've Been

In Chapter 1, we examined some examples of the use of statistics in business. We discussed the role that statistics plays in supporting managerial decision-making. We introduced you to descriptive and inferential statistics and to the five elements of inferential statistics: a population, one or more variables, a sample, an inference, and a measure of reliability for the inference. We described the primary goal of inferential statistics as using sample data to make inferences (estimates, predictions, or other generalizations) about the population from which the sample was drawn.

Where We're Going

Before we make an inference, we must be able to describe and extract information from the sample data. This can be accomplished through both graphical and numerical methods.

Before we can use the information in a sample to make inferences about a population, we must be able to extract the relevant information from the sample. That is, we need methods to summarize and describe the sample measurements. For example, if we look at last year's sales for 100 randomly selected companies, we are unlikely to extract much information by looking at the set of 100 sales figures. We would get a clearer picture of the data by calculating the average sales for all 100 companies, by determining the highest and lowest company sales, by drawing a graph that shows the spread of the 100 sales figures, or, in general, by using some technique that will extract and summarize relevant information from the data and, at the same time, allow us to obtain a clearer understanding of the sample.

In this chapter, we first define four different types of data and then present some graphical and numerical methods for describing data of each type. You will see that graphical methods for describing data are intuitively appealing and can be used to describe either a sample or a population. However, numerical methods for describing data are the keys that unlock the door to population inference-making.

2.1   Types of Data

In Chapter 1, you learned that statistics, both descriptive and inferential, is concerned with measurements of one or more variables of a sample of units drawn from a population. These measurements are referred to as **data**. We will generally classify data as one of four types: **nominal**, **ordinal**, **interval**, or **ratio**.

Definition 2.1

Nominal data are measurements that simply classify the units of the sample (or population) into categories.

Nominal data (also referred to as **categorical data**) are labels or names that identify the category to which each unit belongs. The following are examples of nominal data:

1. The political party affiliation of each individual in a sample of 50 business executives

2. The gender of each individual in a sample of seven applicants for a computer programming job

3. The state in which each of a sample of 100 U.S. firms had its highest sales revenue in 1993.

Note that in each case—political party, gender, and state—the measurement is no more than a categorization of each sample unit. Nominal data are often reported as nonnumerical labels, such as Democrat, woman, and Ohio. Even if the labels are converted to numbers, as they often are for ease of computer entry and analysis, the numerical values are simply codes. They cannot be meaningfully added, subtracted, multiplied, or divided. For example, we might code Democrat = 1, Republican = 2, and Other = 3. These are simply numerical codes for each of the categories into which units may fall and have no further significance.

Definition 2.2

Ordinal data are measurements that enable the units of the sample (or population) to be ordered with respect to the variable of interest.

Ordinal data are measurements that indicate the *relative* amount of a property possessed by the units. The following are examples of ordinal data:

1. The size of car rented by each individual in a sample of 30 business travelers: compact, subcompact, midsize, or full-size

2. A taste-tester's ranking of four brands of barbecue sauce

3. A supervisor's annual ranking of the performance of her 10 employees using a scale of 1 (worst performance) to 10 (best performance)

Note that in each case—size, flavor preference, and performance ranking—more than a categorization of units is involved. In addition to providing a categorization, the measurements actually rank the units. For example, we know that a midsize car is larger than a subcompact and that an employee with a performance ranking of 9 performed better, in the opinion of the supervisor, than one with a ranking of 7. We also know that a taster preferred brand C barbecue sauce to brand A if he gives brand C a higher flavor-preference ranking than brand A.

Ordinal data are said to represent a "higher" level of measurement than nominal data because ordinal data contain all the information of nominal data (i.e., category labels that differentiate units) *plus* an ordering of the units. As with nominal measurements, the distance between ordinal measurements is not meaningful. For example, we do not know whether the difference in size between a full-size and a midsize car is the same as the difference between the midsize and the subcompact. Nor do we know whether the extent of flavor preference between barbecue sauce brands C and A is the same as that between brands A and B if a taster reports her flavor preference as C > A > B > D, where > means "more flavorful than."

As with nominal data, ordinal data can be reported with or without numbers. For example, the automobile sizes are nonnumerically labeled, whereas the supervisor's performance rankings are numerical. Even if numbers are used, we must again be careful: They simply provide an ordering or ranking of the units in the sample or population. The arithmetic operations of addition, subtraction, multiplication, and division are not meaningful for ordinal data.

Definition 2.3

Interval data are measurements that enable the determination of how much more or less of the measured characteristic is possessed by one unit of the sample (or population) than another.

Interval data are always numerical, and the numbers assigned to two units can be subtracted to determine the *difference* between the units with respect to the variable measured. The following are examples of interval data:

1. The temperature (in degrees Fahrenheit) at which each of a sample of 20 pieces of heat-resistant plastic begins to melt

2. The scores of a sample of 150 MBA applicants on the GMAT, a standardized business graduate school entrance exam administered nationwide

3. The time at which the 5 P.M. Washington–to–New York air shuttle arrives at LaGuardia on each of a sample of 30 weekdays

Note that in each case—temperature, score, and arrival time—more than a ranking is involved. The difference between the numerical values assigned to the units is meaningful. For example, the difference between scores of 600 and 580 on the GMAT is the same as that between scores of 520 and 500. Also, the morning shuttle due at 9 A.M. but arriving at 9:20 A.M. is just as late as the afternoon shuttle due at 5:30 P.M. and arriving at 5:50 P.M. Note in each case that the difference is the key, not the numerical measurement itself.

Interval data represent a higher level of measurement than ordinal data, because in addition to ranking the units, interval data reflect the difference between the units with respect to the variable measured. Although adding or subtracting interval data is valid, multiplying or dividing them is not. This is because the zero point (the origin, or 0) does not indicate an absence of the characteristic of interest. For example, the origin on the temperature scale differs for the Fahrenheit and Celsius scales and does not indicate an absence of heat on either scale. Temperatures lower than 0° (e.g., −10°C and −10°F) indicate that less heat is present, so 0° does not mean "no heat." The result is that we cannot say that a temperature of 100°F indicates twice the heat of 50°F. Similarly, since GMAT scores range from 200 to 800, a zero score is not even possible, and thus has no meaning. The result is that a score of 600 cannot be interpreted as being 50% higher than a score of 400.

Most numerical business data are measured on scales for which the origin is meaningful. Thus, most numerical measurements encountered in business are *ratio data*.

> **Definition 2.4**
>
> **Ratio data** are measurements that enable the determination of how many times as much of the measured characteristic is possessed by one unit of the sample (or population) than another.

Ratio data are always numerical, and the ratio between the numbers assigned to two units can be interpreted as the multiple by which the units differ. The following are examples of ratio data:

1. The sales revenue for each firm in a sample of 100 U.S. firms
2. The unemployment rate (reported as a percentage) in the United States for each of the past 60 months
3. The number of female executives employed in each of a sample of 50 manufacturing companies

Note that in each case—dollars of revenue, percentage unemployed, and count of female executives—the scale measures the absolute amount of the characteristic possessed by the unit. The result is that the ratio of measurements between units is meaningful. That is, a company with revenue of $100 million has twice the revenue of a company with $50 million in revenue. Similarly, an unemployment rate of 8% means twice as many unemployed as with a rate of 4%. And a company with 30 female executives has 1.5 times as many as one with 20 female executives.

Ratio data represent the highest level of measurement. The numbers can be used to categorize, rank, differentiate, and measure multiples of one unit with respect to another. All arithmetic operations performed on ratio data are meaningful.

The key to differentiating interval and ratio data is that for ratio data the zero point, or origin, denotes an absence of the characteristic being measured. For example, zero revenue, zero unemployment, and zero female executives mean *absence* of income, unemployment, and female executives, respectively. Most measurement scales utilized in business yield ratio data: measures of monetary value, distance, weight, height, percentages, and numerical counts all usually generate ratio data.

The four types of data are often combined into two classes that are sufficient for most statistical applications. Nominal and ordinal data are often referred to as **qualitative** data, whereas interval and ratio data are called **quantitative** data.

The properties of the four types of data are summarized in the box. As you would expect, the methods for describing and reporting data depend on the type of data analyzed. We devote the remainder of this chapter to graphical methods for describing qualitative and quantitative data.

Types of Data	
Nominal	Classification of sample (or population) units into categories
	Often uses labels rather than numbers
Ordinal	Rank-orders the sample (or population) units
	May be verbal labels or numbers
Interval	Enables comparison of sample (or population) units according to differences between values
	Always numerical, but the zero point on the scale does not indicate an absence of the measured characteristic
Ratio	Enables comparison of sample (or population) units according to multiples of the values
	Always numerical, and the zero point on the scale denotes an absence of the measured characteristic
Qualitative	Includes nominal and ordinal data types
Quantitative	Includes interval and ratio data types

Exercises 2.1 – 2.8

Learning the Mechanics

2.1 a. Explain the difference between nominal and ordinal data.
b. Explain the difference between interval and ratio data.
c. Explain the difference between qualitative and quantitative data.

2.2 Each of the following descriptions of data defines one of the following types: nominal, ordinal, interval, ratio. Match the correct type to each description.
a. Data that enable the units of the sample to be compared by the differences between their numerical values
b. Data that enable the units of the sample to be classified into categories
c. Data that enable the units of the sample to be rank-ordered
d. Data that enable the units of the sample to be compared by computing the ratios of the numerical values

2.3 Suppose you are provided a data set that classifies each sample unit into one of four categories: A, B, C, or D. You plan to create a computer database consisting of these data, and you decide to code the data as A = 1, B = 2, C = 3, and D = 4 for entering them into the computer. Are the data consisting of the classifications A, B, C, and D qualitative or quantitative? After the data are entered as 1, 2, 3, or 4, are they qualitative or quantitative? Explain your answers.

Applying the Concepts

2.4   A food-products company is considering marketing a new snack food. To see how consumers react to the product, the company conducted a taste-test using a sample of 100 shoppers at a suburban shopping mall. The shoppers were asked to taste the snack food and then fill out a short questionnaire that requested the following information:

a. What is your age?

b. Are you the person who typically does the food shopping for your household?

c. How many people are in your family?

d. How would you rate the taste of the snack food on a scale of 1 to 10, where 1 is least tasty?

e. Would you purchase this snack food if it were available on the market?

f. If you answered yes to question e, how often would you purchase it?

Each of these questions defines a variable of interest to the company. Classify the data generated for each variable as nominal, ordinal, interval, or ratio. Justify your classification.

2.5   Classify the following examples of data as nominal, ordinal, interval, or ratio. Justify your classification.

a. Ten college freshmen were asked to indicate the brand of jeans they prefer.

b. Fifteen television cable companies were asked how many hours of sports programming they carry in a typical week.

c. Fifty executives were asked what percentage of their workday is spent in meetings.

d. The number of long-distance phone calls made from each of 100 public telephone booths on a particular day was recorded.

e. The Scholastic Aptitude Test (SAT) scores of 250 incoming freshmen to a small college were compiled.

2.6   Classify the following examples of data as either qualitative or quantitative:

a. The brand of calculator purchased by each of 20 business statistics students

b. The list price of calculators purchased by each of 20 business statistics students

c. The number of automobiles purchased during the past 5 years by each household in a sample of 50 randomly selected households

d. The month indicated by each of 41 randomly selected business firms as the month during which it had the highest sales

e. The depth of tread remaining on each of 137 randomly selected automobile tires after 20,000 miles of wear

2.7   Windows is a computer software product made by Microsoft Corporation. In designing Windows Version 3.1, Microsoft telephoned 60,000 users of Windows 3.0 (an older version) and asked them how the product could be improved (Roberts, 1992). Assume customers were asked the following questions:

I.   Are you the most frequent user of Windows 3.0 in your household?

II.   What is your age?

III.   How would you rate the helpfulness of the Tutorial instructions that accompany Windows 3.0, on a scale of 1 to 10, where 1 is not helpful?

IV.   When using a printer with Windows 3.0, do you most frequently use a dot-matrix printer or another type of printer?

V.   If the speed of Windows 3.0 could be changed, which one of the following would you prefer: slower, unchanged, faster?

VI. How many people in your household have used Windows 3.0 at least once?

Each of these questions defines a variable of interest to the company. Classify the data generated for each variable as nominal, ordinal, interval, or ratio. Justify your classification.

2.8   Classify the examples of data in parts **a–d** as either qualitative or quantitative:
  a. The number of corporate mergers during each of the last 15 years
  b. The change in the Consumer Price Index during each of the last 6 months
  c. The length of time before each of 30 dry-cell batteries goes dead
  d. The American automobile manufacturer that each of 25 service station mechanics indicated as producing the most reliable cars
  e. Classify each of the preceding as nominal, ordinal, interval or ratio data.

2.2   Graphical Methods for Describing Quantitative Data: Histograms and Stem-and-Leaf Displays

Recall from Section 2.1 that quantitative data sets consist of either interval or ratio data. Most business data are quantitative, so that methods for summarizing quantitative data are especially important.

For example, suppose a financial analyst is interested in the amount of resources spent by computer hardware and software companies on research and development (R&D). She samples 50 of these high-technology firms and calculates the amount each spent last year on R&D as a percentage of their total revenues. The results are given in Table 2.1. As numerical measurements made on the sample of 50 units (the firms),

TABLE 2.1   Percentage of Revenues Spent on Research and Development

Company	Percentage	Company	Percentage	Company	Percentage	Company	Percentage
1	13.5	14	9.5	27	8.2	39	6.5
2	8.4	15	8.1	28	6.9	40	7.5
3	10.5	16	13.5	29	7.2	41	7.1
4	9.0	17	9.9	30	8.2	42	13.2
5	9.2	18	6.9	31	9.6	43	7.7
6	9.7	19	7.5	32	7.2	44	5.9
7	6.6	20	11.1	33	8.8	45	5.2
8	10.6	21	8.2	34	11.3	46	5.6
9	10.1	22	8.0	35	8.5	47	11.7
10	7.1	23	7.7	36	9.4	48	6.0
11	8.0	24	7.4	37	10.5	49	7.8
12	7.9	25	6.5	38	6.9	50	6.5
13	6.8	26	9.5				

these percentages represent quantitative data. The analyst's initial objective is to describe these data in order to extract relevant information.

A **relative frequency histogram** for these 50 R&D percentages is shown in Figure 2.1. The horizontal axis of Figure 2.1, which gives the percentage spent on R&D for each company, is divided into intervals commencing with the interval from 5.15 to 6.25 and proceeding in intervals of equal size to 12.85 to 13.95 percent. The vertical axis gives the proportion (or **relative frequency**) of the 50 percentages that fall in each interval. Thus, you can see that the bulk of the companies spend between 6.25% and 10.65% of their revenues on research and development, while only .06 of the companies spend more than 12%. Many other summary statements can be made by further study of the histogram.

FIGURE 2.1 ▶

Relative frequency histogram for the 50 computer companies' R&D percentages

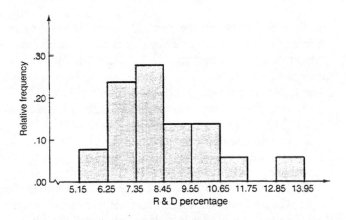

Another graphic representation of these same data, a **stem-and-leaf** display, is shown below. In these displays the **stem** is the portion of the observation to the left of the decimal point, whereas the remaining portion to the right of the decimal point is the **leaf**.

The stems and leaves for the R&D percentages 7.4, 10.5, and 13.2 are shown here:

Stem	Leaf		Stem	Leaf		Stem	Leaf
7	4		10	5		13	2

The stem-and-leaf display for all 50 R&D percentages is shown in Figure 2.2 (page 30). Note that the leaves corresponding to each stem are arranged in ascending order, and a key is included with the display to specify the units of the leaf (and, by implication, the units of the stem).

Stem	Leaf
5	2 6 9
6	0 5 5 5 6 8 9 9 9
7	1 1 2 2 4 5 5 7 7 8 9
8	0 0 1 2 2 2 4 5 8
9	0 2 4 5 5 6 7 9
10	1 5 5 6
11	1 3 7
12	
13	2 5 5

Key: Leaf units are tenths.

Note that although the stem 12 has no leaves (meaning that none of the 50 observations fell in the range from 12.0 to 12.9), we include the 12 stem in the display so that this fact is visually obvious. Note also that the decimal point is not included in the display. When there is no confusion caused by its omission, we can usually obtain a less cluttered graphical description without it.

Several descriptive facts about these data are easily seen in the stem-and-leaf display. Most of the sampled computer companies (37 of 50) spent between 6.0% and 9.9% of their revenues on R&D, and 11 of them spent between 7.0% and 7.9%. Relative to the rest of the sampled companies, three spent a high percentage of revenues on R&D—in excess of 13%.

Both the histogram and stem-and-leaf displays provide useful graphic descriptions of quantitative data. Since most statistical software packages can be used to construct these displays, we will focus on their interpretation rather than their construction.

Histograms can be used to display either the **frequency** or **relative frequency** of the measurements falling into specified intervals (called **measurement classes**). The frequency is just a count of the number of measurements in a class, while the relative frequency is the proportion, or fraction, of measurements in the class. The measurement classes, frequencies, and relative frequencies for the R&D data are shown in Table 2.2.

By looking at a histogram (say, the relative frequency histogram in Figure 2.1), you can see two important facts. First, note the total area under the histogram, and then note the proportion of the total area that falls over a particular interval of the horizontal axis. You will see that the proportion of the total area that falls above an interval is equal to the relative frequency of the measurements that fall in the interval. *

---

*Some histograms are constructed with all class intervals of equal width except the first and last, which are open-ended. The proportionality between area and relative frequency will not hold for such histograms. We will restrict our attention to histograms that have equal-sized class intervals, because later we will want to establish a correspondence between relative frequency histograms and probability distributions.

TABLE 2.2 Measurement Classes, Frequencies, and Relative Frequencies for the R&D Percentage Data

Class	Measurement Class	Class Frequency	Class Relative Frequency	
1	5.15– 6.25	4	$\frac{4}{50}$ =	.08
2	6.25– 7.35	12	$\frac{12}{50}$ =	.24
3	7.35– 8.45	14	$\frac{14}{50}$ =	.28
4	8.45– 9.55	7	$\frac{7}{50}$ =	.14
5	9.55–10.65	7	$\frac{7}{50}$ =	.14
6	10.65–11.75	3	$\frac{3}{50}$ =	.06
7	11.75–12.85	0	$\frac{0}{50}$ =	.00
8	12.85–13.95	3	$\frac{3}{50}$ =	.06
				1.00

For example, the relative frequency for the class interval 5.15–6.25 is .08. Consequently, the rectangle above that interval contains 8% of the total area under the histogram.

Second, you can imagine the appearance of the relative frequency histogram for a very large set of data (say, a population). As the number of measurements in a data set is increased, you can obtain a better description of the data by decreasing the width of the class intervals. When the class intervals become small enough, a relative frequency histogram will (for all practical purposes) appear as a smooth curve (see Figure 2.3).

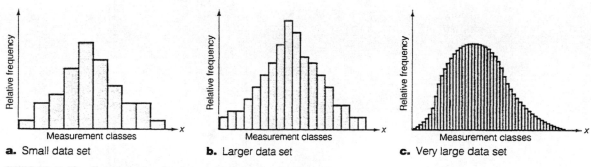

a. Small data set   **b.** Larger data set   **c.** Very large data set

FIGURE 2.3 ▲ The effect of the size of a data set on the outline of a histogram

While histograms provide good visual descriptions, particularly of very large data sets, individual measurements cannot be identified by looking at a histogram. In contrast, each of the original measurements is "visible" in a stem-and-leaf display. The stem-and-leaf display arranges the data in ascending order, which enables easy location of the individual measurements. For example, in Figure 2.2 we can easily see that three of the R&D measurements are equal to 8.2%, whereas that fact is not evident by inspection of the histogram in Figure 2.1. However, stem-and-leaf displays can become unwieldy for very large data sets. A very large number of stems and leaves causes the vertical and horizontal dimensions of the display to become cumbersome, so that the usefulness of the visual display is diminished.

EXAMPLE 2.1

A manufacturer of industrial wheels suspects that profitable orders are being lost because of the long time the firm takes to develop price quotes for potential customers. To investigate this possibility, 50 requests for price quotes were randomly selected from the set of all quotes made last year, and the processing time was determined for each quote. The processing times are displayed in Table 2.3, and each quote was classified according to whether the order was "lost" or not (i.e., whether or not the customer placed an order after receiving a price quote).

TABLE 2.3   Price Quote Processing Times (Days)

Request Number	Processing Time	Lost?	Request Number	Processing Time	Lost?
1	2.36	No	26	3.34	No
2	5.73	No	27	6.00	No
3	6.60	No	28	5.92	No
4	10.05	Yes	29	7.28	Yes
5	5.13	No	30	1.25	No
6	1.88	No	31	4.01	No
7	2.52	No	32	7.59	No
8	2.00	No	33	13.42	Yes
9	4.69	No	34	3.24	No
10	1.91	No	35	3.37	No
11	6.75	Yes	36	14.06	Yes
12	3.92	No	37	5.10	No
13	3.46	No	38	6.44	No
14	2.64	No	39	7.76	No
15	3.63	No	40	4.40	No
16	3.44	No	41	5.48	No
17	9.49	Yes	42	7.51	No
18	4.90	No	43	6.18	No
19	7.45	No	44	8.22	Yes
20	20.23	Yes	45	4.37	No
21	3.91	No	46	2.93	No
22	1.70	No	47	9.95	Yes
23	16.29	Yes	48	4.46	No
24	5.52	No	49	14.32	Yes
25	1.44	No	50	9.01	No

a. Use a statistical software package to create a frequency histogram for these data. Then shade the area under the histogram that corresponds to lost orders.

b. Use a statistical software package to create a stem-and-leaf display for these data. Then shade each leaf of the display that corresponds to a lost order.

c. Compare and interpret the two graphic displays of these data.

Solution

a. We used SAS to generate the relative frequency histogram in Figure 2.4.

FIGURE 2.4 ▶
Frequency histogram for the quote processing time data

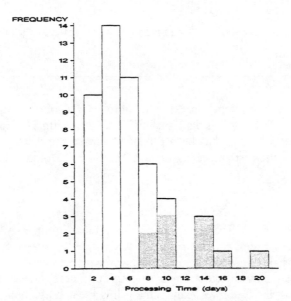

SAS, like most statistical software, offers the user the choice of accepting default class intervals and interval widths, or the user can make his or her own selections. After some experimenting with various numbers of class intervals and interval widths, we used 10 intervals. SAS then created intervals of width 2 days, beginning at 1 day, just below the smallest measurement of 1.25 days, and ending with 21 days, just above the largest measurement of 20.2 days. Note that SAS labels the midpoint of each bar, rather than its endpoints. Thus, the bar labeled "2" represents measurements from 1.00 to 2.99, the bar labeled "4" represents measurements from 3.00 to 4.99, etc. This histogram clearly shows the clustering of the measurements in the lower end of the distribution (between approximately 1 and 7 days), and the relatively few measurements in the upper end of the distribution (greater than 12 days). The shading of the area of the frequency histogram corresponding to lost orders clearly indicates that they lie in the upper tail of the distribution.

b. We used the statistical package SPSS[R] to generate the stem-and-leaf display in Figure 2.5 (page 34).

FIGURE 2.5 ▶

Stem-and-leaf display for the quote processing time data

```
Frequency      Stem &  Leaf

   5.00         1 .  24789
   5.00         2 .  03569
   8.00         3 .  23344699
   6.00         4 .  034469
   6.00         5 .  114579
   5.00         6 .  01467
   5.00         7 .  24557
   1.00         8 .  2
   3.00         9 .  049
   1.00        10 .  0
    .00        11 .
    .00        12 .
   1.00        13 .  4
   4.00 Extremes    (14.1), (14.3), (16.3), (20.2)

Stem width:      1.00
Each leaf:          1 case(s)
```

Note that the stem consists of the number of whole days (units and ten digits), and the leaf is the tenths digit (first digit after the decimal) of each measurement.[*] The hundredths digit has been dropped to make the display more visually effective. Thus, the first processing time in Table 2.3, 2.36 days, is partitioned as follows:

Stem	Leaf
2	3

Note that SPSS also includes a column titled "Frequency" showing the number of measurements corresponding to each stem. Also, note that instead of extending the stems all the way to 20 days to show the largest measurement, SPSS truncates the display after the stem corresponding to 13 days, labels the largest four measurements as "Extremes," and simply lists them horizontally in the last row of the display. Extreme observations that are detached from the remainder of the data are called **outliers**, and they usually receive special attention in statistical analyses. Although outliers may represent legitimate measurements, they are frequently mistakes: incorrectly recorded, miscoded during data entry, or taken from a population different from the one from which the rest of the sample was selected. Stem-and-leaf displays are useful for identifying outliers.

c. As is usually the case for data sets that are not too large (say, fewer than 100 measurements), the stem-and-leaf display provides more detail than the histogram without being unwieldy. For the processing time data, note that the stem-and-leaf display in Figure 2.5 clearly indicates not only that the lost orders are associated with high processing times (as does the histogram in Figure 2.4), but also exactly which of the times correspond to lost orders. Histograms are most useful for displaying very large data sets, when the overall shape of the distribution of measure-

---

[*]In the examples in this section, the stem was formed from the digits to the left of the decimal. This is not always the case. For example, in the following data set the stems could be the tenths digit and the leaves the hundredths digit: .12, .15, .22, .25, .28, .33.

ments is more important than the identification of individual measurements. Nevertheless, the message of both graphical displays is clear: establishing processing time limits may well result in fewer lost orders.

. . . .

While stem-and-leaf displays may generally provide more information than histograms for quantitative (interval or ratio) data, they are not useful for qualitative (nominal or ordinal) data. However, histograms can be used to graph the **frequency** or **relative frequency** corresponding to each classification of the qualitative variable. Histograms for qualitative data are often called **bar charts**, and their usefulness is demonstrated in the Case Study 2.1.

CASE STUDY 2.1   Pareto Analysis

Vilfredo Pareto (1843–1923), an Italian economist, discovered that approximately 80% of the wealth of a country lies with approximately 20% of the people. Others have noted similar findings in other areas: 80% of sales are attributable to 20% of the customers; 80% of customer complaints result from 20% of the components of a product; 80% of defective items produced by a process result from 20% of the types of errors that are made in production (Kane, 1989). These examples illustrate the idea of "the vital few and the trivial many," the **Pareto principle**. As applied to the last example, a "vital few" errors account for most of the defectives produced. The remaining defectives are due to many different errors, the "trivial many."

In general, **Pareto analysis** involves the categorization of items and the determination of which categories contain the most observations. These are the "vital few" categories. Pareto analysis is used in industry today as a problem-identification tool. Managers and workers use it to identify the most important problems or causes of problems that plague them. Knowledge of the "vital few" problems permits management to set priorities and focus their problem-solving efforts.

The primary tool of Pareto analysis is the **Pareto diagram**. The Pareto diagram is simply a frequency or relative frequency histogram, or bar chart, with the bars arranged in descending order of height from left to right across the horizontal axis. That is, the tallest bar is

positioned at the left and the shortest is at the far right. This arrangement locates the most important categories—those with the largest frequencies—at the left of the chart. Since the data are qualitative, there is no inherent numerical order: They can be rearranged to make the display more useful.

Consider the following example from the automobile industry (adapted from Kane, 1989). All cars produced on a particular day were inspected for defects. The defects were categorized by type as follows: body, accessories, electrical, transmission, and engine. The resulting Pareto diagram for these qualitative data is shown in Figure 2.6(a) on page 36. The diagram reveals that most of the defects were found on the bodies of the cars or in their accessories (radio, wipers, etc.).

Sufficient data were collected when the cars were inspected to take the Pareto analysis one step farther. All 70 body defects were further classified as to whether they were paint defects, dents, upholstery defects, windshield defects, or chrome defects. All 50 accessory defects were further classified as to whether they were defects in the air conditioning (A/C) system, the radio, the power steering, the cruise control, or the windshield (W/S) wipers. Two more Pareto diagrams were constructed from these data. They are shown in panels (b) and (c) of Figure 2.6. This decomposition of the original Pareto diagram is called **exploding the Pareto diagram**.

It can be seen that paint defects and dents were the predominant types of body defects and that the accessory with the most problems is the air conditioning system. These are the "vital few" types of defects. Their identification permitted management to target them for special attention by managers, engineers, and assembly-line workers.

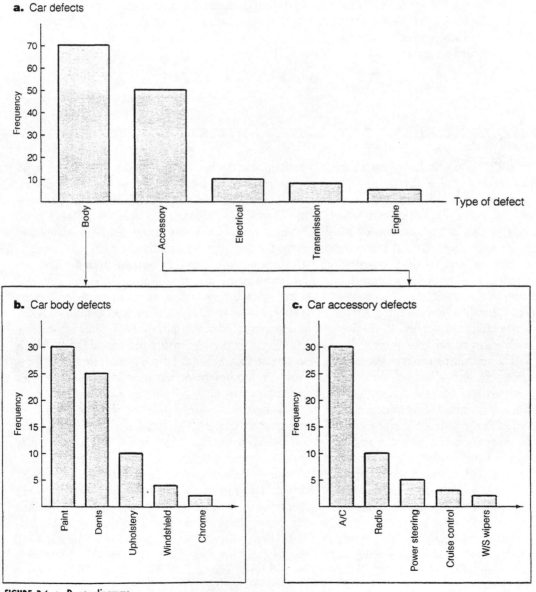

a. Car defects

b. Car body defects

c. Car accessory defects

FIGURE 2.6 ▲ Pareto diagrams

Most statistical software packages can be used to generate histograms and stem-and-leaf displays. Both are useful tools for graphically describing data sets. We recommend generating and comparing both displays when feasible. The histogram will generally be more useful for very large data sets or for qualitative data, whereas the stem-and-leaf display provides useful detail for smaller quantitative data sets.

CASE STUDY 2.3 / Appraising the Market Value of an Asset

The *market value* of an asset is the price negotiated by a willing buyer and a willing seller of the asset, each acting rationally in his or her own self-interest. The *book value* of an asset is the value of the asset as shown in its owner's accounting records. Generally speaking, it is the amount the owner paid for the asset, less any depreciation expense (Davidson, Stickney, and Weil, 1979).

Robert R. Sterling and Raymond Radosevich (1969) examined the hypothesis that accountants generally agree on the book value of a depreciable asset but do not agree on its current market value. A questionnaire was prepared in which the installment purchase of a depreciable asset was described and the respondent was asked to determine the market value of the asset. The questionnaire also contained a series of questions relating to the book value of the asset. These questions

enabled Sterling and Radosevich to calculate a book value for the asset for each of the respondents. The questionnaire was mailed to 500 randomly selected certified public accountants (CPAs) in the United States; 114 and 99 usable book value and market value responses, respectively, were returned.

The frequency distributions of book values and market values obtained from the returned questionnaires appear in Figure 2.7. In both histograms, the intervals from $150 to $200 and $600 to $650 include all responses less than $200 and greater than $600, respectively. The histograms suggest disagreement among the CPAs as to both the book value and the market value of the asset. Thus, Sterling and Radosevich rejected the hypothesis that accountants tend to agree on book values and to disagree on market values.

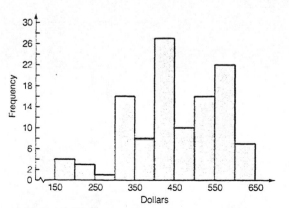

a. Book values   **b.** Market values

FIGURE 2.7 ▲ Frequency histograms for book and market values as assessed by CPAs

Note that decisions based on a visual comparison of histograms (or other graphical descriptions) are risky because they are subject to an unknown probability of error. For example, we might wonder whether dis-agreement among the CPAs really exists or whether the difference we see in the histogram is due to random variation that would be present from sample to sample. We begin to answer questions of this type in Chapter 6.

Exercises 2.9–2.22

Note: Starred exercises (*) require the use of a computer.

Learning the Mechanics

2.9   Graph the relative frequency histogram for the 500 measurements summarized in the accompanying relative frequency table.

Measurement Class	Relative Frequency
.5– 2.5	.10
2.5– 4.5	.15
4.5– 6.5	.25
6.5– 8.5	.20
8.5–10.5	.05
10.5–12.5	.10
12.5–14.5	.10
14.6–16.5	.05

2.10   Refer to Exercise 2.9. Calculate the number of the 500 measurements falling into each of the measurement classes. Then graph a frequency histogram for these data.

2.11   The statistical package Minitab was used to generate the following histogram:

MIDDLE OF INTERVAL	NUMBER OF OBSERVATIONS	
20	1	*
22	3	***
24	2	**
26	3	***
28	4	****
30	7	*******
32	11	***********
34	6	******
36	2	**
38	3	***
40	3	***
42	2	**
44	1	*
46	1	*

a. Is this a frequency histogram or relative frequency histogram? Explain.
b. How many measurement classes were used in the construction of this histogram?
c. How many measurements are there in the data set described by this histogram?

2.12   SAS was used to generate the stem-and-leaf display below. Note that SAS arranges the stems in descending order. Also, the instruction to "Multiply Stem.Leaf by 10**+0.1" indicates that each number should be multiplied by 10. For example, the top number in the display, 5.1, represents an observation of 10(5.1) = 51.

```
Stem Leaf                        #
   5 1                           1
   4 457                         3
   3 00036                       5
   2 1134599                     7
   1 2248                        4
   0 012                         3
     ----+----+----+----+
  Multiply Stem.Leaf by 10**+01
```

a. How many observations were in the original data set?
b. In the bottom row of the stem-and-leaf display, identify the stem, the leaves, and the numbers in the original data set represented by this stem and its leaves.

2.13   Bonds can be issued by the federal government, state and local governments, and U.S. corporations. A *mortgage bond* is a promissory note in which the issuing company pledges certain real assets as security in exchange for a specified amount of money. A *debenture* is an unsecured promissory note, backed only by the general credit of the issuer. The bond price of either a mortgage bond or debenture is negotiated between the asked price (the lowest price anyone will accept) and the bid price (the highest price anyone wants to pay). (See *How the Bond Market Works*, 1988.) The accompanying table contains the bid prices on December 31, 1991, for a sample of 30 publicly traded debenture bonds issued by utility companies.

Utility Company	Bid Price	Utility Company	Bid Price
Gulf States Utilities	108⅜	Indiana & Michigan Electric	98¼
Northern Natural Gas	101⅛	Toledo Edison Co.	105⅛
Indiana Gas	101	Dayton Power and Light	102¼
Appalachian Power	99⅞	Atlantic City Electric	94¼
Empire Gas Corp.	57½	Long Island Lighting	105⅛
Wisconsin Electric Power	100⅜	Portland General Electric	108
Pennsylvania Electric	99⅞	Boston Gas	105⅛
Commonwealth Edison	88	Duquesne Light Co.	69¾
El Paso Natural Gas	106⅜	General Electric Co.	99⅜
Montana Power Co.	100¼	Ohio Power Co.	94⅜
Elizabethtown Water	99⅞	Texas Power and Light	100½
Cascade Natural Gas	109¾	Columbia Gas System	78
Tennessee Gas Pipeline	102⅝	Central Power and Light	108⅛
Western Electric	99¾	Boston Edison	113⅛
Dallas Power and Light	108⅛	Philadelphia Electric	102⅝

Source: *Bond Guide* (a publication of the Standard & Poor Corporation), January 1992.

a. A frequency histogram was generated using a statistical software package. (See the accompanying figure.) Note that the software labels the midpoint of each measurement class rather than the two endpoints, and plots the bars horizontally rather than vertically. Interpret the histogram.

```
price      N =        30

Midpoint  Count

    60       1    ▉
    65       0    ▏
    70       1    ▉
    75       0    ▏
    80       1    ▉
    85       0    ▏
    90       1    ▉
    95       2    ▉▉
   100      12    ▉▉▉▉▉▉▉▉▉▉▉▉
   105       6    ▉▉▉▉▉▉
   110       5    ▉▉▉▉▉
   115       1    ▉

          0.0      3.0      6.0      9.0      12.0     15.0
```

b. Use the histogram to determine the number of bonds in the sample that had a bid price greater than $97.50. What proportion of the total number of bonds is this group?

c. Identify the area under the histogram of part a that corresponds to this proportion.

Applying the Concepts

2.14 Production processes may be classified as *make-to-stock processes* or *make-to-order* processes. Make-to-stock processes are designed to produce a standardized product that can be sold to customers from the firm's inventory. Make-to-order processes are designed to produce products according to customer specifications. The McDonald's and Burger King fast-food chains are classic examples of these two types of processes. McDonald's produces and stocks standardized hamburgers; Burger King—whose slogan is "Your way, right away"—makes hamburgers according to the ingredients specified by the customer (Schroeder, 1993). In general, performance of make-to-order processes is measured by delivery time—the time from receipt of an order until the product is delivered to the customer. The following data set is a sample of delivery times (in days) for a particular make-to-order firm last year. The delivery times marked by an asterisk are associated with customers who subsequently placed additional orders with the firm.

50*	64*	56*	43*	64*
82*	65*	49*	32*	63*
44*	71	54*	51*	102
49*	73*	50*	39*	86
33*	95	59*	51*	68

The Minitab stem-and-leaf display of these data is shown here.

```
Stem-and-leaf of Time      N  = 25
Leaf Unit = 1.0

        3     3 239
        7     4 3499
       (7)    5 0011469
       11     6 34458
        6     7 13
        4     8 26
        2     9 5
        1    10 2
```

a. Circle the individual leaves that are associated with customers who did not place a subsequent order.

b. Concerned that they are losing potential repeat customers because of long delivery times, the management would like to establish a guideline for the maximum tolerable delivery time. Using the stem-and-leaf display, suggest a guideline. Explain your reasoning.

2.15   In order to better understand the interactions that take place between salespeople and customers, Ronald P. Willett and Allan L. Pennington (1966) monitored the interactions of appliance salespeople and customers on the floor of a large department store. Part of their research involved observing the length of time customers and salespeople interacted prior to the close of the sale or the departure of the customer. The data below, adapted from the article, are the lengths of time (in minutes) from the first customer–salesperson contact to the close of the sale or the customer's departure for 132 customers who completed their appliance purchase either at the time they were observed or within the following 2 weeks. Instances where a purchase was made by the customer at the time he or she was observed are denoted with an asterisk.

1.0*	3.2	49.1*	3.3	5.4*	6.0*	7.9*	39.9	1.1	25.4*	14.9
7.4*	12.4	10.9*	20.1*	30.5	27.2*	.9	50.1	48.6	10.0*	40.0
41.3*	26.2	118.4	12.0*	30.5	7.0*	66.1*	105.2*	47.6*	10.1*	12.2*
15.1*	33.3	8.8	30.0*	26.4*	8.4	1.7	12.5	23.0	11.1	21.9
6.1	.7	1.5	13.0	9.0*	7.6	10.9	13.5	8.0*	35.1	41.6
22.3	44.4*	18.4	8.9*	16.9*	34.6*	16.2	98.2	11.0	43.1	31.8
.4*	32.2	37.0	18.0*	14.2	39.2*	8.1*	4.5*	69.1	24.8	15.0*
17.4*	28.7	15.0*	14.2*	20.6*	27.7	7.9	18.7*	8.4	15.9	38.2
11.0*	7.8*	15.0	6.0	77.1	26.0	7.0*	7.4*	3.0	11.1	35.0*
35.4	25.6*	1.9*	40.1	.8	19.2*	42.3	15.5	13.3*	81.0	20.1*
12.8*	14.9	38.1	9.7	17.7*	7.7	42.1	4.1*	17.6*	5.1*	30.0
8.1*	25.1*	29.2	12.3	15.9	60.2*	27.7	10.3	14.0*	30.0*	10.5

SAS was used to construct a relative frequency histogram for each of the following data sets (see page 42):

(1) The complete set of 132 times

(2) The set of times associated with customers who made appliance purchases at the time they were being observed

(3) The set of times associated with customers who made the appliance purchases at a later date

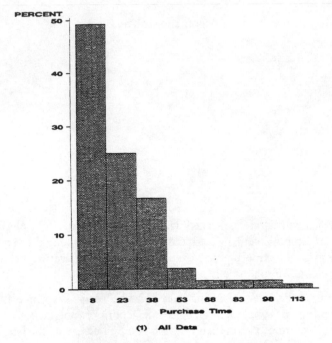

(1) All Data

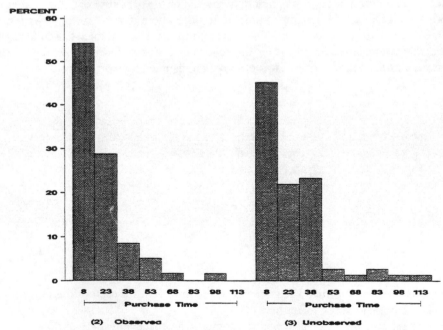

(2) Observed   **(3) Unobserved**

a. Interpret the three histograms. Describe any differences you detect between the histograms of parts (2) and (3).

b. Suggest possible explanations for the differences you noted in part **a.**

2.16 In a manufacturing plant a *work center* is a specific production facility that consists of one or more people and/or machines and is treated as one unit for the purposes of capacity requirements planning and job scheduling. If jobs arrive at a particular work center at a faster rate than they depart, the work center impedes the overall production process and is referred to as a *bottleneck* (Fogarty, Blackstone, and Hoffmann, 1991). The data in the table were collected by an operations manager for use in investigating a potential bottleneck work center.

Number of Items Arriving at Work Center per Hour

155	115	156	156	109	127
150	159	163	148	135	119
172	143	159	140	127	115
166	148	175	122	99	106
151	161	138	171	123	135
148	129	135	125	107	152
140	152	139	111	137	161

The stem-and-leaf displays for the two sets of data are shown below:

Arrivals			Departures	
Stem	Leaf		Stem	Leaf
			9	9
			10	6 7 9
11	5		11	1 5 9
12	9		12	2 3 5 7 7
13	5 8 9		13	5 5 7
14	0 3 8 8		14	0 8
15	0 1 2 5 6 9 9		15	2 6
16	1 3 6		16	1
17	2 5		17	1

Do the stem-and-leaf displays suggest that the work center may be a bottleneck? Explain.

*2.17 The ability to fill a customer's order on time depends to a great extent on being able to estimate how long it will take to produce the product in question. In most production processes, the time required to complete a particular task will be shorter each time the task is undertaken. Furthermore, it has been observed that in most cases the task time will decrease at a decreasing rate the more times the task is undertaken. Thus, in order to estimate how long it will take to produce a particular product, a manufacturer may want to study the relationship between production time per unit and the number of units that have been produced. The line or curve characterizing this relationship is called a *learning curve* (Adler and Clark, 1991). Twenty-five employees, all of whom were performing the same production task for the tenth time, were observed. Each person's task-completion time (in minutes) was recorded. The same 25 employees were observed again the 30th time they performed the same task and the 50th time they performed the task. The resulting completion times are shown in the table.

Tenth Performance		Thirtieth Performance		Fiftieth Performance	
15	19	16	11	10	8
21	20	10	10	5	10
30	22	12	13	7	8
17	20	9	12	9	7
18	19	7	8	8	8
22	18	11	20	11	6
33	17	8	7	12	5
41	16	9	6	9	6
10	20	5	9	7	4
14	22	15	10	6	15
18	19	10	10	8	7
25	24	11	11	14	20
23		9		9	

a. Use a statistical software package to construct a frequency histogram for each of the three data sets.

b. Compare the histograms. Does it appear that the relationship between task completion time and the number of times the task is performed is in agreement with the observations noted above about production processes in general? Explain.

*2.18   When two firms announce plans to merge, it frequently happens that within a few weeks one firm or the other becomes dissatisfied with the consequences of merging and the merger is canceled. Dodd (1980) reported that of 151 merger announcements that he identified, 80 were canceled. Thus, at the time a proposed merger is announced, there exists a great amount of uncertainty concerning whether the merger will take place. This uncertainty may persist for a considerable period of time and it may be many months after the announcement that the merger actually occurs. In her study of 38 mergers that were consummated, Eger (1982) reported the number of *trading days* (days the New York Stock Exchange is open for business) between the merger announcement (defined as the first mention of the potential merger in the *Wall Street Journal*) and the effective date of the merger. These data are listed next:

74	45	55	74	64	97	65	82	92	116
140	62	92	78	45	93	94	57	123	128
92	73	173	116	35	124	64	84	255	277
123	80	143	112	76	214	64	86		

a. Use a statistical software package to construct a stem-and-leaf display for these data.

b. Summarize the information reflected in your stem-and-leaf display concerning the number of trading days between announcement and the effective merger date for this sample of mergers.

2.19   Typically, the more attractive a corporate common stock is to an investor, the higher the stock's price–earnings (P/E) ratio. For example, if investors expect the stock's future earnings per share to increase, the price of the stock will be bid up and a high P/E ratio will result. Thus, the level of a stock's P/E ratio is a function of both the current financial performance of the firm and an investor's expectation of future performance (Spiro, 1982). The table contains the 1986 P/E ratios for samples of firms from the electronics industry and the auto parts industry.

Auto Parts		*Electronics*	
Firm	*P/E Ratio*	*Firm*	*P/E Ratio*
Lear Siegler	9	AMP Inc.	22
Genuine Parts	15	Raytheon	12
Federal–Mogul	12	Intel	85
PPG Industries	13	Avnet	24
Borg–Warner	13	Perkin Elmer	14
Hoover Universal	12	TRW Inc.	15
Libbey–Owens–Ford	8	Motorola	39
Dana	8	Hewlett–Packard	20
Champion Spark Plug	15	Honeywell	12
Dayco	10	American District	27
Sheller–Globe	7	Corning Glass Works	27
Arvin Industries	10	EG&G	19
Allen Group	13	Varian Associates	14
Eaton	9	M/A-Com, Inc.	14
Cummins Engine	10	Harris Corp.	19
Barnes Group	11	Texas Instruments	10
Echlin	14	IT&T	12
Johnson Controls	9	North American Philips	11
Rockwell Int.	9	GTE	8
Snap-on-Tools	14	Tektronix	16

Source: Stock reports (OTC, NYSE, American), Standard & Poor's 1986.

a. Construct a stem-and-leaf display for each of these data sets.

b. What do your stem-and-leaf displays suggest about the level of the P/E ratios of firms in the electronics industry as compared to firms in the auto parts industry? Explain.

2.20 Consider the accompanying **bar chart** (a histogram for qualitative data), which shows 1985 cigarette sales (in billions of cigarettes) by company.

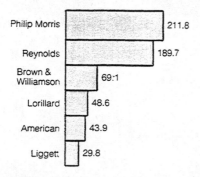

   a. In general, what is described by the bar chart?
   b. Which company sold the most cigarettes in 1985? Approximately how many cigarettes did the company sell?
   c. Convert the bar chart to a relative frequency bar chart. Describe any problems you encounter in making the conversion.

2.21 A large midwestern city conducted a study of commuter traffic patterns and modes of transportation in 1990 and compared the results with those of a similar 1970 study ("In Twin Cities, Free(way)'s a Crowd," 1992). The comparisons will be used by the Metropolitan Council when making decisions about road improvements and mass transit. Some of the general findings were: Due to suburban job growth, most work trips are from suburb to suburb; the average commuting time has increased only 1 minute over the average in 1970. The accompanying table shows additional study findings.

	1970	1990
Drive alone	3,720	8,500
Carpool	1,680	1,000
Use mass transit	360	400
Other	240	100

Data: Metropolitan Council, Minneapolis, MN.

   a. Construct two relative frequency bar charts for these data, one for 1970 and one for 1990.
   b. Combine the bar charts you constructed in part a by plotting the eight relative frequencies on the same bar chart. You can do this by drawing two bars side by side for each category listed on the horizontal axis of your chart. Such a chart facilitates comparison of the two data sets.
   c. *Stacking* is the combining of all the bar charts for any one time period into a single bar, by drawing one on top of the other and distinguishing one from another by the use of colors or patterns. Stack the relative frequencies of the four categories for 1970. Do the same for 1990.
   d. Describe the changes in commuter behavior revealed by these data.

2.22 A research company conducted a written customer survey for a computer manufacturer to evaluate the services provided by its dealerships. Customers who had purchased personal computers were asked which one of the following four items they were least satisfied with: service, technical assistance, training, or the salesperson. Within the indicated category, each customer was asked to select the one aspect with which they were least satisfied. The accompanying table describes their responses.

	No. of Customers
Service	10,002
Timely completion of maintenance/service	6,040
Availability of service, repairs, and maintenance support	1,518
Responsiveness of dealer to your service needs	1,426
Quality of maintenance/service work completed	1,018
Technical Assistance	8,555
Ability of staff to answer technical questions about installation, operations, and applications of the product	6,001
Availability of staff to assist with set-up or operation of the product	2,099
Courtesy of staff providing technical support	455

	No. of Customers	
Training	1,202	
Quality of training provided by the dealer		820
Ability of dealer to provide training to meet your specific needs and level of expertise		212
Availability of individualized training or classroom sessions to assist you in the use of your product		90
Courtesy of the person who provided training		80
Salesperson	4,100	
Salesperson's ability to clearly explain the features and benefits of the product		1,515
Salesperson's understanding of your needs		765
Salesperson's ability to provide solutions to your needs		556
Ease of contacting sales staff		451
Convenience of delivery schedule		410
Condition of product on delivery		300
Courtesy of your salesperson		103

a. How many customers responded to the survey?

b. Construct a Pareto diagram for the four categories. According to your diagram, which category represents the greatest opportunity for increasing customer satisfaction? Explain.

c. For the category you identified in part b, explode the Pareto diagram and identify more specifically (than in part b) how customer satisfaction can be increased.

2.3 Graphical Methods for Describing Quantitative Data Produced Over Time: The Time Series Plot (Optional)

Each of the previous sections has been concerned with describing the information contained in a sample or population of data. Often these data are viewed as having been produced at essentially the same point in time. Thus, time has not been a factor in any of the graphical methods described so far.

Data of interest to managers are often produced and monitored over time. Examples include the daily closing price of their company's common stock, the company's weekly sales volume and quarterly profits, and characteristics—such as weight and length—of products produced by the company.

> **Definition 2.5**
>
> Data that are produced and monitored over time are called **time series data**.

Recall from Section 1.4 that a process is a series of actions or operations that generates output over time. Accordingly, measurements taken of a sequence of units produced by a process—such as a production process—are time series data. In general, any sequence of numbers produced over time can be thought of as being generated by a process.

When measurements are made over time, it is important to record both the numerical value and the time or the time period associated with each measurement. With this information a **time series plot**—sometimes called a **run chart**—can be constructed to describe the time series data and to learn about the process that generated the data. A time series plot is a graph of the measurements (on the vertical axis) plotted against time or against the order in which the measurements were made (on the horizontal axis). The plotted points are usually connected by straight lines to make it easier to see the changes and movement in the measurements over time. For example, Figure 2.8 is a time series plot of a particular company's monthly sales (number of units sold per month). And Figure 2.9 is a time series plot of the weights of 30 one-gallon paint cans that were consecutively filled by the same filling head. Notice that the weights are plotted against the order in which the cans were filled rather than some unit of time. When monitoring production processes, it is often more convenient to record the order rather than the exact time at which each measurement was made.

Time series plots reveal the movement (trend) and changes (variation) in the variable being monitored. Notice how sales trend upward in the summer and how the variation in the weights of the paint cans increases over time. This kind of information would not be revealed by stem-and-leaf displays or histograms, as the following case study illustrates.

FIGURE 2.8 ▶

Time series plot of company sales

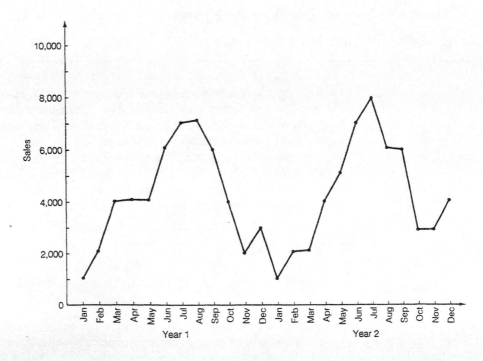

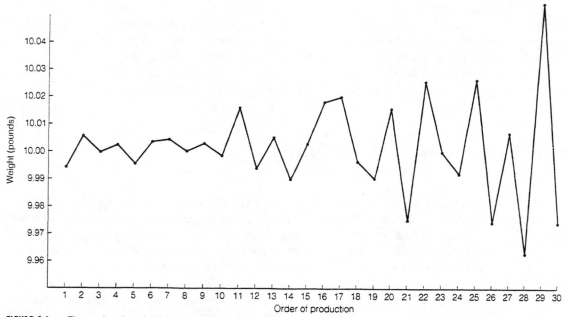

FIGURE 2.9 ▲ Time series plot of paint can weights

W. Edwards Deming is one of America's most famous statisticians. He is best known for the role he played after World War II in teaching the Japanese how to improve the quality of their products by monitoring and continually improving their production processes. In his book *Out of the Crisis* (1986), Deming warns against the knee-jerk (i.e., automatic) use of histograms to display and extract information from data. As evidence he offers the following example.

Fifty camera springs were tested in the order in which they were produced. The elongation of each

spring was measured under the pull of 20 grams. Both a time series plot and a histogram were constructed from the measurements. They are shown in Figure 2.10, which has been reproduced from Deming's book. If you had to predict the elongation measurement of the next spring to be produced (i.e., spring 51) and could use only one of the two plots to guide your prediction, which would you use? Why?

Only the time series plot describes the behavior *over time* of the process that produces the springs. The fact that the elongation measurements are decreasing

FIGURE 2.10 ►
Deming's time series plot
and histogram

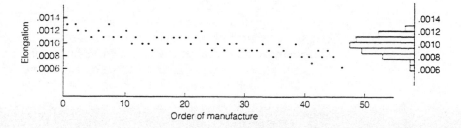

over time can only be gleaned from the time series plot. Because the histogram does not reflect the order in which the springs were produced, it in effect represents all observations as having been produced simultaneously. Using the histogram to predict the elongation of the 51st spring would very likely lead to an overestimate.

The lesson from Deming's example is this: For displaying and analyzing data that have been generated over time by a process, the primary graphical tool is the time series plot, not the histogram.

We cover many other aspects of the statistical analysis of time series data in Chapters 14 and 15.

2.4   Numerical Methods for Measuring Central Tendency

Now that we have presented some graphic techniques for summarizing and describing data sets, we turn to numerical methods for accomplishing this objective. When we speak of a data set, we refer to either a sample or a population. If statistical inference is our goal, we will wish ultimately to use sample numerical descriptive measures to make inferences about the corresponding measures for a population.

As you will see, there are a large number of numerical methods available to describe data sets. Most of these methods measure one of two data characteristics:

1. The **central tendency** of the set of measurements; i.e., the tendency of the data to cluster or to center about certain numerical values.

2. The **variability** of the set of measurements; i.e., the spread of the data.

In this section, we concentrate on measures of central tendency. In the next section, we discuss measures of variability.

The most popular and best understood measure of central tendency for a quantitative data set is the **arithmetic mean** (or simply the **mean**) of a data set.

Definition 2.6

The **mean** of a set of quantitative data is equal to the sum of the measurements divided by the number of measurements contained in the data set.

In everyday terms, the mean is the average value of the data set.

We will denote the measurements of a data set as follows:

$$x_1, x_2, x_3, \ldots, x_n$$

where x_1 is the first measurement in the data set, x_2 is the second measurement in the data set, x_3 is the third measurement in the data set, . . . , and x_n is the nth (and last) measurement in the data set. Thus, if we have five measurements in a set of data, we will write x_1, x_2, x_3, x_4, x_5 to represent the measurements. If the actual numbers are 5, 3, 8, 5, and 4, we have $x_1 = 5$, $x_2 = 3$, $x_3 = 8$, $x_4 = 5$, and $x_5 = 4$.

To calculate the mean of a set of measurements, we must sum them and divide by n, the number of measurements in the set. The sum of measurements x_1, x_2, . . . , x_n is

$$x_1 + x_2 + \cdots + x_n$$

To shorten the notation, we will write this sum as

$$x_1 + x_2 + \cdots + x_n = \sum_{i=1}^{n} x_i$$

where $\sum$ is the symbol for the summation. Verbally translate $\sum_{i=1}^{n} x_i$ as follows: "The sum of the measurements, whose typical member is x_i, beginning with the member x_1 and ending with the member x_n."

Finally, we will denote the mean of a sample of measurements by $\bar{x}$ (read "x-bar"), and represent the formula for its calculation as follows:

$$\bar{x} = \frac{\sum_{i=1}^{n} x_i}{n}$$

EXAMPLE 2.2

Calculate the mean of the following five sample measurements: 5, 3, 8, 5, 6.

Solution

Using the definition of sample mean and the shorthand notation, we find

$$\bar{x} = \frac{\sum_{i=1}^{5} x_i}{5} = \frac{5 + 3 + 8 + 5 + 6}{5} = \frac{27}{5} = 5.4$$

Thus, the mean of this sample is 5.4.*

---

*In the examples given here, $\bar{x}$ is sometimes rounded to the nearest tenth, sometimes the nearest hundredth, sometimes the nearest thousandth. There is no specific rule for rounding when calculating $\bar{x}$ because $\bar{x}$ is specifically defined to be the sum of all measurements divided by n; i.e., it is a specific fraction. When $\bar{x}$ is used for descriptive purposes, it is often convenient to round the calculated value of $\bar{x}$ to the number of significant figures used for the original measurements. When $\bar{x}$ is to be used in other calculations, however, it may be necessary to retain more significant figures.

EXAMPLE 2.3

Refer to Table 2.4. Calculate the mean of the percentages of revenues spent by the 50 companies on research and development.

TABLE 2.4 Percentages of Revenues Spent on Research and Development

Company	Percentage	Company	Percentage	Company	Percentage	Company	Percentage
1	13.5	14	9.5	27	8.2	39	6.5
2	8.4	15	8.1	28	6.9	40	7.5
3	10.5	16	13.5	29	7.2	41	7.1
4	9.0	17	9.9	30	8.2	42	13.2
5	9.2	18	6.9	31	9.6	43	7.7
6	9.7	19	7.5	32	7.2	44	5.9
7	6.6	20	11.1	33	8.8	45	5.2
8	10.6	21	8.2	34	11.3	46	5.6
9	10.1	22	8.0	35	8.5	47	11.7
10	7.1	23	7.7	36	9.4	48	6.0
11	8.0	24	7.4	37	10.5	49	7.8
12	7.9	25	6.5	38	6.9	50	6.5
13	6.8	26	9.5				

Solution

Using the data in Table 2.4, we have

$$\bar{x} = \frac{\sum_{i=1}^{50} x_i}{50} = \frac{13.5 + 8.4 + \cdots + 6.5}{50} = \frac{424.6}{50} = 8.49$$

The average expenditure on research and development for the 50 companies is 8.49% of revenues. Glancing at the relative frequency histogram for these data (Figure 2.11), we note that the mean falls in the middle of this data set.

FIGURE 2.11 ▶

Relative frequency histogram for the 50 computer companies' R&D percentages: The mean

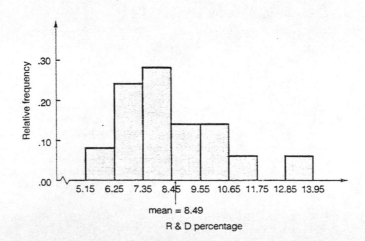

mean = 8.49

R & D percentage

The sample mean will play an important role in accomplishing our objective of making inferences about populations based on sample information. For this reason, it is important to use a different symbol when we want to discuss the **mean of a population**—i.e., the mean of the set of measurements on every unit in the population. We use the Greek letter μ (mu) for the population mean. We will adopt a general policy of using Greek letters to represent population numerical descriptive measures and Roman letters to represent corresponding descriptive measures for the sample.

$$\bar{x} = \text{Sample mean} \qquad \mu = \text{Population mean}$$

The sample mean, $\bar{x}$, will often be used to estimate (make an inference about) the population mean, μ. For example, the percentages of revenues spent on research and development by the population consisting of *all* U.S. companies has a mean equal to some value, μ. Our sample of 50 companies yielded percentages with a mean of $\bar{x} = 8.49$. If, as is usually the case, we did not have access to the measurements for the entire population, we could use $\bar{x}$ as an estimator or approximator for μ. Then we would need to know something about the reliability of our inference. That is, we would need to know how accurately we might expect $\bar{x}$ to estimate μ. In Chapter 7, we will find that this accuracy depends on two factors:

1. *The size of the sample.* The larger the sample, the more accurate the estimate will tend to be.
2. *The variability, or spread, of the data.* All other factors remaining constant, the more variable the data, the less accurate the estimate.

In summary, the mean provides a valuable measure of the central tendency for a set of measurements. It is a very common tool in business and economic research, and therefore the mean will be the focus of much of our discussion of inferential statistics.

CASE STUDY 2.4 / Hotels: A Rational Method for Overbooking

The most outstanding characteristic of the general hotel reservation system is the option of the prospective guest, without penalty, to change or cancel his reservation or even to "no-show" (fail to arrive without notice). Overbooking (taking reservations in excess of the hotel capacity) is practiced widely throughout the industry as a compensating economic measure. This has motivated our research into the problem of determining policies for overbooking which are based on some set of rational criteria.

So said Marvin Rothstein (1974) in an article that appeared in *Decision Sciences*, a journal published by the Decision Sciences Institute. In this paper Rothstein introduces a method for scientifically determining hotel booking policies and applies it to the booking problems of the 133-room Sheraton Pocono Inn at Stroudsburg, Pennsylvania.

From the Sheraton Pocono Inn's records, the number of reservations, walk-ins (people without reservations who expect to be accommodated), cancellations, and no-shows were tabulated for each day during the period August 1–28, 1971. The inn's records for this period included approximately 3,100 guest histories. From the tabulated data, the mean or average number of room reservations per day for each of the seven days of the week was computed, as shown in Table 2.5. In applying his booking policy decision

TABLE 2.5   Mean Number of Room Reservations, August 1–28, 1971, 133 Rooms

Sunday	Monday	Tuesday	Wednesday	Thursday	Friday	Saturday
138	126	149	160	150	150	169

method to the Sheraton's data, Rothstein used the means listed in Table 2.5 to help portray the inn's demand for rooms.

The mean number of Saturday reservations during the period August 1–28, 1971, is 169. This may be interpreted as an estimate of μ, the mean number of rooms demanded via reservations (walk-ins also contribute to the demand for rooms) on a Saturday during 1971. If the reservation data for all Saturdays during 1971 had been tabulated, μ could have been computed. But, since only the August data are available, they were used to estimate μ. Can you think of some problems associated with using August's data to estimate the mean for the entire year?

Another very important measure of central tendency is the **median** of a set of measurements:

Definition 2.7

The **median** of a data set is the middle number when the measurements are arranged in ascending (or descending) order.

The median is of most value in describing large data sets. If the data set is characterized by a relative frequency histogram (see Figure 2.12), the median is the point on the x-axis such that half the area under the histogram lies above the median and half lies below. [*Note:*   In Section 2.2, we observed that the relative frequency associated with a particular interval on the x-axis is proportional to the area under the histogram that lies above the interval.]

FIGURE 2.12 ▶
Location of the median

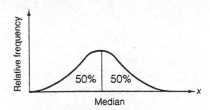

For a small—or even a large but finite—number of measurements, there may be many numbers that satisfy the property indicated in Figure 2.12. For this reason, we will arbitrarily calculate the median of a data set as follows:

Calculating the Median

Arrange the n measurements from the smallest to the largest.

1. If n is odd, the median is the middle number.
2. If n is even, the median is the mean (average) of the middle two numbers.

EXAMPLE 2.4

Consider the following sample of $n = 7$ measurements: 5, 7, 4, 5, 20, 6, 2.

a. Calculate the median of this sample.
b. Eliminate the last measurement (the 2), and calculate the median of the remaining $n = 6$ measurements.

Solution

a. The seven measurements in the sample are first ranked in ascending order:

2, 4, 5, 5, 6, 7, 20

Since the number of measurements is odd, the median is the middle measurement. Thus, the median of this sample is 5.

b. After removing the 2 from the set of measurements, we rank the sample measurements in ascending order as follows:

4, 5, 5, 6, 7, 20

Now the number of measurements is even, so we average the middle two measurements. The median is $(5 + 6)/2 = 5.5$

In certain situations, the median may be a better measure of central tendency than the mean. In particular, the median is less sensitive than the mean to extremely large or small measurements. To illustrate, note that all but one of the measurements in Example 2.4 center about $x = 5$. The single large measurement, $x = 20$, does not affect the value of the median, 5, but it causes the mean, $\bar{x} = 7$, to lie to the right of most of the measurements.

As another example, if you were interested in computing a measure of central tendency of the incomes of a company's employees, the mean might be misleading. If all blue- and white-collar employees' incomes are included in the data set, the high incomes of a few executives will influence the mean more than the median. Thus, the median will often provide a more accurate picture of the typical income for an employee. Similarly, the median yearly sales for a set of companies would locate the middle of the sales data. However, the very large yearly sales of a few companies would

TABLE 2.6	Percentages of Revenues Spent on Research and Development, in Ascending Order		
5.2	7.1	8.2	9.9
5.6	7.2	8.2	10.1
5.9	7.2	8.2	10.5
6.0	7.4	8.4	10.5
6.5	7.5	8.5	10.6
6.5	7.5	8.8	11.1
6.5	7.7	9.0	11.3
6.6	7.7	9.2	11.7
6.8	7.8	9.4	13.2
6.9	7.9	9.5	13.5
6.9	8.0	9.5	13.5
6.9	8.0	9.6	
7.1	8.1	9.7	

greatly influence the mean, making it deceptively large. That is, the mean could exceed a vast majority of the sample measurements, making it a misleading measure of central tendency.

For an example using more measurements, we have arranged the 50 R&D percentages in ascending order in Table 2.6. Since the number of measurements is even, the median equals the mean of the middle two numbers (shaded)—that is, the mean of the 25th and 26th numbers in the ordered list:

$$\frac{8.0 + 8.1}{2} = 8.05$$

Note that the median is smaller than the mean (8.49) for these data. This fact indicates that the data are **skewed** to the right—i.e., there are more extreme measurements in the right tail of the distribution than in the left tail. This affects the mean more than the median, because the extreme values (large or small) are used explicitly in the calculation of the mean. On the other hand, the median is not affected directly by extreme measurements, since the middle measurement(s) is (are) the only one(s) explicitly used to calculate the median. Consequently, if measurements are pulled toward one end of the distribution, the mean will shift toward that tail more than the median. The skewness of the R&D data set is evident in Figure 2.13, where we show the median and mean of the R&D percentages.

FIGURE 2.13 ►
Relative frequency histogram for the R&D percentages: Mean and median

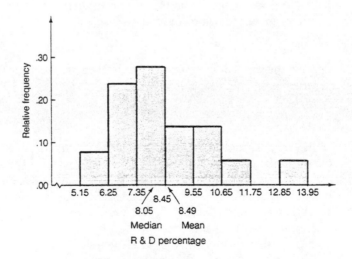

A comparison of the mean and median gives us a general method for detecting skewness in data sets, as shown in the box.

Comparing the Mean and the Median

1. If the median is less than the mean, the data set is skewed to the right:

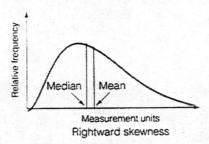

Rightward skewness

2. The median will equal the mean when the data set is symmetric:

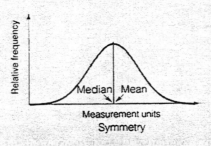

Symmetry

3. If the median is greater than the mean, the data set is skewed to the left:

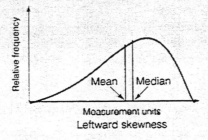

Leftward skewness

George T. Milkovich, Anthony J. Annoni, and Thomas A. Mahoney (1972) explain the delphi technique as follows:

The delphi technique, a set of procedures originally developed by the Rand Corporation in the late 1940's, is designed to obtain the most reliable consensus of opinion of a group of experts. Essentially, the delphi is a series of intensive interrogations of each individual expert (by a series of questionnaires) concerning some primary question interspersed with controlled feedback. The procedures are designed to avoid direct confrontation of the experts with one another.

The interaction among the experts is accomplished through an intermediary who gathers the data requests of the experts and summarizes them along with the experts' answers to the primary question. This mode of controlled interaction among the experts is a deliberate attempt to avoid the disadvantages associated with more conventional use of experts such as in round table discussions or direct confrontation of opposing views. The developers of the delphi argue the procedures are more conducive to independent thought and allow more gradual formulation to a considered opinion.

This article presents a study of the usefulness of the delphi procedure in projecting labor requirements in a low profit margin national retail firm. Seven company executives formed the panel of experts. Five questionnaires submitted at approximately 8-day intervals were used to interrogate the seven experts. On questionnaires 2–5, they were each asked the primary question, "How many buyers will the firm need 1 year from now?" Their individual responses along with the median response of the group for each questionnaire appear in Table 2.7.

TABLE 2.7   Projected Demand for Buyers

Questionnaire	Experts							Median
	A	B	C	D	E	F	G	
2	55	35	33	35	55	33	32	35
3	45	35	41	35	41	34	32	35
4	45	38	41	35	41	34	34	38
5	45	38	41	35	45	34	34	38

Note that the median response increased from 35 on questionnaire 2 to 38 on questionnaires 4 and 5. This increase indicates an upward shift in the distribution of the experts' forecasts as to the number of buyers the firm would need a year from now. If a single number is needed to represent the group's forecast, the median of the last questionnaire—in this case 38—is frequently used.

One conclusion of the study was that the delphi technique provided a better forecast of the actual number of buyers (37) needed by the firm 1 year later than did other more conventional forecasting techniques.

A third measure of central tendency is the **mode** of a set of measurements.

Definition 2.8

The **mode** is the measurement that occurs with greatest frequency in the data set.

Because it emphasizes data concentration, the mode is often used with large data sets to locate the region in which much of the data is concentrated. A retailer of men's clothing would be interested in the modal neck size and sleeve length of potential customers. The modal income class of the laborers in the United States is of interest to the Labor Department. Thus, the mode provides a useful measure of central tendency for many business applications.

Unless a quantitative data set is very large, its mode may not be very meaningful. For example, consider the percentage of revenues spent on research and development (R&D) by 50 companies. These data, first presented in Table 2.1, were analyzed in Section 2.2. A reexamination of the data reveals that three of the measurements are repeated three times: 6.5%, 6.9%, and 8.2%. Thus, there are three modes in the sample, and none is particularly useful as a measure of central tendency.

We can calculate a more meaningful measure by first constructing a relative frequency histogram for the data. The measurement class containing the most measurements is called the **modal class**, and the mode is taken to be the midpoint of this interval. For the R&D data, the modal class is the one corresponding to the interval 7.35 to 8.45, as shown by the shaded rectangle in Figure 2.14. The mode is taken to be the midpoint of this interval, that is, $(7.35 + 8.45)/2 = 7.90$. This modal class (and the mode itself) identifies the area in which the data are most concentrated, and in that sense is a measure of central tendency. However, for most applications involving quantitative data, the mean and median provide more descriptive information than the mode.

FIGURE 2.14 ▶

Relative frequency histogram for the computer companies' R&D percentages: The modal class

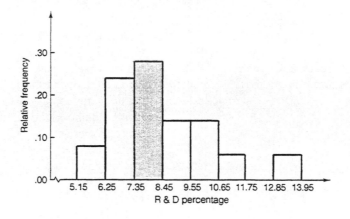

Exercises 2.23–2.34

Learning the Mechanics

2.23 Calculate the mean, median, and mode of the following data: 18, 10, 15, 13, 17, 15, 12, 15, 18, 16, 11.

2.24 Calculate the mean and median of the following grade-point averages: 3.2, 2.5, 2.1, 3.7, 2.8, 2.0.

2.25   Explain the difference between the calculation of the median for an odd and an even number of measurements. Construct one data set consisting of 5 measurements and another consisting of 6 measurements for which the medians are equal.

2.26   Explain how the relationship between the mean and median provides information about the symmetry or skewness of the data's distribution.

2.27   Refer to Case Study 2.5. Practitioners of the delphi technique frequently use the median of the set of responses given by the panel of experts on the last questionnaire to describe "the opinion of the experts." Why do you suppose the median response is used rather than the mean response?

Applying the Concepts

2.28   According to *Consumers' Digest* (Nov.–Dec. 1980), in 1980 sugar was the leading food additive in the U.S. food supply. Sugar may be listed more than once on a product's ingredient list since it goes by different names depending on its source (e.g., sucrose, corn sweetener, fructose, and dextrose). Thus, when you read a product's label you may have to total up the sugar in the product to see how much sweetener it contains. The accompanying table gives a list of candy bars and the percentage of sugar they contain relative to their weight.

Brand	Percentage of Sugar by Weight	Brand	Percentage of Sugar by Weight
Baby Ruth	23.7	Power House	30.6
Butterfinger	29.5	Bit-O-Honey	23.5
Mr. Goodbar	34.2	Chunky	38.4
Milk Duds	36.0	Milk Chocolate Covered Raisinettes	24.7
Mello Mint	79.6	Oh Henry!	31.2
M & M Plain Chocolate Candies	52.2	Borden Cracker Jack	14.7
Mars Chocolate Almond	36.4	Good & Plenty Licorice	28.2
Milky Way	26.8	Nestle's Crunch	43.5
Marathon	36.7	Planter Jumbo Block Peanut Candy	21.5
Snickers	28.0	Switzer Licorice	8.4
3 Musketeers	36.1	Switzer Red Licorice	2.8
Junior Mints	45.3	Tootsie Pop Drops	54.1
Pom Poms	29.5	Tootsie Roll	21.1
Sugar Babies	41.0	Fancy Fruit Lifesavers	77.6
Sugar Daddy	22.0	Spear-O-Mint Lifesavers	67.6
Almond Joy	20.0		

Source: *National Confectioners Association Brand Name Guide to Sugar* (Nelson Hall Paperback).
Secondary Source: *Consumers' Digest*, Nov.–Dec. 1980, p. 11.

a. Calculate the mean percentage of sugar per bar for the candy bars listed.
b. Find the median for the data set.
c. What do the mean and median indicate about the skewness of the data set?
d. Construct a relative frequency histogram for the data set. Indicate the location of the mean, median, and modal class of the data set on your histogram.

2.29   During the 1980s the pharmaceutical industry placed an increased emphasis on producing revolutionary new products. As a result, R&D costs increased and companies took a greater interest in R&D management. The table lists the 1984 R&D expenditures (in millions of dollars) of the world's largest pharmaceutical manufacturers.

Company	R&D Expenditures	Company	R&D Expenditures
Abbott	$110	Pfizer	159
American Home	90	Rhone–Poulenc	110
Bayer	200	Sandoz	181
Boehringer Ingelheim	176	Schering–Plough	129
Bristol–Myers	162	Smith Kline–Beckman	158
Ciba–Geigy	230	Squibb	114
Hoechst	274	Takeda	125
Hoffmann–LaRoche	363	Upjohn	200
Johnson & Johnson	187	Warner–Lambert	162
Merck	290		

Source: *Business Quarterly*, Fall 1985, p. 81.

a. Calculate the mean and median for this data set.
b. What do the mean and median indicate about the skewness of this data set?
c. Will the median of a data set always be equal to an actual value in the data set, as was the case in part a?

2.30   The table lists the mean age for each team in the National Basketball Association (NBA), along with the number of players on each team at the start of the 1982–1983 season. What was the population mean age at the start of the 1982–1983 season? [*Hint:* $\sum_{i=1}^{n} x_i = n\bar{x}$]

Team	Number of Players	Mean Age	Team	Number of Players	Mean Age
1. Indiana	12	24.720	13. San Antonio	12	26.25
2. Portland	12	24.724	14. Los Angeles	13	26.42
3. Golden State	15	24.96	15. New York	14	26.45
4. Dallas	13	25.17	16. Cleveland	14	26.48
5. New Jersey	13	25.26	17. San Diego	13	26.71
6. Kansas City	12	25.27	18. Boston	12	26.94
7. Chicago	12	25.32	19. Seattle	11	27.09
8. Detroit	13	25.65	20. Atlanta	12	27.12
9. Philadelphia	12	25.96	21. Denver	11	27.59
10. Phoenix	13	26.10	22. Houston	12	29.21
11. Washington	13	26.10	23. Milwaukee	13	29.72
12. Utah	11	26.13			

Source: *Basketball Weekly*, Jan. 3, 1983, Vol. 16, No. 5, pp. 10–11.

2.31   According to the U.S. Energy Information Association, the average price of regular unleaded gasoline in the United States as of March 1989 was 14.4 cents per gallon cheaper than the average price of premium gas. The table lists the average price excluding excise tax (in cents per gallon) of regular unleaded gas in each of a sample of 20 states.

State	Price	State	Price
Alaska	92.5	Nevada	64.9
Arkansas	63.3	New Hampshire	74.7
Connecticut	76.8	New York	70.6
Delaware	68.5	North Dakota	72.4
Louisiana	67.6	Oklahoma	64.6
Maine	76.8	Oregon	70.8
Massachusetts	74.9	Pennsylvania	65.5
Michigan	63.9	Texas	64.6
Missouri	63.4	Wisconsin	65.7
Montana	69.0	Wyoming	69.7

Data: U.S. Energy Information Association, *Petroleum Marketing Monthly*, March 1989.
Source: *Statistical Abstract of the United States*, 1989.

a. Calculate the mean, median, and mode of this data set.
b. Eliminate the highest price from the data set and repeat part a. What effect does dropping this measurement have on the measures of central tendency calculated in part a?
c. Arrange the 20 prices in order from lowest to highest. Next, eliminate the lowest two prices and the highest two prices from the data set and calculate the mean of the remaining prices. The result is called an **80% trimmed mean**, since it is calculated using the central 80% of the values in the data set. An advantage of the trimmed mean is that it is not as sensitive as the arithmetic mean to extreme observations in the data set.

2.32   At the end of 1982, McDonald's had 7,300 restaurants and total sales for the year of $7.8 billion. Burger King had 3,400 restaurants and total sales of $2.4 billion. McDonald's opens new restaurants at the rate of 500 per year and Burger King at the rate of 200 per year (*Minneapolis Tribune*, July 3, 1983).
a. Calculate the average sales per restaurant for McDonald's in 1982 and compare it with the average sales per restaurant for Burger King in 1982.
b. On average, how many restaurants did McDonald's open per month? Per week? Per day?

2.33   In 1985, U.S. consumers redeemed 6.49 billion manufacturers' coupons worth a total of $2.24 billion (McCullough, 1986). Find the mean value per coupon.

2.34   In 1972, Kroger Corporation, one of the largest supermarket chains in the United States, made a major strategic decision. Instead of continuing to hold prices high and trying to attract customers with weekend specials and heavy advertising, Kroger decided to emphasize price competition all week long. Its new strategy involved selling "brand-name groceries for less, on average, than its competitors were doing, and to advertise this fact strenuously" ("Keeping Up," 1979). For the situation described, explain what is meant by "on average" in the preceding quote.

2.5   Numerical Methods for Measuring Variability

Measures of central tendency provide only a partial description of a quantitative data set. Our information is incomplete without a measure of the **variability**, or **spread**, of the data set. Note that in describing a data set, we refer to either the sample or the population. Ultimately (in Chapter 7) we will use the sample numerical descriptive measures to make inferences about the corresponding descriptive measures for the population from which the sample was selected.

If you examine the two histograms in Figure 2.15, you will notice that both hypothetical data sets are symmetric, with equal modes, medians, and means. However, in data set 1 in Figure 2.15(a), the measurements occur with almost equal frequency in the measurement classes, whereas in data set 2 in Figure 2.15(b), most of the measurements are clustered about the center. For this reason, a measure of variability is needed, along with a measure of central tendency, to describe a data set.

FIGURE 2.15 ▶

Two hypothetical data sets

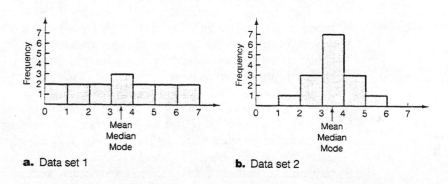

a. Data set 1   **b.** Data set 2

Perhaps the simplest measure of the variability of a quantitative data set is its **range**.

Definition 2.9

The **range** of a data set is equal to the largest measurement minus the smallest measurement.

The range measures the spread of the data by measuring the distance between the smallest and largest measurements. For example, stock A may vary in price during a given year from $32 to $36, whereas stock B may vary from $10 to $58, as shown in

Figure 2.16. The range in price of stock A is \$36 − \$32 = \$4, while that for stock B is \$58 − \$10 = \$48. A comparison of ranges tells us that the price of stock B was much more variable than the price of stock A.

FIGURE 2.16 ▶
Ranges of stock prices for two companies

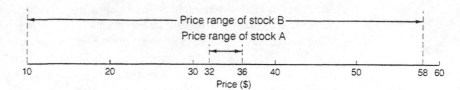

The range is not always a satisfactory measure of variability. For example, suppose we are comparing the profit margin (as a percentage of the total bid price) per construction job for 100 construction jobs for each of two cost estimators working for a large construction company. We find that the profit margins range from −10% (loss) to +40% (profit) for both cost estimators and therefore that the ranges for the two data sets, 40% − (−10%) = 50%, are equal. Because of this, we might be inclined to conclude that there is little or no difference in the performance of the two estimators.

But, suppose the histograms for the two sets of 100 profit margin measurements appear as shown in Figure 2.17. Although the ranges are equal and all central tendency measures are the same for these two symmetric data sets, there is an obvious difference between the two sets of measurements. The difference is that estimator B's profit margins tend to be more stable—i.e., to pile up or to cluster about the center of the data set. In contrast, estimator A's profit margins are more spread out over the range, indicating a higher incidence of some high profit margins, but also a greater risk of losses. Thus, even though the ranges are equal, the profit margin record of estimator A is more variable than that of estimator B, indicating a distinct difference in their cost estimating characteristics. We therefore need to develop more informative numerical measures of variability than the range. In particular, we need a measure that takes into consideration the magnitude of all measurements, not just the largest and smallest.

FIGURE 2.17 ▶
Profit margin histograms for two cost estimators

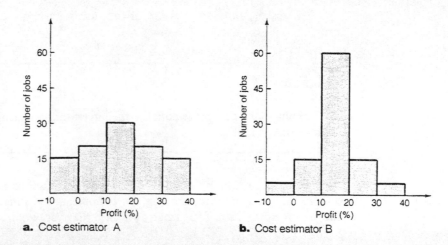

a. Cost estimator A   b. Cost estimator B

CASE STUDY 2.6 / More on the Delphi Technique

You will recall from Case Study 2.5 that the delphi technique is a set of procedures that may be used to obtain a consensus opinion from a group of experts through a series of questionnaires. Case Study 2.5 illustrated the use of the median as a measure of central tendency for the distribution of expert opinions elicited by the questionnaires. As a measure of variability of the data (i.e., the opinions), Milkovich et al. (1972) used the range. Table 2.7, showing the experts' opinions, is repeated here as Table 2.8, with the addition of the range of the distribution of opinions of each questionnaire in the right-hand column.

The range of 23 on questionnaire 2 indicates that at that time the experts' opinions were widely dispersed. The decrease in the range to 11 following questionnaire 4 indicates that as the experts received more information about the firm's needs and learned about one another's opinions, the variability in the distribution of their opinions decreased. Milkovich et al. noted that the decrease in the range was an indication that experts' opinions were converging.

TABLE 2.8	Projected Demand for Buyers								
Questionnaire	Experts							Median	Range
	A	B	C	D	E	F	G		
2	55	35	33	35	55	33	32	35	23
3	45	35	41	35	41	34	32	35	13
4	45	38	41	35	41	34	34	38	11
5	45	38	41	35	45	34	34	38	11

Let us see if we can find a measure of data variability that is more sensitive than the range. Recall that we represent the n measurements in a sample by the symbols x_1, $x_2, \ldots, x_n$, and we represent their mean by $\bar{x}$. What would be the interpretation of $x_1 - \bar{x}$? It is the distance, or **deviation**, between the first sample measurement, x_1, and the sample mean, $\bar{x}$. If we were to calculate this distance for *every* measurement in the sample, we would create a set of distances from the mean:

$$x_1 - \bar{x}, \quad x_2 - \bar{x}, \quad x_3 - \bar{x}, \quad \ldots, \quad x_n - \bar{x}$$

What information do these distance contain? If they tend to be large, the interpretation is that the data are spread out or highly variable. If the distances are mostly small, the data are clustered around the mean $\bar{x}$ and therefore do not exhibit much variability. As a simple example, consider the two samples in Table 2.9 (page 66), which have five measurements (we have ordered the numbers for convenience). You will note that both samples have a mean of 3. However, a glance at the distances shows that sample 1 has greater variability —i.e., more large distances from $\bar{x}$—than sample

2, which is clustered around $\bar{x}$. You can see this clearly by looking at these distances in Figure 2.18. Thus, the distances provide information about the variability of the sample measurements.

TABLE 2.9

	Sample 1	Sample 2
Measurements	1, 2, 3, 4, 5	2, 3, 3, 3, 4
Mean	$\bar{x} = \dfrac{1+2+3+4+5}{5} = \dfrac{15}{5} = 3$	$\bar{x} = \dfrac{2+3+3+3+4}{5} = \dfrac{15}{5} = 3$
Distances from $\bar{x}$	$1-3, \ 2-3, \ 3-3, \ 4-3, \ 5-3$ or $-2, \quad -1, \quad 0, \quad 1, \quad 2$	$2-3, \ 3-3, \ 3-3, \ 3-3, \ 4-3$ or $-1, \quad 0, \quad 0, \quad 0, \quad 1$

FIGURE 2.18 ▶

Distances from the mean for two data sets

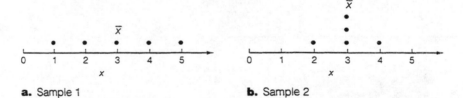

a. Sample 1   **b.** Sample 2

The next step is to condense the information on distances from $\bar{x}$ into a single numerical measure of variability. Simply averaging the distances from $\bar{x}$ will not help. For example, in samples 1 and 2 the negative and positive distances cancel, so that the average distance is 0. Since this is true for any data set—i.e., the sum of the deviations, $\sum_{i=1}^{n} (x_i - \bar{x})$, is always 0—we gain no information by averaging the distances from $\bar{x}$.

There are two methods for dealing with the fact that positive and negative distances from the mean cancel. The first is to treat all the distances as though they were positive, ignoring the sign of the negative distances. We will not pursue this line of thought because the resulting measure of variability (the mean of the absolute values of the distances) presents analytical difficulties beyond the scope of this text. A second method of eliminating the minus signs associated with the distances is to square them. The quantity we can calculate from the squared distances will provide a meaningful description of the variability of a data set.

To use the squared distances calculated from a data set, we first calculate the **sample variance**.

Definition 2.10

The **sample variance** for a sample of n measurements is equal to the sum of the squared distances from the mean divided by $(n - 1)$. In symbols, using s^2 to represent the sample variance,

$$s^2 = \frac{\sum_{i=1}^{n} (x_i - \bar{x})^2}{n - 1}$$

Referring to the two samples in Table 2.9, you can calculate the variance for sample 1 as follows:

$$s^2 = \frac{(1 - 3)^2 + (2 - 3)^2 + (3 - 3)^2 + (4 - 3)^2 + (5 - 3)^2}{5 - 1}$$

$$= \frac{4 + 1 + 0 + 1 + 4}{4} = 2.5$$

The second step in finding a meaningful measure of data variability is to calculate the **standard deviation** of the data set.

Definition 2.11

The **sample standard deviation**, s, is defined as the positive square root of the sample variance, s^2. Thus,

$$s = \sqrt{s^2} = \sqrt{\frac{\sum_{i=1}^{n} (x_i - \bar{x})^2}{n - 1}}$$

The **population variance**, denoted by the symbol σ^2 (sigma squared), is the average of the squared distances of the measurements of *all* units in the population from the mean, μ. σ (sigma) is the square root of this quantity. Since we never really compute σ^2 or σ from the population (the object of sampling is to avoid this costly procedure), we simply denote these two quantities by their respective symbols.

s^2 = Sample variance s = Sample standard deviation

σ^2 = Population variance σ = Population standard deviation

In contrast to the variance, the standard deviation is expressed in the original units of measurement. For example, if the original measurements are in dollars, the variance is expressed in the peculiar units "dollars squared," but the standard deviation is expressed in dollars.

You may wonder why we use the divisor $(n - 1)$ instead of n when calculating the sample variance. Although the use of n may seem logical, since then the sample variance would be the average squared distance from the mean, the use of n tends to underestimate the population variance, σ^2. The use of $(n - 1)$ in the denominator provides the appropriate correction for this tendency.* Since the primary use of sample statistics like s^2 is to estimate population parameters like σ^2, $(n - 1)$ is preferred to n when defining the sample variance.

EXAMPLE 2.5

Calculate the standard deviation of the following sample: 2, 3, 3, 3, 4.

Solution

For this set of data, $\bar{x} = 3$. Then,

$$s = \sqrt{\frac{(2 - 3)^2 + (3 - 3)^2 + (3 - 3)^2 + (3 - 3)^2 + (4 - 3)^2}{5 - 1}}$$

$$= \sqrt{\frac{2}{4}} = \sqrt{.5} = .71$$

As the number of measurements in the sample becomes larger, the sample variance becomes more difficult to calculate. We must calculate the distance between each measurement and the mean, square it, sum the squared distances, and finally divide by $(n - 1)$. Fortunately, as we show in Example 2.8, we can get around this difficulty by using a statistical software package (or most handheld calculators) to compute s^2 and s. However, if you must calculate it by hand, there is a shortcut formula for computing the sample variance.

Appropriate here means that s^2 with a divisor of $(n - 1)$ is an **unbiased** estimator of σ^2. We define and discuss unbiasedness of estimators in Chapter 6.

Shortcut Formula for Sample Variance

$$s^2 = \frac{\left(\begin{array}{c}\text{Sum of squares of}\\\text{sample measurements}\end{array}\right) - \dfrac{\left(\begin{array}{c}\text{Sum of sample}\\\text{measurements}\end{array}\right)^2}{n}}{n-1} = \frac{\displaystyle\sum_{i=1}^{n} x_i^2 - \dfrac{\left(\displaystyle\sum_{i=1}^{n} x_i\right)^2}{n}}{n-1}$$

Note that the formula requires only the sum of the sample measurements, $\sum_{i=1}^{n} x_i$, and the sum of the squares of the sample measurements, $\sum_{i=1}^{n} x_i^2$. Be careful when you calculate these two sums. Rounding the values of x^2 that appear in $\sum_{i=1}^{n} x_i^2$ or rounding the quantity $\left(\sum_{i=1}^{n} x_i\right)^2 / n$ can lead to substantial errors in the calculation of s^2.

. . . .

EXAMPLE 2.6

Use the shortcut formula to compute the variances of these two samples of five measurements each:

    Sample 1: 1, 2, 3, 4, 5   *Sample 2:* 2, 3, 3, 3, 4

Solution

We first work with sample 1. The two quantities needed are

$$\sum_{i=1}^{5} x_i = 1 + 2 + 3 + 4 + 5 = 15$$

and

$$\sum_{i=1}^{5} x_i^2 = 1^2 + 2^2 + 3^2 + 4^2 + 5^2 = 1 + 4 + 9 + 16 + 25 = 55$$

Then the sample variance for sample 1 is

$$s^2 = \frac{\displaystyle\sum_{i=1}^{5} x_i^2 - \dfrac{\left(\displaystyle\sum_{i=1}^{5} x_i\right)^2}{5}}{5-1} = \frac{55 - \dfrac{(15)^2}{5}}{4} = \frac{55-45}{4} = \frac{10}{4} = 2.5$$

Similarly, for sample 2 we get

$$\sum_{i=1}^{5} x_i = 2 + 3 + 3 + 3 + 4 = 15$$

and

$$\sum_{i=1}^{5} x_i^2 = 2^2 + 3^2 + 3^2 + 3^2 + 4^2 = 4 + 9 + 9 + 9 + 16 = 47$$

Then the variance for sample 2 is

$$s^2 = \frac{\sum_{i=1}^{5} x_i^2 - \frac{\left(\sum_{i=1}^{5} x_i\right)^2}{5}}{5 - 1} = \frac{47 - \frac{(15)^2}{5}}{4} = \frac{47 - 45}{4} = \frac{2}{4} = .5$$

EXAMPLE 2.7

The 50 companies' percentages of revenues spent on R&D are repeated here. Calculate the sample variance, s^2, and the standard deviation, s, for these measurements.

13.5	9.5	8.2	6.5	8.4	8.1	6.9	7.5	10.5	13.5
7.2	7.1	9.0	9.9	8.2	13.2	9.2	6.9	9.6	7.7
9.7	7.5	7.2	5.9	6.6	11.1	8.8	5.2	10.6	8.2
11.3	5.6	10.1	8.0	8.5	11.7	7.1	7.7	9.4	6.0
8.0	7.4	10.5	7.8	7.9	6.5	6.9	6.5	6.8	9.5

Solution

The calculation of the sample variance, s^2, would be very tedious for this sample if we tried to use the formula

$$s^2 = \frac{\sum_{i=1}^{50} (x_i - \bar{x})^2}{50 - 1}$$

because it would be necessary to compute all 50 squared distances from the mean. However, for the shortcut formula we need compute only

$$\sum_{i=1}^{50} x_i = 13.5 + 8.4 + \cdots + 6.5 = 424.6$$

and

$$\sum_{i=1}^{50} x_i^2 = (13.5)^2 + (8.4)^2 + \cdots + (6.5)^2 = 3,797.92$$

Then

$$s^2 = \frac{\sum\limits_{i=1}^{50} x_i^2 - \dfrac{\left(\sum\limits_{i=1}^{50} x_i\right)^2}{50}}{50 - 1} = \frac{3{,}797.92 - \dfrac{(424.6)^2}{50}}{49} = 3.9228$$

The standard deviation is

$$s = \sqrt{s^2} = \sqrt{3.9228} = 1.98$$

Notice that we retained all the decimal places in the calculation of the sum of squares of the measurements. This was done to reduce the rounding error in the calculations, even though the original data were accurate to only one decimal place.*

EXAMPLE 2.8

Use a statistical software package to compute the median, mean, variance, and standard deviation of the R&D data given in Example 2.7.

Solution

The SAS/PC printout is shown in Figure 2.19. The median, mean, variance, and standard deviation are shaded on the printout. Although the SAS procedure (PROC

FIGURE 2.19 ▶
SAS/PC printout for mean, median, variance, and standard deviation

```
                           Moments

N                   50    Sum Wgts              50
Mean             8.492    Sum                424.6
Std Dev       1.980604    Variance        3.922792
Skewness      .8546013    Kurtosis        .4192877
USS            3797.92    CSS             192.2168
CV            23.32317    Std Mean        .2800997
T:Mean=0      30.31778    Prob>|T|          0.0001
Sgn Rank         637.5    Prob>|S|          0.0001
Num  ^= 0           50
W:Normal      .9328984    Prob<W            0.009


                     Quantiles(Def=5)

   100% Max       13.5    99%               13.5
    75% Q3         9.6    95%               13.2
    50% Med       8.05    90%               11.2
    25% Q1         7.1    10%                6.5
     0% Min        5.2    5%                 5.9
                          1%                 5.2
```

*The accuracy of the original data has nothing to do with the degree of accuracy used in computing s^2 and s. You should retain twice as many decimal places in s^2 as you want in s. For example, if you want to calculate s to the nearest hundredth, you should calculate s^2 to the nearest ten-thousandth.

UNIVARIATE) generates many other descriptive statistics, some of which we discuss later, we can easily pick out those of interest to us. Note that many decimal places are carried by the program, but when we round to the same number of decimal places used in the previous examples, we find

$$\text{Median} = 8.05 \qquad s^2 = 3.9228$$
$$\bar{x} = 8.49 \qquad s = 1.98$$

The answers are identical to those obtained by hand calculation.

You know that the standard deviation measures the variability of a set of data and you know how to calculate it. But how can we interpret and use the standard deviation? This is the topic of Section 2.6.

Exercises 2.35–2.46

Learning the Mechanics

2.35 The range, variance, and standard deviation provide information about the variation in a data set.
   a. Describe the information each conveys.
   b. Discuss the advantages and disadvantages of using each to measure the variability of a data set.

2.36 Describe the sample variance using words rather than a formula. Do the same with the population variance.

2.37 Given the following information about two data sets, compute $\bar{x}$, the sample variance, and the standard deviation for each:

   a. $n = 25$, $\sum_{i=1}^{n} x_i^2 = 1,000$, $\sum_{i=1}^{n} x_i = 50$ b. $n = 80$, $\sum_{i=1}^{n} x_i^2 = 270$, $\sum_{i=1}^{n} x_i = 100$

2.38 For each of the following data sets, compute $\sum_{i=1}^{n} x_i$, $\sum_{i=1}^{n} x_i^2$, and $\left(\sum_{i=1}^{n} x_i\right)^2$:

   a. 5, 9, 6, 3, 7   b. 3, 1, 4, 3, 0, −2   c. 90, 12, 40, 15
   d. −1, 4, 1, 0, 5   e. 1, 0, 0, 1, 0, 10

2.39 Compute $\bar{x}$, s^2, and s for each of the following data sets:
   a. 10, 1, 0, 0, 20   b. 5, 9, −1, 100

2.40 Compute $\bar{x}$, s^2, and s for each of the following data sets. If appropriate, specify the units in which your answer is expressed.
   a. 3, 1, 10, 10, 4   b. 8 feet, 10 feet, 32 feet, 5 feet   c. −1, −4, −3, 1, −4, −4
   d. 1/5 ounce, 1/5 ounce, 1/5 ounce, 2/5 ounce, 1/5 ounce, 4/5 ounce

2.41 Using only integers between 0 and 10, construct two data sets with at least ten observations each that have the same mean but different variances. Construct dot diagrams for each of your data sets (see Figure 2.18), and mark the mean of each data set on its dot diagram.

2.42 Using only integers between 0 and 10, construct two data sets with at least ten observations each that have the same range but different means. Construct a dot diagram for each of your data sets (see Figure 2.18), and mark the mean of each data set on its dot diagram.

2.43 Can the variance of a data set ever be negative? Explain. Can the variance ever be smaller than the standard deviation? Explain.

Applying the Concepts

2.44 The Consumer Price Index (CPI) measures the price change of a constant market basket of goods and services. The Bureau of Labor Statistics publishes a national CPI (called the U.S. City Average Index) as well as separate indexes for each of 28 different cities in the United States. The national index and some of the city indexes are published monthly; the remainder of the city indexes are published semiannually. The CPI is used in cost-of-living escalator clauses of many labor contracts to adjust wages for inflation (U.S. Department of Labor, 1978). For example, in the printing industry of Minneapolis and St. Paul, hourly wages are adjusted every 6 months (based on October and April values of the CPI) by 4¢ for every point change in the Minneapolis/St. Paul CPI.

The table lists the published values of the U.S. City Average Index and the Chicago Index during 1991 and 1992. The sums and sums of squares for the U.S. City Average Index are $\Sigma x = 3{,}318.1$ and $\Sigma x^2 = 458{,}877.49$, respectively. For the Chicago Index, these quantities are $\Sigma x = 3{,}337.2$ and $\Sigma x^2 = 464{,}169.38$.

Month	U.S. City Average Index	Chicago	Month	U.S. City Average Index	Chicago
January 1991	134.6	135.1	January 1992	138.1	138.9
February	134.8	135.5	February	138.6	139.2
March	135.0	136.2	March	139.3	139.7
April	135.2	136.1	April	139.5	139.8
May	135.6	136.8	May	139.7	140.5
June	136.0	137.3	June	140.2	141.2
July	136.2	137.3	July	140.5	141.4
August	136.6	137.6	August	140.9	141.9
September	137.2	138.3	September	141.3	142.7
October	137.4	138.0	October	141.8	142.1
November	137.8	138.0	November	142.0	142.4
December	137.9	138.3	December	141.9	142.9

Source: U.S. Department of Labor: Labor Statistics, 1991–1993.
Secondary Source: CPI Chicago, pp. 91–93.

a. Calculate the mean values for the U.S. City Average Index and the Chicago Index.
b. Find the ranges of the U.S. City Average Index and the Chicago Index.
c. The standard deviation of the U.S. City Average Index over the 24 months described in the table is 2.43. Calculate the standard deviation for the Chicago Index over the time period described in the table.

d. Which index displays greater variation about its mean over the time period in question? Justify your response.

2.45   To set an appropriate price for a product, it is necessary to be able to estimate its cost of production. One element of the cost is based on the length of time it takes workers to produce the product. The most widely used technique for making such measurements is the **time study**. In a time study, the task to be studied is divided into measurable parts and each is timed with a stopwatch or filmed for later analysis. For each worker, this process is repeated many times for each subtask. Then the average and standard deviation of the time required to complete each subtask are computed for each worker. A worker's overall time to complete the task under study is then determined by adding his or her subtask-time averages (Chase and Aquilano, 1977). The data (in minutes) given in the table are the result of a time study of a production operation involving two subtasks.

| Repetition | Worker A | | Worker B | |
	Subtask 1	Subtask 2	Subtask 1	Subtask 2
1	30	2	31	7
2	28	4	30	2
3	31	3	32	6
4	38	3	30	5
5	25	2	29	4
6	29	4	30	1
7	30	3	31	4

a. Find the overall time it took each worker to complete the manufacturing operation under study.
b. For each worker, find the standard deviation of the seven times for subtask 1.
c. In the context of this problem, what are the standard deviations you computed in part **b** measuring?
d. Repeat part **b** for subtask 2.
e. If you could choose workers similar to A or workers similar to B to perform subtasks 1 and 2, which type would you assign to each subtask? Explain your decisions on the basis of your answers to parts **a–d**.

2.46   The table lists the 1989 profits (in millions of dollars) for a sample of seven airlines.

Airline	Profit
Continental	3.06
Eastern	−852.32
Northwest	355.25
Pan Am	−414.73
Delta	473.17
TWA	−298.55
United	358.09

Source: *Air Transport* (Washington, D.C.:
Air Transport Association of America, 1990).

a. Calculate the range, variance, and standard deviation of the data set.
b. Specify the units in which each of your answers to part **a** is expressed.
c. Suppose Eastern Airlines had a profit of $0 instead of a loss of $852.32 million. Would the range of the data set increase or decrease? Why? Would the standard deviation of the data set increase or decrease? Why?

2.6   Interpreting the Standard Deviation

As we have seen, if we are comparing the variability of two samples selected from a population, the sample with the larger standard deviation is the more variable of the two. Thus, we know how to interpret the standard deviation on a relative or comparative basis, but we have not explained how it provides a measure of variability for a single sample.

One way to interpret the standard deviation as a measure of variability of a data set would be to answer questions such as the following: How many measurements are within 1 standard deviation of the mean? How many measurements are within 2 standard deviations? For a specific data set, we can answer the questions by counting the number of measurements in each of the intervals. However, if we are interested in obtaining a general answer to these questions, the problem is more difficult.

In Table 2.10, we present two sets of guidelines to help answer the questions of how many measurements fall within 1, 2, and 3 standard deviations of the mean. The first set, which applies to any sample, is derived from a theorem proved by the Russian mathematician, Chebyshev. The second set, the Empirical Rule, is based on empirical evidence that has accumulated over time and applies to samples that possess mound-shaped frequency distributions—those that are approximately symmetric, with a clustering of measurements about the midpoint of the distribution (the mean, median, and mode should all be about the same) and that tail off as we move away from the center of the histogram. Thus, the histogram will have the appearance of a mound or bell, as shown in Figure 2.20 on page 76. The percentages given for the various intervals (particularly the interval $\bar{x} - 2s$ to $\bar{x} + 2s$) in Table 2.10 provide remarkably good approximations even when the distribution of the data is slightly skewed or asymmetric.*

TABLE 2.10   Aids to the Interpretation and Use of a Standard Deviation

1. A rule (from Chebyshev's theorem) that applies to any sample of measurements, regardless of the shape of the frequency distribution:
   a. It is possible that none of the measurements will fall within the interval $\bar{x} \pm s$ or $(\bar{x} - s, \bar{x} + s)$—i.e., within 1 standard deviation of the mean.
   b. At least ¾ of the measurements will fall within $(\bar{x} - 2s, \bar{x} + 2s)$—i.e., within 2 standard deviations of the mean.
   c. At least 8/9 of the measurements will fall within $(\bar{x} - 3s, \bar{x} + 3s)$—i.e., within 3 standard deviations of the mean.
   d. Generally, at least $(1 - 1/k^2)$ of the measurements will fall within $(\bar{x} - ks, \bar{x} + ks)$—i.e., within k standard deviations of the mean, where k is any number greater than 1.

---

*Note to the instructor: It is our intention to imply that the Empirical Rule of Table 2.10 not only applies to normal distributions of data, but also applies very well to mound-shaped distributions of large data sets and to distributions that are moderately skewed.

2. A rule of thumb called the Empirical Rule applies to samples with frequency distributions that are mound-shaped:
   a. Approximately 68% of the measurements will fall within the interval $\bar{x} \pm s$ or $(\bar{x} - s, \bar{x} + s)$—i.e., within 1 standard deviation of the mean.
   b. Approximately 95% of the measurements will fall within $(\bar{x} - 2s, \bar{x} + 2s)$—i.e., within 2 standard deviations of the mean.
   c. Essentially all the measurements will fall within $(\bar{x} - 3s, \bar{x} + 3s)$—i.e., within 3 standard deviations of the mean.

FIGURE 2.20 ▶

Histogram of a mound-shaped sample

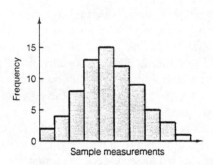

EXAMPLE 2.9

The 50 companies' percentages of revenues spent on R&D are repeated here:

13.5	9.5	8.2	6.5	8.4	8.1	6.9	7.5	10.5	13.5
7.2	7.1	9.0	9.9	8.2	13.2	9.2	6.9	9.6	7.7
9.7	7.5	7.2	5.9	6.6	11.1	8.8	5.2	10.6	8.2
11.3	5.6	10.1	8.0	8.5	11.7	7.1	7.7	9.4	6.0
8.0	7.4	10.5	7.8	7.9	6.5	6.9	6.5	6.8	9.5

We have previously shown that the mean and standard deviation of these data are 8.49 and 1.98, respectively. Calculate the fraction of these measurements that lie within the intervals $\bar{x} \pm s$, $\bar{x} \pm 2s$, and $\bar{x} \pm 3s$, and compare the results with those in Table 2.10.

Solution

We first form the interval

$$(\bar{x} - s, \bar{x} + s) = (8.49 - 1.98, 8.49 + 1.98) = (6.51, 10.47)$$

A check of the measurements reveals that 34 of the 50 measurements, or 68%, are within 1 standard deviation of the mean.
The interval

$$(\bar{x} - 2s, \bar{x} + 2s) = (8.49 - 3.96, 8.49 + 3.96) = (4.53, 12.45)$$

contains 47 of the 50 measurements, or 94%.
The 3 standard deviation interval around $\bar{x}$,

$$(\bar{x} - 3s, \bar{x} + 3s) = (8.49 - 5.94, 8.49 + 5.94) = (2.55, 14.43)$$

contains all the measurements.

In spite of the fact that the distribution of these data is skewed to the right (see Figure 2.13), the percentages within 1, 2, and 3 standard deviations (68%, 94%, and 100%) agree very well with the approximations of 68%, 95%, and 100% given by the Empirical Rule. You will find that unless the distribution is extremely skewed, the mound-shaped approximations will be reasonably accurate. Of course, no matter what the shape of the distribution, Chebyshev's theorem from Table 2.10 assures that at least 75% and at least 89% (8/9) of the measurements will lie within 2 and 3 standard deviations of the mean, respectively.

EXAMPLE 2.10

Chebyshev's theorem and the Empirical Rule (Table 2.10) are useful as a check on the calculation of the standard deviation. For example, suppose we calculated the standard deviation of the R&D percentages to be 3.92. Are there any clues in the data that enable us to judge whether this number is reasonable?

Solution

The range of the R&D percentages is 13.5 − 5.2 = 8.3. From the Empirical Rule we know that most of the measurements (approximately 95% if the distribution is not extremely skewed) will be within 2 standard deviations of the mean. And from Chebyshev's theorem, regardless of the shape of the distribution, almost all of the measurements (at least 8/9) will fall within 3 standard deviations of the mean. Consequently, we would expect the range of measurements to be between 4 (± 2) and 6 (± 3) standard deviations in length (see Figure 2.21). For the R&D data, this means that the standard deviation s should fall between

$$\frac{\text{Range}}{6} = \frac{8.3}{6} = 1.38 \quad \text{and} \quad \frac{\text{Range}}{4} = \frac{8.3}{4} = 2.08$$

FIGURE 2.21 ▶
The relation between the range and the standard deviation

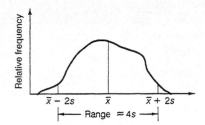

Thus, we would have reason to believe that a calculated standard deviation of 3.92 for these data is too large, since it far exceeds one-fourth the range, 2.08. A check of our work reveals that 3.92 is the variance s^2, not the standard deviation s (see Example 2.7). We "forgot" to take the square root, a common error. The correct value of 1.98 is between one-sixth and one-fourth the range.

In examples and exercises we will sometimes use $s \approx$ range/4 to obtain a crude, and usually conservatively large, approximation for s. However, we stress that this is no substitute for calculating the exact value of s when possible.

Beginning with the following example, we will use the concepts in Chebyshev's theorem and the Empirical Rule to build the foundation for statistical inference-making.

EXAMPLE 2.11

A manufacturer of automobile batteries claims that the average length of useful life for its grade A battery is 60 months. However, the guarantee on this brand is for only 36 months. Assume that the standard deviation of the lifelengths is known to be 10 months and that the frequency distribution of the lifelengths is known to be mound-shaped.

a. Approximately what percentage of the manufacturer's grade A batteries will last more than 50 months, assuming the manufacturer's claim about the mean lifelength is true?

b. Approximately what percentage of the manufacturer's batteries will last less than 40 months, assuming that the manufacturer's claim about the mean lifelength is true?

c. Suppose that your grade A battery lasts 37 months. What would you infer about the manufacturer's claim that the mean lifelength is 60 months?

Solution

Assuming that the distribution of lifelengths is approximately mound-shaped, with a mean of 60 months and a standard deviation of 10 months, it would appear as shown in Figure 2.22. Note that we can take advantage of the fact that mound-shaped distributions are (approximately) symmetric about the mean, so that the percentages given by the Empirical Rule can be split equally between the halves of the distribution on each side of the mean. The approximations given in Figure 2.22 are more dependent on the assumption of a mound-shaped distribution than those given by the Empirical Rule because the approximations in the figure depend on the (approximate) symmetry of the mound-shaped distribution. We saw in Example 2.9 that the Empirical Rule can yield good approximations even for skewed distributions. This will *not* be true of the approximations in Figure 2.22; the distribution must be mound-shaped and (approximately) symmetric.

FIGURE 2.22 ▶

Grade A battery lifelength distribution; manufacturer's claim assumed true

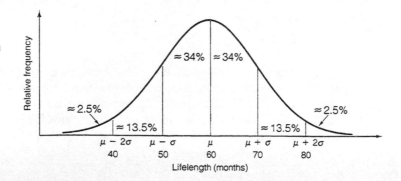

For example, since approximately 68% of the measurements will fall within 1 standard deviation on both sides of the mean, the distribution's symmetry implies that approximately ½ (68%) = 34% of the measurements will fall between the mean and 1 standard deviation on each side. This concept is demonstrated in Figure 2.22. Note that the 2.5% of the measurements beyond 2 standard deviations in each direction from the mean follows from the fact that, if approximately 95% of the measurements fall within 2 standard deviations, then about 5% fall outside 2 standard deviations. If the distribution is approximately symmetric, then about 2.5% fall beyond 2 standard deviations on each side of the mean.

a. Using Figure 2.22, it is easy to see that the percentage of batteries lasting more than 50 months is, approximately, 34% (between 50 and 60 months) plus 50% (greater than 60 months). Thus, approximately (50 + 34)% = 84% of the batteries should last longer than 50 months.

b. The percentage of batteries that last less than 40 months can also be determined from Figure 2.22. Since 40 is 2 standard deviations below the claimed mean of 60 months, approximately 2.5% of the batteries should fail prior to 40 months, assuming the manufacturer's claim is true.

c. If you are so unfortunate that your grade A battery fails at 37 months, one or two inferences can be made: Either your battery was one of the approximately 2.5% that fail prior to 40 months, or the manufacturer's claim is not true. Because the chances are so small that a battery fails before 40 months if the claim is true, you would have good reason to have serious doubts about the manufacturer's claim. A mean smaller than 60 months and/or a standard deviation greater than 10 months would increase the likelihood of a battery's failure prior to 40 months.*

Example 2.11 is our initial demonstration of the statistical inference-making process. At this point you should realize that we will use sample information (in Example 2.11 your battery's failure at 37 months) to make inferences about the population (in Example 2.11, the manufacturer's claim about the mean lifelength for the population of all batteries). We will build on this foundation as we proceed.

CASE STUDY 2.7 / Becoming More Sensitive to Customer Needs

The degree of sensitization on the part of a firm to the needs and wants of its consumers is frequently an important factor in determining the firm's overall success.

Namias (1964) presents a procedure for achieving such sensitivity. The procedure uses the rate of consumer complaints about a product to determine when and

---

*The assumption that the distribution is mound-shaped and symmetric may also be incorrect. However, if the distribution were skewed to the right, as lifelength distributions often tend to be, the percentage of measurements more than 2 standard deviations *below* the mean would be even less than 2.5%.

when not to conduct a search for specific causes of consumer complaints. For simplification, we will discuss Namias's paper as if the procedure described used the number of complaints per 10,000 units of a product sold to determine when and when not to conduct a search for specific causes of consumer complaints. The details of the procedure are discussed in Case Study 2.8.

Namias's procedure, given our simplification, makes use of the **distribution** of the number of consumer complaints received about a product per 10,000 units of the product sold. To visualize such a distribution, imagine that a company produces its product in lots of 10,000 units and keeps track of the number of complaints received about items in each lot. The company's complaint records will show a series of numbers, perhaps 100, 96, 145, 201, etc., each of which is the number of complaints received about a particular lot of 10,000 units. This series of numbers is a quantitative data set from which a relative frequency histogram can be drawn. The histogram constructed from this data set is a representation of the distribution of interest—i.e.,

the distribution of the number of consumer complaints received about a product per 10,000 units of the product sold. It is assumed that this distribution remains stable over time. The variance and standard deviation of this distribution are measures of the variation in the number of consumer complaints received. Namias determined that this distribution was mound-shaped. Accordingly, it can be said that approximately 95% of the time the number of complaints about a product will be within 2 standard deviations of the mean number of complaints. It is upon this fact, as we shall see in Case Study 2.8, that Namias's procedure for determining when it would be worthwhile to conduct a search for specific causes of consumer complaints is founded.

If it could not have been determined that the distribution of the number of complaints was mound-shaped, it would have been necessary for Namias to use Chebyshev's theorem (Table 2.10). In that case, it could have been said only that at least 75% of the time the number of complaints about a product will be within 2 standard deviations of the mean number of complaints.

Exercises 2.47–2.61

Learning the Mechanics

2.47 To what kind of data sets can be Chebyshev's theorem be applied? The Empirical Rule?

2.48 The output from a statistical computer program indicates that the mean and standard deviation of a data set consisting of 200 measurements are $1,500 and $300, respectively.
  a. What are the units of measurement of the variable of interest? Based on the units, are these data nominal, ordinal, interval, or ratio?
  b. What can be said about the number of measurements between $900 and $2,100? Between $600 and $2,400? Between $1,200 and $1,800? Between $1,500 and $2,100?

2.49 For any set of data, what can be said about the percentage of the measurements contained in each of the following intervals?
  a. $\bar{x} - s$ to $\bar{x} + s$ b. $\bar{x} - 2s$ to $\bar{x} + 2s$ c. $\bar{x} - 3s$ to $\bar{x} + 3s$

2.50 As a result of government and consumer pressure, automobile manufacturers in the United States are deeply involved in research to improve their products' gasoline mileage. One manufacturer, hoping to achieve 40 miles per gallon on one of its compact models, measured the mileage obtained by 36 test versions of the model with the following results (rounded to the nearest mile for convenience):

43	35	41	42	42	38	40	41	41
40	40	41	42	36	43	40	38	40
38	45	39	41	42	37	40	40	44
39	40	37	39	41	39	41	37	40

The mean and standard deviation of these data are 40.1 and 2.2, respectively.

a. What are the units in which the mean and standard deviation are expressed?

b. If the manufacturer would be satisfied with a (population) mean of 40 miles per gallon, how would it react to the above test data?

c. Use the information in Table 2.10 to check the reasonableness of the calculated standard deviation, $s = 2.2$.

d. Construct a relative frequency histogram of the data set. Is the data set mound-shaped?

e. What percentage of the measurements would you expect to find within the intervals $\bar{x} \pm s$, $\bar{x} \pm 2s$, and $\bar{x} \pm 3s$?

f. Count the number of measurements that actually fall within the intervals of part e. Express each interval count as a percentage of the total number of measurements. Compare these results with your answers to part e.

2.51 Given a data set with a largest value of 760 and a smallest value of 135, what would you estimate the standard deviation to be? Explain the logic behind the procedure you used to estimate the standard deviation. Suppose the standard deviation is reported to be 25. Is this feasible? Explain.

Applying the Concepts

2.52 A manufacturer of video cassette recorders is disturbed because retailers were complaining that they were not receiving shipments of recorders as fast as they had been promised. The manufacturer decided to run a check on the distribution network. Each of the 50 warehouses owned by the manufacturer throughout the country had been instructed to maintain at least 200 recorders in stock at all times so that a supply would always be readily available for retailers. The manufacturer checked the inventories of 20 of these warehouses and obtained the following numbers of video cassette recorders in stock:

40	10	44	142	14	301	175	0	38	202
220	32	400	78	16	99	0	176	5	86

The mean and standard deviation are 103.9 and 111.3, respectively.

a. Calculate the median. Is the distribution of measurements skewed or symmetric? Explain.

b. Using your answer to part a, would you advise using the Empirical Rule to describe these data? Why?

c. According to Chebyshev's theorem, what percentage of the measurements would you expect to find outside the intervals $\bar{x} \pm s$, $\bar{x} \pm 2s$, and $\bar{x} \pm 3s$?

d. Check the numbers of measurements that actually fall outside the intervals specified in part c. Express each count as a percentage of the total number of measurements. Compare these results with your answers to part c.

2.53 Twenty-five mergers were sampled from the population of mergers that occurred between firms (excluding railroads) listed on the New York Stock Exchange during the period 1958–1980. For each merger, the ratio of the target firm's sales for the preceding year to the bidder firm's sales was calculated. (See Exercise 1.14 for definitions of target and bidder firms.) The 25 sales ratios are listed below (Eger, 1982, p. 133):

.16	.07	.32	.05	.79
.30	.18	.04	.04	.05
.14	.08	.14	.29	.02
.14	.10	.34	.10	.02
.03	.15	.09	.06	.02

For these data, $\Sigma x = 3.72$ and $\Sigma x^2 = 1.2088$.

a. What is the mean sales ratio, $\bar{x}$, for this sample of mergers? Also, find s^2 and s.

b. According to Chebyshev's theorem, what percentage of the measurements would you expect to find in the intervals $\bar{x} \pm .75s$, $\bar{x} \pm 2.5s$, and $\bar{x} \pm 4s$?

c. What percentage of measurements actually fall in the intervals of part **b**? Compare these results with the results of part **b**.

d. What percentage of the mergers involved a target firm with larger sales than the bidder firm?

2.54 Tests have demonstrated that the shelf life of cake mix A has a mound-shaped distribution with a mean of 275 days and a standard deviation of 55 days. Mix B has a shelf life whose distribution is also mound-shaped, but with a mean of 286 days and a standard deviation of 22 days.

a. What percentage of boxes of cake mix A remain fresh for 330 days or more?

b. What percentage of boxes of mix B remain fresh for 330 days or more?

c. Which cake mix is more likely to remain fresh for more than 330 days? Explain.

d. Now assume the shapes of the two shelf-life distributions are unknown. Answer parts **a–c** by applying Chebyshev's theorem.

2.55 A company that bottles sparkling water has determined that it lost an average of 30.4 cases per week last year due to breakage in transit. The standard deviation of the number of cases lost per week was 3.8 cases. With only this information, what can you say about the number of weeks last year that the company lost more than 38 cases due to breakage in transit? Justify your answer.

2.56 A chemical company produces a substance composed of 98% cracked corn particles and 2% zinc phosphide for use in controlling rat populations in sugarcane fields. Production must be carefully controlled to maintain the zinc phosphide at 2% because too much zinc phosphide will damage the sugarcane and too little will be ineffective in controlling the rat population. Records from past production indicate that the distribution of the actual percentage of zinc phosphide present in the substance is approximately mound-shaped, with a mean of 2.0% and a standard deviation of .08%. If the production line is operating correctly and a batch is chosen at random from a day's production, what is the approximate probability that it will contain less than 1.84% zinc phosphide?

2.57 For 50 randomly selected days, the number of vehicles that used a certain road was ascertained by a city engineer. The mean was 385; the standard deviation was 15. Suppose you are interested in the proportion of days that there were between 340 and 430 vehicles using the road. What does Chebyshev's theorem tell you about this proportion?

2.58 A boat dealer has determined that the frequency distribution of the number of outboard motor sales per month over the last five years is mound-shaped, with a sample mean of 30 and a sample variance of 4.

Approximately what percentage of the recorded monthly sales figures of the past five years would be expected to be greater than 34? Less than 26? Greater than 36?

2.59 Solar energy is considered by many to be the energy of the future. A recent survey was taken to compare the cost of solar energy with the cost of gas or electric energy. Results of the survey revealed that the average monthly utility bill of a three-bedroom house using gas or electric energy was $125 and the standard deviation was $15.

    a. If nothing is known about the distribution of utility bills, what can you say about the fraction of all three-bedroom homes with gas or electric energy that have bills between $80 and $170?

    b. If it is reasonable to assume that the distribution of utility bills is mound-shaped, approximately what proportion of three-bedroom homes would have monthly bills less than $110?

    c. Suppose that three houses with solar energy units had the following utility bills: $78, $92, $87. Does this suggest that solar energy units might result in lower utility bills? Explain. [*Note:* We present a statistical method for testing this conjecture in Chapter 7.]

2.60 When it is working properly, a machine that fills 25-pound bags of flour dispenses an average of 25 pounds per fill; the standard deviation of the amount of fill is .1 pound. To monitor the performance of the machine, an inspector weighs the contents of a bag coming off the machine's conveyor belt every half-hour during the day. If the contents of two consecutive bags fall more than 2 standard deviations from the mean (using the mean and standard deviation given above), the filling process is said to be out of control and the machine is shut down briefly for adjustments. The data given in the table are the weights measured by the inspector yesterday. Assume the machine is never shut down for more than 15 minutes at a time. At what times yesterday was the process shut down for adjustment? Justify your answer.

Time	Weight (pounds)	Time	Weight (pounds)
8:00 A.M.	25.10	12:30 P.M.	25.06
8:30	25.15	1:00	24.95
9:00	24.81	1:30	24.80
9:30	24.75	2:00	24.95
10:00	25.00	2:30	25.21
10:30	25.05	3:00	24.90
11:00	25.23	3:30	24.71
11:30	25.25	4:00	25.31
12:00	25.01	4:30	25.15
		5:00	25.20

2.61 A buyer for a lumber company must determine whether to buy a piece of land containing 5,000 pine trees. If 1,000 of the trees are at least 40 feet tall, he will purchase the land; otherwise, he will not. The owner of the land reports that the distribution of the heights of the trees has a mean of 30 feet, and a standard deviation of 3 feet. Based on this information, what should the buyer decide?

2.7   Calculating a Mean and Standard Deviation from Grouped Data (Optional)

If your data have been grouped in classes of equal width and arranged in a frequency table, you can use the following formulas to calculate $\bar{x}$, s^2, and s:

Formulas for Calculating a Mean and Standard Deviation from Grouped Data

$$\bar{x} = \frac{\sum_{i=1}^{k} x_i f_i}{n}$$

$$s^2 = \frac{\sum_{i=1}^{k} (x_i - \bar{x})^2 f_i}{n - 1} \qquad s = \sqrt{s^2}$$

Shortcut formula:
$$s^2 = \frac{\sum_{i=1}^{k} x_i^2 f_i - \frac{\left(\sum_{i=1}^{k} x_i f_i\right)^2}{n}}{n - 1}$$

where x_i = Midpoint of the ith class

f_i = Frequency of the ith class

k = Number of classes

EXAMPLE 2.12

Compute the mean and standard deviation for the companies' R&D percentages based on the groupings used to construct the relative frequency histogram of Figure 2.13.

Solution

The frequency table is repeated in Table 2.11, with a column showing the class midpoints added.

Substituting the class midpoints and frequencies into the formula for the mean of grouped data, we obtain

$$\bar{x} = \frac{\sum_{i=1}^{k} x_i f_i}{n} = \frac{(5.70)(4) + (6.80)(12) + \cdots + (13.40)(3)}{50}$$

$$= \frac{422.5}{50} = 8.45$$

TABLE 2.11   Measurement Classes, Frequencies, and Class Midpoints for the R&D Percentage Data

Class	Measurement Class	Class Midpoint	Class Frequency
1	5.15– 6.25	5.70	4
2	6.25– 7.35	6.80	12
3	7.35– 8.45	7.90	14
4	8.45– 9.55	9.00	7
5	9.55–10.65	10.10	7
6	10.65–11.75	11.20	3
7	11.75–12.85	12.30	0
8	12.85–13.95	13.40	3

Next, using the shortcut formula for calculating the sample variance for grouped data, we obtain

$$s^2 = \frac{\sum\limits_{i=1}^{k} x_i^2 f_i - \dfrac{\left(\sum\limits_{i=1}^{k} x_i f_i\right)^2}{n}}{n-1}$$

$$= \frac{(5.70)^2(4) + (6.80)^2(12) + \cdots + (13.40)^2(3) - \dfrac{(422.5)^2}{50}}{50-1}$$

$$= \frac{3,754.65 - 3,570.125}{49} = 3.7658$$

$$s = \sqrt{3.7658} = 1.94$$

You will note that the sample mean and standard deviation for the grouped data, 8.45 and 1.94, agree well with the exact mean and standard deviation for the 50 measurements, $\bar{x} = 8.49$ and $s = 1.98$. As long as a reasonable number of class intervals is used, the approximations that are based on grouped data will usually be good.

2.8   Measures of Relative Standing

As we have seen, numerical measures of central tendency and variability describe the general nature of a data set (either a sample or a population). We may also be interested in describing the relative location of a particular measurement within a data set.

Descriptive measures of the relationship of a measurement to the rest of the data are called **measures of relative standing**.

One measure of the relative standing of a particular measurement is its **percentile ranking**:

Definition 2.12

Let $x_1, x_2, \ldots, x_n$ be a set of n measurements arranged in increasing (or decreasing) order. The **pth percentile** is a number x such that $p\%$ of the measurements fall below the pth percentile and $(100 - p)\%$ fall above it.

For example, if oil company A reports that its yearly sales are in the 90th percentile of all companies in the industry, the implication is that 90% of all oil companies have yearly sales less than company A's, and only 10% have yearly sales exceeding company A's. This is demonstrated in Figure 2.23.

Another measure of relative standing in popular use is the **z-score**. As you can see in Definition 2.13, the z-score makes use of the mean and standard deviation of the data set in order to specify the location of a measurement:

Definition 2.13

The **sample z-score** for a measurement x is

$$z = \frac{x - \bar{x}}{s}$$

The **population z-score** for a measurement x is

$$z = \frac{x - \mu}{\sigma}$$

Note that the z-score is calculated by subtracting $\bar{x}$ (or μ) from the measurement x and then dividing the result by s (or σ). The result, the z-score, represents the distance between a given measurement, x, and the mean, expressed in standard deviations.

EXAMPLE 2.13

Suppose 200 steelworkers are selected, and the annual income of each is determined. The mean and standard deviation are $\bar{x} = \$24{,}000$ and $s = \$2{,}000$. Suppose Joe Smith's annual income is $22,000. What is his sample z-score?

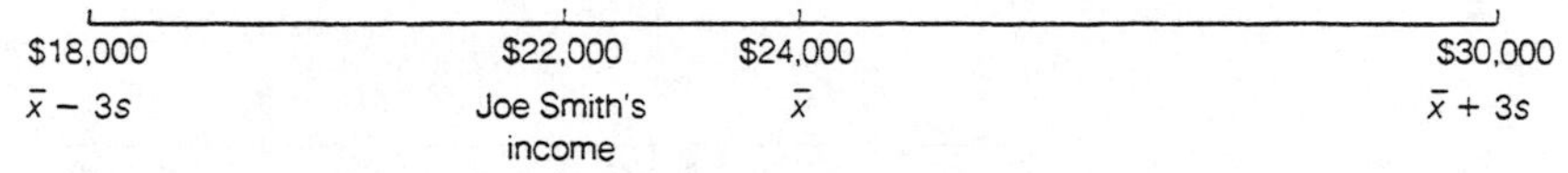

FIGURE 2.24 ▶
Annual income of steelworkers

$18,000 $22,000 $24,000 $30,000
$\bar{x} - 3s$ Joe Smith's $\bar{x}$ $\bar{x} + 3s$
                 income

Solution

Joe Smith's annual income lies below the mean income of the 200 steelworkers (see Figure 2.24). We compute

$$z = \frac{x - \bar{x}}{s} = \frac{\$22{,}000 - \$24{,}000}{\$2{,}000} = -1.0$$

which tells us that Joe Smith's annual income is 1.0 standard deviation *below* the sample mean, or, in short, his sample z-score is -1.0.

The numerical value of the z-score reflects the relative standing of the measurement. A large positive z-score implies that the measurement is larger than almost all other measurements, whereas a large negative z-score indicates that the measurement is smaller than almost every other measurement. If a z-score is 0 or near 0, the measurement is located at or near the mean of the sample or population.

We can be more specific if we know that the frequency distribution of the measurements is mound-shaped. In this case, the following interpretation of the z-scores can be given:

Interpretation of z-Scores for Mound-Shaped Distributions of Data

1. Approximately 68% of the measurements will have a z-score between -1 and 1.

2. Approximately 95% of the measurements will have a z-score between -2 and 2.

3. All or almost all the measurements will have a z-score between -3 and 3.

Note that this interpretation of z-scores is identical to that given in Table 2.10 for samples that exhibit mound-shaped frequency distributions. The statement that a measurement falls in the interval $(\mu - \sigma, \mu + \sigma)$ is identical to the statement that a measurement has a population z-score between -1 and 1, since all measurements between $(\mu - \sigma)$ and $(\mu + \sigma)$ are within 1 standard deviation of μ (see Figure 2.25 on page 88).

FIGURE 2.25 ▶
Population z-scores for a mound-shaped distribution

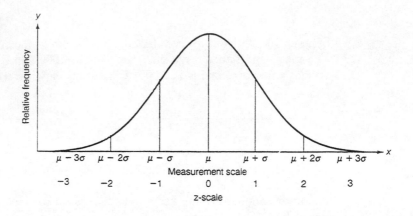

EXAMPLE 2.14

Suppose a female bank employee believes her salary is low as a result of sex discrimination. To substantiate her belief, she collects information on the salaries of her male counterparts in the banking business. She finds that their salaries have a mean of $34,000 and a standard deviation of $2,000. Her salary is $27,000. Does this information support her claim of sex discrimination?

Solution

The analysis might proceed as follows. First, we calculate the z-score for the woman's salary with respect to those of her male counterparts. Thus,

$$z = \frac{\$27,000 - \$34,000}{\$2,000} = -3.5$$

The implication is that the woman's salary is 3.5 standard deviations *below* the mean of the male salary distribution. Furthermore, if a check of the male salary data shows that the frequency distribution is mound-shaped, we can infer that very few salaries in this distribution should have a z-score less than −3, as shown in Figure 2.26. Therefore, a z-score of −3.5 represents either a measurement from a distribution different from the male salary distribution or a very unusual (highly improbable) measurement for the male salary distribution.

FIGURE 2.26 ▶
Male salary distribution

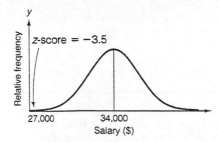

Which of the two situations do you think prevails? Do you think the woman's salary is simply an unusually low one in the distribution of salaries, or do you think her claim of salary discrimination is justified? Most people would probably conclude that her salary does not come from the male salary distribution. However, the careful investigator should require more information before inferring sex discrimination as the cause. We would want to know more about the data collection technique the woman used, and more about her competence at her job. Also, perhaps other factors such as the length of employment should be considered in the analysis.

. . . .

The method of Example 2.14 exemplifies an approach to statistical inference that might be called the **rare event approach**. An experimenter hypothesizes a specific frequency distribution to describe a population of measurements. Then a sample of measurements is drawn from the population. If the experimenter finds it unlikely that the sample came from the hypothesized distribution, the hypothesis is concluded to be false. Thus, in Example 2.14 the woman believes her salary reflects sex discrimination. She hypothesizes that her salary should be just another measurement in the distribution of her male counterparts' salaries if no discrimination exists. However, it is so unlikely that the sample (in this case, her salary) came from the male frequency distribution that she rejects that hypothesis, concluding that the distribution from which her salary was drawn is different from the distribution for the men.

This rare event approach to inference-making is discussed further in later chapters. Proper application of the approach requires a knowledge of probability, the subject of our next chapter.

CASE STUDY 2.8 / Deciding When to Respond to Consumer Complaints

Now we will finish the discussion begun in Case Study 2.7 of a method proposed by Namias (1964) to determine when and when not to conduct a search for specific causes of consumer complaints.

The rate of consumer complaints about a product may change or vary merely as a result of chance or fate, or perhaps because of some specific cause, such as a decline in the quality of the product. Concerning the former, Namias says:

In any operation or production process, variability in the output or product will occur, and no two operational results may be expected to be exactly alike. Complete constancy of consumer rates of complaint is not possible, for the vagaries of fate and chance operate even within the most rigid framework of quality or operation control.

Namias provides a decision rule with which to determine when the observed variation in the rate of consumer complaints is due to chance and when it is due to specific causes. If the observed rate is 2 standard deviations or less away from the mean rate of complaint, it is attributed to chance. If the observed rate is farther than 2 standard deviations above the mean rate, it is attributed to a specific problem in the production or distribution of the product. The reasoning is that if there are no problems with the production and distribution of the product, 95% of the time the rate of complaints should be within 2 standard deviations of the mean rate. If the production and distribution processes were operating normally, it would be very unlikely for a rate higher than 2 standard deviations above the mean to occur. Instead, it is more likely that the high complaint rate is caused by abnormal operation of the production and/or distribution process; that is, something specific is wrong with the process.

Namias recommends searching for the cause (or causes) only if the observed variation in the rate of complaints is determined by the rule to be the result of a specific cause (or causes). The degree of variability due to chance must be tolerated. Namias says,

As long as the results exhibit chance variability, the causes are common, and there is no need to attempt to improve the product by making specific changes. Indeed this may only create more variability, not less, and it may inject trouble where none existed, with waste of time and money. . . . On the other hand, time and money are again wasted through failure to recognize specific conditions when they arise. It is therefore economical to look for a specific cause when there is more variability than is expected on the basis of chance alone.

Namias collected data from the records of a beverage company for a two-week period to demonstrate

the effectiveness of the rule. Consumer complaints concerned chipped bottles that looked dangerous. For one of the firm's brands the mean complaint rate was determined to be 26.01 and the rate 2 standard deviations above the mean was determined to be 48.78 complaints per 10,000 bottles sold. The complaint rate observed during the two weeks under study was 93.12 complaints per 10,000 bottles sold. Since 93.12 is many more than 2 standard deviations above the mean rate, it was concluded that the high rate of complaints must have been caused by some specific problem in the production or distribution of the particular brand of beverage and that a search for the problem would probably be worthwhile. The problem was traced to rough handling of the bottled beverage in the warehouse by newly hired workers. As a result, a training program for new workers was instituted.

In Chapter 13, "Methods of Quality Improvement," we discuss in detail methods for monitoring the variation of a production process and deciding when to take action to improve the process.

Exercises 2.62–2.74

Learning the Mechanics

2.62   What is the 50th percentile of a quantitative data set? What is another name for the 50th percentile?

2.63   In each of the following compute the z-score for the x value, and note whether your result is a sample z-score or a population z-score:
   a. $x = 31$, $s = 7$, $\bar{x} = 24$ b. $x = 95$, $s = 4$, $\bar{x} = 101$
   c. $x = 5$, $\mu = 2$, $\sigma = 1.7$ d. $\mu = 17$, $\sigma = 5$, $x = 14$

2.64   Compare the z-scores to determine which of the following x values lie the greatest distance above the mean and the greatest distance below the mean.
   a. $x = 100$, $\mu = 50$, $\sigma = 25$ b. $x = 1$, $\mu = 4$, $\sigma = 1$
   c. $x = 0$, $\mu = 200$, $\sigma = 100$ d. $x = 10$, $\mu = 5$, $\sigma = 3$

2.65   At the University of Statistics (US), the students are given z-scores at the end of each semester rather than the traditional GPAs. The mean and standard deviation of all students' cumulative GPAs at US, on which the z-scores are based, are 2.7 and .5, respectively.
   a. Translate each of the following z-scores to a corresponding GPA: $z = 2.0$, $z = -1.0$, $z = .5$, $z = -2.5$.
   b. Students with z-scores below -1.6 are put on probation at US. What is the corresponding probationary GPA?

c. The president of US wishes to graduate the top 16% of the students with cum laude honors and the top 2.5% with summa cum laude honors. Where should the limits be set in terms of z-scores? In terms of GPAs? What assumption, if any, did you make about the distribution of the GPAs at US?

2.66 Suppose that 40 and 90 are two elements of a population data set and that their z-scores are -2 and 3, respectively. Using only this information, is it possible to determine the population's mean and standard deviation? If so, find them. If not, explain why it is not possible.

Applying the Concepts

2.67 In 1987 the United States imported merchandise valued at $406 billion and exported merchandise worth $253 billion. The difference between these two quantities (exports minus imports) is referred to as the *merchandise trade balance*. Since more goods were imported than exported in 1987, the merchandise trade balance was a *negative* $153 billion. The accompanying table lists the United States exports to and imports from a sample of ten countries in 1987 (in millions of dollars).

Country	Exports	Imports
Brazil	4,040	7,865
Egypt	2,210	465
France	7,943	10,730
Italy	5,530	11,040
Japan	28,249	84,575
Mexico	14,582	20,271
Panama	743	356
Soviet Union	1,480	425
Sweden	1,894	4,758
Turkey	1,483	821

Source: *Statistical Abstract of the United States: 1989*, pp. 788–791.

a. Calculate the U.S. merchandise trade balance with each of the ten countries. Express your answers in billions of dollars.

b. Use a z-score to identify the relative position of the U.S. trade balance with Japan within the data set you developed in part a. Do the same for the trade balance with the Soviet Union. Write a sentence or two that describes the relative positions of these two trade balances.

2.68 The accompanying table lists the unemployment rate in 1987 for a sample of nine countries.

Country	Percent Unemployed	Country	Percent Unemployed
Australia	8.1	Italy	7.9
Canada	8.9	Japan	2.9
France	11.1	Sweden	1.9
Germany	6.9	United States	6.2
Great Britain	10.3		

Source: *Statistical Abstract of the United States: 1989*, p. 829.

The mean and standard deviation of the nine countries' unemployment rates are 7.1 and 3.1, respectively.
a. Calculate the z-scores of the unemployment rates of the United States, Australia, and Japan.
b. Describe the information conveyed by the sign (positive or negative) of the z-scores you calculated in part a.

2.69   In *Fortune's* 1990 ranking of the 500 largest industrial corporations in the United States, Control Data Corporation ranked 153rd in terms of 1989 sales. In 1985, it ranked 71st. Use percentiles to describe Control Data Corporation's position in each year's sales distribution.

2.70   A parking lot owner's accountant determined the owner's receipts for each of 100 randomly chosen days from the past year. The mean and standard deviation for the 100 days were $360 and $25, respectively. Yesterday's receipts amounted to $370.
a. Find the sample z-score for yesterday's receipts.
b. How many standard deviations away from the mean is the value of yesterday's receipts?
c. Would you consider yesterday's receipts to be unusually high? Why or why not?

2.71   It is known that the frequency distribution of the number of videocassette recorders (VCRs) sold each week by a large department store in Atlanta is mound-shaped, with a mean of 35 and a variance of 9.
a. Approximately what percentage of the measurements in the frequency distribution should fall between 32 and 38? Between 26 and 44?
b. If the z-score for last week's sales was -1.33, how many VCRs did the store sell last week?
c. If it is known that the number of VCRs sold each week by a rival department store has a mound-shaped frequency distribution with a mean of 35 and a standard deviation of 2, for which store is it more likely that more than 41 VCRs will be sold in a week? Why?

2.72   One of the ways the federal government raises money is through the sale of securities such as **Treasury bonds**, **Treasury bills (T-bills)**, and **U.S. savings bonds**. Treasury bonds and bills are marketable (i.e., they can be traded in the securities market) long-term and short-term notes, respectively. U.S. savings bonds are non-marketable notes; they can be purchased and redeemed only from the U.S. Treasury. On June 30, 1983, the interest rate on 3-month T-bills was 8.75%. Within the next week, the *Wall Street Journal* sampled 17 economists and asked them to forecast the interest rate of 3-month T-bills on September 30, 1983. (T-bills are offered for sale weekly by the government, and their interest rates typically vary with each offering.) The forecasts obtained are listed in the table.

Economist	Interest Rate Forecast (%)	Economist	Interest Rate Forecast (%)
Alan Greenspan	8.70	Robert Parry	8.50
Timothy Howard	8.75	John Paulus	9.50
Lacy H. Hunt	9.35	Norman Robertson	8.50
Edward Hyman	7.80	Francis Schott	8.50
David Jones	9.25	Stuart Schweitzer	9.00
Irwin Kellner	8.25	Allen Sinai	9.15
Alan Lerner	9.25	Thomas Thompson	9.25
Donald Maude	7.70	John Wilson	10.00
Anne Parker Mills	8.50		

Source: *Wall Street Journal*, July 5, 1983, p. 2. Reprinted by permission. © Dow Jones & Company, Inc. 1983. All rights reserved.

The mean and standard deviation of the 17 forecasts are 8.82% and .61%, respectively.
a. Calculate the z-scores of Alan Greenspan's forecast and John Wilson's forecast. What do the z-scores tell you about their forecasts relative to the forecasts of the other economists?
b. Write a sentence or two that summarizes the 17 forecasts. In your summary, use a measure of central tendency and a measure of variability.

2.73   The mean and standard deviation of the gross weekly income distribution of a local firm's 120 employees were determined to be $170 and $10, respectively.
a. Approximately what percentage of the employees would be expected to have incomes over $190 per week? Under $160 per week? Over $200 per week?
b. If you were employed by this firm and your weekly income was $185, what would your z-score be, and how many standard deviations would your salary be away from the mean salary?

2.74   Refer to Exercise 2.73. Suppose it is known that the weekly gross income distribution is mound-shaped.
a. Approximately what percentage of the employees would be expected to have incomes over $190 per week? Under $160 per week? Over $200 per week?
b. If you and a friend both worked at the firm and your income was $160 per week and hers was $195 per week, how many standard deviations apart are your incomes?
c. If you randomly chose an employee of this firm, is it more likely that his or her gross income is over $190 per week or under $145 per week? Why?

2.9   Box Plots: Graphical Descriptions Based on Quartiles (Optional)

The **box plot**, a relatively recent introduction to the methodology of descriptive measures, is based on the **quartiles** of a data set. Quartiles are values that partition the data set into four groups, each containing 25% of the measurements. The lower quartile Q_L is the 25th percentile, the middle quartile is the median m (the 50th percentile), and the upper quartile Q_U is the 75th percentile (see Figure 2.27).

FIGURE 2.27 ▶
The quartiles for a data set

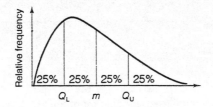

Definition 2.14

The **lower quartile** is the 25th percentile of a data set, the **middle quartile** is the median, and the **upper quartile** is the 75th percentile.

A box plot is based on the **interquartile range (IQR)**, the distance between the lower and upper quartiles:

$$IQR = Q_U - Q_L$$

Definition 2.15

. . . .

The **interquartile range** is the distance between the lower and upper quartiles:

$$IQR = Q_U - Q_L$$

The box plot for the 50 companies' percentages of revenues spent on R&D (Table 2.6) is given in Figure 2.28. The box plot shown there was generated by the Minitab statistical software package for personal computers.* Note that a rectangle (the *box*) is drawn, with the ends of the rectangle (the *hinges*, represented by the "I's" at the ends of the box drawn by the Minitab program) drawn at the quartiles Q_L and Q_U. By definition, then, the "middle" 50% of the observations—those between Q_L and Q_U— fall inside the box. For the R&D data, these quartiles appear to be at (approximately) 7.0 and 9.5 Thus,

$$IQR = 9.5 - 7.0 = 2.5 \quad \text{(approximately)}$$

The median is shown at about 8.0 by a + sign within the box.

FIGURE 2.28 ▶
Minitab box plot for R&D percentages

```
    --------------------------------------------------------------
                    --------------------
    -------------I      +         I----------------------------- *
                    --------------------
    ------+---------+---------+---------+---------+---------+
         6.0       7.5       9.0      10.5      12.0      13.5
    --------------------------------------------------------------
```

To guide the construction of the "tails" of the box plot, two sets of limits, called *inner fences* and *outer fences*, are used. Neither set of fences actually appears on the box plot. Inner fences are located at a distance of 1.5(IQR) from the hinges. Emanating from each hinge of the box are dashed lines called the *whiskers*. The two whiskers will

---

*Although box plots can be generated by hand, the amount of detail required makes them particularly well-suited for computer generation. We will use computer software to generate the box plots in this section.

extend to the most extreme observation inside the inner fences. For example, the inner fence on the lower side of the R&D percentage plot is (approximately):

$$\text{Lower inner fence} = \text{Lower hinge} - 1.5(\text{IQR})$$
$$\approx 7.0 - 1.5(2.5)$$
$$= 7.0 - 3.75 = 3.25$$

The smallest measurement in the data set is 5.2, which is well inside this inner fence. Thus, the lower whisker extends to 5.2. On the upper end, the inner fence is at about $(9.5 + 3.75) = 13.25$. The largest measurement inside this fence is the third largest measurement, 13.2. Note that the longer upper whisker reveals the rightward skewness of the R&D distribution.

Values that are beyond the inner fences receive special attention, because they are extreme values that represent relatively rare occurrences. In fact, for mound-shaped distributions, fewer than 1% of the observations are expected to fall outside the inner fences. As discussed above, none of the R&D measurements fall outside the lower inner fence. However, the two measurements at 13.5 fall outside the upper inner fence which is located at 13.25. These measurements are represented by asterisks (*), and they further emphasize the rightward skewness of the distribution. Note that the box plot does not reveal that there are *two* measurements at 13.5, since only a single symbol is used to represent both observations at that point.

The other pair of imaginary fences, the outer fences, are defined at a distance 3(IQR) from each end of the box. Measurements that fall beyond the outer fences are represented by zeros (0) and are very extreme measurements that require special attention and analysis. Less than one-hundredth of 1% (.01%, or .0001) of the measurements from mound-shaped distributions are expected to fall beyond the outer fences. Since no measurement in the R&D box plot (Figure 2.28) is represented by a 0, we know that none of the measurements fall outside the outer fences.

Generally, any measurements that fall beyond the inner fences, and certainly any that fall beyond the outer fences, are considered potential **outliers**. Outliers are extreme measurements that stand out from the rest of the sample and may be faulty—incorrectly recorded observations or members of a different population from the rest of the sample. At the least, they are very unusual measurements from the same population. For example, the two R&D measurements at 13.5 may be considered outliers, because they exceed the inner fence ("*" representation in Figure 2.28). When we analyze these measurements, we find they are correctly recorded. However, it turns out that both represent R&D expenditures of relatively young and fast-growing companies. Thus, the outlier analysis may have revealed important factors that relate to the R&D expenditures of high-tech companies: their age and rate of growth. Outlier analysis often reveals useful information of this kind, and therefore plays an important role in the statistical inference-making process.

The elements (and nomenclature) of box plots are summarized in the next box. Some aids to the interpretation of box plots are also given.

Elements of a Box Plot

1. A rectangle (the **box**) is drawn with the ends (the **hinges**) drawn at the lower and upper quartiles (Q_L and Q_U). The median of the data is shown in the box, usually by a "+".

2. The points at distances 1.5(IQR) from each hinge mark the **inner fences** of the data set. Horizontal lines (the **whiskers**) are drawn from each hinge to the most extreme measurement inside the inner fence.

3. A second pair of fences, the **outer fences**, exist at a distance of 3 interquartile ranges, 3(IQR), from the hinges. One symbol (usually "*") is used to represent measurements falling between the inner and outer fences, and another (usually "0") is used to represent measurements beyond the outer fences.

4. The symbols used to represent the median and the extreme data points (those beyond the fences) will vary depending on the software you use to construct the box plot. (You may use your own symbols if you are constructing a box plot by hand.) You should consult the program's documentation to determine exactly which symbols are used.

Aids to the Interpretation of Box Plots

1. Examine the length of the box. The IQR is a measure of the sample's variability, and is especially useful for the comparison of two samples (see Example 2.16).

2. Visually compare the lengths of the whiskers. If one is clearly longer, the distribution of the data is probably skewed in the direction of the longer whisker.

3. Analyze any measurements that lie beyond the fences. Fewer than 5% should fall beyond the inner fences, even for very skewed distributions. Measurements beyond the outer fences are probably **outliers**, with one of the following explanations:

   a. The measurement is incorrect. It may have been observed, recorded, or entered into the computer incorrectly.

   b. The measurement belongs to a population different from that from which the rest of the sample was drawn (see Example 2.16).

   c. The measurement may be correct and from the same population as the rest, but represents a rare event. Generally, we accept this explanation only after carefully ruling out all others.

EXAMPLE 2.15

In Example 2.1 we analyzed 50 processing times for the development of price quotes by the manufacturer of industrial wheels. The intent was to determine whether the success or failure in obtaining the order was related to the amount of time to process the price quotes. Each quote that corresponds to "lost" business was so classified. The data are repeated in Table 2.12. Use a statistical software package to draw a box plot for these data.

TABLE 2.12 Price Quote Processing Times (Days)

Request Number	Processing Time	Lost?	Request Number	Processing Time	Lost?
1	2.36	No	26	3.34	No
2	5.73	No	27	6.00	No
3	6.60	No	28	5.92	No
4	10.05	Yes	29	7.28	Yes
5	5.13	No	30	1.25	No
6	1.88	No	31	4.01	No
7	2.52	No	32	7.59	No
8	2.00	No	33	13.42	Yes
9	4.69	No	34	3.24	No
10	1.91	No	35	3.37	No
11	6.75	Yes	36	14.06	Yes
12	3.92	No	37	5.10	No
13	3.46	No	38	6.44	No
14	2.64	No	39	7.76	No
15	3.63	No	40	4.40	No
16	3.44	No	41	5.48	No
17	9.49	Yes	42	7.51	No
18	4.90	No	43	6.18	No
19	7.45	No	44	8.22	Yes
20	20.23	Yes	45	4.37	No
21	3.91	No	46	2.93	No
22	1.70	No	47	9.95	Yes
23	16.29	Yes	48	4.46	No
24	5.52	No	49	14.32	Yes
25	1.44	No	50	9.01	No

Solution

The SAS/PC box plot printout for these data is shown in Figure 2.29 (page 98). Note that the SAS program draws the box plot vertically, and shows a scale for the processing times on the left. SAS uses a horizontal dashed line in the box to represent the median, and a plus (+) sign to represent the mean. (SAS shows the mean in box plots, unlike many other statistical programs.) Also, note that SAS uses the symbol "0" to represent measurements between the inner and outer fences and "*" to represent observations beyond the outer fences.

FIGURE 2.29 ▶
SAS box plot for processing time
data

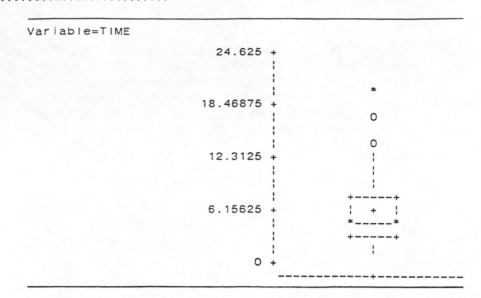

Note that the upper whisker is longer than the lower whisker and that the mean lies above the median; these characteristics reveal the rightward skewness of the data. However, the most important feature of the data is made very obvious by the box plot: There are at least two measurements between the inner and outer fences (in fact, there are three, but two are almost equal and are represented by the same "0") and at least one beyond the outer fence, all on the upper end of the distribution. Thus, the distribution is extremely skewed to the right, and several measurements need special attention in our analysis. We offer an explanation for the outliers in the following example.

EXAMPLE 2.16

The box plot for the 50 processing times (Figure 2.29) does not explicitly reveal the differences, if any, between the set of times corresponding to the success and the set of times corresponding to the failure to obtain the business. Box plots corresponding to the 39 "won" and 11 "lost" bids were generated using the SAS/PC program, and are shown in Figure 2.30. Interpret them.

Solution

The division of the data set into two parts, corresponding to won and lost bids, eliminates any observations that are beyond inner or outer fences. Furthermore, the skewness in the distributions has been reduced, as evidenced by the facts that the upper whiskers are only slightly longer than the lower, and that the means are closer to the medians than for the combined sample. The box plots also reveal that the processing times corresponding to the lost bids tend to exceed those of the won bids. A plausible explanation for the outliers in the combined box plot (Figure 2.29) is that they are from a different population than the bulk of the times. In other words, there are two populations represented by the sample of processing times—one corresponding to lost bids, and the other to won bids.

FIGURE 2.30 ▶

Box plots of processing time data: Won and lost bids

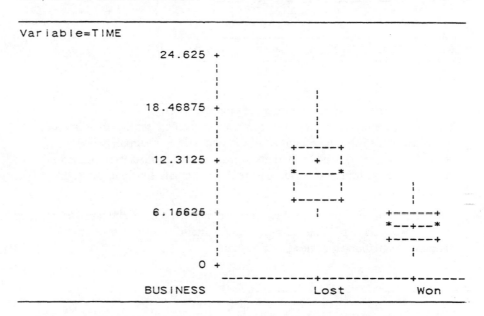

The box plots lend support to the conclusion that the price quote processing time and the success of acquiring the business are related. However, whether the visual differences between the box plots generalize to inferences about the populations corresponding to these two samples is a matter for inferential statistics, not graphical descriptions. We will discuss how to use samples to compare two populations using inferential statistics in Chapter 9.

Exercises 2.75–2.84

Note: Starred (*) exercises require the use of a computer.

Learning the Mechanics

2.75   Define the 25th, 50th, and 75th percentiles of a data set. Explain how they provide a description of the data.

2.76   Suppose a data set consisting of exam scores has a lower quartile $Q_L = 60$, a median $m = 75$, and an upper quartile $Q_U = 85$. The scores on the exam ranged from 18 to 100. Without having the actual scores available to you, construct as much of the box plot as possible.

2.77   Minitab was used to generate the following box plot:

```
     _____  ____
* *  -----------I  +  I--------
                   ----------

 +---------+---------+---------+---------+---------+
0.0      15.0      30.0      45.0      60.0
```

   a. What is the median of the data set (approximately)?
   b. What are the upper and lower quartiles of the data set (approximately)?
   c. What is the interquartile range of the data set (approximately)?
   d. Is the data set skewed to the left, skewed to the right, or symmetric?
   e. What percentage of the measurements in the data set lie to the right of the median? To the left of the upper quartile?

2.78   Minitab was used to generate the accompanying box plots. Compare and contrast the frequency distributions of the two data sets. Your answer should include comparisons of the following characteristics: central tendency, variation, skewness, and outliers.

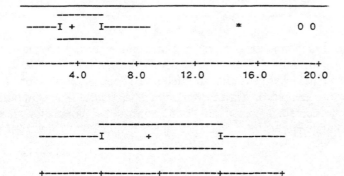

*2.79   Use a statistical software package to construct a box plot for the following set of sample measurements:

1.11	1.39	1.66	1.33	1.30
1.72	1.36	1.26	1.35	1.46
1.55	1.24	1.65	1.40	1.50
1.31	1.41	1.24	1.38	1.28
2.00	1.12	1.25	1.49	2.10
1.86	1.55	1.31	1.14	1.82

*2.80   Consider the following two sample data sets:

Sample A			Sample B		
121	171	158	171	152	170
173	184	163	168	169	171
157	85	145	190	183	185
165	172	196	140	173	206
170	159	172	172	174	169
161	187	100	199	151	180
142	166	171	167	170	188

a. Use a statistical software package to construct a box plot for each data set.
b. Using the information reflected in your box plots, describe the similarities and differences between the two data sets.
c. Identify any outliers that may exist in the two data sets.

Applying the Concepts

2.81   The table contains the top salary offer (in thousands of dollars) received by each member of a sample of 50 undergraduate business majors (excluding accounting majors) who graduated from the Carlson School of Management at the University of Minnesota in 1991–1992.

Salary Offers to 1991–1992 Graduates

23.7	26.1	26.6	27.9	40.0	22.8	26.0	26.5	27.5	37.2
22.0	25.9	26.5	27.5	36.1	21.6	25.7	24.7	27.3	34.8
20.9	25.6	24.6	27.2	32.8	20.7	25.4	25.6	26.9	29.1
19.8	25.3	26.4	26.9	28.9	18.7	24.8	26.4	26.8	28.3
17.5	24.2	26.3	26.7	28.2	14.0	23.9	26.1	26.7	28.1

Source: Placement Office, Carlson School of Management, University of Minnesota.

a. The mean and standard deviation are 26.2 and 4.56, respectively. Find and interpret the z-score associated with the highest salary offer, the lowest salary offer, and the mean salary offer. Would you consider the highest offer to be unusually high? Why or why not?
*b. Use a statistical software package to construct a box plot for this data set. Which salary offers (if any) are potentially faulty observations? Explain.

*2.82   A firm's earnings per share (E/S) of common stock is a measure used by investors to monitor the financial performance of a firm. Thirty firms were sampled from *Fortune*'s 1990 listing of the 500 largest corporations in the United States, and their earnings per share for 1989 are recorded in the table at the top of page 102.

a. Use a statistical software package to construct a box plot for this data set. Identify any outliers that may exist in this data set.
b. For each outlier identified in part a, determine how many standard deviations it lies from the mean of the E/S data set.

Firm	E/S	Firm	E/S
Illinois Tool Works	$3.06	Dow Jones	$ 3.15
Sara Lee	3.50	United Brands	1.70
Reynolds Metals	9.20	Washington Post	15.50
Scott Paper	5.11	Avon Products	.34
Phelps Dodge	7.59	Valhi	.91
Westmoreland Coal	1.39	American Cyanamid	3.12
Avery International	1.96	EG&G	2.40
Warner–Lambert	6.10	Asarco	5.50
Borden	−.41	Snap-on Tools	2.55
General Electric	4.36	McCormick	3.09
Cooper Industries	2.51	Exxon	2.74
Lockheed	.03	Georgia–Pacific	7.42
Kellogg	3.85	Crown Cork & Seal	3.58
FMC	3.79	DuPont (E.I.) de Nemours	3.53
Oxford Industries	.99	Molex	2.28

Source: *Fortune*, Apr. 23, 1990, pp. 337–396.

*2.83 A manufacturer of minicomputer systems is interested in improving its customer support services. As a first step, its marketing department has been charged with the responsibility of summarizing the extent of customer problems in terms of system down time. The 40 most recent customers were surveyed to determine the amount of down time (in hours) they had experienced during the previous month. These data are listed in the table.

Customer Number	Down Time	Customer Number	Down Time	Customer Number	Down Time	Customer Number	Down Time
230	12	240	24	250	4	260	34
231	16	241	15	251	10	261	26
232	5	242	13	252	15	262	17
233	16	243	8	253	7	263	11
234	21	244	2	254	20	264	64
235	29	245	11	255	9	265	19
236	38	246	22	256	22	266	18
237	14	247	17	257	18	267	24
238	47	248	31	258	28	268	49
239	0	249	10	259	19	269	50

a. Use a statistical software package to construct a box plot for these data. Use the information reflected in the box plot to describe the frequency distribution of the data set. Your description should address central tendency, variation, and skewness.

b. Use your box plot to determine which customers are having unusually lengthy down times.

c. Find and interpret the z-scores associated with the customers you identified in part b.

2.84 The accompanying Minitab-generated box plots describe the U.S. Environmental Protection Agency's 1986 automobile mileage estimates for all models manufactured by Ford and Honda.

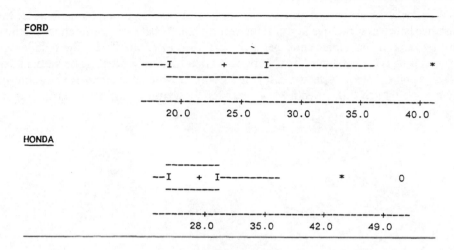

FORD

```
              -------------------
                                   -
        ----I      +      I-------------------        *
              -------------------

        -------+----------+----------+----------+----------+--
           20.0       25.0       30.0       35.0       40.0
```

HONDA

```
              ----------
        --I    +    I----------            *          0
              ----------

        ---------+----------+----------+----------+----
              28.0       35.0       42.0       49.0
```

a. Which manufacturer has the higher median mileage estimate?
b. Which manufacturer's mileage estimates have the greater range?
c. Which manufacturer's mileage estimates have the greater interquartile range?
d. Which manufacturer has the model with the highest mileage estimate? Approximately what is that mileage?

2.10 Distorting the Truth with Descriptive Techniques

While it may be true in telling a story that a picture is worth a thousand words, it is also true that pictures can be used to convey a colored and distorted message to the viewer. So the old adage "Let the buyer (reader) beware" applies. Examine relative frequency histograms, time series plots, and, in general, all graphical descriptions with care. In this section, we mention a few of the pitfalls to watch for when analyzing a chart or graph.

One common way to change the impression conveyed by a graph is to change the scale on the vertical axis, the horizontal axis, or both. For example, if you want to show that the change in firm A's market share over time is moderate, you could pack in a large number of units per inch on the vertical axis. That is, make the distance between successive units on the vertical scale small, as shown in Figure 2.31. You can see that the change in the firm's market share over time appears to be minimal.

FIGURE 2.31 ▶
Firm A's market share, 1980–1990: Packed vertical axis

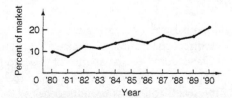

To make the changes in firm A's market share appear large, you could increase the distance between successive units on the vertical axis. That is, you stretch the vertical axis by graphing only a few units per inch, as shown in Figure 2.32. The telltale sign of stretching is a long vertical axis, but this is often hidden by starting the vertical axis at some point above 0, as shown in Figure 2.33(a). Or, the same effect can be achieved by using a broken line called a *scale break* for the vertical axis, as shown in Figure 2.33(b).

FIGURE 232 ►
Firm A's market share, 1980–1990: Stretched vertical axis

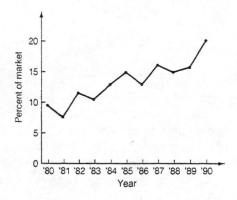

FIGURE 233 ►
Daily stock sales on the New York Stock Exchange from May to July 1979

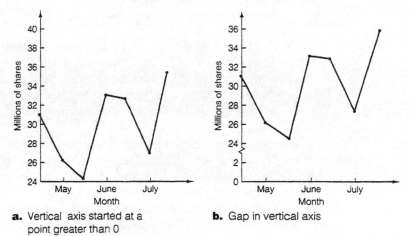

a. Vertical axis started at a point greater than 0

b. Gap in vertical axis

Stretching the horizontal axis (increasing the distance between successive units) may also lead you to incorrect conclusions. For example, Figure 2.34(a) depicts rental income in the United States from the first quarter of 1978 to the first quarter of 1980. If you increase the length of the horizontal axis, as in Figure 2.34(b), the change in the rental income over time seems to be less pronounced.

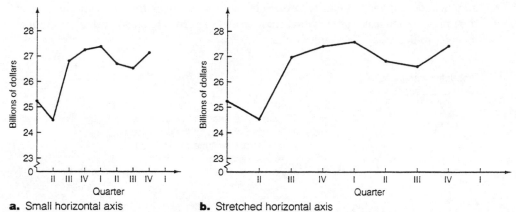

a. Small horizontal axis   **b.** Stretched horizontal axis
FIGURE 2.34 ▲ Rental income from the first quarter of 1978 to the first quarter of 1980

The changes in categories indicated by a bar chart can also be emphasized or deemphasized by stretching or shrinking the vertical axis. Another method of achieving visual distortion with bar charts is by making the width of the bars proportional to their height. For example, look at the bar chart in Figure 2.35(a), which depicts the percentage of a year's total automobile sales attributable to each of the four major manufacturers. Now suppose we make the width as well as the height grow as the market share grows. This is shown in Figure 2.35(b). The reader may tend to equate the *area* of the bars with the relative market share of each manufacturer. In fact, the true relative market share is proportional only to the height of the bars.

FIGURE 2.35 ►
Relative share of the automobile market for each of four major manufacturers

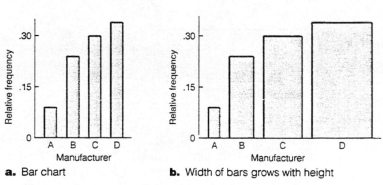

a. Bar chart   **b.** Width of bars grows with height

Sometimes, as noted by Selazny (1975), we do not need to manipulate the graph to distort the impression it creates. Modifying the verbal description that accompanies the graph can change the interpretation that will be made by the viewer. Figure 2.36 (page 106) provides a good illustration of this ploy.

We have presented only a few of the ways that graphs can be used to convey misleading pictures of business phenomena. However, the lesson is clear. Examine all graphical descriptions of data with care. In particular, check the axes and the size of the units on each axis. Ignore visual changes and concentrate on the actual numerical changes indicated by the graph or chart.

FIGURE 2.36 ►

Changing the verbal description to change a viewer's interpretation. Source: Reprinted by permission of the publisher, from "Grappling with Graphics," by Gene Selazny, *Management Review*, Oct. 1975, p. 7. © 1975 American Management Association, New York. All rights reserved.

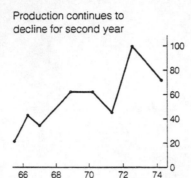

Production continues to decline for second year

For our production, we need not even change the chart, so we can't be accused of fudging the data. Here we'll simply change the title so that for the Senate subcommittee, we'll indicate that we're not doing as well as in the past...

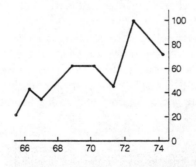

1974: 3rd best year for production

whereas for the general public, we'll tell them that we're still in the prime years.

The information in a data set can also be distorted by using numerical descriptive measures, as Example 2.17 indicates.

EXAMPLE 2.17

Suppose you are considering working for a small firm that presently has a senior member and three junior members. You inquire about the salary you could expect to earn if you join the firm. Unfortunately, you receive two answers:

Answer A: The senior member tells you that an "average employee" earns $57,500.

Answer B: One of the junior members later tells you that an "average employee" earns $45,000.

Which answer can you believe? The confusion exists because the phrase "average employee" has not been clearly defined. Suppose the four salaries paid are $45,000 for each of the three junior members and $95,000 for the senior member. Thus,

$$\bar{x} = \frac{3(\$45,000) + \$95,000}{4} = \frac{\$230,000}{4} = \$57,500$$

Median = \$45,000

You can now see how the two answers were obtained. The senior member reported the mean of the four salaries, and the junior member reported the median. The information you received was distorted because neither person stated which measure of central tendency was being used.

Another distortion of information in a sample occurs when *only* a measure of central tendency is reported. Both a measure of central tendency and a measure of variability are needed to obtain an accurate mental image of a data set.

Suppose you want to buy a new car and are trying to decide which of two models to purchase. Since energy and economy are both important issues, you decide to purchase model A because its EPA mileage rating is 32 miles per gallon in the city, whereas the mileage rating for model B is only 30 miles per gallon in the city.

However, you may have acted too quickly. How much variability is associated with the ratings? As an extreme example, suppose that further investigation reveals that the standard deviation for model A mileages is 5 miles per gallon, whereas that for model B is only 1 mile per gallon. If the mileages form a mound-shaped distribution, they might appear as shown in Figure 2.37. Note that the larger amount of variability associated with model A implies that more risk is involved in purchasing model A. That is, the particular car you purchase is more likely to have a mileage rating that will greatly differ from the EPA rating of 32 miles per gallon if you purchase model A, while a model B car is not likely to vary from the 30 miles per gallon rating by more than 2 miles per gallon.

FIGURE 2.37 ▶
Mileage distributions for two car models

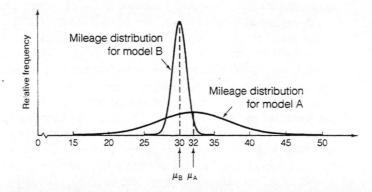

Summary

Data may be classified as one of four types: **nominal, ordinal, interval,** and **ratio.** Nominal data simply classify the sample or population units, whereas ordinal data enable the units to be ranked. Nominal and ordinal data are often referred to collectively as **qualitative.** Interval data are numbers that enable the comparison of sample or population units by calculation of their numerical differences, whereas ratio data enable the comparison using multiples, or ratios, of the numerical values. Interval and ratio data are often referred to collectively as **quantitative.** Since we want to use sample data to make inferences about the population from which it is drawn, it is important for us to be able to describe the data. **Graphic methods** are important and useful tools for describing data sets. Our ultimate goal, however, is to use the sample to make inferences about the population. We are wary of using graphic techniques to accomplish this goal, since they do not lend themselves to a measure of the reliability for an inference. We therefore developed **numerical measures** to describe a data set.

These numerical methods for describing **quantitative** data sets can be grouped as follows:

1. Measures of central tendency
2. Measures of variability

The measures of central tendency we presented were the **mean, median,** and **mode.** The relationship between the mean and median provides information about the **skewness** of the frequency distribution. For making inferences about the population, the sample mean will usually be preferred to the other measures of central tendency. The **range, variance,** and **standard deviation** all represent numerical measures of variability. Of these, the variance and standard deviation are in most common use, especially when the ultimate objective is to make inferences about a population.

The mean and standard deviation may be used to make statements about the fraction of measurements in a given interval. For example, we know that at least 75% of the measurements in a data set lie within 2 standard deviations of the mean. If the frequency distribution of the data set is mound-shaped, approximately 95% of the measurements will lie within 2 standard deviations of the mean.

Measures of relative standing provide still another dimension on which to describe a data set. The objective of these measures is to describe the location of a specific measurement relative to the rest of the data set. By doing so, you can construct a mental image of the relative frequency distribution. **Percentiles** and **z-scores** are important examples of measures of relative standing.

The **rare event** concept of statistical inference means that if the chance that a particular sample came from a hypothesized population is very small, we can conclude either that the sample is extremely rare or that the hypothesized population is not the one from which the sample was drawn. The more unlikely it is that the sample came from the hypothesized population, the more strongly we favor the conclusion that the hypothesized population is not the true one. We need to be able to assess accurately the rarity of a sample, and this requires knowledge of probability, the subject of our next chapter.

Finally, we gave some examples that demonstrated how descriptive statistics may be used to distort the truth. You should be very critical when interpreting graphic or numerical descriptions of data sets.

Supplementary Exercises 2.85–2.126

Note: Starred (*) exercises require the use of a computer. Double-starred exercises (**) refer to optional sections in this chapter.

2.85 Classify the following data as one of four types: nominal, ordinal, interval, or ratio.
  a. The length of time it takes each of 15 telephone installers to hook up a wall phone
  b. The style of music preferred by each of 30 randomly selected radio listeners
  c. The arrival time of the 5 P.M. train from New York to Newark
  d. A sample of 100 customers in a fast-food restaurant asked to rate their hamburger on the following scale: poor, fair, good, excellent
  e. Classify each of the data sets in parts **a–d** as qualitative or quantitative.

2.86 Discuss the conditions under which the median is preferred to the mean as a measure of central tendency.

2.87 Compute $\sum\limits_{i=1}^{n} x_i^2$, $\sum\limits_{i=1}^{n} x_i$, and $\left(\sum\limits_{i=1}^{n} x_i\right)^2$ for each of the following data sets:
  a. 11, 1, 2, 8, 7   **b.** 15, 15, 2, 6, 12   **c.** −1, 2, 0, −4, −8, 13   **d.** 100, 0, 0, 2

2.88 Compute s^2 and s for each of the data sets in Exercise 2.87.

**2.89 A time series plot similar to the one shown here appeared in a recent advertisement for a well-known golf magazine. One person might interpret the plot's message as the longer you subscribe to the magazine, the better golfer you should become. Another person might interpret it as indicating that if you subscribe for 3 years, your game should improve dramatically.

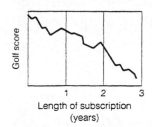

  a. Explain why the plot can be interpreted in more than one way.
  b. How could the plot be altered to rectify the current distortion?

2.90 Explain why we generally prefer the standard deviation to the range as a measure of variability for quantitative data.

2.91   Construct a relative frequency histogram for the data summarized in the accompanying table.

Measurement Class	Relative Frequency	Measurement Class	Relative Frequency
.00– .75	.02	5.25–6.00	.15
.75–1.50	.01	6.00–6.75	.12
1.50–2.25	.03	6.75–7.50	.09
2.25–3.00	.05	7.50–8.25	.05
3.00–3.75	.10	8.25–9.00	.04
3.75–4.50	.14	9.00–9.75	.01
4.50–5.25	.19		

2.92   Compute s^2 for data sets with the following characteristics:

a. $\sum_{i=1}^{n} x_i^2 = 246, \quad \sum_{i=1}^{n} x_i = 63, \quad n = 22$ b. $\sum_{i=1}^{n} x_i^2 = 666, \quad \sum_{i=1}^{n} x_i = 106, \quad n = 25$

c. $\sum_{i=1}^{n} x_i^2 = 76, \quad \sum_{i=1}^{n} x_i = 11, \quad n = 7$

2.93   Climatologists around the world use a 30-year mean as a standard of "normal" temperature or precipitation for a region. These data are regularly used by the tourist, transportation, and construction industries, as well as by farmers. Normals are computed every 10 years. The normals used from 1990–1999 are based on 1961–1990 National Weather Service data ("A Plain Old '30-Year Mean' is Forecaster's Yardstick," 1990). The table contains 1961–1990 temperature data in degrees Fahrenheit for Minnesota.

Year	Mean Daily January Temperature	Year	Mean Daily January Temperature
1961	12.0	1976	11.6
1962	7.1	1977	.3
1963	2.9	1978	5.5
1964	20.0	1979	3.2
1965	10.0	1980	15.3
1966	3.3	1981	18.0
1967	14.6	1982	2.3
1968	14.3	1983	19.6
1969	9.4	1984	12.0
1970	5.6	1985	10.1
1971	6.5	1986	17.5
1972	5.5	1987	21.2
1973	17.4	1988	10.4
1974	11.9	1989	21.2
1975	14.5	1990	26.3

a. What is the "normal" Minnesota temperature for January?

b. What is the standard deviation of the 30 temperatures? What information about the temperatures is conveyed by the standard deviation?

c. According to Chebyshev's theorem, what percentage of the 30 temperatures would be expected to fall within 2 standard deviations of the normal temperature? How many actually fell in that interval?

*2.94   If it is not examined carefully, the graphical description of U.S. peanut production shown here can be misleading.

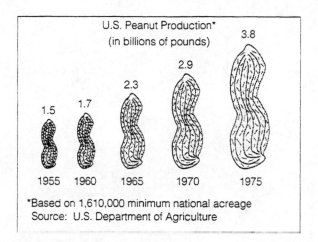

U.S. Peanut Production*
(in billions of pounds)

3.8

2.9

2.3

1.5   1.7

1955   1960   1965   1970   1975

*Based on 1,610,000 minimum national acreage
Source: U.S. Department of Agriculture

a. Explain why the graph may mislead some readers.
b. Construct an undistorted graph of U.S. peanut production for the given years.

2.95   In some locations, radiation levels in homes are measured at well above normal background levels in the environment. As a result many architects and builders are making design changes to assure adequate air exchange so that radioactive radon gas will not be trapped in homes. In one such location, 50 homes' radon levels were measured, and the mean level was 10 ppb (parts per billion), the median was 8 ppb, and the standard deviation was 3 ppb. Background levels in this location are at about 4 ppb.

a. Based on these results, is the distribution of the 50 homes' radon levels symmetric, skewed to the left, or skewed to the right? Why?
b. Use both Chebyshev's theorem and the Empirical Rule to describe the distribution of radon levels. Which do you think is most appropriate in this case? Why?
c. Use the results from part b to approximate the number of homes in this sample with radioactive radon gas levels above the background level.
d. Suppose another home is measured at a location 10 miles from the one sampled, and has a level of 20 ppb. What is the z-score for this measurement relative to the 50 homes sampled in the other location? Is it likely that this new measurement comes from the same distribution of levels as the other 50? Why? How would you confirm your conclusion?

2.96   As part of a study of property values in Minneapolis, the Robinson Appraisal Company sampled 79 apartment buildings and determined, among other things, each building's size, age, and condition as of January 1982. The following data are the ages (in years) of the buildings:

82	67	18	82	21	65	79	13	70	74	65	82	22	21	57	36
62	72	50	69	58	66	82	18	55	23	82	70	82	24	82	10
59	56	19	32	82	13	71	63	19	70	67	15	67	64	23	56
51	70	50	21	18	22	66	69	82	13	73	57	55	14	69	82
18	53	64	82	19	71	72	75	21	79	76	54	70	3	71	

Consider the following computer-generated stem-and-leaf display for these data:

```
Stem Leaf                           #
   8 22222222222                   11
   7 5699                           4
   7 000001112234                  12
   6 5566777999                    10
   6 2344                           4
   5 55667789                       8
   5 00134                          5
   4
   4
   3 6                             1
   3 2                             1
   2
   2 111122334                     9
   1 58888999                      8
   1 03334                         5
   0
   0 3                             1
     ----+----+----+----+
Multiply Stem.Leaf by 10**+1
```

a. Use the display to determine the age that approximately 50% of the buildings exceed.
b. How many buildings are more than 75 years old? Less than 10 years old?

2.97 Various state and national automobile associations regularly survey gasoline stations to determine the current retail price of gasoline. Suppose one such national association decides to survey 200 stations in the United States and intends to determine the price of regular unleaded gasoline at each station.
a. Identify the population of interest.
b. Identify the sample.
c. Identify the variable of interest.
d. In the context of this problem, define the following numerical descriptive measures: μ, σ, $\bar{x}$, s.
e. Suppose the sample of 200 stations is selected, and the mean and standard deviation of their regular

unleaded prices (per gallon) are $1.39 and $.12, respectively. Interpret these descriptive statistics and describe the probable distribution of the 200 prices at the time of the survey.
f. One station in the southeast priced unleaded gasoline at $1.09 per gallon at the time of the survey. Describe the relative standing of this price in the national price distribution as indicated by the sample.

*2.98 Compute the mean and variance of the following data sets:

a. Class	Class Frequency	b.	Class	Class Frequency
1– 5	2		.25– .50	0
6–10	5		.50– .75	5
11–15	12		.75–1.00	12
16–20	6		1.00–1.25	8
			1.25–1.50	6
			1.50–1.75	2

2.99 In experimenting with a new technique for imprinting paper napkins with designs, names, etc., a paper products company discovered that four different results were possible:

  (A) Imprint successful
  (B) Imprint smeared
  (C) Imprint off-center to the left
  (D) Imprint off-center to the right

To test the reliability of the technique, the company imprinted 1,000 napkins and obtained the results shown in the graph.

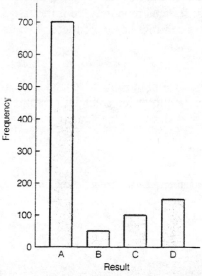

  a. What type of graphical tool is the figure?
  b. What information does the graph convey to you?
  c. From the information provided by the graph, how might you numerically describe the reliability of the imprinting technique?

2.100 The data in the table describe the distribution of rent amounts paid by U.S. apartment dwellers in 1987. Use a relative frequency histogram to describe the data.

Rent (in Dollars)	Percentage of Renters in Rent Class
Less than 350	7%
350–399	12%
400–449	12%
450–499	15%
500–549	11%
550 or more	43%

Source: U.S. Bureau of the Census, *Statistical Abstract of the United States: 1988.*

2.101 Under what circumstances might the standard deviation be preferred to the variance as a measure of the variation in a data set?

2.102 In reference to a particular measurement, what is a measure of relative standing?

2.103 How does a z-score locate a measurement within a set of measurements? Explain.

2.104 In 1985, consumers spent an estimated average of $11,883 for a new car, compared with $5,414 in 1976 (*Minneapolis Star and Tribune*, Mar. 15, 1985). To be able to determine the 1985 average *exactly*, what information is needed?

2.105 Explain why the mode is often an unacceptable measure of central tendency for quantitative data sets.

2.106 A quality control inspector is interested in determining whether a metal lathe used to produce machine bearings is properly adjusted. He plans to do so by using 30 bearings selected randomly from the last 2,000 bearings produced by the machine to estimate the average diameter of bearings being produced. Define and explain the meanings of the following symbols *in the context of this problem:*
a. μ b. $\bar{x}$ c. σ d. s e. $\mu + 2\sigma$

2.107 A manufacturer of industrial wheels is losing many profitable orders because of the long time it takes the firm's marketing, engineering, and accounting departments to develop price quotes for potential customers. To remedy this problem the firm's management would like to set guidelines for the length of time each

Price Quote Processing Times (in Days)

Request Number	Marketing	Engineering	Accounting	Lost?	Request Number	Marketing	Engineering	Accounting	Lost?
1	7.0	6.2	.1	No	26	.6	2.2	.5	No
2	.4	5.2	.1	No	27	6.0	1.8	.2	No
3	2.4	4.6	.6	No	28	5.8	.6	.5	No
4	6.2	13.0	.8	Yes	29	7.8	7.2	2.2	Yes
5	4.7	.9	.5	No	30	3.2	6.9	.1	No
6	1.3	.4	.1	No	31	11.0	1.7	3.3	No
7	7.3	6.1	.1	No	32	6.2	1.3	2.0	No
8	5.6	3.6	3.8	No	33	6.9	6.0	10.5	Yes
9	5.5	9.6	.5	No	34	5.4	.4	8.4	No
10	5.3	4.8	.8	No	35	6.0	7.9	.4	No
11	6.0	2.6	.1	No	36	4.0	1.8	18.2	Yes
12	2.6	11.3	1.0	No	37	4.5	1.3	.3	No
13	2.0	.6	.8	No	38	2.2	4.8	.4	No
14	.4	12.2	1.0	No	39	3.5	7.2	7.0	Yes
15	8.7	2.2	3.7	No	40	.1	.9	14.4	No
16	4.7	9.6	.1	No	41	2.9	7.7	5.8	No
17	6.9	12.3	.2	Yes	42	5.4	3.8	.3	No
18	.2	4.2	.3	No	43	6.7	1.3	.1	No
19	5.5	3.5	.4	No	44	2.0	6.3	9.9	Yes
20	2.9	5.3	22.0	No	45	.1	12.0	3.2	No
21	5.9	7.3	1.7	No	46	6.4	1.3	6.2	No
22	6.2	4.4	.1	No	47	4.0	2.4	13.5	Yes
23	4.1	2.1	30.0	Yes	48	10.0	5.3	.1	No
24	5.8	.6	.1	No	49	8.0	14.4	1.9	Yes
25	5.0	3.1	2.3	No	50	7.0	10.0	2.0	No

department should spend developing price quotes. To help develop these guidelines, 50 requests for price quotes were randomly selected from the set of all price quotes made last year; the processing time was determined for each price quote for each department. These times are displayed in the table. The price quotes are also classified by whether they were "lost" (i.e., whether or not the customer placed an order after receiving the price quote).

a. Stem-and-leaf displays for each of the departments and for the total processing time were produced using Minitab. Note that very high processing times that are "disconnected" from the other times are shown in a list under the heading of "HI" at the bottom of the display. Also, note that the units of the leaves for the total processing time are units (1.0), while the leaf units for each of the three components are tenths (.1). Shade the leaves that correspond to "lost" orders in each of the displays, and interpret each of the displays.

```
Stem-and-leaf of Mkt              Stem-and-leaf of Engr
Leaf Unit = 0.10                  Leaf Unit = 0.10

     6    0 112446                    7    0 4466699
     7    1 3                        14    1 3333788
    14    2 0024699                  19    2 12246
    16    3 25                       23    3 1568
    22    4 001577                   (5)   4 24688
   (10)   5 0344556889              22    5 233
    18    6 0002224799              19    6 01239
     8    7 0038                    14    7 22379
     4    8 07                       9    8
     2    9                          9    9 66
     2   10 0                        7   10 0
     1   11 0                        6   11 3
                                     5   12 023
                                     2   13 0
                                     1   14 4
```

```
Stem-and-leaf of Accnt            Stem-and-leaf of Total
Leaf Unit = 0.10                  Leaf Unit = 1.0

    19    0 1111111111122333444      1    0 1
    (8)   0 55556888                 3    0 33
    23    1 00                       5    0 45
    21    1 79                      11    0 666677
    19    2 0023                    17    0 888999
    15    2                         21    1 0000
    15    3 23                      (5)   1 33333
    13    3 78                      24    1 4444445555
    11    4                         14    1 6677
    11    4                         10    1 8999
    11    5                          6    2 0
    11    5 8                        5    2 3
    10    6 2                        4    2 44
     9    6
     9    7 0                            HI   30, 36
     8    7
     8    8 4

       HI    99, 105, 135, 144,
             182, 220, 300
```

b. Using your results from part a, develop "maximum processing time" guidelines for each department that, if followed, will help the firm reduce the number of lost orders.

2.108   Refer to Exercise 2.107. The means and standard deviations for the processing times are given here.

	Marketing	Engineering	Accounting	Total
$\bar{x}$	4.77	5.04	3.65	13.46
s	2.58	3.84	6.26	6.82

a. Calculate the z-score corresponding to the maximum processing time guideline you developed in Exercise 2.107 for each department, and for the total processing time.
b. Calculate the maximum processing time corresponding to a z-score of 3 for each of the departments. What percentage of the orders exceed these guidelines? How does this agree with Chebyshev's theorem and the Empirical Rule?
c. Repeat part b using a z-score of 2.
d. Compare the percentage of "lost" quotes with corresponding times that exceed at least one of the guidelines in part b to the same percentage using the guidelines in part c. Which set of guidelines would you recommend be adopted? Why?

2.109   What is Pareto analysis?

2.110   A company has roughly the same number of people in each of five departments: Production, Sales, R&D, Maintenance, and Administration. The following table lists the number and type of major injuries that occurred in each department last year.

Type of Injury	Department	Number of Injuries	Type of Injury	Department	Number of Injuries
Burn	Production	3	Cuts	Production	4
	Maintenance	6		Sales	1
Back strain	Production	2		R&D	1
	Sales	1		Maintenance	10
	R&D	1	Broken arm	Production	2
	Maintenance	5		Maintenance	2
	Administration	2	Broken leg	Sales	1
Eye damage	Production	1		Maintenance	1
	Maintenance	2	Broken finger	Administration	1
	Administration	1	Concussion	Maintenance	3
Deafness	Production	1		Administration	1
			Hearing loss	Maintenance	2

a. Construct a Pareto diagram to identify which department or departments have the worst safety record.
b. Explode the Pareto diagram of part a to identify the most prevalent type of injury in the department with the worst safety record.

2.111   One hundred management trainees were given an examination in basic accounting. Their test scores were found to have a mean and variance of 75 and 36, respectively.
a. Make a statement about the percentage of the test scores that would be expected to fall between 69 and 81.

b. If a grade of 63 was required to pass the test, make a statement about the percentage of the trainees who would be expected to fail.

2.112 Redo Exercise 2.111 assuming that the distribution of test scores was determined to be mound-shaped.

2.113 A national chain of automobile oil-change franchises claims that "your hood will be open for less than 12 minutes when we service your car." To check their claim, an undercover consumer reporter from a local television station monitored the "hood time" of 25 consecutive customers at one of the chain's franchises. The resulting data follow. Construct a time series plot for these data and describe in words what it reveals.

Customer Number	Hood Open (Minutes)	Customer Number	Hood Open (Minutes)
1	11.50	14	12.50
2	13.50	15	13.75
3	12.25	16	12.00
4	15.00	17	11.50
5	14.50	18	14.25
6	13.75	19	15.50
7	14.00	20	13.00
8	11.00	21	18.25
9	12.75	22	11.75
10	11.50	23	12.50
11	11.00	24	11.25
12	13.00	25	14.75
13	16.25		

2.114 The vice president in charge of sales for the conglomerate you work for has asked you to evaluate the sales records of two of the firm's divisions. You note that the range of monthly sales for division A over the last 2 years is $50,000 and the range for division B is only $30,000. You compute each division's mean monthly sales for the same time period and discover that both divisions have a mean of $110,000. Assume that is all the information you have about the division's sales records. Would you be willing to say which of the divisions has a more consistent sales record? Why or why not?

2.115 Refer to Exercise 2.114.
  a. Estimate the standard deviation of the monthly sales distribution of division B.
  b. Based on your estimate in part **a**, would you say it is more likely that division B's sales next month will be over $120,000 or under $90,000?
  c. Is it possible for division B's sales next month to be over $160,000? Explain.

2.116 The Age Discrimination in Employment Act mandates that workers 40 years of age or older be treated without regard to age in all phases of employment (hiring, promotions, firing, etc.). Age discrimination cases are of two types: *disparate treatment* and *disparate impact*. In the former, the issue is whether workers have been intentionally discriminated against. In the latter, the issue is whether employment practices adversely affect the protected class (i.e., workers 40 and over) even though no such effect was intended by the employer (Zabell, 1989). During the recession of the early 1990s, a small computer manufacturer laid off 10 of its 20 software engineers. The ages of all the engineers at the time of the lay-off are shown in the table.

Not Laid off: 34 55 42 38 42 32 40 40 46 29
Laid off: 52 35 40 41 40 39 40 64 47 44

a. Find the standard deviation of the 20 ages. Describe how the standard deviation can be used to characterize the set of ages.

b. If a software engineer were selected at random from these 20 to be laid off, what is the probability that the engineer would be 40 or older? [*Note:* We will formally define "probability" in the next chapter.]

c. Find the median age of all 20 engineers and the median age of the 10 who were not laid off.

d. Given your answers to parts b and c (and any other evidence you care to use), does it appear that the company may be vulnerable to a disparate impact claim? Explain.

2.117 Suppose you used the following formula as a measure of the variability (V) of a data set:

$$V = \frac{\sum\limits_{i=1}^{n} (x_i - \bar{x})}{n}$$

What information can be learned about the variability of a data set using this formula? Using the data in part **a** of Exercise 2.87, find V.

2.118 Many firms use on-the-job training to teach their employees computer programming. Suppose you work in the personnel department of a firm that just finished training a group of its employees to program, and you have been requested to review the performance of one of the trainees on the final test that was given to all trainees. The mean and standard deviation of the test scores are 80 and 5, respectively, and the distribution of scores is mound-shaped.

a. The employee in question scored 65 on the final test. Compute the employee's z-score.

b. Approximately what percentage of the trainees will have z-scores equal to or less than the employee of part a?

c. If a trainee were randomly selected from those who had taken the final test, is it more likely that he or she would score 90 or above, or 65 or below?

*2.119 A company that bags and sells wild rice has received numerous complaints from its customers about underfilled bags. Most complaints concern their 5-pound bag. The operations manager suspects that the problem may be due to differences between fill-machine operators. To investigate her suspicion, the manager weighed the last 10 bags filled by machine operator 1 before operator 2 took over at 3:00 P.M. She also weighed the first 10 bags produced by operator 2. The data follow.

Bag Number	Operator Number	Bag Weight (Pounds)	Bag Number	Operator Number	Bag Weight (Pounds)
1	1	5.00	11	2	5.35
2	1	5.10	12	2	4.70
3	1	4.90	13	2	5.05
4	1	5.05	14	2	5.30
5	1	5.05	15	2	4.50
6	1	4.95	16	2	5.40
7	1	5.00	17	2	5.20
8	1	4.90	18	2	5.00
9	1	5.10	19	2	5.20
10	1	5.00	20	2	4.60

a. Construct a time series plot for these data.

b. What do these data reveal about differences in the performances of the two operators?

c. Could such differences account for the customer complaints? Explain.

d. Describe any other filling problems revealed by the plot.

e. Suggest a better plan for selecting the bags to be weighed.

2.120 The advertising expenditures (in thousands of dollars) by media for a recent year are described for the 16 top-selling brandies and cordials by the following Minitab-generated box plots.

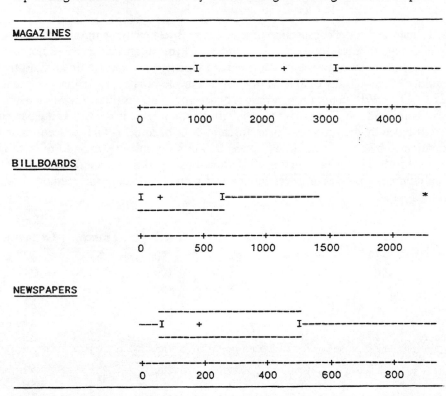

a. For which medium are median expenditures the highest?

b. For which medium is the range of expenditures the largest? The smallest?

c. For which medium is the interquartile range the largest? The smallest?

d. Describe the shape of each data set's frequency distribution.

e. Do any of the media receive advertising expenditures from all 16 brands of brandies and cordials? Explain.

2.121 Chebyshev's theorem (presented in Table 2.10) states that at least $(1 - 1/k^2)$ of a set of measurements will lie within k standard deviations of the mean of the data set. Use Chebyshev's theorem to state the fraction of a set of measurements that will lie:

a. Within 2 standard deviations of the mean μ ($k = 2$).

b. Within 3 standard deviations of the mean.

c. Within 1.5 standard deviations of the mean.

d. More than 2.75 standard deviations of the mean.

**2.122 Calculate the mean and standard deviation of the following data sets:

a. Class	Class Frequency	b. Class	Class Frequency
10–19	15	\$ −99 to \$ −50	20
20–29	12	−49 to 0	55
30–39	8	1 to 50	102
40–49	5	51 to 100	63
50–59	2	101 to 150	18

2.123 Economic theory suggests that the vigor of competition in an industry is related to the number of firms in the industry. As a measure of competitiveness, however, the number of firms in an industry does not take into consideration the extent to which a few firms may dominate that industry. For example, in an industry with 100 firms, each may produce 1% of industry output, or three firms may dominate, producing 75% compared to the other 97 firms' 25%. The *market concentration ratio* is a measure of competitiveness that reflects such inequalities among firms in an industry. The market concentration ratio is usually defined as the percentage of total industry sales contributed by the largest few firms (usually three or four). A high concentration ratio indicates an industry dominated by a few firms. A low concentration ratio indicates an industry with much competition among many firms. The table contains 1970 three-firm market concentration ratios for 12 industries in each of six different countries. Answer the following questions using the methods from this chapter that you deem appropriate.

Industry	United States	Canada	United Kingdom	Sweden	France	West Germany
Brewing	39	89	47	70	63	17
Cigarettes	68	90	94	100	100	94
Fabric weaving	30	67	28	50	23	16
Paints	26	40	40	92	14	32
Petroleum refining	25	64	79	100	60	47
Shoes (except rubber)	17	18	17	37	13	20
Glass bottles	65	100	73	100	84	93
Cement	20	65	86	100	81	54
Ordinary steel	42	80	39	63	84	56
Antifriction bearings	43	89	82	100	80	90
Refrigerators	64	75	65	89	100	72
Storage batteries	54	73	75	100	94	82

Source: F. M. Scherer, Alan Beckenstein, Erich Kaufer, and R. D. Murphy. *The Economics of Multiplant Operation: An International Comparisons Study* (Cambridge, Mass.: Harvard University Press, 1975). Reprinted by permission.

a. For each of the six countries, characterize the magnitude and variability of the sample of 12 market concentration ratios.

b. For each of the 12 industries, characterize the magnitude and variability of the sample of six market concentration ratios.

c. Which nation has on average the most competition within its industries? The least competition?

d. Which are the three most competitive industries? The three least competitive industries?

2.124 The **pie chart** is an alternative graphic technique for describing qualitative data sets. Each category of the data set is assigned one slice of the pie, the size of which is proportional to the relative frequency of the category.

The sequence of pie charts portrays the evolution of the structure of the top 500 firms in the United States and the top 200 firms in the United Kingdom over the period 1950–1980. Describe the trends that are revealed by these pie charts.

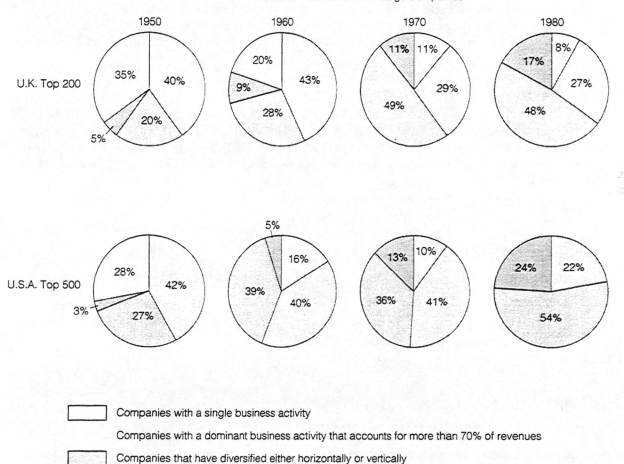

Growth of Diversification of Large Companies

☐ Companies with a single business activity

Companies with a dominant business activity that accounts for more than 70% of revenues

▨ Companies that have diversified either horizontally or vertically

Conglomerates

Source: Adapted from *Long Range Planning*. Vol 19, No 1, 1986, pp. 52-60. Reprinted with permission. Copyright 1986, Pergamon Press, Ltd.

*2.125   *Consumer Reports* is a magazine that contains ratings and reports for consumers on goods, services, health, and personal finances. It is published by Consumers Union, a nonprofit organization established in 1936. Consumers Union reported on the testing of 46 brands of toothpaste ("A Guide to Good Dental Care," 1992). Each was rated on: package design, flavor, cleaning ability, fluoride content, and cost per month (a cost estimate based on brushing with ½ inch of toothpaste twice daily). The data on page 122 are the costs per month for the 46 brands. Costs marked by an asterisk represent those brands that carry the American Dental Association (ADA) seal verifying effective decay prevention.

.58	.66	1.02	1.11	1.77	1.40	.73*	.53*	.57*	1.34
1.29	.89*	.49	.53*	.52	3.90	4.73	1.26	.71*	.55*
.59*	.97	.44*	.74*	.51*	.68*	.67	1.22	.39	.55
.62	.66*	1.07	.64	1.32*	1.77*	.80*	.79	.89*	.64
.81*	.79*	.44*	1.09	1.04	1.12				

a. Use a statistical software package to construct a stem-and-leaf display for the data.
b. Circle the individual leaves that represent those brands that carry the ADA seal.
c. What does the pattern of circles suggest about the costs of those brands approved by the ADA?

*2.126 Newly manufactured tires are rated for traction, heat, and tread wear according to the Uniform Tire Quality Grading System. Traction is rated using and A-B-C system to indicate the tire's braking performance on wet pavement. The tire's ability to dissipate heat is also measured using an A-B-C scale (with A representing the highest rating for both traction and heat). "Tread wear is graded on a number system with the rating for any particular tire expressed as a comparison of that tire with a tire rated at 100. Thus, if the tire tested wore twice as long as the baseline tire, it would carry a rating of 200" (Brand, 1991). Forty new tires, all of the same type and manufactured by the same company, were tested and each tire's tread-wear life in months was recorded. The data are listed below.

48	46	45	48	51	53	49	46	48	47
50	49	43	52	52	50	43	44	43	52
44	47	51	52	45	49	48	43	53	50
53	51	44	43	45	47	53	44	46	53

a. If a tire with a tread-wear rating of 100 lasts 48 months, compute the tread-wear ratings of each of the 40 tires tested. Round the ratings to the nearest whole number.
b. Use a statistical software package to construct a histogram for these 40 ratings.
c. Based on the shape of the histogram, is there reason for concern about the quality of the manufacturing process that is producing these particular tires? Explain.

On Your Own

A number of sources of business data are listed on the following page. Use these and any others you or your instructor can find to select two real business-oriented data sets, one qualitative and one quantitative. Describe both data sets using the graphic and numerical descriptive tools introduced in this chapter. Count the number of observations in your quantitative data set within 1, 2, and 3 standard deviations of the mean of the data and compare the counts with those you would expect using either Chebyshev's theorem or the Empirical Rule.

Be sure to select data of interest to you, since we will be referring to these data sets in **On Your Own** sections of later chapters.

Suggested Secondary Data Sources:*

Annual Reports to Shareholders.

Board of Governors of the Federal Reserve System. *Federal Reserve Bulletin* (monthly).

Business Week (magazine).

Dun & Bradstreet's *Million Dollar Directory* (yearly).

Economic Indicators. Council of Economic Advisors.

Forbes (magazine).

Fortune (magazine).

Handbook of Basic Economic Statistics. Economic Statistics Bureau of Washington, D.C.

Moody's Manuals (set of 8).

Simmons Study of Media and Markets. Simmons Market Research Bureau, Inc.

Sourcebook of Zip Code Demographics.

State Demographics: Population Profiles of the 50 States. Dow Jones-Irwin.

Survey of Buying Power Demographics USA.

Thomas Register of America Manufacturers.

U.S. Bureau of the Census. *Census of Manufacturers* (every 5 years).

U.S. Bureau of the Census. *County Census Patterns* (yearly).

U.S. Bureau of the Census. *Statistical Abstract of the United States* (yearly).

U.S. Department of Commerce, Office of Business Economics, *Business Statistics.*

U.S. Bureau of Commerce, Office of Business Economics. *Survey of Current Business* (monthly).

U.S. Department of Health and Human Services. *Vital Statistics of the United States.*

U.S. Department of Labor. *Monthly Labor Review.*

U.S. Department of Labor, Bureau of Labor Statistics. *Employment and Earnings.*

U.S. Department of Labor, Bureau of Labor Statistics. *National Survey of Professional Administrative, Technical, and Clerical Pay.*

Value Line Investment Survey, Value Line, Inc.

Wall Street Journal (daily).

Your state's statistical abstract.

Guides to Finding Secondary Data*

American Statistical Index: A Comprehensive Guide to the Statistical Publications of the United States Government.

Business Periodical Index.

Business Rankings and Salaries Index. Detroit: Gale Research Co.

Encyclopedia of Business Information Sources. Detroit: Gale Research Co.

Federal Statistical Directory: The Guide to Personnel and Data Sources.

Guide to Bureau of Economic Analysis.

Guide to Special Issues and Indexes of Periodicals.

Houser and Leonard. *Government Statistics for Business Use.*

New York Times Index.

Predicasts F&S Indexes.

Sourcebook of Global Statistics.

Statistical Reference Index: A Selective Guide to American Statistical Publications from Sources Other Than the U.S. Government. Congressional Information Services, Inc.

Statistics Sources, edited by Paul Wasserman. Detroit: Gale Research Co.

U.S. Bureau of the Census. *Directory of Non-federal Statistics for States and Local Areas.*

Wall Street Journal Index.

Your local Chamber of Commerce.

---

*Primary data are data you (or someone in your organization) collect for the study at hand. *Secondary data* are data collected by someone outside the organization for purposes other than the study at hand.

 Many of these sources and guides are now available on computer media, including CD-ROMs and online data services.

Using the Computer

We have supplied a set of data in Appendix C (also available on diskette from the publisher) that will be used as a source for the **Using the Computer** exercises at the end of most chapters. A complete description of the data can be found in Appendix C. Briefly, the data set includes such variables as population size, number of households, average household size, average income, percentage of college graduates, percentage of women in the work force, and purchasing-potential indexes for groceries, sporting goods, and home improvements for each of 1,000 U.S. zip codes.

a. Consider the percentage of women in the work force. Use a statistical software package to generate a stem-and-leaf display and a relative frequency histogram for these 1,000 percentages. Compare the graphical descriptions you obtain, and discuss what each reveals about the distribution of the percentage of women in the work force in the sample of 1,000 zip codes.

b. Repeat part a for one of the census regions, perhaps the one in which you currently reside. Compare the regional distribution to the national distribution you obtained in part a.

c. Finally, repeat part a for the zip codes corresponding to one state, perhaps the one in which you currently reside. Compare the state distribution to the national and regional distributions of parts a and b.

d. Now compute the mean and standard deviation of the same data set over the 1,000 zip codes and over the zip codes in the region you selected. Use the computer to count the number of zip codes' percentages within the intervals $\bar{x} \pm s$, $\bar{x} \pm 2s$, and $\bar{x} \pm 3s$. Compare the results with those given by Chebyshev's theorem and the Empirical Rule (Table 2.10).

References

Adler, Paul S. and Clark, Kim B. "Behind the learning curve: A sketch of the learning process." *Management Science*, Mar. 1991, p. 267.

"A guide to good dental care." *Consumer Reports*, Consumers Union, Sept. 1992, p. 601.

"A plain old '30-year mean' is forecaster's yardstick." *Star Tribune* (Minneapolis). Sept. 2, 1990.

Brand, Paul. "Tire's initial grade loses importance as tread depth starts to wear down." *Star Tribune* (Minneapolis). Sept. 22, 1991.

Chase, R. B. and Aquilano, N. J. *Production and Operations Management*, rev. ed. Homewood, Ill.: Richard D. Irwin, 1977.

Davidson, S., Stickney, C. P., and Weil, R. L. *Financial Accounting*, 2d ed. Chicago: Dryden Press, 1979.

Deming, W. E. *Out of the Crisis.* Cambridge, Mass. M.I.T. Center for Advanced Engineering Study, 1986.

Dodd, P. "Merger proposals, management discretion, and stockholder wealth." *Journal of Financial Economics*, 1980, 8, pp. 105–137.

Eger, C. E. "Corporate mergers: An empirical analysis of the role of risky debt." Unpublished Ph.D. dissertation. School of Management, University of Minnesota, 1982.

Fogarty, D. W., Blackstone, J. H., Jr., and Hoffmann, T. R. *Production and Inventory Management.* Cincinnati, Ohio: South-Western, 1991.

"The *Fortune* 500." *Fortune*, Apr. 23, 1990, pp. 337–396.

Gitlow, H., Gitlow, S., Oppenheim, A., and Oppenheim, R. *Tools and Methods for the Improvement of Quality.* Homewood, Ill.: Irwin, 1989.

How the Bond Market Works. The New York Institute of Finance. New York: 1988.

Huff, D. *How to Lie with Statistics.* New York: Norton, 1954.

Ishikawa, K. *Guide to Quality Control*, 2d ed. White Plains, N.Y.: Kraus International Publications, 1982.

Juran, J. M. *Juran on Planning for Quality*. New York: The Free Press, 1988.

Kane, V. E. *Defect Prevention*. New York: Marcel Dekker, Inc., 1989.

"Keeping up." *Fortune*, Aug. 13, 1979, p. 100.

McCullough, B. "Should you be a coupon clipper?" *Minneapolis Star and Tribune*, Mar. 17, 1986.

Mendenhall, W. *Introduction to Probability and Statistics*, 8th ed. Boston: Duxbury, 1991. Chapter 3.

Milkovich, G. T., Annoni, A. J., and Mahoney, T. A. "The use of the delphi procedures in manpower forecasting." *Management Science*, Dec. 1972, *19*, part 1, pp. 381–388.

Namias, J. "A method to detect specific causes of consumer complaints." *Journal of Marketing Research*, Aug. 1964, pp. 63–68.

Neter, J., Wasserman, W., and Whitmore, G. A. *Applied Statistics*, 2d ed. Boston: Allyn & Bacon, 1982. Chapter 3.

Postlewaite, S. "Salad bars sprout as fast-food battle turns from the burger." *Minneapolis Tribune*, July 3, 1983.

Roberts, Jonathan. "Microsoft speaks: Windows Version 3.1 succeeds by listening to users." *Cue News*. Egghead Software, June 1992, p. 3.

Rothstein, M. "Hotel overbooking as a Markovian sequential decision process." *Decision Sciences*, July 1974, *5*, pp. 389–405.

Schroeder, R. G. *Operations Management*, 4th ed. New York: McGraw-Hill, 1993.

Selazny, G. "Grappling with graphics." *Management Review*, Oct. 1975, p. 7.

Spiro, H. T. *Finance for the Nonfinancial Manager*. New York: Wiley, 1982. Chapter 17.

Sterling, R. R. and Radosevich, R. "A valuation experiment." *Journal of Accounting Research*, Spring 1969, pp. 90–95.

Willett, R. P. and Pennington, A. L. "Customer and salesman: The anatomy of choice and influence in a retail setting." *Science, Technology and Marketing*, Proceedings of the 1966 Fall Conference of the American Marketing Association, Raymond M. Haas (ed.), 1966, pp. 598–616.

U.S. Department of Labor. *The Consumer Price Index: Concepts and Content over the Years*. Bureau of Labor Statistics, Report 517, May 1978.

Zabell, S. L. "Statistical proof of employment discrimination." *Statistics: A Guide to the Unknown*, 3d ed. Pacific Grove, Calif.: Wadsworth, 1989.

CHAPTER THREE
Probability

Contents

3.1 Events, Sample Spaces, and Probability
3.2 Unions and Intersections
3.3 The Additive Rule and Mutually Exclusive Events
3.4 Complementary Events
3.5 Conditional Probability
3.6 The Multiplicative Rule and Independent Events
3.7 Random Sampling

Case Studies

Case Study 3.1 Purchase Patterns and the Conditional Probability of Purchasing
Case Study 3.2 The 1970 Draft Lottery

Where We've Been

In Chapter 1, we identified inference from a sample to a population as one of the major goals of statistics. In Chapter 2, we learned how to describe a set of measurements using graphical and numerical descriptive methods.

Where We're Going

We now begin to consider the problem of making an inference. What permits us to make the inferential jump from sample to population and then to give a measure of reliability for the inference? As you will see, the answer is *probability*. This chapter is devoted to probability—what it is and some of the basic concepts of the theory that surrounds it.

You will recall that statistics is concerned with inferences about a population based on sample information. Understanding how this will be accomplished is easier if you understand the relationship between population and sample. This understanding is enhanced by reversing the statistical procedure of making inferences from sample to population. In this chapter we assume the population *known* and calculate the chances of obtaining various samples from the population. Thus, probability is the "reverse" of statistics: In probability we use the population information to infer the probable nature of the sample.

Probability plays an important role in inference-making. To illustrate, suppose you have an opportunity to invest in an oil exploration company. Past records show that for ten out of ten previous oil drillings (a sample of the company's experiences), all ten resulted in dry wells. What do you conclude? Do you think the chances are better than 50–50 that the company will hit a producing well? Should you invest in this company? We think your answer to these questions will be an emphatic no. If the company's exploratory prowess is sufficient to hit a producing well 50% of the time, a record of ten dry wells out of ten drilled is an event that is just too *improbable*. Do you agree?

As another illustration, suppose you are playing poker with what your opponents assure you is a well-shuffled deck of cards. In three consecutive five-card hands, the person on your right is dealt four aces. Based on this sample of three deals, do you think the cards are being adequately shuffled? Again, we think your answer will be no and that you will reach this conclusion because dealing three hands of four aces is just too improbable, assuming that the cards were properly shuffled.

Note that the conclusion concerning the potential success of the oil drilling company and the conclusion concerning the card shuffling were both based on probabilities—namely, the probabilities of certain sample results. Both situations were contrived so you could easily conclude that the probabilities of the sample results were small. Unfortunately, the probabilities of many observed sample results are not so easy to evaluate. For these cases, we will need the assistance of a theory of probability.

3.1   Events, Sample Spaces, and Probability

Most sets of data that are of interest to the business community are generated by some **experiment**.

Definition 3.1

An **experiment** is an act or process that leads to a single outcome that cannot be predicted with certainty.

Our definition of *experiment* is broader than that used in the physical sciences, where we might picture test tubes, microscopes, and other equipment. Examples of statistical experiments in business are recording whether a customer prefers one of two brands of coffee (say, brand A or brand B), measuring the change in the Dow Jones Industrial Average from one day to the next, recording the weekly sales of a business firm, and counting the number of errors on a page of an accountant's ledger.

A "single outcome" of an experiment is called a **simple event**.

Definition 3.2
....

A **simple event** is an outcome of an experiment that cannot be decomposed into a simpler outcome.

In Table 3.1 we present three examples of experiments and their simple events. We begin with simple coin and dice examples because they are most likely to be familiar to you. Experiment **a** in Table 3.1 is to toss a coin and observe the up face. You will undoubtedly agree that the most basic possible outcomes of this experiment are Observe a head and Observe a tail. Experiment **b** in Table 3.1 is to toss a die and observe the up face. Notice that the simple events Observe a 1, Observe a 2, etc., cannot be decomposed into simpler outcomes. However, the outcome Observe an even number can be decomposed into Observe a 2, Observe a 4, and Observe a 6. Thus, Observe an even number is not a simple event. The reasoning is similar for experiment **c** in Table 3.1.

TABLE 3.1   Experiments and Their Simple Events

a. Experiment: Toss a coin and observe the up face.
    Simple events: 1. Observe a head
                   2. Observe a tail

b. Experiment: Toss a die and observe the up face.
    Simple events: 1. Observe a 1
                   2. Observe a 2
                   3. Observe a 3
                   4. Observe a 4
                   5. Observe a 5
                   6. Observe a 6

c. Experiment: Toss two coins and observe the up faces.
    Simple events: 1. Observe H_1, H_2
                   2. Observe H_1, T_2
                   3. Observe T_1, H_2
                   4. Observe T_1, T_2
(where H_1 means head on coin 1, H_2 means head on coin 2, etc.)

Outcomes such as Observe an even number, which can be decomposed into simpler outcomes (Observe a 2, Observe a 4, Observe a 6), are called **events**.

> **Definition 3.3**
>
> An **event** is a collection of one or more simple events.

Thus, in experiment **b** of Table 3.1, three examples of events are Observe an even number, Observe a number less than 4, and Observe a 6. Note that the last event, Observe a 6, cannot be decomposed into a simpler outcome and so is also a simple event. If the experiment is counting the number of errors on a page of an accountant's ledger, three examples of events are Observe no errors, Observe fewer than five errors, and Observe more than ten errors. Only the first, Observe no errors, is also a simple event. Our goal is to be able to calculate the probability that a particular event will occur when an experiment is performed.

The first step in achieving this goal is to note that simple events have an important property. If the experiment is conducted once, you will observe one and only one simple event. For example, if the experiment is to toss a coin and observe the up face, you cannot Observe a tail and Observe a head on the same toss. Or, if you toss a die and Observe a 2, you cannot Observe a 6 on the same toss. That is, for a single performance of an experiment, one and only one of the simple events will occur. To see that this property does not hold for all events, consider the event Observe an even number. It is possible to Observe an even number and Observe a 2 on the same toss of a die.

The collection of all the simple events of an experiment is called the **sample space.**

> **Definition 3.4**
>
> The **sample space** of an experiment is the collection of all its simple events.

For example, there are six simple events associated with experiment **b** in Table 3.1. These six simple events comprise the sample space for the experiment. Similarly, for experiment **c** in Table 3.1, there are four simple events in the sample space.

A graphical method called a **Venn diagram** is useful for presenting a sample space and its simple events. The sample space is shown as a closed figure, labeled *S*. This figure contains a set of points, called **sample points**, with each point representing a simple event. Figure 3.1 shows the Venn diagram for each of the three experiments in Table 3.1. Note that the number of sample points in a sample space *S* is equal to the number of simple events associated with the respective experiment: two for experiment **a**, six for experiment **b**, and four for experiment **c**.

Now that we have defined the terms *simple event* and *sample space*, we are prepared to define the **probabilities of simple events**. The probability of a simple event is a number that indicates the likelihood that the event will occur when the experiment is performed. This number is usually taken to be the relative frequency of the occur-

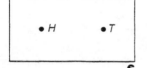

a. Experiment: Observe the up face on a coin

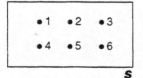

b. Experiment: Observe the up face on a die

c. Experiment: Observe the up faces on two coins

FIGURE 3.1 ▲
Venn diagrams for the three experiments from Table 3.1

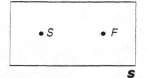

FIGURE 3.2 ▲
Experiment: Invest in a business venture and observe whether it succeeds (S) or fails (F)

rence of a simple event in a very long series of repetitions of the experiment. Or, when this information is not available, we select the number based on experience. For example, if we are assigning probabilities to the two simple events in the coin-toss experiment (Observe a head and Observe a tail), we might reason that if we toss a balanced coin a very large number of times, the simple events Observe a head and Observe a tail will occur with the same relative frequency of .5. Thus, the probability of each simple event is .5.

For some experiments we may assign probabilities to the simple events based on general information about the experiment. For example, if the experiment is to invest in a business venture and to observe whether it succeeds or fails, the sample space would appear as in Figure 3.2.

We are unlikely to be able to assign probabilities to the simple events of this experiment based on a long series of repetitions, since unique factors govern each performance of this kind of experiment. Instead, we may consider factors such as the personnel managing the venture, the general state of the economy at the time, the rate of success of similar ventures, and any other information deemed pertinent. If we finally decide that the venture has an 80% chance of succeeding, we assign a probability of .8 to the simple event Success. This probability can be interpreted as a measure of our degree of belief in the outcome of the business venture.

Such subjective probabilities should be based on expert information and must be carefully assessed. Otherwise, we run the risk of being misled by uninformed and/or biased probability statements. That is, we may be misled on any decisions based on these probabilities or based on any calculations in which they appear. We discuss the assessment of subjective probabilities in more detail in Case Study 19.1.*

No matter how you assign the probabilities to simple events, the probabilities assigned must obey two rules:

1. All simple event probabilities must lie between 0 and 1, inclusive.
2. The probabilities of all the simple events in the sample space must sum to 1.

Recall that an event is a collection of one or more simple events. Let us examine this statement in greater detail. Consider the die-tossing experiment and the event Observe an even number. This event will occur if and only if one of the three simple events, Observe a 2, Observe a 4, or Observe a 6, occurs. Consequently, you can think of the event Observe an even number as the collection of the three simple events, Observe a 2, Observe a 4, and Observe a 6. This event, which we will denote by the symbol A, can be represented in a Venn diagram by a closed figure inside the sample space S. The closed figure A will contain the simple events that constitute event A, as shown in Figure 3.3.

How do you decide which simple events belong to the set associated with an event A? Test each simple event in the sample space S. If event A occurs when a particular simple event occurs, then that simple event is in the event A. For example, in the die-toss experiment, the event Observe an even number (event A) will occur if the

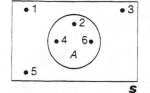

FIGURE 3.3 ▲
Die-toss experiment with event A: Observe an even number

---

*For a text that deals in detail with subjective probabilities, see Winkler (1972) or Lindley (1985).

Bloom County Probabilities

The issue of whether probability should be defined as the relative frequency in a long series of repetitions of an experiment or as a subjective measure of belief is one that has been debated for many years by probabilists, statisticians, and even philosophers. A considerably lighter side of this debate is illustrated in the accompanying Bloom County comic strip.

© 1986, Washington Post Writers Group, reprinted with permission.

simple event Observe a 2 occurs. By the same reasoning, the simple events Observe a 4 and Observe a 6 are in event A.

Now return to our original objective—finding the probability of an event. Consider the problem of finding the probability of observing an even number (event A) in the single toss of a die. You will recall that A will occur if one of the three simple events, toss a 2, 4, or 6, occurs. Since two or more simple events cannot occur at the same time, we can easily calculate the probability of event A by summing the probabilities of the three simple events. If we assume the die is fair (i.e., balanced), then each simple event is equally likely to occur. Accordingly, we would attach a probability equal to ⅙ to each of the simple events, so the probability of observing an even number (event A), denoted by the symbol $P(A)$, would be

$$P(A) = P(\text{Observe a } 2) + P(\text{Observe a } 4) + P(\text{Observe a } 6)$$
$$= \tfrac{1}{6} + \tfrac{1}{6} + \tfrac{1}{6} = \tfrac{1}{2}$$

The previous example leads us to a general procedure for finding the probability of an event A.

The probability of an event A is calculated by summing the probabilities of the simple events in A.

Thus, we can summarize the steps for calculating the probability of any event.

Steps for Calculating Probabilities of Events

1. Define the experiment.
2. List the simple events.
3. Assign probabilities to the simple events.
4. Determine the collection of simple events contained in the event of interest.
5. Sum the simple event probabilities to obtain the event probability.

EXAMPLE 3.1

Consider the experiment of tossing two coins and observing the up faces. Assume both coins are fair.

a. List the simple events and assign them reasonable probabilities.

b. Consider the events

A: {Observe exactly one head} B: {Observe at least one head}

and calculate $P(A)$ and $P(B)$.

Solution

a. The simple events are

$$H_1, H_2 \qquad H_1, T_2 \qquad T_1, H_2 \qquad T_1, T_2$$

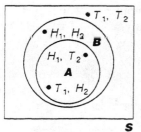

FIGURE 3.4 ▲
Venn diagram of the two-coin toss

where H_1 denotes Observe a head on coin 1, H_2 denotes Observe a head on coin 2, etc. If both coins are fair, we can again use the concept of relative frequency in a long series of experimental repetitions to conclude that each simple event should be assigned a probability of $\frac{1}{4}$.

b. We use a Venn diagram to show the events A: {Observe exactly one head} and B: {Observe at least one head} (Figure 3.4). Using the collection of simple events in A and B, we may calculate the probabilities by adding the appropriate simple event probabilities:

$$P(A) = P(H_1, T_2) + P(T_1, H_2) = \frac{1}{4} + \frac{1}{4} = \frac{1}{2}$$
$$P(B) = P(H_1, H_2) + P(H_1, T_2) + P(T_1, H_2) = \frac{1}{4} + \frac{1}{4} + \frac{1}{4} = \frac{3}{4}$$

EXAMPLE 3.2

A retail computer store owner sells two basic types of microcomputers: IBM personal computers (IBM PCs) and IBM compatibles (PCs that run all or most of the same software as an IBM PC, but that are not manufactured by IBM). One problem facing the owner is deciding how many of each type of PC to stock. One important factor affecting the solution is the proportion of customers who purchase each type of PC. Show how this problem might be formulated in the framework of an experiment, with simple events and a sample space. Indicate how probabilities might be assigned to the simple events.

Solution

Using the term *customer* to refer to a person who purchases one of the two types of PCs, we can define the experiment as the entrance of a customer and the observation of which type of PC is purchased. There are two simple events in the sample space corresponding to this experiment:

Experiment: Observe the type of PC purchased by a customer.
Simple events: 1. *I*: {The customer purchases an IBM PC}
                2. *C*: {The customer purchases an IBM compatible}

The difference between this experiment and the coin-toss experiment becomes apparent when we attempt to assign probabilities to the two simple events. What probability should we assign to the simple event *I*? If you answer .5, you are assuming that the events *I* and *C* should occur with equal likelihood, just as the simple events Heads and Tails in the coin-toss experiment. The assignment of simple event probabilities for the PC purchase experiment is not so easy. Suppose a check of the store's records indicates that 80% of its customers purchase IBM PCs. Then it might be reasonable to assign the probability of the simple event *I* as .8 and that of the simple event *C* as .2. The important points are that simple events are not always equally likely, and that the probabilities of simple events are not always easy to assign, particularly for experiments that represent real applications (as opposed to coin- and die-toss experiments).

EXAMPLE 3.3

A poll of "computer-familiar" adults who do not own a home computer was conducted by *USA Today* (Sept. 25, 1985). Each adult was asked to identify which of 10 electronic appliances was his or her highest-priority purchase, if any. The results are summarized in Table 3.2.

TABLE 3.2   Electronic Appliances of Highest Priority to Purchase by Computer-Familiar Adults

Electronic Appliance	Percent Response[a]	Electronic Appliance	Percent Response[a]
Home computer (HC)	24	Video cassette recorder (VCR)	17
Microwave oven (MO)	13	Video camera (VC)	9
Compact disc player (CDP)	4	Big-screen TV (BSTV)	7
Phone-answering machine (PAM)	6	Movie camera (MC)	3
Car telephone (CT)	5	None (N)	9
Programmable phone (PP)	3		

[a]Response percentages in the *USA Today* article did not add to 100% due to rounding. We have added 1% to the two smallest responses to facilitate the solution to this example.

Source: "Buying a computer is in our budget," *USA Today*, Sept. 25, 1985. Copyright 1985, USA Today. Excerpted with permission.

a. Define the experiment that generated the data in Table 3.2 and list the simple events.

b. Assign probabilities to the simple events.

c. What is the probability that a telephonic appliance is of highest priority?

d. What is the probability that a video appliance is of highest priority?

Solution

a. The experiment is the act of polling a computer-familiar adult. The simple events, the simplest outcomes of the experiment, are the 11 response categories listed in Table 3.2. They are shown in the Venn diagram in Figure 3.5.

FIGURE 3.5 ▶
Venn diagram for electronic appliance poll

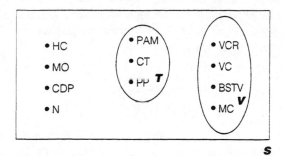

b. In Example 3.1, the simple events were assigned equal probabilities. If we were to assign equal probabilities in this case, each of the response categories would be assigned a probability of $\frac{1}{11}$, or .09. However, you can see by examining Table 3.2 that equal probabilities are not reasonable in this case, because the response percentages were not the same in the 11 classifications. Instead, we assign a probability equal to the actual response percentage in each class, as shown in Table 3.3.

TABLE 3.3   Simple Event Probabilities for Electronic Appliance Poll

Simple Event	Probability
HC	.24
MO	.13
CDP	.04
PAM	.06
CT	.05
PP	.03
VCR	.17
VC	.09
BSTV	.07
MC	.03
N	.09

c. The event T that a telephonic appliance is the highest priority is not a simple event, because it consists of more than one of the response classifications (the simple events). In fact, as shown in Figure 3.5, T consists of three simple events. The probability of T is defined to be the sum of the probabilities of the simple events in T:

$$P(T) = P(PAM) + P(CT) + P(PP) = .06 + .05 + .03 = .14$$

d. The event V that a video appliance is identified as the highest priority purchase consists of four simple events, and the probability of V is the sum of the corresponding simple event probabilities:

$$P(V) = P(VCR) + P(VC) + P(BSTV) + P(MC)$$
$$= .17 + .09 + .07 + .03 = .36$$

EXAMPLE 3.4

You have the capital to invest in two of four ventures, each of which requires approximately the same amount of investment capital. Unknown to you, two of the investments will eventually fail and two will be successful. You research the four ventures because you think that your research will increase your probability of a successful choice over a purely random selection, and you eventually decide on two. What is the lower limit of your probability of selecting the two best out of four? That is, if you used none of the information generated by your research, and selected two ventures at random, what is the probability that you would select the two successful ventures? At least one?

Solution

Denote the two successful enterprises as S_1 and S_2 and the two failing enterprises as F_1 and F_2. The experiment involves a random selection of two out of the four ventures, and each possible pair of ventures represents a simple event. The six simple events that make up the sample space are

1. S_1, S_2 2. S_1, F_1
3. S_1, F_2 4. S_2, F_1
5. S_2, F_2 6. F_1, F_2

The next step is to assign probabilities to the simple events. If we assume that the choice of any one pair is as likely as any other, then the probability of each simple event is $\frac{1}{6}$. Now check to see which simple events result in the choice of two successful ventures. Only one such simple event exists—namely, S_1, S_2. Therefore, the probability of choosing two successful ventures out of the four is

$$P(S_1, S_2) = \frac{1}{6}$$

The event of selecting at least one of the two successful ventures includes all the simple events except F_1, F_2.

$P(\text{Select at least one success})$

$$= P(S_1, S_2) + P(S_1, F_1) + P(S_1, F_2) + P(S_2, F_1) + P(S_2, F_2)$$
$$= \frac{1}{6} + \frac{1}{6} + \frac{1}{6} + \frac{1}{6} + \frac{1}{6} = \frac{5}{6}$$

Therefore, the worst that you could do in selecting two ventures out of four may not be too bad. With a random selection, the probability of selecting two successful ventures will be at least $\frac{1}{6}$ and the probability of selecting at least one successful venture out of two is at least $\frac{5}{6}$.

The preceding examples have one thing in common: The number of simple events in each of the sample spaces was small; hence, the simple events were easy to identify and list. How can we manage this when the simple events run into the thousands or millions? For example, suppose you wish to select five business ventures from a group of 1,000. Then each different group of five ventures would represent a simple event. How can you determine the number of simple events associated with this experiment?

One method of determining the number of simple events for a complex experiment is to develop a counting system. Start by examining a simple version of the experiment. For example, see if you can develop a system for counting the number of ways to select two people from a total of four (this is exactly what was done in Example 3.4). If the ventures are represented by the symbols V_1, V_2, V_3, and V_4, the simple events could be listed in the following pattern:

$$V_1, V_2 \qquad V_2, V_3 \qquad V_3, V_4$$
$$V_1, V_3 \qquad V_2, V_4$$
$$V_1, V_4$$

Note the pattern and now try a more complex situation—say, sampling three ventures out of five. List the simple events and observe the pattern. Finally, see if you can deduce the pattern for the general case. Perhaps you can program a computer to produce the matching and counting for the number of samples of 5 selected from a total of 1,000.

A second method of determining the number of simple events for an experiment is to use **combinatorial mathematics**. This branch of mathematics is concerned with developing counting rules for given situations. For example, there is a simple rule for finding the number of different samples of five ventures selected from 1,000. This rule is given by the formula

$$\binom{N}{n} = \frac{N!}{n!(N-n)!}$$

where N is the number of elements in the population; n is the number of elements in the sample; and the factorial symbol (!) means that, say,

$$n! = n(n-1)(n-2) \cdots \cdots 3 \cdot 2 \cdot 1$$

Thus, $5! = 5 \cdot 4 \cdot 3 \cdot 2 \cdot 1$. (The quantity $0!$ is defined to be equal to 1.)

....

EXAMPLE 3.5

Refer to Example 3.4, in which we selected two ventures from four in which to invest. Use the combinatorial counting rule to determine how many different selections can be made.

Solution

For this example, $N = 4$, $n = 2$, and

$$\binom{4}{2} = \frac{4!}{2!2!} = \frac{4 \cdot 3 \cdot 2 \cdot 1}{(2 \cdot 1)(2 \cdot 1)} = 6$$

You can see that this agrees with the number of simple events obtained in Example 3.4.

....

EXAMPLE 3.6

Suppose you plan to invest equal amounts of money in each of five business ventures. If you have 20 ventures from which to make the selection, how many different samples of five ventures can be selected from the 20?

Solution

For this example, $N = 20$ and $n = 5$. Then the number of different samples of 5 that can be selected from the 20 ventures is

$$\binom{20}{5} = \frac{20!}{5!(20-5)!} = \frac{20!}{5!15!}$$

$$= \frac{20 \cdot 19 \cdot 18 \cdot \cdots \cdot 3 \cdot 2 \cdot 1}{(5 \cdot 4 \cdot 3 \cdot 2 \cdot 1)(15 \cdot 14 \cdot 13 \cdot \cdots \cdot 3 \cdot 2 \cdot 1)} = 15,504$$

The symbol $\binom{N}{n}$, meaning the **number of combinations of N elements taken n at a time,** is just one of a large number of counting rules that have been developed by combinatorial mathematicians. This counting rule applies to situations in which the experiment calls for selecting n elements from a total of N elements, without replacing each element before the next is selected. If you are interested in learning other methods for counting simple events for various types of experiments, you will find a few of the basic counting rules in Appendix A. Others can be found in the references listed at the end of this chapter.

Exercises 3.1 – 3.15

Learning the Mechanics

3.1 What is the difference between a *simple event* and an *event*?

3.2 The diagram describes the sample space of a particular experiment and events A and B.

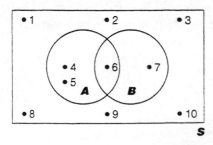

a. What is this type of diagram called?
b. Suppose the simple events are equally likely. Find $P(A)$ and $P(B)$.

c. Suppose $P(1) = P(2) = P(3) = P(4) = P(5) = \frac{1}{20}$ and $P(6) = P(7) = P(8) = P(9) = P(10) = \frac{3}{20}$. Find $P(A)$ and $P(B)$.

3.3 An experiment results in one of the following simple events: $E_1, E_2, E_3, E_4,$ and E_5.
  a. Find $P(E_3)$ if $P(E_1) = .1$, $P(E_2) = .2$, $P(E_4) = .3$, and $P(E_5) = .1$.
  b. Find $P(E_3)$ if $P(E_1) = P(E_3)$, $P(E_2) = .1$, $P(E_4) = .2$, and $P(E_5) = .2$.
  c. Find $P(E_3)$ if $P(E_1) = P(E_2) = P(E_4) = P(E_5) = .1$.

3.4 Compute each of the following:

  a. $\binom{9}{4}$ b. $\binom{7}{2}$ c. $\binom{4}{4}$ d. $\binom{5}{0}$ e. $\binom{6}{5}$

Applying the Concepts

3.5 The population of the amounts of 500 automobile loans made by a bank last year can be described as shown in the table. For the purpose of checking the accuracy of the bank's records, an auditor will randomly select one of these loans for inspection (i.e., each loan has an equal probability of being selected).

Amount of Loan ($)			
Under 2,000	2,000–4,999	5,000–7,999	8,000 or more
35	73	300	92

  a. List the simple events in this experiment.
  b. What is the probability that the loan selected will be for $8,000 or more?
  c. What is the probability that the loan will be for less than $5,000?

3.6 Communications products (telephones, fax machines, etc.) can be designed to operate on either an analog or a digital system. Because of improved accuracy, it is likely that a digital signal will soon replace the current analog signal used in telephone lines. The result will be a flood of new digital products for consumers to choose from (Kozlov, 1992). Suppose a particular firm plans to produce a new fax machine in both analog and digital forms. Concerned with whether the products will succeed or fail in the marketplace, a market analysis is conducted that results in the simple events and associated probabilities of occurrence listed in the table (S_a: analog succeeds, F_a: analog fails, etc.). Find the probability of each of the following events:

  A: {Both new products are successful}
  B: {The analog design is successful}
  C: {The digital design is successful}
  D: {At least one of the two products is successful}

Simple Events	Probabilities
$S_a S_d$	.31
$S_a F_d$	.10
$F_a S_d$	.50
$F_a F_d$	.09

3.7 Of six cars produced at a particular factory between 8 and 10 A.M. last Monday morning, three are known to be "lemons." Three of the six cars were shipped to dealer A and the other three to dealer B. Just by chance, dealer A received all three lemons. What is the probability of this event occurring if, in fact, the three cars shipped to dealer A were selected at random from the six produced?

3.8   A buyer for a large metropolitan department store must choose two firms from the four available to supply the store's fall line of men's pants. The buyer has not dealt with any of the four firms before and considers their products equally suitable. Unknown to the buyer, two of the four firms are having serious financial problems that may result in their not being able to deliver the pants as soon as promised. The firms are identified as G_1 and G_2 (firms in good financial condition) and P_1 and P_2 (firms in poor financial condition).
   a. List each simple event (i.e., list each possible pair of firms that could be selected by the buyer).
   b. Assume the probability of selecting a particular pair from among the four firms is the same for each pair. What is that probability?
   c. Find the probability of each of the following events:

   A: {Buyer selects two firms in poor financial condition}

   B: {Buyer selects at least one firm in poor financial condition}

3.9   Simulate the experiment in Exercise 3.8 by marking four poker chips (or cards), one corresponding to each of the four firms. Mix the chips, randomly draw two, and record the results. Replace the chips. Now repeat the experiment a large number of times (at least 100).
   a. Calculate the proportion of times event A occurs. How does this proportion compare with $P(A)$? Should the proportion equal $P(A)$? Explain.
   b. Calculate the proportion of times event B occurs and compare it with $P(B)$.

3.10   The Value Line Survey, a service for common stock investors, provides its subscribers with up-to-date evaluations of the prospects and risks associated with the purchase of a large number of common stocks. Each stock is ranked 1 (highest) to 5 (lowest) according to Value Line's estimate of the stock's potential for price appreciation during the next 12 months.

Suppose you plan to purchase stock in three electrical utility companies from among seven that possess rankings of 2 for price appreciation. Unknown to you, two of the companies will experience serious difficulties with their nuclear facilities during the coming year. If you randomly select the three companies from among the seven, what is the probability that you select:
   a. None of the companies with prospective nuclear difficulties?
   b. One of the companies with prospective nuclear difficulties?
   c. Both of the companies with prospective nuclear difficulties?

3.11   Approximately 77 million Visa and 60 million Mastercard credit cards had been issued in the United States by the end of 1984. Both were issued by thousands of banks, including Citicorp. Citicorp also issued competing cards of its own: Diners Club, Carte Blanche, and Choice are wholly owned by Citicorp. The accompanying table describes the population of credit cards issued by Citicorp. One Citicorp credit card customer is to be selected at random and the type of credit card will be recorded. (Assume that each customer has only one Citicorp-issued card.)

Credit Card	Number Issued (in millions)	Credit Card	Number Issued (in millions)
Visa and Mastercard	6.0	Carte Blanche	.3
Diners Club	2.2	Choice	1.0

Source: *Fortune*, Feb. 4, 1985, p. 21.

a. List the simple events in this experiment.

b. Find the probability of each simple event.

c. What is the probability that the customer selected uses one of Citicorp's wholly owned credit cards?

3.12 You are a lawyer for a client who has committed a felony, and there are seven judges who could hear your motion to set bail. Four judges are strict, and the other three are lenient. As you walk into the courtroom, judge A (a strict judge) is leaving to go home.

a. What is the probability of drawing a lenient judge for your client?

b. What is the probability of drawing a lenient judge for your client if the probability of getting judge B (a strict judge) is .3, the probability of getting judge C (a strict judge) is .4, and the probabilities of getting any of the other four judges are equally likely?

c. Suppose you know that judge D (a lenient judge) never follows judge A. What is the probability of drawing a lenient judge for your client if the probabilities in part b are valid?

3.13 *Sustainable development* or *sustainable farming* means "finding ways to live and work the Earth without jeopardizing the future" (Schmickle, 1992). Studies were concluded in five midwestern states to develop a profile of a sustainable farmer. Study results revealed that farmers can be classified along a sustainability scale, depending on whether they are likely or unlikely to engage in the following practices: (1) Raise a broad mix of crops; (2) Raise livestock; (3) Use chemicals sparingly; (4) Use techniques for regenerating the soil, such as crop rotation.

a. List the different sets of classifications that are possible.

b. Suppose you are planning to interview farmers across the country to determine the frequency with which they fall into the classification sets you listed for part a. Since no information is yet available, assume initially that there is an equal chance of a farmer falling into any single classification set. Using that assumption, what is the probability that a farmer will be classified as unlikely on all four criteria (i.e., classified as a non-sustainable farmer)?

c. Using the same assumption as in part b, what is the probability that a farmer will be classified as likely on at least three of the criteria (i.e., classified as a near-sustainable farmer)?

3.14 J. D. Power, a market-research firm in Agoura Hills, California, annually surveys thousands of U.S. motor vehicle owners to determine which automobiles and trucks the consumers believe to be the best based on such criteria as repair frequency, mileage, and dealer etiquette. The top three automobiles for 1991 were (in no particular order): Infiniti, Saturn sedan, and Lexus ("GM's Saturn Takes 3rd in New-Car Owner Poll," 1992).

a. List all possible sets of rankings for these three automobiles.

b. Assuming that each set of rankings in part a is equally likely, what is the probability that consumers ranked Saturn first? That consumers ranked Saturn last? That consumers ranked Lexus first and Infiniti second (which is, in fact, what they did)?

3.15 Probabilities are often expressed in terms of **odds**, especially in gambling settings. For example, handicappers for horse races express their belief about the probability of each horse winning a race in terms of odds. If the probability of event E is $P(E)$, then the **odds in favor of** E are $P(E)$ to $[1 - P(E)]$. Thus, if a handicapper assesses a probability of .25 that Snow Chief will win the Belmont Stakes, the odds in favor of Snow Chief are $25/100$ to $75/100$, or 1 to 3. It follows that the **odds against** E are $[1 - P(E)]$ to $P(E)$, or 3 to 1 against a win by Snow Chief. In general, if the odds in favor of event E are a to b, then $P(E) = a/(a + b)$.

a. A second handicapper assesses the probability of a win by Snow Chief to be $1/3$. According to the second handicapper, what are the odds in favor of a Snow Chief win?

b. A third handicapper assesses the odds in favor of Snow Chief to be 1 to 1. According to the third handicapper, what is the probability of a Snow Chief win?

c. A fourth handicapper assesses the odds against Snow Chief winning to be 3 to 2. Find this handicapper's assessment of the probability that Snow Chief will win.

3.2   Unions and Intersections

An event can often be viewed as a composition of two or more other events. Such an event, called a **compound event**, can be formed (composed) in two ways:

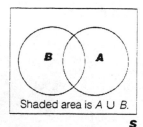

Shaded area is $A \cup B$.

s

Definition 3.5

The **union** of two events A and B is the event that occurs if either A or B or both occur on a single performance of the experiment. We will denote the union of events A and B by the symbol $A \cup B$.

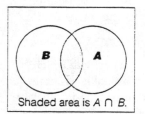

Shaded area is $A \cap B$.

s

Definition 3.6

The **intersection** of two events A and B is the event that occurs if both A and B occur on a single performance of the experiment. We will write $A \cap B$ for the intersection of events A and B.

EXAMPLE 3.7

Consider the die-toss experiment. Define the following events:

   A: {Toss an even number}

   B: {Toss a number less than or equal to 3}

a. Describe $A \cup B$ for this experiment.

b. Describe $A \cap B$ for this experiment.

c. Calculate $P(A \cup B)$ and $P(A \cap B)$ assuming the die is fair.

Solution

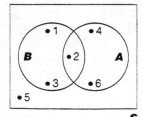

s

a. The **union** of A and B is the event that occurs if we observe an even number, a number less than or equal to 3, or both on a single throw of the die. Consequently, the simple events in the event $A \cup B$ are those for which A occurs, B occurs, or both A and B occur. Testing the simple events in the entire sample space, we find that the collection of simple events in the union of A and B is

$$A \cup B = \{1, 2, 3, 4, 6\}$$

b. The **intersection** of A and B is the event that occurs if we observe *both* an even number and a number less than or equal to 3 on a single throw of the die. Testing the simple events to see which imply the occurrence of *both* events A and B, we see that the intersection contains only one simple event:

$$A \cap B = \{2\}$$

In other words, the intersection of A and B is the simple event Observe a 2.

c. Recalling that the probability of an event is the sum of the probabilities of the simple events of which the event is composed, we have

$$P(A \cup B) = P(1) + P(2) + P(3) + P(4) + P(6)$$
$$= \frac{1}{6} + \frac{1}{6} + \frac{1}{6} + \frac{1}{6} + \frac{1}{6} = \frac{5}{6}$$

and

$$P(A \cap B) = P(2) = \frac{1}{6}$$

EXAMPLE 3.8

Many firms undertake direct marketing campaigns to promote their products. The campaigns typically involve mailing information to millions of households; the responses to the mailings are carefully monitored to determine the demographic characteristics of respondents. By studying tendencies to respond, the firm can better target future mailings to those segments of the population most likely to purchase the products.

Suppose a distributor of mail-order tools is analyzing the results of a recent mailing. The probability of response is believed to be related to income and age of the head of the household. The percentages of the total number of respondents to the mailing are given by income and age classification in Table 3.4.

TABLE 3.4 Percentage of Respondents in Age–Income Classes

		Income		
		<$25,000	$25,000–$50,000	>$50,000
Age	<30 yrs.	5%	12%	10%
	30–50 yrs.	14%	22%	16%
	>50 yrs.	8%	10%	3%

Define the following events:

A: {A respondent's income is more than $50,000}
B: {A respondent's age is 30 years or more}

a. Find P(A) and P(B).   b. Find P(A ∪ B).   c. Find P(A ∩ B).

Solution

Following the steps for calculating probabilities of events (given in the box on page 133), we first note that the objective is to characterize the income and age distribution of respondents to the mailing. To accomplish this, we define the experiment as selecting a respondent from the collection of all respondents, and observing which income and age class he or she occupies. The simple events are the nine different age–income classes:

E_1:　{<30 yrs., <$25,000}

E_2:　{30–50 yrs., <$25,000}

   ⋮　　　⋮

E_9:　{>50 yrs., >$50,000}

Next, we assign probabilities to the simple events. If we blindly select one of the respondents, the probability that he or she will occupy a particular age–income class is just the proportion, or relative frequency, of respondents in that class. These proportions are given (as percentages) in Table 3.4. Thus,

$$P(E_1) = \text{Relative frequency of respondents in}$$
$$\text{age–income class } (<30 \text{ yrs.}, <\$25,000)$$
$$= .05$$
$$P(E_2) = .14$$

and so forth. You may verify that the simple event probabilities add to 1.

a. To find $P(A)$ we first determine the collection of simple events contained in event A. Since A is defined as {>$50,000}, we see from Table 3.4 that A contains the three simple events represented by the last column of the table. In words, the event A consists of the income class (>$50,000) and all three age classes within that income class. The probability of A is the sum of the probabilities of the simple events in A:

$$P(A) = .10 + .16 + .03 = .29$$

Similarly, B consists of the six simple events in the second and third rows of Table 3.4:

$$P(B) = .14 + .22 + .16 + .08 + .10 + .03 = .73$$

b. The union of events A and B, $A \cup B$, consists of all simple events in *either A or B or both A and B*. That is, the union of A and B consists of all respondents whose income exceeds $50,000 *or* whose age is 30 or more. In Table 3.4 this is any simple event found in the third column *or* the last two rows. Thus,

$$P(A \cup B) = .10 + .14 + .22 + .16 + .08 + .10 + .03 = .83$$

c. The intersection of events A and B, $A \cap B$, consists of all simple events in *both A and B*. That is, the intersection of A and B consists of all respondents whose income exceeds $50,000 *and* whose age is 30 or more. In Table 3.4 this is any simple event found in the third column *and* the last two rows (i.e., in the last two rows of the third column). Thus,

$$P(A \cap B) = .16 + .03 = .19$$

3.3   The Additive Rule and Mutually Exclusive Events

In the previous section, we showed how to determine which simple events are contained in a union. Then we showed that the probability of the union can be calculated by adding the probabilities of the simple events in the union. It is also possible to obtain the probability of a union of two events by using the additive rule.

The union of two events will often contain many simple events, since the union occurs if either one or both of the events occur. By studying the Venn diagram in Figure 3.6, you can see that the probability of the union of two events A and B can be obtained by summing $P(A)$ and $P(B)$ and subtracting the probability corresponding to $A \cap B$. Therefore, the formula for calculating the probability of the union of two events is as given in the box.

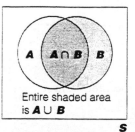

Entire shaded area
is **A ∪ B**

FIGURE 3.6 ▲
Venn diagram of union

> ### Additive Rule of Probability
>
> The probability of the union of events A and B is the sum of the probabilities of events A and B minus the probability of the intersection of events A and B:
>
> $$P(A \cup B) = P(A) + P(B) - P(A \cap B)$$

Note that we must subtract the probability of the intersection because, when we add the probabilities of A and B, the intersection probability is counted twice.

EXAMPLE 3.9

Consider the die-toss experiment. Define the events

A: {Observe an even number}

B: {Observe a number less than or equal to 3}

Assuming the die is fair, calculate the probability of the union of A and B by using the additive rule of probability.

Solution

The formula for the probability of a union requires that we calculate the following:

$$P(A) = P(2) + P(4) + P(6) = \tfrac{1}{6} + \tfrac{1}{6} + \tfrac{1}{6} = \tfrac{3}{6}$$

$$P(B) = P(1) + P(2) + P(3) = \tfrac{1}{6} + \tfrac{1}{6} + \tfrac{1}{6} = \tfrac{3}{6}$$

$$P(A \cap B) = P(2) = \tfrac{1}{6}$$

Now we can calculate the probability of $A \cup B$:

$$P(A \cup B) = P(A) + P(B) - P(A \cap B) = \tfrac{3}{6} + \tfrac{3}{6} - \tfrac{1}{6} = \tfrac{5}{6}$$

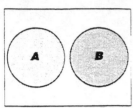

FIGURE 3.7 ▲
Venn diagram of mutually exclusive events

If two events A and B do not intersect—i.e., when $A \cap B$ contains no simple events—we call the events A and B **mutually exclusive** events:

Definition 3.7

Events A and B are **mutually exclusive** if $A \cap B$ contains no simple events.

Figure 3.7 shows a Venn diagram of two mutually exclusive events. The events A and B have no simple events in common; i.e., A and B cannot occur simultaneously, and $P(A \cap B) = 0$. Thus, we have the following important relationship:

If two events A and B are mutually exclusive, the probability of the union of A and B equals the sum of the probabilities of A and B:

$$P(A \cup B) = P(A) + P(B)$$

EXAMPLE 3.10

Consider the experiment of tossing two balanced coins. Find the probability of observing *at least* one head.

Solution

FIGURE 3.8 ▲
Venn diagram for coin toss experiment

Define the events

A: {Observe at least one head}
B: {Observe exactly one head}
C: {Observe exactly two heads}

Note that

$$A = B \cup C$$

and that $B \cap C$ contains no simple events (see Figure 3.8). Thus, B and C are mutually exclusive, so that

$$P(A) = P(B \cup C) = P(B) + P(C) = \tfrac{1}{2} + \tfrac{1}{4} = \tfrac{3}{4}$$

Although Example 3.10 is very simple, the concept of writing events with verbal descriptions that include the phrases "at least" or "at most" as unions of mutually exclusive events is a very useful one. This enables us to find the probability of the event by adding the probabilities of the mutually exclusive events.

3.4   Complementary Events

A very useful concept in the calculation of event probabilities is the notion of **complementary events**:

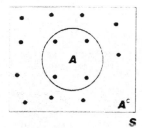

FIGURE 3.9 ▲

Venn diagram of complementary events

Definition 3.8

The **complement** of any event A is the event that A does not occur. We will denote the complement of A by A^c.

Since an event A is a collection of simple events, the simple events included in A^c are just those that are not in A. Figure 3.9 demonstrates this. You will note from the figure that all simple events in S are included in either A or A^c, and that *no* simple event is in both A and A^c. This leads us to conclude that the probabilities of an event and its complement *must sum to 1*:

The sum of the probabilities of complementary events equals 1; i.e.,

$$P(A) + P(A^c) = 1$$

In many probability problems, it will be easier to calculate the probability of the complement of the event of interest than the event itself. Then, since

$$P(A) + P(A^c) = 1$$

we can calculate $P(A)$ by using the relationship

$$P(A) = 1 - P(A^c)$$

EXAMPLE 3.11

Consider the experiment of tossing two fair coins. Calculate the probability of event A: {Observe at least one head} by using the complementary relationship.

Solution

We know that the event A: {Observe at least one head} consists of the simple events

$$A = \{H_1, H_2;\ \ H_1, T_2;\ \ T_1, H_2\}$$

The complement of A is defined as the event that occurs when A does not occur. Therefore,

$$A^c = \{T_1, T_2\}$$

FIGURE 3.10 ▶

Complementary events in the toss of two coins

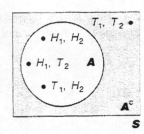

This complementary relationship is shown in Figure 3.10. Assuming the coins are balanced,

$$P(A^c) = P(T_1, T_2) = \tfrac{1}{4} \quad \text{and} \quad P(A) = 1 - P(A^c) = 1 - \tfrac{1}{4} = \tfrac{3}{4}$$

Exercises 3.16–3.31

Learning the Mechanics

3.16 Consider the Venn diagram shown, where $P(E_1) = .13$, $P(E_2) = .05$, $P(E_3) = P(E_4) = .2$, $P(E_5) = .06$, $P(E_6) = .3$, and $P(E_7) = .06$. Find each of the following probabilities.

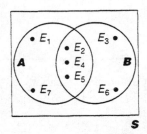

a. $P(A^c)$ **b.** $P(B^c)$ **c.** $P(A^c \cap B)$
d. $P(A \cup B)$ **e.** $P(A \cap B)$ **f.** $P(A^c \cup B^c)$

3.17 What are mutually exclusive events? Give a verbal description, and then draw a Venn diagram.

3.18 Two dice are tossed and the following events are defined:

   A: {The total number of dots on the upper faces of the two dice is equal to 5}
   B: {At least one of the two dice has three dots on the upper face}

a. Identify the simple events in each of the following events: A, B, A ∩ B, and A ∪ B.
b. Find $P(A)$ and $P(B)$ by summing the probabilities of the appropriate simple events.
c. Find $P(A \cap B)$ and $P(A \cup B)$ by summing the probabilities of the appropriate simple events.
d. Find $P(A \cup B)$ using the additive rule. Compare your answer to that for the same event in part c.
e. Are A and B mutually exclusive events? Why?

3.19 Three coins are tossed and the following events are defined:

   A: {Observe at least one head}

   B: {Observe exactly two heads}

   C: {Observe exactly two tails}

Assume that the coins are balanced. Calculate the following probabilities by summing the probabilities of the appropriate simple events:

a. $P(A \cup B)$ **b.** $P(A \cap B)$ **c.** $P(A \cap C)$ **d.** $P(B \cap C)$

e. Are events B and C mutually exclusive?

f. Find $P(B \cup C)$.

3.20 The accompanying table describes the adult population of a small suburb of a large southern city.

		Income		
		Under $20,000	$20,000–$50,000	Over $50,000
	Under 25	950	1,000	50
Age	25–45	450	2,050	1,500
	Over 45	50	950	1,000

A marketing research firm plans to randomly select one adult from this suburb to evaluate a new food product. For this experiment the nine age–income categories are the simple events. Consider the following events:

   A: {Person is under 25}

   B: {Person is between 25 and 45}

   C: {Person is over 45}

   D: {Person has income under $20,000}

   E: {Person has income of $20,000–$50,000}

   F: {Person has income over $50,000}

Convert the frequencies in the table to relative frequencies and use them to calculate the following probabilities:

a. $P(B)$ **b.** $P(F)$ **c.** $P(C \cap F)$ **d.** $P(B \cup C)$ **e.** $P(A^c)$ **f.** $P(A^c \cap F)$

g. Consider each pair of events (A and B, A and C, etc.) and list the pairs of events that are mutually exclusive. Justify your choices.

3.21 Refer to Exercise 3.20 and use the same event definitions to solve the following.

a. Write the event that the person selected is under 25 with an income over $50,000 as an intersection of two of the events defined in Exercise 3.20.

b. Write the event that a person of age 25 or over is selected as the union of two mutually exclusive events.

c. Write the event that a person of age 25 or over is selected as the complement of an event.

3.22 Three fair coins are tossed, and we wish to find the probability of the event A: {Observe at least one head}.
   a. Express A as the union of three mutually exclusive events. Find the probability of A using this expression.
   b. Express A as the complement of an event. Find the probability of A using this expression.

Applying the Concepts

3.23 A state energy agency mailed questionnaires on energy conservation to 1,000 homeowners in the state capital. Five hundred questionnaires were returned. Suppose an experiment consists of randomly selecting and reviewing one of the returned questionnaires. Consider the events:

   A: {The home is constructed of brick}

   B: {The home is more than 30 years old}

   C: {The home is heated with oil}

Describe each of the following events in terms of unions, intersections, and complements (i.e., $A \cup B$, $A \cap B$, A^c, etc.):
   a. The home is more than 30 years old and is heated with oil.
   b. The home is not constructed of brick.
   c. The home is heated with oil or is more than 30 years old.
   d. The home is constructed of brick and is not heated with oil.

3.24 Identifying managerial prospects who are both talented and motivated is difficult. A personnel manager constructed the table shown here to define nine combinations of talent–motivation levels. The numbers in the table are the manager's assessments of the probabilities that a managerial prospect will be classified in the respective categories.

		Talent		
		High	Medium	Low
Motivation	High	.05	.16	.05
	Medium	.19	.32	.05
	Low	.11	.05	.02

Suppose the personnel manager has decided to hire a new manager. Define the following events:

   A: {Prospect places in the high motivation category}

   B: {Prospect places in the high talent category}

   C: {Prospect rates medium or better in both categories}

   D: {Prospect rates low in at least one of the categories}

   E: {Prospect places high in both categories}

   a. Does the sum of the probabilities in the table equal 1?
   b. Find the probability of each event defined above.
   c. Find $P(A \cup B)$, $P(A \cap B)$, and $P(A \cup C)$.
   d. Find $P(A^c)$ and explain what this means from a practical point of view.

e. Consider each pair of events (A and B, A and C, etc.) and list the pairs of events that are mutually exclusive. Justify your choices.

3.25 After completing an inventory of three warehouses, a manufacturer of golf club shafts described its stock of 20,125 shafts with the percentages given in the table. Suppose a shaft is selected at random from the 20,125 currently in stock and the warehouse number and type of shaft are observed.

		Type of Shaft		
		Regular	Stiff	Extra Stiff
Warehouse	1	41%	6%	0%
	2	10%	15%	4%
	3	11%	7%	6%

a. List all the simple events for this experiment.
b. What is the set of all simple events called?
c. Let C be the event that the shaft selected is from warehouse 3. Find P(C) by summing the probabilities of the simple events in C.
d. Let F be the event that the shaft chosen is an extra stiff type. Find P(F).
e. Let A be the event that the shaft selected is from warehouse 1. Find P(A).
f. Let D be the event that the shaft selected is a regular type. Find P(D).
g. Let E be the event that the shaft selected is a stiff type. Find P(E).

3.26 Refer to Exercise 3.25. Define the characteristics of a golf club shaft portrayed by the following events, and then find the probability of each. For each union, use the additive rule to find the probability. Also, determine whether the events are mutually exclusive.
a. A ∩ F   b. C ∪ E   c. C ∩ D   d. A ∪ F   e. A ∪ D

3.27 Refer to Exercise 3.5, in which a bank's loan records were being audited. Suppose each of the 500 automobile loans made by the bank last year is now classified according to two characteristics: amount of loan and length of loan. As before, an auditor is planning to choose one loan at random for inspection.

		Amount of Loan ($)			
		Under 2,000	2,000–4,999	5,000–7,999	8,000 or more
Length of Loan (Months)	12	30	4	0	0
	24	5	18	2	0
	36	0	20	89	4
	42	0	31	95	37
	48	0	0	114	51

a. List the simple events in this experiment.
b. What is the probability that the loan selected will be for $8,000 or more? Does your answer agree with your answer to part b in Exercise 3.5?
c. What is the probability that the loan selected is a 3-year loan for more than $7,999?

d. What is the probability that the loan selected is a 3- or 4-year loan?

e. What is the probability that the loan selected is a 42-month loan for $2,000 or more?

3.28 The long-run success of a business depends on its ability to market products with superior characteristics that maximize consumer satisfaction and that give the firm a competitive advantage (Bagozzi, 1986). Ten new products have been developed by a food products firm. Market research has indicated that the 10 products have the characteristics described by the Venn diagram shown here.

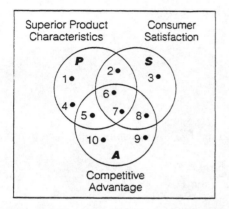

a. Write the event that a product possesses all the desired characteristics as an intersection of the events defined in the Venn diagram. Which products are contained in this intersection?

b. If one of the 10 products were selected at random to be marketed, what is the probability that it would possess all the desired characteristics?

c. Write the event that the randomly selected product would give the firm a competitive advantage or would satisfy consumers as a union of the events defined in the Venn diagram. Find the probability of this union.

d. Write the event that the randomly selected product would possess superior product characteristics and satisfy consumers. Find the probability of this intersection.

3.29 Whether purchases are made by cash or credit card is of concern to merchandisers because they must pay a certain percentage of the sale value to the credit agency. To better understand the relationship between type of purchase (credit or cash) and type of merchandise, a department store analyzed 10,000 sales and placed them in the categories shown in the table. Suppose a single sale is selected at random from the 10,000 and the following events are defined:

A: {Sale was paid by credit card}

B: {Merchandise purchased was women's wear}

C: {Merchandise purchased was men's wear}

D: {Merchandise purchased was sportswear}

		Type of Merchandise			
		Women's Wear	Men's Wear	Sportswear	Household
Type of Purchase	Cash	6%	9%	3%	7%
	Credit Card	41%	9%	22%	3%

Describe the characteristics of a sale implied by the following events, and find the probability of each.

a. $A \cup B$ b. $B \cup C$ c. $B \cap A$ d. $D \cap A$

e. Which pair of events are mutually exclusive? Why?

3.30 Refer to Exercise 3.29. The following events are defined:

A: {Sale was paid by credit card}

B: {Merchandise purchased was women's wear}

a. Describe the events A^c and B^c.   b. Find $P(A^c)$.   c. Find $P(B^c)$.

d. Find the probability that the sale was in neither men's wear nor women's wear.

e. Find the probability that the sale was *not* a credit card purchase in the sportswear department.

3.31 The types of occupations of the 117,342,000 employed workers (age 16 years and older) in the United States in 1989 are described in the table, and their relative frequencies are listed. A worker is to be selected at random from this population and his or her occupation is to be determined. (Assume that each worker in the population has only one occupation.)

Occupation	Relative Frequency
Male worker	.548
Managerial/professional	.142
Technical/sales/administrative	.108
Service	.052
Precision production, craft, and repair	.108
Operators/fabricators	.114
Farming, forestry, and fishing	.024
Female workers	.452
Managerial/professional	.117
Technical/sales/administrative	.200
Service	.080
Precision production, craft, and repair	.010
Operators/fabricators	.040
Farming, forestry, and fishing	.005

Source: *Statistical Abstract of the United States: 1991*, p. 395.

a. What is the probability that the worker will be a male service worker?
b. What is the probability that the worker will be a manager or a professional?
c. What is the probability that the worker will be a female professional or a female operator/fabricator?
d. What is the probability that the worker will not be in a technical/sales/administrative occupation?

3.5   Conditional Probability

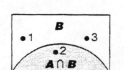

FIGURE 3.11 ▲
Reduced sample space for the die-toss experiment—given that event *B* has occurred

The probabilities we assign to the simple events of an experiment are measures of our belief that they will occur when the experiment is performed. When we assign these probabilities, we should make no assumptions other than those contained in or implied by the definition of the experiment. However, at times we will want to make assumptions other than those implied by the experimental description, and these extra assumptions may alter the probabilities we assign to the simple events of an experiment.

For example, we have shown that the probability of observing an even number (event *A*) on a toss of a fair die is ½. However, suppose you are given the information that on a particular throw of the die the result was a number less than or equal to 3 (event *B*). Would you still believe that the probability of observing an even number on that throw of the die is equal to ½? If you reason that making the assumption that *B* has occurred reduces the sample space from six simple events to three simple events (namely, those contained in event *B*), the reduced sample space is as shown in Figure 3.11.

Since the reduced sample space contains only three simple events (Observe a 1, Observe a 2, Observe a 3), each is assigned a new probability, called a **conditional probability**. Because the simple events for the die-toss experiment are equally likely, each of the three simple events in the reduced sample space is assigned a conditional probability of ⅓. Since the only even number of the three numbers in the reduced sample space *B* is the number 2 and since the die is fair, we conclude that the probability that *A* occurs *given that B occurs* is one in three, or ⅓. We will use the symbol $P(A \mid B)$ to represent the probability of event *A* given that event *B* occurs. For the die-toss example,

$$P(A \mid B) = \frac{1}{3}$$

To get the probability of event *A* given that event *B* occurs, we proceed as follows: We divide the probability of the part of *A* that falls within the reduced sample space *B*—namely, $P(A \cap B)$—by the total probability of the reduced sample space—namely, $P(B)$. Thus, for the die-toss example with event *A*: {Observe an even number} and event *B*: {Observe a number less than or equal to 3}, we find

$$P(A \mid B) = \frac{P(A \cap B)}{P(B)} = \frac{P(2)}{P(1) + P(2) + P(3)} = \frac{\frac{1}{6}}{\frac{3}{6}} = \frac{1}{3}$$

This formula for $P(A \mid B)$ is true in general:

> To find the **conditional probability that event A occurs given that event B occurs,** divide the probability that *both* A and B occur by the probability that B occurs; that is,
>
> $$P(A \mid B) = \frac{P(A \cap B)}{P(B)}$$

This formula adjusts the probability of $A \cap B$ from its original value in the complete sample space S to a conditional probability in the reduced sample space B. If the simple events in the complete sample space are equally likely, then the formula will assign equal probabilities to the simple events in the reduced sample space, as in the die-toss experiment. If, on the other hand, the simple events have unequal probabilities, the formula will assign conditional probabilities proportional to the probabilities in the complete sample space.

EXAMPLE 3.12

Suppose you are interested in the probability of the sale of a large piece of earth-moving equipment. A single prospect is contacted. Let F be the event that the buyer has sufficient money (or credit) to buy the product and let F^c denote the complement of F (the event that the prospect does not have the financial capability to buy the product). Similarly, let B be the event that the buyer wishes to buy the product and let B^c be the complement of that event. Then the four simple events associated with the experiment are shown in Figure 3.12, and their probabilities are given in Table 3.5.

TABLE 3.5 Probabilities of Customer Desire to Buy and Ability to Finance

		Desire	
		To Buy, B	Not to Buy, B^c
Able to Finance	Yes, F	.2	.1
	No, F^c	.4	.3

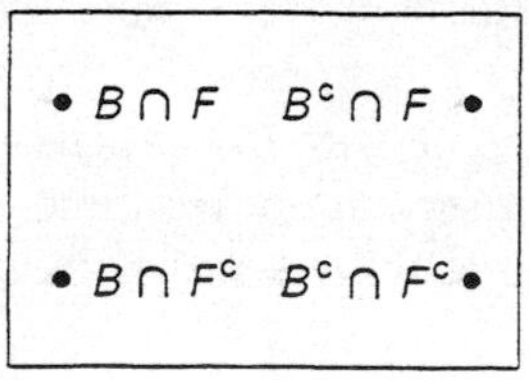

FIGURE 3.12 ▲

Sample space for contacting a sales prospect

Find the probability that a single prospect will buy, given that the prospect is able to finance the purchase.

Solution

Suppose you consider the large collection of prospects for the sale of your product and randomly select one person from this collection. What is the probability that the person selected will buy the product? In order to buy the product, the customer must be financially able and have the desire to buy, so this probability would correspond to

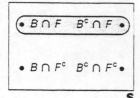

FIGURE 3.13 ▲
Subspace (shaded) containing sample points implying a financially able prospect

the entry in Table 3.5 below B and next to F, or $P(B \cap F) = .2$. This is called the **unconditional probability** of the event $B \cap F$.

In contrast, suppose you know that the prospect selected has the financial capability for purchasing the product. Now you are seeking the probability that the customer will buy given (the condition) that the customer has the financial ability to pay. This probability, the **conditional probability** of B given that F has occurred and denoted by the symbol $P(B \mid F)$, would be determined by considering only the simple events in the reduced sample space containing the simple events $B \cap F$ and $B^c \cap F$—i.e., simple events that imply the prospect is financially able to buy. (This subspace is shaded in Figure 3.13.) From our definition of conditional probability,

$$P(B \mid F) = \frac{P(B \cap F)}{P(F)}$$

where $P(F)$ is the sum of the probabilities of the two simple events corresponding to $B \cap F$ and $B^c \cap F$ (given in Table 3.5). Then

$$P(F) = P(B \cap F) + P(B^c \cap F) = .2 + .1 = .3$$

and the conditional probability that a prospect buys, given that the prospect is financially able, is

$$P(B \mid F) = \frac{P(B \cap F)}{P(F)} = \frac{.2}{.3} = .667$$

As we would expect, the probability that the prospect will buy, given that he or she is financially able, is higher than the unconditional probability of selecting a prospect who will buy.

. . . .

Note in Example 3.12, that the conditional probability formula assigns a probability to the event $(B \cap F)$ in the reduced sample space that is proportional to the probability of the event in the complete sample space. To see this, note that the two simple events in the reduced sample space, $(B \cap F)$ and $(B^c \cap F)$, have probabilities of .2 and .1, respectively, in the complete sample space S. The formula assigns conditional probabilities $\frac{2}{3}$ and $\frac{1}{3}$ (use the formula to check the second one) to these events in the reduced sample space F, so that the conditional probabilities retain the 2 to 1 proportionality of the original simple event probabilities.

EXAMPLE 3.13

The investigation of consumer product complaints by the Federal Trade Commission has generated much interest by manufacturers in the quality of their products. A manufacturer of an electromechanical kitchen aid conducted an analysis of a large number of consumer complaints and found that they fell into the six categories shown in Table 3.6. If a consumer complaint is received, what is the probability that the cause of the complaint was product appearance, given that the complaint originated prior to the end of the guarantee period?

TABLE 3.6   Distribution of Product Complaints

	Reason for Complaint		
	Electrical	Mechanical	Appearance
During Guarantee Period	18%	13%	32%
After Guarantee Period	12%	22%	3%

Solution

Let A represent the event that the cause of a particular complaint was product appearance and let B represent the event that the complaint occurred during the guarantee period. Checking Table 3.6, you can see that (18 + 13 + 32)% = 63% of the complaints occurred during the guarantee time. Hence, $P(B) = .63$. The percentage of complaints that were caused by appearance, A, *and* occurred during the guarantee period, B, is 32%. Therefore, $P(A \cap B) = .32$. Using these probability values, we can calculate the conditional probability $P(A \mid B)$ that the cause of a complaint is appearance given that the complaint occurred prior to the termination of the guarantee time:

$$P(A \mid B) = \frac{P(A \cap B)}{P(B)} = \frac{.32}{.63} = .51$$

Consequently, you can see that slightly more than half of the complaints that occurred during the guarantee period were due to scratches, dents, or other imperfections in the surface of the kitchen devices.

You will see in later chapters that conditional probability plays a key role in many applications of statistics. For example, we may be interested in the probability that a particular stock gains 10% during the next year. We may assess this probability using information such as the past performance of the stock or the general state of the economy at present. However, our probability may change drastically if we assume that the Gross Domestic Product (GDP) will increase by 10% in the next year. We would then be assessing the *conditional probability* that our stock gains 10% in the next year given that the GDP gains 10% in the same year. Thus, the probability of any event that is calculated or assessed based on an assumption that some other event occurs concurrently is a conditional probability.

CASE STUDY 3.1 / Purchase Patterns and the Conditional Probability of Purchasing

In his doctoral dissertation, Alfred A. Kuehn (1958) examined sequential purchase data to gain some insight into consumer brand switching. He analyzed the frozen orange juice purchases of approximately 600 Chicago families during 1950–1952. The data were collected by the *Chicago Tribune* Consumer Panel. Kuehn was interested in determining the influence of a consumer's last four orange juice purchases on the next purchase. Thus, sequences of five purchases were analyzed.

Table 3.7 contains a summary of the data collected for Snow Crop brand orange juice and part of Kuehn's analysis of the data. In the column labeled "Previous Purchase Pattern" an S stands for the purchase of Snow Crop by a consumer and an O stands for the purchase of a brand other than Snow Crop. Thus, for example, SSSO is used to represent the purchase of Snow Crop three times in a row followed by the purchase of some other brand of frozen orange juice. The column labeled "Sample Size" lists the number of occurrences of the purchase sequences in the first column. The column labeled "Frequency" lists the number of times the associated purchase sequence in the first column led to the next purchase (i.e., the fifth purchase in the sequence) being Snow Crop.

The column labeled "Observed Approximate Probability of Purchase" contains the relative frequency with which each sequence of the first column

led to the next purchase being Snow Crop. These relative frequencies, which give approximate probabilities, are computed for each sequence of the first column by dividing the frequency of the sequence by the sample size of the sequence. Notice that these approximate probabilities are really conditional probabilities. For the sequences of five purchases analyzed, each of the entries in the fourth column is the approximate probability that the next purchase is Snow Crop, given that the previous four purchases were as noted in the first column. For example, .806 is the approximate probability that the next purchase will be Snow Crop given that the previous four purchases were also Snow Crop.

An examination of the approximate probabilities in the fourth column indicates that both the most recent brand purchased and the number of times a brand is purchased have an effect on the next brand purchased. It appears that the influence on the next brand of orange juice purchased by the second most recent

| TABLE 3.7   Observed Approximate Probability of Purchasing Snow Crop, Given the Four Previous Brand Purchases |||||
Previous Purchase Pattern S = Snow Crop, O = Other Brand	Sample Size	Frequency	Observed Approximate Probability of Purchase
SSSS	1,047	844	.806
OSSS	277	191	.690
SOSS	206	137	.665
SSOS	222	132	.595
SSSO	296	144	.486
OOSS	248	137	.552
SOOS	138	78	.565
OSOS	149	74	.497
SOSO	163	66	.405
OSSO	181	75	.414
SSOO	256	78	.305
OOOS	500	165	.330
OOSO	404	77	.191
OSOO	433	56	.129
SOOO	557	86	.154
OOOO	8,442	405	.048

purchase is not so strong as the most recent purchase but is stronger than the third most recent purchase. In general, it appears that the probability of a particular consumer purchasing Snow Crop the next time he or she buys orange juice is inversely related to the number of consecutive purchases of another brand he or she made since last purchasing Snow Crop and is directly proportional to the number of Snow Crop purchases among the four purchases.

Kuehn, of course, goes on to conduct a more formal statistical analysis of these data, which we will not pursue here. We simply want you to see that probability is a basic tool for making inferences about populations using sample data.

3.6   The Multiplicative Rule and Independent Events

The probability of an intersection of two events can be calculated using the multiplicative rule, which employs the conditional probabilities we defined in the previous section. Actually, we have already developed the formula in another context. You will recall that the formula for calculating the conditional probability of B given A is

$$P(B \mid A) = \frac{P(A \cap B)}{P(A)}$$

If we multiply both sides of this equation by $P(A)$, we get a formula for the probability of the intersection of events A and B:

Multiplicative Rule of Probability

$P(A \cap B) = P(A)P(B \mid A)$ or, equivalently, $P(A \cap B) = P(B)P(A \mid B)$

The second expression in the box is obtained by multiplying both sides of the equation $P(A \mid B) = P(A \cap B)/P(B)$ by $P(B)$.

Before working an example, we emphasize that the intersection often contains only a few simple events, in which case the probability is easy to calculate by summing the appropriate simple event probabilities.

The formula for calculating intersection probabilities plays a very important role in an area of statistics known as **Bayesian statistics**. (More complete discussions of Bayesian statistics are contained in Chapter 19 and in the references at the end of this chapter.)

EXAMPLE 3.14

Suppose an investment firm is interested in the following events:

A: {Gross Domestic Product gains 10% next year}

B: {Common stock in XYZ Corporation gains 10% next year}

The firm has assigned the following probabilities on the basis of available information:

$P(B \mid A) = .8$ $P(A) = .3$

That is, the investment company believes the probability is .8 that XYZ common stock will gain 10% in the next year *assuming that* the GDP gains 10% in the same time period. In addition, the company believes the probability is only .3 that the GDP will gain 10% in the next year. Use the formula for calculating the probability of an intersection to determine the probability that XYZ common stock *and* the GDP gain 10% in the next year.

Solution

We want to calculate $P(A \cap B)$. The formula is

$$P(A \cap B) = P(A)P(B \mid A) = (.3)(.8) = .24$$

Thus, according to this investment firm, the probability is .24 that both XYZ common stock and the GDP will gain 10% in the next year.

. . . .

In the previous section, we showed that the probability of an event A may be substantially altered by the knowledge that the event B has occurred. However, this will not always be the case. In some instances the assumption that event B has occurred will not alter the probability of event A at all. When this is true, we call events A and B **independent**.

Definition 3.9
. . . .

Events A and B are **independent** if the assumption that B has occurred does not alter the probability that A occurs; i.e., events A and B are independent if

$$P(A \mid B) = P(A)$$

Equivalently, events A and B are **independent** if

$$P(B \mid A) = P(B)$$

Events that are not independent are said to be **dependent**.

EXAMPLE 3.15

Suppose that we decide to change the definition of event B in the die-toss experiment to {Observe a number less than or equal to 4} but we let event A remain {Observe an even number}. Are events A and B independent (assuming a fair die)?

Solution

The Venn diagram for this experiment is shown in Figure 3.14. We first calculate

$$P(A) = \tfrac{1}{2}$$
$$P(B) = P(1) + P(2) + P(3) + P(4) = \tfrac{4}{6} = \tfrac{2}{3}$$
$$P(A \cap B) = P(2) + P(4) = \tfrac{2}{6} = \tfrac{1}{3}$$

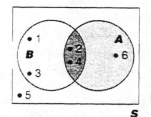

FIGURE 3.14 ▲
Die-toss experiment, Example 3.15

Now assuming B has occurred, the conditional probability of A is

$$P(A \mid B) = \frac{P(A \cap B)}{P(B)} = \frac{1/3}{2/3} = \frac{1}{2} = P(A)$$

Thus, the assumption of the occurrence of event B does not alter the probability of observing an even number—it remains $\frac{1}{2}$. Therefore, the events A and B are independent. Note that if we calculate the conditional probability of B given A, our conclusion is the same:

$$P(B \mid A) = \frac{P(A \cap B)}{P(A)} = \frac{1/3}{1/2} = 2/3 = P(B)$$

EXAMPLE 3.16

Refer to the consumer product complaint study in Example 3.13. The percentages of complaints of various types in the pre- and post-guarantee periods are shown in Table 3.6. Define the following events:

A: {Cause of complaint is product appearance}

B: {Complaint occurred during the guarantee term}

Are A and B independent events?

Solution

Events A and B are independent if $P(A \mid B) = P(A)$. We calculated $P(A \mid B)$ in Example 3.13 to be .51, and from Table 3.6 (page 157) we can see that

$$P(A) = .32 + .03 = .35$$

Therefore, $P(A \mid B) \neq P(A)$, and A and B are not independent events.

To gain an intuitive understanding of independence, think of situations in which the occurrence of one event does not alter the probability that a second event will occur. For example, suppose two small companies are being monitored by a financier for possible investment. If the businesses are in different industries and they are otherwise unrelated, then the success or failure of one company may be *independent* of the success or failure of the other. That is, the event that company A fails may not alter the probability that company B will fail.

As a second example, consider an election poll in which 1,000 registered voters are asked to state their preference between two candidates. One objective of the pollsters is to select a sample of voters so that the responses will be independent. That is, the sample is selected so that the event that one polled voter prefers candidate A does not alter the probability that a second polled voter prefers candidate A.

We will make three final points about independence. The first is that the property of independence, unlike the mutually exclusive property, cannot be shown on or gleaned from a Venn diagram. In general, the only way to check for independence is by performing the calculations of the probabilities in the definition.

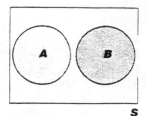

FIGURE 3.15 ▲
Mutually exclusive events are
dependent.

The second point concerns the relationship between the mutually exclusive and independence properties. Suppose that events A and B are mutually exclusive, as shown in Figure 3.15. Are these events independent or dependent? That is, does the assumption that B occurs alter the probability of the occurrence of A? It certainly does, because if we assume that B has occurred, it is impossible for A to have occurred simultaneously. Thus, mutually exclusive events are dependent events.

The third point is that the probability of the intersection of independent events is very easy to calculate. Referring to the formula for calculating the probability of an intersection, we find

$$P(A \cap B) = P(B)P(A \mid B)$$

Thus, since $P(A \mid B) = P(A)$ when A and B are independent, we have the following useful rule:

If events A and B are independent, the probability of the intersection of A and B equals the product of the probabilities of A and B:

$$P(A \cap B) = P(A)P(B)$$

The converse is also true: If $P(A \cap B) = P(A)P(B)$, then events A and B are independent.

In the die-toss experiment, we showed in Example 3.15 that the events A: {Observe an even number} and B: {Observe a number less than or equal to 4} are independent if the die is fair. Thus,

$$P(A \cap B) = P(A)P(B) = (\tfrac{1}{2})(\tfrac{2}{3}) = \tfrac{1}{3}$$

This agrees with the result

$$P(A \cap B) = P(2) + P(4) = \tfrac{2}{6} = \tfrac{1}{3}$$

that we obtained in the example.

EXAMPLE 3.17

Almost every retail business has the problem of determining how much inventory to purchase. Insufficient inventory may result in lost business, and excess inventory will have a detrimental effect on profits. Suppose a retail computer store owner is planning to place an order for personal computers (PCs). She is trying to decide how many IBM PCs and how many IBM compatibles (personal computers that run all or most of the same software as the IBM PC but that are not manufactured by IBM) to order. The owner's records indicate that 80% of the previous PC customers purchased IBM PCs, and 20% purchased compatibles.

a. What is the probability that the next two customers will purchase compatibles?

b. What is the probability that the next 10 customers will purchase compatibles?

Solution

a. Let C_1 represent the event that customer 1 will purchase a compatible, and C_2 the event that customer 2 will purchase a compatible. The event that *both* customers purchase compatibles is the intersection of these events, $C_1 \cap C_2$. From past records, the store owner could reasonably conclude that the probability of C_1 is equal to .2 (based on the fact that 20% of past customers have purchased compatibles), and the same reasoning would apply to C_2. However, in order to compute the probability of the intersection $C_1 \cap C_2$, more information is needed. Either the records must be examined for the occurrence of consecutive purchases of compatibles, or some assumption must be made to enable the calculation of $P(C_1 \cap C_2)$ from the multiplicative rule. It seems reasonable to make the assumption that the two events are independent, since the decision of the first customer is not likely to affect that of the second customer. Assuming independence, we have

$$P(C_1 \cap C_2) = P(C_1)P(C_2) = (.2)(.2) = .04$$

b. To see how to compute the probability that 10 consecutive purchases will be of compatibles, first consider the event that three consecutive customers purchase compatibles. If C_3 represents the event that the third customer purchases a compatible, then we want to compute the probability of the intersection of $C_1 \cap C_2$ with C_3. Again assuming independence of the purchasing decisions, we have

$$P(C_1 \cap C_2 \cap C_3) = P(C_1 \cap C_2)P(C_3) = (.2)^2(.2) = .008$$

Similar reasoning leads to the conclusion that the intersection of 10 such events can be calculated as follows:

$$P(C_1 \cap C_2 \cap \cdots \cap C_{10}) = P(C_1)P(C_2) \cdots \cdots P(C_{10})$$
$$= (.2)^{10}$$
$$= .0000001024$$

Thus, the probability that 10 consecutive customers purchase IBM compatibles is about 1 in 10 million, assuming that the probability of each customer's purchase of a compatible is .2, and that the purchase decisions are independent.

Exercises 3.32–3.47

Learning the Mechanics

3.32 An experiment results in one of three mutually exclusive events, A, B, or C. It is known that $P(A) = .30$, $P(B) = .55$, and $P(C) = .15$. Find each of the following probabilities:
a. $P(A \cup B)$ b. $P(A \cap C)$ c. $P(A \mid B)$ d. $P(B \cup C)$
e. Are B and C independent events? Explain.

3.33 Consider the experiment depicted by the Venn diagram on page 164, with the sample space S containing five simple events. The simple events are assigned the following probabilities: $P(E_1) = .20$, $P(E_2) = .30$, $P(E_3) = .30$, $P(E_4) = .10$, $P(E_5) = .10$.

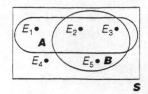

a. Calculate $P(A)$, $P(B)$, and $P(A \cap B)$.

b. Suppose we know that event A has occurred, so that the reduced sample space consists of the three simple events in A—namely, E_1, E_2, and E_3. Use the formula for conditional probability to adjust the probabilities of these three simple events for the knowledge that A has occurred [i.e., $P(E_i \mid A)$]. Verify that the conditional probabilities are in the same proportion to one another as the original simple event probabilities.

c. Calculate the conditional probability $P(B \mid A)$ in two ways: (1) Add the adjusted (conditional) probabilities of the simple events in the intersection $A \cap B$, since these represent the event that B occurs given that A has occurred; (2) Use the formula for conditional probability:

$$P(B \mid A) = \frac{P(A \cap B)}{P(A)}$$

Verify that the two methods yield the same result.

d. Are events A and B independent? Why or why not?

3.34 An experiment results in one of five simple events, with the following probabilities: $P(E_1) = .22$, $P(E_2) = .31$, $P(E_3) = .15$, $P(E_4) = .22$, and $P(E_5) = .10$. The following events have been defined:

$$A = \{E_1, E_3\} \qquad B = \{E_2, E_3, E_4\} \qquad C = \{E_1, E_5\}$$

Find each of the following probabilities:
a. $P(A)$ b. $P(B)$ c. $P(A \cap B)$ d. $P(A \mid B)$ e. $P(B \cap C)$ f. $P(C \mid B)$

3.35 Refer to Exercise 3.34. Which of the following pairs of events are independent? Explain.
a. A and B b. A and C c. B and C

3.36 Three coins are tossed and the following events are defined:

A: {Observe exactly two heads}

B: {Observe at least one head}

C: {Observe at most one head}

D: {Observe at least two tails}

Use the formulas of this section to calculate the following:
a. $P(B \cap C)$ b. $P(B \cup C)$
c. $P(A \cap D)$ d. $P(A \cup D)$
e. $P(B^c \cap C)$ f. $P(A \cap C)$
g. Determine which pairs of events, if any, are independent.

3.37 Defend or refute each of the following statements:
a. Dependent events are always mutually exclusive.
b. Mutually exclusive events are always dependent.

c. Independent events are always mutually exclusive.

d. Mutually exclusive events are always independent.

3.38   If $P(R) = \frac{1}{3}$, $P(S) = \frac{1}{3}$, and events R and S are mutually exclusive, find $P(R \mid S)$ and $P(S \mid R)$.

3.39   Two dice are tossed and the following events are defined:

A: {Sum of the numbers showing is an odd number}

B: {Sum of the numbers showing is 8, 9, 10, or 11}

3.40   Two hundred shoppers at a large suburban mall were asked two questions: (1) Did you see a television ad for the sale at department store X during the past 2 weeks? (2) Did you shop at department store X during the past 2 weeks? The responses to these questions are summarized in the table. One of the 200 shoppers questioned is to be chosen at random.

	Shopped at X	Did Not Shop at X
Saw ad	100	25
Did not see ad	25	50

a. What is the probability that the person selected saw the ad?

b. What is the probability that the person selected saw the ad and shopped at store X?

c. Find the conditional probability that the person shopped at store X given that the person saw the ad.

d. What is the probability that the person selected shopped at store X?

e. Use your answers to parts a, b, and d to check the independence of the events Saw ad and Shopped at X.

f. Are the two events {Did not see ad} and {Did not shop at X} mutually exclusive? Explain.

Applying the Concepts

3.41   Businesses that offer credit to their customers are inevitably faced with the task of collecting unpaid bills. Richard L. Peterson (1986) conducted a study of collection remedies used by creditors. As part of the study he asked samples of creditors in four states about how they deal with past-due bills. Their responses are tallied in the table. "Tough actions" included filing a legal action, turning the debt over to a third party such as an attorney or collection agency, garnishing wages, and repossessing secured property. Suppose one of the creditors questioned is selected at random.

	Wisconsin	Illinois	Arkansas	Louisiana
Take tough action early	0	1	5	1
Take tough action late	37	23	22	21
Never take tough action	9	11	6	15

a. What is the probability that the creditor is from Wisconsin or Louisiana?

b. What is the probability that the creditor is not from Wisconsin or Louisiana?

c. What is the probability that the creditor never takes tough action?

d. What is the probability that the creditor is from Arkansas and never takes tough action?

e. What is the probability that the creditor never takes tough action, given that the creditor is from Arkansas?

f. If the creditor takes tough action early, what is the probability that the creditor is from Arkansas or Louisiana?

g. What is the probability that a creditor from Arkansas never takes tough action?

3.42   A particular automatic sprinkler system for high-rise apartment buildings, office buildings, and hotels has two different types of activation devices for each sprinkler head. One type has a reliability of .91 (i.e., the probability that it will activate the sprinkler when it should is .91). The other type, which operates independently of the first type, has a reliability of .87. Suppose a serious fire starts near a particular sprinkler head.
  a.   What is the probability that the sprinkler head will be activated?
  b.   What is the probability that the sprinkler head will not be activated?
  c.   What is the probability that both activation devices will work properly?
  d.   What is the probability that only the device with reliability .91 will work properly?

3.43   A soft-drink bottler has two quality control inspectors independently check each case of soft drinks for chipped or cracked bottles before the cases leave the bottling plant. Having observed the work of the two trusted inspectors over several years, the bottler has determined that the probability of a defective case getting by the first inspector is .05 and the probability of a defective case getting by the second inspector is .10. What is the probability that a defective case gets by both inspectors?

3.44   The table describes the 67.1 million U.S. long-form federal tax returns filed with the Internal Revenue Service (IRS) in 1989 and the percentage of those returns that were audited by the IRS.

Income	Number of Tax Filers (Millions)	Percentage Audited
Under $25,000	29.1	.5
$25,000–$49,999	25.8	1.0
$50,000–$99,999	10.0	1.0
$100,000 or more	2.2	5.5

Source: *Statistical Abstract of the United States: 1991*, p. 324.

  a.   If a tax filer is randomly selected from this population of tax filers (i.e., each tax filer has an equal probability of being selected), what is the probability that the tax filer was audited?
  b.   If a tax filer is randomly selected from this population of tax filers, what is the probability that the tax filer had an income of $25,000–$49,999 in 1989 *and* was audited? What is the probability that the tax filer had an income of $50,000 or more in 1989 *or* was not audited?

3.45   Even with strong advertising programs, new products are often unsuccessful. A company that produces a variety of household items found that only 18% of the new products it introduced over the last 10 years have become profitable. When two new products were introduced during the same year, only 5% of the time did both products become profitable. Suppose the company plans to introduce two new products, A and B, next year. If the percentages just cited define the probabilities of success, what is the probability that:
  a.   Product A will become profitable?
  b.   Product B will not become profitable?
  c.   At least one of the two products will become profitable?
  d.   Neither of the two products will become profitable?
  e.   Either product A or product B (but not both) will become profitable?

3.46   Refer to Exercise 3.45.
  a.   If product B is profitable, what is the probability that product A becomes profitable?
  b.   If at least one of the products will be profitable, what is the probability that the profitable product is A?

3.47 Total quality management (TQM) is a management philosophy and system of management techniques to improve product and service quality and worker productivity. TQM involves such techniques as teamwork, empowerment of workers, improved communication with customers, evaluation of work processes, and statistical analysis of processes and their output (Benson, 1992). One hundred U.S. companies were surveyed and it was found that 30 had implemented TQM. Among the 100 companies surveyed, 60 reported an increase in sales last year. Of those 60, 20 had implemented TQM. Suppose one of the 100 surveyed companies is to be selected at random for additional analysis.

   a. What is the probability that a firm that implemented TQM is selected? That a firm whose sales increased is selected?

   b. Are the two events {TQM implemented} and {Sales increased} independent or dependent? Explain.

   c. Suppose that instead of 20 TQM-implementers among the 60 firms reporting sales increases, there were 18. Now are the events {TQM implemented} and {Sales increased} independent or dependent? Explain.

3.7   Random Sampling

How a sample is selected from a population is of vital importance in statistical inference because the probability of an observed sample will be used to infer the characteristics of the sampled population. To illustrate, suppose you deal yourself four cards from a deck of 52 cards, and all four cards are aces. Do you conclude that your deck is a ordinary bridge deck, containing only four aces, or do you conclude that the deck is stacked with more than four aces? It depends on how the cards were drawn. If the four aces were always placed on the top of a standard bridge deck, drawing four aces would not be unusual—it would be certain. On the other hand, if the cards were thoroughly mixed, drawing four aces in a sample of four cards would be highly improbable. The point, of course, is that, in order to use the observed sample of four cards to make inferences about the population (the deck of 52 cards), you need to know how the sample was selected from the deck.

One of the simplest and most frequently used sampling procedures (implied in the previous examples and exercises) produces what is known as a **random sample.**

Definition 3.10

If n elements are selected from a population in such a way that every possible combination of n elements in the population has an equal probability of being selected, the n elements are said to be a **random sample.**[*]

---

[*]Strictly speaking, this is a **simple random sample.** There are many different types of random samples. The simple random sample is the most frequently employed. We discuss other types of sampling procedures in Chapter 20.

If a population is not too large and the elements can be marked on slips of paper or poker chips, you can physically mix the slips of paper or chips and remove n elements from the total. Then the elements that appear on the slips or chips selected would indicate the population elements to be included in the sample. Such a procedure would not guarantee a random sample because it is often difficult to achieve a thorough mix, but it provides a reasonably good approximation to random sampling.

Many samplers use a table of random numbers (see Table I in Appendix B) or a statistical software package to generate a random sample. Random-number tables are constructed in such a way that every digit occurs with (approximately) equal probability. To use a table of random numbers, we number the N elements in the population from 1 to N. Then we turn to Table I and haphazardly select a number in the table. Proceeding from this number across the row or down the column (either will do), remove and record n numbers from the table. Use only the necessary number of digits in each random number to identify the element to be included in the sample. If, in the course of recording the n numbers from the table, you obtain a number that has already been selected, simply discard the duplicate, and select a replacement at the end of the sequence. Thus, you may have to select more than n numbers to obtain a random sample of n unique numbers.

We illustrate this procedure with an example.

EXAMPLE 3.18

Suppose you wish to randomly sample five households (we will keep the number in the sample small to simplify our example) from a population of 100,000 households. Use Table I in Appendix B to select a random sample.

TABLE 3.8   Reproduction of Part of Table I of Appendix B: Random Numbers

Row \ Column	1	2	3	4	5	6
1	10480	15011	01536	02011	81647	91646
2	22368	46573	25595	85393	30995	89198
3	24130	48360	22527	97265	76393	64809
4	42167	93093	06243	61680	07856	16376
5	37570	39975	81837	16656	06121	91782
6	77921	06907	11008	42751	27756	53498
7	99562	72905	56420	69994	98872	31016
8	96301	91977	05463	07972	18876	20922
9	89579	14342	63661	10281	17453	18103
10	85475	36857	53342	53988	53060	59533
11	28918	69578	88231	33276	70997	79936
12	63553	40961	48235	03427	49626	69445
13	09429	93969	52636	92737	88974	33488
14	10365	61129	87529	85689	48237	52267
15	07119	97336	71048	08178	77233	13916

Solution

First, number the households in the population from 1 to 100,000. Then, turn to a page of Table I, say, the first page. A reproduction of part of the first page of Table I is shown in Table 3.8. Now, commence with the random number that appears in the third row, second column. This number is 48360. Proceed down the second column to obtain the remaining four random numbers. The five selected random numbers are shaded in Table 3.8. Using the first five digits to represent the households from 1 to 99,999 and the number 00000 to represent household 100,000, you can see that the households numbered

48,360   93,093   39,975   6,907   72,905

should be included in your sample.

CASE STUDY 3.2 / The 1970 Draft Lottery

From 1948 through the early years of the Vietnam War, the Selective Service System drafted men into the military service by age—oldest first, starting with 25-year-olds. A network of local draft boards was used to implement the selection process. Then, on the evening of December 1, 1969, the Selective Service System conducted a lottery to determine the order of selection for 1970 in an attempt to overcome what many believed were inequities in the system. (Such lotteries had been used during World Wars I and II, but it had been 27 years since the last one.)

The objective of the lottery was to randomly order the induction sequence of men between the ages of 19 and 26. To do this, the 366 possible days in a year were written on slips of paper and placed in egg-shaped capsules that were stored in monthly lots. The monthly lots were placed one by one into a wooden box that was ". . . turned end over end several times to mix the numbers" ("Random or not? Judge studies lottery protest," 1970). The capsules were then dumped into a large glass bowl and drawn one by one to obtain the order of induction. All men born on the first day drawn would be inducted first; those born on the second day drawn would be drafted next, etc. Thus, the lottery assigned a rank to each of the 366 birthdays. The results of the lottery are shown in Table 3.9 on page 170.

For a random sequence of numbers to be generated with this procedure, it is necessary for each (re-

maining) capsule in the bowl to have an equal probability of being selected on each draw. That is, by means of thorough mixing, each capsule must have an equal opportunity to come to rest precisely where the sampler's hand closes within the bowl. Although a mixing procedure with this property is almost impossible to achieve, the ideal can be closely approximated. Unfortunately, this was apparently not the case in the 1970 lottery. Even though the sequence of dates in Table 3.9 may appear to be random, there is ample statistical evidence to indicate a nonrandom selection of induction dates.[*]

To obtain an understanding of the problem with the 1970 lottery, we calculated the median rank for each month and plotted the medians in Figure 3.16(a) on page 171. If the sequence of ranks were randomly generated, there should be no relationship between the size of the median ranks and the months of the year. The medians should vary randomly above and below a horizontal line with intercept 183.5 (the median of the integers 1 through 366). However, Figure 3.16(a) reveals a general downward trend in the medians. Men born later in the year we more likely to be drafted before men born early in the year. Furthermore, since not all men between the ages of 19 and 25 would be

[*]We discuss procedures for detecting nonrandomness in Chapter 13.

TABLE 3.9 1970 Draft Lottery Results

No.	Date	No.	Date	No.	Date	No.	Date	No.	Date	No.	Date
1	Sept. 14	62	April 21	123	Dec. 28	184	Sept. 8	245	Aug. 26	306	Jan. 7
2	April 24	63	Sept. 20	124	April 13	185	Nov. 20	246	Sept. 18	307	Aug. 13
3	Dec. 30	64	June 27	125	Oct. 2	186	Jan. 21	247	June 22	308	May 28
4	Feb. 14	65	May 10	126	Nov. 13	187	July 20	248	July 11	309	Nov. 26
5	Oct. 18	66	Nov. 12	127	Nov. 14	188	July 5	249	June 1	310	Nov. 5
6	Sept. 6	67	July 25	128	Dec. 18	189	Feb. 17	250	May 21	311	Aug. 19
7	Oct. 26	68	Feb. 12	129	Dec. 1	190	July 18	251	Jan. 3	312	April 8
8	Sept. 7	69	June 13	130	May 15	191	April 29	252	April 23	313	May 31
9	Nov. 22	70	Dec. 21	131	Nov. 15	192	Oct. 20	253	April 6	314	Dec. 12
10	Dec. 6	71	Sept. 10	132	Nov. 25	193	July 31	254	Oct. 16	315	Sept. 30
11	Aug. 31	72	Oct. 12	133	May 12	194	Jan. 9	255	Sept. 17	316	April 22
12	Dec. 7	73	June 17	134	June 11	195	Sept. 24	256	Mar. 23	317	Mar. 9
13	July 8	74	April 27	135	Dec. 20	196	Oct. 24	257	Sept. 28	318	Jan. 13
14	April 11	75	May 19	136	Mar. 11	197	May 9	258	Mar. 24	319	May 23
15	July 12	76	Nov. 6	137	June 25	198	Aug. 14	259	Mar. 13	320	Dec. 15
16	Dec. 29	77	Jan. 28	138	Oct. 13	199	Jan. 8	260	April 17	321	May 8
17	Jan. 15	78	Dec. 27	139	Mar. 6	200	Mar. 19	261	Aug. 3	322	July 15
18	Sept. 26	79	Oct. 31	140	Jan. 18	201	Oct. 23	262	April 28	323	Mar. 10
19	Nov. 1	80	Nov. 9	141	Aug. 18	202	Oct. 4	263	Sept. 9	324	Aug. 11
20	June 4	81	April 4	142	Aug. 12	203	Nov. 19	264	Oct. 27	325	Jan. 10
21	Aug. 10	82	Sept. 5	143	Nov. 17	204	Sept. 21	265	Mar. 22	326	May 22
22	June 26	83	April 3	144	Feb. 2	205	Feb. 27	266	Nov. 4	327	July 6
23	July 24	84	Dec. 25	145	Aug. 4	206	June 10	267	Mar. 3	328	Dec. 2
24	Oct. 5	85	June 7	146	Nov. 18	207	Sept. 16	268	Mar. 27	329	Jan. 11
25	Feb. 19	86	Feb. 1	147	April 7	208	April 30	269	April 5	330	May 1
26	Dec. 14	87	Oct. 6	148	April 16	209	June 30	270	July 29	331	July 14
27	July 21	88	July 28	149	Sept. 25	210	Feb. 4	271	April 2	332	Mar. 18
28	June 5	89	Feb. 15	150	Feb. 11	211	Jan. 31	272	June 12	333	Aug. 30
29	Mar. 2	90	April 18	151	Sept. 29	212	Feb. 16	273	April 15	334	Mar. 21
30	Mar. 31	91	Feb. 7	152	Feb. 13	213	Mar. 8	274	June 16	335	June 9
31	May 24	92	Jan. 26	153	July 22	214	Feb. 5	275	Mar. 4	336	April 19
32	April 1	93	July 1	154	Aug. 17	215	Jan. 4	276	May 4	337	Jan. 22
33	Mar. 17	94	Oct. 28	155	May 6	216	Feb. 10	277	July 9	338	Feb. 9
34	Nov. 2	95	Dec. 24	156	Nov. 21	217	Mar. 30	278	May 18	339	Aug. 22
35	May 7	96	Dec. 16	157	Dec. 3	218	April 10	279	July 4	340	April 26
36	Aug. 24	97	Nov. 8	158	Sept. 11	219	April 9	280	Jan. 20	341	June 18
37	May 11	98	July 17	159	Jan. 2	220	Oct. 10	281	Nov. 28	342	Oct. 9
38	Oct. 30	99	Nov. 29	160	Sept. 22	221	Jan. 12	282	Nov. 10	343	Mar. 25
39	Dec. 11	100	Dec. 31	161	Sept. 2	222	Jan. 28	283	Oct. 8	334	Aug. 20
40	May 3	101	Jan. 5	162	Dec. 23	223	Mar. 28	284	July 10	345	April 20
41	Dec. 10	102	Aug. 15	163	Dec. 13	224	Jan. 6	285	Feb. 29	346	April 12
42	July 13	103	May 30	164	Jan. 30	225	Sept. 1	286	Aug. 25	347	Feb. 6
43	Dec. 9	104	June 19	165	Dec. 4	226	May 29	287	July 30	348	Nov. 3
44	Aug. 16	105	Dec. 8	166	Mar. 16	227	July 19	288	Oct. 17	349	Jan. 29
45	Aug. 2	106	Aug. 9	167	Aug. 28	228	June 2	289	July 27	350	July 2
46	Nov. 11	107	Nov. 16	168	Aug. 7	229	Oct. 29	290	Feb. 22	351	April 25
47	Nov. 27	108	Mar. 1	169	Mar. 15	230	Nov. 24	291	Aug. 21	352	Aug. 27
48	Aug. 8	109	June 23	170	Mar. 26	231	April 14	292	Feb. 18	353	June 29
49	Sept. 3	110	June 6	171	Oct. 15	232	Sept. 4	293	Mar. 5	354	Mar. 14
50	July 7	111	Aug. 1	172	July 23	233	Sept. 27	294	Oct. 14	355	Jan. 27
51	Nov. 7	112	May 17	173	Dec. 26	234	Oct. 7	295	May 13	356	June 14
52	Jan. 25	113	Sept. 15	174	Nov. 30	235	Jan. 17	296	May 27	357	May 26
53	Dec. 22	114	Aug. 6	175	Sept. 13	236	Feb. 24	297	Feb. 3	358	June 24
54	Aug. 5	115	July 3	176	Oct. 25	237	Oct. 11	298	May 2	359	Oct. 1
55	May 16	116	Aug. 23	177	Sept. 19	238	Jan. 14	299	Feb. 28	360	June 20
56	Dec. 5	117	Oct. 22	178	May 14	239	Mar. 20	300	Mar. 12	361	May 25
57	Feb. 23	118	Jan. 23	179	Feb. 25	240	Dec. 19	301	June 3	362	Mar. 29
58	Jan. 19	119	Sept. 23	180	June 15	241	Oct. 19	302	Feb. 20	363	Feb. 21
59	Jan. 24	120	July 16	181	Feb. 8	242	Sept. 12	303	July 26	364	May 5
60	June 21	121	Jan. 16	182	Nov. 23	243	Oct. 21	304	Dec. 17	365	Feb. 26
61	Aug. 29	122	Mar. 7	183	May 20	244	Oct. 3	305	Jan. 1	366	June 8

FIGURE 3.16 ▶
Median plots for lottery results:
1970 and 1971

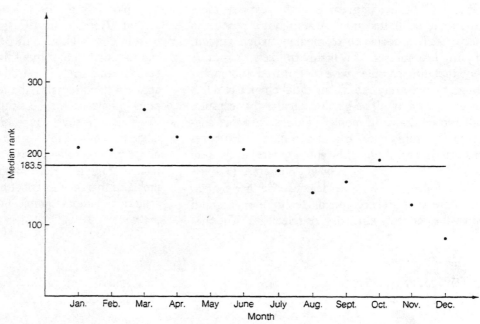

a. 1970 lottery

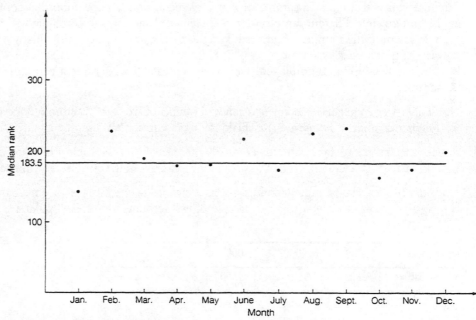

b. 1971 lottery

drafted in 1970, men born earlier in the year were more likely not to be drafted at all. Although it is possible to observe such a sequence of medians when random sampling is employed, it is highly unlikely. It is more likely that the capsules were not mixed thoroughly enough to give every capsule an equal chance of selection on each draw. The graph indicates that capsules tended to be drawn in monthly groups, and thus suggests that monthly lots of capsules in the wooden boxes were not mixed thoroughly enough after they were dumped into the large glass bowl (Williams, 1978).

The following year, the Selective Service System used more sophisticated mixing techniques to guard against the monthly clustering of selections. The me-

dian plot for the 1971 lottery is shown in Figure 3.16(b). [*Note:* The 1971 lottery involved only men born in 1951. Thus, only 365 birthdays were ranked and the sequence of monthly ranked medians should be compared to 183 instead of 183.5.] Note that no apparent trend remains; the new mixing technique appears to have been successful.

This case study emphasizes the value of using a random-number table or a random number generator of a statistical software package in the selection of a random sample. Most important, it points out the problems that may be encountered when attempting to acquire a random sample by a mechanical selection process.

Exercises 3.48–3.54

Learning the Mechanics

3.48 Suppose you wish to draw a sample of $n = 2$ elements from a population that contains $N = 10$ elements.
   a. List all possible different samples of $n = 2$ elements, and also use combinatorial mathematics (see Section 3.1) to count the number of different samples that can be selected. How many different samples of $n = 2$ elements can be selected?
   b. If random sampling is employed, what is the probability of drawing a particular pair of elements in your sample?

3.49 Use Table I of Appendix B to select a random sample of size $n = 20$ from among the digits 0, 1, 2, . . . , 9. (Digits may repeat themselves.) Explain your procedure.

3.50 Suppose that a population contains $N = 200,000$ elements. Use Table I of Appendix B to select a random sample of $n = 10$ elements from the population. Explain how you selected your sample.

3.51 Consider the population of new savings accounts opened in one business day at a bank, as shown in the table. Suppose you wish to draw a random sample of two accounts from this population.

Account Number	0001	0002	0003	0004	0005
Account Balance	$1,000	$12,500	$850	$1,000	$3,450

   a. List all possible different pairs of accounts that could be obtained.
   b. What is the probability of selecting accounts 0001 and 0004?
   c. What is the probability of selecting two accounts that each have a balance of $1,000? That each have a balance other than $1,000?

Applying the Concepts

3.52 To ascertain the effectiveness of their advertising campaigns, firms frequently conduct telephone interviews with consumers. Samples of telephone numbers may be randomly or systematically selected from telephone directories, or a more recent innovation called **random-digit dialing** may be employed. This approach involves using a random-number generator to create the sample of phone numbers to be called. Use the random-number table (Table I of Appendix B) to generate a sample of 10 seven-digit telephone numbers from area code 215. Describe the procedure you used.

3.53 When a company sells shares of stock to investors, the transaction is said to take place in the *primary market*. To enable investors to resell the stock when they wish, *secondary markets* called *stock exchanges* were created. Stock exchange transactions involve buyers and sellers exchanging cash for shares of stock, with none of the proceeds going to the companies that issued the shares (Greenleaf, Foster, and Prinsky, 1982). The results of the previous business day's transactions for stocks traded on the New York Stock Exchange (NYSE) and five regional exchanges—the Midwest, Pacific, Philadelphia, Boston, and Cincinnati stock exchanges—are summarized each business day in the NYSE–Composite Transactions table in the *Wall Street Journal*.
- **a.** Examine the NYSE–Composite Transactions table in a recent issue of the *Wall Street Journal* and explain how to draw a random sample of stocks from the table.
- **b.** Use the procedure you described in part **a** to draw a random sample of 20 stocks from a recent NYSE–Composite Transactions table. For each stock in the sample, list its name (i.e., the abbreviation given in the table), its sales volume, and its closing price.

3.54 The total labor force has increased annually, from 69.6 million in 1960 to 106.9 million in 1980 to 124.8 million in 1990. From 1960 to 1980, the percentage of the labor force age 16–34 steadily increased, and the percentage of the labor force age 35–64 decreased. However, beginning around 1980, with the aging of the baby-boom generation, these percentages began moving in the opposite directions.

Age	Percent in the Labor Force		
	1960	1980	1990
16–34	37.3	51.0	45.7
35–64	58.1	46.1	51.4
65+	4.6	2.9	2.8

Source: *Statistical Abstract of the United States: 1991*, p. 388.

- **a.** If the year were 1990 and one laborer were randomly selected from the labor force, what is the probability that a particular laborer would be selected? What is the probability that the laborer would be between 16 and 34 years of age?
- **b.** Repeat part **a** for the year 1960, and compare the answers.
- **c.** If two laborers were randomly selected from the 1990 labor force, what is the probability of selecting a particular pair of laborers?

Summary

We have developed some of the basic tools of probability that enable us to determine the probabilities of various sample outcomes, given a specific population structure. Although many of the examples we presented were of no practical importance, they accomplished their purpose if you now understand the basic concepts and definitions of probability.

The basic understanding of probability presented in this chapter includes the following concepts: **Experiments** are the basis for the generation of data. The most basic outcomes of experiments, called **simple events**, cannot be predicted with certainty. Therefore, we assign **probabilities** to the simple events, such that they obey two rules: (1) all probabilities must be between 0 and 1, and (2) the simple event probabilities must sum to 1. The collection of all the simple events is called the **sample space** of the experiment.

Unions and **intersections** are useful combinations of events. **Unions** are inclusive: either or both events occur. **Intersections** are limiting: both events occur. **Complements** are exclusive: the event does not occur. The **additive rule** is useful for calculating the probability of unions, and is particularly simple when the events have no intersection, in which case they are said to be **mutually exclusive**.

Conditional probability applies when we have some knowledge about what has occurred, reducing the size of the sample space. The **multiplicative rule** is useful for relating the probability of an intersection to conditional probability. When an intersection probability is equal to the product of the two (unconditional) event probabilities, we say the events are **independent**.

Our primary reason for studying the basics of probability is to enable the quantitative evaluation of alternative explanations (or models) of real data. To be able to rule out some explanations as "unlikely" and to accept others as "probable," we must first be able to quantify "unlikely" and "probable," and the theory of probability will provide the foundation for this endeavor.

In the next several chapters, we will present probability models that can be used to solve practical business problems. You will see that for most applications, we will need to make inferences about unknown aspects of these probability models; i.e., we will need to apply inferential statistics to the problem.

Supplementary Exercises 3.55–3.79

3.55 What are the two rules that probabilities assigned to simple events must obey?

3.56 Are mutually exclusive events also dependent events? Explain.

3.57 Given that $P(A \cap B) = .4$ and $P(A \mid B) = .8$, find $P(B)$.

3.58 Which of the following pairs of events are mutually exclusive? Justify your response.
  a. The Dow Jones Industrial Average increases on Monday.
      A large New York bank decreases its prime interest rate on Monday.
  b. The next sale by a PC retailer is an IBM microcomputer.
      The next sale by a PC retailer is an Apple microcomputer.
  c. You reinvest all your dividend income for 1990 in a limited partnership.
      You reinvest all your dividend income for 1990 in a money market fund.

3.59 A manufacturer of electronic digital watches claims that the probability of its watch running more than 1 minute slow or 1 minute fast after 1 year of use is .05. A consumer protection agency has purchased four of the manufacturer's watches with the intention of testing the claim.

a. Assuming that the manufacturer's claim is correct, what is the probability that all four of the watches are as accurate as claimed?

b. Assuming that the manufacturer's claim is correct, what is the probability that exactly two of the four watches fail to meet the claim?

c. Suppose that three of the four tested watches failed to meet the claim. What inference can be made about the manufacturer's claim? Explain.

d. Suppose that all four tested watches failed to meet the claim. Is it necessarily true that the manufacturer's claim is false? Explain.

3.60 The state legislature has appropriated $1 million to be distributed in the form of grants to individuals and organizations engaged in the research and development of alternative energy sources. You have been hired by the state's energy agency to assemble a panel of five energy experts whose task it will be to determine which individuals and organizations should receive the grant money. You have identified 11 equally qualified individuals who are willing to serve on the panel. How many different panels of five experts could be formed from these 11 individuals?

3.61 A research and development company surveyed all 200 of its employees over the age of 60 and obtained the information given in the table. One of these 200 employees is selected at random.

	Under 20 Years with Company		Over 20 Years with Company	
	Technical Staff	Nontechnical Staff	Technical Staff	Nontechnical Staff
Plan to Retire at Age 65	31	5	45	12
Plan to Retire at Age 68	59	25	15	8

a. What is the probability that the person selected is on the technical staff?

b. If the person selected has over 20 years of service with the company, what is the probability that the person plans to retire at age 68?

c. If the person selected is on the technical staff, what is the probability that the person has been with the company less than 20 years?

d. What is the probability that the person selected has over 20 years with the company, is on the nontechnical staff, and plans to retire at age 65?

3.62 Refer to Exercise 3.61.

a. Consider the events A: {Plan to retire at age 68} and B: {On the technical staff}. Are events A and B independent? Explain.

b. Consider the event D: {Plan to retire at age 68 *and* on the technical staff}. Describe the complement of event D.

c. Consider the event E: {On the nontechnical staff}. Are events B and E mutually exclusive? Explain.

3.63 Two marketing research companies, Richard Saunders International and Marketing Intelligence Service, joined forces to create a consumer preference poll called Acupoll. Acupoll is used to predict whether newly developed products will succeed if they are brought to market. The reliability of the Acupoll has been described as follows: The probability that Acupoll predicts the success of a particular product, given that later the product actually is successful, is .89 (Hall, 1992). A company is considering the introduction of a new product and assesses the product's probability of success to be .90. If this company were to have its product evaluated through Acupoll, what is the probability that Acupoll predicts success for the product and the product actually turns out to be successful?

3.64 The performance of quality inspectors affects both the quality and the cost of outgoing products. A product that passes inspection is assumed to meet quality standards; a product that fails inspection may be reworked, scrapped, or reinspected. Quality engineers at Westinghouse Electric Corporation evaluated inspectors' performances in judging the quality of solder joints by comparing each inspector's classifications of a set of 153 joints with the consensus evaluation of a panel of experts (Meagher and Scazzero, 1985). Suppose the results for a particular inspector are as shown in the table, and that one of the 153 solder joints is to be selected at random.

		Inspector's Judgment	
		Joint Acceptable	Joint Rejectable
Committee's Judgment	Joint Acceptable	101	10
	Joint Rejectable	23	19

a. What is the probability that the inspector judges the joint to be acceptable? That the committee judges the joint to be acceptable?
b. What is the probability that both the inspector and the committee judge the joint to be acceptable? That neither judges the joint to be acceptable?
c. What is the probability that the inspector and the committee disagree? Agree?

3.65 A local country club has a membership of 600 and operates facilities that include an 18-hole championship golf course and 12 tennis courts. Before deciding whether to accept new members, the club president would like to know how many members regularly use each facility. A survey of the membership indicates that 70% regularly use the golf course, 50% regularly use the tennis courts, and 5% use neither of these facilities regularly.
a. Construct a Venn diagram to describe the results of the survey.
b. If one club member is chosen at random, what is the probability that the member uses either the golf course or the tennis courts or both?
c. If one member is chosen at random, what is the probability that the member uses both the golf and the tennis facilities?
d. A member is chosen at random from among those known to use the tennis courts regularly. What is the probability that the member also uses the golf course regularly?

3.66 Insurance companies use *mortality tables* to help them determine how large a premium to charge a particular individual for a particular life insurance policy. The accompanying table shows the probability of survival to age 65 for persons of the specified ages.

Age	Probability of Survival to Age 65	Age	Probability of Survival to Age 65
0	.72	40	.77
10	.74	45	.79
20	.74	50	.81
30	.75	55	.85
35	.76	60	.90

   a. For a person 20 years old, what is the probability that he or she will die before age 65?

   b. Describe in words the trend indicated by the increasing probabilities in the second and fourth columns.

3.67 Explain why the following statement is or is not valid: If an individual is chosen at random from all U.S. citizens living in the 50 states, the probability that this individual lives in New Hampshire is ⅟₅₀.

3.68 A manufacturer of 35-mm cameras knows that a shipment of 30 cameras sent to a large discount store contains six defective cameras. The manufacturer also knows that the store will choose two of the cameras at random, test them, and accept the shipment if neither is defective.

   a. What is the probability that the first camera chosen by the store will be defective?

   b. Given that the first camera chosen passed inspection, what is the probability that the second camera chosen will fail inspection?

   c. What is the probability that the shipment will be accepted?

3.69 The accompanying figure is a schematic representation of a system comprised of three components connected *in series*. The system functions properly only if all three components operate properly. The components could be mechanical or electrical; they could be work stations in an assembly process; or could represent the functions of three different departments in an organization. The probability of failure for each of the components follows: #1 = .12, #2 = .09, #3 = .11.

A System Comprised of Three
Components in Series

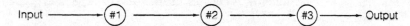

   a. Find the probability that the system operates properly.

   b. What is the probability that at least one of the components will fail and, therefore, that the system will fail?

3.70 To accompanying figure is a representation of a system comprised of two subsystems that are said to operate *in parallel*. Each subsystem has two components that operate in series (refer to Exercise 3.69). The system will operate properly as long as at least one of the subsystems functions properly. The probability of failure for each component in the system is .1. Assume that the components operate independently of each other.

A System Comprised of Two Parallel Subsystems
Subsystem A

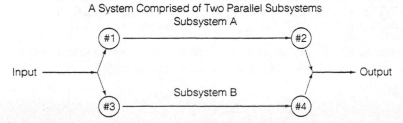

    a. Find the probability that the system operates properly.

    b. Find the probability that exactly one subsystem fails.

    c. Find the probability that the system fails to operate properly.

    d. How many parallel subsystems like the two shown here would be required to guarantee that the system would operate properly more than 99% of the time?

3.71 Your firm has decided to market two new products. The manager of the Marketing Department believes the probability of product A being accepted by the public and product B not being accepted is .3, of product B being accepted and product A not being accepted is .4, and of both products A and B being accepted is .2. Given these probabilities the manager has concluded that the probability of both products failing is .01. Do you agree with this conclusion? Explain.

3.72 Suppose only two daily newspapers are available in your town—a local paper and one from a nearby city—and that 1,000 people in town subscribe to a daily paper. Assume that 65% of the people in town who subscribe to a daily newspaper subscribe to the local paper and 40% of those who subscribe to a daily paper subscribe to the city paper.

    a. Use a Venn diagram to describe the population of newspaper subscribers.

    b. If one of the 1,000 subscribers is chosen at random, what is the probability that he or she subscribes to both newspapers?

3.73 Six people apply for two identical positions in a company. Four are minority applicants and the remainder are nonminority. Define the following events:

        A: {Both persons selected for the positions are nonminority candidates}

        B: {Both persons selected for the positions are minority candidates}

        C: {At least one of the persons selected is a minority candidate}

If all the applicants are equally qualified and the choice is therefore a random selection of two applicants from the six available, find the following:

    a. $P(A)$ **b.** $P(B)$ **c.** $P(C)$ **d.** $P(B \mid C)$

    e. For the purpose of identification, assume that the minority candidates are numbered 1, 2, 3, and 4. Define the event D: {Minority candidate 1 is selected}. Find $P(D \mid C)$.

3.74 Suppose there are 500 applicants for five equivalent positions at a factory and the company is able to narrow the field to 30 equally qualified applicants. Seven of the finalists are minority candidates. Assume that the five who are chosen are selected at random from this final group of 30.

    a. What is the probability that none of the minority candidates is hired?

    b. What is the probability that no more than one minority candidate is hired?

3.75 The probability that a microcomputer salesperson sells a computer to a prospective customer on the first visit to the customer is .4. If the salesperson fails to make the sale on the first visit, the probability that the sale will be made on the second visit is .65. The salesperson never visits a prospective customer more than twice. What is the probability that the salesperson will make a sale to a particular customer?

3.76 A credit counselor claims that the probability that at least two local firms go bankrupt next year is .15, and the probability that exactly two local firms go bankrupt is .20. Can this statement be true? Explain.

3.77 Use a Venn diagram to show that

$$P(A \cap B^c) = P(A) - P(A \cap B)$$

3.78 Use your intuitive understanding of independence to form an opinion about whether each of the following scenarios represents independent events.

   a. The results of consecutive tosses of a coin

   b. The opinions of randomly selected individuals in a pre-election poll

   c. A major-league baseball player's results in two consecutive at-bats

   d. The amount of gain or loss associated with investments in different stocks that are bought on the same day, and sold on the same day 1 month later

   e. The amount of gain or loss associated with investments in different stocks that are bought and sold in different time periods, 5 years apart

   f. The prices bid by two different development firms in response to a building construction proposal issued by a university.

3.79 A fair coin is flipped 20 times and 20 heads are observed. In such cases it is often said that a tail is due on the next flip. Is this statement true or false? Explain.

On Your Own

Obtain a standard bridge deck of 52 cards and think of the cards as the 52 items your firm produces each day. Let the four aces and four kings in the deck represent defective items.

a. If one item is randomly sampled from a day's production, what is the probability of its being defective?

b. Shuffle the cards, draw one, and record whether it is a defective item. Then replace the card and repeat the process. After each draw, recalculate the proportion of the draws that have resulted in a defective item. Construct a graph with the proportion of defectives on the y-axis and the number of draws on the x-axis. Notice how the proportion defective stabilizes as the number of draws increases.

c. Draw a horizontal line on the graph in part **b** at a height equal to the probability you calculated in part **a**. Compare the calculated proportion of defectives to this probability. As the number of draws is increased, does the calculated proportion of defectives more closely approach the actual probability of drawing a defective?

Using the Computer

Suppose a large bank is planning a national mailing to market a major credit card. However, the bank will first test its marketing materials by mailing to a single zip code.

a. If one of the 1,000 zip codes in Appendix C were to be selected randomly for a test mailing, what is the probability that the selected zone is one for which the average income exceeds $35,000?

b. Suppose the zip code were to be selected from the Northeast census region (among those in Appendix C). What is the probability that the selected zone is one for which the average income exceeds $35,000?

c. Are the events described in parts **a** and **b** independent? Why or why not? What are the practical implications of the independence, or dependence, of the events?

References

Bagozzi, R. P. *Principles of Marketing Management*. Chicago: SRA, 1986, p. 215.

Benson, P. George. "Process thinking: The quality catalyst." *Minnesota Management Review*, Carlson School of Management, University of Minnesota, Minneapolis, Fall 1992.

Feller, W. *An Introduction to Probability Theory and Its Applications*, 3d ed. Vol. 1. New York: Wiley, 1968. Chapters 1, 4, and 5.

"GM's Saturn takes 3rd in new-car owner poll." *Star Tribune* (Minneapolis). June 30, 1992.

Greenleaf, J., Foster, R., and Prinsky, R. "Understanding financial data in the *Wall Street Journal*." *Wall Street Journal*, Special Education Edition, 1982, p. 19.

Hall, Trish. "Pollsters think they have trick for product picks." *Star Tribune* (Minneapolis). Dec. 16, 1992.

Kozlov, Alex. "Business products for the technophobic and parsimonious." *Newsweek*, Nov. 16, 1992, p. 7.

Kuehn, A. A. "An analysis of the dynamics of consumer behavior and its implications for marketing management." Unpublished doctoral dissertation, Graduate School of Industrial Administration, Carnegie Institute of Technology, 1958.

Lindley, D. V. *Making Decisions*, 2d ed. London: Wiley, 1985.

Meagher, J. J. and Scazzero, J. A. "Measuring inspector variability." *39th Annual Quality Congress Transactions*, American Society for Quality Control, May 1985, pp. 75–81.

Parzen, E. *Modern Probability Theory and Its Applications*. New York: Wiley, 1960. Chapters 1 and 2.

Peterson, R. L. "Creditors' use of collection remedies." *Journal of Financial Research*, Vol. 9 , No. 1, Spring 1986, pp. 71–86.

Press, S. J. *Bayesian Statistics*. New York: Wiley, 1989.

"Random or not? Judge studies lottery protest." *The National Observer*, Jan. 12, 1970, p. 2.

Schmickle, Sharon. " 'Sustainable' farming viable, study suggests." *Star Tribune* (Minneapolis). June 20, 1992.

Williams, B. *A Sampler on Sampling*. New York: Wiley, 1978. pp. 5–8.

Winkler, R. L. *An Introduction to Bayesian Inference and Decision*. New York: Holt, Rinehart and Winston, 1972. Chapter 2.

Winkler, R. L. and Hays, W. L. *Statistics: Probability, Inference, and Decision*, 2d ed. New York: Holt, Rinehart and Winston, 1975. Chapters 1 and 2.

Appendices

A. REVIEW OF DECIMALS AND PERCENT
B. FINDING THE GREATEST COMMON FACTOR AND LEAST COMMON DENOMINATOR
C. GEOMETRY

Appendix A   Review of Decimals and Percent

> **To Add or Subtract Numbers Containing Decimal Points**
> 1. Align the numbers by the decimal points.
> 2. Add or subtract the numbers as if they were whole numbers.
> 3. Place the decimal point in the sum or difference directly below the decimal points in the numbers being added or subtracted.

EXAMPLE 1   Add $4.6 + 13.813 + 9.02$.

Solution:
```
   4.600
  13.813
+  9.020
 -------
  27.433
```

EXAMPLE 2   Subtract 3.062 from 25.9.

Solution:
```
  25.900
-  3.062
 -------
  22.838
```

> **To Multiply Numbers Containing Decimal Points**
> 1. Multiply as if the factors were whole numbers.
> 2. Determine the total number of digits to the right of the decimal points in the factors.
> 3. Place the decimal point in the product so that the product contains the same number of digits to the right of the decimal as the total found in step 2. For example, if there are a total of three digits to the right of the decimal points in the factors, there must be three digits to the right of the decimal point in the product.

EXAMPLE 3 Multiply 2.34 × 1.9.

Solution:

$$
\begin{array}{r}
2.34 \\
\times\ 1.9 \\
\hline
2106 \\
234 \\
\hline
4.446
\end{array}
$$

2.34 ⟵ two digits to the right of the decimal point
× 1.9 ⟵ one digit to the right of the decimal point
4.446 ⟵ three digits to the right of the decimal point in the product

EXAMPLE 4 Multiply 2.13 × 0.02.

Solution:

$$
\begin{array}{r}
2.13 \\
\times\ 0.02 \\
\hline
0.0426
\end{array}
$$

2.13 ⟵ two digits to the right of the decimal point
× 0.02 ⟵ two digits to the right of the decimal point
0.0426 ⟵ four digits to the right of the decimal point in the product

Note that it was necessary to add a zero preceding the digit 4 in the answer in order to have four digits to the right of the decimal point.

To Divide Numbers Containing Decimal Points

1. Multiply both the dividend and divisor by a power of 10 that will make the divisor a whole number.
2. Divide as if working with whole numbers.
3. Place the decimal point in the quotient directly above the decimal point in the dividend.

To make the divisor a whole number, multiply *both* the dividend and divisor by 10 if the divisor is given in tenths, by 100 if the divisor is given in hundredths, by 1000 if the divisor is given in thousandths, and so on. Multiplying both the numerator and denominator by the same nonzero number is the same as multiplying the fraction by 1. Therefore, the value of the fraction is unchanged.

EXAMPLE 5 Divide $\frac{1.956}{0.12}$.

Solution: Since the divisor, 0.12, is twelve-hundredths, we multiply both the divisor and dividend by 100.

$$\frac{1.956}{0.12} \times \frac{100}{100} = \frac{195.6}{12.}$$

Now divide.

$$
\begin{array}{r}
16.3 \\
12. \overline{)195.6} \\
\underline{12} \\
75 \\
\underline{72} \\
36 \\
\underline{36} \\
0
\end{array}
$$

The decimal point in the answer is placed directly above the decimal point in the dividend. Thus, 1.956/0.12 = 16.3.

EXAMPLE 6 Divide 0.26 by 10.4.

Solution: First, multiply both the dividend and divisor by 10.

$$\frac{0.26}{10.4} \times \frac{10}{10} = \frac{2.6}{104.}$$

Now divide.

$$
\begin{array}{r}
0.025 \\
104\overline{)2.600} \\
\underline{2\ 08} \\
520 \\
\underline{520} \\
0
\end{array}
$$

Note that a zero had to be placed before the digit 2 in the quotient.

$$\frac{0.26}{10.4} = 0.025$$

Percent

The word *percent* means "per hundred." The symbol % means percent. One percent means "one per hundred," or

$$1\% = \frac{1}{100} \quad \text{or} \quad 1\% = 0.01$$

EXAMPLE 7 Convert 16% to a decimal.

Solution: Since $1\% = 0.01$
$$16\% = 16(0.01) = 0.16$$

EXAMPLE 8 Convert 2.3% to a decimal.

Solution: $2.3\% = 2.3(0.01) = 0.023$.

EXAMPLE 9 Convert 1.14 to a percent.

Solution: To change a decimal number to a percent, we multiply the number by 100%.

$$1.14 = 1.14 \times 100\% = 114\%$$

Often you will need to find an amount that is a certain percent of a number. For example, when you purchase an item in a state or county that has a sales tax you must often pay a percent of the item's price as the sales tax. Examples 10 and 11 show how to find a certain percent of a number.

EXAMPLE 10 Find 12% of 200.

Solution: To find a percent of a number, use multiplication. Change 12% to a decimal number, then multiply by 200.

$$(0.12)(200) = 24$$

Thus, 12% of 200 is 24.

EXAMPLE 11   Monroe County in New York State charges an 8% sales tax.

(a) Find the sales tax on a stereo system that cost $580.

(b) Find the total cost of the system, including tax.

Solution: **(a)** The sales tax is 8% of 580.

$$(0.08)(580) = 46.40$$

The sales tax is $46.40

(b) The total cost is the purchase price plus the sales tax:

$$\text{Total cost} = \$580 + \$46.40 = \$626.40$$

Appendix B   Finding the Greatest Common Factor and Least Common Denominator

Prime Factorization   In Section 1.2 we mentioned that to reduce fractions to their lowest terms you can divide both the numerator and denominator by the *greatest common factor* (GCF). One method to find the GCF is to use *prime factorization*. Prime factorization is the process of writing a given number as a product of prime numbers. *Prime numbers* are natural numbers, excluding 1, that can be divided by only themselves and 1. The first ten prime numbers are 2, 3, 5, 7, 11, 13, 17, 19, 23, and 29. Can you find the next prime number? If you answered 31, you answered correctly.

To write a number as a product of primes, we can use a *tree diagram*. Begin by selecting any two numbers whose product is the given number. Then continue factoring each of these numbers into prime numbers, as shown in Example 1.

EXAMPLE 1   Determine the prime factorization of the number 120.

Solution: We will use three different tree diagrams to illustrate the prime factorization of 120.

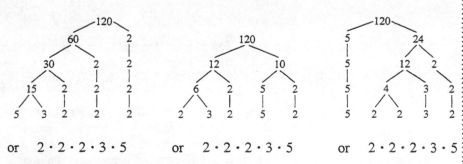

or $2 \cdot 2 \cdot 2 \cdot 3 \cdot 5$ or $2 \cdot 2 \cdot 2 \cdot 3 \cdot 5$ or $2 \cdot 2 \cdot 2 \cdot 3 \cdot 5$

Note that no matter how you start, if you do not make a mistake, you find that the prime factorization of 120 is $2 \cdot 2 \cdot 2 \cdot 3 \cdot 5$. There are other ways 120 can be factored but all will lead to the prime factorization $2 \cdot 2 \cdot 2 \cdot 3 \cdot 5$.

Greatest Common Factor   The greatest common factor (GCF) of two natural numbers is the greatest integer that is a factor of both numbers. We use the GCF when reducing fractions to lowest terms.

To Find the Greatest Common Factor of a Given Numerator and Denominator

1. Write both the numerator and the denominator as a product of primes.
2. Determine all the prime factors that are common to both prime factorizations.
3. Multiply the prime factors found in step 2 to obtain the GCF.

EXAMPLE 2   Consider the fraction $\frac{108}{156}$.

(a) Find the GCF of 108 and 156.

(b) Reduce $\frac{108}{156}$ to lowest terms.

Solution: **(a)** First determine the prime factorizations of both 108 and 156.

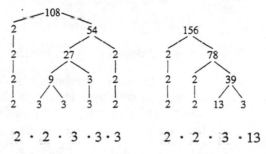

$$2 \cdot 2 \cdot 3 \cdot 3 \cdot 3 \qquad 2 \cdot 2 \cdot 3 \cdot 13$$

There are two 2's and one 3 common to both prime factorizations; thus

$$GCF = 2 \cdot 2 \cdot 3 = 12$$

The greatest common factor of 108 and 156 is 12. Twelve is the greatest integer that divides into both 108 and 156.

(b) To reduce $\frac{108}{156}$, we divide both the numerator and denominator by the GCF, 12.

$$\frac{108 \div 12}{156 \div 12} = \frac{9}{13}$$

Thus, $\frac{108}{156}$ reduces to $\frac{9}{13}$.

Least Common Denominator   When adding two or more fractions, you must write each fraction with a common denominator. The best denominator to use is the *least common denominator* (LCD). The LCD is the smallest number that each denominator divides into. Sometimes the least common denominator is referred to as the *least common multiple* of the denominators.

> To Find the Least Common Denominator of Two or More Fractions
>
> 1. Write each denominator as a product of prime numbers.
> 2. For each prime number, determine the maximum number of times that prime number appears in any of the prime factorizations.
> 3. Multiply all the prime numbers, found in Step 2. Include each prime number the maximum number of times it appears in any of the prime factorizations. The product of all these prime numbers will be the LCD.

Example 3 illustrates the procedure to determine the LCD.

EXAMPLE 3   Consider $\dfrac{7}{108} + \dfrac{5}{156}$.

(a) Determine the least common denominator.

(b) Add the fractions.

Solution: (a) We found in Example 2 that

$$108 = 2 \cdot 2 \cdot 3 \cdot 3 \cdot 3 \quad \text{and} \quad 156 = 2 \cdot 2 \cdot 3 \cdot 13$$

We can see that the maximum number of 2's that appear in either prime factorization is two (there are two 2's in both factorizations), the maximum number of 3's is three, and the maximum number of 13's is one. Multiply as follows:

$$2 \cdot 2 \cdot 3 \cdot 3 \cdot 3 \cdot 13 = 1404$$

Thus, the least common denominator is 1404. This is the smallest number that both 108 and 156 divide into.

(b) To add the fractions, we need to write both fractions with a common denominator. The best common denominator to use is the LCD. Since $1404 \div 108 = 13$, we will multiply $\dfrac{7}{108}$ by $\dfrac{13}{13}$. Since $1404 \div 156 = 9$, we will multiply $\dfrac{5}{156}$ by $\dfrac{9}{9}$.

$$\frac{7}{108} \cdot \frac{13}{13} + \frac{5}{156} \cdot \frac{9}{9} = \frac{91}{1404} + \frac{45}{1404} = \frac{136}{1404} = \frac{34}{351}$$

Thus, $\dfrac{7}{108} + \dfrac{5}{156} = \dfrac{34}{351}$.

TABLES

LIST OF TABLES

C-1. Consumer Price Index of Selected Expenses in Selected Urban Areas

C-2. Comparative Index of Selected Expenses in Selected Urban Areas at Intermediate Standard of Living

C-3. Annual Fire Insurance Premiums for Dwellings

C-4. Short-Term Rates Including Cancellation by the Insured

C-5. Comprehensive and Collision Insurance

C-6. Driver Classifications

C-7. Automobile Liability and Medical Payment Insurance

C-8. Annual Life Insurance Premiums

C-9. Nonforfeiture Options on Typical Life Insurance Policies

C-10. Settlement Options

C-11. Social Security Employee Tax Table

C-12. Federal Income Tax Withholding Table

C-13. MACRS Cost Recovery Factors

C-14. The Number of Each Day of the Year

C-15. Annual Percentage Rate Table for Monthly Payment Plans

C-16. Interest from Day of Deposit

C-17. Interest to Day of Withdrawal

C-18. Compound Amount

C-19. Amount of Annuity

C-20. Sinking Fund

C-21. Present Value

C-22. Present Value of Annuity

C-23. Amortization

C-24. Sum of Months' Digits

C-25. Monthly Payment per $1,000 of Mortgage

C-26. Metric Measures with U.S. Equivalents

C-27. U.S. Measures with Metric Equivalents

C-28. Sample Foreign Currency Exchange Rates

TABLE C-1 · CONSUMER PRICE INDEX OF SELECTED EXPENSES IN SELECTED URBAN AREAS

(1982–84 = 100)

EXPENSE	U.S. URBAN AVERAGE	ATLANTA	CHICAGO	DALLAS	LOS ANGELES	NEW YORK	SEATTLE
Food	147.2	141.1	147.0	142.2	148.5	151.9	146.9
Housing	145.4	140.1	144.8	129.0	151.0	159.9	147.9
Utilities	122.0	132.2	110.7	126.3	143.1	112.4	112.7
Transportation	137.1	123.8	130.3	134.5	140.5	141.8	135.0
Medical care	215.3	227.0	213.2	205.6	215.2	217.6	199.8

Source: U.S. Department of Labor.

TABLE C-2 · COMPARATIVE INDEX OF SELECTED EXPENSES IN SELECTED URBAN AREAS AT INTERMEDIATE STANDARD OF LIVING

U.S. Urban Average = 100

EXPENSE	ATLANTA	CHICAGO	DALLAS	LOS ANGELES	NEW YORK	SEATTLE
Food	98.6	99.3	98.1	110.3	112.8	97.3
Housing	86.8	107.5	93.8	147.9	105.6	132.8
Utilities	110.4	113.2	124.0	91.0	131.0	57.1
Transportation	98.3	108.0	103.2	106.8	95.5	94.7
Medical care	110.4	105.8	113.8	145.5	106.2	124.8
Combined index	97.0	103.5	102.0	121.1	106.0	106.2

Source: American Chamber of Commerce Researchers Association.

TABLE C-3 · ANNUAL FIRE INSURANCE PREMIUMS FOR DWELLINGS

Per $100 of Face Value

TERRITORY	STRUCTURE CLASS A	B	C	D	CONTENTS CLASS A	B	C	D
1	$0.45	$0.56	$0.66	$0.75	$0.51	$0.79	$0.79	$0.98
2	0.58	0.64	0.78	0.80	0.68	0.86	0.91	1.03
3	0.63	0.72	0.85	0.93	0.71	0.89	0.95	1.12

TABLE C-4 SHORT-TERM RATES INCLUDING CANCELLATION BY THE INSURED

MONTHS OF COVERAGE	PERCENT OF ANNUAL PREMIUM CHARGED	MONTHS OF COVERAGE	PERCENT OF ANNUAL PREMIUM CHARGED
1	20%	7	75%
2	30	8	80
3	40	9	85
4	50	10	90
5	60	11	95
6	70	12	100

TABLE C-5 COMPREHENSIVE AND COLLISION INSURANCE

Base Annual Premiums

MODEL CLASS	AGE GROUP	TERRITORY 1			TERRITORY 2			TERRITORY 3		
		COMPRE-HENSIVE	$250 DEDUCT-IBLE COLLISION	$500 DEDUCT-IBLE COLLISION	COMPRE-HENSIVE	$250 DEDUCT-IBLE COLLISION	$500 DEDUCT-IBLE COLLISION	COMPRE-HENSIVE	$250 DEDUCT-IBLE COLLISION	$500 DEDUCT-IBLE COLLISION
(1) A-G	1	$55	$ 82	$ 76	$59	$ 92	$ 80	$73	$100	$ 91
	2,3	52	77	73	56	86	76	58	94	85
	4	49	71	67	51	79	70	54	85	78
(3) J-K	1	63	111	101	69	128	108	75	141	127
	2,3	59	103	95	64	118	101	68	131	118
	4	54	93	86	57	106	91	61	116	105
(4) L-M	1	68	123	112	76	143	120	83	169	142
	2,3	64	125	104	70	133	112	75	138	132
	4	57	102	94	62	117	100	66	129	117
(5) N-O	1	77	140	126	86	164	136	95	183	162
	2,3	70	130	117	77	151	126	85	168	150
	4	62	115	105	68	133	112	73	147	132

TABLE C-6 DRIVER CLASSIFICATIONS

Multiples of Base Annual Automobile Insurance Premiums

			PLEASURE; LESS THAN 3 MILES TO WORK EACH WAY	DRIVES TO WORK, 3 TO 9 MILES EACH WAY	DRIVES TO WORK, 10 MILES OR MORE EACH WAY	USED IN BUSINESS
No young operators	Only operator is female, age 30–64		0.90	1.00	1.30	1.40
	One or more operators age 65 or over		1.00	1.10	1.40	1.50
	All others		1.00	1.10	1.40	1.50
Young females	Age 16	DT[a]	1.40	1.50	1.80	1.90
		No DT	1.55	1.65	1.95	2.05
	Age 20	DT	1.05	1.15	1.45	1.55
		No DT	1.10	1.20	1.50	1.60
Young males (married)	Age 16	DT	1.60	1.70	2.00	2.10
		No DT	1.80	1.90	2.20	2.30
	Age 20	DT	1.45	1.55	1.85	1.95
		No DT	1.50	1.60	1.90	2.00
	Age 21		1.40	1.50	1.80	1.90
	Age 24		1.10	1.20	1.50	1.60
Young unmarried males (not principal operator)	Age 16	DT	2.05	2.15	2.45	2.55
		No DT	2.30	2.40	2.70	2.80
	Age 20	DT	1.60	1.70	2.00	2.10
		No DT	1.70	1.80	2.10	2.20
	Age 21		1.55	1.65	1.95	2.05
	Age 24		1.10	1.20	1.50	1.60
Young unmarried males (owner or principal operator)	Age 16	DT	2.70	2.80	3.10	3.20
		No DT	3.30	3.40	3.70	3.80
	Age 20	DT	2.55	2.65	2.95	3.05
		No DT	2.70	2.80	3.10	3.20
	Age 21		2.50	2.60	2.90	3.00
	Age 24		1.90	2.00	2.30	2.40
	Age 26		1.50	1.60	1.90	2.00
	Age 29		1.10	1.20	1.50	1.60

[a] "DT" indicates completion of a certified driver training course.

TABLE C-7 AUTOMOBILE LIABILITY AND MEDICAL PAYMENT INSURANCE

Base Annual Premiums

	BODILY INJURY				PROPERTY DAMAGE		
COVERAGE	TERRITORY 1	TERRITORY 2	TERRITORY 3	COVERAGE	TERRITORY 1	TERRITORY 2	TERRITORY 3
15/30	$ 81	$ 91	$112	$ 5,000	$83	$ 95	$100
25/25	83	94	115	10,000	85	97	103
25/50	86	97	120	25,000	86	99	104
50/50	88	101	125	50,000	87	101	107
50/100	90	103	129	100,000	90	103	108
100/100	91	104	131	MEDICAL PAYMENT			
100/200	94	108	136				
100/300	95	110	139	$ 1,000	$62	$63	$64
200/300	98	112	141	2,500	65	66	67
300/300	100	115	144	5,000	67	68	69
				10,000	70	72	74

TABLE C-8 ANNUAL LIFE INSURANCE PREMIUMS

Per $1,000 of Face Value for Male Applicants[a]

AGE ISSUED (YEARS)	TERM 10-YEAR	WHOLE LIFE	VARIABLE UNIVERSAL	LIMITED PAYMENT 20-YEAR
18	$ 6.81	$14.77	$18.36	$24.69
20	6.88	15.46	19.81	25.59
22	6.95	16.12	20.28	26.53
24	7.05	16.82	21.33	27.53
25	7.10	17.22	22.17	28.06
26	7.18	17.67	23.43	28.63
28	7.35	18.64	24.79	29.84
30	7.59	19.73	26.05	31.12
35	8.68	23.99	30.87	35.80
40	10.64	28.26	35.55	40.34
45	14.52	33.79	41.24	46.01
50	22.18	40.77	48.11	53.24
55	32.93	51.38	57.62	64.77
60	—	59.32	—	70.86

[a] Because of women's longer life expectancy, premiums for women approximately equal those of men who are 5 years younger.

TABLE C-9 NONFORFEITURE OPTIONS[a] ON TYPICAL LIFE INSURANCE POLICIES

Issued at Age 25

| YEARS IN FORCE | WHOLE LIFE | | | | 20-PAYMENT LIFE | | | | VARIABLE UNIVERSAL |
| | CASH VALUE | PAID-UP INSURANCE | EXT. TERM | | CASH VALUE | PAID-UP INSURANCE | EXT. TERM | | |
			YEARS	DAYS			YEARS	DAYS	CASH VALUE
3	$ 9	$ 19	1	190	$ 32	$ 94	10	84	$ 44
5	31	87	9	200	74	218	19	184	95
10	93	248	18	91	187	507	28	186	321
15	162	387	20	300	319	768	32	164	595
20	251	535	22	137	470	1,000	Life		1,030
40	576	827	—	—	701	—	—	—	2,979

[a] The "cash value" and "paid-up insurance" nonforfeiture values are per $1,000 of life insurance coverage. The time period for "extended term insurance" applies as shown to all policies, regardless of face value. The cash value for variable universal life represents a reasonable estimate of the increase in value, rather than a guaranteed amount.

TABLE C-10 SETTLEMENT OPTIONS

Monthly Installments per $1,000 of Face Value

| OPTIONS 1 AND 2: FIXED AMOUNT OR FIXED NUMBER OF YEARS | | OPTIONS 3 AND 4: INCOME FOR LIFE | | | | |
| | | AGE WHEN ANNUITY BEGINS | | LIFE ANNUITY | LIFE WITH 10 YEARS CERTAIN | LIFE WITH 20 YEARS CERTAIN |
YEARS	AMOUNT	MALE	FEMALE			
10	$9.60	40	45	$4.50	$4.56	$4.44
12	8.52	45	50	5.16	5.07	4.80
14	7.71	50	55	5.30	5.28	5.00
15	6.89	55	60	6.13	6.00	5.46
16	6.43	60	65	6.56	6.31	5.65
18	6.08	65	70	7.22	6.70	5.78
20	5.66					

TABLE C-11 SOCIAL SECURITY EMPLOYEE TAX TABLE

7.65% Employee Tax Deductions

Wages at least	But less than	Tax to be withheld	Wages at least	But less than	Tax to be withheld	Wages at least	But less than	Tax to be withheld	Wages at least	But less than	Tax to be withheld
199.94	200.07	15.30	212.75	212.88	16.28	225.56	225.69	17.26	238.37	238.50	18.24
200.07	200.20	15.31	212.88	213.01	16.29	225.69	225.82	17.27	238.50	238.63	18.25
200.20	200.33	15.32	213.01	213.14	16.30	225.82	225.95	17.28	238.63	238.76	18.26
200.33	200.46	15.33	213.14	213.27	16.31	225.95	226.08	17.29	238.76	238.89	18.27
200.46	200.59	15.34	213.27	213.40	16.32	226.08	226.21	17.30	238.89	239.02	18.28
200.59	200.72	15.35	213.40	213.53	16.33	226.21	226.34	17.31	239.02	239.15	18.29
200.72	200.85	15.36	213.53	213.66	16.34	226.34	226.48	17.32	239.15	239.29	18.30
200.85	200.98	15.37	213.66	213.80	16.35	226.48	226.61	17.33	239.29	239.42	18.31
200.98	201.12	15.38	213.80	213.93	16.36	226.61	226.74	17.34	239.42	239.55	18.32
201.12	201.25	15.39	213.93	214.06	16.37	226.74	226.87	17.35	239.55	239.68	18.33
201.25	201.38	15.40	214.06	214.19	16.38	226.87	227.00	17.36	239.68	239.81	18.34
201.38	201.51	15.41	214.19	214.32	16.39	227.00	227.13	17.37	239.81	239.94	18.35
201.51	201.64	15.42	214.32	214.45	16.40	227.13	227.26	17.38	239.94	240.07	18.36
201.64	201.77	15.43	214.45	214.58	16.41	227.26	227.39	17.39	240.07	240.20	18.37
201.77	201.90	15.44	214.58	214.71	16.42	227.39	227.52	17.40	240.20	240.33	18.38
201.90	202.03	15.45	214.71	214.84	16.43	227.52	227.65	17.41	240.33	240.46	18.39
202.03	202.16	15.46	214.84	214.97	16.44	227.65	227.78	17.42	240.46	240.59	18.40
202.16	202.29	15.47	214.97	215.10	16.45	227.78	227.91	17.43	240.59	240.72	18.41
202.29	202.42	15.48	215.10	215.23	16.46	227.91	228.04	17.44	240.72	240.85	18.42
202.42	202.55	15.49	215.23	215.36	16.47	228.04	228.17	17.45	240.85	240.98	18.43
202.55	202.68	15.50	215.36	215.49	16.48	228.17	228.31	17.46	240.98	241.12	18.44
202.68	202.82	15.51	215.49	215.63	16.49	228.31	228.44	17.47	241.12	241.25	18.45
202.82	202.95	15.52	215.63	215.76	16.50	228.44	228.57	17.48	241.25	241.38	18.46
202.95	203.08	15.53	215.76	215.89	16.51	228.57	228.70	17.49	241.38	241.51	18.47
203.08	203.21	15.54	215.89	216.02	16.52	228.70	228.83	17.50	241.51	241.64	18.48
203.21	203.34	15.55	216.02	216.15	16.53	228.83	228.96	17.51	241.64	241.77	18.49
203.34	203.47	15.56	216.15	216.28	16.54	228.96	229.09	17.52	241.77	241.90	18.50
203.47	203.60	15.57	216.28	216.41	16.55	229.09	229.22	17.53	241.90	242.03	18.51
203.60	203.73	15.58	216.41	216.54	16.56	229.22	229.35	17.54	242.03	242.16	18.52
203.73	203.86	15.59	216.54	216.67	16.57	229.35	229.48	17.55	242.16	242.29	18.53
203.86	203.99	15.60	216.67	216.80	16.58	229.48	229.61	17.56	242.29	242.42	18.54
203.99	204.12	15.61	216.80	216.93	16.59	229.61	229.74	17.57	242.42	242.55	18.55
204.12	204.25	15.62	216.93	217.06	16.60	229.74	229.87	17.58	242.55	242.68	18.56
204.25	204.38	15.63	217.06	217.19	16.61	229.87	230.00	17.59	242.68	242.82	18.57
204.38	204.51	15.64	217.19	217.32	16.62	230.00	230.14	17.60	242.82	242.95	18.58
204.51	204.65	15.65	217.32	217.46	16.63	230.14	230.27	17.61	242.95	243.08	18.59
204.65	204.78	15.66	217.46	217.59	16.64	230.27	230.40	17.62	243.08	243.21	18.60
204.78	204.91	15.67	217.59	217.72	16.65	230.40	230.53	17.63	243.21	243.34	18.61
204.91	205.04	15.68	217.72	217.85	16.66	230.53	230.66	17.64	243.34	243.47	18.62
205.04	205.17	15.69	217.85	217.98	16.67	230.66	230.79	17.65	243.47	243.60	18.63
205.17	205.30	15.70	217.98	218.11	16.68	230.79	230.92	17.66	243.60	243.73	18.64
205.30	205.43	15.71	218.11	218.24	16.69	230.92	231.05	17.67	243.73	243.86	18.65
205.43	205.56	15.72	218.24	218.37	16.70	231.05	231.18	17.68	243.86	243.99	18.66
205.56	205.69	15.73	218.37	218.50	16.71	231.18	231.31	17.69	243.99	244.12	18.67
205.69	205.82	15.74	218.50	218.63	16.72	231.31	231.44	17.70	244.12	244.25	18.68
205.82	205.95	15.75	218.63	218.76	16.73	231.44	231.57	17.71	244.25	244.38	18.69
205.95	206.08	15.76	218.76	218.89	16.74	231.57	231.70	17.72	244.38	244.51	18.70
206.08	206.21	15.77	218.89	219.02	16.75	231.70	231.83	17.73	244.51	244.65	18.71
206.21	206.34	15.78	219.02	219.15	16.76	231.83	231.97	17.74	244.65	244.78	18.72
206.34	206.48	15.79	219.15	219.29	16.77	231.97	232.10	17.75	244.78	244.91	18.73
206.48	206.61	15.80	219.29	219.42	16.78	232.10	232.23	17.76	244.91	245.04	18.74
206.61	206.74	15.81	219.42	219.55	16.79	232.23	232.36	17.77	245.04	245.17	18.75
206.74	206.87	15.82	219.55	219.68	16.80	232.36	232.49	17.78	245.17	245.30	18.76
206.87	207.00	15.83	219.68	219.81	16.81	232.49	232.62	17.79	245.30	245.43	18.77
207.00	207.13	15.84	219.81	219.94	16.82	232.62	232.75	17.80	245.43	245.56	18.78
207.13	207.26	15.85	219.94	220.07	16.83	232.75	232.88	17.81	245.56	245.69	18.79
207.26	207.39	15.86	220.07	220.20	16.84	232.88	233.01	17.82	245.69	245.82	18.80
207.39	207.52	15.87	220.20	220.33	16.85	233.01	233.14	17.83	245.82	245.95	18.81
207.52	207.65	15.88	220.33	220.46	16.86	233.14	233.27	17.84	245.95	246.08	18.82
207.65	207.78	15.89	220.46	220.59	16.87	233.27	233.40	17.85	246.08	246.21	18.83
207.78	207.91	15.90	220.59	220.72	16.88	233.40	233.53	17.86	246.21	246.34	18.84
207.91	208.04	15.91	220.72	220.85	16.89	233.53	233.66	17.87	246.34	246.48	18.85
208.04	208.17	15.92	220.85	220.98	16.90	233.66	233.80	17.88	246.48	246.61	18.86
208.17	208.31	15.93	220.98	221.12	16.91	233.80	233.93	17.89	246.61	246.74	18.87
208.31	208.44	15.94	221.12	221.25	16.92	233.93	234.06	17.90	246.74	246.87	18.88
208.44	208.57	15.95	221.25	221.38	16.93	234.06	234.19	17.91	246.87	247.00	18.89
208.57	208.70	15.96	221.38	221.51	16.94	234.19	234.32	17.92	247.00	247.13	18.90
208.70	208.83	15.97	221.51	221.64	16.95	234.32	234.45	17.93	247.13	247.26	18.91
208.83	208.96	15.98	221.64	221.77	16.96	234.45	234.58	17.94	247.26	247.39	18.92
208.96	209.09	15.99	221.77	221.90	16.97	234.58	234.71	17.95	247.39	247.52	18.93
209.09	209.22	16.00	221.90	222.03	16.98	234.71	234.84	17.96	247.52	247.65	18.94
209.22	209.35	16.01	222.03	222.16	16.99	234.84	234.97	17.97	247.65	247.78	18.95
209.35	209.48	16.02	222.16	222.29	17.00	234.97	235.10	17.98	247.78	247.91	18.96
209.48	209.61	16.03	222.29	222.42	17.01	235.10	235.23	17.99	247.91	248.04	18.97
209.61	209.74	16.04	222.42	222.55	17.02	235.23	235.36	18.00	248.04	248.17	18.98
209.74	209.87	16.05	222.55	222.68	17.03	235.36	235.49	18.01	248.17	248.31	18.99
209.87	210.00	16.06	222.68	222.82	17.04	235.49	235.63	18.02	248.31	248.44	19.00
210.00	210.14	16.07	222.82	222.95	17.05	235.63	235.76	18.03	248.44	248.57	19.01
210.14	210.27	16.08	222.95	223.08	17.06	235.76	235.89	18.04	248.57	248.70	19.02
210.27	210.40	16.09	223.08	223.21	17.07	235.89	236.02	18.05	248.70	248.83	19.03
210.40	210.53	16.10	223.21	223.34	17.08	236.02	236.15	18.06	248.83	248.96	19.04
210.53	210.66	16.11	223.34	223.47	17.09	236.15	236.28	18.07	248.96	249.09	19.05
210.66	210.79	16.12	223.47	223.60	17.10	236.28	236.41	18.08	249.09	249.22	19.06
210.79	210.92	16.13	223.60	223.73	17.11	236.41	236.54	18.09	249.22	249.35	19.07
210.92	211.05	16.14	223.73	223.86	17.12	236.54	236.67	18.10	249.35	249.48	19.08
211.05	211.18	16.15	223.86	223.99	17.13	236.67	236.80	18.11	249.48	249.61	19.09
211.18	211.31	16.16	223.99	224.12	17.14	236.80	236.93	18.12	249.61	249.74	19.10
211.31	211.44	16.17	224.12	224.25	17.15	236.93	237.06	18.13	249.74	249.87	19.11
211.44	211.57	16.18	224.25	224.38	17.16	237.06	237.19	18.14	249.87	250.00	19.12
211.57	211.70	16.19	224.38	224.51	17.17	237.19	237.32	18.15	250.00	250.14	19.13
211.70	211.83	16.20	224.51	224.65	17.18	237.32	237.46	18.16	250.14	250.27	19.14
211.83	211.97	16.21	224.65	224.78	17.19	237.46	237.59	18.17	250.27	250.40	19.15
211.97	212.10	16.22	224.78	224.91	17.20	237.59	237.72	18.18	250.40	250.53	19.16
212.10	212.23	16.23	224.91	225.04	17.21	237.72	237.85	18.19	250.53	250.66	19.17
212.23	212.36	16.24	225.04	225.17	17.22	237.85	237.98	18.20	250.66	250.79	19.18
212.36	212.49	16.25	225.17	225.30	17.23	237.98	238.11	18.21	250.79	250.92	19.19
212.49	212.62	16.26	225.30	225.43	17.24	238.11	238.24	18.22	250.92	251.05	19.20
212.62	212.75	16.27	225.43	225.56	17.25	238.24	238.37	18.23	251.05	251.18	19.21

TABLE C-11 (cont.) SOCIAL SECURITY EMPLOYEE TAX TABLE

7.65% Employee Tax Deductions

Wages at least	But less than	Tax to be withheld	Wages at least	But less than	Tax to be withheld	Wages at least	But less than	Tax to be withheld	Wages at least	But less than	Tax to be withheld
251.18	251.31	19.22	263.99	264.12	20.20	276.80	276.93	21.18	289.61	289.74	22.16
251.31	251.44	19.23	264.12	264.25	20.21	276.93	277.06	21.19	289.74	289.87	22.17
251.44	251.57	19.24	264.25	264.38	20.22	277.06	277.19	21.20	289.87	290.00	22.18
251.57	251.70	19.25	264.38	264.51	20.23	277.19	277.32	21.21	290.00	290.14	22.19
251.70	251.83	19.26	264.51	264.65	20.24	277.32	277.46	21.22	290.14	290.27	22.20
251.83	251.97	19.27	264.65	264.78	20.25	277.46	277.59	21.23	290.27	290.40	22.21
251.97	252.10	19.28	264.78	264.91	20.26	277.59	277.72	21.24	290.40	290.53	22.22
252.10	252.23	19.29	264.91	265.04	20.27	277.72	277.85	21.25	290.53	290.66	22.23
252.23	252.36	19.30	265.04	265.17	20.28	277.85	277.98	21.26	290.66	290.79	22.24
252.36	252.49	19.31	265.17	265.30	20.29	277.98	278.11	21.27	290.79	290.92	22.25
252.49	252.62	19.32	265.30	265.43	20.30	278.11	278.24	21.28	290.92	291.05	22.26
252.62	252.75	19.33	265.43	265.56	20.31	278.24	278.37	21.29	291.05	291.18	22.27
252.75	252.88	19.34	265.56	265.69	20.32	278.37	278.50	21.30	291.18	291.31	22.28
252.88	253.01	19.35	265.69	265.82	20.33	278.50	278.63	21.31	291.31	291.44	22.29
253.01	253.14	19.36	265.82	265.95	20.34	278.63	278.76	21.32	291.44	291.57	22.30
253.14	253.27	19.37	265.95	266.08	20.35	278.76	278.89	21.33	291.57	291.70	22.31
253.27	253.40	19.38	266.08	266.21	20.36	278.89	279.02	21.34	291.70	291.83	22.32
253.40	253.53	19.39	266.21	266.34	20.37	279.02	279.15	21.35	291.83	291.97	22.33
253.53	253.66	19.40	266.34	266.48	20.38	279.15	279.29	21.36	291.97	292.10	22.34
253.66	253.80	19.41	266.48	266.61	20.39	279.29	279.42	21.37	292.10	292.23	22.35
253.80	253.93	19.42	266.61	266.74	20.40	279.42	279.55	21.38	292.23	292.36	22.36
253.93	254.06	19.43	266.74	266.87	20.41	279.55	279.68	21.39	292.36	292.49	22.37
254.06	254.19	19.44	266.87	267.00	20.42	279.68	279.81	21.40	292.49	292.62	22.38
254.19	254.32	19.45	267.00	267.13	20.43	279.81	279.94	21.41	292.62	292.75	22.39
254.32	254.45	19.46	267.13	267.26	20.44	279.94	280.07	21.42	292.75	292.88	22.40
254.45	254.58	19.47	267.26	267.39	20.45	280.07	280.20	21.43	292.88	293.01	22.41
254.58	254.71	19.48	267.39	267.52	20.46	280.20	280.33	21.44	293.01	293.14	22.42
254.71	254.84	19.49	267.52	267.65	20.47	280.33	280.46	21.45	293.14	293.27	22.43
254.84	254.97	19.50	267.65	267.78	20.48	280.46	280.59	21.46	293.27	293.40	22.44
254.97	255.10	19.51	267.78	267.91	20.49	280.59	280.72	21.47	293.40	293.53	22.45
255.10	255.23	19.52	267.91	268.04	20.50	280.72	280.85	21.48	293.53	293.66	22.46
255.23	255.36	19.53	268.04	268.17	20.51	280.85	280.98	21.49	293.66	293.80	22.47
255.36	255.49	19.54	268.17	268.31	20.52	280.98	281.12	21.50	293.80	293.93	22.48
255.49	255.63	19.55	268.31	268.44	20.53	281.12	281.25	21.51	293.93	294.06	22.49
255.63	255.76	19.56	268.44	268.57	20.54	281.25	281.38	21.52	294.06	294.19	22.50
255.76	255.89	19.57	268.57	268.70	20.55	281.38	281.51	21.53	294.19	294.32	22.51
255.89	256.02	19.58	268.70	268.83	20.56	281.51	281.64	21.54	294.32	294.45	22.52
256.02	256.15	19.59	268.83	268.96	20.57	281.64	281.77	21.55	294.45	294.58	22.53
256.15	256.28	19.60	268.96	269.09	20.58	281.77	281.90	21.56	294.58	294.71	22.54
256.28	256.41	19.61	269.09	269.22	20.59	281.90	282.03	21.57	294.71	294.84	22.55
256.41	256.54	19.62	269.22	269.35	20.60	282.03	282.16	21.58	294.84	294.97	22.56
256.54	256.67	19.63	269.35	269.48	20.61	282.16	282.29	21.59	294.97	295.10	22.57
256.67	256.80	19.64	269.48	269.61	20.62	282.29	282.42	21.60	295.10	295.23	22.58
256.80	256.93	19.65	269.61	269.74	20.63	282.42	282.55	21.61	295.23	295.36	22.59
256.93	257.06	19.66	269.74	269.87	20.64	282.55	282.68	21.62	295.36	295.49	22.60
257.06	257.19	19.67	269.87	270.00	20.65	282.68	282.82	21.63	295.49	295.63	22.61
257.19	257.32	19.68	270.00	270.14	20.66	282.82	282.95	21.64	295.63	295.76	22.62
257.32	257.46	19.69	270.14	270.27	20.67	282.95	283.08	21.65	295.76	295.89	22.63
257.46	257.59	19.70	270.27	270.40	20.68	283.08	283.21	21.66	295.89	296.02	22.64
257.59	257.72	19.71	270.40	270.53	20.69	283.21	283.34	21.67	296.02	296.15	22.65
257.72	257.85	19.72	270.53	270.66	20.70	283.34	283.47	21.68	296.15	296.28	22.66
257.85	257.98	19.73	270.66	270.79	20.71	283.47	283.60	21.69	296.28	296.41	22.67
257.98	258.11	19.74	270.79	270.92	20.72	283.60	283.73	21.70	296.41	296.54	22.68
258.11	258.24	19.75	270.92	271.05	20.73	283.73	283.86	21.71	296.54	296.67	22.69
258.24	258.37	19.76	271.05	271.18	20.74	283.86	283.99	21.72	296.67	296.80	22.70
258.37	258.50	19.77	271.18	271.31	20.75	283.99	284.12	21.73	296.80	296.93	22.71
258.50	258.63	19.78	271.31	271.44	20.76	284.12	284.25	21.74	296.93	297.06	22.72
258.63	258.76	19.79	271.44	271.57	20.77	284.25	284.38	21.75	297.06	297.19	22.73
258.76	258.89	19.80	271.57	271.70	20.78	284.38	284.51	21.76	297.19	297.32	22.74
258.89	259.02	19.81	271.70	271.83	20.79	284.51	284.65	21.77	297.32	297.46	22.75
259.02	259.15	19.82	271.83	271.97	20.80	284.65	284.78	21.78	297.46	297.59	22.76
259.15	259.29	19.83	271.97	272.10	20.81	284.78	284.91	21.79	297.59	297.72	22.77
259.29	259.42	19.84	272.10	272.23	20.82	284.91	285.04	21.80	297.72	297.85	22.78
259.42	259.55	19.85	272.23	272.36	20.83	285.04	285.17	21.81	297.85	297.98	22.79
259.55	259.68	19.86	272.36	272.49	20.84	285.17	285.30	21.82	297.98	298.11	22.80
259.68	259.81	19.87	272.49	272.62	20.85	285.30	285.43	21.83	298.11	298.24	22.81
259.81	259.94	19.88	272.62	272.75	20.86	285.43	285.56	21.84	298.24	298.37	22.82
259.94	260.07	19.89	272.75	272.88	20.87	285.56	285.69	21.85	298.37	298.50	22.83
260.07	260.20	19.90	272.88	273.01	20.88	285.69	285.82	21.86	298.50	298.63	22.84
260.20	260.33	19.91	273.01	273.14	20.89	285.82	285.95	21.87	298.63	298.76	22.85
260.33	260.46	19.92	273.14	273.27	20.90	285.95	286.08	21.88	298.76	298.89	22.86
260.46	260.59	19.93	273.27	273.40	20.91	286.08	286.21	21.89	298.89	299.02	22.87
260.59	260.72	19.94	273.40	273.53	20.92	286.21	286.34	21.90	299.02	299.15	22.88
260.72	260.85	19.95	273.53	273.66	20.93	286.34	286.48	21.91	299.15	299.29	22.89
260.85	260.98	19.96	273.66	273.80	20.94	286.48	286.61	21.92	299.29	299.42	22.90
260.98	261.12	19.97	273.80	273.93	20.95	286.61	286.74	21.93	299.42	299.55	22.91
261.12	261.25	19.98	273.93	274.06	20.96	286.74	286.87	21.94	299.55	299.68	22.92
261.25	261.38	19.99	274.06	274.19	20.97	286.87	287.00	21.95	299.68	299.81	22.93
261.38	261.51	20.00	274.19	274.32	20.98	287.00	287.13	21.96	299.81	299.94	22.94
261.51	261.64	20.01	274.32	274.45	20.99	287.13	287.26	21.97			
261.64	261.77	20.02	274.45	274.58	21.00	287.26	287.39	21.98			
261.77	261.90	20.03	274.58	274.71	21.01	287.39	287.52	21.99			
261.90	262.03	20.04	274.71	274.84	21.02	287.52	287.65	22.00			
262.03	262.16	20.05	274.84	274.97	21.03	287.65	287.78	22.01			
262.16	262.29	20.06	274.97	275.10	21.04	287.78	287.91	22.02			
262.29	262.42	20.07	275.10	275.23	21.05	287.91	288.04	22.03			
262.42	262.55	20.08	275.23	275.36	21.06	288.04	288.17	22.04			
262.55	262.68	20.09	275.36	275.49	21.07	288.17	288.31	22.05			
262.68	262.82	20.10	275.49	275.63	21.08	288.31	288.44	22.06			
262.82	262.95	20.11	275.63	275.76	21.09	288.44	288.57	22.07			
262.95	263.08	20.12	275.76	275.89	21.10	288.57	288.70	22.08			
263.08	263.21	20.13	275.89	276.02	21.11	288.70	288.83	22.09			
263.21	263.34	20.14	276.02	276.15	21.12	288.83	288.96	22.10			
263.34	263.47	20.15	276.15	276.28	21.13	288.96	289.09	22.11			
263.47	263.60	20.16	276.28	276.41	21.14	289.09	289.22	22.12			
263.60	263.73	20.17	276.41	276.54	21.15	289.22	289.35	22.13			
263.73	263.86	20.18	276.54	276.67	21.16	289.35	289.48	22.14			
263.86	263.99	20.19	276.67	276.80	21.17	289.48	289.61	22.15			

TABLE C-11 (cont.) SOCIAL SECURITY EMPLOYEE TAX TABLE

7.65% Employee Tax Deductions

Wages at least	But less than	Tax to be withheld	Wages at least	But less than	Tax to be withheld	Wages at least	But less than	Tax to be withheld	Wages at least	But less than	Tax to be withheld
299.94	300.07	22.95	312.75	312.88	23.93	325.56	325.69	24.91	338.37	338.50	25.89
300.07	300.20	22.96	312.88	313.01	23.94	325.69	325.82	24.92	338.50	338.63	25.90
300.20	300.33	22.97	313.01	313.14	23.95	325.82	325.95	24.93	338.63	338.76	25.91
300.33	300.46	22.98	313.14	313.27	23.96	325.95	326.08	24.94	338.76	338.89	25.92
300.46	300.59	22.99	313.27	313.40	23.97	326.08	326.21	24.95	338.89	339.02	25.93
300.59	300.72	23.00	313.40	313.53	23.98	326.21	326.34	24.96	339.02	339.15	25.94
300.72	300.85	23.01	313.53	313.66	23.99	326.34	326.48	24.97	339.15	339.29	25.95
300.85	300.98	23.02	313.66	313.80	24.00	326.48	326.61	24.98	339.29	339.42	25.96
300.98	301.12	23.03	313.80	313.93	24.01	326.61	326.74	24.99	339.42	339.55	25.97
301.12	301.25	23.04	313.93	314.06	24.02	326.74	326.87	25.00	339.55	339.68	25.98
301.25	301.38	23.05	314.06	314.19	24.03	326.87	327.00	25.01	339.68	339.81	25.99
301.38	301.51	23.06	314.19	314.32	24.04	327.00	327.13	25.02	339.81	339.94	26.00
301.51	301.64	23.07	314.32	314.45	24.05	327.13	327.26	25.03	339.94	340.07	26.01
301.64	301.77	23.08	314.45	314.58	24.06	327.26	327.39	25.04	340.07	340.20	26.02
301.77	301.90	23.09	314.58	314.71	24.07	327.39	327.52	25.05	340.20	340.33	26.03
301.90	302.03	23.10	314.71	314.84	24.08	327.52	327.65	25.06	340.33	340.46	26.04
302.03	302.16	23.11	314.84	314.97	24.09	327.65	327.78	25.07	340.46	340.59	26.05
302.16	302.29	23.12	314.97	315.10	24.10	327.78	327.91	25.08	340.59	340.72	26.06
302.29	302.42	23.13	315.10	315.23	24.11	327.91	328.04	25.09	340.72	340.85	26.07
302.42	302.55	23.14	315.23	315.36	24.12	328.04	328.17	25.10	340.85	340.98	26.08
302.55	302.68	23.15	315.36	315.49	24.13	328.17	328.31	25.11	340.98	341.12	26.09
302.68	302.82	23.16	315.49	315.63	24.14	328.31	328.44	25.12	341.12	341.25	26.10
302.82	302.95	23.17	315.63	315.76	24.15	328.44	328.57	25.13	341.25	341.38	26.11
302.95	303.08	23.18	315.76	315.89	24.16	328.57	328.70	25.14	341.38	341.51	26.12
303.08	303.21	23.19	315.89	316.02	24.17	328.70	328.83	25.15	341.51	341.64	26.13
303.21	303.34	23.20	316.02	316.15	24.18	328.83	328.96	25.16	341.64	341.77	26.14
303.34	303.47	23.21	316.15	316.28	24.19	328.96	329.09	25.17	341.77	341.90	26.15
303.47	303.60	23.22	316.28	316.41	24.20	329.09	329.22	25.18	341.90	342.03	26.16
303.60	303.73	23.23	316.41	316.54	24.21	329.22	329.35	25.19	342.03	342.16	26.17
303.73	303.86	23.24	316.54	316.67	24.22	329.35	329.48	25.20	342.16	342.29	26.18
303.86	303.99	23.25	316.67	316.80	24.23	329.48	329.61	25.21	342.29	342.42	26.19
303.99	304.12	23.26	316.80	316.93	24.24	329.61	329.74	25.22	342.42	342.55	26.20
304.12	304.25	23.27	316.93	317.06	24.25	329.74	329.87	25.23	342.55	342.68	26.21
304.25	304.38	23.28	317.06	317.19	24.26	329.87	330.00	25.24	342.68	342.82	26.22
304.38	304.51	23.29	317.19	317.32	24.27	330.00	330.14	25.25	342.82	342.95	26.23
304.51	304.65	23.30	317.32	317.46	24.28	330.14	330.27	25.26	342.95	343.08	26.24
304.65	304.78	23.31	317.46	317.59	24.29	330.27	330.40	25.27	343.08	343.21	26.25
304.78	304.91	23.32	317.59	317.72	24.30	330.40	330.53	25.28	343.21	343.34	26.26
304.91	305.04	23.33	317.72	317.85	24.31	330.53	330.66	25.29	343.34	343.47	26.27
305.04	305.17	23.34	317.85	317.98	24.32	330.66	330.79	25.30	343.47	343.60	26.28
305.17	305.30	23.35	317.98	318.11	24.33	330.79	330.92	25.31	343.60	343.73	26.29
305.30	305.43	23.36	318.11	318.24	24.34	330.92	331.05	25.32	343.73	343.86	26.30
305.43	305.56	23.37	318.24	318.37	24.35	331.05	331.18	25.33	343.86	343.99	26.31
305.56	305.69	23.38	318.37	318.50	24.36	331.18	331.31	25.34	343.99	344.12	26.32
305.69	305.82	23.39	318.50	318.63	24.37	331.31	331.44	25.35	344.12	344.25	26.33
305.82	305.95	23.40	318.63	318.76	24.38	331.44	331.57	25.36	344.25	344.38	26.34
305.95	306.08	23.41	318.76	318.89	24.39	331.57	331.70	25.37	344.38	344.51	26.35
306.08	306.21	23.42	318.89	319.02	24.40	331.70	331.83	25.38	344.51	344.65	26.36
306.21	306.34	23.43	319.02	319.15	24.41	331.83	331.97	25.39	344.65	344.78	26.37
306.34	306.48	23.44	319.15	319.29	24.42	331.97	332.10	25.40	344.78	344.91	26.38
306.48	306.61	23.45	319.29	319.42	24.43	332.10	332.23	25.41	344.91	345.04	26.39
306.61	306.74	23.46	319.42	319.55	24.44	332.23	332.36	25.42	345.04	345.17	26.40
306.74	306.87	23.47	319.55	319.68	24.45	332.36	332.49	25.43	345.17	345.30	26.41
306.87	307.00	23.48	319.68	319.81	24.46	332.49	332.62	25.44	345.30	345.43	26.42
307.00	307.13	23.49	319.81	319.94	24.47	332.62	332.75	25.45	345.43	345.56	26.43
307.13	307.26	23.50	319.94	320.07	24.48	332.75	332.88	25.46	345.56	345.69	26.44
307.26	307.39	23.51	320.07	320.20	24.49	332.88	333.01	25.47	345.69	345.82	26.45
307.39	307.52	23.52	320.20	320.33	24.50	333.01	333.14	25.48	345.82	345.95	26.46
307.52	307.65	23.53	320.33	320.46	24.51	333.14	333.27	25.49	345.95	346.08	26.47
307.65	307.78	23.54	320.46	320.59	24.52	333.27	333.40	25.50	346.08	346.21	26.48
307.78	307.91	23.55	320.59	320.72	24.53	333.40	333.53	25.51	346.21	346.34	26.49
307.91	308.04	23.56	320.72	320.85	24.54	333.53	333.66	25.52	346.34	346.48	26.50
308.04	308.17	23.57	320.85	320.98	24.55	333.66	333.80	25.53	346.48	346.61	26.51
308.17	308.31	23.58	320.98	321.12	24.56	333.80	333.93	25.54	346.61	346.74	26.52
308.31	308.44	23.59	321.12	321.25	24.57	333.93	334.06	25.55	346.74	346.87	26.53
308.44	308.57	23.60	321.25	321.38	24.58	334.06	334.19	25.56	346.87	347.00	26.54
308.57	308.70	23.61	321.38	321.51	24.59	334.19	334.32	25.57	347.00	347.13	26.55
308.70	308.83	23.62	321.51	321.64	24.60	334.32	334.45	25.58	347.13	347.26	26.56
308.83	308.96	23.63	321.64	321.77	24.61	334.45	334.58	25.59	347.26	347.39	26.57
308.96	309.09	23.64	321.77	321.90	24.62	334.58	334.71	25.60	347.39	347.52	26.58
309.09	309.22	23.65	321.90	322.03	24.63	334.71	334.84	25.61	347.52	347.65	26.59
309.22	309.35	23.66	322.03	322.16	24.64	334.84	334.97	25.62	347.65	347.78	26.60
309.35	309.48	23.67	322.16	322.29	24.65	334.97	335.10	25.63	347.78	347.91	26.61
309.48	309.61	23.68	322.29	322.42	24.66	335.10	335.23	25.64	347.91	348.04	26.62
309.61	309.74	23.69	322.42	322.55	24.67	335.23	335.36	25.65	348.04	348.17	26.63
309.74	309.87	23.70	322.55	322.68	24.68	335.36	335.49	25.66	348.17	348.31	26.64
309.87	310.00	23.71	322.68	322.82	24.69	335.49	335.63	25.67	348.31	348.44	26.65
310.00	310.14	23.72	322.82	322.95	24.70	335.63	335.76	25.68	348.44	348.57	26.66
310.14	310.27	23.73	322.95	323.08	24.71	335.76	335.89	25.69	348.57	348.70	26.67
310.27	310.40	23.74	323.08	323.21	24.72	335.89	336.02	25.70	348.70	348.83	26.68
310.40	310.53	23.75	323.21	323.34	24.73	336.02	336.15	25.71	348.83	348.96	26.69
310.53	310.66	23.76	323.34	323.47	24.74	336.15	336.28	25.72	348.96	349.09	26.70
310.66	310.79	23.77	323.47	323.60	24.75	336.28	336.41	25.73	349.09	349.22	26.71
310.79	310.92	23.78	323.60	323.73	24.76	336.41	336.54	25.74	349.22	349.35	26.72
310.92	311.05	23.79	323.73	323.86	24.77	336.54	336.67	25.75	349.35	349.48	26.73
311.05	311.18	23.80	323.86	323.99	24.78	336.67	336.80	25.76	349.48	349.61	26.74
311.18	311.31	23.81	323.99	324.12	24.79	336.80	336.93	25.77	349.61	349.74	26.75
311.31	311.44	23.82	324.12	324.25	24.80	336.93	337.06	25.78	349.74	349.87	26.76
311.44	311.57	23.83	324.25	324.38	24.81	337.06	337.19	25.79	349.87	350.00	26.77
311.57	311.70	23.84	324.38	324.51	24.82	337.19	337.32	25.80	350.00	350.14	26.78
311.70	311.83	23.85	324.51	324.65	24.83	337.32	337.46	25.81	350.14	350.27	26.79
311.83	311.97	23.86	324.65	324.78	24.84	337.46	337.59	25.82	350.27	350.40	26.80
311.97	312.10	23.87	324.78	324.91	24.85	337.59	337.72	25.83	350.40	350.53	26.81
312.10	312.23	23.88	324.91	325.04	24.86	337.72	337.85	25.84	350.53	350.66	26.82
312.23	312.36	23.89	325.04	325.17	24.87	337.85	337.98	25.85	350.66	350.79	26.83
312.36	312.49	23.90	325.17	325.30	24.88	337.98	338.11	25.86	350.79	350.92	26.84
312.49	312.62	23.91	325.30	325.43	24.89	338.11	338.24	25.87	350.92	351.05	26.85
312.62	312.75	23.92	325.43	325.56	24.90	338.24	338.37	25.88	351.05	351.18	26.86

TABLE C-11 (cont.)   SOCIAL SECURITY EMPLOYEE TAX TABLE

7.65% Employee Tax Deductions

Wages at least	But less than	Tax to be withheld	Wages at least	But less than	Tax to be withheld	Wages at least	But less than	Tax to be withheld	Wages at least	But less than	Tax to be withheld
351.18	351.31	26.87	363.99	364.12	27.85	376.80	376.93	28.83	389.61	389.74	29.81
351.31	351.44	26.88	364.12	364.25	27.86	376.93	377.06	28.84	389.74	389.87	29.82
351.44	351.57	26.89	364.25	364.38	27.87	377.06	377.19	28.85	389.87	390.00	29.83
351.57	351.70	26.90	364.38	364.51	27.88	377.19	377.32	28.86	390.00	390.14	29.84
351.70	351.83	26.91	364.51	364.65	27.89	377.32	377.46	28.87	390.14	390.27	29.85
351.83	351.97	26.92	364.65	364.78	27.90	377.46	377.59	28.88	390.27	390.40	29.86
351.97	352.10	26.93	364.78	364.91	27.91	377.59	377.72	28.89	390.40	390.53	29.87
352.10	352.23	26.94	364.91	365.04	27.92	377.72	377.85	28.90	390.53	390.66	29.88
352.23	352.36	26.95	365.04	365.17	27.93	377.85	377.98	28.91	390.66	390.79	29.89
352.36	352.49	26.96	365.17	365.30	27.94	377.98	378.11	28.92	390.79	390.92	29.90
352.49	352.62	26.97	365.30	365.43	27.95	378.11	378.24	28.93	390.92	391.05	29.91
352.62	352.75	26.98	365.43	365.56	27.96	378.24	378.37	28.94	391.05	391.18	29.92
352.75	352.88	26.99	365.56	365.69	27.97	378.37	378.50	28.95	391.18	391.31	29.93
352.88	353.01	27.00	365.69	365.82	27.98	378.50	378.63	28.96	391.31	391.44	29.94
353.01	353.14	27.01	365.82	365.95	27.99	378.63	378.76	28.97	391.44	391.57	29.95
353.14	353.27	27.02	365.95	366.08	28.00	378.76	378.89	28.98	391.57	391.70	29.96
353.27	353.40	27.03	366.08	366.21	28.01	378.89	379.02	28.99	391.70	391.83	29.97
353.40	353.53	27.04	366.21	366.34	28.02	379.02	379.15	29.00	391.83	391.97	29.98
353.53	353.66	27.05	366.34	366.48	28.03	379.15	379.29	29.01	391.97	392.10	29.99
353.66	353.80	27.06	366.48	366.61	28.04	379.29	379.42	29.02	392.10	392.23	30.00
353.80	353.93	27.07	366.61	366.74	28.05	379.42	379.55	29.03	392.23	392.36	30.01
353.93	354.06	27.08	366.74	366.87	28.06	379.55	379.68	29.04	392.36	392.49	30.02
354.06	354.19	27.09	366.87	367.00	28.07	379.68	379.81	29.05	392.49	392.62	30.03
354.19	354.32	27.10	367.00	367.13	28.08	379.81	379.94	29.06	392.62	392.75	30.04
354.32	354.45	27.11	367.13	367.26	28.09	379.94	380.07	29.07	392.75	392.88	30.05
354.45	354.58	27.12	367.26	367.39	28.10	380.07	380.20	29.08	392.88	393.01	30.06
354.58	354.71	27.13	367.39	367.52	28.11	380.20	380.33	29.09	393.01	393.14	30.07
354.71	354.84	27.14	367.52	367.65	28.12	380.33	380.46	29.10	393.14	393.27	30.08
354.84	354.97	27.15	367.65	367.78	28.13	380.46	380.59	29.11	393.27	393.40	30.09
354.97	355.10	27.16	367.78	367.91	28.14	380.59	380.72	29.12	393.40	393.53	30.10
355.10	355.23	27.17	367.91	368.04	28.15	380.72	380.85	29.13	393.53	393.66	30.11
355.23	355.36	27.18	368.04	368.17	28.16	380.85	380.98	29.14	393.66	393.80	30.12
355.36	355.49	27.19	368.17	368.31	28.17	380.98	381.12	29.15	393.80	393.93	30.13
355.49	355.63	27.20	368.31	368.44	28.18	381.12	381.25	29.16	393.93	394.06	30.14
355.63	355.76	27.21	368.44	368.57	28.19	381.25	381.38	29.17	394.06	394.19	30.15
355.76	355.89	27.22	368.57	368.70	28.20	381.38	381.51	29.18	394.19	394.32	30.16
355.89	356.02	27.23	368.70	368.83	28.21	381.51	381.64	29.19	394.32	394.45	30.17
356.02	356.15	27.24	368.83	368.96	28.22	381.64	381.77	29.20	394.45	394.58	30.18
356.15	356.28	27.25	368.96	369.09	28.23	381.77	381.90	29.21	394.58	394.71	30.19
356.28	356.41	27.26	369.09	369.22	28.24	381.90	382.03	29.22	394.71	394.84	30.20
356.41	356.54	27.27	369.22	369.35	28.25	382.03	382.16	29.23	394.84	394.97	30.21
356.54	356.67	27.28	369.35	369.48	28.26	382.16	382.29	29.24	394.97	395.10	30.22
356.67	356.80	27.29	369.48	369.61	28.27	382.29	382.42	29.25	395.10	395.23	30.23
356.80	356.93	27.30	369.61	369.74	28.28	382.42	382.55	29.26	395.23	395.36	30.24
356.93	357.06	27.31	369.74	369.87	28.29	382.55	382.68	29.27	395.36	395.49	30.25
357.06	357.19	27.32	369.87	370.00	28.30	382.68	382.82	29.28	395.49	395.63	30.26
357.19	357.32	27.33	370.00	370.14	28.31	382.82	382.95	29.29	395.63	395.76	30.27
357.32	357.46	27.34	370.14	370.27	28.32	382.95	383.08	29.30	395.76	395.89	30.28
357.46	357.59	27.35	370.27	370.40	28.33	383.08	383.21	29.31	395.89	396.02	30.29
357.59	357.72	27.36	370.40	370.53	28.34	383.21	383.34	29.32	396.02	396.15	30.30
357.72	357.85	27.37	370.53	370.66	28.35	383.34	383.47	29.33	396.15	396.28	30.31
357.85	357.98	27.38	370.66	370.79	28.36	383.47	383.60	29.34	396.28	396.41	30.32
357.98	358.11	27.39	370.79	370.92	28.37	383.60	383.73	29.35	396.41	396.54	30.33
358.11	358.24	27.40	370.92	371.05	28.38	383.73	383.86	29.36	396.54	396.67	30.34
358.24	358.37	27.41	371.05	371.18	28.39	383.86	383.99	29.37	396.67	396.80	30.35
358.37	358.50	27.42	371.18	371.31	28.40	383.99	384.12	29.38	396.80	396.93	30.36
358.50	358.63	27.43	371.31	371.44	28.41	384.12	384.25	29.39	396.93	397.06	30.37
358.63	358.76	27.44	371.44	371.57	28.42	384.25	384.38	29.40	397.06	397.19	30.38
358.76	358.89	27.45	371.57	371.70	28.43	384.38	384.51	29.41	397.19	397.32	30.39
358.89	359.02	27.46	371.70	371.83	28.44	384.51	384.65	29.42	397.32	397.46	30.40
359.02	359.15	27.47	371.83	371.97	28.45	384.65	384.78	29.43	397.46	397.59	30.41
359.15	359.29	27.48	371.97	372.10	28.46	384.78	384.91	29.44	397.59	397.72	30.42
359.29	359.42	27.49	372.10	372.23	28.47	384.91	385.04	29.45	397.72	397.85	30.43
359.42	359.55	27.50	372.23	372.36	28.48	385.04	385.17	29.46	397.85	397.98	30.44
359.55	359.68	27.51	372.36	372.49	28.49	385.17	385.30	29.47	397.98	398.11	30.45
359.68	359.81	27.52	372.49	372.62	28.50	385.30	385.43	29.48	398.11	398.24	30.46
359.81	359.94	27.53	372.62	372.75	28.51	385.43	385.56	29.49	398.24	398.37	30.47
359.94	360.07	27.54	372.75	372.88	28.52	385.56	385.69	29.50	398.37	398.50	30.48
360.07	360.20	27.55	372.88	373.01	28.53	385.69	385.82	29.51	398.50	398.63	30.49
360.20	360.33	27.56	373.01	373.14	28.54	385.82	385.95	29.52	398.63	398.76	30.50
360.33	360.46	27.57	373.14	373.27	28.55	385.95	386.08	29.53	398.76	398.89	30.51
360.46	360.59	27.58	373.27	373.40	28.56	386.08	386.21	29.54	398.89	399.02	30.52
360.59	360.72	27.59	373.40	373.53	28.57	386.21	386.34	29.55	399.02	399.15	30.53
360.72	360.85	27.60	373.53	373.66	28.58	386.34	386.48	29.56	399.15	399.29	30.54
360.85	360.98	27.61	373.66	373.80	28.59	386.48	386.61	29.57	399.29	399.42	30.55
360.98	361.12	27.62	373.80	373.93	28.60	386.61	386.74	29.58	399.42	399.55	30.56
361.12	361.25	27.63	373.93	374.06	28.61	386.74	386.87	29.59	399.55	399.68	30.57
361.25	361.38	27.64	374.06	374.19	28.62	386.87	387.00	29.60	399.68	399.81	30.58
361.38	361.51	27.65	374.19	374.32	28.63	387.00	387.13	29.61	399.81	399.94	30.59
361.51	361.64	27.66	374.32	374.45	28.64	387.13	387.26	29.62	399.94	400.07	30.60
361.64	361.77	27.67	374.45	374.58	28.65	387.26	387.39	29.63	400.07	400.20	30.61
361.77	361.90	27.68	374.58	374.71	28.66	387.39	387.52	29.64	400.20	400.33	30.62
361.90	362.03	27.69	374.71	374.84	28.67	387.52	387.65	29.65	400.33	400.46	30.63
362.03	362.16	27.70	374.84	374.97	28.68	387.65	387.78	29.66	400.46	400.59	30.64
362.16	362.29	27.71	374.97	375.10	28.69	387.78	387.91	29.67	400.59	400.72	30.65
362.29	362.42	27.72	375.10	375.23	28.70	387.91	388.04	29.68	400.72	400.85	30.66
362.42	362.55	27.73	375.23	375.36	28.71	388.04	388.17	29.69	400.85	400.98	30.67
362.55	362.68	27.74	375.36	375.49	28.72	388.17	388.31	29.70	400.98	401.12	30.68
362.68	362.82	27.75	375.49	375.63	28.73	388.31	388.44	29.71	401.12	401.25	30.69
362.82	362.95	27.76	375.63	375.76	28.74	388.44	388.57	29.72	401.25	401.38	30.70
362.95	363.08	27.77	375.76	375.89	28.75	388.57	388.70	29.73	401.38	401.51	30.71
363.08	363.21	27.78	375.89	376.02	28.76	388.70	388.83	29.74	401.51	401.64	30.72
363.21	363.34	27.79	376.02	376.15	28.77	388.83	388.96	29.75	401.64	401.77	30.73
363.34	363.47	27.80	376.15	376.28	28.78	388.96	389.09	29.76	401.77	401.90	30.74
363.47	363.60	27.81	376.28	376.41	28.79	389.09	389.22	29.77	401.90	402.03	30.75
363.60	363.73	27.82	376.41	376.54	28.80	389.22	389.35	29.78	402.03	402.16	30.76
363.73	363.86	27.83	376.54	376.67	28.81	389.35	389.48	29.79	402.16	402.29	30.77
363.86	363.99	27.84	376.67	376.80	28.82	389.48	389.61	29.80	402.29	402.42	30.78

TABLE C-12   FEDERAL INCOME TAX WITHHOLDING TABLE—SINGLE PERSONS

Weekly Payroll Period

If the wages are—		And the number of withholding allowances claimed is—										
At least	But less than	0	1	2	3	4	5	6	7	8	9	10
		The amount of income tax to be withheld is—										
150	155	15	8	1	0	0	0	0	0	0	0	0
155	160	16	9	2	0	0	0	0	0	0	0	0
160	165	17	10	2	0	0	0	0	0	0	0	0
165	170	18	10	3	0	0	0	0	0	0	0	0
170	175	18	11	4	0	0	0	0	0	0	0	0
175	180	19	12	5	0	0	0	0	0	0	0	0
180	185	20	13	5	0	0	0	0	0	0	0	0
185	190	21	13	6	0	0	0	0	0	0	0	0
190	195	21	14	7	0	0	0	0	0	0	0	0
195	200	22	15	8	0	0	0	0	0	0	0	0
200	210	23	16	9	2	0	0	0	0	0	0	0
210	220	25	18	10	3	0	0	0	0	0	0	0
220	230	26	19	12	5	0	0	0	0	0	0	0
230	240	28	21	13	6	0	0	0	0	0	0	0
240	250	29	22	15	8	0	0	0	0	0	0	0
250	260	31	24	16	9	2	0	0	0	0	0	0
260	270	32	25	18	11	3	0	0	0	0	0	0
270	280	34	27	19	12	5	0	0	0	0	0	0
280	290	35	28	21	14	6	0	0	0	0	0	0
290	300	37	30	22	15	8	1	0	0	0	0	0
300	310	38	31	24	17	9	2	0	0	0	0	0
310	320	40	33	25	18	11	4	0	0	0	0	0
320	330	41	34	27	20	12	5	0	0	0	0	0
330	340	43	36	28	21	14	7	0	0	0	0	0
340	350	44	37	30	23	15	8	1	0	0	0	0
350	360	46	39	31	24	17	10	2	0	0	0	0
360	370	47	40	33	26	18	11	4	0	0	0	0
370	380	49	42	34	27	20	13	5	0	0	0	0
380	390	50	43	36	29	21	14	7	0	0	0	0
390	400	52	45	37	30	23	16	8	1	0	0	0
400	410	53	46	39	32	24	17	10	3	0	0	0
410	420	55	48	40	33	26	19	11	4	0	0	0
420	430	56	49	42	35	27	20	13	6	0	0	0
430	440	58	51	43	36	29	22	14	7	0	0	0
440	450	59	52	45	38	30	23	16	9	2	0	0
450	460	61	54	46	39	32	25	17	10	3	0	0
460	470	62	55	48	41	33	26	19	12	5	0	0
470	480	64	57	49	42	35	28	20	13	6	0	0
480	490	66	58	51	44	36	29	22	15	8	0	0
490	500	69	60	52	45	38	31	23	16	9	2	0
500	510	72	61	54	47	39	32	25	18	11	3	0
510	520	75	63	55	48	41	34	26	10	12	5	0
520	530	78	64	57	50	42	35	28	21	14	6	0
530	540	80	67	58	51	44	37	29	22	15	8	1
540	550	83	70	60	53	45	38	31	24	17	9	2
550	560	86	73	61	54	47	40	32	25	18	11	4
560	570	89	75	63	56	48	41	34	27	20	12	5
570	580	92	78	65	57	50	43	35	28	21	14	7
580	590	94	81	68	59	51	44	37	30	23	15	8
590	600	97	84	70	60	53	46	38	31	24	17	10
600	610	100	87	73	62	54	47	40	33	26	18	11
610	620	103	89	76	63	56	49	41	34	27	20	13
620	630	106	92	79	65	57	50	43	36	29	21	14
630	640	108	95	82	68	59	52	44	37	30	23	16
640	650	111	98	84	71	60	53	46	39	32	24	17
650	660	114	101	87	74	62	55	47	40	33	26	19
660	670	117	103	90	76	63	56	49	42	35	27	20
670	680	120	106	93	79	66	58	50	43	36	29	22
680	690	122	109	96	82	69	59	52	45	38	30	23
690	700	125	112	98	85	71	61	53	46	39	32	25
700	710	128	115	101	88	74	62	55	48	41	33	26
710	720	131	117	104	90	77	64	56	49	42	35	28
720	730	134	120	107	93	80	66	58	51	44	36	29
730	740	136	123	110	96	83	69	59	52	45	38	31
740	750	139	126	112	99	85	72	61	54	47	39	32
750	760	142	129	115	102	88	75	62	55	48	41	34
760	770	145	131	118	104	91	78	64	57	50	42	35
770	780	148	134	121	107	94	80	67	58	51	44	37
780	790	150	137	124	110	97	83	70	60	53	45	38
790	800	153	140	126	113	99	86	72	61	54	47	40

TABLE C-12 (cont.) FEDERAL INCOME TAX WITHHOLDING TABLE— MARRIED PERSONS

Weekly Payroll Period

If the wages are—		And the number of withholding allowances claimed is—										
At least	But less than	0	1	2	3	4	5	6	7	8	9	10
		The amount of income tax to be withheld is—										
145	150	4	0	0	0	0	0	0	0	0	0	0
150	155	4	0	0	0	0	0	0	0	0	0	0
155	160	5	0	0	0	0	0	0	0	0	0	0
160	165	6	0	0	0	0	0	0	0	0	0	0
165	170	7	0	0	0	0	0	0	0	0	0	0
170	175	7	0	0	0	0	0	0	0	0	0	0
175	180	8	1	0	0	0	0	0	0	0	0	0
180	185	9	2	0	0	0	0	0	0	0	0	0
185	190	10	2	0	0	0	0	0	0	0	0	0
190	195	10	3	0	0	0	0	0	0	0	0	0
195	200	11	4	0	0	0	0	0	0	0	0	0
200	210	12	5	0	0	0	0	0	0	0	0	0
210	220	14	7	0	0	0	0	0	0	0	0	0
220	230	15	8	1	0	0	0	0	0	0	0	0
230	240	17	10	2	0	0	0	0	0	0	0	0
240	250	18	11	4	0	0	0	0	0	0	0	0
250	260	20	13	5	0	0	0	0	0	0	0	0
260	270	21	14	7	0	0	0	0	0	0	0	0
270	280	23	16	8	1	0	0	0	0	0	0	0
280	290	24	17	10	3	0	0	0	0	0	0	0
290	300	26	19	11	4	0	0	0	0	0	0	0
300	310	27	20	13	6	0	0	0	0	0	0	0
310	320	29	22	14	7	0	0	0	0	0	0	0
320	330	30	23	16	9	1	0	0	0	0	0	0
330	340	32	25	17	10	3	0	0	0	0	0	0
340	350	33	26	19	12	4	0	0	0	0	0	0
350	360	35	28	20	13	6	0	0	0	0	0	0
360	370	36	29	22	15	7	0	0	0	0	0	0
370	380	38	31	23	16	9	2	0	0	0	0	0
380	390	39	32	25	18	10	3	0	0	0	0	0
390	400	41	34	26	19	12	5	0	0	0	0	0
400	410	42	35	28	21	13	6	0	0	0	0	0
410	420	44	37	29	22	15	8	1	0	0	0	0
420	430	45	38	31	24	16	9	2	0	0	0	0
430	440	47	40	32	25	18	11	4	0	0	0	0
440	450	48	41	34	27	19	12	5	0	0	0	0
450	460	50	43	35	28	21	14	7	0	0	0	0
460	470	51	44	37	30	22	15	8	1	0	0	0
470	480	53	46	38	31	24	17	10	2	0	0	0
480	490	54	47	40	33	25	18	11	4	0	0	0
490	500	56	49	41	34	27	20	13	5	0	0	0
500	510	57	50	43	36	28	21	14	7	0	0	0
510	520	59	52	44	37	30	23	16	8	1	0	0
520	530	60	53	46	39	31	24	17	10	3	0	0
530	540	62	55	47	40	33	26	19	11	4	0	0
540	550	63	56	49	42	34	27	20	13	6	0	0
550	560	65	58	50	43	36	29	22	14	7	0	0
560	570	66	59	52	45	37	30	23	16	9	1	0
570	580	68	61	53	46	39	32	25	17	10	3	0
580	590	69	62	55	48	40	33	26	19	12	4	0
590	600	71	64	56	49	42	35	28	20	13	6	0
600	610	72	65	58	51	43	36	29	22	15	7	0
610	620	74	67	59	52	45	38	31	23	16	9	2
620	630	75	68	61	54	46	39	32	25	18	10	3
630	640	77	70	62	55	48	41	34	26	19	12	5
640	650	78	71	64	57	49	42	35	28	21	13	6
650	660	80	73	65	58	51	44	37	29	22	15	8
660	670	81	74	67	60	52	45	38	31	24	16	9
670	680	83	76	68	61	54	47	40	32	25	18	11
680	690	84	77	70	63	55	48	41	34	27	19	12
690	700	86	79	71	64	57	50	43	35	28	21	14
700	710	87	80	73	66	58	51	44	37	30	22	15
710	720	89	82	74	67	60	53	46	38	31	24	17
720	730	90	83	76	69	61	54	47	40	33	25	18
730	740	92	85	77	70	63	56	49	41	34	27	20
740	750	93	86	79	72	64	57	50	43	36	28	21
750	760	95	88	80	73	66	59	52	44	37	30	23
760	770	96	89	82	75	67	60	53	46	39	31	24
770	780	98	91	83	76	69	62	55	47	40	33	26
780	790	99	92	85	78	70	63	56	49	42	34	27
790	800	101	94	86	79	72	65	58	50	43	36	29
800	810	102	95	88	81	73	66	59	52	45	37	30

TABLE C-13 MACRS COST RECOVERY FACTORS

For Property Placed into Service in 1987 and Thereafter

RECOVERY YEAR	3-YR. CLASS	5-YR. CLASS	7-YR. CLASS	10-YR. CLASS
1	0.333333	0.200000	0.142857	0.100000
2	0.444444	0.320000	0.244898	0.180000
3	0.148148	0.192000	0.174927	0.144000
4	0.074074	0.115200	0.124948	0.115200
5	—	0.115200	0.089249	0.092160
6	—	0.057600	0.089249	0.073728
7	—	—	0.089249	0.065536
8	—	—	0.044624	0.065536
9	—	—	—	0.065536
10	—	—	—	0.065536
	—	—	—	0.032768

RECOVERY YEAR(S)	15-YR. CLASS	20-YR. CLASS	27.5-YR. REAL ESTATE	31.5-YR. REAL ESTATE
1	0.050000	0.037500	0.034848	0.030423
2	0.095000	0.072188	0.036364	0.031746
3	0.085500	0.066773	0.036364	0.031746
4	0.076950	0.061765	0.036364	0.031746
5	0.069255	0.057133	0.036364	0.031746
6	0.062330	0.052848	0.036364	0.031746
7	0.059049	0.048884	0.036364	0.031746
8	0.059049	0.045218	0.036364	0.031746
9–15	0.059049	0.044615	0.036364	0.031746
16	0.029525	0.044615	0.036364	0.031746
17–20	—	0.044615	0.036364	0.031746
21	—	0.022308	0.036364	0.031746
22–27	—	—	0.036364	0.031746
28	—	—	0.019697	0.031746
29–31	—	—	—	0.031746
32	—	—	—	0.017196

TABLE C-14   THE NUMBER OF EACH DAY OF THE YEAR*

DAY OF MONTH	JAN.	FEB.	MAR.	APR.	MAY	JUNE	JULY	AUG.	SEPT.	OCT.	NOV.	DEC.	DAY OF MONTH
1	1	32	60	91	121	152	182	213	244	274	305	335	1
2	2	33	61	92	122	153	183	214	245	275	306	336	2
3	3	34	62	93	123	154	184	215	246	276	307	337	3
4	4	35	63	94	124	155	185	216	247	277	308	338	4
5	5	36	64	95	125	156	186	217	248	278	309	339	5
6	6	37	65	96	126	157	187	218	249	279	310	340	6
7	7	38	66	97	127	158	188	219	250	280	311	341	7
8	8	39	67	98	128	159	189	220	251	281	312	342	8
9	9	40	68	99	129	160	190	221	252	282	313	343	9
10	10	41	69	100	130	161	191	222	253	283	314	344	10
11	11	42	70	101	131	162	192	223	254	284	315	345	11
12	12	43	71	102	132	163	193	224	255	285	316	346	12
13	13	44	72	103	133	164	194	225	256	286	317	347	13
14	14	45	73	104	134	165	195	226	257	287	318	348	14
15	15	46	74	105	135	166	196	227	258	288	319	349	15
16	16	47	75	106	136	167	197	228	259	289	320	350	16
17	17	48	76	107	137	168	198	229	260	290	321	351	17
18	18	49	77	108	138	169	199	230	261	291	322	352	18
19	19	50	78	109	139	170	200	231	262	292	323	353	19
20	20	51	79	110	140	171	201	232	263	293	324	354	20
21	21	52	80	111	141	172	202	233	264	294	325	355	21
22	22	53	81	112	142	173	203	234	265	295	326	356	22
23	23	54	82	113	143	174	204	235	266	296	327	357	23
24	24	55	83	114	144	175	205	236	267	297	328	358	24
25	25	56	84	115	145	176	206	237	268	298	329	359	25
26	26	57	85	116	146	177	207	238	269	299	330	360	26
27	27	58	86	117	147	178	208	239	270	300	331	361	27
28	28	59	87	118	148	179	209	240	271	301	332	362	28
29	29		88	119	149	180	210	241	272	302	333	363	29
30	30		89	120	150	181	211	242	273	303	334	364	30
31	31		90		151		212	243		304		365	31

* In leap years, after February 28, add 1 to the tabular number.

TABLE C-15 ANNUAL PERCENTAGE RATE TABLE FOR MONTHLY PAYMENT PLANS

Number of Payments	ANNUAL PERCENTAGE RATE															
	10.00%	10.25%	10.50%	10.75%	11.00%	11.25%	11.50%	11.75%	12.00%	12.25%	12.50%	12.75%	13.00%	13.25%	13.50%	13.75%
	Finance charge per $100 of amount financed															
1	0.83	0.85	0.87	0.90	0.92	0.94	0.96	0.98	1.00	1.02	1.04	1.06	1.08	1.10	1.12	1.15
2	1.25	1.28	1.31	1.35	1.38	1.41	1.44	1.47	1.50	1.53	1.57	1.60	1.63	1.66	1.69	1.73
3	1.67	1.71	1.76	1.80	1.84	1.88	1.92	1.96	2.01	2.05	2.09	2.13	2.17	2.22	2.26	2.30
4	2.09	2.14	2.20	2.25	2.30	2.35	2.41	2.46	2.51	2.57	2.62	2.67	2.72	2.78	2.83	2.88
5	2.51	2.58	2.64	2.70	2.77	2.83	2.89	2.96	3.02	3.08	3.15	3.21	3.27	3.34	3.40	3.46
6	2.94	3.01	3.08	3.16	3.23	3.31	3.38	3.45	3.53	3.60	3.68	3.75	3.83	3.90	3.97	4.05
7	3.36	3.45	3.53	3.62	3.70	3.78	3.87	3.95	4.04	4.12	4.21	4.29	4.38	4.47	4.55	4.64
8	3.79	3.88	3.98	4.07	4.17	4.26	4.36	4.46	4.55	4.65	4.74	4.84	4.94	5.03	5.13	5.22
9	4.21	4.32	4.43	4.53	4.64	4.75	4.85	4.96	5.07	5.17	5.28	5.39	5.49	5.60	5.71	5.82
10	4.64	4.76	4.88	4.99	5.11	5.23	5.35	5.46	5.58	5.70	5.82	5.94	6.05	6.17	6.29	6.41
11	5.07	5.20	5.33	5.45	5.58	5.71	5.84	5.97	6.10	6.23	6.36	6.49	6.62	6.75	6.88	7.01
12	5.50	5.64	5.78	5.92	6.06	6.20	6.34	6.48	6.62	6.76	6.90	7.04	7.18	7.32	7.46	7.60
13	5.93	6.08	6.23	6.38	6.53	6.68	6.84	6.99	7.14	7.29	7.44	7.59	7.75	7.90	8.05	8.20
14	6.36	6.52	6.69	6.85	7.01	7.17	7.34	7.50	7.66	7.82	7.99	8.15	8.31	8.48	8.64	8.81
15	6.80	6.97	7.14	7.32	7.49	7.66	7.84	8.01	8.19	8.36	8.53	8.71	8.88	9.06	9.23	9.41
16	7.23	7.41	7.60	7.78	7.97	8.15	8.34	8.53	8.71	8.90	9.08	9.27	9.46	9.64	9.83	10.02
17	7.67	7.86	8.06	8.25	8.45	8.65	8.84	9.04	9.24	9.44	9.63	9.83	10.03	10.23	10.43	10.63
18	8.10	8.31	8.52	8.75	8.93	9.14	9.35	9.56	9.77	9.98	10.19	10.40	10.61	10.82	11.03	11.24
19	8.54	8.76	8.98	9.20	9.42	9.64	9.86	10.08	10.30	10.52	10.74	10.96	11.18	11.41	11.63	11.85
20	8.98	9.21	9.44	9.67	9.90	10.13	10.37	10.60	10.83	11.06	11.30	11.53	11.76	12.00	12.23	12.46
21	9.42	9.66	9.90	10.15	10.39	10.63	10.88	11.12	11.36	11.61	11.85	12.10	12.34	12.59	12.84	13.08
22	9.86	10.12	10.37	10.62	10.88	11.13	11.39	11.64	11.90	12.16	12.41	12.67	12.93	13.19	13.44	13.70
23	10.30	10.57	10.84	11.10	11.37	11.63	11.90	12.17	12.44	12.71	12.97	13.24	13.51	13.78	14.05	14.32
24	10.75	11.02	11.30	11.58	11.86	12.14	12.42	12.70	12.98	13.26	13.54	13.82	14.10	14.38	14.66	14.95
25	11.19	11.48	11.77	12.06	12.35	12.64	12.93	13.22	13.52	13.81	14.10	14.40	14.69	14.98	15.28	15.57
26	11.64	11.94	12.24	12.54	12.85	13.15	13.45	13.75	14.06	14.36	14.67	14.97	15.28	15.59	15.89	16.20
27	12.09	12.40	12.71	13.03	13.34	13.66	13.97	14.29	14.60	14.92	15.24	15.56	15.87	16.19	16.51	16.83
28	12.53	12.86	13.18	13.51	13.84	14.16	14.49	14.82	15.15	15.48	15.81	16.14	16.47	16.80	17.13	17.46
29	12.98	13.32	13.66	14.00	14.33	14.67	15.01	15.35	15.70	16.04	16.38	16.72	17.07	17.41	17.75	18.10
30	13.43	13.78	14.13	14.48	14.83	15.19	15.54	15.89	16.24	16.60	16.95	17.31	17.66	18.02	18.38	18.74
31	13.89	14.25	14.61	14.97	15.33	15.70	16.06	16.43	16.79	17.16	17.53	17.90	18.27	18.63	19.00	19.38
32	14.34	14.71	15.09	15.46	15.84	16.21	16.59	16.97	17.35	17.73	18.11	18.49	18.87	19.25	19.63	20.02
33	14.79	15.18	15.57	15.95	16.34	16.73	17.12	17.51	17.90	18.29	18.65	19.08	19.47	19.87	20.26	20.66
34	15.25	15.65	16.05	16.44	16.85	17.25	17.65	18.05	18.46	18.86	19.27	19.67	20.08	20.49	20.90	21.31
35	15.70	16.11	16.53	16.94	17.35	17.77	18.18	18.60	19.01	19.43	19.85	20.27	20.69	21.11	21.53	21.95
36	16.16	16.58	17.01	17.43	17.86	18.29	18.71	19.14	19.57	20.00	20.43	20.87	21.30	21.73	22.17	22.60
37	16.62	17.06	17.49	17.93	18.37	18.81	19.25	19.69	20.13	20.58	21.02	21.46	21.91	22.36	22.81	23.25
38	17.08	17.53	17.98	18.43	18.88	19.33	19.78	20.24	20.69	21.15	21.61	22.07	22.52	22.99	23.45	23.91
39	17.54	18.00	18.46	18.93	19.39	19.86	20.32	20.79	21.26	21.73	22.20	22.67	23.14	23.61	24.09	24.56
40	18.00	18.48	18.95	19.43	19.90	20.38	20.86	21.34	21.82	22.30	22.79	23.27	23.76	24.25	24.73	25.22
41	18.47	18.95	19.44	19.93	20.42	20.91	21.40	21.89	22.39	22.88	23.38	23.88	24.38	24.88	25.38	25.88
42	18.93	19.43	19.93	20.43	20.93	21.44	21.94	22.45	22.96	23.47	23.98	24.49	25.00	25.51	26.03	26.55
43	19.40	19.91	20.42	20.94	21.45	21.97	22.49	23.01	23.53	24.05	24.57	25.10	25.62	26.15	26.68	27.21
44	19.86	20.39	20.91	21.44	21.97	22.50	23.03	23.57	24.10	24.64	25.17	25.71	26.25	26.79	27.33	27.88
45	20.33	20.87	21.41	21.95	22.49	23.03	23.58	24.12	24.67	25.22	25.77	26.32	26.88	27.43	27.99	28.55
46	20.80	21.35	21.90	22.46	23.01	23.57	24.13	24.69	25.25	25.81	26.37	26.94	27.51	28.08	28.65	29.22
47	21.27	21.83	22.40	22.97	23.53	24.10	24.68	25.25	25.82	26.40	26.98	27.56	28.14	28.72	29.31	29.89
48	21.74	22.32	22.90	23.48	24.06	24.64	25.23	25.81	26.40	26.99	27.58	28.18	28.77	29.37	29.97	30.57
49	22.21	22.80	23.39	23.99	24.58	25.18	25.78	26.38	26.98	27.59	28.19	28.80	29.41	30.02	30.63	31.34
50	22.69	23.29	23.89	24.50	25.11	25.72	26.33	26.95	27.56	28.18	28.80	29.42	30.04	30.67	31.29	31.92
51	23.16	23.78	24.40	25.02	25.64	26.26	26.89	27.52	28.15	28.78	29.41	30.05	30.68	31.32	31.96	32.60
52	23.64	24.27	24.90	25.53	26.17	26.81	27.45	28.09	28.73	29.38	30.02	30.67	31.32	31.98	32.63	33.29
53	24.11	24.76	25.40	26.05	26.70	27.35	28.00	28.66	29.32	29.98	30.64	31.30	31.97	32.63	33.30	33.97
54	24.59	25.25	25.91	26.57	27.23	27.90	28.56	29.23	29.91	30.58	31.25	31.93	32.61	33.29	33.98	34.66
55	25.07	25.74	26.41	27.09	27.77	28.44	29.13	29.81	30.50	31.18	31.87	32.56	33.26	33.95	34.65	35.35
56	25.55	26.23	26.92	27.61	28.30	28.99	29.69	30.39	31.09	31.79	32.49	33.20	33.91	34.62	35.33	36.04
57	26.03	26.73	27.43	28.13	28.84	29.54	30.25	30.97	31.68	32.39	33.11	33.83	34.56	35.28	36.01	36.74
58	26.51	27.23	27.94	28.66	29.37	30.10	30.82	31.55	32.27	33.00	33.74	34.47	35.21	35.95	36.69	37.43
59	27.00	27.72	28.45	29.18	29.91	30.65	31.39	32.13	32.87	33.61	34.36	35.11	35.86	36.62	37.37	38.13
60	27.48	28.22	28.96	29.71	30.45	31.20	31.96	32.71	33.47	34.23	34.99	35.75	36.52	37.29	38.06	38.83

TABLE C-15 (cont.) ANNUAL PERCENTAGE RATE TABLE FOR MONTHLY PAYMENT PLANS

Number of Payments	ANNUAL PERCENTAGE RATE															
	14.00%	14.25%	14.50%	14.75%	15.00%	15.25%	15.50%	15.75%	16.00%	16.25%	16.50%	16.75%	17.00%	17.25%	17.50%	17.75%
	Finance charge per $100 of amount financed															
1	1.17	1.19	1.21	1.23	1.25	1.27	1.29	1.31	1.33	1.35	1.37	1.40	1.42	1.44	1.46	1.48
2	1.75	1.78	1.82	1.85	1.88	1.91	1.94	1.97	2.00	2.04	2.07	2.10	2.13	2.16	2.19	2.22
3	2.34	2.38	2.43	2.47	2.51	2.55	2.59	2.64	2.68	2.72	2.76	2.80	2.85	2.89	2.93	2.97
4	2.93	2.99	3.04	3.09	3.14	3.20	3.25	3.30	3.36	3.41	3.46	3.51	3.57	3.62	3.67	3.73
5	3.53	3.59	3.65	3.72	3.78	3.84	3.91	3.97	4.04	4.10	4.16	4.23	4.29	4.35	4.42	4.48
6	4.12	4.20	4.27	4.35	4.42	4.49	4.57	4.64	4.72	4.79	4.87	4.94	5.02	5.09	5.17	5.24
7	4.72	4.81	4.89	4.98	5.06	5.15	5.23	5.32	5.40	5.49	5.58	5.66	5.75	5.83	5.92	6.00
8	5.32	5.42	5.51	5.61	5.71	5.80	5.90	6.00	6.09	6.19	6.29	6.38	6.48	6.58	6.67	6.77
9	5.92	6.03	6.14	6.25	6.35	6.46	6.57	6.68	6.78	6.89	7.00	7.11	7.22	7.32	7.43	7.54
10	6.53	6.65	6.77	6.88	7.00	7.12	7.24	7.36	7.48	7.60	7.72	7.84	7.96	8.08	8.19	8.31
11	7.14	7.27	7.40	7.53	7.66	7.79	7.92	8.05	8.18	8.31	8.44	8.57	8.70	8.83	8.96	9.09
12	7.74	7.89	8.03	8.17	8.31	8.45	8.59	8.74	8.88	9.02	9.16	9.30	9.45	9.59	9.73	9.87
13	8.36	8.51	8.66	8.81	8.97	9.12	9.27	9.43	9.58	9.73	9.89	10.04	10.20	10.35	10.50	10.66
14	8.97	9.13	9.30	9.46	9.63	9.79	9.96	10.12	10.29	10.45	10.62	10.78	10.95	11.11	11.28	11.45
15	9.59	9.76	9.94	10.11	10.29	10.47	10.64	10.82	11.00	11.17	11.35	11.51	11.71	11.88	12.06	12.24
16	10.20	10.39	10.58	10.77	10.95	11.14	11.33	11.52	11.71	11.90	12.09	12.28	12.46	12.65	12.84	13.03
17	10.82	11.02	11.22	11.42	11.62	11.82	12.02	12.22	12.42	12.62	12.83	13.03	13.23	13.43	13.63	13.83
18	11.45	11.66	11.87	12.08	12.29	12.50	12.72	12.93	13.14	13.35	13.57	13.78	13.99	14.21	14.42	14.64
19	12.07	12.30	12.52	12.74	12.97	13.19	13.41	13.64	13.86	14.09	14.31	14.54	14.76	14.99	15.22	15.44
20	12.70	12.93	13.17	13.41	13.64	13.88	14.11	14.35	14.59	14.82	15.06	15.30	15.54	15.77	16.01	16.25
21	13.33	13.58	13.82	14.07	14.32	14.57	14.82	15.06	15.31	15.56	15.81	16.05	16.31	16.56	16.81	17.07
22	13.96	14.22	14.48	14.74	15.00	15.26	15.52	15.78	16.04	16.30	16.57	16.83	17.09	17.36	17.62	17.88
23	14.59	14.87	15.14	15.41	15.68	15.96	16.23	16.50	16.78	17.05	17.32	17.60	17.88	18.15	18.43	18.70
24	15.23	15.51	15.80	16.08	16.37	16.65	16.94	17.22	17.51	17.80	18.09	18.37	18.65	18.95	19.24	19.53
25	15.87	16.17	16.46	16.76	17.06	17.35	17.65	17.95	18.25	18.55	18.85	19.15	19.45	19.75	20.05	20.36
26	16.51	16.82	17.13	17.44	17.75	18.06	18.37	18.68	18.99	19.30	19.62	19.93	20.24	20.56	20.87	21.19
27	17.15	17.47	17.80	18.12	18.44	18.76	19.09	19.41	19.74	20.06	20.39	20.71	21.04	21.37	21.69	22.02
28	17.80	18.13	18.47	18.80	19.14	19.47	19.81	20.15	20.48	20.82	21.16	21.50	21.84	22.18	22.52	22.86
29	18.45	18.79	19.14	19.49	19.83	20.18	20.53	20.88	21.23	21.58	21.94	22.29	22.64	22.99	23.35	23.70
30	19.10	19.45	19.81	20.17	20.54	20.90	21.26	21.62	21.99	22.35	22.72	23.08	23.45	23.81	24.18	24.55
31	19.75	20.12	20.49	20.87	21.24	21.61	21.99	22.37	22.74	23.12	23.50	23.88	24.26	24.64	25.02	25.40
32	20.40	20.79	21.17	21.56	21.95	22.33	22.72	23.11	23.50	23.89	23.28	24.68	25.07	25.46	25.86	26.25
33	21.06	21.46	21.85	22.25	22.65	23.06	23.46	23.86	24.26	24.67	25.07	25.48	25.88	26.29	26.70	27.11
34	21.72	22.13	22.54	22.95	23.37	23.78	24.19	24.61	25.03	25.44	25.86	26.28	26.70	27.12	27.54	27.97
35	22.38	22.80	23.23	23.65	24.08	24.51	24.94	25.36	25.79	26.23	26.66	27.09	27.52	27.96	28.39	28.83
36	23.04	23.48	23.92	24.35	24.80	25.24	25.68	26.12	26.57	27.01	27.46	27.90	28.35	28.80	29.25	29.70
37	23.70	24.16	24.61	25.06	25.51	25.97	26.42	26.88	27.34	27.80	28.26	28.72	29.18	29.64	30.10	30.57
38	24.37	24.84	25.30	25.77	26.24	26.70	27.17	27.64	28.11	28.59	29.06	29.53	30.01	30.49	30.96	31.44
39	25.04	25.52	26.00	26.48	26.96	27.44	27.92	28.41	28.89	29.38	29.87	30.36	30.85	31.34	31.83	32.32
40	25.71	26.20	26.70	27.19	27.69	28.18	28.68	29.18	29.68	30.18	30.68	31.18	31.68	32.19	32.69	33.20
41	26.39	26.89	27.40	27.91	28.41	28.92	29.44	29.95	30.46	30.97	31.49	32.01	32.52	33.04	33.56	34.08
42	27.06	27.58	28.10	28.62	29.15	29.67	30.19	30.72	31.25	31.78	32.31	32.84	33.37	33.90	34.44	34.97
43	27.74	28.27	28.81	29.34	29.88	30.42	30.96	31.50	32.04	32.58	33.13	33.67	34.22	34.76	35.31	35.86
44	28.42	28.97	29.52	30.07	30.62	31.17	31.72	32.28	32.83	33.39	33.95	34.51	35.07	35.63	36.19	36.76
45	29.11	29.67	30.23	30.79	31.36	31.92	32.49	33.06	33.63	34.20	34.77	35.35	35.92	36.50	37.08	37.66
46	29.79	30.36	30.94	31.52	32.10	32.68	33.26	33.84	34.43	35.01	35.60	36.19	36.78	37.37	37.96	38.56
47	30.48	31.07	31.66	32.25	32.84	33.44	34.03	34.63	35.23	35.83	36.43	37.04	37.64	38.25	38.86	39.46
48	31.17	31.77	32.37	32.98	33.59	34.20	34.81	35.42	36.03	36.65	37.27	27.88	38.50	39.13	39.75	40.37
49	31.86	32.48	33.09	33.71	34.34	34.96	35.59	36.21	36.84	37.47	38.10	38.74	39.37	40.01	40.65	41.29
50	32.55	33.18	33.82	34.45	35.09	35.73	36.37	37.01	37.65	38.30	38.94	39.59	40.24	40.89	41.55	42.20
51	33.25	33.89	34.54	35.19	35.84	36.49	37.15	37.81	38.46	39.12	39.79	40.45	41.11	41.78	42.45	43.12
52	33.95	34.61	35.27	35.93	36.60	37.27	37.94	38.61	39.28	39.96	40.63	41.31	41.99	42.67	43.36	44.04
53	34.65	35.32	36.00	36.68	37.36	38.04	38.72	39.41	40.10	40.79	41.48	42.17	42.87	43.57	44.27	44.97
54	35.35	36.04	36.73	37.42	38.12	38.82	39.52	40.22	40.92	41.63	42.33	43.04	43.75	44.47	45.18	45.90
55	36.05	36.76	37.46	38.17	38.88	39.60	40.31	41.03	41.74	42.47	43.19	43.91	44.64	45.37	46.10	46.83
56	36.76	37.48	38.20	38.92	39.65	40.38	41.11	41.84	42.57	43.31	44.05	44.79	45.53	46.27	47.02	47.77
57	37.47	38.20	38.94	39.68	40.42	41.16	41.91	42.65	53.40	44.15	44.91	45.66	46.42	47.18	47.94	48.71
58	38.18	38.93	39.68	40.43	41.19	41.95	42.71	43.47	44.23	45.00	45.77	46.54	47.32	48.09	48.87	49.65
59	38.89	39.66	40.42	41.19	41.96	42.74	43.51	44.29	45.07	45.85	46.64	47.42	48.41	49.01	49.80	50.60
60	39.61	40.39	41.17	41.95	42.74	43.53	44.32	45.11	45.91	46.71	47.51	48.31	49.12	49.92	50.73	51.55

TABLE C-15 (cont.) ANNUAL PERCENTAGE RATE TABLE FOR MONTHLY PAYMENT PLANS

Number of Payments	ANNUAL PERCENTAGE RATE															
	18.00%	18.25%	18.50%	18.75%	19.00%	19.25%	19.50%	19.75%	20.00%	20.25%	20.50%	20.75%	21.00%	21.25%	21.50%	21.75%
	Finance charge per $100 of amount financed															
1	1.50	1.52	1.54	1.56	1.58	1.60	1.62	1.65	1.67	1.69	1.71	1.73	1.75	1.77	1.79	1.81
2	2.26	2.29	2.32	2.35	2.38	2.41	2.44	2.48	2.51	2.54	2.57	2.60	2.63	2.66	2.70	2.73
3	3.01	3.06	3.10	3.14	3.18	3.23	3.27	3.31	3.35	3.39	3.44	3.48	3.52	3.56	3.60	3.65
4	3.78	3.83	3.88	3.94	3.99	4.04	4.10	4.15	4.20	4.25	4.31	4.36	4.41	4.47	4.52	4.57
5	4.54	4.61	4.67	4.74	4.80	4.86	4.93	4.99	5.06	5.12	5.18	5.25	5.31	5.37	5.44	5.50
6	5.32	5.39	5.46	5.54	5.61	5.69	5.76	5.84	5.91	5.99	6.06	6.14	6.21	6.29	6.36	6.44
7	6.09	6.18	6.26	6.35	6.43	6.52	6.60	6.69	6.78	6.86	6.95	7.04	7.12	7.21	7.29	7.38
8	6.87	6.96	7.06	7.16	7.26	7.35	7.45	7.55	7.64	7.74	7.84	7.94	8.03	8.13	8.23	8.33
9	7.65	7.76	7.87	7.97	8.08	8.19	8.30	8.41	8.52	8.63	8.73	8.84	8.95	9.06	9.17	9.28
10	8.43	8.55	8.67	8.79	8.91	9.03	9.15	9.27	9.39	9.51	9.63	9.75	9.88	10.00	10.12	10.24
11	9.22	9.35	9.49	9.62	9.75	9.88	10.01	10.14	10.28	10.41	10.54	10.67	10.80	10.94	11.07	11.20
12	10.02	10.16	10.30	10.44	10.59	10.73	10.87	11.02	11.16	11.31	11.45	11.59	11.74	11.88	12.02	12.17
13	10.81	10.97	11.12	11.28	11.43	11.59	11.74	11.90	12.05	12.21	12.36	12.52	12.67	12.83	12.99	13.14
14	11.61	11.78	11.95	12.11	12.28	12.45	12.61	12.78	12.95	13.11	13.28	13.45	13.62	13.79	13.95	14.12
15	12.42	12.59	12.77	12.95	13.13	13.31	13.49	13.67	13.85	14.03	14.21	14.39	14.57	14.75	14.93	15.11
16	13.22	13.41	13.60	13.80	13.99	14.18	14.37	14.56	14.75	14.94	15.13	15.33	15.52	15.71	15.90	16.10
17	14.04	14.24	14.44	14.64	14.85	15.05	15.25	15.46	15.66	15.86	16.07	16.27	16.48	16.68	16.89	17.09
18	14.85	15.07	15.28	15.49	15.71	15.93	16.14	16.36	16.57	16.79	17.01	17.22	17.44	17.66	17.88	18.09
19	15.67	15.90	16.12	16.35	16.58	16.81	17.03	17.26	17.49	17.72	17.95	18.18	18.41	18.64	18.87	19.10
20	16.49	16.73	16.97	17.21	17.45	17.69	17.93	18.17	18.41	18.66	18.90	19.14	19.38	19.63	19.87	20.11
21	17.32	17.57	17.82	18.07	18.33	18.58	18.83	19.09	19.34	19.60	19.85	20.11	20.36	20.62	20.87	21.13
22	18.15	18.41	18.68	18.94	19.21	19.47	19.74	20.01	20.27	20.54	20.81	21.08	21.34	21.61	21.88	22.15
23	18.98	19.26	19.54	19.81	20.09	20.37	20.65	20.93	21.21	21.49	21.77	22.05	22.33	22.61	22.90	23.18
24	19.82	20.11	20.40	20.69	20.98	21.27	21.56	21.86	22.15	22.44	22.74	23.03	23.33	23.62	23.92	24.21
25	20.66	20.96	21.27	21.57	21.87	22.18	22.48	22.79	23.10	23.40	23.71	24.02	24.32	24.63	24.94	25.25
26	21.50	21.82	22.14	22.45	22.77	23.09	23.41	23.73	24.04	24.36	24.68	25.01	25.33	25.65	25.97	26.29
27	22.35	22.68	23.01	23.34	23.67	24.00	24.33	24.67	25.00	25.33	25.67	26.00	26.34	26.67	27.01	27.34
28	23.20	23.55	23.89	24.23	24.58	24.92	25.27	25.61	25.96	26.30	26.65	27.00	27.35	27.70	28.05	28.40
29	24.06	24.41	24.77	25.13	25.49	25.84	26.20	26.56	26.92	27.28	27.64	28.00	28.37	28.73	29.09	29.46
30	24.92	25.29	25.66	26.03	26.40	26.77	27.14	27.52	27.89	28.26	28.64	29.01	29.39	29.77	30.14	30.52
31	25.78	26.16	26.55	26.93	27.32	27.70	28.09	28.47	28.86	29.25	29.64	30.03	30.42	30.81	31.20	31.59
32	26.65	27.04	27.44	27.84	28.24	28.64	29.04	29.44	29.84	30.24	30.64	31.05	31.45	31.85	32.26	32.67
33	27.52	27.93	28.34	28.75	29.16	29.57	29.99	30.40	30.82	31.23	31.65	32.07	32.49	32.91	33.33	33.75
34	28.39	28.81	29.24	29.66	30.09	30.52	30.95	31.37	31.80	32.23	32.67	33.10	33.53	33.96	34.40	34.83
35	29.27	29.71	30.14	30.58	31.02	31.47	31.91	32.35	32.79	33.24	33.68	34.13	34.58	35.03	35.47	35.92
36	30.15	30.60	31.05	31.51	31.96	32.42	32.87	33.33	33.79	34.25	34.71	35.17	35.63	36.09	36.56	37.02
37	31.03	31.50	31.97	32.43	32.90	33.37	33.84	34.32	34.79	35.26	35.74	36.21	36.69	37.16	37.64	38.12
38	31.92	32.40	32.88	33.37	33.85	34.33	34.82	35.30	35.79	36.28	36.77	37.26	37.75	38.24	38.73	39.23
39	32.81	33.31	33.80	34.30	34.80	35.30	35.80	36.30	36.80	37.30	37.81	38.31	38.82	39.32	39.83	40.34
40	33.71	34.22	34.73	35.24	35.75	36.26	36.78	37.29	37.81	38.33	38.85	39.37	39.89	40.41	40.93	41.46
41	34.61	35.13	35.66	36.18	36.71	37.24	37.77	38.30	38.83	39.36	39.89	40.43	40.96	41.50	42.04	42.58
42	35.51	36.05	36.59	37.13	37.67	38.21	38.76	39.30	39.85	40.40	40.95	41.50	42.05	42.60	43.15	43.71
43	36.42	36.97	37.52	38.08	38.63	39.19	39.75	40.31	40.87	41.44	42.00	42.57	43.13	43.70	44.27	44.84
44	37.33	37.89	38.46	39.03	39.60	40.18	40.75	41.33	41.90	42.48	43.06	43.64	44.22	44.81	45.39	45.98
45	38.24	38.82	39.41	39.99	40.58	41.17	41.75	42.35	42.94	43.53	44.13	44.72	45.32	45.92	46.52	47.12
46	39.16	39.75	40.35	40.95	41.55	42.16	42.76	43.37	43.98	44.58	45.20	45.81	46.42	47.03	47.65	48.27
47	40.08	40.69	41.30	41.92	42.54	43.15	43.77	44.40	45.02	45.64	46.27	46.90	47.53	48.16	48.79	49.42
48	41.00	41.63	42.26	42.89	43.52	44.15	44.79	45.43	46.07	46.71	47.35	47.99	48.64	49.28	49.93	50.58
49	41.93	42.57	43.22	43.86	44.51	45.16	45.81	46.46	47.12	47.77	48.43	49.09	49.75	50.41	51.08	51.74
50	42.86	43.52	44.18	44.84	45.50	46.17	46.83	47.50	48.17	48.84	49.52	50.19	50.87	51.55	52.23	52.91
51	43.79	44.47	45.14	45.82	46.50	47.18	47.86	48.55	49.23	49.92	50.61	51.30	51.99	52.69	53.38	54.08
52	44.73	45.42	46.11	46.80	47.50	48.20	48.89	49.59	50.30	51.00	51.71	52.41	53.12	53.83	54.55	54.26
53	45.67	46.38	47.08	47.79	48.50	49.22	49.93	50.65	51.37	52.09	52.81	53.53	54.26	54.98	55.71	56.44
54	46.62	47.34	48.06	48.79	49.51	50.24	50.97	51.70	52.44	53.17	53.91	54.65	55.39	56.14	56.88	57.63
55	47.57	48.30	49.04	49.78	50.52	51.27	52.02	52.77	53.52	54.27	55.02	55.78	56.54	57.30	58.06	58.82
56	48.52	49.27	50.03	50.78	51.54	52.30	53.06	53.83	54.60	55.37	56.14	56.91	57.68	58.46	59.24	60.02
57	49.47	50.24	51.01	51.79	52.56	53.34	54.12	54.90	55.68	56.47	57.25	58.04	58.84	59.63	60.43	61.22
58	50.43	51.22	52.00	52.79	53.58	54.38	55.17	55.97	56.77	57.57	58.38	59.18	59.99	60.80	61.62	62.43
59	51.39	52.20	53.00	53.80	54.61	55.42	56.23	57.05	57.87	58.68	59.51	60.33	61.15	61.98	62.81	63.64
60	52.36	53.18	54.00	54.82	55.64	56.47	57.30	58.13	58.96	59.80	60.64	61.48	62.32	63.17	64.01	64.86

TABLE C-15 (cont.) ANNUAL PERCENTAGE RATE TABLE FOR MONTHLY PAYMENT PLANS

Number of Payments	ANNUAL PERCENTAGE RATE															
	22.00%	22.25%	22.50%	22.75%	23.00%	23.25%	23.50%	23.75%	24.00%	24.25%	24.50%	24.75%	25.00%	25.25%	25.50%	25.75%
	Finance charge per $100 of amount financed															
1	1.83	1.85	1.87	1.90	1.92	1.94	1.96	1.98	2.00	2.02	2.04	2.06	2.08	2.10	2.12	2.15
2	2.76	2.79	2.82	2.85	2.88	2.92	2.95	2.98	3.01	3.04	3.07	3.10	3.14	3.17	3.20	3.23
3	3.69	3.73	3.77	3.82	3.86	3.90	3.94	3.98	4.03	4.07	4.11	4.15	4.20	4.24	4.28	4.32
4	4.62	4.68	4.73	4.78	4.84	4.89	4.94	5.00	5.05	5.10	5.16	5.21	5.26	5.32	5.37	5.42
5	5.57	5.63	5.69	5.76	5.82	5.89	5.95	6.02	6.08	6.14	6.21	6.27	6.34	6.40	6.46	6.53
6	6.61	6.59	6.66	6.74	6.81	6.89	6.96	7.04	7.12	7.19	7.27	7.34	7.42	7.49	7.57	7.64
7	7.47	7.55	7.64	7.73	7.81	7.90	7.99	8.07	8.16	8.24	8.33	8.42	8.51	8.59	8.68	8.77
8	8.42	8.52	8.62	8.72	8.82	8.91	9.01	9.11	9.21	9.31	9.40	9.50	9.60	9.70	9.80	9.90
9	9.39	9.50	9.61	9.72	9.83	9.94	10.04	10.15	10.26	10.37	10.48	10.59	10.70	10.81	10.92	11.03
10	10.36	10.48	10.60	10.72	10.84	10.96	11.08	11.21	11.33	11.45	11.57	11.69	11.81	11.93	12.06	12.18
11	11.33	11.47	11.60	11.73	11.86	12.00	12.13	12.26	12.40	12.53	12.66	12.80	12.93	13.06	13.20	13.33
12	12.31	12.46	12.60	12.75	12.89	13.04	13.18	13.33	13.47	13.62	13.76	13.91	14.05	14.20	14.34	14.49
13	13.30	13.46	13.61	13.77	13.93	14.08	14.24	14.40	14.55	14.71	14.87	15.03	15.18	15.34	15.50	15.66
14	14.29	14.46	14.63	14.80	14.97	15.13	15.30	15.47	15.64	15.81	15.98	16.15	16.32	16.49	16.66	16.83
15	15.29	15.47	15.65	15.83	16.01	16.19	16.37	16.56	16.74	16.92	17.10	17.28	17.47	17.65	17.83	18.02
16	16.29	16.48	16.68	16.87	17.06	17.26	17.45	17.65	17.84	18.03	18.23	18.42	18.62	18.81	19.01	19.21
17	17.30	17.50	17.71	17.92	18.12	18.33	18.53	18.74	18.95	19.16	19.36	19.57	19.78	19.99	20.20	20.40
18	18.31	18.53	18.75	18.97	19.19	19.41	19.62	19.84	20.06	20.28	20.50	20.72	20.95	21.17	21.39	21.61
19	19.33	19.56	19.79	20.02	20.26	20.49	20.72	20.95	21.19	21.42	21.65	21.89	22.12	22.35	22.59	22.82
20	20.35	20.60	20.84	21.09	21.33	21.58	21.82	22.07	22.31	22.56	22.81	23.05	23.30	23.55	23.79	24.04
21	21.38	21.64	21.90	22.16	22.41	22.67	22.93	23.19	23.45	23.71	23.97	24.23	24.49	24.75	25.01	25.27
22	22.42	22.69	22.96	23.23	23.50	23.77	24.04	24.32	24.59	24.86	25.13	25.41	25.68	25.96	26.23	26.50
23	23.46	23.74	24.03	24.31	24.60	24.88	25.17	25.45	25.74	26.02	26.31	26.60	26.88	27.17	27.46	27.75
24	24.51	24.80	25.10	25.40	25.70	25.99	26.29	26.59	26.89	27.19	27.49	27.79	28.09	28.39	28.69	29.00
25	25.56	25.87	26.18	26.49	26.80	27.11	27.43	27.74	28.05	28.36	28.68	28.99	29.31	29.62	29.94	30.25
26	26.62	26.94	27.26	27.59	27.91	28.24	28.56	28.89	29.22	29.55	29.87	30.20	30.53	30.86	31.19	31.52
27	27.68	28.02	28.35	28.69	29.03	29.37	29.71	30.05	30.39	30.73	31.07	31.42	31.76	32.10	32.45	32.79
28	28.75	29.10	29.45	29.80	30.15	30.51	30.86	31.22	31.57	31.93	32.28	32.64	33.00	33.35	33.71	34.07
29	29.82	30.19	30.55	30.92	31.28	31.65	32.02	32.39	32.76	33.13	33.50	33.87	34.24	34.61	34.98	35.36
30	30.90	31.28	31.66	32.04	32.42	32.80	33.18	33.57	33.95	34.33	34.72	35.10	35.49	35.88	36.26	36.65
31	31.98	32.38	32.77	33.17	33.56	33.96	34.35	34.75	35.15	35.55	35.95	36.35	36.75	37.15	37.55	37.95
32	33.07	33.48	33.89	34.30	34.71	35.12	35.53	35.94	36.35	36.77	37.18	37.60	38.01	38.43	38.84	39.26
33	34.17	34.59	35.01	35.44	35.86	36.29	36.71	37.14	37.57	37.99	38.42	38.85	39.28	39.71	40.14	40.58
34	35.27	35.71	36.14	36.58	37.02	37.46	37.90	38.34	38.78	39.23	39.67	40.11	40.56	41.01	41.45	41.90
35	36.37	36.83	37.28	37.73	38.18	38.64	39.09	39.55	40.01	40.47	40.92	41.38	41.84	42.31	42.77	43.23
36	37.49	37.95	38.42	38.89	39.35	39.82	40.29	40.77	41.24	41.71	42.19	42.66	43.14	43.61	44.09	44.57
37	38.60	39.08	39.56	40.05	40.53	41.02	41.50	41.99	42.48	42.96	43.45	43.94	44.43	44.93	45.42	45.91
38	39.72	40.22	40.72	41.21	41.71	42.21	42.71	43.22	43.72	44.22	44.73	45.23	45.74	46.25	46.75	47.26
39	40.85	41.36	41.87	42.39	42.90	43.42	43.93	44.45	44.97	45.49	46.01	46.53	47.05	47.57	48.10	48.62
40	41.98	42.51	43.04	43.56	44.09	44.62	45.16	45.69	46.22	46.76	47.29	47.83	48.37	48.91	49.45	49.99
41	43.12	43.66	44.20	44.75	45.29	45.84	46.39	46.94	47.48	48.04	48.59	49.14	49.69	50.25	50.80	51.36
42	44.26	44.82	45.38	45.94	46.50	47.06	47.62	48.19	48.75	49.32	49.89	50.46	51.03	51.60	52.17	52.74
43	45.41	45.98	46.56	47.13	47.71	48.29	48.87	49.45	50.03	50.61	51.19	51.78	52.36	52.95	53.54	54.13
44	46.56	47.15	47.74	48.33	48.93	49.52	50.11	50.71	51.31	51.91	52.51	53.11	53.71	54.31	54.92	55.52
45	47.72	48.33	48.93	49.54	50.15	50.76	51.37	51.98	52.59	53.21	53.82	54.44	55.06	55.68	56.30	56.92
46	48.89	49.51	50.13	50.75	51.37	52.00	52.63	53.26	53.89	54.52	55.15	55.78	56.42	57.05	57.69	58.33
47	50.06	50.69	51.33	51.97	52.61	53.25	53.89	54.54	55.18	55.83	56.48	57.13	57.78	58.44	59.09	59.75
48	51.23	51.88	52.54	53.19	53.85	54.51	55.16	55.83	56.49	57.15	57.82	58.49	59.15	59.82	60.50	61.17
49	52.41	53.08	53.75	54.42	55.09	55.77	56.44	57.12	57.80	58.48	59.16	59.85	60.53	61.22	61.91	62.60
50	53.59	54.28	54.96	55.65	56.34	57.03	57.73	58.42	59.12	59.81	60.51	61.21	61.92	62.62	63.33	64.03
51	54.78	55.48	56.19	56.89	57.60	58.30	59.01	59.73	60.44	61.15	61.87	62.59	63.31	64.03	64.75	65.47
52	55.98	56.69	57.41	58.13	58.86	59.58	60.31	61.04	61.77	62.50	63.23	63.97	64.70	65.44	66.18	66.92
53	57.18	57.91	58.65	59.38	60.12	60.87	61.61	62.35	63.10	63.85	64.60	65.35	66.11	66.86	67.62	68.38
54	58.38	59.13	59.88	60.64	61.40	62.16	62.92	63.68	64.44	65.21	65.98	66.75	67.52	68.29	69.07	69.84
55	59.59	60.36	61.13	61.90	62.67	63.45	64.23	65.01	65.79	66.57	67.36	68.14	68.93	69.72	70.52	71.31
56	60.80	61.59	62.38	63.17	63.96	64.75	65.54	66.34	67.14	67.94	68.74	69.55	70.36	71.16	71.97	72.79
57	62.02	62.83	63.63	64.44	65.25	66.06	66.87	67.68	68.50	69.32	70.14	70.96	71.78	72.61	73.44	74.27
58	63.25	64.07	64.89	65.71	66.54	67.37	68.20	69.03	69.86	70.70	71.54	72.38	73.22	74.06	74.91	75.76
59	64.48	65.32	66.15	67.00	67.84	68.68	69.53	70.38	71.23	72.09	72.94	73.80	74.66	75.52	76.39	77.25
60	65.71	66.57	67.42	68.28	69.14	70.01	70.87	71.74	72.61	73.48	74.35	75.23	76.11	76.99	77.87	78.76

TABLE C-15 (cont.) ANNUAL PERCENTAGE RATE TABLE FOR MONTHLY PAYMENT PLANS

Number of Payments	ANNUAL PERCENTAGE RATE															
	26.00%	26.25%	26.50%	26.75%	27.00%	27.25%	27.50%	27.75%	28.00%	28.25%	28.50%	28.75%	29.00%	29.25%	29.50%	29.75%
	Finance charge per $100 of amount financed															
1	2.17	2.19	2.21	2.23	2.25	2.27	2.29	2.31	2.33	2.35	2.37	2.40	2.42	2.44	2.46	2.48
2	3.26	3.29	3.32	3.36	3.39	3.42	3.45	3.48	3.51	3.54	3.58	3.61	3.64	3.67	3.70	3.73
3	4.36	4.41	4.45	4.49	4.53	4.58	4.62	4.66	4.70	4.74	4.79	4.83	4.87	4.91	4.96	5.00
4	5.47	5.53	5.58	5.63	5.69	5.74	5.79	5.85	5.90	5.95	6.01	6.06	6.11	6.17	6.22	6.27
5	6.59	6.66	6.72	6.79	6.85	6.91	6.98	7.04	7.11	7.17	7.24	7.30	7.37	7.43	7.49	7.56
6	7.72	7.79	7.87	7.95	8.02	8.10	8.17	8.25	8.32	8.40	8.48	8.55	8.63	8.70	8.78	8.85
7	8.85	8.94	9.03	9.11	9.20	9.29	9.37	9.46	9.55	9.64	9.72	9.81	9.90	9.98	10.07	10.16
8	9.99	10.09	10.19	10.29	10.39	10.49	10.58	10.68	10.78	10.88	10.98	11.08	11.18	11.28	11.38	11.47
9	11.14	11.25	11.36	11.47	11.58	11.69	11.80	11.91	12.03	12.14	12.25	12.36	12.47	12.58	12.69	12.80
10	12.30	12.42	12.54	12.67	12.79	12.91	13.03	13.15	13.28	13.40	13.52	13.64	13.77	13.89	14.01	14.14
11	13.46	13.60	13.73	13.87	14.00	14.13	14.27	14.40	14.54	14.67	14.81	14.94	15.08	15.21	15.35	15.48
12	14.64	14.78	14.93	15.07	15.22	15.37	15.51	15.66	15.81	15.95	16.10	16.25	16.40	16.54	16.69	16.84
13	15.82	15.97	16.13	16.29	16.45	16.61	16.77	16.93	17.09	17.24	17.40	17.56	17.72	17.88	18.04	18.20
14	17.00	17.17	17.35	17.52	17.69	17.86	18.03	18.20	18.37	18.54	18.72	18.89	19.06	19.23	19.41	19.58
15	18.20	18.38	18.57	18.75	18.93	19.12	19.30	19.48	19.67	19.85	20.04	20.22	20.41	20.59	20.78	20.96
16	19.40	19.60	19.79	19.99	20.19	20.38	20.58	20.78	20.97	21.17	21.37	21.57	21.76	21.96	22.16	22.36
17	20.61	20.82	21.03	21.24	21.45	21.66	21.87	22.08	22.29	22.50	22.71	22.92	23.13	23.34	23.55	23.77
18	21.83	22.05	22.27	22.50	22.72	22.94	23.16	23.39	23.61	23.83	24.06	24.28	24.51	24.73	24.96	25.18
19	23.06	23.29	23.53	23.76	24.00	24.23	24.47	24.71	24.94	25.18	25.42	25.65	25.89	26.13	26.37	26.61
20	24.29	24.54	24.79	25.04	25.28	25.53	25.78	26.03	26.28	26.53	26.78	27.04	27.29	27.54	27.79	28.04
21	25.53	25.79	26.05	26.32	26.58	26.84	27.11	27.37	27.63	27.90	28.16	28.43	28.69	28.96	29.22	29.49
22	26.78	27.05	27.33	27.61	27.88	28.16	28.44	28.71	28.99	29.27	29.55	29.82	30.10	30.38	30.66	30.94
23	28.04	28.32	28.61	28.90	29.19	29.48	29.77	30.07	30.36	30.65	30.94	31.23	31.53	31.82	32.11	32.41
24	29.30	29.60	29.90	30.21	30.51	30.82	31.12	31.43	31.73	32.04	32.34	32.65	32.96	33.27	33.57	33.88
25	30.57	30.89	31.20	31.52	31.84	32.16	32.48	32.80	33.12	33.44	33.76	34.08	34.40	34.72	35.04	35.37
26	31.85	32.18	32.51	32.84	33.18	33.51	33.84	34.18	34.51	34.84	35.18	35.51	35.85	36.19	36.52	36.86
27	33.14	33.48	33.83	34.17	34.52	34.87	35.21	35.56	35.91	36.26	36.61	36.96	37.31	37.66	38.01	38.36
28	34.43	34.79	35.15	35.51	35.87	36.23	36.59	36.96	37.32	37.68	38.05	38.41	38.78	39.15	39.51	39.88
29	35.73	36.10	36.48	36.85	37.23	37.61	37.98	38.36	38.74	39.12	39.50	39.88	40.26	40.64	41.02	41.40
30	37.04	37.43	37.82	38.21	38.60	38.99	39.38	39.77	40.17	40.56	40.95	41.35	41.75	42.14	42.54	42.94
31	38.35	38.76	39.16	39.57	39.97	40.38	40.79	41.19	41.60	42.01	42.42	42.83	43.24	43.65	44.06	44.48
32	39.68	40.10	40.52	40.94	41.36	41.78	42.20	42.62	43.05	43.47	43.90	44.32	44.75	45.17	45.60	46.03
33	41.01	41.44	41.88	42.31	42.75	43.19	43.62	44.06	44.50	44.94	45.38	45.82	46.26	46.70	47.15	47.59
34	42.35	42.80	43.25	43.70	44.15	44.60	45.05	45.51	45.96	46.42	46.87	47.33	47.79	48.24	48.70	49.16
35	43.69	44.16	44.62	45.09	45.56	46.02	46.49	46.96	47.43	47.90	48.37	48.85	49.32	49.79	50.27	50.74
36	45.05	45.53	46.01	46.49	46.97	47.45	47.94	48.42	48.91	49.40	49.88	50.37	50.86	51.35	51.84	52.33
37	46.41	46.90	47.40	47.90	48.39	48.89	49.39	49.89	50.40	50.90	51.40	51.91	52.41	52.92	53.42	53.93
38	47.77	48.29	48.80	49.31	49.82	50.34	50.86	51.37	51.89	52.41	52.93	53.45	53.97	54.49	55.02	55.54
39	49.15	49.68	50.20	50.73	51.26	51.79	52.33	52.86	53.39	53.93	54.46	55.00	55.54	56.08	56.62	57.16
40	50.53	51.07	51.62	52.16	52.71	53.26	53.81	54.35	54.90	55.46	56.01	56.56	57.12	57.67	58.23	58.79
41	51.92	52.48	53.04	53.60	54.16	54.73	55.29	55.86	56.42	56.99	57.56	58.13	58.70	59.28	59.85	60.42
42	53.32	53.89	54.47	55.05	55.63	56.21	56.79	57.37	57.95	58.54	59.12	59.71	60.30	60.89	61.48	62.07
43	54.72	55.31	55.90	56.50	57.09	57.69	58.29	58.89	59.49	60.09	60.69	61.30	61.90	62.51	63.11	63.72
44	56.13	56.74	57.35	57.96	58.57	59.19	59.80	60.42	61.03	61.65	62.27	62.89	63.51	64.14	64.76	65.39
45	57.55	58.17	58.80	59.43	60.06	60.69	61.32	61.95	62.59	63.22	63.86	64.50	65.13	65.77	66.42	67.06
46	58.97	59.61	60.26	60.90	61.55	62.20	62.84	63.49	64.15	64.80	65.45	66.11	66.76	67.42	68.08	68.74
47	60.40	61.06	61.72	62.38	63.05	63.71	64.38	65.05	65.71	66.38	67.06	67.73	68.40	69.08	69.75	70.43
48	61.84	62.52	63.20	63.87	64.56	65.24	65.92	66.60	67.29	67.98	68.67	69.36	70.05	70.74	71.44	72.13
49	63.29	63.98	64.68	65.37	66.07	66.77	67.47	68.17	68.87	69.58	70.29	70.99	71.70	72.41	73.13	73.84
50	64.74	65.45	66.16	66.88	67.59	68.31	69.03	69.75	70.47	71.19	71.91	72.64	73.37	74.10	74.83	75.56
51	66.20	66.93	67.66	68.39	69.12	69.86	70.59	71.33	72.07	72.81	73.55	74.29	75.04	75.78	76.53	77.28
52	67.67	68.41	69.16	69.91	70.66	71.41	72.16	72.92	73.67	74.43	75.19	75.95	76.72	77.48	78.25	79.02
53	69.14	69.90	70.67	71.43	72.20	72.97	73.74	74.52	75.29	76.07	76.85	77.62	78.41	79.19	79.97	80.76
54	70.62	71.40	72.18	72.97	73.75	74.54	75.33	76.12	76.91	77.71	78.50	79.30	80.10	80.90	81.71	82.51
55	72.11	72.91	73.71	74.51	75.31	76.12	76.92	77.73	78.55	79.36	80.17	80.99	81.81	82.63	83.45	84.27
56	73.60	74.42	75.24	76.06	76.88	77.70	78.53	79.35	80.18	81.02	81.85	82.68	83.52	84.36	85.20	86.04
57	75.10	75.94	76.77	77.61	78.45	79.29	80.14	80.98	81.83	82.68	83.53	84.39	85.24	86.10	86.96	87.82
58	76.61	77.46	78.32	79.17	80.03	80.89	81.75	82.62	83.48	84.35	85.22	86.10	86.97	87.85	88.72	89.60
59	78.12	78.99	79.87	80.74	81.62	82.50	83.38	84.26	85.15	86.03	86.92	87.81	88.71	89.60	90.50	91.40
60	79.64	80.53	81.42	82.32	83.21	84.11	85.01	85.91	86.81	87.72	88.63	89.54	90.45	91.37	92.28	93.20

Table C-15 (cont.) Annual percentage rate table for monthly payment plans

Number of Payments	ANNUAL PERCENTAGE RATE															
	30.00%	30.25%	30.50%	30.75%	31.00%	31.25%	31.50%	31.75%	32.00%	32.25%	32.50%	32.75%	33.00%	33.25%	33.50%	33.75%
	Finance charge per $100 of amount financed															
1	2.50	2.52	2.54	2.56	2.58	2.60	2.62	2.65	2.67	2.69	2.71	2.73	2.75	2.77	2.79	2.81
2	3.77	3.80	3.83	3.86	3.89	3.92	3.95	3.99	4.02	4.05	4.08	4.11	4.14	4.18	4.21	4.24
3	5.04	5.08	5.13	5.17	5.21	5.25	5.30	5.34	5.38	5.42	5.46	5.51	5.55	5.59	5.63	5.68
4	6.33	6.38	6.43	6.49	6.54	6.59	6.65	6.70	6.75	6.81	6.86	6.91	6.97	7.02	7.08	7.13
5	7.62	7.69	7.75	7.82	7.88	7.95	8.01	8.08	8.14	8.20	8.27	8.33	8.40	8.46	8.53	8.59
6	8.93	9.01	9.08	9.16	9.23	9.31	9.39	9.46	9.54	9.61	9.69	9.77	9.84	9.92	9.99	10.07
7	10.25	10.33	10.42	10.51	10.60	10.68	10.77	10.86	10.95	11.03	11.12	11.21	11.30	11.39	11.47	11.56
8	11.57	11.67	11.77	11.87	11.97	12.07	12.17	12.27	12.37	12.47	12.57	12.67	12.77	12.87	12.97	13.07
9	12.91	13.02	13.13	13.24	13.36	13.47	13.58	13.69	13.80	13.91	14.02	14.14	14.25	14.36	14.47	14.58
10	14.26	14.38	14.50	14.63	14.75	14.87	15.00	15.12	15.24	15.37	15.49	15.62	15.74	15.86	15.99	16.11
11	15.62	15.75	15.89	16.02	16.16	16.29	16.43	16.56	16.70	16.84	16.97	17.11	17.24	17.38	17.52	17.65
12	16.98	17.13	17.28	17.43	17.58	17.72	17.87	18.02	18.17	18.32	18.47	18.61	18.76	18.91	19.06	19.21
13	18.36	18.52	18.68	18.84	19.00	19.16	19.33	19.49	19.65	19.81	19.97	20.13	20.29	20.45	20.62	20.78
14	19.75	19.92	20.10	20.27	20.44	20.62	20.79	20.96	21.14	21.13	21.49	21.66	21.83	22.01	22.18	22.36
15	21.15	21.34	21.52	21.71	21.89	22.08	22.27	22.45	22.64	22.83	23.01	23.20	23.39	23.58	23.76	23.95
16	22.56	22.76	22.96	23.16	23.35	23.55	23.75	23.95	24.15	24.35	24.55	24.75	24.96	25.16	25.36	25.56
17	23.98	24.19	24.40	24.61	24.83	25.04	25.25	25.47	25.68	25.89	26.11	26.32	26.53	26.75	26.96	27.18
18	25.41	25.63	25.86	26.08	26.31	26.54	26.76	26.99	27.22	27.44	27.67	27.90	28.13	28.35	28.58	28.81
19	26.85	27.08	27.32	27.56	27.80	28.04	28.28	28.52	28.76	29.00	29.25	29.49	29.73	29.97	30.21	30.45
20	28.29	28.55	28.80	29.05	29.31	29.56	29.81	30.07	30.32	30.58	30.83	31.09	31.34	31.60	31.86	32.11
21	29.75	30.02	30.29	30.55	30.82	31.09	31.36	31.62	31.89	32.16	32.43	32.70	32.97	33.24	33.51	33.78
22	31.22	31.50	31.78	32.06	32.35	32.63	32.91	33.19	33.48	33.76	34.04	34.33	34.61	34.89	35.18	35.46
23	32.70	33.00	33.29	33.59	33.88	34.18	34.48	34.77	35.07	35.37	35.66	35.96	36.26	36.56	36.86	37.16
24	34.19	34.50	34.81	35.12	35.43	35.74	36.05	36.36	36.67	36.99	37.30	37.61	37.92	38.24	38.55	38.87
25	35.69	36.01	36.34	36.66	36.99	37.31	37.64	37.96	38.29	38.62	38.94	39.27	39.60	39.93	40.26	40.59
26	37.20	37.54	37.88	38.21	38.55	38.89	39.23	39.58	39.92	40.26	40.60	40.94	41.29	41.63	41.97	42.32
27	38.72	39.07	39.42	39.78	40.13	40.49	40.84	41.20	41.56	41.91	42.27	42.63	42.99	43.34	43.70	44.06
28	40.25	40.61	40.98	41.35	41.72	42.09	42.46	42.83	43.20	43.58	43.95	44.32	44.70	45.07	45.45	45.82
29	41.78	42.17	42.55	42.94	43.32	43.71	44.09	44.48	44.87	45.25	45.64	46.03	46.42	46.81	47.20	47.59
30	43.33	43.73	44.13	44.53	44.93	45.33	45.73	46.13	46.54	46.94	47.34	47.75	48.15	48.56	48.96	49.37
31	44.89	45.30	45.72	46.13	46.55	46.97	47.38	47.80	48.22	48.64	49.06	49.48	49.90	50.32	50.74	51.17
32	46.46	46.89	47.32	47.75	48.18	48.61	49.05	49.48	49.91	50.35	50.78	51.22	51.66	52.09	52.53	52.97
33	48.04	48.48	48.93	49.37	49.82	50.27	50.72	51.17	51.62	52.07	52.52	52.97	53.43	53.88	54.33	54.79
34	49.62	50.08	50.55	51.01	51.47	51.94	52.40	52.87	53.33	53.80	54.27	54.74	55.21	55.68	56.15	56.62
35	51.22	51.70	52.17	52.65	53.13	53.61	54.09	54.58	55.06	55.54	56.03	56.51	57.00	57.48	57.97	58.46
36	52.83	53.32	53.81	54.31	54.80	55.30	55.80	56.30	56.80	57.30	57.80	58.30	58.80	59.30	59.81	60.31
37	54.44	54.95	55.46	55.97	56.49	57.00	57.51	58.03	58.54	59.06	59.58	60.10	60.62	61.14	61.66	62.18
38	56.07	56.59	57.12	57.65	58.18	58.71	59.24	59.77	60.30	60.84	61.37	61.90	62.44	62.98	63.52	64.06
39	57.70	58.24	58.79	59.33	59.88	60.42	60.97	61.52	62.07	62.62	63.17	63.72	64.28	64.83	65.39	65.94
40	59.34	59.90	60.47	61.03	61.59	62.15	62.72	63.28	63.85	64.42	64.99	65.56	66.13	66.70	67.27	67.84
41	61.00	61.57	62.15	62.73	63.31	63.89	64.47	65.06	65.64	66.22	66.81	67.40	67.99	68.57	69.16	69.76
42	62.66	63.25	63.85	64.44	65.04	65.64	66.24	66.84	67.44	68.04	68.65	69.25	69.86	70.46	71.07	71.68
43	64.33	64.94	65.56	66.17	66.78	67.40	68.01	68.63	69.25	69.87	70.49	71.11	71.74	72.36	72.99	73.61
44	66.01	66.64	67.27	67.90	68.53	69.17	69.80	70.43	71.07	71.71	72.35	72.99	73.63	74.27	74.91	75.56
45	67.70	68.35	69.00	69.64	70.29	70.94	71.60	72.25	72.90	73.56	74.21	74.87	75.53	76.19	76.85	77.52
46	69.40	70.07	70.73	71.40	72.06	72.73	73.40	74.07	74.74	75.42	76.09	76.77	77.44	78.12	78.80	79.48
47	71.11	71.79	72.47	73.16	73.84	74.53	75.22	75.90	76.60	77.29	77.98	78.67	79.37	80.07	80.76	81.46
48	72.83	73.53	74.23	74.93	75.63	76.34	77.04	77.75	78.46	79.17	79.88	80.59	81.30	82.02	82.74	83.45
49	74.55	75.27	75.99	76.71	77.43	78.15	78.88	79.60	80.33	81.06	81.79	82.52	83.25	83.98	84.72	84.45
50	76.29	77.02	77.76	78.50	79.24	79.98	80.72	81.46	82.21	82.96	83.70	84.45	85.20	85.96	86.71	87.47
51	78.03	78.79	79.54	80.30	81.06	81.81	82.58	83.34	84.10	84.87	85.63	86.40	87.17	87.94	88.71	89.49
52	79.79	80.56	81.33	82.11	82.88	83.66	84.44	85.22	86.00	86.79	87.57	88.36	89.15	89.94	90.73	91.52
53	81.55	82.34	83.13	83.92	84.72	85.51	86.31	87.11	87.91	88.72	89.52	90.33	91.13	91.94	92.75	93.57
54	83.32	84.13	84.94	85.75	86.56	87.38	88.19	89.01	89.83	90.66	91.48	92.30	92.13	93.96	94.79	95.62
55	85.10	85.93	86.75	87.58	88.42	89.25	90.09	90.92	91.76	92.60	93.45	94.29	95.14	95.99	96.83	97.69
56	86.89	87.73	88.58	89.43	90.28	91.13	91.99	92.84	93.70	94.56	95.43	96.29	97.15	98.02	98.89	99.76
57	88.68	89.55	90.41	91.28	92.15	93.02	93.90	94.77	95.65	96.53	97.41	98.30	99.18	100.07	100.96	101.85
58	90.49	91.37	92.26	93.14	94.03	94.92	95.82	96.71	97.61	98.51	99.41	100.31	101.22	102.12	103.03	103.94
59	92.30	93.20	94.11	95.01	95.92	96.83	97.75	98.66	99.58	100.50	101.42	102.34	103.26	104.19	105.12	106.05
60	94.12	95.04	95.97	96.89	97.82	98.75	99.68	100.62	101.56	102.49	103.43	104.38	105.32	106.27	107.21	108.16

TABLE C-15 (cont.) ANNUAL PERCENTAGE RATE TABLE FOR MONTHLY PAYMENT PLANS

Number of Payments	ANNUAL PERCENTAGE RATE															
	34.00%	34.25%	34.50%	34.75%	35.00%	35.25%	35.50%	35.75%	36.00%	36.25%	36.50%	36.75%	37.00%	37.25%	37.50%	37.75%
	Finance charge per $100 of amount financed															
1	2.83	2.85	2.87	2.90	2.92	2.94	2.96	2.98	3.00	3.02	3.04	3.06	3.08	3.10	3.12	3.15
2	4.27	4.30	4.33	4.36	4.40	4.43	4.46	4.49	4.52	4.55	4.59	4.62	4.65	4.68	4.71	4.74
3	5.72	5.76	5.80	5.85	5.89	5.93	5.97	6.02	6.06	6.10	6.14	6.19	6.23	6.27	6.31	6.36
4	7.18	7.24	7.29	7.34	7.40	7.45	7.50	7.56	7.61	7.66	7.72	7.77	7.83	7.88	7.93	7.99
5	8.66	8.72	8.79	8.85	8.92	8.98	9.05	9.11	9.18	9.24	9.31	9.37	9.44	9.50	9.57	9.63
6	10.15	10.22	10.30	10.38	10.45	10.53	10.61	10.68	10.76	10.83	10.91	10.99	11.06	11.14	11.22	11.29
7	11.65	11.74	11.83	11.91	12.00	12.09	12.18	12.27	12.35	12.44	12.53	12.62	12.71	12.80	12.88	12.97
8	13.17	13.27	13.36	13.46	13.56	13.66	13.76	13.86	13.97	14.07	14.17	14.27	14.37	14.47	14.57	14.67
9	14.69	14.81	14.92	15.03	15.14	15.25	15.37	15.48	15.59	15.70	15.82	15.93	16.04	16.15	16.27	16.38
10	16.24	16.36	16.48	16.61	16.73	16.86	16.98	17.11	17.23	17.36	17.48	17.60	17.73	17.85	17.98	18.10
11	17.79	17.93	18.06	18.20	18.34	18.47	18.61	18.75	18.89	19.02	19.16	19.30	19.43	19.57	19.71	19.85
12	19.36	19.51	19.66	19.81	19.96	20.11	20.25	20.40	20.55	20.70	20.85	21.00	21.15	21.31	21.46	21.61
13	20.94	21.10	21.26	21.43	21.59	21.75	21.91	22.08	22.24	22.40	22.56	22.73	22.89	23.05	23.22	23.38
14	22.53	22.71	22.88	23.06	23.23	23.41	23.59	23.76	23.94	24.11	24.29	24.47	24.64	24.82	25.00	25.17
15	24.14	24.33	24.52	24.71	24.89	25.08	25.27	25.46	25.65	25.84	26.03	26.22	26.41	26.60	26.79	26.98
16	25.76	25.96	26.16	26.37	26.57	26.77	26.97	27.17	27.38	27.58	27.78	27.99	28.19	28.39	28.60	28.80
17	27.39	27.61	27.82	28.04	28.25	28.47	28.69	28.90	29.12	29.34	29.55	29.77	29.99	30.20	30.42	30.64
18	29.04	29.27	29.50	29.73	29.96	30.19	30.42	30.65	30.88	31.11	31.34	31.57	31.80	32.03	32.26	32.49
19	30.70	30.94	31.18	31.43	31.67	31.91	32.16	32.40	32.65	32.89	33.14	33.38	33.63	33.87	34.12	34.36
20	32.37	32.63	32.88	33.14	33.40	33.66	33.91	34.17	34.43	34.69	34.95	35.21	35.47	35.73	35.99	36.25
21	34.05	34.32	34.60	34.87	35.14	35.41	35.68	35.96	36.23	36.50	36.78	37.05	37.33	37.60	37.88	38.15
22	35.75	36.04	36.32	36.61	36.89	37.18	37.47	37.76	38.04	38.33	38.62	38.91	39.20	39.49	39.78	40.07
23	37.46	37.76	38.06	38.36	38.66	38.96	39.27	39.57	39.87	40.18	40.48	40.78	41.09	41.39	41.70	42.00
24	39.18	39.50	39.81	40.13	40.44	40.76	41.08	41.40	41.71	42.03	42.35	42.67	42.99	43.31	43.63	43.95
25	40.92	41.25	41.58	41.91	42.24	42.57	42.90	43.24	43.57	43.90	44.24	44.57	44.91	45.24	45.58	45.91
26	42.66	43.01	43.36	43.70	44.05	44.40	44.74	45.09	45.44	45.79	46.14	46.49	46.84	47.19	47.54	47.89
27	44.42	44.78	45.15	45.51	45.87	46.23	46.60	46.96	47.32	47.69	48.05	48.42	48.78	49.15	49.52	49.88
28	46.20	46.57	46.95	47.33	47.70	48.08	48.46	48.84	49.22	49.60	49.98	50.36	50.75	51.13	51.51	51.89
29	47.98	48.37	48.77	49.16	49.55	49.95	50.34	50.74	51.13	51.53	51.93	52.32	52.72	53.12	53.52	53.92
30	49.78	50.19	50.60	51.00	51.41	51.82	52.23	52.65	53.06	53.47	53.88	54.30	54.71	55.13	55.54	55.96
31	51.59	52.01	52.44	52.86	53.29	53.71	54.14	54.57	55.00	55.43	55.85	56.28	56.72	57.15	57.58	58.01
32	53.41	53.85	54.29	54.73	55.17	55.62	56.06	56.50	56.95	57.39	57.84	58.29	58.73	59.18	59.63	60.08
33	55.24	55.70	56.16	56.62	57.07	57.53	57.99	58.45	58.92	59.38	59.84	60.30	60.77	61.23	61.70	62.16
34	57.09	57.56	58.04	58.51	58.99	59.46	59.94	60.42	60.89	61.37	61.85	62.33	62.81	63.30	63.78	64.26
35	58.95	59.44	59.93	60.42	60.91	61.40	61.90	62.39	62.89	63.38	63.88	64.38	64.88	65.37	65.87	66.37
36	60.82	61.33	61.83	62.34	62.85	63.36	63.87	64.38	64.89	65.41	65.92	66.43	66.95	67.47	67.98	68.50
37	62.70	63.22	63.75	64.27	64.80	65.33	65.85	66.38	66.91	67.44	67.97	68.51	69.04	69.57	70.11	70.64
38	64.59	65.14	65.68	66.22	66.76	67.31	67.85	68.40	68.95	69.49	70.04	70.59	71.14	71.69	72.25	72.80
39	66.50	67.06	67.62	68.18	68.74	69.30	69.86	70.43	70.99	71.56	72.12	72.69	73.26	73.83	74.40	74.97
40	68.42	68.99	69.57	70.15	70.13	71.31	71.89	72.47	73.05	73.63	74.22	74.80	75.39	75.98	76.56	77.15
41	70.35	70.94	71.53	72.13	72.73	73.32	73.92	74.52	75.12	75.72	76.32	76.93	77.53	78.14	78.74	79.35
42	72.29	72.90	73.51	74.12	74.74	75.35	75.97	76.59	77.20	77.82	78.44	79.07	79.69	80.31	80.94	81.56
43	74.24	74.87	75.50	76.13	76.76	77.40	78.03	78.67	79.30	79.94	80.58	81.22	81.86	82.50	83.14	83.79
44	76.20	76.85	77.50	78.15	78.80	79.45	80.10	80.76	81.41	82.07	82.72	83.38	84.04	84.70	85.36	86.03
45	78.18	78.84	79.51	80.18	80.85	81.52	82.19	82.86	83.53	84.21	84.88	85.56	86.24	86.92	87.60	88.28
46	80.17	80.85	81.53	82.22	82.91	83.60	84.28	84.98	85.67	86.36	87.06	87.75	88.45	89.15	89.85	90.55
47	82.16	82.87	83.57	84.27	84.98	85.69	86.39	87.10	87.81	88.53	89.24	89.95	90.67	91.39	92.11	92.83
48	84.17	84.89	85.61	86.34	87.06	87.79	88.52	89.24	89.97	90.70	91.44	92.17	92.91	93.64	94.38	95.12
49	86.19	86.93	87.67	88.41	89.16	89.90	90.65	91.40	92.14	92.89	93.65	94.40	95.15	95.91	96.67	97.42
50	88.22	88.98	89.74	90.50	91.26	92.03	92.79	93.56	94.33	95.10	95.87	96.64	97.41	98.19	98.96	99.74
51	90.26	91.04	91.82	92.60	93.38	94.16	94.95	95.74	96.52	97.31	98.10	98.89	99.69	100.48	101.28	102.07
52	92.32	93.11	93.91	94.71	95.51	96.31	97.12	97.92	98.73	99.54	100.35	101.16	101.97	102.79	103.60	104.42
53	94.38	95.20	96.01	96.83	97.65	98.47	99.30	100.12	100.95	101.78	102.61	103.44	104.27	105.10	105.94	106.78
54	96.45	97.29	98.13	98.96	99.80	100.64	101.49	102.33	103.18	104.03	104.87	105.73	106.58	107.43	108.29	109.14
55	98.54	99.39	100.25	101.11	101.97	102.83	103.69	104.55	105.42	106.29	107.16	108.03	108.90	109.77	110.65	111.53
56	100.63	101.51	102.38	103.26	104.14	105.02	105.90	106.79	107.67	108.56	109.45	110.34	111.23	112.13	113.02	113.92
57	102.74	103.63	104.53	105.43	106.32	107.22	108.13	109.03	109.94	110.85	111.75	112.67	113.58	114.49	115.41	116.33
58	104.85	105.77	106.68	107.60	108.52	109.44	110.36	111.29	112.21	113.14	114.07	115.00	115.93	116.87	117.81	118.74
59	106.98	107.91	108.85	109.79	110.73	111.67	112.61	113.55	114.50	115.45	116.40	117.35	118.30	119.26	120.22	121.17
60	109.12	110.07	111.02	111.98	112.94	113.90	114.87	115.83	116.80	117.77	118.74	119.71	120.68	121.66	122.64	123.62

TABLE C-15 (cont.) ANNUAL PERCENTAGE RATE TABLE FOR MONTHLY PAYMENT PLANS

Number of Payments	ANNUAL PERCENTAGE RATE															
	38.00%	38.25%	38.50%	38.75%	39.00%	39.25%	39.50%	39.75%	40.00%	40.25%	40.50%	40.75%	41.00%	41.25%	41.50%	41.75%
	Finance charge per $100 of amount financed															
1	3.17	3.19	3.21	3.23	3.25	3.27	3.29	3.31	3.33	3.35	3.37	3.40	3.42	3.44	3.46	3.48
2	4.77	4.81	4.84	4.87	4.90	4.93	4.96	5.00	5.03	5.06	5.09	5.12	5.15	5.19	5.22	5.25
3	6.40	6.44	6.48	6.53	6.57	6.61	6.65	6.70	6.74	6.78	6.82	6.87	6.91	6.95	7.00	7.04
4	8.04	8.09	8.15	8.20	8.25	8.31	8.36	8.42	8.47	8.52	8.58	8.63	8.69	8.74	8.79	8.85
5	9.70	9.76	9.83	9.89	9.96	10.02	10.09	10.15	10.22	10.28	10.35	10.41	10.48	10.54	10.61	10.68
6	11.37	11.45	11.52	11.60	11.68	11.75	11.83	11.91	11.99	12.06	12.14	12.22	12.29	12.37	12.45	12.52
7	13.06	13.15	13.24	13.33	13.42	13.50	13.59	13.68	13.77	13.86	13.95	14.04	14.13	14.21	14.30	14.39
8	14.77	14.87	14.97	15.07	15.17	15.27	15.37	15.47	15.57	15.67	15.77	15.88	15.98	16.08	16.18	16.28
9	16.49	16.60	16.72	16.83	16.94	17.05	17.17	17.28	17.39	17.51	17.62	17.73	17.85	17.96	18.07	18.19
10	18.23	18.35	18.48	18.61	18.73	18.86	18.98	19.11	19.23	19.36	19.48	19.61	19.74	19.86	19.99	20.12
11	19.99	20.12	20.26	20.40	20.54	20.68	20.81	20.95	21.09	21.23	21.37	21.51	21.65	21.78	21.92	22.06
12	21.76	21.91	22.06	22.21	22.36	22.51	22.66	22.81	22.97	23.12	23.27	23.42	23.57	23.72	23.88	24.03
13	23.54	23.71	23.87	24.04	24.20	24.37	24.53	24.69	24.86	25.02	25.19	25.35	25.52	25.68	25.85	26.01
14	25.35	25.53	25.70	25.88	26.06	26.24	26.41	26.59	26.77	26.95	27.13	27.30	27.48	27.66	27.84	28.02
15	27.17	27.36	27.55	27.74	27.93	28.12	28.32	28.51	28.70	28.89	29.08	29.27	29.47	29.66	29.85	30.04
16	29.01	29.21	29.41	29.62	29.82	30.03	30.23	30.44	30.65	30.85	31.06	31.26	31.47	31.68	31.88	32.09
17	30.86	31.08	31.29	31.51	31.73	31.95	32.17	32.39	32.61	32.83	33.05	33.27	33.49	33.71	33.93	34.15
18	32.73	32.96	33.19	33.42	33.66	33.89	34.12	34.36	34.59	34.83	35.06	35.29	35.53	35.76	36.00	36.23
19	34.61	34.86	35.10	35.35	35.60	35.85	36.09	36.34	36.59	36.84	37.09	37.34	37.59	37.84	38.09	38.34
20	36.51	36.77	37.03	37.30	37.56	37.82	38.08	38.35	38.61	38.87	39.14	39.40	39.66	39.93	40.19	40.46
21	38.43	38.70	38.98	39.26	39.53	39.81	40.09	40.36	40.64	40.92	41.20	41.48	41.76	42.04	42.32	42.60
22	40.36	40.65	40.94	41.23	41.52	41.82	42.11	42.40	42.69	42.99	43.28	43.58	43.87	44.16	44.46	44.75
23	42.31	42.61	42.92	43.23	43.53	43.84	44.15	44.46	44.76	45.07	45.38	45.69	46.00	46.31	46.62	46.93
24	44.27	44.59	44.91	45.23	45.56	45.88	46.20	46.53	46.85	47.17	47.50	47.82	48.15	48.48	48.80	49.13
25	46.25	46.59	46.92	47.26	47.60	47.94	48.28	48.61	48.95	49.29	49.63	49.98	50.32	50.66	51.00	51.34
26	48.24	48.60	48.95	49.30	49.66	50.01	50.36	50.72	51.07	51.43	51.79	52.14	52.50	52.86	53.22	53.58
27	50.25	50.62	50.99	51.36	51.73	52.10	52.47	52.84	53.21	53.58	53.96	54.33	54.70	55.08	55.45	55.83
28	52.28	52.66	53.05	53.43	53.82	54.20	54.59	54.98	55.37	55.76	56.14	56.53	56.92	57.31	57.70	58.10
29	54.32	54.72	55.12	55.52	55.92	56.33	56.73	57.13	57.54	57.94	58.35	58.75	59.16	59.57	59.97	60.38
30	56.37	56.79	57.21	57.63	58.05	58.46	58.88	59.30	59.73	60.15	60.57	60.99	61.42	61.84	62.26	62.69
31	58.44	58.88	59.31	59.75	60.18	60.62	61.05	61.49	61.93	62.37	62.81	63.25	63.69	64.13	64.57	65.01
32	60.53	60.98	61.43	61.88	62.34	62.79	63.24	63.70	64.15	64.61	65.06	65.52	65.98	66.43	66.89	67.35
33	62.63	63.10	63.57	64.03	64.50	64.97	65.44	65.92	66.39	66.86	67.33	67.81	68.28	68.76	69.23	69.71
34	64.75	65.23	65.72	66.20	66.69	67.18	67.66	68.15	68.64	69.13	69.62	70.11	70.61	71.10	71.59	72.09
35	66.88	67.38	67.88	68.38	68.89	69.39	69.90	70.40	70.91	71.42	71.93	72.44	72.95	73.46	73.97	74.48
36	69.02	69.54	70.06	70.58	71.10	71.62	72.15	72.67	73.20	73.72	74.25	74.78	75.30	75.83	76.36	76.89
37	71.18	71.72	72.25	72.79	73.33	73.87	74.41	74.96	75.50	76.04	76.59	77.13	77.68	78.22	78.77	79.32
38	73.35	73.91	74.46	75.02	75.58	76.14	76.69	77.25	77.81	78.38	78.94	79.50	80.07	80.63	81.20	81.76
39	75.54	76.11	76.69	77.26	77.84	78.41	78.99	79.57	80.15	80.73	81.31	81.89	82.47	83.06	83.64	84.23
40	77.74	78.33	78.93	79.52	80.11	80.71	81.30	81.90	82.50	83.09	83.69	84.29	84.90	85.50	86.10	86.70
41	79.96	80.57	81.18	81.79	82.40	83.01	83.63	84.24	84.86	85.48	86.09	86.71	87.33	87.95	88.58	89.20
42	82.19	82.82	83.45	84.07	84.71	85.34	85.97	86.60	87.24	87.87	88.51	89.15	89.79	90.43	91.07	91.71
43	84.43	85.08	85.73	86.37	87.02	87.67	88.33	88.98	89.63	90.29	90.94	91.60	92.26	92.92	93.58	94.24
44	86.69	87.36	88.02	88.69	89.36	90.03	90.70	91.37	92.04	92.72	93.39	94.07	94.74	95.42	96.10	96.78
45	88.96	89.65	90.33	91.02	91.70	92.39	93.08	93.77	94.47	95.16	95.85	96.55	97.24	97.94	98.64	99.34
46	91.25	91.95	92.65	93.36	94.07	94.77	95.48	96.19	96.90	97.62	98.33	99.04	99.76	100.48	101.20	101.91
47	93.55	94.27	94.99	95.72	96.44	97.17	97.90	98.63	99.36	100.09	100.82	101.56	102.29	103.03	103.77	104.50
48	95.86	96.60	97.34	98.09	98.83	99.58	100.33	101.07	101.82	102.58	103.33	104.08	104.84	105.59	106.35	107.11
49	98.18	98.94	99.71	100.47	101.23	102.00	102.77	103.54	104.31	105.08	105.85	106.62	107.40	108.18	108.95	109.73
50	100.52	101.30	102.08	102.87	103.65	104.44	105.22	106.01	106.80	107.59	108.39	109.18	109.98	110.77	111.57	112.37
51	102.87	103.67	104.47	105.28	106.08	106.89	107.69	108.50	109.31	110.12	110.94	111.75	112.57	113.38	114.20	115.02
52	105.24	106.06	106.88	107.70	108.53	109.35	110.18	111.01	111.84	112.67	113.50	114.33	115.17	116.01	116.85	117.69
53	107.61	108.45	109.29	110.14	110.98	111.83	112.68	113.52	114.37	115.23	116.08	116.93	117.79	118.65	119.51	120.37
54	110.00	110.86	111.72	112.59	113.45	114.32	115.19	116.05	116.93	117.80	118.67	119.55	120.42	121.30	122.18	123.06
55	112.40	113.28	114.17	115.05	115.94	116.82	117.71	118.60	119.49	120.38	121.28	122.17	123.07	123.97	124.87	125.77
56	114.82	115.72	116.62	117.53	118.43	119.34	120.25	121.16	122.07	122.98	123.90	124.81	125.73	126.65	127.57	128.49
57	117.25	118.17	119.09	120.01	120.94	121.87	122.80	123.73	124.66	125.59	126.53	127.47	128.40	129.34	130.29	131.23
58	119.68	120.63	121.57	122.51	123.46	124.41	125.36	126.31	127.26	128.22	129.17	130.13	131.09	132.05	133.02	133.98
59	122.13	123.10	124.06	125.03	125.99	126.96	127.93	128.91	129.88	130.86	131.83	132.81	133.79	134.78	135.76	136.75
60	124.60	125.58	126.56	127.55	128.54	129.53	130.52	131.51	132.51	133.51	134.51	135.51	136.51	137.51	138.52	139.52

TABLE C-15 (cont.) ANNUAL PERCENTAGE RATE TABLE FOR MONTHLY PAYMENT PLANS

Number of Payments	ANNUAL PERCENTAGE RATE															
	42.00%	42.25%	42.50%	42.75%	43.00%	43.25%	43.50%	43.75%	44.00%	44.25%	44.50%	44.75%	45.00%	45.25%	45.50%	45.75%
	Finance charge per $100 of amount financed															
1	3.50	3.52	3.54	3.56	3.58	3.60	3.62	3.65	3.67	3.69	3.71	3.73	3.75	3.77	3.79	3.81
2	5.28	5.31	5.34	5.37	5.41	5.44	5.47	5.50	5.53	5.56	5.60	5.63	5.66	5.69	5.72	5.75
3	7.08	7.12	7.17	7.21	7.25	7.29	7.34	7.38	7.42	7.46	7.51	7.55	7.59	7.63	7.68	7.72
4	8.90	8.95	9.01	9.06	9.12	9.17	9.22	9.28	9.33	9.39	9.44	9.49	9.55	9.60	9.66	9.71
5	10.74	10.81	10.87	10.94	11.00	11.07	11.13	11.20	11.26	11.33	11.39	11.46	11.53	11.59	11.66	11.72
6	12.60	12.68	12.76	12.83	12.91	12.99	13.06	13.14	13.22	13.30	13.37	13.45	13.53	13.60	13.68	13.76
7	14.48	14.57	14.66	14.75	14.84	14.93	15.02	15.10	15.19	15.28	15.37	15.46	15.55	15.64	15.73	15.82
8	16.38	16.48	16.58	16.69	16.79	16.89	16.99	17.09	17.19	17.29	17.40	17.50	17.60	17.70	17.80	17.90
9	18.30	18.42	18.53	18.64	18.76	18.87	18.98	19.10	19.21	19.33	19.44	19.55	19.67	19.78	19.90	20.01
10	20.24	20.37	20.49	20.62	20.75	20.87	21.00	21.13	21.25	21.38	21.51	21.63	21.76	21.89	22.02	22.14
11	22.20	22.34	22.48	22.62	22.76	22.90	23.04	23.18	23.32	23.46	23.60	23.74	23.88	24.02	24.16	24.30
12	24.18	24.33	24.49	24.64	24.79	24.94	25.10	25.25	25.40	25.55	25.71	25.86	26.01	26.17	26.32	26.48
13	26.18	26.35	26.51	26.68	26.84	27.01	27.18	27.34	27.51	27.67	27.84	28.01	28.18	28.34	28.51	28.68
14	28.20	28.38	28.56	28.74	28.92	29.10	29.28	29.46	29.64	29.82	30.00	30.18	30.36	30.54	30.72	30.90
15	30.24	30.43	30.62	30.82	31.01	31.20	31.40	31.59	31.79	31.98	32.17	32.37	32.56	32.76	32.95	33.15
16	32.30	32.50	32.71	32.92	33.12	33.33	33.54	33.75	33.96	34.17	34.37	34.58	34.79	35.00	35.21	35.42
17	34.37	34.59	34.82	35.04	35.26	35.48	35.70	35.93	36.15	36.37	36.60	36.82	37.04	37.27	37.49	37.71
18	36.47	36.71	36.94	37.18	37.41	37.65	37.89	38.13	38.36	38.60	38.84	39.08	39.31	39.55	39.79	40.03
19	38.59	38.84	39.09	39.34	39.59	39.84	40.09	40.34	40.60	40.85	41.10	41.35	41.61	41.86	42.11	42.37
20	40.72	40.99	41.25	41.52	41.79	42.05	42.32	42.59	42.85	43.12	43.39	43.66	43.92	44.19	44.46	44.73
21	42.88	43.16	43.44	43.72	44.00	44.28	44.56	44.85	45.13	45.41	45.69	45.98	46.26	46.55	46.83	47.11
22	45.05	45.35	45.64	45.94	46.24	46.53	46.83	47.13	47.43	47.72	48.02	48.32	48.62	48.92	49.22	49.52
23	47.24	47.55	47.87	48.18	48.49	48.80	49.12	49.43	49.74	50.06	50.37	50.69	51.00	51.32	51.63	51.95
24	49.45	49.78	50.11	50.44	50.77	51.09	51.42	51.75	52.08	52.41	52.74	53.07	53.41	53.74	54.07	54.40
25	51.69	52.03	52.37	52.72	53.06	53.40	53.75	54.10	54.44	54.79	55.13	55.48	55.83	56.18	56.53	56.87
26	53.93	54.29	54.65	55.01	55.37	55.73	56.10	56.46	56.82	57.18	57.55	57.91	58.27	58.64	59.00	59.37
27	56.20	56.58	56.95	57.33	57.71	58.08	58.46	58.84	59.22	59.60	59.98	60.36	60.74	61.12	61.50	61.89
28	58.49	58.88	59.27	59.67	60.06	60.45	60.85	61.24	61.64	62.04	62.43	62.83	63.23	63.63	64.02	64.42
29	60.79	61.20	61.61	62.02	62.43	62.84	63.25	63.67	64.08	64.49	64.91	65.32	65.73	66.15	66.57	66.98
30	63.11	63.54	63.97	64.39	64.82	65.25	65.68	66.11	66.54	66.97	67.40	67.83	68.26	68.70	69.13	69.56
31	65.45	65.90	66.34	66.79	67.23	67.68	68.12	68.57	69.02	69.46	69.91	70.36	70.81	71.26	71.71	72.16
32	67.81	68.27	68.73	69.20	69.66	70.12	70.59	71.05	71.51	71.98	72.45	72.91	73.38	73.85	74.32	74.79
33	70.19	70.67	71.15	71.63	72.11	72.59	73.07	73.55	74.03	74.52	75.00	75.48	75.97	76.45	76.94	77.43
34	72.58	73.08	73.58	74.07	74.57	75.07	75.57	76.07	76.57	77.07	77.57	78.07	78.58	79.08	79.59	80.09
35	74.99	75.51	76.02	76.54	77.05	77.57	78.09	78.61	79.12	79.64	80.16	80.68	81.21	81.73	82.25	82.78
36	77.42	77.95	78.49	79.02	79.55	80.09	80.62	81.16	81.70	82.24	82.77	83.31	83.85	84.39	84.94	85.48
37	79.87	80.42	80.97	81.52	82.07	82.63	83.18	83.74	84.29	84.85	85.40	85.96	86.52	87.08	87.64	88.20
38	82.33	82.90	83.47	84.04	84.61	85.18	85.76	86.33	86.90	87.48	88.05	88.63	89.21	89.79	90.37	90.95
39	84.81	85.40	85.99	86.58	87.17	87.76	88.35	88.94	89.53	90.13	90.72	91.32	91.91	92.51	93.11	93.71
40	87.31	87.91	88.52	89.13	89.74	90.35	90.96	91.57	92.18	92.79	93.41	94.02	94.64	95.25	95.87	96.49
41	89.82	90.45	91.07	91.70	92.33	92.96	93.58	94.22	94.85	95.48	96.11	96.75	97.38	98.02	98.65	99.29
42	92.35	93.00	93.64	94.29	94.93	95.58	96.23	96.88	97.53	98.18	98.83	99.49	100.14	100.80	101.45	102.11
43	94.90	95.56	96.23	96.89	97.56	98.22	98.89	99.56	100.23	100.90	101.57	102.25	102.92	103.60	104.27	104.95
44	97.46	98.14	98.83	99.51	100.20	100.88	101.57	102.26	102.95	103.64	104.33	105.03	105.72	106.41	107.11	107.81
45	100.04	100.74	101.45	102.15	102.85	103.56	104.27	104.98	105.69	106.40	107.11	107.82	108.53	109.25	109.96	110.68
46	102.63	103.36	104.08	104.80	105.53	106.25	106.98	107.71	108.44	109.17	109.90	110.63	111.37	112.10	112.84	113.58
47	105.25	105.99	106.73	107.47	108.22	108.96	109.71	110.46	111.21	111.96	112.71	113.46	114.22	114.97	115.73	116.49
48	107.87	108.63	109.39	110.16	110.92	111.69	112.46	113.23	113.99	114.77	115.54	116.31	117.09	117.86	118.64	119.42
49	110.51	111.29	112.08	112.86	113.64	114.43	115.22	116.01	116.80	117.59	118.38	119.17	119.97	120.77	121.56	122.36
50	113.17	113.97	114.77	115.58	116.38	117.19	118.00	118.81	119.62	120.43	121.24	122.06	122.87	123.69	124.51	125.32
51	115.84	116.66	117.48	118.31	119.14	119.96	120.79	121.62	122.45	123.28	124.12	124.95	125.79	126.63	127.46	128.30
52	118.53	119.37	120.21	121.06	121.90	122.75	123.60	124.45	125.30	126.16	127.01	127.87	128.72	129.58	130.44	131.30
53	121.23	122.09	122.95	123.82	124.69	125.56	126.43	127.30	128.17	129.04	129.92	130.80	131.67	132.55	133.43	134.32
54	123.94	124.83	125.71	126.60	127.49	128.38	129.27	130.16	130.16	131.95	132.84	133.74	134.64	135.54	136.44	137.35
55	126.67	127.58	128.48	129.39	130.30	131.21	132.12	133.03	133.95	134.87	135.78	136.70	137.62	138.54	139.47	140.39
56	129.42	130.34	131.27	132.20	133.13	134.06	134.99	135.93	136.86	137.80	138.74	139.68	140.62	141.56	142.51	143.45
57	132.17	133.12	134.07	135.02	135.97	136.92	137.88	138.83	139.79	140.75	141.71	142.67	143.63	144.60	145.56	146.53
58	134.95	135.91	136.88	137.85	138.83	139.80	140.78	141.75	142.73	143.71	144.69	145.68	146.66	147.65	148.63	149.62
59	137.73	138.72	139.71	140.70	141.70	142.69	143.69	144.69	145.69	146.69	147.69	148.70	149.70	150.71	151.72	152.73
60	140.53	141.54	142.55	143.57	144.58	145.60	146.62	147.64	148.66	149.68	150.71	151.73	152.76	153.79	154.82	155.85

TABLE C-16   INTEREST FROM DAY OF DEPOSIT

At 4.5% Compounded Daily (for One Quarter)

QUARTER	1ST MONTH	2ND MONTH	3RD MONTH
1st	January	February	March
2nd	April	May	June
3rd	July	August	September
4th	October	November	December

1ST MONTH		2ND MONTH		3RD MONTH	
DEP. DATE	FACTOR	DEP. DATE	FACTOR	DEP. DATE	FACTOR
1	.0113128	1	.0075277	1	.0037568
2	.0111864	2	.0074018	2	.0036314
3	.0110600	3	.0072759	3	.0035059
4	.0109337	4	.0071500	4	.0033805
5	.0108073	5	.0070241	5	.0032551
6	.0106810	6	.0068983	6	.0031297
7	.0105547	7	.0067724	7	.0030043
8	.0104284	8	.0066466	8	.0028790
9	.0103021	9	.0065208	9	.0027536
10	.0101758	10	.0063950	10	.0026283
11	.0100495	11	.0062692	11	.0025030
12	.0099233	12	.0061434	12	.0023777
13	.0097971	13	.0060177	13	.0022524
14	.0096709	14	.0058919	14	.0021271
15	.0095447	15	.0057662	15	.0020019
16	.0094185	16	.0056405	16	.0018766
17	.0092923	17	.0055148	17	.0017514
18	.0091662	18	.0053891	18	.0016262
19	.0090401	19	.0052635	19	.0015010
20	.0089139	20	.0051378	20	.0013759
21	.0087878	21	.0050122	21	.0012507
22	.0086618	22	.0048866	22	.0011256
23	.0085357	23	.0047610	23	.0010004
24	.0084096	24	.0046354	24	.0008753
25	.0082836	25	.0045099	25	.0007502
26	.0081576	26	.0043843	26	.0006252
27	.0080316	27	.0042588	27	.0005001
28	.0079056	28	.0041333	28	.0003751
29	.0077796	29	.0040078	29	.0002500
30	.0076537	30	.0038823	30	.0001250

TABLE C-17 INTEREST TO DAY OF WITHDRAWAL

At 4.5% Compounded Daily (for One Quarter)

1ST MONTH		2ND MONTH		3RD MONTH	
W/D DATE	FACTOR	W/D DATE	FACTOR	W/D DATE	FACTOR
1	.0001250	1	.0038823	1	.0076537
2	.0002500	2	.0040078	2	.0077796
3	.0003751	3	.0041333	3	.0079056
4	.0005001	4	.0042588	4	.0080316
5	.0006252	5	.0043843	5	.0081576
6	.0007502	6	.0045099	6	.0082836
7	.0008753	7	.0046354	7	.0084096
8	.0010004	8	.0047610	8	.0085357
9	.0011256	9	.0048866	9	.0086618
10	.0012507	10	.0050122	10	.0087878
11	.0013759	11	.0051378	11	.0089139
12	.0015010	12	.0052635	12	.0090401
13	.0016262	13	.0053891	13	.0091662
14	.0017514	14	.0055148	14	.0092923
15	.0018766	15	.0056405	15	.0094185
16	.0020019	16	.0057662	16	.0095447
17	.0021271	17	.0058919	17	.0096709
18	.0022524	18	.0060177	18	.0097971
19	.0023777	19	.0061434	19	.0099233
20	.0025030	20	.0062692	20	.0100495
21	.0026283	21	.0063950	21	.0101758
22	.0027536	22	.0065208	22	.0103021
23	.0028790	23	.0066466	23	.0104284
24	.0030043	24	.0067724	24	.0105547
25	.0031297	25	.0068983	25	.0106810
26	.0032551	26	.0070241	26	.0108073
27	.0033805	27	.0071500	27	.0109337
28	.0035059	28	.0072759	28	.0110600
29	.0036314	29	.0074018	29	.0111864
30	.0037568	30	.0075277	30	.0113128

Tables C-18 through C-23 are printed courtesy of the Financial Publishing Company, Boston, Massachusetts.

	PERIODS	XIV COMPOUND AMOUNT — AMOUNT OF 1 (How $1 left at compound interest will grow.)	XV AMOUNT OF ANNUITY — AMOUNT OF 1 PER PERIOD (How $1 deposited periodically will grow.)	XVI SINKING FUND — SINKING FUND (Periodic deposit that will grow to $1 at future date.)	XVII PRESENT VALUE — PRESENT WORTH OF 1 (What $1 due in the future is worth today.)	XVIII PRESENT VALUE OF ANNUITY — PRESENT WORTH OF 1 PER PERIOD (What $1 payable periodically is worth today.)	XIX AMORTIZATION — PARTIAL PAYMENT (Annuity worth $1 today. Periodic payment necessary to pay off a loan of $1.)	PERIODS
RATE 5/12%	1	1.004 166 6667	1.000 000 0000	1.000 000 0000	.995 850 6224	.995 850 6224	1.004 166 6667	1
	2	1.008 350 6944	2.004 166 6667	.498 960 4990	.991 718 4621	1.987 569 0846	.503 127 1656	2
	3	1.012 552 1557	3.012 517 3611	.331 948 2944	.987 603 4478	2.975 172 5323	.336 114 9611	3
	4	1.016 771 1230	4.025 069 5168	.248 442 9140	.983 505 5082	3.958 678 0405	.252 609 5807	4
	5	1.021 007 6693	5.041 840 6398	.198 340 2633	.979 424 5724	4.938 102 6129	.202 506 9300	5
	6	1.025 261 8680	6.062 848 3091	.164 938 9774	.975 360 5701	5.913 463 1830	.169 105 6440	6
	7	1.029 533 7924	7.088 110 1771	.141 081 3285	.971 313 4308	6.884 776 6138	.145 247 9951	7
	8	1.033 823 5165	8.117 643 9695	.123 188 4527	.967 283 0846	7.852 059 6984	.127 355 1193	8
	9	1.038 131 1145	9.151 467 4860	.109 272 0923	.963 269 4618	8.815 329 1602	.113 438 7590	9
	10	1.042 456 6608	10.189 598 6005	.098 139 2927	.959 272 4931	9.774 601 6533	.102 305 9594	10
	11	1.046 800 2303	11.232 055 2614	.089 030 9010	.955 292 1093	10.729 893 7626	.093 197 5677	11
	12	1.051 161 8979	12.278 855 4916	.081 440 8151	.951 328 2416	11.681 222 0043	.085 607 4818	12
	13	1.055 541 7391	13.330 017 3895	.075 018 6568	.947 380 8216	12.628 602 8259	.079 185 3235	13
	14	1.059 939 8297	14.385 559 1286	.069 514 1559	.943 449 7808	13.572 052 6067	.073 680 8226	14
	15	1.064 356 2457	15.445 498 9583	.064 743 7809	.939 535 0514	14.511 587 6581	.068 910 4475	15
	16	1.068 791 0633	16.509 855 2040	.060 569 8831	.935 636 5657	15.447 224 2238	.064 736 5498	16
	17	1.073 244 3594	17.578 646 2673	.056 887 2019	.931 754 2563	16.378 978 4802	.061 053 8686	17
	18	1.077 716 2109	18.651 890 6268	.053 613 8679	.927 888 0561	17.306 866 5363	.057 780 5346	18
	19	1.082 206 6952	19.729 606 8377	.050 685 2472	.924 037 8982	18.230 904 4344	.054 851 9139	19
	20	1.086 715 8897	20.811 813 5329	.048 049 6329	.920 203 7160	19.151 108 1505	.052 216 2996	20
	21	1.091 243 8726	21.898 529 4226	.045 665 1669	.916 385 4434	20.067 493 5938	.049 831 8335	21
	22	1.095 790 7221	22.989 773 2952	.043 497 6016	.912 583 0141	20.980 076 6080	.047 664 2683	22
	23	1.100 356 5167	24.085 564 0173	.041 518 6457	.908 796 3626	21.888 872 9706	.045 685 3124	23
	24	1.104 941 3356	25.185 920 5340	.039 704 7231	.905 025 4234	22.793 898 3940	.043 871 3897	24
	25	1.109 545 2578	26.290 861 8696	.038 036 0296	.901 270 1311	23.695 168 5251	.042 202 6963	25
	26	1.114 168 3630	27.400 407 1273	.036 495 8081	.897 530 4211	24.592 698 9462	.040 662 4748	26
	27	1.118 810 7312	28.514 575 4904	.035 069 7839	.893 806 2284	25.486 505 1746	.039 236 4506	27
	28	1.123 472 4426	29.633 386 2216	.033 745 7215	.890 097 4889	26.376 602 6635	.037 912 3882	28
	29	1.128 153 5778	30.756 858 6642	.032 513 0733	.886 404 1383	27.263 006 8018	.036 679 7400	29
	30	1.132 854 2177	21.885 012 2419	.031 362 6977	.882 726 1129	28.145 732 9147	.035 529 3644	30
	31	1.137 574 4436	33.017 866 4596	.030 286 6329	.879 063 3489	29.024 796 2636	.034 453 2995	31
	32	1.142 314 3371	34.155 440 9032	.029 277 9122	.875 415 7831	29.900 212 0467	.033 444 5789	32
	33	1.147 073 9802	35.297 755 2403	.028 330 4135	.871 783 3525	30.771 995 3992	.032 497 0801	33
	34	1.151 853 4551	36.444 829 2205	.027 438 7347	.868 165 9942	31.640 161 3934	.031 605 4014	34
	35	1.156 652 8445	37.596 682 6756	.026 598 0913	.864 563 6457	32.504 725 0391	.030 764 7580	35
	36	1.161 472 2313	38.753 335 5200	.025 804 2304	.860 976 2447	33.365 701 2837	.029 970 8971	36
	37	1.166 311 6990	39.914 807 7514	.025 053 3588	.857 403 7291	34.223 105 0129	.029 220 0255	37
	38	1.171 171 3310	41.081 119 4503	.024 342 0825	.853 846 0373	35.076 951 0501	.028 508 7492	38
	39	1.176 051 2116	42.252 290 7814	.023 667 3558	.850 303 1077	35.927 254 1578	.027 834 0225	39
	40	1.180 951 4250	43.428 341 9930	.023 026 4374	.846 774 8790	36.774 029 0368	.027 193 1041	40
	41	1.185 872 0559	44.609 293 4179	.022 416 8536	.843 261 2903	37.617 290 3271	.026 583 5203	41
	42	1.190 813 1895	45.795 165 4738	.021 836 3661	.839 762 2808	38.457 052 6079	.026 003 0328	42
	43	1.195 774 9111	46.985 978 6633	.021 282 9450	.836 277 7900	39.293 330 3979	.025 449 6117	43
	44	1.200 757 3066	48.181 753 5744	.020 754 7448	.832 807 7577	40.126 138 1556	.024 921 4115	44
	45	1.205 760 4620	49.382 510 8810	.020 250 0841	.829 352 1238	40.955 490 2795	.024 416 7508	45
	46	1.210 784 4639	50.588 271 3430	.019 767 4278	.825 910 8287	41.781 401 1082	.023 934 0944	46
	47	1.215 829 3992	51.799 055 8069	.019 305 3712	.822 483 8128	42.603 884 9210	.023 472 0379	47
	48	1.220 895 3550	53.014 885 2061	.018 862 6269	.819 071 0169	43.422 955 9379	.023 029 2936	48
	49	1.225 982 4190	54.235 780 5611	.018 438 0125	.815 672 3820	44.238 628 3199	.022 604 6792	49
	50	1.231 090 6791	55.461 762 9801	.018 030 4402	.812 287 8493	45.050 916 1692	.022 197 1069	50
	51	1.236 220 2236	56.692 853 6592	.017 638 9075	.808 917 3603	45.859 833 5295	.021 805 5741	51
	52	1.241 371 1412	57.929 073 8828	.017 262 4890	.805 560 8567	46.665 394 3862	.021 429 1557	52
	53	1.246 543 5209	59.170 445 0240	.016 900 3292	.802 218 2806	47.467 612 6668	.021 066 9959	53
	54	1.251 737 4523	60.416 988 5449	.016 551 6360	.798 889 5740	48.266 502 2408	.020 718 3026	54
	55	1.256 953 0250	61.668 725 9972	.016 215 6747	.795 574 6795	49.062 076 9203	.020 382 3414	55
	56	1.262 190 3293	62.925 679 0222	.015 891 7634	.792 273 5397	49.854 350 4600	.020 058 4300	56
	57	1.267 449 4556	64.187 869 3514	.015 579 2677	.788 986 0977	50.643 336 5577	.019 745 9344	57
	58	1.272 730 4950	65.455 318 8071	.015 277 5973	.785 712 2964	51.429 048 8542	.019 444 2639	58
	59	1.278 033 5388	66.728 049 3021	.014 986 2016	.782 452 0794	52.211 500 9336	.019 152 8683	59
	60	1.283 358 6785	68.006 082 8408	.014 704 5670	.779 205 3903	52.990 706 3239	.018 871 2336	60
	61	1.288 706 0063	69.289 441 5193	.014 432 2133	.775 972 1729	53.766 678 4969	.018 598 8800	61
	62	1.294 075 6147	70.578 147 5257	.014 168 6915	.772 752 3714	54.539 430 8682	.018 335 3582	62
	63	1.299 467 5964	71.872 223 1404	.013 913 5810	.769 545 9300	55.308 976 7982	.018 080 2477	63
	64	1.304 882 0447	73.171 690 7368	.013 666 4875	.766 352 7934	56.075 329 5916	.017 833 1542	64
	65	1.310 319 0533	74.476 572 7815	.013 427 0410	.763 172 9063	56.838 502 4979	.017 593 7077	65
	66	1.315 778 7160	75.786 891 8348	.013 194 8939	.760 006 2137	57.598 508 7116	.017 361 5606	66
	67	1.321 261 1273	77.102 670 5508	.012 969 7194	.756 852 6609	58.355 361 3725	.017 136 3860	67
	68	1.326 766 3820	78.423 931 6781	.012 751 2097	.753 712 1935	59.109 073 5660	.016 917 8764	68
	69	1.332 294 5753	79.750 698 0600	.012 539 0752	.750 584 7570	59.859 658 3230	.016 705 7419	69
	70	1.337 845 8026	81.082 992 6353	.012 333 0426	.747 470 2974	60.607 128 6204	.016 499 7092	70
	71	1.343 420 1602	82.420 838 4379	.012 132 8540	.744 368 7609	61.351 497 3813	.016 299 5207	71
	72	1.349 017 7442	83.764 258 5981	.011 938 2660	.741 280 0939	62.092 777 4752	.016 104 9327	72
	73	1.354 638 6514	85.113 276 3423	.011 749 0484	.738 204 2428	62.830 981 7180	.015 915 7150	73
	74	1.360 282 9707	86.467 914 9937	.011 564 9834	.735 141 1547	63.566 122 8727	.015 731 6500	74
	75	1.365 950 8249	87.828 197 9728	.011 385 8649	.732 090 7765	64.298 213 6492	.015 552 5316	75
	76	1.371 642 2867	89.194 148 7977	.011 211 4978	.729 053 0554	65.027 266 7046	.015 378 1644	76
	77	1.377 357 4629	90.565 791 0844	.011 041 6967	.726 027 9390	65.753 294 6435	.015 208 3634	77
	78	1.383 096 4523	91.943 148 5472	.010 876 2862	.723 015 3749	66.476 310 0185	.015 042 9529	78
	79	1.388 859 3542	93.326 244 9995	.010 715 0995	.720 015 3111	67.196 325 3296	.014 881 7662	79
	80	1.394 646 2681	94.715 104 3537	.010 557 9781	.717 027 6957	67.913 353 0253	.014 724 6448	80
	81	1.400 457 2943	96.109 750 6218	.010 404 7716	.714 052 4771	68.627 405 5024	.014 571 4382	81
	82	1.406 292 5330	97.510 207 9161	.010 255 3366	.711 089 6037	69.338 495 1061	.014 422 0032	82
	83	1.412 152 0852	98.916 500 4490	.010 109 5368	.708 139 0245	70.046 634 1306	.014 276 2035	83
	84	1.418 036 0522	100.328 652 5342	.009 967 2424	.705 200 6883	70.751 834 8188	.014 133 9091	84
	85	1.423 944 5358	101.746 688 5865	.009 828 3297	.702 274 5443	71.454 109 3632	.013 994 9964	85
	86	1.429 877 6380	103.170 633 1223	.009 692 6807	.699 360 5421	72.153 469 9052	.013 859 3473	86
	87	1.435 835 4615	104.600 510 7603	.009 560 1828	.696 458 6311	72.849 928 5363	.013 726 8494	87
	88	1.441 818 1093	106.036 346 2218	.009 430 7286	.693 568 7613	73.543 497 2976	.013 597 3952	88
	89	1.447 825 6847	107.478 164 3310	.009 304 2155	.690 690 8826	74.234 188 1802	.013 470 8821	89
	90	1.453 858 2917	108.925 990 0157	.009 180 5454	.687 824 9453	74.922 013 1255	.013 347 2121	90
	91	1.459 916 0346	110.379 848 3075	.009 059 6247	.684 970 8999	75.606 984 0254	.013 226 2914	91
	92	1.465 999 0181	111.839 764 3421	.008 941 3636	.682 128 6970	76.289 112 7224	.013 108 0303	92
	93	1.472 107 3473	113.305 763 3602	.008 825 6764	.679 298 2875	76.968 411 0098	.012 992 3431	93
	94	1.478 241 1279	114.777 870 7075	.008 712 4808	.676 479 6224	77.644 890 6322	.012 879 1475	94
	95	1.484 400 4660	116.256 111 8355	.008 601 6983	.673 672 6530	78.318 563 2852	.012 768 3650	95
	96	1.490 585 4679	117.740 512 3014	.008 493 2533	.670 877 3308	78.989 440 6159	.012 659 9200	96
	97	1.496 796 2407	119.231 097 7694	.008 387 0737	.668 093 6074	79.657 534 2233	.012 553 7403	97
	98	1.503 032 8917	120.727 894 0101	.008 283 0899	.665 321 4348	80.322 855 6581	.012 449 7566	98
	99	1.509 295 5288	122.230 926 9018	.008 181 2355	.662 560 7649	80.985 416 4230	.012 347 9022	99
	100	1.515 584 2601	123.740 222 4305	.008 081 4466	.659 811 5501	81.645 227 9731	.012 248 1133	100

RATE 1/2%	PERIODS	XIV COMPOUND AMOUNT — AMOUNT OF 1 — How $1 left at compound interest will grow.	XV AMOUNT OF ANNUITY — AMOUNT OF 1 PER PERIOD — How $1 deposited periodically will grow.	XVI SINKING FUND — SINKING FUND — Periodic deposit that will grow to $1 at future date.	XVII PRESENT VALUE — PRESENT WORTH OF 1 — What $1 due in the future is worth today.	XVIII PRESENT VALUE OF ANNUITY — PRESENT WORTH OF 1 PER PERIOD — What $1 payable periodically is worth today.	XIX AMORTIZATION — PARTIAL PAYMENT — Annuity worth $1 today. Periodic payment necessary to pay off a loan of $1.	PERIODS
	1	1.005 000 0000	1.000 000 0000	1.000 000 0000	.995 024 8756	.995 024 8756	1.005 000 0000	1
	2	1.010 025 0000	2.005 000 0000	.498 753 1172	.990 074 5031	1.985 099 3787	.503 753 1172	2
	3	1.015 075 1250	3.015 025 0000	.331 672 2084	.985 148 7593	2.970 248 1380	.336 672 2084	3
	4	1.020 150 5006	4.030 100 1250	.248 132 7930	.980 247 5217	3.950 495 6597	.253 132 7930	4
	5	1.025 251 2531	5.050 250 6256	.198 009 9750	.975 370 6684	4.925 866 3281	.203 009 9750	5
	6	1.030 377 5094	6.075 501 8788	.164 595 4556	.970 518 0780	5.896 384 4061	.169 595 4556	6
	7	1.035 529 3969	7.105 879 3881	.140 728 5355	.965 689 6298	6.862 074 0359	.145 728 5355	7
	8	1.040 707 0439	8.141 408 7851	.122 828 8649	.960 885 2038	7.822 959 2397	.127 828 8649	8
	9	1.045 910 5791	9.182 115 8290	.108 907 3606	.956 104 6804	8.779 063 9201	.113 907 3606	9
	10	1.051 140 1320	10.228 026 4082	.097 770 5727	.951 347 9407	9.730 411 8608	.102 770 5727	10
	11	1.056 395 8327	11.279 166 5402	.088 659 0331	.946 614 8664	10.677 026 7272	.093 659 0331	11
	12	1.061 677 8119	12.335 562 3729	.081 066 4297	.941 905 3397	11.618 932 0668	.086 066 4297	12
	13	1.066 986 2009	13.397 240 1848	.074 642 2387	.937 219 2434	12.556 151 3103	.079 642 2387	13
	14	1.072 321 1319	14.464 226 3857	.069 136 0860	.932 556 4611	13.488 707 7714	.074 136 0860	14
	15	1.077 682 7376	15.536 547 5176	.064 364 3640	.927 916 8768	14.416 624 6482	.069 364 3640	15
	16	1.083 071 1513	16.614 230 2552	.060 189 3669	.923 300 3749	15.339 925 0231	.065 189 3669	16
	17	1.088 486 5070	17.697 301 4065	.056 505 7902	.918 706 8407	16.258 631 8637	.061 505 7902	17
	18	1.093 928 9396	18.785 787 9135	.053 231 7305	.914 136 1599	17.172 768 0236	.058 231 7305	18
	19	1.099 398 5843	19.879 716 8531	.050 302 5273	.909 588 2188	18.082 356 2424	.055 302 5273	19
	20	1.104 895 5772	20.979 115 4373	.047 666 4520	.905 062 9043	18.987 419 1467	.052 666 4520	20
	21	1.110 420 0551	22.084 011 0145	.045 281 6293	.900 560 1037	19.887 979 2504	.050 281 6293	21
	22	1.115 972 1553	23.194 431 0696	.043 113 7973	.896 079 7052	20.784 058 9556	.048 113 7973	22
	23	1.121 552 0161	24.310 403 2250	.041 134 6530	.891 621 5972	21.675 680 5529	.046 134 6530	23
	24	1.127 159 7762	25.431 955 2411	.039 320 6103	.887 185 6689	22.562 866 2218	.044 320 6103	24
	25	1.132 795 5751	26.559 115 0173	.037 651 8570	.882 771 8098	23.445 638 0316	.042 651 8570	25
	26	1.138 459 5530	27.691 910 5924	.036 111 6289	.878 379 9103	24.324 017 9419	.041 111 6289	26
	27	1.144 151 8507	28.830 370 1453	.034 685 6456	.874 009 8610	25.198 027 8029	.039 685 6456	27
	28	1.149 872 6100	29.974 521 9961	.033 361 6663	.869 661 5532	26.067 689 3561	.038 361 6663	28
	29	1.155 621 9730	31.124 394 6060	.032 129 1390	.865 334 8788	26.933 024 2349	.037 129 1390	29
	30	1.161 400 0829	32.280 016 5791	.030 978 9184	.861 029 7302	27.794 053 9651	.035 978 9184	30
	31	1.167 207 0833	33.441 416 6620	.029 903 0394	.856 746 0002	28.650 799 9653	.034 903 0394	31
	32	1.173 043 1187	34.608 623 7453	.028 894 5324	.852 483 5823	29.503 283 5475	.033 894 5324	32
	33	1.178 908 3343	35.781 666 8640	.027 947 2727	.848 242 3704	30.351 525 9179	.032 947 2727	33
	34	1.184 802 8760	36.960 575 1983	.027 055 8560	.844 022 2591	31.195 548 1771	.032 055 8560	34
	35	1.190 726 8904	38.145 378 0743	.026 215 4958	.839 823 1434	32.035 371 3205	.031 215 4958	35
	36	1.196 680 5248	39.336 104 9647	.025 421 9375	.835 644 9188	32.871 016 2393	.030 421 9375	36
	37	1.202 663 9274	40.532 785 4895	.024 671 3861	.831 487 4814	33.702 503 7207	.029 671 3861	37
	38	1.208 677 2471	41.735 449 4170	.023 960 4464	.827 350 7278	34.529 854 4484	.028 960 4464	38
	39	1.214 720 6333	42.944 126 6640	.023 286 0714	.823 234 5550	35.353 089 0034	.028 286 0714	39
	40	1.220 794 2365	44.158 847 2974	.022 645 5186	.819 138 8607	36.172 227 8641	.027 645 5186	40
	41	1.226 898 2077	45.379 641 5338	.022 036 3133	.815 063 5430	36.987 291 4070	.027 036 3133	41
	42	1.233 032 6987	46.606 539 7415	.021 456 2163	.811 008 5005	37.798 299 9075	.026 456 2163	42
	43	1.239 197 8622	47.839 572 4402	.020 903 1969	.806 973 6323	38.605 273 5398	.025 903 1969	43
	44	1.245 393 8515	49.078 770 3024	.020 375 4086	.802 958 8381	39.408 232 3779	.025 375 4086	44
	45	1.251 620 8208	50.324 164 1539	.019 871 1696	.798 964 0180	40.207 196 3959	.024 871 1696	45
	46	1.257 878 9249	51.575 784 9747	.019 388 9439	.794 989 0727	41.002 185 4686	.024 388 9439	46
	47	1.264 168 3195	52.833 663 8996	.018 927 3264	.791 033 9031	41.793 219 3717	.023 927 3264	47
	48	1.270 489 1611	54.097 832 2191	.018 485 0290	.787 098 4111	42.580 317 7828	.023 485 0290	48
	49	1.276 841 6069	55.368 321 3802	.018 060 8690	.783 182 4986	43.363 500 2814	.023 060 8690	49
	50	1.283 225 8149	56.645 162 9871	.017 653 7580	.779 286 0683	44.142 786 3497	.022 653 7580	50
	51	1.289 641 9440	57.928 388 8020	.017 262 6931	.775 409 0231	44.918 195 3728	.022 262 6931	51
	52	1.296 090 1537	59.218 030 7460	.016 886 7486	.771 551 2668	45.689 746 6396	.021 886 7486	52
	53	1.302 570 6045	60.514 120 8997	.016 525 0686	.767 712 7033	46.457 459 3429	.021 525 0686	53
	54	1.309 083 4575	61.816 691 5042	.016 176 8606	.763 893 2371	47.221 352 5800	.021 176 8606	54
	55	1.315 628 8748	63.125 774 9618	.015 841 3897	.760 092 7732	47.981 445 3532	.020 841 3897	55
	56	1.322 207 0192	64.441 403 8366	.015 517 9735	.756 311 2171	48.737 756 5704	.020 517 9735	56
	57	1.328 818 0543	65.763 610 8558	.015 205 9777	.752 548 4748	49.490 305 0452	.020 205 9777	57
	58	1.335 462 1446	67.092 428 9100	.014 904 8114	.748 804 4525	50.239 109 4977	.019 904 8114	58
	59	1.342 139 4553	68.427 891 0546	.014 613 9240	.745 079 0572	50.984 188 5549	.019 613 9240	59
	60	1.348 850 1525	69.770 030 5099	.014 332 8015	.741 372 1962	51.725 560 7511	.019 332 8015	60
	61	1.355 594 4033	71.118 880 6624	.014 060 9637	.737 683 7774	52.463 244 5285	.019 060 9637	61
	62	1.362 372 3753	72.474 475 0657	.013 797 9613	.734 013 7088	53.197 258 2373	.018 797 9613	62
	63	1.369 184 2372	73.836 847 4411	.013 543 3735	.730 361 8993	53.927 620 1366	.018 543 3735	63
	64	1.376 030 1584	75.206 031 6783	.013 296 8058	.726 728 2580	54.654 348 3946	.018 296 8058	64
	65	1.382 910 3092	76.582 061 8366	.013 057 8882	.723 112 6946	55.377 461 0892	.018 057 8882	65
	66	1.389 824 8607	77.964 972 1458	.012 826 2728	.719 515 1190	56.096 976 2082	.017 826 2728	66
	67	1.396 773 9850	79.354 797 0066	.012 601 6326	.715 935 4418	56.812 911 6499	.017 601 6326	67
	68	1.403 757 8550	80.751 570 9916	.012 383 6600	.712 373 5739	57.525 285 2238	.017 383 6600	68
	69	1.410 776 6442	82.155 328 8466	.012 172 0650	.708 829 4267	58.234 114 6505	.017 172 0650	69
	70	1.417 830 5275	83.566 105 4908	.011 966 5742	.705 302 9122	58.939 417 5627	.016 966 5742	70
	71	1.424 919 6801	84.983 936 0182	.011 766 9297	.701 793 9425	59.641 211 5052	.016 766 9297	71
	72	1.432 044 2785	86.408 855 6983	.011 572 8879	.698 302 4303	60.339 513 9355	.016 572 8879	72
	73	1.439 204 4999	87.840 899 9768	.011 384 2185	.694 828 2889	61.034 342 2244	.016 384 2185	73
	74	1.446 400 5224	89.280 104 4767	.011 200 7037	.691 371 4317	61.725 713 6561	.016 200 7037	74
	75	1.453 632 5250	90.726 504 9991	.011 022 1374	.687 931 7729	62.413 645 4290	.016 022 1374	75
	76	1.460 900 6876	92.180 137 5241	.010 848 3240	.684 509 2267	63.098 154 6557	.015 848 3240	76
	77	1.468 205 1911	93.641 038 2117	.010 679 0785	.681 103 7082	63.779 258 3639	.015 679 0785	77
	78	1.475 546 2170	95.109 243 4028	.010 514 2252	.677 715 1325	64.456 973 4964	.015 514 2252	78
	79	1.482 923 9481	96.584 789 6198	.010 353 5971	.674 343 4154	65.131 316 9118	.015 353 5971	79
	80	1.490 338 5678	98.067 713 5679	.010 197 0359	.670 988 4731	65.802 305 3849	.015 197 0359	80
	81	1.497 790 2607	99.558 052 1357	.010 044 3910	.667 650 2267	66.469 955 6069	.015 044 3910	81
	82	1.505 279 2120	101.055 842 3964	.009 895 5189	.664 328 5791	67.134 284 1859	.014 895 5189	82
	83	1.512 805 6080	102.561 121 6084	.009 750 2834	.661 023 4618	67.795 307 6477	.014 750 2834	83
	84	1.520 369 6361	104.073 927 2164	.009 608 5545	.657 734 7878	68.453 042 4355	.014 608 5545	84
	85	1.527 971 4843	105.594 296 8525	.009 470 2084	.654 462 4754	69.107 504 9110	.014 470 2084	85
	86	1.535 611 3417	107.122 268 3368	.009 335 1272	.651 206 4432	69.758 711 3542	.014 335 1272	86
	87	1.543 289 3984	108.657 879 6784	.009 203 1982	.647 966 6102	70.406 677 9644	.014 203 1982	87
	88	1.551 005 8454	110.201 169 0768	.009 074 3139	.644 742 8957	71.051 420 8601	.014 074 3139	88
	89	1.558 760 8746	111.752 174 9222	.008 948 3717	.641 535 2196	71.692 956 0797	.013 948 3717	89
	90	1.566 554 6790	113.310 935 7968	.008 825 2735	.638 343 5021	72.331 299 5818	.013 825 2735	90
	91	1.574 387 4524	114.877 490 4758	.008 704 9255	.635 167 6638	72.966 467 2455	.013 704 9255	91
	92	1.582 259 3896	116.451 877 9282	.008 587 2381	.632 007 6256	73.598 474 8712	.013 587 2381	92
	93	1.590 170 6866	118.034 137 3178	.008 472 1253	.628 863 3091	74.227 338 1803	.013 472 1253	93
	94	1.598 121 5400	119.624 308 0044	.008 359 5050	.625 734 6359	74.853 072 8162	.013 359 5050	94
	95	1.606 112 1477	121.222 429 5445	.008 249 2984	.622 621 5283	75.475 694 3445	.013 249 2984	95
	96	1.614 142 7085	122.828 541 6922	.008 141 4302	.619 523 9087	76.095 218 2532	.013 141 4302	96
	97	1.622 213 4220	124.442 684 4006	.008 035 8279	.616 441 7002	76.711 659 9535	.013 035 8279	97
	98	1.630 324 4891	126.064 897 8226	.007 932 4222	.613 374 8261	77.325 034 7796	.012 932 4222	98
	99	1.638 476 1116	127.695 222 3118	.007 831 1466	.610 323 2101	77.935 357 9896	.012 831 1466	99
	100	1.646 668 4921	129.333 698 4233	.007 731 9369	.607 286 7762	78.542 644 7658	.012 731 9369	100

	XIV COMPOUND AMOUNT	XV AMOUNT OF ANNUITY	XVI SINKING FUND	XVII PRESENT VALUE	XVIII PRESENT VALUE OF ANNUITY	XIX AMORTIZATION	
PERIODS	AMOUNT OF 1	AMOUNT OF 1 PER PERIOD	SINKING FUND	PRESENT WORTH OF 1	PRESENT WORTH OF 1 PER PERIOD	PARTIAL PAYMENT	PERIODS
	How $1 left at compound interest will grow.	How $1 deposited periodically will grow.	Periodic deposit that will grow to $1 at future date.	What $1 due in the future is worth today.	What $1 payable periodically is worth today.	Annuity worth $1 today. Periodic payment necessary to pay off a loan of $1.	
1	1.005 833 3333	1.000 000 0000	1.000 000 0000	.994 200 4971	.994 200 4971	1.005 833 3333	1
2	1.011 700 6944	2.005 833 3333	.498 545 9078	.988 434 6284	1.982 635 1255	.504 379 2411	2
3	1.017 602 2818	3.017 534 0278	.331 396 4286	.982 702 1989	2.965 337 3245	.337 229 7619	3
4	1.023 538 2951	4.035 136 3096	.247 823 1027	.977 003 0147	3.942 340 3392	.253 656 4360	4
5	1.029 508 9352	5.058 674 6047	.197 680 2380	.971 336 8829	4.913 677 2220	.203 513 5714	5
6	1.035 514 4040	6.088 183 5399	.164 252 6040	.965 703 6118	5.879 380 8338	.170 085 9373	6
7	1.041 554 9047	7.123 697 9439	.140 376 5303	.960 103 0109	6.839 483 8447	.146 209 8636	7
8	1.047 630 6416	8.165 252 8486	.122 470 1817	.954 534 8907	7.794 018 7355	.128 303 5150	8
9	1.053 741 8204	9.212 883 4902	.108 543 6499	.948 999 0628	8.743 017 7983	.114 376 9832	9
10	1.059 888 6476	10.266 625 3106	.097 402 9898	.943 495 3400	9.686 513 1383	.103 236 3231	10
11	1.066 071 3314	11.326 513 9582	.088 288 4181	.938 023 5361	10.624 536 6744	.094 121 7514	11
12	1.072 290 0809	12.392 585 2896	.080 693 4128	.932 583 4658	11.557 120 1402	.086 526 7461	12
13	1.078 545 1063	13.464 875 3705	.074 267 3046	.927 174 9453	12.484 295 0856	.080 100 6379	13
14	1.084 836 6194	14.543 420 4768	.068 759 6155	.921 797 7916	13.406 092 8771	.074 592 9488	14
15	1.091 164 8331	15.628 257 0963	.063 986 6617	.916 451 8226	14.322 544 6997	.069 819 9950	15
16	1.097 529 9613	16.719 421 9293	.059 810 6803	.911 136 8576	15.233 681 5573	.065 644 0136	16
17	1.103 932 2194	17.816 951 8906	.056 126 3232	.905 852 7167	16.139 534 2740	.061 959 6565	17
18	1.110 371 8240	18.920 884 1100	.052 851 6529	.900 599 2213	17.040 133 4953	.058 684 9863	18
19	1.116 848 9929	20.031 255 9339	.049 921 9821	.895 376 1935	17.935 509 6888	.055 755 3154	19
20	1.123 363 9454	21.148 104 9269	.047 285 5607	.890 183 4567	18.825 693 1454	.053 118 8941	20
21	1.129 916 9018	22.271 468 8723	.044 900 4960	.885 020 8351	19.710 713 9805	.050 733 8294	21
22	1.136 508 0837	23.401 385 7740	.042 732 5121	.879 888 1542	20.590 602 1348	.048 565 8454	22
23	1.143 137 7142	24.537 893 8577	.040 753 2939	.874 785 2403	21.465 387 3751	.046 586 6272	23
24	1.149 806 0175	25.681 031 5719	.038 939 2458	.869 711 9208	22.335 099 2958	.044 772 5791	24
25	1.156 513 2193	26.830 837 5894	.037 270 5472	.864 668 0240	23.199 767 3198	.043 103 8806	25
26	1.163 259 5464	27.987 350 8087	.035 730 4272	.859 653 3793	24.059 420 6991	.041 563 7605	26
27	1.170 045 2271	29.150 610 3550	.034 304 5990	.854 667 8170	24.914 088 5161	.040 137 9324	27
28	1.176 870 4909	30.320 655 5821	.032 980 8172	.849 711 1685	25.763 799 6846	.038 814 1506	28
29	1.183 735 5688	31.497 526 0730	.031 748 5252	.844 783 2661	26.608 582 9507	.037 581 8585	29
30	1.190 640 6929	32.681 261 6418	.030 598 5739	.839 883 9431	27.448 466 8938	.036 431 9072	30
31	1.197 586 0970	33.871 902 3347	.029 522 9949	.835 013 0338	28.283 479 9276	.035 356 3282	31
32	1.204 572 0159	35.069 488 4316	.028 514 8157	.830 170 3732	29.113 650 3008	.034 348 1491	32
33	1.211 598 6859	36.274 060 4475	.027 567 9091	.825 355 7978	29.939 006 0986	.033 401 2424	33
34	1.218 666 3449	37.485 659 1334	.026 676 8685	.820 569 1444	30.759 575 2430	.032 510 2019	34
35	1.225 775 2320	38.704 325 4784	.025 836 9055	.815 810 2513	31.575 385 4943	.031 670 2388	35
36	1.232 925 5875	39.930 100 7103	.025 043 7635	.811 078 9574	32.386 464 4516	.030 877 0969	36
37	1.240 117 6534	41.163 026 2978	.024 293 6463	.806 375 1026	33.192 839 5542	.030 126 9796	37
38	1.247 351 6730	42.403 143 9512	.023 583 1570	.801 698 5279	33.994 538 0821	.029 416 4903	38
39	1.254 627 8911	43.650 495 6243	.022 909 2473	.797 049 0749	34.791 587 1570	.028 742 5807	39
40	1.261 946 5538	44.905 123 5154	.022 269 1738	.792 426 5865	35.584 013 7435	.028 102 5071	40
41	1.269 307 9087	46.167 070 0692	.021 660 4606	.787 830 9062	36.371 844 6497	.027 493 7939	41
42	1.276 712 2049	47.436 377 9780	.021 080 8675	.783 261 8786	37.155 106 5283	.026 914 2009	42
43	1.284 159 6927	48.713 090 1829	.020 528 3630	.778 719 3490	37.933 825 8773	.026 361 6964	43
44	1.291 650 6243	49.997 249 8756	.020 001 1001	.774 203 1639	38.708 029 0413	.025 834 4334	44
45	1.299 185 2529	51.288 900 4999	.019 497 3959	.769 713 1704	39.477 742 2117	.025 330 7293	45
46	1.306 763 8336	52.588 085 7528	.019 015 7140	.765 249 2167	40.242 991 4284	.024 849 0474	46
47	1.314 386 6226	53.894 849 5863	.018 554 6487	.760 811 1516	41.003 802 5800	.024 387 9820	47
48	1.322 053 8779	55.209 236 2089	.018 112 9113	.756 398 8251	41.760 201 4051	.023 946 2447	48
49	1.329 765 8588	56.531 290 0868	.017 689 3186	.752 012 0880	42.512 213 4931	.023 522 6519	49
50	1.337 522 8263	57.861 055 9456	.017 282 7817	.747 650 7917	43.259 864 2848	.023 116 1151	50
51	1.345 325 0428	59.198 578 7720	.016 892 2974	.743 314 7887	44.003 179 0735	.022 725 6308	51
52	1.353 172 7723	60.543 903 8148	.016 516 9396	.739 003 9325	44.742 183 0060	.022 350 2729	52
53	1.361 066 2801	61.897 076 5871	.016 155 8519	.734 718 0770	45.476 901 0830	.021 989 1852	53
54	1.369 005 8334	63.258 142 8672	.015 808 2415	.730 457 0774	46.207 358 1604	.021 641 5748	54
55	1.376 991 7008	64.627 148 7006	.015 473 3733	.726 220 7895	46.933 578 9498	.021 306 7067	55
56	1.385 024 1523	66.004 140 4013	.015 150 5647	.722 009 0699	47.655 588 0197	.020 983 8980	56
57	1.393 103 4599	67.389 164 5537	.014 839 1808	.717 821 7762	48.373 409 7959	.020 672 5142	57
58	1.401 229 8967	68.782 268 0136	.014 538 6308	.713 658 7667	49.087 068 5626	.020 371 9641	58
59	1.409 403 7378	70.183 497 9103	.014 248 3636	.709 519 9006	49.796 588 4633	.020 081 6970	59
60	1.417 625 2596	71.592 901 6481	.013 967 8652	.705 405 0379	50.501 993 5012	.019 801 1985	60
61	1.425 894 7403	73.010 526 9077	.013 696 6550	.701 314 0393	51.203 307 5405	.019 529 9884	61
62	1.434 212 4596	74.436 421 6480	.013 434 2836	.697 246 7665	51.900 554 3071	.019 267 6170	62
63	1.442 578 6990	75.870 634 1076	.013 180 3301	.693 203 0819	52.593 757 3890	.019 013 6634	63
64	1.450 993 7414	77.313 212 8066	.012 934 3997	.689 182 8486	53.282 940 2376	.018 767 7331	64
65	1.459 457 8715	78.764 206 5480	.012 696 1223	.685 185 9307	53.968 126 1683	.018 529 4556	65
66	1.467 971 3758	80.223 664 4195	.012 465 1499	.681 212 1929	54.649 338 3611	.018 298 4832	66
67	1.476 534 5421	81.691 635 7953	.012 241 1553	.677 261 5008	55.326 599 8619	.018 074 4886	67
68	1.485 147 6603	83.168 170 3374	.012 023 8307	.673 333 7208	55.999 933 5827	.017 857 1640	68
69	1.493 811 0217	84.653 317 9977	.011 812 8861	.669 428 7199	56.669 362 3026	.017 646 2194	69
70	1.502 524 9193	86.147 129 0194	.011 608 0479	.665 546 3661	57.334 908 6687	.017 441 3812	70
71	1.511 289 6480	87.649 653 9387	.011 409 0582	.661 686 5280	57.996 595 1967	.017 242 3915	71
72	1.520 105 5043	89.160 943 5866	.011 215 6731	.657 849 0751	58.654 444 2718	.017 049 0065	72
73	1.528 972 7864	90.681 049 0909	.011 027 6625	.654 033 8775	59.308 478 1493	.016 860 9958	73
74	1.537 891 7943	92.210 021 8772	.010 844 8082	.650 240 8061	59.958 718 9554	.016 678 1415	74
75	1.546 862 8298	93.747 913 6715	.010 666 9040	.646 469 7327	60.605 188 6880	.016 500 2374	75
76	1.555 886 1963	95.294 776 5013	.010 493 7546	.642 720 5296	61.247 909 2176	.016 327 0879	76
77	1.564 962 1991	96.850 662 6975	.010 325 1746	.638 992 0700	61.886 902 2876	.016 158 5079	77
78	1.574 091 1452	98.415 624 8966	.010 160 9882	.635 287 2278	62.522 189 5154	.015 994 3215	78
79	1.583 273 3436	99.989 716 0418	.010 001 0285	.631 602 8777	63.153 792 3931	.015 834 3618	79
80	1.592 509 1047	101.572 989 3854	.009 845 1370	.627 939 8950	63.781 732 2881	.015 678 4704	80
81	1.601 798 7412	103.165 498 4902	.009 693 1631	.624 298 1557	64.406 030 4438	.015 526 4964	81
82	1.611 142 5672	104.767 297 2314	.009 544 9632	.620 677 5368	65.026 707 9806	.015 378 2966	82
83	1.620 540 8988	106.378 439 7985	.009 400 4011	.617 077 9156	65.643 785 8962	.015 233 7344	83
84	1.629 994 0541	107.998 980 6974	.009 259 3466	.613 499 1704	66.257 285 0667	.015 092 6800	84
85	1.639 502 3527	109.628 974 7514	.009 121 6761	.609 941 1802	66.867 226 2469	.014 955 0094	85
86	1.649 066 1164	111.268 477 1041	.008 987 2714	.606 403 8246	67.473 630 0715	.014 820 6047	86
87	1.658 685 6688	112.917 543 2206	.008 856 0198	.602 886 9838	68.076 517 0553	.014 689 3531	87
88	1.668 361 3352	114.576 228 8894	.008 727 8139	.599 390 5390	68.675 907 5944	.014 561 1472	88
89	1.678 093 4430	116.244 590 2246	.008 602 5509	.595 914 3719	69.271 821 9662	.014 435 8842	89
90	1.687 882 3214	117.922 683 6675	.008 480 1327	.592 458 3647	69.864 280 3310	.014 313 4660	90
91	1.697 728 3016	119.610 565 9889	.008 360 4654	.589 022 4007	70.453 302 7317	.014 193 7987	91
92	1.707 631 7167	121.308 294 2905	.008 243 4594	.585 606 3636	71.038 909 0953	.014 076 7927	92
93	1.717 592 9017	123.015 926 0072	.008 129 0288	.582 210 1378	71.621 119 2331	.013 962 3621	93
94	1.727 612 1936	124.733 518 9089	.008 017 0912	.578 833 6084	72.199 952 8415	.013 850 4246	94
95	1.737 689 9314	126.461 131 1026	.007 907 5681	.575 476 6612	72.775 429 5028	.013 740 9014	95
96	1.747 826 4560	128.198 821 0340	.007 800 3837	.572 139 1827	73.347 568 6854	.013 633 7171	96
97	1.758 022 1104	129.946 647 4900	.007 695 4659	.568 821 0598	73.916 389 7453	.013 528 7993	97
98	1.768 277 2393	131.704 669 6004	.007 592 7452	.565 522 1804	74.481 911 9257	.013 426 0785	98
99	1.778 592 1899	133.472 946 8397	.007 492 1550	.562 242 4329	75.044 154 3586	.013 325 4883	99
100	1.788 967 3110	135.251 539 0296	.007 393 6312	.558 981 7063	75.603 136 0649	.013 226 9645	100

		XIV COMPOUND AMOUNT	XV AMOUNT OF ANNUITY	XVI SINKING FUND	XVII PRESENT VALUE	XVIII PRESENT VALUE OF ANNUITY	XIX AMORTIZATION	
RATE 2/3%	PERIODS	AMOUNT OF 1	AMOUNT OF 1 PER PERIOD	SINKING FUND	PRESENT WORTH OF 1	PRESENT WORTH OF 1 PER PERIOD	PARTIAL PAYMENT	PERIODS
		How $1 left at compound interest will grow.	How $1 deposited periodically will grow.	Periodic deposit that will grow to $1 at future date.	What $1 due in the future is worth today.	What $1 payable periodically is worth today.	Annuity worth $1 today. Periodic payment necessary to pay off a loan of $1.	
	1	1.006 666 6667	1.000 000 0000	1.000 000 0000	.993 377 4834	.993 377 4834	1.006 666 6667	1
	2	1.013 377 7778	2.006 666 6667	.498 338 8704	.986 798 8246	1.980 176 3081	.505 005 5371	2
	3	1.020 133 6296	3.020 044 4444	.331 120 9548	.980 263 7331	2.960 440 0411	.337 787 6215	3
	4	1.026 934 5205	4.040 178 0741	.247 513 8426	.973 771 9203	3.934 211 9614	.254 180 5093	4
	5	1.033 780 7506	5.067 112 5946	.197 351 0518	.967 323 0996	4.901 535 0610	.204 017 7184	5
	6	1.040 672 6223	6.100 893 3452	.163 910 4215	.960 916 9864	5.862 452 0473	.170 577 0882	6
	7	1.047 610 4398	7.141 565 9675	.140 025 3116	.954 553 2977	6.817 005 3450	.146 691 9783	7
	8	1.054 594 5094	8.189 176 4073	.122 112 4018	.948 231 7527	7.765 237 0977	.128 779 0685	8
	9	1.061 625 1394	9.243 770 9167	.108 180 9587	.941 952 0722	8.707 189 1699	.114 847 6254	9
	10	1.068 702 6404	10.305 396 0561	.097 036 5423	.935 713 9790	9.642 903 1489	.103 703 2089	10
	11	1.075 827 3246	11.374 098 6965	.087 919 0542	.929 517 1977	10.572 420 3466	.094 585 7209	11
	12	1.082 999 5068	12.449 926 0211	.080 321 7624	.923 361 4547	11.495 781 8013	.086 988 4291	12
	13	1.090 219 5035	13.532 925 5279	.073 893 8523	.917 246 4781	12.413 028 2794	.080 560 5190	13
	14	1.097 487 6335	14.623 145 0315	.068 384 7420	.911 171 9981	13.324 200 2775	.075 051 4087	14
	15	1.104 804 2178	15.720 632 6650	.063 610 6715	.905 137 7465	14.229 338 0240	.070 277 3382	15
	16	1.112 169 5792	16.825 436 8828	.059 433 8208	.899 143 4568	15.128 481 4808	.066 100 4874	16
	17	1.119 584 0431	17.937 606 4620	.055 748 7980	.893 188 8644	16.021 670 3452	.062 415 4647	17
	18	1.127 047 9367	19.057 190 5051	.052 473 6319	.887 273 7063	16.908 944 0515	.059 140 2986	18
	19	1.134 561 5896	20.184 238 4418	.049 543 6081	.881 397 7215	17.790 341 7730	.056 210 2748	19
	20	1.142 125 3335	21.318 800 0314	.046 906 9553	.875 560 6505	18.665 902 4236	.053 573 6220	20
	21	1.149 739 5024	22.460 925 3649	.044 521 7632	.869 762 2356	19.535 664 6592	.051 188 4299	21
	22	1.157 404 4324	23.610 664 8673	.042 353 7417	.864 002 2208	20.399 666 8800	.049 020 4083	22
	23	1.165 120 4620	24.768 069 2998	.040 374 5640	.858 280 3518	21.257 947 2317	.047 041 2307	23
	24	1.172 887 9317	25.933 189 7618	.038 560 6248	.852 596 3759	22.110 543 6077	.045 227 2915	24
	25	1.180 707 1846	27.106 077 6935	.036 892 0952	.846 950 0423	22.957 493 6500	.043 558 7619	25
	26	1.188 578 5659	28.286 784 8782	.035 352 1973	.841 341 1017	23.798 834 7517	.042 018 8640	26
	27	1.196 502 4230	29.475 363 4440	.033 926 6385	.835 769 3063	24.634 604 0580	.040 593 3052	27
	28	1.204 479 1058	30.671 865 8670	.032 603 1681	.830 234 4102	25.464 838 4682	.039 269 8348	28
	29	1.212 509 9665	31.876 344 9728	.031 371 2253	.824 736 1691	26.289 574 6373	.038 037 8920	29
	30	1.220 592 3596	33.088 853 9392	.030 221 6572	.819 274 3402	27.108 848 9774	.036 888 3238	30
	31	1.228 729 6420	34.309 446 2988	.029 146 4919	.813 848 6823	27.922 697 6597	.035 813 1586	31
	32	1.236 921 1729	35.538 175 9408	.028 138 7543	.808 458 9559	28.731 156 6156	.034 805 4209	32
	33	1.245 167 3141	36.775 097 1138	.027 192 3143	.803 104 9231	29.534 261 5387	.033 858 9810	33
	34	1.253 468 4295	38.020 264 4279	.026 301 7634	.797 786 3474	30.332 047 8861	.032 968 4301	34
	35	1.261 824 8857	39.273 732 8574	.025 462 3110	.792 502 9941	31.124 550 8802	.032 128 9777	35
	36	1.270 237 0516	40.535 557 7431	.024 669 6988	.787 254 6299	31.911 805 5101	.031 336 3655	36
	37	1.278 705 2986	41.805 794 7947	.023 920 1289	.782 041 0221	32.693 846 5323	.030 586 7958	37
	38	1.287 230 0006	43.084 500 0934	.023 210 2032	.776 861 9435	33.470 708 4767	.029 876 8698	38
	39	1.295 861 5340	44.371 730 0940	.022 536 8720	.771 717 1624	34.242 425 6392	.029 203 5386	39
	40	1.304 450 2775	45.667 541 6279	.021 897 3907	.766 606 4527	35.009 032 0919	.028 564 0573	40
	41	1.313 146 6127	46.971 991 9055	.021 289 2824	.761 529 5888	35.770 561 6807	.027 955 9491	41
	42	1.321 900 9235	48.285 138 5182	.020 710 3061	.756 486 3465	36.527 048 0272	.027 376 9728	42
	43	1.330 713 5963	49.607 039 4416	.020 158 4294	.751 476 5031	37.278 524 5303	.026 825 0960	43
	44	1.339 585 0203	50.937 753 0379	.019 631 8043	.746 499 8375	38.025 024 3678	.026 298 4710	44
	45	1.348 515 5871	52.277 338 0581	.019 128 7475	.741 556 1300	38.766 580 4978	.025 795 4142	45
	46	1.357 505 6910	53.625 853 6452	.018 647 7218	.736 645 1623	39.503 225 6601	.025 314 3885	46
	47	1.366 555 7289	54.983 359 3362	.018 187 3209	.731 766 7175	40.234 992 3776	.024 854 9876	47
	48	1.375 666 1004	56.349 915 0651	.017 746 2557	.726 920 5803	40.961 912 9579	.024 412 9223	48
	49	1.384 837 2078	57.725 581 1655	.017 323 3423	.722 106 5367	41.684 019 4946	.023 990 0089	49
	50	1.394 069 4558	59.110 418 3733	.016 917 4915	.717 324 3742	42.401 343 8688	.023 584 1582	50
	51	1.403 363 2522	60.504 487 8291	.016 527 6996	.712 573 8817	43.113 917 7505	.023 194 3663	51
	52	1.412 719 0072	61.907 851 0813	.016 153 0401	.707 854 8493	43.821 772 5998	.022 819 7068	52
	53	1.422 137 1339	63.320 570 0885	.015 792 6563	.703 167 0689	44.524 939 6687	.022 459 3230	53
	54	1.431 618 0481	64.742 707 2224	.015 445 7551	.698 510 3333	45.223 450 0020	.022 112 4218	54
	55	1.441 162 1685	66.174 325 2706	.015 111 6010	.693 884 4371	45.917 334 4391	.021 778 2677	55
	56	1.450 769 9163	67.615 487 4390	.014 789 5111	.689 289 1759	46.606 623 6150	.021 456 1777	56
	57	1.460 441 7157	69.066 257 3553	.014 478 8503	.684 724 3469	47.291 347 9679	.021 145 5170	57
	58	1.470 177 9938	70.526 699 0710	.014 179 0274	.680 189 7486	47.971 537 7105	.020 845 6941	58
	59	1.479 979 1804	71.996 877 0648	.013 889 4913	.675 685 1807	48.647 222 8912	.020 556 1580	59
	60	1.489 845 7083	73.476 856 2452	.013 609 7276	.671 210 4444	49.318 433 3356	.020 276 3943	60
	61	1.499 778 0130	74.966 701 9535	.013 339 2556	.666 765 3421	49.985 198 6778	.020 005 9223	61
	62	1.509 776 5331	76.466 479 9666	.013 077 6257	.662 349 6776	50.647 548 3554	.019 744 2923	62
	63	1.519 841 7100	77.976 256 4997	.012 824 4166	.657 963 2559	51.305 511 6113	.019 491 0833	63
	64	1.529 973 9881	79.496 098 2097	.012 579 2337	.653 605 8834	51.959 117 4947	.019 245 9004	64
	65	1.540 173 8147	81.026 072 1977	.012 341 7065	.649 277 3676	52.608 394 8623	.019 008 3731	65
	66	1.550 441 6401	82.566 246 0124	.012 111 4868	.644 977 5175	53.253 372 3798	.018 778 1535	66
	67	1.560 777 2177	84.116 687 6525	.011 888 2475	.640 706 1432	53.894 078 5229	.018 554 9141	67
	68	1.571 183 1038	85.677 465 5702	.011 671 6805	.636 463 0561	54.530 541 5791	.018 338 3471	68
	69	1.581 657 6578	87.248 648 6740	.011 461 4956	.632 248 0690	55.162 789 6481	.018 128 1622	69
	70	1.592 202 0422	88.830 306 3318	.011 257 4192	.628 060 9957	55.790 850 6438	.017 924 0859	70
	71	1.602 816 7225	90.422 508 3740	.011 059 1933	.623 901 6514	56.414 752 2952	.017 725 8600	71
	72	1.613 502 1673	92.025 325 0965	.010 866 5739	.619 769 8523	57.034 522 1475	.017 533 2406	72
	73	1.624 258 8484	93.638 827 2638	.010 679 3307	.615 665 4162	57.650 187 5637	.017 345 9973	73
	74	1.635 087 2407	95.263 086 1122	.010 497 2455	.611 588 1618	58.261 775 7256	.017 163 9121	74
	75	1.645 987 8224	96.898 173 3530	.010 320 1120	.607 537 9091	58.869 313 6347	.016 986 7787	75
	76	1.656 961 0745	98.544 161 1753	.010 147 7347	.603 514 4792	59.472 828 1139	.016 814 4013	76
	77	1.668 007 4817	100.201 122 2498	.009 979 9281	.599 517 6946	60.072 345 8085	.016 646 5948	77
	78	1.679 127 5315	101.869 129 7315	.009 816 5166	.595 547 3788	60.667 893 1873	.016 483 1832	78
	79	1.690 321 7151	103.548 257 2630	.009 657 3330	.591 603 3564	61.259 496 5437	.016 323 9996	79
	80	1.701 590 5265	105.238 578 9781	.009 502 2188	.587 685 4534	61.847 181 9970	.016 168 8854	80
	81	1.712 934 4634	106.940 169 5046	.009 351 0262	.583 793 4967	62.430 975 4937	.016 017 6898	81
	82	1.724 354 0265	108.653 103 9680	.009 203 6027	.579 927 3146	63.010 902 8083	.015 870 2694	82
	83	1.735 849 7200	110.377 457 9945	.009 059 8209	.576 086 7364	63.586 989 5447	.015 726 4876	83
	84	1.747 422 0514	112.113 307 7144	.008 919 5477	.572 271 5924	64.159 261 1371	.015 586 2144	84
	85	1.759 071 5318	113.860 729 7659	.008 782 6593	.568 481 7143	64.727 742 8514	.015 449 3260	85
	86	1.770 798 6753	115.619 801 2976	.008 649 0375	.564 716 9348	65.292 459 7862	.015 315 7042	86
	87	1.782 603 9998	117.390 599 9729	.008 518 5696	.560 977 0875	65.853 436 8737	.015 185 2363	87
	88	1.794 488 0265	119.173 203 9728	.008 391 1481	.557 262 0075	66.410 698 8812	.015 057 8147	88
	89	1.806 451 2800	120.967 691 9992	.008 266 6701	.553 571 5306	66.964 270 4118	.014 933 3367	89
	90	1.818 494 2885	122.774 143 2792	.008 145 0375	.549 905 4940	67.514 175 9057	.014 811 7042	90
	91	1.830 617 5838	124.592 637 5678	.008 026 1564	.546 263 7357	68.060 439 6414	.014 692 8231	91
	92	1.842 821 7010	126.423 255 1516	.007 909 9371	.542 646 0951	68.603 085 7365	.014 576 6038	92
	93	1.855 107 1790	128.266 076 8526	.007 796 2936	.539 052 4123	69.142 138 1489	.014 462 9603	93
	94	1.867 474 5602	130.121 184 0316	.007 685 1437	.535 482 5288	69.677 620 6777	.014 351 8104	94
	95	1.879 924 3906	131.988 658 5918	.007 576 4085	.531 936 2869	70.209 556 9646	.014 243 0752	95
	96	1.892 457 2199	133.868 582 9824	.007 470 0126	.528 413 5300	70.737 970 4946	.014 136 6793	96
	97	1.905 073 6013	135.761 040 2023	.007 365 8835	.524 914 1027	71.262 884 5973	.014 032 5501	97
	98	1.917 774 0920	137.666 113 8036	.007 263 9517	.521 437 8503	71.784 322 4477	.013 930 6184	98
	99	1.930 559 2526	139.583 887 8957	.007 164 1506	.517 984 6196	72.302 307 0672	.013 830 8173	99
	100	1.943 429 6477	141.514 447 1483	.007 066 4163	.514 554 2578	72.816 861 3250	.013 733 0830	100

		XIV COMPOUND AMOUNT	XV AMOUNT OF ANNUITY	XVI SINKING FUND	XVII PRESENT VALUE	XVIII PRESENT VALUE OF ANNUITY	XIX AMORTIZATION	
RATE 3/4%	PERIODS	AMOUNT OF 1	AMOUNT OF 1 PER PERIOD	SINKING FUND	PRESENT WORTH OF 1	PRESENT WORTH OF 1 PER PERIOD	PARTIAL PAYMENT	PERIODS
		How $1 left at compound interest will grow.	How $1 deposited periodically will grow.	Periodic deposit that will grow to $1 at future date.	What $1 due in the future is worth today.	What $1 payable periodically is worth today.	Annuity worth $1 today. Periodic payment necessary to pay off a loan of $1.	
	1	1.007 500 0000	1.000 000 0000	1.000 000 0000	.992 555 8313	.992 555 8313	1.007 500 0000	1
	2	1.015 056 2500	2.007 500 0000	.498 132 0050	.985 167 0782	1.977 722 9094	.505 632 0050	2
	3	1.022 669 1719	3.022 556 2500	.330 845 7866	.977 833 3282	2.955 556 2377	.338 345 7866	3
	4	1.030 339 1907	4.045 225 4219	.247 205 0123	.970 554 1719	3.926 110 4096	.254 705 0123	4
	5	1.038 066 7346	5.075 564 6125	.197 022 4155	.963 329 2029	4.889 439 6125	.204 522 4155	5
	6	1.045 852 2351	6.113 631 3471	.163 568 9074	.956 158 0178	5.845 597 6303	.171 068 9074	6
	7	1.053 696 1269	7.159 483 5822	.139 674 8786	.949 040 2162	6.794 637 8464	.147 174 8786	7
	8	1.061 598 8478	8.213 179 7091	.121 755 5241	.941 975 4006	7.736 613 2471	.129 255 5241	8
	9	1.069 560 8392	9.274 778 5569	.107 819 2858	.934 963 1768	8.671 576 4239	.115 319 2858	9
	10	1.077 582 5455	10.344 339 3961	.096 671 2287	.928 003 1532	9.599 579 5771	.104 171 2287	10
	11	1.085 664 4146	11.421 921 9416	.087 550 9398	.921 094 9411	10.520 674 5182	.095 050 9398	11
	12	1.093 806 8977	12.507 586 3561	.079 951 4768	.914 238 1550	11.434 912 6731	.087 451 4768	12
	13	1.102 010 4494	13.601 393 2538	.073 521 8798	.907 432 4119	12.342 345 0850	.081 021 8798	13
	14	1.110 275 5278	14.703 403 7032	.068 011 4632	.900 677 3319	13.243 022 4169	.075 511 4632	14
	15	1.118 602 5942	15.813 679 2310	.063 236 3908	.893 972 5378	14.136 994 9547	.070 736 3908	15
	16	1.126 992 1137	16.932 281 8252	.059 058 7855	.887 317 6554	15.024 312 6101	.066 558 7855	16
	17	1.135 444 5545	18.059 273 9389	.055 373 2118	.880 712 3131	15.905 024 9232	.062 873 2118	17
	18	1.143 960 3887	19.194 718 4934	.052 097 6643	.874 156 1420	16.779 181 0652	.059 597 6643	18
	19	1.152 540 0916	20.338 678 8821	.049 167 4020	.867 648 7762	17.646 829 8414	.056 667 4020	19
	20	1.161 184 1423	21.491 218 9738	.046 530 6319	.861 189 8523	18.508 019 6937	.054 030 6319	20
	21	1.169 893 0234	22.652 403 1161	.044 145 4266	.854 779 0097	19.362 798 7034	.051 645 4266	21
	22	1.178 667 2210	23.822 296 1394	.041 977 4817	.848 415 8905	20.211 214 5940	.049 477 4817	22
	23	1.187 507 2252	25.000 963 3605	.039 998 4587	.842 100 1395	21.053 314 7335	.047 498 4587	23
	24	1.196 413 5294	26.188 470 5857	.038 184 7423	.835 831 4040	21.889 146 1374	.045 684 7423	24
	25	1.205 386 6309	27.384 884 1151	.036 516 4956	.829 609 3340	22.718 755 4714	.044 016 4956	25
	26	1.214 427 0306	28.590 270 7459	.034 976 9335	.823 433 5821	23.542 189 0535	.042 476 9335	26
	27	1.223 535 2333	29.804 697 7765	.033 551 7578	.817 303 8036	24.359 492 8571	.041 051 7578	27
	28	1.232 711 7476	31.028 233 0099	.032 228 7125	.811 219 6562	25.170 712 5132	.039 728 7125	28
	29	1.241 957 0857	32.260 944 7574	.030 997 2323	.805 180 8001	25.975 893 3134	.038 497 2323	29
	30	1.251 271 7638	33.502 901 8431	.029 848 1608	.799 186 8984	26.775 080 2118	.037 348 1608	30
	31	1.260 656 3021	34.754 173 6069	.028 773 5226	.793 237 6163	27.568 317 8281	.036 273 5226	31
	32	1.270 111 2243	36.014 829 9090	.027 766 3397	.787 332 6216	28.355 650 4497	.035 266 3397	32
	33	1.279 637 0585	37.284 941 1333	.026 820 4795	.781 471 5847	29.137 122 0344	.034 320 4795	33
	34	1.289 234 3364	38.564 578 1918	.025 930 5313	.775 654 1784	29.912 776 2128	.033 430 5313	34
	35	1.298 903 5940	39.853 812 5282	.025 091 7023	.769 880 0778	30.682 656 2907	.032 591 7023	35
	36	1.308 645 3709	41.152 716 1222	.024 299 7327	.764 148 9606	31.446 805 2513	.031 799 7327	36
	37	1.318 460 2112	42.461 361 4931	.023 550 8228	.758 460 5068	32.205 265 7581	.031 050 8228	37
	38	1.328 348 6628	43.779 821 7043	.022 841 5732	.752 814 3988	32.958 080 1569	.030 341 5732	38
	39	1.338 311 2778	45.108 170 3671	.022 168 9329	.747 210 3214	33.705 290 4783	.029 668 9329	39
	40	1.348 348 6123	46.446 481 6449	.021 530 1561	.741 647 9617	34.446 938 4400	.029 030 1561	40
	41	1.358 461 2269	47.794 830 2572	.020 922 7650	.736 127 0091	35.183 065 4492	.028 422 7650	41
	42	1.368 649 6861	49.153 291 4841	.020 344 5175	.730 647 1555	35.913 712 6046	.027 844 5175	42
	43	1.378 914 5588	50.521 941 1703	.019 793 3804	.725 208 0948	36.638 920 6994	.027 293 3804	43
	44	1.389 256 4180	51.900 855 7290	.019 267 5051	.719 809 5233	37.358 730 2227	.026 767 5051	44
	45	1.399 675 8411	53.290 112 1470	.018 765 2073	.714 451 1398	38.073 181 3625	.026 265 2073	45
	46	1.410 173 4099	54.689 787 9881	.018 284 9493	.709 132 6449	38.782 314 0074	.025 784 9493	46
	47	1.420 749 7105	56.099 961 3980	.017 825 3242	.703 863 7419	39.486 167 7493	.025 325 3242	47
	48	1.431 405 3333	57.520 711 1085	.017 385 0424	.698 614 1359	40.184 781 8852	.024 885 0424	48
	49	1.442 140 8733	58.952 116 4418	.016 962 9194	.693 413 5344	40.878 195 4195	.024 462 9194	49
	50	1.452 956 9299	60.394 257 3151	.016 557 8657	.688 251 6470	41.566 447 0665	.024 057 8657	50
	51	1.463 854 1068	61.847 214 2450	.016 168 8770	.683 128 1856	42.249 575 2521	.023 668 8770	51
	52	1.474 833 0126	63.311 068 3518	.015 795 0265	.678 042 8641	42.927 618 1163	.023 295 0265	52
	53	1.485 894 2602	64.785 901 3645	.015 435 4571	.672 995 3986	43.600 613 5149	.022 935 4571	53
	54	1.497 038 4672	66.271 795 6247	.015 089 3754	.667 985 5073	44.268 599 0222	.022 589 3754	54
	55	1.508 266 2557	67.768 834 0919	.014 756 0455	.663 012 9105	44.931 611 9327	.022 256 0455	55
	56	1.519 578 2526	69.277 100 3476	.014 434 7843	.658 077 3305	45.589 689 2633	.021 934 7843	56
	57	1.530 975 0895	70.796 678 6002	.014 124 9564	.653 178 4918	46.242 867 7551	.021 624 9564	57
	58	1.542 457 4027	72.327 653 6897	.013 825 9704	.648 316 1209	46.891 183 8760	.021 325 9704	58
	59	1.554 025 8332	73.870 111 0923	.013 537 2749	.643 489 9463	47.534 673 8224	.021 037 2749	59
	60	1.565 681 0269	75.424 136 9255	.013 258 3552	.638 699 6986	48.173 373 5210	.020 758 3552	60
	61	1.577 423 6346	76.989 817 9525	.012 988 7305	.633 945 1103	48.807 318 6312	.020 488 7305	61
	62	1.589 254 3119	78.567 241 5871	.012 727 9510	.629 225 9159	49.436 544 5471	.020 227 9510	62
	63	1.601 173 7192	80.156 495 8990	.012 475 5953	.624 541 8520	50.061 086 3991	.019 975 5953	63
	64	1.613 182 5221	81.757 669 6183	.012 231 2684	.619 892 6571	50.680 979 0562	.019 731 2684	64
	65	1.625 281 3911	83.370 852 1404	.011 994 5997	.615 278 0715	51.296 257 1278	.019 494 5997	65
	66	1.637 471 0015	84.996 133 5315	.011 765 2411	.610 697 8387	51.906 954 9655	.019 265 2411	66
	67	1.649 752 0340	86.633 604 5329	.011 542 8650	.606 151 7000	52.513 106 6655	.019 042 8650	67
	68	1.662 125 1743	88.283 356 5669	.011 327 1633	.601 630 4045	53.114 746 0700	.018 827 1633	68
	69	1.674 591 1131	89.945 481 7412	.011 117 8458	.597 160 6992	53.711 906 7692	.018 617 8458	69
	70	1.687 150 5464	91.620 072 8543	.010 914 6388	.592 715 3342	54.304 622 1035	.018 414 6388	70
	71	1.699 804 1755	93.307 223 4007	.010 717 2839	.588 303 0613	54.892 925 1647	.018 217 2839	71
	72	1.712 552 7068	95.007 027 5762	.010 525 5372	.583 923 6340	55.476 848 7987	.018 025 5372	72
	73	1.725 396 8521	96.719 580 2830	.010 339 1681	.579 576 8079	56.056 425 6067	.017 839 1681	73
	74	1.738 337 3285	98.444 977 1351	.010 157 9586	.575 262 3404	56.631 687 9471	.017 657 9586	74
	75	1.751 374 8585	100.183 314 4636	.009 981 7021	.570 979 9905	57.202 667 9375	.017 481 7021	75
	76	1.764 510 1699	101.934 689 3221	.009 810 2030	.566 729 5191	57.769 397 4566	.017 310 2030	76
	77	1.777 743 9962	103.699 199 4920	.009 643 2760	.562 510 6889	58.331 908 1455	.017 143 2760	77
	78	1.791 077 0762	105.476 943 4882	.009 480 7450	.558 322 2644	58.890 230 4099	.016 980 7450	78
	79	1.804 510 1542	107.268 020 5644	.009 322 4429	.554 167 0118	59.444 398 4218	.016 822 4429	79
	80	1.818 043 9804	109.072 530 7186	.009 168 2112	.550 041 6991	59.994 440 1209	.016 668 2112	80
	81	1.831 679 3102	110.890 574 6990	.009 017 8990	.545 947 0959	60.540 387 2168	.016 517 8990	81
	82	1.845 416 9051	112.722 254 0092	.008 871 3627	.541 882 9736	61.082 270 1903	.016 371 3627	82
	83	1.859 257 5319	114.567 670 9143	.008 728 4658	.537 849 1053	61.620 119 2956	.016 228 4658	83
	84	1.873 201 9633	116.426 928 4462	.008 589 0783	.533 845 2658	62.153 964 5614	.016 089 0783	84
	85	1.887 250 9781	118.300 130 4095	.008 453 0761	.529 871 2316	62.683 835 7930	.015 953 0761	85
	86	1.901 405 3604	120.187 381 3876	.008 320 3410	.525 926 7807	63.209 762 5736	.015 820 3410	86
	87	1.915 665 9006	122.088 786 7480	.008 190 7604	.522 011 6930	63.731 774 2666	.015 690 7604	87
	88	1.930 033 3949	124.004 452 6486	.008 064 2266	.518 125 7499	64.249 900 0165	.015 564 2266	88
	89	1.944 508 6453	125.934 486 0435	.007 940 6367	.514 268 7344	64.764 168 7509	.015 440 6367	89
	90	1.959 092 4602	127.878 994 6888	.007 819 8926	.510 440 4311	65.274 609 1820	.015 319 8926	90
	91	1.973 785 6536	129.838 087 1490	.007 701 9003	.506 640 6264	65.781 249 8085	.015 201 9003	91
	92	1.988 589 0460	131.811 872 8026	.007 586 5700	.502 869 1081	66.284 118 9166	.015 086 5700	92
	93	2.003 503 4639	133.800 461 8486	.007 473 8158	.499 125 6656	66.783 244 5822	.014 973 8158	93
	94	2.018 529 7398	135.803 965 3125	.007 363 5552	.495 410 0900	67.278 654 6722	.014 863 5552	94
	95	2.033 668 7129	137.822 495 0523	.007 255 7096	.491 722 1737	67.770 376 8458	.014 755 7096	95
	96	2.048 921 2282	139.856 163 7652	.007 150 2033	.488 061 7108	68.258 438 5567	.014 650 2033	96
	97	2.064 288 1375	141.905 084 9934	.007 046 9638	.484 428 4971	68.742 867 0538	.014 546 9638	97
	98	2.079 770 2985	143.969 373 1309	.006 945 9217	.480 822 3296	69.223 689 3834	.014 445 9217	98
	99	2.095 368 5757	146.049 143 4294	.006 847 0104	.477 243 0071	69.700 932 3905	.014 347 0104	99
	100	2.111 083 8400	148.144 512 0051	.006 750 1657	.473 690 3296	70.174 622 7201	.014 250 1657	100

RATE 5/6%	PERIODS	XIV COMPOUND AMOUNT	XV AMOUNT OF ANNUITY	XVI SINKING FUND	XVII PRESENT VALUE	XVIII PRESENT VALUE OF ANNUITY	XIX AMORTIZATION	PERIODS
		AMOUNT OF 1	AMOUNT OF 1 PER PERIOD	SINKING FUND	PRESENT WORTH OF 1	PRESENT WORTH OF 1 PER PERIOD	PARTIAL PAYMENT	
		How $1 left at compound interest will grow.	How $1 deposited periodically will grow.	Periodic deposit that will grow to $1 at future date.	What $1 due in the future is worth today.	What $1 payable periodically is worth today.	Annuity worth $1 today. Periodic payment necessary to pay off a loan of $1.	
	1	1.008 333 3333	1.000 000 0000	1.000 000 0000	.991 735 5372	.991 735 5372	1.008 333 3333	1
	2	1.016 736 1111	2.008 333 3333	.497 925 3112	.983 539 3757	1.975 274 9129	.506 258 6445	2
	3	1.025 208 9120	3.025 069 4444	.330 570 9235	.975 410 9511	2.950 685 8640	.338 904 2569	3
	4	1.033 752 3196	4.050 278 3565	.246 896 6110	.967 349 7036	3.918 035 5677	.255 229 9444	4
	5	1.042 366 9223	5.084 030 6761	.196 694 3285	.959 355 0780	4.877 390 6456	.205 027 6619	5
	6	1.051 053 3133	6.126 397 5984	.163 228 0609	.951 426 5236	5.828 817 1692	.171 561 3942	6
	7	1.059 812 0909	7.177 450 9117	.139 325 2301	.943 563 4945	6.772 380 6637	.147 658 5635	7
	8	1.068 643 8584	8.237 263 0027	.121 399 5474	.935 765 4491	7.708 146 1127	.129 732 8807	8
	9	1.077 549 2238	9.305 906 8610	.107 458 6298	.928 031 8503	8.636 177 9630	.115 791 9631	9
	10	1.086 528 8007	10.383 456 0849	.096 307 0477	.920 362 1656	9.556 540 1286	.104 640 3810	10
	11	1.095 583 2074	11.469 984 8856	.087 184 0730	.912 755 8667	10.469 295 9953	.095 517 4064	11
	12	1.104 713 0674	12.565 568 0930	.079 582 5539	.905 212 4298	11.374 508 4251	.087 915 8872	12
	13	1.113 919 0097	13.670 281 1604	.073 151 3850	.897 731 3353	12.272 239 7605	.081 484 7183	13
	14	1.123 201 6681	14.784 200 1701	.067 639 7768	.890 312 0681	13.162 551 8285	.075 973 1102	14
	15	1.132 561 6820	15.907 401 8382	.062 863 8171	.882 954 1171	14.045 505 9457	.071 197 1505	15
	16	1.141 999 6960	17.039 963 5201	.058 685 5716	.875 656 9757	14.921 162 9213	.067 018 9050	16
	17	1.151 516 3601	18.181 963 2161	.054 999 5613	.868 420 1411	15.789 583 0625	.063 332 8946	17
	18	1.161 112 3298	19.333 479 5763	.051 723 7467	.861 243 1152	16.650 826 1777	.060 057 0800	18
	19	1.170 788 2659	20.494 591 9061	.048 793 3600	.854 125 4035	17.504 951 5811	.057 126 6933	19
	20	1.180 544 8348	21.665 380 1720	.046 156 5868	.847 066 5159	18.352 018 0970	.054 489 9201	20
	21	1.190 382 7084	22.845 925 0067	.043 771 4822	.840 065 9661	19.192 084 0631	.052 104 8155	21
	22	1.200 302 5643	24.036 307 7151	.041 603 7277	.833 123 2722	20.025 207 3354	.049 937 0610	22
	23	1.210 305 0857	25.236 610 2794	.039 624 9730	.826 237 9559	20.851 445 2913	.047 958 3063	23
	24	1.220 390 9614	26.446 915 3651	.037 811 5930	.819 409 5430	21.670 854 8343	.046 144 9263	24
	25	1.230 560 8861	27.667 306 3264	.036 143 7427	.812 637 5634	22.483 492 3977	.044 477 0760	25
	26	1.240 815 5601	28.897 867 2125	.034 604 6299	.805 921 5504	23.289 413 9481	.042 937 9632	26
	27	1.251 155 6898	30.138 682 7726	.033 179 9504	.799 261 0418	24.088 674 9898	.041 513 2837	27
	28	1.261 581 9872	31.389 838 4624	.031 857 4433	.792 655 5786	24.881 330 5684	.040 190 7767	28
	29	1.272 095 1704	32.651 420 4496	.030 626 5389	.786 104 7060	25.667 435 2745	.038 959 8723	29
	30	1.282 695 9635	33.923 515 6200	.029 478 0768	.779 607 9729	26.447 043 2474	.037 811 4102	30
	31	1.293 385 0965	35.206 211 5835	.028 404 0786	.773 164 9318	27.220 208 1793	.036 737 4119	31
	32	1.304 163 3057	36.499 596 6800	.027 397 5630	.766 774 1390	27.986 983 3183	.035 730 8963	32
	33	1.315 031 3332	37.803 759 9857	.026 452 3952	.760 438 1544	28.747 421 4727	.034 785 7286	33
	34	1.325 989 9277	39.118 791 3189	.025 563 1620	.754 153 5415	29.501 575 0142	.033 896 4953	34
	35	1.337 039 8437	40.444 781 2465	.024 725 0688	.747 920 8677	30.249 495 8819	.033 058 4022	35
	36	1.348 181 8424	41.781 821 0903	.023 933 8539	.741 739 7035	30.991 235 5853	.032 267 1872	36
	37	1.359 416 6911	43.130 002 9327	.023 185 7160	.735 609 6233	31.726 845 2086	.031 519 0494	37
	38	1.370 745 1635	44.489 419 6238	.022 477 2543	.729 530 2049	32.456 375 4135	.030 810 5877	38
	39	1.382 168 0399	45.860 164 7873	.021 805 4166	.723 501 0296	33.179 876 4431	.030 138 7500	39
	40	1.393 686 1069	47.242 332 8272	.021 167 4560	.717 521 6823	33.897 398 1254	.029 500 7893	40
	41	1.405 300 1578	48.636 018 9341	.020 560 8934	.711 591 7510	34.608 989 8764	.028 894 2267	41
	42	1.417 010 9924	50.041 319 0919	.019 983 4860	.705 710 8275	35.314 700 7039	.028 316 8193	42
	43	1.428 819 4174	51.458 330 0843	.019 433 1996	.699 878 5066	36.014 579 2105	.027 766 5329	43
	44	1.440 726 2458	52.887 149 5017	.018 908 1849	.694 094 3867	36.708 673 5972	.027 241 5182	44
	45	1.452 732 2979	54.327 875 7475	.018 406 7569	.688 358 0694	37.397 031 6666	.026 740 0902	45
	46	1.464 838 4004	55.780 608 0454	.017 927 3772	.682 669 1598	38.079 700 8264	.026 260 7105	46
	47	1.477 045 3870	57.245 446 4458	.017 468 6383	.677 027 2659	38.756 728 0923	.025 801 9717	47
	48	1.489 354 0986	58.722 491 8329	.017 029 2501	.671 431 9992	39.428 160 0915	.025 362 5834	48
	49	1.501 765 3828	60.211 845 9315	.016 608 0276	.665 882 9745	40.094 043 0660	.024 941 3609	49
	50	1.514 280 0943	61.713 611 3142	.016 203 8808	.660 379 8094	40.754 422 8754	.024 537 2141	50
	51	1.526 899 0951	63.227 891 4085	.015 815 8050	.654 922 1250	41.409 345 0003	.024 149 1383	51
	52	1.539 623 2542	64.754 790 5036	.015 442 8729	.649 509 5455	42.058 854 5458	.023 776 2062	52
	53	1.552 453 4480	66.294 413 7578	.015 084 2272	.644 141 6980	42.702 996 2438	.023 417 5605	53
	54	1.565 390 5600	67.846 867 2058	.014 739 0741	.638 818 2129	43.341 814 4566	.023 072 4074	54
	55	1.578 435 4814	69.412 257 7658	.014 406 6773	.633 538 7235	43.975 353 1801	.022 740 0107	55
	56	1.591 589 1104	70.990 693 2472	.014 086 3535	.628 302 8663	44.603 656 0464	.022 419 6868	56
	57	1.604 852 3530	72.582 282 3576	.013 777 4670	.623 110 2806	45.226 766 3270	.022 110 8003	57
	58	1.618 226 1226	74.187 134 7106	.013 479 4261	.617 960 6089	45.844 726 9359	.021 812 7594	58
	59	1.631 711 3403	75.805 360 8332	.013 191 6792	.612 853 4964	46.457 580 4323	.021 525 0125	59
	60	1.645 308 9348	77.437 072 1734	.012 913 7114	.607 788 5915	47.065 369 0238	.021 247 0447	60
	61	1.659 019 8426	79.082 381 1082	.012 645 0416	.602 765 5453	47.668 134 5690	.020 978 3749	61
	62	1.672 845 0079	80.741 400 9508	.012 385 2198	.597 784 0118	48.265 918 5808	.020 718 5532	62
	63	1.686 785 3830	82.414 245 9587	.012 133 8245	.592 843 6481	48.858 762 2289	.020 467 1579	63
	64	1.700 841 9278	84.101 031 3417	.011 890 4606	.587 944 1138	49.446 706 3427	.020 223 7939	64
	65	1.715 015 6106	85.801 873 2695	.011 654 7572	.583 085 0715	50.029 791 4143	.019 988 0905	65
	66	1.729 307 4073	87.516 888 8801	.011 426 3660	.578 266 1867	50.608 057 6009	.019 759 6993	66
	67	1.743 718 3024	89.246 196 2875	.011 204 9593	.573 487 1273	51.181 544 7282	.019 538 2927	67
	68	1.758 249 2882	90.989 914 5898	.010 990 2290	.568 747 5642	51.750 292 2924	.019 323 5624	68
	69	1.772 901 3657	92.748 163 8781	.010 781 8846	.564 047 1711	52.314 339 4636	.019 115 2179	69
	70	1.787 675 5437	94.521 065 2437	.010 579 6522	.559 385 6243	52.873 725 0878	.018 912 9856	70
	71	1.802 572 8399	96.308 740 7874	.010 383 2735	.554 762 6026	53.428 487 6904	.018 716 6069	71
	72	1.817 594 2802	98.111 313 6273	.010 192 5044	.550 177 7877	53.978 665 4781	.018 525 8378	72
	73	1.832 740 8992	99.928 907 9076	.010 007 1143	.545 630 8638	54.524 296 3419	.018 340 4476	73
	74	1.848 013 7401	101.761 648 8068	.009 826 8848	.541 121 5178	55.065 417 8598	.018 160 2181	74
	75	1.863 413 8546	103.609 662 5469	.009 651 6095	.536 649 4392	55.602 067 2989	.017 984 9428	75
	76	1.878 942 3033	105.473 076 4014	.009 481 0926	.532 214 3198	56.134 281 6188	.017 814 4259	76
	77	1.894 600 1559	107.352 018 7048	.009 315 1485	.527 815 8544	56.662 097 4732	.017 648 4819	77
	78	1.910 388 4905	109.246 618 8606	.009 153 6014	.523 453 7399	57.185 551 2131	.017 486 9347	78
	79	1.926 308 3946	111.157 007 3511	.008 996 2839	.519 127 6759	57.704 678 8890	.017 329 6173	79
	80	1.942 360 9645	113.083 315 7457	.008 843 0375	.514 837 3646	58.219 516 2535	.017 176 3708	80
	81	1.958 547 3059	115.025 676 7103	.008 693 7111	.510 582 5103	58.730 098 7638	.017 027 0444	81
	82	1.974 868 5335	116.984 224 0162	.008 548 1612	.506 362 8201	59.236 461 5840	.016 881 4945	82
	83	1.991 325 7712	118.959 092 5497	.008 406 2511	.502 178 0034	59.738 639 5874	.016 739 5844	83
	84	2.007 920 1527	120.950 418 3209	.008 267 8507	.498 027 7720	60.236 667 3594	.016 601 1840	84
	85	2.024 652 8206	122.958 338 4736	.008 132 8360	.493 911 8400	60.730 579 1994	.016 466 1693	85
	86	2.041 524 9275	124.982 991 2942	.008 001 0887	.489 829 9240	61.220 409 1234	.016 334 4220	86
	87	2.058 537 6352	127.024 516 2216	.007 872 4960	.485 781 7428	61.706 190 8662	.016 205 8294	87
	88	2.075 692 1155	129.083 053 8568	.007 746 9503	.481 767 0176	62.187 957 8838	.016 080 2836	88
	89	2.092 989 5498	131.158 745 9723	.007 624 3486	.477 785 4720	62.665 743 3558	.015 957 6819	89
	90	2.110 431 1294	133.251 735 5221	.007 504 5927	.473 836 8318	63.139 580 1876	.015 837 9260	90
	91	2.128 018 0554	135.362 166 6514	.007 387 5886	.469 920 8249	63.609 501 0125	.015 720 9219	91
	92	2.145 751 5392	137.490 184 7069	.007 273 2465	.466 037 1817	64.075 538 1942	.015 606 5798	92
	93	2.163 632 8021	139.635 936 2461	.007 161 4803	.462 185 6348	64.537 723 8290	.015 494 8136	93
	94	2.181 663 0754	141.799 569 0481	.007 052 2076	.458 365 9188	64.996 089 7478	.015 385 5409	94
	95	2.199 843 6010	143.981 232 1235	.006 945 3496	.454 577 7707	65.450 667 5184	.015 278 6830	95
	96	2.218 175 6310	146.181 075 7246	.006 840 8308	.450 820 9296	65.901 488 4480	.015 174 1641	96
	97	2.236 660 4280	148.399 251 3556	.006 738 5785	.447 095 1008	66.348 583 5488	.015 071 9118	97
	98	2.255 299 2649	150.635 911 7836	.006 638 5232	.443 400 1357	66.791 983 7205	.014 971 8566	98
	99	2.274 093 4254	152.891 211 0484	.006 540 5963	.439 735 6717	67.231 719 3922	.014 873 9317	99
	100	2.293 044 2039	155.165 304 4738	.006 444 7397	.436 101 4926	67.667 820 8848	.014 778 0730	100

RATE 1% PERIODS	XIV COMPOUND AMOUNT — AMOUNT OF 1 — How $1 left at compound interest will grow.	XV AMOUNT OF ANNUITY — AMOUNT OF 1 PER PERIOD — How $1 deposited periodically will grow.	XVI SINKING FUND — SINKING FUND — Periodic deposit that will grow to $1 at future date.	XVII PRESENT VALUE — PRESENT WORTH OF 1 — What $1 due in the future is worth today.	XVIII PRESENT VALUE OF ANNUITY — PRESENT WORTH OF 1 PER PERIOD — What $1 payable periodically is worth today.	XIX AMORTIZATION — PARTIAL PAYMENT — Annuity worth $1 today. Periodic payment necessary to pay off a loan of $1.	PERIODS
1	1.010 000 0000	1.000 000 0000	1.000 000 0000	.990 099 0099	.990 099 0099	1.010 000 0000	1
2	1.020 100 0000	2.010 000 0000	.497 512 4378	.980 296 0494	1.970 395 0593	.507 512 4378	2
3	1.030 301 0000	3.030 100 0000	.330 022 1115	.970 590 1479	2.940 985 2072	.340 022 1115	3
4	1.040 604 0100	4.060 401 0000	.246 281 0939	.960 980 3445	3.901 965 5517	.256 281 0939	4
5	1.051 010 0501	5.101 005 0100	.196 039 7996	.951 465 6876	4.853 431 2393	.206 039 7996	5
6	1.061 520 1506	6.152 015 0601	.162 548 3667	.942 045 2353	5.795 476 4746	.172 548 3667	6
7	1.072 135 3521	7.213 535 2107	.138 628 2829	.932 718 0547	6.728 194 5293	.148 628 2829	7
8	1.082 856 7056	8.285 670 5628	.120 690 2920	.923 483 2225	7.651 677 7518	.130 690 2920	8
9	1.093 685 2727	9.368 527 2684	.106 740 3628	.914 339 8242	8.566 017 5760	.116 740 3628	9
10	1.104 622 1254	10.462 212 5411	.095 582 0766	.905 286 9547	9.471 304 5307	.105 582 0766	10
11	1.115 668 3467	11.566 834 6665	.086 454 0757	.896 323 7175	10.367 628 2482	.096 454 0757	11
12	1.126 825 0301	12.682 503 0132	.078 848 7887	.887 449 2253	11.255 077 4735	.088 848 7887	12
13	1.138 093 2804	13.809 328 0433	.072 414 8197	.878 662 5993	12.133 740 0728	.082 414 8197	13
14	1.149 474 2132	14.947 421 3238	.066 901 1717	.869 962 9696	13.003 703 0423	.076 901 1717	14
15	1.160 968 9554	16.096 895 5370	.062 123 7802	.861 349 4748	13.865 052 5172	.072 123 7802	15
16	1.172 578 6449	17.257 864 4924	.057 944 5968	.852 821 2622	14.717 873 7794	.067 944 5968	16
17	1.184 304 4314	18.430 443 1373	.054 258 0551	.844 377 4873	15.562 251 2667	.064 258 0551	17
18	1.196 147 4757	19.614 747 5687	.050 982 0479	.836 017 3142	16.398 268 5809	.060 982 0479	18
19	1.208 108 9504	20.810 895 0444	.048 051 7536	.827 739 9150	17.226 008 4959	.058 051 7536	19
20	1.220 190 0399	22.019 003 9948	.045 415 3149	.819 544 4703	18.045 552 9663	.055 415 3149	20
21	1.232 391 9403	23.239 194 0347	.043 030 7522	.811 430 1687	18.856 983 1349	.053 030 7522	21
22	1.244 715 8598	24.471 585 9751	.040 863 7185	.803 396 2066	19.660 379 3415	.050 863 7185	22
23	1.257 163 0183	25.716 301 8348	.038 885 8401	.795 441 7887	20.455 821 1302	.048 885 8401	23
24	1.269 734 6485	26.973 464 8532	.037 073 4722	.787 566 1274	21.243 387 2576	.047 073 4722	24
25	1.282 431 9950	28.243 199 5017	.035 406 7534	.779 768 4430	22.023 155 7006	.045 406 7534	25
26	1.295 256 3150	29.525 631 4967	.033 868 8776	.772 047 9634	22.795 203 6640	.043 868 8776	26
27	1.308 208 8781	30.820 887 8117	.032 445 5287	.764 403 9241	23.559 607 5881	.042 445 5287	27
28	1.321 290 9669	32.129 096 6898	.031 124 4356	.756 835 5684	24.316 443 1565	.041 124 4356	28
29	1.334 503 8766	33.450 387 6567	.029 895 0198	.749 342 1470	25.065 785 3035	.039 895 0198	29
30	1.347 848 9153	34.784 891 5333	.028 748 1132	.741 922 9178	25.807 708 2213	.038 748 1132	30
31	1.361 327 4045	36.132 740 4486	.027 675 7309	.734 577 1463	26.542 285 3676	.037 675 7309	31
32	1.374 940 6785	37.494 067 8531	.026 670 8857	.727 304 1053	27.269 589 4729	.036 670 8857	32
33	1.388 690 0853	38.869 008 5316	.025 727 4378	.720 103 0745	27.989 692 5474	.035 727 4378	33
34	1.402 576 9862	40.257 698 6170	.024 839 9694	.712 973 3411	28.702 665 8885	.034 839 9694	34
35	1.416 602 7560	41.660 275 6031	.024 003 6818	.705 914 1991	29.408 580 0876	.034 003 6818	35
36	1.430 768 7836	43.076 878 3592	.023 214 3098	.698 924 9496	30.107 505 0373	.033 214 3098	36
37	1.445 076 4714	44.507 647 1427	.022 468 0491	.692 004 9006	30.799 509 9379	.032 468 0491	37
38	1.459 527 2361	45.952 723 6142	.021 761 4958	.685 153 3670	31.484 663 3048	.031 761 4958	38
39	1.474 122 5085	47.412 250 8503	.021 091 5951	.678 369 6702	32.163 032 9751	.031 091 5951	39
40	1.488 863 7336	48.886 373 3588	.020 455 5980	.671 653 1389	32.834 686 1140	.030 455 5980	40
41	1.503 752 3709	50.375 237 0924	.019 851 0232	.665 003 1078	33.499 689 2217	.029 851 0232	41
42	1.518 789 8946	51.878 989 4633	.019 275 6260	.658 418 9186	34.158 108 1403	.029 275 6260	42
43	1.533 977 7936	53.397 779 3580	.018 727 3705	.651 899 9194	34.810 008 0597	.028 727 3705	43
44	1.549 317 5715	54.931 757 1515	.018 204 4058	.645 445 4648	35.455 453 5245	.028 204 4058	44
45	1.564 810 7472	56.481 074 7231	.017 705 0455	.639 054 9156	36.094 508 4401	.027 705 0455	45
46	1.580 458 8547	58.045 885 4703	.017 227 7499	.632 727 6392	36.727 236 0793	.027 227 7499	46
47	1.596 263 4432	59.626 344 3250	.016 771 1103	.626 463 0091	37.353 699 0884	.026 771 1103	47
48	1.612 226 0777	61.222 607 7682	.016 333 8354	.620 260 4051	37.973 959 4935	.026 333 8354	48
49	1.628 348 3385	62.834 833 8459	.015 914 7393	.614 119 2129	38.588 078 7064	.025 914 7393	49
50	1.644 631 8218	64.463 182 1844	.015 512 7309	.608 038 8247	39.196 117 5311	.025 512 7309	50
51	1.661 078 1401	66.107 814 0062	.015 126 8048	.602 018 6383	39.798 136 1694	.025 126 8048	51
52	1.677 688 9215	67.768 892 1463	.014 756 0329	.596 058 0577	40.394 194 2271	.024 756 0329	52
53	1.694 465 8107	69.446 581 0678	.014 399 5570	.590 156 4928	40.984 350 7199	.024 399 5570	53
54	1.711 410 4688	71.141 046 8784	.014 056 5826	.584 313 3592	41.568 664 0791	.024 056 5826	54
55	1.728 524 5735	72.852 457 3472	.013 726 3730	.578 528 0784	42.147 192 1576	.023 726 3730	55
56	1.745 809 8192	74.580 981 9207	.013 408 2440	.572 800 0776	42.719 992 2352	.023 408 2440	56
57	1.763 267 9174	76.326 791 7399	.013 101 5595	.567 128 7898	43.287 121 0250	.023 101 5595	57
58	1.780 900 5965	78.090 059 6573	.012 805 7272	.561 513 6532	43.848 634 6782	.022 805 7272	58
59	1.798 709 6025	79.870 960 2539	.012 520 1950	.555 954 1121	44.404 588 7903	.022 520 1950	59
60	1.816 696 6986	81.669 669 8564	.012 244 4477	.550 449 6159	44.955 038 4062	.022 244 4477	60
61	1.834 863 6655	83.486 366 5550	.011 978 0036	.544 999 6197	45.500 038 0260	.021 978 0036	61
62	1.853 212 3022	85.321 230 2205	.011 720 4123	.539 603 5839	46.039 641 6099	.021 720 4123	62
63	1.871 744 4252	87.174 442 5227	.011 471 2520	.534 260 9742	46.573 902 5840	.021 471 2520	63
64	1.890 461 8695	89.046 186 9480	.011 230 1271	.528 971 2615	47.102 873 8456	.021 230 1271	64
65	1.909 366 4882	90.936 648 8174	.010 996 6665	.523 733 9223	47.626 607 7679	.020 996 6665	65
66	1.928 460 1531	92.846 015 3056	.010 770 5215	.518 548 4379	48.145 156 2058	.020 770 5215	66
67	1.947 744 7546	94.774 475 4587	.010 551 3641	.513 414 2950	48.658 570 5008	.020 551 3641	67
68	1.967 222 2021	96.722 220 2133	.010 338 8859	.508 330 9851	49.166 901 4860	.020 338 8859	68
69	1.986 894 4242	98.689 442 4154	.010 132 7961	.503 298 0051	49.670 199 4911	.020 132 7961	69
70	2.006 763 3684	100.676 336 8395	.009 932 8207	.498 314 8565	50.168 514 3476	.019 932 8207	70
71	2.026 831 0021	102.683 100 2079	.009 738 7009	.493 381 0461	50.661 895 3936	.019 738 7009	71
72	2.047 099 3121	104.709 931 2100	.009 550 1925	.488 496 0852	51.150 391 4789	.019 550 1925	72
73	2.067 570 3052	106.757 030 5221	.009 367 0646	.483 659 4903	51.634 050 9692	.019 367 0646	73
74	2.088 246 0083	108.824 600 8273	.009 189 0987	.478 870 7825	52.112 921 7516	.019 189 0987	74
75	2.109 128 4684	110.912 846 8356	.009 016 0881	.475 129 4876	52.587 051 2393	.019 016 0881	75
76	2.130 219 7530	113.021 975 3040	.008 847 8369	.469 435 1362	53.056 486 3755	.018 847 8369	76
77	2.151 521 9506	115.152 195 0570	.008 684 1593	.464 787 2636	53.521 273 6391	.018 684 1593	77
78	2.173 037 1701	117.303 717 0076	.008 524 8791	.460 185 4095	53.981 459 0486	.018 524 8791	78
79	2.194 767 5418	119.476 754 1776	.008 369 8290	.455 629 1183	54.437 088 1670	.018 369 8290	79
80	2.216 715 2172	121.671 521 7194	.008 218 8501	.451 117 9389	54.888 206 1059	.018 218 8501	80
81	2.238 882 3694	123.888 236 9366	.008 071 7914	.446 651 4247	55.334 857 5306	.018 071 7914	81
82	2.261 271 1931	126.127 119 3060	.007 928 5090	.442 229 1334	55.777 086 6639	.017 928 5090	82
83	2.283 883 9050	128.388 390 4990	.007 788 8662	.437 850 6271	56.214 937 2910	.017 788 8662	83
84	2.306 722 7440	130.672 274 4040	.007 652 7328	.433 515 4724	56.648 452 7634	.017 652 7328	84
85	2.329 789 9715	132.978 997 1481	.007 519 9845	.429 223 2400	57.077 676 0034	.017 519 9845	85
86	2.353 087 8712	135.308 787 1196	.007 390 5030	.424 973 5049	57.502 649 5083	.017 390 5030	86
87	2.376 618 7499	137.661 874 9908	.007 264 1754	.420 765 8465	57.923 415 3547	.017 264 1754	87
88	2.400 384 9374	140.038 493 7407	.007 140 8937	.416 599 8480	58.340 015 2027	.017 140 8937	88
89	2.424 388 7868	142.438 878 6781	.007 020 5551	.412 475 0970	58.752 490 2997	.017 020 5551	89
90	2.448 632 6746	144.863 267 4648	.006 903 0612	.408 391 1852	59.160 881 4849	.016 903 0612	90
91	2.473 119 0014	147.311 900 1395	.006 788 3178	.404 347 7081	59.565 229 1929	.016 788 3178	91
92	2.497 850 1914	149.785 019 1409	.006 676 2351	.400 344 2654	59.965 573 4584	.016 676 2351	92
93	2.522 828 6933	152.282 869 3323	.006 566 7268	.396 380 4608	60.361 953 9192	.016 566 7268	93
94	2.548 056 9803	154.805 698 0256	.006 459 7105	.392 455 9018	60.754 409 8210	.016 459 7105	94
95	2.573 537 5501	157.353 755 0059	.006 355 1073	.388 570 1998	61.142 980 0207	.016 355 1073	95
96	2.599 272 9256	159.927 292 5559	.006 252 8414	.384 722 9701	61.527 702 9908	.016 252 8414	96
97	2.625 265 6548	162.526 565 4815	.006 152 8403	.380 913 8318	61.908 616 8226	.016 152 8403	97
98	2.651 518 3114	165.151 831 1363	.006 055 0343	.377 142 4077	62.285 759 2303	.016 055 0343	98
99	2.678 033 4945	167.803 349 4477	.005 959 3566	.373 408 3245	62.659 167 5548	.015 959 3566	99
100	2.704 813 8294	170.481 382 9422	.005 865 7431	.369 711 2123	63.028 878 7671	.015 856 7431	100

	XIV COMPOUND AMOUNT	XV AMOUNT OF ANNUITY	XVI SINKING FUND	XVII PRESENT VALUE	XVIII PRESENT VALUE OF ANNUITY	XIX AMORTIZATION	
RATE 1 1/6%	AMOUNT OF 1	AMOUNT OF 1 PER PERIOD	SINKING FUND	PRESENT WORTH OF 1	PRESENT WORTH OF 1 PER PERIOD	PARTIAL PAYMENT	
PERIODS	How $1 left at compound interest will grow.	How $1 deposited periodically will grow.	Periodic deposit that will grow to $1 at future date.	What $1 due in the future is worth today.	What $1 payable periodically is worth today.	Annuity worth $1 today. Periodic payment necessary to pay off a loan of $1.	PERIODS
1	1.011 666 6667	1.000 000 0000	1.000 000 0000	.988 467 8748	.988 467 8748	1.011 666 6667	1
2	1.023 469 4444	2.011 666 6667	497 100 2486	.977 068 7395	1.965 536 6143	.508 766 9152	2
3	1.035 409 9213	3.035 136 1111	329 474 5156	.965 801 0605	2.931 337 6748	.341 141 1823	3
4	1.047 489 7037	4 070 546 0324	245 667 2869	.954 663 3217	3.886 000 9965	257 333 9536	4
5	1.059 710 4169	5.118 035 7361	195 387 4595	.943 654 0248	4.829 655 0212	.207 054 1261	5
6	1.072 073 7051	6 177 746 1530	161 871 3322	.932 771 6884	5.762 426 7096	173 537 9989	6
7	1.084 581 2317	7.249 819 8582	.137 934 4618	.922 014 8485	6.684 441 5581	.149 601 1284	7
8	1.097 234 6794	8.334 401 0898	.119 984 6263	.911 382 0578	7.595 823 6159	.131 651 2929	8
9	1.110 035 7506	9.431 635 7692	106 026 1469	.900 871 8858	8.496 695 5017	.117 692 8136	9
10	1.122 986 1677	10.541 671 5199	.094 861 6164	.890 482 9184	9.387 178 4202	.106 528 2831	10
11	1.136 087 6730	11.664 657 6876	.085 729 0481	.880 213 7579	10.267 392 1781	.097 395 7148	11
12	1.149 342 0292	12.800 745 3606	.078 120 4509	.870 063 0227	11.137 455 2007	.089 787 1176	12
13	1.162 751 0195	13.950 087 3898	.071 684 1387	.860 029 3469	11.997 484 5477	.083 350 8054	13
14	1.176 316 4481	15.112 838 4094	066 168 9071	.850 111 3808	12.847 595 9285	.077 835 5737	14
15	1.190 040 1400	16.289 154 8575	.061 390 5392	.840 307 7900	13.687 903 7185	073 057 2059	15
16	1.203 923 9416	17.479 194 9975	.057 210 8727	.830 617 2553	14.518 520 9738	.068 877 5394	16
17	1.217 969 7210	18.683 118 9391	.053 524 2538	.821 038 4731	15.339 559 4469	.065 190 9205	17
18	1.232 179 3677	19.901 088 6601	.050 248 5074	.811 570 1546	16.151 129 6015	.061 915 1740	18
19	1.246 554 7937	21.133 268 0278	.047 318 7582	.802 211 0260	16.953 340 6275	.058 985 4249	19
20	1.261 097 9329	22.379 822 8214	.044 683 1062	.792 959 8280	17.746 300 4556	.056 349 7729	20
21	1.275 810 7421	23.640 920 7544	.042 299 5369	.783 815 3160	18.530 115 7716	.053 966 2036	21
22	1.290 695 2008	24.916 731 4965	.040 133 6748	.774 776 2596	19.304 892 0312	.051 800 3415	22
23	1.305 753 3115	26.207 426 6973	.038 157 1228	.765 841 4428	20.070 733 4740	.049 823 7895	23
24	1.320 987 1001	27.513 180 0087	.036 346 2166	.757 009 6634	20.827 743 1374	.048 012 8833	24
25	1.336 398 6163	28.834 167 1088	.034 681 0780	.748 279 7332	21.576 022 8706	.046 347 7447	25
26	1.351 989 9335	30.170 565 7251	.033 144 8873	739 650 4776	22.315 673 3482	.044 811 5539	26
27	1.367 763 1494	31.522 555 6586	.031 723 3162	731 120 7357	23.046 794 0839	.043 389 9828	27
28	1.383 720 3861	32.890 318 8079	.030 404 0835	722 689 3598	23.769 483 4437	.042 070 7502	28
29	1.399 863 7906	34.274 039 1940	.029 176 6020	714 355 2156	24.483 838 6593	.040 843 2687	29
30	1.416 195 5348	35.673 902 9846	.028 031 6959	.706 117 1819	25.189 955 8412	.039 698 3626	30
31	1.432 717 8161	37 090 098 5194	.026 961 3736	.697 974 1501	25.887 929 9913	.038 628 0402	31
32	1.449 432 8572	38.522 816 3355	.025 958 6420	.689 925 0248	26.577 855 0161	.037 625 3087	32
33	1.466 342 9072	39.972 249 1927	.025 017 3563	.681 968 7230	27.259 823 7391	.036 684 0230	33
34	1.483 450 2412	41.438 592 1000	.024 132 0940	.674 104 1743	27.933 927 9135	.035 798 7607	34
35	1.500 757 1606	42.922 042 3412	.023 298 0526	.666 330 3206	28.600 258 2341	.034 964 7193	35
36	1.518 265 9942	44.422 799 5018	.022 510 9631	.658 646 1159	29.258 904 3500	.034 177 6298	36
37	1.535 979 0975	45.941 065 4960	.021 767 0180	.651 050 5264	29.909 954 8764	.033 433 6847	37
38	1.553 896 8536	47 477 044 5934	.021 062 8106	.643 542 5303	30.553 497 4067	.032 729 4773	38
39	1.572 027 6735	49.030 943 4470	.020 395 2837	.636 121 1172	31.189 618 5239	.032 061 9503	39
40	1.590 367 9964	50.602 971 1206	.019 761 6855	.628 785 2889	31.818 403 8128	.031 428 3522	40
41	1.608 922 2897	52.193 339 1170	.019 159 5329	.621 534 0582	32.439 937 8709	.030 826 1996	41
42	1.627 693 0497	53.802 261 4067	.018 586 5793	.614 366 4496	33.054 304 3205	.030 253 2460	42
43	1.646 661 8020	55.429 954 4564	.018 040 7870	.607 281 4988	33.661 585 8193	.029 707 4536	43
44	1.665 894 1013	57.076 637 2584	.017 520 3034	.600 278 2525	34.261 864 0718	.029 186 9700	44
45	1.685 329 5325	58.742 531 3598	.017 023 4407	.593 355 7685	34.855 219 8403	.028 690 1074	45
46	1.704 991 7104	60.427 860 8923	.016 548 6579	.586 513 1155	35.441 732 9559	.028 215 3246	46
47	1.724 883 2804	62.132 852 6027	.016 094 5451	.579 749 3728	36.021 482 3287	.027 761 2118	47
48	1.745 006 9186	63.857 735 8831	.015 659 8098	.573 063 6305	36.594 545 9592	.027 326 4765	48
49	1.765 365 3327	65.602 742 8017	.015 243 2651	.566 454 9889	37.161 000 9481	.026 909 9318	49
50	1.785 961 2616	67.368 108 1344	.014 843 8189	.559 922 5591	37.720 923 5072	.026 510 4856	50
51	1.806 797 4763	69.154 069 3960	.014 460 4650	.553 465 4620	38.274 388 9692	.026 127 1317	51
52	1.827 876 7802	70.960 866 8723	.014 092 2743	.547 082 8290	38.821 471 7982	.025 758 9410	52
53	1.849 202 0093	72.788 743 6524	.013 738 3880	.540 773 8013	39.362 245 5996	.025 405 0546	53
54	1.870 776 0327	74.637 945 6617	.013 398 0108	.534 537 5302	39.896 783 1297	.025 064 6774	54
55	1.892 601 7531	76.508 721 6944	.013 070 4053	.528 373 1764	40.425 156 3062	.024 737 0719	55
56	1.914 682 1069	78.401 323 4475	.012 754 8867	.522 279 9108	40.947 436 2170	.024 421 5534	56
57	1.937 020 0648	80.316 005 5544	.012 450 8184	.516 256 9135	41.463 693 1304	.024 117 4851	57
58	1.959 618 6322	82.253 025 6192	.012 157 6075	.510 303 3741	41.973 996 5045	.023 824 2742	58
59	1.982 480 8496	84.212 644 2514	.011 874 7013	.504 418 4917	42.478 414 9963	.023 541 3680	59
60	2.005 609 7020	86.195 125 1010	.011 601 3642	.498 601 4745	42.977 016 4708	.023 268 2508	60
61	2.029 008 5738	88.200 734 8939	.011 337 7740	.492 851 5399	43.469 868 0106	.023 004 4407	61
62	2.052 680 3405	90.229 743 4677	.011 082 8199	.487 167 9142	43.957 035 9248	.022 749 4866	62
63	2.076 628 2778	92.282 423 8081	.010 836 2997	.481 549 8328	44.438 585 7577	.022 502 9664	63
64	2.100 855 6077	94.359 052 0859	.010 597 8174	.475 996 5399	44.914 582 2977	.022 264 4840	64
65	2.125 365 5898	96.459 907 6935	.010 367 0014	.470 507 2882	45.385 089 5857	.022 033 6681	65
66	2.150 161 5216	98.585 273 2833	.010 143 5028	465 081 3392	45.850 170 9249	.021 810 1695	66
67	2.175 246 7394	100.735 434 8049	.009 926 9934	459 717 9630	46.309 888 8879	.021 593 6601	67
68	2.200 624 6180	102.910 681 5443	.009 717 1643	.454 416 4379	46.764 305 3258	.021 383 8310	68
69	2.226 298 5719	105.111 306 1623	.009 513 7244	.449 176 0506	47.213 481 3764	.021 180 3911	69
70	2.252 272 0552	107.337 604 7342	.009 316 3994	.443 996 0962	47.657 477 4725	.020 983 0661	70
71	2.278 548 5625	109.589 876 7895	.009 124 9304	.438 875 8776	48.096 353 3501	.020 791 5971	71
72	2.305 131 6291	111.868 425 3520	.008 939 0728	.433 814 7060	48.530 168 0561	.020 605 7395	72
73	2.332 024 8314	114.173 556 9811	.008 758 5955	.428 811 9005	48.958 979 9566	.020 425 2621	73
74	2.359 231 7878	116.505 581 8126	.008 583 2797	.423 866 7880	49.382 846 7446	.020 249 9464	74
75	2.386 756 1587	118.864 813 6004	.008 412 9186	.418 978 7031	49.801 825 4477	.002 079 5853	75
76	2.414 601 6472	121.251 569 7591	.008 247 3159	.414 146 9882	50.215 972 4360	.019 913 9826	76
77	2.442 771 9997	123.666 171 4062	.008 086 2858	.409 370 9933	50.625 343 4293	.019 752 9524	77
78	2.471 271 0064	126.108 943 4060	.007 929 6517	.404 650 0758	51.029 993 5051	.019 596 3184	78
79	2.500 102 5015	128.580 214 4124	.007 777 2463	.399 983 6004	51.429 977 1055	.019 443 9130	79
80	2.529 270 3640	131.080 316 9139	.007 628 9105	.395 370 9395	51.825 348 0450	.019 295 5771	80
81	2.558 778 5182	133.609 587 2779	.007 484 4928	.390 811 4723	52.216 159 5173	.019 151 1595	81
82	2.588 630 9343	136.168 365 7961	.007 343 8496	.386 304 5855	52.602 464 1027	.019 010 5163	82
83	2.618 831 6285	138.756 996 7304	.007 206 8438	.381 849 6726	52.984 313 7754	.018 873 5105	83
84	2.649 384 6642	141.375 828 3589	.007 073 3449	.377 446 1344	53.361 759 9097	.018 740 0116	84
85	2.680 294 1519	144.025 213 0231	.006 943 2688	.373 093 3783	53.734 853 2880	.018 609 8954	85
86	2.711 564 2504	146.705 507 1750	.006 816 3767	.368 790 8188	54.103 644 1068	.018 483 0434	86
87	2.743 199 1666	149.417 071 4254	.006 692 6757	.364 537 8769	54.468 181 9837	.018 359 3423	87
88	2.775 203 1569	152.160 270 5920	.006 572 0178	.360 333 9804	54.828 515 9641	.018 238 6844	88
89	2.807 580 5271	154.935 473 7489	.006 454 2998	.356 178 5638	55.184 694 5279	.018 120 9665	89
90	2.840 335 6332	157.743 054 2760	.006 339 4233	.352 071 0680	55.536 765 5960	.018 006 0900	90
91	2.873 472 8823	160.583 389 9092	.006 227 2941	.348 010 9404	55.884 776 5364	.017 893 9608	91
92	2.906 996 7326	163.456 862 7915	.006 117 8225	.343 997 6347	56.228 774 1710	.017 784 4887	92
93	2.940 911 6944	166.363 859 5241	.006 010 9209	.340 030 6109	56.568 804 7819	.017 677 5876	93
94	2.975 222 3309	169.304 771 2185	.005 906 5081	.336 109 3353	56.904 914 1172	.017 573 1748	94
95	3.009 933 2581	172.279 993 5494	.005 804 5045	.332 233 2804	57.237 147 3976	.017 471 1712	95
96	3.045 049 1461	175.289 926 8075	.005 704 8344	.328 401 9246	57.565 549 3222	.017 371 5010	96
97	3.080 574 7195	178.334 975 9536	.005 607 4250	.324 614 7525	57.890 164 0746	.017 274 0917	97
98	3.116 514 7579	181.415 550 6730	.005 512 2066	.320 871 2545	58.211 035 3291	.017 178 8733	98
99	3.152 874 0967	184.532 065 4309	.005 419 1184	.317 170 9270	58.528 206 2561	.017 085 7790	99
100	3.189 657 6278	187.684 939 5276	.005 328 0780	.313 513 2722	58.841 719 5283	.016 994 7447	100

RATE 1 1/4%		XIV COMPOUND AMOUNT	XV AMOUNT OF ANNUITY	XVI SINKING FUND	XVII PRESENT VALUE	XVIII PRESENT VALUE OF ANNUITY	XIX AMORTIZATION	
	PERIODS	AMOUNT OF 1	AMOUNT OF 1 PER PERIOD	SINKING FUND	PRESENT WORTH OF 1	PRESENT WORTH OF 1 PER PERIOD	PARTIAL PAYMENT	PERIODS
		How $1 left at compound interest will grow.	How $1 deposited periodically will grow.	Periodic deposit that will grow to $1 at future date.	What $1 due in the future is worth today.	What $1 payable periodically is worth today.	Annuity worth $1 today. Periodic payment necessary to pay off a loan of $1.	
	1	1.012 500 0000	1.000 000 0000	1.000 000 0000	.987 654 3210	.987 654 3210	1.012 500 0000	1
	2	1.025 156 2500	2.012 500 0000	.496 894 4099	.975 461 0578	1.963 115 3788	.509 394 4099	2
	3	1.037 970 7031	3.037 656 2500	.329 201 1728	.963 418 3287	2.926 533 7074	.341 701 1728	3
	4	1.050 945 3369	4.075 626 9531	.245 361 0233	.951 524 2752	3.878 057 9826	.257 861 0233	4
	5	1.064 082 1536	5.126 572 2900	.195 062 1084	.939 777 0619	4.817 835 0446	.207 562 1084	5
	6	1.077 383 1805	6.190 654 4437	.161 533 8102	.928 174 8760	5.746 009 9206	.174 033 8102	6
	7	1.090 850 4703	7.268 037 6242	.137 588 7209	.916 715 9269	6.662 725 8475	.150 088 7209	7
	8	1.104 486 1012	8.358 888 0945	.119 633 1365	.905 398 4463	7.568 124 2938	.132 133 1365	8
	9	1.118 292 1774	9.463 374 1957	.105 670 5546	.894 220 6877	8.462 344 9815	.118 170 5546	9
	10	1.132 270 8297	10.581 666 3731	.094 503 0740	.883 180 9262	9.345 525 9077	.107 003 0740	10
	11	1.146 424 2150	11.713 937 2028	.085 368 3935	.872 277 4579	10.217 803 3656	.097 868 3935	11
	12	1.160 754 5177	12.860 361 4178	.077 758 3123	.861 508 6004	11.079 311 9660	.090 258 3123	12
	13	1.175 263 9492	14.021 115 9356	.071 320 9993	.850 872 6918	11.930 184 6578	.083 820 9993	13
	14	1.189 954 7486	15.196 379 8848	.065 805 1462	.840 368 0906	12.770 552 7485	.078 305 1462	14
	15	1.204 829 1829	16.386 334 6333	.061 026 4603	.829 993 1759	13.600 545 9244	.073 526 4603	15
	16	1.219 889 5477	17.591 163 8162	.056 846 7221	.819 746 3466	14.420 292 2710	.069 346 7221	16
	17	1.235 138 1670	18.811 053 3639	.053 160 2341	.809 626 0213	15.229 918 2924	.065 660 2341	17
	18	1.250 577 3941	20.046 191 5310	.049 884 7873	.799 630 6384	16.029 548 9307	.062 384 7873	18
	19	1.266 209 6116	21.296 768 9251	.046 955 4797	.789 758 6552	16.819 307 5859	.059 455 4797	19
	20	1.282 037 2317	22.562 978 5367	.044 320 3896	.780 008 5483	17.599 316 1342	.056 820 3896	20
	21	1.298 062 6971	23.845 015 7684	.041 937 4854	.770 378 8132	18.369 694 9474	.054 437 4854	21
	22	1.314 288 4808	25.143 078 4655	.039 772 3772	.760 867 9636	19.130 562 9110	.052 272 3772	22
	23	1.330 717 0868	26.457 366 9463	.037 796 6561	.751 474 5320	19.882 037 4430	.050 296 6561	23
	24	1.347 351 0504	27.788 084 0331	.035 986 6480	.742 197 0686	20.624 234 5116	.048 486 6480	24
	25	1.364 192 9385	29.135 435 0836	.034 322 4667	.733 034 1418	21.357 268 6534	.046 822 4667	25
	26	1.381 245 3503	30.499 628 0221	.032 787 2851	.723 984 3376	22.081 252 9910	.045 287 2851	26
	27	1.398 510 9172	31.880 873 3724	.031 366 7693	.715 046 2594	22.796 299 2504	.043 866 7693	27
	28	1.415 992 3036	33.279 384 2895	.030 048 6329	.706 218 5278	23.502 517 7784	.042 548 6329	28
	29	1.433 692 2074	34.695 376 5932	.028 822 2841	.697 499 7805	24.200 017 5587	.041 322 2841	29
	30	1.451 613 3600	36.129 068 8006	.027 678 5434	.688 888 6721	24.888 906 2308	.040 178 5434	30
	31	1.469 758 5270	37.580 682 1606	.026 609 4159	.680 383 8737	25.569 290 1045	.039 109 4159	31
	32	1.488 130 5086	39.050 440 6876	.025 607 9056	.671 984 0728	26.241 274 1773	.038 107 9056	32
	33	1.506 732 1400	40.538 571 1962	.024 667 8650	.663 687 9731	26.904 962 1504	.037 167 8650	33
	34	1.525 566 2917	42.045 303 3361	.023 783 8693	.655 494 2944	27.560 456 4448	.036 283 8693	34
	35	1.544 635 8703	43.570 869 6278	.022 951 1141	.647 401 7723	28.207 858 2171	.035 451 1141	35
	36	1.563 943 8187	45.115 505 4982	.022 165 3285	.639 409 1578	28.847 267 3749	.034 665 3285	36
	37	1.583 493 1165	46.679 449 3169	.021 422 7035	.631 515 2176	29.478 782 5925	.033 922 7035	37
	38	1.603 286 7804	48.262 942 4334	.020 719 8308	.623 718 7334	30.102 501 3259	.033 219 8308	38
	39	1.623 327 8652	49.866 229 2138	.020 053 6519	.616 018 5021	30.718 519 8281	.032 553 6519	39
	40	1.643 619 4635	51.489 557 0790	.019 421 4139	.608 413 3355	31.326 933 1635	.031 921 4139	40
	41	1.664 164 7068	53.133 176 5424	.018 820 6327	.600 902 0597	31.927 835 2233	.031 320 6327	41
	42	1.684 966 7656	54.797 341 2492	.018 249 0606	.593 483 5158	32.521 318 7390	.030 749 0606	42
	43	1.706 028 8502	56.482 308 0148	.017 704 6589	.586 156 5588	33.107 475 2978	.030 204 6589	43
	44	1.727 354 2108	58.188 336 8650	.017 185 5745	.578 920 0581	33.686 395 3558	.029 685 5745	44
	45	1.748 946 1384	59.915 691 0758	.016 690 1188	.571 772 8968	34.258 168 2527	.029 190 1188	45
	46	1.770 807 9652	61.664 637 2143	.016 216 7499	.564 713 9722	34.822 882 2249	.028 716 7499	46
	47	1.792 943 0647	63.435 445 1795	.015 764 0574	.557 742 1948	35.380 624 4196	.028 264 0574	47
	48	1.815 354 8531	65.228 388 2442	.015 330 7483	.550 856 4886	35.931 480 9083	.027 830 7483	48
	49	1.838 046 7887	67.043 743 0973	.014 915 6350	.544 055 7913	36.475 536 6995	.027 415 6350	49
	50	1.861 022 3736	68.881 789 8860	.014 517 6251	.537 339 0531	37.012 875 7526	.027 017 6251	50
	51	1.884 285 1532	70.742 812 2596	.014 135 7117	.530 705 2376	37.543 580 9902	.026 635 7117	51
	52	1.907 838 7177	72.627 097 4128	.013 768 9655	.524 153 3211	38.067 734 3114	.026 268 9655	52
	53	1.931 686 7016	74.534 936 1305	.013 416 5272	.517 682 2925	38.585 416 6038	.025 916 5272	53
	54	1.955 832 7854	76.466 622 8321	.013 077 6012	.511 291 1530	39.096 707 7568	.025 577 6012	54
	55	1.980 280 6952	78.422 455 6175	.012 751 4497	.504 978 9166	39.601 686 6734	.025 251 4497	55
	56	2.005 034 2039	80.402 736 3127	.012 437 3877	.498 744 6090	40.100 431 2824	.024 937 3877	56
	57	2.030 097 1315	82.407 770 5166	.012 134 7780	.492 587 2681	40.593 018 5505	.024 634 7780	57
	58	2.055 473 3456	84.437 867 6481	.011 843 0276	.486 505 9438	41.079 524 4943	.024 343 0276	58
	59	2.081 166 7624	86.493 340 9937	.011 561 5837	.480 499 6976	41.560 024 1919	.024 061 5837	59
	60	2.107 181 3470	88.574 507 7561	.011 289 9301	.474 567 6026	42.034 591 7945	.023 789 9301	60
	61	2.133 521 1138	90.681 689 1031	.011 027 5846	.468 708 7433	42.503 300 5378	.023 527 5846	61
	62	2.160 160 1277	92.815 210 2168	.010 774 0962	.462 922 2156	42.966 222 7534	.023 274 0962	62
	63	2.187 192 5043	94.975 400 3445	.010 529 0422	.457 207 1265	43.423 429 8799	.023 029 0422	63
	64	2.214 532 4106	97.162 592 8489	.010 292 0267	.451 562 5941	43.874 992 4739	.022 792 0267	64
	65	2.242 214 0657	99.377 125 2595	.010 062 6779	.445 987 7472	44.320 980 2212	.022 562 6779	65
	66	2.270 241 7416	101.619 339 3252	.009 840 6465	.440 481 7257	44.761 461 9468	.022 340 6465	66
	67	2.298 619 7633	103.889 581 0668	.009 625 6043	.435 043 6797	45.196 505 6265	.022 125 6043	67
	68	2.327 352 5104	106.188 200 8301	.009 417 2421	.429 672 7700	45.626 178 3966	.021 917 2421	68
	69	2.356 444 4168	108.515 553 3405	.009 215 2689	.424 368 1679	46.050 546 5645	.021 715 2689	69
	70	2.385 899 9720	110.871 997 7572	.009 019 4100	.419 129 0548	46.469 675 6193	.021 519 4100	70
	71	2.415 723 7216	113.257 897 7292	.008 829 4063	.413 954 6220	46.883 630 2412	.021 329 4063	71
	72	2.445 920 2681	115.673 621 4508	.008 645 0133	.408 844 0711	47.292 474 3123	.021 145 0133	72
	73	2.476 494 2715	118.119 541 7190	.008 456 9997	.403 796 6134	47.696 270 9258	.020 956 9997	73
	74	2.507 450 4499	120.596 035 9904	.008 292 1465	.398 811 4701	48.095 082 3958	.020 792 1465	74
	75	2.538 793 5805	123.103 486 4403	.008 123 2468	.393 887 8717	48.488 970 2675	.020 623 2468	75
	76	2.570 528 5003	125.642 280 0208	.007 959 1042	.389 025 0584	48.877 995 3259	.020 459 1042	76
	77	2.602 660 1065	128.212 808 5211	.007 799 5328	.384 222 2799	49.262 217 6058	.020 299 5328	77
	78	2.635 193 3578	130.815 468 6276	.007 644 3559	.379 478 7950	49.641 696 4008	.020 144 3559	78
	79	2.668 133 2748	133.450 661 9854	.007 493 4061	.374 793 8716	50.016 490 2724	.019 993 4061	79
	80	2.701 484 9408	136.118 795 2603	.007 346 5240	.370 166 7868	50.386 657 0592	.019 846 5240	80
	81	2.735 253 5025	138.820 280 2010	.007 203 5584	.365 596 8264	50.752 253 8856	.019 703 5584	81
	82	2.769 444 1713	141.555 533 7035	.007 064 3653	.361 083 2854	51.113 337 1710	.019 564 3653	82
	83	2.804 062 2234	144.324 977 8748	.006 928 8076	.356 625 4670	51.469 962 6380	.019 428 8076	83
	84	2.839 113 0012	147.129 040 0983	.006 796 7547	.352 222 6835	51.822 185 3215	.019 296 7547	84
	85	2.874 601 9137	149.968 153 0995	.006 668 0824	.347 874 2553	52.170 059 5768	.019 168 0824	85
	86	2.910 534 4377	152.842 755 0132	.006 542 6719	.343 579 5114	52.513 639 0882	.019 042 6719	86
	87	2.946 916 1181	155.753 289 4509	.006 420 4101	.339 337 7890	52.852 976 8772	.018 920 4101	87
	88	2.983 752 5696	158.700 205 5690	.006 301 1891	.335 148 4336	53.188 125 3108	.018 801 1891	88
	89	3.021 049 4767	161.683 958 1386	.006 184 9055	.331 010 7986	53.519 136 1094	.018 684 9055	89
	90	3.058 812 5952	164.705 007 6154	.006 071 4608	.326 924 2456	53.846 060 3550	.018 571 4608	90
	91	3.097 047 7526	167.763 820 2106	.005 960 7608	.322 888 1438	54.168 948 4988	.018 460 7608	91
	92	3.135 760 8495	170.860 867 9632	.005 852 7152	.318 901 8704	54.487 850 3692	.018 352 7152	92
	93	3.174 957 8602	173.996 628 8127	.005 747 2378	.314 964 8103	54.802 815 1794	.018 247 2378	93
	94	3.214 644 8334	177.171 586 6729	.005 644 2459	.311 076 3558	55.113 891 5352	.018 144 2459	94
	95	3.254 827 8938	180.386 231 5063	.005 543 6604	.307 235 9070	55.421 127 4422	.018 043 6604	95
	96	3.295 513 2425	183.641 059 4001	.005 445 4053	.303 442 8711	55.724 570 3133	.017 945 4053	96
	97	3.336 707 1605	186.936 572 6426	.005 349 4080	.299 696 6628	56.024 266 9761	.017 849 4080	97
	98	3.378 415 9975	190.273 279 8007	.005 255 5987	.295 996 7040	56.320 263 6801	.017 755 5987	98
	99	3.420 646 1975	193.651 695 7982	.005 163 9104	.292 342 4237	56.612 606 1038	.017 663 9104	99
	100	3.463 404 2749	197.072 341 9957	.005 074 2788	.288 733 2580	56.901 339 3618	.017 574 2788	100

PERIODS	XIV COMPOUND AMOUNT — AMOUNT OF 1 — How $1 left at compound interest will grow.	XV AMOUNT OF ANNUITY — AMOUNT OF 1 PER PERIOD — How $1 deposited periodically will grow.	XVI SINKING FUND — SINKING FUND — Periodic deposit that will grow to $1 at future date.	XVII PRESENT VALUE — PRESENT WORTH OF 1 — What $1 due in the future is worth today.	XVIII PRESENT VALUE OF ANNUITY — PRESENT WORTH OF 1 PER PERIOD — What $1 payable periodically is worth today.	XIX AMORTIZATION — PARTIAL PAYMENT — Annuity worth $1 today. Periodic payment necessary to pay off a loan of $1.	PERIODS
1	1.015 000 0000	1.000 000 0000	1.000 000 0000	.985 221 6749	.985 221 6749	1.015 000 0000	1
2	1.030 225 0000	2.015 000 0000	.496 277 9156	.970 661 7486	1.955 883 4235	.511 277 9156	2
3	1.045 678 3750	3.045 225 0000	.328 382 9602	.956 316 9937	2.912 200 4173	.343 382 9602	3
4	1.061 363 5506	4.090 903 3750	.244 444 7860	.942 184 2303	3.854 384 6476	.259 444 7860	4
5	1.077 284 0039	5.152 266 9256	.194 089 3231	.928 260 3254	4.782 644 9730	.209 089 3131	5
6	1.093 443 2639	6.229 550 9295	.160 525 2146	.914 542 1925	5.697 187 1655	.175 525 2146	6
7	1.109 844 9129	7.322 994 1935	.136 556 1645	.901 026 7907	6.598 213 9561	.151 556 1645	7
8	1.126 492 5866	8.432 839 1064	.118 584 0246	.887 711 1238	7.485 925 0799	.133 584 0246	8
9	1.143 389 9754	9.559 331 6929	.104 609 8234	.874 592 2102	8.360 517 3201	.119 609 8234	9
10	1.160 540 8250	10.702 721 6683	.093 434 1779	.861 667 2317	9.222 184 5519	.108 434 1779	10
11	1.177 948 9374	11.863 262 4934	.084 293 8442	.848 933 2332	10.071 117 7851	.099 293 8442	11
12	1.195 618 1715	13.041 211 4308	.076 679 9929	.836 387 4219	10.907 505 2070	.091 679 9929	12
13	1.213 552 4440	14.236 829 6022	.070 240 3574	.824 027 0166	11.731 532 2236	.085 240 3574	13
14	1.231 755 7307	15.450 382 0463	.064 723 3186	.811 849 2775	12.543 381 5011	.079 723 3186	14
15	1.250 232 0667	16.682 137 7770	.059 944 3557	.799 851 5049	13.343 233 0060	.074 944 3557	15
16	1.268 985 5477	17.932 369 8436	.055 765 0778	.788 031 0393	14.131 264 0453	.070 765 0778	16
17	1.288 020 3309	19.201 355 3913	.052 079 6569	.776 385 2604	14.907 649 3057	.067 079 6569	17
18	1.307 340 6358	20.489 375 7221	.048 805 7818	.764 911 5866	15.672 560 8924	.063 805 7818	18
19	1.326 950 7454	21.796 716 3580	.045 878 4701	.753 607 4745	16.426 168 3669	.060 878 4701	19
20	1.346 855 0066	23.123 667 1033	.043 245 7359	.742 470 4182	17.168 638 7851	.058 245 7359	20
21	1.367 057 8316	24.470 522 1099	.040 865 4950	.731 497 9490	17.900 136 7341	.055 865 4950	21
22	1.387 563 6991	25.837 579 9415	.038 703 3152	.720 687 6345	18.620 824 3685	.053 703 3152	22
23	1.408 377 1546	27.225 143 6407	.036 730 7520	.710 037 0783	19.330 861 4468	.051 730 7520	23
24	1.429 502 8119	28.633 520 7953	.034 924 1020	.699 543 9195	20.030 405 3663	.049 924 1020	24
25	1.450 945 3541	30.063 023 6072	.033 263 4539	.689 205 8320	20.719 611 1984	.048 263 4539	25
26	1.472 709 5344	31.513 968 9613	.031 731 9599	.679 020 5242	21.398 631 7225	.046 731 9599	26
27	1.494 800 1774	32.986 678 4957	.030 315 2680	.668 985 7381	22.067 617 4606	.045 315 2680	27
28	1.517 222 1801	34.481 478 6732	.029 001 0765	.659 099 2494	22.726 716 7100	.044 001 0765	28
29	1.539 980 5128	35.998 700 8533	.027 778 7802	.649 358 8664	23.376 075 5763	.042 778 7802	29
30	1.563 080 2205	37.538 681 3661	.026 639 1883	.639 762 4299	24.015 838 0062	.041 639 1883	30
31	1.586 526 4238	39.101 761 5865	.025 574 2954	.630 307 8127	24.646 145 8189	.040 574 2954	31
32	1.610 324 3202	40.688 288 0103	.024 577 0970	.620 992 9189	25.267 138 7379	.039 577 0970	32
33	1.634 479 1850	42.298 612 3305	.023 641 4375	.611 815 6837	25.878 954 4216	.038 641 4375	33
34	1.658 996 3727	43.933 091 5155	.022 761 8855	.602 774 0726	26.481 728 4941	.037 761 8855	34
35	1.683 881 3183	45.592 087 8882	.021 933 6303	.593 866 0814	27.075 594 5755	.036 933 6303	35
36	1.709 139 5381	47.275 969 2065	.021 152 3955	.585 089 7353	27.660 684 3109	.036 152 3955	36
37	1.734 776 6312	48.985 108 7446	.020 414 3672	.576 440 0000	28.237 137 3599	.035 414 3673	37
38	1.760 798 2806	50.719 885 3758	.019 716 1329	.567 924 2256	28.805 051 6255	.034 716 1329	38
39	1.787 210 2548	52.480 683 6564	.019 054 6298	.559 531 2568	29.364 582 8822	.034 054 6298	39
40	1.814 018 4087	54.267 893 9113	.018 427 1017	.551 262 3219	29.915 845 2042	.033 427 1017	40
41	1.841 228 6848	56.081 912 3199	.017 831 0610	.543 115 5881	30.458 960 7923	.032 831 0610	41
42	1.868 847 1151	57.923 141 0047	.017 264 2571	.535 089 2494	30.994 050 0417	.032 264 2571	42
43	1.896 879 8218	59.791 988 1198	.016 724 6488	.527 181 5265	31.521 231 5681	.031 724 6488	43
44	1.925 333 0191	61.688 867 9416	.016 210 3801	.519 390 6665	32.040 622 2346	.031 210 3804	44
45	1.954 213 0144	63.614 200 9607	.015 719 7604	.511 714 9423	32.552 337 1770	.030 719 7604	45
46	1.983 526 2096	65.568 413 9751	.015 251 2458	.504 152 6526	33.056 489 8295	.030 251 2458	46
47	2.013 279 1028	67.551 940 1848	.014 803 4238	.496 702 1207	33.553 191 9503	.029 803 4238	47
48	2.043 478 2893	69.565 219 2875	.014 374 9996	.489 361 6953	34.042 553 6456	.029 374 9996	48
49	2.074 130 4637	71.608 697 5768	.013 964 7841	.482 129 7491	34.524 683 3947	.028 964 7841	49
50	2.105 242 4206	73.682 828 0405	.013 571 6832	.475 004 6789	34.999 688 0736	.028 571 6832	50
51	2.136 821 0569	75.788 070 4611	.013 194 6887	.467 984 9053	35.467 672 9789	.028 194 6887	51
52	2.168 873 3728	77.924 891 5180	.012 832 8700	.461 068 8722	35.928 741 8511	.027 832 8700	52
53	2.201 406 4734	80.093 764 8908	.012 485 3664	.454 255 0465	36.382 996 8977	.027 485 3664	53
54	2.234 427 5705	82.295 171 3642	.012 151 3812	.447 541 9178	36.830 538 8154	.027 151 3812	54
55	2.267 943 9840	84.529 598 9346	.011 830 1756	.440 927 9978	37.271 466 8132	.026 830 1756	55
56	2.301 963 1438	86.797 542 9186	.011 521 0635	.434 411 8205	37.705 878 6337	.026 521 0635	56
57	2.336 492 5909	89.099 506 0624	.011 223 4068	.427 991 9414	38.133 870 5751	.026 223 4068	57
58	2.371 539 9798	91.435 998 6534	.010 936 6116	.421 666 9373	38.555 537 5124	.025 936 6116	58
59	2.407 113 0795	93.807 538 6332	.010 660 1241	.415 435 4062	38.970 972 9186	.025 660 1241	59
60	2.443 219 7757	96.214 651 7126	.010 393 4274	.409 295 9667	39.380 268 8853	.025 393 4274	60
61	2.479 868 0723	98.657 871 4883	.010 136 0387	.403 247 2579	39.783 516 1432	.025 136 0387	61
62	2.517 066 0934	101.137 739 5607	.009 887 5059	.397 287 9388	40.180 804 0820	.024 887 5059	62
63	2.554 822 0848	103.654 805 6541	.009 647 4061	.391 416 6884	40.572 220 7704	.024 647 4061	63
64	2.593 144 4161	106.209 627 7389	.009 415 3423	.385 632 2054	40.957 852 9758	.024 415 3423	64
65	2.632 041 5823	108.802 772 1550	.009 190 9423	.379 933 2073	41.337 786 1830	.024 190 9423	65
66	2.671 522 2061	111.434 813 7373	.008 973 8563	.374 318 4308	41.712 104 6138	.023 973 8563	66
67	2.711 595 0392	114.106 335 9434	.008 763 7552	.368 786 6313	42.080 891 2451	.023 763 7552	67
68	2.752 268 9647	116.817 930 9825	.008 560 3297	.363 336 5826	42.444 227 8277	.023 560 3297	68
69	2.793 552 9992	119.570 199 9472	.008 363 2878	.357 967 0764	42.802 194 9042	.023 363 2878	69
70	2.835 456 2942	122.363 752 9464	.008 172 3548	.352 676 9226	43.154 871 8268	.023 172 3548	70
71	2.877 988 1386	125.199 209 2406	.007 987 2709	.347 464 9484	43.502 336 7751	.022 987 2709	71
72	2.921 157 9607	128.077 197 3793	.007 807 7911	.342 329 9984	43.844 666 7735	.022 807 7911	72
73	2.964 975 3301	130.998 355 3399	.007 633 6836	.337 270 9344	44.181 937 7079	.022 633 6836	73
74	3.009 449 9601	133.963 330 6700	.007 464 7293	.332 286 6349	44.514 224 3428	.022 464 7293	74
75	3.054 591 7095	136.972 780 6301	.007 300 7206	.327 375 9949	44.841 600 3377	.022 300 7206	75
76	3.100 419 5851	140.027 372 3395	.007 141 4609	.322 537 9260	45.164 138 2638	.022 141 4609	76
77	3.146 916 7439	143.127 782 9246	.006 986 7637	.317 771 3557	45.481 909 6195	.021 986 7637	77
78	3.194 120 4950	146.274 699 6685	.006 836 4523	.313 075 2273	45.794 984 8468	.021 836 4523	78
79	3.242 032 3025	149.468 820 1635	.006 690 3586	.308 448 4998	46.103 433 3466	.021 690 3586	79
80	3.290 662 7870	152.710 852 4660	.006 548 3231	.303 890 1476	46.407 323 4941	.021 548 3231	80
81	3.340 022 7288	156.001 515 2530	.006 410 1941	.299 399 1602	46.706 722 6543	.021 410 1941	81
82	3.390 123 0697	159.341 537 9818	.006 275 8275	.294 974 5421	47.001 697 1964	.021 275 8275	82
83	3.440 974 9158	162.731 661 0515	.006 145 0857	.290 615 3124	47.292 312 5088	.021 145 0857	83
84	3.492 589 5395	166.172 635 9673	.006 017 8380	.286 320 5048	47.578 633 0136	.021 017 8380	84
85	3.544 978 3826	169.665 225 5068	.005 893 9597	.282 089 1673	47.860 722 1808	.020 893 9597	85
86	3.598 153 0583	173.210 203 8894	.005 773 3319	.277 920 3619	48.138 642 5427	.020 773 3319	86
87	3.652 125 3542	176.808 356 9477	.005 655 8413	.273 813 1644	48.412 455 7071	.020 655 8413	87
88	3.706 907 2345	180.460 482 3019	.005 541 3795	.269 766 6644	48.682 222 3715	.020 541 3794	88
89	3.762 510 8430	184.167 389 5365	.005 429 8429	.265 779 9650	48.948 002 3365	.020 429 8429	89
90	3.818 948 5057	187.929 900 3795	.005 321 1330	.261 852 1822	49.209 854 5187	.020 321 1330	90
91	3.876 232 7333	191.748 848 8852	.005 215 1552	.257 982 4455	49.467 836 9642	.020 215 1552	91
92	3.934 376 2243	195.625 081 6185	.005 111 8190	.254 169 8971	49.722 006 8613	.020 111 8190	92
93	3.993 391 8676	199.559 457 8428	.005 011 0379	.250 413 6917	49.972 420 5530	.020 011 0379	93
94	4.053 292 7457	203.552 849 7104	.004 912 7291	.246 712 9968	50.219 133 5498	.019 912 7291	94
95	4.114 092 1368	207.606 142 4561	.004 816 8132	.243 066 9919	50.462 200 5416	.019 816 8132	95
96	4.175 803 5189	211.720 234 5929	.004 723 2141	.239 474 8688	50.701 675 4105	.019 723 2142	96
97	4.238 440 5717	215.896 038 1118	.004 631 8500	.235 935 8314	50.937 611 2419	.019 631 8590	97
98	4.302 017 1803	220.134 478 6835	.004 542 6778	.232 449 0949	51.170 060 3368	.019 542 6778	98
99	4.366 547 4380	224.436 495 8637	.004 455 6033	.229 013 8866	51.399 074 2235	.019 455 6033	99
100	4.432 045 6495	228.803 043 3017	.004 370 5712	.225 629 4450	51.624 703 6684	.019 370 5712	100

	PERIODS	XIV COMPOUND AMOUNT — AMOUNT OF 1 — How $1 left at compound interest will grow.	XV AMOUNT OF ANNUITY — AMOUNT OF 1 PER PERIOD — How $1 deposited periodically will grow.	XVI SINKING FUND — SINKING FUND — Periodic deposit that will grow to $1 at future date.	XVII PRESENT VALUE — PRESENT WORTH OF 1 — What $1 due in the future is worth today.	XVIII PRESENT VALUE OF ANNUITY — PRESENT WORTH OF 1 PER PERIOD — What $1 payable periodically is worth today.	XIX AMORTIZATION — PARTIAL PAYMENT — Annuity worth $1 today. Periodic payment necessary to pay off a loan of $1.	PERIODS
	1	1.017 500 0000	1.000 000 0000	1.000 000 0000	.982 800 9828	.982 800 9828	1.017 500 0000	1
	2	1.035 306 2500	2.017 500 0000	.495 662 9492	.965 897 7718	1.948 698 7546	.513 162 9492	2
	3	1.053 424 1094	3.052 806 2500	.327 567 4635	.949 285 2794	2.897 984 0340	.345 067 4635	3
	4	1.071 859 0313	4.106 230 3594	.243 532 3673	.932 958 5056	3.830 942 5396	.261 032 3673	4
	5	1.090 616 5643	5.178 089 3907	.193 121 4246	.916 912 5362	4.747 855 0757	.210 621 4246	5
	6	1.109 702 3542	6.268 705 9550	.159 522 5565	.901 142 5417	5.648 997 6174	.177 022 5565	6
	7	1.129 122 1454	7.378 408 3092	.135 530 5857	.885 643 7756	6.534 641 3930	.153 030 5857	7
	8	1.148 881 7830	8.507 530 4546	.117 542 9233	.870 411 5731	7.405 052 9661	.135 042 9233	8
	9	1.168 987 2142	9.656 412 2376	.103 558 1306	.855 441 3495	8.260 494 3156	.121 058 1306	9
	10	1.189 444 4904	10.825 399 4517	.092 375 3442	.840 728 5990	9.101 222 9146	.109 875 3442	10
	11	1.210 259 7690	12.014 843 9421	.083 230 3778	.826 268 8934	9.927 491 8080	.100 730 3778	11
	12	1.231 439 3149	13.225 103 7111	.075 613 7738	.812 057 8805	10.739 549 6884	.095 113 7738	12
	13	1.252 989 5030	14.456 543 0261	.069 172 8305	.798 091 2830	11.537 640 9714	.086 672 8305	13
	14	1.274 916 8193	15.709 532 5290	.063 655 6179	.784 364 8973	12.322 005 8687	.081 155 6179	14
	15	1.297 227 8636	16.984 449 3483	.058 877 3872	.770 874 5919	13.092 880 4607	.076 377 3872	15
	16	1.319 929 3512	18.281 677 2119	.054 699 5764	.757 616 3066	13.850 496 7672	.072 199 5764	16
	17	1.343 028 1149	19.601 606 5631	.051 016 2265	.744 586 0507	14.595 082 8179	.068 516 2265	17
	18	1.366 531 1069	20.944 634 6779	.047 744 9244	.731 779 9024	15.326 862 7203	.065 244 9244	18
	19	1.390 445 4012	22.311 165 7848	.044 820 6073	.719 194 0073	16.046 056 7276	.062 320 6073	19
	20	1.414 778 1958	23.701 611 1860	.042 191 2246	.706 824 5772	16.752 881 3048	.059 691 2246	20
	21	1.439 536 8142	25.116 389 3818	.039 814 6399	.694 667 8891	17.447 549 1939	.057 314 6399	21
	22	1.464 728 7084	26.555 926 1960	.037 656 3782	.682 720 2841	18.130 269 4780	.055 156 3782	22
	23	1.490 361 4608	28.020 654 9044	.035 687 9596	.670 978 1662	18.801 247 6442	.053 187 9596	23
	24	1.516 442 7864	29.511 016 3652	.033 885 6510	.659 438 0012	19.460 685 6454	.051 385 6510	24
	25	1.542 980 5352	31.027 459 1516	.032 229 5163	.648 096 3157	20.108 781 9611	.049 729 5163	25
	26	1.569 982 6945	32.570 439 6868	.030 702 6865	.636 949 6960	20.745 731 6571	.048 202 6865	26
	27	1.597 457 3917	34.140 422 3813	.029 290 7917	.625 994 7872	21.371 726 4443	.046 790 7917	27
	28	1.625 412 8960	35.737 879 7730	.027 981 5145	.615 228 2921	21.986 954 7364	.045 481 5145	28
	29	1.653 857 6217	37.363 292 6690	.026 764 2365	.604 646 9701	22.591 601 7066	.044 264 2365	29
	30	1.682 800 1301	39.017 150 2907	.025 629 7549	.594 247 6365	23.185 849 3431	.043 129 7549	30
	31	1.712 249 1324	40.699 950 4208	.024 570 0545	.584 027 1612	23.769 876 5042	.042 070 0545	31
	32	1.742 213 4922	42.412 199 5532	.023 578 1216	.573 982 4680	24.343 858 9722	.041 078 1216	32
	33	1.772 702 2283	44.154 413 0453	.022 647 7928	.564 110 5336	24.907 969 5059	.040 147 7928	33
	34	1.803 724 5173	45.927 115 2736	.021 773 6297	.554 408 3869	25.462 377 8928	.039 273 6297	34
	35	1.835 289 6963	47.730 839 7909	.020 950 8151	.544 873 1075	26.007 251 0003	.038 450 8151	35
	36	1.867 407 2660	49.566 129 4873	.020 175 0673	.535 501 8255	26.542 752 8258	.037 675 0673	36
	37	1.900 086 8932	51.433 536 7533	.019 442 5673	.526 291 7204	27.069 044 5462	.036 942 5673	37
	38	1.933 338 4138	53.333 623 6465	.018 749 8979	.517 240 0201	27.586 284 5663	.036 249 8979	38
	39	1.967 171 8361	55.266 962 0603	.018 093 9926	.508 344 0001	28.094 628 5664	.035 593 9926	39
	40	2.001 597 3432	57.234 133 8963	.017 472 0911	.499 600 9829	28.594 229 5493	.034 972 0911	40
	41	2.036 625 2967	59.235 731 2395	.016 881 7026	.491 008 3370	29.085 237 8863	.034 381 7026	41
	42	2.072 266 2394	61.272 356 5362	.016 320 5735	.482 563 4762	29.567 801 3625	.033 820 5735	42
	43	2.108 530 8986	63.344 622 7756	.015 786 6596	.474 263 8586	30.042 065 2211	.033 286 6596	43
	44	2.145 430 1893	65.453 153 6742	.015 278 1026	.466 106 9864	30.508 172 2075	.032 778 1026	44
	45	2.182 975 2176	67.598 583 8635	.014 793 2093	.458 090 4043	30.966 262 6117	.032 293 2093	45
	46	2.221 177 2839	69.781 559 0811	.014 330 4336	.450 211 6996	31.416 474 3113	.031 830 4336	46
	47	2.260 047 8864	72.002 736 3650	.013 888 3611	.442 468 5008	31.858 942 8121	.031 388 3611	47
	48	2.299 598 7244	74.262 784 2514	.013 465 6950	.434 858 4774	32.293 801 2895	.030 965 6950	48
	49	2.339 841 7021	76.562 382 9758	.013 061 2445	.427 379 3390	32.721 180 6285	.030 561 2445	49
	50	2.380 788 9319	78.902 224 6779	.012 673 9139	.420 028 8344	33.141 209 4629	.030 173 9139	50
	51	2.422 452 7382	81.283 013 6097	.012 302 6935	.412 804 7513	33.554 014 2142	.029 802 6935	51
	52	2.464 845 6611	83.705 466 3479	.011 946 6511	.405 704 9152	33.959 719 1294	.029 446 6511	52
	53	2.507 980 4602	86.170 312 0090	.011 604 9249	.398 727 1894	34.358 446 3188	.029 104 9249	53
	54	2.551 870 1182	88.678 292 4691	.011 276 7169	.391 869 4736	34.750 315 7925	.028 776 7169	54
	55	2.596 527 8453	91.230 162 5874	.010 961 2871	.385 129 7038	35.135 445 4963	.028 461 2871	55
	56	2.641 967 0826	93.826 690 4326	.010 657 9481	.378 505 8514	35.513 951 3477	.028 157 9481	56
	57	2.688 201 5065	96.468 657 5152	.010 366 0611	.371 995 9228	35.885 947 2705	.027 866 0611	57
	58	2.735 245 0329	99.156 859 0217	.010 085 0310	.365 597 9585	36.251 545 2290	.027 585 0310	58
	59	2.783 111 8210	101.892 104 0546	.009 814 3032	.359 310 0329	36.610 855 2619	.027 314 3032	59
	60	2.831 816 2778	104.675 215 8756	.009 553 3598	.353 130 2535	36.963 985 5154	.027 053 3598	60
	61	2.881 373 0627	107.507 032 1534	.009 301 7171	.347 056 7602	37.311 042 2755	.026 801 7171	61
	62	2.931 797 0913	110.388 405 2161	.009 058 9224	.341 087 7250	37.652 130 0005	.026 558 9224	62
	63	2.983 103 5404	113.320 202 3073	.008 824 5518	.335 221 3513	37.987 351 3519	.026 324 5518	63
	64	3.035 307 8523	116.303 305 8477	.008 598 2079	.329 455 8736	38.316 807 2072	.026 098 2079	64
	65	3.088 425 7398	119.338 613 7001	.008 379 5175	.323 789 5563	38.640 596 7817	.025 879 5175	65
	66	3.142 473 1902	122.427 039 4398	.008 168 1302	.318 220 6942	38.958 817 4759	.025 668 1302	66
	67	3.197 466 4710	125.569 512 6300	.007 963 7165	.312 747 6110	39.271 565 0869	.025 463 7165	67
	68	3.253 422 1343	128.766 979 1010	.007 765 9661	.307 368 6594	39.578 933 7463	.025 265 9661	68
	69	3.310 357 0216	132.020 401 2353	.007 574 5869	.302 082 2206	39.881 015 9669	.025 074 5869	69
	70	3.368 288 2695	135.330 758 2569	.007 389 3032	.296 886 7033	40.177 902 6702	.024 889 3032	70
	71	3.427 233 3142	138.699 046 5264	.007 209 8549	.291 780 5438	40.469 683 2139	.024 709 8549	71
	72	3.487 209 8972	142.126 279 8406	.007 035 9964	.286 762 2052	40.756 445 4191	.024 535 9964	72
	73	3.548 236 0704	145.613 489 7378	.006 867 4956	.281 830 1771	41.038 275 5962	.024 367 4956	73
	74	3.610 330 2016	149.161 725 8083	.006 704 1327	.276 982 9750	41.315 258 5712	.024 204 1327	74
	75	3.673 510 9802	152.772 056 0099	.006 545 6997	.272 219 1401	41.587 477 7112	.024 045 6997	75
	76	3.737 797 4223	156.445 566 9901	.006 391 9996	.267 537 2384	41.855 014 9496	.023 891 9996	76
	77	3.803 208 8772	160.183 364 4124	.006 242 8455	.262 935 8608	42.117 950 8104	.023 742 8455	77
	78	3.869 765 0326	163.986 573 2896	.006 098 0602	.258 413 6224	42.376 364 4329	.023 598 0602	78
	79	3.937 485 9206	167.856 338 3222	.005 957 4754	.253 969 1621	42.630 333 5949	.023 457 4754	79
	80	4.006 391 9242	171.793 824 2428	.005 820 9310	.249 601 1421	42.879 934 7370	.023 320 9310	80
	81	4.076 503 7829	175.800 216 1671	.005 688 2751	.245 308 2478	43.125 242 9848	.023 188 2751	81
	82	4.147 842 5991	179.876 719 9500	.005 559 3631	.241 089 1870	43.366 332 1718	.023 059 3631	82
	83	4.220 429 8446	184.024 562 5491	.005 434 0572	.236 942 6899	43.603 274 8617	.022 934 0572	83
	84	4.294 287 3669	188.244 992 3937	.005 312 2263	.232 867 5085	43.836 142 3702	.022 812 2263	84
	85	4.369 437 3958	192.539 279 7606	.005 193 7454	.228 862 4162	44.065 004 7865	.022 693 7454	85
	86	4.445 902 5502	196.908 717 1564	.005 078 4953	.224 926 2076	44.289 930 9941	.022 578 4953	86
	87	4.523 705 8449	201.354 619 7067	.004 966 3623	.221 057 6979	44.510 988 6920	.022 466 3623	87
	88	4.602 870 6972	205.878 325 5515	.004 857 2379	.217 255 7227	44.728 244 4147	.022 357 2379	88
	89	4.683 420 9344	210.481 196 2487	.004 751 0182	.213 519 1378	44.941 763 5525	.022 251 0182	89
	90	4.765 380 8007	215.164 617 1830	.004 647 6043	.209 846 8185	45.151 610 3711	.022 147 6043	90
	91	4.848 774 9647	219.929 997 9837	.004 546 9013	.206 237 6595	45.357 848 0305	.022 046 9013	91
	92	4.933 628 5266	224.778 772 9485	.004 448 8187	.202 690 5744	45.560 538 6049	.021 948 8187	92
	93	5.019 967 0258	229.712 401 4751	.004 353 2695	.199 204 4957	45.759 743 1007	.021 853 2695	93
	94	5.107 816 4488	234.732 368 5009	.004 260 1709	.195 778 3742	45.955 521 4749	.021 760 1709	94
	95	5.197 203 2366	239.840 184 9496	.004 169 4431	.192 411 1786	46.147 932 6534	.021 669 4431	95
	96	5.288 154 2933	245.037 388 1863	.004 081 0099	.189 101 8954	46.337 034 5488	.021 581 0099	96
	97	5.380 696 9934	250.325 542 4795	.003 994 7981	.185 849 5286	46.522 884 0775	.021 494 7981	97
	98	5.474 859 1908	255.706 239 4729	.003 910 7376	.182 653 0994	46.705 537 1769	.021 410 7376	98
	99	5.570 669 2266	261.181 098 6637	.003 828 7610	.179 511 6456	46.885 048 8225	.021 328 7610	99
	100	5.668 155 9381	266.751 767 8903	.003 748 8036	.176 424 2217	47.061 473 0442	.021 248 8036	100

	XIV COMPOUND AMOUNT	XV AMOUNT OF ANNUITY	XVI SINKING FUND	XVII PRESENT VALUE	XVIII PRESENT VALUE OF ANNUITY	XIX AMORTIZATION	
RATE 2% PERIODS	AMOUNT OF 1 — How $1 left at compound interest will grow	AMOUNT OF 1 PER PERIOD — How $1 deposited periodically will grow.	SINKING FUND — Periodic deposit that will grow to $1 at future date.	PRESENT WORTH OF 1 — What $1 due in the future is worth today.	PRESENT WORTH OF 1 PER PERIOD — What $1 payable periodically is worth today.	PARTIAL PAYMENT — Annuity worth $1 today Periodic payment necessary to pay off a loan of $1	PERIODS
1	1.020 000 0000	1.000 000 0000	1.000 000 0000	.980 392 1569	.980 392 1569	1.020 000 0000	1
2	1.040 400 0000	2.020 000 0000	.495 049 5050	.961 168 7812	1.941 560 9381	.515 049 5050	2
3	1.061 208 0000	3.060 400 0000	.326 754 6726	.942 322 3345	2.883 883 2726	.346 754 6726	3
4	1.082 432 1600	4.121 608 0000	.242 623 7527	.923 845 4260	3.807 728 6987	.262 623 7527	4
5	1.104 080 8032	5.204 040 1600	.192 158 3941	.905 730 8098	4.713 459 5085	.212 158 3941	5
6	1.126 162 4193	6.308 120 9632	.158 525 8123	.887 971 3822	5.601 430 8907	.178 525 8123	6
7	1.148 685 6676	7.434 283 3825	.134 511 9561	.870 560 1786	6.471 991 0693	.154 511 9561	7
8	1.171 659 3810	8.582 969 0501	.116 509 7991	.853 490 3712	7.325 481 4405	.136 509 7991	8
9	1.195 092 5686	9.754 628 4311	.102 515 4374	.836 755 2659	8.162 236 7064	.122 515 4374	9
10	1.218 994 4200	10.949 720 9997	.091 326 5279	.820 348 2999	8.982 585 0062	.111 326 5279	10
11	1.243 374 3084	12.168 715 4197	.082 177 9428	.804 263 0391	9.786 848 0453	.102 177 9428	11
12	1.268 241 7946	13.412 089 7281	.074 559 5966	.788 493 1756	10.575 341 2209	.094 559 5966	12
13	1.293 606 6305	14.680 331 5227	.068 118 3527	.773 032 5251	11.348 373 7460	.088 118 3527	13
15	1.319 478 7631	15.973 938 1531	.062 601 9702	.757 875 0246	12.106 248 7706	.082 601 9702	14
15	1.345 868 3383	17.293 416 9162	.057 825 4723	.743 014 7300	12.849 263 5006	.077 825 4723	15
16	1.372 785 7051	18.639 285 2545	.053 650 1259	.728 445 8137	13.577 709 3143	.073 650 1259	16
17	1.400 241 4192	20.012 070 9596	.049 969 8408	.714 162 5625	14.291 871 8768	.069 969 8408	17
18	1.428 246 2476	21.412 312 3788	.046 702 1022	.700 159 3750	14.992 031 2517	.066 702 1022	18
19	1.456 811 1725	22.840 558 6264	.043 781 7663	.686 430 7598	15.678 462 0115	.063 781 7663	19
20	1.485 947 3960	24.297 369 7989	.041 156 7181	.672 971 3331	16.351 433 3446	.061 156 7181	20
21	1.515 666 3439	25.783 317 1949	.038 784 7689	.659 775 8168	17.011 209 1614	.058 784 7689	21
22	1.545 979 6708	27.298 983 5388	.036 631 4005	.646 839 0361	17.658 048 1974	.056 631 4005	22
23	1.576 899 2642	28.844 963 2096	.034 668 0976	.634 155 9177	18.292 204 1151	.054 668 0976	23
24	1.608 437 2495	30.421 862 4738	.032 871 0973	.621 721 4879	18.913 925 6031	.052 871 0973	24
25	1.640 605 9945	32.030 299 7232	.031 220 4384	.609 530 8705	19.523 456 4736	.051 220 4384	25
26	1.673 418 1144	33.670 905 7177	.029 699 2308	.597 579 2848	20.121 035 7584	.049 699 2308	26
27	1.706 886 4766	35.344 323 8321	.028 293 0862	.585 862 0440	20.706 897 8024	.048 293 0862	27
28	1.741 024 2062	37.051 210 3087	.026 989 6716	.574 374 5529	21.281 272 3553	.046 989 6716	28
29	1.775 844 6903	38.792 234 5149	.025 778 3552	.563 112 3068	21.844 384 6620	.045 778 3552	29
30	1.811 361 5841	40.568 079 2052	.024 649 9223	.552 070 8890	22.396 455 5510	.044 649 9223	30
31	1.847 588 8158	42.379 440 7893	.023 596 3472	.541 245 9696	22.937 701 5206	.043 596 3472	31
32	1.884 540 5921	44.227 029 6051	.022 610 6073	.530 633 3035	23.468 334 8241	.042 610 6073	32
33	1.922 231 4039	46.111 570 1972	.021 686 5311	.520 228 7289	23.988 563 5530	.041 686 5311	33
34	1.960 676 0320	48.033 801 6011	.020 818 6728	.510 028 1656	24.498 591 7187	.040 818 6728	34
35	1.999 889 5527	49.994 477 6331	.020 002 2092	.500 027 6134	24.998 619 3320	.040 002 2092	35
36	2.039 887 3437	51.994 367 1858	.019 232 8526	.490 223 1504	25.488 842 4824	.039 232 8526	36
37	2.080 685 0906	54.034 254 5295	.018 506 7789	.480 610 9317	25.969 453 4141	.038 506 7789	37
38	2.122 298 7924	56.114 939 6201	.017 820 6662	.471 107 1000	26.440 560 6021	.037 820 6662	38
39	2.164 744 7682	58.237 238 4125	.017 171 1439	.461 948 2235	26.902 588 8256	.037 171 1439	39
40	2.208 039 6636	60.401 983 1807	.016 555 7478	.452 890 4152	27.355 479 2407	.036 555 7478	40
41	2.252 200 4569	62.610 022 8444	.015 971 8836	.444 010 2110	27.799 489 4517	.035 971 8836	41
42	2.297 244 4660	64.862 223 3012	.015 417 2945	.435 304 1284	28.234 793 5801	.035 417 2945	42
43	2.343 189 3553	67.159 467 7673	.014 889 9334	.426 768 7533	28.661 562 3334	.034 889 9334	43
44	2.390 053 1425	69.502 657 1226	.014 387 9391	.418 400 7386	29.079 963 0720	.034 387 9391	44
45	2.437 854 2053	71.892 710 2651	.013 909 6161	.410 196 8025	29.490 159 8745	.033 909 6161	45
46	2.486 611 2894	74.330 564 4704	.013 453 4159	.402 153 7280	29.892 313 6025	.033 453 4159	46
47	2.536 343 5152	76.817 175 7598	.013 017 9220	.394 268 3607	30.286 581 9632	.033 017 9220	47
48	2.587 070 3855	79.353 519 2750	.012 601 8355	.386 537 6086	30.673 119 5718	.032 601 8355	48
49	2.638 811 7932	81.940 589 6605	.012 203 9639	.378 958 4398	31.052 078 0115	.032 203 9639	49
50	2.691 588 0291	84.579 401 4537	.011 823 2097	.371 527 8821	31.423 605 8937	.031 823 2097	50
51	2.745 419 7897	87.270 989 4828	.011 458 5615	.364 243 0217	31.787 848 9153	.031 458 5615	51
52	2.800 328 1854	90.016 409 2724	.011 109 0856	.357 101 0017	32.144 949 9170	.031 109 0856	52
53	2.856 334 7492	92.816 737 4579	.010 773 9189	.350 099 0212	32.495 048 9382	.030 773 9189	53
54	2.913 461 4441	95.673 072 2070	.010 452 2618	.343 234 3345	32.838 283 2728	.030 452 2618	54
55	2.971 730 6730	98.586 533 6512	.010 143 3732	.336 504 2496	33.174 787 5223	.030 143 3732	55
56	3.031 165 2865	101.558 264 3242	.009 846 5645	.329 906 1270	33.504 693 6494	.029 846 5645	56
57	3.091 788 5922	104.589 429 6107	.009 561 1957	.323 437 3794	33.828 131 0288	.029 561 1957	57
58	3.153 624 3641	107.681 218 2029	.009 286 6706	.317 095 4700	34.145 226 4988	.029 286 6706	58
59	3.216 696 8513	110.834 842 5669	.009 022 4335	.310 877 9118	34.456 104 4106	.029 022 4335	59
60	3.281 030 7884	114.051 539 4183	.008 767 9658	.304 782 2665	34.760 886 6770	.028 767 9658	60
61	3.346 651 4041	117.332 570 2066	.008 522 7827	.298 806 1436	35.059 692 8206	.028 522 7827	61
62	3.413 584 4322	120.679 221 6108	.008 286 4306	.292 947 1996	35.352 640 0202	.028 286 4306	62
63	3.481 856 1209	124.092 806 0430	.008 058 4849	.287 203 1389	35.639 843 1571	.028 058 4849	63
64	3.551 493 2433	127.574 662 1638	.007 838 5471	.281 571 7028	35.921 414 8599	.027 838 5471	64
65	3.622 523 1081	131.126 155 4071	.007 626 2436	.276 050 6890	36.197 465 5489	.027 626 2436	65
66	3.694 973 5703	134.748 678 5153	.007 421 2231	.270 637 9304	36.468 103 4793	.027 421 2231	66
67	3.768 873 0417	138.443 652 0856	.007 223 1553	.265 331 3043	36.733 434 7837	.027 223 1553	67
68	3.844 250 5025	142.212 525 1273	.007 031 7294	.260 128 7297	36.993 563 5134	.027 031 7294	68
69	3.921 135 5126	146.056 775 6298	.006 846 6526	.255 028 1664	37.248 591 6798	.026 846 6526	69
70	3.999 558 2228	149.977 911 1424	.006 667 6485	.250 027 6141	37.498 619 2939	.026 667 6485	70
71	4.079 549 3873	153.977 469 3652	.006 494 4567	.245 125 1119	37.743 744 4058	.026 494 4567	71
72	4.161 140 3751	158.057 018 7526	.006 326 8307	.240 318 7371	37.984 063 1429	.026 326 8307	72
73	4.244 363 1826	162.218 159 1276	.006 164 5380	.235 606 6050	38.219 669 7480	.026 164 5380	73
74	4.329 250 4462	166.462 522 3102	.006 007 3582	.230 986 8677	38.450 656 6157	.026 007 3582	74
75	4.415 835 4551	170.791 772 7564	.005 855 0830	.226 457 7134	38.677 114 3291	.025 855 0830	75
76	4.504 152 1642	175.207 608 2115	.005 707 5147	.222 017 3661	38.899 131 6952	.025 707 5147	76
77	4.594 235 2075	179.711 760 3757	.005 564 4661	.217 664 0844	39.116 795 7796	.025 564 4661	77
78	4.686 119 9117	184.305 995 5833	.005 425 7595	.213 396 1612	39.330 191 9408	.025 425 7595	78
79	4.779 842 3099	188.992 115 4949	.005 291 2260	.209 211 9227	39.539 403 8635	.025 291 2260	79
80	4.875 439 1561	193.771 957 8048	.005 160 7055	.205 109 7282	39.744 513 5917	.025 160 7055	80
81	4.972 947 9392	198.647 396 9609	.005 034 0453	.201 087 9688	39.945 601 5605	.025 034 0453	81
82	5.072 406 8980	203.620 344 9001	.004 911 1006	.197 145 0674	40.142 746 6279	.024 911 1006	82
83	5.173 855 0360	208.692 751 7981	.004 791 7333	.193 279 4779	40.336 026 1058	.024 791 7333	83
84	5.277 332 1367	213.866 606 8341	.004 675 8118	.189 489 6842	40.525 515 7900	.024 675 8118	84
85	5.382 878 7794	219.143 938 9708	.004 563 2108	.185 774 2002	40.711 289 9902	.024 563 2108	85
86	5.490 536 3550	224.526 817 7502	.004 453 8110	.182 131 5688	40.893 421 5590	.024 453 8110	86
87	5.600 347 0821	230.017 354 1052	.004 347 4981	.178 560 3616	41.071 981 9206	.024 347 4981	87
88	5.712 354 0237	235.617 701 1873	.004 244 1633	.175 059 1780	41.247 041 0986	.024 244 1633	88
89	5.826 601 1042	241.330 055 2111	.004 143 7027	.171 626 6451	41.418 667 7437	.024 143 7027	89
90	5.943 133 1263	247.156 656 3153	.004 046 0169	.168 261 4168	41.586 929 1605	.024 046 0169	90
91	6.061 995 7888	253.099 789 4416	.003 951 0108	.164 962 1733	41.751 891 3339	.023 951 0108	91
92	6.183 235 7046	259.161 785 2304	.003 858 5936	.161 727 6209	41.913 618 9548	.023 858 5936	92
93	6.306 900 4187	265.345 020 9350	.003 768 6782	.158 556 4911	42.072 175 4458	.023 768 6782	93
94	6.433 038 4271	271.651 921 3537	.003 681 1814	.155 447 5403	42.227 622 9862	.023 681 1814	94
95	6.561 699 1956	278.084 959 7808	.003 596 0233	.152 399 5493	42.380 022 5354	.023 596 0233	95
96	6.692 933 1795	284.646 658 9764	.003 513 1275	.149 411 3228	42.529 433 8582	.023 513 1275	96
97	6.826 791 8431	291.339 592 1559	.003 432 4205	.146 481 6891	42.675 915 5473	.023 432 4205	97
98	6.963 327 6800	298.166 383 9991	.003 353 8321	.143 609 4991	42.819 525 0464	.023 353 8321	98
99	7.102 594 2336	305.129 711 6790	.003 277 2947	.140 793 6265	42.960 318 6729	.023 277 2947	99
100	7.244 646 1183	312.232 305 9126	.003 202 7435	.138 032 9672	43.098 351 6401	.023 202 7435	100

		XIV COMPOUND AMOUNT	XV AMOUNT OF ANNUITY	XVI SINKING FUND	XVII PRESENT VALUE	XVIII PRESENT VALUE OF ANNUITY	XIX AMORTIZATION	
RATE 2 1/4%	PERIODS	AMOUNT OF 1 How $1 left at compound interest will grow.	AMOUNT OF 1 PER PERIOD How $1 deposited periodically will grow.	SINKING FUND Periodic deposit that will grow to $1 at future date.	PRESENT WORTH OF 1 What $1 due in the future is worth today.	PRESENT WORTH OF 1 PER PERIOD What $1 payable periodically is worth today.	PARTIAL PAYMENT Annuity worth $1 today. Periodic payment necessary to pay off a loan of $1.	PERIODS
	1	1.022 500 0000	1.000 000 0000	1.000 000 0000	.977 995 1100	.977 995 1100	1.022 500 0000	1
	2	1.045 506 2500	2.022 500 0000	.494 437 5773	.956 474 4352	1.934 469 5453	.516 937 5773	2
	3	1.069 030 1406	3.068 006 2500	.325 944 5772	.935 427 3205	2.869 896 8658	.348 444 5772	3
	4	1.093 083 3188	4.137 036 3906	.241 718 9277	.914 843 3453	3.784 740 2110	.264 218 9277	4
	5	1.117 677 6935	5.230 119 7094	.191 200 2125	.894 712 3181	4.679 452 5291	.213 700 2125	5
	6	1.142 825 4416	6.347 797 4029	.157 534 9584	.875 024 2720	5.554 476 8011	.180 034 9584	6
	7	1.168 030 0140	7.490 622 8444	.133 500 2470	.855 769 4591	6.410 246 2602	.156 000 2470	7
	8	1.194 831 1418	8.659 161 8584	.115 484 6181	.836 938 3464	7.247 184 6066	.137 984 6181	8
	9	1.221 714 8425	9.853 993 0003	.101 481 7039	.818 521 6101	8.065 706 2167	.123 981 7039	9
	10	1.249 203 4265	11.075 707 8428	.090 287 6831	.800 510 1322	8.866 216 3489	.112 787 6831	10
	11	1.277 310 5036	12.324 911 2692	.081 136 4868	.782 894 9948	9.649 111 3436	.103 636 4868	11
	12	1.306 049 9899	13.602 221 7728	.073 517 4015	.765 667 4765	10.414 778 8202	.096 017 4015	12
	13	1.335 436 1147	14.908 271 7627	.067 076 8561	.748 819 0480	11.163 597 8681	.089 576 8561	13
	14	1.365 483 4272	16.243 707 8773	.061 562 2989	.732 341 3672	11.895 939 2354	.084 062 2989	14
	15	1.396 206 8044	17.609 191 3046	.056 788 5250	.716 226 2760	12.612 165 5113	.079 288 5250	15
	16	1.427 621 4575	19.005 398 1089	.052 616 6300	.700 465 7956	13.312 631 3069	.075 116 6300	16
	17	1.459 742 9402	20.433 019 5664	.048 940 3926	.685 052 1228	13.997 683 4298	.071 440 3926	17
	18	1.492 587 1564	21.892 762 5066	.045 677 1958	.669 977 6262	14.667 661 0560	.068 177 1958	18
	19	1.526 170 3674	23.385 349 6630	.042 761 8152	.665 234 8423	15.322 895 8983	.065 261 8152	19
	20	1.560 509 2007	24.911 520 0304	.040 142 0708	.640 816 4717	15.963 712 3700	.062 642 0708	20
	21	1.595 620 6577	26.472 029 2311	.037 775 7214	.626 715 3757	16.590 427 7457	.060 275 7214	21
	22	1.631 522 1225	28.067 649 8888	.035 628 2056	.612 924 5728	17.203 352 3185	.058 128 2056	22
	23	1.668 231 3703	29.699 172 0113	.033 670 9724	.599 437 2350	17.802 789 5536	.056 170 9724	23
	24	1.705 766 5761	31.367 403 3816	.031 880 2289	.586 246 6846	18.389 036 2382	.054 380 2289	24
	25	1.744 146 3240	33.073 169 9577	.030 235 9889	.573 346 3908	18.962 382 6291	.052 735 9889	25
	26	1.783 389 6163	34.817 316 2817	.028 721 3406	.560 729 9666	19.523 112 5957	.051 221 3406	26
	27	1.823 515 8827	36.600 705 8980	.027 321 8774	.548 391 1654	20.071 503 7610	.049 821 8774	27
	28	1.864 544 9901	38.424 221 7807	.026 025 2506	.536 323 8781	20.607 827 6392	.048 525 2506	28
	29	1.906 497 2523	40.288 766 7708	.024 820 8143	.524 522 1302	21.132 349 7693	.047 320 8143	29
	30	1.949 393 4405	42.195 264 0232	.023 699 3422	.512 980 0784	21.645 329 8478	.046 199 3422	30
	31	1.993 254 7929	44.144 657 4637	.022 652 7978	.501 692 0082	22.147 021 8560	.045 152 7978	31
	32	2.038 103 0258	46.137 912 2566	.021 674 1493	.490 652 3308	22.637 674 1868	.044 174 1493	32
	33	2.083 960 3439	48.176 015 2824	.020 757 2169	.479 855 5802	23.117 529 7670	.043 257 2169	33
	34	2.130 849 4516	50.259 975 6262	.019 896 5477	.469 296 4110	23.586 826 1780	.042 396 5477	34
	35	2.178 793 5643	52.390 825 0778	.019 087 3115	.458 969 5951	24.045 795 7731	.041 587 3115	35
	36	2.227 816 4194	54.569 618 6421	.018 325 2151	.448 870 0197	24.494 665 7928	.040 825 2151	36
	37	2.277 942 2889	56.797 435 0615	.017 606 4289	.438 992 6843	24.933 658 4771	.040 106 4289	37
	38	2.329 195 9904	59.075 377 3504	.016 927 5262	.429 332 6985	25.362 991 1756	.039 427 5262	38
	39	2.381 602 9002	61.404 573 3408	.016 285 4319	.419 885 2798	25.782 876 4554	.038 785 4319	39
	40	2.435 188 9654	63.786 176 2410	.015 677 3781	.410 645 7504	26.193 522 2057	.038 177 3781	40
	41	2.489 980 7171	66.221 365 2064	.015 100 8666	.401 609 5358	26.595 131 7416	.037 600 8666	41
	42	2.546 005 2833	68.711 345 9235	.014 553 6372	.392 772 1622	26.987 903 9037	.037 053 6372	42
	43	2.603 290 4022	71.257 351 2068	.014 033 6398	.384 129 2540	27.372 033 1577	.036 533 6398	43
	44	2.661 864 4362	73.860 641 6090	.013 539 0105	.375 676 5320	27.747 709 6897	.036 039 0105	44
	45	2.721 756 3860	76.522 506 0452	.013 068 0508	.367 409 8112	28.115 119 5009	.035 568 0508	45
	46	2.782 995 9047	79.244 262 4312	.012 619 2101	.359 324 9988	28.474 444 4997	.035 119 2101	46
	47	2.845 613 2126	82.027 258 3359	.012 191 0694	.351 410 0917	28.825 862 5913	.034 691 0694	47
	48	2.909 639 6121	84.872 871 6484	.011 782 3279	.343 685 1753	29.169 547 7666	.034 282 3279	48
	49	2.975 106 5034	87.782 511 2605	.011 391 7908	.336 122 4208	29.505 670 1874	.033 891 7908	49
	50	3.042 046 3997	90.757 617 7639	.011 018 3588	.328 726 0839	29.834 396 2713	.033 518 3588	50
	51	3.110 492 4437	93.799 664 1636	.010 661 0190	.321 492 5026	30.155 888 7739	.033 161 0190	51
	52	3.180 478 5237	96.910 156 6073	.010 318 8359	.314 418 0954	30.470 306 8693	.032 818 8359	52
	53	3.252 039 2904	100.090 635 1309	.009 990 9447	.307 499 3598	30.777 806 2291	.032 490 9447	53
	54	3.325 210 1745	103.342 674 4214	.009 676 5446	.300 732 8703	31.078 539 0994	.032 176 5446	54
	55	3.400 027 4034	106.667 884 5958	.009 374 8930	.294 115 2765	31.372 654 3760	.031 874 8930	55
	56	3.476 528 0200	110.067 911 9993	.009 085 3000	.287 643 3022	31.660 297 6782	.031 585 3000	56
	57	3.554 749 9004	113.544 440 0192	.008 807 1243	.281 313 7430	31.941 611 4212	.031 307 1243	57
	58	3.634 731 7732	117.099 189 9197	.008 539 7687	.275 123 4651	32.216 734 8863	.031 039 7687	58
	59	3.716 513 2381	120.733 921 6929	.008 282 6764	.269 069 4035	32.485 804 2898	.030 782 6764	59
	60	3.800 134 7859	124.450 434 9310	.008 035 3275	.263 148 5609	32.748 952 8506	.030 535 3275	60
	61	3.885 637 8186	128.250 569 7169	.007 797 2363	.257 358 0057	33.006 310 8563	.030 297 2363	61
	62	3.973 064 6695	132.136 207 5355	.007 567 9484	.251 694 8711	33.258 005 7275	.030 067 9484	62
	63	4.062 458 6246	136.109 272 2051	.007 347 0380	.246 156 3532	33.504 162 0807	.029 847 0380	63
	64	4.153 863 9437	140.171 730 8297	.007 134 1061	.240 739 7097	33.744 901 7904	.029 634 1061	64
	65	4.247 325 8824	144.325 594 7734	.006 928 7780	.235 442 2589	33.980 344 0493	.029 428 7780	65
	66	4.342 890 7148	148.572 920 6558	.006 730 7016	.230 261 3779	34.210 605 4272	.029 230 7016	66
	67	4.440 605 7558	152.915 811 3705	.006 539 5461	.225 194 5016	34.435 799 9288	.029 039 5461	67
	68	4.540 519 3853	157.356 417 1264	.006 354 9998	.220 239 1214	34.656 039 0501	.028 854 9998	68
	69	4.642 681 0715	161.896 936 5117	.006 176 7691	.215 392 7837	34.871 431 8339	.028 676 7691	69
	70	4.747 141 3956	166.539 617 5832	.006 004 5773	.210 653 0892	35.082 084 9231	.028 504 5773	70
	71	4.853 952 0770	171.286 758 9788	.005 838 1629	.206 017 6912	35.288 102 6143	.028 338 1629	71
	72	4.963 165 9988	176.140 711 0559	.005 677 2792	.201 484 2946	35.489 586 9088	.028 177 2792	72
	73	5.074 837 2337	181.103 877 0546	.005 521 6929	.197 050 6548	35.686 637 5637	.028 021 6929	73
	74	5.189 021 0715	186.178 714 2883	.005 371 1833	.192 714 5768	35.879 352 1405	.027 871 1833	74
	75	5.305 774 0456	191.367 735 3598	.005 225 5413	.188 473 9138	36.067 826 0543	.027 725 5413	75
	76	5.425 153 9616	196.673 509 4054	.005 084 5689	.184 326 5660	36.252 152 6203	.027 584 5689	76
	77	5.547 219 9258	202.098 663 3670	.004 948 0782	.180 270 4802	36.432 423 1006	.027 448 0782	77
	78	5.672 032 3741	207.645 883 2928	.004 815 8913	.176 303 6482	36.608 726 7487	.027 315 8913	78
	79	5.799 653 1025	213.317 915 6669	.004 687 8388	.172 424 1058	36.781 150 8545	.027 187 8388	79
	80	5.930 145 2973	219.117 568 7694	.004 563 7600	.168 629 9323	36.949 780 7868	.027 063 7600	80
	81	6.063 573 5665	225.047 714 0667	.004 443 5021	.164 919 2492	37.114 700 0360	.026 943 5021	81
	82	6.200 003 9717	231.111 287 6332	.004 326 9198	.161 290 2193	37.275 990 2552	.026 826 9198	82
	83	6.339 504 0611	237.311 291 6050	.004 213 8745	.157 741 0457	37.433 731 3010	.026 713 8745	83
	84	6.482 142 9025	243.650 795 6661	.004 104 2345	.154 269 9714	37.588 001 2723	.026 604 2345	84
	85	6.627 991 1178	250.132 938 5686	.003 997 8741	.150 875 2776	37.738 876 5500	.026 497 8741	85
	86	6.777 120 9179	256.760 929 6863	.003 894 6735	.147 555 2837	37.886 431 8337	.026 394 6735	86
	87	6.929 606 1386	263.538 050 6043	.003 794 5185	.144 308 3460	38.030 740 1797	.026 294 5185	87
	88	7.085 522 2767	270.467 656 7429	.003 697 2998	.141 132 8567	38.171 873 0363	.026 197 2998	88
	89	7.244 946 5279	277.553 179 0196	.003 602 9132	.138 027 2437	38.309 900 2800	.026 102 9132	89
	90	7.407 957 8248	284.798 125 5475	.003 511 2591	.134 989 9694	38.444 890 2494	.026 011 2591	90
	91	7.574 636 8759	292.206 083 3724	.003 422 2422	.132 019 5300	38.576 909 7794	.025 922 2422	91
	92	7.745 066 2056	299.780 720 2482	.003 335 7716	.129 114 4547	38.706 024 2341	.025 835 7716	92
	93	7.919 330 1952	307.525 786 4538	.003 251 7598	.126 273 3054	38.832 297 5395	.025 751 7598	93
	94	8.097 515 1246	315.445 116 6490	.003 170 1236	.123 494 6752	38.955 792 2147	.025 670 1236	94
	95	8.279 709 2149	323.542 631 7736	.003 090 7828	.120 777 1884	39.076 569 4031	.025 590 7828	95
	96	8.466 002 6722	331.822 340 9885	.003 013 6609	.118 119 4997	39.194 688 9028	.025 513 6609	96
	97	8.656 487 7324	340.288 343 6608	.002 938 6843	.115 520 2931	39.310 209 1959	.025 438 6843	97
	98	8.851 258 7063	348.944 831 3932	.002 865 7825	.112 978 2818	39.423 187 4776	.025 365 7825	98
	99	9.050 412 0272	357.796 090 0995	.002 794 8880	.110 492 2071	39.533 679 6847	.025 294 8880	99
	100	9.254 046 2979	366.846 502 1267	.002 725 9358	.108 080 8382	39.641 740 5229	.025 225 9358	100

	XIV COMPOUND AMOUNT	XV AMOUNT OF ANNUITY	XVI SINKING FUND	XVII PRESENT VALUE	XVIII PRESENT VALUE OF ANNUITY	XIX AMORTIZATION	
P E R I O D S	AMOUNT OF 1 — How $1 left at compound interest will grow.	AMOUNT OF 1 PER PERIOD — How $1 deposited periodically will grow.	SINKING FUND — Periodic deposit that will grow to $1 at future date.	PRESENT WORTH OF 1 — What $1 due in the future is worth today.	PRESENT WORTH OF 1 PER PERIOD — What $1 payable periodically is worth today.	PARTIAL PAYMENT — Annuity worth $1 today. Periodic payment necessary to pay off a loan of $1.	P E R I O D S
1	1.025 000 0000	1.000 000 0000	1.000 000 0000	.975 609 7561	.975 609 7561	1.025 000 0000	1
2	1.050 625 0000	2.025 000 0000	.493 827 1605	.951 814 3962	1.927 424 1523	.518 827 1605	2
3	1.076 890 6250	3.075 625 0000	.325 137 1672	.928 599 4109	2.856 023 5632	.350 137 1672	3
4	1.103 812 8906	4.152 515 6250	.240 817 8777	.905 950 6448	3.761 974 2080	.265 817 8777	4
5	1.131 408 2129	5.256 328 5156	.190 246 8609	.883 854 2876	4.645 828 4956	.215 246 8609	5
6	1.159 693 4182	6.387 736 7285	.156 549 9711	.862 296 8660	5.508 125 3616	.181 549 9711	6
7	1.188 685 7537	7.547 430 1467	.132 495 4296	.841 265 2351	6.349 390 5967	.157 495 4296	7
8	1.218 402 8975	8.736 115 9004	.114 467 3458	.820 746 5708	7.170 137 1675	.139 467 3458	8
9	1.248 862 9699	9.954 518 7979	.100 456 8900	.800 728 3618	7.970 865 5292	.125 456 8900	9
10	1.280 084 5442	11.203 381 7679	.089 258 7632	.781 198 4017	8.752 063 9310	.114 258 7632	10
11	1.312 086 6578	12.483 466 3121	.080 105 9558	.762 144 7822	9.514 208 7131	.105 105 9558	11
12	1.344 888 8242	13.795 552 9699	.072 487 1270	.743 555 8850	10.257 764 5982	.097 487 1270	12
13	1.378 511 0449	15.140 441 7941	.066 048 2708	.725 420 3757	10.983 184 9738	.091 048 2708	13
14	1.412 973 8210	16.518 952 8390	.060 536 5249	.707 727 1958	11.690 912 1696	.085 536 5249	14
15	1.448 298 1665	17.931 926 6599	.055 766 4561	.690 465 5568	12.381 377 7264	.080 766 4561	15
16	1.484 505 6207	19.380 224 8264	.051 598 9886	.673 624 9335	13.055 002 6599	.076 598 9886	16
17	1.521 618 2612	20.864 730 4471	.047 927 7699	.657 195 0571	13.712 197 7170	.072 927 7699	17
18	1.559 658 7177	22.386 348 7083	.044 670 0805	.641 165 9093	14.353 363 6264	.069 670 0805	18
19	1.598 650 1856	23.946 007 4260	.041 760 6151	.625 527 7164	14.978 891 3428	.066 760 6151	19
20	1.638 616 4403	25.544 657 6116	.039 147 1287	.610 270 9429	15.589 162 2856	.064 147 1287	20
21	1.679 581 8513	27.183 274 0519	.036 787 3273	.595 386 2857	16.184 548 5714	.061 787 3273	21
22	1.721 571 3976	28.862 855 9032	.034 646 6061	.580 864 6690	16.765 413 2404	.059 646 6061	22
23	1.764 610 6825	30.584 427 3008	.032 696 3781	.566 697 2380	17.332 110 4784	.057 696 3781	23
24	1.808 725 9496	32.349 037 9833	.030 912 8204	.552 875 3542	17.884 985 8326	.055 912 8204	24
25	1.853 944 0983	34.157 763 9329	.029 275 9210	.539 390 5894	18.424 376 4220	.054 275 9210	25
26	1.900 292 7008	36.011 708 0312	.027 768 7467	.526 234 7214	18.950 611 1434	.052 768 7467	26
27	1.947 800 0183	37.912 000 7320	.026 376 8722	.513 399 7282	19.464 010 8717	.051 376 8722	27
28	1.996 495 0188	39.859 800 7503	.025 087 9327	.500 877 7836	19.964 888 6553	.050 087 9327	28
29	2.046 407 3942	41.856 295 7690	.023 891 2685	.488 661 2523	20.453 549 9076	.048 891 2685	29
30	2.097 567 5791	43.902 703 1633	.022 777 6407	.476 742 6852	20.930 292 5928	.047 777 6407	30
31	2.150 006 7686	46.000 270 7424	.021 739 0025	.465 114 8148	21.395 407 4076	.046 739 0025	31
32	2.203 756 9378	48.150 277 5109	.020 768 3123	.453 770 5510	21.849 177 9586	.045 768 3123	32
33	2.258 850 8612	50.354 034 4487	.019 859 3819	.442 702 9766	22.291 880 9352	.044 859 3819	33
34	2.315 322 1327	52.612 885 3099	.019 006 7508	.431 905 3430	22.723 786 2783	.044 006 7508	34
35	2.375 205 1861	54.928 207 4426	.018 205 5823	.421 371 0664	23.145 157 3447	.043 205 5823	35
36	2.432 535 3157	57.301 412 6287	.017 451 5767	.411 093 7233	23.556 251 0680	.042 451 5767	36
37	2.493 348 6986	59.733 947 9444	.016 740 8992	.401 067 0471	23.957 318 1151	.041 740 8992	37
38	2.555 682 4161	62.227 296 6430	.010 070 1180	.391 284 9240	24.348 603 0391	.041 070 1180	38
39	2.619 574 4765	64.782 979 0591	.015 436 1534	.381 741 3893	24.730 344 4284	.040 436 1534	39
40	2.685 063 8384	67.402 553 5356	.014 836 2332	.372 430 6237	25.102 775 0521	.039 836 2332	40
41	2.752 190 4343	70.087 617 3740	.014 267 8555	.363 346 9499	25.466 122 0020	.039 267 8555	41
42	2.820 995 1952	72.839 807 8083	.013 728 7567	.354 484 8292	25.820 606 8313	.038 728 7567	42
43	2.891 520 0751	75.660 803 0035	.013 216 8833	.345 838 8578	26.166 445 6890	.038 216 8833	43
44	2.963 808 0770	78.552 323 0786	.012 730 3683	.337 403 7637	26.503 849 4527	.037 730 3683	44
45	3.037 903 2789	81.516 131 1556	.012 267 5106	.329 174 4036	26.833 023 8563	.037 267 5106	45
46	3.113 850 8609	84.554 034 4345	.011 826 7568	.321 145 7596	27.154 169 6159	.036 826 7568	46
47	3.191 697 1324	87.667 885 2954	.011 406 6855	.313 312 9362	27.467 482 5521	.036 406 6855	47
48	3.271 489 5607	90.859 582 4277	.011 005 9938	.305 671 1573	27.773 153 7094	.036 005 9938	48
49	3.353 276 7997	94.131 071 9884	.010 623 4847	.298 215 7632	28.071 369 4726	.035 623 4847	49
50	3.437 108 7197	97.484 348 7881	.010 258 0569	.290 942 2080	28.362 311 6805	.035 258 0569	50
51	3.523 036 4377	100.921 457 5078	.009 908 6956	.283 846 0566	28.646 157 7371	.034 908 6956	51
52	3.611 112 3486	104.444 493 9455	.009 574 4635	.276 922 9820	28.923 080 7191	.034 574 4635	52
53	3.701 390 1574	108.055 606 2942	.009 254 4944	.270 168 7629	29.193 249 4821	.034 254 4944	53
54	3.793 924 9113	111.756 996 4515	.008 947 9856	.263 579 2809	29.456 828 7630	.033 947 9856	54
55	3.888 773 0341	115.550 921 3628	.008 654 1932	.257 150 5180	29.713 979 2810	.033 654 1932	55
56	3.985 992 3599	119.439 694 3969	.008 372 4260	.250 878 5541	29.964 857 8351	.033 372 4260	56
57	4.085 642 1689	123.425 686 7568	.008 102 0412	.244 759 5650	30.209 617 4001	.033 102 0412	57
58	4.187 783 2231	127.511 328 9257	.007 842 4404	.238 789 8195	30.448 407 2196	.032 842 4404	58
59	4.292 477 8037	131.699 112 1489	.007 593 0656	.232 965 6776	30.681 372 8972	.032 593 0656	59
60	4.399 789 7488	135.991 589 9526	.007 353 3060	.227 283 5073	30.908 656 4851	.032 353 3060	60
61	4.509 784 4925	140.391 379 7014	.007 122 9445	.221 740 0857	31.130 396 5708	.032 122 9445	61
62	4.622 529 1048	144.901 164 1940	.006 901 2558	.216 331 7910	31.346 728 3617	.031 901 2558	62
63	4.738 092 3325	149.523 693 2988	.006 687 9033	.211 055 4058	31.557 783 7676	.031 687 9033	63
64	4.856 544 6408	154.261 785 6313	.006 482 4869	.205 907 7130	31.763 691 4805	.031 482 4869	64
65	4.977 958 2568	159.118 330 2721	.006 284 6311	.200 885 5736	31.964 577 0542	.031 284 6311	65
66	5.102 407 2132	164.096 288 5289	.006 093 9830	.195 985 9255	32.160 562 9797	.031 093 9830	66
67	5.229 967 3936	169.198 695 7421	.005 910 2110	.191 205 7810	32.351 768 7607	.030 910 2110	67
68	5.360 716 5784	174.428 663 1356	.005 733 0027	.186 542 2253	32.538 310 9860	.030 733 0027	68
69	5.494 734 4929	179.789 379 7140	.005 562 0638	.181 992 4150	32.720 303 4010	.030 562 0638	69
70	5.632 102 8552	185.284 114 2069	.005 397 1168	.177 553 5756	32.897 856 9766	.030 397 1168	70
71	5.772 905 4266	190.916 217 0620	.005 237 8997	.173 223 0006	33.071 079 9772	.030 237 8997	71
72	5.917 228 0622	196.689 122 4886	.005 084 1652	.168 998 0493	33.240 078 0265	.030 084 1652	72
73	6.065 158 7638	202.606 350 5508	.004 935 6794	.164 876 1457	33.404 954 1722	.029 935 6794	73
74	6.216 787 7329	208.671 509 3146	.004 792 2211	.160 854 7763	33.565 808 9485	.029 792 2211	74
75	6.372 207 4262	214.888 297 0474	.004 653 5806	.156 931 4891	33.722 740 4375	.029 653 5806	75
76	6.531 512 6118	221.260 504 4736	.004 519 5594	.153 103 8918	33.875 844 3293	.029 519 5594	76
77	6.694 800 4271	227.792 017 0855	.004 389 9695	.149 369 6505	34.025 213 9798	.029 389 9695	77
78	6.862 170 4378	234.486 817 5126	.004 264 6321	.145 726 4883	34.170 940 4681	.029 264 6321	78
79	7.033 724 6988	241.348 987 9504	.004 143 3776	.142 172 1837	34.313 112 6518	.029 143 3776	79
80	7.209 567 8162	248.382 712 6492	.004 026 0451	.138 704 5695	34.451 817 2213	.029 026 0451	80
81	7.389 807 0116	255.592 280 4654	.003 912 4812	.135 321 5312	34.587 138 7525	.028 912 4812	81
82	7.574 552 1869	262.982 087 4770	.003 802 5404	.132 021 0060	34.719 159 7585	.028 802 5404	82
83	7.763 915 9916	270.556 639 6640	.003 696 0838	.128 800 9815	34.847 960 7400	.028 696 0838	83
84	7.958 013 8914	278.320 555 6556	.003 592 9793	.125 659 4941	34.973 620 2342	.028 592 9793	84
85	8.156 964 2387	286.278 569 5470	.003 493 1011	.122 594 6284	35.096 214 8626	.028 493 1011	85
86	8.360 888 3446	294.435 533 7856	.003 396 3292	.119 604 5155	35.215 819 3781	.028 396 3292	86
87	8.569 910 5533	302.796 422 1303	.003 302 5489	.116 687 3322	35.332 506 7104	.028 302 5489	87
88	8.784 158 3171	311.366 332 6835	.003 211 6510	.113 841 2997	35.446 348 0101	.028 211 6510	88
89	9.003 762 2750	320.150 491 0006	.003 123 5311	.111 064 6827	35.557 412 6928	.028 123 5311	89
90	9.228 856 3319	329.154 253 2756	.003 038 0893	.108 355 7880	35.665 768 4808	.028 038 0893	90
91	9.459 577 7402	338.383 109 6075	.002 955 2302	.105 712 9639	35.771 481 4447	.027 955 2302	91
92	9.696 067 1837	347.842 687 3477	.002 874 8628	.103 134 5989	35.874 616 0436	.027 874 8628	92
93	9.938 468 8633	357.538 754 5314	.002 796 8996	.100 619 1209	35.975 235 1645	.027 796 8996	93
94	10.186 930 5849	367.477 223 3947	.002 721 2571	.098 164 9960	36.073 400 1605	.027 721 2571	94
95	10.441 603 8495	377.664 153 9796	.002 647 8552	.095 770 7278	36.169 170 8882	.027 647 8552	95
96	10.702 643 9457	388.105 757 8290	.002 576 6173	.093 434 8564	36.262 605 7446	.027 576 6173	96
97	10.970 210 0444	398.808 401 7748	.002 507 4697	.091 155 9574	36.353 761 7021	.027 507 4697	97
98	11.244 466 2955	409.778 611 8191	.002 440 3421	.088 932 6414	36.442 694 3435	.027 440 3421	98
99	11.525 576 9279	421.023 077 1146	.002 375 1667	.086 763 5526	36.529 457 8961	.027 375 1667	99
100	11.813 716 3511	432.548 654 0425	.002 311 8787	.084 647 3684	36.614 105 2645	.027 311 8787	100

	XIV COMPOUND AMOUNT	XV AMOUNT OF ANNUITY	XVI SINKING FUND	XVII PRESENT VALUE	XVIII PRESENT VALUE OF ANNUITY	XIX AMORTIZATION	
P E R I O D S	AMOUNT OF 1 How $1 left at compound interest will grow.	AMOUNT OF 1 PER PERIOD How $1 deposited periodically will grow.	SINKING FUND Periodic deposit that will grow to $1 at future date.	PRESENT WORTH OF 1 What $1 due in the future is worth today.	PRESENT WORTH OF 1 PER PERIOD What $1 payable periodically is worth today.	PARTIAL PAYMENT Annuity worth $1 today. Periodic payment necessary to pay off a loan of $1.	P E R I O D S
1	1.030 000 0000	1.000 000 0000	1.000 000 0000	.970 873 7864	.970 873 7864	1.030 000 0000	1
2	1.060 900 0000	2.030 000 0000	.492 610 8374	.942 595 9091	1.913 469 6955	.522 610 8374	2
3	1.092 727 0000	3.090 900 0000	.323 530 3633	.915 141 6594	2.828 611 3549	.353 530 3633	3
4	1.125 508 8100	4.183 627 0000	.239 027 0452	.888 487 0479	3.717 098 4028	.269 027 0452	4
5	1.159 274 0743	5.309 135 8100	.188 354 5714	.862 608 7844	4.579 707 1872	.218 354 5714	5
6	1.194 052 2965	6.468 409 8843	.154 597 5005	.837 484 2567	5.417 191 4439	.184 597 5005	6
7	1.229 873 8654	7.662 462 1808	.130 506 3538	.813 091 5113	6.230 282 9552	.160 506 3538	7
8	1.266 770 0814	8.892 336 0463	.112 456 3888	.789 409 2343	7.019 692 1895	.142 456 3888	8
9	1.304 773 1838	10.159 106 1276	.098 433 8570	.766 416 7323	7.786 108 9219	.128 433 8570	9
10	1.343 916 3793	11.463 879 3115	.087 230 5066	.744 093 9149	8.530 202 8368	.117 230 5066	10
11	1.384 233 8707	12.807 795 6908	.078 077 4478	.722 421 2766	9.252 624 1134	.108 077 4478	11
12	1.425 760 8868	14.192 029 5615	.070 462 0855	.701 379 8802	9.954 003 9936	.100 462 0855	12
13	1.468 533 7135	15.617 790 4484	.064 029 5440	.680 951 3400	10.634 955 3336	.094 029 5440	13
14	1.512 589 7249	17.086 324 1618	.058 526 3390	.661 117 8058	11.296 073 1394	.088 526 3390	14
15	1.557 967 4166	18.598 913 8867	.053 766 5805	.641 861 9474	11.937 935 0868	.083 766 5805	15
16	1.604 706 4391	20.156 881 3033	.049 610 8493	.623 166 9392	12.561 102 0260	.079 610 8493	16
17	1.652 847 6323	21.761 587 7424	.045 952 5294	.605 016 4458	13.166 118 4718	.075 952 5294	17
18	1.702 433 0612	23.414 435 3747	.042 708 6959	.587 394 6076	13.753 513 0795	.072 708 6959	18
19	1.753 506 0531	25.116 868 4359	.039 813 8806	.570 286 0268	14.323 799 1063	.069 813 8806	19
20	1.806 111 2347	26.870 374 4890	.037 215 7076	.553 675 7542	14.877 474 8605	.067 215 7076	20
21	1.860 294 5717	28.676 485 7236	.034 871 7765	.537 549 2759	15.415 024 1364	.064 871 7765	21
22	1.916 103 4089	30.536 780 2954	.032 747 3948	.521 892 5009	15.936 916 6372	.062 747 3948	22
23	1.973 586 5111	32.452 883 7042	.030 813 9027	.506 691 7484	16.443 608 3857	.060 813 9027	23
24	2.032 794 1065	34.426 470 2153	.029 047 4159	.491 933 7363	16.935 542 1220	.059 047 4159	24
25	2.093 778 9297	36.459 264 3218	.027 427 8710	.477 605 5693	17.413 147 6913	.057 427 8710	25
26	2.156 591 2675	38.553 042 2515	.025 938 2903	.463 694 7274	17.876 842 4187	.055 938 2903	26
27	2.221 289 0056	40.709 633 5190	.024 564 2103	.450 189 0558	18.327 031 4745	.054 564 2103	27
28	2.287 927 6757	42.930 922 5246	.023 293 2334	.437 076 7532	18.764 108 2277	.053 293 2334	28
29	2.356 565 5060	45.218 850 2003	.022 114 6711	.424 346 3623	19.188 454 5900	.052 114 6711	29
30	2.427 262 4712	47.575 415 7063	.021 019 2593	.411 986 7595	19.600 441 3495	.051 019 2593	30
31	2.500 080 3453	50.002 678 1775	.019 998 9288	.399 987 1452	20.000 428 4946	.049 998 9288	31
32	2.575 082 7557	52.502 758 5228	.019 046 6183	.388 337 0341	20.388 765 5288	.049 046 6183	32
33	2.652 335 2384	55.077 841 2785	.018 156 1219	.377 026 2467	20.765 791 7755	.048 156 1219	33
34	2.731 905 2955	57.730 176 5169	.017 321 9633	.366 044 8997	21.131 836 6752	.047 321 9633	34
35	2.813 862 4544	60.462 081 8124	.016 539 2916	.355 383 3978	21.487 220 0731	.046 539 2916	35
36	2.898 278 3280	63.275 944 2668	.015 803 7942	.345 032 4251	21.832 252 4981	.045 803 7942	36
37	2.985 226 6778	66.174 222 5948	.015 111 6244	.334 982 9369	22.167 235 4351	.045 111 6244	37
38	3.074 783 4782	69.159 449 2726	.014 459 3401	.325 226 1524	22.492 461 5874	.044 459 3401	38
39	3.167 026 9825	72.234 232 7508	.013 843 8516	.315 753 5460	22.808 215 1334	.043 843 8516	39
40	3.262 037 7920	75.401 259 7333	.013 262 3779	.306 556 8408	23.114 771 9742	.043 262 3779	40
41	3.359 898 9258	78.663 297 5253	.012 712 4089	.297 628 0008	23.412 399 9750	.042 712 4089	41
42	3.460 695 8935	82.023 196 4511	.012 191 6731	.288 959 2240	23.701 359 1990	.042 191 6731	42
43	3.564 516 7703	85.483 892 3446	.011 698 1103	.280 542 9360	23.981 902 1349	.041 698 1103	43
44	3.671 452 2734	89.048 409 1149	.011 229 8469	.272 371 7825	24.254 273 9174	.041 229 8469	44
45	3.781 595 8417	92.719 861 3884	.010 785 1757	.264 438 6238	24.518 712 5412	.040 785 1757	45
46	3.895 043 7169	96.501 457 2300	.010 362 5378	.256 736 5279	24.775 449 0691	.040 362 5378	46
47	4.011 895 0284	100.396 500 9469	.009 960 5065	.249 258 7650	25.024 707 8341	.039 960 5065	47
48	4.132 251 8793	104.408 395 9753	.009 577 7738	.241 998 8009	25.266 706 6350	.039 577 7738	48
49	4.256 219 4356	108.540 647 8546	.009 213 1383	.234 950 2922	25.501 656 9272	.039 213 1383	49
50	4.383 906 0187	112.796 867 2902	.008 865 4944	.228 107 0798	25.729 764 0070	.038 865 4944	50
51	4.515 423 1993	117.180 773 3089	.008 533 8232	.221 463 1843	25.951 227 1913	.038 533 8232	51
52	4.650 885 8952	121.696 196 5082	.008 217 1837	.215 012 8003	26.166 239 9915	.038 217 1837	52
53	4.790 412 4721	126.347 082 4035	.007 914 7059	.208 750 2915	26.374 990 2830	.037 914 7059	53
54	4.934 124 8463	131.137 494 8756	.007 625 5841	.202 670 1859	26.577 660 4690	.037 625 5841	54
55	5.082 148 5917	136.071 619 7218	.007 349 0710	.196 767 1708	26.774 427 6398	.037 349 0710	55
56	5.234 613 0494	141.153 768 3135	.007 084 4726	.191 036 0882	26.965 463 7279	.037 084 4726	56
57	5.391 651 4409	146.388 381 3629	.006 831 1432	.185 471 9303	27.150 935 6582	.036 831 1432	57
58	5.553 400 9841	151.780 032 8038	.006 588 4819	.180 069 8352	27.331 005 4934	.036 588 4819	58
59	5.720 003 0136	157.333 433 7879	.006 355 9281	.174 825 0827	27.505 830 5761	.036 355 9281	59
60	5.891 603 1040	163.053 436 8015	.006 132 9587	.169 733 0900	27.675 563 6661	.036 132 9587	60
61	6.068 351 1972	168.945 039 9056	.005 919 0847	.164 789 4978	27.840 353 0739	.035 919 0847	61
62	6.250 401 7331	175.013 391 1027	.005 713 8485	.159 989 7163	28.000 342 7902	.035 713 8485	62
63	6.437 913 7851	181.263 792 8358	.005 516 8216	.155 329 8216	28.155 672 6118	.035 516 8216	63
64	6.631 051 1986	187.701 706 6209	.005 327 6021	.150 805 6521	28.306 478 2639	.035 327 6021	64
65	6.829 982 7346	194.332 757 8195	.005 145 8128	.146 413 2544	28.452 891 5184	.035 145 8128	65
66	7.034 882 2166	201.162 740 5541	.004 971 0995	.142 148 7907	28.595 040 3091	.034 971 0995	66
67	7.245 928 6831	208.197 622 7707	.004 803 1288	.138 008 5347	28.733 048 8438	.034 803 1288	67
68	7.463 306 5436	215.443 551 4539	.004 641 5871	.133 988 8686	28.867 037 7124	.034 641 5871	68
69	7.687 205 7399	222.906 857 9975	.004 486 1787	.130 086 2802	28.997 123 9926	.034 486 1787	69
70	7.917 821 9121	230.594 063 7374	.004 336 6251	.126 297 3594	29.123 421 3521	.034 336 6251	70
71	8.155 356 5695	238.511 885 6495	.004 192 6632	.122 618 7956	29.246 040 1476	.034 192 6632	71
72	8.400 017 2666	246.667 242 2190	.004 054 0446	.119 047 3743	29.365 087 5220	.034 054 0446	72
73	8.652 017 7846	255.067 259 4856	.003 920 5345	.115 579 9751	29.480 667 4971	.033 920 5345	73
74	8.911 578 3181	263.719 277 2701	.003 791 9109	.112 213 5680	29.592 881 0651	.033 791 9109	74
75	9.178 925 6676	272.630 855 5882	.003 667 9634	.108 945 2117	29.701 826 2768	.033 667 9634	75
76	9.454 293 4377	281.809 781 2559	.003 548 4929	.105 772 0502	29.807 598 3270	.033 548 4929	76
77	9.737 922 2408	291.264 074 6936	.003 433 3105	.102 691 3109	29.910 289 6379	.033 433 3105	77
78	10.030 059 9080	301.001 996 9344	.003 322 2371	.099 700 3018	30.009 989 9397	.033 322 2371	78
79	10.330 961 7053	311.032 056 8424	.003 215 1027	.096 796 4095	30.106 786 3492	.033 215 1027	79
80	10.640 890 5564	321.363 018 5477	.003 111 7457	.093 977 0966	30.200 763 4458	.033 111 7457	80
81	10.960 117 2731	332.003 909 1041	.003 012 0127	.091 239 8996	30.292 003 3455	.033 012 0127	81
82	11.288 920 7913	342.964 026 3772	.002 915 7577	.088 582 4268	30.380 585 7723	.032 915 7577	82
83	11.627 588 4151	354.252 947 1685	.002 822 8417	.086 002 3561	30.466 588 1284	.032 822 8417	83
84	11.976 416 0675	365.880 535 5836	.002 733 1325	.083 497 4332	30.550 085 5616	.032 733 1325	84
85	12.335 708 5495	377.856 951 6511	.002 646 5042	.081 065 4691	30.631 151 0307	.032 646 5042	85
86	12.705 779 8060	390.192 660 2006	.002 562 8365	.078 704 3389	30.709 855 3696	.032 562 8365	86
87	13.086 953 2002	402.898 440 0067	.002 482 0151	.076 411 9795	30.786 267 3491	.032 482 0151	87
88	13.479 561 7962	415.985 393 2069	.002 403 9306	.074 186 3879	30.860 453 7370	.032 403 9306	88
89	13.883 948 6501	429.464 955 0031	.002 328 4787	.072 025 6193	30.932 479 3563	.032 328 4787	89
90	14.300 467 1096	443.348 903 6532	.002 255 5599	.069 927 7857	31.002 407 1421	.032 255 5599	90
91	14.729 481 1229	457.649 370 7628	.002 185 0789	.067 891 0541	31.070 298 1962	.032 185 0789	91
92	15.171 365 5566	472.378 851 8856	.002 116 9449	.065 913 6448	31.136 211 8409	.032 116 9449	92
93	15.626 506 5233	487.550 217 4422	.002 051 0708	.063 993 8299	31.200 205 6708	.032 051 0708	93
94	16.095 301 7190	503.176 723 9655	.001 987 3733	.062 129 9319	31.262 335 6027	.031 987 3733	94
95	16.578 160 7705	519.272 025 6844	.001 925 7729	.060 320 3223	31.322 655 9250	.031 925 7729	95
96	17.075 505 5936	535.850 186 4550	.001 866 1932	.058 563 4197	31.381 219 3446	.031 866 1932	96
97	17.587 770 7615	552.925 692 0486	.001 808 5613	.056 857 6890	31.438 077 0336	.031 808 5613	97
98	18.115 403 8843	570.513 462 8101	.001 752 8070	.055 201 6398	31.493 278 6734	.031 752 8070	98
99	18.658 866 0008	588.628 866 6944	.001 698 8633	.053 593 8250	31.546 872 4985	.031 698 8633	99
100	19.218 631 9809	607.287 732 6952	.001 646 6659	.052 032 8399	31.598 905 3383	.031 646 6659	100

	XIV COMPOUND AMOUNT	XV AMOUNT OF ANNUITY	XVI SINKING FUND	XVII PRESENT VALUE	XVIII PRESENT VALUE OF ANNUITY	XIX AMORTIZATION	
RATE 3 1/2% PERIODS	AMOUNT OF 1 *How $1 left at compound interest will grow.*	AMOUNT OF 1 PER PERIOD *How $1 deposited periodically will grow.*	SINKING FUND *Periodic deposit that will grow to $1 at future date.*	PRESENT WORTH OF 1 *What $1 due in the future is worth today.*	PRESENT WORTH OF 1 PER PERIOD *What $1 payable periodically is worth today.*	PARTIAL PAYMENT *Annuity worth $1 today. Periodic payment necessary to pay off a loan of $1.*	PERIODS
1	1.035 000 0000	1.000 000 0000	1.000 000 0000	.966 183 5749	.966 183 5749	1.035 000 0000	1
2	1.071 225 0000	2.035 000 0000	.491 400 4914	.933 510 7004	1.899 694 2752	.526 400 4914	2
3	1.108 717 8750	3.106 225 0000	.321 934 1806	.901 942 7057	2.801 636 9809	.356 934 1806	3
4	1.147 523 0006	4.214 942 8750	.237 251 1395	.871 442 2277	3.673 079 2086	.272 251 1395	4
5	1.187 686 3056	5.362 465 8756	.186 481 3732	.841 973 1669	4.515 052 3755	.221 481 3732	5
6	1.229 255 3263	6.550 152 1813	.152 668 2087	.813 500 6443	5.328 553 0198	.187 668 2087	6
7	1.272 279 2628	7.779 407 5076	.128 544 4938	.785 990 9607	6.114 543 9805	.163 544 4938	7
8	1.316 809 0370	9.051 686 7704	.110 476 6465	.759 411 5562	6.873 955 5367	.145 476 6465	8
9	1.362 897 3533	10.368 495 8073	.096 446 0051	.733 730 9722	7.607 686 5089	.131 446 0051	9
10	1.410 598 7606	11.731 393 1606	.085 241 3679	.708 918 8137	8.316 605 3226	.120 241 3679	10
11	1.459 969 7172	13.141 991 9212	.076 091 9658	.684 945 7137	9.001 551 0363	.111 091 9658	11
12	1.511 068 6573	14.601 961 6385	.068 483 9493	.661 783 2983	9.663 334 3346	.103 483 9493	12
13	1.563 956 0604	16.113 030 2958	.062 061 5726	.639 404 1529	10.302 738 4875	.097 061 5726	13
14	1.618 694 5225	17.676 986 3562	.056 570 7287	.617 781 7903	10.920 520 2778	.091 570 7287	14
15	1.675 348 8308	19.295 680 8786	.051 825 0694	.596 890 6186	11.517 410 8964	.086 825 0694	15
16	1.733 986 0398	20.971 029 7094	.047 684 8306	.576 705 9117	12.094 116 8081	.082 684 8306	16
17	1.794 675 5512	22.705 015 7492	.044 043 1317	.557 203 7794	12.651 320 5876	.079 043 1317	17
18	1.857 489 1955	24.499 691 3004	.040 816 8408	.538 361 1396	13.189 681 7271	.075 816 8408	18
19	1.922 501 3174	26.357 180 4960	.037 940 3252	.520 155 6904	13.709 837 4175	.072 940 3252	19
20	1.989 788 8635	28.279 681 8133	.035 361 0768	.502 565 8844	14.212 403 3020	.070 361 0768	20
21	2.059 431 4737	30.269 470 6768	.033 036 5870	.485 570 9028	14.697 974 2048	.068 036 5870	21
22	2.131 511 5753	32.328 902 1505	.030 932 0742	.469 150 6308	15.167 124 8355	.065 932 0742	22
23	2.206 114 4804	34.460 413 7257	.029 018 8042	.453 285 6336	15.620 410 4691	.064 018 8042	23
24	2.283 328 4872	36.666 528 2061	.027 272 8303	.437 957 1339	16.058 367 6030	.062 272 8303	24
25	2.363 244 9843	38.949 856 6933	.025 674 0354	.423 146 9893	16.481 514 5923	.060 674 0354	25
26	2.445 958 5587	41.313 101 6776	.024 205 3963	.408 837 6708	16.890 352 2631	.059 205 3963	26
27	2.531 567 1083	43.759 060 2363	.022 852 4103	.395 012 2423	17.285 364 5054	.057 852 4103	27
28	2.620 171 9571	46.290 627 3446	.021 602 6452	.381 654 3404	17.667 018 8458	.056 602 6452	28
29	2.711 877 9756	48.910 799 3017	.020 445 3825	.368 748 1550	18.035 767 0008	.055 445 3825	29
30	2.806 793 7047	51.622 677 2772	.019 371 3316	.356 278 4106	18.392 045 4114	.054 371 3316	30
31	2.905 031 4844	54.429 470 9819	.018 372 3998	.344 230 3484	18.736 275 7598	.053 372 3998	31
32	3.006 707 5863	57.334 502 4663	.017 441 5048	.332 589 7086	19.068 865 4684	.052 441 5048	32
33	3.111 942 3518	60.341 210 0526	.016 572 4221	.321 342 7136	19.390 208 1820	.051 572 4221	33
34	3.220 860 3342	63.453 152 4044	.015 759 6583	.310 476 0518	19.700 684 2338	.050 759 6583	34
35	3.333 590 4459	66.674 012 7386	.014 998 3473	.299 976 8617	20.000 661 0955	.049 998 3473	35
36	3.450 266 1115	70.007 603 1845	.014 284 1628	.289 832 7166	20.290 493 8121	.049 284 1628	36
37	3.571 025 4254	73.457 869 2959	.013 613 2454	.280 031 6102	20.570 525 4223	.048 613 2454	37
38	3.696 011 3162	77.028 894 7213	.012 982 1414	.270 561 9422	20.841 087 3645	.047 982 1414	38
39	3.825 371 7113	80.724 906 0365	.012 387 7506	.261 412 5046	21.102 499 8691	.047 387 7506	39
40	3.959 259 7212	84.550 277 7478	.011 827 2823	.252 572 4682	21.355 072 3373	.046 827 2823	40
41	4.097 833 8114	88.509 537 4690	.011 298 2174	.244 031 3702	21.599 103 7075	.046 298 2174	41
42	4.241 257 9948	92.607 371 2804	.010 798 2765	.235 779 1017	21.834 882 8092	.045 798 2765	42
43	4.389 702 0246	96.848 629 2752	.010 325 3914	.227 805 8953	22.062 688 7046	.045 325 3914	43
44	4.543 341 5955	101.238 331 2998	.009 877 6816	.220 102 3143	22.282 791 0189	.044 877 6816	44
45	4.702 358 5513	105.781 672 8953	.009 453 4334	.212 659 2409	22.495 450 2598	.044 453 4334	45
46	4.866 941 1006	110.484 031 4467	.009 051 0817	.205 467 8656	22.700 918 1254	.044 051 0817	46
47	5.037 284 0392	115.350 972 5473	.008 669 1944	.198 519 6769	22.899 437 8023	.043 669 1944	47
48	5.213 588 9805	120.388 256 5864	.008 306 4580	.191 806 4511	23.091 244 2535	.043 306 4580	48
49	5.396 064 5948	125.601 845 5670	.007 961 6665	.185 320 2426	23.276 564 4961	.042 961 6665	49
50	5.584 926 8557	130.997 910 1618	.007 633 7096	.179 053 3745	23.455 617 8706	.042 633 7096	50
51	5.780 399 2956	136.582 837 0175	.007 321 5641	.172 998 4295	23.628 616 3001	.042 321 5641	51
52	5.982 713 2710	142.363 236 3131	.007 024 2854	.167 148 2411	23.795 764 5412	.042 024 2854	52
53	6.192 108 2354	148.345 949 5840	.006 740 9997	.161 495 8851	23.957 260 4263	.041 740 9997	53
54	6.408 832 0237	154.538 057 8195	.006 470 8979	.156 034 6716	24.113 295 0978	.041 470 8979	54
55	6.633 141 1445	160.946 889 8432	.006 213 2297	.150 758 1368	24.264 053 2346	.041 213 2297	55
56	6.865 301 0846	167.580 030 9877	.005 967 2981	.145 660 0355	24.409 713 2702	.040 967 2981	56
57	7.105 586 6225	174.445 332 0722	.005 732 4549	.140 734 3339	24.550 447 6040	.040 732 4549	57
58	7.354 282 1543	181.550 918 6948	.005 508 0966	.135 975 2018	24.686 422 8058	.040 508 0966	58
59	7.611 682 0297	188.905 200 8491	.005 293 6605	.131 377 0066	24.817 799 8124	.040 293 6605	59
60	7.878 090 9008	196.516 882 8788	.005 088 6213	.126 934 3059	24.944 734 1182	.040 088 6213	60
61	8.153 824 0823	204.394 973 7796	.004 892 4882	.122 641 8414	25.067 375 9597	.039 892 4882	61
62	8.439 207 9252	212.548 797 8619	.004 704 8020	.118 494 5328	25.185 870 4924	.039 704 8020	62
63	8.734 580 2025	220.988 005 7870	.004 525 1325	.114 487 4713	25.300 357 9637	.039 525 1325	63
64	9.040 290 5096	229.722 585 9896	.004 353 0765	.110 615 9143	25.410 973 8780	.039 353 0765	64
65	9.356 700 6775	238.762 876 4992	.004 188 2558	.106 875 2795	25.517 849 1575	.039 188 2558	65
66	9.684 185 2012	248.119 577 1767	.004 030 3148	.103 261 1396	25.621 110 2971	.039 030 3148	66
67	10.023 131 6832	257.803 762 3779	.003 878 9193	.099 769 2170	25.720 879 5141	.038 878 9193	67
68	10.373 941 2921	267.826 894 0611	.003 733 7550	.096 395 3788	25.817 274 8928	.038 733 7550	68
69	10.737 029 2374	278.200 835 3532	.003 594 5255	.093 135 6316	25.910 410 5245	.038 594 5255	69
70	11.112 825 2607	288.937 864 5906	.003 460 9517	.089 986 1175	26.000 396 6420	.038 460 9517	70
71	11.501 774 1448	300.050 689 8512	.003 332 7702	.086 943 1087	26.087 339 7507	.038 332 7702	71
72	11.904 336 2399	311.552 463 9960	.003 209 7323	.084 003 0036	26.171 342 7543	.038 209 7323	72
73	12.320 988 0083	323.456 800 2359	.003 091 6030	.081 162 3223	26.252 505 0766	.038 091 6030	73
74	12.752 222 5885	335.777 788 2442	.002 978 1601	.078 417 7027	26.330 922 7794	.037 978 1601	74
75	13.198 550 3791	348.530 010 8327	.002 869 1934	.075 765 8964	26.406 688 6757	.037 869 1934	75
76	13.660 499 6424	361.728 561 2119	.002 764 5038	.073 203 7646	26.479 892 4403	.037 764 5038	76
77	14.138 617 1299	375.389 060 8543	.002 663 9029	.070 728 2750	26.550 620 7153	.037 663 9029	77
78	14.633 468 7294	389.527 677 9842	.002 567 2117	.068 336 4976	26.618 957 2128	.037 567 2117	78
79	15.145 640 1350	404.161 146 7136	.002 474 2606	.066 025 6015	26.684 982 8143	.037 474 2606	79
80	15.675 737 5397	419.306 786 8486	.002 384 8887	.063 792 8517	26.748 775 6660	.037 384 8887	80
81	16.224 388 3536	434.982 524 3883	.002 298 9429	.061 635 6055	26.810 411 2715	.037 298 9429	81
82	16.792 241 9450	451.206 912 7419	.002 216 2781	.059 551 3097	26.869 962 5812	.037 216 2781	82
83	17.379 970 4141	467.999 154 6878	.002 136 7560	.057 537 4973	26.927 500 0785	.037 136 7560	83
84	17.988 269 3786	485.379 125 1019	.002 060 2452	.055 591 7848	26.983 091 8632	.037 060 2452	84
85	18.617 858 8068	503.367 394 4805	.001 986 6205	.053 711 8694	27.036 803 7326	.036 986 6205	85
86	19.269 483 8651	521.985 253 2873	.001 915 7629	.051 895 5260	27.088 699 2585	.036 915 7629	86
87	19.943 915 8003	541.254 737 1524	.001 847 5589	.050 140 6048	27.138 839 8633	.036 847 5589	87
88	20.641 952 8533	561.198 652 9527	.001 781 9002	.048 445 0288	27.187 284 8921	.036 781 9002	88
89	21.364 421 2032	581.840 605 8060	.001 718 6838	.046 806 7911	27.234 091 6832	.036 718 6838	89
90	22.112 175 9453	603.205 027 0092	.001 657 8111	.045 223 9527	27.279 315 6359	.036 657 8111	90
91	22.886 102 1034	625.317 202 9546	.001 599 1884	.043 694 6403	27.323 010 2762	.036 599 1884	91
92	23.687 115 6770	648.203 305 0580	.001 542 7259	.042 217 0438	27.365 227 3200	.036 542 7259	92
93	24.516 164 7257	671.890 420 7350	.001 488 3379	.040 789 4143	27.406 016 7343	.036 488 3379	93
94	25.374 230 4911	696.406 585 4607	.001 435 9428	.039 410 0621	27.445 426 7965	.036 435 9428	94
95	26.262 328 5583	721.780 815 9519	.001 385 4621	.038 077 3547	27.483 504 1512	.036 385 4621	95
96	27.181 510 0579	748.043 144 5102	.001 336 8213	.036 789 7147	27.520 293 8659	.036 336 8213	96
97	28.132 862 9099	775.224 654 5680	.001 289 9487	.035 545 6181	27.555 839 8040	.036 289 9487	97
98	29.117 513 1117	803.357 517 4779	.001 244 7758	.034 343 5923	27.590 183 0763	.036 244 7758	98
99	30.136 626 0706	832.475 030 5896	.001 201 2372	.033 182 2148	27.623 365 2911	.036 201 2372	99
100	31.191 407 9831	862.611 656 6603	.001 159 2702	.032 060 1109	27.655 425 4020	.036 159 2702	100

	XIV COMPOUND AMOUNT	XV AMOUNT OF ANNUITY	XVI SINKING FUND	XVII PRESENT VALUE	XVIII PRESENT VALUE OF ANNUITY	XIX AMORTIZATION	
RATE 3 3/4% PERIODS	AMOUNT OF 1 — How $1 left at compound interest will grow.	AMOUNT OF 1 PER PERIOD — How $1 deposited periodically will grow.	SINKING FUND — Periodic deposit that will grow to $1 at future date.	PRESENT WORTH OF 1 — What $1 due in the future is worth today.	PRESENT WORTH OF 1 PER PERIOD — What $1 payable periodically is worth today.	PARTIAL PAYMENT — Annuity worth $1 today. Periodic payment necessary to pay off a loan of $1.	PERIODS
1	1.037 500 0000	1.000 000 0000	1.000 000 0000	.963 855 4217	.963 855 4217	1.037 500 0000	1
2	1.076 406 2500	2.037 500 0000	.490 797 5460	.929 017 2739	1.892 872 6956	.528 297 5460	2
3	1.116 771 4844	3.113 906 2500	.321 140 0472	.895 438 3363	2.788 311 0319	.358 640 0472	3
4	1.158 650 4150	4.230 677 7344	.236 368 7482	.863 073 0952	3.651 384 1271	.273 868 7482	4
5	1.202 099 8056	5.389 328 1494	.185 551 8856	.831 877 6822	4.483 261 8093	.223 051 8856	5
6	1.247 178 5483	6.591 427 9550	.151 712 1945	.801 809 8141	5.285 071 6234	.189 212 1945	6
7	1.293 947 7439	7.838 606 5033	.127 573 6956	.772 828 7365	6.057 900 3599	.165 073 6956	7
8	1.342 470 7843	9.132 554 2472	.109 498 3915	.744 895 1677	6.802 795 5276	.146 998 3915	8
9	1.392 813 4387	10.475 025 0315	.095 465 1657	.717 971 2460	7.520 766 7736	.132 965 1657	9
10	1.445 043 9426	11.867 838 4702	.084 261 3423	.692 020 4781	8.212 787 2517	.121 761 3423	10
11	1.499 233 0905	13.312 882 4128	.075 115 2131	.667 007 6897	8.879 794 9414	.112 615 2131	11
12	1.555 454 3314	14.812 115 5033	.067 512 3010	.642 898 9780	9.522 693 9194	.105 012 3010	12
13	1.613 783 8688	16.367 569 8346	.061 096 4248	.619 661 6656	10.142 355 5850	.098 596 4248	13
14	1.674 300 7639	17.981 353 7034	.055 613 1655	.597 264 2560	10.739 619 8409	.093 113 1655	14
15	1.737 087 0425	19.655 654 4673	.050 875 9452	.575 676 3913	11.315 296 2322	.088 375 9452	15
16	1.802 227 8066	21.392 741 5098	.046 744 8270	.554 868 8109	11.870 165 0431	.084 244 8270	16
17	1.869 811 3494	23.194 969 3165	.043 112 7968	.534 813 3117	12.404 978 3548	.080 612 7968	17
18	1.939 929 2750	25.064 780 6658	.039 896 6188	.515 482 7101	12.920 461 0649	.077 396 6188	18
19	2.012 676 6228	27.004 709 9408	.037 030 5773	.496 850 8049	13.417 311 8698	.074 530 5773	19
20	2.088 151 9961	29.017 386 5636	.034 462 0973	.478 892 3421	13.896 204 2118	.071 962 0973	20
21	2.166 457 6960	31.105 538 5597	.032 148 6155	.461 582 9803	14.357 787 1921	.069 648 6155	21
22	2.247 699 8596	33.271 996 2557	.030 055 3051	.444 899 2581	14.802 686 4502	.067 555 3051	22
23	2.331 988 6043	35.519 696 1153	.028 153 3940	.428 818 5620	15.231 505 0123	.065 653 3940	23
24	2.419 438 1770	37.851 684 7196	.026 418 9033	.413 319 0959	15.644 824 1082	.063 918 9033	24
25	2.510 167 1086	40.271 122 8966	.024 831 6890	.398 379 8515	16.043 203 9597	.062 331 6890	25
26	2.604 298 3752	42.781 290 0052	.023 374 7042	.383 980 5798	16.427 184 5395	.060 874 7042	26
27	2.701 959 5643	45.385 588 3804	.022 033 4259	.370 101 7636	16.797 286 3031	.059 533 4259	27
28	2.803 283 0479	48.087 547 9447	.020 795 4043	.356 724 5915	17.154 010 8946	.058 295 4043	28
29	2.908 406 1622	50.890 830 9926	.019 649 9051	.343 830 9315	17.497 841 8261	.057 149 9051	29
30	3.017 471 3933	53.799 237 1548	.018 587 6242	.331 403 3075	17.829 245 1336	.056 087 6242	30
31	3.130 626 5706	56.816 708 5481	.017 600 4564	.319 424 8747	18.148 670 0083	.055 100 4564	31
32	3.248 025 0670	59.947 335 1187	.016 681 3087	.307 879 3973	18.456 549 4056	.054 181 3087	32
33	3.369 826 0070	63.195 360 1856	.015 823 9465	.296 751 2263	18.753 300 6319	.053 323 9465	33
34	3.496 194 4822	66.565 186 1926	.015 022 8679	.286 025 2784	19.039 325 9102	.051 522 8679	34
35	3.627 301 7753	70.061 380 6748	.014 273 1986	.275 687 0153	19.315 012 9255	.051 773 1986	35
36	3.763 325 5919	73.688 682 4501	.013 570 6050	.265 722 4244	19.580 735 3499	.051 070 6050	36
37	3.904 450 3016	77.452 008 0420	.012 911 2211	.256 117 9994	19.836 853 3493	.050 411 2211	37
38	4.050 867 1879	81.356 458 3436	.012 291 5872	.246 860 7223	20.083 714 0716	.049 791 5872	38
39	4.202 774 7074	85.407 325 5315	.011 708 5975	.237 938 0456	20.321 652 1172	.049 208 5975	39
40	4.360 378 7590	89.610 100 2389	.011 159 4563	.229 337 8753	20.550 989 9925	.048 659 4563	40
41	4.523 892 9624	93.970 478 9979	.010 641 6399	.221 048 5545	20.772 038 5470	.048 141 6399	41
42	4.693 538 9485	98.494 371 9603	.010 152 8644	.213 058 8477	20.985 097 3947	.047 652 8644	42
43	4.869 546 6591	103.187 910 9088	.009 691 0577	.205 357 9255	21.190 455 3202	.047 191 0577	43
44	5.052 154 6588	108.057 457 5679	.009 254 3358	.197 935 3499	21.388 390 6701	.046 754 3358	44
45	5.241 610 4585	113.109 612 2267	.008 840 9816	.190 781 0601	21.579 171 7302	.046 340 9816	45
46	5.438 170 8507	118.351 222 6852	.008 449 4269	.183 885 3592	21.763 057 0893	.045 949 4269	46
47	5.642 102 2576	123.789 393 5359	.008 078 2365	.177 238 9004	21.940 295 9897	.045 578 2365	47
48	5.853 681 0923	129.431 495 7935	.007 726 0947	.170 832 6751	22.111 128 6648	.045 226 0947	48
49	6.073 194 1332	135.285 176 8857	.007 391 7928	.164 658 0001	22.275 786 6649	.044 891 7928	49
50	6.300 938 9132	141.358 371 0189	.007 074 2185	.158 706 5061	22.434 493 1709	.044 574 2185	50
51	6.537 224 1225	147.659 309 9321	.006 772 3464	.152 970 1264	22.587 463 2973	.044 272 3464	51
52	6.782 370 0270	154.196 534 0546	.006 485 2301	.147 441 0856	22.734 904 3829	.043 985 2301	52
53	7.036 708 9031	160.978 904 0816	.006 211 9941	.142 111 8898	22.877 016 2727	.043 711 9941	53
54	7.300 585 4869	168.015 612 9847	.005 951 8278	.136 975 3154	23.013 991 5882	.043 451 8278	54
55	7.574 357 4427	175.316 198 4716	.005 703 9795	.132 024 4004	23.146 015 9886	.043 203 9795	55
56	7.858 395 8468	182.890 555 9143	.005 467 7509	.127 252 4341	23.273 268 4227	.042 967 7509	56
57	8.153 085 6910	190.748 951 7611	.005 242 4928	.122 652 9486	23.395 921 3713	.042 742 4928	57
58	8.458 826 4045	198.902 037 4521	.005 027 6006	.118 219 7095	23.514 141 0808	.042 527 6006	58
59	8.776 032 3946	207.360 863 8566	.004 822 5108	.113 946 7079	23.628 087 7887	.042 322 5108	59
60	9.105 133 6094	216.136 896 2512	.004 626 6973	.109 828 1522	23.737 915 9409	.042 126 6973	60
61	9.446 576 1198	225.242 029 8606	.004 439 6687	.105 858 4600	23.843 774 4009	.041 939 6687	61
62	9.800 822 7243	234.688 605 9804	.004 260 9653	.102 032 2506	23.945 806 6515	.041 760 9653	62
63	10.168 353 5764	244.489 428 7047	.004 090 1564	.098 344 3379	24.044 150 9894	.041 590 1564	63
64	10.549 666 8355	254.657 782 2811	.003 926 8386	.094 789 7233	24.138 940 7126	.041 426 8386	64
65	10.945 279 3419	265.207 449 1166	.003 770 6332	.091 363 5887	24.230 304 3013	.041 270 6332	65
66	11.355 727 3172	276.152 728 4585	.003 621 1846	.088 061 2903	24.318 365 5916	.041 121 1846	66
67	11.781 567 0916	287.508 455 7757	.003 478 1586	.084 878 3521	24.403 243 9438	.040 978 1586	67
68	12.223 375 8575	299.290 022 8673	.003 341 2407	.081 810 4599	24.485 054 4036	.040 841 2407	68
69	12.681 752 4522	311.513 398 7248	.003 210 1348	.078 853 4553	24.563 907 8589	.040 710 1348	69
70	13.157 318 1691	324.195 151 1770	.003 084 5619	.076 003 3304	24.639 911 1893	.040 584 5619	70
71	13.650 717 6005	337.352 469 3461	.002 964 2587	.073 256 2221	24.713 167 4114	.040 464 2587	71
72	14.162 619 5105	351.003 186 9466	.002 848 9770	.070 608 4068	24.783 775 8182	.040 348 9770	72
73	14.693 717 7421	365.165 806 4571	.002 738 4820	.068 056 2957	24.851 832 1139	.040 238 4820	73
74	15.244 732 1575	379.859 524 1992	.002 632 5521	.065 596 4296	24.917 428 5435	.040 132 5521	74
75	15.816 409 6134	395.104 256 3567	.002 530 9775	.063 225 4743	24.980 654 0179	.040 030 9775	75
76	16.409 524 9739	410.920 665 9701	.002 433 5598	.060 940 2162	25.041 594 2341	.039 933 5598	76
77	17.024 882 1604	427.330 190 9440	.002 340 1108	.058 737 5578	25.100 331 7919	.039 840 1108	77
78	17.663 315 2414	444.355 073 1044	.002 250 4525	.056 614 5135	25.156 946 3054	.039 750 4525	78
79	18.325 689 5630	462.018 388 3458	.002 164 4160	.054 568 2058	25.211 514 5113	.039 664 4160	79
80	19.012 902 9216	480.344 077 9088	.002 081 8410	.052 595 8610	25.264 110 3723	.039 581 8410	80
81	19.725 886 7811	499.356 980 8303	.002 002 5754	.050 694 8058	25.314 805 1781	.039 502 5754	81
82	20.465 607 5354	519.082 867 6115	.001 926 4747	.048 862 4634	25.363 667 6416	.039 426 4747	82
83	21.233 067 8180	539.548 475 1469	.001 853 4016	.047 096 3503	25.410 763 9919	.039 353 4016	83
84	22.029 307 8612	560.781 542 9649	.001 783 2256	.045 394 0726	25.456 158 0645	.039 283 2256	84
85	22.855 406 9060	582.810 850 8261	.001 715 8225	.043 753 3230	25.499 911 3874	.039 215 8225	85
86	23.712 484 6650	605.666 257 7321	.001 651 0743	.042 171 8776	25.542 083 2650	.039 151 0743	86
87	24.601 702 8399	629.378 742 3970	.001 588 8684	.040 647 5928	25.582 730 8578	.039 088 8684	87
88	25.524 266 6964	653.980 445 2369	.001 529 0977	.039 178 4027	25.621 909 2606	.039 029 0977	88
89	26.481 426 6975	679.504 711 9333	.001 471 6601	.037 762 3159	25.659 671 5764	.038 971 6601	89
90	27.474 480 1987	705.986 138 6308	.001 416 4584	.036 397 4129	25.696 068 9893	.038 916 4584	90
91	28.504 773 2061	733.460 618 8294	.001 363 3997	.035 081 8438	25.731 150 8331	.038 863 3997	91
92	29.573 702 2013	761.965 392 0356	.001 312 3956	.033 813 8253	25.764 964 6584	.038 812 3956	92
93	30.682 716 0339	791.539 094 2369	.001 263 3615	.032 591 6389	25.797 556 2973	.038 763 3615	93
94	31.833 317 8852	822.221 810 2708	.001 216 2168	.031 413 6278	25.828 969 9251	.038 716 2168	94
95	33.027 067 3058	854.055 128 1559	.001 170 8846	.030 278 1955	25.859 248 1205	.038 670 8846	95
96	34.265 582 3298	887.082 195 4618	.001 127 2913	.029 183 8029	25.888 431 9234	.038 627 2913	96
97	35.550 541 6672	921.347 777 7916	.001 085 3665	.028 128 9666	25.916 560 8900	.038 585 3665	97
98	36.883 668 9797	956.898 319 4588	.001 045 0431	.027 112 2570	25.943 673 1470	.038 545 0431	98
99	38.266 825 2414	993.782 006 4385	.001 006 2569	.026 132 2959	25.969 805 4429	.038 506 2569	99
100	39.701 831 1880	1032.048 831 6799	.000 968 9464	.025 187 7551	25.994 993 1980	.038 468 9464	100

RATE 4%

PERIODS	XIV COMPOUND AMOUNT — AMOUNT OF 1 (How $1 left at compound interest will grow.)	XV AMOUNT OF ANNUITY — AMOUNT OF 1 PER PERIOD (How $1 deposited periodically will grow.)	XVI SINKING FUND (Periodic deposit that will grow to $1 at future date.)	XVII PRESENT VALUE — PRESENT WORTH OF 1 (What $1 due in the future is worth today.)	XVIII PRESENT VALUE OF ANNUITY — PRESENT WORTH OF 1 PER PERIOD (What $1 payable periodically is worth today.)	XIX AMORTIZATION — PARTIAL PAYMENT (Annuity worth $1 today. Periodic payment necessary to pay off a loan of $1.)	PERIODS
1	1.040 000 0000	1.000 000 0000	1.000 000 0000	.961 538 4615	.961 538 4615	1.040 000 0000	1
2	1.081 600 0000	2.040 000 0000	.490 196 0784	.924 556 2130	1.886 094 6746	.530 196 0784	2
3	1.124 864 0000	3.121 600 0000	.320 348 5392	.888 996 3587	2.775 091 0332	.360 348 5392	3
4	1.169 858 5600	4.246 464 0000	.235 490 0454	.854 804 1910	3.629 895 2243	.275 490 0454	4
5	1.216 652 9024	5.416 322 5600	.184 627 1135	.821 927 1068	4.451 822 3310	.224 627 1135	5
6	1.265 319 0185	6.632 975 4624	.150 761 9025	.790 314 5257	5 242 136 8567	.190 761 9025	6
7	1.315 931 7792	7.898 294 4809	.126 609 6120	.759 917 8132	6.002 054 6699	.166 609 6120	7
8	1.368 569 0504	9.214 226 2601	.108 527 8320	.730 690 2050	6.732 744 8750	.148 527 8320	8
9	1.423 311 8124	10.582 795 3105	.094 492 9927	.702 586 7356	7.435 331 6105	.134 492 9927	9
10	1.480 244 2849	12.006 107 1230	.083 290 9443	.675 564 1688	8.110 895 7794	.123 290 9443	10
11	1.539 454 0563	13.486 351 4079	.074 149 0393	.649 580 9316	8.760 476 7109	.114 149 0393	11
12	1.601 032 2186	15.025 805 4642	.066 552 1727	.624 597 0496	9.385 073 7605	.106 552 1727	12
13	1.665 073 5073	16.626 837 6828	.060 143 7278	.600 574 0861	9.985 647 8466	.100 143 7278	13
14	1.731 676 4476	18.291 911 1901	.054 668 9731	.577 475 0828	10.563 122 9295	.094 668 9731	14
15	1.800 943 5055	20.023 587 6377	.049 941 1004	.555 264 5027	11.118 387 4322	.089 941 1004	15
16	1.872 981 2457	21.824 531 1432	.045 819 9992	.533 908 1757	11.652 295 6079	.085 819 9992	16
17	1.947 900 4956	23.697 512 3889	.042 198 5221	.513 373 2459	12.165 668 8537	.082 198 5221	17
18	2.025 816 5154	25.645 412 8845	.038 993 3281	.493 628 1210	12.659 296 9747	.078 993 3281	18
19	2.106 849 1760	27.671 229 3998	.036 138 6184	.474 642 4240	13.133 939 3988	.076 138 6184	19
20	2.191 123 1430	29.778 078 5758	.033 581 7503	.456 386 9462	13.590 326 3450	.073 581 7503	20
21	2.278 768 0688	31.969 201 7189	.031 280 1054	.438 833 6021	14.029 159 9471	.071 280 1054	21
22	2.369 918 7915	34.247 969 7876	.029 198 8111	.421 955 3867	14.451 115 3337	.069 198 8111	22
23	2.464 715 5432	36.617 888 5791	.027 309 0568	.405 726 3333	14.856 841 6671	.067 309 0568	23
24	2.563 304 1649	39.082 604 1223	.025 586 8313	.390 121 4743	15.246 963 1414	.065 586 8313	24
25	2.665 836 3315	41.645 908 2872	.024 011 9628	.375 116 8023	15.622 079 9437	.064 011 9628	25
26	2.772 469 7847	44.311 744 6187	.022 567 3805	.360 689 2329	15.982 769 1766	.062 567 3805	26
27	2.883 368 5761	47.084 214 4034	.021 238 5406	.346 816 5701	16.329 585 7467	.061 238 5406	27
28	2.998 703 3192	49.967 582 9796	.020 012 9752	.333 477 4713	16.663 063 2180	.060 012 9752	28
29	3.118 651 4519	52.966 286 2987	.018 879 9342	.320 651 4147	16.983 714 6327	.058 879 9342	29
30	3.243 397 5100	56.084 937 7507	.017 830 0991	.308 318 6680	17.292 033 3007	.057 830 0991	30
31	3.373 133 4104	59.328 335 2607	.016 855 3524	.296 460 2577	17.588 493 5583	.056 855 3524	31
32	3.508 058 7468	62.701 468 6711	.015 948 5897	.285 057 9401	17.873 551 4984	.055 948 5897	32
33	3.648 381 0967	66.209 527 4180	.015 103 5665	.274 094 1731	18.147 645 6715	.055 103 5665	33
34	3.794 316 3406	69.857 908 5147	.014 314 7715	.263 552 0896	18.411 197 7611	.054 314 7715	34
35	3.946 088 9942	73.652 224 8553	.013 577 3224	.253 415 4707	18.664 613 2318	.053 577 3224	35
36	4.103 932 5540	77.598 313 8495	.012 886 8780	.243 668 7219	18.908 281 9537	.052 886 8780	36
37	4.268 089 8561	81.702 246 4035	.012 239 5655	.234 296 8479	19.142 578 8016	.052 239 5655	37
38	4.438 813 4504	85.970 336 2596	.011 631 9191	.225 285 4307	19.367 864 2323	.051 631 9191	38
39	4.616 365 9884	90.409 149 7100	.011 060 8274	.216 620 6064	19.584 484 8388	.051 060 8274	39
40	4.801 020 6279	95.025 515 6984	.010 523 4893	.208 289 0447	19.792 773 8834	.050 523 4893	40
41	4.993 061 4531	99.826 536 3264	.010 017 3765	.200 277 9276	19.993 051 8110	.050 017 3765	41
42	5.192 783 9112	104.819 597 7794	.009 540 2007	.192 574 9303	20.185 626 7413	.049 540 2007	42
43	5.400 495 2676	110.012 381 6906	.009 089 8859	.185 168 2023	20.370 794 9436	.049 089 8859	43
44	5.616 515 0783	115.412 876 9582	.008 664 5444	.178 046 3483	20.548 841 2919	.048 664 5444	44
45	5.841 175 6815	121.029 392 0365	.008 262 4558	.171 198 4118	20.720 039 7038	.048 262 4558	45
46	6.074 822 7087	126.870 567 7180	.007 882 0488	.164 613 8575	20.884 653 5613	.047 882 0488	46
47	6.317 815 6171	132.945 390 4267	.007 521 8855	.158 282 5553	21.042 936 1166	.047 521 8855	47
48	6.570 528 2418	139.263 206 0438	.007 180 6476	.152 194 7647	21.195 130 8814	.047 180 6476	48
49	6.833 349 3714	145.833 734 2855	.006 857 1240	.146 341 1199	21.341 472 0013	.046 857 1240	49
50	7.106 683 3463	152.667 083 6570	.006 550 2004	.140 712 6153	21.482 184 6167	.046 550 2004	50
51	7.390 950 6801	159.773 767 0032	.006 258 8497	.135 300 5917	21.617 485 2083	.046 258 8497	51
52	7.686 588 7073	167.164 717 6834	.005 982 1236	.130 096 7228	21.747 581 9311	.045 982 1236	52
53	7.994 052 2556	174.851 306 3907	.005 719 1451	.125 093 0027	21.872 674 9337	.045 719 1451	53
54	8.313 814 3459	182.845 358 6463	.005 469 1025	.120 281 7333	21.992 956 6671	.045 469 1025	54
55	8.646 366 9197	191.159 172 9922	.005 231 2426	.115 655 5128	22.108 612 1799	.045 231 2426	55
56	8.992 221 5965	199.805 539 9119	.005 004 8662	.111 207 2239	22.219 819 4037	.045 004 8662	56
57	9.351 910 4603	208.797 761 5083	.004 789 3234	.106 930 0229	22.326 749 4267	.044 789 3234	57
58	9.725 986 8787	218.149 671 9687	.004 584 0087	.102 817 3297	22.429 566 7564	.044 584 0087	58
59	10.115 026 3539	227.875 658 8474	.004 388 3581	.098 862 8171	22.528 429 5735	.044 388 3581	59
60	10.519 627 4081	237.990 685 2013	.004 201 8451	.095 060 4010	22.623 489 9745	.044 201 8451	60
61	10.940 412 5044	248.510 312 6094	.004 023 9779	.091 404 2318	22.714 894 2062	.044 023 9779	61
62	11.378 029 0045	259.450 725 1137	.003 854 2964	.087 888 6844	22.802 782 8906	.043 854 2964	62
63	11.833 150 1647	270.828 754 1183	.003 692 3701	.084 508 3504	22.887 291 2410	.043 692 3701	63
64	12.306 476 1713	282.661 904 2830	.003 537 7955	.081 258 0292	22.968 549 2702	.043 537 7955	64
65	12.798 735 2182	294.968 380 4544	.003 390 1939	.078 132 7204	23.046 681 9905	.043 390 1939	65
66	13.310 684 6269	307.767 115 6725	.003 249 2100	.075 127 6157	23.121 809 6063	.043 249 2100	66
67	13.843 112 0120	321.077 800 2994	.003 114 5099	.072 238 0921	23.194 047 6984	.043 114 5099	67
68	14.396 836 4925	334.920 912 3114	.002 985 7795	.069 459 7039	23.263 507 4023	.042 985 7795	68
69	14.972 709 9522	349.317 748 8039	.002 862 7231	.066 788 1768	23.330 295 5791	.042 862 7231	69
70	15.571 618 3502	364.290 458 7560	.002 745 0623	.064 219 4008	23.394 514 9799	.042 745 0623	70
71	16.194 483 0843	379.862 077 1063	.002 632 5344	.061 749 4238	23.456 264 4038	.042 632 5344	71
72	16.842 262 4076	396.056 560 1905	.002 524 8919	.059 374 4460	23.515 638 8498	.042 524 8919	72
73	17.515 952 9039	412.898 822 5981	.002 421 9008	.057 090 8135	23.572 729 6632	.042 421 9008	73
74	18.216 591 0201	430.414 775 5021	.002 323 3403	.054 895 0130	23.627 624 6762	.042 323 3403	74
75	18.945 254 6609	448.631 366 5221	.002 229 0015	.052 783 6663	23.680 408 3425	.042 229 0015	75
76	19.703 064 8473	467.576 621 1830	.002 138 6869	.050 753 5253	23.731 161 8678	.042 138 6869	76
77	20.491 187 4412	487.279 686 0303	.002 052 2095	.048 801 4666	23.779 963 3344	.042 052 2095	77
78	21.310 834 9389	507.770 873 4716	.001 969 3922	.046 924 4871	23.826 887 8215	.041 969 3922	78
79	22.163 268 3364	529.081 708 4104	.001 890 0672	.045 119 6992	23.872 007 5207	.041 890 0672	79
80	23.049 799 0699	551.244 976 7468	.001 814 0755	.043 384 3261	23.915 391 8468	.041 814 0755	80
81	23.971 791 0327	574.294 775 0167	.001 741 2661	.041 715 6982	23.957 107 5450	.041 741 2661	81
82	24.930 662 6740	598.266 566 8494	.001 671 4957	.040 111 2483	23.997 218 7933	.041 671 4957	82
83	25.927 889 1809	623.197 229 5233	.001 604 6284	.038 568 5079	24.035 787 3013	.041 604 6284	83
84	26.965 004 7482	649.125 118 7043	.001 540 5351	.037 085 1038	24.072 872 4050	.041 540 5351	84
85	28.043 604 9381	676.090 123 4525	.001 479 0928	.035 658 7537	24.108 531 1587	.041 479 0928	85
86	29.165 349 1356	704.133 728 3906	.001 420 1848	.034 287 2631	24.142 818 4218	.041 420 1848	86
87	30.331 963 1010	733.299 077 5262	.001 363 7001	.032 968 5222	24.175 786 9441	.041 363 7001	87
88	31.545 241 6251	763.631 040 6272	.001 309 5329	.031 700 5022	24.207 487 4462	.041 309 5329	88
89	32.807 051 2901	795.176 282 2523	.001 257 5828	.030 481 2521	24.237 968 6983	.041 257 5828	89
90	34.119 333 3417	827.983 333 5424	.001 207 7538	.029 308 8962	24.267 277 5945	.041 207 7538	90
91	35.484 106 6754	862.102 666 8841	.001 159 9547	.028 181 6310	24.295 459 2255	.041 159 9547	91
92	36.903 470 9424	897.586 773 5595	.001 114 0984	.027 097 7221	24.322 556 9476	.041 114 0984	92
93	38.379 609 7801	934.490 244 5018	.001 070 1021	.026 055 5020	24.348 612 4496	.041 070 1021	93
94	39.914 794 1713	972.869 854 2819	.001 027 8867	.025 053 3673	24.373 665 8169	.041 027 8867	94
95	41.511 385 9381	1012.784 648 4532	.000 987 3767	.024 089 7763	24.397 755 5932	.040 987 3767	95
96	43.171 841 3757	1054.296 034 3913	.000 948 5002	.023 163 2464	24.420 918 8396	.040 948 5002	96
97	44.898 715 0307	1097.467 875 7670	.000 911 1884	.022 272 3523	24.443 191 1919	.040 911 1884	97
98	46.694 663 6319	1142.366 590 7976	.000 875 3757	.021 415 7234	24.464 606 9153	.040 875 3757	98
99	48.562 450 1772	1189.061 254 4296	.000 840 9996	.020 592 0417	24.485 198 9570	.040 840 9996	99
100	50.504 948 1843	1237.623 704 6067	.000 808 0000	.019 800 0401	24.504 998 9972	.040 808 0000	100

653

	XIV COMPOUND AMOUNT	XV AMOUNT OF ANNUITY	XVI SINKING FUND	XVII PRESENT VALUE	XVIII PRESENT VALUE OF ANNUITY	XIX AMORTIZATION	
PERIODS	AMOUNT OF 1 — How $1 left at compound interest will grow.	AMOUNT OF 1 PER PERIOD — How $1 deposited periodically will grow.	SINKING FUND — Periodic deposit that will grow to $1 at future date.	PRESENT WORTH OF 1 — What $1 due in the future is worth today.	PRESENT WORTH OF 1 PER PERIOD — What $1 payable periodically is worth today.	PARTIAL PAYMENT — Annuity worth $1 today. Periodic payment necessary to pay off a loan of $1.	PERIODS
1	1.045 000 0000	1.000 000 0000	1.000 000 0000	.956 937 7990	.956 937 7990	1.045 000 0000	1
2	1.092 025 0000	2.045 000 0000	.488 997 5550	.915 729 9512	1.872 667 7503	.533 997 5550	2
3	1.141 166 1250	3.137 025 0000	.318 773 3601	.876 296 6041	2.748 964 3543	.363 773 3601	3
4	1.192 518 6006	4.278 191 1250	.233 743 6479	.838 561 3436	3.587 525 6979	.278 743 6479	4
5	1.246 181 9377	5.470 709 7256	.182 791 6395	.802 451 0465	4.389 976 7444	.227 791 6395	5
6	1.302 260 1248	6.716 891 6633	.148 878 3875	.767 895 7383	5.157 872 4827	.193 878 3875	6
7	1.360 861 8305	8.019 151 7881	.124 701 4680	.734 828 4577	5.892 700 9404	.169 701 4680	7
8	1.422 100 6128	9.380 013 6186	.106 609 6533	.703 185 1270	6.595 886 0674	.151 609 6533	8
9	1.486 095 1404	10.802 114 2314	.092 574 4700	.672 904 4277	7.268 790 4951	.137 574 4700	9
10	1.552 969 4217	12.288 209 3718	.081 378 8217	.643 927 6820	7.912 718 1771	.126 378 8217	10
11	1.622 853 0457	13.841 178 7936	.072 248 1817	.616 198 7388	8.528 916 9159	.117 248 1817	11
12	1.695 881 4328	15.464 031 8393	.064 666 1886	.589 663 8649	9.118 580 7808	.109 666 1886	12
13	1.772 196 0972	17.159 913 2721	.058 275 3528	.564 271 6410	9.682 852 4218	.103 275 3528	13
14	1.851 944 9216	18.932 109 3693	.052 820 3160	.539 972 8622	10.222 825 2840	.097 820 3160	14
15	1.935 282 4431	20.784 054 2909	.048 113 8061	.516 720 4423	10.739 545 7263	.093 113 8061	15
16	2.022 370 1530	22.719 336 7340	.044 015 3694	.494 469 3228	11.234 015 0491	.089 015 3694	16
17	2.113 376 8099	24.741 706 8870	.040 417 5833	.473 176 3854	11.707 191 4346	.085 417 5833	17
18	2.208 478 7664	26.855 083 6970	.037 236 8975	.452 800 3688	12.159 991 8034	.082 236 8975	18
19	2.307 860 3108	29.063 562 4633	.034 407 3443	.433 301 7884	12.593 293 5918	.079 407 3443	19
20	2.411 714 0248	31.371 422 7742	.031 876 1443	.414 642 8597	13.007 936 4515	.076 876 1443	20
21	2.520 241 1560	33.783 136 7990	.029 600 5669	.396 787 4255	13.404 723 8770	.074 600 5669	21
22	2.633 652 0080	36.303 377 9550	.027 545 6461	.379 700 8857	13.784 424 7627	.072 545 6461	22
23	2.752 166 3483	38.937 029 9629	.025 682 4930	.363 350 1298	14.147 774 8925	.070 682 4930	23
24	2.876 013 8340	41.689 196 3113	.023 987 0299	.347 703 4735	14.495 478 3660	.068 987 0299	24
25	3.005 434 4565	44.565 210 1453	.022 439 0280	.332 730 5967	14.828 208 9627	.067 439 0280	25
26	3.140 679 0071	47.570 644 6018	.021 021 3674	.318 402 4849	15.146 611 4476	.066 021 3674	26
27	3.282 009 5624	50.711 323 6089	.019 719 4616	.304 691 3731	15.451 302 8206	.064 719 4616	27
28	3.429 699 9927	53.993 333 1713	.018 520 8051	.291 570 6919	15.742 873 5126	.063 520 8051	28
29	3.584 036 4924	57.423 033 1640	.017 414 6147	.279 015 0162	16.021 888 5288	.062 414 6147	29
30	3.745 318 1345	61.007 069 6564	.016 391 5429	.267 000 0155	16.288 888 5443	.061 391 5429	30
31	3.913 857 4506	64.752 387 7909	.015 443 4459	.255 502 4072	16.544 390 9515	.060 443 4459	31
32	4.089 981 0359	68.666 245 2415	.014 563 1962	.244 499 9112	16.788 890 8627	.059 563 1962	32
33	4.274 030 1825	72.756 226 2774	.013 744 5281	.233 971 2069	17.022 862 0695	.058 744 5281	33
34	4.466 361 5407	77.030 256 4599	.012 981 9119	.223 895 8917	17.246 757 9613	.057 981 9119	34
35	4.667 347 8100	81.496 618 0005	.012 270 4478	.214 254 4419	17.461 012 4031	.057 270 4478	35
36	4.877 378 4615	86.163 965 8106	.011 605 7796	.205 028 1740	17.666 040 5772	.056 605 7796	36
37	5.096 860 4922	91.041 344 2720	.010 984 0206	.196 199 2096	17.862 239 7868	.055 984 0206	37
38	5.326 219 2144	96.138 204 7643	.010 401 6920	.187 750 4398	18.049 990 2266	.055 401 6920	38
39	5.565 899 0790	101.464 423 9787	.009 855 6712	.179 665 4926	18.229 655 7192	.054 855 6712	39
40	5.816 364 5376	107.030 323 0577	.009 343 1466	.171 928 7011	18.401 584 4203	.054 343 1466	40
41	6.078 100 9418	112.846 687 5953	.008 861 5804	.164 525 0728	18.566 109 4931	.053 861 5804	41
42	6.351 615 4842	118.924 788 5371	.008 408 6759	.157 440 2611	18.723 549 7542	.053 408 6759	42
43	6.637 438 1810	125.276 404 0213	.007 982 3492	.150 660 5369	18.874 210 2911	.052 982 3492	43
44	6.936 122 8991	131.913 842 2022	.007 580 7056	.144 172 7626	19.018 383 0536	.052 580 7056	44
45	7.248 248 4296	138.849 965 1013	.007 202 0184	.137 964 3661	19.156 347 4198	.052 202 0184	45
46	7.574 419 6089	146.098 213 5309	.006 844 7107	.132 023 3169	19.288 370 7366	.051 844 7107	46
47	7.915 268 4913	153.672 633 1398	.006 507 3395	.126 338 1023	19.414 708 8389	.051 507 3395	47
48	8.271 455 5734	161.587 901 6311	.006 188 5821	.120 897 7055	19.535 606 5444	.051 188 5821	48
49	8.643 671 0742	169.859 357 2045	.005 887 2235	.115 691 5842	19.651 298 1286	.050 887 2235	49
50	9.032 636 2725	178.503 028 2787	.005 602 1459	.110 709 6500	19.762 007 7785	.050 602 1459	50
51	9.439 104 9048	187.535 664 5512	.005 332 3191	.105 942 2488	19.867 950 0273	.050 332 3191	51
52	9.863 864 6255	196.974 769 4560	.005 076 7923	.101 380 1424	19.969 330 1697	.050 076 7923	52
53	10.307 738 5337	206.838 634 0815	.004 834 6867	.097 014 4903	20.066 344 6600	.049 834 6867	53
54	10.771 586 7677	217.146 372 6152	.004 605 1886	.092 836 8328	20.159 181 4928	.049 605 1886	54
55	11.256 308 1722	227.917 959 3829	.004 387 5437	.088 839 0745	20.248 020 5673	.049 387 5437	55
56	11.762 842 0400	239.174 267 5551	.004 181 0518	.085 013 4684	20.333 034 0357	.049 181 0518	56
57	12.292 169 9318	250.937 109 5951	.003 985 0622	.081 352 6013	20.414 386 6370	.048 985 0622	57
58	12.845 317 5787	263.229 279 5269	.003 798 9695	.077 849 3793	20.492 236 0163	.048 798 9695	58
59	13.423 356 8698	276.074 597 1056	.003 454 2558	.074 497 0137	20.566 733 0299	.048 622 2094	59
60	14.027 407 9289	289.497 953 9753	.003 454 2558	.071 289 0083	20.638 022 0382	.048 454 2558	60
61	14.658 641 2857	303.525 361 9042	.003 294 6176	.068 219 1467	20.706 241 1849	.048 294 6176	61
62	15.318 280 1435	318.184 003 1899	.003 142 8356	.065 281 4801	20.771 522 6650	.048 142 8356	62
63	16.007 602 7500	333.502 283 3335	.002 998 4802	.062 470 3159	20.833 992 9808	.047 998 4802	63
64	16.727 944 8738	349.509 886 0835	.002 861 1494	.059 780 2066	20.893 773 1874	.047 861 1494	64
65	17.480 702 3931	366.237 830 9572	.002 730 4661	.057 205 9393	20.950 979 1267	.047 730 4661	65
66	18.267 334 0008	383.718 533 3503	.002 606 0769	.054 742 5256	21.005 721 6523	.047 606 0769	66
67	19.089 364 0308	401.985 867 3511	.002 487 6496	.052 385 1920	21.058 106 8443	.047 487 6496	67
68	19.948 385 4122	421.075 231 3819	.002 374 8725	.050 129 3703	21.108 236 2147	.047 374 8725	68
69	20.846 062 7557	441.023 616 7941	.002 267 4523	.047 970 6893	21.156 206 9040	.047 267 4523	69
70	21.784 135 5797	461.869 679 5498	.002 165 1129	.045 904 9659	21.202 111 8699	.047 165 1129	70
71	22.764 421 6808	483.653 815 1295	.002 067 5946	.043 928 1970	21.246 040 0668	.047 067 5946	71
72	23.788 820 6565	506.418 236 8104	.001 974 6524	.042 036 5521	21.288 076 6190	.046 974 6524	72
73	24.859 317 5860	530.207 057 4668	.001 886 0556	.040 226 3657	21.328 302 9847	.046 886 0556	73
74	25.977 986 8774	555.066 375 0528	.001 801 5863	.038 494 1298	21.366 797 1145	.046 801 5863	74
75	27.146 996 2869	581.044 361 9302	.001 721 0390	.036 836 4879	21.403 633 6024	.046 721 0390	75
76	28.368 611 1198	608.191 358 2171	.001 644 2194	.035 250 2276	21.438 883 8301	.046 644 2194	76
77	29.645 198 6202	636.559 969 3368	.001 570 9439	.033 732 2753	21.472 616 1053	.046 570 9439	77
78	30.979 232 5581	666.205 167 9570	.001 501 0391	.032 279 6892	21.504 895 7946	.046 501 0391	78
79	32.373 298 0232	697.184 400 5151	.001 434 3408	.030 889 6548	21.535 785 4494	.046 434 3408	79
80	33.830 096 4342	729.557 698 5382	.001 370 6935	.029 559 4783	21.565 344 9276	.046 370 6935	80
81	35.352 450 7738	763.387 794 9725	.001 309 9502	.028 286 5821	21.593 631 5097	.046 309 9502	81
82	36.943 311 0586	798.740 245 7462	.001 251 9715	.027 068 4996	21.620 700 0093	.046 251 9715	82
83	38.605 760 0562	835.683 556 8048	.001 196 6252	.025 902 8704	21.646 602 8797	.046 196 6252	83
84	40.343 019 2587	874.289 316 8610	.001 143 7861	.024 787 4358	21.671 390 3155	.046 143 7861	84
85	42.158 455 1254	914.632 336 1198	.001 093 3355	.023 720 0343	21.695 110 3497	.046 093 3355	85
86	44.055 585 6060	956.790 791 2452	.001 045 1606	.022 698 5974	21.717 808 9471	.046 045 1606	86
87	46.038 086 9583	1000.846 376 8512	.000 999 1543	.021 721 1458	21.739 530 0929	.045 999 1543	87
88	48.109 800 8714	1046.884 463 8095	.000 955 2152	.020 785 7855	21.760 315 8784	.045 955 2152	88
89	50.274 741 9106	1094.994 264 6809	.000 913 2468	.019 890 7038	21.780 206 5822	.045 913 2468	89
90	52.537 105 2966	1145.269 006 5916	.000 873 1573	.019 034 1663	21.799 240 7485	.045 873 1573	90
91	54.901 275 0350	1197.806 111 8882	.000 834 8597	.018 214 5132	21.817 455 2617	.045 834 8597	91
92	57.371 832 4115	1252.707 386 9232	.000 798 2710	.017 430 1562	21.834 885 4179	.045 798 2710	92
93	59.953 564 8701	1310.079 219 3347	.000 763 3126	.016 679 5753	21.851 564 9932	.045 763 3126	93
94	62.651 475 2893	1370.032 784 2048	.000 729 9095	.015 961 3161	21.867 526 3093	.045 729 9095	94
95	65.470 791 6772	1432.684 259 4940	.000 697 9905	.015 273 9867	21.882 800 2960	.045 697 9905	95
96	68.416 977 3027	1498.155 051 1712	.000 667 4877	.014 616 2552	21.897 416 5512	.045 667 4877	96
97	71.495 741 2813	1566.572 028 4739	.000 638 3364	.013 986 8471	21.911 403 3983	.045 638 3364	97
98	74.713 049 6390	1638.067 769 7552	.000 610 4754	.013 384 5427	21.924 787 9409	.045 610 4754	98
99	78.075 136 8727	1712.780 819 3942	.000 583 8459	.012 808 1748	21.937 596 1157	.045 583 8459	99
100	81.588 518 0320	1790.855 956 2670	.000 558 3922	.012 256 6266	21.949 852 7423	.045 558 3922	100

		XIV COMPOUND AMOUNT	XV AMOUNT OF ANNUITY	XVI SINKING FUND	XVII PRESENT VALUE	XVIII PRESENT VALUE OF ANNUITY	XIX AMORTIZATION	
RATE 5%	PERIODS	AMOUNT OF 1 How $1 left at compound interest will grow.	AMOUNT OF 1 PER PERIOD How $1 deposited periodically will grow.	SINKING FUND Periodic deposit that will grow to $1 at future date.	PRESENT WORTH OF 1 What $1 due in the future is worth today.	PRESENT WORTH OF 1 PER PERIOD What $1 payable periodically is worth today.	PARTIAL PAYMENT Annuity worth $1 today. Periodic payment necessary to pay off a loan of $1.	PERIODS
	1	1.050 000 0000	1.000 000 0000	1.000 000 0000	.952 380 9524	.952 380 9524	1.050 000 0000	1
	2	1.102 500 0000	2.050 000 0000	.487 804 8780	.907 029 4785	1.859 410 4308	.537 804 8780	2
	3	1.157 625 0000	3.152 500 0000	.317 208 5646	.863 837 5985	2.723 248 0294	.367 208 5646	3
	4	1.215 506 2500	4.310 125 0000	.232 011 8326	.822 702 4748	3.545 950 5042	.282 011 8326	4
	5	1.276 281 5625	5.525 631 2500	.180 974 7981	.783 526 1665	4.329 476 6706	.230 974 7981	5
	6	1.340 095 6406	6.801 912 8125	.147 017 4681	.746 215 3966	5.075 692 0673	.197 017 4681	6
	7	1.407 100 4227	8.142 008 4531	.122 819 8184	.710 681 3301	5.786 373 3974	.172 819 8184	7
	8	1.477 455 4438	9.549 108 8758	.104 721 8136	.676 839 3620	6.463 212 7594	.154 721 8136	8
	9	1.551 328 2160	11.026 564 3196	.090 690 0800	.644 608 9162	7.107 821 6756	.140 690 0800	9
	10	1.628 894 6268	12.577 892 5355	.079 504 5750	.613 913 2535	7.721 734 9292	.129 504 5750	10
	11	1.710 339 3581	14.206 787 1623	.070 388 8915	.584 679 2891	8.306 414 2183	.120 388 8915	11
	12	1.795 856 3260	15.917 126 5204	.062 825 4100	.556 837 4182	8.863 251 6364	.112 825 4100	12
	13	1.885 649 1423	17.712 982 8465	.056 455 7652	.530 321 3506	9.393 572 9871	.106 455 7652	13
	14	1.979 931 5994	19.598 631 9888	.051 023 9695	.505 067 9530	9.898 640 9401	.101 023 9695	14
	15	2.078 928 1794	21.578 563 5882	.046 342 2876	.481 017 0981	10.379 658 0382	.096 342 2876	15
	16	2.182 874 5884	23.657 491 7676	.042 269 9080	.458 111 5220	10.837 769 5602	.092 269 9080	16
	17	2.292 018 3178	25.840 366 3560	.038 699 1417	.436 296 6876	11.274 066 2478	.088 699 1417	17
	18	2.406 619 2337	28.132 384 6738	.035 546 2223	.415 520 6549	11.689 586 9027	.085 546 2223	18
	19	2.526 950 1954	30.539 003 9075	.032 745 0104	.395 733 9570	12.085 320 8597	.082 745 0104	19
	20	2.653 297 7051	33.065 954 1029	.030 242 5872	.376 889 4829	12.462 210 3425	.080 242 5872	20
	21	2.785 962 5904	35.719 251 8080	.027 996 1071	.358 942 3646	12.821 152 7072	.077 996 1071	21
	22	2.925 260 7199	38.505 214 3984	.025 970 5086	.341 849 8711	13.163 002 5783	.075 970 5086	22
	23	3.071 523 7559	41.430 475 1184	.024 136 8219	.325 571 3058	13.488 573 8841	.074 136 8219	23
	24	3.225 099 9437	44.501 998 8743	.022 470 9008	.310 067 9103	13.798 641 7943	.072 470 9008	24
	25	3.386 354 9409	47.727 098 8180	.020 952 4573	.295 302 7717	14.093 944 5660	.070 952 4573	25
	26	3.555 672 6879	51.113 453 7589	.019 564 3207	.281 240 7350	14.375 185 3010	.069 564 3207	26
	27	3.733 456 3223	54.669 126 4468	.018 291 8599	.267 848 3190	14.643 033 6200	.068 291 8599	27
	28	3.920 129 1385	58.402 582 7692	.017 122 5304	.255 093 6371	14.898 127 2571	.067 122 5304	28
	29	4.116 135 5954	62.322 711 9076	.016 045 5149	.242 946 3211	15.141 073 5782	.066 045 5149	29
	30	4.321 942 3752	66.438 847 5030	.015 051 4351	.231 377 4487	15.372 451 0269	.065 051 4351	30
	31	4.538 039 4939	70.760 789 8782	.014 132 1204	.220 359 4749	15.592 810 5018	.064 132 1204	31
	32	4.764 941 4686	75.298 829 3721	.013 280 4189	.209 866 1666	15.802 676 6684	.063 280 4189	32
	33	5.003 188 5420	80.063 770 8407	.012 490 0437	.199 872 5396	16.002 549 2080	.062 490 0437	33
	34	5.253 347 9691	85.066 959 3827	.011 755 4454	.190 354 7996	16.192 904 0076	.061 755 4454	34
	35	5.516 015 3676	90.320 307 3518	.011 071 7072	.181 290 2854	16.374 194 2929	.061 071 7072	35
	36	5.791 816 1360	95.836 322 7194	.010 434 4571	.172 657 4146	16.546 851 7076	.060 434 4571	36
	37	6.081 406 9428	101.628 138 8554	.009 839 7945	.164 435 6330	16.711 287 3405	.059 839 7945	37
	38	6.385 477 2899	107.709 545 7982	.009 284 2282	.156 605 3647	16.867 892 7053	.059 284 2282	38
	39	6.704 751 1544	114.095 023 0881	.008 764 6242	.149 147 9664	17.017 040 6717	.058 764 6242	39
	40	7.039 988 7121	120.799 774 2425	.008 278 1612	.142 045 6823	17.159 086 3540	.058 278 1612	40
	41	7.391 988 1477	127.839 762 9546	.007 822 2924	.135 281 6022	17.294 367 9562	.057 822 2924	41
	42	7.761 587 5551	135.231 751 1023	.007 394 7131	.128 839 6211	17.423 207 5773	.057 394 7131	42
	43	8.149 666 9329	142.993 338 6575	.006 993 3328	.122 704 4011	17.545 911 9784	.056 993 3328	43
	44	8.557 150 2795	151.143 005 5903	.006 616 2506	.116 861 3344	17.662 773 3128	.056 616 2506	44
	45	8.985 007 7935	159.700 155 8699	.006 261 7347	.111 296 5089	17.774 069 8217	.056 261 7347	45
	46	9.434 258 1832	168.685 163 6633	.005 928 2036	.105 996 6752	17.880 066 4968	.055 928 2036	46
	47	9.905 971 0923	178.119 421 8465	.005 614 2109	.100 949 2144	17.981 015 7113	.055 614 2109	47
	48	10.401 269 6469	188.025 392 9388	.005 318 4306	.096 142 1090	18.077 157 8203	.055 318 4306	48
	49	10.921 333 1293	198.426 662 5858	.005 039 6453	.091 563 9133	18.168 721 7336	.055 039 6453	49
	50	11.467 399 7858	209.347 995 7151	.004 776 7355	.087 203 7270	18.255 925 4606	.054 776 7355	50
	51	12.040 769 7750	220.815 395 5008	.004 528 6697	.083 051 1685	18.338 976 6291	.054 528 6697	51
	52	12.642 808 2638	232.856 165 2759	.004 294 4966	.079 096 3510	18.418 072 9801	.054 294 4966	52
	53	13.274 948 6770	245.498 973 5397	.004 073 3368	.075 329 8581	18.493 402 8382	.054 073 3368	53
	54	13.938 696 1108	258.773 922 2166	.003 864 3770	.071 742 7220	18.565 145 5602	.053 864 3770	54
	55	14.635 630 9164	272.712 618 3275	.003 666 8637	.068 326 4019	18.633 471 9621	.053 666 8637	55
	56	15.367 412 4622	287.348 249 2439	.003 480 0978	.065 072 7637	18.698 544 7258	.053 480 0978	56
	57	16.135 783 0853	302.715 661 7060	.003 303 4300	.061 974 0607	18.760 518 7865	.053 303 4300	57
	58	16.942 572 2396	318.851 444 7913	.003 136 2568	.059 022 9149	18.819 541 7014	.053 136 2568	58
	59	17.789 700 8515	335.794 017 0309	.002 978 0161	.056 212 2999	18.875 754 0013	.053 070 0101	59
	60	18.679 185 8941	353.583 717 8825	.002 828 1045	.053 535 5237	18.929 289 5251	.052 828 1845	60
	61	19.613 145 1888	372.262 903 7766	.002 686 2736	.050 986 2131	18.980 275 7382	.052 686 2736	61
	62	20.593 802 4483	391.876 048 9654	.002 551 8273	.048 558 2982	19.028 834 0363	.052 551 8273	62
	63	21.623 492 5707	412.469 851 4137	.002 424 4196	.046 245 9983	19.075 080 0346	.052 424 4196	63
	64	22.704 667 1992	434.093 343 9844	.002 303 6520	.044 043 8079	19.119 123 8425	.052 303 6520	64
	65	23.839 900 5592	456.798 011 1836	.002 189 1514	.041 946 4837	19.161 070 3262	.052 189 1514	65
	66	25.031 895 5871	480.637 911 7428	.002 080 5683	.039 949 0321	19.201 019 3583	.052 080 5683	66
	67	26.283 490 3665	505.669 807 3299	.001 977 5751	.038 046 6972	19.239 066 0555	.051 977 5751	67
	68	27.597 664 8848	531.953 297 6964	.001 879 8643	.036 234 9497	19.275 301 0052	.051 879 8643	68
	69	28.977 548 1291	559.550 962 5812	.001 787 1473	.034 509 4759	19.309 810 4812	.051 787 1473	69
	70	30.426 425 5355	588.528 510 7103	.001 699 1530	.032 866 1676	19.342 676 6487	.051 699 1530	70
	71	31.947 746 8123	618.954 936 2458	.001 615 6265	.031 301 1120	19.373 977 7607	.051 615 6265	71
	72	33.545 134 1529	650.902 683 0581	.001 536 3280	.029 810 5828	19.403 788 3435	.051 536 3280	72
	73	35.222 390 8605	684.447 817 2110	.001 461 0318	.028 391 0313	19.432 179 3748	.051 461 0318	73
	74	36.983 510 4036	719.670 208 0715	.001 389 5254	.027 039 0774	19.459 218 4522	.051 389 5254	74
	75	38.832 685 9238	756.653 718 4751	.001 321 6085	.025 751 5023	19.484 969 9545	.051 321 6085	75
	76	40.774 320 2199	795.486 404 3989	.001 257 0925	.024 525 2403	19.509 495 1947	.051 257 0925	76
	77	42.813 036 2309	836.260 724 6188	.001 195 7993	.023 357 3717	19.532 852 5664	.051 195 7993	77
	78	44.953 688 0425	879.073 760 8497	.001 137 5610	.022 245 1159	19.555 097 6823	.051 137 5610	78
	79	47.201 372 4446	924.027 448 8922	.001 082 2189	.021 185 8247	19.576 283 5069	.051 082 2189	79
	80	49.561 441 0668	971.228 821 3368	.001 029 6235	.020 176 9759	19.596 460 4828	.051 029 6235	80
	81	52.039 513 1202	1020.790 262 4037	.000 979 6332	.019 216 1675	19.615 676 6503	.050 979 6332	81
	82	54.641 488 7762	1072.829 775 5239	.000 932 1143	.018 301 1119	19.633 977 7622	.050 932 1143	82
	83	57.373 563 2150	1127.471 264 3001	.000 886 9406	.017 429 6304	19.651 407 3925	.050 886 9406	83
	84	60.242 241 3758	1184.844 827 5151	.000 843 9924	.016 599 6480	19.668 007 0405	.050 843 9924	84
	85	63.254 353 4445	1245.087 068 8908	.000 803 1567	.015 809 1885	19.683 816 2291	.050 803 1567	85
	86	66.417 071 1168	1308.341 422 3354	.000 764 3265	.015 056 3700	19.698 872 5991	.050 764 3265	86
	87	69.737 924 6726	1374.758 493 4521	.000 727 4005	.014 339 4000	19.713 211 9992	.050 727 4005	87
	88	73.224 820 9062	1444.496 418 1247	.000 692 2828	.013 656 5715	19.726 868 5706	.050 692 2828	88
	89	76.886 061 9515	1517.721 239 0310	.000 658 8825	.013 006 2585	19.739 874 8292	.050 658 8825	89
	90	80.730 365 0491	1594.607 300 9825	.000 627 1136	.012 386 9129	19.752 261 7421	.050 627 1136	90
	91	84.766 883 3016	1675.337 666 0317	.000 596 8946	.011 797 0599	19.764 058 8020	.050 596 8946	91
	92	89.005 227 4667	1760.104 549 3332	.000 568 1481	.011 235 2951	19.775 294 0971	.050 568 1481	92
	93	93.455 488 8400	1849.109 776 7999	.000 540 8008	.010 700 2811	19.785 994 3782	.050 540 8008	93
	94	98.128 263 2820	1942.565 265 6399	.000 514 7832	.010 190 7439	19.796 185 1221	.050 514 7832	94
	95	103.034 676 4461	2040.693 528 9219	.000 490 0295	.009 706 4704	19.805 890 5925	.050 490 0295	95
	96	108.186 410 2684	2143.728 205 3680	.000 466 4770	.009 243 3061	19.815 133 8976	.050 466 4770	96
	97	113.595 730 7818	2251.914 615 6364	.000 444 0666	.008 803 1477	19.823 937 0453	.050 444 0666	97
	98	119.275 517 3209	2365.510 346 4182	.000 422 7418	.008 383 9502	19.832 320 9955	.050 422 7418	98
	99	125.239 293 1870	2484.785 863 7391	.000 402 4492	.007 984 7145	19.840 305 7100	.050 402 4492	99
	100	131.501 257 8463	2610.025 156 9261	.000 383 1381	.007 604 4900	19.847 910 2000	.050 383 1381	100

RATE 6% PERIODS	XIV COMPOUND AMOUNT — AMOUNT OF 1 — How $1 left at compound interest will grow.	XV AMOUNT OF ANNUITY — AMOUNT OF 1 PER PERIOD — How $1 deposited periodically will grow.	XVI SINKING FUND — SINKING FUND — Periodic deposit that will grow to $1 at future date.	XVII PRESENT VALUE — PRESENT WORTH OF 1 — What $1 due in the future is worth today.	XVIII PRESENT VALUE OF ANNUITY — PRESENT WORTH OF 1 PER PERIOD — What $1 payable periodically is worth today.	XIX AMORTIZATION — PARTIAL PAYMENT — Annuity worth $1 today. Periodic payment necessary to pay off a loan of $1.	PERIODS
1	1.060 000 0000	1.000 000 0000	1.000 000 0000	.943 396 2264	.943 396 2264	1.060 000 0000	1
2	1.123 600 0000	2.060 000 0000	.485 436 8932	.889 996 4400	1.833 392 6664	.545 436 8932	2
3	1.191 016 0000	3.183 600 0000	.314 109 8128	.839 619 2830	2.673 011 9495	.374 109 8128	3
4	1.262 476 9600	4.374 616 0000	.228 591 4924	.792 093 6632	3.465 105 6127	.288 591 4924	4
5	1.338 225 5776	5.637 092 9600	.177 396 4004	.747 258 1729	4.212 363 7856	.237 396 4004	5
6	1.418 519 1123	6.975 318 5376	.143 362 6285	.704 960 5404	4.917 324 3260	.203 362 6285	6
7	1.503 630 2590	8.393 837 6499	.119 135 0181	.665 057 1136	5.582 381 4396	.179 135 0181	7
8	1.593 848 0745	9.897 467 9088	.101 035 9426	.627 412 3713	6.209 793 8110	.161 035 9426	8
9	1.689 478 9590	11.491 315 9834	.087 022 2350	.591 898 4635	6.801 692 2745	.147 022 2350	9
10	1.790 847 6965	13.180 794 9424	.075 867 9582	.558 394 7769	7.360 087 0514	.135 867 9582	10
11	1.898 298 5583	14.971 642 6389	.066 792 9381	.526 787 5254	7.886 874 5768	.126 792 9381	11
12	2.012 196 4718	16.869 941 1973	.059 277 0294	.496 969 3636	8.383 843 9404	.119 277 0294	12
13	2.132 928 2601	18.882 137 6691	.052 960 1053	.468 839 0222	8.852 682 9626	.112 960 1053	13
14	2.260 903 9558	21.015 065 9292	.047 584 9090	.442 300 9644	9.294 983 9270	.107 584 9090	14
15	2.396 558 1931	23.275 969 8850	.042 962 7640	.417 265 0607	9.712 248 9877	.102 962 7640	15
16	2.540 351 6847	25.672 528 0781	.038 952 1436	.393 646 2837	10.105 895 2715	.098 952 1436	16
17	2.692 772 7858	28.212 879 7628	.035 444 8042	.371 364 4186	10.477 259 6901	.095 444 8042	17
18	2.854 339 1529	30.905 652 5485	.032 356 5406	.350 343 7911	10.827 603 4812	.092 356 5406	18
19	3.025 599 5021	33.759 991 7015	.029 620 8604	.330 513 0105	11.158 116 4917	.089 620 8604	19
20	3.207 135 4722	36.785 591 2035	.027 184 5570	.311 804 7269	11.469 921 2186	.087 184 5570	20
21	3.399 563 6005	39.992 726 6758	.025 004 5467	.294 155 4027	11.764 076 6213	.085 004 5467	21
22	3.603 537 4166	43.392 290 2763	.023 045 5685	.277 505 0969	12.041 581 7182	.083 045 5685	22
23	3.819 749 6616	46.995 827 6929	.021 278 4847	.261 797 2612	12.303 378 9794	.081 278 4847	23
24	4.048 934 6413	50.815 577 3545	.019 679 0050	.246 978 5483	12.550 357 5278	.079 679 0050	24
25	4.291 870 7197	54.864 511 9957	.018 226 7182	.232 998 6305	12.783 356 1583	.078 226 7182	25
26	4.549 382 9629	59.156 382 7155	.016 904 3467	.219 810 0288	13.003 166 1870	.076 904 3467	26
27	4.822 345 9407	63.705 765 6784	.015 697 1663	.207 367 9517	13.210 534 1387	.075 697 1663	27
28	5.111 686 6971	68.528 111 6191	.014 592 5515	.195 630 1431	13.406 164 2818	.074 592 5515	28
29	5.418 387 8990	73.639 798 3162	.013 579 6135	.184 556 7388	13.590 721 0206	.073 579 6135	29
30	5.743 491 1729	79.058 186 2152	.012 648 9115	.174 110 1309	13.764 831 1515	.072 648 9115	30
31	6.088 100 6433	84.801 677 3881	.011 792 2196	.164 254 8405	13.929 085 9920	.071 792 2196	31
32	6.453 386 6819	90.889 778 0314	.011 002 3374	.154 957 3967	14.084 043 3887	.071 002 3374	32
33	6.840 589 9828	97.343 164 7133	.010 272 9350	.146 186 2233	14.230 229 6119	.070 272 9350	33
34	7.251 025 2758	104.183 754 5961	.009 598 4254	.137 911 5314	14.368 141 1433	.069 598 4254	34
35	7.686 086 7923	111.434 779 8719	.008 973 8590	.130 105 2183	14.498 246 3616	.068 973 8590	35
36	8.147 251 9999	119.120 866 6642	.008 394 8348	.122 740 7720	14.620 987 1336	.068 394 8348	36
37	8.636 087 1198	127.268 118 6640	.007 857 4274	.115 793 1811	14.736 780 3147	.067 857 4274	37
38	9.154 252 3470	135.904 205 7839	.007 358 1240	.109 238 8501	14.846 019 1648	.067 358 1240	38
39	9.703 507 4879	145.058 458 1309	.006 893 7724	.103 055 5190	14.949 074 6838	.066 893 7724	39
40	10.285 717 9371	154.761 965 6188	.006 461 5359	.097 222 1877	15.046 296 8715	.066 461 5359	40
41	10.902 861 0134	165.047 683 5559	.006 058 8551	.091 719 0450	15.138 015 9165	.066 058 8551	41
42	11.557 032 6742	175.950 544 5692	.005 683 4152	.086 527 4010	15.224 543 3175	.065 683 4152	42
43	12.250 454 6346	187.507 577 2434	.005 333 1178	.081 629 6235	15.306 172 9410	.065 333 1178	43
44	12.985 481 9127	199.758 031 8780	.005 006 0565	.077 009 0788	15.383 182 0198	.065 006 0565	44
45	13.764 610 8274	212.743 513 7907	.004 700 4958	.072 650 0743	15.455 832 0942	.064 700 4958	45
46	14.590 487 4771	226.508 124 6181	.004 414 8527	.068 537 8060	15.524 369 9002	.064 414 8527	46
47	15.465 916 7257	241.098 612 0952	.004 147 6805	.064 658 3075	15.589 028 2077	.064 147 6805	47
48	16.393 871 7293	256.564 528 8209	.003 897 6549	.060 998 4033	15.650 026 6110	.063 897 6549	48
49	17.377 504 0330	272.958 400 5502	.003 663 5619	.057 545 6635	15.707 572 2746	.063 663 5619	49
50	18.420 154 2750	290.335 904 5832	.003 444 2864	.054 288 3618	15.761 860 6364	.063 444 2864	50
51	19.525 363 5315	308.756 058 8582	.003 238 8028	.051 215 4357	15.813 076 0721	.063 238 8028	51
52	20.696 885 3434	328.281 422 3897	.003 046 1669	.048 316 4488	15.861 392 5208	.063 046 1669	52
53	21.938 698 4640	348.978 307 7331	.002 865 5076	.045 581 5554	15.906 974 0762	.062 865 5076	53
54	23.255 020 3718	370.917 006 1970	.002 696 0209	.043 001 4674	15.949 975 5436	.062 696 0209	54
55	24.650 321 5941	394.172 026 5689	.002 536 9634	.040 567 4221	15.990 542 9657	.062 536 9634	55
56	26.129 340 8898	418.822 348 1630	.002 387 6472	.038 271 1529	16.028 814 1186	.062 387 6472	56
57	27.697 101 3432	444.951 689 0528	.002 247 4350	.036 104 8612	16.064 918 9798	.062 247 4350	57
58	29.358 927 4238	472.648 790 3959	.002 115 7359	.034 061 1898	16.098 980 1696	.062 115 7359	58
59	31.120 463 0692	502.007 717 8197	.001 992 0012	.032 133 1979	16.131 113 3676	.061 992 0012	59
60	32.987 690 8533	533.128 180 8889	.001 875 7215	.030 314 3377	16.161 427 7052	.061 875 7215	60
61	34.966 952 3045	566.115 871 7422	.001 766 4228	.028 598 4318	16.190 026 1370	.061 766 4228	61
62	37.064 969 4428	601.082 824 0467	.001 663 6642	.026 979 6526	16.217 005 7896	.061 663 6642	62
63	39.288 867 6094	638.147 793 4895	.001 567 0351	.025 452 5025	16.242 458 2921	.061 567 0351	63
64	41.646 199 6659	677.436 661 0989	.001 476 1528	.024 011 7948	16.266 470 0869	.061 476 1528	64
65	44.144 971 6459	719.082 860 7649	.001 390 6603	.022 652 6366	16.289 122 7235	.061 390 6603	65
66	46.793 669 9446	763.227 832 4107	.001 310 2248	.021 370 4119	16.310 493 1354	.061 310 2248	66
67	49.601 290 1413	810.021 502 3554	.001 234 5351	.020 160 7659	16.330 653 9013	.061 234 5351	67
68	52.577 367 5498	859.622 792 4967	.001 163 3009	.019 019 5905	16.349 673 4918	.061 163 3009	68
69	55.732 009 6028	912.200 160 0465	.001 096 2506	.017 943 0099	16.367 616 5017	.061 096 2506	69
70	59.075 930 1790	967.932 169 6493	.001 033 1302	.016 927 3678	16.384 543 8695	.061 033 1302	70
71	62.620 485 9897	1027.008 099 8283	.000 973 7022	.015 969 2149	16.400 513 0844	.060 973 7022	71
72	66.377 715 1491	1089.628 585 8180	.000 917 7439	.015 065 2971	16.415 578 3816	.060 917 7439	72
73	70.360 378 0580	1156.006 300 9670	.000 865 0472	.014 212 5444	16.429 790 9260	.060 865 0472	73
74	74.582 000 7415	1226.366 679 0251	.000 815 4168	.013 408 0608	16.443 198 9868	.060 815 4168	74
75	79.056 920 7860	1300.948 679 7666	.000 768 6698	.012 649 1140	16.455 848 1007	.060 768 6698	75
76	83.800 336 0332	1380.005 600 5526	.000 724 6347	.011 933 1264	16.467 781 2271	.060 724 6347	76
77	88.828 356 1951	1463.805 936 5857	.000 683 1507	.011 257 6664	16.479 038 8935	.060 683 1507	77
78	94.158 057 5669	1552.634 292 7808	.000 644 0667	.010 620 4400	16.489 659 3335	.060 644 0667	78
79	99.807 541 0209	1646.792 350 3477	.000 607 2411	.010 019 2830	16.499 678 6165	.060 607 2411	79
80	105.795 993 4821	1746.599 891 3686	.000 572 5410	.009 452 1538	16.509 130 7703	.060 572 5410	80
81	112.143 753 0910	1852.395 884 8507	.000 539 8414	.008 917 1262	16.518 047 8965	.060 539 8414	81
82	118.872 378 2765	1964.539 637 9417	.000 509 0251	.008 412 3832	16.526 460 2797	.060 509 0251	82
83	126.004 720 9731	2083.412 016 2182	.000 479 9819	.007 936 2106	16.534 396 4903	.060 479 9819	83
84	133.565 004 2315	2209.416 737 1913	.000 452 6081	.007 486 9911	16.541 883 4814	.060 452 6081	84
85	141.578 904 4854	2342.981 741 4228	.000 426 8066	.007 063 1992	16.548 946 6806	.060 426 8066	85
86	150.073 638 7545	2484.560 645 9082	.000 402 4856	.006 663 3954	16.555 610 0760	.060 402 4856	86
87	159.078 057 0798	2634.634 284 6626	.000 379 5593	.006 286 2221	16.561 896 2981	.060 379 5593	87
88	168.622 740 5045	2793.712 341 7424	.000 357 9467	.005 930 3982	16.567 826 6963	.060 357 9467	88
89	178.740 104 9348	2962.335 082 2469	.000 337 5715	.005 594 7153	16.573 421 4116	.060 337 5715	89
90	189.464 511 2309	3141.075 187 1818	.000 318 3623	.005 278 0333	16.578 699 4450	.060 318 3623	90
91	200.832 381 9048	3330.539 698 4127	.000 300 2516	.004 979 2767	16.583 678 7217	.060 300 2516	91
92	212.882 324 8190	3531.372 080 3174	.000 283 1761	.004 697 4308	16.588 376 1525	.060 283 1761	92
93	225.655 264 3082	3744.254 405 1365	.000 267 0759	.004 431 5385	16.592 807 6910	.060 267 0759	93
94	239.194 580 1667	3969.909 669 4447	.000 251 8949	.004 180 6967	16.596 988 3878	.060 251 8949	94
95	253.546 254 9767	4209.104 249 6113	.000 237 5802	.003 944 0535	16.600 932 4413	.060 237 5802	95
96	268.759 030 2753	4462.650 504 5880	.000 224 0821	.003 720 8052	16.604 653 2465	.060 224 0821	96
97	284.884 572 0918	4731.409 534 8633	.000 211 3535	.003 510 1936	16.608 163 4401	.060 211 3535	97
98	301.977 646 4173	5016.294 106 9551	.000 199 3504	.003 311 5034	16.611 474 9435	.060 199 3504	98
99	320.096 305 2023	5318.271 753 3724	.000 188 0310	.003 124 0598	16.614 599 0033	.060 188 0310	99
100	339.302 083 5145	5638.368 058 5748	.000 177 3563	.002 947 2262	16.617 546 2295	.060 177 3563	100

656

		XIV COMPOUND AMOUNT	XV AMOUNT OF ANNUITY	XVI SINKING FUND	XVII PRESENT VALUE	XVIII PRESENT VALUE OF ANNUITY	XIX AMORTIZATION	
	P E R I O D S	AMOUNT OF 1 — How $1 left at compound interest will grow.	AMOUNT OF 1 PER PERIOD — How $1 deposited periodically will grow.	SINKING FUND — Periodic deposit that will grow to $1 at future date.	PRESENT WORTH OF 1 — What $1 due in the future is worth today.	PRESENT WORTH OF 1 PER PERIOD — What $1 payable periodically is worth today.	PARTIAL PAYMENT — Annuity worth $1 today. Periodic payment necessary to pay off a loan of $1.	P E R I O D S
	1	1.070 000 0000	1.000 000 0000	1.000 000 0000	.934 579 4393	.934 579 4393	1.070 000 0000	1
	2	1.144 900 0000	2.070 000 0000	.483 091 7874	.873 438 7283	1.808 018 1675	.553 091 7874	2
	3	1.225 043 0000	3.214 900 0000	.311 051 6657	.816 297 8769	2.624 316 0444	.381 051 6657	3
	4	1.310 796 0100	4.439 943 0000	.225 228 1167	.762 895 2120	3.387 211 2565	.295 228 1167	4
	5	1.402 551 7307	5.750 739 0100	.173 890 6944	.712 986 1795	4.100 197 4359	.243 890 6944	5
	6	1.500 730 3518	7.153 290 7407	.139 795 7998	.666 342 2238	4.766 539 6598	.209 795 7998	6
	7	1.605 781 4765	8.654 021 0925	.115 553 2196	.622 749 7419	5.389 289 4016	.185 553 2196	7
	8	1.718 186 1798	10.259 802 5690	.097 467 7625	.582 009 1046	5.971 298 5062	.167 467 7625	8
	9	1.838 459 2124	11.977 988 7489	.083 486 4701	.543 933 7426	6.515 232 2488	.153 486 4701	9
	10	1.967 151 3573	13.816 447 9613	.072 377 5027	.508 349 2921	7.023 581 5409	.142 377 5027	10
	11	2.104 851 9523	15.783 599 3186	.063 356 9048	.475 092 7964	7.498 674 3373	.133 356 9048	11
	12	2.252 191 5890	17.888 451 2709	.055 901 9887	.444 011 9592	7.942 686 2966	.125 901 9887	12
	13	2.409 845 0002	20.140 642 8598	.049 650 8481	.414 964 4479	8.357 650 7444	.119 650 8481	13
	14	2.578 534 1502	22.550 487 8600	.044 344 9386	.387 817 2410	8.745 467 9855	.114 344 9386	14
	15	2.759 031 5407	25.129 022 0102	.039 794 6247	.362 446 0196	9.107 914 0051	.109 794 6247	15
	16	2.952 163 7486	27.888 053 5509	.035 857 6477	.338 734 5978	9.446 648 6029	.105 857 6477	16
	17	3.158 815 2110	30.840 217 2995	.032 425 1931	.316 574 3905	9.763 222 9934	.102 425 1931	17
	18	3.379 932 2757	33.999 032 5105	.029 412 6017	.295 863 9163	10.059 086 9097	.099 412 6017	18
	19	3.616 527 5350	37.378 964 7862	.026 753 0148	.276 508 3330	10.335 595 2427	.096 753 0148	19
	20	3.869 684 4625	40.995 492 3212	.024 392 9257	.258 419 0028	10.594 014 2455	.094 392 9257	20
	21	4.140 562 3749	44.865 176 7837	.022 289 0017	.241 513 0867	10.835 527 3323	.092 289 0017	21
	22	4.430 401 7411	49.005 739 1586	.020 405 7732	.225 713 1652	11.061 240 4974	.090 405 7732	22
	23	4.740 529 8630	53.436 140 8997	.018 713 9263	.210 946 8833	11.272 187 3808	.088 713 9263	23
	24	5.072 366 9534	58.176 670 7627	.017 189 0207	.197 146 6199	11.469 334 0007	.087 189 0207	24
	25	5.427 432 6401	63.249 037 7160	.015 810 5172	.184 249 1775	11.653 583 1783	.085 810 5172	25
	26	5.807 352 9249	68.676 470 3562	.014 561 0279	.172 195 4930	11.825 778 6713	.084 561 0279	26
	27	6.213 867 6297	74.483 823 2811	.013 425 7340	.160 930 3673	11.986 709 0386	.083 425 7340	27
	28	6.648 838 3638	80.697 690 9108	.012 391 9283	.150 402 2124	12.137 111 2510	.082 391 9283	28
	29	7.114 257 0492	87.346 529 2745	.011 448 6518	.140 562 8154	12.277 674 0664	.081 448 6518	29
	30	7.612 255 0427	94.460 786 3237	.010 586 4035	.131 367 1172	12.409 041 1835	.080 586 4035	30
	31	8.145 112 8956	102.073 041 3664	.009 796 9061	.122 773 0067	12.531 814 1902	.079 796 9061	31
	32	8.715 270 7983	110.218 154 2621	.009 072 9155	.114 741 1277	12.646 555 3179	.079 072 9155	32
	33	9.325 339 7542	118.933 425 0604	.008 408 0653	.107 234 6988	12.753 790 0168	.078 408 0653	33
	34	9.978 113 5370	128.258 764 8146	.007 796 7381	.100 219 3447	12.854 009 3615	.077 796 7381	34
	35	10.676 581 4846	138.236 878 3516	.007 233 9596	.093 662 9390	12.947 672 3004	.077 233 9596	35
	36	11.423 942 1885	148.913 459 8363	.006 715 3097	.087 535 4570	13.035 207 7574	.076 715 3097	36
	37	12.223 618 1417	160.337 402 0248	.006 236 8480	.081 808 8383	13.117 016 5957	.076 236 8480	37
	38	13.079 271 4117	172.561 020 1665	.005 795 0515	.076 456 8582	13.193 473 4539	.075 795 0515	38
	39	13.994 820 4105	185.640 291 5782	.005 386 7616	.071 455 0077	13.264 928 4616	.075 386 7616	39
	40	14.974 457 8392	199.635 111 9887	.005 009 1389	.066 780 3810	13.331 708 8426	.075 009 1389	40
	41	16.022 669 8880	214.609 569 8279	.004 659 6245	.062 411 5710	13.394 120 4137	.074 659 6245	41
	42	17.144 256 7801	230.632 239 7158	.004 335 9072	.058 328 5711	13.452 448 9847	.074 335 9072	42
	43	18.344 354 7547	247.776 496 4959	.004 035 8953	.054 512 6832	13.506 961 6680	.074 035 8953	43
	44	19.628 459 5875	266.120 851 2507	.003 757 6913	.050 946 4329	13.557 908 1009	.073 757 6913	44
	45	21.002 451 7587	285.749 310 8382	.003 499 5710	.047 613 4887	13.605 521 5896	.073 499 5710	45
	46	22.472 623 3818	306.751 762 5969	.003 259 9650	.044 498 5876	13.650 020 1772	.073 259 9650	46
	47	24.045 707 0185	329.224 385 9787	.003 037 4421	.041 587 4650	13.691 607 6423	.073 037 4421	47
	48	25.728 906 5098	353.270 092 9972	.002 830 6953	.038 866 7898	13.730 474 4320	.072 830 6953	48
	49	27.529 929 9655	378.998 999 5070	.002 638 5294	.036 324 1026	13.766 798 5346	.072 638 5294	49
	50	29.457 025 0631	406.528 929 4724	.002 459 8495	.033 947 7594	13.800 746 2940	.072 459 8495	50
	51	31.519 016 8175	435.985 954 5355	.002 293 6519	.031 726 8780	13.832 473 1720	.072 293 6519	51
	52	33.725 347 9947	467.504 971 3530	.002 139 0147	.029 651 2878	13.862 124 4598	.072 139 0147	52
	53	36.086 122 3543	501.230 319 3477	.001 995 0908	.027 711 4839	13.889 835 9437	.071 995 0908	53
	54	38.612 150 9191	537.316 441 7021	.001 861 1007	.025 898 5831	13.915 734 5269	.071 861 1007	54
	55	41.315 001 4835	575.928 592 6212	.001 736 3264	.024 204 2833	13.939 938 8102	.071 736 3264	55
	56	44.207 051 5873	617.243 594 1047	.001 620 1059	.022 620 8255	13.962 559 6357	.071 620 1059	56
	57	47.301 545 1984	661.450 645 6920	.001 511 8286	.021 140 9584	13.983 700 5941	.071 511 8286	57
	58	50.612 653 3623	708.752 190 8905	.001 410 9304	.019 757 9051	14.003 458 4991	.071 410 9304	58
	59	54.155 539 0977	759.364 844 2528	.001 316 8900	.018 465 3318	14.021 923 8310	.071 316 8900	59
	60	57.946 426 8345	813.520 383 3505	.001 229 2255	.017 257 3195	14.039 181 1504	.071 229 2255	60
	61	62.002 676 7130	871.466 810 1850	.001 147 4906	.016 128 3360	14.055 309 4864	.071 147 4906	61
	62	66.342 864 0829	933.469 486 8980	.001 071 2723	.015 073 2112	14.070 382 6976	.071 071 2723	62
	63	70.986 864 5687	999.812 350 9808	.001 000 1877	.014 087 1132	14.084 469 8108	.071 000 1877	63
	64	75.955 945 0885	1070.799 215 5495	.000 933 8819	.013 165 5264	14.097 635 3372	.070 933 8819	64
	65	81.272 861 2447	1146.755 160 6379	.000 872 0257	.012 304 2303	14.109 939 5675	.070 872 0257	65
	66	86.961 961 5318	1228.028 021 8826	.000 814 3137	.011 499 2806	14.121 438 8481	.070 814 3137	66
	67	93.049 298 8390	1314.989 983 4144	.000 760 4621	.010 746 9912	14.132 185 8394	.070 760 4621	67
	68	99.562 749 7577	1408.039 282 2534	.000 710 2075	.010 043 9171	14.142 229 7564	.070 710 2075	68
	69	106.532 142 2408	1507.602 032 0111	.000 663 3050	.009 386 8384	14.151 616 5948	.070 663 3050	69
	70	113.989 392 1976	1614.134 174 2519	.000 619 5272	.008 772 7461	14.160 389 3409	.070 619 5272	70
	71	121.968 649 6515	1728.123 566 4495	.000 578 6623	.008 198 8282	14.168 588 1691	.070 578 6623	71
	72	130.506 455 1271	1850.092 216 1010	.000 540 5136	.007 662 4562	14.176 250 6253	.070 540 5136	72
	73	139.641 906 9860	1980.598 671 2281	.000 504 8978	.007 161 1740	14.183 411 7993	.070 504 8978	73
	74	149.416 840 4750	2120.240 578 2140	.000 471 6446	.006 692 6860	14.190 104 4854	.070 471 6446	74
	75	159.876 019 3082	2269.657 418 6890	.000 440 5951	.006 254 8468	14.196 359 3321	.070 440 5951	75
	76	171.067 340 6598	2429.533 437 9973	.000 411 6017	.005 845 6512	14.202 204 9833	.070 411 6017	76
	77	183.042 054 5060	2600.600 778 6571	.000 384 5265	.005 462 2254	14.207 668 2087	.070 384 5265	77
	78	195.854 998 3214	2783.642 833 1631	.000 359 2415	.005 105 8181	14.212 774 0268	.070 359 2415	78
	79	209.564 848 2039	2979.497 831 4845	.000 335 6270	.004 771 7926	14.217 545 8194	.070 335 6270	79
	80	224.234 387 5782	3189.062 679 6884	.000 313 5718	.004 459 6193	14.222 005 4387	.070 313 5718	80
	81	239.930 794 7087	3413.297 067 2666	.000 292 9719	.004 167 8685	14.226 173 3072	.070 292 9719	81
	82	256.725 950 3383	3653.227 861 9752	.000 273 7305	.003 895 2042	14.230 068 5114	.070 273 7305	82
	83	274.696 766 8619	3909.953 812 3135	.000 255 7575	.003 640 3778	14.233 708 8892	.070 255 7575	83
	84	293.925 540 5423	4184.650 579 1754	.000 238 9686	.003 403 2222	14.237 111 1114	.070 238 9686	84
	85	314.500 328 3802	4478.576 119 7177	.000 223 2853	.003 179 6469	14.240 290 7583	.070 223 2853	85
	86	336.515 351 3669	4793.076 448 0980	.000 208 6343	.002 971 6326	14.243 262 3909	.070 208 6343	86
	87	360.071 425 9625	5129.591 799 4648	.000 194 9473	.002 777 2268	14.246 039 6177	.070 194 9473	87
	88	385.276 425 7799	5489.663 225 4273	.000 182 1605	.002 595 5390	14.248 635 1567	.070 182 1605	88
	89	412.245 775 5845	5874.939 651 2073	.000 170 2145	.002 425 7374	14.251 060 8941	.070 170 2145	89
	90	441.102 979 8754	6287.185 426 7918	.000 159 0537	.002 267 0443	14.253 327 9384	.070 159 0537	90
	91	471.980 188 4667	6728.288 406 6672	.000 148 6262	.002 118 7330	14.255 446 6714	.070 148 6262	91
	92	505.018 801 6594	7200.268 595 1339	.000 138 8837	.001 980 1243	14.257 426 7957	.070 138 8837	92
	93	540.370 117 7755	7705.287 396 7933	.000 129 7810	.001 850 5835	14.259 277 3792	.070 129 7810	93
	94	578.196 026 0198	8245.657 514 5688	.000 121 2760	.001 729 5172	14.261 006 8965	.070 121 2760	94
	95	618.669 747 8412	8823.853 540 5886	.000 113 3292	.001 616 3713	14.262 623 2677	.070 113 3292	95
	96	661.976 630 1901	9442.523 288 4298	.000 105 9039	.001 510 6273	14.264 133 8951	.070 105 9039	96
	97	708.314 994 3034	10104.499 918 6199	.000 098 9658	.001 411 8013	14.265 545 6963	.070 098 9658	97
	98	757.897 043 9046	10812.814 912 9233	.000 092 4829	.001 319 4404	14.266 865 1367	.070 092 4829	98
	99	810.949 836 9780	11570.711 956 8279	.000 086 4251	.001 233 1219	14.268 098 2586	.070 086 4251	99
	100	867.716 325 5664	12381.661 793 8059	.000 080 7646	.001 152 4504	14.269 250 7090	.070 080 7646	100

RATE 7 1/2%

PERIODS	XIV COMPOUND AMOUNT — AMOUNT OF 1 — How $1 left at compound interest will grow.	XV AMOUNT OF ANNUITY — AMOUNT OF 1 PER PERIOD — How $1 deposited periodically will grow.	XVI SINKING FUND — SINKING FUND — Periodic deposit that will grow to $1 at future date.	XVII PRESENT VALUE — PRESENT WORTH OF 1 — What $1 due in the future is worth today.	XVIII PRESENT VALUE OF ANNUITY — PRESENT WORTH OF 1 PER PERIOD — What $1 payable periodically is worth today.	XIX AMORTIZATION — PARTIAL PAYMENT — Annuity worth $1 today. Periodic payment necessary to pay off a loan of $1.	PERIODS
1	1.075 000 0000	1.000 000 0000	1.000 000 0000	.930 232 5581	.930 232 5581	1.075 000 0000	1
2	1.155 625 0000	2.075 000 0000	.481 927 7108	.865 332 6122	1.795 565 1704	.556 927 7108	2
3	1.242 296 8750	3.230 625 0000	.309 537 6282	.804 960 5695	2.600 525 7399	.384 537 6282	3
4	1.335 469 1406	4.472 921 8750	.223 567 5087	.748 800 5298	3.349 326 2696	.298 567 5087	4
5	1.435 629 3262	5.808 391 0156	.172 164 7178	.696 558 6324	4.045 884 9020	.247 164 7178	5
6	1.543 301 5256	7.244 020 3418	.138 044 8912	.647 961 5185	4.693 846 4205	.213 044 8912	6
7	1.659 049 1401	8.787 321 8674	.113 800 3154	.602 754 9009	5.296 601 3214	.188 800 3154	7
8	1.783 477 8256	10.446 371 0075	.095 727 0232	.560 702 2334	5.857 303 5548	.170 727 0232	8
9	1.917 238 6625	12.229 848 8331	.081 767 1595	.521 583 4729	6.378 887 0277	.156 767 1595	9
10	2.061 031 5622	14.147 087 4955	.070 685 9274	.485 193 9283	6.864 080 9560	.145 685 9274	10
11	2.215 608 9293	16.208 119 0577	.061 697 4737	.451 343 1891	7.315 424 1451	.136 697 4737	11
12	2.381 779 5990	18.423 727 9870	.054 277 8313	.419 854 1294	7.735 278 2745	.129 277 8313	12
13	2.560 413 0690	20.805 507 5860	.048 064 1963	.390 561 9808	8.125 840 2554	.123 064 1963	13
14	2.752 444 0491	23.365 920 6550	.042 797 3721	.363 313 4706	8.489 153 7259	.117 797 3721	14
15	2.958 877 3528	26.118 364 7041	.038 287 2363	.337 966 0191	8.827 119 7450	.113 287 2363	15
16	3.180 793 1543	29.077 242 0569	.034 391 1571	.314 386 9945	9.141 506 7396	.109 391 1571	16
17	3.419 352 6408	32.258 035 2112	.031 000 0282	.292 453 0182	9.433 959 7577	.106 000 0282	17
18	3.675 804 0889	35.677 387 8520	.028 028 9578	.272 049 3192	9.706 009 0770	.103 028 9578	18
19	3.951 489 3956	39.353 191 9410	.025 410 8994	.253 069 1342	9.959 078 2111	.100 410 8994	19
20	4.247 851 1002	43.304 681 3365	.023 092 1916	.235 413 1481	10.194 491 3592	.098 092 1916	20
21	4.566 439 9328	47.552 532 4368	.021 029 3742	.218 988 9749	10.413 480 3341	.096 029 3742	21
22	4.908 922 9277	52.118 972 3695	.019 186 8710	.203 710 6744	10.617 191 0085	.094 186 8710	22
23	5.277 092 1473	57.027 895 2972	.017 535 2780	.189 498 3017	10.806 689 3102	.092 535 2780	23
24	5.672 874 0583	62.304 987 4445	.016 050 0795	.176 277 4900	10.982 966 8002	.091 050 0795	24
25	6.098 339 6127	67.977 861 5029	.014 710 6716	.163 979 0605	11.146 945 8607	.089 710 6716	25
26	6.555 715 0837	74.076 201 1156	.013 499 6124	.152 538 6609	11.299 484 5215	.088 499 6124	26
27	7.047 393 7149	80.631 916 1992	.012 402 0369	.141 896 4287	11.441 380 9503	.087 402 0369	27
28	7.575 948 2436	87.679 309 9142	.011 405 1993	.131 996 6779	11.573 377 6282	.086 405 1993	28
29	8.144 144 3618	95.255 258 1578	.010 498 1081	.122 787 6073	11.696 165 2355	.085 498 1081	29
30	8.754 955 1890	103.399 402 5196	.009 671 2358	.114 221 0301	11.810 386 2656	.084 671 2358	30
31	9.411 576 8281	112.154 357 7086	.008 916 2831	.106 252 1210	11.916 638 3866	.083 916 2831	31
32	10.117 445 0903	121.565 934 5367	.008 225 9887	.098 839 1823	12.015 477 5689	.083 225 9887	32
33	10.876 253 4720	131.683 379 6269	.007 593 9728	.091 943 4254	12.107 420 9943	.082 593 9728	33
34	11.691 972 4824	142.559 633 0990	.007 014 6084	.085 528 7678	12.192 949 7622	.082 014 6084	34
35	12.568 870 4186	154.251 605 5814	.006 482 9147	.079 561 6445	12.272 511 4067	.081 482 9147	35
36	13.511 535 7000	166.820 476 0000	.005 994 4680	.074 010 8321	12.346 522 2388	.080 994 4680	36
37	14.524 900 8775	180.332 011 7000	.005 545 3271	.068 847 2857	12.415 369 5244	.080 545 3271	37
38	15.614 268 4433	194.856 912 5775	.005 131 9709	.064 043 9867	12.479 413 5111	.080 131 9709	38
39	16.785 338 5766	210.471 181 0208	.004 751 2443	.059 575 8016	12.538 989 3127	.079 751 2443	39
40	18.044 238 9698	227.256 519 5974	.004 400 3138	.055 419 3503	12.594 408 6629	.079 400 3138	40
41	19.397 556 8925	245.300 758 5672	.004 076 6282	.051 552 8840	12.645 961 5469	.079 076 6282	41
42	20.852 373 6595	264.698 315 4597	.003 777 8858	.047 956 1711	12.693 917 7181	.078 777 8858	42
43	22.416 301 6839	285.550 689 1192	.003 502 0052	.044 610 3918	12.738 528 1098	.078 502 0052	43
44	24.097 524 3102	307.966 990 8031	.003 247 1012	.041 498 0388	12.780 026 1487	.078 247 1012	44
45	25.904 838 6335	332.064 515 1134	.003 011 4630	.038 602 8268	12.818 628 9755	.078 011 4630	45
46	27.847 701 5310	357.969 353 7469	.002 793 5352	.035 909 6064	12.854 538 5819	.077 793 5352	46
47	29.936 279 1458	385.817 055 2779	.002 591 9020	.033 404 2850	12.887 942 8669	.077 591 9020	47
48	32.181 500 0818	415.753 334 4237	.002 405 2724	.031 073 7535	12.919 016 6203	.077 405 2724	48
49	34.595 112 5879	447.934 834 5055	.002 232 4676	.028 905 8172	12.947 922 4375	.077 232 4676	49
50	37.189 746 0320	482.529 947 0934	.002 072 4102	.026 889 1323	12.974 811 5698	.077 072 4102	50
51	39.978 976 9844	519.719 693 1254	.001 924 1141	.025 013 1463	12.999 824 7161	.076 924 1141	51
52	42.977 400 2582	559.698 670 1098	.001 786 6757	.023 268 0431	13.023 092 7591	.076 786 6757	52
53	46.200 705 2776	602.676 070 3681	.001 659 2661	.021 644 6912	13.044 737 4504	.076 659 2661	53
54	49.665 758 1734	648.876 775 6457	.001 541 1247	.020 134 5965	13.064 872 0469	.076 541 1247	54
55	53.390 690 0364	698.542 533 8191	.001 431 5521	.018 729 8572	13.083 601 9040	.076 431 5521	55
56	57.394 991 7892	751.933 223 8555	.001 329 9053	.017 423 1230	13.101 025 0270	.076 329 9053	56
57	62.699 616 1734	809.328 215 6447	.001 235 5927	.016 207 5563	13.117 232 5833	.076 235 5927	57
58	66.327 087 3864	871.027 831 8180	.001 148 0689	.015 076 7965	13.132 309 3798	.076 148 0689	58
59	71.301 618 9403	937.354 919 2044	.001 066 8318	.014 024 9270	13.146 334 3068	.076 066 8318	59
60	76.649 240 3609	1008.656 538 1447	.000 991 4178	.013 046 4437	13.159 380 7505	.075 991 4178	60
61	82.397 933 3879	1085.305 778 5056	.000 921 3993	.012 136 2267	13.171 516 9772	.075 921 3993	61
62	88.577 778 3920	1167.703 711 8935	.000 856 3816	.011 289 5132	13.182 806 4904	.075 856 3816	62
63	95.221 111 7714	1256.281 490 2855	.000 795 9999	.010 501 8728	13.193 308 3632	.075 795 9999	63
64	102.362 695 1543	1351.502 602 0569	.000 739 9172	.009 769 1840	13.203 077 5471	.075 739 9172	64
65	110.039 897 2908	1453.865 297 2112	.000 687 8216	.009 087 6130	13.212 165 1601	.075 687 8216	65
66	118.292 889 5877	1563.905 194 5020	.000 639 4249	.008 453 5935	13.220 618 7536	.075 639 4249	66
67	127.164 856 3067	1682.198 084 0897	.000 594 4603	.007 863 8079	13.228 482 5615	.075 594 4603	67
68	136.702 220 5297	1809.362 940 3964	.000 552 6807	.007 315 1701	13.235 797 7316	.075 552 6807	68
69	146.954 887 0695	1946.065 160 9261	.000 513 8574	.006 804 8094	13.242 602 5411	.075 513 8574	69
70	157.976 503 5997	2093.020 047 9956	.000 477 7785	.006 330 0553	13.248 932 5963	.075 477 7785	70
71	169.824 741 3696	2250.996 551 5952	.000 444 2477	.005 888 4235	13.254 821 0198	.075 444 2477	71
72	182.561 596 9724	2420.821 292 9649	.000 413 0829	.005 477 6033	13.260 298 6231	.075 413 0829	72
73	196.253 716 7453	2603.382 889 9373	.000 384 1156	.005 095 4449	13.265 394 0680	.075 384 1156	73
74	210.972 745 5012	2799.636 606 6826	.000 357 1892	.004 739 9487	13.270 134 0168	.075 357 1892	74
75	226.795 701 4138	3010.609 352 1837	.000 332 1587	.004 409 2546	13.274 543 2714	.075 332 1587	75
76	243.805 379 0198	3237.405 053 5975	.000 308 8894	.004 101 6322	13.278 644 9036	.075 308 8894	76
77	262.090 782 4463	3481.210 432 6173	.000 287 2564	.003 815 4718	13.282 460 3755	.075 287 2564	77
78	281.747 591 1296	3743.301 215 0636	.000 267 1439	.003 549 2761	13.286 009 6516	.075 267 1439	78
79	302.878 660 4645	4025.048 806 1934	.000 248 4442	.003 301 6522	13.289 311 3038	.075 248 4442	79
80	325.594 559 9993	4327.927 466 6579	.000 231 0575	.003 071 3044	13.292 382 6082	.075 231 0575	80
81	350.014 151 9993	4653.522 026 6573	.000 214 8910	.002 857 0273	13.295 239 6355	.075 214 8910	81
82	376.265 213 3992	5003.536 178 6566	.000 199 8587	.002 657 6996	13.297 897 3354	.075 199 8587	82
83	404.485 104 4042	5379.801 392 0558	.000 185 8805	.002 472 2789	13.300 369 6143	.075 185 8805	83
84	434.821 487 2345	5784.286 496 4600	.000 172 8822	.002 299 7944	13.302 669 4087	.075 172 8822	84
85	467.433 098 7771	6219.107 983 6945	.000 160 7948	.002 139 3436	13.304 808 7522	.075 160 7948	85
86	502.490 581 1854	6686.541 082 4716	.000 149 5542	.001 990 0871	13.306 798 8393	.075 149 5542	86
87	540.177 374 7743	7189.031 663 6569	.000 139 1008	.001 851 2438	13.308 650 0831	.075 139 1008	87
88	580.690 677 8823	7729.209 038 4312	.000 129 3793	.001 722 0872	13.310 372 1703	.075 129 3793	88
89	624.242 478 7235	8309.899 716 3136	.000 120 3384	.001 601 9416	13.311 974 1119	.075 120 3384	89
90	671.060 664 6278	8934.142 195 0371	.000 111 9302	.001 490 1782	13.313 464 2901	.075 111 9302	90
91	721.390 214 4749	9605.202 859 6649	.000 104 1102	.001 386 2123	13.314 850 5025	.075 104 1102	91
92	775.494 480 5605	10326.593 074 1397	.000 096 8374	.001 289 4998	13.316 140 0023	.075 096 8374	92
93	833.656 566 6025	11102.087 554 7002	.000 090 0732	.001 199 5347	13.317 339 5370	.075 090 0732	93
94	896.180 809 0977	11935.744 121 3027	.000 083 7820	.001 115 8463	13.318 455 3833	.075 083 7820	94
95	963.394 369 7800	12831.924 930 4004	.000 077 9306	.001 037 9965	13.319 493 3798	.075 077 9306	95
96	1035.648 947 5135	13795.319 300 1804	.000 072 4884	.000 965 5782	13.320 458 9579	.075 072 4884	96
97	1113.322 618 5770	14830.968 247 6940	.000 067 4265	.000 898 2122	13.321 357 1702	.075 067 4265	97
98	1196.821 814 9703	15944.290 866 2710	.000 062 7184	.000 835 5463	13.322 192 7164	.075 062 7184	98
99	1286.583 451 0931	17141.112 681 2414	.000 058 3393	.000 777 2523	13.322 969 9688	.075 058 3393	99
100	1383.077 209 9251	18427.696 132 3345	.000 054 2661	.000 723 0254	13.323 692 9942	.075 054 2661	100

		XIV COMPOUND AMOUNT	XV AMOUNT OF ANNUITY	XVI SINKING FUND	XVII PRESENT VALUE	XVIII PRESENT VALUE OF ANNUITY	XIX AMORTIZATION	
PERIODS		AMOUNT OF 1 How $1 left at compound interest will grow.	AMOUNT OF 1 PER PERIOD How $1 deposited periodically will grow.	SINKING FUND Periodic deposit that will grow to $1 at future date	PRESENT WORTH OF 1 What $1 due in the future is worth today.	PRESENT WORTH OF 1 PER PERIOD What $1 payable periodically is worth today.	PARTIAL PAYMENT Annuity worth $1 today. Periodic payment necessary to pay off a loan of $1	PERIODS
1		1.080 000 0000	1.000 000 0000	1.000 000 0000	.925 925 9259	.925 925 9259	1.080 000 0000	1
2		1.166 400 0000	2.080 000 0000	.480 769 2308	.857 338 8203	1.783 264 7462	.560 769 2308	2
3		1.259 712 0000	3.246 400 0000	.308 033 5140	.793 832 2410	2.577 096 9872	.388 033 5140	3
4		1.360 488 9600	4.506 112 0000	.221 920 8045	.735 029 8528	3.312 126 8400	.301 920 8045	4
5		1.469 328 0768	5.866 600 9600	.170 456 4546	.680 583 1970	3.992 710 0371	.250 456 4546	5
6		1.586 874 3229	7.335 929 0368	.136 315 3862	.630 169 6269	4.622 879 6640	.216 315 3862	6
7		1.713 824 2688	8.922 803 3597	.112 072 4014	.583 490 3953	5.206 370 0592	.192 072 4014	7
8		1.850 930 2103	10.636 627 6285	.094 014 7606	.540 268 8845	5.746 638 9437	.174 014 7606	8
9		1.999 004 6271	12.487 557 8388	.080 079 7092	.500 248 9671	6.246 887 9109	.160 079 7092	9
10		2.158 924 9973	14.486 562 4659	.069 029 4887	.463 193 4881	6.710 081 3989	.149 029 4887	10
11		2.331 638 9971	16.645 487 4632	.060 076 3421	.428 882 8592	7.138 964 2583	.140 076 3421	11
12		2.518 170 1168	18.977 126 4602	.052 695 0169	.397 113 7586	7.536 078 0169	.132 695 0169	12
13		2.719 623 7262	21.495 296 5771	.046 521 8052	.367 697 9247	7.903 775 9416	.126 521 8052	13
14		2.937 193 6243	24.214 920 3032	.041 296 8528	.340 461 0414	8.244 236 9830	.121 296 8528	14
15		3.172 169 1142	27.152 113 9275	.036 829 5449	.315 241 7050	8.559 478 6879	.116 829 5449	15
16		3.425 942 6433	30.324 283 0417	.032 976 8720	.291 890 4676	8.851 369 1555	.112 976 8720	16
17		3.700 018 0548	33.750 225 6850	.029 629 4315	.270 268 9514	9.121 638 1069	.109 629 4315	17
18		3.996 019 4992	37.450 243 7398	.026 702 0959	.250 249 0291	9.371 887 1360	.106 702 0959	18
19		4.315 701 0591	41.446 263 2390	.024 127 6275	.231 712 0640	9.603 599 2000	.104 127 6275	19
20		4.660 957 1438	45.761 964 2981	.021 852 2088	.214 548 2074	9.818 147 4074	.101 852 2088	20
21		5.033 833 7154	50.422 921 4420	.019 832 2503	.198 655 7476	10.016 803 1550	.099 832 2503	21
22		5.436 540 4126	55.456 755 1573	.018 032 0684	.183 940 5070	10.200 743 6621	.098 032 0684	22
23		5.871 463 6456	60.893 295 5699	.016 422 1692	.170 315 2843	10.371 058 9464	.096 422 1692	23
24		6.341 180 7372	66.764 759 2155	.014 977 9616	.157 699 3373	10.528 758 2837	.094 977 9616	24
25		6.848 475 1962	73.105 939 9527	.013 678 7791	.146 017 9049	10.674 776 1886	.093 678 7791	25
26		7.396 353 2119	79.954 415 1490	.012 507 1267	.135 201 7638	10.809 977 9524	.092 507 1267	26
27		7.988 061 4689	87.350 768 3609	.011 448 0962	.125 186 8183	10.935 164 7707	.091 448 0962	27
28		8.627 106 3864	95.338 829 8297	.010 488 9057	.115 913 7207	11.051 078 4914	.090 488 9057	28
29		9.317 274 8973	103.965 936 2161	.009 618 5350	.107 327 5192	11.158 406 0106	.089 618 5350	29
30		10.062 656 8891	113.283 211 1134	.008 827 4334	.099 377 3325	11.257 783 3431	.088 827 4334	30
31		10.867 669 4402	123.345 868 0025	.008 107 2841	.092 016 0487	11.349 799 3918	.088 107 2841	31
32		11.737 082 9954	134.213 537 4427	.007 450 8132	.085 200 0451	11.434 999 4368	.087 450 8132	32
33		12.676 049 6350	145.950 620 4381	.006 851 6324	.078 888 9306	11.513 888 3674	.086 851 6324	33
34		13.690 133 6059	158.626 670 0732	.006 304 1101	.073 045 3061	11.586 933 6736	.086 304 1101	34
35		14.785 344 2943	172.316 803 6790	.005 803 2646	.067 634 5427	11.654 568 2163	.085 803 2646	35
36		15.968 171 8379	187.102 147 9733	.005 344 6741	.062 624 5766	11.717 192 7928	.085 344 6741	36
37		17.245 625 5849	203.070 319 8112	.004 924 4025	.057 985 7190	11.775 178 5119	.084 924 4025	37
38		18.625 275 6317	220.315 945 3961	.004 538 9361	.053 690 4806	11.828 868 9925	.084 538 9361	38
39		20.115 297 6822	238.941 221 0278	.004 185 1297	.049 713 4080	11.878 582 4004	.084 185 1297	39
40		21.724 521 4968	259.056 518 7100	.003 860 1615	.046 030 9333	11.924 613 3337	.083 860 1615	40
41		23.462 483 2165	280.781 040 2068	.003 561 4940	.042 621 2345	11.967 234 5683	.083 561 4940	41
42		25.339 481 8739	304.243 523 4233	.003 286 8407	.039 464 1061	12.006 698 6743	.083 286 8407	42
43		27.366 640 4238	329.583 005 2972	.003 034 1370	.036 540 8389	12.043 239 5133	.083 034 1370	43
44		29.555 971 6577	356.949 645 7210	.002 801 5156	.033 834 1101	12.077 073 6234	.082 801 5156	44
45		31.920 449 3903	386.505 617 3787	.002 587 2845	.031 327 8797	12.108 401 5032	.082 587 2845	45
46		34.474 085 3415	418.426 066 7690	.002 389 9085	.029 007 2961	12.137 408 7992	.082 389 9085	46
47		37.232 012 1688	452.900 152 1105	.002 207 9922	.026 858 6075	12.164 267 4067	.082 207 9922	47
48		40.210 573 1423	490.132 164 2793	.002 040 2660	.024 869 0810	12.189 136 4877	.082 040 2660	48
49		43.327 418 9937	530.342 737 4217	.001 885 5731	.023 026 9268	12.212 163 4145	.081 885 5731	49
50		46.901 612 5132	573.770 156 4154	.001 742 8582	.021 321 2286	12.233 484 6431	.081 742 8582	50
51		50.653 741 5143	620.671 768 9286	.001 611 1575	.019 741 8783	12.253 226 5214	.081 611 1575	51
52		54.706 040 8354	671.325 510 4429	.001 489 5903	.018 279 5169	12.271 506 0383	.081 489 5903	52
53		59.082 524 1023	726.031 551 2783	.001 377 3506	.016 925 4786	12.288 431 5169	.081 377 3506	53
54		63.809 126 0304	785.114 075 3806	.001 273 7003	.015 671 7395	12.304 103 2564	.081 273 7003	54
55		68.913 856 1129	848.923 201 4111	.001 177 9629	.014 510 8699	12.318 614 1263	.081 177 9629	55
56		74.426 964 6019	917.837 057 5239	.001 089 5180	.013 435 9906	12.332 050 1170	.081 089 5180	56
57		80.381 121 7701	992.264 022 1259	.001 007 7963	.012 440 7321	12.344 490 8490	.081 007 7963	57
58		86.811 611 5117	1072.645 143 8959	.000 932 2748	.011 519 1964	12.356 010 0454	.080 932 2748	58
59		93.756 540 4326	1159.456 755 4076	.000 862 4729	.010 665 9226	12.366 675 9680	.080 862 4729	59
60		101.257 063 6672	1253.213 295 8402	.000 797 9488	.009 875 8542	12.376 551 8222	.080 797 9488	60
61		109.357 628 7606	1354.470 359 5074	.000 738 2960	.009 144 3095	12.385 696 1317	.080 738 2960	61
62		118.106 239 0614	1463.827 988 2680	.000 683 1404	.008 466 9532	12.394 163 0049	.080 683 1404	62
63		127.554 738 1864	1501.934 227 3295	.000 632 1375	.007 839 7715	12.402 002 8564	.080 632 1375	63
64		137.759 117 2413	1709.488 965 5158	.000 584 9701	.007 259 0477	12.409 261 9040	.080 584 9701	64
65		148.779 846 6206	1847.248 082 7571	.000 541 3458	.006 721 3404	12.415 983 2445	.080 541 3458	65
66		160.682 234 3502	1996.027 929 3777	.000 500 9950	.006 223 4634	12.422 206 7079	.080 500 9950	66
67		173.536 813 0982	2156.710 163 7279	.000 463 6692	.005 762 4661	12.427 969 1739	.080 463 6692	67
68		187.419 758 1461	2330.246 976 8261	.000 429 1391	.005 335 6167	12.433 304 7907	.080 429 1391	68
69		202.413 338 7978	2517.666 734 9722	.000 397 1932	.004 940 3859	12.438 245 1766	.080 397 1932	69
70		218.606 405 9016	2720.080 073 7700	.000 367 6362	.004 574 4314	12.442 819 6079	.080 367 6362	70
71		236.094 918 3737	2938.686 479 6716	.000 340 2881	.004 235 5846	12.447 055 1925	.080 340 2881	71
72		254.982 511 8436	3174.781 398 0453	.000 314 9823	.003 921 8376	12.450 977 0301	.080 314 9823	72
73		275.381 112 7911	3429.763 909 8889	.000 291 5653	.003 631 3311	12.454 608 3612	.080 291 5653	73
74		297.411 601 8144	3705.145 022 6800	.000 269 8950	.003 362 3436	12.457 970 7048	.080 269 8950	74
75		321.204 529 9596	4002.556 624 4944	.000 249 8403	.003 113 2811	12.461 083 9860	.080 249 8403	75
76		346.900 892 3563	4323.761 154 4540	.000 231 2801	.002 882 6677	12.463 966 6537	.080 231 2801	76
77		374.652 963 7448	4670.662 046 8103	.000 214 1024	.002 669 1368	12.466 635 7904	.080 214 1024	77
78		404.625 200 8444	5045.315 010 5551	.000 198 2037	.002 471 4229	12.469 107 2134	.080 198 2037	78
79		436.995 216 9120	5449.940 211 3995	.000 183 4883	.002 288 3546	12.471 395 5679	.080 183 4883	79
80		471.954 834 2649	5886.935 428 3115	.000 169 8677	.002 118 8468	12.473 514 4147	.080 169 8677	80
81		509.711 221 0081	6358.890 262 5764	.000 157 2601	.001 961 8952	12.475 476 3099	.080 157 2601	81
82		550.488 118 6866	6868.601 483 5825	.000 145 5900	.001 816 5696	12.477 292 8796	.080 145 5900	82
83		594.527 168 1815	7419.089 602 2691	.000 134 7874	.001 682 0089	12.478 974 8885	.080 134 7874	83
84		642.089 341 6361	8013.616 770 4506	.000 124 7876	.001 557 4157	12.480 532 3042	.080 124 7876	84
85		693.456 488 9669	8655.706 112 0867	.000 115 5307	.001 442 0515	12.481 974 3557	.080 115 5307	85
86		748.933 008 0843	9349.162 601 0536	.000 106 9615	.001 335 2329	12.483 309 5886	.080 106 9615	86
87		808.847 648 7310	10098.095 609 1379	.000 099 0286	.001 236 3268	12.484 545 9154	.080 099 0286	87
88		873.555 460 6295	10906.943 257 8690	.000 091 6847	.001 144 7470	12.485 690 6624	.080 091 6847	88
89		943.439 897 4799	11780.498 718 4985	.000 084 8860	.001 059 9509	12.486 750 6133	.080 084 8860	89
90		1018.915 089 2783	12723.938 615 9783	.000 078 5920	.000 981 4360	12.487 732 0494	.080 078 5920	90
91		1100.428 296 4205	13742.853 705 2566	.000 072 7651	.000 908 7371	12.488 640 7865	.080 072 7651	91
92		1188.462 560 1342	14843.282 001 6771	.000 067 3705	.000 841 4232	12.489 482 2097	.080 067 3705	92
93		1283.539 564 9449	16031.744 561 8113	.000 062 3762	.000 779 0956	12.490 261 3053	.080 062 3762	93
94		1386.222 730 1405	17315.284 126 7562	.000 057 7524	.000 721 3848	12.490 982 6901	.080 057 7524	94
95		1497.120 548 5517	18701.506 856 8967	.000 053 4716	.000 667 9489	12.491 650 6389	.080 053 4716	95
96		1616.890 192 4359	20198.627 405 4485	.000 049 5083	.000 618 4712	12.492 269 1101	.080 049 5083	96
97		1746.241 407 8307	21815.517 597 8843	.000 045 8389	.000 572 6585	12.492 841 7686	.080 045 8389	97
98		1885.940 720 4572	23561.759 005 7151	.000 042 4417	.000 530 2394	12.493 372 0080	.080 042 4417	98
99		2036.815 978 0938	25447.699 726 1723	.000 039 2963	.000 490 9624	12.493 862 9704	.080 039 2963	99
100		2199.761 256 3413	27484.515 704 2661	.000 036 3841	.000 454 5948	12.494 317 5652	.080 036 3841	100

		XIV COMPOUND AMOUNT	XV AMOUNT OF ANNUITY	XVI SINKING FUND	XVII PRESENT VALUE	XVIII PRESENT VALUE OF ANNUITY	XIX AMORTIZATION	
	P E R I O D S	AMOUNT OF 1 — How $1 left at compound interest will grow.	AMOUNT OF 1 PER PERIOD — How $1 deposited periodically will grow.	SINKING FUND — Periodic deposit that will grow to $1 at future date.	PRESENT WORTH OF 1 — What $1 due in the future is worth today.	PRESENT WORTH OF 1 PER PERIOD — What $1 payable periodically is worth today.	PARTIAL PAYMENT — Annuity worth $1 today. Periodic payment necessary to pay off a loan of $1.	P E R I O D S
1		1.090 000 0000	1.000 000 0000	1.000 000 0000	.917 431 1927	.917 431 1927	1.090 000 0000	1
2		1.188 100 0000	2.090 000 0000	.478 468 8995	.841 679 9933	1.759 111 1859	.568 468 8995	2
3		1.295 029 0000	3.278 100 0000	.305 054 7573	.772 183 4801	2.531 294 6660	.395 054 7573	3
4		1.411 581 6100	4.573 129 0000	.218 668 6621	708 425 2111	3.239 719 8771	.308 668 6621	4
5		1.538 623 9549	5.984 710 6100	.167 092 4570	.649 931 3863	3.889 651 2634	.257 092 4570	5
6		1.677 100 1108	7.523 334 5649	.132 919 7833	.596 267 3265	4.485 918 5902	.222 919 7833	6
7		1.828 039 1208	9.200 434 6757	.108 690 5168	.547 034 2448	5.032 952 8351	.198 690 5168	7
8		1.992 562 6417	11.028 473 7966	.090 674 3778	.501 866 2797	5.534 819 1147	.180 674 3778	8
9		2.171 893 2794	13.021 036 4382	.076 798 8021	.460 427 7795	5.995 246 8943	.166 798 8021	9
10		2.367 363 6746	15.192 929 7177	.065 820 0899	.422 410 8069	6.417 657 7012	.155 820 0899	10
11		2.580 426 4053	17.560 293 3923	.056 946 6567	.387 532 8504	6.805 190 5515	.146 946 6567	11
12		2.812 664 7818	20.140 719 7976	.049 650 6585	.355 534 7251	7.160 725 2766	.139 650 6585	12
13		3.065 804 6121	22.953 384 5794	.043 566 5597	.326 178 6469	7.486 903 9235	.133 566 5597	13
14		3.341 727 0272	26.019 189 1915	.038 433 1730	.299 246 4650	7.786 150 3885	.128 433 1730	14
15		3.642 482 4597	29.360 916 2188	.034 058 8827	.274 538 0413	8.060 688 4299	.124 058 8827	15
16		3.970 305 8811	33.003 398 6784	.030 299 9097	.251 869 7627	8.312 558 1925	.120 299 9097	16
17		4.327 633 4104	36.973 704 5595	.027 046 2485	.231 073 1768	8.543 631 3693	.117 046 2485	17
18		4.717 120 4173	41.301 337 9699	.024 212 2907	.211 993 7402	8.755 625 1094	.114 212 2907	18
19		5.141 661 2548	46.018 458 3871	.021 730 4107	.194 489 6699	8.950 114 7793	.111 730 4107	19
20		5.604 410 7678	51.160 119 6420	.019 546 4750	.178 430 8898	9.128 545 6691	.109 546 4750	20
21		6.108 807 7369	56.764 530 4098	.017 616 6348	.163 698 0640	9.292 243 7331	.107 616 6348	21
22		6.658 600 4332	62.873 338 1466	.015 904 9930	.150 181 7101	9.442 425 4432	.105 904 9930	22
23		7.257 874 4722	69.531 938 5798	.014 381 8800	.137 781 3854	9.580 206 8286	.104 381 8800	23
24		7.911 083 1747	76.789 813 0520	.013 022 5607	.126 404 9408	9.706 611 7694	.103 022 5607	24
25		8.623 080 6604	84.700 896 2267	.011 806 2505	.115 967 8356	9.822 579 6049	.101 806 2505	25
26		9.399 157 9198	93.323 976 8871	.010 715 3599	.106 392 5097	9.928 972 1146	.100 715 3599	26
27		10.245 082 1326	102.723 134 8069	.009 734 9054	.097 607 8070	10.026 579 9217	.099 734 9054	27
28		11.167 139 5246	112.968 216 9396	.008 852 0473	.089 548 4468	10.116 128 3685	.098 852 0473	28
29		12.172 182 0818	124.135 356 4641	.008 055 7226	.082 154 5384	10.198 282 9069	.098 055 7226	29
30		13.267 678 4691	136.307 538 5459	.007 336 3514	.075 371 1361	10.273 654 0430	.097 336 3514	30
31		14.461 769 5314	149.575 217 0150	.006 685 5995	.069 147 8313	10.342 801 8743	.096 685 5995	31
32		15.763 328 7892	164.036 986 5464	.006 096 1861	.063 438 3773	10.406 240 2517	.096 096 1861	32
33		17.182 028 3802	179.800 315 3356	.005 561 7255	.058 200 3462	10.464 440 5979	.095 561 7255	33
34		18.728 410 9344	196.982 343 7158	.005 076 5971	.053 394 8130	10.517 835 4109	.095 076 5971	34
35		20.413 967 9185	215.710 754 6502	.004 635 8375	.048 986 0670	10.566 821 4779	.094 635 8375	35
36		22.251 225 0312	236.124 722 5687	.004 235 0500	.044 941 3459	10.611 762 8237	.094 235 0500	36
37		24.253 835 2840	258.375 947 5999	.003 870 3293	.041 230 5925	10.652 993 4163	.093 870 3293	37
38		26.436 680 4595	282.629 782 8839	.003 538 1975	.037 826 2317	10.690 819 6480	.093 538 1975	38
39		28.815 981 7009	309.066 463 3434	.003 235 5500	.034 702 9648	10.725 522 6128	.093 235 5500	39
40		31.409 420 0540	337.882 445 0443	.002 959 6092	.031 837 5824	10.757 360 1952	.092 959 6092	40
41		34.236 267 8588	369.291 865 0983	.002 707 8853	.029 208 7912	10.786 568 9865	.092 707 8853	41
42		37.317 531 9661	403.528 132 9572	.002 478 1420	.026 797 0562	10.813 366 0426	.092 478 1420	42
43		40.676 109 8431	440.845 664 9233	.002 268 3675	.024 584 4552	10.837 950 4978	.092 268 3675	43
44		44.336 959 7290	481.521 774 7664	.002 076 7493	.022 554 5461	10.860 505 0439	.092 076 7493	44
45		48.327 286 1046	525.858 734 4954	.001 901 6514	.020 692 2441	10.881 197 2880	.091 901 6514	45
46		52.676 741 8540	574.186 020 6000	.001 741 5959	.018 983 7102	10.900 180 9981	.091 741 5959	46
47		57.417 648 6209	626.862 762 4540	.001 595 2455	.017 416 2479	10.917 597 2460	.091 595 2455	47
48		62.585 236 9967	684.280 411 0748	.001 461 3892	.015 978 2090	10.933 575 4550	.091 461 3892	48
49		68.217 908 3264	746.865 648 0716	.001 338 9289	.014 658 9074	10.948 234 3624	.091 338 9289	49
50		74.357 520 0758	815.083 556 3980	.001 226 8681	.013 448 5389	10.961 682 9013	.091 226 8681	50
51		81.049 696 8826	889.441 076 4738	.001 124 3016	.012 338 1091	10.974 021 0104	.091 124 3016	51
52		88.344 169 6021	970.490 773 3565	.001 030 4065	.011 319 3661	10.985 340 3765	.091 030 4065	52
53		96.295 144 8663	1058.834 942 9585	.000 944 4343	.010 384 7396	10.995 725 1160	.090 944 4343	53
54		104.961 707 9042	1155.130 087 8248	.000 865 7034	.009 527 2840	11.005 252 4000	.090 865 7034	54
55		114.408 261 6156	1260.091 795 7290	.000 793 5930	.008 740 6275	11.013 993 0276	.090 793 5930	55
56		124.705 005 1610	1374.500 057 3447	.000 727 5373	.008 018 9243	11.022 011 9519	.090 727 5373	56
57		135.928 455 6255	1499.205 062 5057	.000 667 0202	.007 356 8113	11.029 368 7632	.090 667 0202	57
58		148.162 016 6318	1635.133 518 1312	.000 611 5709	.006 749 3682	11.036 118 1314	.090 611 5709	58
59		161.496 598 1287	1783.295 534 7630	.000 560 7595	.006 192 0809	11.042 310 2123	.090 560 7595	59
60		176.031 291 9602	1944.792 132 8917	.000 514 1938	.005 680 8082	11.047 991 0204	.090 514 1938	60
61		191.874 108 2367	2120.823 424 8519	.000 471 5150	.005 211 7506	11.053 202 7710	.090 471 5150	61
62		209.142 777 9780	2312.697 533 0886	.000 432 3955	.004 781 4226	11.057 984 1936	.090 432 3955	62
63		227.965 627 9960	2521.840 311 0665	.000 396 5358	.004 386 6262	11.062 370 8198	.090 396 5358	63
64		248.482 534 5156	2749.805 939 0625	.000 363 6620	.004 024 4277	11.066 395 2475	.090 363 6620	64
65		270.845 962 6220	2998.288 473 5782	.000 333 5236	.003 692 1355	11.070 087 3831	.090 333 5236	65
66		295.222 099 2580	3269.134 436 2002	.000 305 8914	.003 387 2803	11.073 474 6634	.090 305 8914	66
67		321.792 088 1912	3564.356 535 4582	.000 280 5555	.003 107 5966	11.076 582 2600	.090 280 5555	67
68		350.753 376 1285	3886.148 623 6495	.000 257 3242	.002 851 0061	11.079 433 2660	.090 257 3242	68
69		382.321 179 9800	4236.901 999 7779	.000 236 0215	.002 615 6019	11.082 048 8695	.090 236 0215	69
70		416.730 086 1782	4619.223 179 7579	.000 216 4866	.002 399 6348	11.084 448 5027	.090 216 4866	70
71		454.235 793 9343	5035.953 265 9361	.000 198 5721	.002 201 4998	11.086 650 0025	.090 198 5721	71
72		495.117 015 3883	5490.189 059 8704	.000 182 1431	.002 019 7246	11.088 669 7270	.090 182 1431	72
73		539.677 546 7733	5985.306 075 2587	.000 167 0758	.001 852 9583	11.090 522 6853	.090 167 0758	73
74		588.248 525 9829	6524.983 622 0220	.000 153 2571	.001 699 9618	11.092 222 6471	.090 153 2571	74
75		641.190 893 3213	7113.232 148 0149	.000 140 5831	.001 559 5979	11.093 782 2450	.090 140 5831	75
76		698.898 073 7203	7754.423 041 3362	.000 128 9587	.001 430 8238	11.095 213 0689	.090 128 9587	76
77		761.798 900 3551	8453.321 115 0565	.000 118 2967	.001 312 6824	11.096 525 7512	.090 118 2967	77
78		830.360 801 3870	9215.120 015 4116	.000 108 5173	.001 204 2958	11.097 730 0470	.090 108 5173	78
79		905.093 273 5119	10045.480 816 7986	.000 099 5473	.001 104 8585	11.098 834 9055	.090 099 5473	79
80		986.551 668 1279	10950.574 090 3105	.000 091 3194	.001 013 6317	11.099 848 5372	.090 091 3194	80
81		1075.341 318 2595	11937.125 758 4384	.000 083 7723	.000 929 9373	11.100 778 4745	.090 083 7723	81
82		1172.122 036 9028	13012.467 076 6979	.000 076 8494	.000 853 1535	11.101 631 6280	.090 076 8494	82
83		1277.613 020 2241	14184.589 113 6007	.000 070 4990	.000 782 7096	11.102 414 3376	.090 070 4990	83
84		1392.598 192 0442	15462.202 133 8247	.000 064 6738	.000 718 0822	11.103 132 4198	.090 064 6738	84
85		1517.932 029 3282	16854.800 325 8690	.000 059 3303	.000 658 7910	11.103 791 2108	.090 059 3303	85
86		1654.545 911 9677	18372.732 355 1972	.000 054 4285	.000 604 3954	11.104 395 6063	.090 054 4285	86
87		1803.455 044 0448	20027.278 267 1649	.000 049 9319	.000 554 4912	11.104 950 0975	.090 049 9319	87
88		1965.765 998 0089	21830.733 311 2098	.000 045 8070	.000 508 7075	11.105 458 8050	.050 045 8070	88
89		2142.684 937 8297	23796.499 309 2187	.000 042 0230	.000 466 7042	11.105 925 5092	.090 042 0230	89
90		2335.526 582 2343	25939.184 247 0483	.000 038 5517	.000 428 1690	11.106 353 6782	.090 038 5517	90
91		2545.723 974 6354	28274.710 829 2827	.000 035 3673	.000 392 8156	11.106 746 4937	.090 035 3673	91
92		2774.839 132 3526	30820.434 803 9181	.000 032 4460	.000 360 3813	11.107 106 8750	.090 032 4460	92
93		3024.574 654 2644	33595.273 936 2708	.000 029 7661	.000 330 6250	11.107 437 5000	.090 029 7661	93
94		3296.786 373 1482	36619.848 590 5351	.000 027 3076	.000 303 3257	11.107 740 8257	.090 027 3076	94
95		3593.497 146 7315	39916.634 963 6833	.000 025 0522	.000 278 2804	11.108 019 1060	.090 025 0522	95
96		3916.911 889 9373	43510.132 110 4148	.000 022 9832	.000 255 3032	11.108 274 4093	.090 022 9832	96
97		4269.433 960 0317	47427.044 000 3521	.000 021 0850	.000 234 2231	11.108 508 6324	.090 021 0850	97
98		4653.683 016 4345	51696.477 960 3838	.000 019 3437	.000 214 8836	11.108 723 5159	.090 019 3437	98
99		5072.514 487 9137	56350.160 976 8183	.000 017 7462	.000 197 1409	11.108 920 6568	.090 017 7462	99
100		5529.040 791 8259	61422.675 464 7320	.000 016 2806	.000 180 8632	11.109 101 5200	.090 016 2806	100

		XIV COMPOUND AMOUNT	XV AMOUNT OF ANNUITY	XVI SINKING FUND	XVII PRESENT VALUE	XVIII PRESENT VALUE OF ANNUITY	XIX AMORTIZATION		
RATE 10%	P E R I O D S	AMOUNT OF 1 — How $1 left at compound interest will grow.	AMOUNT OF 1 PER PERIOD — How $1 deposited periodically will grow.	SINKING FUND — Periodic deposit that will grow to $1 at future date.	PRESENT WORTH OF 1 — What $1 due in the future is worth today.	PRESENT WORTH OF 1 PER PERIOD — What $1 payable periodically is worth today.	PARTIAL PAYMENT — Annuity worth $1 today. Periodic payment necessary to pay off a loan of $1.	P E R I O D S	
	1	1.100 000 0000	1.000 000 0000	1.000 000 0000	.909 090 9091	.909 090 9091	1.100 000 0000	1	
	2	1.210 000 0000	2.100 000 0000	.476 190 4762	.826 446 2810	1.735 537 1901	.576 190 4762	2	
	3	1.331 000 0000	3.310 000 0000	.302 114 8036	.751 314 8009	2.486 851 9910	.402 114 8036	3	
	4	1.464 100 0000	4.641 000 0000	.215 470 8037	.683 013 4554	3.169 865 4463	.315 470 8037	4	
	5	1.610 510 0000	6.105 100 0000	.163 797 4808	.620 921 3231	3.790 786 7694	.263 797 4808	5	
	6	1.771 561 0000	7.715 610 0000	.129 607 3804	.564 473 9301	4.355 260 6995	.229 607 3804	6	
	7	1.948 717 1000	9.487 171 0000	.105 405 4997	.513 158 1182	4.868 418 8177	.205 405 4997	7	
	8	2.143 588 8100	11.435 888 1000	.087 444 0176	.466 507 3802	5.334 926 1979	.187 444 0176	8	
	9	2.357 947 6910	13.579 476 9100	.073 640 5391	.424 097 6184	5.759 023 8163	.173 640 5391	9	
	10	2.593 742 4601	15.937 424 6010	.062 745 3949	.385 543 2894	6.144 567 1057	.162 745 3949	10	
	11	2.853 116 7061	18.531 167 0611	.053 963 1420	.350 493 8995	6.495 061 0052	.153 963 1420	11	
	12	3.138 428 3767	21.384 283 7672	.046 763 3151	.318 630 8177	6.813 691 8229	.146 763 3151	12	
	13	3.452 271 2144	24.522 712 1439	.040 778 5238	.289 664 3797	7.103 356 2026	.140 778 5238	13	
	14	3.797 498 3358	27.974 983 3583	.035 746 2232	.263 331 2543	7.366 687 4569	.135 746 2232	14	
	15	4.177 248 1694	31.772 481 6942	.031 473 7769	.239 392 0494	7.606 079 5063	.131 473 7769	15	
	16	4.594 972 9864	35.949 729 8636	.027 816 6207	.217 629 1358	7.823 708 6421	.127 816 6207	16	
	17	5.054 470 2850	40.544 702 8499	.024 664 1344	.197 844 6689	8.021 553 3110	.124 664 1344	17	
	18	5.559 917 3135	45.599 173 1349	.021 930 2222	.179 858 7899	8.201 412 1009	.121 930 2222	18	
	19	6.115 909 0448	51.159 090 4484	.019 546 8682	.163 507 9908	8.364 920 0917	.119 546 8682	19	
	20	6.727 499 9493	57.274 999 4933	.017 459 6248	.148 643 6280	8.513 563 7198	.117 459 6248	20	
	21	7.400 249 9443	64.002 499 4426	.015 624 3898	.135 130 5709	8.648 694 2907	.115 624 3898	21	
	22	8.140 274 9387	71.402 749 3868	.014 005 0630	.122 845 9736	8.771 540 2643	.114 005 0630	22	
	23	8.954 302 4326	79.543 024 3255	.012 571 8127	.111 678 1578	8.883 218 4221	.112 571 8127	23	
	24	9.849 732 6758	88.497 326 7581	.011 299 7764	.101 525 5980	8.984 744 0201	.111 299 7764	24	
	25	10.834 705 9434	98.347 059 4339	.010 168 0722	.092 295 9982	9.077 040 0182	.110 168 0722	25	
	26	11.918 176 5377	109.181 765 3773	.009 159 0386	.083 905 4529	9.160 945 4711	.109 159 0386	26	
	27	13.109 994 1915	121.099 941 9150	.008 257 6423	.076 277 6844	9.237 223 1556	.108 257 6423	27	
	28	14.420 993 6106	134.209 936 1065	.007 451 0132	.069 343 3495	9.306 566 5051	.107 451 0132	28	
	29	15.863 092 9717	148.630 929 7171	.006 728 0747	.063 039 4086	9.369 605 9137	.106 728 0747	29	
	30	17.449 402 2689	164.494 022 6889	.006 079 2483	.057 308 5533	9.426 914 4670	.106 079 2483	30	
	31	19.194 342 4958	181.943 424 9578	.005 496 2140	.052 098 6848	9.479 013 1518	.105 496 2140	31	
	32	21.113 776 7454	201.137 767 4535	.004 971 7167	.047 362 4407	9.526 375 5926	.104 971 7167	32	
	33	23.225 154 4199	222.251 544 1989	.004 499 4063	.043 056 7643	9.569 432 3569	.104 499 4063	33	
	34	25.547 669 8619	245.476 698 6188	.004 073 7064	.039 142 5130	9.608 574 8699	.104 073 7064	34	
	35	28.102 436 8481	271.024 368 4806	.003 689 7051	.035 584 1027	9.644 158 9726	.103 689 7051	35	
	36	30.912 680 5329	299.126 805 3287	.003 343 0638	.032 349 1843	9.676 508 1569	.103 343 0638	36	
	37	34.003 948 5862	330.039 485 8616	.003 029 9405	.029 408 3494	9.705 916 5063	.103 029 9405	37	
	38	37.404 343 4448	364.043 434 4477	.002 746 9250	.026 734 8631	9.732 651 3694	.102 746 9250	38	
	39	41.144 777 7893	401.447 777 8925	.002 490 9840	.024 304 4210	9.756 955 7903	.102 490 9840	39	
	40	45.259 255 5682	442.592 555 6818	.002 259 4144	.022 094 9282	9.779 050 7185	.102 259 4144	40	
	41	49.785 181 1250	487.851 811 2499	.002 049 8028	.020 086 2983	9.799 137 0168	.102 049 8028	41	
	42	54.763 699 2375	537.636 992 3749	.001 859 9911	.018 260 2712	9.817 397 2880	.101 859 9911	42	
	43	60.240 069 1612	592.400 691 6124	.001 688 0466	.016 600 2465	9.833 997 5345	.101 688 0466	43	
	44	66.264 076 0774	652.640 760 7737	.001 532 2365	.015 091 1332	9.849 088 6678	.101 532 2365	44	
	45	72.890 483 6851	718.904 836 8510	.001 391 0047	.013 719 2120	9.862 807 8798	.101 391 0047	45	
RATE 12%	1	1.120 000 0000	1.000 000 0000	1.000 000 0000	.892 857 1429	.892 857 1429	1.120 000 0000	1	
	2	1.254 400 0000	2.120 000 0000	.471 698 1132	.797 193 8776	1.690 051 0204	.591 698 1132	2	
	3	1.404 928 0000	3.374 400 0000	.296 348 9806	.711 780 2478	2.401 831 2682	.416 348 9806	3	
	4	1.573 519 3600	4.779 328 0000	.209 234 4363	.635 518 0784	3.037 349 3466	.329 234 4363	4	
	5	1.762 341 6832	6.352 847 3600	.157 409 7319	.567 426 8557	3.604 776 2023	.277 409 7319	5	
	6	1.973 822 6852	8.115 189 0432	.123 225 7184	.506 631 1212	4.111 407 3235	.243 225 7184	6	
	7	2.210 681 4074	10.089 011 7284	.099 117 7359	.452 349 2153	4.563 756 5389	.219 117 7359	7	
	8	2.475 963 1763	12.299 693 1358	.081 302 8414	.403 883 2280	4.967 639 7668	.201 302 8414	8	
	9	2.773 078 7575	14.775 656 3121	.067 678 8888	.360 610 0250	5.328 249 7918	.187 678 8888	9	
	10	3.105 848 2083	17.548 735 0696	.056 984 1642	.321 973 2366	5.650 223 0284	.176 984 1642	10	
	11	3.478 549 9933	20.654 583 2779	.048 415 4043	.287 476 1041	5.937 699 1325	.168 415 4043	11	
	12	3.895 975 9925	24.133 133 2712	.041 436 8076	.256 675 0929	6.194 374 2255	.161 436 8076	12	
	13	4.363 493 1117	28.029 109 2638	.035 677 1951	.229 174 1901	6.423 548 4156	.155 677 1951	13	
	14	4.887 112 2851	32.392 602 3754	.030 871 2461	.204 619 8126	6.628 168 2282	.150 871 2461	14	
	15	5.473 565 7593	37.279 714 6605	.026 824 2396	.182 696 2613	6.810 864 4895	.146 824 2396	15	
	16	6.130 393 6504	42.753 280 4197	.023 390 0180	.163 121 6618	6.973 986 1513	.143 390 0180	16	
	17	6.866 040 8884	48.883 674 0701	.020 456 7275	.145 644 3409	7.119 630 4922	.140 456 7275	17	
	18	7.689 965 7950	55.749 714 9585	.017 937 3114	.130 039 5901	7.249 670 0824	.137 937 3114	18	
	19	8.612 761 6904	63.439 680 7535	.015 763 0049	.116 106 7769	7.365 776 8592	.135 763 0049	19	
	20	9.646 293 0933	72.052 442 4440	.013 878 7800	.103 666 7651	7.469 443 6243	.333 878 7800	20	
	21	10.803 848 2645	81.698 735 5372	.012 240 0915	.092 559 6117	7.562 003 2360	.132 240 0915	21	
	22	12.100 310 0562	92.502 583 8017	.010 810 5088	.082 642 5104	7.644 645 7464	.130 810 5088	22	
	23	13.552 347 2629	104.602 893 8579	.009 559 9650	.073 787 9557	7.718 433 7022	.129 559 9650	23	
	24	15.178 628 9345	118.155 241 1209	.008 463 4417	.065 882 1033	7.784 315 8055	.128 463 4417	24	
	25	17.000 064 4066	133.333 870 0554	.007 499 9698	.058 823 3066	7.843 139 1121	.127 499 9698	25	
	26	19.040 072 1354	150.333 934 4620	.006 651 8581	.052 520 8094	7.895 659 9215	.126 651 8581	26	
	27	21.324 880 7917	169.374 006 5974	.005 904 0937	.046 893 5798	7.942 553 5013	.125 904 0937	27	
	28	23.883 866 4867	190.698 887 3891	.005 243 8691	.041 869 2677	7.984 422 7690	.125 243 8691	28	
	29	26.749 930 4651	214.582 753 8758	.004 660 2068	.037 383 2747	8.021 806 0438	.124 660 2068	29	
	30	29.959 922 1209	241.332 684 3409	.004 143 6576	.033 377 9239	8.055 183 9677	.124 143 6576	30	
	31	33.555 112 7754	271.292 606 4618	.003 686 0570	.029 801 7177	8.084 985 6854	.123 686 0570	31	
	32	37.581 726 3085	304.847 719 2373	.003 280 3263	.026 608 6766	8.111 594 3620	.123 280 3263	32	
	33	42.091 533 4655	342.429 445 5457	.002 920 3096	.023 757 7469	8.135 352 1089	.122 920 3096	33	
	34	47.142 517 4813	384.520 979 0112	.002 600 6383	.021 212 2740	8.156 564 3830	.122 600 6383	34	
	35	52.799 619 5791	431.663 496 4926	.002 316 6193	.018 939 5304	8.175 503 9134	.122 316 6193	35	
	36	59.135 573 9286	484.463 116 0717	.002 064 1406	.016 910 2950	8.192 414 2084	.122 064 1406	36	
	37	66.231 842 8000	543.598 690 0003	.001 839 5924	.015 098 4777	8.207 512 6860	.121 839 5924	37	
	38	74.179 663 9360	609.830 532 8003	.001 639 7998	.013 480 7803	8.220 993 4697	.121 639 7998	38	
	39	83.081 223 6084	684.010 196 7363	.001 461 9665	.012 036 4140	8.233 029 8836	.121 461 9665	39	
	40	93.050 970 4414	767.091 420 3447	.001 303 6256	.010 746 7982	8.243 776 6818	.121 303 6256	40	
	41	104.217 086 8943	860.142 390 7861	.001 162 5982	.009 595 3555	8.253 372 0373	.121 162 5982	41	
	42	116.723 137 3216	964.359 477 6804	.001 036 9577	.008 567 2817	8.261 939 3190	.121 036 9577	42	
	43	130.729 913 8002	1081.082 615 0020	.000 924 9987	.007 649 3587	8.269 588 6777	.120 924 9987	43	
	44	146.417 503 4563	1211.812 528 8023	.000 825 2102	.006 829 7845	8.276 418 4623	.120 825 2102	44	
	45	163.987 603 8710	1358.230 032 2586	.000 736 2523	.006 098 0219	8.282 516 4842	.120 736 2523	45	

		XIV COMPOUND AMOUNT	XV AMOUNT OF ANNUITY	XVI SINKING FUND	XVII PRESENT VALUE	XVIII PRESENT VALUE OF ANNUITY	XIX AMORTIZATION	
RATE	PERIODS	AMOUNT OF 1 — How $1 left at compound interest will grow.	AMOUNT OF 1 PER PERIOD — How $1 deposited periodically will grow.	SINKING FUND — Periodic deposit that will grow to $1 at future date.	PRESENT WORTH OF 1 — What $1 due in the future is worth today.	PRESENT WORTH OF 1 PER PERIOD — What $1 payable periodically is worth today.	PARTIAL PAYMENT — Annuity worth $1 today. Periodic payment necessary to pay off a loan of $1.	PERIODS
14%	1	1.140 000 0000	1.000 000 0000	1.000 000 0000	.877 192 9825	.877 192 9825	1.140 000 0000	1
	2	1.299 600 0000	2.140 000 0000	.467 289 7196	.769 467 5285	1.646 660 5109	.607 289 7196	2
	3	1.481 544 0000	3.439 600 0000	.290 731 4804	.674 971 5162	2.321 632 0271	.430 731 4804	3
	4	1.688 960 1600	4.921 144 0000	.203 204 7833	.592 080 2774	2.913 712 3045	.343 204 7833	4
	5	1.925 414 5824	6.610 104 1600	.151 283 5465	.519 368 6644	3.433 080 9689	.291 283 5465	5
	6	2.194 972 6239	8.535 518 7424	.117 157 4957	.455 586 5477	3.888 667 5165	.257 157 4957	6
	7	2.502 268 7913	10.730 491 3663	.093 192 3773	.399 637 3225	4.288 304 8391	.233 192 3773	7
	8	2.852 586 4221	13.232 760 1576	.075 570 0238	.350 559 0549	4.638 863 8939	.215 570 0238	8
	9	3.251 948 5212	16.085 346 5797	.062 168 3838	.307 507 9429	4.946 371 8368	.202 168 3838	9
	10	3.707 221 3141	19.337 295 1008	.051 713 5408	.269 743 8095	5.216 115 6463	.191 713 5408	10
	11	4.226 232 2981	23.044 516 4150	.043 394 2714	.236 617 3768	5.452 733 0231	.183 394 2714	11
	12	4.817 904 8198	27.270 748 7131	.036 669 3269	.207 559 1024	5.660 292 1255	.176 669 3269	12
	13	5.492 411 4946	32.088 653 5329	.031 163 6635	.182 069 3881	5.842 361 5136	.171 163 6635	13
	14	6.261 349 1038	37.581 065 0275	.026 609 1448	.159 709 9896	6.002 071 5032	.166 609 1448	14
	15	7.137 937 9784	43.842 414 1313	.022 808 9630	.140 096 4821	6.142 167 9852	.162 808 9630	15
	16	8.137 249 2954	50.980 352 1097	.019 615 4000	.122 891 6509	6.265 059 6362	.159 615 4000	16
	17	9.276 464 1967	59.117 601 4051	.016 915 4359	.107 799 6938	6.372 859 3300	.156 915 4359	17
	18	10.575 169 1843	68.394 065 6018	.014 621 1516	.094 561 1349	6.467 420 4649	.154 621 1516	18
	19	12.055 692 8700	78.969 234 7861	.012 663 1593	.082 948 3640	6.550 368 8288	.152 663 1593	19
	20	13.743 489 8719	91.024 927 6561	.010 986 0016	.072 761 7228	6.623 130 5516	.150 986 0016	20
	21	15.667 578 4539	104.768 417 5280	.009 544 8612	.063 826 0726	6.686 956 6242	.149 544 8612	21
	22	17.861 039 4375	120.435 995 9819	.008 303 1654	.055 987 7830	6.742 944 4072	.148 303 1654	22
	23	20.361 584 9587	138.297 035 4193	.007 230 8130	.049 112 0903	6.792 056 4976	.147 230 8130	23
	24	23.212 206 8529	158.658 620 3780	.006 302 8406	.043 080 7810	6.835 137 2786	.146 302 8406	24
	25	26.461 915 8123	181.870 827 2310	.005 498 4079	.037 790 1588	6.872 927 4373	.145 498 4079	25
	26	30.166 584 0261	208.332 743 0433	.004 800 0136	.033 149 2621	6.906 076 6994	.144 800 0136	26
	27	34.389 905 7897	238.499 327 0694	.004 192 8839	.029 078 3001	6.935 154 9995	.144 192 8839	27
	28	39.204 492 6003	272.889 232 8591	.003 664 4905	.025 507 2808	6.960 662 2803	.143 664 4905	28
	29	44.693 121 5643	312.093 725 4594	.003 204 1657	.022 374 8077	6.983 037 0879	.143 204 1657	29
	30	50.950 158 5833	356.786 847 0237	.002 802 7939	.019 627 0243	7.002 664 1122	.142 802 7939	30
	31	58.083 180 7850	407.737 005 6070	.002 452 5613	.017 216 6880	7.019 880 8002	.142 452 5613	31
	32	66.214 826 0949	465.820 186 3920	.002 146 7511	.015 102 3579	7.034 983 1581	.142 146 7511	32
	33	75.484 901 7482	532.035 012 4868	.001 879 5755	.013 247 6823	7.048 230 8404	.141 879 5755	33
	34	86.052 787 9929	607.519 914 2350	.001 646 0366	.011 620 7740	7.059 851 6144	.141 646 0366	34
	35	98.100 178 3119	693.572 702 2279	.001 441 8099	.010 193 6614	7.070 045 2758	.141 441 8099	35
	36	111.834 203 2756	791.672 880 5398	.001 263 1480	.008 941 8082	7.078 987 0840	.141 263 1480	36
	37	127.490 991 7342	903.507 083 8154	.001 106 7982	.007 843 6914	7.086 830 7755	.141 106 7982	37
	38	145.339 730 5769	1030.998 075 5495	.000 969 9339	.006 880 4311	7.093 711 2065	.140 969 9339	38
	39	165.687 292 8577	1176.337 806 1264	.000 850 0959	.006 035 4659	7.099 746 6724	.140 850 0959	39
	40	188.883 513 8578	1342.025 098 9841	.000 745 1425	.005 294 2683	7.105 040 9407	.140 745 1425	40
	41	215.327 205 7979	1530.908 612 8419	.000 653 2069	.004 644 0950	7.109 685 0357	.140 653 2069	41
	42	245.473 014 6096	1746.235 818 6398	.000 572 6603	.004 073 7675	7.113 758 8033	.140 572 6603	42
	43	279.839 236 6549	1991.708 833 2494	.000 502 0814	.003 573 4803	7.117 332 2836	.140 502 0814	43
	44	319.016 729 7866	2271.548 069 9043	.000 440 2284	.003 134 6318	7.120 466 9154	.140 440 2284	44
	45	363.679 071 9567	2590.564 799 6909	.000 386 0162	.002 749 6771	7.123 216 5925	.140 386 0162	45
15%	1	1.150 000 0000	1.000 000 0000	1.000 000 0000	.869 565 2174	.869 565 2174	1.150 000 0000	1
	2	1.322 500 0000	2.150 000 0000	.465 116 2791	.756 143 6673	1.625 708 8847	.615 116 2791	2
	3	1.520 875 0000	3.472 500 0000	.287 976 9618	.657 516 2324	2.283 225 1171	.437 976 9618	3
	4	1.749 006 2500	4.993 375 0000	.200 265 3516	.571 753 2456	2.854 978 3627	.350 265 3516	4
	5	2.011 357 1875	6.742 381 2500	.148 315 5525	.497 176 7353	3.352 155 0980	.298 315 5525	5
	6	2.313 060 7656	8.753 738 4375	.114 236 9066	.432 327 5959	3.784 482 6939	.264 236 9066	6
	7	2.660 019 8805	11.066 799 2031	.090 360 3636	.375 937 0399	4.160 419 7338	.240 360 3636	7
	8	3.059 022 8625	13.726 819 0836	.072 850 0896	.326 901 7738	4.487 321 5077	.222 850 0896	8
	9	3.517 876 2919	16.785 841 9461	.059 574 0150	.284 262 4120	4.771 583 9197	.209 574 0150	9
	10	4.045 557 7357	20.303 718 2381	.049 252 0625	.247 184 7061	5.018 768 6259	.199 252 0625	10
	11	4.652 391 3961	24.349 275 9738	.041 068 9830	.214 943 2227	5.233 711 8486	.191 068 9830	11
	12	5.350 250 1055	29.001 667 3698	.034 480 7761	.186 907 1502	5.420 618 9988	.184 480 7761	12
	13	6.152 787 6213	34.351 917 4753	.029 110 4565	.162 527 9567	5.583 146 9554	.179 110 4565	13
	14	7.075 705 7645	40.504 705 0966	.024 688 4898	.141 328 6580	5.724 475 6134	.174 688 4898	14
	15	8.137 061 6292	47.580 410 8611	.021 017 0526	.122 894 4852	5.847 370 0986	.171 017 0526	15
	16	9.357 620 8735	55.717 472 4902	.017 947 6914	.106 864 7697	5.954 234 8684	.167 947 6914	16
	17	10.761 264 0046	65.075 093 3638	.015 366 8623	.092 925 8867	6.047 160 7551	.165 366 8623	17
	18	12.375 453 6053	75.836 357 3683	.013 186 2874	.080 805 1189	6.127 965 8740	.163 186 2874	18
	19	14.231 771 6460	88.211 810 9736	.011 336 3504	.070 265 3208	6.198 231 1948	.161 336 3504	19
	20	16.366 537 3929	102.443 582 6196	.009 761 4704	.061 100 2789	6.259 331 4737	.159 761 4704	20
	21	18.821 518 0019	118.810 120 0126	.008 416 7914	.053 130 6773	6.312 462 1511	.158 416 7914	21
	22	21.644 745 7022	137.631 638 0145	.007 265 7713	.046 200 5890	6.358 662 7401	.157 265 7713	22
	23	24.891 457 5575	159.276 383 7166	.006 278 3947	.040 174 4252	6.398 837 1653	.156 278 3947	23
	24	28.625 176 1911	184.167 841 2741	.005 429 8286	.034 934 2828	6.433 771 4481	.155 429 8296	24
	25	32.918 952 6198	212.793 017 4653	.004 699 4023	.030 377 6372	6.464 149 0853	.154 699 4023	25
	26	37.856 795 5128	245.711 970 0851	.004 069 8058	.026 415 3367	6.490 564 4220	.154 069 8058	26
	27	43.535 314 8397	283.568 765 5978	.003 526 4815	.022 969 8580	6.513 534 2800	.153 526 4815	27
	28	50.065 612 0656	327.104 080 4375	.003 057 1309	.019 973 7896	6.533 508 0695	.153 057 1309	28
	29	57.575 453 8755	377.169 692 5031	.002 651 3265	.017 368 5127	6.550 876 5822	.152 651 3265	29
	30	66.211 771 9568	434.745 146 3786	.002 300 1982	.015 103 0545	6.565 979 6367	.152 300 1982	30
	31	76.143 537 7503	500.956 918 3354	.001 996 1796	.013 133 0909	6.579 112 7276	.151 996 1796	31
	32	87.565 068 4128	577.100 456 0857	.001 732 8006	.011 420 0790	6.590 532 8066	.151 732 8006	32
	33	100.699 828 6748	664.665 524 4985	.001 504 5161	.009 930 5035	6.600 463 3101	.151 504 5161	33
	34	115.804 802 9760	765.365 353 1733	.001 306 5655	.008 635 2204	6.609 098 5305	.151 306 5655	34
	35	133.175 523 4224	881.170 156 1493	.001 134 8546	.007 508 8873	6.616 607 4178	.151 134 8546	35
	36	153.151 851 9358	1014.345 679 5717	.000 985 8572	.006 529 4672	6.623 136 8851	.150 985 8572	36
	37	176.124 629 7261	1167.497 531 5074	.000 856 5329	.005 677 7976	6.628 814 6627	.150 856 5329	37
	38	202.543 324 1850	1343.622 161 2335	.000 744 2569	.004 937 2153	6.633 751 8980	.150 744 2569	38
	39	232.924 822 8128	1546.165 485 4186	.000 646 7613	.004 293 2307	6.638 045 1287	.150 646 7613	39
	40	267.863 546 2347	1779.090 308 2314	.000 562 0850	.003 733 2441	6.641 778 3728	.150 562 0850	40
	41	308.043 078 1699	2046.953 854 4661	.000 488 5308	.003 246 2992	6.645 024 6720	.150 488 5308	41
	42	354.249 539 8954	2354.996 932 6360	.000 424 6290	.002 822 8689	6.647 847 5408	.150 424 6290	42
	43	407.386 970 8797	2709.246 472 5314	.000 369 1063	.002 454 6686	6.650 302 2094	.150 369 1063	43
	44	468.495 016 5117	3116.633 443 4111	.000 320 8590	.002 134 4944	6.652 436 7038	.150 320 8590	44
	45	538.769 268 9884	3585.128 459 9227	.000 278 9300	.001 856 0821	6.654 292 7860	.150 278 9300	45

		XIV COMPOUND AMOUNT	XV AMOUNT OF ANNUITY	XVI SINKING FUND	XVII PRESENT VALUE	XVIII PRESENT VALUE OF ANNUITY	XIX AMORTIZATION	
RATE 16%	PERIODS	AMOUNT OF 1 — How $1 left at compound interest will grow.	AMOUNT OF 1 PER PERIOD — How $1 deposited periodically will grow.	SINKING FUND — Periodic deposit that will grow to $1 at future date.	PRESENT WORTH OF 1 — What $1 due in the future is worth today.	PRESENT WORTH OF 1 PER PERIOD — What $1 payable periodically is worth today.	PARTIAL PAYMENT — Annuity worth $1 today. Periodic payment necessary to pay off a loan of $1.	PERIODS
	1	1.160 000 0000	1.000 000 0000	1.000 000 0000	.862 068 9655	.862 068 9655	1.160 000 0000	1
	2	1.345 600 0000	2.160 000 0000	.462 962 9630	.743 162 9013	1.605 231 8668	.622 962 9630	2
	3	1.560 896 0000	3.505 600 0000	.285 257 8731	.640 657 6735	2.245 889 5404	.445 257 8731	3
	4	1.810 639 3600	5.066 496 0000	.197 375 0695	.552 291 0979	2.798 180 6382	.357 375 0695	4
	5	2.100 341 6576	6.877 135 3600	.145 409 3816	.476 113 0154	3.274 293 6537	.305 409 3816	5
	6	2.436 396 3228	8.977 477 0176	.111 389 8702	.410 442 2547	3.684 735 9083	.271 389 8702	6
	7	2.826 219 7345	11.413 873 3404	.087 612 6771	.353 829 5299	4.038 565 4382	.247 612 6771	7
	8	3.278 414 8920	14.240 093 0749	.070 224 2601	.305 025 4568	4.343 590 8950	.230 224 2601	8
	9	3.802 961 2747	17.518 507 9669	.057 082 4868	.262 952 9800	4.606 543 8750	.217 082 4868	9
	10	4.411 435 0786	21.321 469 2416	.046 901 0831	.226 683 6034	4.833 227 4785	.206 901 0831	10
	11	5.117 264 6912	25.732 904 3202	.038 860 7515	.195 416 8995	5.028 644 3780	.198 860 7515	11
	12	5.936 027 0418	30.850 169 0114	.032 414 7333	.168 462 8444	5.197 107 2224	.192 414 7333	12
	13	6.885 791 3685	36.786 196 0533	.027 184 1100	.145 226 5900	5.342 333 8124	.187 184 1100	13
	14	7.987 517 9875	43.671 987 4218	.022 897 9733	.125 195 3362	5.467 529 1486	.182 897 9733	14
	15	9.265 520 8655	51.659 505 4093	.019 357 5218	.107 927 0140	5.575 456 1626	.179 357 5218	15
	16	10.748 004 2040	60.925 026 2748	.016 413 6162	.093 040 5293	5.668 496 6919	.176 413 6162	16
	17	12.467 684 8766	71.673 030 4787	.013 952 2494	.080 207 3528	5.748 704 0447	.173 952 2494	17
	18	14.462 514 4569	84.140 715 3553	.011 884 8526	.069 144 2697	5.817 848 3144	.171 884 8526	18
	19	16.776 516 7700	98.603 229 8122	.010 141 6556	.059 607 1290	5.877 455 4435	.170 141 6556	19
	20	19.460 759 4531	115.379 746 5821	.008 667 0324	.051 385 4561	5.928 840 8996	.168 667 0324	20
	21	22.574 480 9656	134.840 506 0353	.007 416 1691	.044 297 8070	5.973 138 7065	.167 416 1691	21
	22	26.186 397 9201	157.414 987 0009	.006 352 6353	.038 187 7646	6.011 326 4711	.166 352 6353	22
	23	30.376 221 5874	183.601 384 9211	.005 446 5820	.032 920 4867	6.044 246 9579	.165 446 5820	23
	24	35.236 417 0414	213.977 606 5085	.004 673 3862	.028 379 7299	6.072 626 6878	.164 673 3862	24
	25	40.874 243 7680	249.214 023 5498	.004 012 6153	.024 465 2844	6.097 091 9723	.164 012 6153	25
	26	47.414 122 7708	290.088 267 3178	.003 447 2266	.021 090 7624	6.118 182 7347	.163 447 2266	26
	27	55.000 382 4142	337.502 390 0886	.002 962 9420	.018 181 6918	6.136 364 4265	.162 962 9420	27
	28	63.800 443 6004	392.502 772 5028	.002 547 7527	.015 673 8722	6.152 038 2987	.162 547 7527	28
	29	74.008 514 5765	456.303 216 1032	.002 191 5252	.013 511 9588	6.165 550 2575	.162 191 5252	29
	30	85.849 876 9088	530.311 730 6798	.001 885 6833	.011 648 2403	6.177 198 4978	.161 885 6833	30
	31	99.585 857 2142	616.161 607 5885	.001 622 9508	.010 041 5865	6.187 240 0843	.161 622 9508	31
	32	115.519 594 3684	715.747 464 8027	.001 397 1408	.008 656 5401	6.195 896 6244	.161 397 1408	32
	33	134.002 729 4674	831.267 059 1711	.001 202 9828	.007 462 5346	6.203 359 1590	.161 202 9828	33
	34	155.443 166 1822	965.269 788 6385	.001 035 9798	.006 433 2194	6.209 792 3784	.161 035 9798	34
	35	180.314 072 7713	1120.712 954 8207	.000 892 2891	.005 545 8788	6.215 338 2573	.160 892 2891	35
	36	209.164 324 4147	1301.027 027 5920	.000 768 6235	.004 780 9300	6.220 119 1873	.160 768 6235	36
	37	242.630 616 3211	1510.191 352 0067	.000 662 1677	.004 121 4914	6.224 240 6787	.160 662 1677	37
	38	281.451 514 9324	1752.821 968 3278	.000 570 5086	.003 553 0098	6.227 793 6885	.160 570 5086	38
	39	326.483 757 3216	2034.273 483 2602	.000 491 5760	.003 062 9395	6.230 856 6281	.160 491 5760	39
	40	378.721 158 4931	2360.757 240 5818	.000 423 5929	.002 640 4651	6.233 497 0932	.160 423 5929	40
	41	439.316 543 8520	2739.478 399 0749	.000 365 0330	.002 276 2630	6.235 773 3562	.160 365 0330	41
	42	509.607 190 8683	3178.794 942 9269	.000 314 5846	.001 962 2957	6.237 735 6519	.160 314 5846	42
	43	591.144 341 4072	3688.402 133 7952	.000 271 1201	.001 691 6342	6.239 427 2861	.160 271 1201	43
	44	685.727 436 0324	4279.546 475 2025	.000 233 6696	.001 458 3054	6.240 885 5915	.160 233 6696	44
	45	795.443 825 7976	4965.273 911 2349	.000 201 3988	.001 257 1598	6.242 142 7513	.160 201 3988	45
RATE 18%	1	1.180 000 0000	1.000 000 0000	1.000 000 0000	.847 457 6271	.847 457 6271	1.180 000 0000	1
	2	1.392 400 0000	2.180 000 0000	.458 715 5963	.718 184 4298	1.565 642 0569	.638 715 5963	2
	3	1.643 032 0000	3.572 400 0000	.279 923 8607	.608 630 8727	2.174 272 9296	.459 923 8607	3
	4	1.938 777 7600	5.215 432 0000	.191 738 6709	.515 788 8752	2.690 061 8047	.371 738 6709	4
	5	2.287 757 7568	7.154 209 7600	.139 777 8418	.437 109 2162	3.127 171 0209	.319 777 8418	5
	6	2.699 554 1530	9.441 967 5168	.105 910 1292	.370 431 5392	3.497 602 5601	.285 910 1292	6
	7	3.185 473 9006	12.141 521 6698	.082 361 9994	.313 925 0332	3.811 527 5933	.262 361 9994	7
	8	3.758 859 2027	15.326 995 5704	.065 244 3589	.266 038 1637	4.077 565 7571	.245 244 3589	8
	9	4.435 453 8592	19.085 854 7731	.052 394 8239	.225 456 0710	4.303 021 8280	.232 394 8239	9
	10	5.233 835 5538	23.521 308 6323	.042 514 6413	.191 064 4669	4.494 086 2949	.222 514 6413	10
	11	6.175 925 9535	28.755 144 1860	.034 776 3862	.161 919 0398	4.656 005 3347	.214 776 3862	11
	12	7.287 592 6251	34.931 070 1395	.028 627 8089	.137 219 5252	4.793 224 8599	.208 627 8089	12
	13	8.599 359 2976	42.218 662 7646	.023 686 2073	.116 287 7332	4.909 512 5931	.203 686 2073	13
	14	10.147 243 9712	50.818 022 0622	.019 678 0583	.098 548 9265	5.008 061 5196	.199 678 0583	14
	15	11.973 747 8860	60.965 266 0334	.016 402 7825	.083 516 0394	5.091 577 5590	.196 402 7825	15
	16	14.129 022 5055	72.939 013 9195	.013 710 3046	.070 776 3046	5.162 353 8635	.193 710 3046	16
	17	16.672 246 5565	87.068 036 4250	.011 485 2711	.059 979 9191	5.222 333 7827	.191 485 2711	17
	18	19.673 250 9367	103.740 282 9814	.009 639 4570	.050 830 4399	5.273 164 2226	.189 639 4570	18
	19	23.214 436 1053	123.413 533 9181	.008 102 8390	.043 076 6440	5.316 240 8666	.188 102 8390	19
	20	27.393 034 6042	146.627 970 0234	.006 819 9812	.036 505 6305	5.352 746 4971	.186 819 9812	20
	21	32.323 780 8330	174.021 004 6276	.005 746 4327	.030 936 9750	5.383 683 4721	.185 746 4327	21
	22	38.142 061 3829	206.344 785 4605	.004 846 2577	.026 217 7754	5.409 901 2476	.184 846 2577	22
	23	45.007 632 4318	244.486 846 8434	.004 090 1996	.022 218 4538	5.432 119 7013	.184 090 1996	23
	24	53.109 006 2695	289.494 479 2752	.003 454 2973	.018 829 1981	5.450 948 8994	.183 454 2973	24
	25	62.668 827 3981	342.603 485 5448	.002 918 8261	.015 956 9475	5.466 905 8470	.182 918 8261	25
	26	73.948 980 3297	405.272 112 9429	.002 467 4779	.013 522 8369	5.480 428 6839	.182 467 4779	26
	27	87.259 796 7891	479.221 093 2726	.002 086 7195	.011 460 0313	5.491 888 7152	.182 086 7195	27
	28	102.966 560 2111	566.480 890 0616	.001 765 2846	.009 711 8909	5.501 600 6061	.181 765 2846	28
	29	121.500 541 0491	669.447 450 2727	.001 493 7692	.008 230 4160	5.509 831 0221	.181 493 7692	29
	30	143.370 638 4379	790.947 991 3218	.001 264 3056	.006 974 9288	5.516 805 9509	.181 264 3056	30
	31	169.177 353 3568	934.318 629 7597	.001 070 2987	.005 910 9566	5.522 716 9076	.181 070 2987	31
	32	199.629 276 9610	1103.495 983 1165	.000 906 2108	.005 009 2853	5.527 726 1928	.180 906 2108	32
	33	235.562 546 8139	1303.125 260 0775	.000 767 3859	.004 245 1570	5.531 971 3499	.180 767 3859	33
	34	277.963 805 2405	1538.687 806 8914	.000 649 9044	.003 597 5907	5.535 568 9406	.180 649 9044	34
	35	327.997 290 1837	1816.651 612 1319	.000 550 4633	.003 048 8057	5.538 617 7462	.180 550 4633	35
	36	387.036 802 4168	2144.648 902 3156	.000 466 2768	.002 583 7336	5.541 201 4799	.180 466 2768	36
	37	456.703 426 8518	2531.685 704 7324	.000 394 9937	.002 189 6048	5.543 391 0846	.180 394 9937	37
	38	538.910 043 6852	2988.389 131 5843	.000 334 6284	.001 855 5973	5.545 246 6819	.180 334 6284	38
	39	635.913 851 5485	3527.299 175 2694	.000 283 5030	.001 572 5401	5.546 819 2219	.180 283 5030	39
	40	750.378 344 8272	4163.213 026 8179	.000 240 1991	.001 332 6611	5.548 151 8830	.180 240 1991	40
	41	885.446 446 8961	4913.591 371 6451	.000 203 5171	.001 129 3738	5.549 281 2568	.180 203 5171	41
	42	1044.826 807 3374	5799.037 818 5413	.000 172 4424	.000 957 0964	5.550 238 3532	.180 172 4424	42
	43	1232.895 632 6582	6843.864 625 8787	.000 146 1163	.000 811 0987	5.551 049 4519	.180 146 1163	43
	44	1454.816 846 5366	8076.760 258 5369	.000 123 8120	.000 687 3717	5.551 736 8236	.180 123 8120	44
	45	1716.683 878 9132	9531.577 105 0735	.000 104 9144	.000 582 5184	5.552 319 3420	.180 104 9144	45

TABLE C-24 SUM OF MONTHS' DIGITS

NUMBER OF MONTHS	SUM: 1 THROUGH LARGEST MONTH
6	21
9	45
10	55
12	78
15	120
18	171
24	300
36	666

TABLE C-25 MONTHLY PAYMENT PER $1,000 OF MORTGAGE[a]

RATE	20 YEARS	25 YEARS	30 YEARS
8%	$8.37	$7.72	$7.34
$8\frac{1}{4}$	8.53	7.89	7.52
$8\frac{1}{2}$	8.68	8.06	7.69
$8\frac{3}{4}$	8.84	8.23	7.87
9	9.00	8.40	8.05
$9\frac{1}{4}$	9.16	8.57	8.23
$9\frac{1}{2}$	9.33	8.74	8.41
$9\frac{3}{4}$	9.49	8.92	8.60
10	9.66	9.09	8.78
11	10.33	9.81	9.53

[a] Monthly payments including principal and interest.

TABLE C-26 METRIC MEASURES WITH U.S. EQUIVALENTS

LENGTH	WEIGHT	LIQUID CAPACITY
1 millimeter = 0.039 inch	1 gram[a] = 0.035 ounce	1 liter[b] = 33.8 ounces
1 centimeter = 0.394 inch	1 kilogram = 2.20 pounds	= 2.11 pints
1 decimeter = 3.94 inches		= 1.06 quarts
1 meter = 39.37 inches	TEMPERATURE	= 0.264 gallon
= 3.28 feet		
= 1.09 yards	$C = \frac{5}{9}(F - 32)$	
1 kilometer = 0.621 mile	or $C = (F - 32) \div 1.8$	

[a] 1 gram is defined as the weight of 1 cubic centimeter of pure water at 4° Celsius.
[b] 1 liter is defined as the capacity of a cube that is 1 decimeter long on each edge.

TABLE C-27 U.S. MEASURES WITH METRIC EQUIVALENTS

LENGTH	WEIGHT	LIQUID CAPACITY
1 inch = 2.54 centimeters	1 ounce = 28.4 grams	1 ounce = 0.030 liter
1 foot = 0.305 meter	1 pound = 454 grams	1 pint = 0.473 liter
1 yard = 0.914 meter	= 0.454 kilograms	1 quart = 0.946 liter
1 mile = 1.61 kilometers		1 gallon = 3.79 liters

TEMPERATURE

$$F = \frac{9}{5}C + 32$$
$$\text{or} \quad F = 1.8C + 32$$

TABLE C-28 SAMPLE FOREIGN CURRENCY EXCHANGE RATES

COUNTRY AND CURRENCY	$1 U.S. IN FOREIGN CURRENCY	FOREIGN CURRENCY IN U.S. DOLLARS
Britain (£)	0.6371	1.5695
Canada (C$)	1.3570	0.7369
France (F)	5.0800	0.1969
Germany (DM)	1.4380	0.6954
Japan (¥)	86.5500	0.011554
Mexico (N$)	5.9200	0.168919

Answers

Chapter 1

Exercise Set 1.2

1. $\frac{1}{4}$ **3.** $\frac{2}{3}$ **5.** $\frac{1}{2}$ **7.** $\frac{3}{7}$ **9.** $\frac{5}{8}$ **11.** lowest terms **13.** $\frac{4}{3}$ or $1\frac{1}{3}$ **15.** $\frac{10}{7}$ or $1\frac{3}{7}$ **17.** (a) **19.** (b) **21.** $\frac{3}{8}$ **23.** $\frac{5}{14}$
25. $\frac{1}{12}$ **27.** $\frac{5}{4}$ or $1\frac{1}{4}$ **29.** $\frac{5}{16}$ **31.** 6 **33.** $\frac{4}{9}$ **35.** $\frac{16}{65}$ **37.** $\frac{19}{14}$ or $1\frac{5}{14}$ **39.** 12 **41.** 1 **43.** 2 **45.** $\frac{5}{7}$ **47.** $\frac{1}{6}$
49. 1 **51.** $\frac{7}{13}$ **53.** $\frac{37}{30}$ or $1\frac{7}{30}$ **55.** $\frac{1}{5}$ **57.** $\frac{4}{15}$ **59.** $\frac{3}{56}$ **61.** $\frac{29}{24}$ or $1\frac{5}{24}$ **63.** $\frac{9}{28}$ **65.** $\frac{93}{20}$ or $4\frac{13}{20}$ **67.** $\frac{23}{6}$ or $3\frac{5}{6}$
69. $\frac{52}{15}$ or $3\frac{7}{15}$ **71.** $\frac{81}{20}$ or $4\frac{1}{20}$ **73.** $\frac{5}{6}$ **75.** $\frac{11}{12}$ **77.** $20\frac{1}{4}$ yd **79.** $13\frac{11}{16}$ in **81.** $8\frac{7}{16}$ ft **83.** $11\frac{7}{8}$ ft
85. 297 min or 4 hr 57 min **87.** $\frac{25}{16}$ or $1\frac{9}{16}$ in **89.** 5 mg **91.** (a) yes (b) $\frac{5}{8}$ in **93.** (a) $\frac{5}{16}$ (b) $\frac{20}{9}$ or $2\frac{2}{9}$
(c) $\frac{29}{24}$ or $1\frac{5}{24}$ (d) $\frac{11}{24}$ **95.** A general term for any collection of numbers, variables, grouping symbols, and operations.
97. (b). In part (a) we have divided out common factors from *two* fractions.

Group Activity/Challenge Problems

1. (b) Rice and water 1 cup, salt $\frac{3}{8}$ tsp, butter $1\frac{1}{2}$ tsp **3.** 3 **5.** $\frac{427}{90}$ or $4\frac{67}{90}$

Exercise Set 1.3

1. $\{\ldots, -3, -2, -1, 0, 1, 2, 3, \ldots\}$ **3.** $\{1, 2, 3, 4, \ldots\}$ **5.** $\{1, 2, 3, 4, \ldots\}$ **7.** T **9.** T **11.** F **13.** F
15. T **17.** T **19.** F **21.** F **23.** T **25.** T **27.** T **29.** F **31.** T **33.** T **35.** T **37.** F **39.** (a) 7, 9
(b) 7, 0, 9 (c) $-6, 7, 0, 9$ (d) $-6, 7, 12.4, -\frac{9}{5}, -2\frac{1}{4}, 0, 9, 0.35$ (e) $\sqrt{3}, \sqrt{7}$ (f) $-6, 7, 12.4, -\frac{9}{5}, -2\frac{1}{4}, \sqrt{3}, 0, 9,$
$\sqrt{7}, 0.35$ **41.** (a) 5 (b) 5 (c) -300 (d) $5, -300$ (e) $\frac{1}{2}, 4\frac{1}{2}, \frac{5}{12}, -1.67, 5, -300, -9\frac{1}{2}$ (f) $\sqrt{2}, -\sqrt{2}$ (g) $\frac{1}{2},$
$\sqrt{2}, -\sqrt{2}, 4\frac{1}{2}, \frac{5}{12}, -1.67, 5, -300, -9\frac{1}{2}$ **43.** $-\frac{2}{3}, \frac{1}{2}, 6.3$ **45.** $-\sqrt{7}, \sqrt{3}, \sqrt{6}$ **47.** $-5, 0, 4$ **49.** $-13, -5, -1$
51. $1.5, 3, 6\frac{1}{4}$ **53.** $-7, 1, 5$

Cumulative Review Exercises

56. $\frac{14}{3}$ **57.** $5\frac{1}{3}$ **58.** $\frac{49}{40}$ or $1\frac{9}{40}$ **59.** $\frac{70}{27}$ or $2\frac{16}{27}$

Group Activity/Challenge Problems

1. (a) no (b) Infinite set **3.** (a) and (b) an infinite number **5.** $A \cup B = \{a, b, c, d, g, h, i, j, m, p\}$, $A \cap B = \{b, c, d\}$

Exercise Set 1.4

1. 4 **3.** 15 **5.** 0 **7.** -8 **9.** -65 **11.** $2 < 3$ **13.** $-3 < 0$ **15.** $\frac{1}{2} > -\frac{2}{3}$ **17.** $0.2 < 0.4$ **19.** $-\frac{1}{2} > -1$
21. $4 > -4$ **23.** $-2.1 < -2$ **25.** $\frac{5}{9} > -\frac{5}{9}$ **27.** $-\frac{3}{2} < \frac{3}{2}$ **29.** $0.49 > 0.43$ **31.** $5 > -7$ **33.** $-0.006 > -0.007$

35. $-5 < -2$ **37.** $-\frac{2}{3} > -3$ **39.** $-\frac{1}{2} > -\frac{3}{2}$ **41.** $8 > |-7|$ **43.** $|0| < \frac{2}{3}$ **45.** $|-3| < |-4|$ **47.** $4 < |-\frac{9}{2}|$
49. $|-\frac{6}{2}| > |-\frac{2}{6}|$ **51.** $=$ **53.** $<$ **55.** $<$ **57.** $4, -4$ **59.** $2, -2$
61. The distance between 0 and the number on the number line.

CUMULATIVE REVIEW EXERCISES

62. $\frac{31}{24}$ or $1\frac{7}{24}$ **63.** $\{0, 1, 2, 3, \ldots\}$ **64.** $\{1, 2, 3, 4, \ldots\}$ **65. (a)** 5   **(b)** 5, 0   **(c)** 5, -2, 0   **(d)** 5, -2, 0, $\frac{1}{3}$, $-\frac{5}{9}$, 2.3
(e) $\sqrt{3}$ **(f)** 5, -2, 0, $\frac{1}{3}$, $\sqrt{3}$, $-\frac{5}{9}$, 2.3

GROUP ACTIVITY/CHALLENGE PROBLEMS

1. less than   **3.** 3, -3 **5. (a)** x **(b)** $-x$ **(c)** $|x| = \begin{cases} x, & x \geq 0 \\ -x, & x < 0 \end{cases}$

EXERCISE SET 1.5

1. -12 **3.** 40   **5.** 0   **7.** $-\frac{5}{3}$ **9.** $-\frac{3}{5}$ **11.** -0.63 **13.** $-3\frac{1}{5}$ **15.** 3.1   **17.** 7   **19.** 1   **21.** -6 **23.** 0   **25.** 0
27. -10 **29.** 0   **31.** -10 **33.** 0   **35.** -6 **37.** 3   **39.** -9 **41.** 9   **43.** -27 **45.** -44 **47.** -26 **49.** 5
51. -20 **53.** -31 **55.** 91   **57.** -140 **59.** -98 **61.** 266   **63.** -373 **65.** -452 **67.** -1300 **69.** -22
71. -3880 **73.** -1267 **75.** -2050 **77.** $-14,559$ **79.** -1215 **81.** -7494 **83.** 7458   **85.** True   **87.** False
89. False   **91.** $174   **93.** $1927   **95.** 54 ft   **97.** increased by 92 million people

CUMULATIVE REVIEW EXERCISES

101. 1   **102.** $\frac{43}{16}$ or $2\frac{11}{16}$ **103.** $|-3| > 2$ **104.** $8 > |-7|$

GROUP ACTIVITY/CHALLENGE PROBLEMS

1. -22 **2.** -10 **3.** 20   **4.** 55   **5.** 210   **6.** 5050

EXERCISE SET 1.6

1. 3   **3.** -1 **5.** 0   **7.** -3 **9.** -6 **11.** 6   **13.** -6 **15.** 6   **17.** -8 **19.** 2   **21.** 2   **23.** 9   **25.** 0
27. -18 **29.** -2 **31.** 0   **33.** 0   **35.** 0   **37.** -1 **39.** -5 **41.** -41 **43.** -3 **45.** -180 **47.** -110
49. -10 **51.** 220   **53.** 0   **55.** -46 **57.** -18 **59.** -16 **61.** 10   **63.** -2 **65.** 13   **67.** 0   **69.** -4
71. 11   **73.** 81   **75.** 99   **77.** -595 **79.** 847   **81.** 1712   **83.** 196   **85.** -448 **87.** 116.1   **89.** 0   **91.** -69
93. -1670 **95.** 97.32   **97.** 7   **99.** -2 **101.** -15 **103.** -2 **105.** 0   **107.** 43   **109.** -6 **111.** -9 **113.** 35
115. -21 **117.** -12 **119.** -3 **121.** 18   **123.** 12   **125.** -22 **127.** 326 boxes   **129.** $1246   **131.** 100°
133. (b) 8   **135. (a)** 148 mi   **(b)** 12 mi

CUMULATIVE REVIEW EXERCISES

137. $\{\ldots, -3, -2, -1, 0, 1, 2, 3, \ldots\}$ **138.** The set of rational numbers together with the set of irrational numbers forms
the set of real numbers.   **139.** $|-3| > -5$ **140.** $|-6| < |-7|$

GROUP ACTIVITY/CHALLENGE PROBLEMS

1. -5 **3.** 50   **4. (a)** 7 units   **(b)** $5 - (-2)$ **5.** 253 ft.   **7.** 0

EXERCISE SET 1.7

1. 12   **3.** -9 **5.** -32 **7.** -9 **9.** 12   **11.** 36   **13.** 96   **15.** 81   **17.** -10 **19.** 36   **21.** 0   **23.** -1
25. -120 **27.** 84   **29.** -90 **31.** 360   **33.** $-\frac{3}{10}$ **35.** $\frac{14}{27}$ **37.** 4   **39.** $-\frac{15}{28}$ **41.** 3   **43.** 4   **45.** 4   **47.** -4
49. -18 **51.** 5   **53.** 6   **55.** 5   **57.** -1 **59.** -4 **61.** 0   **63.** 16   **65.** 0   **67.** -3 **69.** -6 **71.** 5   **73.** $-\frac{3}{4}$

75. $\frac{3}{80}$ **77.** 1 **79.** $-\frac{144}{5}$ **81.** -30 **83.** 9 **85.** 5 **87.** 60 **89.** 0 **91.** -45 **93.** -20 **95.** -1 **97.** 0
99. undefined **101.** 0 **103.** 0 **105.** 0 **107.** undefined **109.** -1440 **111.** -4 **113.** -16 **115.** -9
117. 2550 **119.** 17,052 **121.** 0 **123.** -199.5 **125.** undefined **127.** 0 **129.** -172.8 **131.** 7027.2
133. True **135.** True **137.** True **139.** False **141.** False **143.** True **145.** True
147. Each pair of negative numbers has a positive product.

CUMULATIVE REVIEW EXERCISES

149. $\frac{25}{7}$ or $3\frac{4}{7}$ **150.** -2 **151.** -3 **152.** 3

GROUP ACTIVITY/CHALLENGE PROBLEMS

1. 81 **3.** $\frac{8}{27}$ **9.** 1

EXERCISE SET 1.8

1. 25 **3.** 8 **5.** 27 **7.** 216 **9.** -8 **11.** -1 **13.** 27 **15.** -36 **17.** 36 **19.** 16 **21.** 4 **23.** 16 **25.** -16
27. -64 **29.** 225 **31.** 80 **33.** 32 **35.** -75 **37.** x^2y^2 **39.** xy^3z **41.** y^2z^3 **43.** x^2y^2z **45.** a^2x^2y **47.** xy^2z^3
49. $3xy^2$ **51.** xxy **53.** $xyyy$ **55.** $xyyzzz$ **57.** $3 \cdot 3yz$ **59.** $2 \cdot 2 \cdot 2xxxy$ **61.** $(-2)(-2)yyyz$ **63.** 9, -9
65. 16, -16 **67.** 4, -4 **69.** 49, -49 **71.** 1, -1 **73.** $\frac{1}{4}$, $-\frac{1}{4}$ Calculator answers sometimes vary in the last digit displayed and some calculators do not display a 0 before a decimal number between -1 and 1. **75.** 243 **77.** -8 **79.** -32
81. $-15,625$ **83.** 1296 **85.** 592.704 **87.** -12.167 **89.** 0.0625 **91.** 0.0256 **93.** 0.197530864 **95.** False
97. False **99.** True **101.** True **103.** True **105.** Any nonzero number will be positive when squared.
107. Positive; an even number of negative numbers are being multiplied. **109.** Any real number except 0 raised to the zero power equals 1.

CUMULATIVE REVIEW EXERCISES

110. 18 **111.** -5 **112.** 10,364 **113.** $\frac{10}{3}$ or $3\frac{1}{3}$ **114.** 0

GROUP ACTIVITY/CHALLENGE PROBLEMS

1. (a) 2^5 (b) 3^5 (c) 2^7 (d) x^{m+n} **3.** (a) 2^6 (b) 3^6 (c) 4^4 (d) x^{mn}

EXERCISE SET 1.9

1. 23 **3.** 8 **5.** 13 **7.** -10 **9.** 16 **11.** 29 **13.** -13 **15.** -2 **17.** 12 **19.** 10 **21.** 7 **23.** 36 **25.** 121
27. $\frac{1}{2}$ **29.** -5 **31.** 12 **33.** 9 **35.** 169 **37.** 156 **39.** 25 **41.** 129.81 **43.** 26.04 **45.** $\frac{71}{112}$ **47.** $\frac{1}{4}$ **49.** $\frac{170}{9}$
51. $[(6 \cdot 3) - 4] - 2$, 12 **53.** $9[[(20 \div 5) + 12] - 8]$, 72 **55.** $(\frac{4}{5} + \frac{3}{7}) \cdot \frac{2}{3}$, $\frac{86}{105}$ **57.** 2 **59.** 10 **61.** 3 **63.** -7
65. -25 **67.** 75 **69.** -20 **71.** 0 **73.** -5 **75.** 21 **77.** 33 **79.** -18 **81.** -3 **83.** 49 **85.** 5 **87.** 28
89. 4 **91.** -8 **93.** 20 **95.** -47 **97.** -50 **99.** 38 **103.** (b) -91

CUMULATIVE REVIEW EXERCISES

104. 144 **105.** (a) 25 (b) -25 **106.** 16 **107.** -16

GROUP ACTIVITY/CHALLENGE PROBLEMS

1. 160 **2.** 177 **3.** -312 **5.** $12 - (4 - 6) + 10$ **7.** $30 + (15 \div 5) + 10 \div 2$

EXERCISE SET 1.10

1. Distributive property **3.** Commutative property of multiplication **5.** Distributive property **7.** Associative property of multiplication **9.** Distributive property **11.** $4 + 3$ **13.** $(-6 \cdot 4) \cdot 2$ **15.** $(y)(6)$ **17.** $1 \cdot x + 1 \cdot y$ or $x + y$

19. $3y + 4x$ **21.** $5(x + y)$ **23.** $3(x + 2)$ **25.** $3x + (4 + 6)$ **27.** $(x + y)3$ **29.** $4x + 4y + 12$ **31.** Commutative property of addition   **33.** Distributive property   **35.** Commutative property of addition   **37.** Distributive property   **39.** yes   **41.** no

CUMULATIVE REVIEW EXERCISES

44. $\frac{49}{15}$ or $3\frac{4}{15}$ **45.** $\frac{23}{16}$ or $1\frac{7}{16}$ **46.** 45   **47.** -25

GROUP ACTIVITY/CHALLENGE PROBLEMS

1. Commutative property of addition

CHAPTER 1 REVIEW EXERCISES

1. $\frac{1}{2}$ **2.** $\frac{9}{25}$ **3.** $\frac{25}{36}$ **4.** $\frac{7}{6}$ or $1\frac{1}{6}$ **5.** $\frac{19}{72}$ **6.** $\frac{17}{15}$ or $1\frac{2}{15}$ **7.** $\{1, 2, 3, \ldots\}$ **8.** $\{0, 1, 2, 3, \ldots\}$ **9.** $\{\ldots, -3, -2, -1, 0, 1, 2, 3, \ldots\}$ **10.** {quotient of two integers, denominator not 0}   **11.** {all numbers that can be represented on the real number line}   **12. (a)** 3, 426   **(b)** 3, 0, 426   **(c)** 3, -5, -12, 0, 426   **(d)** 3, -5, -12, 0, $\frac{1}{2}$, -0.62, 426, $-3\frac{1}{4}$ **(e)** $\sqrt{7}$ **(f)** 3, -5, -12, 0, $\frac{1}{2}$, -0.62, $\sqrt{7}$, 426, $-3\frac{1}{4}$ **13. (a)** 1   **(b)** 1   **(c)** -8, -9,   **(d)** -8, -9, 1   **(e)** -2.3, -8, -9, $1\frac{1}{2}$, 1, $-\frac{3}{17}$ **(f)** -2.3, -8, -9, $1\frac{1}{2}$, $\sqrt{2}$, $-\sqrt{2}$, 1, $-\frac{3}{17}$ **14.** $>$ **15.** $<$ **16.** $>$ **17.** $>$ **18.** $<$ **19.** $>$ **20.** $<$ **21.** $>$ **22.** $<$ **23.** $=$ **24.** 3   **25.** -9 **26.** 0   **27.** -5 **28.** -3 **29.** -6 **30.** -6 **31.** -5 **32.** 8   **33.** -2 **34.** -9 **35.** -10 **36.** 5   **37.** -5 **38.** 4   **39.** -12 **40.** 5   **41.** -4 **42.** -12 **43.** -7 **44.** 6   **45.** 6   **46.** -1 **47.** 9   **48.** -28 **49.** 27   **50.** -36 **51.** -6 **52.** $-\frac{6}{35}$ **53.** $-\frac{6}{11}$ **54.** $\frac{15}{56}$ **55.** 0   **56.** 48   **57.** 12   **58.** -70 **59.** -60 **60.** -24 **61.** 144   **62.** -5 **63.** -3 **64.** -4 **65.** 18   **66.** 0   **67.** 0   **68.** -8 **69.** 5   **70.** 9   **71.** $-\frac{3}{32}$ **72.** $-\frac{3}{4}$ **73.** $\frac{56}{27}$ **74.** $-\frac{35}{9}$ **75.** 1   **76.** 0   **77.** 0   **78.** Undefined   **79.** Undefined   **80.** Undefined   **81.** 0   **82.** 24   **83.** -8 **84.** 1   **85.** 3   **86.** -8 **87.** 18   **88.** -2 **89.** -4 **90.** 10   **91.** 1   **92.** 15   **93.** -4 **94.** 16   **95.** 36   **96.** 729   **97.** 1   **98.** 81   **99.** 16   **100.** -27 **101.** -1 **102.** -32 **103.** $\frac{4}{49}$ **104.** $\frac{9}{25}$ **105.** $\frac{8}{125}$ **106.** x^2y **107.** xy^2 **108.** x^3y^2 **109.** y^2z^2 **110.** $2^2 \cdot 3^3xy^2$ **111.** $5 \cdot 7^2x^2y$ **112.** x^2y^2z **113.** xxy **114.** $xzzz$ **115.** $yyyz$ **116.** $2xxxyy$ **117.** -9 **118.** -16 **119.** -27 **120.** -16 **121.** 23   **122.** -2 **123.** 23   **124.** 22   **125.** 26   **126.** -19 **127.** -39 **128.** -3 **129.** -4 **130.** -60 **131.** 10   **132.** 20   **133.** 20   **134.** 114   **135.** 9   **136.** 14   **137.** 2   **138.** 26   **139.** 9   **140.** 0   **141.** -3 **142.** -11 **143.** -3 **144.** 21   **145.** 3   **146.** -335 **147.** 353.6   **148.** -2.88 **149.** 117.8   **150.** 78,125   **151.** 729   **152.** -74.088 **153.** 58   **154.** 1   **155.** Associative property of addition   **156.** Commutative property of multiplication   **157.** Distributive property   **158.** Commutative property of multiplication   **159.** Commutative property of addition   **160.** Associative property of addition   **161.** Commutative property of addition

CHAPTER 1 PRACTICE TEST

1. (a) 42   **(b)** 42, 0   **(c)** -6, 42, 0, -7, -1 **(d)** -6, 42, $-3\frac{1}{2}$, 0, 6.52, $\frac{5}{9}$, -7, -1 **(e)** $\sqrt{5}$ **(f)** -6, 42, $-3\frac{1}{2}$, 0, 6.52, $\sqrt{5}$, $\frac{5}{9}$, -7, -1 **2.** $<$ **3.** $>$ **4.** -12 **5.** -11 **6.** 16   **7.** -14 **8.** 8   **9.** -24 **10.** $\frac{16}{63}$ **11.** -2 **12.** -69 **13.** -2 **14.** 12   **15.** 81   **16.** $\frac{27}{125}$ **17.** $2^25^2y^2z^3$ **18.** $2 \cdot 2 \cdot 3 \cdot 3 \cdot 3xxxxyy$ **19.** 26   **20.** 10   **21.** 11   **22.** Commutative property of addition   **23.** Distributive property   **24.** Associative property of addition   **25.** Commutative property of multiplication

Chapter 2

EXERCISE SET 2.1

1. $5x$ **3.** $-x$ **5.** $x + 9$ **7.** $3x$ **9.** $4x - 7$ **11.** $2x + 3$ **13.** $5x + 8$ **15.** $5x + 3y + 3$ **17.** $2x - 4$ **19.** $x + 8$ **21.** $-8x + 2$ **23.** $-2x + 11$ **25.** $3x - 6$ **27.** $-5x + 3$ **29.** $6y + 6$ **31.** $4x - 10$ **33.** $3x - 4$

35. $x + \frac{5}{12}$ **37.** $48.5x + 8.3$ **39.** $x + \frac{1}{8}y$ **41.** $-4x - 8.3$ **43.** $-2x + 7$ **45.** $7x - 16$ **47.** $7x - 1$

49. $x - 8$ **51.** $21.72x - 7.11$ **53.** $-\frac{23}{20}x - 5$ **55.** $2x + 12$ **57.** $5x + 20$ **59.** $-2x + 8$ **61.** $-x + 2$

63. $x - 4$ **65.** $\frac{1}{4}x - 3$ **67.** $-1.8x + 3$ **69.** $-x + 3$ **71.** $0.8x - 0.2$ **73.** $x - y$ **75.** $-2x + 6y - 8$

77. $14.26x - 10.58y + 8.28$ **79.** $x - 8y + \frac{1}{2}$ **81.** $x + 3y - 9$ **83.** $x - 4 - 2y$ **85.** $3x - 8$ **87.** $2x - 5$

89. $14x + 18$ **91.** $4x - 2y + 3$ **93.** $y + 3$ **95.** $7x + 3$ **97.** $x - 9$ **99.** $6x - 12$ **101.** $-x - 2$

103. $-x + 6$ **105.** $8x - 19$ **107.** $x + 6.8$ **109.** $3x$ **111.** $x + 15$ **113.** $0.2x + 4y + 0.4$ **115.** $-6x + 3y - 3$

117. $x - 5$ **119.** $\frac{1}{6}x - \frac{10}{3}$ **121.** The signs of all the terms inside the parentheses are changed when the parentheses are removed. **123.** (a) $2x^2$, $3x$, -5; The terms are the part of the expression that are added or subtracted. (b) The factors of $2x^2$ are $1, 2, x, 2x, x^2$ and $2x^2$. Note that $1 \cdot 2x^2 = 2x^2$, $2 \cdot x^2 = 2x^2$ and $x \cdot 2x = 2x^2$. Expressions that are multiplied are factors of the product.

Cumulative Review Exercises

124. 7 **125.** -16 **127.** -12

Group Activity/Challenge Problems

1. $18x - 25y + 3$ **3.** $6x^2 + 5y^2 + 3x + 7y$ **5.** (a) $3x^2$, $-10x$, 8 (b) positive factors of $3x^2$: $1, 3, x, 3x, x^2, 3x^2$ (c) Factors of 8: $1, 2, 4, 8, -1, -2, -4, -8$

Exercise Set 2.2

1. solution **3.** not solution **5.** solution **7.** not solution **9.** solution **11.** solution **13.** $x + 5 = 8, x = 3$
15. $12 = x + 3, x = 9$ **17.** $10 = x + 7, x = 3$ **19.** $x + 6 = 4 + 11, x = 9$ **21.** 4 **23.** -10 **25.** -9
27. -61 **29.** 22 **31.** 43 **33.** -12 **35.** 72 **37.** -26 **39.** -58 **41.** 12 **43.** -12 **45.** 3 **47.** -9
49. 53 **51.** 3 **53.** 5 **55.** 1 **57.** 17 **59.** -26 **61.** -36 **63.** -47.5 **65.** 46.5 **67.** -21.58 **69.** 0
71. 720 **73.** (a) The number or numbers that make the equation a true statement. (b) To find the solutions to an equation. **77.** (a) Get the variable by itself on one side of the equation. **79.** Subtract 3

Cumulative Review Exercises

80. 18 **81.** -8 **82.** $2x - 13$ **83.** $10x - 32$

Group Activity/Challenge Problems

1. (a) yes (b) yes (c) yes **3.** (a) $2x = 8$ (b) $x = 4$ **5.** (a) $20 = 4x$ (b) $5 = x$ (or $x = 5$)

Exercise Set 2.3

1. $2x = 10, x = 5$ **3.** $6 = 3x, x = 2$ **5.** $2x = 5, x = \frac{5}{2}$ **7.** $4 = 3x, x = \frac{4}{3}$ **9.** 3 **11.** 8 **13.** -2 **15.** -12

17. 5 **19.** 3 **21.** $-\frac{3}{2}$ **23.** 6 **25.** 2 **27.** 49 **29.** $-\frac{1}{3}$ **31.** 6 **33.** $\frac{10}{13}$ **35.** 2 **37.** -1 **39.** $-\frac{3}{40}$ **41.** -75

43. 125 **45.** -35 **47.** 20 **49.** -5 **51.** 12 **53.** -16 **55.** -36 **57.** 6 **59.** -20.2 **61.** $-\frac{5}{4}$ **63.** 9

65. (a) $-a$ (b) -5 (c) 5 **67.** Divide by -2 **69.** Multiply by $\frac{1}{4}, \frac{3}{20}$

Cumulative Review Exercises

71. -4 **72.** 0 **73.** $-11x + 38$ **74.** -57

Group Activity/Challenge Problems

1. (a) 4 (b) $2x + 6 = 14$ (c) $x = 4$ **3.** (a) 1 (b) $6 = 2x + 4$ (c) $x = 1$

EXERCISE SET 2.4

1. $2x + 4 = 16, x = 6$ **3.** $30 = 2x + 12, x = 9$ **5.** $3x + 10 = 4, x = -2$ **7.** $5 + 3x = 12, x = \frac{7}{3}$ **9.** 3 **11.** -6

13. 5 **15.** $\frac{12}{5}$ **17.** -12 **19.** 3 **21.** $\frac{11}{3}$ **23.** $-\frac{19}{16}$ **25.** -2.9 **27.** 5 **29.** $-\frac{7}{6}$ **31.** 3 **33.** 20 **35.** 6.8

37. 32 **39.** 0 **41.** 0 **43.** -1 **45.** 0 **47.** $-\frac{7}{6}$ **49.** 1 **51.** -4 **53.** 4 **55.** 3 **57.** 0.6 **59.** -1 **61.** 6

63. 2.1 **65.** -3.6 **67.** Addition property **69. (b)** 5

CUMULATIVE REVIEW EXERCISES

70. $\frac{49}{40}$ or $1\frac{9}{40}$ **71.** 64 **72.** Isolate the variable on one side of the equation. **73.** Divide both sides of the equation by -4.

GROUP ACTIVITY/CHALLENGE PROBLEMS

1. $\frac{35}{6}$ **2.** $\frac{4}{5}$ **3.** -4

4. (a) **(b)** $2x + 2 = 8$ **(c)** \$3

5. (a) **(b)** $3x + 6 = 42$ **(c)** \$12 **7. (a)** $2x = x + 3$ **(b)** $x = 3$

9. (a) $2x + 3 = 4x + 2$ **(b)** $x = \frac{1}{2}$

EXERCISE SET 2.5

1. $2x = x + 6, x = 6$ **3.** $5 + 2x = x + 19, x = 14$ **5.** $5 + x = 2x + 5, x = 0$ **7.** $2x + 8 = x + 4, x = -4$ **9.** 5

11. 1 **13.** $\frac{3}{5}$ **15.** 3 **17.** 2 **19.** 1 **21.** 4.16 **23.** 4 **25.** $-\frac{17}{7}$ **27.** No solution **29.** $\frac{34}{5}$ **31.** -4 **33.** 25

35. All real numbers **37.** All real numbers **39.** 0 **41.** All real numbers **43.** $-\frac{112}{15}$ **45.** 14 **47.** $-\frac{5}{3}$ **49.** 12

51. 16 **53.** $-\frac{10}{3}$ **57.** You will obtain a false statement. **59. (b)** -8.

CUMULATIVE REVIEW EXERCISES

60. 0.131687243 **61.** Numbers or letters multiplied together are factors; numbers or letters added or subtracted are terms.
62. $7x - 10$ **63.** $\frac{10}{7}$ **64.** -3

GROUP ACTIVITY/CHALLENGE PROBLEMS

1. $\frac{1}{4}$ **3.** -4 **5. (a)** **(b)** $3x = x + 20$ **(c)** 10 lbs

EXERCISE SET 2.6

1. 5:8 **3.** 2:1 **5.** 25:4 **7.** 5:3 **9.** 1:3 **11.** 6:1 **13.** 13:32 **15.** 8:1 **17. (a)** 5.3:3.6 **(b)** about 1.47:1
19. (a) 20,000:165 **(b)** about 121.21:1 **21.** 16 **23.** 45 **25.** -100 **27.** 5 **29.** -30 **31.** 6 **33.** 384 mi
35. 7 gal **37.** 1.27 ft **39.** 260 in or 21.67 ft **41.** 24 tsp **43.** 340 trees **45.** 0.55 mL **47.** 96 sec or 1 min 36 sec
49. about 261,200 thousand people or 261,200,000 people **51.** 4.75 ft **53.** 2.9 sq. yd **55.** 10.5 in **57.** 15.63 mi
59. \$0.83 **61.** 5 points **63.** 2,033,898.3 lire **65.** 32 in **67.** 11.2 ft **69.** 5.6 in **71.** yes, her ratio is 2.12:1
75. You need a given ratio and one of the two parts of a second ratio.

CUMULATIVE REVIEW EXERCISES

76. Commutative property of addition **77.** Associative property of multiplication **78.** Distributive property **79.** $\frac{3}{4}$

GROUP ACTIVITY/CHALLENGE PROBLEMS

1. (a) 750:10,000 **(b)** 0.075:1 **2.** $\frac{1}{3}$ cup flour, $\frac{2}{3}$ tsp nutmeg, $\frac{2}{3}$ tsp cinnamon, $\frac{1}{6}$ tsp salt, $1\frac{1}{3}$ tbsp butter, 1 cup sugar

3. 0.625 cc   **5. (a)** about 140,920,000 people   **(b)** about 48,780,000 people   **(c)** about 92,140,000 people

EXERCISE SET 2.7

1. $x > 4$ **3.** $x \geq -2$ **5.** $x > -5$ **7.** $x < 10$

9. $x \leq -4$ **11.** $x > -\frac{3}{2}$ **13.** $x \leq 1$ **15.** $x < -3$

17. $x < \frac{3}{2}$ **19.** $x > \frac{35}{9}$ **21.** $x > -\frac{8}{3}$ **23.** $x \leq -\frac{11}{3}$

25. $x \geq -6$ **27.** $x < 1$ **29.** $x < 2$ **31.** All real numbers

33. $x > \frac{3}{4}$ **35.** $x > \frac{23}{10}$ **37.** No solution   **39.** $x \geq -\frac{7}{11}$

41. All real numbers   **43.** The inequality has no solution.   **45.** When multiplying or dividing by a negative number

CUMULATIVE REVIEW EXERCISES

47. -9 **48.** -25 **49.** $\frac{14}{5}$ or $2\frac{4}{5}$ **50.** 500 kwh

GROUP ACTIVITY/CHALLENGE PROBLEMS

1. $x \geq -2$ **4. (a)** $10   **(c)** $160

CHAPTER 2 REVIEW EXERCISES

1. $2x + 8$ **2.** $3x - 6$ **3.** $8x - 6$ **4.** $-2x - 8$ **5.** $-x - 2$ **6.** $-x + 2$ **7.** $-16 + 4x$ **8.** $18 - 6x$
9. $20x - 24$ **10.** $-6x + 15$ **11.** $36x - 36$ **12.** $-4x + 12$ **13.** $-3x - 3y$ **14.** $-6x + 4$ **15.** $-3 - 2y$
16. $-x - 2y + z$ **17.** $3x + 9y - 6z$ **18.** $-4x + 6y - 14$ **19.** $5x$ **20.** $7y + 2$ **21.** $-2y + 7$ **22.** $5x + 1$
23. $6x + 3y$ **24.** $-3x + 3y$ **25.** $6x + 8y$ **26.** $6x + 3y + 2$ **27.** $-x - 1$ **28.** $3x + 3y + 6$ **29.** 3
30. $-12x + 3$ **31.** $5x + 6$ **32.** $-2x$ **33.** $5x + 7$ **34.** $-10x + 12$ **35.** $5x + 3$ **36.** $4x - 4$ **37.** $22x - 42$
38. $3x - 3y + 6$ **39.** $-x + 5y$ **40.** $3x + 2y + 16$ **41.** 3   **42.** $-x - 2y + 4$ **43.** 2   **44.** -8 **45.** 11
46. -27 **47.** 2   **48.** $\frac{11}{2}$ **49.** -2 **50.** -3 **51.** 12   **52.** 1   **53.** 6   **54.** -3 **55.** $-\frac{21}{5}$ **56.** -5 **57.** -19
58. -1 **59.** $\frac{2}{3}$ **60.** $\frac{1}{5}$ **61.** $\frac{9}{2}$ **62.** $\frac{10}{7}$ **63.** -3 **64.** -1 **65.** -8 **66.** $-\frac{23}{5}$ **67.** -10 **68.** $-\frac{4}{3}$
69. No solution   **70.** All real numbers   **71.** $\frac{17}{3}$ **72.** $-\frac{20}{7}$ **73.** 3:4   **74.** 5:12   **75.** 1:1   **76.** 3   **77.** 3   **78.** 9
79. $\frac{135}{4}$ **80.** -4 **81.** -24 **82.** 36   **83.** 90   **84.** 40 in   **85.** 1 ft   **86.** $x \geq 2$ **87.** $x < 3$

88. $x \geq -\frac{12}{5}$ **89.** No solution   **90.** All real numbers   **91.** $x < -3$

92. $x \leq \frac{9}{5}$ **93.** $x > \frac{8}{5}$ **94.** $x < -\frac{5}{3}$ **95.** $x \leq \frac{5}{11}$

96. No solution   **97.** All real numbers   **98.** 240 calories   **99.** 110 copies   **100.** $6\frac{1}{3}$ in
101. 9.45 ft.   **102.** approximately $0.3209   **103.** 57.3°   **104.** 192 bottles

CHAPTER 2 PRACTICE TEST

1. $4x - 8$ **2.** $-x - 3y + 4$ **3.** $2x + 4$ **4.** $-x + 10$ **5.** $-6x + y - 6$ **6.** $7x - 5y + 3$ **7.** $8x - 1$
8. 4   **9.** -2 **10.** 2   **11.** -1 **12.** $-\frac{1}{7}$ **13.** No solution   **14.** All real numbers   **15.** -45

16. $x > -7$ **17.** $x \leq 12$ **18.** No solution   **19.** $\frac{32}{3}$ or $10\frac{2}{3}$ ft
20. 150 gal

CUMULATIVE REVIEW TEST

1. $\frac{16}{25}$ **2.** $\frac{1}{2}$ **3.** $>$ **4.** -6 **5.** -8 **6.** 7 **7.** 3 **8.** 1 **9.** Associative Property of Addition **10.** $10x + y$

11. $3x + 16$ **12.** 3 **13.** -40 **14.** 2 **15.** -1 **16.** 6 **17.** $x > 10$

18. $x \geq -12$ **19.** 158.4 lbs **20.** \$42

Chapter 3

EXERCISE SET 3.1

1. 25 **3.** 22 **5.** 126 **7.** 12.56 **9.** 10 **11.** 6 **13.** 1080 **15.** 56 **17.** 5 **19.** 60 **21.** 16 **23.** 6

25. $y = -2x + 8, 4$ **27.** $y = \dfrac{2x + 4}{6}, 4$ **29.** $y = \dfrac{-3x + 6}{2}, 0$ **31.** $y = \dfrac{4x - 20}{5}, -\dfrac{4}{5}$ **33.** $y = \dfrac{3x + 18}{6}, 3$

35. $y = \dfrac{-x + 8}{2}, 6$ **37.** $t = \dfrac{d}{r}$ **39.** $p = \dfrac{i}{rt}$ **41.** $d = \dfrac{C}{\pi}$ **43.** $b = \dfrac{2A}{h}$ **45.** $w = \dfrac{P - 2l}{2}$ **47.** $n = \dfrac{m - 3}{4}$

49. $b = y - mx$ **51.** $r = \dfrac{I - P}{Pt}$ **53.** $d = \dfrac{3A - m}{2}$ **55.** $b = d - a - c$ **57.** $y = \dfrac{-ax + c}{b}$ **59.** $h = \dfrac{V}{\pi r^2}$

61. 35 **63.** 10°C **65.** 95°F **67.** $P = 10$ **69.** $K = 4$ **71.** 30 **73.** \$1440 **75.** \$5000 **77.** 30 in

79. 24 sq cm **81.** 50.24 sq in **83.** 25.12 in **85.** 8 ft **87.** (a) 62.1 ft (b) 124.2 ft **89.** 18,237.12 cu in

91. When you multiply a unit by the same unit you get a square unit. **93.** (a) $\pi = \dfrac{C}{2r}$ or $\pi = \dfrac{C}{d}$ (b) π or about 3.14

CUMULATIVE REVIEW EXERCISES

94. 0 **95.** 3:2 **96.** 1620 min or 27 hrs **97.** $x \leq -17$

GROUP ACTIVITY/CHALLENGE PROBLEMS

1. (a) $A = d^2 - \pi \left(\dfrac{d}{2}\right)^2$ (b) 3.44 sq ft (c) 7.74 sq ft **2.** (a) $V = 18x^3 - 3x^2$ (b) 6027 cu cm (c) $S = 54x^2 - 8x$

(d) 2590 sq cm **4.** (a) diameter: approximately 142 ft, radius: approximately 71 ft (b) approximately 134 ft (c) approximately 14,095 sq ft (d) approximately 1,691,455 cu ft

EXERCISE SET 3.2

1. $x + 5$ **3.** $4x$ **5.** $0.70x$ **7.** $0.10c$ **9.** $0.16p$ **11.** $6x - 3$ **13.** $\frac{3}{4}x + 7$ **15.** $2(x + 8)$ **17.** $4x$ **19.** $0.23x$

21. $8.20b$ **23.** $300n$ **25.** $25x$ **27.** $12x$ **29.** $16c$ **31.** $275x + 25y$ **33.** Six less than a number. **35.** One more than four times a number. **37.** Seven less than five times a number. **39.** Four times a number, decreased by two.
41. Three times a number subtracted from two. **43.** Twice the difference of a number and one. **45.** Martin's salary is x; Eileen's salary is $x + 45$. **47.** One number is x; the second number is $x/3$. **49.** The first consecutive even integer is x; the second consecutive even integer is $x + 2$. **51.** One number is x; the second number is $x + 12$ (or $x - 12$). **53.** One number is x; the other number is $(x/2) + 3$. **55.** One number is x; the second number is $3x - 4$. **57.** The first consecutive odd integer is x; the second consecutive odd integer is $x + 2$. **59.** One number is x; the second number is $x - 0.15x$.
61. $c, c - 0.10c$ **63.** $p, p - 0.50p$ **65.** $w, 2w$ **67.** $m, m + 0.15m$ **69.** $x + 5x = 18$ **71.** $x + (x + 1) = 47$
73. $2x - 8 = 12$ **75.** $\frac{1}{5}(x + 10) = 150$ **77.** $x + (2x - 8) = 1000$ **79.** $x + 0.08x = 92$ **81.** $x - 0.25x = 65$
83. $x - 0.20x = 215$ **85.** $x + (2x - 3) = 21$ **87.** $40t = 180$ **89.** $15y = 215$ **91.** $25q = 150$ **93.** Three more than a number is six. **95.** Three times a number, decreased by one, is four more than twice the number **97.** Four times the difference of a number and one is six. **99.** Six more than five times a number is the difference of six times the number and one **101.** The sum of a number and the number increased by four is eight **103.** The sum of twice a number and the number increased by three is five

CUMULATIVE REVIEW EXERCISES

107. 3.35 tsp   **108.** $\frac{1}{6}$ cup   **109.** 15   **110.** $y = \dfrac{3x-6}{2}$ $\left(\text{or } y = \dfrac{3}{2}x - 3\right)$, 6

GROUP ACTIVITY/CHALLENGE PROBLEMS

1. (a) $86,400d + 3600h + 60m + s$ **(b)** 368,125 sec   **3.** $30 = 6t$ **5.** $40,000y = 1,000,000$
7. $20 + 0.60m = 30 + 0.45m$

EXERCISE SET 3.3

1. $x + (x + 1) = 45$; 22, 23   **3.** $x + (x + 2) = 68$; 33, 35   **5.** $x + (3x - 5) = 43$; 12, 31
7. $x + (x + 2) + (x + 4) = 87$; 27, 29, 31   **9.** $(2x - 8) - x = 17$; 25, 42   **11.** $x + (5x + 3) = 69$; Vector, 11 mpg;
Geo, 58 mpg   **13.** $x + (15x + 6) = 22$;   Mexico, 1; Canada, 21   **15.** $x - 0.06x = 65,800$; \$70,000
17. $20x = 15$; 75%   **19.** $1500 + 2x = 3100$; 800   **21.** $2000 + 0.02x = 2400$; \$20,000   **23.** $0.08x = 60$; \$750
25. $x + 0.08x = 37,800$; \$35,000   **27.** $x + 0.07x = 1.50$; \$1.40   **29.** $x + 3x + 3x = 210,000$; each child, \$90,000;
charity, \$30,000   **31.** $4000 - 300x = 2000$; about 6.67 yr.   **33.** $x - 0.60x = 24$; 60 gal   **35.** $15 + 5x = 65$; 10 mph
37. $x + 0.90x = 110,000$; about 57,895 people   **39.** $x + 0.07x + 0.15x = 20$; \$16.39   **41.** $x - 0.10x - 20 = 250$;
\$300   **43.** $x + 15x = 4$; $\frac{1}{4}$ or 0.25 gal oil and $3\frac{3}{4}$ or 3.75 gal gas   **45.** $x - 0.01x = 2.362$; about 2.386 million
47. (a) about 42 months or 3.5 yr **(b)** Citibank   **49. (a)** 18.75 mo or about 1.56 yr **(b)** Countrywide   **51. (a)** 9.2 mo
(b) \$325.50 per month

CUMULATIVE REVIEW EXERCISES

54. $\frac{17}{12}$ **55.** Associative property of addition   **56.** Commutative property of multiplication   **57.** Distributive property
58. 56 lb   **59.** $b = 2M - a$

GROUP ACTIVITY/CHALLENGE PROBLEMS

3. n
  $4n$
  $4n + 6$
  $(4n + 6)/2 = 2n + 3$
  $2n + 3 - 3 = 2n$
4. about 185.7% increase   **6.** about 251,476.2 people per sq mi

EXERCISE SET 3.4

1. 9.5 in   **3.** $A = 47°, B = 133°$ **5.** 50°, 60°, 70°   **7.** 4m, 4m, 2m   **9.** $w = 48$ ft, $l = 72$ ft
11. two smaller angles, 69°; two larger angles, 111°   **13.** $w = 2\frac{2}{3}$ ft, $h = 4\frac{2}{3}$ ft   **15.** $h = 3$ ft, $l = 9$ ft
17. The area remains the same.   **19.** The volume becomes eight times as great.

CUMULATIVE REVIEW EXERCISES

22. <   **23.** >   **24.** -8 **25.** $-2x - 4y + 6$ **26.** $y = \dfrac{-2x + 9}{3}$ or $y = -\frac{2}{3}x + 3$, 1

GROUP ACTIVITY/CHALLENGE PROBLEMS

2. $ac + ad + bc + bd$ **3. (a)** 342.56 ft   **(b)** 192 ft

CHAPTER 3 REVIEW EXERCISES

1. 12.56   **2.** 48   **3.** 20   **4.** 300   **5.** 240   **6.** 28.26   **7.** 113.04   **8.** 20   **9.** 21   **10.** -11 **11.** -8 **12.** 15
13. 4.5   **14.** $y = 2x - 12$, 8   **15.** $y = \dfrac{3x + 4}{2}$, 5   **16.** $y = \dfrac{3x - 5}{2}$, -7 **17.** $y = -3x - 10$, -10

18. $y = \dfrac{-3x - 6}{2}, 6$ **19.** $y = \dfrac{4x - 3}{3}, \dfrac{5}{3}$ **20.** $m = \dfrac{F}{a}$ **21.** $h = \dfrac{2A}{b}$ **22.** $t = \dfrac{i}{pr}$ **23.** $w = \dfrac{P - 2l}{2}$

24. $y = \dfrac{2x - 6}{3}$ **25.** $B = 2A - C$ **26.** $h = \dfrac{V}{\pi r^2}$ **27.** \$180   **28.** 6 in   **29.** 29 and 33   **30.** 127 and 128

31. 38 and 7   **32.** \$8000   **33.** \$2000   **34.** \$650   **35. (a)** 166.7 mo or 13.9 yr   **(b)** Mellon Bank

36. (a) 27.4 mo or 2.3 yr   **(b)** yes   **37.** 45°, 55°, 80°   **38.** 30°, 40°, 150°, 140°   **39.** $w = 15.5$ ft, $l = 19.5$ ft

40. 103 and 105   **41.** \$450   **42.** \$12,000   **43.** 42°, 50°, 88°   **44.** 8 years   **45.** 70°, 70°, 110°, 110°

46. (a) 500 copies   **(b)** King Kopie by \$5

PRACTICE TEST

1. 18 ft   **2.** 145   **3.** 100.48   **4.** $R = \dfrac{P}{I}$ **5.** $y = \dfrac{3x - 6}{2}$ **6.** $a = 3A - b$ **7.** $c = \dfrac{D - Ra}{R}$ or $c = \dfrac{D}{R} - a$

8. 56 and 102   **9.** 13, 14, and 15   **10.** \$16.39   **11.** 15, 30, 30 in   **12.** 50°, 50°, 130°, 130°

Chapter 7

EXERCISE SET 7.1

1. (a) 53.5% **(b)** No, only percents are indicated **(c)** No **(d)** No **3. (a)** $2.7 million **(b)** $0.54 million
(c) State Fair 1993 revenue: $3.6 million

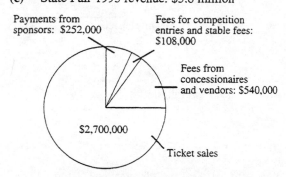

Payments from sponsors: $252,000

Fees for competition entries and stable fees: $108,000

Fees from concessionaires and vendors: $540,000

$2,700,000

Ticket sales

5. (a) 15 years **(b)** 23 years, five hundredths of a second
(d) 9.82 sec **7. (a)** decreased by 14,464 **(b)** increased by 5554
(c) 1950: 67,148; 1991: 55,247 **9. (a)** 30,000 **(b)** 60,000
(c) 160,000 **(d)** about 960,000 **11. (a)** 31%, 20%, 18.5%
(b) It has varied between 18.5% and 14% but has remained relatively
stable. **(c)** It has varied between 31% and 35%. It increased up until
1990–1991, then began decreasing. **13. (a)** $320,000 **(b)** after
1989 **(c)** $450,000 **(d)** $650,000 **(e)** 144% **(f)** 28.8%
15. (a) 3 billion **(b)** 7 billion **(c)** 800 million **(d)** 1 billion
(e) 2 billion **(f)** The world population is expected to increase from
about 5 billion to 11 billion from 1990 to 2100, with the poorest
accounting for most of the increase.

CUMULATIVE REVIEW EXERCISES

22. $\dfrac{18}{5}x - \dfrac{7}{6}$ **23.** $3x + 2 + \dfrac{10}{x-2}$ **24.** $4(x+2)(x-2)$ **25.** $\dfrac{5}{12}$

GROUP ACTIVITY/CHALLENGE PROBLEMS

1. Disney's Income, 1992

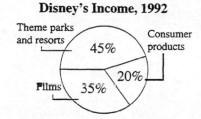

Disney's Income, 1992

Theme parks and resorts 45%

Consumer products 20%

Films 35%

3. (a) 92%, 80%, 77%, 59%, 30%, 15%, 2%
b)

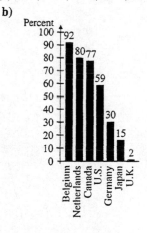

4.

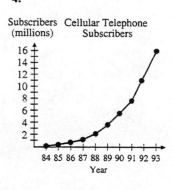

Subscribers (millions) Cellular Telephone Subscribers

84 85 86 87 88 89 90 91 92 93
Year

EXERCISE SET 7.2

1. I **3.** III **5.** II **7.** I **9.** III **11.** II **13.** $A(3, 1), B(-3, 0), C(1, -3), D(-2, -3), E(0, 3), F(\frac{3}{2}, -1)$
15.

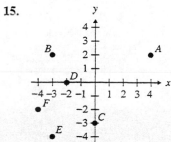

17.

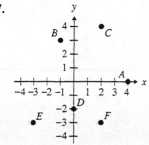

19. (3, 1) not on line

21. (a) $(0, 1)$, $(-1, 0)$, $(2, 3)$

(b)

23. (a) $(2, 0)$, $(\frac{2}{3}, -2)$, $(\frac{4}{3}, -1)$

(b)

25. (a) $(1, \frac{1}{2})$, $(0, 1)$, $(-2, 2)$

(b)

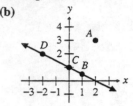

27. The x coordinate   **29. (a)** x axis   **(b)** y axis   **31.** axis is singular, axes is plural
33. An illustration of the set of points whose coordinates satisfy the equation.   **35.** a straight line   **37.** $ax + by = c$

CUMULATIVE REVIEW EXERCISES

39. $-8x^2 - x + 4$ **40.** $6x^3 - 17x^2 + 22x - 15$ **41.** $(x + 3y)(x - 2)$ **42.** $\dfrac{-x - 5}{(x + 2)(x + 1)}$

GROUP ACTIVITY/CHALLENGE PROBLEMS

1.

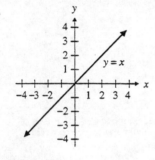

3.

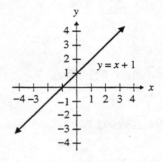

EXERCISE SET 7.3

1. 2   **3.** $\frac{11}{2}$ **5.** 3   **7.** -1 **9.** $\frac{8}{3}$ **11.** $-\frac{17}{2}$

13.

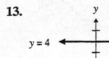

15.

17.

19.

21.

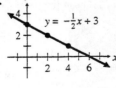

23.

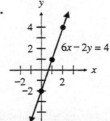

25.

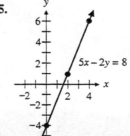

27.

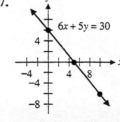

29.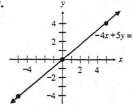

31.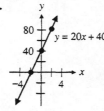

33.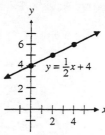

35.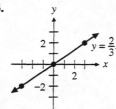

37.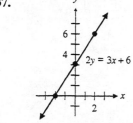

39.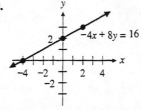

41.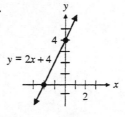

43.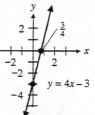

45.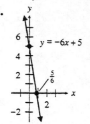

47.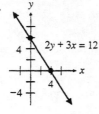

49.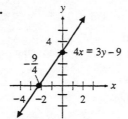

51.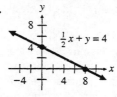

53.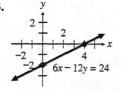

55.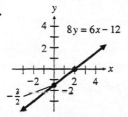

57.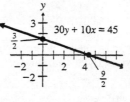

59.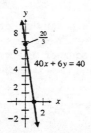

61.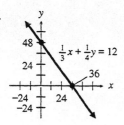

63.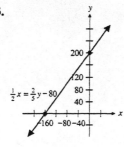

65. $x = -3$
67. $y = 3$

69. (a) $C = m + 25$
(b)

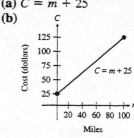

(c) $75   **(d)** $35

71. (a)

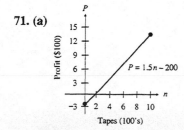

(b) $550   **(c)** 800 tapes

73. x intercept: substitute 0 for y and find the corresponding value of x; y intercept: substitute 0 for x and find the corresponding value of y.   **75.** a horizontal line
77. You may not be able to read the exact answers from a graph.
79. 5, 4   **81.** 6, 4

CUMULATIVE REVIEW EXERCISES

83. 5   **84.** 4.5 mph, 7.5 mph   **85.** $\frac{1}{2}$, -12 **86.** 6, 8

GROUP ACTIVITY/CHALLENGE PROBLEMS

1. (a) 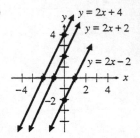   **3. (a)** 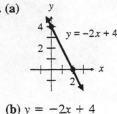   **5.**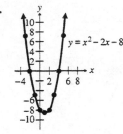

(b) $y = -2x + 4$

(b) They appear to be parallel lines

EXERCISE SET 7.4

1. 5   **3.** $\frac{1}{2}$ **5.** 0   **7.** 0   **9.** undefined   **11.** $-\frac{5}{9}$ **13.** -2 **15.** $m = 2$ **17.** $m = -\frac{3}{2}$ **19.** $m = -\frac{3}{2}$ **21.** $m = \frac{7}{4}$
23. $m = 0$ **25.** slope is undefined
27. The ratio of the vertical change to the horizontal change between any two points on the line.
29. The values of y increase as the values of x increase.
31. Lines that rise from left to right have a positive slope. Lines that fall from left to right have a negative slope.
33. No, since we cannot divide by 0. We say that the slope of a vertical line is undefined.

CUMULATIVE REVIEW EXERCISES

34. (a) An equation that contains only one variable and that variable has an exponent of 1.
(b) $2x + 3 = 5x - 6$ (answers will vary)
35. (a) An equation that contains only one variable and the greatest exponent on that variable is 2.
(b) $x^2 + 2x - 3 = 0$ (answers will vary)   **36. (a)** An equation that contains only one variable and one or more fractions.
(b) $\frac{x}{3} + \frac{x}{4} = 12$ (answers will vary)   **37. (a)** An equation that contains two variables and the exponent on both variables is 1.   **(b)** $y = 3x - 2$ (answers will vary)

GROUP ACTIVITY/CHALLENGE PROBLEMS

1. $\frac{225}{68}$ **3.** 7
5. (a)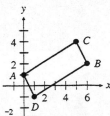

(b) $AC, m = \frac{3}{5}$
  $CB, m = -2$
  $DB, m = \frac{3}{5}$
  $AD, m = -2$

(c) yes

EXERCISE SET 7.5

1. 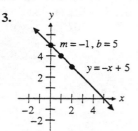 $m = 2, b = -1$ $y = 2x - 1$

3. 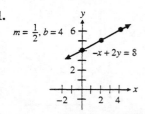 $m = -1, b = 5$ $y = -x + 5$

5. 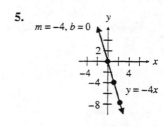 $m = -4, b = 0$ $y = -4x$

7. 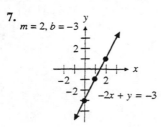 $m = 2, b = -3$ $-2x + y = -3$

9. 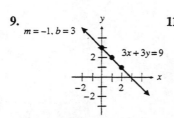 $m = -1, b = 3$ $3x + 3y = 9$

11. 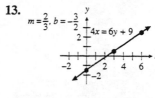 $m = \frac{1}{2}, b = 4$ $-x + 2y = 8$

13. 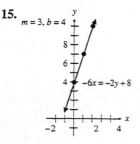 $m = \frac{2}{3}, b = -\frac{3}{2}$ $4x = 6y + 9$

15. $m = 3, b = 4$ $-6x = -2y + 8$

17. $m = \frac{3}{8}, b = -1$ $-3x + 8y = -8$

19. $m = \frac{3}{2}, b = 2$ $3x = 2y - 4$

21. $y = 2x$
23. $y = -3x - 5$
25. $y = \frac{1}{3}x + 5$
27. $y = 2x - 1$
29. Yes
31. Yes
33. No
35. No

37. $y = 5x + 4$
39. $y = -2x - 3$
41. $y = \frac{1}{2}x - \frac{9}{2}$
43. $y = \frac{3}{5}x + 7$
45. $y = 3x + 10$
47. $y = -\frac{3}{2}x$
49. $y = \frac{1}{2}x - 2$
51. $y = 5.2x - 1.6$

53.
x	y
0	-2
2	1
4	4

$3x - 2y = 4$

55.
x	y
0	2
3	4
-3	0

$2x - 3y = -6$

57. Compare their slopes. If the slopes are the same but their y intercepts are different then the lines are parallel.

59. (a) $ax + by = c$
(b) $y = mx + b$
(c) $y - y_1 = m(x - x_1)$

61. (b) 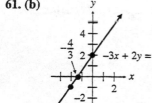 $-3x + 2y = 4$

CUMULATIVE REVIEW EXERCISES

62. $3x^2 - 3x - 1 + \dfrac{6}{3x + 2}$ **63.** $1.5 L$ **64.** $\dfrac{x - 2}{2x + 1}$ **65.** $\dfrac{4(2x - 1)}{(x - 2)(x + 2)}$ **66.** $5, 6$ **67.** $b = 8$ ft, $h = 9$ ft

GROUP ACTIVITY/CHALLENGE PROBLEMS

3. Yes   **4.** $y = \dfrac{3}{4}x + 2$ **5.** $y = -\dfrac{2}{5}x + \dfrac{13}{10}$

EXERCISE SET 7.6

1. function, domain $\{1, 2, 3, 4, 5\}$, range $\{1, 2, 3, 4, 5\}$ **3.** relation, domain $\{1, 2, 3, 5, 7\}$, range $\{-2, 0, 2, 4, 5\}$
5. relation, domain $\{0, 1, 3, 5\}$, range $\{-4, -1, 0, 1, 2\}$ **7.** relation, domain $\{0, 1, 4\}$, range $\{-3, 0, 2, 5\}$

9. function, domain {0, 1, 2, 3, 4}, range {3}   **11. (a)** {(1, 4), (2, 5), (3, 5), (4, 7)}   **(b)** Function
13. (a) {(−4, 5), (0, 7), (6, 9), (6, 3)}   **(b)** Not function   **15.** Function   **17.** Function   **19.** Not function   **21.** Function
23. Not function   **25.** Function   **27. (a)** 7   **(b)** −1   **29. (a)** 0   **(b)** 5   **31. (a)** 5   **(b)** 15   **33. (a)** 3   **(b)** 5
35.

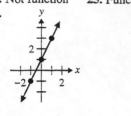

37.

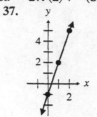

39.

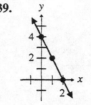

41.

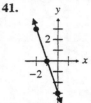

43. (a)

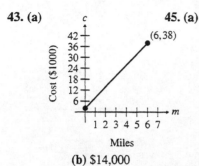

Miles

(b) $14,000

45. (a)

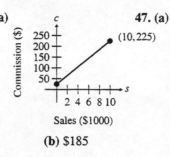

Sales ($1000)

(b) $185

47. (a)

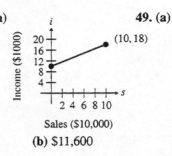

Sales ($10,000)

(b) $11,600

49. (a)

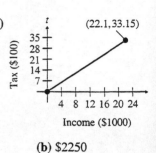

Income ($1000)

(b) $2250

51. A relation in which no two ordered pairs have the same first coordinate and a different second coordinate.
53. The set of values that represent the dependent variable.   **55.** No, each *x* must have a unique *y* for it to be a function.
57. Yes, each *x* may have a unique value of *y*.   **59.** yes   **61.** no

Cumulative Review Exercises

63. $\dfrac{7}{2}$ **64.** $53.57   **65.** $x < -1$, ⟵───○───   **66.** $w = \dfrac{A - 2l}{2}$
                                                              −1

Group Activity/Challenge Problems

3. (a) 0   **(b)** 5

Exercise Set 7.7

1.

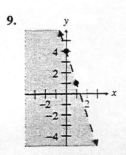

3.

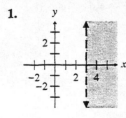

5.

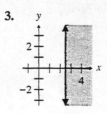

7.

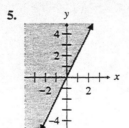

9.

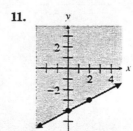

11.

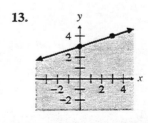

13.

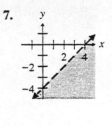

15.
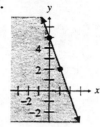

17.
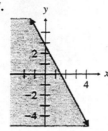

19.
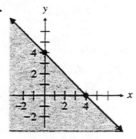

21.
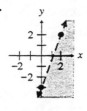

23.
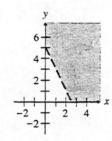

25. The points on the line satisfy the equal (=) part of the inequality.

CUMULATIVE REVIEW EXERCISES

27. $x > 3$,   **28.** $1250   **29.** $F = \frac{9}{5}C + 32$ **30.** $m = \frac{6}{5}, b = -\frac{9}{5}$

GROUP ACTIVITY/CHALLENGE PROBLEMS

4. (a) 1   **(b)** 2   **(c)** $x > 2$,

5.
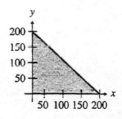

7. (a) $2x + y \le 10$

(d)
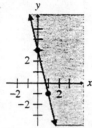

(b)
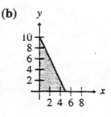

CHAPTER 7 REVIEW EXERCISES

1. (a) 38%
   (b) 62%
   (c) $101.6 billion
   (d) Major Cards' Amount Charged in 1993

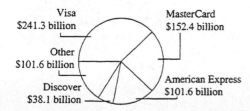

2. (a) 48%   **(b)** 18%   **(c)** greater, by about 30%   **(d)** superstores
3. (a) 68%, 10%   **(b)** about the third quarter of 1991   **(c)** about 94%
(d) about 87%   **4. (a)** about 135 per 100,000; about 350 per 100,000; increase of about 215 per 100,000
(b) 25%, 60%   **(c)** 100%   **(d)** 100%

5.
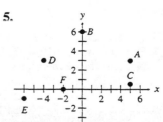

6. No
7. b, d
8. (a) -1 **(b)** -4
   (c) $\frac{16}{3}$ **(d)** $\frac{8}{3}$

9.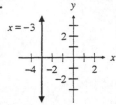

10.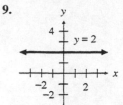

11.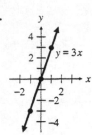

12.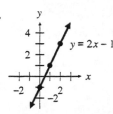

13.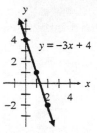

14.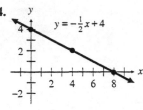

15.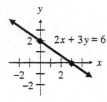

16.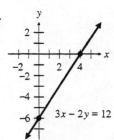

17.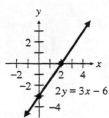

18.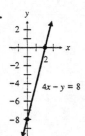

19.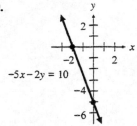

20.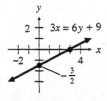

21.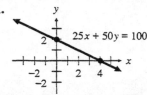

22.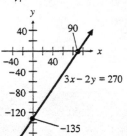

23.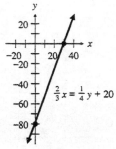

24. $-\frac{12}{5}$ **25.** $-\frac{1}{12}$ **26.** -2 **27.** 0 **28.** undefined   **29.** The ratio of the vertical change to the horizontal change between any two points on the line.   **30.** $-\frac{5}{7}$ **31.** $\frac{9}{4}$ **32.** $\frac{1}{4}$ **33.** $m = -1, b = 4$ **34.** $m = -4, b = \frac{1}{2}$

35. $m = -\frac{2}{3}, b = \frac{8}{3}$ **36.** $m = -\frac{1}{2}, b = \frac{3}{2}$ **37.** $m = \frac{3}{2}, b = 3$ **38.** $m = -\frac{3}{5}, b = \frac{12}{5}$ **39.** $m = -\frac{9}{7}, b = \frac{15}{7}$

40. Slope is undefined, no y intercept   **41.** $m = 0, b = -3$ **42.** $y = 2x + 2$ **43.** $y = x - \frac{5}{2}$ **44.** $y = -\frac{1}{2}x + 2$

45. Yes   **46.** No   **47.** Yes   **48.** Yes   **49.** $y = 2x - 2$ **50.** $y = -3x + 2$ **51.** $y = -\frac{2}{3}x + 4$ **52.** $y = 2$

53. $x = 3$ **54.** $y = -2x - 4$ **55.** $y = -\frac{7}{2}x - 4$ **56.** $x = -4$
57. Function, domain $\{0, 1, 2, 4, 6\}$, range $\{-3, -1, 2, 4, 5\}$ **58.** Not function, domain $\{3, 4, 6, 7\}$, range $\{0, 1, 2, 5\}$
59. Not function, domain $\{3, 4, 5, 6\}$, range $\{-3, 1, 2\}$ **60.** Function, domain $\{-2, 3, 4, 5, 9\}$, range $\{-2\}$
61. (a) $\{(1, 3), (4, 5), (7, 2), (9, 2)\}$ **(b)** Function   **62. (a)** $\{(4, 1), (6, 3), (6, 5), (8, 7)\}$ **(b)** Not function
63. Function   **64.** Not function   **65.** Function   **66.** Function   **67. (a)** 2 **(b)** -19 **68. (a)** 11 **(b)** -37
69. (a) -4 **(b)** -8 **70. (a)** 12 **(b)** 76

71.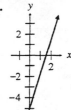

72.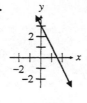

73.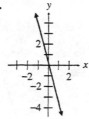

74.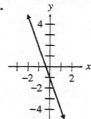

75. (a)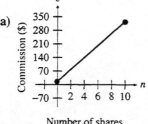

Number of shares
(1000's)

(b) $55

76. (a)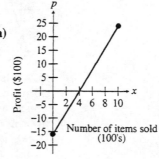

Number of items sold
(100's)

(b) $0

77.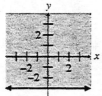

78.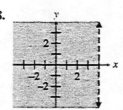

79.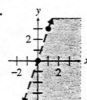

80.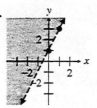

81.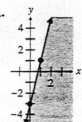

82.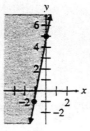

83.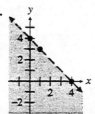

84.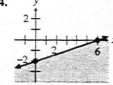

CHAPTER 7 PRACTICE TEST

1. (a) 36.7% **(b)** 5.7% **(c)** $0.8112 billion or $811.2 million **2.** a, b **3.** $-\frac{4}{3}$ **4.** $m = \frac{4}{9}, b = -\frac{5}{3}$ **5.** $y = -x - 1$

6. $y = 3x$ **7.** $y = -\frac{3}{7}x + \frac{2}{7}$ **8.** Yes, the slope of both lines is $\frac{3}{2}$ and y intercepts are different.

9.

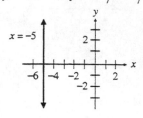

10.

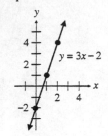

11.

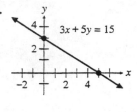

12.

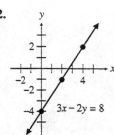

13. A relation in which no two ordered pairs have the same first element and a different second element.
14. (a) Not function **(b)** domain $\{1, 3, 5, 6\}$, range $\{-4, 0, 2, 3, 5\}$
15. (a) Function **(b)** Not function

16.

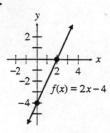

17.

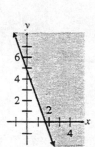

18.

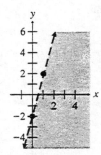

Chapter 8

EXERCISE SET 8.1

1. c **3.** a **5.** a **7.** a, c **9.** a, c **11.** Consistent—one solution **13.** Dependent—infinite number of solutions
15. Consistent—one solution **17.** Dependent—infinite number of solutions **19.** One solution **21.** No solution
23. One solution **25.** Infinite number of solutions **27.** No solution **29.** No solution
31.

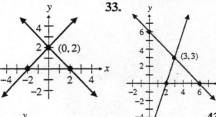

33.

35.

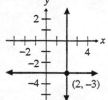

37.

39.

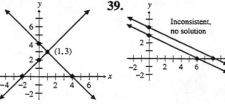

41.

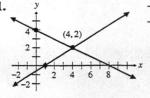

43.

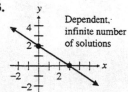

45.

47.

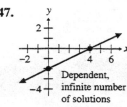

49.

51.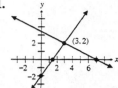

53.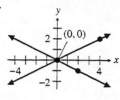

55.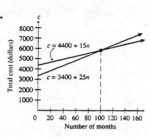

57.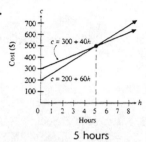

5 hours

59. The lines will be parallel since the slopes are the same but the y intercepts are different.

61. Write both equations in slope-intercept form and then compare their slopes and y intercepts. If the slopes are different there is one solution. If the slopes are the same but the y intercepts are different there is no solution. If both the slopes and y intercepts are the same there are an infinite number of solutions.

CUMULATIVE REVIEW EXERCISES

63. (a) 6   **(b)** 6, 0   **(c)** 6, -4, 0   **(d)** 6, -4, 0, $2\frac{1}{2}$, $-\frac{9}{5}$, 4.22   **(e)** $\sqrt{3}$, $-\sqrt{7}$ **(f)** 6, -4, 0, $\sqrt{3}$, $2\frac{1}{2}$, $-\frac{9}{5}$, 4.22, $-\sqrt{7}$

64. $(x + 3)(y - 4)$ **65.** $(2x + 3)(4x - 5)$ **66.** $\dfrac{-x - 6}{x + 3}$ **67.** -6

GROUP ACTIVITY/CHALLENGE PROBLEMS

1. 0   **2.** an infinite number

EXERCISE SET 8.2

1. $(2, 1)$ **3.** $(-1, -1)$ **5.** Inconsistent—no solution   **7.** $(4, -9)$ **9.** Dependent—infinite number of solutions
11. $(-1, 2)$ **13.** Dependent—infinite number of solutions   **15.** $(2, 1)$ **17.** Inconsistent—no solution   **19.** $(-1, 0)$
21. $\left(-\dfrac{59}{37}, \dfrac{9}{37}\right)$ **23. (a)** 4 hr   **(b)** 74°F   **25. (a)** 3 hr   **(b)** 295 mile marker
27. You will obtain a false statement, such as $3 = 0$.

CUMULATIVE REVIEW EXERCISES

29. -27 **30.** -27 **31.** -81 **32.** 81   **33.** 6 eggs   **34.** $5\frac{1}{3}$ in.   **35.** $\dfrac{9y^4}{x^2}$ **36.** $576x^{14}y^{19}$ **37.** 10

GROUP ACTIVITY/CHALLENGE PROBLEMS

1. (a) $x = \dfrac{d - b}{a - c}$ **(b)** $x = 2$ **(c)** $(2, 8)$ **3. (a)** $(300, 1800)$ **(b)** x value remains the same, but the y value is halved.
(c) $(300, 900)$ **5.** $(4, 2, -1)$

EXERCISE SET 8.3

1. $(6, 2)$ **3.** $(-2, 3)$ **5.** $\left(4, \frac{11}{2}\right)$ **7.** Inconsistent—no solution   **9.** $(-8, -26)$ **11.** $(4, -2)$ **13.** $(5, 4)$
15. $\left(\frac{3}{2}, -\frac{1}{2}\right)$ **17.** Dependent—infinite number of solutions   **19.** $\left(\frac{2}{5}, \frac{8}{5}\right)$ **21.** Inconsistent—no solution   **23.** $(0, 0)$
25. $\left(10, \frac{15}{2}\right)$ **27.** $\left(\frac{31}{28}, -\frac{23}{28}\right)$ **29.** $\left(\frac{20}{39}, -\frac{16}{39}\right)$ **31.** $\left(\frac{14}{5}, -\frac{12}{5}\right)$ **33.** You will obtain a false statement like $0 = 6$.
35. (b) $(4, 1)$

CUMULATIVE REVIEW EXERCISES

36. $\dfrac{64y^3}{x^6z^{12}}$ **37.** 22 days   **38.** $\dfrac{2x + 3}{2x + 1}$ **39.** $\dfrac{x^2 - 18x - 3}{(x + 1)(x - 1)(x - 15)}$

GROUP ACTIVITY/CHALLENGE PROBLEMS

3. $(8, -1)$ **4.** $(-\frac{105}{41}, \frac{447}{82})$ **6.** $(1, 2, 3)$

EXERCISE SET 8.4

1. $x + y = 26, x = 2y + 2; 8, 18$ **3.** $a + b = 90, b = a + 18; a = 36°, b = 54°$
5. $a + b = 180, a = b + 52; a = 116°, b = 64°$ **7.** $l = w + 100, 2l + 2w = 800; l = 250$ ft, $w = 150$ ft
9. $x + y = 14, 480x + 460y = 6560$; 6 Eagles, 8 Maple Leafs   **11.** $B = 5M, 37B + 75M = 7800$; 150 shares BancOne,
30 shares Microsoft   **13.** $k + c = 4.5, k - c = 3.2$; 3.85 mph, kayak; 0.65 mph, current
15. $c = 50 + 0.85p, c = 100 + 0.80p$; \$1000   **17. (a)** $c = 0.40s, c = 1.00s - 1500$; \$2500
(b) $1500n = 6000$; 4 months   **19.** $x + y = 12{,}500, 0.1x + 0.0525y = 1200$; \$11,447.37 at 10%
21. $T = J + 4, 3T = 3.2J$; Jill's boat, 60 mph; Teresa's boat, 64 mph
23. $U = D + 100, 3U + 3D = 2700$; Delta, 400 mph; United, 500 mph   **25.** $M = P + 0.3, 5M = 8P$; 0.5 hour
27. $x + y = 10, 0.25x + 0.50y = 0.40(10)$; $4L$ of 25%, $6L$ of 50%   **29.** $x + y = 30, 5x + 7y = 160$; 25 lb, \$5; 5 lb, \$7
31. $x + y = 8, 12x + 6y = 10(8)$; $2\frac{2}{3}$ oz drink, $5\frac{1}{3}$ oz juice

CUMULATIVE REVIEW EXERCISES

33. 234   **34.** $\dfrac{1}{9x^8}$ **35. (a)** yes, third   **(b)** yes, fourth   **(c)** No, a polynomial cannot have a negative exponent on the
variable.   **36.** $2x - 3 + \dfrac{2}{x + 4}$

GROUP ACTIVITY/CHALLENGE PROBLEMS

1. 45 min   **3.** $9t = d, 5t = d - \dfrac{1}{2}$; 1.125 mi
4. $x + y = 300, 0.7x + 0.4y = 0.6(300)$, or $[0.3x + 0.6y = 0.4(300)]$; 200 g of first alloy, 100 g of second alloy

EXERCISE SET 8.5

1. 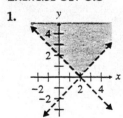   **3.** 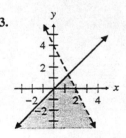   **5.** 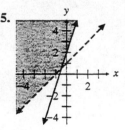   **7.** 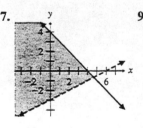   **9.**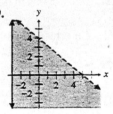

11. 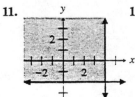   **13.** 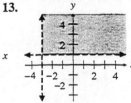   **15.** 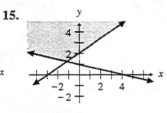   **17.** No

CUMULATIVE REVIEW EXERCISES

18. $3x^3 - 10x^2 + 29x - 28$ **19.** $(x - 3)(y + 1)$ **20.** $(x - 6)(x - 7)$ **21.** $(3x - 2)(2x + 1)$

Group Activity/Challenge Problems

1.

3.
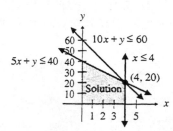

Chapter 8 Review Exercises

1. c   **2.** a   **3.** Consistent, one   **4.** Inconsistent, none   **5.** Dependent, infinite number of solutions   **6.** Consistent, one
7. No solution   **8.** One solution   **9.** Infinite number of solutions   **10.** One solution

11.
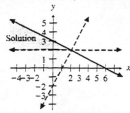

12.
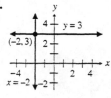

13.

14.
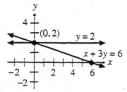

15.
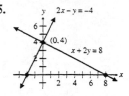

16.

17.
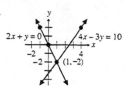

18.
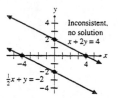

19. $(5, 2)$ **20.** $(-3, 2)$ **21.** $(2, 1)$ **22.** $(5, 4)$ **23.** $(5, 2)$ **24.** $(-18, 6)$ **25.** No solution

26. Infinite number of solutions   **27.** $(\frac{5}{2}, -1)$ **28.** $(\frac{20}{9}, \frac{26}{9})$ **29.** $(8, -2)$ **30.** $(1, -2)$ **31.** $(26, -16)$ **32.** $(-7, 19)$

33. $(\frac{32}{13}, \frac{8}{13})$ **34.** $(-1, \frac{13}{3})$ **35.** No solution   **36.** $(\frac{7}{5}, \frac{13}{5})$ **37.** Infinite number of solutions   **38.** $(-\frac{78}{7}, -\frac{48}{7})$

39. $x + y = 48, y = 2x - 3$; 17, 31   **40.** $p + w = 600, p - w = 530$; 565 mph, plane; 35 mph, wind
41. $c = 20 + 0.50$ m, $c = 35 + 0.40$ m; 150 mi   **42.** $x + y = 16,000, 0.04x + 0.06y = 760$; \$10,000 at 4%, \$6000 at 6%
43. $A = R + 6, 5A + 5R = 600$; Ron 57 mph, Audra 63 mph   **44.** $G + A = 40$; $0.6G + 0.45A = 20.25$; 15 lb of Green
Turf, 25 lb of Agway   **45.** $x + y = 6$; $0.3x + 0.5y = 0.4(6)$; 3 liters of each

46.
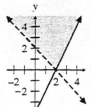

47.
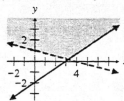

48.
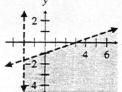

49.
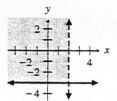

Chapter 8 Practice Test

1. b   **2.** Inconsistent—no solution   **3.** Consistent—one solution   **4.** Dependent—infinite number of solutions
5. No solution   **6.** One solution   **7.**
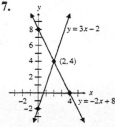
8.
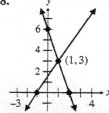

9. $\left(\frac{7}{2}, -\frac{5}{2}\right)$ **10.** $(3, 1)$ **11.** $(5, -5)$ **12.** $\left(\frac{44}{19}, \frac{48}{19}\right)$ **13.** $c = 40 + 0.08x, c = 45 + 0.03x;$ 100 mi

14. $x + y = 20, 6x + 4.5y = 5(20);$ $13\frac{1}{3}$ lb of peanuts, $6\frac{2}{3}$ lb of cashews.

15.

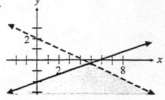

CUMULATIVE REVIEW TEST

1. $\frac{8}{3}$ **2.** 2   **3.** $3, \frac{4}{3}$ **4.** $\frac{85}{4}$ **5.** $\frac{1}{2}$ **6.** $\frac{20}{3} \approx 6.67$ in   **7.** $2x^{23}y^{17}$ **8.** $(3x - 4)(2x - 1)$ **9.** $\dfrac{x - 33}{(x + 3)(x - 3)(x - 6)}$

10. $\dfrac{(x - 4)(x + 4)}{(2x - 3)(x + 3)}$ **11.**

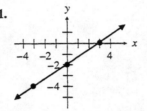

12.

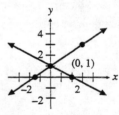

13.

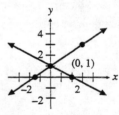

14. No solution, the lines are parallel (same slope)   **15.**

16. $\left(\frac{34}{11}, \frac{-8}{11}\right)$ **17.** 60 min   **18. (a)** \$500,000 **(b)** PCR   **19.** $6\frac{2}{3}$ L of 20%, $3\frac{1}{3}$ L of 35%   **20.** $\frac{300}{11} \approx 27.3$ min

CHAPTER 3

REVIEW OF PERCENT

SECTION 1

1. 0.35; $\dfrac{7}{20}$ **3.** 0.16; $\dfrac{4}{25}$

5. 0.03; $\dfrac{3}{100}$ **7.** 0.5225; $\dfrac{209}{400}$

9. 0.045; $\dfrac{9}{200}$ **11.** 2.50; $\dfrac{5}{2}$ *or* $2\dfrac{1}{2}$

13. 1.375; $\dfrac{11}{8}$ *or* $1\dfrac{3}{8}$ **15.** 0.008; $\dfrac{1}{125}$

17. 0.0175; $\dfrac{7}{400}$ **19.** 1.45; $\dfrac{29}{20}$ *or* $1\dfrac{9}{20}$

21. 0.0075; $\dfrac{3}{400}$ **23.** 0.004; $\dfrac{1}{250}$

25. 0.00375; $\dfrac{3}{800}$ **27.** 0.016; $\dfrac{2}{125}$

29. 0.875; $\dfrac{7}{8}$ **31.** 0.125; $\dfrac{1}{8}$

33. 7%   **35.** 35%

37. 36%   **39.** 16.5%

41. 211%   **43.** 106%

45. 0.1%   **47.** 50%

49. 0.5%   **51.** 310%

53. 460%   **55.** 3%

57. $44\dfrac{4}{9}$% *or* $44.\overline{4}$%   **59.** 60%

61. 175%   **63.** 480%

SECTION 2

Part One

1.	6	**3.**	108		**5.**	19.5
7.	222	**9.**	33		**11.**	27
13.	25%	**15.**	$18\frac{3}{4}\%$ or 18.75%		**17.**	35%
19.	3%	**21.**	$22\frac{2}{9}\%$ or $22.2\overline{2}\%$		**23.**	320
25.	75	**27.**	800		**29.**	21
31.	125	**33.**	900		**35.**	750

Part Two

37. 40% **39.** 20%

41. 60% **43.** $22\frac{2}{9}\%$ or $22.2\overline{2}\%$

45. $28\frac{4}{7}\%$ or 28.57% **47.** $\frac{1}{2}\%$ or 0.5%

Part Three

49.	60	**51.**	48
53.	72	**55.**	648
57.	66	**59.**	63

SECTION 3

Part One

1.	4%	**3.**	37.5%	**5.**	$393.26
7.	$1,125	**9.**	123,600	**11.**	48
13.	$6.80	**15.**	$25	**17.**	$44\frac{4}{9}\%$ or $44.\overline{4}\%$
19.	3%	**21.**	20%	**23.**	28
25.	30	**27.**	30 million	**29.**	6,400
31.	$36				

Part Two

33.	$1,215	**35.**	6%	**37.**	$800
39.	$46,000	**41.**	10%	**43.**	24%
45.	500	**47.**	40%	**49.**	Answers will vary.

CHAPTER 15

SIMPLE INTEREST

SECTION 1

1. a. $45.00; $545   b. $22.50; $522.50   c. $78; $858
    d. $63; $963   e. $49; $889
3. a. $545; $45   c. $858; $78   e. $889; $49
5. 9%   7.   9 months   9.   16%
11. $7,000   13. 10%

SECTION 2

1. a. 58 days   b. 214 days   c. 222 days
    d. 243 days   e. 121 days   f. 143 days
    g. 153 days   h. 152 days
3. a. September 10   b. December 4
    c. November 16   d. December 26
    e. October 12   f. February 28
5. a. December 2; 61 days   b. November 7; 123 days
    c. September 12; 244 days d. October 18; 122 days
    e. May 3; 90 days

SECTION 3

1. a. $72.00; $71.01   b. $50.00; $49.32
3. $50.60; $49.91; $49.50
5. a. $60   b. $30   c. $90   d. $45
7. a. $35.00   b. $105.00 c. $52.50   d. $210.00
9. a. $12.00   b. $36.00   c. $43.20
11. a. $25.00   b. $18.75   c. $50.00
13. a. $64.40   b. 32.20   c. $46.00
15. a. $38.40   b. $9.60   c. $28.80

SECTION 4

1.   a. $1,200   b. Stanley L. Warren

       c. North Austin State Bank   d. August 30, 19XX

       e. September 29, 19XX   f. $1,200

       g. 9%   h. 30 days

       i. $8.88   j. $1,208.88

3.   a. 45 days; $7.50; $407.50   b. 12/30; $26; $676

       c. 11/13; $24.60; $744.60   d. $1,080; 1/16; $1,116

5. $54; $1,514   **7.** $2,417   **9.** $5,120

11.   12%   **13.**   146 days   **15.**   180 days *or* 6 months

17. $1,300   **19.** $5,000

SECTION 5

1.   a. $900   b. $800

3.   a. $1,260.00; $1,211.54   b. $1,515.00; $1,503.72

5.   a. $2,135.00; $2,082.93   b. $2,687.50; $2,647.78

7. $4,000

9. $2,000   **11.** $3,781.46   **13.** $14,909.09

15. $1,523.76   **17.** $6,332.82   **19.** $128,000 (best offer)

CHAPTER 18

COMPOUND INTEREST

SECTION 1

		NO. OF PERIODS	RATE PER PERIOD
1.	a.	5	7%
	b.	36	0.5
	c.	12	4.25
	d.	36	2
	e.	16	2.75

3. a. $5,849.29   b. $5,858.30
$849.29 $858.30

5. a. $2,590.06   b. $2,604.52
$590.06 $604.52

7. a. $8,241.80   b. $8,243.02   **9.** Interest accumulates faster the more often it is compounded.
$241.80 $243.02

SECTION 2

1. a. $5,849.30   b. $5,858.30
$849.30 $858.30

3. a. $2,590.06   b. $2,604.52
$590.06 $604.52

5. a. $8,241.80   b. $8,243.02
$241.80 $243.02

7. a. $344.94   b. $8,785.83   c. $2,457.92
$44.94 $2,385.83 $957.92

d. $9,834.82   e. $1,627.85
$5,034.82 $727.85

9. a. $901.73   b. $1,803.46   c. $3,606.91
$101.73 $203.46 $406.91

d. Doubling the principal doubles the interest at the same interest rate and time.

695

11. a. $1,126.99   b. $1,268.99   c. $1,604.71   d. No
        $126.99 $268.99 $604.71

13. a. $1,552.97   b. $2,411.71   c. $5,816.36   d. No
        $552.97 $1,411.71 $4,816.36

15. a. $830.38   b. $169.62   c. $1,037.97   d. $68.35

17. a. $1,015.08   b. $484.92   c. $1,552.96   d. $68.04

19. a. $1,035.51   b. $264.49   c. $1,523.16   d. $258.67

Section 3

1. a. (1) $9.54   b. (1) $1.63   c. (1) $7.52
        (2) $1,009.54   (2) $501.63   (2) $1,507.52

        d. (1) $20.35
        (2) $2,020.35

3. a. (1) $113.13   b. (1) $50.91
        (2) $112.50   (2) $50.63

5. a. (1) $16.65   b. (1) $53.50
        (2) $1,916.65   (2) $5,853.50

7. a. (1) $82.88   b. (1) $72.14
        (2) $7,182.88   (2) $6,272.14

9. a. (1) $42.58   b. (1) $59.50   c. (1) $97.93
        (2) $3,742.58   (2) $5,159.50   (2) $8,097.93

Section 4

1. a. $698.93; $301.07   b. $3,039.25; $1,060.75

        c. $6,315.27; $1,684.73   d. $529.70; $970.30

        e. $1,858.57; $1,141.43

3. a. $21,742.93   b. $28,257.07

5. a. $25,069.35   b. $4,930.65

7. a. $63,079.46   b. $16,920.54

9. a. $7,680.51   b. $6,294.10

11. a. $8,100.00   b. $6,014.01

13. a. $10,450.00   b. $10,192.52

CHAPTER 19

ANNUITIES

SECTION 1

		MATURITY VALUE	TOTAL DEPOSITS	TOTAL INTEREST EARNED
1.	a.	$ 1,810.34	$ 1,600	$ 210.34
	b.	27,908.01	24,000	3,908.01
	c.	17,690.81	12,800	4,890.81
	d.	95,007.03	72,000	23,007.03
	e.	30,653.59	24,000	6,653.59

3. a. $2,608.24   b. $2,400.00   c. $208.24

5. a. $8,376.43   b. $7,200.00   c. $1,176.43

7. a. $7,500.00   b. $10,789.28   c. $3,289.28

9. a. $80,000.00   b. $93,196.43   c. $13,196.43

SECTION 2

1.
a. (1) $12,462.21
   (2) $20,000.00
   (3) $7,537.79

b. (1) $78,161.32
   (2) $86,400.00
   (3) $8,238.68

c. (1) $42,921.60
   (2) $50,000.00
   (3) $7,078.40

d. (1) $29,179.73
   (2) $33,600.00
   (3) $4,420.27

e. (1) 26,379.36
   (2) $36,000.00
   (3) $9,620.64

3.
a. (1) $85,900.56; $13,900.56
   (2) $60,091.22; $11,908.78

b. (1) $77,520.90; $13,520.90
   (2) $52,220.01; $11,779.99

c. (1) $357,964.51; $57,964.51
   (2) $252,509.97; $47,490.03

5. a. $6,522.47   b. $7,200.00   c. $677.53

7. a. $6,838.17   b. $7,200.00   c. $361.83

9.   a. $103,000   b. $64,000   c. $56,000

11.   a. $4,400   b. $3,500   c. $1,300

13.   a. $176,000.00   b. $143,230.95

15.   a. $490,000.00   b. $248,467.08

CHAPTER 20

SINKING FUNDS AND AMORTIZATION

SECTION 1, PAGE 509

		PERIODIC PAYMENT	TOTAL DEPOSITS	TOTAL INTEREST
1.	a.	$ 491.54	$ 15,729.28	$ 4,270.72
	b.	391.47	7,829.40	2,170.60
	c.	544.39	32,663.40	7,336.60
	d.	1,044.59	62,675.40	67,324.60
	e.	3,703.72	311,112.48	88,887.52

		PURCHASE PRICE	PREMIUM (P) OR DISCOUNT (D)	ANNUAL INTEREST	CURRENT YIELD
3.	a.	$1,050.00	$50.00 (P)	$ 52.50	5.00%
	b.	920.00	80.00 (D)	57.50	6.25
	c.	1,000.00	0 (par)	72.50	7.25
	d.	962.50	37.50 (D)	77.00	8.00
	e.	1,012.50	12.50 (P)	101.25	10.00

5.   a. $3,727.98   b. $44,735.76   c. $5,264.24

7.   a. $108,527.83   b. $868,222.64   c. $131,777.36

Note: Answers were obtained by mentally moving decimal in factor.

9.   a. $10,032.96   b. $601,977.60   c. $98,022.40

11.   a. $940   b. $60 (discount)   c. $282,000

       d. $94   e. 10%   f. $28,200

13.   a. $572.34   b. $3,547.92

SECTION 2, PAGE 519

		PAYMENT	TOTAL REPAID	TOTAL INTEREST
1.	a.	$24,556.60	$736,698.00	$336,698.00
	b.	4,528.93	362,314.40	182,314.40
	c.	1,296.81	93,370.32	23,370.32
	d.	12,454.56	298,909.44	98,909.44
	e.	1,159.97	69,598.20	9,598.20

		MONTHLY PAYMENT	TOTAL OF PAYMENTS	TOTAL INTEREST
3.	a.	$1,279.50	$ 307,080	$157,080
	b.	685.60	205,680	125,680
	c.	2,012.50	724,500	474,500
	d.	3,512.00	1,264,320	864,320

5.   a. $1,485.09   b. $14,105.40

7.   a. $2,130.53   b. $18,176.96

9.   a. $2,435.74   b. $104,859.20

   c. $202,859.20

11.   a. $4,383.30   b. $65,597.60

   c. $365,597.60

13.   a. $2,571; $2,469   b. $771,300; $888,840

   c. $791,300; $908,840   d. $117,540

15.   a. $2,308.73   b. $1,114.97

SECTION 3, PAGE 522

1.   a. 1. $18,729.81   b. 1. $9,923.38

   2. $8,729.81   2. $2,923.38

3.   a. 1. $5,339.08   b. 1. $4,937.84

   2. $4,660.92   2. $2,062.16

5.   a. 1. $458.20   b. 1. $97.78

   2. $7,331.20   2. $5,866.80

   3. $2,668.80   3. $1,133.20

7.   a. 1. $858.20   b. 1. $138.61

   2. $13,731.20   2. $8,316.60

   3. $3,731.20   3. $1,316.60

9. a. 1. $152,710.85   b. 1. $9,202.53
       2. $80,000.00   2. $7,200.00
       3. $72,710.85   3. $2,002.53
11. a. 1. $46,407.32   b. 1. $5,703.45
       2. $80,000.00   2. $7,200.00
       3. $33,592.68   3. $1,496.55
13. a. $4,435.93   b. $564.07
15. a. $145,784.22   b. $25,784.22
17. a. $5,381.33   b. $37,626.60
19. a. $36,673.79   b. $48,000.00   c. $11,326.21
21. a. $370.05   b. $13,321.80   c. $1,678.20
23. a. $5,632.47   b. $632.47

Answers to Selected Exercises

Chapter 2

2.3. Qualitative; qualitative **2.5a.** Nominal **b.** Ratio **c.** Ratio **d.** Ratio **e.** Interval **2.7.** I: Nominal, II: Ratio, III: Ordinal, IV: Nominal, V: Ordinal, VI: Ratio **2.11a.** Frequency histogram **b.** 14 **c.** 49 **2.13b.** 24; .8 **2.23.** 14.545; 15; 15 **2.29a.** 180; 162 **b.** Skewed to the right **c.** No **2.31a.** 70.01; 68.75; two modes: 64.6 and 76.8 **b.** 68.83; 69; two modes: 64.6 and 76.8 **c.** 69.0125 **2.33.** \$.35 **2.37a.** 2; 37.5; 6.124 **b.** 1.25; 1.835; 1.355 **2.39a.** 6.2; 77.2; 8.786 **b.** 28.25; 2,304.92; 48.010 **2.43.** No; yes **2.45a.** A: 33.14; B: 34.57 **b.** A: 3.98; B: .98 **d.** A: .82; B: 2.12 **2.47.** Any data set; mound-shaped data sets **2.49a.** At least 0% **b.** At least 75% **c.** At least 88.9% **2.51.** No · **2.53a.** .1488; .0273; .1652 **b.** Cannot say anything; at least 84%; at least 93.75% **c.** 68%; 96%; 100% **d.** 0% **2.55.** At most 13 **2.57.** At least .889 **2.59a.** At least .889 **b.** ≈.16 **c.** Yes **2.61.** Do not buy **2.63a.** 1; sample **b.** −1.5; sample **c.** 1.765; population **d.** −.6; population **2.65a.** 3.7; 2.2; 2.95; 1.45 **b.** 1.9 **c.** Cum laude: $z > 1$, GPA > 3.2; summa cum laude: $z > 2$, GPA > 3.7; mound-shaped distribution **2.67a.** Brazil: −3.825; Egypt: 1.745; France: −2.787; Italy: −5.510; Japan: −56.326; Mexico: −5.689; Panama: .387; Soviet Union: 1.055; Sweden: −2.864; Turkey: .622 **b.** −2.81; .48 **2.69.** 1989: 69.4th percentile; 1985: 85.8th percentile **2.71a.** ≈68%; ≈100% **b.** 31 **c.** Original **2.73a.** At most 25%; cannot be determined; at most 11.1% **b.** 1.5; 1.5 **2.77a.** 39 **b.** 45; 31.5 **c.** 13.5 **d.** Skewed to the left **e.** 50%; 75% **2.81a.** 3.03; −2.68; 0 **2.83b.** Customers 238, 264, 268, and 269 **c.** Customer 238: 1.92; Customer 264: 3.14; Customer 268: 2.06; Customer 269: 2.13 **2.85a.** Ratio **b.** Nominal **c.** Interval **d.** Ordinal **e.** (a) Quantitative; (b) Qualitative; (c) Quantitative; (d) Qualitative **2.87a.** 239; 29; 841 **b.** 634; 50; 2,500 **c.** 254; 2; 4 **d.** 10,404; 102; 10,404 **2.93a.** 11.65 **b.** 6.6441 **c.** At least 75%; 96.7% **2.95a.** Skewed to the right **c.** Empirical rule: ≈49; Chebyshev: at least 38 **d.** 3.33; no **2.97f.** −2.5 **2.99a.** Frequency bar chart **2.111a.** At least 0% **b.** At most 25% **2.115a.** \$7,500 **b.** Over 120,000 **c.** Yes, but very unlikely **2.117a.** None; $V = 0$ for all data sets **2.121a.** At least .75 **b.** At least .889 **c.** At least .56 **d.** At least .87 **2.123a.** U.S.: $\bar{x} = 41.08$, $s^2 = 330.08$; Canada: $\bar{x} = 70.83$, $s^2 = 529.24$; United Kingdom: $\bar{x} = 60.42$, $s^2 = 634.27$; Sweden: $\bar{x} = 83.42$, $s^2 = 511.17$; France: $\bar{x} = 66.33$, $s^2 = 1,051.88$; West Germany: $\bar{x} = 56.08$, $s^2 = 907.17$ **b.** Brewing: $\bar{x} = 54.17$, $s^2 = 640.97$; cigarettes: $\bar{x} = 91.00$, $s^2 = 142.00$; fabric weaving: $\bar{x} = 35.67$, $s^2 = 365.07$; paints: $\bar{x} = 40.67$, $s^2 = 727.47$; petroleum refining: $\bar{x} = 62.50$, $s^2 = 666.70$; shoes: $\bar{x} = 20.33$, $s^2 = 71.87$; glass bottles: $\bar{x} = 85.83$, $s^2 = 210.97$; cement: $\bar{x} = 67.67$, $s^2 = 805.07$; ordinary steel: $\bar{x} = 60.67$, $s^2 = 352.67$; antifriction bearings: $\bar{x} = 80.67$, $s^2 = 390.27$; refrigerators: $\bar{x} = 77.50$, $s^2 = 202.70$; storage batteries: $\bar{x} = 79.67$, $s^2 = 269.87$ **c.** U.S., Sweden **d.** Shoes, fabric weaving, and paints; cigarettes, glass bottles, and antifriction bearings

Chapter 3

3.3a. .3 **b.** .25 **c.** .6 **3.5a.** {under 2,000, 2,000–4,999, 5,000–7,999, 8,000 or more} **b.** .184 **c.** .216 **3.7.** 1/20 **3.11a.** {Visa or MasterCard, Diners Club, Carte Blanche, Choice} **b.** P(Visa or MasterCard) = .632; P(Diners Club) = .232; P(Carte Blanche) = .032; P(Choice) = .105 **c.** .368 **3.13b.** 1/16 **c.** 5/16 **3.15a.** 1 to 2 **b.** 1/2 **c.** .4 **3.19a.** 7/8 **b.** 3/8 **c.** 3/8 **d.** 0 **e.** Yes **f.** 3/4 **3.21a.** $A \cap F$ **b.** $B \cup C$ **c.** A^c **3.23a.** $B \cap C$ **b.** A^c **c.** $C \cup B$ **d.** $A \cap C^c$ **3.25a.** {(R, 1), (R, 2), (R, 3), (S, 1), (S, 2), (S, 3), (E, 1), (E, 2), (E, 3)} **b.** Sample space **c.** .24 **d.** .10 **e.** .47 **f.** .62 **g.** .28 **3.27b.** .184; yes **c.** .008 **d.** .556 **e.** .326 **3.29a.** .81 **b.** .65 **c.** .41 **d.** .22 **e.** B and C; B and D; C and D **3.31a.** .052 **b.** .259 **c.** .157 **d.** .692 **3.33a.** $P(A) = .8$; $P(B) = .70$; $P(A \cap B) = .60$ **b.** $P(E_1 \mid A) = .25$; $P(E_2 \mid A) = .375$; $P(E_3 \mid A) = .375$ **c.** $P(B \mid A) = .75$ **d.** No **3.35a.** No **b.** No **c.** No **3.37a.** No **b.** Yes

c. No   d. No   **3.39.** No   **3.41a.** .550   b. .450   c. .272   d. .040   e. .182   f. .857   g. .182   **3.43.** .005
3.45a. .18   b. .82   c. .31   d. .69   e. .26   **3.47a.** .3; .6   b. Dependent   c. Independent   **3.51a.** {(0001, 0002), (0001, 0003), (0001, 0004), (0001, 0005), (0002, 0003), (0002, 0004), (0002, 0005), (0003, 0004), (0003, 0005), (0004, 0005)}   b. $\frac{1}{10}$ c. $\frac{1}{10}$ d. $\frac{3}{10}$ **3.57.** .5   **3.59a.** .8145   b. .0135   c. Evidence to indicate claim is incorrect
d. No   **3.61a.** .75   b. .2875   c. .6   d. .06   **3.63.** .801   **3.65b.** .95   c. .25   d. .5   **3.69a.** .7127   b. .2873
3.71. No   **3.73a.** $\frac{1}{15}$ b. $\frac{6}{15}$ c. $\frac{14}{15}$ d. $\frac{6}{14}$ e. $\frac{5}{14}$ **3.75.** .79   **3.79.** False

Chapter 4

4.3a. Continuous   b. Discrete   c. Continuous   d. Discrete   **4.11a.** {(HHH), (HHT), (HTH), (THH), (HTT), (THT), (TTH), (TTT)}   b. $p(0) = \frac{1}{8}$; $p(1) = \frac{3}{8}$; $p(2) = \frac{3}{8}$; $p(3) = \frac{1}{8}$ **4.13a.** Not valid   b. Valid   c. Not valid   d. Not valid
4.15b. .56; .32   **4.17a.** .729; .001   b. .243; .027   c. Yes   **4.19a.** 3.85   **4.21a.** 60; 250; 15.8113   c. (23.38, 91.62); 1
4.23a. Expected total loss is $2,450 for both firms   b. A: $\sigma = 661.44$; B: $\sigma = 701.78$; greater risk is B   **4.25a.** .8   b. No

4.27a.

Disease	Hepatitis	Cirrhosis	Gallstone	Pancreatic cancer
Cost	$700	$1,110	$3,320	$16,450
p(cost)	.4	.1	.45	.05

b. $2,707.50

c.

Disease	Hepatitis	Cirrhosis
Cost	$700	$1,110
p(cost)	.8	.2

d. $782.00   **4.29a.**

Cost	$1,000	$2,000	$3,000
p(cost)	.25	.25	.50

b. .25   c. $2,250   d. $2,250   **4.31a.** Discrete   b. Binomial   d. 2.4; 1.2   **4.33a.** .21875   b. .0250   c. .1296
4.35a. .09767   b. .99869   c. .22884   **4.37a.** .5   b. $p < .5$ c. $p > .5$ d. .5; $p < .5$; $p > .5$ **4.39a.** .006; .046
b. .0293; .0003   c. .0662; .0019   d. .8992   **4.41b.** 2.4; 1.470   c. Binomial with $p = .9$, $q = .1$, and $n = 24$; $E(y) = 21.6$; $\sigma = 1.470$ **4.43a.** 1   b. .998   c. .537   d. .009   e. 0   f. 0   g. 0   h. 1   **4.45a.** 520; 13.491   b. No   c. No
4.47a. .265   b. .647   c. .981   d. Increases   **4.49b.** 5; 2.236; (.5278, 9.4722)   c. .961   **4.51a.** 2   b. No   **4.53** .193; .660   **4.55.** .224; .050; .05^8; hours are independent   **4.57.** .632   **4.59a.** .2734   b. .4096   c. .3432   **4.61a.** .084
b. .073   c. .028   **4.63a.** Discrete   b. Continuous   c. Continuous   d. Continuous   **4.65a.** $497,000
b. 6.606×10^{11} **4.67a.** A: 4.6; B: 3.7   b. A: $46,000; B: $55,550   c. A: $\sigma^2 = 1.34$, $\sigma = 1.16$; B: $\sigma^2 = 1.21$, $\sigma = 1.10$ d. A: .95; B: .95   **4.69.** .3028   **4.71.** .036   **4.73a.** .34272   b. .004   **4.75a.** 5; 4   b. .617   c. .006

Chapter 5

5.1a. $f(x) = \frac{1}{25}$; $20 \le x \le 45$ b. 32.5; 52.0833   c. 1   **5.3a.** $f(x) = \frac{1}{4}$, $3 \le x \le 7$ b. 5; 1.333   c. .577
5.5a. 0   b. 1   c. 1   **5.9b.** .5; .2; .2; 0   **5.11.** .4444   **5.13a.** .2789   b. .9544   c. .0819   d. .9974   e. .4878
f. .4878   **5.15a.** 0   b. .8413   c. .8413   d. .1587   **5.17a.** .6826   b. .95   c. .90   d. .9544   **5.19a.** −.81   b. .55
c. 1.43   d. .21   e. −2.05   f. .50   **5.21a.** 1.25 below   b. 1.875 above   c. 0   d. 1.5 above   **5.23a.** .0456; .0026
b. .6826; .9544   c. 1,008.4; 987.2   **5.25.** 182   **5.27a.** .2843   b. .0228   c. 71.64   **5.29a.** .1151   b. .6554
c. $10.50   **5.31a.** XYZ   b. ABC: $105; XYZ: $107   c. ABC   **5.33.** 5.068   **5.35a.** .367879   b. .082085   c. .000553
d. .223130   **5.37a.** .999447   b. .999955   c. .981684   d. .632121   **5.39a.** .018316   b. .950213   c. .383401
5.41. .223130   **5.43a.** .367879; .212248   b. .049787   c. Less   d. 40.6   **5.45a.** $R(x) = e^{-.5x}$ b. .135335   c. .367879
d. No   e. 820.85; 3,934.69   f. 37 days   **5.49a.** Yes   b. 17.5; 5.25   c. .902   d. .9049   **5.51a.** .4880   b. .2334
c. 0   **5.53a.** .0559   c. No   **5.55b.** ≈0   c. No   d. Yes   **5.57a.** $f(x) = \frac{1}{80}$, $10 \le x \le 90$ b. 50; 23.094   d. .625
e. 0   f. .875   g. .577   h. .1875   **5.59a.** .3300   b. .0918   c. .9245   d. .0255   **5.61a.** −.13   b. .02   c. 1.04
d. −.69   **5.63a.** .451188   b. .406570   c. 0   d. .877544   e. .273870   f. 0   **5.65a.** .0918   b. 0   c. Lower by 4.87
decibels   **5.67.** $9.6582   **5.69a.** 13.33 weeks   b. .860708; .637628   c. .593430   **5.71.** From high to low: a. Bank 3, bank 1, bank 2   b. Bank 3, bank 1, bank 2   c. Bank 1, bank 3, bank 2   **5.73a.** .0548   b. .6006   c. .3446
d. $6,503.80   **5.75a.** .8264   b. 17   c. .6217   d. 0; −157